TORTS:
PERSONAL INJURY
LITIGATION

FOURTH EDITION

The West Legal Studies Series

Your options keep growing with West Legal Studies

Each year our list continues to offer you more options for every area of the law to meet your course or on-the-job reference requirements. We now have over 140 titles from which to choose in the following areas:

Administrative Law	Family Law
Alternative Dispute Resolution	Federal Taxation
Bankruptcy	Intellectual Property
Business Organizations/Corporations	Introduction to Law
Civil Litigation and Procedure	Introduction to Paralegalism
CLA Exam Preparation	Law Office Management
Client Accounting	Law Office Procedures
Computer in the Law Office	Legal Research, Writing, and Analysis
Constitutional Law	Legal Terminology
Contract Law	Paralegal Employment
Criminal Law and Procedure	Real Estate Law
Document Preparation	Reference Materials
Environmental Law	Torts and Personal Injury Law
Ethics	Will, Trusts, and Estate Administration

You will find unparalleled, practical support

Each book is augmented by instructor and student supplements to ensure the best learning experience possible. We also offer custom publishing and other benefits such as West's Student Achievement Award. In addition, our sales representatives are ready to provide you with dependable service.

We want to hear from you

Our best contributions for improving the quality of our books and instructional materials is feedback from the people who use them. If you have a question, concern, or observation about any of our materials, or you have a product proposal or manuscript, we want to hear from you. Please contact your local representative or write us at the following address:

West Legal Studies, 3 Columbia Circle, P.O. Box 15015, Albany, NY 12212-5015

For additional information point your browser at
www.westlegalstudies.com

WEST
TM
THOMSON LEARNING

TORTS: PERSONAL INJURY LITIGATION

FOURTH EDITION

WILLIAM P. STATSKY

WEST
THOMSON LEARNING

Australia Canada Mexico Singapore Spain United Kingdom United States

WEST LEGAL STUDIES

Torts, Personal Injury Litigation, Fourth Edition
by William P. Statsky

Business Unit Director:
Susan L. Simpfenderfer

Acquisitions Editor:
Joan M. Gill

Developmental Editor:
Rhonda Dearborn

Editorial Assistant:
Lisa Flatley

Executive Marketing Manager:
Donna J. Lewis

Channel Manager:
Nigar Hale

Executive Production Manager:
Wendy A. Troeger

Production Editor:
Betty L. Dickson

Cover Design:
John Walker Design

For permission to use material from this text or product, contact
us by
Tel: (800) 730-2214
Fax (800) 730-2215
www.thomsonrights.com

Library of Congress Cataloging-in-Publication Data

Statsky, William P.
  Torts, personal injury litigation/William P. Statsky.—4th ed.
    p. cm.
  Includes bibliographical references and index.
  ISBN-13 978-0-7668-1230-7
  ISBN-10 0-7668-1230-8
    1. Personal injuries—United States. 2. Torts—United States.
    3. Actions and defenses—United States. I. Title

KF1257 .S73 2001
346.7303'23—dc21   00-035171

NOTICE TO THE READER

Publisher does not warrant or guarantee any of the products described herein or perform any independent analysis in connection with any of the product information contained herein. Publisher does not assume, and expressly disclaims, any obligation to obtain and include information other than that provided to it by the manufacturer.

The reader is notified that this text is an educational tool, not a practice book. Since the law is in constant change, no rule or statement of law in this book should be relied upon for any service to any client. The reader should always refer to standard legal sources for the current rule or law. If legal advice or other expert assistance is required, the services of the appropriate professional should be sought.

The Publisher makes no representation or warranties of any kind, including but not limited to, the warranties of fitness for particular purpose or merchantability, nor are any such representations implied with respect to the material set forth herein, and the publisher takes no responsibility with respect to such material. The publisher shall not be liable for any special, consequential, or exemplary damages resulting, in whole or part, from the readers' use of, or reliance upon, this material.

Dedication

For Pat, Jessie, Gabe, Randy, Pani, Kila, and Kora

CONTENTS IN BRIEF

CHAPTER 1   INRODUCTION TO TORT LAW AND PRACTICE   1

CHAPTER 2   LEGAL ANALYSIS IN TORT LAW   27

CHAPTER 3   TORT LITIGATION AND PARALEGAL ROLES   49

CHAPTER 4   FORESEEABILITY IN TORT LAW   95

CHAPTER 5   BATTERY   105

CHAPTER 6   ASSAULT   119

CHAPTER 7   FALSE IMPRISONMENT AND FALSE ARREST   131

CHAPTER 8   MISUSE OF LEGAL PROCESS   147

CHAPTER 9   INFLICTION OF EMOTIONAL DISTRESS   159

CHAPTER 10   CONVERSION AND TRESPASS TO CHATTELS   179

CHAPTER 11   STRICT LIABILITY   191

CHAPTER 12   NEGLIGENCE: A SUMMARY   205

CHAPTER 13   NEGLIGENCE: ELEMENT I: DUTY   213

CHAPTER 14   NEGLIGENCE: ELEMENT II: BREACH OF DUTY (UNREASONABLENESS)   229

CHAPTER 15   NEGLIGENCE: ELEMENT III: PROXIMATE CAUSE   265

CHAPTER 16   NEGLIGENCE: ELEMENT IV: DAMAGES   285

CHAPTER 17   NEGLIGENCE: DEFENSES   303

CHAPTER 18   MEDICAL MALPRACTICE AND LEGAL MALPRACTICE   321

CHAPTER 19   PRODUCTS LIABILITY   345

CHAPTER 20   MASS TORT LITIGATION   387

CHAPTER 21   SURVIVAL AND WRONGFUL DEATH   425

CHAPTER 22   TORTS AGAINST AND WITHIN THE FAMILY   433

CHAPTER 23   TORTS CONNECTED WITH LAND   445

CHAPTER 24   DEFAMATION   475

CHAPTER 25   INVASION OF PRIVACY   499

CHAPTER 26   MISREPRESENTATION, TORTIOUS INTERFERENCE, AND OTHER TORTS   513

CHAPTER 27   ADDITIONAL TORT DEFENSES   535

CHAPTER 28   WORKERS' COMPENSATION   567

CHAPTER 29   SETTLEMENT   585

APPENDIX A   BASIC MEDICAL ANATOMY   633

APPENDIX B   SURVEY OF NEGLIGENCE LAW IN THE UNITED STATES   653

APPENDIX C   AUTOMOBILE ACCIDENT AND INVESTIGATION CHECKLIST   661

APPENDIX D   SAMPLE ACCIDENT REPORT
              FILED WITH POLICE
              DEPARTMENT   671

APPENDIX E   RESOURCES: STATE AGENCIES
              RELEVANT TO A TORTS
              PRACTICE   675

APPENDIX F   VERDICTS AND
              SETTLEMENTS   683

APPENDIX G   AUTOMOBILE INSURANCE 687

APPENDIX H   LEGAL NURSE   693

APPENDIX I   DISABLING INJURIES AND
              DEATH: SOME STATISTICS 695

APPENDIX J   "DO YOU SELDOMLY
              SWEAR . . ."   701

GLOSSARY   705

CONTENTS

CHAPTER 1   **INTRODUCTION TO TORT LAW AND PRACTICE**   **1**

SCOPE   2

DEFINITIONS AND PURPOSES   3

ELEMENTS OF ALL THE TORTS   4

CATEGORIES OF TORTS   4

INTRODUCTION TO CAUSATION   10

THE RELATIONSHIP BETWEEN TORT LAW AND OTHER AREAS OF THE LAW   10

SOURCES OF TORT LAW   12

CHAPTER 2   **LEGAL ANALYSIS IN TORT LAW**   **27**

STRUCTURE OF LEGAL ANALYSIS   28

ISSUE   29

RULE   30

APPLICATION   31

CONCLUSION   46

CHAPTER 3   **TORT LITIGATION AND PARALEGAL ROLES**   **49**

OVERVIEW   50

LIABILITY, DAMAGES, AND COLLECTIBILITY   51

ALTERNATIVE DISPUTE RESOLUTION (ADR)   52

INTRODUCTION TO FACT GATHERING   53

ACHIEVING SPECIFICITY AND COMPREHENSIVENESS   56

TAKING A WITNESS STATEMENT   62

TORT COMPLAINTS   63

DISCOVERY   73

TRIAL AND APPEAL   88

ENFORCEMENT   91

CHAPTER 4   **FORESEEABILITY IN TORT LAW**   **95**

INTRODUCTION   96

DEFINING FORESEEABILITY   96

		Foreseeability Spectrum	96
		Objective Standard	97
		Phrasing the Foreseeability Question	98
		Foreseeability Determination "Formula"	99
		Review of Steps to Determine Foreseeability	103
Chapter 5	Battery		105
		Introduction	106
		Act	110
		Person	110
		Intent	110
		Harmful or Offensive Contact	113
		Consent and Privilege	117
Chapter 6	Assault		119
		Introduction	120
		Act	123
		Apprehension	123
		Harmful or Offensive	124
		Transferred Intent	125
		Assault and Civil Rights	126
Chapter 7	False Imprisonment and False Arrest		131
		Introduction	132
		False Imprisonment	132
		False Arrest	143
Chapter 8	Misuse of Legal Proceedings		147
		Introduction	148
		Malicious Prosecution	148
		Wrongful or Unjustified Civil Proceedings	154
		Abuse of Process	156
Chapter 9	Infliction of Emotional Distress		159
		Introduction	160
		Intentional Infliction of Emotional Distress	160
		Tort Law and the Impeachment of the President	167
		Media Defendants and the Constitution	171
		Negligent Infliction of Emotional Distress	172

CHAPTER 10   **CONVERSION AND TRESPASS TO CHATTELS**   **179**

     INTRODUCTION   179
     DAMAGES   183
     KIND OF INTERFERENCE   184
     MISTAKE DEFENSE   186

CHAPTER 11   **STRICT LIABILITY**   **191**

     INTRODUCTION   192
     ANIMALS   192
     STRICT LIABILITY FOR ABNORMALLY DANGEROUS CONDITIONS OR ACTIVITIES   195

CHAPTER 12   **NEGLIGENCE: A SUMMARY**   **205**

     INTRODUCTION   206
     NEGLIGENCE AND BREACH OF DUTY   206
     NEGLIGENCE AND INSURANCE   206
     SHORTHAND DEFINITION   207
     NEGLIGENCE CHECKLIST   207

CHAPTER 13   **NEGLIGENCE: ELEMENT I: DUTY**   **213**

     GENERAL RULE ON DUTY   214
     UNFORESEEABLE PLAINTIFF   215
     NONFEASANCE AND SPECIAL RELATIONSHIPS   217
     GRATUITOUS UNDERTAKING   223
     PROTECTION FOR THE GOOD SAMARITAN   227

CHAPTER 14   **NEGLIGENCE: ELEMENT II: BREACH-OF-DUTY (UNREASONABLENESS)**   **229**

     STANDARD OF CARE: REASONABLENESS   230
     BREACH-OF-DUTY (UNREASONABLENESS) EQUATION   232
     OBJECTIVE OR SUBJECTIVE STANDARD?   237
     RES IPSA LOQUITUR   240
     CUSTOM AND USAGE   246
     VIOLATION OF A STATUTE   247
     COMPLIANCE WITH A STATUTE   254
     GROSS NEGLIGENCE (UNREASONABLENESS) AND WILLFUL, WANTON, AND RECKLESS CONDUCT   254
     VICARIOUS LIABILITY   255

CHAPTER 15   NEGLIGENCE: ELEMENT III: PROXIMATE CAUSE   265

INTRODUCTION   266
CAUSE IN FACT   266
CUT-OFF TEST OF PROXIMATE CAUSE   273
OVERVIEW OF STEPS NEEDED TO ANALYZE PROXIMATE CAUSE   279

CHAPTER 16   NEGLIGENCE: ELEMENT IV: DAMAGES   285

KINDS OF DAMAGES   286
PRESENT VALUE   287
PAIN AND SUFFERING   293
SOFTWARE   294
PROPERTY DAMAGE   295
DOCTRINE OF AVOIDABLE CONSEQUENCES   296
COLLATERAL SOURCE RULE   298
JOINT TORTFEASORS   298
RELEASE   300
CONTRIBUTION   300
INDEMNITY   301

CHAPTER 17   NEGLIGENCE: DEFENSES   303

INTRODUCTION   304
CONTRIBUTORY NEGLIGENCE   305
LAST CLEAR CHANCE   307
COMPARATIVE NEGLIGENCE   309
ASSUMPTION OF THE RISK   309

CHAPTER 18   MEDICAL MALPRACTICE AND LEGAL MALPRACTICE   321

MEDICAL MALPRACTICE   322
LEGAL MALPRACTICE   335

CHAPTER 19   PRODUCTS LIABILITY   345

PRODUCTS LIABILITY IN THE MEDIA   346
CATEGORIES OF DEFECTS   347
NEGLIGENCE   348
MISREPRESENTATION   355
WARRANTY AND STRICT LIABILITY   355
EXPRESS WARRANTY   355
SALE VERSUS SERVICE   357
IMPLIED WARRANTIES   359
STRICT LIABILITY IN TORT   364
REFORM   380
PARALEGAL ROLES   380

CHAPTER 20 MASS TORT LITIGATION 387
    INTRODUCTION 388
    SOLICITATION OF CLIENTS 390
    CLASS ACTIONS 392
    JUNK SCIENCE AND CAUSATION 396
    ASBESTOS 397
    BREAST IMPLANTS 401
    TOBACCO 406
    PARALEGAL ROLES IN MASS TORT LITIGATION 411

CHAPTER 21 SURVIVAL AND WRONGFUL DEATH 425
    INTRODUCTION 426
    SURVIVAL OF TORTS UNRELATED TO DEATH 426
    WRONGFUL DEATH 428
    AVOIDING DOUBLE RECOVERY 429

CHAPTER 22 TORTS AGAINST AND WITHIN THE FAMILY 433
    TORTS DERIVED FROM OTHER TORTS 434
    TORTS NOT DERIVED FROM OTHER TORTS 435
    PRENATAL INJURIES 438
    WRONGFUL LIFE, BIRTH, PREGNANCY 438
    WRONGFUL ADOPTION 442
    INTRAFAMILY TORT IMMUNITY 442

CHAPTER 23 TORTS CONNECTED WITH LAND 445
    INTRODUCTION 446
    TRESPASS TO LAND 446
    NUISANCE 451
    TRADITIONAL NEGLIGENCE LIABILITY 462

CHAPTER 24 DEFAMATION 475
    INTRODUCTION 476
    DEFAMATORY STATEMENT 481
    EXTRINSIC FACTS 484
    FALSITY OF THE STATEMENT 484
    OF AND CONCERNING THE PLAINTIFF 488
    PUBLICATION 488
    REPUBLICATION 489
    CYBERSPACE DEFAMATION 490
    DAMAGES 491
    PRIVILEGE 493
    SLAPP SUITS 495
    "VEGGIE LIBEL" 496

CHAPTER 25	**INVASION OF PRIVACY**	**499**
	FOUR TORTS	500
	INTRUSION	503
	APPROPRIATION	507
	PUBLIC DISCLOSURE OF PRIVATE FACT	508
	FALSE LIGHT	509
	MEDIA DEFENDANTS	510
CHAPTER 26	**MISREPRESENTATION, TORTIOUS INTERFERENCE, AND OTHER TORTS**	**513**
	MISREPRESENTATION	514
	INTERFERENCE WITH CONTRACT RELATIONS	523
	INTERFERENCE WITH PROSPECTIVE ADVANTAGE	527
	TORTIOUS INTERFERENCE WITH EMPLOYMENT (WRONGFUL DISCHARGE)	528
	DISPARAGEMENT	529
	INJURIOUS FALSEHOOD	530
	PRIMA FACIE TORT	531
	BAD FAITH LIABILITY	532
	DRAM SHOP LIABILITY	532
CHAPTER 27	**ADDITIONAL TORT DEFENSES**	**535**
	INTRODUCTION	536
	CONSENT IN TORT LAW	536
	SELF-HELP PRIVILEGES	543
	SOVEREIGN IMMUNITY	554
	OFFICIAL IMMUNITY: THE PERSONAL LIABILITY OF GOVERNMENT EMPLOYEES	559
	CHARITABLE IMMUNITY	564
	INTRAFAMILY TORT IMMUNITY	564
CHAPTER 28	**WORKERS' COMPENSATION**	**567**
	INTRODUCTION	568
	ON-THE-JOB INJURIES AT COMMON LAW	568
	WORKERS' COMPENSATION STATUTES	569
	INJURIES AND DISEASES COVERED	570
	FILING A CLAIM	580
	BENEFITS AVAILABLE	582
	TORT CLAIMS AGAINST THIRD PARTIES	582
	REFORM	583
CHAPTER 29	**SETTLEMENT**	**585**
	INTRODUCTION	586
	PARALEGAL ROLES DURING SETTLEMENT	586
	SETTLEMENT PRECIS	586
	SETTLEMENT BROCHURE	589

APPENDIX A	BASIC MEDICAL ANATOMY	633
APPENDIX B	SURVEY OF NEGLIGENCE LAW IN THE UNITED STATES	653
APPENDIX C	AUTOMOBILE ACCIDENT AND INVESTIGATION CHECKLIST	661
APPENDIX D	SAMPLE ACCIDENT REPORT FILED WITH POLICE DEPARTMENT	671
APPENDIX E	RESOURCES: STATE AGENCIES RELEVANT TO A TORTS PRACTICE	675
APPENDIX F	VERDICTS AND SETTLEMENTS	683
APPENDIX G	AUTOMOBILE INSURANCE	687
APPENDIX H	LEGAL NURSE	693
APPENDIX I	DISABLING INJURIES AND DEATH: SOME STATISTICS	695
APPENDIX J	"DO YOU *SELDOMLY* SWEAR . . ?"	701
GLOSSARY		705

TABLE OF CASES

Chapter 5

Garratt v. Dailey, 46 Wash. 2d 197, 279 P.2d 1091 (Washington State 1955) 111
Brzoska v. Olson, 668 A.2d 1355 (Delaware 1995) 114

Chapter 6

Allen v. Walker, 569 So. 2d 350 (Alabama 1990) 126
Lucero v. Trosch, 904 F. Supp. 1336 (S.D. Alabama 1995) 127

Chapter 7

The Limited Stores, Inc. v. Wilson-Robinson, 317 Ark. 80, 876 S.W.2d 248 (Arkansas 1994) 138
Andrews v. Piedmont Air Lines, 297 S.C. 367, 377 S.E.2d 127 (South Carolina 1989) 142

Chapter 8

Raine and Highfield v. Drasin and Fadel, 621 S.W.2d 895 (Kentucky 1981) 155
Routh Wrecker Service, Inc. v. Washington, 335 Ark. 232, 980 S.W.2d 240 (Arkansas 1998) 157

Chapter 9

Paula Corbin Jones v. William Jefferson Clinton and Danny Ferguson, 990 F. Supp. 657 (E.D.
   Arkansas 1998) 168
Thing v. La Chusa, 48 Cal. 3d 644, 771 P.2d 814 (California 1989) 175

Chapter 10

Russell-Vaughn Ford, Inc. v. E.W. Rouse, 281 Ala. 567, 206 So. 2d 371 (Alabama 1968) 185
Moore v. The Regents of the University of California, 51 Cal. 3d 120, 793 P.2d 479, 271
   Cal. Rptr. 146 (California 1990) 187

Chapter 11

Nardi v. Gonzalez, 165 Misc. 2d 336, 630 N.Y.S.2d 215 (Yonkers, New York 1995) 193
Foster v. Preston Mill Co., 44 Wash. 2d 440, 268 P.2d 645 (Washington State 1954) 202

Chapter 13

Soldano v. O'Daniels, 141 Cal. App. 3d 443, 190 Cal. Rptr. 310 (California 1983) 220
Riss v. City of New York, 22 N.Y.2d 579, 240 N.E.2d 860, 293 N.Y.S.2d 897 (New York 1968) 224

Chapter 14

Ward v. Forrester Day Care, Inc., 547 So. 2d 410 (Alabama 1989) 245
Potts v. Fidelity Fruit & Produce Co., Inc., 165 Ga. App. 546, 301 S.E.2d 903 (Georgia 1983) 252

Chapter 15

Parra v. Tarasco, Inc. d/b/a Jiminez Restaurant, 230 Ill. App. 3d 819, 595 N.E.2d 1186
   (Illinois 1992) 272
Mussivand v. David, 45 Ohio St. 3d 314, 544 N.E.2d 265 (Ohio 1989) 281
Gaines-Tabb v. ICI Explosives, USA, Inc., 160 F.3d 613 (10th Circuit 1998) 282

Chapter 16

O'Shea v. Riverway Towing Co., 677 F.2d 1194 (7th Circuit 1982) 290
Keans v. Bottiarelli, 35 Conn. App. 239, 645 A.2d 1029 (Connecticut 1994) 297

Chapter 17

Wagenblast v. Odessa School District No. 105–157–166J, 110 Wash. 2d 845, 758 P.2d 968 (Washington State 1988) 311
Knight v. Jewett, 3 Cal. 4th 296, 834 P.2d 696, 11 Cal. Rptr. 2d 2 (California 1992) 316

Chapter 18

Fein v. Permanente Medical Group, 38 Cal. 3d 137, 211 Cal. Rptr. 368, 695 P.2d 665 (California 1985) 327
Smith v. Lewis, 13 Cal. 3d 349, 118 Cal. Rptr. 621, 530 P.2d 589 (California 1975) 339

Chapter 19

MacPherson v. Buick Motor Co., 217 N.Y. 382, 111 N.E. 1050 (New York 1916) 350
Ressallat v. Burglar & Fire Alarms, Inc., 79 Ohio App. 3d 43, 606 N.E.2d 1001 (Ohio 1992) 362
Riley v. Becton Dickinson Vascular Access, Inc., 913 F. Supp. 879 (E.D. Pennsylvania 1995) 373

Chapter 20

In re Breast Implant Litigation, 11 F. Supp. 2d 1217 (D. Colorado 1998) 403

Chapter 21

Cassano v. Durham, 180 N.J. Super. 620, 436 A.2d 118 (New Jersey 1981) 430

Chapter 22

Franklin v. Hill, 264 Ga. 302, 444 S.E.2d 778 (Georgia 1994) 437
Berman v. Allen, 80 N.J. 421, 404 A.2d 8 (New Jersey 1979) 439

Chapter 23

Armory Park Neighborhood Assn. v. Episcopal Community Services, 148 Ariz. 1, 712 P.2d 914 (Arizona 1985) 460
Donnell v. California Western School of Law, 200 Cal. App. 3d 715, 246 Cal. Rptr. 199 (California 1988) 469

Chapter 24

Van Duyn v. Smith, 173 Ill. App. 3d 523, 527 N.E.2d 1005 (Illinois 1988) 482
Jeffrey Becker, Steven Becker, and Thomas Becker v. Kathleen Zellner and Associates, 292 Ill. App. 3d 116, 684 N.E.2d 1378 (Illinois 1997) 492

Chapter 25

Hamberger v. Eastman, 106 N.H. 107, 206 A.2d 239, 11 A.L.R. 3d 1288 (New Hampshire 1964) 504
Smyth v. The Pillsbury Co., 914 F. Supp. 97 (E.D. Pennsylvania 1996) 505
Peoples Bank and Trust Co. of Mountain Home, Conservator of the Estate of Nellie Mitchell, an Aged Person v. Globe International Publishing, Inc. doing business as "Sun", 978 F.2d 1065 (8th Circuit 1992) 510

Chapter 26

Dushkin and Others v. Desai, 18 F. Supp. 2d 117 (D. Massachusetts 1998) 519
Vokes v. Arthur Murray, Inc., 212 So. 2d 906 (Florida 1968) 521
Texaco, Inc. v. Pennzoil Co., 729 S.W.2d 768 (Texas 1987) 526

Chapter 27

Peterson v. Sorlien, 299 N.W.2d 123 (Minnesota 1980) 541
Katko v. Briney, 183 N.W.2d 657 (Iowa 1971) 550
Conn and Najera v. Gabbert, 119 S. Ct. 1292, 143 L. Ed. 2d 399 (1999) 562

Chapter 28

Colvin v. Industrial Indemnity, 83 Or. App. 73, 730 P.2d 585 (Oregon 1986) 574
Seitz v. L&R Industries, Inc., 437 A.2d 1345 (Rhode Island 1981) 578

TABLE OF FIGURES

1–1   Costs of Unintentional Injuries by Class, 1997 ($ Billions)
1–2   Types of Tort Cases in the Nation's 75 Largest Counties, 1992
1–3   Torts and Related Causes of Action: The Elements
1–4   Categories of Primary Authority in a Tort Case
1–5   Excerpt from a Court Opinion on a Torts Issue
1–6   Excerpt from a Page in a Statutory Code on a Torts Issue
1–7   Excerpt from an Administrative Regulation on a Torts Issue
1–8   Excerpt from a Page in a Volume of *Corpus Juris Secundum* on a Torts Issue
1–9   Excerpt from a Page in a Volume of *American Jurisprudence 2d* on a Torts Issue
1–10   Excerpt from a Page of a Legal Treatise on a Torts Issue
1–11   Excerpt from a Page from the *Index to Legal Periodicals and Books* That Provides
       Citations to Legal Periodical Literature on a Torts Issue
1–12   Excerpt from the First Page of an Annotation on a Torts Issue
1–13   Internet Sites Relevant to Tort Law
2–1   Legal Analysis in Tort Law
2–2   Connecting Facts to Elements in a Torts Case
2–3   Heading of a Legal Memorandum
3–1   Overview of Tort Litigation with Paralegal Roles
3–2   Guides for Fact Gathering in a Torts Practice
3–3   Fact Versions
3–4   The Spectrum of Believability
3–5   Fact Particularization
3–6   Beginning of a Witness Statement
3–7   Structure of a Negligence Complaint
3–8   How to Avoid Abusing a Standard Form
3–9   Sample Complaint
3–10   Sample Complaint
3–11   Sample Complaint
3–12   Sample Complaint
3–13   Sample Complaint
3–14   Pretrial Discovery Devices with Paralegal Roles
3–15   Sample Interrogatories
3–16   *Subpoena Duces Tecum* for Deposition
3–17   Request for Production of Documents and Things; Entry on Land for Inspection and
       Other Purposes
3–18   Request for Admissions
3–19   Flow Chart of Jury Trial, Appeal, and Enforcement Process
3–20   Trial Graphic Designed by a Paralegal in a Torts Case
3–21   Informal Investigative Techniques to Discover the Assets of a Judgment Debtor
4–1   Foreseeability Spectrum: How Foreseeable, If at All?
4–2   Foreseeability Determination "Formula"
6–1   Doctrine of Transferred Intent
7–1   Comparison of Peace Officer's and Private Citizen's Privilege to Arrest Without a
       Warrant
8–1   Probable Cause in Malicious Prosecution Suits
10–1   Factors Considered by a Court to Determine Whether an Interference with a Chattel
       Is Serious Enough for Conversion
12–1   Coverage of Negligence Topics
13–1   Duty in the Law of Negligence

13–2 Foreseeable and Unforeseeable Plaintiffs
13–3 Negligence: When Is a Duty Owed?
13–4 Misfeasance and Nonfeasance
13–5 Duty in Nonfeasance Cases
13–6 Special Relationships That Create a Duty to Use Reasonable Care in Nonfeasance Cases
14–1 Factors to Be Assessed in the Determination of Reasonableness
14–2 Reasonableness by Comparison
14–3 Perfect/Reasonable/Unreasonable Persons
14–4 Breach-of-Duty Equation
14–5 Objective and Subjective Standards
14–6 Elements of a Res Ipsa Loquitur Case
14–7 Spectrum of Likelihood
14–8 How to Determine Whether the Violation of a Statute Will Become the Standard of Care in a Negligence Action
14–9 Vicarious Unreasonableness
14–10 Checklist of Factors Used to Determine Scope of Employment
14–11 Liability for Torts of Independent Contractors
15–1 The Tests of Proximate Cause
15–2 Weight of the Evidence on Cause in Fact: Eight Possibilities
16–1 Jury Instructions on Damages
16–2 Software to Help Calculate Damages
17–1 Breach-of-Duty Equation
18–1 Largest Medical Malpractice Claims (1985–1998)
18–2 Sample Medical Malpractice Interrogatories Sent by a Defendant Hospital to Plaintiff(s)
18–3 Professional Liability Claims Against Law Firms by Error Group (1987–1991)
18–4 Mistakes of Attorneys
19–1 Consumer Products Involved in Injuries: Estimates of Cases Treated in Hospital Emergency Rooms: 1996–1997
19–2 Categories of Defects in Products
19–3 Status: Who Is the Plaintiff? Who Is the Defendant?
19–4 Examples of Trial Exhibits in a Products Liability Case That Paralegals Help Prepare, Order, and Manage
19–5 Sample Products Liability Complaint
19–6 Sample Products Liability Answer
20–1 Categories of Mass Tort Litigation
20–2 Threshold Requirements for a Class Action in Federal Court Under FRCP 23
20–3 Asbestos Cases in Federal Court: 1993–1996
20–4 Notice Printed in Newspapers of Tobacco Class Action Filed Against Liggett Group in Alabama State Court on Behalf of Smokers Nationwide
22–1 Intrafamily Torts
23–1 Private Nuisance: An Overview
23–2 Spectrum of Interference
23–3 Standard of Care Owed by Occupiers of Land to Persons Outside the Land
23–4 Trespasser, Licensee, Invitee
23–5 Breach-of-Duty Equation
24–1 Photo of Becker Brothers
25–1 Factors a Court Will Consider When Deciding Whether Plaintiff Was Engaged in a Private Activity
27–1 Elements of Consent
27–2 Overview of the Privilege of Self Defense
27–3 Overview of the Privilege of Defense of Others
27–4 Overview of the Privilege of Necessity
27–5 Overview of the Privilege of Defense of Property
27–6 Overview of the Privilege of Recapture of Chattels (Personal Property)
27–7 Federal Tort Claims Act
27–8 Sample Federal Tort Claims Act Complaint
27–9 Official Immunity of Government Employees for Common Law Torts and for Violations of the Civil Rights Act
28–1 Benefits/Disadvantages of Workers' Compensation (WC)
28–2 Filing a Claim
28–3 Example of a Schedule of Weeks of Benefits
29–1 Paralegal Roles During Settlement

Tens of thousands of injuries occur every day on the road, at work, in department stores, on the playground, and at home. The incidence of property damage is even higher. Although most of these mishaps never find their way into the legal system, many of them constitute potential torts. This is one of the reasons that tort law has a large impact on our lives. In addition to providing compensation to victims, one of the major objectives of tort law is behavior modification. A premise of tort litigation is that one of the most effective ways to force people to avoid injuring others is to hang the threat of a lawsuit over their heads. These are some of the dynamics we will explore in this book.

It is an exciting time to study tort law. Throughout the country there is considerable controversy on whether our system of tort litigation is causing more societal ills than it is solving. Horror stories abound on the editorial pages of our morning newspapers. An example is the seventeen-year-old Michigan high school student who sued Nintendo and Toys 'R Us where she bought a Nintendo video game machine. Her suit claims that she has an inflamed thumb from playing too much Nintendo. Her doctor calls her condition, "Nintendinitis," which prevents her from writing, from typing—and, of course, from playing video games! Such cases have prompted calls for reform. The chapters of this book will help place these calls in perspective.

Tort law is one of the first subjects taught to future attorneys in law school because the course can provide an excellent insight into the legal system, the practice of law, and legal analysis. Paralegal students can also gain this insight. In a personal-injury practice of law, the attorney-paralegal team makes an important contribution. In many offices, the team is inseparable. To achieve this work environment, one of the first steps is to understand the principles of tort law that the attorney applies in a personal-injury practice. This understanding is one of our major goals.

CHAPTER FORMAT

Each chapter includes features designed to assist students in understanding the material:

- A chapter outline at the beginning of each chapter provides a preview of the major topics in each chapter.
- Figures and tables are used extensively to clarify concepts and present detailed information in an organized chart form.
- Assignments are included within most chapters that ask students to apply concepts to particular fact situations.
- A chapter summary at the end of each chapter provides a concise review of the main concepts discussed.
- Key terms are printed in bold face type the first time they appear in each chapter. Also, a list of key terms is found at the end of each chapter to help students review important terminology introduced in that chapter.
- Examples are used extensively to highlight critical legal doctrines and practices.

- Prior to the discussion of every major tort in a chapter you will find a comprehensive checklist of definitions, defenses, relationships, paralegal roles, and research references for the tort. The checklist is designed to provide the "big picture" by making connections between the particular tort examined in the chapter and related material on other torts discussed in other chapters. The checklist will also serve as an on-the-job refresher for the individual torts.

CHANGES IN THE FOURTH EDITION

- Many new and revised examples and assignments are included.
- A new chapter on mass torts has been added with an emphasis on the themes of asbestos, breast implants, and tobacco products. In addition the chapter covers the ethical problem of attorney solicitation in mega-fee cases and the use of junk science in the courtroom.
- Extended discussion on paralegal roles in tort litigation is provided in Chapters 3, 20, and 29 as well as within the comprehensive checklists provided for every major tort throughout the book.
- The material on medical malpractice has been expanded into its own chapter along with legal malpractice.
- The number of extended case studies has been increased from 30 to 49. Among the controversial issues discussed in these court opinions are AIDS, the Oklahoma bombing, computer torts, assistance to the homeless, new age religions, invasion of privacy, defamation by the media, "veggie" libel, breast implants, defamation of paralegals, billion dollar verdicts and settlements, attacks on abortion clinics, civil rights torts, biomedical research, and the alleged tort committed by President Clinton that became part of his historic impeachment and Senate trial.
- The chapters give greater attention to the role of constitutional law and torts, particularly in the areas of civil rights, defamation, invasion of privacy, and intentional infliction of emotional distress.
- A new section on tort law on the Internet has been added to Chapter 1. In addition, the comprehensive checklists on the major torts throughout the book now include online references to the law governing specific torts.
- Expanded coverage on tort reform is found in the chapters on medical malpractice, products liability, and workers' compensation.
- New material on the use of computers in a torts practice has been added such as software for the calculation of damages discussed in Chapter 16.
- New material on torts committed through e-mail and the Internet has been added to Chapters 24 and 25.
- More material on alternative dispute resolution has been added, particularly in Chapter 3.
- The most important features of the five chapters on civil procedure in a torts case have been consolidated in Chapter 3 in conjunction with a greater emphasis on the role of paralegals in tort litigation.
- The main negligence chapters now come after most of the chapters on the intentional torts in order to take advantage of the analytical foundation that intentional torts provide for negligence.
- Legal research assignments have been cut back in order to concentrate on legal analysis, investigation, and drafting assignments.
- New material on the purposes of tort law and the creation of tort law by statute has been added to Chapter 1.
- The legal research material that was in Chapter 2 has been consolidated and moved to the end of Chapter 1.
- A greater variety of sample tort complaints has been included in Chapter 3.
- The comprehensive interviewing and investigation in an automobile case has been moved from Chapter 4 to Appendix C at the end of the book.

- A new chapter on strict liability has been added (Chapter 11) covering areas other than products liability, which is covered in Chapters 19 and 20.
- The negligence chapters now include the special statutory protection for the Good Samaritan against tort liability.
- In the negligence, products liability, and mass tort chapters, greater attention is given to risk-benefit analysis in determining whether there has been a breach of duty.
- Chapter 17 on negligence defenses includes greater coverage on the impact of comparative negligence on assumption of risk and the other defenses to negligence.
- Appendix E is new to the text and lists state agencies relevant to a torts practice.
- Appendix H now includes a position paper that seeks to distinguish the role of traditional paralegals from that of the relatively new position of legal nurse or legal nurse consultant in personal injury litigation.

TEACHING AIDS AND SUPPLEMENTS

- **Instructor's Manual with Test Bank** and overhead masters accompanies this text. The Instructor's Manual by William Statsky contains suggested answers to the assignments in the text, as well as teaching suggestions. The Test Bank was also prepared by William Statsky. The Test Bank contains true/false, multiple-choice, and discussion questions for each chapter. The questions are designed to test a student's knowledge of major chapter concepts.
- **Computerized Test Bank**—The Test Bank found in the Instructor's Manual is also available in a computerized format on CD-ROM. The platforms supported include Windows™ 3.1 and 95, Windows™ NT, and Macintosh. Features include:

  Multiple methods of question selection
  Multiple outputs—that is, print, ASCII, and RTF
  Graphic support (black and white)
  Random questioning output
  Special character support
- **Survival Manual for Paralegal Students,** written by Bradene Moore and Kathleen Reed of the University of Toledo, provides tips for making the most of paralegal courses. ISBN 0-314-22111-5.
- **Strategies and Tips for Paralegal Educators,** written by Anita Tebbe of Johnson County Community College, provides teaching strategies specifically designed for paralegal educators. It concentrates on how to teach and is organized in three parts: the WHO of Paralegal education—students and teachers; the WHAT of paralegal education—goals and objectives; and the HOW of paralegal education—methods of instruction, methods of evaluation, and other aspects of teaching. A copy of this pamphlet is available to each adopter of a West text. ISBN 0-314-04971-1.
- **WESTLAW®** West's on-line computerized legal research system offers students hands-on experience with a system commonly used in law offices. Qualified adopters can receive 10 free hours of WESTLAW®. WESTLAW® can be accessed with Macintosh and IBM PC and compatibles. A modem is required.
- **West's Paralegal Video Library** includes:
  - ABA Mock Trial Video—Anatomy of a Trial: A Contracts Case ISBN #0-314-07343-44
  - ABA Mock Trial Video—Product Liability ISBN #0-314-07342-6

These videos are available free to qualified adopters.

- **Web page** Come visit our Web site at *www.westlegalstudies.com,* where you will find a page dedicated to this text with sample material, hotlinks, and content updates. You will also find valuable information about our other West Legal Studies texts.

ACKNOWLEDGMENTS

Valuable contributions have been made to this edition by the team at West Legal Studies, an imprint of Delmar, a division of Thomson Learning. My thanks to Joan Gill, Acquisitions Editor, Rhonda Dearborn, Developmental Editor, Lisa Flatley, Editorial Assistant, and Betty Dickson, Production Editor.

A word of thanks, also, to the reviewers who made valuable suggestions for improving this text.

Laura Barnard
Lakeland Community College, OH

Mardy Chaplin, J.D.
Cuyahoga Community College, OH

John DeLeo
Central PA College, PA

Bob Diotalevi
The College of West Virginia, WV

Anne Dobmeyer
Bay Path College, MA

Paul Guymon
William Rainey Harper College, IL

Gail Krebs
Bryant and Stratton College, VA

Richard Mann
University of OK, OK

Christopher Sadler
Denver Paralegal Institute, CO

Jean Volk
Middlesex County College, NJ

Thomas Wright
Roger Williams University, RI

Please note the Internet resources are of a time sensitive nature and URL addresses may often change or be deleted.

Contact us at westlegalstudies@delmar.com.

Introduction to Tort Law and Practice

CHAPTER OUTLINE

- Scope
- Definitions and Purposes
- Elements of All the Torts
- Categories of Torts
- Introduction to Causation
- Relationship Between Tort Law and Other Areas of the Law
- Sources of Tort Law

SCOPE

Unintentional injuries take a staggering toll on society. In 1997, for example, the total economic cost of unintentional injuries amounted to $478 billion according to the National Safety Council. This included medical expenses, vehicle damage, wage and productivity losses, other employer costs, fire losses, and administrative expenses such as police and legal costs. (See Figure 1–1.) In addition, lost quality of life from these injuries is valued at $1,052 billion. This brings the total annual cost of unintentional injuries to $1.5 trillion.

Some of these injuries lead to tort litigation, which brings us to the subject of this book. For an overview of the types of tort cases filed in court, the kinds of harm alleged, and the amount of time taken to process the cases through the courts, see Figure 1–2. Our goal is to understand the law behind these statistics and the roles played by paralegals in a legal system designed to identify who should be compensated for losses that have been suffered.

FIGURE 1–1 Costs of unintentional injuries by class, 1997 ($ billions).

Cost	Total[a]	Motor-Vehicle	Work	Home	Other
Total	$478.3	$200.3	$127.7	$99.9	$66.1
Wage and productivity losses	238.4	70.2	63.4	63.7	44.5
Medical expenses	76.3	21.9	20.7	21.9	12.9
Administrative expenses[b]	82.4	56.2	26.5	4.5	3.9
Motor-vehicle damage	49.8	49.8	2.0		
Employer cost	21.3	2.2	11.9	4.3	3.4
Fire loss	10.1		3.2	5.5	1.4

Source: National Safety Council, *Accident Facts, 1998 edition.*
[a]Duplication between work and motor-vehicle, which amounted to $15.7 billion, was eliminated in the total.
[b]Includes the administrative cost of public and private insurance and police and legal costs.

FIGURE 1–2
Types of tort cases in state courts in the nation's 75 largest counties, 1992.

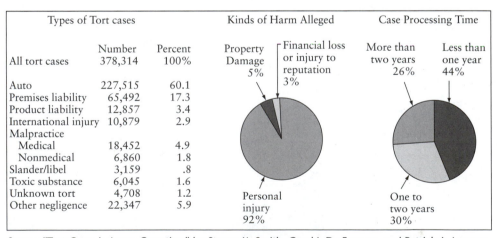

Types of Tort cases	Number	Percent
All tort cases	378,314	100%
Auto	227,515	60.1
Premises liability	65,492	17.3
Product liability	12,857	3.4
International injury	10,879	2.9
Malpractice		
Medical	18,452	4.9
Nonmedical	6,860	1.8
Slander/libel	3,159	.8
Toxic substance	6,045	1.6
Unknown tort	4,708	1.2
Other negligence	22,347	5.9

Kinds of Harm Alleged: Property Damage 5%; Financial loss or injury to reputation 3%; Personal injury 92%

Case Processing Time: More than two years 26%; Less than one year 44%; One to two years 30%

Source: "Tort Cases in Large Counties," by Steven K. Smith, Carol J. De Frances, and Patrick A. Langan, *Bureau of Justice Statistics Special Report,* 1995; *Bulletin,* 1997.

DEFINITIONS AND PURPOSES

When someone harms or damages the person or property of another, the primitive instinct of the victim is to strike back. Our legal system functions as a check against this instinct so that the peace of the realm is not disturbed. We ask everyone to resolve conflicts by seeking a **remedy** in court. In the medical world, a remedy is something that cures or treats an ailment. In the law, a remedy is a means by which the enforcement of a right is sought or the violation of a right is compensated for or otherwise redressed.

There are two kinds of disputes over which courts have **jurisdiction:** criminal disputes and civil disputes. (Jurisdiction is the authority or power of a court to resolve a dispute.) These disputes are based on the two major categories of law:

- **criminal law:** the law that governs crimes alleged by the government
- **civil law:** the law that governs rights and duties between private persons or between private persons and the government concerning matters other than the commission of a crime[1]

Criminal law covers those wrongs that are serious enough to be classified as crimes, e.g., murder, burglary. Civil law covers civil wrongs, which essentially consists of everything other than criminal wrongs. Tort law is one of the branches of civil law. Another familiar branch is contract law.

The word **tort** comes from the Latin word "tortus," meaning twisted, and from the French word "tort," meaning injury or wrong. The modern definition of tort is a civil wrong (other than a breach of contract) that causes injury or other damage for which our legal system deems it just to provide a remedy such as compensation. Although torts are different from crimes and breaches of contract, we will see later that there can be a close relationship among them. For example, a person's conduct may constitute both a crime and a tort.

> **EXAMPLE:**   When Mary isn't looking, Jim takes jewelry out of Mary's purse. For this action, Jim may face prosecution for larceny (resolved in a criminal court proceeding) and liability for the tort of conversion (resolved in a civil court proceeding).

When a crime is committed, public order is disrupted; therefore, the primary focus of criminal law is to vindicate a *public* wrong. The primary focus of tort law, however, is to vindicate a *private* wrong.

There are four major purposes of tort law:[2]

1. Peace: to provide a peaceful means for adjusting the rights of parties who might otherwise "take the law into their own hands." A courtroom is a neutral setting where the allegations can be aired in order to reach a rational resolution that the parties and the community can accept.
2. Deterrence: to deter wrongful conduct. Tort litigation takes place in public. The media is free to report what occurs in court. News that certain conduct forced someone into court and led to the payment of a large money judgment (called **damages**) can encourage the public to avoid that kind of conduct for fear of being subjected to a similar fate. This is sometimes called the "behavior modification" purpose of tort law. It has the effect of

---

[1]Civil law also refers to the legal system and kind of law that exists in many Western European countries other than England. See footnote 4.
[2]Adapted from John W. Wade et al., *Torts* 1 (9th ed. 1994).

encouraging socially responsible behavior such as making safer automobiles and removing ice from your sidewalk.

3. Restoration: to restore injured parties to their original position, insofar as this is possible, by compensating them for their injury. This is sometimes referred to as being **made whole.** Of course, it is often impossible to restore someone to the condition that existed before the injury occurred. If you negligently break my leg, I may never be restored to full health. Yet by providing compensation (damages), I am being made as whole as is humanly possible.

4. Justice: to identify those who should be held accountable for the harm that resulted. A tort case can involve one or more victims and one or more defendants alleged to have a role in causing the victim's injury. The law of torts is designed to sort through the involvement of all of the participants in order to identify who is culpable or blameworthy and to determine who, in fairness, should be made to pay.

Someone has suffered a loss due to an injury. The overriding question of tort law—and the theme of this book—is whether that loss should be shifted to someone else in light of the peace, deterrence, restoration, and justice objectives of tort law.

ELEMENTS OF ALL THE TORTS

Every tort is a **cause of action,** which is simply a legally acceptable reason for bringing a suit. When you **state a tort cause of action,** you list the facts that give you a right to judicial relief against the **tortfeasor**—the wrongdoer who is alleged to have committed the tort. Causes of action are rules. Every rule can be broken down into the component parts that we call **elements.** (As we will see in Chapter 2, the complete definition of an element is as follows: a portion of a rule that is one of the preconditions of the applicability of the entire rule.) The elements of the torts and related causes of action that we will study in this book are listed in Figure 1–3. For each cause of action listed in Figure 1–3, you are told what elements must be supported by facts in order to "state" the cause of action.[3]

CATEGORIES OF TORTS

There are three main categories of torts:

- intentional torts
- negligence
- strict liability torts

These categories are not ironclad. There are some torts that overlap the categories, as we will see.

Intentional Torts

An **intentional tort** is a tort in which a person either desired to bring about the result or knew with substantial certainty that the result would follow from what the person did or failed to do. Some of the major intentional torts are battery, assault, trespass, and false imprisonment. Many of the cases asserting these torts are relatively

(Cont. on page 8)

---

[3]When a party has offered sufficient evidence covering every element of a cause of action, that party has presented what is called a **prima facie case** that will entitle the party to prevail unless the other side offers convincing counterevidence.

Figure 1–3   Torts and related causes of action: The elements
(the page numbers in the first column tell you where the cause of action is discussed in this book).

The Cause of Action	Its Elements
1. Abuse of Process (p. 156)	i. Use of civil or criminal proceedings ii. Improper or ulterior purpose
2. Alienation of Affections (p. 436)	i. Intent to diminish the material relationship between spouses ii. Affirmative conduct iii. Affections between spouses are in fact alienated iv. Causation

3. Assault (Civil) (p. 119)	i. Act
	ii. Intent to cause either:
	  a. an imminent harmful or offensive contact, or
	  b. an apprehension of an imminent harmful or offensive contact
	iii. Apprehension of an imminent harmful or offensive contact to the plaintiff's person
	iv. Causation

4. Battery (Civil) (p. 105)	i. Act
	ii. Intent to cause either:
	  a. an imminent harmful or offensive contact, or
	  b. an apprehension of an imminent harmful or offensive contact
	iii. Harmful or offensive contact with the plaintiff's person
	iv. Causation

5. Civil Rights Violation (p. 560)	i. A person acting under color of state law ii. Deprives someone of a federal right
6. Conversion (p. 180)	i. Personal property (chattel) ii. Plaintiff is in possession of the chattel or is entitled to immediate possession iii. Intent to exercise dominion or control over the chattel iv. Serious interference with plaintiff's possession v. Causation
7. Criminal Conversation (p. 436)	Defendant has sexual relations with the plaintiff's spouse (adultery)

Defamation (two torts) (p. 475)
 8. Libel
	i. Written defamatory statement by the defendant
	ii. Of and concerning the plaintiff
	iii. Publication of the statement
	iv. Damages:
	  a. In some states, special damages never have to be proven in a libel case
	  b. In other states, only libel on its face does not require special damages. In these states, libel per quod requires special damages
	v. Causation

9. Slander	i. Oral defamatory statement by the defendant
	ii. Of and concerning the plaintiff
	iii. Publication of the statement
	iv. Damages:
	  a. Special damages are not required if the slander is slander per se
	  b. Special damages must be proven if the slander is not slander per se
	v. Causation

10. Disparagement (p. 529)	i. False statement of fact ii. Disparaging the plaintiff's business or property iii. Publication iv. Intent v. Special damages vi. Causation

Figure 1–3 (Continued)

The Cause of Action	Its Elements

11. Enticement of a Child or Abduction of a Child (p. 436)	i. Intent to interfere with a parent's custody over his or her child
	ii. Affirmative conduct by the defendant:
	   a. to abduct or force the child from the parent's custody, or
	   b. to entice or encourage the child to leave the parent, or
	   c. to harbor the child and encourage him or her to stay away from the parent's custody
	iii. The child leaves the custody of the parent
	iv. Causation

12. Enticement of Spouse (p. 436)	i. Intent to diminish the marital relationship between the spouses
	ii. Affirmative conduct by the defendant:
	   a. to entice or encourage the spouse to leave the plaintiff's home, or
	   b. to harbor the spouse and encourage him or her to stay away from the plaintiff's home
	iii. The spouse leaves the plaintiff's home
	iv. Causation

13. False Imprisonment (p. 132)	i. An act that completely confines the plaintiff within fixed boundaries set by the defendant ii. Intent to confine plaintiff or a third person iii. Causation of the confinement iv. Plaintiff was either conscious of the confinement or suffered actual harm by it
14. Intentional Infliction of Emotional Distress (p. 160)	i. An act of extreme or outrageous conduct ii. Intent to cause severe emotional distress iii. Severe emotional distress is suffered iv. Causation
15. Interference with Contract Relations (p. 523)	i. An existing contract ii. Interference with the contract by defendant iii. Intent iv. Damages v. Causation
16. Interference with Prospective Advantage (p. 527)	i. Reasonable expectation of an economic advantage ii. Interference with this expectation iii. Intent iv. Damages v. Causation
Invasion of Privacy (four torts)	
17. Appropriation (p. 507)	i. The use of the plaintiff's name, likeness, or personality ii. For the benefit of the defendant
18. False Light (p. 509)	i. Publicity ii. Placing the plaintiff in a false light iii. Highly offensive to a reasonable person
19. Intrusion (p. 503)	i. An act of intrusion into a person's private affairs or concerns ii. Highly offensive to a reasonable person
20. Public Disclosure of Private Fact (p. 508)	i. Publicity ii. Concerning the private life of the plaintiff iii. Highly offensive to a reasonable person
21. Malicious Prosecution (p. 148)	i. Initiation or procurement of the initiation of criminal proceedings ii. Without probable cause iii. With malice iv. The criminal proceedings terminate in favor of the accused

Figure 1–3 (Continued)

The Cause of Action	Its Elements
22. Misrepresentation (p. 514)	i. Statement of fact ii. Statement is false iii. Scienter (intent to mislead) iv. Justifiable reliance v. Actual damages
23. Negligence (p. 205)	i. Duty ii. Breach of duty iii. Proximate cause iv. Damages
Nuisance (two torts) (p. 451)	
24. Private Nuisance	An unreasonable interference with the use and enjoyment of private land
25. Public Nuisance	An unreasonable interference with a right that is common to the general public
26. Prima Facie Tort (p. 531)	i. Infliction of harm ii. Intent to do harm (malice) iii. Special damages iv. Causation
27. Seduction (p. 436)	The defendant has sexual relations with the plaintiff's daughter, with or without consent
28. Strict Liability for Harm Caused by Animals (p. 193)	Domestic Animals: i. Owner has reason to know the animal has a specific propensity to cause harm ii. Harm caused by the animal was due to that specific propensity Wild Animals: i. Keeping a wild animal ii. Causes harm
29. Strict Liability for Abnormally Dangerous Conditions or Activities (p. 195)	i. Existence of an abnormally dangerous condition or activity ii. Knowledge of the condition or activity iii. Damages iv. Causation
30. Strict Liability in Tort (p. 364)	i. Seller ii. A defective product that is unreasonably dangerous to person or property iii. User or consumer iv. Physical harm (damages) v. Causation
31. Trespass to Chattels (p. 180)	i. Personal property (chattel) ii. Plaintiff is in possession of the chattel or is entitled to immediate possession iii. Intent to dispossess or to intermeddle with the chattel iv. Dispossession or intermeddling v. Causation
32. Trespass to Land (p. 446)	i. An act ii. Intrusion on land iii. In possession of another iv. Intent to intrude v. Causation of the intrusion

Figure 1–3 (Continued)

The Cause of Action	Its Elements
Warranty (three causes of action)	
33. Breach of Express Warranty (p. 355)	i. A statement of fact that is false ii. Made with the intent or expectation that the statement will reach the plaintiff iii. Reliance on the statement by the plaintiff iv. Damage v. Causation
34. Breach of Implied Warranty of Fitness for a Particular Purpose (p. 360)	i. Sale of goods ii. Seller has reason to know the buyer's particular purpose in buying the goods iii. Seller has reason to know that the buyer is relying on the seller's skill or judgment in buying the goods iv. The goods are not fit for the particular purpose v. Damage vi. Causation
35. Breach of Implied Warranty of Merchantability (p. 359)	i. Sale of goods ii. By a merchant of goods of that kind iii. The goods are not merchantable iv. Damage v. Causation

straightforward. An easy battery case, for example, occurs when one person punches another in the nose. Other cases, however, are not so easy:

> **EXAMPLE:** Jim rides his bicycle through a large puddle of water directly in front of a bench where Mary is sitting. The water splashes on Mary who now sues Jim for battery. *Mary v. Jim* (battery)

When we study battery, we will see that this intentional tort can be committed by using an object such as a stick or water to make an offensive contact with someone. In the battery case of *Mary v. Jim,* a main issue will be whether Jim desired to hit Mary with the water or knew with substantial certainty that this would happen by riding through the water.

It is often difficult to get into someone's head to prove desire. Hence, plaintiffs use the alternative test of substantially certain knowledge. Compare the following two cases:

- I place a lighted match to the newspaper you are reading, which then catches fire. Assume that I was just joking around; I didn't want the newspaper to go up in flames.
- I light a cigarette in a room full of gasoline vapors, which then explode. Assume that I did not want this explosion to occur.

In the first case, a jury would probably conclude that I had substantially certain knowledge that your newspaper would catch fire when I placed a lighted match to it. To reach this result, the jury would rely on common sense and the everyday experience of all adults. The jury, however, might not conclude that I had substantially certain knowledge that the explosion would result in the second case. I may have been stupid to light a cigarette in that room, but stupidity or carelessness is not the same as substantially certain knowledge.

In the case of *Mary v. Jim,* suppose that the jury believes Jim when he asserts that he never wanted to splash Mary (perhaps because he never saw anyone on the bench) or that he did not know with substantial certainty that he would splash her (perhaps because he was riding the bike so slowly). In short, the jury believes Jim when he says that he splashed Mary by accident. If the jury accepts this version of the facts, there is no intentional tort because the element of intent has not been proven. There is, however, another tort that Jim may have committed: negligence.

Negligence

Negligence is harm caused by the failure to use reasonable care. An example might be colliding with someone while driving under the influence of medication that causes drowsiness. A critical distinction between a case of negligence and a case of an intentional tort is the distinction between an unreasonable risk of harm and the substantial certainty of harm:

- negligence: The heart of a plaintiff's negligence case is to show that the defendant created an *unreasonable risk of harm*.
- intentional tort: The heart of a plaintiff's intentional tort case is to show that the defendant wanted the harm to result or knew that there was a *substantial certainty of harm* based on what the defendant did or failed to do.

In our bicycle example of *Mary v. Jim,* assume that Mary does not sue for battery because of the difficulty of proving intent. Instead, she sues Jim under a negligence cause of action. Now the question will be whether Jim was so careless in riding the bike near the bench that he created an unreasonable risk of splashing people with water. The answer may depend on a variety of facts (which a paralegal might be asked to help uncover through interviewing and investigation) such as:

- how fast Jim was riding,
- how deep was the puddle,
- whether Jim knew his riding through other puddles in the area was causing splashes,
- how visible to Jim was Mary on the bench, etc.

A jury might believe Jim that he never wanted (desired) to splash Mary and that he did not have substantially certain knowledge that he would splash her, but still come to the conclusion that he created an unreasonable risk of splashing her. Hence, he committed negligence. In later chapters, we will examine other examples of this important distinction between negligence and intentional torts.

Strict Liability

The general meaning of **strict liability** (also called **absolute liability** or **liability without fault**) is responsibility regardless of blameworthiness or fault. If the defendant engages in a certain kind of conduct that causes harm, liability will result irrespective of intent, negligence, or innocence. An example would be performing an abnormally dangerous activity such as blasting. If the plaintiff is injured because of the explosion of the defendant's dynamite, the latter will be responsible (i.e., **liable**), regardless of whether the defendant desired to injure the plaintiff or knew with substantial certainty that the plaintiff or anyone else would be injured (intent), and regardless of whether the defendant acted unreasonably in setting off the explosive (negligence). As we will see, however, it is sometimes difficult to distinguish strict liability from negligence, especially in the area of products liability.

One final caution about definitions of legal terminology: use the definitions as points of departure only. The most dangerous definitions are the ones that give the appearance of universality. The meaning of a word or phrase may change when the context changes. In the practice of law, great care is needed to *localize* all definitions by determining what a particular court in your state meant by a word or phrase. Also, keep in mind that as courts struggle to do justice, they sometimes stretch the definitions to accommodate the result they want to reach on the facts before them. Again, consider all definitions as no more than starting points from which you need to make further inquiry.

INTRODUCTION TO CAUSATION

In Chapter 15 we will study causation extensively. Since causation will be referred to throughout the book, a brief introduction is in order here. There are two main tests that are used to determine whether something has in fact caused something else:

- **but-for test:** Without (i.e., "but for") the act or omission, the event would not have occurred.
- **substantial factor test:** The act or omission had a significant role in bringing about the event.

Either test is sufficient to establish causation, or to establish what we call **cause in fact.** The but-for test is used when there is only one alleged cause of an event in question. The substantial factor test is used primarily when more than one causal entity is alleged.

> **EXAMPLES:**   George fires his gun at Bill. Bill's left arm is paralyzed in the area hit by the bullet. But for the gunshot wound, Bill's arm would not have been paralyzed. Therefore, George's act of firing the gun caused the paralysis—it was a cause in fact of the paralysis.
> Two companies, Ajax Manufacturing Co. and Winthrop, Inc., pour chemicals into a county stream. After this dumping of chemicals by both companies, the stream is no longer suitable for fishing.

- The dumping of chemicals by Ajax into the stream had a significant role in making it unsuitable for fishing. Therefore, Ajax was a substantial factor in making it unsuitable. Ajax was a cause in fact of the pollution that made the stream unsuitable for fishing.
- The dumping of chemicals by Winthrop into the stream had a significant role in making it unsuitable for fishing. Therefore, Winthrop was a substantial factor in making it unsuitable. Winthrop was a cause in fact of the pollution that made the stream unsuitable for fishing.

Again, we will have a lot more to say about these two tests for causation in Chapter 15.

RELATIONSHIP BETWEEN TORT LAW AND OTHER AREAS OF THE LAW

The study of tort law will involve us in many other areas of the law:

Contract Law

When you buy a toaster, you have entered a contract of purchase. If the appliance explodes in your face when you try it for the first time, you may have an action for a breach of contract *and* an action for a tort. Most of the law of products liability grows out of such situations. Furthermore, it can be a tort to cause or induce someone to breach a contract.

Criminal Law

When Ted punches Bob in the face, two wrongs have probably been committed. Bob has been *personally* injured. He can bring a tort action against Ted for civil battery. In addition, as we have seen, the public has been injured. The public peace has been violated. The state prosecutor can bring a criminal action against Ted for a crime that might be called "battery" or "assault and battery." The tort action and the criminal action are separate proceedings. We need to examine the relationship between torts and crimes. For example, is it a tort to encourage the prosecutor to bring a criminal action that turns out to be groundless? We will answer this question when we study the tort called malicious prosecution.

Civil Procedure Law

A tort may lead to a lawsuit where civil procedure law governs jurisdiction, pleadings, discovery, trial, and appeal. We will review some of these topics with an emphasis on paralegal roles during the different stages of tort litigation. We will also cover alternative dispute resolution such as mediation and arbitration.

Family Law

There are a number of tort doctrines that are designed to protect aspects of the family. Examples include damages for loss of consortium and suits for wrongful adoption. In addition, family members can commit torts against each other. Whether they are allowed to sue for such torts depends on the scope of the intrafamily tort immunity in the state.

Constitutional Law

To deprive someone of federal civil rights under color of state law can be what is called a constitutional tort. In the law of defamation, the constitution has set new limits on the right to sue the media and, in the process, has revolutionized the law of libel and slander.

Estate Law

What happens when the wrongdoer dies before being sued by the injured party? Can the wrongdoer's estate be sued? Suppose the injured party dies before suing the wrongdoer. Can the estate of the injured party sue the wrongdoer? If so, what happens to the assets collected in the suit? We will examine these questions under the topic of survival and wrongful death.

State and Local Government Law

Can a city or state be sued in tort? Can a tort action be brought against the United States government? Answers to such questions involve the doctrine of sovereign immunity.

Real Property Law

There are a number of torts that are committed by or against landowners and land occupiers. Such torts sometimes raise questions like these: What is land? What is the possession of land?

Insurance Law

Insurance law has a major impact on tort litigation, particularly on the question of whether the parties will settle their dispute. Also, in many states, insurance companies can be sued for "bad faith" in how they handle claims made against them.

Environmental Law

Environmental rules and regulations can have an important impact on certain negligence and nuisance cases as well as in the area of mass tort litigation.

SOURCES OF TORT LAW

Where does tort law come from? Who writes the rules for establishing tort liability through litigation? Where are these rules found? These are our concerns in this section. Although many of these themes may be covered in a legal research course, it is helpful to reinforce them in the context of tort litigation.

Primary Authority

Primary authority is any law that a court could rely on in reaching a decision. Examples include court opinions (also called cases and decisions), statutes, constitutions, administrative regulations, administrative decisions, charters, ordinances, and rules of court. See Figure 1–4 for the definitions of these categories of primary authority and examples of how they could be involved in tort litigation.

FIGURE 1–4 Categories of primary authority involved in a tort case.

Category	Definition	Example
(a) Opinion	A court's written explanation of how it applied the law to the facts before it to resolve a legal dispute. Also called a case or a decision. (Most tort law is created in opinions.)	The case of *Smith v. Jones* rules that Jones negligently injured Smith in an automobile collision.
(b) Statute	A law passed by the legislature declaring, commanding, or prohibiting something.	Davis is injured in one of the elevators at Macy's Department Store. In the suit, Davis alleges that Macy's violated § 236 of the state's statutory code, which requires a monthly safety inspection of all elevators.
(c) Constitution	The fundamental law that creates the branches of government and identifies basic rights and obligations.	A story in *Time* magazine links Harris with the illegal drug trade. Harris sues for libel. *Time* argues that the suit violates the First Amendment right to freedom of the press.
(d) Administrative Regulation	A law of an administrative agency designed to explain or carry out the statutes and executive orders that govern the agency.	Simpson suffers food poisoning after eating a product of General Foods Inc. The suit alleges that General Foods failed to follow § 137.3, a regulation of the Food and Drug Administration on proper food labeling.
(e) Administrative Decision	An administrative agency's resolution of a controversy involving the application of administrative regulations, statutes, or executive orders that govern the agency.	In *Perry v. Commissioner,* the State Workers' Compensation Board rules that Perry is not entitled to benefits because his injury did not arise out of his employment.
(f) Charter	The fundamental law of a municipality or other local unit of government, authorizing it to perform designated governmental functions.	Adams can sue Portland for the injury caused by a city police officer because § 26 of the Portland charter waives sovereign immunity for injuries wrongfully caused by municipal employees within the scope of employment.
(g) Ordinance	A law passed by the local legislative branch of government (e.g., city council, county commission) that declares, commands, or prohibits something. (Same as a statute, but at the local level.)	Kelly sues Parker for trespass when Parker's cows damage Kelly's land. Parker argues that Kelly did not have the kind of fencing around his land required by § 22(g) of the County Ordinance on farm animal control.
(h) Rules of Court	The procedural laws that govern the mechanics of litigation (practice and procedure) before a particular court. Also called court rules.	Richardson sues his doctor for negligence. Under Superior Court Rule 38, all medical malpractice cases must be first heard by a magistrate, who must prepare a pretrial order before the case can commence in Superior Court.

Opinions   Court opinions (referred to as case law) are the foundation of tort law. In fact, the major way in which tort law comes into existence is through what is called **common law**. This is judge-made law created in the absence of statutes or other controlling law.[4] In effect, the courts create tort law when there is a vacuum. If, for example, the court has a dispute before it that is not governed by any statute or constitutional provision, the court can create law to govern that dispute. What it creates is called the common law. An example is invasion of privacy, which, as we will see in Chapter 25, consists of four separate torts. The courts created privacy tort law at a time when there were few or no statutes in this area. When a court creates common law, it relies primarily on the customs and values of the community from time immemorial. Very often these customs and values are described and enforced in old opinions, which are heavily referred to (i.e., cited) by modern courts in the continuing process of developing the common law.

Court opinions are printed in volumes called **reporters.** For example, in Figure 1–5 you will find the first page of the opinion called *Austria v. Bike Athletic Co.*, printed in volume 810 of the Pacific Reporter, 2d Series. This is a products liability case in which a high school student sued a helmet manufacturer after being severely injured in the head during football practice. Hundreds of thousands of tort opinions such as this can be found in the many sets of reporter volumes in the law library.

Statutes   The statutes passed by legislatures affect tort litigation in three significant ways:

Statutes Can Change the Common Law   Generally, statutes are superior in authority to court opinions. If the legislature desires to change the common law that has been developed by the courts, it can pass a statute making this change. Such a law is called a statute in **derogation of the common law.**

Statutes Can Define the Standard of Care   When a defendant is sued for negligence, one of the claims often made by the plaintiff is that the defendant violated a statute, e.g., a traffic statute or a license statute. In such cases, the court must examine the relationship between the common law of negligence and the statute that has allegedly been violated. As we will see in Chapter 14, the specific question is whether

---

[4]There are four interrelated meanings of the term *common law,* the last of which will be our main concern in this book.

At the broadest level, common law simply means case law—court opinions—as opposed to statutory law. In this sense, all case law develops and is part of the common law.

The term common law also refers to the legal system of England, America, and countries adopting or based on this legal system. Its counterpart is the *civil law* system of many Western European countries other than England, e.g., France. The origins of civil law include the jurisprudence of the Roman Empire set forth in the Code of Justinian. (Louisiana is unique in that its state law is in large measure based on the civil law—the **Code Napoléon**—unlike that of the remaining forty-nine common law states.) Although there is overlap between the two systems, there is generally a greater reliance on case law in common law systems than in civil law systems. The latter tend to place a greater emphasis on code or statutory law than common law systems.

More narrowly, common law refers to all of the case law *and* statutory law in England and the American colonies before the American Revolution. The phrase **at common law** will often refer to this colonial period, although the phrase also means the common law that existed before it was changed by statute.

The most prevalent definition of common law is judge-made law in the absense of statutes or other controlling law.

FIGURE 1–5
Excerpt from a court opinion on a torts issue: *Austria v. Bike Athletic Co.,* 810 P.2d 1312, 107 Or. App. 57 (1991).

1312 Or. 810 Pacific Reporter, 2d Series

107 Or.App. 57

John Austria, as guardian ad litem for Richard Austria, a minor, and John Austria and Perla Austria, husband and wife, Respondents.

v.

BIKE ATHLETIC CO., a foreign corporation, Colgate-Palmolive Co., a foreign corporation, and Kendall Research Center, a foreign entity, Appellants,

and

Renato Pizarro, M.D., Defendant

A8707–044789; CA A63376.

Court of Appeals of Oregon.

Argued and Submitted Nov. 21, 1990.

Decided May 1, 1991.

Parents of football player severely injured by blow to head during football practice brought suit against designer and manufacturer of football helmet, alleging defective design. The Circuit Court, Multnomah County, Richard L. Unis, J., entered judgment for plaintiffs, and defendants appealed. The Court of Appeals, Deits, J., held that there was evidence from which jury could conclude that player's injuries were caused by defects in football helmet.

Affirmed.

1. Products Liability 60
In order to prove that football player's injuries were caused by defects in football helmet, it was not necessary to prove amount of force received by player as result of blow, amount of force that he would have received had he been wearing helmet of alternative design or amount of force required to cause type of head injury he suffered.

2. Products Liability 83
Evidence, when combined with inferences drawn therefrom, was sufficient to allow jury to conclude that defective helmet caused football player's head injury; there was evidence about how and why player was struck, what a football helmet is supposed to do to reduce consequences of collision, that hematoma resulted from precisely the kind of trauma that helmets are designed to prevent, that properly designed helmet would have greatly reduced likelihood of hematoma and that helmet was not adequately designed to reduce that likelihood.

3. Products Liability 88
There was sufficient proof to submit to jury allegation that football helmet was improperly designed or manufactured so that it would allow energy of blow to be transmitted to head of user without absorbing sufficient amounts of energy so as to prevent closed head injuries.

James N. Westwood, Portland, argued the cause for appellants.

W. Eugene Hallman, Pendleton, argued the cause for respondents.

Before RICHARDSON, P.J., and NEWMAN and DEITS, JJ.

DEITS, Judge.

Richard Austria was severely injured by a blow to the head during football practice. Through his guardian ad litem, he sued the designer and manufacturer of the football helmet that he was wearing, alleging that its defective design was the cause of his injury. The jury returned a verdict for plaintiffs and defendants appeal, arguing, primarily, that the trial court erred in denying their motions for directed verdict, because there was insufficient evidence of causation. We affirm.

In September, 1985, Richard Austria was a sixteen year old high school junior. He was injured during football practice when the knee of another player forcefully struck the front of his helmet. Although he was dazed by the collision, he walked off the field on his own and seemed to suffer few ill effects. Approximately two weeks later, however, he experienced severe headaches. On October 1, he collapsed during football practice. A CT scan indicated that Richard had a subdural hematoma....

---

the statute will be used by the court to define the standard of care to which the defendant will be held.

Statutes Can Create New Torts Occasionally the legislature will create an entirely new tort cause of action. The state of Minnesota, for example, recently decided that the traditional torts did not sufficiently cover the harm caused when one person coerces another into prostitution. Consequently, the Minnesota legislature created the following new cause of action:

Minnesota Statutes Annotated § 611A.81. Cause of action for coercion for use in prostitution

Subdivision 1. Cause of action created.
(a) An individual has a cause of action against a person who:
(1) coerced the individual into prostitution;
(2) coerced the individual to remain in prostitution;

(3) used coercion to collect or receive any of the individual's earnings derived from prostitution. . . .

Subdivision 2. Damages.

A person against whom a cause of action may be maintained under subdivision 1 is liable for the following damages that resulted from the plaintiff's being used in prostitution or to which the plaintiff's use in prostitution proximately contributed:

(1) economic loss, including damage, destruction, or loss of use of personal property; loss of past or future income or earning capacity; and income, profits, or money owed to the plaintiff from contracts with the person; and

(2) damages for death. . ., personal injury, disease, and mental and emotional harm, including medical, rehabilitation, and burial expenses; and pain and suffering, including physical impairment.

This cause of action for coerced prostitution did not exist at common law. It is a creation of the legislature.

In the same manner, the legislature could pass a statute that creates a new defense to an existing cause of action or could set limits on the amount and kind of damages that can be awarded for certain torts that are successfully established. For example, some states have statutes that limit the amount of damages that can be awarded in a medical malpractice case.

Statutes are printed in volumes called **statutory codes.** For example, in Figure 1–6 you will find the beginning of § 2-621 in *Illinois Annotated Statutes.* This section of the statute provides some of the requirements for bringing products liability litigation against manufacturers and other defendants.

Administrative Regulations In a number of areas, administrative agencies and their regulations have a large role in tort litigation. At the state level, the best example is the workers' compensation agency or board that covers occupational accidents. At the federal level, an example of an important agency is the United States Consumer Product Safety Commission, as we will see when we examine products liability.

Administrative regulations are printed in volumes often called **administrative code** or **code of regulations.** For example, in Figure 1–7 you will find § 1118.1 in *Code of Federal Regulations.* This section covers investigations conducted by the United States Consumer Product Safety Commission on products alleged to be unsafe, such as athletic equipment used in school sports.

110 ¶ 2–621   CODE OF CIVIL PROCEDURE
Code of Civ.Proc. § 2–621

2–621. Product liability actions

§ 2–621. Product liability actions. (a) In any product liability action based in whole or in part on the doctrine of strict liability in tort commenced or maintained against a defendant or defendants other than the manufacturer, that party shall upon answering or otherwise pleading file an affidavit certifying the correct identity of the manufacturer of the product allegedly causing injury, death or damage. The commencement of a product liability action based in whole or in part on the doctrine of strict liability in tort against such defendant or defendants shall toll the applicable statute of limitation and statute of repose relative to the defendant or defendants for purposes of asserting a strict liability in tort cause of action.

(b) Once the plaintiff has filed a complaint against the manufacturer or manufacturers, and the manufacturer or manufacturers have or are required to have answered or otherwise pleaded, the court shall order the dismissal of a strict liability in tort claim against the certifying defendant or defendants, provided the certifying defendant or defendants are not within the categories set forth in subsection (c) of this Section. Due diligence shall be exercised by the certifying defendant or defendants in providing the plaintiff with the correct identity of the manufacturer or manufacturers, and due diligence shall be exercised by the plaintiff in filing an action and obtaining jurisdiction over the manufacturer or manufacturers. . . .

FIGURE 1–6
Excerpt from a page in a statutory code on a torts issue: *Illinois Annotated Statutes,* chapter 110, section 2-621 (Smith-Hurd 1983).

FIGURE 1-7 Excerpt from an administrative regulation on a torts issue: 16 Code of Federal Regulations § 1118.1 (1993).

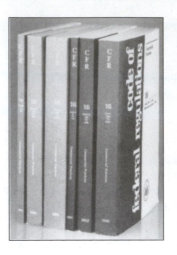

Consumer Product Safety Commission

PART 1118—INVESTIGATIONS, INSPECTIONS AND INQUIRIES UNDER THE CONSUMER PRODUCT SAFETY ACT
Subpart A—Procedures for Investigations, Inspections, and Inquiries
Sec.
1118.1 Definitions, initiation of investigations, inspections, and inquiries and delegations.
1118.2 Conduct and scope of inspections.
1118.3 Compulsory processes and service.
1118.4 Subpoenas.
1118.5 Investigational hearings.
1118.6 Depositions.
1118.7 Rights of witnesses at investigational hearings and of deponents at depositions.
1118.8 General or special orders seeking information.
1118.9 Motions to limit or quash subpoenas and general or special orders and delegation to modify terms for compliance.
1118.10 Remedies for failure to permit authorized investigation.

1118.11 Nonexclusive delegation of power.
Subpart A—Procedures for Investigations, Inspections, and Inquiries
§1118.1 Definitions, initiation of investigations, inspections, and inquiries and delegations.
(a) *Definitions.* For the purpose of these rules, the following definitions apply:
(1) *Act* means Consumer Product Safety Act (15 U.S.C. 2051, et seq.).
(2) *Commission* means the Consumer Product Safety Commission.
(3) *Firm* means a manufacturer, private labeler, distributor, or retailer of a consumer product, except as otherwise provided by section 16(b) of the Act.
(4) *Investigation* is an undertaking by the Commission to obtain information for implementing, enforcing, or determining compliance with the Consumer Product Safety Act and the regulations, rules, and orders issued under the Act.

Secondary Authority

Secondary authority is any nonlaw that a court could rely on to reach its decision. Examples include legal encyclopedias, legal treatises, legal periodical literature, and annotations. There are two main values of secondary authorities. First, they often contain extensive footnotes that will lead you to court opinions and other primary authorities on the tort (or other) topic you are examining. Second, they are usually written in a clear, basic writing style. Since they often cover the fundamentals, they are excellent starting points for the novice who needs a quick overview or summary of the law. This background can be very valuable in understanding the sometimes more difficult-to-read primary authority.

Courts can rely on secondary authority, although they are not required to do so. Secondary authority can only be **persuasive authority,** which means that the court is free to accept or reject the authority in rendering its decision.[5] When a dispute is in litigation, the main focus of the court is on the primary authority that applies. Secondary authority is of interest to the court when the legal issue before the court is a difficult one or when it is relatively novel. Otherwise, courts generally prefer that parties do not cite secondary authority in documents submitted to the court and exchanged among the parties during litigation.

Assume that you are working on a products liability case and that you want to find relevant discussions of the law in secondary authority. Here are some examples of law books you might use:

Legal Encyclopedia A **legal encyclopedia** is a multivolume set of books that alphabetically summarizes almost every legal topic. Two of the major legal encyclopedias are *Corpus Juris Secundum* (see Figure 1–8 for a sample page) and *American Jurisprudence 2d* (see Figure 1–9 for a sample page), both published by Thomson.

---

[5]When a court is required to follow an authority, the authority is called **mandatory authority.** Only primary authority can be mandatory authority. Not all primary authority, however, is mandatory authority.

72 C.J.S.Supp.

Assuming facts favorable to plaintiff suing a cigarette manufacturer for cancer or death resulting from cancer because of cigarette smoking, recovery might be grounded on negligence,[67] fraud for misrepresentation,[68] implied warranty,[69] or strict liability in tort.[70] While a manufacturer of cigarettes is strictly liable for foreseeable harm resulting from a defective condition in the product when the consumer uses the product for the purposes for which it was manufactured and marketed,[71] there is no absolute liability for the harmful effects of which no developed skill or foresight can avoid.[72] Thus the manufacturer of cigarettes cannot be held absolutely liable for cancer, or a consumer's death from cancer, allegedly caused by smoking cigarettes,[73] where plaintiff's claim negatives scientific foreseeability, peculiar defects in cigarettes, and cancer consequences to a substantial segment of the public.[74]

§66. Toys, Games, and Athletic or Recreational Equipment

The concept of products liability applies to a manufacturer of toys, games, and athletic or recreational equipment.

PRODUCTS LIABILITY §§65–66

Library References

Products Liability 60.

The concept of products liability applies to a manufacturer of toys, games, and athletic or recreational equipment.[75] Thus, the manufacturer may be liable under the doctrine of strict liability in tort for injury caused by a defective condition unreasonably dangerous to the user or consumer of such products.[76] Liability may also be grounded on negligence.[77] The manufacturer is not an insurer of safety of the equipment[78] and does not guarantee that it will not wear out and will last forever.[79] The manufacturer should anticipate the reasonably foreseeable risks in the use of the product.[80]

The manufacturer of toys, games, and athletic or recreational equipment, is under a duty to test and inspect the products for safety before marketing them,[81] but a wholesaler or retailer has been held not to have a duty to inspect products packaged by, and received from, a reputable manufacturer.[82] While a manufacturer has a . . . .

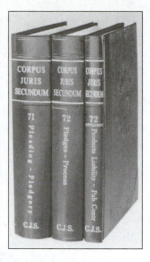

FIGURE 1–8 Excerpt from a page in a volume of *Corpus Juris Secundum* on a torts issue: 72 *Corpus Juris Secundum* Supplement § 66 (1975).

67. U.S.—Lartigue v. R. J. Reynolds Tobacco Co., C.A.La., 317 F.2d 19, certiorari denied 84 S.Ct. 137, 375 U.S. 865, 11 L.Ed.2d 32.

68. U.S.—Lartigue v. R. J. Reynolds Tobacco CO., C.A.La., 317 F.2d 19, certiorari denied 84 S.Ct. 137, 375 U.S. 865, 11 L.Ed.2d 92.

69. U.S.—Lartigue v. R. J. Reynolds Tobacco Co., C.A.La., 317 F.2d 19, certiorari denied 84 S.Ct. 137, 375 U.S. 865, 11 L.Ed.2d 92.

70. U.S.—Lartigue v. R. J. Reynolds Tobacco Co., C.A.La., 317 F.2d 19, certiorari denied 84 S.Ct. 137, 375 U.S. 865, 11 L.Ed.2d 92.

71. U.S.—Lartigue v. R. J. Reynolds Tobacco Co., C.A.La., 317 F.2d

18, certiorari denied 84 S.Ct. 137, 375 U.S. 865, 11 L.Ed.2d 92.

72. U.S.—Lartigue v. R. J. Reynolds Tobacco Co., C.A.La., 317 F.2d 19, certiorari denied 84 S.Ct. 137, 375 U.S. 865, 11 L.Ed.2d 92.

73. U.S.—Hudson v. R. J. Reynolds Tobacco Co., C.A.La., 427 F.2d 541—Green v. American Tobacco Co., C.A.Fla., 409 F.2d 1166, certiorari denied 90 S.Ct. 912, 397 U.S. 911, 25 L.Ed.2d93—Lartigue v. R. J. Reynolds Tobacco Co., C.A.La., 317 F.2d 19, certiorari denied 84 S.Ct. 137, 375 U.S. 865, 11 L.Ed.2d 92.

74. U.S.—Hudson v. R. J. Reynolds Tobacco Co., C.A.La., 427 F.2d

541.

75. Ind.—Dudley Sports Co. v. Schmitt, 279 N.E.2d 266, 151 Ind.App.217.

Golf cart

Purchaser of allegedly defective golf carts could maintain action against manufacturer to recover for loss of his bargain and cost of making repairs, even though parts were purchased from a dealer and not directly from the manufacturer.

Mich.—Cova v. Harley Davidson Motor Co., 812 N.W.2d 800, 26 Mich.App.602.

76. Baseball sunglasses

U.S.—Filler v. Rayex Corp., C.A.Ind., 435 F.2d 336.

---

§ 1. GENERALLY; "PRODUCTS LIABILITY" DEFINED

The term "products liability," a phrase almost unknown to the legal profession in earlier years, is now almost universally applied to the liability of a manufacturer, processor, or nonmanufacturing seller for injury to the person or property of a buyer or third party caused by a product which has been sold. The subject matter of products liability was formerly dealt with under such legal classifications as "negligence," "torts," or "sales." Particularly in light of the development of the doctrine of strict liability in tort, however,[1] it is clear that "products liability" has become a legal heading or subject in its own right.

The paradigmatic products liability action is one where a product which is reasonably certain to place life and limb in peril, and is distributed without reinspection, causes bodily harm, and a manufacturer is liable regardless of whether it is negligent because public policy demands that responsibility be fixed wherever it will most effectively reduce the hazards to life and health inherent in defective products that reach the market.[2] Typically, the term "products liability" covers any liability of a manufacturer or other seller or a product, where personal injury or damage to some other property is caused by a defect in the product.[3] The manufacturer's duty of care includes protection against property damage, which traditionally means damages to other property caused by a defective product; such damage is so akin to personal injury that the two are treated alike.[4]

Products liability may also include any liability arising because some defect causes loss or destruction of the product itself.[5] . . .

FIGURE 1–9
Excerpt from a page in a volume of *American Jurisprudence 2d* on a torts issue: 63 *American Jurisprudence 2d* § 1 (1996).

[1] §§ 517 et seq.

[2] East River S.S. Corp. v Transamerica Delaval, 476 US 858, 90 L Ed 2d 865, 106 S Ct 2295, CCH Prod Liab Rep ¶ 11008, 1986 AMC 2027, 1 UCCRS2d 609 (not followed on other grounds by Washington Water Co. v Graybar Elec. Co., 112 Wash 2d 847, 774 P2d 1199, CCH Prod Liab Rep ¶ 12233).

[3] Greenman v Yuba Power Products, Inc., 59 Gal 2d 57, 27 Cal Rptr 697, 377 P2d 897, 13 ALR3d 1049 (which first judicially applied the doctrine of strict liability in tort).

[4] East River S.S. Corp. v Transamerica Delaval, 476 US 858, 90 L Ed 2d 865, 106 S Ct 2295, CCH Prod Liab Rep ¶ 11008, 1986 AMC 2027, 1 UCCRS2d 609 (not followed on other grounds by Washington Water Power Co. v Graybar Elec. Co., 112 Wash 2d 847, 774 P2d 1199, CCH Prod Liab Rep ¶ 12233).

[5] See, for example, Gherna v Ford Motor Co. (1st Dist) 246 Cal App 2d 639, 55 Cal Rptr 94 (an action for the sudden destruction of a car by fire because of an alleged defect therein).

Legal Treatise A legal treatise is a book written by a private individual (or by a public official writing as a private citizen) that provides a summary or commentary on a legal topic. Perhaps the most famous and widely used legal treatise is *Prosser and Keeton on the Law of Torts* (see Figure 1–10 for a sample page).

Another extremely important legal treatise is *Restatement of Torts*, published by a private organization of scholars, the American Law Institute. Many courts are greatly influenced by the *Restatement*, particularly when these courts are dealing with questions or issues that are relatively new for their states. Products liability litigation is a major example of this; a large number of courts have agreed with and have adopted positions of the *Restatement* on strict liability in tort. These positions are found within the volumes of *Restatement (Second) of Torts* (1965, 1977, 1979).

FIGURE 1–10
Excerpt from a page of a legal treatise on a torts issue: W. Page Keeton et al., *Prosser and Keeton on the Law of Torts* § 95 (5th ed. 1984).

Chapter 17

PRODUCTS LIABILITY

Table of Sections

Sec.
95. Theories of Recovery and Types of Losses.
95A. Warranty and Intangible Economic Losses.
96. Negligence and Liability for Physical Harm to Persons and Tangible Things.
97. Strict Liability in Warranty for Physical Harm to Persons and Tangible Things.
98. Strict Liability in Tort for Physical Harm to Persons and Tangible Things.
99. Meaning of Dangerously Defective or Unsafe Products.
100. Parties.
101. Summary—Interests Protected and Theories of Recovery.
102. Contributory Negligence, Misuse, and Other Intervening Misconduct.
103. Proof.
104. Other Suppliers.
104A. Real Estate Transactions.

§95. Theories of Recovery and Types of Losses

Products liability is the name currently given to the area of the law involving the liability of those who supply goods or products for the use of others to purchasers, users, and bystanders for losses of various kinds resulting from so-called defects in those products.

At the very outset, it is important to make a distinction between two types of product conditions that can result in some kind of loss either to the purchaser or a third person. One is a dangerous condition of the product or, if one prefers, a product hazard;[1] the other is the inferior condition or . . . .

1. A recent government estimate placed the number of consumer product injuries (both in and out of the home) at 36 million for 1977. See Prod.Saf. & Liab.Rep. (BNA), June 29, 1979, 511. The total cost of such injuries to the nation has been estimated at $20 billion or more per year. Owen, Punitive Damages in Products Liability Litigation, 1976, 74 Mich.L.Rev. 1258–59 n. 2.

677

As we will see in Chapter 19, some controversial changes were made in the most recent addition to the field *Restatement (Third) of Torts: Products Liability* (1998).

Legal Periodical Literature   A **legal periodical** is an ongoing publication (e.g., published six times a year) containing articles, case notes, and other information on legal topics. When published by law schools, legal periodicals are often called **law reviews** or **law journals,** e.g., *Harvard Law Review, Yale Law Journal.* Two of the main indexes to legal periodical literature are the *Current Law Index* and the *Index to Legal Periodicals and Books.* See Figure 1–11 for a sample page from the *Index to Legal Periodicals and Books.*

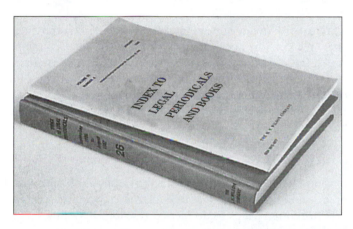

FIGURE 1–11
Excerpt from a page from the *Index to Legal Periodicals and Books* that provides citations to legal periodical literature on a torts issue.

SUBJECT AND AUTHOR INDEX   199

Prodan, Pamela
The legal framework for Hydro-Quebec imports, 28
  Tulsa L.J. 435–75 Spr '93
Products liability
      See also
      Strict liability
      Tobacco industry
Apportionment of damages—Third Circuit predicts Pennsylvania courts would not allow jury to apportion liability in a cigarette smoking, asbestos exposure case—Borman v. Raymark Industries, Inc., 960 F.2d 327 (1992). R.K. Shuter, student author. 66 *Temp.L.Rev.* 223–38 Spr '93
Cipollone v. Liggett Group, Inc. [112 S.Ct. 2608 (1992)]: one step closer to exterminating the FIFRA presumption controversy. C. E. Boeh, student author. 81 *Ky.L.J.* 749–78 Spr '92/'93
Constitutional law—pre-emption—the Federal Cigarette Labeling and Advertising Act's express pre-emption provision defines the pre-emptive reach of the Act and must be construed narrowly. Cipollone v. Liggett Group, Inc., 112 S.Ct. 2608 (1992). M. A. Bakris, student author. 70 *U.Det.Mercy L.Rev.* 487–512 Wint '93.
Dangerous products and injured bystanders. R.F. Cochran, Jr. 81 *Ky.L.J.* 687–725 Spr '92/'93

Drugs
  California
Kill or cure? Pogash. 13 *Cal.Law.* 48–51 + Je/'93
  Motor vehicles
The tide has turned. L. E. Cohen. 29 *Trial* 75–9 Ja '93
  Alaska
Products liability in Alaska—a practitioner's overview. T. A. Matthews. 10 *Alaska L.Rev.* 1–32 Je'93
  California
Don't kill the messenger 'till you read the message: products liability verdicts in six California counties, 1970–1990. S. Daniels, J. Martin. 16 *Just.Sys.J.* 69–95 '93
  European Community countries
The asbestos problem and the European Economic Community. E. R. Bothwell, student author. 31 *Column. J. Transnat'l L.* 205–30 '93
  Michigan
Uniform Commercial Code—Article 2—the economic loss doctrine bars an action in tort and a buyer's sole remedy is found under Article 2, where a product purchased for commercial purposes causes economic loss. Neibarger v. Universal Cooperatives, Inc., 486 N.W.2d 612 (Mich.1992). C. W. Fabian, student author. 70 *U.Det.Mercy L.Rev.* 513–29 Wint '93

FIGURE 1–12
Excerpt from the first page of an annotation on a torts issue: Lee R. Russ, *Products Liability: Competitive Sports Equipment*, 76 *American Law Reports*, 4th 201 (1990).

Products Liability—Sports   76 ALR4th
76 ALR4th 201

ANNOTATION

PRODUCTS LIABILITY: COMPETITIVE SPORTS EQUIPMENT

by

Lee R. Russ, J.D.

§7. Football helmets—liability of manufacturers and sellers
[a] Failure to protect against spinal injury—liability supportable

In the following products liability cases involving claims that a football helmet was defective in failing to protect its wearer against injuries to the spine, the courts held that, under the particular circumstances presented, there was sufficient evidence of liability to support a judgment in favor of the plaintiff or to reverse a judgment in favor of the manufacturer of the helmet at issue.

Finding several evidentiary rulings to have been erroneous, the court in Galindo v. Rid-

dell, Inc. (1982, 3d Dist) 107 Ill App 3d 139, 62 Ill Dec. 849, 437 NE2d 376, CCH Prod Liab Rep ¶ 9374, reversed a judgment for the maker of a "TK-2" football helmet who was sued by a high school football player for spinal injuries sustained while attempting to make a tackle in a varsity football game. The helmet consisted of a plastic shell on the outside, with a grey rubber pad and cloth strap suspension system on the inside. The plaintiff was paralyzed from the neck down as a result of a dislocation fracture at the fifth and sixth cervical vertebrae. The plaintiff sued on theories of strict liability. . . .

Annotations An **annotation** is a set of notes and commentary on issues in court opinions. The major annotations are published by Thomson in books called *American Law Reports*. These books print the annotations and the court opinions that contain the issues treated in the annotations. The main units of *American Law Reports* are A.L.R., A.L.R.2d, A.L.R.3d, A.L.R.4th, A.L.R.5th, and A.L.R. Fed. Annotations provide excellent leads to case law on thousands of issues. For an example, see Figure 1–12.

Tort Law Online

It is now possible to obtain a great deal of **online** information that is relevant to a torts practice. In addition to research into cases, statutes, and other primary authority, a law firm often needs to do factual research. Examples include obtaining information about the manufacturer of a product, the weather conditions on the day of an accident, the assets of a defendant, or the location of a potential witness. "Nearly anything you can imagine is out there," commented one researcher.[6]

The two major commercial online services, for which you pay a subscription fee, are WESTLAW and LEXIS-NEXIS. An important jury verdict database in both of these services allows you to search court records to find out what jury verdicts have been returned for certain bodily injuries caused by specific products. Such information can be invaluable in deciding whether to settle a case and in making a presentation to a liability insurance company.

In addition to these fee-based, online services, you can obtain a great deal of information on the **Internet** through the **World Wide Web.** Most of it is free once you have the basic connection to the Internet. Greater care is needed, however, when using information found on the Internet. Unlike services such as WESTLAW and LEXIS-NEXIS, the Internet is not centrally regulated or monitored. Consequently, you cannot have the same assurance in the accuracy and quality of material obtained from the Internet sites that you can for material obtained from the fee-based services or, indeed, from traditional bound volumes. Nevertheless, the vast resources of the Internet are useful as starting points. See Figure 1–13 for several Internet sites relevant to tort law.

---

[6]Samuels, David (1998, August 2). The White House Shamus, *New York Times Magazine*, p. 40.

FIGURE 1–13
Internet sites relevant to tort law.

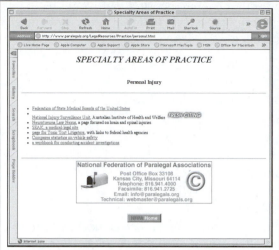

National Federation of Paralegal Associations
Personal Injury Law Links
http://paralegals.org/LegalResources/Practice/
personal.html

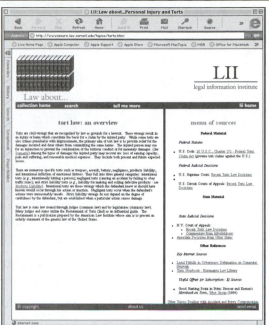

Legal Information Institute of Cornell Law School
Torts Links
http://www.law.cornell.edu/topics/torts.html

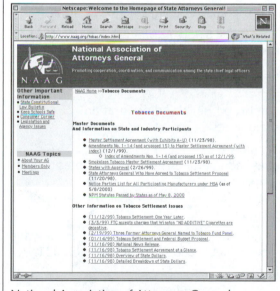

National Association of Attorneys General
http://www.naag.org/tobac/index.html

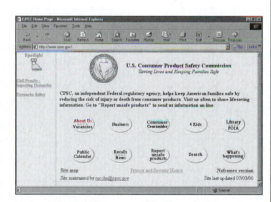

United States Consumer Product Safety
Commission
http://www.cpsc.gov

Here are some additional Internet sites that would be of interest to someone in a law office doing work on personal injury or property damage cases. The sites are clustered into five categories:

Torts, Accidents, and Injuries

Factual Research

Tort Litigation Planning

General Legal Sites

Medical Sites

Torts, Accidents, and Injuries

- American Tort Reform Association
http://www.atra.org

- Emory Law Library, Electronic Reference Desk, Tort Law Links
http://www.law.emory.edu/LAW/refdesk/subject/tort.html

- FindLaw [find law firms practicing tort law]
http://firms.findlaw.com/firms/pract46.html

- Hieros Gamos, Guide to Tort Law
http://www.hg.org/torts.html

- Junk Science Review
http://www.junkscience.com

- Jurist: The Law Professors' Page, Torts Course Outlines
http://jurist.law.pitt.edu/sg_torts.htm

- LawJournal Extra
http://www.ljx.com/practice/negligence/index.html

- National Highway Traffic Safety Administration (NHTSA)
http://www.nhtsa.dot.gov

- National Transportation Safety Board
http://www.ntsb.gov

- Occupational Safety and Health Administration
http://www.osha.gov

- Products Liability Sites
http://ublib.buffalo.edu/libraries/units/law/remotesites/liability.html
http://www.productslaw.com
http://www.ljx.com/practice/productliability/index.html
http://www.cpsc.gov

- Rand Institute, Understanding Mass Personal Injury Litigation
http://www.rand.org/publications/RB/RB9021/RB9021.word.html

- Tobacco Litigation
http://www.tobacco-litigation.net
http://www.house.gov/commerce/TobaccoDocs/documents.html
http://stic.neu.edu/settlement/6-20-settle.htm
http://www.naag.org/tobac/index.html

- Toxic Torts
http://www.toxlaw.com
http://www.toxlaw.com/toxtalk

- United States Consumer Product Safety Commission
http://www.cpsc.gov

- World Wide Web Virtual Library: Law: Torts
http://www.law.indiana.edu/law/v-lib/tort.html
http://www.law.indiana.edu/v-lib

- Workers' Compensation
  http://www.law.cornell.edu/topics/workers_compensation.html
  http://www.dol.gov/dol.esa/public/regs/statutes/owcp/stwclaw/stwclaw.htm
  http://www.prairielaw.com/wc

Factual Research
- Chemical Manufacturers Association
  http://www.cmahq.com

- Database America [information about parties and witnesses; people finder]
  http://www.databaseamerica.com

- Hoover's Online [company profiles]
  http://www.hoovers.com

- InvestQuest [annual reports for public companies]
  http://www.investquest.com

- Kelly Blue Book Web Site [value of motor vehicles]
  http://www.kbb.com

- KnowX [public records information on businesses, court filings, etc.]
  http://www.knowx.com

- People Finders
  http://www.whowhere.lycos.com
  http://www.isleuth.com
  http://www.theultimates.com
  http://bigfoot.com
  http://people.yahoo.com
  http://infospace.com
  http://www.switchboard.com

- Social Security Death Index
  http://www.ancestry.com/ssdi/advanced.htm

- Webagator [investigative resources on the web]
  http://www.inil.com/users/dguss/wgator.htm

Tort Litigation Planning
- Association of Trial Lawyers of America
  http://www.atlanet.org

- CataLaw, Negligence and Malpractice Law [choose "Negligence and Malpractice" topic]
  http://www.catalaw.com

- Defense Research Institute
  http://www.dri.org

- DepoConnect [depositions for plaintiff attorneys from other cases]
  http://www.depoconnect.com

- Directory of Expert Witnesses and Consultants
  http://www.expertpages.com

- Federation of Insurance and Corporate Counsel
  http://www.thefederation.org

- Frankenfeld Report Newsletter [calculation of damages]
  http://www.frankenfeld.com/newsletter

- Hiero Gamos [finding expert witnesses]
  http://www.hg.org/expert-serv.html

- Mediation Information and Resource Center
  http://www.mediate.com

- National Association of Professional Process Servers
  http://www.napps.org/napps.htm

- National Directory of Expert Witnesses
  http://www.claims.com

- Yearbook of Experts and Authorities
  http://www.yearbooknews.com

General Legal Sites

- Center for Information Law and Policy
  http://www.law.vill.edu

- Cornell's Legal Information Institute
  http://www.law.cornell.edu

- FindLaw
  http://www.findlaw.com

- GPO Access [Official Federal Government Information]
  http://www.access.gpo.gov/su_docs

- Hiero Gamos
  http://www.hg.org

- Internet Legal Resource Guide
  http://www.ilrg.com

- LawCrawler
  http://lawcrawler.findlaw.com

- Law Engine
  http://www.fastsearch.com/law/main.htm

- LawGuru
  http://www.lawguru.com/search/lawsearch.html

- Thomas [Library of Congress]
  http://thomas.loc.gov

Medical Sites (for information on injuries and diseases)

- Alternative Medicine HomePage
  http://www.pitt.edu/~cbw/altm.html

- American Medical Association
  http://www.ama-assn.org

- Anatomy Sites
  http://www.ama-assn.org/insight/gen_hlth/atlas/atlas.htm
  http://www.vh.org/Providers/Textbooks/BrainAnatomy/BrainAnatomy.html

- Centers for Disease Control
  http://www.cdc.gov

- Forensic Information Services [Zeno's Forensic Page]
  http://www.bart.nl:80/~geradts/forensic.html

- Healthfinder
  http://www.healthfinder.gov

- Internet Drug Index
  http://www.rxlist.com

- Internet Grateful Med [access to numerous resources such as MEDLINE]
  http://igm.nlm.nih.gov

- Martindale's Health Science Guide
  http://www-sci.lib.uci.edu/HSG/HSGuide.html

- Mayo Clinic
  http://www.mayohealth.org

- Mediconsult [general medical search engine]
  http://www.mediconsult.com

- Med Engine
  http://www.fastsearch.com/med/main.htm

- Medical Abbreviations
  http://www.accused.com/contents/authors/Medabrev.html

- MEDLINE
  http://www.nlm.nih.gov/databases/freemedl.html

- Medscape [medical search engine]
  www.medscape.com

- MedWeb [medical search engine]
  http://www.medweb.emory.edu

- National Institutes of Health
  http://www.nih/health

- National Library of Medicine
  http://www.nlm.nih.gov

- National Patient Safety Foundation
  http://www.npsf.org

- PubMed [National Library of Medicine's search service to MEDLINE]
  http://www.ncbi.nlm.nih.gov/PubMed

Another useful resource on the Internet is the mailing lists, called **listservs.** A listserv is a program that allows online mailing lists (e-mail lists) to be managed automatically. Joining or subscribing to a listserv is free. When you subscribe to one that relates to the law, you can ask research or "I need help" questions that are read by potentially thousands of other members of the list. Here is an example of the kind of question a paralegal might post on a listserv:

> I am a personal injury paralegal in a law firm in Boston. We are trying to locate a 1969 Pontiac Skylark to use in an accident reconstruction. We need to test the car. The manufacturer wasn't much help. I've tried used-car dealers and even some large junk yards. So far no luck. Anyone got any ideas where I might check?

This message was read by paralegals and others all over the country—everyone who was a subscriber to this listserv. Almost instantly responses started flowing onto the list so that everyone could read them. They offered practical suggestions on how to locate a 1969 Pontiac Skylark. Listservs can be an excellent way to obtain and share legal information. For a catalog of every major listserv on the Internet, all of which are free, and how to subscribe, see http://www.lawguru.com/subscribe/listtool.html and http://www.liszt.com.

**ASSIGNMENT
1.1**

When answering the following questions, give the full name and Internet address of the sites you use, the dates you visited the sites, and, if provided, the dates the sites were last updated. You can use any of the sites listed in this chapter as well as links within them.

a. Find a reference to a court opinion written by a state court in your state on any tort topic. What is the name of the opinion? What tort did it cover? What court wrote it?

b. Find a discussion of any disease that you select. Include a definition of the disease.

c. Find a federal regulation on air bags. Quote a line from the regulation.

SUMMARY

A remedy is a means by which the enforcement of a right is sought or the violation of a right is compensated for or otherwise redressed. Criminal law governs a suit brought by the government for the commission of a crime. Civil law governs a suit between private persons or between private persons and the government over a matter other than the commission of a crime. Tort law is one of the branches of the civil law. A tort is a civil wrong (other than a breach of contract) that causes injury or other damage for which our legal system deems it just to provide a remedy such as compensation. There are four major purposes of tort law: to provide a peaceful means for adjusting the rights of parties, to deter wrongful conduct, to try to restore injured parties to their original position, and to identify who in fairness should be responsible for the harm that resulted.

A cause of action is a legally acceptable reason for bringing a suit. Tort causes of action have elements. To state a tort cause of action is to list the facts that support each element of the tort. There are three main categories of torts: intentional torts (the actor desires the result or knows with substantial certainty that it will occur), negligence (the actor creates an unreasonable risk of harm), and strict liability torts (the actor engages in certain conduct for which the law imposes liability regardless of intent or reasonableness). The two tests for causation (cause in fact) are the but-for test and the substantial factor test.

Primary authority is any law that a court can rely on in reaching a decision. The major primary authorities are court opinions, statutes, constitutions, administrative regulations, administrative decisions, charters, ordinances, and rules of court. Common law is judge-made law in the absence of statutes or other controlling law. Statutes can change the common law, define the standard of care in negligence cases, and create new torts and defenses. Secondary authority is any nonlaw that a court can rely on to reach a decision. Examples include legal encyclopedias, legal treatises, legal periodical literature, and annotations. Secondary authority is helpful in finding and explaining primary authority. Courts also like to see references to secondary authority on difficult or novel legal issues. There is a great deal of legal and factual information relevant to a torts litigation practice that is available online from commercial, fee-based services and from the Internet through the World Wide Web.

KEY TERMS

remedy   3
jurisdiction   3
criminal law   3
civil law   3
tort   3
damages   3
made whole   4
cause of action   4
state a tort cause of action   4
tortfeasor   4
elements   4
prima facie case   4
intentional tort   4
negligence   9
strict liability   9
absolute liability   9
liability without fault   9

liable   9
but-for test   10
substantial factor test   10
cause in fact   10
primary authority   12
opinion   12
statute   12
constitution   12
administrative regulation   12
administrative decision   12
charter   12
ordinance   12
rules of court   12
common law   13
Code Napoléon   13
at common law   13
reporters   13

derogation of the common law   13
statutory codes   15
administrative code   15
code of regulations   15
secondary authority   16
persuasive authority   16
mandatory authority   16
legal encyclopedia   16
legal treatise   18
legal periodical   19
law reviews   19
law journals   19
annotation   20
online   20
Internet   20
World Wide Web   20
listserv   25

Legal Analysis in Tort Law

CHAPTER OUTLINE

- Structure of Legal Analysis
- Issue
- Rule
- Application
- Conclusion

STRUCTURE OF LEGAL ANALYSIS

The foundation of all the other skills in the delivery of legal services is the skill of **legal analysis,** also referred to as **legal reasoning.** There is no better way to *mis*prepare oneself to work in a law office than by memorizing a lot of law or by learning to go through the steps of a task by rote. The danger is somewhat similar to signing a contract without understanding the fine print. The fact that it is frequently done makes it no less dangerous.

This chapter will present an introduction to the fundamentals of legal analysis, a skill that attorneys learn and perfect in three grueling years of law school and in a lifetime of diligent practice. Given the vast scope of the topic, our coverage in this chapter is limited to the basics. Paralegals can increase their effectiveness as part of the torts-litigation team by understanding the specific purpose and general framework of legal analysis. This understanding is our goal in this chapter.

We begin with a definition: *Legal analysis* is the application of primary authority to facts in order to solve a legal problem. Figure 1–4 in Chapter 1 defined the major categories of primary authority such as court opinions or case law (containing the common law), statutes, constitutions, administrative regulations, administrative decisions, charters, and ordinances. For now, we will refer to any primary authority as a rule. In tort law, these rules (particularly opinions and statutes) define the tort causes of action (see the list in Figure 1–3 of Chapter 1) and their defenses.

Here is a more comprehensive definition of legal analysis:

Legal analysis is the application of one or more rules to the facts presented by a client in order to answer a legal question that will:
(1) avoid a legal dispute from arising,
(2) resolve a legal dispute that has arisen, or
(3) prevent a legal dispute from becoming worse.

The central legal dispute in tort law centers on the determination of who, if anyone, is **liable** (i.e., legally responsible) for an injury or harm that has occurred. Legal analysis helps us make this determination.

One of the benefits of effective legal analysis is that it will enable you to perform other critical skills such as those listed in Legal Analysis Guideline #1:

LEGAL ANALYSIS GUIDELINE #1

- *Additional Fact Finding.* Legal analysis will help you identify further facts you need to try to obtain through client interviewing and field investigation.
- *Advocacy.* Legal analysis will help you:
  (a) make the most reasonable argument on how a rule applies to the facts in a manner most helpful to the client of the law office where you work, and
  (b) make the most reasonable argument on how a rule applies to the facts in a manner most helpful to the *opponent* of the client of your office.
- *Prediction.* Legal analysis will help you make an educated guess of what a particular court (or other tribunal such as an administrative agency) might decide if it must determine how a rule applies to the facts.

Legal analysis always has four components. To remember them, use the acronym **IRAC,** which stands for Issue, Rule, Application (also called Analysis), and Conclusion:

Issue: Identify the legal issue to be resolved in the client's case.
Rule: State the rule that is at the center of the issue.
Application: Apply the rule to the facts of the client's case. Do this from the perspective of the client and from the perspective of the client's

opponent. (The latter perspective is the *counteranalysis*, which is the position of the other side on how the rule applies to the facts.)

Conclusion: State the conclusion of whether the rule applies to the facts.

These four components of IRAC constitute the structure of legal analysis. If a problem in the client's case involves more than one rule, each is "IRAC-ed" in the same manner.

IRAC can be used in memos, in essay exam answers, or in your head—in short, whenever you are doing legal analysis. If you write out your analysis in a law office, you usually do so in a document called a **memorandum of law** (also called a **legal memorandum**). It is a written explanation of how the law might apply to a set of facts. If the audience of the memorandum is someone in your office such as a supervisor, the memorandum is called an **interoffice memorandum of law.**[1] Often the organization of the memorandum of law (or **memo** for short) consists of four parts corresponding to the four components of IRAC. Some of the essay examinations you take in school can often follow the same organizational format, although your examination answer may not be as formally structured as a memo. Even less formal will be the legal analysis you will do in your head. Wherever you do legal analysis, you will use the same analytical structure outlined in Legal Analysis Guideline #2, which corresponds to IRAC:

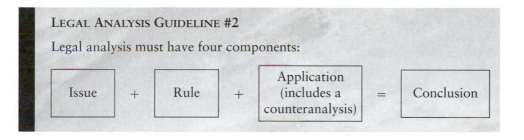

LEGAL ANALYSIS GUIDELINE #2

Legal analysis must have four components:

| Issue | + | Rule | + | Application (includes a counteranalysis) | = | Conclusion |

ISSUE

A **legal issue** (also called a **question of law**) is a question of whether one or more rules apply to facts. During informal discussions in a law office, you will often find that attorneys and paralegals phrase legal issues very broadly, almost in shorthand. For example:

- Will the seller win?
- Was Tom negligent?
- What causes of action can the company raise?
- What trespass defenses are worth checking?

Although broad issue statements such as these can be good starting points, you need to *narrow* the issue as much as possible. There are several ways of doing this. One is by rephrasing the issue so that it specifically refers to no more than one cause of action (such as a single tort) or no more than one defense. By this standard, only the second question—"Was Tom negligent?"—is sufficient. The question, "Who will win?", might be rephrased as:

- Was the seller negligent?
- Is the seller strictly liable in tort?
- Did the seller commit misrepresentation?

---

[1]If the audience is someone outside the office such as a hearing officer or judge, it might be called a hearing memorandum, a points and authorities memorandum, or a trial memorandum.

And the question, "What trespass defenses are worth checking?", becomes:

- Did the plaintiff consent to the entry on the land? and
- Was the defendant's entry protected by the privilege of necessity?

> **LEGAL ANALYSIS GUIDELINE #3**
>
> If the question or issue is stated broadly, rephrase it narrower so that the focus of the issue is only one tort cause of action or one defense.

As we will see later when we study elements, it is often necessary to make an even narrower statement of the issue.

RULE

The second component of legal analysis is a statement of the **rule** to be applied to the facts. As we said earlier, the rules are the primary authorities we defined in Figure 1–4 in Chapter 1 such as court opinions or case law (containing the common law), statutes, constitutions, administrative regulations, administrative decisions, charters, and ordinances. Suppose, for example, that the rule we were applying is the common law of negligence. After presenting the legal issue that mentions this rule, we would provide a fuller statement of this rule:

> Negligence is harm caused by the failure to use reasonable care.

This is the rule that we will apply to the facts in order to reach a conclusion. Attorneys often use these conclusions to formulate the legal advice they provide to clients. See Figure 2–1. The predominant rules that are applied in a personal injury practice

FIGURE 2–1
Legal analysis in tort law.

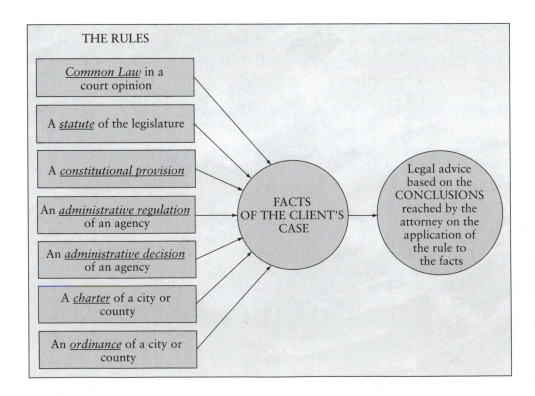

THE RULES

- _Common Law_ in a court opinion
- A _statute_ of the legislature
- A _constitutional provision_
- An _administrative regulation_ of an agency
- An _administrative decision_ of an agency
- A _charter_ of a city or county
- An _ordinance_ of a city or county

FACTS OF THE CLIENT'S CASE

Legal advice based on the CONCLUSIONS reached by the attorney on the application of the rule to the facts

are the torts listed in Figure 1–3 in Chapter 1, which are based mainly on common law and statutory law, although the other categories of rules can have important roles as well.

APPLICATION

We now come to the heart of legal analysis: **application** in which you explain the extent to which the rule applies to the facts. We will examine this subject through the following topics:

1. preliminary assessment
2. legal analysis and legal research
3. legal analysis, investigation, and interviewing
4. breaking a rule down into its elements
5. definitions of the elements
6. connecting facts with elements of the rule
7. legal analysis and further research, investigation, and interviewing
8. factor analysis
9. counteranalysis
10. length of legal analysis

1. Preliminary Assessment

The starting point in legal analysis is always a set of facts. In the law office, these facts come from the initial client interview. (In school, the facts come from the teacher's **hypothetical,** given orally in class or in a written question.[2]) Your first responsibility is to make a preliminary assessment of the facts. This is done in your mind or on paper before you start giving a formal answer. The preliminary assessment has the following focus: What rules *appear* to apply to this fact situation? You are searching for reasonable categories of *possibilities.*

Of course, you must be guided by the question asked by your supervisors or teachers. There are two kinds of such questions:

- the open-ended question
- the directed question

The open-ended question broadly asks, in effect, who is liable for what. What torts have been committed? What defenses are available? What remedies can be used? Make a list of possible causes of action and defenses. You are not looking for *the* answer yet; you are searching for possibilities that need to be further explored. As indicated earlier, every separate tort should be formulated into a separate issue. The same is true of every defense. If there is a reasonable possibility that the tort or defense might apply, include it in the list you make for the preliminary assessment. Obviously, this preliminary assessment cannot be done unless you know a fair amount of tort law. At a minimum, you must know the basic elements of the major tort causes of action (see Figure 1–3 at the beginning of Chapter 1).

The directed question is more specific or narrow. (Was Dr. Davis the proximate cause of Smith's death? Did the accountant intend to deceive the broker? Did Franklin violate the "due diligence" provision of § 23.5 of the statutory code?) The directed question focuses on one of the *elements* of a rule in contention and makes that element the centerpiece of a more narrow issue. We will examine elements in greater detail later in the chapter.

---

[2]As a noun, *hypothetical* means a set of facts that are assumed to exist for purposes of discussion. (The teacher asked the students to analyze the hypothetical she gave them.) As an adjective, it means assumed or based on conjecture. (The lawyer asked the witness a hypothetical question.)

> **LEGAL ANALYSIS GUIDELINE #4**
>
> Do a preliminary assessment of open-ended questions in order to list the possible tort causes of action and defenses that might be involved in the fact situation. Do a preliminary assessment of directed questions by focusing on the elements of the tort, defense, or other rule that will probably be most in contention.

This preliminary assessment of the open-ended or directed question has three purposes:

- to help you organize your thinking about the next stage of legal analysis
- to help you decide what legal research must be done
- to help you decide what further facts you must check through field investigation and further client interviewing

2. Legal Analysis and Legal Research

Once you have done a preliminary assessment, you have before you a list of the torts and defenses that might be applicable to the facts of the problem, or a list of elements that are most likely to be in dispute. When you are working on a client's case, the next step is to take this information to the law library. Legal research must be undertaken to locate the latest court opinions, statutes, rules of court, etc. You need to determine what *your state* has said about the problem you are analyzing. Your guide in undertaking this research is the list of possibilities that you compiled through a preliminary assessment of the legal analysis problem. While doing the research, the likelihood is that you will come across new options that need to be added to your list. Other tort causes of action and defense possibilities, for example, might be revealed by this research.

Following the research,

- You are in a position to evaluate the validity of your preliminary assessment. Did you initially identify the right torts and defenses? Did you initially identify the elements of the torts or defenses that will pose the most difficulty in litigation? Your preliminary assessment must be revised according to what you uncover in the law library.
- You have before you research notes containing citations to the major court opinions, statutes, regulations, etc. These are all rules that must be subjected to the IRAC legal analysis process.

3. Legal Analysis, Investigation, and Interviewing

During the initial stages of legal analysis, you will find yourself saying: "In order to provide an answer to the problem, I need to know more facts." This should happen often while you are still doing your preliminary assessment and legal research. It is rare that the initial client interview will have given you every fact that you need. The same is true of a fact situation in a school exam.

Assume, for example, that you are analyzing an automobile accident case. In your preliminary assessment and initial research, you are pursuing the possibility of a negligence action. You know that it will be important to determine the foreseeability of the accident. As you start the legal analysis, you realize that foreseeability is a complex topic involving the examination of numerous factors:

- condition of the road
- weather
- visibility
- speed of defendant's car and other cars

- posted speed limit
- other traffic signals
- distance between the two cars
- distractions
- time of day
- defendant's and plaintiff's familiarity with the area
- when defendant first saw plaintiff
- whether anyone used a horn before the accident
- etc.

As you read negligence opinions in the library, you may come across other factors that courts considered relevant to the foreseeability of the accidents discussed in the opinions. For example, you may read an opinion in which the court emphasized the extent to which the defendant knew about prior similar accidents in the area. Also, as you think more carefully about what foreseeability means, other factors may come to you.

The likelihood is that your initial statement of facts is not adequate to enable you to give an intelligent answer to the question of whether the accident in question was foreseeable; you simply do not have enough facts. The deeper you go in the legal analysis and research of the problem, the wider the gap may become between the facts you have and the facts you need to discover. *Indeed, this is one of the functions of legal analysis: to help you identify facts you need to pursue through investigation and additional client interviewing.* Analysis and research regularly feed into field investigation and interviewing in this way.

Of course, if you are taking an examination in school, you do not have the opportunity to obtain more facts through investigation and interviewing. All you have is the set of facts in the exam question. What do you do when you feel that more facts are needed to answer the exam question? First, you answer the question as best you can with the facts that you have. Second, while you are analyzing the facts that you have, you also point out what further facts you need to know in order to answer the question, and why you need to know these facts. For example, you might say, "We are not told in the facts how close the defendant's car was to the plaintiff's car just before the accident. The distance could have a significant bearing on foreseeability. The closer they were, the more foreseeable the accident was or should have been." In other words, you discuss the facts that you *do not have* when they would be relevant to the analysis. You must be reasonable in discussing missing facts. There must be a logical reason why you need the fact. That reason must always be related to the rule under discussion. If the rule you are analyzing is the foreseeability of the accident, it is logical to inquire about the factors that go into a determination of foreseeability. Common sense is also a guide. If, for example, you are not told how fast the defendant was driving, logic and common sense would tell you that questions about speed must be raised because of its high relevance to foreseeability.

4. Breaking a Rule Down into Its Elements

One of the most important skills in legal analysis is the ability to break down a rule— any rule—into its elements. An **element** is a portion of a rule that is one of the preconditions of the applicability of the entire rule. If one of the elements of the rule does not apply, the entire rule cannot apply. These rules are the categories of primary authority we discussed earlier, particularly the common law and statutory law that have given us the tort causes of action and their defenses. These causes of action and defenses are rules that tell us when someone is liable for the harm they caused.

Element analysis is important in many areas of the law. Here are some examples:

- In drafting a tort complaint in some states, a plaintiff makes sure that the facts alleged cover every element of the tort.
- When giving instructions to a jury, judges must cover all the elements of the tort and all the elements of the defenses raised.

- When conducting a deposition, attorneys frequently organize questions around the elements of the torts and defenses in the case.
- The organization of a memorandum of law often follows the list of elements of the torts and defenses.
- An exam answer is often effectively organized around the list of elements of the rules being discussed.

A major characteristic of sloppy legal analysis is that it fails to take the reader through the elements of a rule clearly. Suppose that you are analyzing the following statute:

> § 100. A company that keeps or suffers to be kept upon premises owned or occupied by it within 50 yards of an inhabited building of another more than 50 pounds of nitroglycerine shall be subject to a fine of $500 per day.

The first step is to break this rule down into its elements:

1. a company
2. keeps or suffers to be kept more than 50 pounds of nitroglycerine
3. upon premises owned or occupied by the company
4. within 50 yards of an inhabited building of another

The fine of $500 will not apply until each of these four elements is established. It is the nature of an element that if one of the elements falls, the entire rule falls. For example, if a neighbor (not engaged in a business of any kind) keeps 51 pounds of nitroglycerine within 50 yards of another, there is no fine, since the first element calls for a *company*.

> **LEGAL ANALYSIS GUIDELINE #5**
>
> The legal analysis of a rule begins when you break it down into its elements. An element is a portion of a rule that is one of the preconditions to the applicability of the entire rule.

Some rules are already broken down for you into their elements. See, for example, Figure 1–3 in Chapter 1, which lists the elements of all the major tort causes of action. For many other rules, however, *you* must break them into their elements. This is particularly true of statutes and administrative regulations.

Use logic and common sense as your guide. In § 100, for example, notice that in the second element, we have included "nitroglycerine" with the verbs "keeps or suffers to be kept," even though "nitroglycerine" does not appear until the end of § 100. This is done because it is impractical to discuss a verb separate from its object. (Keep what?) Do not be reluctant to re-group words and phrases in a sentence so that the elements will consist of logical units. Often the more complex the rule, the more unraveling you will have to do to achieve such units.

When a rule states *alternative* conditions, the alternatives should be kept in the same element. Hence, when you see "or," "either," or like words, be alert to the existence of alternatives. The second and third elements in the nitroglycerine statute contain alternatives ("keeps or suffers to be kept") ("owned or occupied"). When the alternatives deal with the same topic, they should be kept together so that the element is a self-contained unit.

> **LEGAL ANALYSIS GUIDELINE #6**
>
> Keep alternative conditions covering the same topic within one element.

There are often two parts in a rule:

- the conditions of the applicability of the rule
- the consequences of the applicability of the rule

The consequence of violating the nitroglycerine statute is a $500 fine. Other kinds of consequences might be stated in the rule such as:

- the granting of an injunction
- the waiver of an obligation
- the establishment of a particular tort
- the establishment of a particular defense to a tort

When identifying the elements of a rule, focus on the conditions (or preconditions) of the rule's applicability. The consequences follow if all the elements are met. Do not include consequences as one of the elements of the rule.

Not all rules, however, state consequences. Some rules simply make affirmations or provide definitions. For example, an administrative regulation might state that "helmets must be worn on job sites" without specifying the penalty or other consequence that will result if this rule is violated. Other administrative regulations in the same code may establish the penalty or consequence. Or the code may be silent on what happens if there is a violation.

ASSIGNMENT

2.1

The following rules are quotations from statutes, administrative regulations, and opinions. Break them into their elements.

a. An owner of premises is prohibited from willfully or intentionally injuring a trespasser by means of force that either takes life or inflicts great bodily injury.

b. Privacy is invaded only if the information sought is of a confidential nature and the defendant's conduct was unreasonably intrusive.

c. The term *safety belt interlock* means any system designed to prevent starting or operation of a motor vehicle if one or more occupants of such vehicle are not using safety belts.

d. The constitutional guarantees require, we think, a federal rule that prohibits a public official from recovering damages for a defamatory statement relating to his official conduct unless he proves that the statement was made with actual malice—that is, with knowledge that it was false or with reckless disregard of whether it was false or not.

e. In short, where an internal operation is indicated, surgeons may lawfully perform, and it is their duty to perform, such operation as good surgery demands, even when it means an extension of the operation further than was originally contemplated, and for so doing they are not to be held in damages as for an unauthorized operation.

f. When the mental or physical condition (including the blood group) of a party, or of a person in the custody or under the legal control of parties, is in controversy, the court in which the action is pending may order the party to submit to a physical or mental examination by a physician or to produce for examination the person in his custody or legal control. The order may be made only on motion for good cause shown and upon notice to the person to be examined and to all parties and shall specify the time, place, manner, conditions, and scope of the examination and the persons by whom it is to be made.

5. Definitions of the Elements

As indicated earlier, one of the most important observations you need to learn to make in legal analysis is, "In order to answer your question, I need the following additional facts because. . . ." We come now to another critical inquiry that the student of legal analysis must constantly make: *What is the definition of that word or phrase?* Legal analysis, in large manner consists of the application of definitions to facts. More precisely, it consists of the application of definitions of the *elements* of the rules to facts. Hence, once you have broken a rule into its elements, the next step is to seek definitions of the major words and phrases in those elements.

Refer back to the nitroglycerine example (§100) discussed earlier. The definitional questions that need to be asked are as follows:

- What is a "company"?
- What is meant by "keeps or suffers to be kept"?
- What are "premises"?
- What does "owned or occupied" mean?
- What is an "inhabited building"?
- What does "another" mean?
- What is "nitroglycerine"?

You must challenge the elements by demanding of yourself and of others that definitions be provided. The same is true if you are listening to a lecture or discussion about the law: Insist that the major terms be defined.

You will note that we did not list a number of words and phrases from the nitroglycerine statute as definitional questions, such as "or," "more than 50 pounds," "upon," "within 50 yards." They do not appear to be unclear and in need of definitions. There may, however, be circumstances where there *will* be a need to have such words or phrases defined. It would not be unusual for a court to spend time defining a conjunction or a preposition! Trespass, for example, requires an intrusion, or an entry *on* land. Litigation has been necessary to define what is meant by "on." If you throw a rock across someone's land and the rock never touches the ground, has there been an entry *on* the land? The answer depends on the definition of "on" as well as the definition of "land."

Your goal is to define every *major* word and phrase in an element. The two tests to use to determine whether something is major are common sense and whether you anticipate that the word or phrase will be disputed by the parties. When in doubt about whether something is major, provide the definition.

In applying these two tests, you may decide that words such as "nitroglycerine" and "premises" do *not* need to be defined. Both parties may agree, for example, that the substance that exploded was nitroglycerine and that this occurred on premises. If so, time does not have to be wasted defining such terms. Be careful, however, in coming to such conclusions. If you must err, do so on the side of providing too many definitions.

Legal Analysis Guideline #7

Define every major word and phrase in every element of a rule, so that the definitions can be applied to the facts. When in doubt about whether a word or phrase is major, resolve the doubt in favor of providing a definition. Whenever you anticipate a dispute over a word or phrase in an element, that word or phrase is always major.

You may think it is an easy task to know when to ask for a definition. Quite the contrary. Time and again you will see and hear people analyzing the law without defining major terms. *They make the assumption that readers or listeners already know the definitions of the words or phrases being used or that the definitions are obvious from the context of the analysis.* That is a dangerous assumption to make. You are urged to avoid making this assumption in your own analysis, even though you will be surrounded by courts, legislatures, lawyers, teachers, paralegals, etc. who regularly make the assumption. Sloppy analysis does not cease to be sloppy simply because it appears that everyone is doing it!

To be sure, there is such a thing as shorthand analysis, in which people communicate through short summarizations of legal principles without providing all the definitions. Such analysis plays an important role in a busy law office. In your own career, however, it is much too early to attempt such summarizations. You must first learn how to do complete analysis before you start using shorthand analysis. Also, when people talk shorthand *to you,* do not be reluctant to slow them down so that you can better understand what is being said. This understanding comes primarily when you inquire about definitions. Take the risk that someone will think that you do not know a lot of law. At this stage in your career, you don't.

Of course, simply because you have a definition, you are not home free. Often you will need a definition of the definition. Suppose that you are given the following definition of hazardous substance: "Any substance that is toxic, corrosive, or an irritant." Although it is helpful to have this definition, you obviously cannot stop there. What is "toxic"? What is "corrosive"? What is an "irritant"?

LEGAL ANALYSIS GUIDELINE #8

Provide definitions for the major words or phrases contained *within* definitions.

It is important that you train your ears and eyes to recognize legal analysis that fails to provide definitions of major words or phrases. For example, suppose you hear or read the following:

> The defendant acted reasonably because every safety precaution was taken before the fireworks were exploded, e.g., the area was roped off, the fireworks were inspected for defects, extra personnel were added. Furthermore, the explosion was not the proximate cause of the injury suffered by the plaintiff. The case should be dismissed.

Such a passage should give you intellectual indigestion. There are a number of significant concepts that are not defined: "reasonably," "safety precaution," "exploded," "inspected," "defects," "proximate cause," etc. The author of the passage assumes that you know what they mean. Again, this is a dangerous assumption to make in the law.

ASSIGNMENT 2.2

Examine the following passages taken from legal analysis found in memos, court opinions, appellate briefs, etc. Identify words or phrases, if any, in each passage that are not defined and that you think may have to be defined:

a. The interest in emotional and mental tranquility is not one that the law will protect from invasion in its own right.

b. Each tenant in common is equally entitled to share in the possession of the entire property and neither may exclude the other from any part of it.

c. It is not enough that the act itself is intentionally done even though the actor realizes or should realize that it contains a very grave risk of bringing about the contact or apprehension. They must realize that to a substantial certainty the contact or apprehension will result.

   d. In that case, judgment for the plaintiffs was reversed where it appeared that the odors emanating from defendant's building were necessarily incident to its operation, that the business was properly operated, and that plaintiffs were not substantially injured. It appeared that disinterested witnesses had not found the odors particularly offensive. The Appellate Court said, "In the instant case, we have nothing more than unpleasant and disagreeable odors, and those only occasionally perhaps sickening to a few who seem to be unduly sensitive or might we say allergic to such smells."

Having recognized the need for definitions, the next question is: Where do you get them? Can you go to a standard nonlegal dictionary such as *Webster's?* It is important to understand that there are many **terms of art** in the law. A term of art is a word or phrase that has a special or technical meaning. In the law of battery, for example, the word "act" means a voluntary movement of the body, and in the law of defamation, "publication" means a communication to at least one person other than the plaintiff. To obtain the definition of a term of art, you would *not* go to *Webster's.* Unfortunately, you will not always know whether a word or phrase is a term of art or whether its ordinary "lay" definition was intended. To be safe:

- Know the "lay" definition of the word or phrase (check it in *Webster's* or another standard nontechnical dictionary).
- Assume, however, that the word or phrase is a term of art until you establish for yourself otherwise.
- Use the basic research techniques (listed after Guideline #9) to determine whether the word or phrase is a term of art, and if so, what it means.

> **LEGAL ANALYSIS GUIDELINE #9**
>
> Assume that all words and phrases in the law are terms of art until you satisfy yourself that a nontechnical meaning was intended. Know the nontechnical as well as the technical definition of such words and phrases.

Basic Techniques of Locating Definitions

Here are some ways to try to locate definitions of a word or phrase in an element of a rule that needs a definition.

If the word or phrase is in an element of a statute, follow steps 1 through 5:

1. Check whether there is a definitions section in the statutory code. The legislature may have defined the word or phrase in another statute (often called a definitions section) that is part of the same cluster of statutes.
2. Check whether the word or phrase has been interpreted or defined in court opinions. Examine the Notes to Decisions that follow the text of the statute in the annotated code. Also Shepardize the statute. (When you shepardize something, you use the set of books called *Shepard's Citations* to obtain information such as whether any opinions have discussed it.)
3. Check whether an agency has written administrative regulations that define the word or phrase.
4. Check whether an agency has written administrative decisions that define or interpret the word or phrase.
5. Check whether the legislative history of the statute gives any clues to the meaning intended by the legislature for the word or phrase.

If the word or phrase is in an element of a common law rule such as a tort cause of action, you need to find court opinions that have interpreted or defined the word or phrase. To find such opinions, follow steps 6 through 10:

6. Check the digests, such as the *American Digest System* and the digest that covers the state court opinions of your state.

7. Check annotations in *A.L.R., A.L.R.2d, A.L.R.3d, A.L.R.4th, A.L.R.5th,* and *A.L.R. Fed.* Annotations provide extensive references to court opinions.

8. Check the legal encyclopedias such as *Corpus Juris Secundum* and *American Jurisprudence 2d.* The footnotes in them will often lead you to court opinions.

9. Check the footnotes in legal periodical literature for leads to court opinions.

10. Check the footnotes in legal treatises for leads to court opinions.

Use **CALR** (computer-assisted legal research), if available. For example, if you have access to WESTLAW, the question (or query) **conversion /s defin!** will lead you to any court opinion, statute, or other document in the database you select that explicitly gives a definition of conversion.[3] The Internet may be another source for legal materials. See Figure 1–13 at the end of Chapter 1.

6. Connecting Facts with Elements of the Rule

Let's recap: You have identified a series of rules, each rule has been broken down into its elements, and the definitions of the major words and phrases in the elements have been obtained. For each rule, the next step is to connect the facts of the problem with the elements of the rule. This connection is what is meant by applying a rule to the facts. (See Legal Analysis Guideline #2 and the earlier discussion of IRAC.) In your mind or on paper, make a series of columns, one column per element. In each column, place those facts that are relevant to the element covered by that column. (A fact is relevant if it helps to establish that the element applies or if it helps to establish that the element does not apply.) To illustrate, we will briefly examine the tort of trespass to land. Although we will not cover this tort in any depth until Chapter 23, you will be given enough information about the tort here so that you can follow the illustration. This legal analysis technique—connecting facts with elements—can be used when you want to apply any tort, or indeed, any rule, to a set of facts. Assume that you are analyzing the following facts:

Tom lives in a residential neighborhood. He plants a new tree along the edge of his property, two feet from Jim's land. He finishes planting at 7 A.M. on a Tuesday morning. Before Tom goes to work at 8 A.M., he turns on his hose in front of the tree to water it. He sees that the water quickly collects around the tree and starts draining toward Jim's land. Tom decides to leave the hose on while he is at work. When he returns at 6 P.M. that day, Jim's yard is flooded by the water. Jim sues Tom for trespass to land. What result?

The elements of trespass to land are:

- an act
- intrusion on land
- in possession of another
- intent to intrude
- causation of the intrusion

Once you have obtained the definitions of the major words or phrases in these elements, the next step is to line up the facts of the problem with each of the elements. It is recommended that you do this on paper. When you acquire practice in doing it, you will eventually do it in your head. Make five columns to correspond with the five

---

[3]The query **conversion /s defin!** asks the computer to find any document, e.g., a court opinion, in which the word "conversion" and the words "define" or "definition" are used in the same sentence. See William P. Statsky, *Legal Research and Writing: Some Starting Points,* 257 (5th ed. 1999).

FIGURE 2–2 Connecting facts to elements in a tort case: *Jim v. Tom* (trespass to land)

Act	Intrusion on Land	In Possession of Another	Intent to Intrude	Causation of the Intrusion
• Tom decided to keep the hose on. • There is no indication in the facts that anyone coerced or forced Tom to turn on the hose and to leave it on when he left for work.	• The water from the hose flooded Jim's yard.	• The yard and land (where the water went) was Jim's. • We do not know if Jim was living on the land, or whether anyone else was claiming the land.	• Tom saw the water start draining toward Jim's land. • We do not know whether Tom wanted the water to go on Jim's land. • The tree was two feet from Jim's yard. • The water collected quickly. • We do not know whether the land was flat or inclined toward (or away from) Jim's land. • Tom decided to leave the hose on while he is at work. • Ten hours passed with the hose on. • We do not know whether Tom saw the water go onto Jim's land.	• The yard was flooded from Tom's hose. • There is no indication that the water came from any other source.

elements of trespass to land. Under each column, make a note of the facts that are relevant to that column. A fact is relevant to an element if it may help to prove or disprove that element. Facts that are relevant to more than one element should be repeated under each appropriate column. If you need more facts to help you analyze an element, make a note of the missing facts under the column for that element. (See Figure 2–10.)

> **LEGAL ANALYSIS GUIDELINE #10**
>
> Before you start writing your final analysis of a problem, make a row of columns with headings to cover each element of the rule being analyzed (e.g., the tort or defense). Under each column heading, make a list of every fact that may be relevant to proving that the element does or does not apply. If one fact is relevant to more than one element, place the fact in the appropriate column for each of the elements involved. If there are missing facts you need to know, make a list of them in the appropriate column(s). The columns will become a checklist of what you need to discuss when you begin your written analysis.

You are now ready to write your legal analysis of the trespass problem. Your guide or checklist will be the information you collected under the columns. Assume that you are writing an answer to an examination question of whether Tom committed trespass to land in the hypothetical we have been examining. (Later we will point out some of the differences between this answer and an interoffice legal memorandum.) Notice that the discussion of each element begins with the definition of the element. You are not expected to know these definitions; they will be covered in Chapter 23. For now, simply note the detailed connection made between the definition of an element and the facts listed under the column for that element. Note also that the organization of the analysis follows the listing of the elements.

Model Answer: *Jim v. Tom* (Trespass to Land)   There are five elements to trespass to land:

- an act
- intrusion on land
- in possession of another
- intent to intrude
- causation of the intrusion

Act   An act is a voluntary movement of the body. There is no indication in the facts that Tom was coerced into turning on the hose. Everything that Tom did appeared voluntary, as indicated by the fact that he decided to keep the hose on. People who decide things usually act under their own willpower. Tom will concede that the first element applies.

Intrusion on Land   Intrusion means physically going on land. Water is a physical thing that went on the surface of Jim's land, since we are told, the "yard was flooded by the water." Tom will concede that the hose water is something physical that entered the land, and that the second element applies.

In Possession of Another   Possession means actual occupancy of the land with the intent to have exclusive control over it, or the right to immediate occupancy when no one else is actually occupying it with intent to control it. We are told that the land is "Jim's." We do not know, however, whether Jim or anyone else was occupying the land at the time of Tom's intrusion. For example, we do not know whether Jim had a tenant living on the land at the time. Hence, we cannot tell from the facts whether Jim was in possession. I will assume, however, that Jim was in possession, since the facts indicate that Jim owned the land and there is no indication that anyone else was occupying it with the intent to control it. Hence, the third element has been established.

Intent to Intrude   This element poses the most difficulty. Intent to intrude is the desire to intrude or the knowledge with substantial certainty that the intrusion will result from what the defendant does or fails to do. The facts do not tell us whether Tom wanted the water from his hose to enter Jim's yard. Jim would argue, however, that there was an intent to intrude, because Tom knew with substantial certainty that the water would physically enter his land. Presumably, Tom knew that the new tree was two feet from the property line. He knew, therefore, that the water would not have far to travel. He saw the water quickly collect around the tree and start draining toward Jim's land. Tom knew, therefore, that all the water was not being absorbed into his own land. He knew that the water was headed toward Jim's land. (The facts do not tell us if the land was flat or on an incline.) Tom knew that the water was going to run from 8 A.M. until he returned from work—some ten hours later. Furthermore, since the water collected "quickly," Tom probably had it turned on high. Since Tom knew that the water was headed toward Jim's land two feet away and that it would be kept on high for ten hours, Jim will argue that Tom knew with substantial certainty that the water would enter Jim's land. Therefore, Tom intended the entry or intrusion.

Tom disagrees. The facts do not say that he desired the water to enter. Nor do they say that he saw the water enter. He may have been negligent in causing the water to enter, or maybe even reckless, but there was no intent to have it enter. There may have been carelessness in allowing the water to drain into Jim's yard, but there was no knowledge with substantial certainty that it would enter. Tom admits that it may have been stupid to leave the water on, but there was no intent.

Causation of the Intrusion   There are two definitions of causation: "but for" and substantial factor. Plaintiff must establish causation by either definition. "But for" what the defendant did, the harm would not have occurred; or, the defendant was a substantial factor in producing the harm. Jim argues that "but for" Tom's leaving the hose on for ten hours, his land would not have been flooded. The facts say that the land was flooded "by the water," referring to the water from the hose. There is no indication that the water came from any other source. (Since no other causal entity is involved, Jim does not need to use the substantial factor test. But it would be easy to show that Tom was a substantial factor in producing the flooding.) Tom will concede that he caused the intrusion on Jim's land.

Conclusion   I believe that Jim will win this case. The only element in contention is intent. I do not think that Tom can deny that he knew with substantial certainty that the water would enter Jim's land. He saw the water go toward the yard even before he left for a long time with the hose on. Hence, I think Jim has the stronger argument on intent.

The characteristics of this model answer are outlined in Legal Analysis Guideline #11.

LEGAL ANALYSIS GUIDELINE #11

1. The analysis is organized according to the elements of the rule (here, trespass to land). The columns were used as a checklist in writing the answer.
2. Definitions of the major words and phrases in the elements are provided at the beginning of the discussion of each element.
3. The definitions are then applied to the facts. This is done by making a *specific* connection between the language of the definition and the facts. Simply restating rules without an extensive discussion of facts is weak analysis.
4. Most of the discussion centers on the elements that are most likely to be in contention (here, the element of intent).
5. The writer is not afraid of identifying missing facts where they are relevant to a particular element.
6. If assumptions must be made about missing facts, they are labeled as assumptions (see the discussion on possession).
7. For each element, the positions of both sides are provided, even if one of the positions amounts to a concession on an element (here, most of the counteranalysis centers on the element of intent).
8. The writer's conclusion is provided at the end of the analysis.

ASSIGNMENT

2.3

Mary and Cindy are walking on the sidewalk beside Lena's home. The home is seven inches from the sidewalk. Suddenly Mary and Cindy start a violent argument. They are shouting at each other. Mary pushes Cindy. Cindy loses her balance and falls on Lena's home. Lena sues Mary and Cindy for trespass to land.

a. Analyze Lena's action against Mary.
b. Analyze Lena's action against Cindy.

Do the column exercise for each case and write your answer according to the guidelines discussed thus far in this chapter. (Do not do any legal research on the problem.)

MEMO TO: Supervisor's name
FROM: Your name
DATE: Today's date

RE: Jim v. Tom
Trespass to Land
OFFICE FILE NO.
99-82105

You have asked me to prepare a memo on whether Tom committed trespass to land against Jim.

Issue:

Did Tom commit trespass to land when he flooded Jim's land after leaving his hose on for an extended period of time, knowing that the water was headed toward Jim's land two feet away?
Yes.

Conclusion: Yes

Analysis: There are five elements to trespass to land in this state according to the recent state supreme court opinion of *Johnson v. Allen,* 487 P.2d 55 (Ct. App. 1999), which held that . . .

FIGURE 2–3
Heading of a legal memorandum.

In the model answer for the case involving Jim v. Tom, the analysis was done in the format of a school examination. A number of major differences would exist in the answer if you were presenting it as a legal memorandum. First of all, there would be a heading to the memo (see Figure 2–3).

The major difference between an exam answer and a legal memorandum is that the memo is supported by research from the law library. For example, court opinions and statutes are cited and applied as authority for the elements of the torts or defenses, as well as for the definitions of the major words and phrases in the elements. No such research is given in the exam answer. The format of the analysis, however, is the same: Rules are broken down into their elements, definitions are given, specific connections between definitions and facts are made, most of the analysis is devoted to the elements most in contention, etc.

It is usually a good idea to begin a legal memorandum with a statement of the assignment that the supervisor has given you. This was done in Figure 2–3 ("You have asked me to prepare a . . . "). Note also that the legal issue is stated at the beginning of the memo just after the statement of the assignment. The issue in Figure 2–3 contains some of the critical facts of the case. There are some supervisors, however, who prefer a much shorter statement of the issue, e.g., "Has there been a trespass to land?"

The issue is stated at the beginning of the memo, but is usually written last, after the analysis has been done. First, you do all your thinking and research. You then write out your analysis by the elements. When you finish the analysis, you will have a better idea of how you want to phrase the issue. At that time, insert it at the beginning of the memo. Of course, the memo may have a number of issues. For long and relatively complex memos, it is recommended that you insert all of the issues at the beginning of the memo so that they serve as a kind of table of contents of what is to come.[4]

There is also a brief conclusion stated after the issue. This summary conclusion should not replace the longer conclusion that will go at the end of the memo and at the end of your analysis of each issue.

[4]On the variety of formats for a memorandum of law, see William Statsky and John Wernet, *Case Analysis and Fundamentals of Legal Writing* 180 ff. (4th ed. 1994).

7. Legal Analysis and Further Research, Investigation, and Interviewing

It must be emphasized that you will often find yourself rewriting the legal memorandum. New facts may be uncovered, e.g., through discovery. The ongoing research may raise factual gaps that need to be pursued through further investigation and client interviewing. You may even be asked to do research and investigation while the trial is going on, due to the facts revealed by witnesses on the stand. Analysis, legal research, and fact gathering constantly feed into each other as the client's case unfolds.

8. Factor Analysis

Thus far we have concentrated on the analysis of the *elements* of rules. Elements are preconditions to the applicability of a rule; if one of the elements does not apply, the entire rule does not apply. We now turn to a different kind of analysis: *factor* analysis.

A **factor** is simply a consideration that a court will examine to help it decide whether an element applies. A factor is not a precondition of applicability. It is simply one of a series of items a court will weigh. In negligence, for example, the court must determine the foreseeability of the accident. As we will see in Chapter 4, this determination is based on a large number of factors. The court will weigh facts and observations that center on:

- the area
- the activity
- the people
- preparation
- assumptions about human nature
- historical data
- specific sensory data
- common sense

We will also be examining other rules in this book for which a factor analysis will be required.

No one factor will usually be determinative for a court. All of the factors are examined and weighed. The question is not "Was the fire foreseeable?", but "How foreseeable or unforeseeable was the fire?" Factor analysis is most often used when the court is considering the *degree* or the *extent* of something. Hence there is a need to carefully explore everything before concluding where something falls on the scale.

You do a factor analysis by listing the factors that a court will consider and by examining one factor at a time in much the same way that you would analyze each element. State the factor, define it, list the specific facts that appear to support or not to support the applicability of the factor, integrate questions about missing facts into the discussion of each factor, etc.

LEGAL ANALYSIS GUIDELINE #12

Factors are often used by courts to help decide whether a rule (or an element within a rule) applies. Examine each factor separately and then make a collective assessment of how the totality of factors helps to establish or disestablish the rule (or an element within the rule).

Factor analysis and element analysis are not limited to the application of rules to facts. Almost every major decision you make involves elements and factors, e.g., picking someone to marry, buying a car. When people look for a house, they consider space, neighborhood, area schools, affordability, etc. If an item is essential, it is an element. Suppose, for example, that you will not buy a house with fewer than three bedrooms. This is a precondition to the entire purchase in the same manner as any single element of a rule is a precondition to the applicability of the entire rule. A house hunter may also want a large yard and a bus line within walking distance. But if these are not preconditions, they are simply factors to be considered, no one of which is necessarily dispositive or essential.

Identify one of the major decisions in your life. List the elements (preconditions) and the factors (considerations) that went into your decision.

In the remainder of the course, think about your answer to this assignment. Ask yourself whether the use of elements and factors in a court's application of rules to facts is significantly similar to the process we all go through in making major life decisions.

9. Counteranalysis

In discussing the model answer in the trespass case, we looked at the need for a counteranalysis—what the other side will say. Students of law tend to identify with clients for whom they are working, or with the side they think should win. *The more you personally believe in an argument, the greater the danger that you will have a weak counteranalysis to that argument.* This is not to say that you must invent a counterargument for the sake of having one. The safest state of mind you can have is to assume that there is a better counterargument than the one you have identified to date. Keep thinking. The worst kind of analysis hits the reader over the head with only one perspective. The test of whether to include a counterargument is whether a reasonable advocate would present that argument. When in doubt, include it.

> **LEGAL ANALYSIS GUIDELINE #13**
>
> To construct a counteranalysis, put yourself in the shoes of the opponent and ask whether he or she would warmly embrace or would raise objections to the conclusions you reached in applying any of the elements to the facts. The objections to your arguments constitute the counteranalysis.

10. Length of Legal Analysis

There are two basic kinds of legal analysis:

- conclusory
- demonstrative

Conclusory Legal Analysis   The following is an example of conclusory legal analysis:

> Reasonable care is the conduct of an ordinary prudent person under the same or similar circumstances. The truck driver, Ed, took his eyes off the road and it was at this time that his truck swerved into the opposite lane. It cannot be said that the driver was unreasonable simply because he took his eyes off the road in this manner.

This analysis begins with a rule containing the definition of reasonable care. The application of this rule to the facts is conclusory because we are told only that the truck driver was not unreasonable; we are not told *why* he was not unreasonable. Conclusory analysis fails to give any reasons why a rule applies or does not apply to the facts, or gives only cursory reasons.

Demonstrative Analysis   The following is an example of demonstrative legal analysis:

> Reasonable care is the conduct of an ordinary prudent person under the same or similar circumstances. The truck driver, Ed, took his eyes off the road and it was at this time that his truck swerved into the opposite lane. The truck driver will argue that it is not uncommon for a truck driver to take his eyes off the road. Ordinary and prudent truck drivers do not keep their eyes on the road every second. For example, truck drivers look at their gas gauges, their rearview mirrors, etc. Trucks are designed with instrument panels that can be checked only by being looked at, at least momentarily. Hence, it cannot be said that the truck driver acted unreasonably simply because he took his eyes off the road. We need to determine why he took his eyes off the road in order to. . . .

This analysis also begins with a rule containing the definition of reasonable care. The analysis is demonstrative, however, because we are taken through at least some of the steps the writer used to conclude that the truck driver was reasonable (or was not unreasonable). We are given *reasons* for this conclusion. For elements in contention, demonstrative analysis will be essential. Such analysis takes the reader by the hand to point out why a rule applies to the facts in a certain way. The assumption of the author of demonstrative analysis is that an argument is rarely, if ever, self-evident.

How long should your answer or memo be? Common sense is an important guide. The more complex the issues being analyzed, the longer the analysis must be. Also, what has your supervisor told you? Has a page limitation been set? Is the analysis needed in a few hours? Will the supervisor have only ten or fifteen minutes to read your analysis before dashing off to court? Questions such as these are relevant to the length of what you write. You do not want to belabor the obvious in your writing, nor write something so long that no one will want to read it.

Early in your legal career, it is recommended that you be demonstrative as often as you can. Conclusory analysis is shorthand analysis. Before you learn how to "talk in shorthand," you should learn how to be demonstrative.

> **LEGAL ANALYSIS GUIDELINE #14**
>
> Whether you provide conclusory or demonstrative analysis depends on the complexity of the problem and the instructions of your supervisor. When in doubt, be demonstrative.

CONCLUSION

The fourth and final component of legal analysis (via IRAC) is the conclusion. In the model answer for the trespass case, you saw an example of a conclusion. It gives your own personal opinion as to which side has the better legal argument on a question. You will also be predicting how a particular court will rule on the question.

Another function of the conclusion is to list the next steps that should be taken to:

- initiate a lawsuit
- do further investigation on . . .
- do further research on . . .
- etc.

Generally, the conclusion should be brief and should not raise arguments that were not discussed in the analysis or counteranalysis.

> **LEGAL ANALYSIS GUIDELINE #15**
>
> State a brief conclusion of your personal views at the end of the analysis and counteranalysis. Tell the reader which side you think has the strongest position. Include any next steps you recommend. Do not state any new arguments in the conclusion.

Throughout this book there are many legal analysis assignments that ask you to apply rules to sets of facts in the manner in which this chapter has covered this skill. The general instructions for these assignments are as follows:

General Instructions for the Legal Analysis Assignment

1. The most important part of legal analysis is *fact* analysis. Carefully read each fact in this assignment. Give detailed attention to *every* word covering *every* fact. Hence, the first instruction is to know the facts thoroughly.
2. Review the material in this introductory chapter on legal analysis. Give particular attention to the fifteen legal analysis guidelines in this chapter (some of which are repeated and summarized here).
3. Most of the legal analysis assignments will ask you to apply an entire tort or defense, or will ask you to apply one of the elements of the tort or defense.
4. The rules you will be applying will be found on the pages immediately preceding the assignment. Do not do any legal research for the assignment.
5. Place a heavy emphasis on the application of definitions of words or phrases in the elements. All of the arguments in your analysis should relate to the definitions of these words or phrases. In effect, it is these definitions that you will be applying to the facts. In your application, draw specific, explicit connections between the language of the element (or the definitions of the words or phrases in the element) and the individual facts of the problem you are analyzing.
6. Where reasonably possible, try to stretch the definition of a word phrase to fit the facts of the assignment.
7. When you need more facts to do the analysis and counteranalysis, state what facts you need, explain why you need them, and integrate these missing facts into your writing, always making clear that such facts are assumptions only.
8. Use the example of the trespass analysis in this chapter as a model.
9. Use demonstrative rather than conclusory analysis for anything in contention.
10. There are times when two advocates will agree on how a certain rule (or more accurately, how the definition of an element in a rule) applies to the facts, *but such times are rare.* Give both sides of the analytical picture. If you think that one of the parties will concede an argument, say so. For most arguments, however, put yourself in the shoes of both advocates and argue

both sides. Do not hit the reader over the head with an analysis that insists on one interpretation. Resist the temptation of constantly telling the reader that an argument "clearly" points in one direction. Legal analysis is rarely that clear.

SUMMARY

Legal analysis is the application of primary authority (consisting of rules) to facts in order to solve a legal problem. This can occur by avoiding a legal dispute, resolving it, or preventing it from becoming worse. The structure of legal analysis consists of a statement of the *issue,* a statement of the *rule,* the *application* of the rule to the facts (including a counteranalysis), and a *conclusion* on how the rule applies to the facts (IRAC). The issue is a question of how one or more rules apply to the facts. It should be phrased as narrowly as possible. The focus of an issue should be one tort cause of action or one defense. The main rules in tort litigation are court opinions containing common law, statutes, constitutions, administrative regulations, administrative decisions, charters, and ordinances.

Your preliminary analysis should make broad or general issues out of every possible tort cause of action and defense. Then try to narrow the issues to be more specific by focusing on the element(s) of the rule in contention. Next, undertake legal research on the issues you have identified during the preliminary analysis. While going through these steps, you will often be identifying additional facts that you will need to try to uncover through further client interviewing and investigation. Next break down every rule under examination into its elements, noting each of the elements that have words or phrases that require definitions. Do legal research to obtain such definitions. Then line up your facts with each of the elements of the rules under analysis—connect the facts with the elements. Your written analysis should be organized by elements of the rules. Most of the writing should focus on the elements that will probably raise the most contention. Where needed, a factor analysis is also undertaken. The perspective of the other side is presented as a counteranalysis. Avoid conclusory analysis early in your career. For elements in contention, provide demonstrative analysis. The conclusion in an exam answer or in an interoffice legal memorandum of law should state your personal opinion on which side has the better legal argument, your prediction of what a court might decide, and any next steps you recommend.

KEY TERMS

Legal analysis   28
legal reasoning   28
liable   28
IRAC   28
memorandum of law   29
legal memorandum   29

interoffice memorandum
  of law   29
memo   29
legal issue   29
question of law   29
rule   30

application   31
hypothetical   31
element   33
terms of art   38
CALR   39
factor   44

CHAPTER

3

Tort Litigation and Paralegal Roles

CHAPTER OUTLINE

- Overview
- Liability, Damages, and Collectibility
- Alternative Dispute Resolution (ADR)
- Introduction to Fact Gathering
- Achieving Specificity and Comprehensiveness
- Taking a Witness Statement
- Tort Complaints
- Discovery
- Trial and Appeal
- Enforcement

OVERVIEW

This chapter presents a summary of the major steps involved in tort litigation plus many of the tasks paralegals perform during those steps. For an overview, see the chart in Figure 3–1. Note that this chart includes an "Agency Stage." Most tort cases do not have this stage; they begin immediately in court. An important exception is workers' compensation, which begins by filing a claim in an administrative agency (see Chapter 29). Another exception is a tort claim asserted against the government that is not barred by sovereign immunity (see Chapter 27). The first step is often to make the claim within a designated administrative agency of the government.

This chapter will also introduce you to two of the important categories of assignments in the book: designing an investigation strategy in a torts case and drafting a torts complaint. When you are given these assignments later in the book, you will be referred back to this chapter for general instructions in completing them.

FIGURE 3–1 Overview of tort litigation with paralegal roles.

Event	Definitions	Role of Litigation Assistant

I. Agency Stage
   1. Someone protests an action taken by the *administrative agency*
   2. *Agency hearing*
   3. *Intra-agency appeal* to a commission, board of appeals, director, or secretary within the agency. (If no agency is involved, the litigation begins in court at the pretrial stage.)
	Administrative agency: a governmental body whose primary function is to carry out or administer statutes passed by the legislature and enacted into law.
	Agency hearing: a proceeding, similar to a trial, in which the hearing examiner of the agency listens to evidence and legal arguments before deciding the case.
	Intra-agency appeal: a review within the agency of an earlier decision to determine if that decision was correct.
		a. Open case file
		b. Interview client
		c. Conduct investigation
		d. Organize and manage case file

II. Pretrial Stage
   4. Plaintiff files a *complaint*
   5. Clerk issues a *summons*
   6. *Service of process* on defendant
   7. Defendant files an *answer*
   8. *Discovery* (there are six discovery devices; they are described in Figure 3–14)
   9. Pretrial *motions*
  10. *Settlement* efforts
  11. *Voir dire*
	Complaint: a pleading in which the plaintiff states claim(s) against the defendant
	Summons: a court notice requiring the defendant to appear and answer the complaint
	Service of process: a formal notification to a defendant that a suit has been instituted against him or her and that he or she must respond to it
	Answer: a pleading in which the defendant gives a response to the plaintiff's complaint
	Discovery: methods by which one party obtains information from the other party about the litigation before trial
	Motion: a formal request to the court, such as a motion to dismiss
	Settlement: a resolution of the dispute, making the trial unnecessary
	Voir dire: a preliminary examination to assess someone's qualifications (here, to be a juror, if the case will be tried before a jury)
		a.–d. Same as above if case does not begin at an agency
		e. Perform legal research
		f. Help draft complaint and other pleadings
		g. Schedule discovery
		h. Draft discovery requests and motions
		i. Summarize and digest discovery data; perform other discovery tasks (see Figure 3–14)
		j. Assemble trial notebook
		k. Arrange exhibits
		l. Continue investigation

FIGURE 3–1   (Continued)

Event	Definitions	Role of Litigation Assistant

III. Trial Stage
12. *Opening statement* of plaintiff
13. *Opening statement* of defendant
14. Plaintiff presents its case:
    (a) *evidence* introduced
    (b) *direct examination*
    (c) *cross-examination*
15. *Motions* to dismiss
16. Defendant presents its case:
    (a) *evidence* introduced
    (b) *direct examination*
    (c) *cross-examination*
17. Closing arguments to jury by attorneys
18. *Charge* to jury
19. *Verdict* of jury
20. *Judgment* of court
	Opening statement: a summary of the facts the attorney will try to prove during the trial
	Evidence: that which is offered to help prove or disprove a fact involved in the dispute
	Direct examination: questioning by an attorney of his or her own witness
	Cross-examination: questioning of a witness by an attorney for the other side
	Charge: the judge's instructions to the jury on how it should go about reaching its verdict
	Verdict: the results of the jury's deliberation
	Judgment: the final conclusion of a court
		a. Coordinate scheduling of witnesses
		b. Help evaluate prospective jurors during voir dire
		c. Take notes during trial
		d. Assist attorney with documents and exhibits

IV. Appeal Stage **21.** Filing of *notice of appeal* **22.** Filing of *appellant's appellate brief* **23.** Filing of *appellee's appellate brief* **24.** Filing of appellant's reply brief **25.** Oral argument by attorneys **26.** Judgment of court	**Notice of appeal:** a statement of the intention to seek a review of the trial court's judgment **Appellant:** the party bringing the appeal because of dissatisfaction with the trial court's judgment **Appellee:** the party against whom the appeal is brought **Appellate brief:** a party's written argument covering the issues on appeal relating to claimed errors that occurred during the trial	a. Draft and file notice of appeal b. Order trial transcript c. Summarize and digest trial testimony relevant to appeal issues
V. Enforcement Stage **27.** *Posttrial discovery* **28.** *Execution* by sheriff	**Posttrial discovery:** steps taken after a trial designed to help the winning party (the **judgment creditor**) enforce the judgment against the losing party (the **judgment debtor**), e.g., deposition of judgment debtor to help identify his or her assets **Execution:** the process of carrying out or enforcing a judgment	a. Investigate judgment debtor's assets b. Schedule posttrial discovery c. Arrange for sheriff to begin execution

LIABILITY, DAMAGES, AND COLLECTIBILITY

Once a new client walks into a law office with a personal injury case, the three initial concerns of the office are liability, damages, and collectibility.

Liability

Assume the client claims that the defendant injured the client. Under our system, this does not automatically make the defendant responsible even if the client can prove that the defendant caused the injury. *We are not responsible for every harm we cause.* We are responsible:

- if the harm was wrongful because it was intentional or negligent, or
- if the harm results from a special category of conduct that leads to strict liability regardless of whether it was intentional, negligent, or innocent.

The law makes us *liable* only for harm that falls within these categories. **Liability** means being legally responsible for something. In the law of torts, liability occurs when a plaintiff has successfully established a **cause of action,** which is a legally acceptable reason for bringing a suit. To state a cause of action, the plaintiff alleges a set of facts that gives him or her a right to judicial relief.

For our purposes, the causes of action are the thirty-five torts and related causes of action outlined in Figure 1–3 of Chapter 1 and examined throughout the chapters of this book. Each cause of action consists of its own elements. In order to make a preliminary assessment of whether the client "has a case," the office must decide whether enough facts can eventually be established to support the elements of any of these causes of action. If it can, liability will follow.

Damages

Damages consist of an amount of money awarded to the plaintiff upon establishing a cause of action against the defendant for personal injury or other harm. The amount in damages can range from $1 (which would be considered **nominal**—in name only—**damages**) to millions of dollars. How much is awarded depends primarily on the extent of the harm proven. An attorney will probably turn away a case where liability is clear, but where the harm suffered is relatively small. For example, it may be easy to establish liability against a bottling company that left a nail in its soda bottle. But if the plaintiff suffered no significant injury upon discovering the nail, the case may not be worth litigating. Most personal injury attorneys are paid a **contingent fee.** They take a percentage of the award *if* an award is given, or a percentage of the settlement *if* the case is settled. In short, the attorney is paid contingent on the client's receiving something. But even a large percentage of a small amount is not very attractive to an attorney. Of course, the client can always offer to pay the lawyer an hourly fee rather than a contingent fee. Few clients, however, are willing to do so when the injury suffered is comparatively small. Hence, the question of damages will be a major topic of discussion with a new client.

Collectibility

The attorney may feel that the prospects for establishing liability are very good and that the injury suffered is so substantial that the likelihood of a high damages award is also very good. A dream case for every **PI** (personal injury) attorney? Not necessarily. What good is a multimillion-dollar judgment against a bankrupt defendant with no liability insurance? (At the end of this chapter, we will discuss collection and other enforcement themes.) During the initial contact with a new client, the office will start compiling information on the financial health of prospective defendants. The question is whether a defendant's pockets are deep or shallow. A **deep pocket** is a person who has resources from which a judgment can be collected. The resources can include cash, other property, insurance policy, etc. A **shallow pocket** is a person without such resources.

ALTERNATIVE DISPUTE RESOLUTION (ADR)

Litigation can be an expensive and costly process. If the parties cannot resolve the dispute on their own and would like to avoid litigation, an increasingly popular option is **alternative dispute resolution (ADR).** Many disputants try ADR before resorting to traditional litigation. In some kinds of cases, e.g., medical malpractice, disputants may be required to try ADR before being allowed to have a court trial. ADR may take several forms:

Arbitration: Both sides agree to submit their dispute to a neutral third party who will listen to the evidence and make a decision. They can also agree on whether the decision of the arbitrator will be binding or advisory. The arbitrator is usually a professional arbitrator hired through organizations such as the American Arbitration Association. An arbitration proceeding is not as formal as a court trial. Generally, the decision of an arbitrator is not appealable to a court. If a party is dissatisfied, he or she must go to court and start all over again rather than appeal a particular arbitration decision.

Rent-a-Judge: This is actually another form of arbitration. A retired judge is hired by both sides to listen to the evidence and to make a decision, which has no more or less validity than any other arbitrator's decision.

Mediation: Both sides agree to submit their dispute to a neutral third party who will help the disputants reach a negotiated settlement on their own. The mediator does not render a decision, although sometimes he or she may make suggestions or recommendations.

Med-Arb: First, mediation is tried. If it is not successful, the proceeding becomes an arbitration, and the mediator switches roles. He or she then makes a decision as an arbitrator.

Neighborhood Justice Center (NJC): In many localities, an NJC exists to offer mediation and arbitration services for disputes involving ongoing relationships in the community, such as between landlord and tenant or among neighbors. The NJC could be sponsored by the government, a foundation, or an existing community organization.

Summary Jury Trial: The parties use an advisory jury, which often comes from the regular pool of jurors in the county. The attorneys present their evidence to this jury in an abbreviated format. The jury deliberates and renders a nonbinding advisory verdict. Attorneys then question the jurors on the strengths and weaknesses of each side's presentation. The parties use all of this information in deciding whether they should settle and, if so, for what.

Paralegals have many roles in assisting attorneys who have cases in ADR. For example, a paralegal can organize files, schedule discovery and ADR itself, conduct investigations, summarize or digest data from discovery, help prepare the client for ADR, and assist the attorney during the ADR proceeding in much the same fashion as paralegals assist attorneys during regular trials.

In addition, some paralegals have become arbitrators and mediators themselves. In most states, you do not have to be an attorney to conduct arbitration or mediation. Service companies are available that offer arbitration and mediation services to parties involved in disputes. A few of these companies hire people with paralegal training and experience to be arbitrators or mediators.

INTRODUCTION TO FACT GATHERING

Later in Chapter 20, a senior paralegal makes the following observation about paralegals in tort litigation:

> Whether you are the legal assistant project manager or the newest legal assistant on the team, you are the keeper of the facts.

There are two major categories of facts that a paralegal helps an office collect early in a tort case: background facts on the client and the facts needed to establish a

prima facie case. A prima facie case is established when a party alleges enough facts to cover every element of a cause of action.

Background Facts

Law firms differ on the amount of background information they seek from every client. The following checklist of questions will give you some idea of the kind of background information that can be sought.

- name of client
- ever used other names (aliases)?
- ever been through a formal change-of-name procedure?
- birth name
- other married names
- current address and phone (home)
- length of time lived at this address
- current address and phone (work)
- prior residences
- nationality/citizenship/place of birth
- addresses and phones where spouse (or closest relative) can be reached
- date of birth
- religion, race (may be relevant in jury selection process)
- how was client referred to this office?
- has client hired any other attorney on this case?
- has client spoken to any other attorney about this case?
- if client is a minor, is there a legal guardian?
- marital status
- prior marriages (information on divorces or annulments)
- date of present marriage
- date of divorce(s) or annulment(s)
- names of children, if any
- ages/addresses
- name of other parent of each child
- current status of property settlement, alimony/lump sum/child support payments
- current employer(s) of client and spouse
- job title/salary
- length of employment there
- prior employment history
- self-employment/business ventures
- tax data (filing status, gross income, availability of copies of returns, etc.)
- real property client owns in own name
- real property owned in joint names
- personal property (cash, bank accounts, furniture, motor vehicles, etc.)
- education
- prior litigation involvement (dates, courts, attorneys, outcomes, etc.)
- present state of health
- names and addresses of doctors currently treating client
- nature of treatment
- medical problems for which no treatment has yet been sought
- prior medical history (for the last _____ years)
- prior hospital treatment (dates, addresses, doctors, care provided, outcomes)
- name of every insurance company (past/present) that has covered medical care
- list of every insurance claim client has ever filed for medical care
- names of people who could verify client's prior medical condition

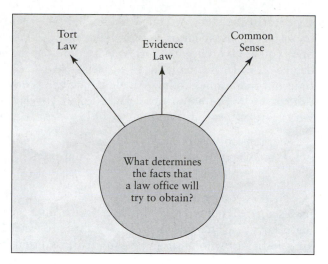

FIGURE 3–2
Guides for fact gathering in a torts practice.

Prima Facie Case

A law office uses three fact-gathering guides to determine the facts it will seek through interviewing and investigation to try to establish a prima facie case: tort law, evidence law, and common sense. (See Figure 3–2.) **Legal interviewing** is the process of gathering facts from a client (or from a prospective client if the office has not yet decided whether to take the case) in order to solve or avoid a legal problem. **Legal investigation** is the process of gathering additional facts and verifying presently known facts in order to solve or avoid a legal problem. The facts investigated are usually from a source other than the client.

Tort Law Tort law consists of the elements of the major torts and related causes of action outlined in Figure 1–3 of Chapter 1 plus the defenses to them. These causes of action and defenses are also outlined in the checklists called, "Definitions, Relationships, Paralegal Roles, and Research References" found throughout the chapters of the book. Knowing the elements of these torts—and the elements of their defenses—will provide direction for all interviewing and investigation efforts of the office.

Evidence Law A general understanding of the law of evidence will be of assistance when asking questions during interviewing and in verifying facts through investigation. Assume, for example, that a client tells you that he or she suffered $100,000 in lost wages due to an injury that may now be litigated. Some of the evidentiary questions related to these facts are as follows:

- Are there documents (e.g., past wage receipts) that will help document the loss?
- Are these documents **admissible** in court? (Something is admissible if a trial judge will allow a jury to consider it.)
- Are witnesses available to testify about the wage loss?
- Are these witnesses **competent** to testify and would their testimony be admissible? (A witness is competent to give testimony if he or she understands the obligation to tell the truth, has a basic ability to communicate, and has knowledge of the topic of his or her proposed testimony.)

It is not enough to know that a $100,000 loss has been suffered. The evidentiary context of this fact must be considered as the interviewer interviews and the investigator investigates. They need to ask additional questions and pursue additional facts that will help minimize any evidentiary problems that could arise during a trial.

Common Sense Although a knowledge of evidence law and of tort law is important to investigation, *it is probably not as important as common sense*. In fact, once you are working in a law practice, you will be surprised to discover the high degree to which so many legal problems are solved by the use of common sense. Indeed, you must be careful to avoid letting your knowledge of law interfere with the exercise of your common sense! The most effective attorneys and paralegals are those who came to the study and practice of law *already equipped* with:

- a sense of responsibility
- inquisitiveness
- common sense

Facts do not have legs that simply walk into the office to reveal themselves. Common sense tells interviewers and investigators that they must be aggressive and imaginative in going after the facts. This reality is reflected in the following comments by an investigator who must investigate road conditions in an accident case:

> Sometimes I don't know what I am looking for until I find it. You've got to keep an open mind in this business. I need to find out the road conditions on the day of the accident. I can call the client—that's OK as a starter. I'm going to get a copy of the newspaper for the day of the accident to see if it has a weather report. I think copies of old newspapers are available. Also, there must be some way to get a governmental weather bureau to give us something official. I'm going to check the Internet. I think I'll also give Fred a call. He once had a case like this. Maybe he can give me a lead. I wonder if the city highway department keeps a record of road conditions and road repairs. I can always ask my supervisor if she wants me to go to some of the people who live in that area to see what they might be able to tell me about the road. Sometimes you can turn up good leads just by talking to people.

Someone with this kind of determination would be a prized employee in any law office.

ACHIEVING SPECIFICITY AND COMPREHENSIVENESS

Two of the major characteristics of effective fact gathering are specificity and comprehensiveness. There are a number of techniques that will help you achieve both. Checklists can be particularly helpful. There are a number of them in this book. For example:

- Appendix C contains an extensive checklist on collecting facts for an automobile accident case.
- All of the chapters in the book that cover the major torts contain a checklist called, "Definitions, Relationships, Paralegal Roles, and Research References." It lists the categories of facts that need to be established to prove the elements of each of the torts and their defenses.
- The sample interrogatories for any tort case that we will examine in Figure 3–15 later in this chapter will also suggest questions that could be asked in an interview and pursued through investigation.
- The sample interrogatories for a medical malpractice case we will examine in Figure 18–2 in Chapter 18 will accomplish the same purpose.

In addition to checklists, there are other methods discussed in the book for achieving comprehensiveness and specificity. For example:

- The legal analysis discussion in Chapter 2 shows how to identify further facts that need to be pursued, particularly in a follow-up legal interview with a client.

- The foreseeability discussion in Chapter 4 presents guidelines for formulating numerous factual questions when foreseeability is an issue, as it is in a great many tort cases.

We turn now to two additional techniques: organizing facts into versions and fact particularization.

Starting Point:

All the facts you presently have on the case.

Procedure:

- Arrange the facts chronologically.
- Place a number before each fact that must be established in a legal proceeding.

State the Following Versions of Each Fact:

- Version I: The client's
- Version II: The opponent's (as revealed to you or as you assume it might be)
- Version III: A witness's
- Version IV: Another witness's
- Version V: Any other reasonable version (e.g., from your own deductions)

As to Each Version:

- State precisely (with quotations if possible) what the version is.
- State the evidence or indications that tend to support the version according to persons presenting the version.
- State the evidence or indications that tend to contradict this version.
- Determine how you will verify whether the evidence or indications exist.

FIGURE 3–3   Fact versions.

Fact Versions

People perceive events differently. Consequently, everyone will not always have the same version of what happened. In fact, it is healthy for the interviewer and investigator to anticipate the presence of multiple versions for every important fact. This process is outlined in Figure 3–3.

Of course, all versions of facts are not of equal weight. Some versions are more believable—have more **credibility**—than others. Interviewers and investigators must be constantly evaluating the believability of all the evidence they are helping the office assemble.

The **burden of proof** is the standard that tells the trier of fact, usually the jury, how believable a party's evidence must be on a fact in order to accept that fact as true. In the vast majority of tort cases, the burden of proof is **preponderance of the evidence.** This standard is met when a party proves it is *more likely than not* that his or her version of a fact is true. (Figure 3–4 presents this standard along with others.)

> **EXAMPLE:**   Ted is suing Mary for negligence. One of Ted's arguments is that Mary failed to make a right-turn signal just before the accident. Mary swears she did make it.

Under the preponderance standard, a juror can accept whichever version of this fact is more likely true than not. This is the equivalent of accepting whichever version the juror believes more than disbelieves. To agree with Mary, a juror does not have to conclude that Ted was lying. The juror simply must be able to say, "I believe Mary more than I believe Ted." This is the meaning of preponderance of the evidence.

Although preponderance is the minimum standard that must be met, your goal in gathering facts is always to go as far beyond the minimum as possible. For safety,

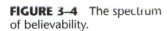

FIGURE 3–4 The spectrum of believability.

How Convincing Is the Version of the Fact?	Use of This Standard
Totally Believable: The evidence leaves no doubt whatsoever that the version of the fact is true.	This is never the standard used at trial. It may be that the trier of fact will conclude that a version of the fact offered by a party is totally believable, but it is never *required* that the evidence meet this standard to be accepted as true at trial.
Beyond a Reasonable Doubt: There may be some doubt that the version of the fact is true, but none of these doubts are reasonable.	This is the standard used in a criminal trial. The prosecution must prove the existence of every fact necessary to constitute the crime beyond a reasonable doubt. This standard is *not* used in tort cases.
Clear and Convincing: There is a high probability that the version of the fact is true.	Only rarely is this high standard of believability used in tort cases. One example of its use is the requirement in a defamation case against a media defendant that the plaintiff prove by clear and convincing evidence that the defendant knew the statement about the plaintiff was false or was reckless with regard to its truth or falsity (actual malice). The standard is also used in many contract or will cases to prove fraud or duress.
Preponderance of the Evidence: It is more likely than not that the version of the fact is true.	This is the standard of believability that is used in the vast majority of tort cases.
Fifty/Fifty Possibility: The evidence is evenly balanced on the fact. It is as likely that the version of the fact is true as it is that the version is false.	If the evidence establishes a fifty/fifty possibility of truth, then the fact cannot be established as true. The trier of fact would be acting on mere speculation or conjecture (guessing) if only a fifty/fifty possibility is shown.
A Possibility: The evidence establishes no more than a possibility that the version of the fact is true.	Anything is possible. Hence, to show a mere possibility is never enough to establish a version of a fact. The trier of fact would again be dealing in mere speculation or conjecture (guessing).
Highly Unbelievable: There is a high probability that the version of the fact is false.	Obviously enough to establish the falsity of a version of a fact.
Totally Unbelievable: The evidence leaves no doubt whatsoever that the version of the fact is false.	Obviously enough to establish the falsity of a version of a fact.

you keep digging for facts in the hope of finding evidence that will make your version as believable as possible.

Fact Particularization

Perhaps the most effective technique for developing the skill of competent fact gathering is called **fact particularization.** It is one of the most important skills that you can develop.

The hallmark of the professional is to view people, objects, and events as unique. The bureaucrat or administrator, on the other hand, sees people, objects, and events in categories. The focus of the professional is on differences and individuality. The focus of the bureaucrat is on similarities and groupings.[1]

Professionalism in fact gathering means to *particularize* the facts so that there is an exploration of all or almost all the details that make the facts unique. (See Figure 3–5). Fact particularization involves collecting more facts in order to obtain a comprehensive picture of what happened. Your main guide in accomplishing particularization is common sense.

You *particularize* a fact you already have:
1. by assuming that what you know about this fact is woefully inadequate,
2. by assuming that there is more than one version of this fact, and
3. by asking a large number of basic who, what, where, how, when, and why questions about the fact, which, if answered, will provide as comprehensive a picture of that fact as is possible at this time.

FIGURE 3–5 Fact particularization.

EXAMPLE: You are working on an automobile negligence case. Two cars collide on a two-lane street. They were driven by Ed Smith and Sam Jones. Jones is a client of your law office. One of the facts in the file is that, according to Jones, Smith's car "veered into Jones's lane moments before the collision." Your job is to particularize this fact. *Design an investigation strategy consisting of questions you would like answered in order to obtain a much more detailed picture of what happened.* This is done by elaborating on the facts already collected. You ask the following commonsense questions: who, what, where, how, when, and why.

- What does Jones mean by veering into the other lane?
- How much veering was done? An inch? A foot? The entire car in the other lane? How much of an angle was there?
- Who saw this happen? The file tells us that Smith's car veered, "according to Jones." Did Jones see this happen himself? Who else saw it, if anyone? Any passengers in Jones's car? Any passengers in Smith's car? Were there bystanders? Has the neighborhood been checked for witnesses, e.g., people who live or work in the area, people who frequently sit on public benches in the area?
- Were the police called after the accident? If so, who was the officer? Was a report made? If so, what does it say, if anything, about the car veering into the other lane? Where is this report? How can you obtain a copy?
- How fast was Jones's car going at the time of the veering? Who would be able to substantiate the speed? Who might have a different version of how fast Jones was going?
- How fast was Smith's car going at the time of the veering? Who would be able to substantiate the speed? Who might have a different version of how fast Smith was going?
- Have there been other accidents in the area? If so, how similar have they been to this one?
- What was the condition of the road at the time Smith started to veer? At the time of the collision?
- What was the weather at the time?
- How was visibility?
- What kind of a road is it? Straight? Curved at the area of the collision? Any inclines? Any hills that could affect speed and visibility?

---

[1]William Statsky & Philip Lang, *The Legal Paraprofessional as Advocate and Assistant: Roles, Training Concepts and Materials,* 159 (1971).

- What kind of area is it? Residential? Commercial?
- Is there anything in the area that would distract drivers, e.g., potholes?
- Where is the nearest traffic light, stop sign, or other traffic signal? How, if at all, did they affect traffic at the time of the accident?
- What is the speed limit of the area?
- What kind of car was Smith driving? Were there any mechanical problems with the car? Would these problems help cause the veering? What prior accidents has Smith had, if any?
- What kind of car was Jones driving? Were there any mechanical problems with the car? What prior accidents has Jones had, if any?
- Etc.

This list of questions is by no means exhaustive. Many more could be asked to try to complete the picture of what happened and to collect as many new and substantiating facts as possible on what happened. You need to develop the *habit* of generating such factual questions. Not all of the questions will turn out to be productive. Some—or perhaps many—will lead to dead ends. Be willing to take this risk.

Throughout the chapters of this book, there are a number of investigation strategy assignments in which you will be asked to particularize facts relevant to the area of law discussed in the chapters. Here are the general instructions for this assignment:

General Instructions for the
Investigation Strategy Assignments

| **Objectives of Assignment:** | • To demonstrate the close connection between common sense and fact gathering |
| | • To assist you in developing an investigation plan based on the need for more factual detail |

1. The starting point is a set of facts that you are given in the assignment. Assume that you have entered the case after these facts have been collected by someone else.
2. Assume further that these facts are inadequate because *many* more facts are needed.
3. Closely examine the facts you have. Are they arranged chronologically? If not, rearrange them chronologically so that the facts tell a story with a beginning, middle, and ending. There will be many gaps in the story. Your task will be to identify these gaps and to raise the questions that the investigator should pursue in order to try to fill or close the gaps. These questions will become the investigator's plan for further investigation.
4. The focus of these questions will be on what you *don't* know about the facts that you have.
5. Isolate the facts that you have into small clusters of facts, e.g., the soda bottle exploded. For each small set of facts that you identify or isolate in this way, make a *large* list of questions that fall into two categories:
   - questions that you would ask in order to obtain additional facts that will help you compile a much more detailed picture of what happened; to aid you in this list, ask the basic who, what, where, how, when, and why questions about every fact
   - questions that you would ask in order to obtain additional facts that will help you substantiate (or prove) the facts that you already have

   There is no rigid formula to follow in order to make these lists of questions. The goal is a specific and comprehensive list of questions, that, if answered, would provide as complete a picture of what happened as possible. Do not worry about the answers to these questions. The need now is to identify the questions that will later become the strategy or plan for the investigator.
6. Be scrupulous about dates. Ask questions about the dates you have and also about the dates that are missing.

7. Do a "people analysis" of the facts. Make a list of every person who is involved or who could be involved in the facts. Assume that each person potentially has a different version of the facts (see Figure 3–3). Structure your questions for this assignment around these different versions.

8. Preceding most of the assignments there will be a discussion of some legal principles governing certain torts or defenses. Include questions that would be relevant to the elements of these torts or defenses. (On generating such questions, see also the section on legal analysis, investigation, and interviewing in Chapter 2 on legal analysis.) If there is no such discussion, simply ask the basic who-what-where-etc. questions that you would like answered as a matter of common sense, in order to obtain a complete picture of what happened.

9. The list of questions in this assignment does not have to be written in any particular order. You select your own format of presenting the questions so that they are readable. A possible model for writing out your questions would be to cluster all the questions under the elements of the tort or defense being examined in the chapter.

ASSIGNMENT 3.1

Assume you are working on the following cases. Prepare an investigation strategy. Follow the general instructions for the investigation strategy assignments, except for instruction 8. There is no need to examine elements at this time.

a. Mr. Flint was in the XYZ Supermarket, on his way out. He slipped on a wet floor just inside the exit door.

b. George and Ted are students in the same class. One day during a break, George said to Ted in a very loud voice, "You are a thief."

ASSIGNMENT 3.2

The Hazard Interview

In this assignment you will be interviewing someone about a hazard. Ask a friend, a neighbor, a relative, another student, or another employee about a hazard where they live, work, study, or play. The hazard should have the following characteristics:

- It should be a hazard about which the interviewee has personal knowledge.
- It should be a hazard about which you (the interviewer) have *no* personal knowledge.
- It should be a hazard that involves a specific thing, object, or condition—preferably relating to a building, an appliance, a motor vehicle, a sidewalk, a street area, etc. It should not deal with anything as general or vague as "the hazards of city living," "the hazards of smoking," etc.

After you conduct the interview, prepare a report on the interview. The report will be evaluated according to the following criteria:

- factual detail
- organization (no particular organization is required; select an organization that will make the memo easy to read)
- spelling, grammar, and composition (including the structure and sequencing of sentences and paragraphs)

Type the memo—double-spaced with generous margin space. There is no minimum or maximum length for the memo. The length should be appropriate for the nature of the hazard being described.

TAKING A WITNESS STATEMENT

There are four major kinds of **witness statements:**

1. Handwritten statement
2. Recorded statement in question-and-answer format (on audio or video tape)
3. Responses to a questionnaire that is mailed to the witness to answer
4. Statement taken in question-and-answer format before a court reporter

The most common kind of statement is the first, which we will consider here.

In a handwritten statement, the investigator writes down what the witness says, or the witness writes out the statement himself or herself. There is no formal structure to which the written statement must conform. The major requirements for the statement are clarity and accuracy.

The statement should begin by identifying (1) the witness (name, address, place of work, names of relatives, and other identifying data that may be helpful in locating the witness later); (2) the date and place of the taking of the statement; and (3) the name of the person to whom the statement is being made. See the example of the beginning of a witness statement in Figure 3–6.

Then comes the body of the statement, in which the witness provides information about the event or circumstance in question (an accident that was observed, what the witness did and saw just before a fire, where the witness was on a certain date, etc.). It is often useful to have the witness present the facts in a chronological order, particularly when many facts are involved in the statement. It is important that the witness give detailed facts that demonstrate the witness was in a good position to observe the event. This will lend credibility to the statement.

At the end of the statement, the witness should say that he or she is making the statement of his or her own free will, without any pressure or coercion from anyone. The witness then signs the statement. The signature goes on the last page. Each of the other pages is also signed or initialed. If others have watched the witness make and sign the statement, they should also sign an **attestation clause,** which simply states that they observed the witness sign the statement.

Before the witness signs, he or she should read the entire statement and make any corrections that need to be made. Each correction should be initialed by the witness. Each page should be numbered with the total number of pages indicated each time. For example, if there are four pages, the page numbers would be "1 of 4," "2 of 4," "3 of 4," and "4 of 4." The investigator should not try to correct any spelling or grammatical mistakes made by the witness. The statement should exist exactly as the witness spoke or wrote it. Just before the signature of the witness at the end of the statement, the witness should say (in writing), "I have read all _____ pages of this statement, and the facts within it are accurate to the best of my knowledge."

Investigators sometimes use various tricks of the trade to achieve a desired effect. For example, if the investigator is writing out the statement as the witness speaks, the investigator may *intentionally* make an error of fact. When the witness reads over the statement, the investigator makes sure that the witness catches the error and initials the correction. This becomes added evidence that the witness carefully read the

FIGURE 3–6 Beginning of a witness statement.

Statement of John Wood

I am John Wood. I am 42 years old and live at 3416 34th Street, N.W., Nashua, New Hampshire 03060. I work at the Deming Chemical Plant at region circle, Nashua. My home phone is 966-3954. My work phone is 297-9700 x301. I am married to Patricia Wood. We have two children, Jessica (twenty-two years old) and Gabriel (eighteen years old). I am making this statement to Rose Thompson, a paralegal at Fields, Smith and Farrell. This statement is being given on March 13, 1986 at my home, 3416 34th Street, NW.

On February 15, 1986, I was standing on the corner of . . . .

statement. The witness might later try to claim that he or she did not read the statement. The initialed correction helps rebut this position.

Witness statements are generally not admitted into evidence at trial. They might be admitted to help the attorney demonstrate that the pretrial statement of the witness is inconsistent with the testimony of this witness during the trial itself. The main value of witness statements is thoroughness and accuracy in case preparation. Trials can occur years after the events that led to litigation. Witnesses may disappear or forget. Witness statements taken soon after the event can sometimes be helpful in tracking down witnesses and in helping them recall the details of the event.

ASSIGNMENT

3.3

Select any member of the class and take a witness statement from this person. The statement should concern some accident in which the witness was a participant or an observer. The witness, however, should not be a party to any litigation growing out of the accident. You write out the statement from what the witness says in response to your questions. Do not submit a statement handwritten by the witness except for his or her signature, initials, etc. Assume that you (the investigator-paralegal) work for the law firm of Davis and Davis, which represents someone else involved in the accident.

TORT COMPLAINTS

One of the assignments in many of the chapters of this book is the torts complaint-drafting assignment. You will be given a set of facts and asked to draft a torts complaint that would be acceptable in the state courts of your state. The general instructions for this assignment are here in Chapter 3. Before presenting these instructions, we need to examine complaints in the context of pleadings that are drafted and filed in the pretrial stage of torts litigation.

Pleadings are formal, pretrial documents filed by parties to litigation that contain their claims, defenses, or other responses. The function of the pleadings is to help define the controversy and give everyone involved, including the court, notice of what the controversy is all about. The major pleadings are as follows:

Complaint (also called a **petition**): The plaintiff's statement of claims (causes of action) against the defendant.

Answer: The defendant's response to the complaint. The allegations of the complaint are admitted or denied, and defenses are presented.

Reply: The plaintiff's response to the affirmative allegations in the answer. (Required in a minority of states.)

Counterclaim: The defendant's statement of a claim (cause of action) against the plaintiff. Counterclaims are often stated in the defendant's answer.

Cross-claim: The defendant's statement of a claim (cause of action) against a co-defendant.

Third-party Complaint: A complaint filed by the defendant against a third party who is not now in the suit. This complaint alleges that the third party may be liable for all or part of the damages the plaintiff may win from the defendant.

One of the most common challenges to pleadings is the **demurrer.** It states that even if all the facts alleged by the other side can be proven at trial, those facts do not legally add up to or constitute the necessary elements of a claim or cause of action. (Some states and the federal courts no longer use the term *demurrer*. In its place, motions are used that have the same effect, e.g., motion to dismiss for failure to state a claim on which relief can be granted.)

We turn now to our main focus in this section, the complaint. The following discussion presents an overview of the main components of a complaint as illustrated in the sample found in Figure 3–7.[2]

Caption

The **caption** is the heading of the pleading. It should contain the name of the court, the name of the parties, and the number assigned to the case by the court.

Designation of the Pleading

The title of the pleading should be clearly stated at the top. In Figure 3–7, the pleading is a Complaint for Negligence.

Statement of Jurisdiction

Every state does not require a statement of the court's **subject matter jurisdiction**— its power or authority to hear this kind of case. A complaint filed in federal court, however, usually contains a statement of the United States District Court's subject matter jurisdiction.

For purposes of determining **venue**—the place of the trial—the complaint may also have to allege the residence of the parties and where the accident or wrong allegedly occurred.

Body

The claims of the plaintiff are presented in the body of the complaint. A claim is a cause of action. Every separate cause of action used by the plaintiff should be stated in a separate "count," e.g., Count I, Count II, or simply as First Cause of Action, Second Cause of Action, etc. The paragraphs should be consecutively numbered. Each paragraph should contain a single fact or a closely related small grouping of facts.

With what factual detail must the complaint state the cause of action? There are two main schools of thought on this question.

Fact Pleading

In **fact pleading**, there must be a statement of the ultimate facts that set forth the cause of action. Not every detail that the plaintiff intends to try to prove at trial is pleaded. The complaint need not contain a catalog of the evidence that the plaintiff will eventually introduce at the trial. Only the ultimate facts are pleaded. There is, however, no satisfactory definition of an ultimate fact. Generally, it is one that is essential to the establishment of an element of a cause of action.

The complaint must *not* state conclusions of law, such as "Jones assaulted Smith" or Jones "violated section 23 of the state code." The problem, however, is that it is as difficult to define a conclusion of law as it is to define an ultimate fact. Some statements are mixed statements of fact and law—for example, "Jones negligently drove his car into. . . . " As a matter of common sense and practicality, if the conclusion of law (here, "negligently") is also a convenient way of stating facts, it will be permitted.

The only reliable guide for a pleader is to determine what the prior decisions of the courts in the state have concluded are proper and improper statements of fact in a complaint.

Notice Pleading

Under the federal system and under states that have followed the lead of the federal courts, the goal of the complaint is to say enough to notify or inform the defendant of the nature of the claims against him or her. This is the essence

---

[2]Adapted from MacDonald, Pick, DeWitt & Volz, *Wisconsin Practice Methods* 239 (2d ed. 1959).

Caption

STATE OF _____   COUNTY OF _____

_____ COURT

John Doe, Plaintiff

　　　　v.　　　　　　　　　　　　　　　　Civil Action No. _____

Richard Roe, Defendant

Designation of Pleading →

COMPLAINT FOR NEGLIGENCE

Statement of Jurisdiction →

Plaintiff alleges that:

Body

　　1. The jurisdiction of this court is based on section _____, title _____ of the [State] Code.

　　2. Plaintiff is a plumber, residing at 107 Main Street in the City of _____, _____ County, State of _____ .

　　3. Upon information and belief, defendant is a traveling salesman, residing at 5747 Broadway Street in the City of Chicago, Cook County, Illinois.

　　4. On or about the second day of January, 1989 an automobile driven by defendant, on Highway 18 in the vicinity of Verona, _____, struck an automobile being driven by the plaintiff on said highway.

　　5. Defendant was negligent in the operation of said automobile at the aforesaid time and place as to:

　　a. Speed,

　　b. Lookout,

　　c. Management and control.

　　6. As a result of said negligence of defendant, his automobile struck plaintiff's automobile and caused the following damage:

　　a. Plaintiff was subjected to great pain and suffering.

　　b. Plaintiff necessarily incurred medical and hospital expense.

　　c. Plaintiff suffered a loss of income.

　　d. Plaintiff's automobile was damaged.

Prayer for Relief →

　　Wherefore plaintiff demands judgment in the amount of one hundred thousand dollars ($100,000), together with the costs and disbursements of this action.

　　　　　　　　　　　　　　　　_____

　　　　　　　　　　　　　　　　　　　Plaintiff's Attorney

Subscription →

　　　　　　　　　　　　　　　　　　　1 Main Street

　　　　　　　　　　　　　　　_____ , _____

State of _____

　　　　　　　　　　　　　　　　　　　　ss

County of _____

Verification

　　John Doe, being first duly sworn on oath according to law, deposes and says that he has read the foregoing complaint and that the matters stated therein are true to the best of his knowledge, information, and belief.

　　　　　　　　　　　　　　　　_____

　　　　　　　　　　　　　　　　　　　　John Doe

Subscribed and sworn to before me on this_____ day of _____, 19 _____ .

　　　　　　　　　　　　　　　　_____

　　　　　　　　　　　　　　　　　　　Notary Public

My commission expires:

FIGURE 3–7
Structure of a negligence complaint.

of **notice pleading.** There is no requirement that ultimate facts be alleged. The plaintiff must simply provide a "short and plain statement of the claim showing the pleader is entitled to relief."

It is not improper to fail to plead an ultimate fact. The critical point is that the complaint will not be thrown out if it *fails* to plead an ultimate fact or if it *includes* conclusions of law—as long as the complaint gives adequate notice of the nature of the claim. The technicalities of pleading facts, conclusions of law, etc. are unimportant in notice pleading.

Notice pleading does not necessarily require a different kind of pleading from fact pleading; notice pleading is simply more liberal or tolerant in what is acceptable.

When the plaintiff lacks personal knowledge of a fact being alleged, the fact should be stated "upon information and belief," as in the third paragraph of Figure 3–7.

There are times when the law requires specificity in the pleading. For example, allegations of fraud must be stated with specificity or particularity. Also, when special damages are required in defamation cases, the facts must be pleaded with some specificity.

Prayer for Relief

In the **prayer for relief,** the complaint asks for a specific amount of damages or for some other form of relief such as an injunction against a nuisance. If the prayer asks for damages, the clause requesting it is called the **ad damnum clause.** In the event that the defendant fails to appear and answer the complaint, a **default judgment** is entered against the defendant. (This is a judgment that is granted against a party who fails to appear or to file an answer before the deadline.) The relief given in a default judgment cannot exceed what the plaintiff requested in the prayer for relief.

Subscription

The **subscription** is the signature of the attorney who prepared the complaint and who represents the plaintiff. If the plaintiff prepared the complaint and is acting as his or her own attorney, then the plaintiff signs the complaint.

Verification

A **verification** is an affidavit that is submitted with the pleading. It is signed by parties on whose behalf the pleading was prepared, who swear that they have read the pleading and that it is true to the best of their knowledge, information, and belief. (Not all states require that complaints be verified.)

In Figures 3–9 to 3–13, you will find other examples of tort complaints. It is frequently helpful to examine sample documents, or what are called *standard* forms. Caution is needed, however, in the use of such forms. See Figure 3–8 on avoiding abuse of standard forms.

Figures 3–10 to 3–13 are from *West's Legal Forms Revised Second Edition*, vol. 11 by Lawrence R. Ahern III and Nancy MacLean, §§ 18.63–18.67 (1994). See also Figure 19–5 in Chapter 19 for a sample products liability complaint.

ASSIGNMENT 3.4

a. Assume that you want to draft a complaint for negligence in your state. Select any court in your state with subject matter jurisdiction over negligence actions. Examine your state code and the rules of court governing that court in order to identify the requirements for such a complaint. (You may or may not

1. A standard form is an example of the document or instrument you need to draft, such as a pleading, contract, or other agreement.
2. Standard forms are found in a number of places—for example, in formbooks, manuals, practice texts, in some statutory codes, and in some court rules.
3. Most standard forms are written by private attorneys. Occasionally, however, a standard form will be written by the legislature or by the court as the suggested or required format to use.
4. Considerable care must be exercised in the use of a standard form. Such forms can be deceptive in that they appear to require little more than filling in the blanks. The intelligent use of these forms usually requires much more.
5. The cardinal rule is: *adapt* the form to the particulars of the client's case.
6. Do not be afraid of changing the printed language in the form if you have a good reason. Whenever you make such a change, bring it to your supervisor for approval.
7. You should never use a standard form unless and until you have satisfied yourself that you know the meaning of *every* word and phrase on the form. This includes **boilerplate,** which is standard language often used in the same kind of document. The great temptation of most form users is to ignore what they do not understand because the form has been used so often in the past without any apparent difficulty. Do not give in to this temptation. Find out what everything means by:
    • Using a legal dictionary
    • Asking your supervisor
    • Asking other knowledgeable people
    • Doing other legal research
8. You need to know whether the entire form or any part of it has ever been litigated in court. To find out, do some legal research in the area of the law relevant to the form.
9. Once you have found a form that appears useful, look around for another form that attempts to serve the same purpose. Analyze the different or alternative forms available. Which one is preferable? Why? The important point is: keep questioning the validity of the form. Be very skeptical about the use of any form.
10. Do not leave any blank spaces on the form. If a question does not apply, make a notation to indicate this, such as N.A. (not applicable).
11. If the form was written for another state, be sure that the form can be adapted to the law of your state.
12. Occasionally you may go to an old case file to find a document that might be used as a model for a similar document you need to draft on a current case. All the above cautions apply to the adaptation of documents from closed case files.

FIGURE 3–8   How to avoid abusing a standard form.

find rules specifically governing complaints to be filed in negligence actions; the rules may refer more generally to civil actions.) Identify whatever requirements you can find as to the caption, statement of jurisdiction, statement of claim, verification, etc. You do not have to draft a complaint for this assignment. You must simply cite and summarize whatever requirements you find on the format of a complaint for negligence in your state.

b. Examine the complaints found in Figures 3–7 and 3–9 to 3–13. Assume that all of these complaints are to be filed in state courts of your state. What defects in form, if any, do you find in these complaints in the light of the requirements for complaints in your state? What, if anything, is missing from these forms? Review your answer to part *a* of this assignment on negligence complaints in your state. For the other causes of action covered in the complaints, e.g., slander, you will have to determine whether there are any other requirements on format imposed by your state, that differ from those governing negligence complaints. Do not concentrate on the substantive law of torts dealt with in the complaints. Focus on the procedural law of format. (The substantive law of these torts will be covered in later chapters.)

FIGURE 3–9 Sample complaint.

SUPERIOR COURT OF ALASKA FIRST JUDICIAL DISTRICT AT JUNEAU

B-E-C-K CONSTRUCTORS, a Joint
Venture Consisting of Koon-Boen,
Inc. and Cummins-Egge, Inc.,

Plaintiff,

vs.

STATE OF ALASKA,
DEPARTMENT OF HIGHWAYS,

Defendant.

NO. 72–361

COMPLAINTS FOR DAMAGES
FILED in the Superior Court
State of Alaska, First District
at Juneau
OCT. 5 1972
D. V. Dungan, Clerk
By B. Marlow, Deputy

Plaintiff alleges:

1. Plaintiff is and at all times material hereto was a joint venture consisting of Koon-Boen, Inc. and Cummins-Egge, Inc., both of which are foreign corporations holding certificates of authority to transact business in the state of Alaska, and both of which have paid their last annual corporation tax and have filed annual reports for the current year and have complied with all the laws relative to the contractor's registration in the state of Alaska.

2. Plaintiff is general contractor for defendant for the construction of bridges on Copper River at Flagg Point and Round Island, project number ER-38(1) to be constructed in accordance with plans and specifications furnished by defendant.

3. An existing bridge at Flagg Point which had undergone earthquake damage paralleled the work and with the knowledge of defendant and by its invitation plaintiff used it in connection with its work. Said bridge was inherently dangerous in that some of its foundations were in extremely bad repair, but defendant negligently failed to disclose this dangerous situation although it knew from previous investigations of the dangerous condition and negligently failed to include in its specifications any warning as to said dangerous condition.

4. Defendant impliedly warranted the safety of said bridge by permitting and inviting plaintiff to use the same in its construction activities.

5. On or about the 21st day of July, 1971, while plaintiff was making use of said existing bridge, the same collapsed precipitating equipment and personnel of plaintiff into the river, causing loss of life and equipment and thereafter changing the conditions under which the remainder of the contract had to be performed because said bridge became thereafter unavailable, thereby substantially increasing the costs to plaintiff of the completion of the job and substantially delaying completion.

6. Plaintiff has duly made claim in accordance with the provisions of the contract for its extra costs by reason of the changed conditions and the negligence and breach of warranty by defendant, but defendant has declined to entertain said claim and all remedies under the contract have been exhausted by plaintiff.

7. Plaintiff has been damaged by the collapse of said bridge and the changed conditions under which it has thereafter had to perform its contract in the sum of $908,488, and its subcontractor, Central Construction Company, has been damaged in a sum exceeding $449,702, for which amount it has asserted a claim against plaintiff.

Wherefore, plaintiff prays for judgment against defendant in the sum of $1,358,190, or such larger sum as may be proved at the trial, together with plaintiff's costs and disbursements incurred herein, and plaintiff's reasonable attorneys fee.

Dated September 28, 1972.

ROBERTSON, MONAGLE,
EASTAUGH & BRADLEY
Coattorneys for Plaintiff
By _____
    J. B. BRADLEY

LYCETTE, DIAMOND &
SYLVESTER
Coattorneys for Plaintiff
By _____
    LYLE L. IVERSEN

LAW OFFICES
LYCETTE, DIAMOND
& SYLVESTER
HOGE BUILDING, SEATTLE
98104 MAIN 3-1330

FIGURE 3–10

[Caption]

COMPLAINT FOR ASSAULT AND FALSE IMPRISONMENT

Plaintiff states:

1. [*Jurisdictional allegation, if needed or desired.*]
2. [*Venue allegation, if needed or desired.*]
3. On [*date*], plaintiff purchased merchandise on credit from defendant.
4. Prior to [*date*], through no fault and on account of illness, plaintiff became temporarily unable to make the payments due to defendant in timely fashion.
5. On [*date*], defendant's credit manager, _____ , acting within the course and scope of employment, demanded that plaintiff come to the credit manager's office that day to discuss plaintiff's account.
6. Shortly after plaintiff arrived at the credit manager's office, the credit manager, while acting within the course and scope of employment, shouted at and threatened plaintiff, putting plaintiff in fear for [*his/her*] safety. The credit manager refused to permit plaintiff to leave the office until plaintiff paid all the money then in plaintiff's pockets.
7. As a result of these actions by defendant's credit manager, plaintiff was deprived of liberty, suffered fright, humiliation, mental anguish and distress, was subjected to scorn and ridicule by those knowing of the detention, was injured in credit, and was prevented from attending to business during the time of the imprisonment, all to [*his/her*] damage in the amount of $_____ .

THEREFORE, plaintiff demands judgment against defendant in the amount of $_____ plus costs; and plaintiff prays for such other and further relief as is just and proper.

_____
Attorney for Plaintiff

Several assignments in this book will ask you to draft complaints on the torts being discussed. The general instructions for these assignments are as follows:

**General Instructions for the Complaint-Drafting
Assignments in Personal Injury Litigation**

Objectives of Assignment:
- To introduce some of the basic principles of complaint drafting
- To show how complaint drafting can help increase your understanding of substantive tort law

1. The goal is to write a personal injury complaint that would be acceptable in a trial court of your state.
2. Go to your statutory code and read everything you can about complaints, about pleadings in civil actions generally, and about complaints and pleadings on the particular torts involved in the assignment.
3. Go to the rules of court used in the court before which you expect to bring the complaint you will be drafting. Read everything you can about complaints and pleadings in civil actions generally and about complaints and pleadings on the particular torts involved in this assignment. If the case can be brought in more than one court, select one.
4. In some state codes and in some sets of rules of court there are standard form complaints that may be helpful. Be careful, however, when using standard forms. See "How to Avoid Abusing a Standard Form" in Figure 3–8.
5. There are many practice texts or manuals written by attorneys. These books often have standard form complaints. See "How to Avoid Abusing a Standard Form" in Figure 3–8.
6. For more on the procedural aspects of complaints, review the discussion on Figure 3–7.

FIGURE 3–11 Sample complaint.

[Caption]

COMPLAINT FOR INTENTIONAL INFLICTION OF DISTRESS

Plaintiffs _____ and _____ , by their undersigned attorney, state:

1. [*Jurisdictional allegation, if needed or desired.*]

2. [*Venue allegation, if needed or desired.*]

3. Plaintiffs are the owners of real property improved by premises _____ , which is their home, and legally described as _____ .

4. On [*date*], plaintiffs signed a deed of trust on their home in favor of defendant _____ in return for a loan of $_____ , payable on the following terms: _____ .

5. Plaintiffs made payments as follows: $_____ on [*date*]; $_____ on [*date*]; $_____ on [*date*]; [etc.].

6. The unpaid balance of the loan as of [*date*], was $_____ .

7. On [*date*], plaintiffs became temporarily unable to make further payments of $_____ per month on the loan because of the following facts, which plaintiffs fully explained to defendant on [*date*]: _____ .

8. Plaintiffs also explained to defendant, on [*date*], that plaintiff _____ suffered from chronic hypertension, which could result in life-threatening complications as a result of sudden stress, and that plaintiff _____ was then pregnant.

9. Nevertheless, on [*date*], defendant came to plaintiffs' home, and threatened to commence foreclosure proceedings against them immediately if they did not pay $_____ by [*date*]; and over a period of _____ defendant continued the same and similar tactics and courses of conduct in order to obtain payments, which he well knew that plaintiffs could not afford to make; defendant also well knew that his tactics and courses of conduct were likely to cause mental distress and resulting physical injuries to plaintiffs.

10. As a direct and proximate result of defendant's actions, both plaintiffs suffered extreme mental anguish, worry and distress about their inability to pay the amounts demanded and consequently about the immediate prospect of losing their home through foreclosure.

11. On [*date*], as a consequence of his extreme mental anguish, worry and distress, plaintiff _____ suffered both a stroke and complete, irreversible renal (kidney) failure, resulting in his permanent disability, loss of earnings and of earning capacity, and medical expenses; and, on [*date*], as a consequence of her extreme mental anguish, worry and distress, plaintiff _____ suffered a miscarriage, resulting in further mental and physical distress and medical expenses; both plaintiffs have become unable to perform fully their functions as father and husband and as mother and wife, respectively, and each of them has been deprived of the assistance, comfort, companionship and consortium of the other—all to their damage in the total amount of $_____ .

12. [*Punitive damages, if any, for defendant's malicious actions in reckless and wanton disregard for plaintiffs' rights, and defendant's intent to cause plaintiffs mental and physical distress.*]

THEREFORE, plaintiffs demand judgment against defendant in the amount of $_____ , plus costs; and plaintiffs pray for such other and further relief as is just and proper.

_____
Attorney for Plaintiff

7. In the complaint-drafting assignments of this book, you will often need additional facts to do the complaint, e.g., the full names of the parties, their addresses, some of the basic facts that prompted the plaintiff to file the complaint, etc. Whatever facts are missing should be made up by you as long as your facts are consistent with the limited facts provided in the assignment.

8. The caption of the complaint should conform to local practice. Normally, it contains:

   a. the name of the court

   b. the parties' names and litigation capacity (plaintiff, defendant, etc.)

   c. the docket number assigned by the court, which will usually be a number such as Civil Action No. 90-6483. (You make up this number.)

FIGURE 3–12   Sample complaint.

[Caption]

COMPLAINT FOR DEFAMATION
(libel and slander)

Plaintiff states:

1. [*Jurisdictional allegation, if needed or desired.*]

2. [*Venue allegation, if needed or desired.*]

3. On [*date*], defendant came to plaintiff's place of employment, in the presence and hearing of plaintiff's employer and co-workers, stated words to the effect that plaintiff is "in the habit of obtaining goods and credit on false representations," is "in the habit of making false promises about payment of his bills" and, "refuses to pay his just debts," is "a deadbeat," and other similar words of like effect.

4. On [*date*], defendant published similar words of like effect in a letter to plaintiff's brother, _____ ; and on [*date*], defendant published similar words of like effect in a notice posted on the front door of plaintiff's home.

5. Defendant's statements were false.

6. As a result of defendant's publications of these defamatory statements, plaintiff has been greatly injured in his credit and reputation and suffered great pain and anguish, to plaintiff's damage in the sum of $_____ .

THEREFORE, plaintiff demands judgment against defendant in the amount of $_____ plus costs; and plaintiff prays for such other and further relief as is just and proper.

_____
Attorney for Plaintiff

9. The designation of the pleading should be given. Place a title on the pleading, e.g., COMPLAINT FOR SLANDER.

10. If your state requires a statement of jurisdiction, provide it early in the complaint. This is the statutory cite that gives the court the subject matter jurisdiction over this kind of complaint.

11. If residency, place of the alleged wrong, etc. must be alleged in order to establish proper venue, make the necessary statements.

12. Number each paragraph of the complaint separately. Limit the amount of information you place in each paragraph to a single topic, such as the statement of jurisdiction. When you are alleging facts, limit each paragraph to one fact or to a small cluster of related facts.

13. Complaints often have more than one legal theory. For example, a products liability complaint may sue on the theories of strict liability, negligence, breach of warranty, and misrepresentation. Each theory is a separate cause of action. Cover each theory separately in the complaint under the heading, CAUSE OF ACTION FOR . . . or FIRST CAUSE OF ACTION, or FIRST COUNT, or COUNT 1, etc.

14. The complaint should be written in readable English. Avoid excessive language and long recitations of facts. Be brief and concise.

15. The body of the complaint covers the claims made. You will have to determine whether your state is a fact-pleading state or a notice-pleading state. When in doubt, use fact pleading so that ultimate facts are alleged for each element of the tort or cause of action involved.

16. Where do you obtain the law on the causes of action alleged in the complaint? Use the elements of torts listed in this book unless your instructor tells you otherwise.

17. Where the same facts need to be used to allege elements in more than one cause of action, repetition can be avoided by cross-referencing to the facts mentioned earlier in the complaint. Facts reused in this way are said to be *incorporated*. This can be done with ease if the paragraphs are numbered as

FIGURE 3–13 Sample complaint.

[*Caption*]

COMPLAINT FOR INVASION OF PRIVACY
(public disclosure of private fact)

Plaintiff states:

1. [*Jurisdictional allegation, if needed or desired.*]
2. [*Venue allegation, if needed or desired.*]
3. On [*date*], plaintiff purchased from defendant the following merchandise: _____
_____
4. The terms of payment for the merchandise were as follows: _____
_____ .
5. Plaintiff made payments as follows: $_____ on [*date*]; $_____ on [*date*];
$_____ on [*date*]; [etc.].
6. The unpaid balance for the merchandise as of [*date*], was $_____ , or less
than _____% of the total purchase price.
7. On [*date*], plaintiff became temporarily unable to make further payment for the
merchandise because of the following facts, which plaintiff fully explained to defendant
on [*date*]: _____
8. Thereafter, beginning on [*date*], and continuing up to the present, defendant
has invaded plaintiff's right to privacy and solitude by, without plaintiff's consent, doing the following, among other things:
   (a) Publishing in the _____ newspaper on [*date*], the following notice:
_____ .
   (b) Posting on the front and rear doors of plaintiff's home, in large bold-face print,
the following notice: _____
_____ .
   (c) Posting on the front display-window of defendant's store, located at _____ ,
the following notice: _____
_____ .
   (d) Telephoning certain of plaintiff's friends and neighbors on numerous occasions
and discussing plaintiff's financial affairs with them.
   (e) Visiting plaintiff's home both late at night and early in the morning on numerous occasions and using loud and abusive language which could be heard by plaintiff's
neighbors.
   (f) Visiting plaintiff's place of employment on numerous occasions and using loud
and abusive language, which could be heard by plaintiff's employer and co-workers.
9. As a result , plaintiff has been exposed to public ridicule, contempt and disgrace
and plaintiff's standing in the community has been injured, causing severe mental anguish and distress, all to plaintiff's damage in the amount of $_____ .
10. [*Special damages, if any, such as for medical care and treatment, loss of employment, expenses for moving to a new home, etc.*]
11. [*Punitive damages, if any, for defendant's malicious actions in reckless and wanton
disregard for plaintiff's rights, and defendant's intent to harass and vex plaintiff.*]
   THEREFORE, plaintiff demands judgment against defendant in the amount of
$_____ plus costs; and plaintiff prays for such other and further relief as is just and
proper.

_____
Attorney for Plaintiff

---

indicated in instruction #12. (For example: "Plaintiff refers to paragraph numbers 6–9 above and incorporates them here.")

18. Very rarely is there a need to give citations to statutes, cases, etc. in a complaint. The one exception is the citation to the law (usually a statute) giving the court subject matter jurisdiction. See instruction #10. If needed, this citation should be given in the complaint.

19. Do not fill the complaint with overstatements. At the trial, the allegations in the complaint must be proven. Do not plead facts in the complaint that cannot be proven at trial. On the other hand, you do not have to limit yourself to facts you will be able to prove beyond a reasonable doubt.

20. Use a separate paragraph for the prayer for relief in which you state what you want. This will usually be a specific amount in damages, although other remedies can also be sought, e.g., an injunction. In some courts, there are jurisdictional limits on the amount in damages that can be claimed. If so, be sure your statement of damages is within these limits.
21. The verification is a sworn statement that the contents of the complaint are true. Check the law in your state to determine whether your tort complaint must be verified.

DISCOVERY

Discovery consists of a series of out-of-court, pretrial devices designed to help attorneys prepare for trial. The six formal discovery devices are:

1. written interrogatories
2. oral deposition
3. written deposition
4. production of documents and things; entry on land for inspection
5. physical or mental examination
6. request for admission

All are designed to force an exchange of pretrial information about the litigation. The major objectives of discovery are as follows:

1. Information Gathering

At the beginning of a relatively complex suit, there is a great deal that each side does not know about the other's case. Who are the parties? What is their background? What facts are being alleged to support claims and defenses? What witnesses might be called at trial? What documents or other physical things are involved in the claims or defenses? Rather than wait and be surprised at trial, each side uses discovery to obtain answers to such questions beforehand. Every claim (cause of action) and every defense has elements. Discovery is a way of obtaining more facts that both sides are likely to use to prove or disprove these elements at trial.

2. Strategy Formulation

A major objective of gathering the information is to formulate strategies for settlement and for trial. What a person says during discovery can usually be used against that person at trial if there are inconsistencies. One way to **impeach** (i.e., discredit) a witness at trial is to introduce into evidence inconsistent statements the witness made during discovery. In addition, discovery gives attorneys the chance to observe each other's skills. Strategies are based in part on perceived strengths and weaknesses of opposing counsel. Discovery is one place to gather these perceptions. More important, attorneys use discovery to "size up" parties and other witnesses on both sides in order to determine how well they present their position, how well they communicate. Attorneys may decide not to use witnesses at trial based on how they "come across" during deposition. Finally, attorneys may want to use discovery to let the other side know how strong their case is, and how correspondingly weak the other side's case is, as a strategy to pressure the other side into a favorable settlement.

3. Case Valuation

How much is this case "really" worth? What are the chances of a judgment imposing liability? What are the chances of a high damages award? What obstacles will exist in overcoming expected objections to crucial evidence? How much time, effort, and money will be needed to win this case? These questions are uppermost in the attorney's mind from the moment the client walks in the door. They are also of paramount importance during discovery, where an attorney may begin to obtain clear answers to these questions for the first time.

Very often attorneys will present data obtained from discovery to insurance carriers in order to help the latter decide whether to settle, and, if so, for how much. (See Chapter 29 on the settlement brochure.)

4. Narrowing the Focus of the Trial

Once the parties have been through discovery, they may be able to agree on what is *not* in dispute. In effect, they stipulate such matters out of the trial. The request for admissions, for example, is a discovery device designed to exert pressure for such agreements that have the effect of narrowing the trial so that time does not have to be wasted on matters the parties are not contesting. Absent such pressure, one party may force another to prove something solely for the purpose of harassment.

5. Preserving Evidence

Suppose it is impossible for witnesses to appear at trial, e.g., due to other commitments or illness. If their testimony has been obtained through discovery, the discovery testimony can sometimes be introduced at trial in substitute for an actual appearance at trial. Normally, such a substitution is not allowed. The major exception is when the testimony would otherwise be unobtainable.

6. Laying a Foundation for Summary Judgment

One of the early motions made by a party at trial is often the **motion for summary judgment.** The basis of the motion is that there is no need to go to trial because there are no genuine issues of material fact. In support of the motion, attorneys will refer to what is revealed through discovery. Hence, as attorneys go through discovery, an important objective will be to determine whether a basis exists for a summary judgment motion.

The chart in Figure 3–14 describes the six discovery devices. It also lists paralegal roles for each. The outline of the law in the chart is based on the Federal Rules of Civil Procedure (FRCP), which governs procedure in the main trial courts within the federal court system, the United States District Courts. Many states have adopted discovery rules that are closely based on the Federal Rules of Civil Procedure.

Following Figure 3–14, there are sample interrogatories in Figure 3–15. They cover a typical personal injury case involving an automobile collision.[4] Of course, all interrogatories for such cases will not be this extensive. Some attorneys will want to use a much shorter version of the questions and rely instead on other discovery devices to obtain the kind of detail sought here. Indeed, in some states a much shorter version may be *required.*

In addition to being a guide for drafting interrogatories, the sample questions in Figure 3–15 have a number of other advantages:

- The questions can serve as a guide for investigators in a personal injury case.
- The questions can serve as a guide for the legal interviewer conducting an intake interview of new clients.
- The questions can serve as a guide for the attorney preparing for and conducting a deposition.

For another set of interrogatories geared to a medical malpractice case, see Figure 18–2 in Chapter 18.

---

[4]The interrogatories are adapted from those found in W. Smith, "Form Interrogatories in Personal Injury Actions," 32 *Insurance Counsel Journal* 453, 458ff (1965). Reprinted with permission granted by the International Association of Insurance Counsel.

FIGURE 3–14 Pretrial discovery devices with paralegal roles.

Discovery Device	Description	Who Must Submit to Device?	How Initiated	Time Limits	Legitimate Reasons for Not Complying	Sanctions for Noncompliance	Role of the Litigation Assistant	Federal Rules of Civil Procedure
1: Written interrogatories (For a sample set of interrogatories for an automobile negligence case, see Figure 3–15 in this chapter. For a sample set used in a medical malpractice case see Figure 18–2 in Chapter 18.)	A series of written questions is sent by one party to the other. (There may be a maximum number of questions that can be asked, e.g., 25, unless the court grants permission to ask more.) The attorney for the party receiving the questions prepares written answers, which are returned to the sending party. The answers are given under oath, i.e., the answering party swears the answers are true.	Parties only. Nonparty witnesses do not have to answer and cannot send interrogatories.	No court order is involved. The parties begin the process by simply sending the questions to each other.	Parties must usually wait until after the action has been commenced before sending the questions. States differ on how much time the receiving party has to answer, e.g., 30 days, 45 days.	**a.** The question is improper because it is not reasonably calculated to lead to admissible evidence. **b.** The answer to the question is protected by privilege (e.g., attorney/client privilege, doctor/patient privilege). **c.** The question will lead to annoyance, embarrassment, or undue burden. **d.** The answer to the question is protected by the **attorney work-product rule.** This rule protects ideas, memos, etc. prepared in anticipation of litigation by attorneys and their assistants.	**a.** Go to court to move that the other side be ordered to answer. **b.** Ask the court to require the noncomplying party to pay the expenses of the motion listed in (a) above. **c.** Ask the court to rule that the other side be deemed to have admitted the matters involved in the questions not answered, or answered incompletely or evasively. **d.** Ask the court for a contempt order. Parties disobeying court orders imposing sanctions may be held in contempt.	**a.** Prepare a draft of the interrogatories. **b.** Prepare a draft of answers to interrogatories received from the other side. **c.** Read all pleadings, interview reports, and investigation reports as background for the drafting tasks listed in (a) and (b) above. **d.** Arrange conference with client to go over questions and answers. **e.** Draft motions, e.g., to compel a response to interrogatories. **f.** Index and digest interrogatories and answers for office file. **g.** Enter the dates in office tickler to serve as reminders.	FRCP #33 (interrogatories to parties) FRCP #37 (sanctions for noncompliance)
2: Oral deposition	A deposition is a question-and-answer session usually conducted in the office of one of the attorneys. The attorney asks the questions and all answers are **transcribed** (recorded word for word) by a stenographer or	A deposition can be taken of a party to the suit. It is also possible to take the deposition of a nonparty witness. The party being *deposed* (i.e., asked questions) is called the **deponent.**	A court order is generally not needed. The deponent is simply sent a notice of the time and place of the deposition. Some courts allow a **subpoena duces tecum** to be served if the requesting party	Parties must usually wait until the action has been commenced before taking a deposition. (A court order may be needed to take the deposition sooner, e.g., because the the deponent may not be available after	**a.** The question is improper because it is not reasonably calculated to lead to admissible evidence. **b.** The answer to the question is protected by privilege (e.g., attorney/client privilege, doctor/	**a.** Go to court to move that the deponent be forced to appear at the deposition, to answer a question that was objected to, or to bring documents or other materials to the deposition as requested.	**a.** Schedule time and place for the deposition. **b.** Prepare subpoena duces tecum. **c.** Prepare a list of suggested questions for attorney to ask deponent. **d.** Arrange for scheduling and	FRCP #30 (oral depositions) FRCP #37 (sanctions)

FIGURE 3-14 Continued

Discovery Device	Description	Who Must Submit to Device?	How Initiated	Time Limits	Legitimate Reasons for Not Complying	Sanctions for Noncompliance	Role of the Litigation Assistant	Federal Rules of Civil Procedure
2: Oral deposition— Continued	court reporter who administers an oath to the deponent. (The proceeding might also be recorded on video or audio tape recorder). The opposing attorney is allowed cross-examination questions. If the deponent refuses to answer a question, the deposition moves on to other matters after the reason for the refusal and the objection thereto is noted in the record. (Later, a court may be asked to compel the answer.) Once the transcript is typed, the deponent reads it and signs it if accurate, or states why it is inaccurate.		wants the deponent to bring documents or materials to the deposition. (See Figure 3–16.) Such a subpoena is used mainly when the deponent bringing such documents or materials is a nonparty witness. Note: some states will not allow more than 10 depositions in the litigation without special court permission.	the action has commenced.)	patient privilege). **c.** The question will lead to annoyance, embarrassment, oppression, or undue burden. **d.** The answer to the question is protected by the attorney work-product rule.	payment of stenographer or reporter. **b.** Ask the court to require the deponent to pay the expenses of the motion listed in (a) above. **c.** Ask the court to rule that the other side be deemed to have admitted the matters involved in the deposition questions not answered or answered incompletely or evasively. **d.** If the court makes any of the above orders, the deponent may be held in contempt for continued noncompliance.	payment of stenographer or reporter. **e.** Order transcript of deposition. **f.** Read all pleadings, interview reports, investigation reports, and prior answers to interrogatories, if any, in order to prepare indexes, digests, and draft questions for the attorney. **g.** Take notes at the deposition. **h.** Draft motions, e.g., to force compliance by other side. **i.** Read transcript of deposition to index it, digest it, compare it to interrogatory answers, look for inconsistencies, etc. **j.** Make entries in office tickler on due dates.	
3: Written deposition	Same as oral deposition, except that both attorneys are not present. The attorneys prepare the questions on behalf of their clients who are the deponents. But the questions are asked by a stenographer or reporter.	Same as oral deposition.	Same as oral deposition.	Same as oral deposition.	Same as oral deposition.	Same as oral deposition.	Same as oral deposition.	FRCP #31 (depositions on written questions)

FIGURE 3–14 Continued

Discovery Device	Description	Who Must Submit to Device?	How Initiated	Time Limits	Legitimate Reasons for Not Complying	Sanctions for Noncompliance	Role of the Litigation Assistant	Federal Rules of Civil Procedure
4: Production of documents and things; entry on land for inspection and other purposes (For example, see Figure 3–17.)	A party wants to inspect, test, or copy documents (e.g., photos, drawings) or other tangible things, or go upon land to inspect, photograph, or measure. This is allowed as long as the requesting party proceeds in a reasonable time and manner. If a party has made a statement about the case, e.g., to the insurance adjuster, this discovery device may be a way to obtain a copy of the statement.	This device is directed at parties only. The party must be in possession or control of the document, thing, or land in question. If you want a *nonparty* to turn over documents and other materials, you can seek a deposition of this nonparty and use a *subpoena duces tecum* to specify what should be brought to the deposition.	In most courts, no court order is needed to start the process. A party simply sends a notice to the other party making a request for access to the document, thing, etc. Some courts, however, require a court order and a showing of good cause to use this discovery device.	Parties must usually wait until the action is commenced. After the request is made, the other side has a designated time, e.g., 30 days, in which to respond to the request and allow the inspection, copying, etc.	**a.** The inspection, copying, or testing is improper because it is not reasonably calculated to lead to admissible evidence. **b.** The items to be inspected, copied, or tested are protected by privilege, e.g., attorney/client privilege, doctor/patient privilege. **c.** The inspection, copying, or testing will lead to annoyance, embarrassment, oppression, or undue burden. **d.** The items to be inspected, copied, or tested are protected by the attorney work-product rule.	**a.** Go to court to move that the inspection, copying, etc., be ordered against a noncooperating party. **b.** Ask the court to require the other side to pay the expenses of the above motion, listed in (a). **c.** Ask the court to rule that the other side is deemed to have admitted the matters related to the document, thing, etc. in a manner favorable to the requesting party. **d.** If the court makes any of the orders that are not obeyed, the nonconforming party may be held in contempt.	**a.** Prepare a draft of a request for production of documents, things, etc. specifying what you want to copy, inspect, or test, and when you want to do so. **b.** Arrange who will do the inspecting, copying, etc., payment of costs involved, etc. **c.** Draft a motion to compel the inspection, copying, etc. **d.** File, digest, and index the report(s) that come back from the inspection. **e.** Enter scheduled dates for inspection, copying, etc. in the office tickler.	FRCP #34 (production of documents, etc.) FRCP #37 (sanctions)
5: Physical or mental examination	The person to be examined is given the name and address of the doctor who will conduct the physical or mental exam. Some states do not allow that person's own attorney to be present. All parties, includ-	Limited to parties only and to persons under the control of parties, e.g., the child of a party. (In a few courts, the employees of a party can also be forced to undergo a physical or mental examination.)	A court order is required. There must be a showing of *good cause* for the examination. (Parties, however, may informally agree to have the exam done without asking for a court order.)	The court must approve the time and place of the exam unless the parties mutually agree on their own.	**a.** The person to be examined is not within the control of the responding party. **b.** The person's mental or physical condition is not in controversy. **c.** There is no *good cause* for the examination.	Ask a court to rule that the party who refused to submit to the ordered examination be deemed to have admitted matters that are in controversy (concerning the physical or mental examination) in a	**a.** Schedule doctor's appointment and payment. **b.** Enter appointment date in office tickler. **c.** Prepare court motion to order the examination. **d.** Prepare court motion to have matters relevant	FRCP #35 (physical or mental examination) FRCP #37 (sanctions)

FIGURE 3–14 Continued

Discovery Device	Description	Who Must Submit to Device?	How Initiated	Time Limits	Legitimate Reasons for Not Complying	Sanctions for Noncompliance	Role of the Litigation Assistant	Federal Rules of Civil Procedure
5: Physical or mental examination—Continued	ing the person examined, are given a copy of the doctor's report.				**d.** The examination would be unduly burdensome.	manner favorable to the requesting party.	to the examination be deemed admitted for failure to submit to examination.	
6: Request for admissions (For example, see Figure 3–18.)	One party sends the other statements of fact and asks that the truth of the statements be admitted so that the requesting party does not have to prove the facts at trial. A similar request may be made to admit the genuineness of certain documents or other things. The responding party must either agree to the admission or disagree, with reasons why he or she is denying the request for admission.	Limited to parties only.	No court order is involved. The requests for admission are simply sent to the other party.	The requests are made after the suit has begun. The responding party has a set number of days in which to reply, e.g., 30.	**a.** The requests for admission call for matters protected by privilege, e.g., attorney/client privilege, doctor/patient privilege. **b.** The requests for admission will lead to annoyance, embarrassment, oppression, or undue burden. **c.** The requests for admission call for matters protected by the attorney work-product rule.	**a.** Ask a court to rule that the party who failed to respond to the request within the designated time be deemed to have made the admissions. **b.** Ask the court to require the offending party to pay the expenses the aggrieved party had to bear in proving the truth of the facts or the genuineness of the documents or things at trial.	**a.** Read everything in the file (interview and investigation reports, interrogatory answers, deposition transcript, etc.) in order to prepare a list of facts the other side will be requested to admit. **b.** File, index, and digest the responses from the other side in the office file. **c.** Enter due dates in office tickler.	FRCP #36 (requests for admission) FRCP #37 (sanctions)

STATE OF _____
County of _____
Civil Court Branch

Dennis Diamond   Plaintiff
346 Redgrove Street
City of _____ ,   CIVIL ACTION NO. _____
State of _____
                    V.
Janet McDonald   Defendant
781 4th Street
City of _____ ,
State of _____

Interrogatories to Plaintiff

Pursuant to section _____ , _____ hereby submits the following interrogatories to _____ . These interrogatories are to be answered by _____ under oath and served on the attorney for _____ within _____ days.

Instructions:

A. All information is to be divulged that is in the possession of individuals or corporate parties, their attorneys, investigators, agents, employees, or other representatives of the named parties and their attorneys.

B. A "medical practitioner" as used in these interrogatories is meant to include any medical doctor, osteopathic physician, podiatrist, doctor of chiropractic, naturopathic physician, or other person who performs any form of healing art.

C. Where an individual interrogatory calls for an answer that involves more than one part, each part of the answer should be clearly set out so that it is understandable.

D. Where the terms "you," "plantiff," or "defendant" are used, they are meant to include every individual party, and separate answers should be given for each person named as a party, if requested.

E. Where the terms "accident" or "the accident" are used, they are meant to mean the incident or occurrence that is the basis of this lawsuit, unless otherwise specified.

Name

1. State your full name, age, and place of birth.

2. Have you ever been known by any other name? If so, give the other name or names and state where and when you used such names.

3. Has your name ever been legally changed? If so, state when, where, and through what procedure.

Residence

4. State your present residence address and the period during which you have resided at this address.

5. List all other addresses at which you have resided during the past ten years and the dates of the use of each.

Marriage

6. Are you married at the present time? If so:
a. give your spouse's full name.
b. if a female, your spouse's birth name if different.
c. your spouse's address for the five years before your marriage,
d. the date and place of your marriage,
e. state whether your spouse is now living with you,
f. if not, state when the separation occurred, and
g. your spouse's present address.

7. If you were previously married, state for each previous spouse:
a. the name and present residence address of each spouse:
b. the dates of commencement and termination of each marriage,

FIGURE 3–15 Sample interrogatories.

FIGURE 3–15 Continued

c. the place where you were married to each spouse,
d. the manner in which each marriage was terminated,
e. if any marriage was terminated by divorce, state for each such divorce the county and state or place where the action was filed and the ground alleged in said action and whether the divorce was filed by you.

Past Employment

8. For the ten years immediately preceding the date of the incident referred to in the complaint, state:
   a. names and addresses of each of your employers,
   b. dates of commencement and termination of each employment,
   c. detailed description of the services or other work performed for each employment,
   d. your average weekly wages or earnings from each employment,
   e. whether a physical examination was required, and if so, state the date, place, and person giving the physical examination,
   f. whether you gave your employer any statements or representations in writing or answered in writing any questions concerning your physical condition,
   g. names of your immediate boss or other superior to whom you were responsible at each of the places of employment listed above.

Present Employment

9. What was your business or occupation at the time of the incident referred to in the complaint? Are you still engaged in such business or occupation? If not, state:
   a. when you ceased working in such business or occupation,
   b. your present business or occupation, the date entered, and present income from such business or occupation,
   c. any other business or occupation prior to your present one, the dates entered and income from such businesses or occupations.
10. Have you lost any time from your business or occupation since the incident referred to in the complaint? If so, state:
    a. the cause of such loss of time,
    b. the number of days lost and the dates,
    c. the amount of any wages or income lost.
11. If employed at the time of the incident referred to in the complaint, state:
    a. the name and address of the employer,
    b. the position held and the nature of the work performed,
    c. average weekly wages for the preceding year.
12. If employed since the incident referred to in the complaint, state:
    a. name and address of present employer,
    b. position held and nature of work being performed,
    c. hours worked per week,
    d. present weekly wages, earnings, income, or profit,
    e. name of your immediate boss or other superior to whom you are responsible,
    f. whether a physical examination was required, and, if so, state the date, place, and person giving the examination,
    g. whether you gave your employer any statements or representations in writing or answered in writing any questions concerning your physical condition.

Social Security, Workers' Compensation, or Other Disability Payments

13. What is your social security number?
14. Have you ever drawn social security benefits for disability? If so, state:
    a. your residence at the time,
    b. the social security office through which you filed your claim,
    c. the nature and extent of the disability,
    d. the length of time of such disability and the beginning date.
15. Are you now receiving or have you ever received any disability pension, income, or insurance or any workers' compensation from any agency, company, person, corporation, state, or government? If so, state:
    a. the nature of any such payment,

FIGURE 3–15   Continued

   b. dates you received the payments,
   c. for what injuries or disability you received the payments, and how such injury occurred or disability arose,
   d. by whom they were paid,
   e. whether you now have any present disability as a result of such injuries or disability,
   F. if so, the nature and extent of such disability.
   g. whether you had any disability at the time of the incident referred to in the complaint,
   h. if so, the nature and extent of such disability.

Income and Tax Returns

16. With respect to each of the past five years, state:
   a. your yearly gross income,
   b. your yearly net income,
   c. the name and address of the person, firm, or corporation having custody of any papers pertaining to your income.
17. Did you file income tax returns with the Internal Revenue Service (IRS) for any of the past five years or with any state tax authority or department? If so state:
   a. the IRS office with which each federal return was filed,
   b. the amount reported in each federal return as earned income,
   c. the years filed,
   d. the amount of tax shown to be due on each federal return,
   e. the state tax authority or department with whom state returns were filed,
   f. the years filed,
   g. the amount of tax shown to be due on each state return.

Education

18. State the name and address of each school, college, or educational institution you have attended or completed, listing the courses of study, dates of attendance, and dates of completion (if completed).

Armed Forces

19. Have you ever served in the armed forces or performed military services for any branch of any governmental agency? If so state:
   a. the name of each organization and the particular branch for which you performed services,
   b. the dates and places of services,
   c. your serial or identification number,
   d. a detailed description of the services performed,
   e. whether a physical exam was required, and if so, the dates and places of the exams,
   f. the date of termination of the services,
   g. a detailed description of reasons the services were discontinued.
20. Have you ever been rejected for military service for physical reasons? If so, state:
   a. the date thereof,
   b. the condition for which rejected,
   c. the agency rejecting you.
21. Have you ever received a discharge from military or government service for physical reasons? If so state:
   a. the date thereof,
   b. the condition for which discharged,
   c. the agency discharging you.

Hobbies and Recreation

22. List all hobbies and forms of recreation in which you have participated in the last ten years.
23. State all social clubs, lodges, or associations of any nature in which you have participated or of which you were a member in the last ten years.

FIGURE 3–15 Continued

Other Claims

24. Have you made claim for any benefits under any medical pay coverage or policy of insurance relating to injuries arising out of the incident involved in the complaint? If so, state:
    a. the name of the insurance company or organization to which the claim was made,
    b. the date of the claim,
    c. the claim number and policy number.
25. Have you ever made claim for any benefits under any insurance policy, or against any person, firm, or corporation for personal injuries or physical condition you have not heretofore listed in your answers to these interrogatories? If so, state:
    a. the injury or condition for which such claim was made,
    b. the name and address of the person, firm, or corporation to which or against which it was made,
    c. the date it was made,
    d. the nature and amount of any payment received.

Prior or Subsequent Injuries and Diseases

26. Have you ever suffered any injuries in any accident either prior or subsequent to the incident referred to in the complaint? If so, state:
    a. date and place of such injury,
    b. detailed description of all the injuries you received,
    c. name and addresses of any hospitals rendering treatment,
    d. names and addresses of all medical practitioners rendering treatment,
    e. nature and extent of recovery, and, if any permanent disability was suffered, the nature and extent of the permanent disability,
    f. if you were compensated in any manner for any such injury, state the names and addresses of each and every person or organization paying such compensation and the amount thereof.
27. Have you ever had any serious illness, sickness, disease, or surgical operations, either prior or subsequent to the incident referred to in the complaint? If so, state:
    a. date and place,
    b. detailed description of your symptoms,
    c. names and addresses of any hospitals rendering treatment,
    d. names and addresses of all medical practitioners rendering treatment,
    e. approximate date of your recovery,
    f. if you did not recover fully, give the date your condition became stationary and a description of your condition at that time.

Life Insurance

28. Have you ever been turned down or rated by any company for accident, health, or life insurance? If so, state:
    a. the name and address of such company or companies,
    b. the date thereof,
    c. the reason stated by the company or companies.

Weight

29. Please give your average weight for the two years preceding the injuries complained of, your weight at the time of such injuries, and your weight at this time.

Crimes or Imprisonment

30. Have you ever been convicted, by plea of guilty, by plea of no contest, or by trial, of any crime other than traffic violations? If so, state:
    a. the nature of the offense,
    b. the date,
    c. the county and state in which you were convicted,
    d. the sentence given you.
31. Have you ever entered or been committed to any institution, either public or private, for the treatment or observation of mental conditions, alcoholism, narcotic addiction, or disorders of any kind? If so, state:

FIGURE 3–15   Continued

  a. the name and address of such institution,
  b. the length of your stay and the dates thereof,
  c. the purpose or reason for your entry into such institution,
  d. the name and address of each of the doctors who treated you for such condition.

Traffic Violations

 32. Please list all violations of the motor vehicle or traffic laws or ordinances to which you have pleaded guilty or no contest and to which you have been found guilty. For each violation, state the date, the court in which the case was heard, and the nature of the violation charged.

Driver's License

 33. At the time of the incident referred to in the complaint, did you have a valid license to operate a motor vehicle? If so, state:
  a. the state issuing it,
  b. the expiration date,
  c. the number of such license,
  d. whether there were any restrictions on said license, and, if so, the nature of the restrictions.
 34. Have you ever had a license to operate a motor vehicle suspended or revoked? If so, state:
  a. when and where it was suspended or revoked,
  b. the period of the suspension or revocation,
  c. the reasons for the suspension or revocation,
  d. whether the suspension or revocation was lifted, and if so, when.

Purpose of Trip

 35. State the point of origin and the point of destination of the particular travel in which you were engaged on the date and time of the incident referred to in the complaint, and state the following:
  a. the date and time on which you left your point of origin,
  b. the names and addresses of all passengers who may have been with you between the point of origin and the point of accident,
  c. the date, time, and specific location of each place you may have stopped between the point of origin and the point of accident,
  d. the number of miles between the point of origin and the point of accident,
  e. the estimated time you were expecting to arrive at your intended point of destination,
  f. the purpose of your travel.

Facts of Accident

 36. State in detail the manner in which you assert the incident referred to in the complaint occurred, specifying the speed, position, direction, and location of each vehicle involved during its approach to, at the time of, and immediately after the collision.

Preceding Forty-Eight Hours

 37. Did you consume any alcoholic beverage of any type, or any sedative, tranquilizer, or other drug, medicine, or pill during the forty-eight hours immediately preceding the incident referred to in the complaint? If so, state:
  a. the nature, amount, and type of item consumed,
  b. the amount of time during which consumed,
  c. the names and addresses of any and all persons who have any knowledge as to the consumption of these items.

Repairs to Vehicle

 38. State whether the vehicle in which you were riding was repaired. If so, state:
  a. the date thereof,
  b. the name and address of the person or corporation making such repairs,
  c. the nature of the repairs,
  d. the cost of the repairs,

FIGURE 3–15 Continued

    e. if written records or memoranda were made of the repairs, state where and when they were made, the names and addresses of the persons making them, their present whereabouts, and the name and address of the persons now in possession or custody of them.

  39. If the vehicle was not repaired, state whether an estimate of the necessary repairs was made. If so, state:

    a. the name and address of the person making such estimate,

    b. if it was written, the name and address of any person presently having custody of a copy thereof.

Statements by Plaintiff

  40. State whether you have made any statement or statements in any form to any person regarding any of the events or happenings referred to in your complaint. If so, state:

    a. the name and addresses of the person or persons to whom such statements were made,

    b. the date such statements were made,

    c. the form of the statement, whether written, oral, taken by recording device, by court reporter, or by stenographer,

    d. whether such statements, if written, were signed,

    e. the names and addresses of the persons presently having custody of such statements.

Witnesses

  41. State the full name and last known address, giving the street, street number, city, and state of every witness known to you or to your attorneys who has any knowledge regarding the facts and circumstances surrounding the incident referred to in the complaint or your alleged injuries including, but not limited to, eyewitnesses to such event, as well as medical witnesses and other persons having any knowledge thereof.

  42. If any of the witnesses listed above or whom you propose to use at the trial are related to you or to each other, please state the nature of such relationship.

Defendant's Statement

  43. State the full name and last known address, giving the street, street number, city, and state, of every witness known to you or to your attorneys who claims to have seen or heard the defendant make any statement or statements pertaining to any of the events or happenings alleged in your complaint.

  44. For each individual whose name you have given in the answer to the preceding interrogatory, state:

    a. the location or locations where the defendant made any such statement or statements,

    b. the name and address of the person or persons in whose presence the defendant made any such statement or statements,

    c. the time and date on which the defendant made any such statement or statements,

    d. the name and address of any other person present at the time and place the defendant made such statement or statements,

    e. whether you or anyone acting on your behalf obtained statements in any form from any persons who claim to be able to testify to the statement or statements made by the defendant.

  45. If the answer to question 44(e) is in the affirmative, state:

  a. the names and addresses of the persons from whom any such statements were taken,

  b. the date on which said statements were taken,

  c. the names and addresses of the employers of the persons who took such statements,

  d. the names and addresses of the persons having custody of such statements,

  e. whether such statements were written, oral, taken by recording device, by court reporter, or by stenographer.

Written Statements of Witnesses

  46. State whether you, your attorney, your insurance carrier, or anyone acting on your or their behalf obtained statements in any form from any persons regarding any of the events or happenings that occurred at the scene of the incident referred to in the complaint immediately before, at the time of, or immediately after said incident. If so, state:

FIGURE 3–15   Continued

a. the name and address of the person from whom any such statements were taken,
b. the dates on which such statements were taken,
c. the names and addresses of the persons and employers of such persons who took such statements,
d. the names and addresses of the persons having custody of such statements,
e. whether such statements were written, oral, taken by recording device, by court reporter, or by stenographer.

Expert and Medical Evidence

47. State the names and addresses of any and all proposed expert witnesses, and the technical field in which you claim they are an expert.

48. Do you intend to rely on any medical text in your cross-examination of this defendant's medical experts? If so, state:
a. the exact title of each medical text on which you intend to rely,
b. the name and address of the publisher of each such medical text,
c. the date on which each such medical text was published,
d. the name of the author of each such medical text.

Diagrams, Photos, Surveys, and Other Descriptions

49. Do you, your attorney, your insurance carrier, or anyone acting on your or their behalf, have or know of any photographs, motion pictures, maps, drawings, diagrams, measurements, surveys, or other descriptions concerning the events and happenings alleged in the complaint, the scene of the accident, or the areas or persons or vehicles involved made either before, after, or at the time of the events in question, including any photographs or other recordings made of the plaintiff at any time since the incident referred to in the complaint? If so, as to each such item, state:
a. its nature,
b. its specific subject matter,
c. the date it was made or taken,
d. the name and last known address of the person making or taking it,
e. what each such item purports to show, illustrate, or represent,
f. the name and address of the person having custody of such item.

Injuries

50. Please state in detail the nature of the injury or injuries you allege you suffered as a result of the incident referred to in the complaint.

51. With respect to the injuries allegedly suffered, state:
a. the extent and nature of any disability,
b. the location of any pain suffered and the duration and intensity of such pain,
c. whether you suffered any restraint of your normal activities due to the injuries allegedly suffered, and, if so, describe in detail the nature of such restraint and the date you suffered the pain.

52. If you receive any treatment with respect to the injuries allegedly suffered, state:
a. the name and address of each hospital at which you were treated or admitted,
b. the dates on which said treatment was rendered, including the dates of entry and discharge into and from said hospital or hospitals,
c. the cost and expenses imposed by each of the hospitals listed above,
d. the name and address of each medical practitioner who examined, treated, or conferred with you with respect to the injuries alleged,
e. the cost and expenses of such examinations or treatments by the medial practitioner listed above.

53. State the treatment, procedures, or operation performed in connection with the alleged injuries at any hospital and give the name of the hospital and the name of the medical practitioners giving the treatment or performing the procedures, and the dates upon which they were given or performed.

54. Since the date of the incident referred to in your complaint, have you been treated by or examined by or conferred with or consulted with any other medical practitioner whose name you have not heretofore supplied? If so, state:
a. the name and address of each medical practitioner who examined, treated, conferred, or consulted with you and the dates of the same,
b. the condition for which the examination, treatment, or attention was rendered.

FIGURE 3–15 Continued

55. If you have incurred any medical bills in connection with the alleged injuries not heretofore listed, please state:
   a. the total amount of each such bill,
   b. the person to whom such amount was paid,
   c. the service or thing for which the bill was rendered.
56. If you are still receiving medical services or treatment of any nature whatsoever, state:
   a. the name or names of the person or persons serving or treating you,
   b. the approximate frequency of said service or treatment.
57. State the dates following your discharge from the hospital during which you were confined:
   a. to your bed,
   b. to your home.

Orthopedic Appliances
58. Have you worn any brace or other type of orthopedic appliance? If so, state:
   a. the name of the medical practitioner who fitted or prescribed said appliance,
   b. the nature of the appliance and its cost,
   c. when you started wearing said appliance,
   d. when you stopped wearing said appliance,
   e. was said appliance worn constantly or intermittently during the foregoing period? If both, state the period in which it was worn constantly.
59. At the time of the incident referred to in the complaint, did you have any condition for which you wore eyeglasses or for which eyeglasses had been prescribed for you? If so, state:
   a. the nature of the condition,
   b. whether you were wearing glasses at the time in question,
   c. the name and address of the person who prescribed eyeglasses for you.

Medicine
60. Please list all medicine purchased or used by you in connection with the treatment of the injuries complained of, the cost thereof, and the store from which purchased or obtained.

Charge Based on the Incident Complained of
61. Were you charged with any violation of law arising out of the incident referred to in your complaint? If so, state:
   a. the plea entered by you to such charge,
   b. the court in which the charge was heard,
   c. the nature of the charge,
   d. whether the testimony at any trial on said charge was transcribed or recorded in any manner whatsoever.
62. If such testimony was recorded, state by whom it was recorded and whether a transcript has been made of such recording.
   a. If a transcript has been made, state who has possession of the transcript at this time,
   b. If there was a hearing or trial on any such charge, state:
   (1) the date of the hearing or trial,
   (2) the names and addresses of the person or persons who were subpoenaed or who appeared as witnesses,
   (3) the final disposition of the hearing or trial.

Other Actions
63. Have you ever been involved in any other legal action, either as a defendant or as a plaintiff? If so, state:
   a. the date and place each action was filed, giving the name of the court, the name of the other party or parties involved, the court docket number of the action, and the names of the attorneys representing each party,
   b. a description of the nature of each action,

FIGURE 3–15   Continued

c. the result of each action, whether there was an appeal, the result of the appeal, whether the case was reported, and, if so, the name, volume number, and page citation of the report.

Losses Not Otherwise Covered

64. Have you sustained any additional financial losses as a result of the incident complained of, other than those covered by the preceding interrogatories? If so, state:

a. the nature and amount of such losses,

b. the date thereof,

c. the names and addresses of any persons to whom any money claimed for additional losses was paid.

Witnesses and Exhibits

65. List the names, addresses, official titles (if any), and other identification of all witnesses, including expert witnesses, who, it is contemplated, will be called upon to testify in support of your claim in this action, indicating the nature and substance of the testimony that is expected to be given by each witness, and state the relationship, if any, of each witness to the plaintiff(s).

66. List specifically and in detail each exhibit you propose to utilize at the trial in this matter. This interrogatory is directed both to exhibits you have already decided to use at the trial and exhibits you might use.

67. With reference to each exhibit listed in the previous interrogatory, state the source of the exhibit, the nature of the exhibit (e.g., whether the exhibit is documentary, a picture, etc.), who prepared the exhibit, and the date on which it was prepared.

Continuing Interrogatories

68. These interrogatories shall be deemed continuing so as to require supplemental answers if you or your attorneys obtain further information between the time answers are served and the time of trial.

FIGURE 3–16   *Subpoena Duces Tecum* for deposition.

THE STATE OF FLORIDA

To: _____

You are commanded to appear before a person authorized by law to take depositions at _____ in _____ , Florida, on _____ , 19____ , at _____ , for the taking of your deposition in this action and to have with you at that time and place the following: _____ _____ .

If you fail to appear, you may be in contempt of court.

You are subpoenaed to appear by the following attorneys and unless excused from this subpoena by these attorneys or the court, you shall respond to this subpoena as directed.

Witness my hand and the seal of this Court on _____ , 19____ .

(Name of the Clerk)
As Clerk of the Court
By _____
As Deputy Clerk

_____

Attorney for _____
_____

Address

FIGURE 3–17 Request for production of documents and things; entry on land for inspection and other purposes.

Plaintiff A. B. requests defendant C. D. to respond within _____ days to the following requests:

(1) That defendant produce and permit plaintiff to inspect and to copy each of the following documents:

[*Here list the documents either individually or by category and describe each of them.*]

[*Here state the time, place, and manner of making the inspection and performance of any related acts.*]

(2) That defendant produce and permit plaintiff to inspect and to copy, test, or sample each of the following objects:

[*Here list the objects either individually or by category and describe each of them.*]

[*Here state the time, place, and manner of making the inspection and performance of any related acts.*]

(3) That defendant permit plaintiff to enter [*here describe the real property to be entered*] and to inspect and to photograph, test, or sample [*here describe the portion of the property and the objects to be inspected*].

[*Here state the time, place, and manner of making the inspection and performance of any related acts.*]

Signed: _____
Attorney for Plaintiff
Address: _____

FIGURE 3–18 Request for admissions.

Plaintiff A. B. requests defendant C. D. within 30 days [or within such other time as the court may have ordered], after service of this request, to make the following admissions for the purpose of this action only and subject to all pertinent objections to admissibility which may be interposed at the trial:

1. That each of the following documents, a copy of which is attached to this request, is genuine.

[*Here list and describe each document.*]

2. That each of the following statements is true.

[*Here list the statements.*]

Signed _____
Attorney for Plaintiff
Address _____
Telephone Number _____

TRIAL AND APPEAL

Trial

The major events in a jury trial are presented in the flow chart of Figure 3–19. (In a jury trial, the jury resolves the factual disputes and the trial judge resolves the legal disputes; in a nonjury trial, the judge decides both.) The flow chart also includes the appeal and enforcement process. (See the glossary at the end of this book for the definition of any terms used in the chart with which you are unfamiliar.)

The role of paralegals at trials depends, in part, on the involvement that they have had with the case up to trial. If the involvement has been minimal, then they may not have much to do to assist the attorney at trial. If, on the other hand, they have been working closely with the attorney on the case all along, their role at trial could include a number of tasks:

- Monitoring all the files, documents, and evidence that the attorney will need to plan and to replan strategy as outlined in the trial notebook

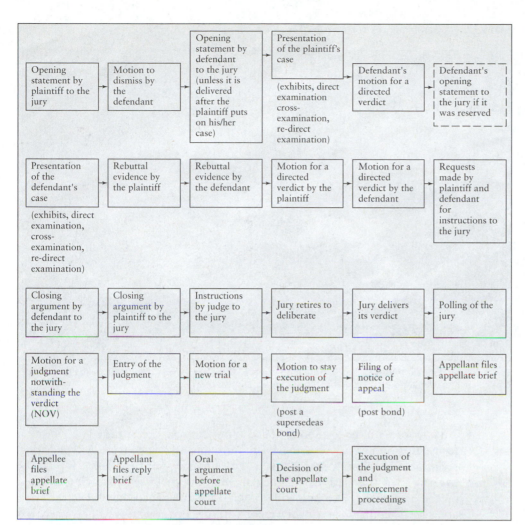

FIGURE 3–19
Flow chart of jury trial, appeal, and enforcement process.

- Helping design trial exhibits. (See Figure 3–20 for an example.)
- Doing some spot legal research on issues that come up during the trial that require an answer fairly quickly
- Preparing preliminary drafts of certain motions and other documents that are required during the course of the trial
- Assuring the presence of witnesses; assisting the attorney in preparing them for direct examination and in anticipating what may be asked of them on cross-examination

FIGURE 3–20 Trial graphic designed by a paralegal in a torts case.

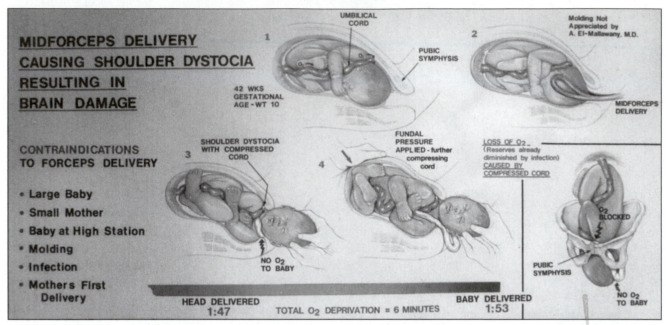

Illustration created by paralegal Kathleen Young, Litigation Visuals, Inc., that helped win a $3.9 million verdict. "Illustrations really do help the jury know where they are going in calculating damages." 11 *Legal Assistant Today* 28 (November/December, 1993).

- Taking notes on the testimony of certain witnesses. The attorney may be able to use these notes in preparing for other segments of the trial. A typed transcript of the testimony may not be available until after the trial.
- Making suggestions to the attorney on what questions to ask a witness based on the paralegal's close following of what has happened thus far in the trial, and based on his or her involvement with the documents and files prepared during the pretrial stage.

In many courts, only attorneys can sit at counsel's table during a trial. Yet, in some courts a paralegal is allowed to sit with the attorneys if permission of the presiding judge is obtained. The paralegal does not take an active role in the trial. He or she provides general assistance (e.g., note taking, organizing trial documents) for the attorney. While at the table, the paralegal is sometimes said to be sitting in the **second chair.** This phrase, however, is more accurately used to refer to another attorney who assists the lead attorney who is the "first chair." When a nonattorney such as a paralegal is allowed to sit at counsel's table, it might be more accurate to refer to him or her as being in the "third chair."

If the office is about to begin a very important and potentially complex trial, it may decide to conduct a **shadow trial** first. A shadow trial is a mock (i.e., pretend) trial designed to give the participants "stand-up" practice and feedback. For example, the office might hire some strangers to play the roles of jurors and conduct part of the trial in front of them. Attorneys in the office would be assigned the roles of opposing counsel. "Jury" deliberations would take place in front of everyone. After the trial, there would be a freewheeling discussion of the strengths and weaknesses of the case. In effect, the shadow trial acts as a kind of focus group in preparation for the real trial. (Since actual opposing attorneys and witnesses are not involved, a mock trial is different from the summary jury trial discussed earlier under ADR—alternative dispute resolution.) Litigation paralegals often have a large role in helping organize shadow trials, e.g., hiring the jurors, holding an orientation session for them before the proceedings, acting as a nonvoting juror to keep the deliberations moving along and on track.

Appeal

After the trial, the losing attorney plans appeal strategies. He or she must review all of the documents and testimony in the trial in order to identify grounds for an appeal. The paralegal may be asked to go back over the record and do the following:

- Make a list of every time I objected to something during the trial. Include the page number where my objection is found, a brief summary of what my objection was, and the ruling of the judge on my objection.
- Make a list of every time opposing counsel made reference to a particular topic, such as the plaintiff's prior involvement in other litigation.
- Make a list of every time the judge asked questions of witnesses.

Other paralegal tasks can include:

- Researching the legislative history of relevant statutes.
- Shepardizing cases and conducting cite checking.
- Reading over appellate briefs to cross-check the accuracy of quoted testimony from the typed transcript of the trial.
- Monitoring the typing, printing, and filing of appellate briefs.

ENFORCEMENT

Judgments are not self-executing. After the court announces its final decision, the loser (now called the judgment debtor) rarely walks over to the winner (the judgment creditor) with a check for the amount of the damages awarded. One of the first tasks of a paralegal working for the attorney that represented the judgment creditor is often to compile a list of the assets of the judgment debtor. The following information is needed for each asset:

- A description of the asset. Be specific as to quantity, color, size or other measurements, function, component parts, or any other data relevant to the kind of asset in question.
- Location. Where is the asset? Give the exact addresses and names of people who have possession of the asset or who recently had possession, including, of course, the judgment debtor.
- A record of how the judgment debtor obtained his or her interest in the asset. If by purchase, how much was paid, when was it acquired, etc.?
- Current fair market value of the asset. If the asset was sold on the open market today, how much would it probably bring?

How do you go about locating the assets of the uncooperative judgment debtor? There are some formal procedures that can be of assistance in discovering assets. Before discussing these, some thoughts will be presented on *informal* investigative techniques. See Figure 3–21.

The judgment creditor has just been through a trial and perhaps an appeal with the judgment debtor. A good deal is already known about the latter. This data must be organized and evaluated at two levels. First, the data contain specific information on the possible assets and other debts of the judgment debtor. Second, the data tell you a lot about the lifestyle of the judgment debtor. One's lifestyle can be an excellent clue to available assets. See the categories of Figure 3–21.

We now turn to the more formal methods of posttrial discovery of assets and liabilities that might be available. Four major devices will be discussed, some of which overlap. These devices are often begun by the judgment creditor's service of a subpoena on the judgment debtor or on anyone else who may have information on the financial condition of the judgment debtor.

FIGURE 3–21
Informal investigative techniques to discover the assets of a judgment debtor.

I. Financial Data That You Already Have about the Judgment Debtor from the Litigation to Date

A. Data in the Office Case File

1. Notes on the reasons why the attorney for the judgment creditor (JC) agreed to take the case initially. What led the attorney to believe that the judgment debtor (JD) was not judgment proof?
2. Notes on the intake interview of the client. What did the client say or imply about the financial status of the JD?
3. Notes on preliminary investigations done by the law firm.
4. Notes on early negotiations with opposing counsel to settle the case. What was said about the JD? Did you learn about liability insurance limits?
5. Pleadings, e.g., the responses given in the answer to the complaint.
6. Correspondence in the file.
7. Data obtained through pretrial discovery:
   • answers to interrogatories
   • deposition transcripts of the JD and other witnesses
   • the contents of documents obtained through a motion to produce
   • the answers to requests for admissions
   • the results of physical and mental examinations
8. Transcripts of direct, cross, and re-direct examination of the JD and other witnesses who testified about the JD's past.
9. Exhibits introduced at trial, whether or not they were admitted into evidence, e.g., police reports on the accident, prior convictions.
10. Motions and briefs filed by the JD.

B. Other Direct or Indirect Financial Data Based on Appearances as Clues to Lifestyle

1. Did the JD hire an expensive law firm?
2. How well did the JD dress? What kind of car did he or she drive?
3. Did the JD appear successful and prominent in business?
4. What educational level was demonstrated?
5. To what kind of lifestyle did the JD's family appear to be accustomed?
6. What level of integrity and openness was demonstrated? Did the JD appear to be secretive?
7. Was it expensive for the defendant to defend this suit? Did the defendant use extensive resources, e.g., expert witnesses, demonstrations? Do you know who paid these expenses?

II. Leads to Additional Financial Data about Judgment Debtor

A. Data in Public Records

1. Telephone directory (how many phone numbers are listed?).
2. Land records in county offices.
3. Prior litigation brought by or against the JD as revealed in court clerks' offices, e.g., breach-of-contract actions, divorce proceedings, bankruptcy proceedings.
4. Index bureaus on prior claims made by the JD.
5. Credit bureaus with data on the JD or on the JD's business.
6. Motor vehicle registration.
7. Government license offices.
8. Secretary of state's office for incorporation papers, financial statements.
9. Newspaper stories on the JD or on the JD's business.
10. Obituary column, if JD is deceased.
11. Government consumer protection agencies that might list consumer complaints against JD's business.
12. Government offices where liens and mortgages are filed (including filings pursuant to the Uniform Commercial Code).

B. Other Leads

1. Interviews with neighbors.
2. Interviews with clients or other business associates of the JD.
3. Site visit to residencies.
4. Site visit to places of business.

Posttrial Deposition

Earlier in Figure 3–14, we examined the *pretrial* deposition used by attorneys to help prepare for trial. The procedures for the *posttrial* deposition are often very similar, including the availability of protection from the court against undue harassment by the judgment creditor who is using the deposition to discover assets.

Production of Documents

In a motion for production of documents, the judgment creditor is looking for bank statements, balance sheets, tax returns, dividend and royalty statements, separation agreements (check alimony and property division terms), antenuptial agreements, wills, insurance policies, trust instruments, mortgages, deeds, financial statements filed to obtain loans, etc.

Written Interrogatories

Much of the same information can be sought by sending written questions, which often must be answered under oath.

Supplementary Proceedings

The judgment creditor may be able to ask the court to order the judgment debtor to appear at a court hearing in order to answer questions about available assets and finances. In some states, such a hearing can be used in addition to the precding three discovery devices.

SUMMARY

Paralegals perform a large number of roles assisting attorneys during the five stages of litigation: agency (if the case begins in an administrative agency), pretrial, trial, appeal, and enforcement. Three of the initial concerns about the case of a new client are liability, damages, and collectibility. Alternative dispute resolution (ADR) where paralegals can provide assistance includes arbitration, rent-a-judge, mediation, med-arb, neighborhood justice center, and summary jury trial.

A law office needs considerable background information about a prospective client. There are three guides to the facts needed to establish a prima facie case: tort law, evidence law, and common sense. Every important fact should be viewed from the perspectives of different versions of that fact. The believability of each version must be weighed within the context of the main standard of proof in tort cases: preponderance of the evidence. Fact particularization will help achieve comprehensiveness and specificity in fact gathering. Witness statements are important even if they are not admitted at trial. They help everyone recall events that may have taken place a long time ago.

The major pleadings are the complaint or petition, answer, reply, counterclaim, cross-claim, and third-party complaint. The major components of a complaint are the caption, designation of pleading, statement of subject matter jurisdiction, body, prayer for relief, subscription, and verification. Most courts allow notice pleading rather than require fact pleading. There are six discovery devices to help parties prepare for trial: written interrogatories; oral deposition; written deposition; production of documents and things, entry on land for inspection and other purposes; physical or mental examination; and requests for admission.

Paralegal roles during pretrial, trial, appeal, and enforcement include drafting motions; indexing and digesting discovery data; monitoring files, documents, and evidence; helping design trial exhibits; legal research; drafting and filing briefs; identifying and investigating the assets of the judgment debtor; etc.

KEY TERMS

administrative agency   50

agency hearing   50

intra-agency appeal   50

complaint   50

summons   50

service of process   50

answer   50

discovery   50

motion   50

settlement   50

voir dire   50

opening statement   51

evidence   51

direct examination   51

cross-examination   51

charge   51

verdict   51

judgment   51

notice of appeal   51

appellant   51

appellee   51

appellate brief   51

posttrial discovery   51

judgment creditor   51

judgment debtor   51

execution   51

liability   52

cause of action   52

damages   52

nominal damages   52

contingent fee   52

PI   52

deep pocket   52

shallow pocket   52

alternative dispute resolution
    (ADR)   52

arbitration   53

rent-a-judge   53

mediation   53

med-arb   53

neighborhood justice center
    (NJC)   53

summary jury trial   53

prima facie case   54

legal interviewing   55

legal investigation   55

admissible   55

competent   55

credibility   57

burden of proof   57

preponderance of the
    evidence   57

fact particularization   58

witness statements   62

attestation clause   62

pleadings   63

petition   63

reply   63

counterclaim   63

cross-claim   63

third-party complaint   63

demurrer   63

caption   64

subject matter jurisdiction   64

venue   64

fact pleading   64

notice pleading   66

prayer for relief   66

ad damnum clause   66

default judgment   66

subscription   66

verification   66

boilerplate   67

impeach   73

motion for summary
    judgment   74

written interrogatories   75

transcribed   75

deponent   75

subpoena duces tecum   75

attorney work-product rule   75

oral deposition   75

written deposition   76

production of documents
    and things; entry on
    land for inspection
    and other purposes   77

physical or mental
    examination   77

requests for admission   78

second chair   90

shadow trial   90

CHAPTER

4

Foreseeability in Tort Law

CHAPTER OUTLINE

- Introduction
- Defining Foreseeability
- Foreseeability Spectrum
- Objective Standard
- Phrasing the Foreseeability Question
- Foreseeability Determination "Formula"
- Review of Steps to Determine Foreseeability

INTRODUCTION

Foreseeability is a critical concept in tort law. In three of the elements of negligence, for example, foreseeability often plays a major role:

- duty
- breach of duty
- proximate cause

In later chapters we will discover that foreseeability is relevant to some of the intentional and strict-liability torts as well as to negligence. Before studying any of these torts, we need to spend some time analyzing the concept of foreseeability. Given its critical importance, we will be referring back to this discussion throughout the remainder of the book.

The central question of this chapter is: How do we determine foreseeability? This question is explored through the following topics:

- the meaning of foreseeability
- the spectrum of foreseeability
- foreseeability as an objective standard
- phrasing the foreseeability question
- the foreseeability determination "formula"

The legal consequences of foreseeability will be considered in later chapters. For now, our concern is the nature of foreseeability itself.

DEFINING FORESEEABILITY

In everyday language, foresee means "to see or know beforehand." **Foreseeable,** the adjective, simply describes that which one can see or know beforehand. From a legal perspective, however, the emphasis is on the *extent* to which something can be known beforehand. It is important to understand that the question, "Is it foreseeable?", is less significant than the question, "How foreseeable is it?" Or, to combine the two questions: "How foreseeable is it, if at all?" Foreseeability is primarily a question of the *extent* to which something is predictable or "occurable."

It is also important to understand that foreseeability is determined *before the fact.* If you want to know, for example, whether a fire was foreseeable, you mentally turn the clock back to the period of time *before* the fire occurred and ask: how likely was it, if at all, that a fire would occur? This determination is not made on the basis of what happens after the fact. An event or result is not foreseeable simply because it happened.

FORESEEABILITY SPECTRUM

To assess the foreseeability of an event or result, you must pinpoint it on a scale or **spectrum of foreseeability.** Figure 4–1 presents this spectrum. The threshold question is whether the event or result was foreseeable in any shape, fashion, or form. If the answer is no, the inquiry is ended. If, however, the answer is yes, then the next and most important inquiry is *how* foreseeable was the event or result. Where on the spectrum did it fall before it happened?

The categories on the spectrum are not mutually exclusive. There is no scientific or measurable distinction among all the items on the spectrum. The categories are rough approximations on the higher-to-lower ranges of "occurability."

FIGURE 4–1
Foreseeability spectrum: How foreseeable, if at all?

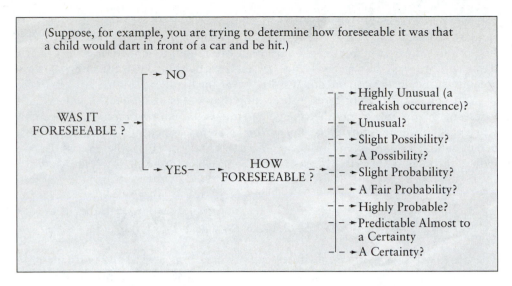

(Suppose, for example, you are trying to determine how foreseeable it was that a child would dart in front of a car and be hit.)

WAS IT FORESEEABLE?
— NO
— YES → HOW FORESEEABLE?
— → Highly Unusual (a freakish occurrence)?
— → Unusual?
— → Slight Possibility?
— → A Possibility?
— → Slight Probability?
— → A Fair Probability?
— → Highly Probable?
— → Predictable Almost to a Certainty
— → A Certainty?

Note the last item on the spectrum: foreseeability to a certainty. When something is that foreseeable, the law says that you *intended* the event or result to occur. **Intent** has two meanings in the law: the desire to have something happen or the **knowledge with substantial certainty** that it will happen from what you do or fail to do. If you pull the trigger of a gun aimed at a crowd a few feet in front of where you are standing, you cannot claim that you did not intend to shoot the person who was hit. You may have hoped and prayed that no one would be hit, but a court will probably find that you had substantially certain knowledge that someone would be hit. In the eyes of the law, you intended this result. You have committed a battery.

OBJECTIVE STANDARD

When foreseeability is an issue in the law, we often ask two questions:

- Was the event or result foreseeable to the defendant? (You answer this question by applying a **subjective standard.**)
- Would the event or result have been foreseeable to a reasonable person? (You answer this question by applying an **objective standard.**)

In most cases, the second question is asked only when the answer to the first question is no.

A subjective standard simply means that everything is measured solely by what the defendant actually knew or understood. Suppose, for example, we want to know whether it was foreseeable that Ted Vinson's dog would bite the mail carrier last Monday morning. Assume that the dog has bitten mail carriers (and others) in the past and that the dog runs loose in the front yard where the mailbox is located. Assume further that Ted is totally oblivious of the dog's biting habits and believes he owns the most gentle and friendly dog in the world. He has forgotten that the dog has bitten people before. By a subjective standard, the Monday bite was not foreseeable to Ted. He may have been silly in thinking the dog is harmless, but if he honestly believed the dog would not bite anyone, then the Monday bite was not foreseeable to him.

Suppose, however, we apply an objective standard to the dog bite case. An objective standard measures something by reference to what a **reasonable person** under the same or similar circumstances would have known or understood. What do we mean by a reasonable person? We will spend a great deal of time on this topic in later chapters. For now, suffice it to say that a reasonable person is an ordinary, prudent person.

Would a reasonable person have foreseen that the dog would bite the mail carrier last Monday? An ordinary, prudent person would *not* have been oblivious of this dog's prior biting habit and would have understood that an untied dog with such a habit will probably bite again. Hence, by an objective standard, the bite was foreseeable, particularly since the dog was kept near the mailbox.

If a defendant did not foresee something that a reasonable person would have foreseen, we are able to say that the defendant *should have foreseen* it. We cannot reach this conclusion, however, until we make an assessment of what a reasonable person would have foreseen—using an objective standard. This is the process that we will go through in most of the cases in this book when foreseeability is an issue.

PHRASING THE FORESEEABILITY QUESTION

There are two ways to phrase the foreseeability question: general and particular. Assume that Mary Jefferson crashes her car into a lamp post by a local beach two weeks after Christmas. She claims that Mrs. X is responsible for the crash because of how she disposed of her Christmas tree. Compare the following two foreseeability questions concerning this case:

A. Was harm foreseeable to Mrs. X when she allowed Tommy to take the Christmas tree she had just thrown into the garbage two weeks after Christmas, which led to Mary Jefferson's injury?
B. When Mrs. X allowed ten-year-old Tommy to take the Christmas tree that she had just thrown into the garbage two weeks after Christmas, how foreseeable was it to Mrs X:
   1. that an older child, Ted, would steal the tree from Tommy,
   2. that Ted would organize a tree-collection project so that the trees could be burned together at a big bonfire at a local beach,
   3. that about thirty children would drag the trees across busy streets to get to the beach,
   4. that traffic would be interrupted, and
   5. that Mary Jefferson would be injured when she crashed her car into a lamp post in an effort to avoid hitting Ted crossing the street with Mrs. X's tree?

The first statement is a very general phrasing of the foreseeability question: Was harm foreseeable? The second statement, however, is highly particularized. Everything is segmented into events that raise a series of isolated foreseeability subquestions.

When do you use a general foreseeability question and when do you use a particularized one? The answer, in part, is governed by the following advocacy principles:

Advocacy Principles: Arguments on Foreseeability

- The party who wants to reach the conclusion that something was *foreseeable* will seek to phrase the foreseeability question in the most broad, *generalized* form possible. (In our Christmas tree case, Mary Jefferson wants to argue that the injury she suffered was foreseeable to Mrs. X; therefore, she will phrase the foreseeability question broadly. See question A.)
- The party who wants to reach the conclusion that something was *unforeseeable* will seek to phrase the foreseeability question in the most narrow, *particularized* form possible. (Mrs. X wants to argue that the injury Mary Jefferson suffered was unforeseeable; therefore, she will phrase the foreseeability question narrowly. See question B.)

A particularized statement of the foreseeability question itemizes the major chain of events that led up to the accident or injury. The more events listed, the more self-evident the answer becomes: a particularized question is stacked in favor of *un*foreseeability. After reading all the events in the question, we are often inclined to say that all of it could not possibly have been foreseen. Care must be used, however, not to overparticularize the question to the point of absurdity.

Later, we will learn what the courts have said on how foreseeable something must be in given areas of tort law such as proximate cause in negligence. Knowing the law, however, will not eliminate the need for advocacy in the statement of the foreseeability question. The more an advocate wants to conclude that something was very foreseeable on the foreseeability spectrum, the more generalized the advocate will try to make the foreseeability question. The more an advocate wants to conclude that there was low foreseeability, the more particularized the advocate will try to make the foreseeability question.

ASSIGNMENT 4.1

You are a paralegal who works in the office of Smith & Smith. The firm represents Dan in a suit by Pete who claims that Dan caused Pete to suffer a seizure. Pete is represented by Karen Wilson, Esq. Read the following fact situation carefully. Focus on the foreseeability of Pete's seizure. First, phrase the foreseeability question that Karen Wilson would try to use on behalf of Pete. Her phrasing will be broad and generalized. Next, phrase the foreseeability question that Smith & Smith would try to use on behalf of Dan. Its phrasing will be narrow and particularized. Assume that Dan wants to reach the conclusion that the seizure was very unforeseeable and that Pete wants to reach the conclusion that an injury was foreseeable.

Dan has a weekend job operating a ferris wheel at the state fair. Pete buys a ticket and gets on. Soon after the ride begins, Dan notices that Pete is throwing objects onto the people below. Dan decides to stop the wheel in order to remove Pete. When Dan grabs the brake lever, he immediately notices that it is stuck. He has an emergency brake, but is very reluctant to use it because it might cause the entire wheel to come to a jolting halt. He fears that some of the riders could be thrown out. The more he thinks about it, the more frantic he becomes. This is only his first week on the job. While he stands there thinking about what to do, some of the people on the ground, who have been hit by the objects Pete threw on them, begin shouting at Dan to do something. Dan becomes more and more dizzy as he tries to think of what to do. Someone in the crowd yells out at Dan to turn the electricity off as a way to stop the wheel. Dan thinks it is a good idea, but by this time, he is so confused that he does not know what to do. Suddenly, he dashes away from the crowd so that he can try to collect his thoughts. Luckily, he spots his boss at the other end of the fair. He runs toward her for help. When he reaches her, he is so upset and frantic that it takes his boss close to a minute to figure out what he is talking about. When the boss finally does understand, she goes to the still-turning ferris wheel and stops it safely by skillfully using the emergency brake. When Pete gets off this twenty-eight-minute ride, he suffers a seizure. Later, he sues Dan.

FORESEEABILITY DETERMINATION "FORMULA"

It is probably accurate to say that you will rarely have enough facts to determine how foreseeable something was or was not. Hence, determining foreseeability requires a probing for further facts. Questions need to be asked about the facts that you do not have, and often, about the facts that you do have. For this reason, effective interviewing and investigation are critical to reaching intelligent conclusions about foreseeability.

FIGURE 4–2
Foreseeability determination "formula."

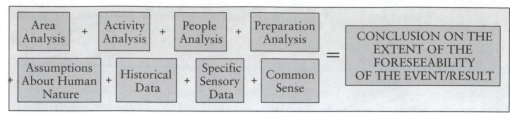

The foreseeability "formula" in Figure 4–2 is designed to provide a framework for asking the right questions about foreseeability. The starting point in the use of the formula is to identify the subject matter of the foreseeability question. What is the event or result whose foreseeability or unforeseeability you want to assess? As pointed out earlier, the subject matter of the foreseeability inquiry can be stated in *generalized* terms (e.g., was any harm or injury of any kind foreseeable), or in very *particularized* terms (e.g., was it foreseeable that customers in a department store would run toward an exit because of a light failure during the day, push each other in an effort to get out, and then fail to. . .). After you have identified the question, you then apply the "formula."

There are eight factors to consider:

area	human nature
activity	history
people	sensory data
preparation	common sense

The factors may appear complicated. In fact, however, the list is simply a detailed overview of the process we naturally go through whenever we want to determine whether something is foreseeable. Examine each of the eight factors separately, even though there will be considerable overlap among them. As you focus on each factor, ask yourself factual questions that relate to foreseeability. Do not, however, expect definitive answers at this point. The "formula" is not a mathematical equation. It is no more than an aid to give you some direction as you try to place an event or result on the foreseeability spectrum. Later, you will want to pursue answers to the questions during client interviews and field investigation.

Area Analysis

The nature of the area can sometimes be very important. If, for example, a child is hit by a car, it is important to know whether the accident occurred in a residential area, near a school, at a playground, etc. From the nature of the area, how foreseeable is it that children will be around? If an accident occurs in a supermarket, it is equally important to assess the area. It is usually a crowded, closed area with many products stacked on shelves or on the floor. What is foreseeable given these conditions? A rotted tree branch falls and hits the plaintiff. Where did this occur? In the country? In a city? A suburb? A zoo? A park? How, if at all, would the area affect the foreseeability of what happened? An explosion occurs in a university lab. A lab is a place for experiments and the storage of chemicals. Danger is usually more foreseeable in a lab than in other areas.

Activity Analysis

Area and activity are intimately related. What specific activities were going on at the time of the accident or event whose foreseeability we are assessing? Swimming? Driving? Walking? Running? Eating? Selling? Dynamiting? What occurs during this activity? What is frequently foreseeable? Occasionally foreseeable? Rarely foreseeable? Examine the nature of the activity or activities themselves. What does human experience tell you (or what should it tell you) about what might be anticipated from this activity?

People Analysis

What kind of people were involved in the activities that led to the event or result whose foreseeability is being examined? How would you characterize them, and does this characterization tell you something about what should have been foreseeable by them or by others interacting with them? Were they children? Adults? Trespassers? Doctors? Mechanics or others with special knowledge and skills? What is normally expected from such people? What precautions do they usually take or fail to take? We have certain expectations from certain classes or kinds of people. What are the expectations in this case? Do these expectations help us determine what should have been foreseeable?

Preparation Analysis

What do people usually do before they engage in the activity you listed? Is any long-term preparation needed, e.g., training, testing? Short-term preparation, e.g., checking equipment, looking out for obstacles? No preparation? The data received from any preparation will usually be very relevant to foreseeability.

Assumptions About Human Nature

This factor is very similar to the people analysis except that it is more general. What kind of behavior is usually expected of anyone engaged in the kind of activity in question? In driving a car, for example, can you assume that other drivers will *not* always obey all traffic laws? When people are in danger, can you assume that they will act in self-defense? Can you assume that people will gravitate toward pleasurable, attractive things or events? Can you assume that many people will not read five pages of fine-print instructions? Such assumptions, when they can be made, are often relevant to what might be anticipated from people.

This is not to say that any of these assumptions are to be condoned or that they justify conduct in any way. The law that applies to conduct is a separate matter that will be considered in later chapters. Here we are limiting ourselves to a consideration of the extent of foreseeability, independent of any legal consequences.

Historical Data

The more something has occurred in the past, the more foreseeable is its reoccurrence. Have incidents of a similar nature occurred in the past? If so, under what circumstances? How often? How well known were they? A customer sues a grocery store owner for injuries received when opening a can of tuna. We want to know if this injury was foreseeable to the owner of the store. Has the owner had similar complaints about this tuna brand in the past? Has the owner heard of problems other stores have had? Is this the first time the owner became aware of such a problem? Historical data can be quite relevant to foreseeability.

Specific Sensory Data

What did the eyes, ears, nose, fingers, feet, etc. tell the parties just before the incident? Did any of this sensory data provide signs of what might happen? Are certain things foreseeable in certain kinds of weather? (Was this kind of weather foreseeable?) Visibility is often relevant to foreseeability. What factors affected visibility, e.g., weather, time of day, and presence of obstructions? Were there distractions that prevented people from being aware of a danger? If so, were these distractions foreseeable?

Common Sense

Common sense is a catchall factor. All of the other factors should have led you to questions and observations grounded in common sense. Here we simply reinforce the central role of this factor and ask ourselves to what extent something was or was not foreseeable based on common sense.

> **EXAMPLE:** Jones builds a swimming pool in his backyard. The use of the pool is restricted to Jones family members and guests who are present when an adult is there to supervise. One hot, summer night, a neighbor's child opens an unlocked door of a fence that surrounds the Jones yard and goes into the pool. (There is no separate fence around the pool.) The child knows he is not supposed to be there without an adult. No one else is at the pool. The child drowns.
>
> **Foreseeability question (general):** Was it foreseeable that someone would be injured in the pool?
>
> **Foreseeability question (particular):** Was it foreseeable that a neighbor's child would violate a rule of the owner of the pool not to use it unless an adult was present, open a closed fence door to get to the pool, and drown in it?

From the facts, it appears that Jones built his pool in a residential area. If so, it certainly was foreseeable that children would be in the area. Jones should have anticipated that children would be drawn to the pool. The neighbor's child used the pool while no one was around. (We need to know how old the child was.) It would help to know whether people use each other's pools in this way in the neighborhood. If it is common, then it is more foreseeable to Jones that a child would use his pool without permission or supervision in spite of his rule to the contrary. Why did he impose this rule? Because of prior pool trespassing in the neighborhood? Swimming is generally considered a dangerous activity, particularly for children. It is foreseeable, however, that children will not be able to fully protect themselves in water, hence the need to take additional precautions when children could be swimming.

There was no separate fence around Jones's pool; there was simply an unlocked door to a fence around the yard. Was it foreseeable to Jones that this might be an inadequate precaution? Again, this may depend on the frequency with which children have made unauthorized use of pools in the area and the extent to which Jones knew about this or should have known about it. Are other pools in the area left unlocked and unguarded at night? Should Jones have checked on this? It is true that Jones had a rule that adults must be present. But is this rule enough? Shouldn't Jones have assumed that a child would *not* obey such a rule? Has any child ever violated this rule in the past? Have there ever been children using the Jones pool without adults present? If so, then Jones was on notice that it could happen again and that additional precautions would be needed. What steps did Jones take, if any, to make sure that neighborhood children and their parents knew about his rule?

We also need to know whether there have been any recent swimming pool accidents in the area. The drowning took place at night. (We do not know whether any of the Jones family members were at home at the time.) Common sense tells us that a child will be tempted to use an easily accessible swimming pool in the summer and that drowning is a fair probability when there is no supervision.

ASSIGNMENT

4.2

a. You have just read a series of facts and factual questions relevant to whether the swimming pool tragedy was foreseeable. Categorize each of these facts and questions under the eight categories of the foreseeability determination formula. Specify what falls under area analysis, activity analysis, people analysis, preparation analysis, assumptions about human nature, historical data, specific sensory data, and common sense. Place a fact or a question under more than one category if there is overlap.

b. Under each of these eight areas, what additional questions would you want to ask to enable you to determine whether the tragedy was foreseeable? (See General Instructions for the Investigation Strategy Assignment in Chapter 3.)

REVIEW OF STEPS TO DETERMINE FORESEEABILITY

1. Turn the clock back to the time before the event/result in question occurred—foreseeability is determined *before* the fact.
2. Decide how broadly (generalized) or narrowly (particularized) you want to phrase the foreseeability question.
3. Apply the factors in the foreseeability determination formula that are applicable to the situation.
4. From the range of "highly unusual" to "a certainty," draw your conclusion of where the event/result falls on the foreseeability spectrum.
5. Give a counteranalysis. If both sides are not going to agree on the extent to which the event/result was foreseeable, state the other side.

ASSIGNMENT

4.3

Assess the foreseeability of the events listed in the following situations. Go through the five steps just listed. Include a large number of factual questions you would raise, and state how these factual questions might be relevant to the foreseeability of the result or event in question.

a. The ABC Company manufactures kitchen stoves. Smith buys one of the stoves. There is no heat in Smith's kitchen. Hence, Smith often turns the stove on, opens the oven door, and rests his feet on the door while sitting on a chair in front of the stove. One day, the stove collapses forward onto Smith while he is warming his feet in this way. Smith is severely injured. Was this injury foreseeable to the ABC Company?

b. A hobo hitching a ride on a railroad train falls off and injures himself. Was this injury foreseeable to the railroad?

c. Examine the facts of Assignment 4.1. Was the injury foreseeable to Dan's boss?

ASSIGNMENT

4.4

Accidents happen to all of us throughout our lives. Think of an event in your life involving an accident that was somewhat of a surprise to you when it occurred. It can be a major or a minor accident. In class the teacher will select one student to be interviewed by the rest of the class (i.e., to be the interviewee) in order to determine how foreseeable the accident was to you (subjective standard) and how foreseeable it would have been to a reasonable person (objective standard).

Instructions to interviewee: If you are selected, start by telling the class what the accident was. The class will then ask you questions relevant to foreseeability. (Feel free to change any facts to preserve privacy.)

Instructions to class: Assume that each of you is conducting the interview. Start asking questions of the interviewee in class. Your questions should cover the eight categories of area, activity, people, preparation, assumptions about human nature, historical data, specific sensory data, and common sense. When the teacher indicates that the interview is over, write down your answers to the two following questions. The teacher will then lead a class discussion on the differences and similarities in the answers among the students in the class.

a. Was the accident foreseeable to the interviewee? Where on the foreseeability spectrum would you place it?
b. Would the accident have been foreseeable to a reasonable person? Where on the foreseeability spectrum would you place it?

SUMMARY

Foreseeability means the extent to which we can see or know something beforehand. It is determined before the fact; something is not foreseeable simply because it happened. The spectrum of foreseeability ranges from highly unusual to a virtual certainty. (If something falls into the latter category, it was intended.) When foreseeability is an issue, we ask if the event or result was foreseeable to the defendant (answered by using a subjective standard). If not, we often ask if the event or result would have been foreseeable to a reasonable person (answered by applying an objective standard). Advocates tend to generalize the foreseeability question when they want to argue that something was foreseeable; they particularize the question when they are hoping for a finding of unforeseeability. Assessing foreseeability requires an analysis of the area involved, the activity undertaken, the people involved, the preparation involved, assumptions about human nature, historical data, specific sensory data, and common sense.

KEY TERMS

foreseeable 96
spectrum of foreseeability 96
intent 97

knowledge with substantial
   certainty 97
subjective standard 97

objective standard 97
reasonable person 97

Battery

CHAPTER OUTLINE

- Introduction
- Act
- Person
- Intent
- Harmful or Offensive Contact
- Consent and Privilege

INTRODUCTION

Battery—civil battery—is a harmful or offensive contact with a person that results from the defendant's intent to cause the contact or to cause an apprehension of imminent contact. The easiest case is when the defendant punches the plaintiff in the nose. Many make the mistake of saying that the punch was an "assault." Although the words *battery* and *assault* are sometimes confused, we need to keep the concepts separate. As we will see in the next chapter, assault is a separate tort that does not require actual contact with the plaintiff. By the time you finish studying this chapter and the next one, you should know why Sleeping Beauty, if she woke up angry, could have sued the kissing prince for battery, but not for assault.

Battery is frequently committed, but rarely litigated. A major reason for this is that most batterers are not **deep pockets,** meaning individuals who have enough resources from which a plaintiff can collect a judgment. The vast majority of people who commit intentional torts such as battery are **shallow pockets**—individuals without assets. Furthermore, liability insurance policies generally do not cover intentional torts, whereas they do cover the most common cause of injury, automobile negligence. For most victims of battery, therefore, the cost and hassle of suing under a battery cause of action is simply not worth it. If, however, the person committing battery has assets, i.e., is a deep pocket, a battery suit is likely. Sports figures or other celebrities, for example, are relatively common defendants in battery actions.

Of course, criminal law may be an option. The same conduct can constitute both a criminal battery and a civil battery. (Criminal battery is sometimes called "assault" or "assault and battery.") Our focus in this chapter is civil battery, which is a tort. Criminal battery is a crime prosecuted by the state.

Before beginning our study of the substantive law of civil battery, you will find a comprehensive checklist of definitions, defenses, relationships, paralegal roles, and research references for this tort. It is designed to make connections between the battery chapter and related material discussed in other chapters and in other courses in the curriculum. It can also serve as an on-the-job checklist after graduation. We will provide a comparable checklist at the beginning of our discussion of every major tort in this book.

 Battery Checklist

Definitions, Relationships, Paralegal Roles, and Research References

Category
Battery is an intentional tort.

Interest Protected by This Tort
The right to be free from a harmful or offensive bodily contact.

Elements
  i. Act
 ii. Intent to cause either:
    a. an imminent harmful or offensive contact, or
    b. an apprehension of an imminent harmful or offensive contact
 iii. Harmful or offensive contact with the plaintiff's person
 iv. Causation of the harmful or offensive contact

Definitions of Major Words/Phrases in the Elements
  Act: A voluntary movement of the defendant's body.
  Intent: Either
    a. the desire to bring about the consequences of the act (i.e., the desire to cause the contact or the apprehension of an imminent contact), or
    b. the substantially certain knowledge that the consequences (i.e., the contact or the apprehension) will follow from the act.

Battery Checklist Continued

Harmful: Involving physical damage, impairment, pain, or illness to the body.

Offensive: Offending the personal dignity of an ordinary person who is not unduly sensitive.

Person: One's body, something attached to the body, or something so closely associated with the body as to be identified with it.

Causation: Either

a. but for the defendant's act, the consequences would not have occurred (i.e., the contact would not have occurred), or

b. the defendant's act was a substantial factor in bringing about the consequences (i.e., the contact).

Major Defense and Counterargument Possibilities That Need to Be Explored

1. There was no voluntary movement of the defendant's body (no act).
2. The defendant had no desire to make contact with the plaintiff, nor any substantially certain knowledge that such contact would result from what the defendant did (no intent).
3. The contact was neither harmful nor offensive.
4. But for what the defendant did, the contact would have resulted anyway. The defendant was not a substantial factor in producing the contact. (No causation.)
5. The plaintiff consented to the defendant's contact (on the defense of consent, see Chapter 27).
6. The contact resulted while the defendant was defending him- or herself from the plaintiff (on self-defense and other self-help privileges, see Chapter 27).
7. The contact occurred while the defendant was defending someone else from the plaintiff (on the defense of others and other self-help privileges, see Chapter 27).
8. The contact occurred while the defendant was defending property or recapturing chattels from the plaintiff (on the privileges of necessity, defense of property, recapture of property, and other self-help privileges, see Chapter 27).
9. The contact occurred while the defendant was disciplining the plaintiff (on discipline and other self-help privileges, see Chapter 27).
10. The contact occurred while the defendant was arresting the plaintiff (on the privilege of arrest, see Chapter 7).
11. The plaintiff's suit against the government for a battery committed by a government employee may be barred by sovereign immunity (on sovereign immunity, see Chapter 27).
12. The plaintiff's suit against the government employee for battery may be barred by public official immunity (on official immunity, see Chapter 27).
13. The plaintiff's suit against the charitable organization for a battery committed by someone working for the organization may be barred by charitable immunity (on charitable immunity, see Chapter 27).
14. The plaintiff's suit against a family member for battery may be barred by intrafamily immunity (on intrafamily immunity, see Chapter 22).
15. The plaintiff failed to take reasonable steps to mitigate the harm caused when the defendant committed battery; therefore, damages should not cover the aggravation of the harm caused by the plaintiff (on the doctrine of avoidable consequences, see Chapter 16).

Damages

The plaintiff can recover compensatory damages for the contact, including pain and suffering, medical bills, and loss of wages. Since the defendant often acts out of hatred and malice in committing the battery, punitive damages are commonly awarded as well. (On the categories of damages, see Chapter 16.)

Relationship to Criminal Law

The same act of the defendant can constitute a *civil* battery (for which the plaintiff recovers damages) and a *criminal* battery (for which the state collects a fine or imposes jail or imprisonment). The crime may be called assault and battery, aggravated assault, assault with intent to kill, etc.

Other Torts and Related Actions

Assault: If there was no contact, but the plaintiff was placed in apprehension of a contact, the tort of assault may have been committed.

False Imprisonment: While committing the tort of false imprisonment, battery may also have been committed if contact was made with the plaintiff's person during or just before the confinement.

Battery Checklist Continued

Negligence: (a) There may have been a harmful or offensive contact that was not intentional, hence no battery. Yet if the contact was due to unreasonable conduct by the defendant, negligence should be explored. (b) A doctor must have informed consent before making contact with a part of the patient's body. The failure to obtain such consent is a battery in some states. In most states, however, as we will see in Chapter 18, the patient must sue under a negligence cause of action in such cases.

Wrongful Death: A wrongful death action can be brought by the survivors of the deceased if death resulted from the battery.

Federal Law

a. Under the Federal Tort Claims Act, the United States Government will *not* be liable for a battery committed by one of its federal employees within the scope of employment (respondeat superior) *unless* the federal employee is an investigative or law enforcement officer. (See Figure 27–7 in Chapter 27.)

b. There may be liability under the Civil Rights Act if the battery was committed while the defendant was depriving the plaintiff of federal rights under color of law. (See Figure 27–9 in Chapter 27.)

Employer-Employee (Agency) Law

An employee who commits a battery is personally liable for this tort. His or her employer will *also* be liable for battery if the conduct of the employee was within the scope of employment (respondeat superior). The employee must be furthering a business objective of the employer at the time. Intentional torts such as battery, however, are often outside the scope of employment. If so, only the employee is liable for the battery. (On the factors that determine the scope of employment, see Figure 14–10 in Chapter 14.)

Paralegal Roles in Battery Litigation

(See also Figures 3–1, 3–14, and 29–1 in Chapters 3 and 29.)

Fact finding (help the office collect facts relevant to prove the elements of battery, the elements of available defenses, and extent of injuries or other damages):
- client interviewing
- field investigation
- online research (e.g., find newspaper accounts of a public brawl)

File management (help the office control the volume of paperwork in a battery litigation):
- open client file
- enter case data in computer database
- maintain file documents

Litigation assistance (help the trial attorney prepare for a battery trial and appeal, if needed):
- draft discovery requests
- draft answers to discovery requests
- draft pleadings
- digest and index discovery documents
- help prepare, order, and manage trial exhibits (visuals or demonstratives)
- prepare trial notebook
- draft notice of appeal
- order trial transcript
- cite check briefs
- perform legal research

Collection/enforcement (help the trial attorney for the judgment creditor to collect the damages award or to enforce other court orders at the conclusion of the battery case):
- draft postjudgment discovery requests
- field investigation to monitor compliance with judgment
- online research (e.g., location of defendant's business assets)

Research References for Battery

Digests
In the digests of West, look for case summaries on battery under key topics such as:

Assault and Battery	Damages
Torts	Death

Battery Checklist Continued

Corpus Juris Secundum
In this legal encyclopedia, see the discussion under topic headings such as:

Assault and Battery	Damages
Torts	Death

American Jurisprudence 2d
In this legal encyclopedia, see the discussion under topic headings such as:

Assault and Battery	Damages
Torts	Death

Legal Periodical Literature
There are two index systems to use to try to locate legal periodical literature on battery:

INDEX TO LEGAL PERIODICALS AND BOOKS (ILP)	CURRENT LAW INDEX (CLI)
See literature in *ILP* under subject headings such as:	See literature in *CLI* under subject headings such as:
Assault and Battery	Assault and Battery
Damages	Torts
Federal Tort Claims Act	Damages
Personal Injuries	Personal Injuries
Torts	
Wrongful Death	

Example of a legal periodical article you will find by using *ILP* or *CLI:*

> *Smoker Battery: An Antidote to Second-Hand Smoke* by Donald B. Ezra, 63 Southern California Law Review 1061 (1991).

A.L.R., A.L.R.2d, A.L.R.3d, A.L.R.4th, A.L.R.5th, A.L.R. Fed.
Use the *ALR Index* to locate annotations on battery. In this index, check subject headings such as:

Assault and Battery
Damages
Torts

Example of an annotation on battery you can locate through this index:

> *Civil Liability of Insane or Other Disordered Person for Assault or Battery,* by C. R. McCorkle, 77 A.L.R.2d 625 (1961).

Words and Phrases
In this multivolume legal dictionary, look up *battery, harmful, offensive, apprehension,* and every other word or phrase connected with the tort discussed in this chapter. The dictionary will give you definitions of these words or phrases from court opinions.

CALR: Computer-Assisted Legal Research

> Example of a query you could ask on WESTLAW or on LEXIS to try to find cases, statutes, or other legal materials on battery: **battery /p damages**

> Example of search terms you could use on an Internet legal search engine such as LawCrawler (http://lawcrawler.findlaw.com) to find cases, statutes, or other legal materials on battery: **civil AND battery AND tort**

> Example of search terms you could use on an Internet general search engine such as Alta Vista (http://www.altavista.com) to find cases, statutes, or other legal materials on battery: +**civil** +**battery** +**tort**

> More Internet sites to check for materials on battery and other torts:
> Jurist: (http://jurist.law.pitt.edu/sg_torts.htm)
> LawGuru: (http://www.lawguru.com/search/lawsearch.html)
> See also Torts Law Online at the end of Chapter 1.

ACT

There must be an **act** by the defendant that leads to contact with the plaintiff's person. An act is a voluntary movement of the body. Not all harmful or offensive contacts are the result of acts. For example, if Dan's arm hits Linda during a sleep walk, no battery exists because there is no act—no voluntary movement of Dan's body that caused the contact.

PERSON

The definition of **person** is broad. It means one's body, anything attached to one's body, or anything so closely associated with one's body as to be identified with it. A kick in the shin is clearly a contact with the body. So is a yank on a tie or other item of clothing worn by the plaintiff. The following cases also illustrate the broader definition of person:

- the defendant knocks off the plaintiff's hat
- the defendant pulls a plate out of the plaintiff's hand
- the defendant stabs or shoots a horse while the plaintiff is riding it

The hat, plate, and horse are so closely associated with the body in these cases as to be practically identified with it at the time of the contact. There does not have to be contact with the physical body.

Consciousness

The tort of battery is designed to protect the personal integrity of one's body against intentional invasions, which can occur even if one does know it at the time. The plaintiff does not have to be conscious of the invasion.

■ **EXAMPLE:** Jim kisses Lena while she is asleep or under anesthesia.

Lena has been battered by Jim.

INTENT

For purposes of battery, **intent** is the desire to bring about **imminent** harmful or offensive contact or to bring about an imminent apprehension of that contact. Imminent means immediate in the sense of no significant delay. In most cases, intent is not difficult to prove, because it is clear that the defendant wants to make contact with the plaintiff, e.g., the defendant picks up a bucket of water and pours it on the plaintiff's head. It is more difficult to prove intent when the defendant does not want contact to occur, but merely wants the plaintiff to think it will occur.

EXAMPLE: Mary throws a hammer at George. She aims it several feet above George's head, hoping to scare him. Unfortunately, it hits him in the eye.

Mary can accurately say that she did not intend to hit George, but this is not a defense. She wanted him to think he was about to be hit. She intended to cause an **apprehension** (i.e., an understanding or awareness) of an imminent contact. This is sufficient to establish the element of intent.

Suppose that there is no desire to cause a contact or even an apprehension of one.

> **EXAMPLE:** Fred throws a stone through an open window of a crowded moving bus. His purpose is to have it pass through another open window at the other side of the bus without anyone noticing. One of the passengers, however, is hit by the stone.

Did Fred intend to hit the passenger? In general, intent is the desire to bring about the consequences of an act or the **knowledge with substantial certainty** that the consequences will follow from the act. If Fred had substantially certain knowledge that a passenger would be hit (or would have an apprehension of being hit), then he intended that result. Note, however, that merely being careless or even reckless is not enough to establish intent. There must be substantially certain knowledge. If all you can show is carelessness or recklessness, the tort to bring is *negligence* in creating an unreasonable risk of injuring someone, not the intentional tort of battery.

CASE

Garratt v. Dailey
46 Wash. 2d 197, 279 P.2d 1091 (1955)
Supreme Court of Washington

Background: *Ruth Garratt suffered a fractured hip from a fall that occurred when five-year-old Brian Dailey removed the chair Garratt was about to use. She sued Dailey for battery. The trial court found for Dailey. The boy did not have the intent to commit battery. The case is now on appeal before the Supreme Court of Washington.*

Decision on Appeal: *The case is sent back (remanded) to the trial court to clarify its finding on intent.*

OPINION OF COURT

Justice HILL delivered the opinion of the court:

The liability of an infant for an alleged battery is presented to this court for the first time. Brian Dailey (age five years, nine months) was visiting with Naomi Garratt, an adult and a sister of the plaintiff, Ruth Garratt, likewise an adult, in the back yard of the plaintiff's home, on July 16, 1951. It is plaintiff's contention that she came out into the back yard to talk with Naomi and that, as she started to sit down in a wood and canvas lawn chair, Brian deliberately pulled it out from under her. . . . The trial court . . . adopted instead Brian Dailey's version of what happened, and made the following findings:

"III. . . . that while Naomi Garratt and Brian Dailey were in the back yard the plaintiff, Ruth Garratt, came out of her house into the back yard. Some time subsequent thereto defendant, Brian Dailey, picked up a lightly built wood and canvas lawn chair which was then and there located in the back yard of the above described premises, moved it sideways a few feet and seated himself therein, at which time he discovered the plaintiff, Ruth Garratt, about to sit down at the place where the lawn chair had formerly been, at which time he hurriedly got up from the chair and attempted to move it toward Ruth Garratt to aid her in sitting down in the chair; that due to the defendant's small size and lack of dexterity he was unable to get the lawn chair under the plaintiff in time to prevent her from falling to the ground. That plaintiff fell to the ground and sustained a fracture of her hip, and other injuries. . . .

"IV. That the preponderance of the evidence in this case establishes that when the defendant, Brian Dailey, moved the chair in question *he did not have any wilful or unlawful purpose in doing so; that he did not have any intent to injure the plaintiff, or any intent to bring about any unauthorized or offensive contact with her person* or any objects appurtenant thereto; that the circumstances which immediately preceded the fall of the plaintiff established that the defendant, *Brian Dailey, did not have purpose, intent or design to perform a prank or to effect an assault and battery upon the person of the plaintiff.*" (Italics ours, for a purpose hereinafter indicated.) . . .

It is urged that Brian's action in moving the chair constituted a battery. A definition (not all-inclusive but sufficient for our purpose) of a battery is the intentional infliction of a harmful bodily contact upon another. The rule that determines liability for battery is given in 1 *Restatement, Torts,* 29, § 13, as:

"An act which, directly or indirectly, is the legal cause of a harmful contact with another's person makes the actor liable to the other, if

"(a) the act is done with the intention of bringing about a harmful or offensive contact or an apprehension thereof to the other or a third person. . . .

In the comment on clause (a), the *Restatement* says:

"Character of actor's intention. In order that an act may be done with the intention of bringing about a harmful or offensive contact or an apprehension thereof to a particular person, . . . the act must be done for the purpose of causing the contact or apprehension or with knowledge on the part of the actor that such contact or apprehension is substantially certain to be produced." See, also, *Prosser on Torts* 41, § 8.

We have here the conceded volitional act of Brian, i.e., the moving of a chair. Had the plaintiff proved to the satisfaction of the trial court that Brian moved the chair while she was in the act of sitting down, Brian's action would patently have been for the purpose or with the intent of causing the plaintiff's bodily contact with the ground, and she would be entitled to a judgment against him for the resulting damages. *Vosburg v. Putney,* 1891, 80 Wis. 523, 50 N.W. 403. . . .

After the trial court determined that the plaintiff had not established her theory of a battery (i.e., that Brian had pulled the chair out from under the plaintiff while she was in the act of sitting down), it then became concerned with whether a battery was established under the facts as it found them to be.

In this connection, we quote another portion of the comment on the "Character of actor's intention," relating to clause (a) of the rule from the *Restatement* heretofore set forth:

"It is not enough that the act itself is intentionally done and this, even though the actor realizes or should realize that it contains a very grave risk of bringing about the contact or apprehension. Such realization may make the actor's conduct negligent or even reckless but unless he realizes that to a substantial certainty, the contact or apprehension will result, the actor has not that intention which is necessary to make him liable under the rule stated in this section."

A battery would be established if, in addition to plaintiff's fall, it was proved that, when Brian moved the chair, he knew with substantial certainty that the plaintiff would attempt to sit down where the chair had been. If Brian had any of the intents which the trial court found, in the italicized portions of the findings of fact quoted above, that he did not have, he would of course have had the knowledge to which we have referred. The mere absence of any intent to injure the plaintiff or to play a prank on her or to embarrass her, or to commit an assault and battery on her would not absolve him from liability if in fact he had such knowledge. *Mercer v. Corbin,* 1889, 117 Ind. 450, 20 N.E. 132. Without such knowledge, there would be nothing wrongful about Brian's act in moving the chair and, there being no wrongful act, there would be no liability.

While a finding that Brian had no such knowledge can be inferred from the findings made, we believe that before the plaintiff's action in such a case should be dismissed there should be no question but that the trial court had passed upon that issue; hence, the case should be remanded for clarification of the findings to specifically cover the question of Brian's knowledge, because intent could be inferred therefrom. If the court finds that he had such knowledge the necessary intent will be established and the plaintiff will be entitled to recover, even though there was no purpose to injure or embarrass the plaintiff. *Vosburg v. Putney,* supra. If Brian did not have such knowledge, there was no wrongful act by him and the basic premise of liability on the theory of a battery was not established.

It will be noted that the law of battery as we have discussed it is the law applicable to adults, and no significance has been attached to the fact that Brian was a child less than six years of age when the alleged battery occurred. The only circumstance where Brian's age is of any consequence is in determining what he knew, and there his experience, capacity, and understanding are of course material. . . .

The remand for clarification gives the plaintiff an opportunity to secure a judgment even though the trial court did not accept her version of the facts, if from all the evidence, the trial court can find that Brian knew with substantial certainty that the plaintiff intended to sit down where the chair had been before he moved it, and still without reference to motivation. . . .

The cause is remanded for clarification, with instructions to make definite findings on the issue of whether Brian Dailey knew with substantial certainty that the plaintiff would attempt to sit down where the chair which he moved had been, and to change the judgment if the findings warrant it. . . .

Remanded for clarification.

ASSIGNMENT **5.1**	

a. What was wrong with the trial court's findings of fact? Didn't the trial court find that there was no intent to cause an offensive contact?

b. Suppose that Brian Dailey was not aware of the presence of Ruth Garratt until he heard her fall just after he took the chair. Would he have the required intent for battery under the guidelines of *Garratt v. Dailey?*

c. Two three-year-old children are standing on the edge of a bed. One says to the other, "Don't push me off." The other says, "I will so," and does so. Has there been a battery under the guidelines of *Garratt v. Dailey?*

d. Smith is an adult who suffers from severe paranoid schizophrenia that involves delusions of persecution, grandeur, and auditory hallucinations. He hits a stranger with a stick because he believed the stranger was Hitler coming to harm him. Has there been a battery under the guidelines of *Garratt v. Dailey?*

Transferred Intent

It is no defense to argue that the person hit is not the one the defendant intended to hit.

> **EXAMPLE:** Helen fires a gun at Paul. She misses him, but strikes Rich, whom she did not see.

Helen has battered Rich. Under the rule of **transferred intent,** her intent to hit Paul is transferred to Rich. (For more on transferred intent, see Figure 6–1 in Chapter 6.)

Motive

Motive is irrelevant. If the defendant intends a harmful or offensive contact, a battery has been committed, even if the defendant was trying to help the plaintiff through the contact.

> **EXAMPLE:**   On a rainy night, John falls off the curb. When a passerby tries to help, John says, "Don't touch me." Nevertheless, the passerby lifts John to carry him out of the rain.

The passerby has battered John. The fact that the motive may have been to be of help is no defense. As long as the contact is harmful or offensive (see next section), the tort has been committed. When we study medical malpractice in Chapter 18, we will see that treatment by a doctor without the informed consent of the patient is a battery in some states. Here again, the fact that the doctor had a benevolent motive would not be a defense. Most states, however, prefer that patients use negligence as the cause of action when they are treated without their informed consent.

HARMFUL OR OFFENSIVE CONTACT

Contact is **harmful** if it brings about physical damage, impairment, pain, or illness. It is **offensive** if it offends the personal dignity of an ordinary person who is not unduly sensitive.

Any physical damage, impairment, pain, or illness—no matter how trivial or slight—is considered harmful. The jury award that the plaintiff can recover for modest harm may be nominal, but even technical violations will give rise to a cause of action for battery.

If there is no harmful contact, the plaintiff may still be able to recover if the contact is offensive. An **objective standard** is used to determine when contact is offensive. The test is whether a reasonable person—someone not unduly sensitive—would be offended by the contact. If not, there is no battery, even though the plaintiff considered the contact offensive.

> **EXAMPLE:**   In a noisy, crowded subway, Jim approaches Cecile, a stranger. He gently taps her on the shoulder and says, "Would you please tell me the time?" Cecile is absolutely outraged by this contact, and screams.

A reasonable person would not consider this contact offensive, even though Cecile clearly does. In city life, a reasonable person expects a certain amount of contact as part of everyday living.

There is an exception to this rule when the defendant knows that the plaintiff has peculiar—even unreasonable—sensibilities about being touched. In such a case, the court will find the contact to be offensive even though someone of ordinary sensibilities would not be offended by it. The test of offensiveness is no longer objective when the defendant has such knowledge.

> **EXAMPLE:** Same situation involving Jim and Cecile, except that she is not a stranger, and Jim knows that she would be angered by the tap.

Here the contact is offensive. Jim's knowledge of her idiosyncrasy makes it so. (Depending on the severity of the circumstances, she may even have an action for the separate tort of intentional infliction of emotional distress. See Chapter 9.)

CASE

Brzoska v. Olson
668 A.2d 1355 (1995)
Supreme Court of Delaware

Background: *The death of Delaware dentist, Raymond Owens, from AIDS in 1991 made national news. Six hundred and thirty of his former patients took tests for HIV, which causes AIDS. None tested positive. Nevertheless, thirty-eight of the former patients sued for battery based on "offensive touching" during treatment. In the Superior Court, the plaintiffs lost; the judge ruled they had no basis for recovery for "fear of AIDS" in the absence of an underlying physical injury. He granted summary judgment against them and thereby avoided a trial on the battery claim. The case is now on appeal before the Supreme Court of Delaware.*

Decision on Appeal: *Judgment is affirmed. There was no battery.*

OPINION OF COURT

Justice WALSH delivered the opinion for the majority:

In this appeal from the Superior Court, we confront the question of whether a patient may recover damages for treatment by a health care provider afflicted with Acquired Immunodeficiency Syndrome ("AIDS") absent a showing of a resultant physical injury or exposure to disease. . . . We conclude that the Superior Court correctly ruled that, under the circumstances of Dr. Owens' treatment, there can be no recovery for fear of contracting a disease in the absence of a showing that any of the plaintiffs had suffered physical harm. Specifically, plaintiffs cannot recover under battery as a matter of law because they could not show that their alleged offense was reasonable in the absence of being actually exposed to a disease-causing agent. . . .

Prior to his death, Dr. Owens had been engaged in the general practice of dentistry in the Wilmington area for almost 30 years. Although plaintiffs have alleged that Dr. Owens was aware that he had AIDS for at least ten years, it is clear from the record that it was in March, 1989, that Dr. Owens was advised by his physician that he was HIV-positive. Dr. Owens continued to practice, but his condition had deteriorated by the summer of 1990. Toward the end of 1990, he exhibited open lesions, weakness, and memory loss. In February, 1991, his physician recommended that Dr. Owens discontinue his practice because of deteriorating health. Shortly thereafter, on February 23, Dr. Owens was

hospitalized. He remained hospitalized until his death on March 1, 1991.

Shortly after Dr. Owens' death, the Delaware Division of Public Health (the "Division") undertook an evaluation of Dr. Owens' practice and records, in part to determine if his patients had been placed at risk through exposure to HIV. The Division determined that Dr. Owens' equipment, sterilization procedures and precautionary methods were better than average and that he had ceased doing surgery since being diagnosed as HIV-positive in 1989.[1] Although the Division determined that the risk of patient exposure was "very small," it notified all patients treated by Dr. Owens from the time of his 1989 diagnosis until his death that their dentist had died from AIDS and that there was a possibility that they were exposed to HIV. The Division also advised the former patients that they could participate in a free program of HIV testing and counseling. Some patients availed themselves of the Division's testing while others secured independent testing. Of the 630 former patients of

---

[1] . . . On July 12, 1991, four months after Dr. Owens died from AIDS, the CDC [Centers for Disease Control] issued comprehensive guidelines concerning the practice of HIV-infected HCWs [health care workers] with their patients. *Recommendations for Preventing Transmission of Human Immunodeficiency Virus and Hepatitis B Virus to Patients During Exposure-Prone Invasive Procedures,* 40 Morbidity & Mortality Weekly Report RR-8, 1-9 (1991). In light of its determination that the risk of doctor-to-patient transmission of HIV is at most a small one, the CDC recommended that HIV-positive HCWs not be barred from performing most procedures. Instead, it recommended strict adherence to universal precautions, an approach to infection control where all human blood and certain human body fluids be treated as if infectious for HIV and other blood-borne pathogens. Such precautions include hand-washing, wearing protective barriers such as gloves and masks, and care in the use of needles and other sharp instruments. Id. If followed, the CDC concluded that the practice of HIV-infected HCWs who perform invasive procedures should not be restricted. It also recommended that HIV-positive HCWs obtain the approval of a review panel of experts and the consent of the patient before performing "exposure-prone" procedures. . . . Federal law now conditions federal funding to the states upon their adoption and enforcement of the CDC guidelines. 42 U.S.C. § 300ee-2. OSHA [Occupational Safety and Health Administration] regulations now also compel adherence to universal precautions. 29 C.F.R. § 1910.1030. Delaware has adopted standards analogous to the CDC guidelines. . . .

Dr. Owens who have been tested, none have tested positive for HIV. . . .

In their Superior Court action, the plaintiffs alleged that each of them had been patients of Dr. Owens in 1990 or 1991. Each claimed to have received treatment, including teeth extraction, reconstruction and cleaning, during which their gums bled. The plaintiffs alleged that Dr. Owens was HIV-positive and that he exhibited open lesions and memory loss at the time of such treatment. The plaintiffs did not allege the contraction of any physical ailment or injury as a result of their treatment, but claimed to have suffered "mental anguish" from past and future fear of contracting AIDS. They also alleged embarrassment in going for medical testing to a State clinic which they found to be "an uncomfortable environment." Plaintiffs sought compensation and punitive damages for mental anguish, the cost of medical testing and monitoring, and reimbursement for monies paid to Dr. Owens for dental treatment. . . .

Under the *Restatement (Second) of Torts,* "[a]n actor is subject to liability to another for battery if (a) he acts intending to cause a harmful or offensive contact with the person . . . and (b) a harmful contact with the person of the other directly or indirectly results." *Restatement (Second) of Torts* § 18 (1965); see also W. Page Keeton, et al., *Prosser and Keeton on Torts,* § 9 at 39 (5th ed. 1984) (hereafter "Prosser and Keeton") ("A harmful or offensive contact with a person, resulting from an act intended to cause the plaintiff or third person to suffer such a contact, or apprehension that such contact is imminent, is a battery."). . . .

The intent necessary for battery is the intent to make contact with the person, not the intent to cause harm. . . . In addition, the contact need not be harmful, it is sufficient if the contact offends the person's integrity. . . . "Proof of the technical invasion of the integrity of the plaintiff's person by even an entirely harmless, yet offensive, contact entitles the plaintiff to vindication of the legal right by the award of nominal damages." *Prosser and Keeton,* § 9 at 40. The fact that a person does not discover the offensive nature of the contact until after the event does not, *ipso facto,* preclude recovery. . . .

Although a battery may consist of any unauthorized touching of the person which causes offense or alarm, the test for whether a contact is "offensive" is not wholly subjective. The law does not permit recovery for the extremely sensitive who become offended at the slightest contact. Rather, for a bodily contact to be offensive, it must offend a *reasonable* sense of personal dignity. *Restatement (Second) of Torts* § 19 (1965). "In order for a contact [to] be offensive to a reasonable sense of personal dignity, it must be one which would offend the ordinary person and as such one not unduly sensitive as to his personal dignity. It must, therefore, be a contact which is unwarranted by the social usages prevalent at the time and place at which it is inflicted." Id. at comment a; *Prosser and Keeton,* § 9, at 42. The propriety of the contact is therefore assessed by an objective "reasonableness" standard.

Plaintiffs contend that the "touching" implicit in the dental procedures performed by Dr. Owens was offensive because he was HIV-positive. We must therefore determine whether the performance of dental procedures by an HIV-infected dentist, standing alone, may constitute offensive bodily contact for purposes of battery, i.e., would such touching offend a *reasonable* sense of personal dignity?

. . . HIV is transmitted primarily through direct blood-to-blood contact or by the exchange of bodily fluids with an infected individual. In a dental setting, the most probable means of transmission is through the exchange of bodily fluids between the dentist and patient by percutaneous (through the skin) contact, by way of an open wound, non-intact skin or mucous membrane, with infected blood or blood-contaminated bodily fluids. During invasive dental procedures, such as teeth extraction, root canal and periodontal treatments, there is a risk that the dentist may suffer a percutaneous injury to the hands, such as a puncture wound caused by a sharp instrument or object during treatment, and expose the dentist and patient to an exchange of blood or other fluids. Robert S. Klein, et al., *Low Occupational Risk of Human Immunodeficiency Virus Infection Among Dental Professionals,* 318 New England Journal of Medicine 86 (1988). Although the use of gloves as a protective barrier during invasive dental procedures reduces the risk of exposure of HIV, their use cannot prevent piercing injuries to the hands caused by needles, sharp instruments or patient biting. *Transmission of Human Immunodeficiency Virus in a Dental Practice,* 116 Annals in Medicine 798, 803 (1992).

The risk of HIV transmission from a health care worker to a patient during an invasive medical procedure is very remote.[2] In fact, even a person who is *exposed* to HIV holds a slim chance of infection. The CDC has estimated that the theoretical risk of HIV transmission from an HIV-infected health care worker to patient following actual percutaneous exposure to HIV-infected blood is, by any measure, less than one percent.

Here, plaintiffs have alleged no injuries which stem from their exposure to HIV. Instead, plaintiff's alleged "injuries" arise solely out of their *fear* that they have been exposed to HIV. In essence, they claim mental anguish damages for their "fear of AIDS.". . . As earlier noted, the offensive character of a contact in a battery case is assessed by a "reasonableness" standard. In a "fear of AIDS" case in which battery is alleged, therefore, we examine the overall reasonableness of the plaintiffs' fear in contracting the disease to determine whether the contact or touching was offensive. Since HIV causes AIDS, any assessment of the fear of contracting AIDS must, ipso facto, relate to the exposure to HIV. Moreover, because HIV is transmitted only through fluid-to-fluid contact or exposure, the reasonableness of a plaintiff's fear of AIDS should be measured by whether or not there was a channel of infection or actual exposure of the plaintiff to the virus.[3] It is unreasonable for a person to fear infection when that person has not been exposed to a disease. . . . Such fear is based on uninformed apprehension, not reality. In such circumstances, the fear of contracting AIDS is *per se*

---

[2]The CDC estimates that the probability of HIV transmission from a dentist to patient during a dental procedure in which the patient bleeds ranges from one in 263,158 and one in 2,631,579. . . . The only known instance of HIV transmission from a health care worker to a patient occurred in the well-publicized Kimberly Bergalis case in which a Florida dentist (Dr. Acer) infected as many as five of his patients. . . . To date, medical experts have been unable to scientifically determine how the dentist infected his patients.

[3]Of the jurisdictions that have addressed the issue of recovery under any claim for the fear of AIDS, the great majority require proof of actual exposure to HIV for plaintiffs to recover damages for emotional distress caused by fear of contracting AIDS. . . .

unreasonable without proof of actual exposure to HIV. In our view, the mere fear of contracting AIDS, in the absence of actual exposure to HIV, is not sufficient to impose liability on a health care provider. AIDS phobia, standing alone, cannot form the basis for recovery of damages, even under a battery theory because the underlying causation/harm nexus is not medically supportable.

AIDS is a disease that spawns widespread public misperception based upon the dearth of knowledge concerning HIV transmission. Indeed, plaintiffs rely upon the degree of public misconception about AIDS to support their claim that their fear was reasonable. To accept this argument is to contribute to the phobia. Were we to recognize a claim for the fear of contracting AIDS based upon a mere allegation that one *may* have been exposed to HIV, totally unsupported by any medical evidence or factual proof, we would open a Pandora's Box of "AIDS-phobia" claims by individuals whose ignorance, unreasonable suspicion or general paranoia cause them apprehension over the slightest of contact with HIV-infected individuals or objects. Such plaintiffs would recover for their fear of AIDS, no matter how irrational. See James C. Maroulis, *Can HIV-Negative Plaintiffs Recover Emotional Distress Damages for Their Fear of AIDS?*, 62 Fordham Law Review 225, 261 (1993) ("Allowing juries to decide whether the plaintiff's fear is reasonable even where there is no evidence of exposure invites jury speculation and may allow recovery based on ignorance or unreasonable fear of the disease."). We believe the better approach is to assess the reasonableness of a plaintiff's fear of AIDS according to the plaintiff's *actual*—not *potential*—exposure to HIV.

In sum, we find that, without actual exposure to HIV, the risk of its transmission is so minute that any fear of contracting AIDS is *per se* unreasonable. We therefore hold, *as a matter of law,* that the incidental touching of a patient by an HIV-infected dentist while performing ordinary, consented-to dental procedures is insufficient to sustain a battery claim in the absence of a channel for HIV infection. In other words, such contact is "offensive" only if it results in actual exposure to the HIV virus. We therefore adopt an "actual exposure" test, which requires a plaintiff to show "actual exposure" to a disease-causing agent as a prerequisite to prevail on a claim based upon fear of contracting disease. Attenuated and speculative allegations of exposure to HIV do not give rise to a legally cognizable claim in Delaware. . . .

In this case, the material facts are not in dispute. Even viewing the facts from plaintiffs' vantage point, the record fails to establish actual exposure to HIV. Plaintiffs argue to the contrary, noting that Dr. Owens exhibited lesions on his arms, legs, and elbow, and that he was known to have cut himself on at least one occasion while working on a patient. They have not, however, averred that the wound or lesions of Dr. Owens ever came into contact with the person of any of

the plaintiffs, nor have they identified which patient was present during Dr. Owens' injury or even whether that patient was a plaintiff in this action. In fact, nothing in this record suggests any bleeding from Dr. Owens or that any wound or lesions ever came into contact with a break in the skin or mucous membrane of any of the plaintiffs. Plaintiffs have failed to demonstrate any evidence of actual exposure to potential HIV transmission beyond mere unsupported supposition. . . .[4]

Although Dr. Owens presumably came into contact with the bodily fluids of some of the plaintiffs who bled during their dental procedures, there is no indication that the plaintiffs were actually exposed to a disease-causing agent. Again, HIV transmission requires fluid-to-fluid contact. In this case, plaintiffs have not been exposed to HIV, but rather, they have been exposed only to an HIV-infected dentist. Plaintiffs merely hypothesize as to how a possible exposure to HIV could have occurred without offering any substantiating evidence to that effect. Plaintiffs have shown nothing except that their risk of HIV infection was theoretical and remote. As such, plaintiffs' claims do not rise above mere speculation. . . .

In conclusion, the tort of battery requires a harmful or offensive contact, and "offensive" conduct is tested by a reasonableness standard. We hold that the fear of contracting a disease without exposure to a disease-causing agent is *per se* unreasonable. Thus, absent actual exposure to HIV, plaintiffs cannot recover for fear of contracting AIDS. . . .

The judgment of the Superior Court [on the battery claim] is affirmed. . . .

Justice DUFFY, . . . dissenting:

The [focus of the] majority opinion . . . is on so-called "AIDS-phobia" claims which are based on fear of the virus and nothing more. But that is not this case. . . . Here there is much more than the "phobia" which the majority condemns as arising from ignorance, unreasonable suspicion, general paranoia or fragile sensibility. Indeed, there is an abundance of evidence from which a jury could conclude that the fears of plaintiffs— or some of them—that they may have contracted a fatal disease were reasonable. . . . [P]laintiffs have offered evidence to show that the contacts were offensive because the possibility of the transmission of AIDS (at the time of treatment) was greater than a statistical average because of: Dr. Owens' health, his open lesions and where they were, the stage or progression of his disease at the time of patient contact, the advice given by his own physician to stop treating patients, his casual attitude with respect to washing, and whether or not Dr. Owens complied with the advised precautions. . . .

---

[4]Contact permitting the passage of fluids is essential to any claim of battery in an AIDS setting. In this case, we read the complaint as lacking any such allegation. Our ruling today is not intended, however, to foreclose a claim of battery where it is alleged that a wound or lesion of an AIDS-infected health care provider came into actual contact with a break in the skin or mucous membrane of a patient.

ASSIGNMENT

5.2

a. Did the court say it did not believe the patients' statement that they felt the contact with the dentist was offensive?

b. The court says that these plaintiffs were unreasonably sensitive to find the contact with the dentist to be offensive. Would the case be different if Dr. Owens knew one of the patients was very sensitive about surface-skin contact with an infected person? Would this change the result of the court as to this patient?

c. A healthy person spits in the face of the plaintiff, a stranger. No injuries result from this act, but the plaintiff sues for battery. Was the contact offensive? If so, how does this case differ from the *Brzoska* case?

d. In January of 2001, a disease breaks out among people who live in the Southwest section of the city. Many of those infected die. No one knows what is causing the disease. Mary Smith does not live in this section. On June 4, 2001, she is on a bus in the city. John Davis is running for County Supervisor. He walks up to Mary and offers to shake her hand. She does so. Later when she learns that John lives in the Southwest section of the city and has the disease, she sues him for battery. Does *Brzoska* apply? Assume that Mary does not contract the disease.

e. Tom and Linda are drug addicts. Tom knows that he has AIDS, but Linda does not know this. They have sexual relations and share each other's drug needles. Has either of them committed a battery?

CONSENT AND PRIVILEGE

Consent is a complete defense. There is no liability for battery if the plaintiff permitted the contact.

> **EXAMPLE:** The plaintiff offers her arm to a doctor who is inoculating everyone in line.

The plaintiff cannot later say that the doctor battered her. She consents to the contact if certain conditions are met, e.g., she has the capacity to consent, she voluntarily does so, and she knows what she is consenting to. For an extensive discussion of consent, see Chapter 27.

Similarly, if the plaintiff has a **privilege** to cause a contact with the plaintiff, the latter cannot win a suit for battery. The privileges include self-defense, the defense of others, the defense of property, discipline, and arrest. The elements of these privileges are discussed in Chapters 7 and 27.

ASSIGNMENT

5.3

a. Bill is behind the steering wheel of his parked car. He sees Helen take a baseball bat and swing it at the windshield directly in front of him. The windshield cracks but does not shatter. Has a battery been committed? Why or why not? What other torts, if any, might have been committed?

b. Ed throws a snowball at Dan's house, knowing that Dan is inside. The moment Dan hears the snowball, he is afraid that he will be hit. Battery?

c. Sam makes a batch of cookies with poison in them. He leaves them in a hall next to a telephone booth. A stranger eats one after making a call. Has Sam battered the stranger? If not, has another tort been committed?

d. Diane and Bob are walking across the street. Bob is daydreaming and doesn't see a car about to hit him. Diane pushes him away from the path of the car into safety. But he falls and breaks his ankle from the push. Bob sues Diane for battery. What result?

(See General Instructions for the Legal Analysis Assignment in Chapter 2.)

ASSIGNMENT

5.4

a. Select any of the fact situations presented in the problems of Assignment 5.3. Draft a complaint for the plaintiff in the case. (See General Instructions for the Complaint-Drafting Assignment in Chapter 3.)

b. In the case discussed in the text in which Fred threw a stone through the window of a moving bus, do you think that intent can be proven? What further facts would you like to have? (See General Instructions for the Investigation Strategy Assignment in Chapter 3.)

SUMMARY

Battery is a harmful or offensive contact with a person that results from the defendant's intent to cause either imminent contact or apprehension of imminent contact. There must be a voluntary movement of the defendant's body—an act. There must be actual contact with the person of the plaintiff. The plaintiff's person can include the plaintiff's body, anything attached to it, or anything so closely associated with the body as to be identified with it. The plaintiff does not have to be aware of the contact. The intent must be either the desire to bring about the contact or an imminent apprehension of the contact.

The law presumes the defendant had the requisite intent if he or she knew with substantial certainty that the contact or apprehension would result from his or her act. If the defendant intended to make contact with one person but in fact hit another, the law will transfer the intent to cover the latter. The defendant's motive is not relevant, even if it was to help (and even if the defendant does in fact help) the plaintiff through the contact.

The contact is harmful if it brings about physical damage, impairment, pain, or illness. It is offensive if it offends the personal dignity of an ordinary person who is not unduly sensitive. This objective test of offensiveness is used unless the defendant has reason to know that the plaintiff has an overly sensitive reaction to contact.

Consent and privilege are defenses to the cause of action of battery.

KEY TERMS

battery 106
deep pockets 106
shallow pockets 106
act 110
person 110
intent 110

imminent 110
apprehension 110
knowledge with substantial
    certainty 111
transferred intent 112
motive 113

harmful 113
offensive 113
objective standard 113
consent 117
privilege 117

CHAPTER

6

Assault

CHAPTER OUTLINE

- Introduction
- Act
- Apprehension
- Harmful or Offensive
- Transferred Intent
- Assault and Civil Rights

INTRODUCTION

Assault is an act that intentionally causes an apprehension of a harmful or offensive contact. Phrased another way, it means intentionally causing an awareness of a battery. The average citizen thinks of assault as an unwanted, and usually violent, contact with someone. But the tort of assault does not require actual contact. If someone hits you with a stick, a battery has been committed against you. If you were aware of the stick coming at you, an assault has also been committed against you. The contact and the apprehension (awareness) of the contact constitute separate torts. In criminal law, assault often means a violent contact; in the law of torts, however, it is the apprehension of a harmful or offensive contact.

For a sample complaint asserting a cause of action for assault, see Figure 3–10 in Chapter 3.

 Assault Checklist

Definitions, Relationships, Paralegal Roles, and Research References

Category
Assault is an intentional tort.

Interest Protected by This Tort
The right to be free from the apprehension of a harmful or offensive contact.

Elements of This Tort
  i. Act
  ii. Intent to cause either:
    a. an imminent harmful or offensive contact, or
    b. an apprehension of an imminent harmful or offensive contact
  iii. Apprehension of an imminent harmful or offensive contact to the plaintiff's person
  iv. Causation

Definitions of Major Words/Phrases in the Elements
Act: A voluntary movement of the defendant's body.
Intent: Either:
a. the desire to bring about the consequence of the act (i.e., the desire to cause the apprehension), or
b. the substantially certain knowledge that the consequence (i.e., the apprehension) will follow from the act.
Apprehension: Anticipation, knowledge, or belief (fear is *not* required).
Imminent: Immediate in the sense of no significant delay (something can be imminent without being instantaneous).
Harmful: Involving physical impairment, pain, or illness.
Offensive: Offending the personal dignity of an ordinary person who is not unduly sensitive.
Causation: Either:
a. but for the defendant's act, the consequence would not have occurred (i.e., the apprehension would not have occurred), or
b. the defendant's act was a substantial factor in bringing about the consequence (i.e., the apprehension).

Major Defense and Counterargument Possibilities That Need to Be Explored
1. Defendant's conduct was involuntary (no act).
2. Defendant did not desire a contact or apprehension, or know with substantial certainty that the apprehension would result from what he or she did (no intent).
3. There was no apprehension.
4. The apprehension pertained to a future contact (no imminence).
5. The apprehension would have occurred even if the defendant did not do what he or she did. The defendant was not a substantial factor in producing the apprehension. (No causation.)
6. The plaintiff consented to the conduct of the defendant that led to the apprehension (on the defense of consent, see Chapter 27).

Assault Checklist Continued

7. The apprehension resulted while the defendant was defending him- or herself from the plaintiff (on self-defense and other self-help privileges, see Chapter 27).
8. The apprehension occurred while the defendant was defending someone else from the plaintiff (on the defense of others and other self-help privileges, see Chapter 27).
9. The apprehension occurred while the defendant was defending property or recapturing chattels from the plaintiff (on the privileges of necessity, defense of property, recapture of property, and other self-help privileges, see Chapter 27).
10. The apprehension occurred while the defendant was disciplining plaintiff (on discipline and other self-help privileges, see Chapter 27).
11. The apprehension occurred while the defendant was arresting the plaintiff (on the privilege of arrest, see Chapter 7).
12. The plaintiff's suit against the government for an assault committed by a government employee may be barred by sovereign immunity (on sovereign immunity, see Chapter 27).
13. The plaintiff's suit against the government employee for assault may be barred by public official immunity (on official immunity, see Chapter 27).
14. The plaintiff's suit against the charitable organization for assault committed by someone working for the organization may be barred by charitable immunity (on charitable immunity, see Chapter 27).
15. The plaintiff's suit against a family member for assault may be barred by intrafamily immunity (on intrafamily immunity, see Chapter 27).

Damages

The plaintiff can recover compensatory damages for the apprehension, including pain and suffering, medical bills, and loss of wages. If the defendant acts out of hatred and malice in committing the assault, punitive damages are often awarded as well. (On the categories of damages, see Chapter 16.)

Relationship to Criminal Law

The same act of the defendant can constitute a *civil* assault (for which the plaintiff recovers damages) and a *criminal* assault (for which the state collects a fine or imposes jail or imprisonment). The word "assault" in criminal law is often used interchangeably with the word "battery."

Other Torts and Related Actions

Battery: The defendant may intend to batter the plaintiff, but fail to do so. If, in the process, the plaintiff is aware of the attempted battery, the tort of assault is probably committed.

False Imprisonment: If the plaintiff is aware of the defendant's attempt to confine the plaintiff, there may be an apprehension of contact, and hence an assault as well as false imprisonment.

Intentional Infliction of Emotional Distress: Assaults frequently accompany this tort.

Negligence: If the defendant does not intentionally cause apprehension in the plaintiff, the defendant may be negligent in causing it. For the negligence action to succeed, there must be actual harm in addition to the apprehension.

Wrongful Death: A wrongful-death action can be brought by the survivors of the plaintiff if death results from the assault.

Federal Law

a. Under the Federal Tort Claims Act, the United States Government will *not* be liable for an assault committed by one of its federal employees within the scope of employment (respondeat superior) *unless* the federal employee is an investigative or law enforcement officer. (See Figure 27–7 in Chapter 27.)
b. There may be liability under the Civil Rights Act if the assault was committed while the defendant was depriving the plaintiff of federal rights under color of law. (See Figure 27–9 in Chapter 27.)
c. There may be liability under the federal Free Access to Clinic Entrances Act (FACE) for assaults committed against people seeking or providing "reproductive health services." See discussion of FACE and the case of *Lucero v. Trosch* at the end of this chapter.

Employer-Employee (Agency) Law

An employee who commits an assault is personally liable for this tort. His or her employer will *also* be liable for assault if the conduct of the employee was within the scope of employment (respondeat superior). The employee must be furthering a business objective of

Assault Checklist Continued

the employer at the time. Intentional torts such as assault, however, are often outside the scope of employment. If so, only the employee is liable for the assault. (On the factors that determine the scope of employment, see Figure 14–10 in Chapter 14.)

Paralegal Roles in Assault Litigation
(See also Figures 3–1, 3–14, and 29–1 in Chapters 3 and 29.)

Fact finding (help the office collect facts relevant to prove the elements of assault, the elements of available defenses, and extent of injuries or other damages):
- client interviewing
- field investigation
- online research

File management (help the office control the volume of paperwork in an assault litigation):
- open client file
- enter case data in computer database
- maintain file documents

Litigation assistance (help the trial attorney prepare for an assault trial and appeal, if needed):
- draft discovery requests
- draft answers to discovery requests
- draft pleadings
- digest and index discovery documents
- help prepare, order, and manage trial exhibits (visuals or demonstratives)
- prepare trial notebook
- draft notice of appeal
- order trial transcript
- cite check briefs
- perform legal research

Collection/enforcement (help the trial attorney for the judgment creditor to collect the damages award or to enforce other court orders at the conclusion of the assault case):
- draft postjudgment discovery requests
- field investigation to monitor compliance with judgment
- online research (e.g., location of defendant's business assets)

Research References for Assault

Digests
In the digests of West, look for case summaries on assault under key topics such as:

Assault and Battery	Damages
Torts	

Corpus Juris Secundum
In this legal encyclopedia, see the discussions under topic headings such as:

Assault and Battery	Damages
Torts	

American Jurisprudence 2d
In this legal encyclopedia, see the discussions under topic headings such as:

Assault and Battery	Damages
Torts	

Legal Periodical Literature
There are two index systems to use to try to locate legal periodical literature on assault:

INDEX TO LEGAL PERIODICALS AND BOOKS (ILP)	CURRENT LAW INDEX (CLI)
See literature in *ILP* under subject headings such as:	See literature in *CLI* under subject headings such as:
Assault and Battery	Assault and Battery
Damages	Torts
Federal Tort Claims Act	Damages
Personal Injuries	Personal Injuries
Torts	
Wrongful Death	

Assault Checklist Continued

Example of a legal periodical article you will find by using *ILP* or *CLI:*

> *Respondeat Superior and the Intentional Tort: A Short Discourse on How to Make Assault and Battery a Part of the Job* by J. Terry Griffith, 45 University of Cincinnati Law Review 235 (1976).

A.L.R., A.L.R.2d, A.L.R.3d, A.L.R.4th, A.L.R.5th, A.L.R. Fed.
Use the *ALR Index* to locate annotations on assault. In this index, check subject headings such as:

> Assault and Battery   Damages
> Torts

Example of an annotation on assault you can locate through this index:

> *Federal Tort Claims Act Provision Exempting from Coverage Claim Arising out of Assault, Battery, False Imprisonment, False Arrest, Malicious Prosecution, etc.* by W. J. Dunn, 23 A.L.R.2d 574 (1952).

Words and Phrases
In this multivolume legal dictionary, look up *assault, apprehension, imminent, harmful, offensive, transferred intent,* and every other word or phrase connected with assault discussed in this chapter. The dictionary will give you definitions of these words or phrases from court opinions.

CALR: Computer-Assisted Legal Research
Example of a query you could ask on WESTLAW or on LEXIS to try to find cases, statutes, or other legal materials on assault: **assault/p damages**

Example of search terms you could use on an Internet legal search engine such as Law-Crawler (http://lawcrawler.findlaw.com) to find cases, statutes, or other legal materials on assault: **civil AND assault AND tort**

Example of search terms you could use on an Internet general search engine such as Alta Vista (http://www.altavista.com) to find cases, statutes, or other legal materials on assault: **+civil +assault +tort**

More Internet sites to check for materials on assault and other torts:
Jurist: (http://jurist.law.pitt.edu/sg_torts.htm)
LawGuru: (http://www.lawguru.com/search/lawsearch.html)
See also Tort Law Online at the end of Chapter 1.

ACT

The apprehension of a harmful or offensive contact must be caused by an **act,** which is a voluntary movement of the body.

> **EXAMPLE:**   A stranger pushes Jim, who then falls toward Ed. When Ed sees Jim coming, he quickly gets out of the way.

Ed, concerned about being hit by Jim, clearly had an apprehension of a harmful or offensive contact. But Jim did not commit an act that caused this apprehension. Because of the stranger's push, Jim involuntarily moved toward Ed. The stranger committed an act; Jim did not.

APPREHENSION

Apprehension is an understanding, awareness, anticipation, belief, or knowledge of something. It is not the equivalent of fear, although fear certainly qualifies as apprehension.

EXAMPLES:

- Greg (a 300-pound wrestler) swings his fist at Martha (a seventy-year-old, petite widow) because she called him a "bum" at a match. Terrified, Martha ducks just in time to avoid his punch.
- Later, Martha raises her newspaper to strike Greg in the stomach. Laughing, Greg steps back to avoid Martha's swing.

Greg and Martha have assaulted each other. Both had an awareness—an apprehension—of a harmful or offensive contact. Martha was afraid; Greg was not. But fear or intimidation is not required.

Greg laughed. Doesn't this mean he didn't think Martha was going to do something harmful or offensive? It depends on the meaning of harmful and offensive. This brings us to the third element of assault.

HARMFUL OR OFFENSIVE

As we saw in Chapter 5 on battery, **harmful** means bringing about physical damage, impairment, pain, or illness; and **offensive** means offending the dignity of an ordinary person who is not unduly sensitive. A smack on the stomach with a newspaper could cause pain, no matter how slight. Also, it is hardly a friendly gesture. Furthermore, most people would take offense at being hit under these circumstances. Greg may have thought it was all a big joke. Yet note that he stepped back to avoid the newspaper. To him, the idea of a fight with an old lady may have been ludicrous, but he clearly didn't appreciate being hit. Most people wouldn't. He was not *afraid* of a harmful or offensive contact, but he surely had an *apprehension* of one, however minor it might have been.

Reasonable

The plaintiff must be **reasonable** in claiming that he or she experienced an apprehension of the contact. The plaintiff may actually feel that a harmful or offensive contact is coming, but if this concern is peculiar or excessive, there is no tort of assault. There may, however, be an exception if the defendant knows that the plaintiff is unreasonably sensitive but proceeds to cause the apprehension anyway.

Imminent

The apprehension must be of an **imminent** harmful or offensive contact. A future or **conditional threat** is not enough.

EXAMPLE: On Monday, Ted calls Don on the phone and says, "If you don't pay your debt to me by this Friday, I'll be by Saturday to kill you." When Don hangs up the phone, he breaks out in a sweat because he knows Ted can be very violent.

There is no doubt that Don apprehends a very dangerous harmful and offensive contact. Yet it is not an imminent contact. It is scheduled to happen in the future (Saturday), and is conditional (on not paying the debt by Friday). Imminent means immediate, without significant delay. Verbal threats alone are often not sufficient when they explicitly relate to future conduct. Furthermore, the defendant must have the **apparent present ability** to carry out the threat. If the defendant points a toy gun at the plaintiff and threatens to shoot, there is no imminent apprehension if the plaintiff knows that the gun is a toy that is incapable of firing anything.

a. Recall the example given in the text of the stranger pushing Jim, who then falls toward Ed. When Ed sees Jim coming toward him, he quickly gets out of the way. As we said in the text, Jim did not commit an assault on Ed. What torts, if any, did the stranger commit?

b. Several Ku Klux Klan members in white robes march on the sidewalk five feet in front of a black person's house for about thirty minutes. The black person is terrified. Have the KKK members assaulted this person?

c. Sam puts an unloaded gun on the table in front of Mary and says, "This is for you if you don't cooperate." Mary knows the gun is unloaded but is terrified because Sam has thrown things at her in the past. Did Sam assault Mary with the gun?

(See General Instructions for the Legal Analysis Assignment in Chapter 2.)

TRANSFERRED INTENT

Assume that the defendant intends to assault one person, but in fact assaults the plaintiff, whom the defendant never knew existed. In spite of this mistake, the plaintiff has been assaulted by the defendant. This result is due to the doctrine of **transferred intent.** The defendant's intent to assault one person has been transferred to another person—the unintended plaintiff. Assault is not the only intentional tort that protects unintended plaintiffs through transferred intent. There are four others: battery, false imprisonment, trespass to land, and trespass to chattels.

In addition to unintended plaintiffs, there also can be unintended torts that are subject to a similar transfer under the doctrine of transferred intent. For an overview of unintended plaintiffs and unintended torts involving these five torts, see Figure 6–1.

FIGURE 6–1   Doctrine of transferred intent: What to do about an unintended plaintiff and/or an unintended tort?

Unintended Plaintiff

a. Defendant (D) intends to commit one of the following five torts against P$_1$:
   Assault
   Battery
   False Imprisonment
   Trespass to Land
   Trespass to Chattel
b. In fact, this tort is committed against P$_2$.
c. D did not intend to commit this tort against P$_2$.

Result: The law will transfer D's intent from P$_1$ to P$_2$ in order to make D liable for this tort to P$_2$.

Examples:

• D wants to lock Mary in a room. D mistakes Fran for Mary and falsely imprisons Fran. Fran can sue D for false imprisonment.
• D throws a rock, intending to hit Paul's car. The rock misses Paul's car and hits Bill's van. Bill can sue D for trespass to chattels.

In the above two examples, it is irrelevant that D did not intend to commit any tort against Fran or Bill. They are unintended plaintiffs to whom D is liable under the doctrine of transferred intent.

Unintended Tort

a. Defendant (D) intends to commit acts that would constitute one of the following five torts:
   Assault
   Battery
   False Imprisonment
   Trespass to Land
   Trespass to Chattel
b. In fact, D commits one of the other four torts.
c. D did not intend to commit the tort that occurred.

Result: The law will transfer D's intent from the tort D intended to commit to the tort that in fact resulted in order to make D liable for the latter tort.

Example:

• D wants to lock Joe in a room. D does not succeed because the door to the room has no lock. By mistake, however, D causes Joe to be in apprehension of being hit. Joe can sue D for assault.

In the above example, it is irrelevant that D did not intend to commit assault against Joe. An unintended tort has been committed for which D is liable under the doctrine of transferred intent.

CASE

Allen v. Walker
569 So. 2d 350 (1990)
Supreme Court of Alabama

Background: *Kathryn Allen and Richard Walker both work for Gulf States Paper Company. Following an argument, she sued him for assault. The lower court granted Walker a summary judgment. The case is now on appeal before the Supreme Court of Alabama.*

Decision on Appeal: *Judgment for Kathryn Allen. There is sufficient evidence to support an action for assault.*

OPINION OF COURT

Justice ALMON delivered the opinion of the court. . . .

Kathryn and Walker were employed at Gulf States' plant in Demopolis and were members of the same union. During a conversation concerning the proper method of filing a grievance against Gulf States with the union, Walker allegedly shook his finger at Kathryn's face. Kathryn told Walker that the last man who pointed his finger at her "was sorry that he did it." Walker then allegedly stated that he would "whip [Kathryn's] ass anytime, anywhere." The conversation then ended and Kathryn returned to work. The next day she and Walker had a second confrontation, during which Walker allegedly repeated his earlier threat. Following that second incident Kathryn became "agitated and upset" and reported Walker's threats to her supervisor.

"An assault consists of '. . . an intentional, unlawful, offer to touch the person of another in a rude or angry manner under such circumstances as to create in the mind of the party alleging the assault a well-founded fear of an imminent battery, coupled with the apparent present ability to effectuate the attempt, if not prevented.' *Western Union Telegraph Co. v. Hill*, 25 Ala. App. 540, 542, 150 So. 709, 710 (1933)." *Holcombe v. Whitaker*, 294 Ala. 430, 435, 318 So.2d 289, 294 (1975). Words standing alone cannot constitute an assault. However, they may give meaning to an act, and when both are taken together they may create a well-founded fear of a battery in the mind of the person at whom they are directed, thereby constituting an assault.

Kathryn argues that Walker's alleged threats, when combined with the fact that he shook his finger in her face during their first conversation, created a question for the jury on the issue of assault. . . .

[W]e cannot say that, as a matter of law, Walker's acts and threats could not create a reasonable or well-founded apprehension of imminent physical harm. There was evidence that, after Walker's first alleged threat, Allen walked away. That evidence is not conclusive, however, as to whether she discounted the threat or whether she left to avoid the threatened harm. She also testified that, after the second alleged assault the next day, she had to leave work because she was so frightened and upset. . . .

[W]e conclude that Kathryn presented sufficient evidence that Walker's alleged threats created a well-founded fear of imminent harm and created a jury question on her claim of assault. Therefore, the summary judgment on that claim will be reversed. . . .

ASSIGNMENT
6.2

a. If someone says he can or will harm you "anytime, anywhere," isn't this a threat to do something to you in the future *if* you keep bothering him? Isn't that what Walker meant? Why did the court say otherwise?

b. Kathryn told Walker that the last man who pointed his finger at her "was sorry that he did it." If she pointed her finger at Walker when she said this, would he have an assault case against her?

ASSAULT AND CIVIL RIGHTS

In Chapter 27 we will examine the Civil Rights Act, which is a federal statute that gives someone a right to damages for being deprived of federal rights under color of law. (See Figure 27–9 in Chapter 27.) There are other statutes that also provide similar remedies for civil rights violations. An example is the federal Free Access to Clinic Entrances Act (**FACE**). Between 1977 and 1993, over 1,000 acts of violence were committed against abortion providers. Thousands of clinic blockades also occurred. In response, Congress passed FACE, which provides a remedy for anyone who is a victim of assault or other attack while seeking or providing "reproductive health services." 18 U.S.C.A. § 248. The statute provides that "civil remedies" will be available against anyone who:

> "by force or threat of force or by physical obstruction, intentionally injures, intimidates or interferes with or attempts to injure, intimidate or interfere with any person because that person is or has been, or in order to intimidate such person or any other person or any class of persons from obtaining or providing reproductive health services. . . ." § 248(a)(1).

The following case interprets this provision. After you read the case, one of the assignment questions asks you to compare the apprehension element of civil assault and the threats prohibited by FACE.

CASE

Lucero v. Trosch
904 F. Supp. 1336 (1995)
United States District Court, S.D. Alabama

Background: *Father David Trosch is an antiabortion activist. On a television talk show (Geraldo), he appeared with Dr. Bruce Lucero. On the show, Trosch said that he would kill an abortion doctor if Trosch had a gun in his hand. He also said that Dr. Lucero, who performed abortions, "should be dead." Based on these statements, Lucero sued Trosch for violating the Free Access to Clinic Entrances Act (FACE). Trosch moved to dismiss on the ground that the complaint against him does not state a cause of action. His position is that there is no need for a trial because even if he said what Lucero alleges, FACE has not been violated. Furthermore, Trosch asserts that FACE is unconstitutional. The court must now rule on Trosch's motion to dismiss.*

Decision of Court: *The motion to dismiss is denied. The case should go to trial. If Lucero can prove his allegations, FACE has been violated. Also, FACE is constitutional.*

OPINION OF COURT

Chief Judge BUTLER delivered the opinion of the court . . .:

Plaintiff Bruce Lucero, M.D. ("Lucero") is a physician who provides reproductive health services, including abortions, at the New Woman All Women Health Care Clinic in Birmingham, Alabama. On October 5, 1994, Lucero and defendant Fr. David Trosch ("Trosch") appeared as guests on the *Geraldo Show,* which was filmed in New York, New York. Transcripts of the show indicate that Trosch's responses to questions posed by the program's host included the following:

Q: Father David Trosch, would you murder an abortion doctor if you had the gun in your hand?

A: No, I would not murder him, but I would kill him, there's a difference. . . .

Q: Sitting along side you, Dr. Bruce Lucero, a doctor who admits to performing abortions—

A: —he is a mass murder—

Q: —would you kill him?

A: He is a mass murderer and should be dead. Absolutely.

Q: He should be dead?

A: Should be dead. . . .

Q: Father Trosch, do you have the courage to say that you would kill him?

A: He deserves to be dead, [a]bsolutely.

Geraldo Show Transcript (Exhibit A to Defendant's Brief), at 2, 3.

Two months previously, in August 1994, Trosch appeared on the *Shelly Stewart Show,* which was filmed in Birmingham, Alabama. The tenor of Trosch's remarks on *Shelly Stewart* was generally similar to that of his comments on *Geraldo,* as he asserted that those who provide abortions should be killed and suggested that he could possibly kill one who performed abortions.[1] Lucero was not present at the show's taping, and none of Trosch's statements on *Shelly Stewart* made specific reference to Lucero.

---

[1] In particular, the following exchange took place on *Shelly Stewart:*

Q: If everyone listened to you, there would be people by the hundreds, by the thousands killed, wouldn't you say?

A: No, not at all. I believe if 20, 30, 40 doctors, abortionists, their staffs were killed, the rest of them would get out of the business. . . .

Q: Would you possibly yourself, pull the trigger and kill someone for performing an abortion?

A: Let me put it this way, Elijah slit the throats of 450 profits [sic] of Al because of the evil they did, and they were not even murderers, so if Elijah could do it I suppose I could.

Q: You could kill?

A: In defense of innocent human beings, yes.

First Amended Complaint (containing excerpts of *Shelly Stewart Show* transcript), at 5.

Lucero and the business at which he works, New Woman All Women Health Care Clinic, brought this action in the Northern District of Alabama, alleging that Trosch's conduct on the *Geraldo Show* and the *Shelly Stewart Show* violated the Free Access to Clinic Entrances Act. . . .

The Access Act creates a civil right of action against anyone who "by force or threat of force or by physical obstruction, intentionally injures, intimidates or interferes with or attempts to injure, intimidate or interfere with any person because that person is or has been, or in order to intimidate such person or any other person or any class of persons from, obtaining or providing reproductive health services." 18 U.S.C. § 248(a)(1).

Trosch contends that his words on the *Geraldo Show* did not rise to the level of force, threats of force, or physical obstruction sufficient to trigger the Access Act right of action, and that Lucero's claim for relief under the Act must be dismissed on that basis. In the alternative, Trosch contends that the Access Act is inapplicable because the statute excludes expressive conduct protected by the First Amendment.

Although the Access Act itself does not specifically define the term "threat of force," the Eleventh Circuit has elaborated on the term slightly, construing it as a "threat of physical force placing a person in reasonable apprehension of bodily harm." *Cheffer v. Reno*, 55 F.3d 1517, 1521 (11th Cir. 1995); see also *U.S. v. Brock*, 863 F. Supp. 851, 857 (E.D. Wis. 1994) (the Access Act is limited to "true threats", meaning those which could reasonably produce in victim a fear that threat would be carried out). Moreover, the court may obtain guidance from the multitude of cases defining the terms "threat" or "threat of force" in the context of analogous statutory provisions. These opinions indicate that a threat is a statement made "under such circumstances that a reasonable person would construe [it] as a serious expression of an intention to inflict bodily harm upon or to take the life of the persons named in the statute." *U.S. v. Callahan*, 702 F.2d 964, 965 (11th Cir. 1983) (interpreting 18 U.S.C. § 871). In the Eleventh Circuit, the test is an objective one which does not turn on the speaker's actual intentions. Id. at 965-66.

The court is unwilling to conclude as a matter of law that Trosch's statements, as set forth in Lucero's complaint, do not constitute threats of force actionable under the Access Act. See *U.S. v. Stobo*, 251 F. 689 (D.C. Del. 1918) (whether statement that "The President ought to be shot and I would like to be the one to do it" constituted a threat was a question for jury); *U.S. v. Stickrath*, 242 F.151 (D.C. Ohio 1917) (statement that President ought to be killed and that if he had the opportunity to do it, speaker would do so himself constituted threat). According to the complaint, Trosch said that Lucero "should be dead" and that he would kill an abortion doctor if he had a gun in his hand. Given the complaint's allegations of Trosch's words and the context in which they were spoken, the court cannot hold that a reasonable recipient could not have interpreted them as a serious expression of an intent to inflict bodily harm or death upon him.

Trosch argues that his statements on the *Geraldo Show* could not be construed as threats under the Access Act because: (1) they did not indicate any conduct by Trosch; (2) they did not express any intent to engage in future actions; and (3) they were not directed at Lucero. This argument must fail. Trosch has presented no case law stating that the three criteria outlined above are essential components of a threat; indeed, the weight of the precedents cited previously is at odds with such a legal construction of the term threat. More fundamentally, Trosch's contentions are meritless because they merely advance one interpretation of his statements on *Geraldo*. Based on the allegations before the court, other reasonable interpretations are possible. The court cannot foreclose the possibility that a reasonable recipient of Trosch's comments could have construed his remarks as satisfying all three of the articulated criteria.[2] The fact that Trosch did not expressly state to Lucero that he was going to kill Lucero at some future time does not preclude a reasonable factfinder from determining that a threat was in fact made to Lucero. See *U.S. v. Malik*, 16 F.3d 45, 50 (2d Cir. 1994) (threatening nature of communication may arise from reasonable connotations derived from its ambience); *U.S. v. Gilbert*, 884 F.2d 454, 457 (9th Cir. 1989) (the fact that a threat is subtle does not render it any less of a threat); *U.S. v. Cox*, 957 F.2d 264, 266 (6th Cir. 1992) (a specific individual as a target of the threat need not be identified as such).

Trosch next contends that . . . his statements which aired on the *Geraldo Show* constituted protected speech under the First Amendment; therefore, he claims, Lucero is barred from invoking the civil remedies which would otherwise be available to him under the Access Act.

It is widely recognized that true threats of force are not cloaked in the protections afforded other types of speech by the First Amendment. See *Watts v. U.S.*, 394 U.S. 705, 707, 89 S.Ct. 1399, 1401 (1969) (holding that "[w]hat is a threat must be distinguished from what is constitutionally protected speech"); *American Life League, Inc. v. Reno*, 47 F.3d 642, 648 (4th Cir. 1995) (threats of force targeted by the Access Act are not protected by First Amendment). In fact, there are numerous federal statutes which proscribe threats and threats of force. These statutes have been upheld routinely against First Amendment challenges, with courts adopting the rationale that threats are not protected speech. . . . If Trosch's remarks on the *Geraldo Show* were threats of force, then they cannot receive First Amendment protection. . . .

For all of the foregoing reasons, defendant's motion to dismiss the complaint for failure to state a claim upon which relief can be granted is DENIED. . . .

---

[2]Indeed . . . the facts can support the conclusion that Trosch's comments constituted statements of intent to kill Lucero in the future, and that such statements were directed at Lucero who was, after all, sitting next to Trosch at the time that he expressed such sentiments on the *Geraldo Show*.

a. The court said in footnote 2 that "the facts can support the conclusion that Trosch's comments constituted statements of intent to kill Lucero in the future." Make an argument that this conclusion of the court is accurate. Make an argument that it is not.

b. Would the court have reached the same result if the only comment made by Trosch was, "my conscience does not allow killing, but you, Dr. Lucero, should be stopped by any means possible"?

c. Threats can constitute civil assault. They also can constitute a violation of FACE. What is the difference?

d. Did Father Trosch's comments constitute civil assault? Why or why not?

SUMMARY

An assault is an act (usually an attempted battery) that causes apprehension of an imminent harmful or offensive contact. There is no requirement that the plaintiff fear—he or she need only be aware of—a coming harmful or offensive contact. "Harmful" means bringing about physical damage, impairment, pain, or illness; "offensive" means offending the dignity of an ordinary person who is not unduly sensitive.

The plaintiff must be reasonable in claiming that he or she experienced the apprehension. Furthermore, the apprehension must pertain to an imminent (not a future or conditional) harmful or offensive contact.

If the defendant intends to assault one person, but mistakenly assaults another, the defendant is liable for assault to the unintended plaintiff. This doctrine of transferred intent also covers the intentional torts of battery, false imprisonment, trespass to land, and trespass to chattels. In addition, under this doctrine, the defendant's intent to commit one of these five torts will also make the defendant liable for one of the other four unintended torts that results from what the defendant did.

The federal Free Access to Clinic Entrances Act (FACE) provides a civil cause of action for a person who has been threatened or otherwise attacked while seeking or providing reproductive health services.

KEY TERMS

assault 120	offensive 124	apparent present ability 124
act 123	reasonable 124	transferred intent 125
apprehension 123	imminent 124	FACE 126
harmful 124	conditional threat 124	

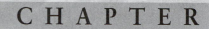

CHAPTER

7

False Imprisonment and False Arrest

CHAPTER OUTLINE

- Introduction
- False Imprisonment
- False Arrest

INTRODUCTION

The tort of **false imprisonment** covers much more than prisons and jails. It protects the right of everyone to move about freely. The most obvious example of this tort is being locked in a room. But imprisonment is not limited to forcing a person to remain within an enclosed structure. It is possible to falsely imprison someone in an area where there are no walls. Recently, a celebrity brought a false imprisonment suit against *paparazzi*—photographers who stalk celebrities for photographs outside restaurants, in parking lots, on the sidewalk, on the freeway, etc. To understand how such conduct might constitute false imprisonment, we need to explore the broader dimension of this intentional tort.

For a sample complaint asserting a cause of action for false imprisonment, see Figure 3–10 in Chapter 3.

FALSE IMPRISONMENT

 False Imprisonment Checklist

Definitions, Relationships, Paralegal Roles, and Research References

Category
False imprisonment is an intentional tort.

Interest Protected by This Tort
The right to be free from intentional restraints on one's freedom of movement.

Elements of This Tort
 i. An act that completely confines the plaintiff within fixed boundaries set by the defendant
 ii. Intent to confine the plaintiff or a third party
 iii. Causation of the confinement
 iv. The plaintiff was either conscious of the confinement or suffered actual harm by it

Definitions of Major Words/Phrases in These Elements
 Act: A volitional movement of the defendant's body by words or other conduct.
 Confine: To restrain the plaintiff's freedom of movement:
 a. by physical barriers, or
 b. by physical force, or
 c. by the threat of present physical force, or
 d. by asserting legal authority to confine, or
 e. by refusing to release the plaintiff.
 Complete: A total confinement where the plaintiff knows of no safe or inoffensive means of escape.
 Intent to Confine: The desire to confine the plaintiff or the knowledge with substantial certainty that the defendant's act will result in the confinement.
 Causation: But for the defendant's act, the plaintiff would not have been confined, or the defendant was a substantial factor in producing the confinement.
 Harmed: Actual damage or injury in addition to the confinement itself.

Major Defense and Counterargument Possibilities That Need to Be Explored
 1. There was no confinement.
 2. The confinement was not total; there was a safe and inoffensive means of escape that the plaintiff did not take.
 3. The threat of force related to the future.
 4. The confinement was accidental. It may have been negligently or recklessly caused, but it was not intentional.

False Imprisonment Checklist Continued

5. The defendant was not a substantial factor in producing the confinement.
6. The plaintiff either did not know about the confinement or was not physically harmed by it.
7. The plaintiff consented to the confinement by the defendant (on the defense of consent, see Chapter 27).
8. The confinement resulted while the defendant was defending him- or herself from the plaintiff (on self-defense and other self-help privileges, see Chapter 27).
9. The confinement occurred while the defendant was defending someone else from the plaintiff (on the defense of others and other self-help privileges, see Chapter 27).
10. The confinement occurred while the defendant was legitimately defending property or recapturing chattels from the plaintiff (on the privileges of necessity, defense of property, recapture of property, and other self-help privileges, see Chapter 27).
11. The confinement occurred while the defendant was detaining plaintiff for investigation to determine whether the plaintiff had stolen property or services (shopkeeper's privilege, covered in this chapter).
12. The confinement occurred while the defendant was disciplining the plaintiff (on discipline and other self-help privileges, see Chapter 27).
13. The confinement occurred while the defendant was arresting the plaintiff (privilege of arrest, covered in this chapter).
14. The plaintiff's suit against the government for false imprisonment committed by a government employee may be barred by sovereign immunity (on sovereign immunity, see Chapter 27).
15. The plaintiff's suit against the government employee for false imprisonment may be barred by public official immunity (on official immunity, see Chapter 27).
16. The plaintiff's suit against the charitable organization for a false imprisonment committed by someone working for the organization may be barred by charitable immunity (on charitable immunity, see Chapter 27).
17. The plaintiff's suit against a family member for false imprisonment may be barred by intrafamily immunity (on intrafamily immunity, see Chapter 22).
18. The plaintiff failed to take reasonable steps to mitigate the harm caused when the defendant committed false imprisonment; therefore, damages should not cover the aggravation of the harm caused by the plaintiff (on the doctrine of avoidable consequences, see Chapter 16).

Damages

The plaintiff does not have to prove actual harm to establish a prima facie case of false imprisonment (unless the plaintiff was unaware of the confinement). In most cases, the confinement is harm enough. Once the elements of false imprisonment have been proven, the jury will be allowed to consider compensatory damages for humiliation, injury to plaintiff's reputation, illness or other physical discomfort, loss of earnings or other damage to personal property due to the confinement, etc. If the defendant acted out of hatred or malice, punitive damages are also possible.

Relationship to Criminal Law

In many states, false imprisonment is also a crime if the confinement is serious enough. The crime may be called false imprisonment, abduction, kidnapping, etc.

Relationship to Other Torts

Assault: An assault may also be committed if the defendant puts the plaintiff in apprehension of a harmful or offensive contact while falsely imprisoning him or her.

Battery: It is common for the defendant to touch the plaintiff while falsely imprisoning him or her. If this touching was without consent, the defendant may also be liable for a battery.

Defamation: Defamation may occur during the false imprisonment. For example, the defendant may use derogatory language while confining the plaintiff. Also, the very act of being confined may be a derogatory "communication," especially if the defendant is a police officer and the confinement is seen by others.

Intentional Infliction of Emotional Distress: This tort may also be committed if the intent of the defendant who falsely imprisoned the plaintiff was to subject the plaintiff to severe emotional trauma by the confinement.

False Imprisonment Checklist Continued

Malicious Prosecution: If the defendant has instigated an unlawful arrest of the plaintiff, the defendant may be liable for false imprisonment and for malicious prosecution if the defendant acted with malice, without probable cause, and if the criminal case terminated favorably to the plaintiff.

Negligence: The defendant may have caused the confinement of the plaintiff by carelessness or recklessness rather than with the intent to confine him or her, e.g., the defendant accidentally, but carelessly or recklessly, locks the plaintiff in a room. If so, there is no false imprisonment, but there may be negligence if the plaintiff has suffered actual harm in addition to the confinement itself.

Federal Law

a. Under the Federal Tort Claims Act, the United States Government will *not* be liable for a false imprisonment committed by one of its federal employees within the scope of employment (respondeat superior) *unless* the federal employee is an investigative or law enforcement officer. (See Figure 27–7 in Chapter 27.)

b. There may be liability under the Civil Rights Act if the false imprisonment was committed while the defendant was depriving the plaintiff of federal rights under color of law. (See Figure 27–9 in Chapter 27.)

Employer-Employee (Agency) Law

An employee who commits false imprisonment is personally liable for this tort. His or her employer will *also* be liable for false imprisonment if the conduct of the employee was within the scope of employment (respondeat superior). The employee must be furthering a business objective of the employer at the time. Intentional torts such as false imprisonment, however, are often outside the scope of employment. If so, only the employee is liable for the false imprisonment. (On the factors that determine the scope of employment, see Figure 14–10 in Chapter 14.)

Paralegal Roles in False Imprisonment Litigation

(See also Figures 3–1, 3–14, and 29–1 in Chapters 3 and 29.)

Fact finding (help the office collect facts relevant to prove the elements of false imprisonment, the elements of available defenses, and extent of injuries or other damages):
• client interviewing
• field investigation
• online research

File management (help the office control the volume of paperwork in a false imprisonment litigation):
• open client file
• enter case data in computer database
• maintain file documents

Litigation assistance (help the trial attorney prepare for a false imprisonment trial and appeal, if needed):
• draft discovery requests
• draft answers to discovery requests
• draft pleadings
• digest and index discovery documents
• help prepare, order, and manage trial exhibits (visuals or demonstratives)
• prepare trial notebook
• draft notice of appeal
• order trial transcript
• cite check briefs
• perform legal research

Collection/enforcement (help the trial attorney for the judgment creditor to collect the damages award or to enforce other court orders at the conclusion of the false imprisonment case):
• draft postjudgment discovery requests
• field investigation to monitor compliance with judgment
• online research (e.g., location of defendant's business assets)

False Imprisonment Checklist Continued

Research References for False Imprisonment

Digests
In the digests of West, look for case summaries on false imprisonment under key topics such as:

False Imprisonment	Torts
Arrest	Damages

Corpus Juris Secundum
In this legal encyclopedia, look for discussions under topic headings such as:

False Imprisonment	Torts
Arrest	Damages

American Jurisprudence 2d
In this legal encyclopedia, look for discussions under topic headings such as:

False Imprisonment	Torts
Arrest	Damages

Legal Periodical Literature
There are two index systems to use to try to locate legal periodical literature on false imprisonment:

INDEX TO LEGAL PERIODICALS AND BOOKS (ILP)	CURRENT LAW INDEX (CLI)
See literature in *ILP* under subject headings such as:	See literature in *CLI* under subject headings such as:
False Imprisonment	False Imprisonment
Arrest	Arrest
Damages	Tort
Torts	Damages
Personal Injuries	Duress
	Personal Injuries
	Privileges and Immunities

Example of a legal periodical article on this tort you will find by using *ILP* or *CLI*:

> *"Nowhere to Go and Chose to Stay"; Using the Tort of False Imprisonment to Redress Involuntary Confinement of the Elderly in Nursing Homes and Hospitals* by Cathrael Kazin, 137 University of Pennsylvania Law Review 903 (1989).

A.L.R., A.L.R.2d, A.L.R.3d, A.L.R.4th, A.L.R.5th, A.L.R. Fed.
Use the *ALR Index* to locate annotations on false imprisonment. In this index, check subject headings such as:

False Imprisonment	Shoplifting
Arrest	Torts
Privileges and Immunities	Damages

Example of an annotation on false imprisonment you can locate through this index:

> *Liability of Attorney Acting for Client for False Imprisonment or Malicious Prosecution of Third Party,* 27 A.L.R.3d 1113 by J. Kraut (1969).

Words and Phrases
In this multivolume legal dictionary, look up *false imprisonment, confinement, false arrest,* and every other word or phrase connected with the torts discussed in this chapter. The dictionary will give you definitions of these words or phrases from court opinions.

CALR: Computer-Assisted Legal Research
Example of a query you could ask on WESTLAW to try to find cases, statutes, or other legal materials on false imprisonment: **"false imprisonment" /p damages**

Example of a query you could ask on LEXIS to try to find cases, statutes, or other legal materials on false imprisonment: **false imprisonment /p damages**

Example of search terms you could use on an Internet legal search engine such as Law-Crawler (http://lawcrawler.findlaw.com) to find cases, statutes, or other legal materials on false imprisonment: **"false imprisonment"**

Example of search terms you could use on an Internet general search engine such as Alta Vista (http://www.altavista.com) to find cases, statutes, or other legal materials on false imprisonment: **"false imprisonment" -crime**

More Internet sites to check for materials on false imprisonment and other torts:
Jurist: (http://jurist.law.pitt.edu/sg_torts.htm)
LawGuru: (http://www.lawguru.com/search/lawsearch.html)
See also Tort Law Online at the end of Chapter 1.

Confinement

The first element of false imprisonment is an act that completely confines the plaintiff within fixed boundaries set by the defendant. The word "imprisonment" is very misleading. To commit this tort, you do not have to place someone behind bars without authority. Such an act will constitute false imprisonment, as will an illegal delay in releasing someone from jail or prison. But false imprisonment is not limited to such extreme situations. It can also occur when there is a **confinement** of one's freedom of movement. This confinement or restraint can happen in five ways:

Confinement by Physical Barrier   Tangible, physical restraints or barriers are imposed on the plaintiff.

> **EXAMPLES:**
>
> • The defendant locks the plaintiff in a room.
> • The defendant takes away the plaintiff's wheelchair.
> • The defendant takes away the plaintiff's ladder that is necessary to climb out of a deep ditch.

Confinement by Physical Force Against the Plaintiff, the Plaintiff's Immediate Family, or the Plaintiff's Property

> **EXAMPLES:**
>
> • If the defendant grabs or holds the plaintiff, confinement results from physical force on the plaintiff's body.
> • The plaintiff can also be confined if the defendant uses physical force on the plaintiff's child or other members of his or her immediate family. Suppose that the defendant ties up the plaintiff's son. The plaintiff may be able to escape, but it is highly unlikely that he or she will do so while the child is in danger. Hence, the defendant has confined *both* the child and the plaintiff. The physical force used against the child has also resulted in the confinement of the parent.
> • Finally, suppose that the defendant uses physical force against the plaintiff's valuable property, such as by seizing the plaintiff's watch. The plaintiff stays in order to try to get the watch back. (As we will see in Chapter 27, the plaintiff has a **privilege to recapture** such property.)

In the last two examples, the parent who remains because his or her child is tied up and the plaintiff who remains to see about a watch that has been taken, have "agreed" to stay, but they have done so under such severe **duress** that the confinement is not voluntary. The confinement is imposed on the plaintiffs as effectively in these situations as when actual physical force is used on a plaintiff's body.

Confinement by Threat of Present Physical Force Against the Plaintiff, Against the Plaintiff's Immediate Family, or Against the Plaintiff's Property   A plaintiff's freedom of movement is certainly restricted if the defendant threatens present force or violence against the plaintiff, against a member of the plaintiff's immediate family, or against the plaintiff's valuable property if the plaintiff tries to escape or move out of an area designated by the defendant. If the plaintiff submits to the threat and remains, a confinement has occurred for purposes of establishing the first element of the tort of false imprisonment. The plaintiff does not have to be reasonable in submitting as long as the defendant has the intent to confine the plaintiff through the threat of immediate physical force.[1]

Confinement by Asserted Legal Authority   Here the defendant claims the legal authority or right to confine or arrest the plaintiff. Confinement occurs when the plaintiff is taken into custody. If the defendant does not have the privilege of arresting the plaintiff, as defined later in the chapter, the first element of false imprisonment has been met. No physical force or touching need be used as long as the plaintiff has reason to believe that such force will be used if the plaintiff either moves outside an area designated by the defendant or fails to follow the defendant.

Confinement by Refusal to Release   Assume that the plaintiff has been validly confined, e.g., imprisoned. At the time when the plaintiff has a right to be released, he or she has been improperly confined if the defendant interferes with the release.

Confinement in any of the five ways must be complete or total, meaning that the plaintiff must know of no safe or inoffensive means of escape out of the fixed boundaries set by the defendant. There is no confinement, for example, if the defendant blocks the plaintiff's path when there is a clear and accessible way around the defendant. Nor is there confinement when the defendant locks all the doors of a house if the plaintiff is able to escape by climbing out of a window that is very close to the ground and if the inconvenience in climbing out is slight. A different result would follow, however, if the plaintiff had little or no clothing on, or would have substantial difficulty climbing out because of age or illness.

Finally, there is no set length of time that the confinement must last. A person can be confined for a brief or a prolonged period.

A great many false imprisonment cases result from detention in shops and department stores when a customer is suspected of stealing merchandise or services. A **shopkeeper's privilege** gives a shopkeeper the right to detain someone temporarily for the sole purpose of investigating whether theft has occurred. Reasonable force can be used to carry out this temporary investigation. The shopkeeper must be reasonable in suspecting that the person has committed the crime. If it turns out that the person is innocent and that the shopkeeper has made a mistake, the latter is still protected if the mistake was reasonable.

Every state has a shopkeeper's privilege in one form or another. The privilege may have been created by the courts as part of the **common law** or by the legislature as part of its statutory code. One of the states with a statute is New York. Here is its statute. Note that New York extends the privilege to cover detention or confinement for the purpose of questioning someone suspected of using recording devices in a theater. Not all states would grant the privilege for this purpose.

§ 218   In any action for false arrest, false imprisonment, unlawful detention, defamation of character, assault, trespass, or invasion of civil rights, brought by any person by reason of having been detained on or in the immediate vicinity of the premises of (a) a retail mercantile establishment for the purpose of investigation or questioning as to . . . the ownership of any merchandise, or (b) a motion picture theater for the purposes of investigation or questioning as to the unauthorized operation of a recording device in a motion picture theater, it shall be a defense to such action that the person was detained in a reasonable manner and for not more than a reasonable time to permit such investigation or questioning by . . . the owner of the retail mercantile establishment or motion picture theater, his authorized

---

[1] *Restatement (Second) of Torts* § 40 comment d (1965).

employee or agent, and that such . . . owner, employee or agent had reasonable grounds to believe that the person so detained was . . . attempting to commit larceny on such premises of such merchandise or was engaged in the unauthorized operation of a recording device in a motion picture theater. As used in this section, "reasonable grounds" shall include, but not be limited to, knowledge that a person (i) has concealed possession of unpurchased merchandise of a retail mercantile establishment, or (ii) has possession of an item designed for the purpose of overcoming detection of security markings attachments placed on merchandise offered for sale at such an establishment, or (iii) has possession of a recording device in a theater in which a motion picture is being exhibited and a "reasonable time" shall mean the time necessary to permit the person detained to make a statement or to refuse to make a statement, and the time necessary to examine employees and records of the mercantile establishment relative to the ownership of the merchandise, or possession of such an item or device. . . . N.Y. General Business Law § 218 (McKinney, 1998).

The following example demonstrates the operation of the privilege.

> **EXAMPLE:** George is a store clerk at Macy's. He sees Fred, a teenager, take a watch from the counter, put it in his pocket, and walk out the door without paying. In the parking lot, George orders Fred to the back room of the store. After about ten minutes of questioning, George concludes that Fred stole the watch. As Fred breaks down and cries, George spends about an hour lecturing Fred about the morality of stealing. He then calls the police. Later, Fred sues Macy's for false imprisonment.

The store can raise the defense of shopkeeper's privilege to cover the time when Fred was escorted to the back room and questioned about payment for the watch. The privilege, however, would *not* cover the period after George completed his investigation of Fred. There is no shopkeeper's privilege to lecture thieves about the morality of what they are doing. During the time of the lecture, Fred was falsely imprisoned.

ASSIGNMENT
7.1

Jim is soliciting religious contributions in Leo's department store. Leo tells Jim that this is not allowed in the store. Jim nevertheless continues. Leo and four of his security guards surround Jim and tell him to come to the manager's office. Jim does so. In the manager's office, Leo shouts at Jim and tells him, "you've got thirty seconds to get out the back door." Jim leaves and sues Leo for false imprisonment. Discuss Jim's chances of winning. (See General Instructions for the Legal Analysis Assignment in Chapter 2.)

CASE

The Limited Stores, Inc. v. Wilson-Robinson
317 Ark. 80, 876 S.W.2d 248 (1994)
Supreme Court of Arkansas

Background: *Perrylyn Wilson-Robinson was a customer in The Limited Stores, Inc. (referred to as Stores in the opinion). As she was walking out the front door, the sensor alarm went off. When employees asked her to come back for questioning, she agreed. After determining that there was no theft, she was told she* *could go. She then sued Stores for false imprisonment and won. She was awarded $6,850 in compensatory damages and $23,650 in punitive damages. The case is now on appeal before the Supreme Court of Arkansas where Wilson-Robinson is the appellee and Stores is the appellant.*

Decision on Appeal: *The judgment is reversed. There was no false imprisonment.*

OPINION OF COURT

Justice HAYS delivered the opinion of the court . . .:

Ms. Wilson-Robinson testified that she was shopping in The Limited Stores in North Little Rock. As she left the store the alarm on the sensormatic device sounded. Although she heard the alarm she continued out into the mall, thinking the alarm did not pertain to her. Two female employees from the store approached her. Ms. Wilson-Robinson testified "[t]hey asked if I would return to the store because when I left out the buzzer went off." "I said, 'Well, sure,' because I hadn't done anything."

When the two employees and Ms. Wilson-Robinson reentered the store the alarm did not go off. One of the employees then asked if she had a calculator in her bag. She said, " 'Yes, I have a calculator,' and I opened up my bag. I said, 'See, you know, here's the calculator.' " At that point one of the employees waved the calculator in front of the device but the alarm did not go off. The employee then said: "Well, okay, you know, it is fine. You can leave now." Ms. Wilson-Robinson asked to meet with the store manager and, after speaking with her, she left.

Ms. Wilson-Robinson testified there were other people leaving the store when she heard the alarm and she felt she was stopped because "I'm a heavy set black female, and I carry a large purse." In explaining why she returned to the store, she testified: "When they stopped me on the mall, my impression was that they were accusing me of taking something, so I really didn't have a choice, so I said, 'Sure, I will go back,' because I knew I hadn't done anything. And, if I hadn't gone back, then the consequences was saying, well, maybe she is guilty. So I went back to the store because I didn't do anything." . . .

A merchant may detain, for a reasonable length of time, a person he or she has reasonable cause to believe is shoplifting. See *Arkansas Code Annotated* § 5-36-116 (Repl. 1993); 7 Speiser, Krause and Gans, *The American Law of Torts* § 27.18 (1990). However, whether Stores had grounds to detain Ms. Wilson-Robinson pursuant to the statute is not the issue. Rather, Stores contends Ms. Wilson-Robinson was not detained. Simply put, Stores contends the detention or imprisonment requirement of the tort was not met.

False imprisonment has been defined as the unlawful violation of the personal liberty of another, consisting of *detention* without sufficient legal authority. *Headrick v. Wal-Mart Stores, Inc.*, 293 Ark. 433, 738 S.W.2d 418 (1987). Any express or implied threat of force whereby one is deprived of his liberty or compelled to go where one does not wish to go is an imprisonment. *Pettijohn v. Smith* et al., 255 Ark. 780, 502 S.W.2d 618 (1973). Stores submits there was no detention, imprisonment or arrest. Ms. Wilson-Robinson contends there was a detention because *two* employees went after [her] and there was an "implied threat of arrest."

It is well established that the restraint constituting a false imprisonment may be by threats of force which intimidate the plaintiff into compliance with orders. *Restatement (Second) of Torts* § 40 (1965); Prosser and Keeton, *Prosser and Keeton on Torts* § 11 (5th ed. 1984). Although the plaintiff is not required to incur the risk of personal violence by resisting until force is actually used, it is essential that the restraint be against the plaintiff's will. 1 Harper, James and Gray, *The Law of Torts* § 3.8 (2nd ed. 1986). Submission to the mere verbal direction of another, unaccompanied by force or threats of any character, does not constitute false imprisonment. *Faniel v. Chesapeake & Potomac Telephone Co.*, 404 A.2d 147 (D.C. 1979). If one agrees of one's own free choice to surrender freedom of motion, as by accompanying another voluntarily to clear oneself of suspicion, rather than yielding to the constraint of a threat, then there is no imprisonment. . . .

[T]here is no evidence that Ms. Wilson-Robinson was threatened. She simply responded voluntarily to a request occasioned by the alarm. Nor is the testimony . . . that the employees believed Ms. Wilson-Robinson had shoplifted telling, so long as she was not forcibly detained.

Although the appellee contends there was an "implied threat of arrest," threats of future action, such as calling the police and having the person arrested, are not ordinarily sufficient in themselves to effect an unlawful imprisonment. *Morales v. Lee*, 668 S.W.2d 867 (Tex. App. 4 Dist.1984); Prosser and Keeton, supra. Even where the confinement is attributable to the threat of *physical* force, the submission must be responsive to a threat to apply "physical force to the other's person immediately upon the other's going or attempting to go beyond the area in which the actor intends to confine him." *Restatement (Second) of Torts* § 40. Submission to the threat to apply physical force at a time appreciably later than that at which the other attempts to go beyond the given area is not confinement. *Restatement (Second) of Torts* § 40, comment b. Consequently, even if the store employees had threatened to call the police in the instant case, there would not have been a confinement.

We find the appellee failed to establish the detention element of false imprisonment. Although it is generally a jury question as to what was reasonably to be understood and implied from the defendant's conduct, the appellee did not testify or allege that she had any fear of force. See Prosser and Keeton, supra. In fact, she testified repeatedly that she was "*asked*" if she would return to the store, responding, "Well, sure." When she returned to the store, she was not detained by any threat of force, she was "*asked*" if she had a calculator. There is no imprisonment when one agrees to surrender her freedom of motion. *Pounders v. Trinity Court Nursing Home*, 265 Ark. 1, 576 S.W.2d 934 (1979). In sum, there is insufficient evidence to establish a tort of false imprisonment. . . .

Reversed and dismissed.

a. The court said there was no confinement. Assume that the court reached the conclusion that there was a confinement because Perrylyn Wilson-Robinson did not voluntarily return to the store. Now would she have won the case?

b. Would this court reach the same result if three employees surrounded Perrylyn Wilson-Robinson and asked her to return to the store?

c. Would this court reach the same result if each of the employees wore coats with badges that said "Store Security"?

d. Is it relevant that Perrylyn Wilson-Robinson is black? Assume that the employees would not have stopped her if she was white. Would the court have found that there was false imprisonment?

e. The court said, "even if the store employees had threatened to call the police in the instant case, there would not have been a confinement." Do you know why this statement is dictum?

Intent

False imprisonment is an intentional tort. To establish **intent,** the defendant must desire to confine or know with substantial certainty that confinement will result from what he or she does. If the defendant is merely negligent or reckless in causing the confinement, the intentional tort of false imprisonment has not been committed. The tort of **negligence** might be possible. A negligence suit, however, requires proof of actual damages, whereas for false imprisonment, no more damages than the confinement itself need be shown. (See, however, an exception in the next section on causation covering cases in which the plaintiff was unaware of the confinement.)

> **EXAMPLE:** The defendant locks up an old building and carelessly or even recklessly fails to check whether anyone is still inside. This is not enough to establish intent to confine, because the defendant neither desired nor knew with substantial certainty that someone would be confined.

The doctrine of **transferred intent** applies. If the defendant intends to confine one person, but mistakenly confines a plaintiff whom the defendant never even knew existed, the requisite intent has been established. The defendant's intent to confine one person is transferred to another person who is in fact confined by the defendant's intentional conduct. (On transferred intent, see Figure 6–1 in Chapter 6.)

Causation

To establish the element of **causation,** the plaintiff must be able to show that either:

- but for the act of the defendant the plaintiff would not have been confined, or
- the defendant was a substantial factor in producing the plaintiff's confinement.

The defendant need not be the sole cause of the confinement.

> **EXAMPLE:** A citizen makes a complaint about a person to a police officer. The latter makes an arrest of the person—a false arrest, because the privilege to arrest, to be discussed later, does not apply.

The question arises whether the citizen who made the complaint to the police officer is liable for the false imprisonment that resulted from the false arrest. Was the citizen a substantial factor in the false arrest? The answer depends on whether the citizen instigated the arrest, as opposed to simply reporting the facts to the police officer who made up his or her own mind on whether to arrest. **Instigation** consists of insisting, directing, encouraging, or participating in the arrest. There must be persuasion or influencing of some kind in order for the citizen to have been a substantial factor in producing the arrest by the police officer. Without this instigation, the citizen has not caused the confinement.

Consciousness or Harm

The courts are split on whether the plaintiff must *know* that he or she is being confined. Some courts do not require consciousness of the confinement. The tort of false imprisonment can exist even if the plaintiff was ignorant of the confinement.

> **EXAMPLE:** Sam walks into a room to sleep. After he falls asleep, someone locks the door to the room for one hour. By the time Sam wakes up, however, the door has been unlocked.

Sam was unaware that he had been confined for one hour. In some states, this is not relevant. False imprisonment has still been committed. Other states require consciousness of confinement. These states, however, make an exception if the victim suffered actual harm (e.g., an illness) during the confinement. If such harm can be shown, recovery will be allowed even though the victim was unaware of the confinement. In general, actual harm is not an element of false imprisonment. The confinement itself is sufficient. In cases where the plaintiff was unaware of the confinement, however, some states require a showing of actual harm.

ASSIGNMENT

7.3

In each of the following four situations, determine whether false imprisonment has been committed. (See General Instructions for the Legal Analysis Assignment in Chapter 2.)

a. Luis is driving a car down the highway. His two-year-old son, Fred, is in the back seat playing. It is a three-lane highway going one way; Luis is in the middle lane. Dan's car is in the far right lane. Luis gives a right-turn signal. He wants to go to the far right lane in order to make a right turn. Dan is driving to the immediate right of Luis. Dan refuses to yield, forcing Luis to miss his turn. Luis loses fifteen minutes in taking an alternate route to where he was headed. Luis and Fred sue Dan for false imprisonment.

b. Mary calls John on the phone and threatens to kill him by 2 P.M. tomorrow unless John goes downtown to pay a debt that John owes Mary's company. John does so. He later sues Mary for false imprisonment.

c. Jane is one of the guests on the talk show called, "How Nasty Can You Get?" She says she was invited on the show to receive a surprise on the air. She thought the surprise might be that she was going to receive a free trip to Germany to visit her husband who was stationed at a military base there. Instead she was told by her sister, Ann, that Jane's husband was the father of Ann's recently born baby. Jane was stunned and disgusted. She immediately stood up and tried to take her microphone off so that she could leave. Because the wire was attached through Jane's clothes, she was unable to disconnect the wire. After about five minutes, a stagehand helped her remove the microphone so that she could leave. She now brings a false imprisonment suit against the TV station for inviting her on the program under false pretenses and for the five minutes of humiliation when she could not unhook the microphone.

d. Paul Richardson is a photographer for the SinSational Daily News. He is in the parking lot of the Fillmore Maternity Clinic waiting for Sally Starr to emerge with her first-born child. Sally is an international recording artist. Suddenly he spots her coming out through a side door. He sees Sally's husband help her into a car. Paul quickly gets into his own car and races toward the exit where Sally's car is headed. Paul blocks this exit, jumps out of his car, goes over to Sally's car, and takes her picture through the car window. He then gets back into his own car and drives it out of the way of the exit. Sally's husband drives through. Paul follows behind through city streets for over three hours. Sally's husband wants to stop and confront Paul. But Sally says, "No, don't stop. I'm too sick to stop. He's got us trapped on this road." Finally Paul gives up and returns without obtaining any more pictures. Sally and her husband now sue Paul for false imprisonment.

ASSIGNMENT

7.4

Pick any of the plaintiffs in Assignment 7.3. Draft a false imprisonment complaint for this plaintiff. (See General Instructions for the Complaint-Drafting Assignment in Chapter 3.)

CASE

Andrews v. Piedmont Air Lines
297 S.C. 367, 377 S.E.2d 127 (1989)
Court of Appeals of South Carolina

Background: *Clarence Andrews was not allowed to board an airplane due to the restrictions the airline imposed on customers in wheelchairs. He sued for false imprisonment. The lower court granted summary judgment for the airlines. The case is now before the Court of Appeals of South Carolina.*

Decision on Appeal: *Judgment for the airlines. There was no false imprisonment.*

OPINION OF COURT

PER CURIAM.

. . . Clarence Andrews sued Piedmont Air Lines for an incident which occurred after Piedmont denied him boarding on a flight due to his physical incapacity to travel unaccompanied. . . . In 1984, Andrews, a diabetic who had previously suffered a stroke, was admitted to Greenville Memorial Hospital for circulatory problems in his right leg. As a result of the stroke, his speech was slurred, he drooled, and his left side was paralyzed. Unfortunately, the treatment for his leg was unsuccessful and it had to be amputated above the knee. During the recovery period, the hospital contacted Andrews' daughter in Florida and asked if her father could live with her. She agreed and the hospital arranged the trip.

A hospital social worker, Andrew Irwin, telephoned Piedmont and reserved a seat for Andrews. Piedmont informed Irwin that the airline had guidelines governing travel by unaccompanied physically handicapped passengers. Under the guidelines, Piedmont would accept the passenger if he (1) could use the lavatory without assistance, (2) was able

to sit in a normal sitting position with the seatbelt properly fastened, and (3) required no assistance eating.

In December 1984, the hospital discharged Andrews and took him by ambulance to the Greenville/Spartanburg Airport. He was placed in an airport wheelchair and taken to the Piedmont ticket counter. He purchased a ticket and was wheeled to the gate area to wait for his flight. While waiting to embark, Andrews asked other passengers for cigarettes and asked a passenger to tie his leg to the wheelchair. The supervisor of airport security notified Milton Ward, the Piedmont station manager, of a potential problem at the departure gate.

When Ward arrived at the gate, he found Andrews slumped over in the wheelchair with saliva drooling out of the side of his mouth. Ward questioned Andrews about his ability to go to the bathroom by himself. He received a negative answer. Since Andrews did not meet Piedmont's guidelines, Ward kept him off the flight. Andrews was removed from the passenger waiting area to an area adjacent to the Piedmont office and ticket counter. Piedmont telephoned the hospital to come get Andrews.

Upon receipt of Piedmont's call, Irwin went to the airport and found Andrews in a wheelchair. He called the hospital requesting an ambulance and remained with Andrews, one and a half to two hours, until it arrived. Andrews returned to the hospital and alternate travel plans were arranged. . . .

False imprisonment is depriving the plaintiff of his liberty without lawful justification. In order to establish a cause of action, the evidence must prove: (1) that the defendant restrained the plaintiff; (2) that the restraint was intentional; and (3) that the restraint was unlawful.

The facts of the case do not support a cause of action for false imprisonment. Assuming Piedmont restrained Andrews, there is no evidence that the restraint was unlawful. Common carriers have a higher duty of care towards noticeably handicapped passengers. See *Singletary v. Atlantic Coast Line Railroad Co.,* 217 S.C. 212, 60 S.E.2d 305 (1950). Due to his physical condition, Andrews was not ambulatory. Piedmont placed Andrews in the area adjacent to the ticket counter so they could periodically check on him and find him when the ambulance arrived. There is no evidence that he protested waiting there or that he asked to be moved to another location. Further, after Irwin arrived, Andrews did not leave in Irwin's personal car, but chose to wait for the ambulance in this same area. In light of Andrews' condition, the alleged restraint was reasonable and it might well have been a breach of Piedmont's duty if they had not detained him until Irwin arrived. The trial court correctly granted the motion for summary judgment on the cause of action for false imprisonment.

ASSIGNMENT

7.5

a. Was Andrews restrained by the airline? Was he confined by Greenville Memorial Hospital?
b. Assume Andrews met all the requirements for boarding the airplane. Would it have been false imprisonment for the airline to refuse to allow him to board?

FALSE ARREST

One way to commit false imprisonment is to make a **false arrest.** An arrest is false when it is not privileged. Private citizens as well as peace officers have a privilege to arrest. A summary of the privilege each enjoys is presented in Figure 7–1.

Throughout this discussion, our concern is the **personal liability** of the individual making the arrest. When someone is personally liable for a wrong, the consequence is that an adverse judgment is paid out of the pocket of the wrongdoer. When the defendant is a peace officer, a separate question arises as to whether the government that employs the officer is *also* liable for the tort on a theory of **respondeat superior.** The answer depends upon whether the government has waived its sovereign immunity for this kind of claim. Sovereign immunity is considered in Chapter 27.

Peace Officer's Privilege to Arrest

When a **peace officer** has a **warrant** to arrest someone, the arrest is privileged as long as the warrant is **fair on its face.** Courts differ on the meaning of this phrase. Most courts will give it a broad interpretation in order to protect the peace officer. A warrant is not fair on its face if it is obviously defective, e.g., the warrant does not name the party to be arrested or does not state the crime charged. An officer is not required to be an attorney who knows how to analyze the warrant in all its technicalities. The officer is required, however, to be able to recognize blatant irregularities such as these.

If the officer arrests the wrong person under the warrant, the privilege is lost in most states. In some states, however, the privilege is not lost if the officer's mistake was reasonable under the circumstances.

An officer may also make an arrest without a warrant. As Figure 7–1 shows, the principles of the privilege to arrest without a warrant differ depending on why the arrest is being made:

- criminal arrest for a felony
- criminal arrest for a misdemeanor
- civil arrest for treatment or protection rather than for the commission of an alleged crime

FIGURE 7–1   Comparison of Peace Officer's and Private Citizen's Privilege to Arrest without a Warrant.

Elements of Privilege

Peace Officer's Privilege	Private Citizen's Privilege
1. Criminal Arrest: Felony a. The peace officer has reasonable grounds to believe a felony has been committed. b. The peace officer has reasonable grounds to suspect that the person arrested by the peace officer probably committed the felony. c. The peace officer uses reasonable force in making the arrest or in preventing the person from fleeing. Notes: • States differ on whether deadly force can be used to make the arrest or to prevent fleeing. • Deadly force can be used if the peace officer's life becomes endangered while making the arrest or preventing fleeing (self-defense). • A reasonable mistake on any of the three elements will still protect the officer. **2. Criminal Arrest: Misdemeanor** a. The misdemeanor must be a breach of the peace. b. The misdemeanor must be committed in the presence of the officer. c. The arrest must be made immediately or in fresh pursuit. d. Reasonable force is used to make the arrest or to prevent fleeing. Notes: • The peace officer's privilege to arrest for a misdemeanor is the same as that of a private citizen. • In most states, a mistake on the first three elements will not protect the peace officer, even if the mistake is reasonable. • The officer can use deadly force only if the officer's life is in danger in making the arrest or in preventing fleeing (self-defense). • Statutes may exist in a state to extend the privilege to arrest for misdemeanors not committed in the officer's presence and for misdemeanors that are not breaches of the peace. **3. Civil Arrest** a. The officer must reasonably believe that an insane or mentally ill person poses a serious threat of danger to him- or herself or to others. b. Reasonable force is used to bring the person to the authorities for medical attention.	**1. Criminal Arrest: Felony** a. A felony has in fact been committed. b. The felony committed is the one for which the citizen has made the arrest. c. The citizen has reasonable grounds to suspect that the person arrested by the citizen probably committed the felony. d. The citizen uses reasonable force in making the arrest or in preventing the person from fleeing. Notes: • States differ on whether deadly force can be used to make the arrest or to prevent fleeing. • Deadly force can be used if the citizen's life becomes endangered while making the arrest or preventing fleeing (self-defense). • A reasonable mistake on any of the four elements will not protect the citizen. Some states, however, have passed statutes that say the privilege is not lost if the citizen has reasonable grounds to believe that a felony has been committed by the person arrested—a reasonable mistake will protect the citizen in these states. **2. Criminal Arrest: Misdemeanor** a. The misdemeanor must be a breach of the peace. b. The misdemeanor must be committed in the presence of the citizen. c. The arrest must be made immediately or in fresh pursuit. d. Reasonable force is used to make the arrest or to prevent fleeing. Notes: • The citizen's privilege to arrest for a misdemeanor is the same as that of a peace officer. • In most states, a mistake on the first three elements will not protect the citizen, even if the mistake was reasonable. • The citizen can use deadly force only if the citizen's own life was in danger in making the arrest or in preventing fleeing (self-defense). • Statutes may exist in a state to extend the privilege to arrest for misdemeanors not committed in the citizen's presence and for misdemeanors that are not breaches of the peace. **3. Civil Arrest** a. The citizen must reasonably believe that an insane or mentally ill person poses a serious threat of danger to him- or herself or to others. b. Reasonable force is used to bring the person to the authorities for medical attention.

Major Definitions
- **Warrant:** a written order issued by an authorized government body directing the arrest of a person.
- **Peace Officer:** a person appointed by the government to keep the peace.
- **Arrest:** taking another into custody to bring before the proper authorities.
- **Felony:** a serious crime that is defined as a felony by the government. The common definition is a crime punishable by incarceration for a term exceeding a year.
- **Misdemeanor:** a less serious crime that is defined as a misdemeanor by the government. The common definition is a crime punishable by incarceration of a year or less, or a crime that is less serious than a felony.

FIGURE 7–1   Continued

- **Breach of the Peace:** an offense committed by violence or by acts likely to cause immediate disturbance of the public order.
- **Fresh pursuit:** promptly, without undue delay.
- **Civil Arrest:** arrest for the purpose of treatment or protection, and not because of the alleged commission of a crime.

Paralegal Investigation Tasks
Relevant to the Privilege to Arrest

- What crime was reported? To whom?
- What evidence existed that a crime had been committed? Who was aware of this evidence?
- What evidence led X (the person who arrested Y) to conclude that Y committed this crime? Did anyone else reach this conclusion? If so, on what basis?
- Were there any other suspects?
- What did other people say to X about Y?
- Was X present when Y committed the crime? Did X see Y commit the crime? Did anyone witness the crime?
- Did X know Y before the incident leading to the arrest? If so, how?
- Did Y have a reputation for criminal behavior in the area?
- What did Y say to X before and during the arrest? What did X say to Y? Did Y admit to X that Y committed a crime?
- How soon after X concluded that Y committed a crime did X arrest Y?
- What caused the delay, if any?
- Did Y resist the arrest? If so, how? What force, if any, did X use to make the arrest? Why did X think this force was needed? Was less force possible? Why or why not?
- What are the physical differences between X and Y, e.g., age, weight, bodily strength?
- Where did X take Y after the arrest and how long did it take to get there?
- If X made a civil arrest, what indications were there that Y's mental condition was a threat to the safety of Y or to anyone else?

ASSIGNMENT
7.6

At a rock concert, a police officer smells marijuana coming from a section where Mary and her seven friends are sitting. The officer arrests all of them. The officer thinks that one or two are doing the smoking, but he wants to take them all in for questioning so that he can find out which ones are guilty. Mary tries to run away. The officer shoots her. An investigation reveals that none of the arrested individuals possessed or used any drugs. The police officer is sued for false arrest, false imprisonment, and battery. What result based on the principles in Figure 7–1? (See General Instructions for the Legal Analysis Assignment in Chapter 2.)

Private Citizen's Privilege to Arrest

The privilege of a **private citizen** to make an arrest without a warrant must be considered under the same three categories covered in Figure 7–1 for peace officers:

- criminal arrest for a felony
- criminal arrest for a misdemeanor
- criminal arrest for treatment or protection rather than for the commission of an alleged crime

---

ASSIGNMENT
7.7

For this assignment, the facts are the same as in Assignment 7.6, except that the person who made the arrests, did the shooting, and is sued is a private citizen, rather than a peace officer. What result based on the principles in Figure 7–1? (See General Instructions for the Legal Analysis Assignment in Chapter 2.)

ASSIGNMENT

7.8

Sam is a private citizen. Someone has just stolen his $200 watch, but he is not sure who did it. Len, a stranger, comes up to Sam and tells him that he just saw a woman named Cindy steal the watch. Len points Cindy out to Sam as she is about to board a train. Sam follows the train in his car until Cindy gets off. He arrests her immediately. When she resists, he pushes her into his car. At the trial, Cindy is found innocent of the crime. Cindy now sues Sam for false arrest, false imprisonment, and battery. Does Sam have any defense? Prepare an investigation strategy. (See General Instructions for the Investigation Strategy Assignment in Chapter 3.)

SUMMARY

False imprisonment is an intentional confinement within fixed boundaries set by the defendant. The confinement can be by physical barriers; by physical force or threat of physical force against the plaintiff, against his or her immediate family, or against his or her property; by asserted legal authority; or by a refusal to release someone who was initially confined properly. The confinement must be complete or total. Shopkeepers have a limited privilege to detain someone temporarily to investigate whether merchandise has been stolen.

The defendant must desire to confine the plaintiff or know with substantial certainty that the confinement will result from what the defendant does. The plaintiff must either be aware of the confinement or suffer physical harm as a result of it.

An arrest is false when it is unprivileged. A peace officer has a privilege to arrest someone if the officer is acting on a warrant that is fair on its face. If no warrant exists, the peace officer has a privilege to make a felony arrest if there are reasonable grounds to believe the plaintiff committed the felony and if the officer uses reasonable force; to make a misdemeanor arrest if the misdemeanor is a breach of the peace, if it is committed in the officer's presence, if the arrest is made immediately or in fresh pursuit, and if the officer uses reasonable force; or to make a civil arrest if the officer reasonably believes the insane or mentally ill plaintiff poses a serious danger to him- or herself or to others, and if the officer uses reasonable force.

A private citizen has a privilege to make a felony arrest if a felony has in fact been committed, if it is the felony the citizen arrested the plaintiff for, if the citizen has reasonable grounds to believe the plaintiff committed the felony, and if the citizen uses reasonable force; to make a misdemeanor arrest if the misdemeanor is a breach of the peace, if it is committed in the citizen's presence, if the arrest is made immediately or in fresh pursuit, and if the citizen uses reasonable force; or to make a civil arrest if the citizen reasonably believes the insane or mentally ill plaintiff poses a serious danger to him- or herself or to others, and if the citizen uses reasonable force.

KEY TERMS

false imprisonment 132	transferred intent 140	fair on its face 143
confinement 136	causation 140	arrest 144
privilege to recapture 136	instigation 140	felony 144
duress 136	false arrest 143	misdemeanor 144
shopkeeper's privilege 137	personal liability 143	breach of the peace 145
common law 137	respondeat superior 143	fresh pursuit 145
intent 140	peace officer 143	civil arrest 145
negligence 140	warrant 143	private citizen 145

Misuse of Legal Proceedings

CHAPTER OUTLINE

- Introduction
- Malicious Prosecution
- Wrongful or Unjustified Civil Proceedings
- Abuse of Process

INTRODUCTION

Think of the devastating feeling you would have if:

- a police officer comes to your home or your place of employment to tell you that you are under arrest for a crime (e.g., passing a forged check) that you know you did not commit; or
- a process server comes to your home or place of employment to hand you a summons and complaint notifying you that you are the defendant in a civil action (e.g., negligence) that you know is frivolous.

You would not be able to close the door and refuse to cooperate with the police or refuse to accept the summons and complaint. Once the system is set in motion, the process must go forward to the next step. The costs to you can be substantial: damage to reputation, disruption in schedule, expense of defending yourself, emotional stress, etc. Surprisingly, it is relatively easy for a criminal or civil proceeding to be launched. Essentially, all that is needed is an allegation by someone against you.

Since you cannot walk away from legal proceedings that have been commenced, what remedy do you have once you are able to convince the system that the criminal or civil case against you was groundless? You can bring a tort action. Three torts are possible: **malicious prosecution, wrongful civil proceedings,** and **abuse of process.** These torts are our concern in this chapter.

We begin with malicious prosecution. It primarily covers wrongful *criminal* proceedings launched against you. Wrongful *civil* proceedings may also be covered under the tort of malicious prosecution or a state may have a separate tort called "malicious civil prosecution" or "wrongful civil proceedings" to cover civil matters. At the end of the chapter, we will examine abuse of process, a distinct tort that covers legal proceedings that are properly initiated, but for an improper purpose.

This is a delicate area of the law. We want to provide some protection against defendants who have been subjected to wrongful legal proceedings. At the same time, we do not want to discourage the public at large from filing grievances. Arguably, people will be less inclined to complain to the police or to the courts if they know that they might end up being sued themselves for the torts of malicious prosecution, wrongful civil proceedings, or abuse of process if they turn out to be wrong. One way in which the system tries to balance these concerns is to make these torts available, but relatively difficult to win.

MALICIOUS PROSECUTION

 Malicious Prosecution Checklist

Definitions, Relationships, Paralegal Roles, and Research References

Category
Malicious prosecution is an intentional tort.

Interest Prosecuted by This Tort
The right to be free from unreasonable or unjustifiable criminal litigation brought against you. Secondarily, the tort protects your interest in not having your reputation harmed by such litigation. (The tort may also cover unjustified civil proceedings, although many states have a separate tort to cover the latter.)

Elements of This Tort
    i. Initiation or procurement of the initiation of criminal proceedings
    ii. Without probable cause

Malicious Prosecution Checklist Continued

   iii. With malice
   iv. The criminal proceedings terminate in favor of the accused

Definitions of Major Words/Phrases in These Elements

Initiation: Instigation, urging, inciting, exertion of pressure to begin something.
Criminal Proceedings: Formal action commenced by criminal justice officials.
Probable Cause: A suspicion based on the appearance of circumstances that are strong enough to allow a reasonable person to believe that a criminal charge against an individual is true.
Malice: An improper motive. If the primary motive for initiating criminal proceedings is not the desire to bring the accused to justice, then the motive is improper.
Terminate in Favor of the Accused: The ending of the criminal proceedings expressly or by fair implication shows that the accused is innocent of the charge.

Major Defense and Counterargument Possibilities That Need to Be Explored

1. Criminal proceedings never actually began.
2. The accuser did not instigate the prosecution, but simply gave the facts to the authorities who decided to prosecute without urging from the accuser.
3. There was probable cause.
4. The primary purpose of the accuser was to bring the accused to justice (i.e., to use the court for its *proper* purpose).
5. The criminal proceedings have not yet terminated.
6. The criminal proceedings did not terminate in favor of the accused.
7. The plaintiff's suit against the government for malicious prosecution may be barred by sovereign immunity (on sovereign immunity, see Chapter 27).
8. The plaintiff's suit against the government employee for malicious prosecution may be barred by public official immunity, e.g., prosecutors have an absolute immunity (on official immunity, see Chapter 27).
9. The criminal case against the plaintiff began when the defendant arrested the plaintiff (on the privilege of arrest, see Chapter 7).
10. The plaintiff's suit against the charitable organization for malicious prosecution committed by someone working for the organization may be barred by charitable immunity (on charitable immunity, see Chapter 27).
11. The plaintiff's suit against a family member for malicious prosecution may be barred by intrafamily immunity (on intrafamily immunity, see Chapter 22).

Damages

Malicious prosecution (unlike negligence) does not require proof of actual damages. There can be recovery for the humiliation and mental suffering. Other compensatory damages include the costs of defending the underlying criminal case, medical bills, and loss of business or employment. Punitive damages are often possible when the defendant (the accuser in the criminal case) acted out of hatred for the accused. (On the categories of damages, see Chapter 16.)

Relationship to Criminal Law

One of the main purposes of the malicious prosecution tort is to provide a remedy against a person who has unjustifiably caused the criminal justice system "to go after you" because of an accusation that you have committed a crime.

Relationship to Other Torts

Abuse of Process: Abuse of process is the improper use of legal proceedings that may have been properly initiated. If proceedings have been properly initiated, there is no malicious prosecution, but there may be abuse of process if the proceedings are used for an improper goal, e.g., to coerce the accused to pay a debt.
Battery: If the accused was touched, e.g., as part of an arrest, as criminal proceedings were initiated, the tort of battery as well as malicious prosecution may have been committed.
Defamation: Defamation (libel or slander) as well as malicious prosecution may be committed when the accuser initiates criminal proceedings against the accused. Things are probably said or written that are derogatory of the accused's character.
Disparagement: In the process of initiating criminal proceedings against the accused, the accuser may utter false statements injurious to the accused's business or property. The tort of disparagement as well as malicious prosecution may have been committed.

Malicious Prosecution Checklist Continued

False Imprisonment: The accused may have been improperly restrained in his or her liberty while being maliciously prosecuted.

Intentional Infliction of Emotional Distress: It may be that the objective of the accuser was to subject the accused to severe emotional trauma by initiating criminal proceedings against the accused. A court might consider such conduct sufficiently outrageous so that the tort of intentional infliction of emotional distress is committed along with malicious prosecution.

Wrongful Civil Proceedings: Malicious prosecution covers wrongful criminal proceedings. It may also cover wrongful civil proceedings. In some states, however, wrongful civil proceedings is covered by a separate tort, sometimes called wrongful civil proceedings.

Federal Law

a. Under the Federal Tort Claims Act, the United States Government will *not* be liable for malicious prosecution committed by one of its federal employees within the scope of employment (respondeat superior) *unless* the federal employee is an investigative or law enforcement officer. (See Figure 27–7 in Chapter 27.)

b. There may be liability under the Civil Rights Act if the malicious prosecution was committed while the defendant was depriving the plaintiff of federal rights under color of law. (See Figure 27–9 in Chapter 27.)

Employer-Employee (Agency) Law

An employee who commits malicious prosecution is personally liable for this tort. His or her employer will *also* be liable for malicious prosecution if the conduct of the employee was within the scope of employment (respondeat superior). The employee must be furthering a business objective of the employer at the time. Intentional torts such as malicious prosecution, however, are often outside the scope of employment. If so, only the employee is liable for the malicious prosecution. (On the factors that determine scope of employment, see Figure 14–10 in Chapter 14.)

Paralegal Roles in Malicious Prosecution Litigation

(See also Figures 3–1, 3–14, and 29–1 in Chapters 3 and 29.)

Fact finding (help the office collect facts relevant to prove the elements of malicious prosecution, the elements of available defenses, and extent of injuries or other damages):
- client interviewing
- field investigation
- online research (e.g., court records)

File management (help the office control the volume of paperwork in a malicious prosecution litigation):
- open client file
- enter case data in computer database
- maintain file documents

Litigation assistance (help the trial attorney prepare for a malicious prosecution trial and appeal, if needed):
- draft discovery requests
- draft answers to discovery requests
- draft pleadings
- digest and index discovery documents
- help prepare, order, and manage trial exhibits (visuals or demonstratives)
- prepare trial notebook
- draft notice of appeal
- order trial transcript
- cite check briefs
- perform legal research

Collection/enforcement (help the trial attorney for the judgment creditor to collect the damages award or to enforce other court orders at the conclusion of the malicious prosecution case):
- draft postjudgment discovery requests
- field investigation to monitor compliance with judgment
- online research (e.g., location of defendant's business assets)

Malicious Prosecution Checklist Continued

Research References for Malicious Prosecution

Digests of West such as the American Digest System
In these digests, check key topics such as:

Malicious Prosecution	Arrest (especially key number 63.4 on
False Imprisonment	probable cause)
Torts	Damages
Extortion	Compromise and Settlement
Indictment and Information	Attorney and Client (especially key
	number 159)

Corpus Juris Secundum
In this legal encyclopedia, see the discussions under topic headings such as:

Malicious Prosecution	Indictment and Information
Malice	Arrest
False Imprisonment	Damages
Agency	Accord and Satisfaction
Torts	Compromise and Settlement
Extortion	

American Jurisprudence 2d
In this legal encyclopedia, see the discussions under topic headings such as:

Malicious Prosecution	Master and Servant
Abuse of Process	Damages
Attachment and Garnishment	Arrest
(see sections 596ff)	Criminal Law
Executions (sections 750ff)	Extortion, Blackmail and Threats
Malice	Indictment and Information
False Imprisonment	Compromise and Settlement
Torts	Prosecuting Attorneys

Legal Periodical Literature
There are two index systems to use to locate articles on this tort:

INDEX TO LEGAL PERIODICALS AND BOOKS (ILP)	CURRENT LAW INDEX (CLI)
See literature in *ILP* under subject headings such as:	See literature in *CLI* under subject headings such as:
Malicious Prosecution	Malicious Prosecution
Damages	False Imprisonment
False Imprisonment	Torts
Master and Servant	Damages
Personal Injuries	Personal Injuries
Settlements	Employers' Liability
Torts	

Example of a legal periodical article on malicious prosecution you can locate by using these index systems:

Damages for Injury to Feelings in Malicious Prosecution and Abuse of Process by A.M. Witte, 15 Cleveland Marshall Law Review 15 (1969).

A.L.R., A.L.R.2d, A.L.R.3d, A.L.R.4th, A.L.R.5th, A.L.R. Fed.
Use the *ALR Index* to find annotations relevant to malicious prosecution. In this index, check headings such as:

Malicious Prosecution	Libel and Slander
Malice	Master and Servant
Malicious Use of Process	Federal Tort Claims Act
Torts	Criminal Law
Damages	

Malicious Prosecution Checklist Continued

Example of an annotation on malicious prosecution you can locate by using this index:

Malicious Prosecution: Effect of Grand Jury Indictment on Issue of Probable Cause by J.D. Perovich, 28 A.L.R.3d 748 (1969).

Words and Phrases
In this multivolume legal dictionary, look up *malicious prosecution, probable cause, malice, nolle prosequi, abuse of process,* and every other word or phrase discussed in this chapter. The dictionary will give you definitions of these words or phrases from court opinions.

CALR: Computer-Assisted Legal Research

Example of a query you could ask on WESTLAW to try to find cases, statutes, or other legal materials on malicious prosecution: **"malicious prosecution"/p damages**

Example of search terms you could use on an Internet legal search engine such as LawCrawler (http://lawcrawler.findlaw.com) to find cases, statutes, or other legal materials on malicious prosecution: **"malicious prosecution"**

Example of search terms you could use on an Internet general search engine such as Alta Vista (http://www.altavista.com) to find cases, statutes, or other legal materials on malicious prosecution: **+"malicious prosecution" +tort -crime**

More Internet sites to check for materials on malicious prosecution and other torts:
Jurist: (http://jurist.law.pitt.edu/sg_torts.htm)
LawGuru: (http://www.lawguru.com/search/lawsearch.html)
See also Tort Law Online at the end of Chapter 1.

Initiation or Procurement of the Initiation of Criminal Proceedings

The first element of malicious prosecution is that the wrongdoer initiates or procures the initiation of criminal proceedings.

> **EXAMPLE:** Dan calls the police to complain that Linda stole his car. The police then arrest Linda. After an investigation, she is indicted for grand larceny.

In many states, Dan would be called the complaining witness. By his specific accusation, he has set official action in motion against Linda who will become the defendant in a criminal case. To **initiate** means to instigate, urge on, or incite. The instigator in the criminal case later becomes the defendant in the civil case of malicious prosecution brought by whoever was accused in the criminal case. The two separate proceedings are as follows:

State v. Linda (criminal case of grand larceny)

Linda v. Dan (civil case of malicious prosecution)

Without Probable Cause

The legal proceedings must be initiated without **probable cause.** Probable cause is a suspicion based on the appearance of circumstances that are strong enough to allow a reasonable person to believe that a criminal charge against a person is true. If there *is* probable cause, then the tort of malicious prosecution cannot succeed no matter how much ill will or malice the initiator may have against the accused.

Some of the factors that a court will use to determine whether probable cause exists are outlined in Figure 8–1.

With Malice

Malice, for purposes of this tort, means doing something for an improper motive. It does not necessarily require a showing of hatred or ill will. The proper motive for ini-

> **Factors Considered by the Court in Determining Whether the Accuser Had Probable Cause to Initiate the Criminal Process against the Accused.**
>
> 1. Did the accuser honestly believe that the accused committed the crime charged?
> 2. Did the accuser have first-hand knowledge/observation of what the accused allegedly did?
> 3. If the accuser used second-hand knowledge/observation, how reliable was the source used? If, for example, an informer gave information to the accuser (which the latter used in initiating the criminal case against the accused), what was the informer's reputation for reliability? Did the accuser check into this before initiating the criminal case?
> 4. What was the accused's reputation in the community? Notorious? The type of person who would commit this kind of crime? Or an honest, upright citizen?
> 5. Did the accuser know of the accused's reputation? If not, was there time to find out?
> 6. Did the accuser first confront the accused before going to the authorities? If not, why not? Impractical? No time? Danger to the accuser? Fear the accused would flee?
> 7. Was there any time for the accuser to do any further informal or formal investigation before contacting the authorities? If there was time, was it practical to use it?
> 8. Did the accuser seek the advice of his or her own attorney on whether there was a basis for the accuser to initiate criminal proceedings against the accused? If so, and if the advice was that the accuser should go to the authorities, did the accuser give the attorney all the relevant facts known to the accuser so that the attorney could provide informed advice?
> 9. Was there any other information that was reasonably available to the accuser that should have been obtained by the accuser before he or she initiated the criminal case against the accused?

FIGURE 8–1 Probable cause in malicious prosecution suits.

tiating criminal proceedings is to bring an alleged criminal to justice. If this is not the initiator's primary purpose, then he or she is acting with malice. Examples of improper (and hence malicious) purposes are to exert pressure on the accused to pay a debt, to return property, or to vote a certain way in an election. Often the initiator has more than one motive. If the primary motive is proper, the contemporaneous presence of improper incidental motives will not lead to the conclusion that the proceeding was initiated with malice.

Criminal Proceedings Terminate in Favor of the Accused

The criminal proceedings must be over, and the accused must have won the case. Most states require the victory to be on the merits, rather than be a mere technical or procedural victory. If the accused did not win the case, the strong likelihood is that the initial prosecution against the accused was made with probable cause rather than with malice. Examples of criminal proceedings that terminate in favor of the accused would include a verdict of not guilty, a discharge of the case because the grand jury fails to indict, and a **nolle prosequi** (i.e., a statement by the district attorney that he or she is unwilling to prosecute).

The malicious prosecution case is not necessarily won, however, just because the criminal proceedings end in favor of the accused. As we have seen, the accused must also show that there was no probable cause. Winning the criminal case does not necessarily mean that there was no probable cause.

> **EXAMPLE:** While walking in the corridor, Mary overhears Fred say on a cell phone that he is going to "bomb a federal building." They were in a federal building at the time. He was carrying a suspicious suitcase and acting erratically when Mary heard him talking. In a panic, she immediately calls the police and demands that Fred be arrested. Fred is tried but found not guilty because he convinced the jury that the statement he actually made was that "anyone who would bomb a federal building should be executed." Mary had misunderstood what he was saying. Fred now sues Mary for malicious prosecution.

The criminal proceedings certainly terminated in favor of the accused—Fred was acquitted. In the malicious prosecution case, however, he must show that Mary had no probable cause to instigate his arrest and prosecution. But Mary did have probable cause based on what she thought she heard, the suspicious suitcase, and the erratic behavior. She simply made a reasonable mistake in failing to hear Fred correctly. Hence, Fred loses the malicious prosecution case for failure to establish that Mary acted without probable cause. This is a case in which there was probable cause to believe that an innocent person committed a crime.

ASSIGNMENT

8.1

Elaine arrives home one night to find that her home has been burglarized. She calls the police. When questioned by the police, she says she does not know who did it, but that her uncle Bob recently threatened to harm her. The police conduct an investigation of Bob. He is indicted for burglary. At his trial, Elaine testifies that he once threatened her. The jury is deadlocked, and a mistrial is declared. The District Attorney (D.A.) is unsure whether to reprosecute him. By this time, Elaine is convinced Bob is guilty of the burglary. She urges the D.A. to retry Bob for the burglary. She constantly calls the D.A. Once she carries a sign outside the D.A.'s office urging prosecution. The D.A.'s decision, however, is to drop the charges. After the case is dismissed, Bob sues Elaine for malicious prosecution. What result? (See General Instructions for the Legal Analysis Assignment in Chapter 2.)

WRONGFUL OR UNJUSTIFIED CIVIL PROCEEDINGS

The tort of malicious prosecution covers wrongful criminal litigation. Suppose that wrongful civil proceedings are initiated.

> **EXAMPLE:** Charles files a complaint against Ted for negligence. Ted is served with process, which orders Ted to file an answer within thirty days. After a trial, Ted is found not liable for negligence.

Charles has initiated civil proceedings that have terminated in favor of Ted. Many states will now allow Ted to assert a tort action against Charles for bringing wrongful civil proceedings. The action may still be called malicious prosecution, although this term is more appropriate when the underlying proceedings are criminal.

Generally, the same elements apply for the causes of action of wrongful civil proceedings and wrongful criminal proceedings. The defendant must maliciously initiate civil proceedings without probable cause, and the proceedings must terminate in favor of the person charged in the civil proceedings. (The latter was the defendant in the civil proceedings case and is now the plaintiff in the wrongful civil proceedings case.) Probable cause here means a reasonable belief that good grounds exist for initiating the civil proceeding. Some courts impose an additional requirement for parties bringing wrongful civil proceedings suits: they must show some special interference with person or property as a result of the wrongful civil proceedings. Evidence of such a special injury or grievance is not required of parties suing because of wrongful criminal proceedings.

CASE

Raine and Highfield v. Drasin and Fadel
621 S.W.2d 895 (1981)
Supreme Court of Kentucky

Background: *Robert Browning sued a hospital and Doctors Drasin and Fadel for medical malpractice. Browning was represented by two attorneys, Raine and Highfield. The doctors won the malpractice case by a voluntary dismissal (an "agreed order of dismissal") which meant that Browning agreed to terminate his suit. Since the dismissal was with prejudice, the same claims could not be brought again on the same facts. The doctors then sued Raine and Highfield for malicious prosecution. The trial court found that both attorneys committed malicious prosecution (wrongful civil proceedings). The Court of Appeals affirmed the judgment against Raine, but dismissed all claims against Highfield. The case is now before the Supreme Court of Kentucky on appeal.*

Decision on Appeal: *Judgment affirmed. Raine committed malicious prosecution; Highfield did not.*

OPINION OF COURT

Justice STEPHENS delivered the opinion of the court . . .

On July 19, 1975, Robert Browning . . . suffered a massive heart attack at his home. He was taken, unconscious, to Sts. Mary and Elizabeth Hospital. Following treatment in the emergency room, he was examined by Dr. James Fitzpatrick. During his initial examination of Browning, Dr. Fitzpatrick discovered an injury to Browning's shoulder. He ordered X-rays taken which revealed that the shoulder was fractured. Dr. Fitzpatrick then called in Dr. Fadel, an orthopedic surgeon, to treat the shoulder. Dr. Drasin, a radiologist, had read the X-ray but never saw or treated Browning.

Following his release from the hospital, Browning contacted attorney Raine regarding a possible suit for the fracture of his shoulder. On September 15, 1975, Raine visited the hospital and reviewed its records which clearly showed that the fracture of the shoulder occurred before Drs. Drasin and Fadel were involved.

On November 21, 1975, a complaint was filed in the Jefferson Circuit Court against the hospital for allegedly breaking Browning's shoulder. Raine prepared the complaint, but because he represented another hospital he did not wish to sign the complaint. At his request attorney James H. Highfield, a long-time associate of Raine's, with space in his office, signed it. He did so without reading it and without investigating any of the facts. In March of 1976, the attorneys served interrogatories on the hospital, the answers to which revealed that . . . both doctors were contacted after Browning's shoulder injury was discovered. On May 24, 1976, the deposition of Dr. Fitzpatrick was taken. It is clearly shown that the deponent told the attorneys that the injury occurred before he saw Browning in the emergency room and moreover that, after he discovered the injury, he then called in Drs. Fadel and Drasin. In spite of this clear and cumulative evidence, on July 15, 1976, Raine filed an amended complaint (signed by Highfield), in which the two doctors were joined as parties defendant, and were charged with malpractice in that they

negligently broke Browning's shoulder. Highfield did not read the amended complaint.

[Soon thereafter, however, an order for voluntary dismissal was entered. It was an "agreed order of dismissal" that dismissed the medical malpractice case against the doctors with prejudice, meaning that the case could not be brought against them again.]

Subsequent to the dismissal, the doctors filed this suit against both attorneys, alleging malicious prosecution. . . . At the trial, no evidence was introduced by the doctors concerning any out-of-pocket expenses. They did testify as to their embarrassment, humiliation, mortification and mental anguish at having been publicly accused of malpractice. Dr. Fadel testified that he suffered an acute anxiety reaction.

Both doctors stated that the malpractice accusation (even though specious), became a permanent part of their professional and insurance records. The attorneys testified that they had no evidence to implicate the doctors. Raine had access to and was aware of this fact even when he filed the malpractice action. . . . [The trial court found that attorneys Raine and Highfield had committed malicious prosecution. On appeal, the judgment against Raine was affirmed, but reversed as to Highfield.]

On this appeal Raine argues that the order of dismissal was not a favorable determination of the action, thus eliminating a key ingredient in a malicious prosecution action . . . [and] that the testimony of an expert concerning violations of an ethical code was improperly admitted in evidence. . . . [T]he doctors argue [on appeal] that the dismissal of the . . . claim against Highfield was improper. . . .

The doctrine of malicious prosecution is an old one in our Commonwealth. Historically, it has not been favored in the law. Public policy requires that all persons be able to freely resort to the courts for redress of a wrong, and the law should and does protect them when they commence a civil or criminal action in good faith and upon reasonable grounds. It is for this reason that one must strictly comply with the prerequisites of maintaining an action for malicious prosecution.

Generally speaking, there are six basic elements necessary to the maintenance of an action for malicious prosecution, in response to both criminal prosecutions and civil action. They are: (1) the institution or continuation of original judicial proceedings, either civil or criminal, or of administrative or disciplinary proceedings, (2) by, or at the instance, of the plaintiff, (3) the termination of such proceedings in defendant's favor, (4) malice in the institution of such proceeding, (5) want or lack of probable cause for the proceeding, and (6) the suffering of damage as a result of the proceeding. With these principles in mind, we will examine the arguments.

IS AN AGREED ORDER OF DISMISSAL A FAVORABLE TERMINATION OF THE MALPRACTICE ACTION?

Shortly after the malpractice action against the doctors was filed, the order of dismissal was filed. It was, by its terms, an "agreed order of dismissal." The order provided that the amended complaint against the doctors was dismissed, with prejudice. It was signed by the plaintiff, Browning, and by his counsel, Raine and Highfield, and by counsel for the doctors. The document did not entail any compromise or settlement; it simply and effectively terminated the lawsuit as far as the defendant doctors were concerned. The dismissal declared, in effect, that there was no malpractice on the part of the defendants.

The purpose of this prerequisite to a malicious prosecution suit is to show that the action against the defendant was unsuccessful. The basis for the requirement is that courts will not tolerate inconsistent judgments on the same action between the same parties. In Kentucky, no particular form of termination in civil actions has been required. Since the order of dismissal effectively terminates the litigation, with respect to the doctors, . . . the order constituted a favorable termination so as to support this action. . . .

WAS THE TESTIMONY OF AN EXPERT CONCERNING THE ATTORNEYS' POSSIBLE VIOLATION OF ETHICAL CODE PROPERLY ADMITTED?

The deposition of Professor David Leibson, a member of the Ethics Committee of the Louisville Bar Association, was apparently read to the jury. Professor Leibson stated that, in his opinion, the actions of both Raine and Highfield did not comply with the standard of care for ordinary and prudent lawyers. Raine complains that the admission was improper. We believe that such evidence was properly introduced to show one of the key ingredients of a malicious prosecution action; viz., lack of probable cause. . . .

[WAS THE REVERSAL AGAINST HIGHFIELD PROPER?]

Attorney Highfield, it will be remembered, signed the complaint and amended complaint without reading them. He literally knew nothing about the allegations therein, the parties therein, the factual background or the law. The evidence shows that he was a long-time friend, associate of attorney Raine and has space in Raine's office. Undoubtedly, he signed the documents as a convenience and as a favor to Raine. . . . [S]uch action does not constitute malice. At worst it was a breach of ethics, and at least, it was poor judgment on his part.

The only evidence, relative to probable cause and malice against Highfield, is his signing the amended complaint. He was given a plausible reason why Raine did not want to sign the complaint, and based on years of fellowship and association, he signed it. . . . [T]his is not sufficient evidence, as a matter of law, for a jury to find the necessary malice upon which to base a malicious prosecution action.

[The decision affirming the malicious prosecution claim against Raine but reversing it against Highfield is affirmed.]

ASSIGNMENT

8.2

a. The court does not like malicious prosecution cases. They have "not been favored in the law." Why?

b. Raine did not want to sign the complaint "because he represented another hospital." Why would this make any difference?

c. Do you agree with the dismissal of all claims against attorney Highfield? What message does this send out to attorneys? Suppose that an attorney brings a case solely to pressure the defendant to settle. The attorney refuses to do any research or investigation on the case. Does this refusal mean that the attorney, like Highfield, will win a malicious prosecution suit brought against him or her later by the defendant? What's the difference between this attorney and Highfield?

ABUSE OF PROCESS

The elements of the tort of abuse of process are:

    i. Use of civil or criminal proceedings, and
    ii. Improper or ulterior motive.

Some states also require a showing of injury to person or property beyond mere injury to name or reputation.

Unlike malicious prosecution, abuse of process involves a civil or criminal case that was *properly* initiated. Probable cause may exist, and the proceeding does not have to terminate in favor of the person now bringing the abuse-of-process action. Yet, the civil or criminal proceeding was used for an improper or ulterior motive.

EXAMPLE: Bob and Mary are married, but have been separated for over five years. They have two children. Mary believes that she is the better parent and tells Bob that if he does not agree to give her full custody,

> she will tell the Internal Revenue Service that he has been cheating on his business taxes for years. Bob refuses. Mary tells the IRS, which begins a criminal fraud case against Bob. He is convicted. He then sues Mary for abuse of process.

Bob would win. Mary had an ulterior motive in initiating the criminal case against Bob. She was using the courts for a purpose for which they are not designed. She may have had probable cause to accuse Bob of tax fraud, but it is improper to initiate a criminal tax proceeding against someone in order to gain agreement on a child custody matter.

CASE

Routh Wrecker Service, Inc. v. Washington
335 Ark. 232, 980 S.W.2d 240 (1998)
Supreme Court of Arkansas

Background: *Codney Washington, an African-American, purchased a used car from Ronald Routh for $400. When Washington stopped payment on the check, Routh notified the police who arrested Washington. A probable cause hearing was held in municipal court at which time he was bound over to the circuit court. Eventually the criminal charge evaporated when the prosecuting attorney declined to file charges. Washington then sued Routh for abuse of process. Washington won a verdict and judgment of $76,000 ($1,000 in compensatory damages and $75,000 in punitive damages to punish the defendant). The case is now on appeal before the Supreme Court of Arkansas where Routh argues that there was no abuse of process and that the punitive damages were excessive.*

Decision on Appeal: *The judgment is affirmed. There was an abuse of process and the punitive damages were justified.*

OPINION OF COURT
Justice BROWN delivered the opinion of the court . . .:
The facts are these. On Saturday, June 11, 1994, Washington and a friend attended a car auction sponsored by Routh. At the auction, Washington purchased a 1988 Ford Escort for $400 and paid Routh by check. Because the car was blocked by other cars, Washington did not take the car with him that day. Routh representatives told him he could leave the car on the lot for five business days. When he returned for the car on the following Monday, the Escort's battery, spare tire, and some tools were missing. Washington left the car on the lot and stopped payment on the $400 check. He later testified that he expected Routh to contact him to resolve the matter because he still intended to purchase the car.

On June 29, 1994, Ronald Routh, general manager of Routh Wrecker, contacted the prosecuting attorney's office and swore out an affidavit for a warrant of arrest for Washington. He averred in the affidavit that Washington had stopped payment on the check but had not returned the Escort to the premises nor the documentation for sale. On July 11, 1994, Little Rock police officers arrested Washington at his place of employment, First Commercial Bank in Little Rock. They handcuffed him at the bank, led him to a police car, booked him at the police station, and put him in a holding cell. After the arrest, Frank Washington, Washington's father, called Routh. Routh told him that all he wanted was his money and that he would drop the charges if he was paid.

Washington advised his father not to pay the $400. Immediately after the arrest, Washington's attorney contacted Routh and told him that the car was still on the lot, which Routh verified. Routh explained to the attorney that storage charges on the vehicle had accrued and should be paid.

Routh did not drop the charges. On September 19, 1994, at the probable cause hearing in municipal court, the municipal judge found probable cause for a theft arrest based on Routh's testimony that Washington was given the car keys and legal documents and then stopped payment on the check. The case was certified to circuit court, where charges were not filed by the prosecuting attorney.

[Washington then filed a civil complaint against Routh for abuse of process. After a jury verdict in Washington's favor for $1,000 in compensatory damages and $75,000 in punitive damages, the trial court entered judgment for Washington. Routh has now appealed.]

This court has stated that the test of abuse of process is whether a judicial process is used to extort or coerce. See *Cordes v. Outdoor Living Ctr., Inc.*, 301 Ark. 26, 781 S.W.2d 31 (1989). The elements of the tort are: (1) a legal procedure set in motion in proper form, even with probable cause and ultimate success; (2) the procedure is perverted to accomplish an ulterior purpose for which it was not designed; and (3) a willful act is perpetrated in the use of process which is not proper in the regular conduct of the proceeding. See *Wynn v. Remet*, 321 Ark. 227, 902 S.W.2d 213 (1995); *Harmon v. Carco Carriage Corp.*, 320 Ark. 322, 895 S.W.2d 938 (1995). In short, the key to the tort is the improper use of process after its issuance in order to accomplish a purpose for which the process was not designed. See *Union Nat'l Bank v. Kutait*, 312 Ark. 14, 846 S.W.2d 652 (1993). Thus, it is the purpose for which the process is used, once issued, that is important in reaching a conclusion. . . . [T]he use of criminal prosecution to extort payment of money or recovery of property is a classic example of the tort of abuse of process. . . .

Routh initiated a proceeding against Washington that caused his arrest. Washington's father testified that he spoke to Ron Routh after the arrest and Routh's response was that all he wanted was his money and he would drop the charges. Routh admitted that although he knew the car was on the lot, he did not ask to drop the charges. Instead, he allowed the case to proceed to a probable-cause hearing in municipal court, after which it was bound over to circuit court. Routh knew that Washington did not have the odometer statement which is necessary to obtain the actual certificate of title to the car. He further knew that Washington did not have the car itself, and he later admitted that he did not know who had the keys to the car. However, at the probable-cause hearing, Routh testified that Washington had failed to return the keys and the legal paperwork. This inconsistency between Routh's knowledge and testimony in municipal court was emphasized by Washington at the civil trial.

We conclude that after the arrest warrant, Routh allowed the case to proceed to a hearing in municipal court for the coercive purpose of collecting the $400. [We affirm the trial court's judgment that there was an abuse of process and turn now to the separate question of the propriety of the award of punitive damages, which depends on whether the defendant acted with malice.]

The circumstances in this case are egregious and nightmarish. Washington, a young African-American male, was arrested at work at the bank in front of his peers and supervisor. The testimony was that he was humiliated, suffered emotional distress, and was frightened about what might happen to him. After the arrest, he suffered migraine headaches and could not sleep or eat. He lost 30 pounds.

Several witnesses testified to the dramatic and negative changes to him, including a loss of interest in social activities and depression. His psychologist, Dr. James Moneypenney, testified that because of Washington's status as a young African-American, the arrest struck at the core of his identity and that "something important has been taken from him and I think he is going to continue to suffer from that."

Even after he found the Escort on his lot, Routh did nothing to stop the proceedings against Washington. He did not inform the prosecuting attorney that the car was on his lot until the day of the probable-cause hearing. At the hearing, he testified that Washington had failed to return the paperwork or keys to him, implying that Washington had converted this property, if not the car itself. In point of fact, Washington never had the keys to the car in his possession, never took the car from the lot, and never had all the necessary paperwork to obtain title to the Escort. We conclude that malice can certainly be inferred from Routh's statement to Washington's father that if he got paid, he would drop the charges. We hold that the jury's punitive award was not excessive. . . .

We affirm. . . .

ASSIGNMENT

8.3

a. Would the court have reached the same conclusion on abuse of process if, instead of filing criminal charges, Routh simply sued Washington for breach of contract for failing to pay the $400?

b. Did Routh also commit malicious prosecution?

SUMMARY

Malicious prosecution requires initiating, or procuring the initiation of, criminal proceedings against an accused. There must be no probable cause to initiate the proceedings. This means that a reasonable person would not have suspected that the accused was guilty. Malice is also required, meaning that the primary purpose in initiating the proceedings was improper because the purpose was something other than to bring someone to justice. Finally, the legal proceedings must terminate in favor of the accused, usually on the merits.

Initiating wrongful civil proceedings is a tort in many states. The defendant must maliciously initiate civil proceedings without probable cause, and the proceedings must terminate in favor of the person charged in the civil proceedings. Some courts also require the defendant to show that he or she suffered a special injury or grievance as a result of the wrongdoing civil proceedings.

Abuse of process covers criminal or civil litigation that is properly initiated because probable cause exists, but it is used for an improper motive or purpose. The civil or criminal litigation does not have to terminate in favor of the defendant in the litigation.

KEY TERMS

malicious prosecution   148
wrongful civil proceedings   148
abuse of process   148

initiate   152
probable cause   152
malice   152

nolle prosequi   153

Infliction of Emotional Distress

CHAPTER OUTLINE

- Introduction
- Intentional Infliction of Emotional Distress
- Tort Law and the Impeachment of the President
- Media Defendants and the Constitution
- Negligent Infliction of Emotional Distress

INTRODUCTION

Emotional distress can be damaging to a person. Our concern in this chapter is whether the sufferer can bring a tort action against the person who caused this suffering. When someone commits a traditional tort such as battery, false imprisonment, or negligence, there is usually little difficulty recovering for the emotional distress (called **pain and suffering**) that results from this tort. In fact, damages for pain and suffering often constitute the largest portion of a successful plaintiff's judgment. Suppose, however, that the defendant causes mental distress without committing one of these traditional torts. For example, George is emotionally upset when Mary refuses to date him and tells him that she never wants to see him again as long as she lives. Although this statement could cause George enormous pain and suffering (in fact, an emotional breakdown), Mary has not committed a tort. The facts do not fit any of the traditional torts.

A floodgate of litigation would result if every victim of every emotional distress is allowed to sue. The filing of claims could turn into "unlimited liability for emotional distress," according to Judge Eagleson of the Supreme Court of California in the *Thing v. La Chusa* case that we will read later in the chapter. Courts are also concerned about the filing of fraudulent lawsuits because it is fairly easy to fabricate a claim of emotional distress.

One of the ways the law has dealt with these concerns is to create a new tort called **intentional infliction of emotional distress** (also called the tort of **outrage**). To prevent this tort from opening a floodgate of litigation, the tort is relatively difficult to win, as President Bill Clinton discovered to his relief in the famous case of *Jones v. Clinton* that we will study. After we examine the boundaries of this narrow intentional tort, we need to determine when *negligently* inflicted emotional distress can also be a basis of recovery.

For a sample complaint asserting a cause of action for intentional infliction of emotional distress, see Figure 3–11 in Chapter 3.

INTENTIONAL INFLICTION OF EMOTIONAL DISTRESS

 Intentional Infliction of Emotional Distress Checklist

Definitions, Relationships, Paralegal Roles, and Research References

Category
Intentional infliction of emotional distress is an intentional tort. Some courts have expanded it to include recovery for reckless infliction of emotional distress.

Interest Protected by This Tort
The right to be free from emotional distress that is intentionally (or recklessly) caused by someone else.

Elements of This Tort
   i. An act of extreme or outrageous conduct
   ii. Intent to cause severe emotional distress
   iii. Severe emotional distress is suffered
   iv. Defendant is the cause of this distress

Definitions of Major Words/Phrases in These Elements
   Act: Voluntary movement of the defendant's body.
   Extreme or outrageous conduct: Atrocious and totally intolerable behavior—shocking conduct.

Intentional Infliction of Emotional Distress Checklist Continued

Intent: The desire to inflict severe emotional distress on the plaintiff or the knowledge with substantial certainty that such distress will result from what the defendant does. (In some states, recklessness, or wanton and willful conduct, will be sufficient.)

Severe emotional distress: Substantial mental anguish.

Cause: "But for" what the defendant did, the plaintiff would not have suffered severe emotional distress, or the defendant was a substantial factor in producing such distress.

Major Defense and Counterargument Possibilities That Need to Be Explored

1. The defendant did not act voluntarily.
2. The defendant's conduct may have been unpleasant and wrongful, but it was not extreme or outrageous.
3. The defendant did not desire the plaintiff to suffer severe emotional distress nor know with substantial certainty that such distress would result from what the defendant did (no intent). In a state where recklessness can be a substitute for intent, the defendant did not recklessly cause such distress.
4. The plaintiff may have been embarrassed or upset, but did not suffer severe emotional distress.
5. The plaintiff may have suffered severe emotional distress, but a reasonable person would not have reacted in this way.
6. The plaintiff suffered severe emotional distress because he or she is unusually sensitive and the defendant had no reason to know of this sensitivity.
7. "But for" what the defendant did, the plaintiff would still have suffered severe emotional distress; the defendant was not a substantial factor in producing plaintiff's emotional distress (no causation).
8. The plaintiff consented to the defendant's conduct that led to the severe emotional distress (on the defense of consent, see Chapter 27).
9. The plaintiff's severe emotional distress resulted while the defendant was defending himself or herself from the plaintiff (on self-defense and other self-help privileges, see Chapter 27).
10. The plaintiff's severe emotional distress occurred while the defendant was defending someone else from the plaintiff (on the defense of others and other self-help privileges, see Chapter 27).
11. The plaintiff's severe emotional distress occurred while the defendant was defending property or recapturing chattels from the plaintiff (on necessity, defense of property, recapture of property, and other self-help privileges, see Chapter 27).
12. The plaintiff's severe emotional distress occurred while the defendant was disciplining the plaintiff (on discipline and other self-help privileges, see Chapter 27).
13. The plaintiff's severe emotional distress occurred while the defendant was arresting the plaintiff (on the privilege of arrest, see Chapter 7).
14. The plaintiff's suit against the government for intentional infliction of emotional distress committed by a government employee may be barred by sovereign immunity (on sovereign immunity, see Chapter 27).
15. The plaintiff's suit against the government employee for intentional infliction of emotional distress may be barred by public official immunity (on official immunity, see Chapter 27).
16. The plaintiff's suit against the charitable organization for intentional infliction of emotional distress committed by someone working for the organization may be barred by charitable immunity (on charitable immunity, see Chapter 27).
17. The plaintiff's suit against a family member for intentional infliction of emotional distress may be barred by intrafamily immunity (on intrafamily immunity, see Chapter 22).
18. The plaintiff failed to take reasonable steps to mitigate the harm caused when the defendant committed intentional infliction of emotional distress; therefore, damages should not cover the aggravation of the harm caused by the plaintiff (on the doctrine of avoidable consequences, see Chapter 16).

Damages

The plaintiff can recover compensatory damages for the mental distress suffered as well as for any physical harm or illness that may have resulted from the defendant's conduct. Punitive damages are also likely if the defendant acted out of hatred or malice. (On the categories of damages, see Chapter 16.)

Intentional Infliction of Emotional Distress Checklist Continued

Relationship to Criminal Law

The defendant's conduct may also constitute the crime of extortion, criminal assault, breach of the peace, criminal battery, etc.

Other Torts and Related Actions

Abuse of process: While using the criminal process for an improper purpose, the defendant may have intended to cause the plaintiff severe emotional distress.

Assault: While intending to cause severe emotional distress in the plaintiff, the defendant may have intentionally placed the plaintiff in apprehension of an imminent harmful or offensive contact.

Battery: While intending to cause severe emotional distress in the plaintiff, the defendant may have intentionally made harmful or offensive contact with the plaintiff.

Conversion: Defendant may have intended to have the plaintiff suffer severe emotional distress by destroying plaintiff's personal property.

Defamation: While intentionally causing the plaintiff to suffer severe emotional distress, the defendant may have published derogatory statements that injured the reputation of the plaintiff.

False imprisonment: By intentionally locking the plaintiff up or otherwise restricting his or her movement, the defendant may have had the intent to cause the plaintiff severe emotional distress.

False light (invasion of privacy): By giving unreasonable publicity to false private facts, the defendant may have had the intent to cause the plaintiff severe emotional distress.

Intrusion (invasion of privacy): By unreasonably intruding on the plaintiff's privacy, the defendant may have had the intent to cause the plaintiff severe emotional distress.

Malicious prosecution: The defendant may have initiated legal proceedings against the plaintiff with the intent to cause the plaintiff severe emotional distress.

Negligence: If the defendant negligently caused physical harm to the plaintiff, the latter can also recover for resulting emotional distress that was not intended. Some states also allow recovery for negligent infliction of emotional distress.

Trespass to land: While trespassing on the plaintiff's land, the defendant may have had the intent to subject the plaintiff to severe emotional distress.

Wrongful death: If the plaintiff died as a result of intentional infliction of emotional distress, designated survivors may be able to bring a wrongful death action.

Federal Law

a. Under the Federal Tort Claims Act, there is no explicit exclusion that says the United States Government will not be liable for intentional infliction of emotional distress committed by one of its federal employees within the scope of employment (respondeat superior). (See Figure 27–7 in Chapter 27.)

b. There may be liability under the Civil Rights Act if the intentional infliction of emotional distress was committed while the defendant was depriving the plaintiff of federal rights under color of law. (See Figure 27–9 in Chapter 27.)

Employer-Employee (Agency) Law

An employee who commits intentional infliction of emotional distress is personally liable for this tort. His or her employer will *also* be liable for the tort if the conduct of the employee was within the scope of employment (respondeat superior). The employee must be furthering a business objective of the employer at the time. Intentional torts such as intentional infliction of emotional distress, however, are often outside the scope of employment. If so, only the employee is liable for the tort. (On the factors that determine the scope of employment, see Figure 14–10 in Chapter 14.)

Paralegal Roles in Intentional Infliction of Emotional Distress Litigation

(See also Figures 3–1, 3–14, and 29–1 in Chapters 3 and 29.)

Fact finding (help the office collect facts relevant to prove the elements of intentional infliction of emotional distress, the elements of available defenses, and extent of injuries or other damages):
- client interviewing
- field investigation
- online research

Intentional Infliction of Emotional Distress Checklist Continued

File management (help the office control the volume of paperwork in an intentional infliction of emotional distress litigation):

- open client file
- enter case data in computer database
- maintain file documents

Litigation assistance (help the trial attorney prepare for an intentional infliction of emotional distress trial and appeal, if needed):
- draft discovery requests
- draft answers to discovery requests
- draft pleadings
- digest and index discovery documents
- help prepare, order, and manage trial exhibits (visuals or demonstratives)
- prepare trial notebook
- draft notice of appeal
- order trial transcript
- cite check briefs
- perform legal research

Collection/enforcement (help the trial attorney for the judgment creditor to collect the damages award or to enforce other court orders at the conclusion of the intentional infliction of emotional distress case):
- draft postjudgment discovery requests
- field investigation to monitor compliance with judgment
- online research (e.g., location of defendant's business assets)

Research References for Intentional Infliction of Emotional Distress

Digests

In the digests of West, look for case summaries on this tort under key topics such as:

Torts	Death
Threats	Damages

Corpus Juris Secundum

In this legal encyclopedia, look for discussions on this tort under topic headings such as:

Torts	Telegraph, telephone, radio
Threats and unlawful	and television
communications	Death
Damages	

American Jurisprudence 2d

In this legal encyclopedia, look for discussions on this tort under topic headings such as:

Torts	Damages
Fright, shock and	Death
mental disturbance	

Legal Periodical Literature

There are two index systems to use to try to locate articles on this tort:

INDEX TO LEGAL PERIODICALS AND BOOKS (ILP)	CURRENT LAW INDEX (CLI)
See literature in *ILP* under subject headings such as:	See literature in *CLI* under subject headings such as:
Torts	Privacy, Right of
Collection	Mental Distress
Agencies	Negligence
Damages	Damages
Negligence	Torts
Personal Injuries	Personal Injuries
Privacy	Death by
Wrongful Death	Wrongful Act
	Collection Agencies

Intentional Infliction of Emotional Distress Checklist Continued

Example of legal periodical literature you can locate through the *ILP* or *CLI* on this tort:

Intentional Infliction of Mental Distress—Seventeen Years Later by Arthur J. Sabin, 66 Illinois Bar Journal 248 (1978).

A.L.R., A.L.R.2d, A.L.R.3d, A.L.R.4th, A.L.R.5th, A.L.R. Fed.
Use the *ALR Index* to locate annotations on this tort. In this index, check subject headings such as:

Mental Anguish	Torts
Shock	Death
Emotional Disturbance	Intentional Tort
Debtors and Creditors	

Example of an annotation you can locate through this index on this tort:

Recovery by Debtor, under Tort of Intentional or Reckless Infliction of Emotional Distress, for Damages Resulting from Collection Methods by Joel E. Smith, 87 A.L.R.3d 201 (1978).

Words and Phrases
In this multivolume legal dictionary, look up *intentional infliction of emotional distress, emotional distress, outrageous, reckless, negligent infliction of emotional distress,* and every other word or phrase connected with the tort(s) discussed in this chapter. The dictionary will give you definitions of these words or phrases from court opinions.

CALR: Computer-Assisted Legal Research
Example of a query you could ask on WESTLAW to try to find cases, statutes, or other legal materials on this tort: **"intentional infliction of emotional distress"/p damages**

Example of a query you could ask on LEXIS to try to find cases, statutes, or other legal materials on this tort: **intentional infliction of emotional distress/p damages**

Example of search terms you could use on an Internet legal search engine such as LawCrawler (http://lawcrawler.findlaw.com) to find cases, statutes, or other legal materials on this tort: **"intentional infliction of emotional distress"**

Example of search terms you could use on an Internet general search engine such as Alta Vista (http://www.altavista.com) to find cases, statutes, or other legal materials on this tort: **"intentional infliction of emotional distress"**

More Internet sites to check for materials on intentional infliction of emotional distress and other torts:
Jurist: (http://jurist.law.pitt.edu/sg_torts.htm)
LawGuru: (http://www.lawguru.com/search/lawsearch.html)
See also Tort Law Online at the end of Chapter 1.

Extreme or Outrageous Conduct

The conduct of the defendant must be so **extreme or outrageous** that it would be regarded as atrocious and totally intolerable. Avoid the mistake of concluding that it is atrocious and intolerable to commit any intentional tort, and that therefore, any battery, assault, false imprisonment, or malicious prosecution is *also* the tort of intentional infliction of emotional distress. This is not always so. As indicated in the chart, it is possible for the tort of intentional infliction of emotional distress to be committed simultaneously with other torts. This, however, is not necessarily the case. The act required for intentional infliction of emotional distress must shock the conscience of society.

> **EXAMPLES:**
>
> - playing a practical joke on a mother by telling her that her son has just committed suicide
> - putting a knife to the throat of a ten-year-old child as a threat
> - surrounding a debtor and threatening to kill him and to destroy all of his business machinery if he does not pay a debt
> - pushing a pregnant woman down a flight of stairs or threatening to do so

If the defendant knows that the plaintiff is vulnerable because of age, mental illness, or physical illness, it is usually easier to establish that the conduct was extreme or outrageous. Yet, vulnerability in this sense is not required. It would be extreme or outrageous, for example, for a defendant to drive a car at a high rate of speed on the sidewalk in order to scare a pedestrian directly in front of the car, whether the pedestrian is on crutches or is a healthy boxer.

As we will see elsewhere in this book, common carriers, innkeepers, and public utilities are more likely to be found liable for a tort than other categories of defendants. This is particularly true with the tort of intentional infliction of emotional distress. For most defendants, the first element of this tort is not established by mere insults, threats, or obscenities directed at the plaintiff—they are not atrocious enough. Yet, such conduct might be sufficient if the defendant is a hotel or a public transit facility.

ASSIGNMENT

9.1

Has extreme or outrageous conduct taken place in the following cases? (See General Instructions for the Legal Analysis Assignment in Chapter 2.)

a. A creditor threatens to force the debtor into involuntary bankruptcy if a debt is not paid immediately.

b. The principal of the school suspects that a student has been smoking marijuana in the restroom. The principal threatens to use the student as an example of delinquency before the entire school assembly if the student does not confess to smoking the marijuana.

c. Defendant pretends to be a police detective and threatens to arrest the plaintiff for espionage if the plaintiff does not turn over letters received by the plaintiff from a friend in Asia.

d. A bus driver tells a seventy-five-year-old passenger that her hat is so ridiculous that she would look better bald.

Intent

In most states, the defendant must have the **intent** to cause the severe emotional distress. This means that the defendant must either desire such a consequence or know with substantial certainty that it will result from what he or she does.

In a few states, **recklessness** (or willful and wanton conduct) is enough. In such states, the second element is met if the defendant knows that his or her conduct creates a very great risk that the plaintiff will suffer severe emotional distress. The following is a classic example of the kind of case that meets this standard:

> **EXAMPLE:** Bob is a good friend of Mary's. He attempts to commit suicide with a knife in Mary's kitchen. She suffers severe emotional distress upon seeing the blood and gore.

Mary sues Bob for intentional infliction of emotional distress. In a state that requires intent, Mary loses because there is no indication that Bob desired Mary to suffer this distress or that Bob knew with certainty that it would result. Mary has a better chance in a state where recklessness will suffice, because a strong argument can be made that Bob knew he created a very great risk that Mary would suffer this distress.

The line between desiring something or knowing something with substantial certainty (intent), and knowing that you create a very great risk of something (recklessness) is often very difficult to draw. Yet the line may have to be drawn in a state where recklessness is not enough to establish the second element of this tort.

If the defendant is merely *negligent* in causing the severe emotional distress, there is no intentional infliction of emotional distress. In the next section, we will consider the question of whether the plaintiff might be able to recover under a theory of negligence.

What happens if the defendant intends to cause severe emotional distress in one person, but in fact causes such distress in another person whom the defendant had no intent to bother? What happens if two individuals suffer severe emotional distress, even though defendant's intent was directed at only one of them? Rodney, for example, intentionally terrifies Mary and then maims her. Mary's mother suffers severe emotional distress because of this injury and the way it was brought about. Can both Mary and her mother sue Rodney for intentional infliction of emotional distress? Mary certainly can. In most states, however, her mother cannot sue unless the defendant either desired to cause her severe emotional distress or knew with substantial certainty that it would result from what he did. The doctrine of **transferred intent** (see Figure 6–1 in Chapter 6) does not apply to this tort. If, however, Rodney knew that the mother was present when he terrified and maimed Mary, a good argument can be made that he was at least reckless in creating a very grave risk that the mother would suffer severe emotional distress along with the daughter. In those states where recklessness is sufficient, the mother would be able to sue for intentional infliction of emotional distress if she could convince a jury that Rodney knew that he was creating this very grave risk.

Even states that accept recklessness, however, are reluctant to permit third persons to sue under this tort, and sometimes impose the requirements that the third person be a close relative of the person whom the defendant intends to injure, that this third person be present at the time of the act, and that the defendant know this third person is present.

Whether the mother can sue under a theory of negligence will be considered in the next section of this chapter.

Severe Emotional Distress

It is not enough that the defendant commit an outrageous act intended to cause **severe emotional distress** in the plaintiff. The plaintiff must in fact experience such distress. Minor inconvenience or annoyance is not enough. There must be severe fright, horror, grief, humiliation, embarrassment, anger, worry, or nausea. The severity of these feelings is, of course, measured by their intensity and duration as well as other factors, such as the relative size and weight of the plaintiff and defendant, and how the defendant approached the plaintiff. It is not necessary in the vast majority of states that the plaintiff suffer any **physical injury** or harm as a result of what the defendant did. Such physical illness or harm, if it exists, will increase the damages and help to prove that the plaintiff is telling the truth about the severity of the emotional distress that is alleged, but the plaintiff need not prove physical illness or harm in order to establish the tort.

Suppose the plaintiff is unusually sensitive and experiences severe emotional distress even though anyone else would not, e.g., the plaintiff goes into shock when the defendant plays a practical joke by telling the plaintiff that one of his flowers has just died. If the defendant knew of this vulnerability and still proceeded with the intent to cause severe emotional distress, the third element of the tort is established. Otherwise, the test is objective: the plaintiff will not be able to recover unless an ordinary person, not unduly sensitive, would have suffered severe emotional distress from what the defendant did.

ASSIGNMENT

9.2

For months Tom has been having difficulty finding work. Finally he gets a job at the XYZ gym as a judo instructor. It is the first time he has had a job in over a year and a half. A collection agency has been after Tom to pay a $500 debt. An employee of the agency calls Tom and says, "I understand that you now have a job and that you have had to go through a lot to get it. Don't do anything silly, which might cost you that job. Don't make me call your new boss to let him know that you're the kind of guy who doesn't pay his debts. You've got one week to pay up or else." Tom is terrified at the thought of losing his job. He has many sleepless nights worrying about the possibility that the collection agency might call his boss. Tom sues the agency for intentional infliction of emotional distress. What result? (See General Instructions for the Legal Analysis Assignment in Chapter 2.)

Causation

Plaintiff can use either of the following tests to establish **causation:**

- But for what the defendant did, the plaintiff would not have suffered severe emotional distress.
- The defendant was a substantial factor in producing the plaintiff's severe emotional distress.

The second test is used when there is more than one potential cause of the severe emotional distress. The plaintiff is not required to prove causation by the but-for test. The broader substantial factor test is sufficient.

TORT LAW AND THE IMPEACHMENT OF THE PRESIDENT

In 1999, Congress impeached and tried the president of the United States for only the second time in American history. One of the articles of impeachment against President Bill Clinton was that he lied when he gave a deposition in a sexual harassment and tort case that was filed against him by Paula Corbin Jones. Her tort cause of action was intentional infliction of emotional distress, called the tort of outrage in Arkansas. During the deposition the president gave in this case, he answered "none" when asked whether there were any female employees of the federal government with whom he had had sexual relations. In particular, he denied having such relations with Monica Lewinsky, a White House intern. A special prosecutor and almost all Republicans in Congress charged that his answers were intentionally false. They believed that lying in a deposition was one of the "high crimes and misdemeanors" that should lead to his removal from office. Ultimately, the Senate as a whole disagreed when it failed to convict the president by the required two-thirds vote. By acquitting the president, the Senate was saying either that it did not believe the president lied, or that even if he did, the lie and the other charges were not serious enough to remove him from office.

The president also won the sexual harassment and tort case when the trial court judge, Susan Webber Wright, ruled that his conduct did not constitute sexual harassment nor the tort of outrage. In a stinging rebuke, however, Judge Wright ruled that he *did* lie during his deposition and held him in civil contempt. One of the consequences of the lie was that the legal team of Jones had to spend extra time preparing its case. Hence the judge ordered the president to pay a fine of $90,000 for reasonable legal fees covering this time. The fee request included $60 an hour for the work of two paralegals on the Jones legal team.

In the meantime, Jones was set to appeal Judge Wright's ruling that the president did not commit sexual harassment nor the tort of outrage. The president did not relish the prospect of fighting the appeal, particularly since the appeal would have taken place before the impeachment proceeding in Congress was concluded. Hence the president decided that the safest legal and political strategy was to settle the case to prevent the appeal from going forward. He agreed to pay Jones $850,000 in exchange for her decision to drop her appeal of Judge Wright's ruling against her on the sexual harassment and tort claims.

For our purposes, we need to examine why the court ruled that there was no intentional infliction of emotional distress. Here is the opinion of Judge Wright on this issue.

CASE

Paula Corbin Jones v. William Jefferson Clinton and Danny Ferguson
990 F. Supp. 657 (1998)
United States District Court, Eastern District, Arkansas

Background: *Paula Corbin Jones, an Arkansas state clerical worker, alleges that when President Clinton was Governor in 1991, he made a sexual advance toward her in a Little Rock hotel, which she rejected. After Governor Clinton became President, Jones sued him and a state trooper (Danny Ferguson) in a federal trial court, the United States District Court in Arkansas. Her claims were sexual harassment and intentional infliction of emotional distress, which is called the tort of outrage in Arkansas. (Loss-of-reputation claims such as defamation were also included but later dropped.) The President argued that he should not have to defend the suit until after he left office. The United States Supreme Court disagreed (117 S. Ct. 1636) and the case proceeded. After depositions were taken of the plaintiff, the defendants, and others, the President made a motion for summary judgment, asking that the case be dismissed without a trial. His position was that even if the plaintiff proved everything she alleged, his conduct constituted neither sexual harassment nor intentional infliction of emotional distress (outrage).*

Decision of Court: *The President's motion for summary judgment is granted. (1) There was no sexual harassment. The plaintiff's refusal to submit to unwelcome sexual advances or requests for sexual favors did not result in retaliation or other tangible job detriment and this single incident did not amount to a hostile work environment. (2) The plaintiff has not stated a claim for the tort of intentional infliction of emotional distress (outrage). The excerpts from the opinion below cover the tort claim only.*

OPINION OF COURT

Judge Susan Webber WRIGHT delivered the opinion of the court . . .:

This lawsuit is based on an incident that is said to have taken place on the afternoon of May 8, 1991, in a suite at the Excelsior Hotel in Little Rock, Arkansas. President Clinton was Governor of the State of Arkansas at the time, and plaintiff was a State employee with the Arkansas Industrial Development Commission ("AIDC"), having begun her State employment on March 11, 1991. [Danny] Ferguson was an Arkansas State Police officer assigned to the Governor's security detail.

According to the record, then-Governor Clinton was at the Excelsior Hotel on the day in question delivering a speech at an official conference being sponsored by the AIDC. Plaintiff states that she and another AIDC employee, Pamela Blackard, were working at a registration desk for the AIDC when a man approached the desk and informed her and Blackard that he was Trooper Danny Ferguson, the Governor's bodyguard. She states that Ferguson made

small talk with her and Blackard and that they asked him if he had a gun as he was in street clothes and they "wanted to know." Ferguson acknowledged that he did and, after being asked to show the gun to them, left the registration desk to return to the Governor. The conversation between plaintiff, Blackard, and Ferguson lasted approximately five minutes and consisted of light, friendly banter; there was nothing intimidating, threatening, or coercive about it.

Upon leaving the registration desk, Ferguson apparently had a conversation with the Governor about the possibility of meeting with plaintiff, during which Ferguson states the Governor remarked that plaintiff had "that come-hither look," i.e. "a sort of [sexually] suggestive appearance from the look or dress." Ferguson Deposition at 50; Plaintiff's Statement of Material Facts, ¶ 3; President's Deposition at 109.[1] He states that "some time later" the Governor asked him to "get him a room, that he was expecting a call from the White House and . . . had several phone calls that he needed to make," and asked him to go to the car and get his briefcase containing the phone messages. Ferguson states that upon obtaining the room, the Governor told him that if plaintiff wanted to meet him, she could "come up."

Plaintiff states that Ferguson later reappeared at the registration desk, delivered a piece of paper to her with a four-digit number written on it, and said that the Governor would like to meet with her in this suite number. She states that she, Blackard, and Ferguson talked about what the Governor could want and that Ferguson stated, among other things, "We do this all the time." Thinking that it was an honor to be asked to meet the Governor and that it might lead to an enhanced employment opportunity, plaintiff states that she agreed to the meeting and that Ferguson escorted her to the floor of the hotel upon which the Governor's suite was located.

Plaintiff states that upon arriving at the suite and announcing herself, the Governor shook her hand, invited her in, and closed the door. She states that a few minutes of small talk ensued, which included the Governor asking her about her job and him mentioning that Dave Harrington, plaintiff's ultimate superior within the AIDC and a Clinton appointee, was his "good friend." Plaintiff states that the Governor then "unexpectedly reached over to [her], took her hand, and pulled her toward him, so that their bodies were close to each other." She states she removed her hand from his and retreated several feet, but that the

---

[1]Ferguson states that plaintiff informed him that she would like to meet the Governor, remarking that she thought the Governor "was good-looking [and] had sexy hair," Ferguson Deposition at 50, while plaintiff states that Ferguson asked her if she would like to meet the Governor and that she was "excited" about the possibility, Plaintiff's Deposition at 101.

Governor approached her again and, while saying, "I love the way your hair flows down your back" and "I love your curves," put his hand on her leg, started sliding it toward her pelvic area, and bent down to attempt to kiss her on the neck, all without her consent. Plaintiff states that she exclaimed, "What are you doing?," told the Governor that she was "not that kind of girl," and "escaped" from the Governor's reach "by walking away from him." She states she was extremely upset and confused and, not knowing what to do, attempted to distract the Governor by chatting about his wife. Plaintiff states that she sat down at the end of the sofa nearest the door, but that the Governor approached the sofa where she had taken a seat and, as he sat down, "lowered his trousers and underwear, exposed his penis (which was erect) and told [her] to 'kiss it.' " She states that she was "horrified" by this and that she "jumped up from the couch" and told the Governor that she had to go, saying something to the effect that she had to get back to the registration desk. Plaintiff states that the Governor, "while fondling his penis," said, "Well, I don't want to make you do anything you don't want to do," and then pulled up his pants and said, "If you get in trouble for leaving work, have Dave call me immediately and I'll take care of it." She states that as she left the room (the door of which was not locked), the Governor "detained" her momentarily, "looked sternly" at her, and said, "You are smart. Let's keep this between ourselves."

Plaintiff states that the Governor's advances to her were unwelcome, that she never said or did anything to suggest to the Governor that she was willing to have sex with him, and that during the time they were together in the hotel suite, she resisted his advances although she was "stunned by them and intimidated by who he was." She states that when the Governor referred to Dave Harrington, she "understood that he was telling her that he had control over Mr. Harrington and over her job, and that he was willing to use that power." She states that from that point on, she was "very fearful" that her refusal to submit to the Governor's advances could damage her career and even jeopardize her employment.

Plaintiff states that when she left the hotel suite, she was in shock and upset but tried to maintain her composure. She states she saw Ferguson waiting outside the suite but that he did not escort her back to the registration desk and nothing was said between them. Ferguson states that five or ten minutes after plaintiff exited the suite he joined the Governor for their return to the Governor's Mansion and that the Governor, who was working on some papers that he had spread out on the desk, said, "She came up here, and nothing happened."

Plaintiff states she returned to the registration desk and told Blackard some of what had happened. Blackard states that plaintiff was shaking and embarrassed. Following the Conference, plaintiff states she went to the workplace of a friend, Debra Ballentine, and told her of the incident as well. Ballentine states that plaintiff was upset and crying. Later that same day, plaintiff states she told her sister, Charlotte Corbin Brown, what had happened and, within the next two days, also told her other sister, Lydia Corbin

Cathey, of the incident. Brown's observations of plaintiff's demeanor apparently are not included in the record. Cathey, however, states that plaintiff was "bawling" and "squalling," and that she appeared scared, embarrassed, and ashamed.

Ballentine states that she encouraged plaintiff to report the incident to her boss or to the police, but that plaintiff declined, pointing out that her boss was friends with the Governor and that the police were the ones who took her to the hotel suite. Ballentine further states that plaintiff stated she did not want her fiancé to know of the incident and that she "just want[ed] this thing to go away." Plaintiff states that what the Governor and Ferguson had said and done made her "afraid" to file charges. . . .

The President moves for summary judgment on the [ground that the] claim of intentional infliction of emotional distress or outrage fails because . . . plaintiff did not as a result of the alleged conduct suffer emotional distress so severe that no reasonable person could endure it. . . . The President and Ferguson both argue that there are no genuine issues of material fact with respect to any of these issues and that they are entitled to summary judgment as a matter of law. . . .

Arkansas recognizes a claim of intentional infliction of emotional distress based on sexual harassment. *Davis v. Tri-State Mack Distribs., Inc.,* 981 F.2d 340, 342 (8th Cir. 1992) (citing *Hale v. Ladd,* 308 Ark. 567, 826 S.W.2d 244 (1992)). To establish a claim of intentional infliction of emotional distress, a plaintiff must prove that: (1) the defendant intended to inflict emotional distress or knew or should have known that emotional distress was the likely result of his conduct; (2) the conduct was extreme and outrageous and utterly intolerable in a civilized community; (3) the defendant's conduct was the cause of the plaintiff's distress; and (4) the plaintiff's emotional distress was so severe in nature that no reasonable person could be expected to endure it. *Croom v. Younts,* 323 Ark. 95, 913 S.W.2d 283, 286 (1996).

The President argues that the alleged conduct of which plaintiff complains was brief and isolated; did not result in any physical harm or objective symptoms of the requisite severe distress; did not result in distress so severe that no reasonable person could be expected to endure it; and he had no knowledge of any special condition of plaintiff that would render her particularly susceptible to distress. He argues that plaintiff has failed to identify the kind of clear cut proof that Arkansas courts require for a claim of outrage and that he is therefore entitled to summary judgment. The Court agrees.

One is subject to liability for the tort of outrage or intentional infliction of emotional distress if he or she willfully or wantonly causes severe emotional distress to another by extreme and outrageous conduct. In *M.B.M. Co. v. Counce,* 268 Ark. 269, 280, 596 S.W.2d 681, 687 (1980), the Arkansas Supreme Court stated that "[b]y extreme and outrageous conduct, we mean conduct that is so outrageous in character, and so extreme in degree, as to go beyond all possible bounds of decency, and to be regarded as atrocious, and utterly intolerable in civilized society." Whether conduct is "extreme and outrageous" is determined by looking at "the conduct at issue; the period of time over which the conduct took place; the relation between plaintiff and defendant; and defendant's knowledge that plaintiff is particularly susceptible to emotional distress by reason of some physical or mental peculiarity." *Doe v. Wright,* 82 F.3d 265, 269 (8th Cir. 1996) (citing *Hamaker,* 51 F.3d 108, 111 (8th Cir. 1995)). The tort is clearly not intended to provide legal redress for every slight insult or indignity that one must endure. *Manning v. Metropolitan Life Ins. Co.,* 127 F.3d 686, 690 (8th Cir. 1997) (citing *Hamaker,* 51 F.3d at 110). The Arkansas courts take a strict approach and give a narrow view to claims of outrage, and merely describing conduct as outrageous does not make it so.

Plaintiff seems to base her claim of outrage on her erroneous belief that the allegations she has presented are sufficient to constitute criminal sexual assault. She states that "Mr. Clinton's outrageous conduct includes offensive language, an offensive proposition, offensive touching (constituting sexual assault under both federal and state definitions), and *actual exposure of an intimate private body part,*" and that "[t]here are few more outrageous acts than a criminal sexual assault followed by unwanted exposure, coupled with a demand for oral sex by the most powerful man in the state against a very young, low-level employee." Plaintiff's Opposition to Defendant Clinton's Motion for Summary Judgment at 66 (emphasis in original).

While the Court will certainly agree that plaintiff's allegations describe offensive conduct, the Court . . . has found that the Governor's alleged conduct does not constitute sexual assault. Rather, the conduct as alleged by plaintiff describes a mere sexual proposition or encounter, albeit an odious one, that was relatively brief in duration, did not involve any coercion or threats of reprisal, and was abandoned as soon as plaintiff made clear that the advance was not welcome. The Court is not aware of any authority holding that such a sexual encounter or proposition of the type alleged in this case, without more, gives rise to a claim of outrage. Cf. *Croom,* 913 S.W.2d at 287 (use of wine and medication by a vastly older relative to foist sex on a minor cousin went "beyond a mere sexual encounter" and offended all sense of decency).

Moreover, notwithstanding the offensive nature of the Governor's alleged conduct, plaintiff admits that she never missed a day of work following the alleged incident, she continued to work at AIDC another nineteen months (leaving only because of her husband's job transfer), she continued to go on a daily basis to the Governor's Office to deliver items and never asked to be relieved of that duty, she never filed a formal complaint or told her supervisors of the incident while at AIDC, she never consulted a psychiatrist, psychologist, or incurred medical bills as a result of the alleged incident, and she acknowledges that her two subsequent contacts with the Governor involved comments made "in a light vein" and nonsexual contact that was done in a "friendly fashion." Further, despite earlier claiming that she suffered marital discord and humiliation, plaintiff stated in her deposition that she was not claiming damages to her marriage as a result of the Governor's alleged conduct and she acknowledged the request to drop her claim of injury to reputation by stating, "I didn't really care if it was dropped or not personally." Plaintiff's actions and statements in this case do not portray someone who experienced emotional distress so severe in nature that no reasonable person could be expected to endure it. Cf. *Hamaker,* 51 F.3d 108 (no claim of outrage where plaintiff, who had a speech impediment and an I.Q. of between 75 and 100, was "red-faced and angry," had an "increased heart rate and blood pressure," and had trouble sleeping four days after incident involving "rather nasty" practical joke).

Nevertheless, plaintiff submits a declaration from a purported expert with a Ph.D. in education and counseling, Patrick J. Carnes, who, after a 3.5 hour meeting with plaintiff and her husband a mere four days prior to the filing of President Clinton's motion for summary judgment, opines that her alleged encounter with Governor Clinton in 1991, "and the ensuing events," have caused plaintiff to suffer severe emotional distress and "consequent sexual aversion." The Court does not credit this declaration.

In *Angle v. Alexander,* 328 Ark. 714, 945 S.W.2d 933 (1997), the Arkansas Supreme Court noted that absent physical harm, courts look for more in the way of extreme outrage as an assurance that the mental disturbance claimed is not fictitious. In that case, the plaintiffs offered their own testimony that they had experienced emotional distress, thoughts of death, fear, anger, and worry, but little else. In concluding that there was no evidence of extreme emotional distress required to prevail on an outrage claim, the Court found it significant that none had seen a physician or mental health professional for these concerns. The Court did not allow the fact that one plaintiff "on the advice of her attorney, spoke to a psychologist," to overcome her failure of proof on this point. Id. at 937 n. 3.

Aside from other deficiencies with the Carnes' declaration (including the fact that the substance of this declaration apparently was not disclosed in accordance with rules governing pre-trial discovery), the opinions stated therein are vague and conclusory and, as in *Angle,* do not suffice to overcome plaintiff's failure of proof on her claim of outrage. Cf. *Crenshaw v. Georgia-Pacific Corp.,* 915 F. Supp. 93, 99 (W.D. Ark. 1995) (affidavit prepared after opposing motion for summary judgment filed detailing symptoms of weight loss, lack of sleep, headache, worry, and nausea, failed to present sufficient evidence of emotional distress).

In sum, plaintiff's allegations fall far short of the rigorous standards for establishing a claim of outrage under Arkansas law and the Court therefore grants the President's motion for summary judgment on this claim. For the foregoing reasons, the Court finds that the President's and Ferguson's motions for summary judgment should both be and hereby are granted. There being no remaining issues, the Court will enter judgment dismissing this case.

a. The *Jones* decision on the tort of outrage was clearly incorrect. Right? Explain.

b. The *Jones* decision on the tort of outrage was clearly correct. Right? Explain.

c. Did the court dismiss the tort claim because the President's conduct was not serious enough or because the court did not think the plaintiff was telling the truth about what happened?

d. The court says that the case of *Croom v. Younts,* which reached a different decision, is distinguishable from the facts of the *Jones* case. Do you agree?

MEDIA DEFENDANTS AND THE CONSTITUTION

The First Amendment of the United States Constitution gives special protection to newspapers, magazines, TV, theater, and other media entities when they are sued because of something they publish. This includes a suit for intentional infliction of emotional distress. In a famous case that reached the United States Supreme Court, Reverend Jerry Falwell asserted this tort against *Hustler Magazine* and its publisher, Larry Flynt, after the magazine printed a crude parody about him. Falwell was the host of a nationally syndicated television show and the founder and president of a political organization formerly known as the Moral Majority. Here is the Court's description of Falwell's grievance:

> Petitioner Hustler Magazine, Inc., is a magazine of nationwide circulation. Respondent Jerry Falwell, a nationally known minister who has been active as a commentator on politics and public affairs, sued petitioner and its publisher, petitioner Larry Flynt, to recover damages for . . . intentional infliction of emotional distress. . . . The inside front cover of the November 1983 issue of Hustler Magazine featured a "parody" of an advertisement for Campari Liqueur that contained the name and picture of respondent and was entitled "Jerry Falwell talks about his first time." This parody was modeled after actual Campari ads that included interviews with various celebrities about their "first times." Although it was apparent by the end of each interview that this meant the first time they sampled Campari, the ads clearly played on the sexual double entendre of the general subject of "first times." Copying the form and layout of these Campari ads, Hustler's editors chose respondent as the featured celebrity and drafted an alleged "interview" with him in which he states that his "first time" was during a drunken incestuous rendezvous with his mother in an outhouse. The Hustler parody portrays respondent and his mother as drunk and immoral, and suggests that respondent is a hypocrite who preaches only when he is drunk. In small print at the bottom of the page, the ad contains the disclaimer, "ad parody—not to be taken seriously." The magazine's table of contents also lists the ad as "Fiction; Ad and Personality Parody." *Hustler Magazine and Larry C. Flynt v. Jerry Falwell,* 485 U.S. 46, 47–8, 108 S. Ct. 876, 887–8, 99 L. Ed. 2d 41, 47 (1988).

The question before the Court was whether Falwell had to prove an additional element of the tort because he was suing a media defendant. The Court concluded that he did. It is not enough to show that the defendant acted outrageously. When a public official or a public figure such as Falwell sues the media for intentional infliction of emotional distress, there must be proof that the media published a false statement of fact with **actual malice** (also called constitutional malice). This means that the media knew the statement was false or that it published the statement in reckless disregard of whether it was true or false. This is a standard that is very difficult for most plaintiffs to meet. It would, therefore, tend to discourage an onslaught of tort claims against the media and thereby help ensure the robust exchange of ideas that the First Amendment is designed to encourage.

In the *Hustler* case, the Court ruled against Falwell because the ad parody could not reasonably be understood as describing actual facts about Falwell. Given the context of the publication, the caricature was simply not reasonably believable. Therefore, the magazine did not publish a false statement of fact about Falwell, and, by definition could not have acted with actual malice. Consequently, the plaintiff cannot assert the tort of intentional infliction of emotional distress.

When the media is sued for something it publishes, the more common tort asserted against it is libel. This is the area of tort law that gave birth to the Supreme Court's imposition of the actual malice standard for media defendants. When we discuss defamation in Chapter 24, we will provide a fuller treatment of actual malice, particularly when the plaintiff is a public official or a public figure.

NEGLIGENT INFLICTION OF EMOTIONAL DISTRESS

Traditional Negligence

A traditional negligence action alleges that the defendant caused physical harm or injury for which damages can be recovered (see Chapter 12). The plaintiff can also recover damages for the emotional distress (*pain and suffering*) that accompany this physical harm or injury.

> **EXAMPLE:** Dan negligently drives his car into Rose, a pedestrian crossing the street. She suffers a broken back.

Rose can recover damages for the injury to her back (a direct physical injury) as well as for the pain and suffering she experienced during and since the accident.

Suppose, however, a person suffers emotional distress but no direct or immediate physical injury.

> **EXAMPLES:** Case A. Bob negligently drives his car past Mary, a pedestrian crossing the street. She is not hit, but is extremely distressed by the way Bob was driving.
>
> Case B. Bob negligently drives his car past Mary, a pedestrian crossing the street. She is not hit, but is extremely distressed by the way Bob was driving. Two days after this incident, Mary develops ulcers brought on by her memories of Bob's driving.
>
> Case C. Bob negligently drives his car past Mary, a pedestrian crossing the street. His car runs into and kills another pedestrian. Mary is not hit, but is extremely distressed by witnessing the death.

If Bob intentionally caused Mary's distress in any of these cases, she may be able to sue him for intentional infliction of emotional distress. Suppose, however, that he negligently caused Mary's emotional distress in Cases A, B, or C. When emotional distress is negligently caused, we need to determine whether there can be a suit for **negligent infliction of emotional distress (NIED)**. Several variations are possible:

- The plaintiff does not suffer physical harm or injury along with the emotional distress (Case A).

- The plaintiff suffers emotional distress now and physical harm or injury at a later time (Case B).
- The plaintiff suffers emotional distress from witnessing someone else's injury and may or may not also suffer physical harm or injury (Case C).

No Physical Harm or Injury

We begin our discussion with Case A. Assume that the defendant's negligently driven car just misses the plaintiff. The latter suffers no *physical* harm or injury at any time, but does suffer substantial fright, anxiety, or other emotional distress. There can be no recovery according to the traditional rule. Courts take the position that the emotional distress is too trivial if it does not grow out of or cause a physical harm or injury, e.g., a heart attack. Courts are also concerned that it would be too easy to fabricate the emotional distress if it were not connected to physical harm or injury. A small number of courts provide an exception to this rule in certain kinds of cases, e.g., the defendant is a telegraph company that has negligently misdelivered a message (e.g., of death) to the wrong relative; the defendant is a funeral home that has negligently handled the body of the deceased. Relatives suffering emotional distress in such cases *can* recover even if they did not also suffer direct physical harm or injury. These are exceptions, however. In the vast majority of other cases, recovery is denied.

Later Physical Harm or Injury

Next we examine the case in which the negligence of the defendant causes emotional distress that *later* leads to physical harm or injury (Case B). The negligence does not directly produce this harm or injury. The classic case is the woman who suffers a miscarriage due to anxiety two weeks after the defendant *almost* hit her while negligently driving a truck close to the sidewalk. Assuming that the plaintiff can establish the causal link between the emotional distress and the physical harm or injury (not an easy task), can there be recovery? Courts answer this question differently; considerable confusion exists.

- Some courts will deny recovery unless the emotional distress and physical harm or injury are simultaneous.
- Most courts will allow recovery, but only if there is some **physical impact** on the plaintiff at the time of the defendant's negligence; the impact need not be substantial (a slight jar, or smoke in the face will be sufficient); the impact itself does not have to produce any physical harm or injury as long as harm or injury is caused by the emotional distress.
- Some courts allow recovery even if there is no impact as long as the evidence is strong enough to establish the causal connection between the emotional distress and the physical harm or injury that later develops.
- Some courts will allow recovery, but only if the plaintiff is in the **zone of danger** of physical impact due to the defendant's negligence even if there is no actual impact on the plaintiff.

When recovery is denied, it is sometimes based on the theory that the defendant owed no duty to the plaintiff to prevent the injury that resulted (see Chapter 13 on duty), or that the defendant was not the proximate cause of the injury (see Chapter 15 on proximate cause).

Witnessing Someone Else's Injury

The situation becomes even more complicated when the plaintiff is a witness to an injury negligently caused to someone else (Case C). What happens when the plaintiff suffers emotional distress in such a case (e.g., the plaintiff witnesses her son being hit by the defendant's negligently driven truck) and there is no impact on the plaintiff?

Can the plaintiff recover damages if he or she has a physical injury caused by the emotional distress? Can the plaintiff recover damages if no physical injury results from the emotional distress? Again, the courts do not handle these questions in the same way.

- Some courts deny recovery in all such cases.
- Some courts will allow recovery but only if the plaintiff suffered a physical injury and was close enough to also be in the zone of danger when he or she witnessed the other person being injured.
- Some courts will allow recovery but only if the plaintiff suffered a physical injury, was close enough to also be in the zone of danger, and was very closely related to the person the plaintiff witnessed being injured.
- Some courts will allow recovery even if the plaintiff did not suffer a physical injury as long as the emotional distress from witnessing the injury was foreseeable and was serious or severe.

When recovery is denied, it is sometimes based on the theory that the defendant owed no duty to the plaintiff witnessing the accident (see Chapter 13), or that the defendant was not the proximate cause of what the plaintiff suffered by witnessing someone else's injury (see Chapter 15).

ASSIGNMENT 9.4

In the following situations, determine whether there can be recovery for negligent infliction of emotional distress (NIED). (See General Instructions for the Legal Analysis Assignment in Chapter 2.)

a. Eight-year-old Johnny is on his first trip to Disneyland. While walking through the park, he is shocked to see Mickey Mouse remove his mask to get a drink of water at a fountain. Johnny is traumatized to learn that the character he idolized is not real. Johnny sues the person in the costume and Disneyland for NIED.

b. Mary is a passenger on a flight across the country. Suddenly the plane jerks. Mary looks out the window and sees that part of the wing has broken off. The pilot announces that everyone should be prepared for an emergency landing. Forty-five minutes of terror later, the plane lands safely in a farm field. Mary sues the airline for NIED.

c. While eating a sandwich, Bill senses something strange in the mustard. He immediately spits out what is in his mouth and discovers very small glass particles in the mustard. Bill suffers great anxiety at the thought of the glass in his mouth. He sues the manufacturer of the mustard for NIED.

d. Helen and Laura work for the railroad. Due to Laura's negligence, Helen's foot is trapped for a few seconds on a track with a train approaching directly at her. At the last moment, Helen is able to move out of the way. Helen is numb from fright. At home that night and for three nights thereafter, she suffers excruciating anguish at the thought of almost being hit by a train. Helen sues Laura for NIED.

e. Fred is on a hill overlooking his house. He watches a huge truck being carelessly driven by Jim heading right for his house. Fred knows that there is no one in the house, but is extremely concerned because he just had $50,000 in repairs made on the front of the house. Jim smashes into the front of the house. Fred is frantic. He starts running toward the house, trips, and has a heart attack. Fred sues Jim for NIED.

CASE

Thing v. La Chusa
48 Cal. 3d 644, 771 P.2d 814 (1989)
Supreme Court of California

Background: *Maria Thing's son, John, was injured in an automobile accident that was negligently caused by the defendant, James V. La Chusa. The son sued the defendant separately for his injuries. Maria Thing brought her own suit for negligent infliction of emotional distress (NIED) based on the distress she suffered when she came to the scene of the accident and saw the condition of her son. She did not observe the accident itself. There was no physical impact on her and she suffered no physical injury herself at the scene. The trial court dismissed her claim by granting a summary judgment for the defendant because she did not contemporaneously perceive the accident. On appeal, however, the Court of Appeals reversed and allowed her to recover for NIED. The case is now on further appeal before the Supreme Court of California.*

Decision on Appeal: *Judgment for the defendant. The decision of the Court of Appeals is reversed. Maria Thing has failed to establish negligent infliction of emotional distress since she did not witness the accident.*

OPINION OF COURT

Justice EAGLESON delivered the opinion of the court . . .

On December 8, 1980, John Thing, a minor, was injured when struck by an automobile operated by defendant James V. La Chusa. His mother, plaintiff Maria Thing, was nearby, but neither saw nor heard the accident. She became aware of the injury to her son when told by a daughter that John had been struck by a car. She rushed to the scene where she saw her bloody and unconscious child, whom she believed was dead, lying in the roadway. Maria sued defendant, alleging that she suffered great emotional disturbance, shock, and injury to her nervous system as a result of these events, and that the injury to John and emotional distress she suffered were proximately caused by defendant's negligence. . . .

The impact of personally observing the injury-producing event in most, although concededly not all, cases distinguishes the plaintiff's resultant emotional distress from the emotion felt when one learns of the injury or death of a loved one from another, or observes pain and suffering but not the traumatic cause of the injury. Greater certainty and a more reasonable limit on the exposure to liability for negligent conduct is possible by limiting the right to recover for negligently caused emotional distress to plaintiffs who personally and contemporaneously perceive the injury-producing event and its traumatic consequences.*

Similar reasoning justifies limiting recovery to persons closely related by blood or marriage since, in common experience, it is more likely that they will suffer a greater degree of emotional distress than a disinterested witness to negligently caused pain and suffering or death. Such limi-

tations are indisputably arbitrary since it is foreseeable that in some cases unrelated persons have a relationship to the victim or are so affected by the traumatic event that they suffer equivalent emotional distress. As we have observed, however, drawing arbitrary lines is unavoidable if we are to limit liability and establish meaningful rules for application by litigants and lower courts.

No policy supports extension of the right to recover for NIED to a larger class of plaintiffs. Emotional distress is an intangible condition experienced by most persons, even absent negligence, at some time during their lives. Close relatives suffer serious, even debilitating, emotional reactions to the injury, death, serious illness, and evident suffering of loved ones. These reactions occur regardless of the cause of the loved one's illness, injury, or death. That relatives will have severe emotional distress is an unavoidable aspect of the "human condition." The emotional distress for which monetary damages may be recovered, however, ought not to be that form of acute emotional distress or the transient emotional reaction to the occasional gruesome or horrible incident to which every person may potentially be exposed in an industrial and sometimes violent society. Regardless of the depth of feeling or the resultant physical or mental illness that results from witnessing violent events, persons unrelated to those injured or killed may not now recover for such emotional upheaval even if negligently caused. Close relatives who witness the accidental injury or death of a loved one and suffer emotional trauma may not recover when the loved one's conduct was the cause of that emotional trauma. The overwhelming majority of "emotional distress" which we endure, therefore, is not compensable.

Unlike an award of damages for intentionally caused emotional distress which is punitive, the award for NIED simply reflects society's belief that a negligent actor bears some responsibility for the effect of his conduct on persons other than those who suffer physical injury. In identifying those persons and the circumstances in which the defendant will

---

*"[A] distinction between distress caused by personal observation of the injury and by hearing of the tragedy from another is justified because compensation should be limited to abnormal life experiences which cause emotional distress. While receiving news that a loved one has been injured or has died may cause emotional distress, it is the type of experience for which in a general way one is prepared, an experience which is common. By contrast few persons are forced to witness the death or injury of a loved one or to suddenly come upon the scene without warning in situations where tortious conduct is involved. In the present case, for example, while it is common to visit a loved one in a hospital and to be distressed by the loved one's pain and suffering, it is highly uncommon to witness the apparent neglect of the patient's immediate medical needs by medical personnel." (*Ochoa v. Superior Court* (1985) 39 Cal. 3d 159, 165, fn. 6, 703 P.2d 1.)

be held to redress the injury, it is appropriate to restrict recovery to those persons who will suffer an emotional impact beyond the impact that can be anticipated whenever one learns that a relative is injured, or dies, or the emotion felt by a "disinterested" witness. The class of potential plaintiffs should be limited to those who because of their relationship suffer the greatest emotional distress. When the right to recover is limited in this manner, the liability bears a reasonable relationship to the culpability of the negligent defendant. . . . Even if it is "foreseeable" that persons other than closely related percipient witnesses may suffer emotional distress, this fact does not justify the imposition of what threatens to become unlimited liability for emotional distress on a defendant whose conduct is simply negligent. . . .

We conclude, therefore, that a plaintiff may recover damages for emotional distress caused by observing the negligently inflicted injury of a third person if, but only if, said plaintiff: (1) is closely related to the injury victim;* (2) is present at the scene of the injury-producing event at the time it occurs and is then aware that it is causing injury to the victim; and (3) as a result suffers serious emotional distress—a reaction beyond that which would be anticipated in a disinterested witness and which is not an abnormal response to the circumstances. . . .†

The merely negligent actor does not owe a duty the law will recognize to make monetary amends to all persons who may have suffered emotional distress on viewing or learning about the injurious consequences of his conduct. . . .

The undisputed facts establish that [Maria Thing] was not present at the scene of the accident in which her son was injured. She did not observe defendant's conduct and was not aware that her son was being injured. She could not, therefore, establish a right to recover for the emotional distress she suffered when she subsequently learned of the accident and observed its consequences. The order granting summary judgment was proper. The judgment of the Court of Appeal is reversed.

---

*In most cases no justification exists for permitting recovery for NIED by persons who are only distantly related to the injury victim. Absent exceptional circumstances, recovery should be limited to relatives residing in the same household, or parents, siblings, children, and grandparents of the victim.

†As explained by the Hawaii Supreme Court, "serious mental distress may be found where a reasonable [person] normally constituted, would be unable to adequately cope with the mental distress engendered by the circumstances of the case." (*Rodrigues v. State* (1970) 52 Hawaii 156, 173, 472 P.2d 509, 519–520.)

ASSIGNMENT

9.5

Jim Nester drowns while swimming in a pool operated by Fun Center, Inc. The death is solely due to the negligence of Fun Center, Inc. Jim was at the pool with his stepfather, Frank Carter. (Frank married Jim's mother a month before Jim's death. Frank had lived with the mother about three weeks before the marriage.) Jim was accidentally pushed into the pool by a careless lifeguard. Frank did not see this, but he heard a stranger scream when Jim fell in the water. When he heard the scream, Fred looked over in the direction of Jim. Since people had gathered around, he was not certain what had happened. He walked over and saw Jim being pulled from the water. Frank gasped in horror when he saw Jim's face turn blue. As a lifeguard started carrying Jim to an ambulance, Frank panicked. He felt dizzy and almost fainted. He has been unable to sleep because of Jim's death. After the funeral, Frank sued Fun Center, Inc. for negligent infliction of emotional distress. What are his chances of success? Does the *Thing* case apply?

SUMMARY

The tort of intentional infliction of emotional distress requires an act of extreme or outrageous conduct. It must shock the conscience. For defendants such as common carriers and innkeepers, however, courts sometimes say that less severe conduct will suffice. In most states, there must be intent to cause the severe emotional distress; in some states, recklessness is enough. The defendant's intent to cause distress in one person will not be transferred to another person who suffered the distress if the defendant did not intend to harm the latter. The plaintiff must in fact suffer severe emotional distress. Physical illness or harm is not required. The test of whether the distress was severe is an objective test unless the defendant is aware of (and takes advantage of) the plaintiff's unusual susceptibility to such distress. The plaintiff must show either that but for what the defendant did the distress would not have resulted, or that the defendant was a substantial factor in producing it.

When a media defendant is sued for intentional infliction of emotional distress and the plaintiff is a public official or public figure, the plaintiff must prove that the media published a false statement of fact and either knew the statement was false or published it in reckless disregard of whether it was true or false (actual malice).

In a standard negligence action, the plaintiff can recover for emotional distress arising out of direct and immediate physical harm or injury. With few exceptions, if the plaintiff never suffers physical harm or injury, courts deny recovery for the negligently caused emotional distress. If this distress later results in physical harm or injury, courts sometimes grant recovery. It may depend on whether there was some physical impact on the plaintiff or whether the plaintiff was in the zone of danger of impact. If the plaintiff witnesses someone else's injury, recovery may depend on whether the plaintiff suffered a physical injury, was also in the zone of danger, was closely related to the person whose injury the plaintiff witnessed, suffered serious or severe emotional distress that was foreseeable, etc.

KEY TERMS

pain and suffering   160

intentional infliction of emotional distress   160

outrage   160

extreme or outrageous   164

intent   165

recklessness   165

transferred intent   166

severe emotional distress   166

physical injury   166

causation   167

actual malice   171

negligent infliction of emotional distress (NIED)   172

physical impact   173

zone of danger   173

C H A P T E R

10

Conversion and Trespass to Chattels

CHAPTER OUTLINE

- Introduction
- Damages
- Kind of Interference
- Mistake Defense

INTRODUCTION

If someone accidently damages your personal property (also called a **chattel**) e.g., a motorist dents the right fender of your car in a collision, you may be able to sue for negligence. Suppose, however, that the interference is *intentional* rather than accidental, e.g., someone steals your fountain pen from your bag or decides to "borrow" your car for an hour without your permission. Your remedy in such cases is the tort of **conversion** or the tort of **trespass to chattels.** The major distinction between the two torts is the degree of interference that is involved. If the interference is relatively minor, the tort to use is trespass to chattels. A more serious interference justifies an action for conversion.

 Conversion and Trespass to Chattels Checklist

Definitions, Relationships, Paralegal Roles, and Research References

Category of These Torts
They are both intentional torts.

Interests Protected by These Torts
Conversion: The right to be free from serious intentional interferences with personal property.
Trespass to Chattels: The right to be free from intentional interferences with personal property resulting in dispossession or intermeddling.

Elements of These Torts
Conversion:

    i. Personal property (chattel)
    ii. The plaintiff is in possession of the chattel or is entitled to immediate possession
    iii. Intent to exercise dominion or control over the chattel
    iv. Serious interference with plaintiff's possession
    v. Causation (of element iv)

Trespass to Chattels:

    i. Personal property (chattel)
    ii. The plaintiff is in possession of the chattel or is entitled to immediate possession
    iii. Intent to dispossess or to intermeddle with the chattel
    iv. Dispossession or intermeddling
    v. Causation (of element iv)

Definitions of Major Words/Phrases in the Elements
Chattel: Tangible or intangible property other than land or things attached to land.
Intent: The desire to exercise control or dominion over the chattel, or the knowledge with substantial certainty that this control or dominion will result from what the defendant does (for conversion). The desire to dispossess or to intermeddle, or the knowledge with substantial certainty that dispossession or intermeddling will result from what the defendant does (for trespass to chattels).
Control: Exerting power over something.
Dominion: Asserting supreme power or authority over something.
Dispossess: To take physical control of the chattel without the consent of the person who has possession, but without exercising dominion over the chattel.
Intermeddle: Make physical contact with the chattel.
Causation: But for what the defendant did, the serious interference with the chattel would not have occurred, or the defendant was a substantial factor in producing the serious interference (for conversion). But for what the defendant did, the plaintiff would not have been dispossessed of the chattel or had it intermeddled with, or the defendant was a substantial factor in producing the dispossession or intermeddling (for trespass to chattel).

Major Defense and Counterargument Possibilities That Need to Be Explored
    1. The property involved was not personal property (not a chattel).
    2. The plaintiff was not in possession or entitled to immediate possession.
    3. There was no intent to exercise dominion or control (for conversion), nor to dispossess or intermeddle (for trespass to chattels).

Conversion and Trespass to Chattels Checklist Continued

4. The interference was not serious enough.
5. The defendant's control over the chattel was trivial. There was no impairment. The plaintiff was not deprived of the use of the chattel for a substantial time.
6. The defendant did not cause the interference with the plaintiff's possession of the chattel.
7. The plaintiff consented to what the defendant did to the chattel and the defendant did not exceed that consent (on the defense of consent, see Chapter 27).
8. The interference with the plaintiff's property occurred while the defendant was defending the defendant's own property against the plaintiff (on the privilege of defense of property and other self-help privileges, see Chapter 27).
9. The interference with the plaintiff's property occurred while the defendant was recapturing the defendant's own property from the plaintiff (on the recapture of property and other self-help privileges, see Chapter 27).
10. The interference with the plaintiff's property occurred while the defendant was protecting person or property (on necessity and other self-help privileges, see Chapter 27).
11. The interference with the plaintiff's property occurred while the defendant was abating a nuisance (on abating a nuisance and other self-help privileges, see Chapters 23 and 27).
12. The plaintiff's suit against the government for conversion or trespass to chattels committed by a government employee may be barred by sovereign immunity (on sovereign immunity, see Chapter 27).
13. The plaintiff's suit against the government employee for conversion or trespass to chattels may be barred by public official immunity (on official immunity, see Chapter 27).
14. The plaintiff's suit against the charitable organization for conversion or trespass to chattels committed by someone working for the organization may be barred by charitable immunity (on charitable immunity, see Chapter 27).
15. The plaintiff failed to take reasonable steps to mitigate the harm caused when the defendant committed trespass to chattels; therefore, damages should not cover the aggravation of the harm caused by the plaintiff (on the doctrine of avoidable consequences, see Chapter 16).

Damages
In conversion, the plaintiff recovers the full fair market value of the chattel at the time and place of the conversion. In trespass to chattels, the plaintiff's recovery is limited to harm or injury caused the chattel, e.g., repair costs and cost of renting a substitute. If malice or hatred existed, punitive damages are also possible.

Relationship to Criminal Law
A number of crimes may also be involved in addition to these torts: theft or larceny, embezzlement, false pretenses, receiving stolen property, robbery, extortion, blackmail, burglary, etc.

Relationship to Other Torts
Misrepresentation: The defendant's interference with the chattel of plaintiff may have occurred through misrepresentation, so that this tort plus conversion or trespass to chattels are committed.
Negligence: If the plaintiff cannot establish that the interference with his or her property was intentional, he or she may be able to show negligence if there was unreasonable conduct by the defendant and actual harm to the property.

Federal Law
a. Under the Federal Tort Claims Act, the United States Government will be liable for claims arising out of conversion or trespass to chattels committed by one of its federal employees within the scope of employment (respondeat superior). (See Figure 27–7 in Chapter 27.)
b. There may be liability under the Civil Rights Act if the conversion or trespass to chattels was committed while the defendant was depriving the plaintiff of federal rights under color of law. (See Figure 27–9 in Chapter 27.)

Employer-Employee (Agency) Law
An employee who commits conversion or trespass to chattels is personally liable for this tort. His or her employer will *also* be liable for these torts if the conduct of the employee was

Conversion and Trespass to Chattels Checklist Continued

within the scope of employment (respondeat superior). The employee must be furthering a business objective of the employer at the time. (On the factors that determine the scope of employment, see Figure 14–10 in Chapter 14.)

Paralegal Roles in Conversion or Trespass to Chattels Litigation
(See also Figures 3–1, 3–14, and 29–1 in Chapters 3 and 29.)

Fact finding (help the office collect facts relevant to prove the elements of conversion or trespass to chattels, the elements of available defenses, and extent of injuries or other damages):
- client interviewing
- field investigation
- online research (e.g., blue book value of a used car)

File management (help the office control the volume of paperwork in a conversion or trespass to chattels litigation):
- open client file
- enter case data in computer database
- maintain file documents

Litigation assistance (help the trial attorney prepare for a conversion or trespass to chattels trial and appeal, if needed):
- draft discovery requests
- draft answers to discovery requests
- draft pleadings
- digest and index discovery documents
- help prepare, order, and manage trial exhibits (visuals or demonstratives)
- prepare trial notebook
- draft notice of appeal
- order trial transcript
- cite check briefs
- perform legal research

Collection/enforcement (help the trial attorney for the judgment creditor to collect the damages award or enforce other court orders at the conclusion of the conversion or trespass to chattels case):
- draft postjudgment discovery requests
- field investigation to monitor compliance with judgment
- online research (e.g., location of defendant's business assets)

Research References for Conversion and Trespass to Chattels

Digests
In the digests of West, look for case summaries on these torts under key topics such as:

Conversion	Bailments
Trover and Conversion	Torts
Property	Damages

Corpus Juris Secundum
In this legal encyclopedia, see the discussion under topic headings such as:

Conversion	Bailments
Trover and Conversion	Torts
Property	Damages

American Jurisprudence 2d
In this legal encyclopedia, see the discussion under topic headings such as:

Conversion	Abandoned, Lost and Unclaimed Property
Property	Damages
Bailments	Torts

Legal Periodical Literature
There are two index systems to use to locate legal periodical literature on these torts:

Conversion and Trespass to Chattels Checklist Continued

INDEX TO LEGAL PERIODICALS *AND BOOKS (ILP)*	*CURRENT LEGAL INDEX* *(CLI)*

See literature in *ILP* under subject
headings such as:
  Conversion
  Personal Property
  Property
  Torts
  Damages
  Bailments
	See literature in *CLI* under subject
	headings such as:
	  Personal Property
	  Torts
	  Property
	  Bailments
	  Intangible Property
	  Damages
	  Fraudulent Conveyances

Example of a legal periodical article you will find by using *ILP* or *CLI*:

> *Commercial Exploitation of DNA and the Tort of Conversion: A Physician May Not Destroy a Patient's Interest in Her Body-Matter* by Aaron C. Lichtman, 34 New York Law School Law Review 531 (1989).

A.L.R., A.L.R.2d, A.L.R.3d, A.L.R.4th, A.L.R.5th, A.L.R. Fed.
Use the *ALR Index* to locate annotations on these torts. In this index, check subject headings such as:

Trover and Conversion	Property Damages
Conversion	Personal Property
Damages	Torts

Example of an annotation you can locate through these subject headings on these torts:

Punitive or Exemplary Damages for Conversion of Personality by One Other Than Chattel Mortgagee or Conditional Seller by E. LeFevre, 54 A.L.R.2d 1361 (1957).

Words and Phrases
In this multivolume legal dictionary, look up *conversion, trespass to chattels, chattels, dispossession, dominion, bona fide purchaser,* and every other word or phrase connected with conversion and trespass to chattels discussed in this chapter. The dictionary will give you definitions of these words or phrases from court opinions.

CALR: Computer-Assisted Legal Research
Example of a query you could ask on WESTLAW or on LEXIS to try to find cases, statutes, or other legal materials on conversion and trespass to chattels: **conversion /p damages**

Example of search terms you could use on an Internet legal search engine such as LawCrawler (http://lawcrawler.findlaw.com) to find cases, statutes, or other legal materials on conversion and trespass to chattels: **conversion AND tort AND damages**

Example of search terms you could use on an Internet general search engine such as Alta Vista (http://www.altavista.com) to find cases, statutes, or other legal materials on conversion and trespass to chattels: **+conversion +tort +damages**

More Internet sites to check for materials on conversion, trespass to chattels, and other torts:
Jurist: (http://jurist.law.pitt.edu/sg_torts.htm)
LawGuru: (http://www.lawguru.com/search/lawsearch.html)
See also Tort Law Online at the end of Chapter 1.

DAMAGES

A successful plaintiff in an action for trespass to chattels can recover the cost of repairs or the cost of temporarily renting a replacement for the chattel. For major or aggravated interferences, the plaintiff can sue for conversion, for which the recovery is the full value of the chattel at the time it was converted. In effect, the party that interfered with the chattel is forced to buy it—even if this wrongdoer later offers to return the chattel in its original condition.

FIGURE 10–1
Factors considered by a court to determine whether an interference with a chattel is serious enough for conversion.[1]

- The extent and duration of the defendant's exercise of control or dominion over the chattel; the more substantial and lengthy the interference, the more likely it will constitute conversion.
- Whether the defendant intended to assert a right in the chattel that was inconsistent with the plaintiff's right of control.
- Whether the defendant acted in good faith or bad faith when interfering with the chattel.
- Whether the interference caused any damage or harm to the chattel.
- Whether the plaintiff suffered any inconvenience or expense as a result of the interference.

[1]W. Page Keeton et al., *Prosser and Keeton on the Law of Torts* 90 (5th ed. 1984). *Restatement (Second) of Torts* §222A (1965).

KIND OF INTERFERENCE

When is an interference serious enough for conversion? There is no absolute answer to this question that will cover every case. The court will consider a number of factors, no one of which is conclusive. The factors are outlined in Figure 10–1.

In general, neither **dispossession** (taking physical control of a chattel without consent but without exercising dominion over it) nor **intermeddling** (making physical contact with a chattel) are serious enough interferences for conversion. Both, however, would constitute trespass to chattels.

Dispossession

> **EXAMPLE:** Dan takes Jim's book for an afternoon and reads it without permission. No damage is done to the book. It is returned. Dan never claims that he owned the book. Jim did not need the book while Dan had it.

Intermeddling

> **EXAMPLE:** Tom is sitting in the park with his new puppy. Paula comes over and starts petting it, even though Tom asks her to stop. The dog growls a little, but is not harmed.

In the intermeddling example, what if Paula accidently got a little ink on the white fur of the puppy? The case is still not serious enough to constitute conversion. In a trespass-to-chattels action, Tom would be limited to recovering any cost associated with cleaning the dog. Suppose, however, that the ink could not be removed or could be removed only by subjecting the dog to a painful chemical procedure. Now the interference may be serious enough to constitute the tort of conversion.

ASSIGNMENT

10.1

Has conversion or trespass to chattels been committed in any of the following cases? (See General Instructions for the Legal Analysis Assignment in Chapter 2.)

a. After an argument, Susan places all of her boyfriend's belongings on the sidewalk in front of Susan's home. The boyfriend watches Susan do this. He sues her for converting his belongings.

b. Same facts as in *a,* except that the boyfriend does not learn about the removal of the belongings until he comes home from work on the day Susan placed them on the sidewalk.

c. George orders a very expensive meal at a restaurant where he is dining alone. He puts his silk jacket on the chair next to where he is sitting and goes to make a phone call in the hall. While away, Ralph, another patron, comes over to George's table. He tries on George's jacket in order to help decide whether he wants to buy one like it. He also pours a few drops of wine from George's glass into an empty glass Ralph brings over. Ralph wants to taste the wine in order to decide whether to order the same wine. George sues Ralph for converting his jacket and his meal.

d. Mary lies to her boyfriend, John, about her use of birth control. When she becomes pregnant, he sues her for converting his semen.

CASE

Russell-Vaughn Ford, Inc. v. E. W. Rouse
281 Ala. 567, 206 So. 2d 371 (1968)
Supreme Court of Alabama

Background: *E. W. Rouse sued Russell-Vaughn Ford for conversion when the dealer failed to return the keys to Rouse's car, a Falcon, which he was negotiating to trade for a new car. The trial court found for Rouse and awarded him $5,000, an amount that included punitive damages. The case is now on appeal before the Supreme Court of Alabama. At the trial, the dealer was the defendant and is now the appellant, the party bringing the appeal. Rouse was the plaintiff at the trial and on appeal is the appellee, the party against whom an appeal is brought. The dealer argued that it converted the keys, not the Falcon.*

Decision on Appeal: *The judgment for Rouse is affirmed. The dealer committed conversion of the Falcon.*

OPINION OF COURT

Justice SIMPSON delivered the opinion of the court . . .

On April 24, 1962, the appellee went to the place of business of Russell-Vaughn Ford, Inc., to discuss trading his Falcon automobile in on a new Ford. He talked with one of the salesmen for a while who offered to trade a new Ford for the Falcon, plus $1,900. The trade was not consummated on this basis, but Mr. Rouse went to his house and picked up his wife and children and returned to the dealer. With his wife and children there Mr. Rouse discussed further the trade but no deal was made that night.

The following night he returned with a friend where further discussions on the trade were had. At the time of this visit one of the salesmen, Virgil Harris, asked Mr. Rouse for the keys to his Falcon. The keys were given to him and Mr. Rouse, his friend, and appellant Parker [another salesman] looked at the new cars for a time and then proceeded with the negotiations with regard to the trade. The testimony indicates that in this conversation the salesman offered to trade a new Ford for the Falcon, plus $2,400. The plaintiff declined to trade on this basis.

At this stage of the negotiations, Mr. Rouse asked for the return of the keys to the Falcon. The evidence is to the effect that both salesmen to whom Rouse had talked said that they did not know where the keys were. Mr. Rouse then asked several people who appeared to be employees of Russell-Vaughn for the keys. He further asked several people in the building if they knew where his keys were. The testimony indicates that there were a number of people around who were aware of the fact that the appellee was seeking to have the keys to his car returned. Several mechanics and salesmen were, according to plaintiff's testimony, sitting around on cars looking at him and laughing at him.

After a period of time the plaintiff called the police department of the City of Birmingham. In response to his call Officer Montgomery came to the showroom of Russell-Vaughn Ford and was informed by the plaintiff that he was unable to get his keys back. Shortly after the arrival of the policeman, according to the policeman's testimony, the salesman Parker threw the keys to Mr. Rouse with the statement that he was a cry baby and that "they just wanted to see him cry a while."

The evidence is abundant to the effect that Mr. Rouse made a number of efforts to have his keys returned to him. He talked to the salesmen, to the manager, to mechanics, etc. and was met in many instances with laughter as if the entire matter was a "big joke" . . . .

The appellants have . . . argued that the facts of this case do not make out a case of conversion. It is argued that the conversion if at all, [is] a conversion of the keys to the automobile, not of the automobile itself. It is further contended that there was not under the case here presented a conversion at all. We are not persuaded that the law of Alabama supports this proposition. As noted in *Long-Lewis Hardware Co. v. Abston,* 235 Ala. 599, 180 So. 261,

"It has been held by this court that 'the fact of conversion does not necessarily import an acquisition of property in the defendant.' Howton v. Mathias, 197 Ala. 457, 73 So. 92, 95. The conversion may consist, not only in an appropriation of the property to one's own use, but in its destruction, or in exercising dominion over it in exclusion or defiance of plaintiff's right. McGill v. Hollman, 208 Ala. 9, 93 So. 848, 31 A.L.R. 941, 948." (Emphasis added.)

It is not contended that the plaintiff here had no right to demand the return of the keys to his automobile. Rather, the appellants seem to be arguing that there was no conversion which the law will recognize under the facts of this case because the defendants did not commit sufficient acts to amount to a conversion. We cannot agree. A remarkable admission in this regard was elicited by the plaintiff in examining one of the witnesses for the defense. It seems that according to salesman for Russell-Vaughn Ford, Inc. it is a rather usual practice in the automobile business to "lose keys" to cars belonging to potential customers. We see nothing in our cases which requires in a conversion case that the plaintiff prove that the defendant appropriated the property to his own use; rather, as noted in the cases referred to above, it is enough that he show that the defendant exercised dominion over it in exclusion or defiance of the right of the plaintiff. We think that has been done here. The jury so found and we cannot concur that a case for conversion has not been made on these facts.

Further, appellants argue that there was no conversion since the plaintiff could have called his wife at home, who had another set of keys and thereby gained the ability to move his automobile. We find nothing in our cases which would require the plaintiff to exhaust all possible means of gaining possession of a chattel which is withheld from him

by the defendant, after demanding its return. On the contrary, it is the refusal, without legal excuse, to deliver a chattel, which constitutes a conversion. *Compton v. Sims,* 209 Ala. 287, 96 So. 185.

We find unconvincing the appellants' contention that if there were a conversion at all, it was the conversion of the automobile keys, and not of the automobile. In *Compton v. Sims,* supra, this court sustained a finding that there had been a conversion of cotton where the defendant refused to deliver to the plaintiff "warehouse tickets" which would have enabled him to gain possession of the cotton. The court spoke of the warehouse tickets as a symbol of the cotton and found that the retention of them amounted to a conversion of the cotton. So here, we think that the withholding from the plaintiff after demand of the keys to his automobile, without which he could not move it, amounted to a conversion of the automobile.

It is next argued by appellants that the amount of the verdict is excessive. It is not denied that punitive damages are recoverable here in the discretion of the jury. In *Roan v. McCaleb,* 264 Ala. 31, 84 So.2d 358, this court held:

> "If the conversion was committed in known violation of the law and of plaintiff's rights with circumstances of insult, or contumely, or malice, punitive damages were recoverable in the discretion of the jury."

We think that the evidence justifies the jury's conclusion that these circumstances existed in this case. . . . We are clear to the conclusion that the evidence supports the verdict of the jury. . . .

Affirmed.

ASSIGNMENT

10.2

a. Would this case have reached the same result if the dealer made Rouse wait an hour in the showroom before returning the keys?

b. Sam owns a house on Main Street. He is outside his home in a wheelchair. A neighbor locks all the doors to Sam's house. Sam is not able to get into his house until the next day when he hires someone to force his way in. Has the neighbor converted Sam's house? The furnishings and other personal belongings in the house?

c. Bill and Fred have an argument over money. Bill takes Fred's wallet. In the wallet, there is a garage ticket that Fred needs to obtain his car. The garage will not return the car without the ticket or written proof that Fred owns the car. It takes Fred four days to obtain the documents needed to prove the car is his. Has Bill converted the car? Has the garage?

MISTAKE DEFENSE

It is not a defense that the defendant acted in good faith or made a reasonable **mistake,** although this is one of the overall factors that the court will take into consideration in determining whether the interference is serious enough for conversion.

> **EXAMPLE:**   Lena steals Sam's rifle. She offers to sell the rifle to Ed, who has no idea where she got it. Ed buys it for $200. Lena disappears. When Sam finds out what happened, he demands that Ed return the rifle. Ed refuses. Sam then sues Ed for conversion.

Sam will win. It is no defense that Ed is a **bona fide purchaser** who bought the rifle thinking that Lena had the right to sell it. Ed intended to exercise total ownership and control over the gun when he bought it. This was in full contradiction to Sam's rights in the rifle. (A bona fide purchaser is someone who purchases property for value without notice of defects in the title of the seller to the property.)

ASSIGNMENT 10.3

Ted grows valuable and expensive orchids in his backyard. It is the end of the growing season. He has two orchids remaining from his most expensive variety. He cuts one and places it in a basket in the yard next to the one still growing. Later that afternoon, Janice, one of Ted's houseguests, mistakenly thinks Ted is throwing away the orchid in the basket. She takes it from the basket and also cuts the one still growing. She puts them both in her suitcase. The next morning she wonders whether she made a mistake in taking the orchids without asking Ted. When Ted finds out what Janice did, he sues her for conversion. What result? (See General Instructions for the Legal Analysis Assignment in Chapter 2.)

CASE

Moore v. The Regents of the University of California
51 Cal. 3d 120, 793 P.2d 479, 271 Cal. Rptr. 146 (1990)
Supreme Court of California

Background: *John Moore underwent treatment for hairy-cell leukemia at the UCLA Medical Center, which is operated by the Regents of the University of California. The doctors withdrew blood, skin, bone marrow aspirate, sperm, and his spleen. Unknown to Moore, the defendants were using his cells in research on regulating the immune system through the techniques of recombinant DNA. The research was successful. The defendants established a cell line from Moore's T-lymphocytes and applied for a patent on the cell line, which they received. Some biotechnology reports predict a potential market of over three billion dollars in this area. When Moore found out what role his cells played in this development, he sued for breach of a duty to disclose and for conversion. The trial court ruled against Moore. The case is now on appeal before the Supreme Court of California.*

Decision on Appeal: *The use of excised human cells in medical research does not amount to a conversion. Moore, however, can sue for breach of a physician's fiduciary duty to disclose information needed by a patient to make an informed consent to treatment.*

OPINION OF COURT
Justice PANELLI delivered the opinion of the court . . .
Moore . . . attempts to characterize the invasion of his rights as a conversion—a tort that protects against interfer-

ence with possessory and ownership interests in personal property. He theorizes that he continued to own his cells following their removal from his body, at least for the purpose of directing their use, and that he never consented to their use in potentially lucrative medical research. Thus, to complete Moore's argument, defendants' unauthorized use of his cells constitutes a conversion. As a result of the alleged conversion, Moore claims a proprietary interest in each of the products that any of the defendants might ever create from his cells or the patented cell line. . . .

In effect, what Moore is asking us to do is to impose a tort duty on scientists to investigate the consensual pedigree of each human cell sample used in research. To impose such a duty, which would affect medical research of importance to all of society, implicates policy concerns far removed from the traditional, two-party ownership disputes in which the law of conversion arose. Invoking a tort theory originally used to determine whether the loser or the finder of a horse had the better title, Moore claims ownership of the results of socially important medical research, including the genetic code for chemicals that regulate the functions of every human being's immune system. . . .

"To establish a conversion, plaintiff must establish an actual interference with his *ownership* or *right of possession.* . . . Where plaintiff neither has title to the property alleged to have been converted, nor possession thereof, he cannot maintain an action for conversion." (*Del E. Webb Corp. v. Structural Materials Co.* (1981) 123 Cal. App. 3d 593, 610–611.)

Since Moore clearly did not expect to retain possession of his cells following their removal, to sue for their conversion he must have retained an ownership interest in them. But . . . California statutory law . . . drastically limits a patient's control over excised cells. Pursuant to Health and Safety Code section 7054.4, "[n]otwithstanding any other provision of law, recognizable anatomical parts, human tissues, anatomical human remains, or infectious waste following conclusion of scientific use shall be disposed of by interment, incineration, or any other method determined by the state department [of health services] to protect the public health and safety." Clearly the Legislature did not specifically intend this statute to resolve the question of whether a patient is entitled to compensation for the nonconsensual use of excised cells. A primary object of the statute is to ensure the safe handling of potentially hazardous biological waste materials. Yet one cannot escape the conclusion that the statute's practical effect is to limit, drastically, a patient's control over excised cells. By restricting how excised cells may be used and requiring their eventual destruction, the statute eliminates so many of the rights ordinarily attached to property that one cannot simply assume that what is left amounts to "property" or "ownership" for purposes of conversion law.

It may be that some limited right to control the use of excised cells does survive the operation of this statute. There is, for example, no need to read the statute to permit "scientific use" contrary to the patient's expressed wish. A fully informed patient may always withhold consent to treatment by a physician whose research plans the patient does not approve. That right, however . . . is protected by the fiduciary-duty and informed-consent theories.

Finally, the subject matter of the Regents' patent—the patented cell line and the products derived from it—cannot be Moore's property. This is because the patented cell line is both factually and legally distinct from the cells taken from Moore's body. Federal law permits the patenting of organisms that represent the product of "human ingenuity," but not naturally occurring organisms. . . . It is this *inventive effort* that patent law rewards, not the discovery of naturally occurring raw materials. Thus, Moore's allegations that he owns the cell line and the products derived from it are inconsistent with the patent, which constitutes an authoritative determination that the cell line is the product of invention. . . .

[A competent patient does have a right] to make autonomous medical decisions. That right . . . is grounded in well-recognized and long-standing principles of fiduciary duty and informed consent. This policy weighs in favor of providing a remedy to patients when physicians act with undisclosed motives that may affect their professional judgment. . . . [But we should] not threaten with disabling civil liability innocent parties who are engaged in socially useful activities, such as researchers who have no reason to be-

lieve that their use of a particular cell sample is, or may be, against a donor's wishes. . . .

We need not, however, make an arbitrary choice between liability and nonliability. Instead, an examination of the relevant policy considerations suggests an appropriate balance: Liability based upon existing disclosure obligations, rather than an unprecedented extension of the conversion theory, protects patients' rights of privacy and autonomy without unnecessarily hindering research.

To be sure, the threat of liability for conversion might help to enforce patients' rights indirectly. This is because physicians might be able to avoid liability by obtaining patients' consent, in the broadest possible terms, to any conceivable subsequent research use of excised cells. Unfortunately, to extend the conversion theory would utterly sacrifice the other goal of protecting innocent parties. . . . [It] would impose liability on all those into whose hands the cells come, whether or not the particular defendant participated in, or knew of, the inadequate disclosures that violated the patient's right to make an informed decision. In contrast to the conversion theory, the fiduciary-duty and informed-consent theories protect the patient directly, without punishing innocent parties or creating disincentives to the conduct of socially beneficial research. . . .

[T]he theory of liability that Moore urges us to endorse threatens to destroy the economic incentive to conduct important medical research. If the use of cells in research is a conversion, then with every cell sample a researcher purchases a ticket in a litigation lottery. . . .

If the scientific users of human cells are to be held liable for failing to investigate the consensual pedigree of their raw materials, we believe the Legislature should make that decision. Complex policy choices affecting all society are involved, and "[l]egislatures, in making such policy decisions, have the ability to gather empirical evidence, solicit the advice of experts, and hold hearings at which all interested parties present evidence and express their views. . . ." (*Foley v. Interactive Data Corp.* (1988) 47 Cal. 3d 654, 694, 765 P.2d 373.)

Finally, there is no pressing need to impose a judicially created rule of strict liability, since enforcement of physicians' disclosure obligations will protect patients against the very type of harm with which Moore was threatened. So long as a physician discloses research and economic interests that may affect his judgment, the patient is protected from conflicts of interest. Aware of any conflicts, the patient can make an informed decision to consent to treatment, or to withhold consent and look elsewhere for medical assistance. As already discussed, enforcement of physicians' disclosure obligations protects patients directly, without hindering the socially useful activities of innocent researchers.

For these reasons, we hold that the allegations of Moore's . . . complaint state a cause of action for breach of fiduciary duty or lack of informed consent, but not conversion. . . .

a. The doctors that treated Moore had a conflict of interest. What was the conflict?

b. In most states, you have the right to make a gift of your eyes or other organs. Is the decision in *Moore* inconsistent with this right?

c. Assume that after the UCLA Medical Center doctor extracts blood, skin, bone marrow aspirate, and sperm from Moore (plus his spleen), a doctor from another hospital breaks into the UCLA Medical Center and steals everything extracted from Moore. The doctors and researchers in this other hospital then use it in their own research, which leads to the patent. Do the UCLA doctor and the UCLA Medical Center have an action for conversion? If so, who would the plaintiff be? John Moore? UCLA?

SUMMARY

The torts of conversion and trespass to chattels are designed to provide a remedy for intentional interferences with personal property. If the interference is serious, conversion is the appropriate remedy, requiring the wrongdoer to pay the plaintiff the full value of the chattel converted. Trespass to chattels covers less serious interferences. If the act constituting interference is intentional, it is no defense that the interference was an innocent mistake, as in the case of a bona fide purchaser.

KEY TERMS

chattel   180

conversion   180

trespass to chattels   180

dispossession   184

intermeddling   184

mistake   186

bona fide purchaser   187

11

Strict Liability

CHAPTER OUTLINE

- Introduction
- Animals
- Strict Liability for Abnormally Dangerous Conditions or Activities

INTRODUCTION

As we saw in Chapter 1, there are three main categories of torts: intentional torts, negligence, and strict liability torts. **Strict liability** (sometimes referred to as **absolute liability** or **liability without fault**) means responsibility regardless of blameworthiness or fault. Persons who engage in certain kinds of activity will be liable or responsible for the harm that results even if they acted with the greatest of care to avoid the harm. The normal method of demonstrating blameworthiness or fault is for the plaintiff to show that the defendant's conduct fit within one of the intentional torts or was unreasonable (negligent). For some activities, however, the blameworthiness or fault of the defendant is irrelevant. As a matter of social policy, the law says that when designated activities cause harm, the defendant must pay—whether the defendant acted innocently, intentionally, or negligently. The same is true for harm that results from certain conditions that exist on the defendant's land.

In this chapter we will consider two categories of harm that lead to strict liability: harm caused by animals and harm caused by abnormally dangerous conditions or activities. In Chapter 19 on products liability, we will examine the separate tort called **strict liability in tort,** which covers harm caused by a defective product irrespective of the blameworthiness or fault of the manufacturer or distributor of the product.

One final point before we begin: there is some overlap among the three categories of torts studied in this book. For example, some of the intentional torts will lead to liability even though it may be difficult to find blameworthiness or fault in the defendant's conduct. Also, as we will see later, it is sometimes difficult to distinguish between negligence and the tort called strict liability in tort. Nevertheless, categorizing torts is useful as a starting point in studying tort law. Be prepared, however, to find an absence of rigid boundary lines among the various torts.

ANIMALS

The Centers for Disease Control and Prevention estimates that each year dogs bite 4.7 million people, 800,000 of whom require medical treatment. Half of all children are bitten by a dog before their twelfth birthday.[1] When a dog or other animal causes harm, the owner might be liable under several possible theories of recovery. The cause of action might be an intentional tort or negligence.

> **EXAMPLES:** Mary knows that her dog is aggressive around strangers. One day in the park, she guides her dog close to the leg of a stranger so that the dog will take a bite. The dog does so. Mary has committed a battery because she intended a harmful or offensive contact (see Chapter 5).
>
> Mary knows that her dog is aggressive around strangers. To prevent the dog from bothering anyone, she keeps the dog on a leash. One day in a crowded park, however, she carelessly drops the leash so that she can read a newspaper on the bench. A stranger walking by is bitten by the dog. Mary has committed negligence because her failure to use reasonable care caused harm (see Chapter 14).

What about strict liability? Can a pet owner be strictly liable for harm caused by an animal even if no intentional tort or negligence has been committed? The answer depends, in part, on whether the animal is wild or domestic.

---

[1] Jane E. Brody, *Heeding the Warnings From Dangerous Dogs,* N.Y. Times, May 18, 1999, at D8.

Wild Animals

A **wild animal** is an animal in the state of nature, e.g., lion, bear, monkey. In most states, an owner (or keeper) of a wild animal will be strictly liable for any harm it causes whether or not the owner knew of the animal's dangerous propensities, irrespective of how well trained the animal may have been, and regardless of how much care the owner took to prevent harm to others by the animal.

Domestic Animals

A **domestic animal** is an animal that has been domesticated or habituated to live among humans, e.g., dog, cat, horse. An owner (or keeper) of a domestic animal will be strictly liable for the harm it causes if two elements can be established:

  i.   owner has reason to know the animal has a specific propensity to cause harm, and
  ii. harm caused by the animal was due to that specific propensity.

> **EXAMPLE:**   George knows that his dog, Fido, likes to bite joggers. Fido has never bothered anyone else. One day the dog bites Tom, a jogger. A few hours later, Fido knocks down Mary, a neighbor, while she is gardening.

In most states, George will be strictly liable to Tom since biting was a known propensity. There was no known propensity, however, for knocking people down. Therefore, there would be no strict liability to Mary. If she wants to recover, she must show that George was negligent in failing to prevent Fido from knocking her down or that he intended this result.

Occasionally, you will see the phrase, "every dog is entitled to one free bite." The implication of this statement is that an owner won't know about the propensity of the dog to bite until the dog has claimed its first human victim. Yet, this is not accurate. There might be other evidence of this propensity, e.g., the dog's inclination to lunge toward everyone with its mouth wide open. Another reason the first bite may not be "free" is that an owner might be subject to negligence liability for failing to control an obviously feisty and aggressive dog even if the dog has never bitten anyone.

A few states have passed special statutes that impose strict liability for harm caused by domestic animals with no known dangerous propensities. In effect, such statutes treat domestic animals the same as wild animals.

ASSIGNMENT

11.1

Sam knows that his dog bites other dogs. One day Sam's dog bites a stranger, the first time it has ever attacked a human. Is Sam subject to strict liability? (See General Instructions for the Legal Analysis Assignment in Chapter 2.)

CASE

Nardi v. Gonzalez
165 Misc. 2d 336, 630 N.Y.S.2d 215 (1995)
City Court of Yonkers

Background: *A 110-pound German shepherd injures two small dogs. The owners of the small dogs, the Nardis, sue the owner of the German shepherd, Mrs. Gonzalez, for strict liability.*

Decision of Court: *Mrs. Gonzalez is strictly liable.*

OPINION OF COURT
   Judge DICKERSON delivered the opinion of the court:
   Bianca and Pepe are diminutive, curly coated Bichon Frises and are, respectively, 9 years old and 3 years old. Bianca and Pepe are owned by the plaintiffs, Dusolina and

Alfred Nardi ["the Nardis"], . . . Ace is a large 5 year old German Shepherd weighing 110 pounds. Ace is owned by the defendant, Maureen Gonzalez [Mrs. Gonzalez], . . . On March 24, 1993 and again on June 16, 1994, Mrs. Gonzalez allowed Ace to run loose without a leash. On these two occasions Ace entered onto the Nardis' property and viciously attacked Bianca causing severe injuries. On both occasions, Bianca was taken to a veterinarian for treatment of the wounds inflicted by Ace. The veterinarian bills were $392 for the March 24, 1993 attack and $182 for the June 16, 1994 attack.

On June 22, 1994 the Nardis commenced a lawsuit before this Court seeking damages for the injuries sustained by Bianca and themselves. After a trial held on October 26, 1994, this Court (Smith, J.) found Ace and its owner Mrs. Gonzalez responsible ["Considering the disparate sizes of the animals and all the circumstances. . . ."] for the injuries inflicted upon Bianca ["Ace bit (Bianca) causing bite wounds and bleeding"] and awarded damages of $524.

On February 4, 1995, Pepe, the younger Bichon Frise, was with his owner, Alfred Nardi, who was in his driveway shoveling snow. Ace suddenly appeared, sniffed Pepe and then, without provocation, viciously attacked and mauled Pepe. Alfred Nardi chased Ace away and took Pepe to the veterinarian. Pepe remained hospitalized for four days undergoing surgery. The photographs introduced at trial show a 10 inch gash held together with surgical staples running from Pepe's stomach to his back. The veterinarian bills for Pepe's hospitalization, care and treatment were $819, considerably more than those incurred by Bianca just the year before.

In this action, the plaintiffs seek damages to include the costs of veterinarian services [$819], two days lost wages in caring for Pepe [$156] and all other appropriate damages. In response Mrs. Gonzalez stated that she had built a fence around her backyard to keep Ace enclosed. Unfortunately, Ace escaped from the enclosure on February 4, 1995, went to the Nardi's house and mauled Pepe. Based upon the facts of this case the Court finds that plaintiffs have stated a cognizable cause of action for strict liability for injuries caused by a vicious and dangerous dog.

Dogs can be wonderful companions and loyal guardians. On occasion, however, dogs can also be vicious animals that annoy and wound men, women and children. . . . *Coleman v. Blake,* 128 N.Y.S.2d 780, 781–782 (1954) ("Mrs. Coleman proffered the dog a bit of cheese. Man's best friend rewarded her affection by taking a bite out of her proboscis, and in so doing nipped a beautiful friendship in its origin. . .", damages of $7,500 for injuries, medical expenses and loss of earnings); *Fontecchio v. Esposito,* 108 A.D.2d 780, 485 N.Y.S.2d 113 (1985) (dog bites woman, damages of $240,000 and $70,000 reversed as excessive); *Zager v. Dimilia,* 138 Misc. 2d 448, 524 N.Y.S.2d 968 (1988) (McDuff bites Tucker, damages limited to veterinarian bills, no punitive damages without evidence of prior known bites); *Corso v. Crawford Dog and Cat Hospital, Inc.,* 97 Misc. 2d 530, 415 N.Y.S.2d 182, 183 (1979) ("a pet is not just a thing but occupies a special place somewhere in between a person and a piece of personal property", damages of $700); *Fowler v. Town of Ticonderoga,* 131 A.D.2d 919, 516 N.Y.S.2d 368 (1987) (dog shot by Dog Control Officer, no damages for owner's psychic trauma).

Some dogs can be more vicious and dangerous than others. For example, German Shepherds are large, intelligent and strong and, if trained properly, can serve as trusted guard dogs and police dogs. Without proper training, however, German Shepherds can be vicious, indeed [see e.g., *Ford v. Steindon,* 35 Misc. 2d 339, 232 N.Y.S.2d 473, 474 (1962) (vicious German Shepherd attacks man, "the dog . . . was a German Shepherd colloquially known as a police dog . . . It has been said that with respect to such dogs 'it is a matter of common knowledge that the court can almost take judicial knowledge of the fact that police dogs are, by nature, vicious, inheriting the wild and untamed characteristics of their wolf ancestors' "); *DiGrazia v. Castronova,* 48 A.D.2d 249, 368 N.Y.S.2d 898 (1975) (vicious German Shepherd [*Sam*] attacks six year old boy); *Lagoda v. Dorr,* 28 A.D.2d 208, 284 N.Y.S.2d 130 (1967) (vicious German Shepherd attacks boy on bicycle knocking him to ground); *Strunk v. Zoltanski,* 62 N.Y.2d 572, 479 N.Y.S.2d 175, 468 N.E.2d 13 (1984) (dangerous German Shepherd bites infant on mouth and arms); *Application of Fugazy,* 82 Misc. 2d 135, 368 N.Y.S.2d 652 (Harrison Town Ct. West. Cty. 1974) (two dangerous German Shepherds [Kelly & Murphy] attack, bite and chase fifteen year old boy)].

New York recognizes a cause of action which imposes strict liability [no proof of negligence necessary] upon owners for injuries inflicted by their vicious dogs, the owners having knowledge thereof and viciousness being defined as prior bites and/or mischievous propensities [see e.g., *Wheaton v. Guthrie,* 89 A.D.2d 809, 453 N.Y.S.2d 480 ("strict liability 'vicious dog' cause of action . . . the proof established that (the dog) had a vicious propensity known to the defendant. A vicious propensity is the tendency of a dog to do an act which might endanger another . . ."); *Morales v. Quinones,* 72 A.D.2d 519, 420 N.Y.S.2d 899, 900 (1979) ("Liability in vicious propensity or dog bite cases is 'absolute' . . . and is not dependent upon proof of negligence in the manner of keeping the animal. . . The keeping of the animal, knowing its vicious propensities is the gravamen of the offense. . ."); *Lagoda v. Dorr,* supra, 28 A.D.2d at 209, 284 N.Y.S.2d, at 132 ("The doctrine that every dog is entitled to 'one free bite', if it ever prevailed in this State, is no longer followed. . . The gravamen of the action is the knowledge of the owner that the dog was possessed of vicious or mischievous propensities. . ."); *Coleman v. Blake,* supra, at 128 N.Y.S.2d 781 ("Knowing dog's waspish nature and a bite of record. . ."); *Fox v. Martin,* 174 A.D.2d 875, 571 N.Y.S.2d 161, 162 (1991) (cause of action requires evidence of prior bites or vicious propensities and owner's knowledge thereof)].

In this case Mrs. Gonzalez knew full well that Ace possessed vicious propensities since on two prior occasions Ace had viciously attacked Bianca causing substantial injuries for which this Court (Smith, J.) found her liable and responsible. That Mrs. Gonzalez thereafter constructed a fence to enclose Ace is of no significance [see *Lynch v. Nacewicz,* 511 N.Y.S.2d 121, 122 (1987) ("Liability is not dependent upon proof of negligence in the manner of keeping or confining the animal. . .")] since, in fact, Ace escaped on February 4, 1995 and viciously attacked and mauled Pepe. All of the elements of a strict liability cause of action-vicious dog are met herein and the Court finds Mrs. Gonzalez strictly liable for all appropriate damages.

The Court awards the following damages to the plaintiffs. First, damages will include the $819 veterinarian bills for Pepe's hospitalization, care and treatment; second, damages will include $156 lost wages incurred by Alfred Nardi in caring for Pepe; third, this Court finds defendant's misconduct to be morally culpable [see e.g., *Walker v. Sheldon,* 10 N.Y.2d 401, 223 N.Y.S.2d 488, 490, 179 N.E.2d 497 (1961)]. Ace was a dangerous instrumentality and defendant knew of the dog's vicious propensities. Punitive damages are appropriate in this case and are needed to deter other dog owners from failing to protect humans and other animals from vicious and dangerous dogs. Further, such damages will encourage defendant to take appropriate measures in the future to protect her neighbors from Ace or similar like minded dogs. The Court awards plaintiffs punitive damages of $1,000.

Ordered accordingly.

ASSIGNMENT 11.2

a. Does the court say that all owners of German shepherds will always be strictly liable for the harm they cause?

b. Do you agree with the award of punitive damages against Mrs. Gonzalez? What could she have done to avoid punitive damages so that she would pay only the vet bills and lost wages?

c. Reread the facts of Assignment 11.1. How would *Nardi v. Gonzalez* apply to Sam? Would he be strictly liable for the harm his dog caused the stranger? Give arguments for both sides on the applicability of *Nardi.*

STRICT LIABILITY FOR ABNORMALLY DANGEROUS CONDITIONS OR ACTIVITIES

Next we examine those conditions or activities causing harm that can lead to strict liability. The tort is called **strict liability for abnormally dangerous conditions or activities** and sometimes, absolute liability for abnormally dangerous conditions or activities. It is important to keep in mind that the defendant is not necessarily home free if the plaintiff fails to establish that the condition or activity of the defendant qualifies for strict liability status. The plaintiff may still be able to win by showing that the defendant committed other torts such as trespass to land, nuisance, or negligence in maintaining the condition or engaging in the activity.

Most of the cases on strict liability for abnormally dangerous conditions or activities involve the way in which the defendant uses or abuses his or her land. It is also possible, however, to commit this tort while on someone else's land, e.g., transporting a large quantity of explosives over a neighbor's land or over a public highway.

 Strict Liability for Abnormally Dangerous Conditions or Activities Checklist

Definitions, Relationships, Paralegal Roles, and Research References

Category
Strict liability for abnormally dangerous conditions or activities is a strict liability tort (neither negligence nor intent must be shown).

Interest Protected by This Tort
The right to be free from harm caused by abnormally dangerous conditions or activities.

Elements of This Tort
  i. Existence of an abnormally dangerous condition or activity
  ii. Knowledge of the condition or activity
  iii. Damages
  iv. Causation

Strict Liability for Abnormally Dangerous Conditions or Activities Checklist Continued

Definitions of Major Words/Phrases in the Elements

Abnormal: Unusual or non-natural for the area.

Dangerous: Creating a substantial likelihood of great harm to persons or property, which cannot be eliminated by the use of reasonable care by the defendant.

Proximate Cause: The defendant is the cause in fact of the harm that results. The kind of harm that results was foreseeable by the defendant, or should have been foreseeable. The plaintiff was within the class of people who were foreseeably endangered by the condition or activity.

Major Defenses and Counterargument Possibilities That Need to Be Explored

1. The condition or activity was not abnormally dangerous. (NOTE: The objective of the defendant is to try to force the plaintiff to prove negligence. This is accomplished if the plaintiff fails to show that the condition or activity was abnormally dangerous. Items 2 to 5 below try to establish that the condition or activity was not abnormally dangerous.)
2. The condition or activity was usual or natural for the environment in question.
3. The likelihood of serious harm from the condition or activity was small.
4. The danger in the condition or activity could have been eliminated by the use of reasonable care. (Defendant does not admit, however, that such care was not used.)
5. The value of the condition or activity to the community outweighed any possible danger.
6. A statute required or authorized the condition or activity.
7. The defendant was not aware of the condition or activity.
8. The defendant was not the cause in fact of the harm suffered by the plaintiff.
9. The kind of harm that resulted was not foreseeable.
10. The person injured was not a foreseeable plaintiff.
11. The plaintiff was aware of the danger, understood it, and unreasonably encountered it (assumption of the risk).
12. The plaintiff consented to what the defendant did (on the defense of consent, see Chapter 27).
13. The plaintiff's suit against the government for strict liability for abnormally dangerous conditions or activities committed by a government employee may be barred by sovereign immunity (on sovereign immunity, see Chapter 27).
14. The plaintiff's suit against the government employee for strict liability for abnormally dangerous conditions or activities may be barred by public official immunity (on official immunity, see Chapter 27).
15. The plaintiff's suit against the charitable organization for strict liability for abnormally dangerous conditions or activities committed by someone working for the organization may be barred by charitable immunity (on charitable immunity, see Chapter 27).
16. The plaintiff failed to take reasonable steps to mitigate the harm caused when the defendant committed strict liability for abnormally dangerous conditions or activities; therefore, damages should not cover the aggravation of the harm caused by the plaintiff (on the doctrine of avoidable consequences, see Chapter 16).

Damages

The plaintiff can recover compensatory damages for the harm caused by the defendant's condition or activity. Punitive damages may also be possible if the plaintiff can show that the defendant was malicious or reckless in allowing the harm to occur. (On the categories of damages, see Chapter 16.)

Relationship to Criminal Law

There may be a criminal statute that prohibits the defendant from maintaining the condition or engaging in the activity involved, e.g., a statute making it a crime to explode fireworks in public areas. The consequences of violating such a statute may include criminal penalties as well as civil liability for the strict liability tort under discussion in this chapter.

Other Torts and Related Actions

Negligence: If the condition or activity of the defendant does not qualify for strict liability status because the condition or activity is not abnormally dangerous, the

Strict Liability for Abnormally Dangerous Conditions or Activities Checklist Continued

plaintiff may be able to show that the defendant was negligent in connection with the condition or activity.

Nuisance: Nuisance should be considered when the condition or activity of the defendant interferes with the use and enjoyment of the plaintiff's land. In some states, there is liability for an absolute nuisance on the same facts that would constitute strict liability for an abnormally dangerous condition or activity.

Trespass to Land: This tort is used when there is an entry of a physical object on the land of the plaintiff due to the abnormally dangerous condition or activity of the defendant.

Wrongful Death: This action can be brought by the survivors of the plaintiff if death results from the abnormally dangerous condition or activity of the defendant.

Federal Law

Under the Federal Tort Claims Act, the United States Government will *not* be liable for a claim based on strict liability for abnormally dangerous conditions or activities committed by one of its federal employees. (See Figure 27–7 in Chapter 27.)

Employer-Employee (Agency) Law

An employee who commits strict liability for abnormally dangerous conditions or activities is personally liable for this tort. His or her employer will *also* be liable for this tort if the conduct of the employee was within the scope of employment (respondeat superior). The employee must be furthering a business objective of the employer at the time. (On the factors that determine the scope of employment, see Figure 14–10 in Chapter 14.)

Paralegal Roles in Litigation for Strict Liability for Abnormally Dangerous Conditions or Activities

(See also Figures 3–1, 3–14, and 29–1 in Chapters 3 and 29.)

Fact finding (help the office collect facts relevant to prove the elements of strict liability for abnormally dangerous conditions or activities, the elements of available defenses, and extent of injuries or other damages):
- client interviewing
- field investigation
- online research (e.g., records on weather conditions on the date of the accident)

File management (help the office control the volume of paperwork in a litigation of a case asserting strict liability for abnormally dangerous conditions or activities):
- open client file
- enter case data in computer database
- maintain file documents

Litigation assistance (help the trial attorney prepare for a trial and appeal, if needed):
- draft discovery requests
- draft answers to discovery requests
- draft pleadings
- digest and index discovery documents
- help prepare, order, and manage trial exhibits (visuals or demonstratives)
- prepare trial notebook
- draft notice of appeal
- order trial transcript
- cite check briefs
- perform legal research

Collection/enforcement (help the trial attorney for the judgment creditor to collect the damages award or to enforce other court orders at the conclusion of the case):
- draft postjudgment discovery requests
- field investigation to monitor compliance with judgment
- online research (e.g., location of defendant's business assets)

Strict Liability for Abnormally Dangerous Conditions or Activities Checklist Continued

Research References for This Tort

Digests
In the digests of West, look for case summaries on this tort under key topics such as:

Explosives	Damages
Trespass	Torts
Waters and Water Courses	Death
	Nuisance

Corpus Juris Secundum
In this legal encyclopedia, see the discussion under topic headings such as:

Explosives	Damages
Trespass	Torts
Waters and Water Courses	Death
	Nuisance

American Jurisprudence 2d
In this legal encyclopedia, see the discussion under topic headings such as:

Explosions and Explosives	Damages
Waters	Torts
Premises Liability	Death
Adjoining Landowners	Nuisance

Legal Periodical Literature
There are two main index systems to use to locate legal periodical literature on this tort:

INDEX TO LEGAL PERIODICALS AND BOOKS (ILP)	*CURRENT LAW INDEX (CLI)*
See literature in *ILP* under subject headings such as:	See literature in *CLI* under subject headings such as:
Water and Water Courses	Strict Liability
Liability without Fault	Explosives
Animals	Water
Fires and Fire Prevention	Damages
Trespass	Torts
Real Property	Real Property
Torts	Liability for Landslide Damages
Damages	Liability for Condition and
Adjoining Landowners	Use of Land

Example of a legal periodical article you will find by using *ILP* or *CLI*:

Common Carriers and Risk Distribution: Absolute Liability for Transporting Hazardous Materials by James R. Roberts, 67 Kentucky Law Journal 441 (1978–79).

A.L.R., A.L.R.2d, A.L.R.3d, A.L.R.4th, A.L.R.5th, A.L.R. Fed.
Use the *ALR Index* to locate annotations on this tort. In this index, check subject headings such as:

Absolute Liability	Torts
Floods and Flooding	Damages
Explosions and Explosives	Water

Example of an annotation you can locate through this index:

Liability for Property Damage caused by Vibrations, or the like, Without Blasting or Explosion by T. S. Tellier, 79 A.L.R.2d 966 (1961).

Words and Phrases
In this multivolume legal dictionary, look up *abnormally dangerous* and every other word or phrase connected with strict liability for abnormally dangerous conditions

**Strict Liability for Abnormally Dangerous
Conditions or Activities Checklist** Continued

or activities discussed in this chapter. The dictionary will give you definitions of these words or phrases from court opinions.

CALR: Computer-Assisted Legal Research

Example of a query you could ask on WESTLAW to try to find cases or other legal materials on this tort: **"strict liability for abnormally dangerous activities" /p damages**

Example of a query you could ask on LEXIS to try to find cases or other legal materials on this tort: **strict liability for abnormally dangerous activities /p damages**

Example of search terms you could use on an Internet legal search engine such as LawCrawler (http://lawcrawler.findlaw.com) to find cases, statutes, or other legal materials on this tort: **"strict liability for abnormally dangerous activities"**

Example of search terms you could use on an Internet general search engine such as Alta Vista (http://www.altavista.com) to find cases, statutes, or other legal materials on this tort: **"strict liability for abnormally dangerous activities"**

More Internet sites to check for materials on strict liability for abnormally dangerous conditions or activities and other torts:
Jurist: (http://jurist.law.pitt.edu/sg_torts.htm)
LawGuru: (http://www.lawguru.com/search/lawsearch.html)
See also Tort Law Online at the end of Chapter 1.

Abnormally Dangerous Condition or Activity

The first element is the existence of an **abnormally dangerous condition or activity.** Some conditions or activities are so dangerous to persons or property that the defendant will be liable for the harm they cause even if the defendant neither intended the harm nor was negligent in producing the harm. It is not a defense for the defendant to show that he or she acted reasonably or used the greatest of care—strict liability will still be imposed.

A great deal of the law in this area stems from a famous English case, *Rylands v. Fletcher.*[2] The defendants built a reservoir on their land. The plaintiff owned a mine nearby. The mine was flooded when water from the defendant's reservoir broke through and reached the mine. The rule from this case, which was eventually accepted in most American states, is as follows:

If the defendant knows he or she is engaging in:

(a) a non-natural or abnormal use of land,
(b) that creates an increased danger to persons or property,

the defendant will be strictly liable for harm caused by this use. The plaintiff will not have to prove negligence.

In short, there is strict liability for abnormally dangerous conditions or activities. (As we will see later, however, there are foreseeability requirements that must also be met before a court will impose strict liability.)

The determination of what is abnormal or non-natural will, of course, depend on the environment. The following are examples that have been found to be abnormally dangerous:

• storing large quantities of inflammable liquids in an urban area
• blasting in a residential area
• extensive pile driving
• emitting noxious gases from a factory in a residential area

---

[2]L.R. 3 H.L. 330 (1868).

The activity or condition must be unusual for the area and present a serious threat of harm. The following are examples of cases that were *not* found to be abnormally dangerous because they did not meet both criteria:

- electric wiring in a business
- gasoline stored at a gas station underground
- a small amount of dynamite stored in a factory
- an oil well dug in a Texas field

Although damage caused by such activities may not be considered abnormally dangerous enough to qualify for strict liability status, a plaintiff may still be able to recover under other theories. If the defendant acted unreasonably, a negligence case is possible, perhaps with the help of res ipsa loquitur (see Chapter 14). Nuisance and trespass to land should also be explored (see Chapter 23).

Is airplane flying an abnormally dangerous activity? Suppose a plane crashes onto someone's land, causing substantial damage to people and property below. Strict liability? Years ago, many courts would say yes. As aviation has become more common and accepted, however, modern courts are inclined to say no. A plaintiff, therefore, must establish negligence or some other tort in order to recover.

Statutes often play a role in this area of strict liability. A statute, for example, might require or simply authorize a common carrier to transport dangerous substances. In such cases, strict liability is usually not applied when damage results from the activity. Liability will result only if negligence can be shown. On the other hand, there may be statutes that prohibit certain activity, e.g., blasting in certain areas or selling drugs to minors. It is sometimes unclear what civil consequences, if any, the legislature intended for a violation of such statutes. Research into the legislative history of the statute must be undertaken. A court might interpret the statute as calling for strict liability, negligence liability, or no civil liability at all for its violation.

The *Restatement of Torts* lists a number of factors that a court should analyze in determining whether something is abnormally dangerous:[3]

- the degree of risk of some harm to people, land, or chattels of others
- the likelihood that the harm that results from the activity will be great
- the inability to eliminate the risk by the exercise of reasonable care
- the extent to which the activity is not a matter of common usage
- the inappropriateness of the activity to the place where the activity is carried on
- the extent to which the value of the activity to the community is outweighed by its dangerous attributes

None of these factors is usually conclusive in deciding whether an activity is abnormally dangerous. The factors are simply aids for a court to determine the extent of the abnormality and the extent of the danger posed by the defendant. (On the meaning of factors in legal analysis, see Legal Analysis Guideline #12 in Chapter 2.)

In balancing these factors, if a court tips the scale against strict liability, it does not necessarily mean that the defendant has won the case. It simply means that the plaintiff must try to fit the facts of the case under the elements of other torts: negligence, nuisance, trespass to land, etc.

ASSIGNMENT

11.3

In each of the following situations, assume that the object or activity in question has resulted in damage or harm to someone. Do you think a court will impose strict liability? Why or why not? (See General Instructions for the Legal Analysis Assignment in Chapter 2.)

a. Tom is moving his own barn. He places it on a huge truck platform and drives it on a public highway. It crashes into a bridge.
b. The XYZ Company has installed a large steam boiler in its factory. It explodes.

---

[3]*Restatement (Second) of Torts* § 520 (1965).

c. The large lake on Linda's land overflows into neighboring land after a thunderstorm.

d. From an army base in Florida, scientists send up a satellite. Unfortunately it lands in Newark, New Jersey.

e. Fred knows that he is HIV positive. Yet, he continues to have unprotected sex with others who are unaware of Fred's HIV status.

f. A bystander is shot when a handgun accidentally goes off during a robbery. The bystander sues the manufacturer of the handgun for engaging in an abnormally dangerous activity.

Knowledge of the Condition or Activity

A defendant will not be strictly liable for an abnormally dangerous condition or activity of which the defendant is unaware. The plaintiff must establish knowledge on the part of the defendant.

Causation: Cause in Fact and Proximate Cause

The harm that the plaintiff's person or property has suffered must have been caused by the defendant's abnormally dangerous condition or activity. The **cause-in-fact** tests are as follows:

- **but for** the defendant's conduct, the plaintiff would not have been harmed, or
- the defendant's conduct was a **substantial factor** in producing the harm suffered by the plaintiff

The second test is used when there is more than one cause factor involved.

Once cause in fact has been established, **proximate cause** must be explored. When we study proximate cause in Chapter 15, we will learn that the rules of proximate cause establish a cutoff point beyond which the defendant will not be liable for the harm he or she caused in fact. Proximate cause, therefore, is more of a policy question than a causation question.

The harm that results must be within the type of harm that was initially foreseeable, and the individual injured must be part of the group or class of people that were included in the foreseeable risk posed by the abnormally dangerous activity. The foreseeability of both is required in order to establish proximate cause. In a moment, we will study the famous mink case (*Foster v. Preston Mill*). This case teaches that some consequences (e.g., a mink killing its young) are so unforeseeable that the condition or activity of the defendant (e.g., dynamite blasting near the mink) is not considered unusually dangerous for those consequences.

The proximate cause rules for strict liability are not as broad as the proximate cause rules for negligence (see Chapter 15). A court is more willing to find proximate cause in a negligence case than in a strict liability case involving abnormally dangerous activities. Unforeseeable **intervening causes** such as an **act of God** or an act of a third person are more likely to cut off liability in a strict liability case than in a negligence case. Courts are willing to limit the extent of liability in this way when there is an absence of fault in a defendant who is strictly liable. No such reluctance is shown toward defendants who are negligent or intentional wrongdoers. Suppose, for example, that the defendant maintains a lake that is abnormally dangerous. An unusual frost results in leakage, causing damage to neighboring land. In many courts, this act of God (the frost) would cut off the defendant's *strict liability,* whereas if the defendant had been careless in maintaining the lake, the act of God would probably not terminate *negligence* liability.

Defenses

Contributory negligence on the part of the plaintiff is not a defense to the tort of maintaining an abnormally dangerous condition or activity. This is so with all strict liability torts—the negligence of the plaintiff will not defeat liability. Suppose, for example, that Tom carelessly walks into an area where construction blasting is occurring. Tom fails to realize that blasting is going on, but if he had been exercising reasonable care for his own safety, he should have realized this. Tom is injured by the blasting. There is clear contributory negligence. This is not a defense, however, when the plaintiff is suing under the strict liability tort of maintaining an abnormally dangerous condition or activity.

If, however, the plaintiff knows of and understands the danger posed by the defendant and voluntarily proceeds to encounter it, then the plaintiff has assumed the risk of the danger. **Assumption of the risk** *is* a defense to a strict liability tort. To avoid permitting a defendant to use this defense as an unfair weapon against a plaintiff, however, the defendant must establish that the plaintiff's assumption of the risk was unreasonable. A plaintiff has a right to the reasonable use and enjoyment of his or her property. A defendant cannot encircle the plaintiff's land with a dangerous condition or activity and then assert assumption of the risk when the plaintiff uses his or her land and is injured because of the condition or activity. The defendant must show that this use was unreasonable, and courts are reluctant to make such a finding when the defendant has prevented the plaintiff from making ordinary and reasonable use of his or her property.

CASE

Foster v. Preston Mill Co.
44 Wash. 2d 440, 268 P.2d 645 (1954).
Supreme Court of Washington

Background: *Blasting for road construction frightened mother mink owned by B. W. Foster, which caused the mink to kill their kittens. Foster brought this action against the company doing the blasting (Preston Mill) to recover damages on the theory of absolute liability. The trial court found for Foster in the sum of $1,953.68. The case is now on appeal before the Supreme Court of Washington where Preston Mill is the appellant and Foster is the respondent.*

Decision on Appeal: *Judgment reversed. Absolute liability does not extend this far.*

OPINION OF COURT

Justice HAMLEY delivered the opinion of the court . . . :

Respondent's mink ranch is located in a rural area one and one-half miles east of North Bend, in King County, Washington. The ranch occupies seven and one half acres on which are located seven sheds for growing mink. The cages are of welded wire, but have wood roofs covered with composition roofing. The ranch is located about two blocks from U.S. highway No. 10, which is a main east-west thoroughfare across the state. Northern Pacific Railway Company tracks are located between the ranch and the highway, and Chicago, Milwaukee, St. Paul & Pacific Railroad Company tracks are located on the other side of the highway about fifteen hundred feet from the ranch.

The period of each year during which mink kittens are born, known as the whelping season, begins about May 1st. The kittens are born during a period of about two and one-half weeks, and are left with their mothers until they are six weeks old. During this period, the mothers are very excitable. If disturbed by noises, smoke, or dogs and cats, they run back and forth in their cages and frequently destroy their young. However, mink become accustomed to disturbances of this kind, if continued over a period of time. This explains why the mink in question were apparently not bothered, even during the whelping season, by the heavy traffic on U.S. highway No. 10, and by the noise and vibration caused by passing trains. There was testimony to the effect that mink would even become accustomed to the vibration and noise of blasting, if it were carried on in a regular and continuous manner.

Appellant and several other companies have been engaged in logging in the adjacent area for more than fifty years. Early in May, 1951, appellant began the construction of a road to gain access to certain timber which it desired to cut. The road was located about two and one-quarter miles southwest of the mink ranch, and about twenty-five hundred feet above the ranch, along the side of what is known as Rattlesnake Ledge.

It was necessary to use explosives to build the road. The customary types of explosives were used, and the customary methods of blasting were followed. The most powder used in one shooting was one hundred pounds, and usually the charge was limited to fifty pounds. The procedure used was to set off blasts twice a day—at noon and at the end of the work day.

Roy A. Peterson, the manager of the ranch in 1951, testified that the blasting resulted in "a tremendous vibration, is all. Boxes would rattle on the cages." The mother mink would then run back and forth in their cages and many of them would kill their kittens. Peterson also testified that on two occasions the blasts had broken windows.

Appellant's expert, Professor Drury Augustus Pfeiffer, of the University of Washington, testified as to tests made with a pin seismometer, using blasts as large as those used by appellant. He reported that no effect on the delicate apparatus was shown at distances comparable to those involved in this case. He said that it would be impossible to break a window at two and one-fourth miles with a hundred-pound shot, but that it could cause vibration of a lightly-supported cage. It would also be audible. Charles E. Erickson, who had charge of the road construction for appellant in 1951, testified that there was no glass breakage in the portable storage and filing shed which the company kept within a thousand feet of where the blasting was done. There were windows on the roof as well as on the sides of this shed.

Before the 1951 whelping season had far progressed, the mink mothers, according to Peterson's estimate, had killed thirty-five or forty of their kittens. He then told the manager of appellant company what had happened. He did not request that the blasting be stopped. After some discussion, however, appellant's manager indicated that the shots would be made as light as possible. The amount of explosives used in a normal shot was then reduced from nineteen or twenty sticks to fourteen sticks.

Officials of appellant company testified that it would have been impractical to entirely cease road-building during the several weeks required for the mink to whelp and wean their young. Such a delay would have made it necessary to run the logging operation another season, with attendant expense. It would also have disrupted the company's log production schedule and consequently the operation of its lumber mill.

In this action, respondent sought and recovered judgment only for such damages as were claimed to have been sustained as a result of blasting operations conducted after appellant received notice that its activity was causing loss of mink kittens.

The primary question presented by appellant's assignments of error is whether, on these facts, the judgment against appellant [Preston Mill] is sustainable on the theory of absolute liability.

The modern doctrine of strict liability for dangerous substances and activities stems from Justice Blackburn's decision in *Rylands v. Fletcher,* L.R. 3 H.L. 330 (1868). *Prosser on Torts,* 449, § 59. As applied to blasting operations, the doctrine has quite uniformly been held to establish liability, irrespective of negligence, for property damage sustained as a result of casting rocks or other debris on adjoining or neighboring premises. *Patrick v. Smith,* 75 Wash. 407, 134 P. 1076. . . . However . . . strict liability should be confined to consequences which lie within the extraordinary risk whose existence calls for such responsibility. *Prosser on Torts,* 458, § 60; 3 *Restatement of Torts,* 41, § 519. . . . This restriction which has been placed upon the application of the doctrine of absolute liability is based upon considerations of policy. As Professor Prosser has said:

"It is one thing to say that a dangerous enterprise must pay its way within reasonable limits, and quite another to say that it must bear responsibility for every extreme of harm that it may cause. . . . *Prosser on Torts,* 457, § 60.

Applying this principle to the case before us, the question comes down to this: Is the risk that any unusual vibration or noise may cause wild animals, which are being raised for commercial purposes, to kill their young, one of the things which make the activity of blasting ultrahazardous?

We have found nothing in the decisional law which would support an affirmative answer to this question. The decided cases, as well as common experience, indicate that the thing which makes blasting ultrahazardous is the risk that property or persons may be damaged or injured by coming into direct contact with flying debris, or by being directly affected by vibrations of the earth or concussions of the air.

Where, as a result of blasting operations, a horse has become frightened and has trampled or otherwise injured a person, recovery of damages has been upheld on the theory of negligence. *Klein v. Phelps Lumber Co.,* 75 Wash. 500, 135 P. 226. Contra: *Uvalde Construction Co. v. Hill,* 142 Tex. 19, 175 S.W.2d 247, where a milkmaid was injured by a frightened cow. But we have found no case where recovery of damages caused by a frightened farm animal has been sustained on the ground of absolute liability.

If, however, the possibility that a violent vibration, concussion, or noise might frighten domestic animals and lead to property damages or personal injuries be considered one of the harms which makes the activity of blasting ultrahazardous, this would still not include the case we have here.

The relatively moderate vibration and noise which appellant's blasting produced at a distance of two and a quarter miles was no more than a usual incident of the ordinary life of the community. See 3 *Restatement of Torts,* 48, § 522, comment a. The trial court specifically found that the blasting did not unreasonably interfere with the enjoyment of their property by nearby landowners, except in the case of respondent's mink ranch.

It is the exceedingly nervous disposition of mink, rather than the normal risks inherent in blasting operations, which therefore must, as a matter of sound policy, bear the responsibility for the loss here sustained . . . . [T]he policy of the law does not impose the rule of strict liability to protect against harms incident to the . . . extraordinary and unusual use of land. . . .

It is our conclusion that the risk of causing harm of the kind here experienced, as a result of the relatively minor vibration, concussion, and noise from distant blasting, is not the kind of risk which makes the activity of blasting ultrahazardous. The doctrine of absolute liability is therefore inapplicable under the facts of this case, and respondent is not entitled to recover damages. The judgment is reversed.

ASSIGNMENT

11.4

a. What other theories of recovery could Foster try to use against Preston Mill Co. to recover for the damages the blasting did to its mink kittens?

b. A company blasts in an area. This excites a horse, which then runs into and kills a prize cow. The owner of the cow sues the blasting company on a theory of absolute liability. What result? Does *Foster* apply?

SUMMARY

Strict liability is the imposition of liability or responsibility for harm whether or not the person causing the harm displayed any fault or moral impropriety. In most states, an owner of a wild animal will be strictly liable for any harm it causes whether or not the owner knew of the animal's dangerous propensities and irrespective of how careful the owner was in trying to prevent any harm from occurring. In most states, an owner of a domestic animal will be strictly liable for the harm it causes if the owner had reason to know the animal had specific propensities to harm others, and the harm caused by the animal was due to that specific propensity.

A condition or activity is abnormal (for purposes of establishing strict liability for abnormally dangerous conditions or activities) if it is unusual or non-natural for the area. It is dangerous when it poses a substantial likelihood of great harm to persons or property that cannot be eliminated by the use of reasonable care by the defendant. If the abnormal condition or activity does not meet this definition of "dangerous," there can be no strict liability. In order to recover, the plaintiff must establish that the defendant created a nuisance, caused a trespass to land, or acted negligently with the condition or activity. For strict liability, the defendant must know that the condition or activity is dangerous, must be the cause in fact of the harm, and must be the proximate cause of the harm. For proximate cause, the harm that results must be within the type of harm that was initially foreseeable, and the plaintiff must be part of the group within the foreseeable risk posed by the abnormally dangerous condition or activity. Some consequences are so unforeseeable that the condition or activity of the defendant is not considered unusually dangerous for those consequences. Contributory negligence is not a defense, but unreasonable assumption of risk is.

KEY TERMS

strict liability 192
absolute liability 192
liability without fault 192
strict liability in tort 192
wild animals 193
domestic animals 193

strict liability for abnormally dangerous conditions or activities 195
abnormally dangerous condition or activity 199
Rylands v. Fletcher 199
cause in fact 201

but for 201
substantial factor 201
proximate cause 201
intervening causes 201
act of God 201
contributory negligence 201
assumption of the risk 202

CHAPTER

12

Negligence:
A Summary

CHAPTER OUTLINE

- Introduction
- Negligence and Breach of Duty
- Negligence and Insurance
- Shorthand Definition
- Negligence Checklist

INTRODUCTION

Negligence is the largest of the three major categories of torts (the other two being the intentional torts and the various kinds of strict liability). Negligence has been called a "catchall" tort in that it encompasses a wide variety of unreasonable actions and inactions that cause injury or other loss. This chapter is an overview of negligence. Elsewhere, more specific negligence topics will be treated. (See Figure 12–1.)

FIGURE 12–1 Coverage of Negligence Topics.

Topic	Where Covered in This Book
Foreseeability	p. 95
Duty	p. 213
Breach of Duty	p. 229
Proximate Cause	p. 265
Damages	p. 285
Employer Liability	p. 257
Medical Malpractice	p. 322
Legal Malpractice	p. 335
Owners and Occupiers of Land	p. 445
Manufacturers and Retailers (products liability)	p. 345
Wrongful Death	p. 425
Negligent Infliction of Emotional Distress	p. 172
Defenses	p. 303

NEGLIGENCE AND BREACH OF DUTY

The word "negligence" is used in two different senses. It can mean the entire tort or only one of its elements. In this book, **negligence** means the entire tort that exists when all four elements are present: duty, breach of duty, proximate cause, and damages. You will also sometimes see the word negligence used in the narrower sense of **unreasonableness,** which is another way of phrasing the breach-of-duty element. Hence the statement, "he acted negligently" either means that one of the elements (**breach of duty**) has been established, or that the tort has been committed. In this book, we mean the latter.

NEGLIGENCE AND INSURANCE

It is commonly assumed by the public that if a driver hits a pedestrian on the street, the driver is responsible and must pay for the injury or other loss suffered by the pedestrian. This is not necessarily so. We must be careful to distinguish **insurance** law from negligence law. The injured party may be automatically compensated if the terms of an insurance policy so provide. For many insurance policies, all that is needed is a covered injury, a covered person, and causation. Much more is needed to trigger the law of negligence. You are not considered negligent simply because you cause an injury. The hallmark of negligence is **fault**—sometimes referred to as **culpability** or wrongfulness. The fault or wrong involved may be simple carelessness or momentary unreasonableness. But a lapse of some kind is required. We are *not* liable for every injury that we cause. We are liable under the law of negligence for those injuries we wrongfully cause in the sense that our conduct fell below a minimum standard of conduct when we caused the injury. One of our main objectives in the following chapters is to explore what this standard is. An important first step in achieving this objective is to avoid the trap of equating negligence with causation or with insurance.

SHORTHAND DEFINITION

A shorthand definition of the tort of negligence is *injury or other loss caused by unreasonable conduct*. In the vast majority of negligence cases that are litigated, the sole questions before the court are:

- Was the defendant's conduct unreasonable?
- Did this unreasonableness cause the plaintiff's injury or other loss?

In the next seven chapters, we will examine these questions along with a large number of others. As we do so, it is important that you not lose sight of the general definition of negligence as *injury or other loss caused by unreasonable conduct*. This definition will suffice for most negligence cases. While we must look at a maze of special rules in the law of negligence, there is a danger of thinking that the maze is the norm. It isn't.

NEGLIGENCE CHECKLIST

Before we begin a detailed study of the law of negligence, briefly examine the negligence checklist containing an overview of definitions, relationships, paralegal roles, and research references for this tort. You may want to refer back to this checklist while you are studying the next seven chapters that cover specific negligence issues.

 Negligence Checklist:
Definitions, Relationships, Paralegal Roles, and Research References

Category
Negligence is a category unto itself. It covers harm that is neither intentional nor the basis of strict liability.

Interest Protected by This Tort
The right to be free from injury or other loss to person or property caused by unreasonable conduct.

Elements of This Tort
   i. Duty
   ii. Breach of duty
   iii. Proximate cause
   iv. Damages

Definitions of Major Words/Phrases in the Elements
   Duty: The obligation to use reasonable care to avoid risks of injuring the person or property of others (see Chapter 13).
   Breach of duty: Unreasonable conduct (the foreseeability of an accident causing serious injury outweighed the burden or inconvenience on the defendant to take precautions against the injury, and the defendant failed to take those precautions) (see Chapter 14).

Negligence Checklist Continued

Proximate cause: The defendant is the cause in fact of the plaintiff's injury, the injury was the foreseeable consequence of the original risk, and there is no policy reason why the defendant should not be liable for what he or she caused in fact (see Chapter 15).
Damages: Actual harm or loss (see Chapter 16).

Major Defenses and Counterargument Possibilities That Need to Be Explored

1. The defendant owed the plaintiff no duty.
2. The injury was not foreseeable.
3. A serious injury was not foreseeable.
4. The burden or inconvenience on the defendant to avoid the injury outweighed the risk of the injury occurring. The burden or inconvenience of avoidance was substantial, whereas the risk of injury was minimal.
5. The activity of the defendant had significant social importance or utility, which justified his or her taking the risks of injury that might be caused by that activity.
6. The defendant was not the cause in fact of the plaintiff's injury. Under the two tests to determine cause in fact: (a) it cannot be said that "but for" what the defendant did or failed to do, the injury to the plaintiff would not have occurred; (b) the defendant was not a substantial factor in producing the plaintiff's injury.
7. The plaintiff's injury was not within the original risk created by the defendant. (There was no proximate cause.)
8. The plaintiff's injury was produced by a superseding intervening cause. (There was no proximate cause.)
9. The plaintiff's injury was produced by an intervening cause that was highly extraordinary. (There was no proximate cause.)
10. The plaintiff suffered no actual harm or loss due to the unreasonable conduct of the defendant. (There were no damages.)
11. The plaintiff was unreasonable in taking risks for his or her own safety and this helped cause the injury (contributory negligence).
12. The harm caused the plaintiff by his or her own negligence exceeded the minimum threshold established by the comparative negligence statute.
13. The plaintiff assumed the risk of his or her own injury.
14. The plaintiff failed to take reasonable steps to mitigate the harm caused by the defendant's negligence; therefore, damages should not cover the aggravation of the harm caused by the plaintiff (on the doctrine of avoidable consequences, see Chapter 16).
15. The plaintiff's suit against the government for negligence committed by a government employee may be barred by sovereign immunity (on sovereign immunity, see Chapter 27).
16. The plaintiff's suit against the government employee for negligence may be barred by public official immunity (on official immunity, see Chapter 27).
17. The plaintiff's suit against the charitable organization for negligence committed by someone working for the organization may be barred by charitable immunity (on charitable immunity, see Chapter 27).
18. The plaintiff's suit against a family member for negligence may be barred by intrafamily immunity (on intrafamily immunity, see Chapter 22).

Damages
Negligence requires proof of actual harm. Without it, the negligence case fails and no compensatory damages can be awarded. Nominal damages are not allowed in a negligence action. In general, punitive damages are not allowed for ordinary negligence. Recklessness or malice of some kind is usually the basis for an award of punitive damages. (On the categories of damages, see Chapter 16.)

Relationship to Criminal Law
There are some crimes based on negligence, e.g., negligent homicide. More than ordinary negligence, however, is usually required. Negligence in criminal law requires at least recklessness.

Relationship to Other Torts
If you are not able to prove one of the intentional torts, explore the possibility of negligence. For example, if you cannot establish the tort of battery because you cannot prove

Negligence Checklist Continued

that the defendant had the intent to cause a harmful or offensive contact, you may be able to establish the tort of negligence if you can prove that the harmful or offensive contact was caused by the defendant's unreasonable conduct. The same may be true of other intentional torts, such as conversion and false imprisonment. Whenever you are having difficulty establishing an intentional tort, determine whether the defendant created an unreasonable risk of the same injury occurring. If so, negligence may be an alternative cause of action. Finally, explore negligence as an alternative to strict liability torts.

Federal Law

a. Under the Federal Tort Claims Act, the United States Government will be liable for negligence committed by one of its federal employees within the scope of employment (respondeat superior) as long as the employee's conduct did not involve discretion at the planning level. (See Figure 27–7 in Chapter 27.)

b. There may be liability under the Civil Rights Act if the negligence was committed while the defendant was depriving the plaintiff of federal rights under color of law. (See Figure 27–9 in Chapter 27.)

c. Under the Consumer Product Safety Act, penalties can be imposed for violations of the rules of the Consumer Product Safety Commission (CPSC) concerning dangerous products on the market.

Employer-Employee (Agency) Law

An employee who commits negligence is personally liable for this tort. His or her employer will *also* be liable for negligence: (a) vicariously, if the conduct of the employee was within the scope of employment (respondeat superior), or (b) independently, if the employer was careless in hiring or supervising an incompetent employee who posed a risk of injuring others. (On the factors that determine the scope of employment, see Figure 14–10 in Chapter 14.)

Paralegal Roles in Negligence Litigation

(See also Figures 3–1, 3–14, and 29–1 in Chapters 3 and 29.)

Fact finding (help the office collect facts relevant to prove the elements of negligence, the elements of available defenses, and the extent of injuries or other damages):
- client interviewing
- field investigation
- online research (e.g., records on weather conditions on the date of the accident)

File management (help the office control the volume of paperwork in a negligence litigation):
- open client file
- enter case data in computer database
- maintain file documents

Litigation assistance (help the trial attorney prepare for a negligence trial and appeal, if needed):
- draft discovery requests
- draft answers to discovery requests
- draft pleadings
- digest and index discovery documents
- help prepare, order, and manage trial exhibits (visuals or demonstratives)
- prepare trial notebook
- draft notice of appeal
- order trial transcript
- cite check briefs
- perform legal research

Collection/enforcement (help the trial attorney for the judgment creditor to collect the damages award or to enforce other court orders at the conclusion of the negligence case):
- draft postjudgment discovery requests
- field investigation to monitor compliance with judgment
- online research (e.g., location of defendant's business assets)

Negligence Checklist Continued

Research References for Negligence

Digests

In the digests of West, look for case summaries on negligence under key topics such as:

Negligence	Automobiles
Damages	Landlord and Tenant
Products Liability	Health and Environment
Master and Servant	Innkeepers
Physicians and Surgeons	Highways
Death	Nuisance
Animals	Contribution
Drugs and Narcotics	Carriers
Explosives	Telecommunications
Torts	

Corpus Juris Secundum

In this legal encyclopedia, see the discussions on negligence under topic headings such as:

Negligence	Landlord and Tenant
Damages	Health and Environment
Products Liability	Inns, Hotels and Eating Places
Master and Servant	Highways
Physicians and Surgeons	Nuisance
Death	Contribution
Animals	Carriers
Drugs and Narcotics	Telegraphs, Telephones,
Explosives	Radio and Television
Motor Vehicles	

American Jurisprudence 2d

In this legal encyclopedia, see the discussions on negligence under topic headings such as:

Negligence	Drugs, Narcotics and Poisons
Products Liability	Master and Servant
Premises Liability	Automobiles and Highway Traffic
Hospitals and Asylums	Occupations, Trades and Professions
Damages	Hotels, Motels and Restaurants
Contribution	Landlord and Tenant
Amusements and Exhibitions	Highways, Streets and Bridges
Animals	Physicians and Surgeons
Carriers	Health
Death	

Legal Periodical Literature

There are two index systems to use to locate legal periodical literature on negligence:

INDEX TO LEGAL PERIODICALS AND BOOKS (ILP)	**CURRENT LAW INDEX (CLI)**
See literature in *ILP* under subject headings such as:	See literature in *CLI* under subject headings such as:
Negligence	Negligence
Accidents	Automobiles
Act of God	Bailments
Automobile Insurance	Contribution
Contributory Negligence	Damages
Damages	Death by Wrongful Act
Highways and Streets	Exemplary Damages
Inns and Innkeepers	Drugs
Joint Tortfeasors	Employers' Liability
Landlord and Tenant	Food
Last Clear Chance	Hospitals

Negligence Checklist Continued

Master and Servant	Informed Consent
Motor Vehicles	Joint Tortfeasors
Nuisance	Landlord and Tenant
Products Liability	Liability for Condition and Use of Land
Personal Injuries	Malpractice
Proximate Cause	Products Liability
Physicians and Surgeons	Respondeat Superior
Res Ipsa Loquitur	Personal Injuries
Traffic Accidents	Physicians
Vicarious Liability	Tort Liability
Wrongful Death	

Example of a legal periodical article you will find on negligence by using *ILP* or *CLI*:

Emergency Room Negligence by Steven E. Pegalis and Harvey F. Wachsman, 16 Trial 50 (May, 1980).

A.L.R., A.L.R.2d, A.L.R.3d, A.L.R.4th, A.L.R.5th, A.L.R. Fed.
Use the *ALR Index* to locate annotations on negligence. In this index, check subject headings such as:

Neglience	Landlord and Tenant
Aggravated Negligence	Products Liability
Attractive Nuisance	Rescue Doctrine
Comparative Negligence	Malpractice
Concurrent Negligence	Hospitals
Contributory Negligence or	Master and Servant
Assumption of Risk	Res Ipsa Loquitur
Corporate Officers, Directors	Mitigation or Aggravation
and Agents	of Damages
Governmental Immunity or Privilege	Federal Tort Claims Act
Gross Negligence	Health and Accident Insurance
Imputed Negligence and Liability	Policies and Provisions

Example of an annotation on negligence you can locate through the *ALR Index*:

Modern Development of Comparative Negligence Doctrine Having Applicability to Negligence Actions Generally by Thomas R. Trenkner, 78 A.L.R.3d 339 (1977).

Words and Phrases
In this multivolume legal dictionary, look up *negligence, duty, breach of duty, proximate cause, damages, contributory negligence, comparative negligence, assumption of the risk,* and every other word or phrase connected with negligence discussed in the next seven chapters. The dictionary will give you definitions of these words or phrases from court opinions.

CALR: Computer-Assisted Legal Research
Example of a query you could ask on WESTLAW or on LEXIS to try to find cases, statutes, or other legal materials on negligence: **negligence/p damages**

Example of search terms you could use on an Internet legal search engine such as LawCrawler (http://lawcrawler.findlaw.com) to find cases, statutes, or other legal materials on negligence: **negligence AND tort**

Example of search terms you could use on an Internet general search engine such as Alta Vista (http://www.altavista.com) to find cases, statutes, or other legal materials on negligence: **+negligence tort**

More Internet sites to check for materials on negligence and other torts:
Jurist: (http://jurist.law.pitt.edu/sg_torts.htm)
LawGuru: (http://www.lawguru.com/search/lawsearch.html)
See also Tort Law Online at the end of Chapter 1.

SUMMARY

Negligence is the largest of the three major categories of torts. It covers injury or other loss caused by unreasonableness. (The other two categories are intentional torts and strict liability torts.) The broad meaning of negligence is the tort that has been committed when all four of its elements are established (duty, breach of duty, proximate cause, and damages). More narrowly, it refers to the second element of the tort: breach of duty. In the vast majority of negligence cases, defendants are liable for the injury or other loss they wrongfully cause. Insurance, on the other hand, provides compensation for every covered injury or loss caused by the insured. A shorthand definition of negligence is injury or other loss caused by unreasonable conduct.

KEY TERMS

negligence 206	breach of duty 206	fault 206
unreasonableness 206	insurance 206	culpability 206

CHAPTER

13

Negligence: Element I: Duty

CHAPTER OUTLINE

- General Rule on Duty
- Unforeseeable Plaintiff
- Nonfeasance and Special Relationships
- Gratuitous Undertaking
- Protection for the Good Samaritan

GENERAL RULE ON DUTY

What is a **duty?** In its broadest sense:

> A duty is an obligation or a requirement to conform to a standard of conduct prescribed by law.

From this broad definition, we come to a series of very specific interrelated questions:

- Who owes this duty?
- To whom is the duty owed?
- When does the duty arise?
- What is the standard of conduct to which there must be conformity?—i.e., duty to do what?

All of these questions can be answered by the **general rule on duty,** which is outlined at the beginning of Figure 13–1. This general rule will be adequate to cover the vast majority of automobile collision cases, on-the-job mishaps, and similar occurrences. The chart will also outline those circumstances that call for limitations on or modifications of the general rule on duty.

FIGURE 13–1 Duty in the law of negligence.

> **General Rule on Duty:**
>
> Whenever one's conduct creates a foreseeable risk of injury or damage to someone else's person or property, a duty of care arises to take reasonable precautions to prevent that injury or damage.
>
> **Exceptions and Special Circumstances:**
>
> **1.** The unforeseeable plaintiff, p. 215
>   **a.** Zone-of-danger test of duty
>   **b.** World-at-large test of duty
> **2.** Nonfeasance and the special relationship, p. 217
> **3.** Gratuitous undertaking, p. 222

We begin with a simple application of the general rule:

> **EXAMPLE:** You are driving down the road late at night. It is raining and the road is slippery.

These facts trigger the application of the general rule on duty. It is foreseeable that someone may be injured when you are driving under such conditions. Therefore, you owe a duty to take reasonable precautions to prevent such an injury—to slow down, turn on the headlights, watch extra carefully for pedestrians and other cars, keep a safe distance between your car and the car in front of you, etc. The more foreseeable the injury, the greater is the need for precautions.

Under the general rule, the duty is to use **reasonable care,** which will be discussed at length in the next chapter when we examine **breach of duty,** or unreasonableness. In the vast majority of cases, this duty is triggered by the **foreseeability** of injury or damage. We have already looked at foreseeability in tort law in Chapter 4, and we will examine it again when we discuss breach of duty and proximate cause. (A foreseeability analysis is needed to determine the applicability of three elements: duty, breach of duty, and proximate cause. In most cases, the foreseeability analysis is the same in all three elements. This is why foreseeability was treated separately in Chapter 4, with particular emphasis on the factors that go into the determination of foreseeability.)

For the remainder of this chapter, we will focus on those exceptions and special circumstances that have posed problems with the general rule on duty stated in Figure 13–1.

UNFORESEEABLE PLAINTIFF

Consider the sequence of events in Figure 13–2, based on the famous *Palsgraf* case.[1] A railroad conductor carelessly pushes a passenger onto a train. (We will call this passenger, Plaintiff #1.) This causes the passenger to drop an unmarked package, which explodes. The blast causes a scale to hit a bystander. (We will call this bystander, Plaintiff #2.)

FIGURE 13–2   Foreseeable and unforeseeable plaintiffs.

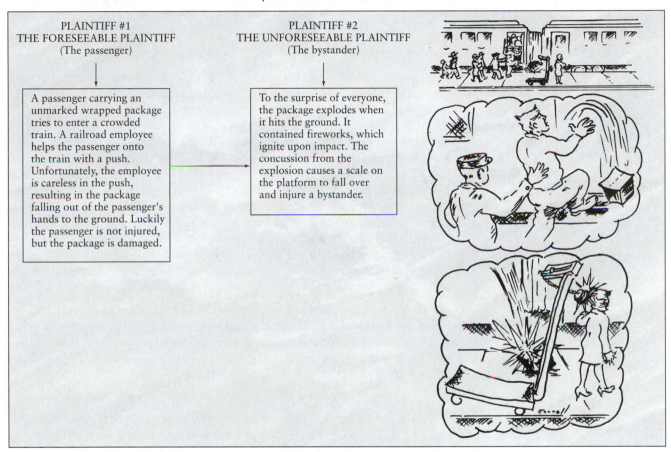

PLAINTIFF #1
THE FORESEEABLE PLAINTIFF
(The passenger)

A passenger carrying an unmarked wrapped package tries to enter a crowded train. A railroad employee helps the passenger onto the train with a push. Unfortunately, the employee is careless in the push, resulting in the package falling out of the passenger's hands to the ground. Luckily the passenger is not injured, but the package is damaged.

PLAINTIFF #2
THE UNFORESEEABLE PLAINTIFF
(The bystander)

To the surprise of everyone, the package explodes when it hits the ground. It contained fireworks, which ignite upon impact. The concussion from the explosion causes a scale on the platform to fall over and injure a bystander.

Plaintiff #1 is a **foreseeable plaintiff** who will have no trouble suing the railroad for the negligence of its employee. A duty is clearly owed to the passenger. Since the employee carelessly pushed the passenger, some harm was foreseeable to the passenger's property or to the person of the passenger. What about the bystander, Plaintiff #2? At the time the employee pushed the passenger onto the train, no one could foresee danger to the bystander from the falling package. Plaintiff #2 is an **unforeseeable plaintiff.** An essential question in Plaintiff #2's negligence suit against the railroad is whether a *duty* was owed to this plaintiff. If not, then the first element of negligence cannot be established and hence the entire negligence cause of action will fall. How then do we determine whether a duty is owed to a person in Plaintiff #2's position? Two major tests have been proposed: the **Cardozo test,** or zone-of-danger test, and the **Andrews test,** or world-at-large test.[2] (See Figure 13–3.) States differ on which of these two tests is followed.

---

[1]*Palsgraf v. Long Island R.R.,* 248 N.Y. 339, 162 N.E. 99, 59 A.L.R. 1253 (1928). This is one of the most famous tort cases in American legal history.
[2]Cardozo wrote the majority opinion in the *Palsgraf* case (supra note 1); Andrews wrote the dissenting opinion.

FIGURE 13–3 Negligence: When is a duty owed?

Zone-of-Danger Test (the Cardozo test)

A duty is owed to a specific person (plaintiff) in the **zone of danger**, as determined by the test of foreseeability.

World-at-Large Test (the Andrews test)

A duty is owed to anyone in the **world at large** (any plaintiff) IF:
1. the plaintiff (who sues) suffers injury as a result of
2. unreasonable conduct of the defendant toward anyone, whether or not the plaintiff who sues was in the zone of danger. This plaintiff does not have to have been in the zone of danger as long as *someone* (in the world at large) was in this zone because of the action or inaction of the defendant.

A number of points should be made about these two tests:

- The two tests focus only on the element of duty. All of the other elements of negligence must also be analyzed to determine whether the cause of action has been established.
- The Andrews test is broader than the Cardozo test. More plaintiffs can establish duty under the Andrews test because they do not have to be in the foreseeable zone of danger in order to be owed a duty. They only have to be injured as a result of the defendant's unreasonable conduct that created, and placed *someone* in, the zone of danger.
- A choice between the two tests must be made when the facts involve a chain of events and an unanticipated person—the unforeseeable plaintiff. The two tests give two different standards on whether such a person is owed a duty. If, however, the facts do not involve a chain of events, then the great likelihood is that both tests would produce the *same* result on whether a duty is owed (i.e., it would make no difference in such cases which test is used).

Let us now apply the two different tests to the fact situation in Figure 13–2 involving the passenger whose package was damaged and the bystander on whom the scale fell. What would happen in a state that has adopted the zone-of-danger (Cardozo) test? How does this compare with the outcome in a state that has adopted the world-at-large (Andrews) test?

1. Zone-of-danger state:
   Would a duty be owed to the passenger? YES, as we have already seen. When the employee carelessly pushed the passenger, it was foreseeable that some injury or damage would result to this passenger. Hence, the passenger was in the zone of danger.
   Would a duty be owed to the bystander? NO. Pushing the passenger created no foreseeable risk to a bystander since there was no indication to the employee that there were fireworks or any other dangerous object in the passenger's unmarked package. The bystander was outside the zone of danger.
2. World-at-large state:
   Would a duty be owed to the passenger? YES. The two-part test has been met: the passenger suffered injury or damage (to the package) as a result of unreasonable conduct (the careless push) directed at someone (here, the passenger). Although it is not necessary for the passenger to have been in the zone of danger under this test, in fact, the passenger was within this zone.
   Would a duty be owed to the bystander? YES. The two-part test has been met: the bystander suffered an injury (the scale fell on the bystander) as a result of unreasonable conduct (the careless push) directed at someone (here, the passenger). Under this test, it is not necessary that the bystander be in the zone of danger as long as someone was in this zone as a result of the defendant's unreasonable conduct. The passenger is the "someone" who was in the zone of danger.

Helen and Grace are on a subway train on the way home from an office where they work together. Both are standing near one of the doors of the crowded train. Suddenly, the door opens while the train is moving and Helen falls out. Moments later, the train stops when the driver realizes what has happened. (Assume that the reason the door opened was negligent maintenance by the subway.) Grace watches in horror as Helen falls out the door. When the train stops, Grace immediately climbs down through the open door onto the tracks in order to try to help Helen. As Grace searches in the dark, she slips on a live rail and dies from electrocution. Luckily, Helen finds her way to safety with only minor injury. Helen and Grace's estate now bring separate negligence actions against the subway. Focus solely on the issue of duty:

a. In a zone-of-danger (Cardozo) state, did the subway owe a duty to Helen? Explain. To Grace? Explain.

b. In a world-at-large (Andrews) state, did the subway owe a duty to Helen? Explain. To Grace? Explain.

(See also general Instructions for the Legal Analysis Assignment in Chapter 2.)

NONFEASANCE AND SPECIAL RELATIONSHIPS

Most negligence liability is based on **affirmative conduct** that is improper or unreasonable. This is called **misfeasance**. With limited exceptions, negligence liability cannot be based on a mere omission or failure to act, called **nonfeasance**.[3] Only if a **special relationship** existed between the plaintiff and defendant will nonfeasance by the defendant lead to negligence. Compare the two situations in Figure 13–4.

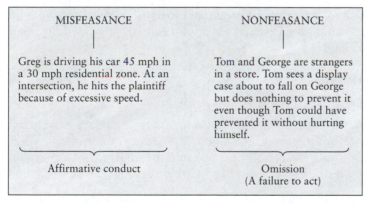

MISFEASANCE	NONFEASANCE
Greg is driving his car 45 mph in a 30 mph residential zone. At an intersection, he hits the plaintiff because of excessive speed.	Tom and George are strangers in a store. Tom sees a display case about to fall on George but does nothing to prevent it even though Tom could have prevented it without hurting himself.
Affirmative conduct	Omission (A failure to act)

FIGURE 13–4
Misfeasance and nonfeasance.

When Greg (in Figure 13–4) is sued by the plaintiff for negligence in the first situation, there will not be a problem establishing the existence of a duty. In such cases of misfeasance, there is almost never a duty problem. Affirmative conduct by Greg (his driving) created a risk of foreseeable injury to the plaintiff. It is very easy to establish the existence of a duty when affirmative conduct (alone or in combination with inaction) creates such a risk. The vast majority of negligence cases fall into the misfeasance category.

Now let us focus on the second hypothetical in Figure 13–4, involving Tom and George. Here we have *non*feasance. There was no affirmative conduct by Tom. He did nothing to create or increase the risk of injury to George. Rather, there was an

---

[3]Do not confuse the following three words. *Nonfeasance* is the omission of an act, the failure to act. *Misfeasance* is improper or unreasonable action. **Malfeasance** is wrongful or illegal actions by a public official.

omission, a failure to act. In most states, there is no duty in such situations to exercise any kind of care unless a special relationship exists between the parties. These special relationships will be outlined later in Figure 13–6.

In most cases involving strangers such as Tom and George, there is no such special relationship, and hence no duty to act with reasonable care. It is surprising to many to learn that *you have no duty to assist someone simply because it is possible for you to give assistance without harming yourself.* Nor does the mere foreseeability of injury give rise to a duty to give aid. According to the American Law Institute:

> The fact that the actor realizes or should realize that action on his part is necessary for another's aid or protection does not of itself impose upon him a duty to take such action.[4]

The classic example is the stranger who refuses to lift a finger to save the life of a drowning victim even though the stranger would be under no jeopardy in making the effort. There is *no* requirement in our law to be a **Good Samaritan.** In fact, if someone voluntarily decides to be a Good Samaritan and renders assistance, even though there was no initial duty to do so, the Good Samaritan can be sued for negligence if he or she fails to use reasonable care in rendering this free assistance! Although special statutory protection for the Good Samaritan has recently been enacted, the fear of being sued continues to discourage many potential Good Samaritans from rendering assistance. (We will discuss this area of the law later in the section on Gratuitous Undertaking.)

Most accidents involve *both* conduct and omissions; for example, while driving on the highway (affirmative conduct), the defendant failed to slow down at the intersection and failed to use the horn to warn the inattentive plaintiff (omissions). This example would be considered a *mis*feasance case of negligence, even though there were components of *non*feasance in it. Generally, if there was *some* affirmative conduct that helped cause the injury, you will not need to worry about the existence or nonexistence of a special relationship even though omissions were involved. The nonfeasance case usually arises when all the defendant "did" was to "decide" to do nothing to help the plaintiff. Here the special relationship will be critical. Without it, the plaintiff's negligence case falls because there is no duty to act.

In addition to the presence of a special relationship, the defendant's duty depends on the foreseeability of injury and the opportunity to do something about it, as diagrammed in Figure 13–5.

FIGURE 13–5
Duty in nonfeasance cases.

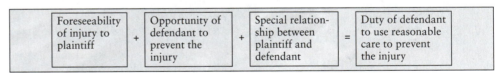

| Foreseeability of injury to plaintiff | + | Opportunity of defendant to prevent the injury | + | Special relationship between plaintiff and defendant | = | Duty of defendant to use reasonable care to prevent the injury |

The duty is *not* to prevent the injury. The duty arising from the special relationship is simply to use *reasonable care* to avoid the injury. The duty does not guarantee anything. Here are some examples of what reasonable care might entail:

- taking reasonable steps in advance to try to make the area safe
- taking reasonable steps to try to prevent third persons under the defendant's control from injuring the plaintiff
- taking reasonable steps immediately after the injury to try to prevent aggravation of the injury

What are the special relationships? The main ones are outlined in Figure 13–6.

A good deal of controversy has recently centered around the problem of controlling the conduct of third parties who are not part of the special relationship itself.

> **EXAMPLE:** Tom is a patient of Dr. Edward Smith, a therapist. During a session, Tom tells Dr. Smith that he is going to kill his girlfriend. The latter is not a patient of Dr. Smith. The next day, Tom carries out his threat and kills his girlfriend.

---

[4]*Restatement (Second) of Torts* § 314 (1965).

FIGURE 13–6
Special relationships that
create a duty to use
reasonable care in
nonfeasance cases.

Principle

In nonfeasance cases, there is no duty to use reasonable care (and hence no negligence) unless the plaintiff fits within one of the following categories of special relationships. If none of the relationships exist, there is no duty to act, and hence omissions (nonfeasance) by the defendant cannot constitute negligence. This applies only to nonfeasance cases. If the defendant has engaged in affirmative conduct, there is usually a duty to use reasonable care whether or not a special relationship exists between plaintiff and defendant.

Special Relationships

1. Common Carrier/Passenger

Example: A passenger on a bus becomes ill or is in danger because of what another passenger is doing. The bus driver has a duty to use reasonable care to help the passenger in trouble even though the driver did not cause the trouble. This duty arises because of the special relationship the law imposes between a bus company or other common carrier and a passenger.

2. Innkeeper/Guest

Example: A hotel guest becomes ill or is injured on the premises. Hotel employees have a duty to use reasonable care to help the guest regardless of who caused the difficulty. This duty arises because of the special relationship the law imposes between a hotel or other innkeeper and a guest.

3. Employer/Employee

Example: An employee is injured on the job. The employer has a duty to use reasonable care to help the employee no matter who caused the injury. This duty arises because of the special relationship the law imposes between employer and employee. (See Chapter 28 on the system of workers' compensation that covers such injuries.)

4. Possessor of Land/Invitee

Example: A customer in a department store becomes ill or is in danger because of what another customer is doing. A store employee has a duty to use reasonable care to help the customer in trouble even though the store did not cause the trouble. This duty arises because of the special relationship the law imposes between owners or other possessors of land such as a department store and invitees on the land such as customers. (For more on duties owed invitees, see Chapter 23.)

5. Parent/Child

Example: A child falls off a chair at home while playing and is in pain on the floor. A parent has a duty to use reasonable care to aid the injured child even if the fall was not the fault of the parent. This duty arises because of the special relationship the law imposes between parents and their children. (On whether a child can sue his or her parent in tort, see intrafamily tort immunity in Chapter 22.)

6. School/Student

Example: One student injures another in a violent attack during a gym class. A school employee has a duty to use reasonable care to aid the injured student even if no school employee was at fault in causing the injury. This duty arises because of the special relationship the law imposes between a school and its students.

7. Jail or Prison/Inmate

Example: An inmate becomes sick in jail or prison. Employees at the institution have a duty to use reasonable care to aid the inmate even if the institution was not at fault in causing the sickness. This duty arises because of the special relationship the law imposes between jails or prisons and their inmates.

The girlfriend's estate now brings a negligence action against Dr. Smith. Again, we have a nonfeasance problem. We have omissions: Dr. Smith did not warn the girlfriend of Tom's threat, he did not tell the police of the threat, he did not tell the girlfriend's family about the threat, etc. The question is whether Dr. Smith owed a *duty* to the girlfriend. He engaged in no affirmative conduct toward the girlfriend that placed her in danger or that increased the danger she was in because of Tom. Hence, we do not have misfeasance. There was no special relationship between Dr. Smith and the girlfriend. The traditional result, therefore, in such situations is that there is no duty and hence no liability for negligence. It should be noted, however, that not all states follow this traditional rule. Some states, and the *Restatement,*[5] will say that a duty of reasonable care *would* be owed by the doctor to the girlfriend in such a case.

California is one of the states that takes this position. It did so in the famous case of *Tarasoff v. Regents of University of California,* 17 Cal. 3d 425, 551 P.2d 334 (1976). This case is discussed in the *Soldano* case, to which we will be turning in a moment.

---

[5]*Restatement (Second) of Torts* § 315 (1965).

ASSIGNMENT

13.2

Dr. George Donovan is treating an AIDS patient, Kevin Smith. Kevin tells Dr. Donovan that he no longer uses protection in his sexual relations with his roommate, whom Dr. Donovan has never met, and with Paul Grondon, who is also a patient of Dr. Donovan. By remaining silent about Kevin's sexual practices, could Dr. Donovan be sued for negligence by anyone who contracts AIDS from Kevin? (See General Instructions for the Legal Analysis Assignment in Chapter 2.)

CASE

Soldano v. O'Daniels
141 Cal. App. 3d 443, 190 Cal. Rptr. 310 (1983)
California Court of Appeals, Fifth District

Background: *On August 9, 1977, Darrell Soldano was shot and killed at Happy Jack's Saloon. The defendant, O'Daniels, owns the Circle Inn, an eating establishment across the street from Happy Jack's. A patron at Happy Jack's Saloon came into the Circle Inn and informed a Circle Inn bartender that a man had been threatened at Happy Jack's. He asked the bartender either to call the police or to allow him to use the Circle Inn phone to call the police. The bartender refused even though it would have been convenient to grant either request and would have cost the defendant nothing. The victim's son sued the defendant for negligence, alleging that the Circle Inn employee (the bartender) breached a legal duty owed to the decedent. At the trial, the court granted the defendant a summary judgment. The plaintiff has now appealed to the California Court of Appeals for the Fifth District.*

Decision on Appeal: *The trial court judgment is reversed. The defendant had a duty to call the police or to allow the phone to be used for this purpose.*

OPINION OF COURT

Justice ANDREEN delivered the opinion of the court . . .

Does a business establishment incur liability . . . if it denies use of its telephone to a good samaritan who explains an emergency situation occurring without and wishes to call the police? . . .

There is a distinction, well rooted in the common law, between action and nonaction. It has found its way into the prestigious *Restatement Second of Torts* (hereafter cited as *"Restatement"*), which provides in section 314: "The fact that the actor realizes or should realize that action on his part is necessary for another's aid or protection does not of itself impose upon him a duty to take such action." . . .

Defendant argues that the request that its employee call the police is a request that it *do* something. He points to the established rule that one who has not created a peril ordinarily does not have a duty to take affirmative action to assist an imperiled person. It is urged that the alternative request of the patron from Happy Jack's Saloon that he be allowed to use defendant's telephone so that he personally could make the call is again a request that the defendant do something—assist another to give aid. . . .

The refusal of the law to recognize the moral obligation of one to aid another when he is in peril and when such aid may be given without danger and at little cost in effort has been roundly criticized. Prosser describes the case law sanctioning such inaction as a "refus[al] to recognize the moral obligation of common decency and common humanity" and characterizes some of these decisions as "shocking in the extreme. . . ." (Prosser, *Law of Torts* (4th ed. 1971) § 56, pp. 340–341.) . . .

As noted in *Tarasoff v. Regents of University of California,* (1976) 17 Cal. 3d 425, 435, 551 P.2d 334, the courts have increased the instances in which affirmative duties are imposed not by direct rejection of the common law rule, but by expanding the list of special relationships which will justify departure from that rule. For instance, California courts have found special relationships in *Ellis v. D'Angelo* (1953) 116 Cal. App. 2d 310, 253 P.2d 675 (upholding a cause of action against parents who failed to warn a babysitter of the violent proclivities of their child), *Johnson v. State of California* (1968) 69 Cal. 2d 782, 447 P.2d 352 (upholding suit against the state for failure to warn foster parents of the dangerous tendencies of their ward), *Morgan v. County of Yuba* (1964) 230 Cal. App.2d 938, 41 Cal. Rptr. 508 (sustaining cause of action against a sheriff who had promised to warn decedent before releasing a dangerous prisoner, but failed to do so).

And in *Tarasoff,* a therapist was told by his patient that he intended to kill Tatiana Tarasoff [the patient's girlfriend]. The therapist and his supervisors predicted the patient presented a serious danger of violence. In fact he did, for he carried out his threat. The court held the patient-therapist relationship was enough to create a duty to exercise reasonable care to protect others from the foreseeable result of the patient's illness.

Section 314A of the *Restatement* lists other special relationships which create a duty to render aid, such as that of a common carrier to its passengers, an innkeeper to his guest, possessors of land who hold it open to the public, or one who has a custodial relationship to another. A duty may be created by an undertaking to give assistance. (See *Rest. 2d Torts*, § 321 et seq.)

Here there was no special relationship between the defendant and the deceased. It would be stretching the concept beyond recognition to assert there was a relationship between the defendant and the patron from Happy Jack's Saloon who wished to summon aid. But this does not end the matter. It is time to re-examine the common law rule of nonliability for nonfeasance in the special circumstances of the instant case. . . .

The [California] Supreme Court has identified certain factors to be considered in determining whether a duty is owed to third persons. These factors include: "the foreseeability of harm to the plaintiff, the degree of certainty that the plaintiff suffered injury, the closeness of the connection between the defendant's conduct and the injury suffered, the moral blame attached to the defendant's conduct, the policy of preventing future harm, the extent of the burden to the defendant and consequences to the community of imposing a duty to exercise care with resulting liability for breach, and the availability, cost, and prevalence of insurance for the risk involved." (*Rowland v. Christian* (1968) 69 Cal. 2d 108, 113, 70 Cal. Rptr. 97, 443 P.2d 561.)

We examine those factors in reference to this case. (1) The harm to the decedent was abundantly foreseeable; it was imminent. The employee was expressly told that a man had been threatened. The employee was a bartender. As such he knew it is foreseeable that some people who drink alcohol in the milieu of a bar setting are prone to violence. (2) The certainty of decedent's injury is undisputed. (3) There is arguably a close connection between the employee's conduct and the injury: the patron wanted to use the phone to summon the police to intervene. The employee's refusal to allow the use of the phone prevented this anticipated intervention. If permitted to go to trial, the plaintiff may be able to show that the probable response time of the police would have been shorter than the time between the prohibited telephone call and the fatal shot. (4) The employee's conduct displayed a disregard for human life that can be characterized as morally wrong:* he was callously indifferent to the possibility that Darrell Soldano would die as the result of his refusal to allow a person to use the telephone. Under the circumstances before us the bartender's burden was minimal and exposed him to no risk: all he had to do was allow the use of the telephone. It would have cost him or his employer nothing. It could have saved a life. (5) Finding a duty in these circumstances would promote a policy of preventing future harm. A citizen would not be required to summon the police but would be required, in circumstances such as those before us, not to impede another who has chosen to summon aid. (6) We have no information on the question of the availability, cost, and prevalence of insurance for the risk, but note that the liability which is sought to be imposed here is that of employee negligence, which is covered by many insurance policies. (7) The extent of the burden on the defendant was minimal. . . .

As the Supreme Court has noted, the reluctance of the law to impose liability for nonfeasance, as distinguished from misfeasance, is in part due to the difficulties in setting standards and of making rules workable.

Many citizens simply "don't want to get involved." No rule should be adopted which would require a citizen to open up his or her house to a stranger so that the latter may use the telephone to call for emergency assistance. As Mrs. Alexander in Anthony Burgess' *A Clockwork Orange* learned to her horror, such an action may be fraught with danger. It does not follow, however, that use of a telephone in a public portion of a business should be refused for a legitimate

---

*The moral right of plaintiff's decedent to have the defendant's bartender permit the telephone call is so apparent that legal philosophers treat such rights as given and requiring no supporting argument. (See Dworkin, *Taking Rights Seriously* (Harv. U. Press 1978) p. 99.) The concept flows from the principle that each member of a community has a right to have each other member treat him with a minimal respect due a fellow human being. (Id. at p. 98.)

emergency call. Imposing liability for such a refusal would not subject innocent citizens to possible attack by the "good samaritan," for it would be limited to an establishment open to the public during times when it is open to business, and to places within the establishment ordinarily accessible to the public. Nor would a stranger's mere assertion that an "emergency" situation is occurring create the duty to utilize an accessible telephone because the duty would arise if and only if it were clearly conveyed that there exists an imminent danger of physical harm. (See *Rest. 2d Torts,* supra, § 327.)

Such a holding would not involve difficulties in proof, overburden the courts or unduly hamper self-determination or enterprise.

A business establishment such as the Circle Inn is open for profit. The owner encourages the public to enter, for his earnings depend on it. A telephone is a necessary adjunct to such a place. It is not unusual in such circumstances for patrons to use the telephone to call a taxicab or family member.

We acknowledge that defendant contracted for the use of his telephone, and its use is a species of property. But if it exists in a public place as defined above, there is no privacy or ownership interest in it such that the owner should be permitted to interfere with a good faith attempt to use it by a third person to come to the aid of another. . . .

We conclude that the bartender owed a duty to the plaintiff's decedent to permit the patron from Happy Jack's to place a call to the police or to place the call himself. It bears emphasizing that the duty in this case does not require that one must go to the aid of another. That is not the issue here. The employee was not the good samaritan intent on aiding another. The patron was.

It would not be appropriate to await legislative action in this area. The rule was fashioned in the common law tradition, as were the exceptions to the rule. To the extent this opinion expands the reach of section 327 of the *Restatement,* it represents logical and needed growth, the hallmark of the common law. . . . "Although the Legislature may of course speak to the subject, in the common law system the primary instruments of this evolution are the courts, adjudicating on a regular basis the rich variety of individual cases brought before them." (*Rodriguez v. Bethlehem Steel Corp.* (1974) 12 Cal. 3d 382, 394, 525 P.2d 669.) . . .

The creative and regenerative power of the law has been strong enough to break chains imposed by outmoded former decisions. What the courts have power to create, they also have power to modify, reject and re-create in response to the needs of a dynamic society. The exercise of this power is an imperative function of the courts and is the strength of the common law. . . .

The possible imposition of liability on the defendant in this case is not a global change in the law. It is but a slight departure from the "morally questionable" rule of nonliability for inaction absent a special relationship. . . . It is a logical extension of *Restatement* section 327 which imposes liability for negligent interference with a third person who the defendant knows is attempting to render necessary aid. However small it may be, it is a step which should be taken.

We conclude there are sufficient justiciable issues to permit the case to go to trial and therefore reverse.

ASSIGNMENT
13.3

a. Do you think the courts should provide a forum to redress every moral wrong? Should every moral duty be backed up by a legal duty? Does the *Soldano* court take this position?

b. What if the only phone at the Circle Inn were a pay phone. The Good Samaritan asks the bartender to let him borrow money for the emergency call. The bartender has the change readily available, but refuses to let him borrow the money. Does *Soldano* apply?

c. Your house is on fire. You do not have a phone. You run across the street and ask your neighbor to call 911 for help. The neighbor, who has never liked you, refuses. Later you sue the neighbor for refusing your request. Does *Soldano* apply?

GRATUITOUS UNDERTAKING

Question: If you do something that you do not have to do, is there a duty to do it with reasonable care?

An **undertaking** is simply doing something. The undertaking is **gratuitous** if there was no obligation to do it—the defendant did it for free. Many undertakings are not for free. Rather, they result from "payment" of one kind or another. In the law of contracts, this payment is often referred to as **consideration.** A homeowner may enter a contract with an electrician to re-wire a house for a set fee. The work of the electrician on the wiring is an undertaking supported by consideration. There is no duty problem here. The electrician has the duty to perform the undertaking (the re-wiring) with reasonable care. Suppose, however, that the undertaking is *not* supported by consideration. Suppose that the undertaking is gratuitous.

> **EXAMPLE:**
>
> - An electrician agrees to re-wire a house for $3,000. While doing this job, he discovers a broken water valve in the bathroom. On his own, as a goodwill gesture, the electrician decides to fix the valve. Because of his inexperience with plumbing, the electrician causes additional damage to the pipes. Working on the pipes was a gratuitous undertaking. Did the electrician have a *duty* to use reasonable care in trying to fix the water valve?
>
> - Phil is an off-duty lifeguard driving by a lake in another state. He sees a small, unattended child drowning close to the shore. Phil stops his car and decides to help. While Phil is carrying the child out of the water, the child's arm is broken due to Phil's carelessness in holding the child. Phil did not have a duty to come to the aid of the child because no special relationship existed between them. Phil's act of help was a gratuitous undertaking. Did Phil owe a *duty* to use reasonable care in helping the child?

The answer to both questions is *yes*. Even though there may be no duty to do anything, if you decide to do something, you have the duty to do it reasonably. The duty arises from a gratuitous undertaking. The defendants (the electrician and Phil in the preceding examples) are said to have assumed the duty on their own.

A final dimension of this problem must be considered. Suppose a defendant, again someone who has no special relationship with plaintiff, makes a gratuitous **promise** to the plaintiff.

> **EXAMPLE:**   Richard is injured on the road. A passerby sees Richard and says, "Don't do anything. Lie still. I'll get help." Soon another stranger comes by and asks Richard if he needs any help. He says, "No, someone has just gone for help." In fact, the original passerby did nothing, thinking (foolishly) that someone else would probably help Richard.

Did the original passerby owe Richard a *duty* to perform his gratuitous promise with reasonable care? The traditional answer has been no. More modern cases, however, are beginning to find that a duty does exist as long as there has been **reliance** by plaintiff on the defendant's promise. Such was clearly the case with Richard, who did not seek further help because of the first passerby's promise. The promise increased the risk to Richard since it discouraged him from seeking further help.

ASSIGNMENT

13.4

a. ABC Realty Company leases space to Jones, who uses it as a grocery store. The lease agreement provides that all repairs and maintenance are the responsibility of Jones. One day, an officer of the ABC Realty Company tells Jones that the company is thinking about installing smoke detectors to replace the rusty sprinkler system. Two days later, a customer is injured in Jones's store due to a fire. The sprinkler system did not work and smoke detectors had not been installed. Did ABC Realty Company owe a duty of reasonable care to the customer? (See General Instructions for the Legal Analysis Assignment in Chapter 2.)

b. The B & O Railroad (RR) has a track that crosses a county street. For years, the RR stationed one of its employees at this crossing in order to warn oncoming traffic using the county street of an approaching train. There is no law that requires the RR to keep this employee at this crossing. You may assume that if the RR had never placed an employee at this crossing, a claim of negligence against the RR would not be successful. In fact, however, the RR had an employee at this crossing for years. As a train approached, the employee stepped out onto the county street and warned all traffic to stop. The employee lived in the area, and hence knew many of the automobile drivers that used the crossing. For the last three years, the RR had been experiencing declining business and never had more than two trains crossing the county street on any given day. The poor business also led to employee layoffs. On December 3rd, the employee who had worked the county street crossing was laid off. She was not replaced. Hence, no RR employee now works at the county street crossing. In the view of the RR, the sound of an oncoming train would be warning enough to cars approaching the county street. On December 6th of the same year, Peter Blanchard was driving his truck on the county street in question. He was making a delivery from a neighboring state. He crashed into one of the RR trains at the point where the county street and the RR track meet. At all times Peter was driving very carefully. It was a rainy night, and hence he did not hear the oncoming train. You may assume that Peter will be able to establish that the accident would not have happened if the RR employee (who was laid off on 12/3) had been on duty at the time of the accident. Peter Blanchard brings a negligence action against the B & O RR for its failure to have the employee present to warn traffic of oncoming trains at the crossing. Discuss the element of duty. (See General Instructions for the Legal Analysis Assignment in Chapter 2.)

c. Rich is driving down the road carefully. Suddenly a storm begins. Visibility is very poor. Rich unavoidably hits a pedestrian, who suffers a broken leg. Rich gets out of the car and runs toward the pedestrian. When Rich sees the injury, he panics. He does not know what to do. Hours go by without Rich doing anything. The pedestrian dies. Did Rich owe the pedestrian a duty? Give an argument that he did. Give an argument that he did not. (See General Instructions for the Legal Analysis Assignment in Chapter 2.)

ASSIGNMENT

13.5

Prepare a negligence complaint for the estate of the pedestrian against Rich on the facts of Assignment 13.4(c). (See General Instructions for the Complaint Drafting Assignment in Chapter 3.)

CASE

Riss v. City of New York
22 N.Y.2d 579, 240 N.E.2d 860, 293 N.Y.S.2d 897 (1968)
Court of Appeals of New York

Background: *For more than six months, Linda Riss was terrorized by a rejected suitor, Burton Pugach. This miscreant, masquerading as a respectable attorney, repeatedly threatened to have Linda killed or maimed if she did not yield to him: "If I can't have you, no one else will have you, and when I get through with you, no one else will want you." In fear for her life, she contacted the police in February of 1959. One detective told her that she would have to be hurt before the police could do anything. On June 14, 1959 Linda became engaged to another man. At a party held to celebrate the event, she received a phone call warning her that it was her "last chance." Completely distraught, she called the police, begging for help, but was refused. The next day Pugach carried out his dire threats in the very manner he had foretold by having a hired thug throw lye in Linda's face. She was blinded in one eye, lost a good portion of her vision in the other, and her face was permanently scarred.*

After this attack, the authorities concluded that there was some basis for Linda's fears, and for the next three and one-half years, she was given around-the-clock protection. She sued the city for negligence. The trial court dismissed the complaint. The Appellate Division affirmed. The plaintiff now appeals to the Court of Appeals of New York.

Decision on Appeal: *The judgment for the city is affirmed. The city is not liable to an assault victim for failure to supply police protection upon request.*

OPINION OF COURT

Judge BREITEL delivered the opinion of the court . . .

This appeal presents, in a very sympathetic framework, the issue of the liability of a municipality for failure to provide special protection to a member of the public who was repeatedly threatened with personal harm and eventually suffered dire personal injuries for lack of such protection. [The] . . . case involves the provision of a governmental service to protect the public generally from external hazards and particularly to control the activities of criminal wrongdoers. The amount of protection that may be provided is limited by the resources of the community and by a considered legislative-executive decision as to how those resources may be deployed. For the courts to proclaim a new and general duty of protection in the law of tort, even to those who may be the particular seekers of protection based on specific hazards, could and would inevitably determine how the limited police resources of the community should be allocated and without predictable limits. This is quite different from the predictable allocation of resources and liabilities when public hospitals, rapid transit systems, or even highways are provided.

Before such extension of responsibilities should be dictated by the indirect imposition of tort liabilities, there should be a legislative determination that that should be the scope of public responsibility. . . . When one considers the greatly increased amount of crime committed throughout the cities, but especially in certain portions of them, with a repetitive and predictable pattern, it is easy to see the consequences of fixing municipal liability upon a showing of probable need for and request for protection. To be sure these are grave problems at the present time, exciting high priority activity on the part of the national, state and local governments, to which the answers are neither simple, known, or presently within reasonable controls. To foist a presumed cure for these problems by judicial innovation of a new kind of liability in tort would be foolhardy indeed and an assumption of judicial wisdom and power not possessed by the courts. . . .

For all of these reasons, there is no warrant in judicial tradition or in the proper allocation of the powers of government for the courts, in the absence of legislation, to carve out an area of tort liability for police protection to members of the public. Quite distinguishable, of course, is the situation where the police authorities undertake responsibilities to particular members of the public and expose them, without adequate protection, to the risks which then materialize into actual losses (*Schuster v. City of New York*, 5 N.Y.S.2d 75, 180 N.Y.S.2d 265, 154 N.E.2d 534).

Accordingly, the order of the Appellate Division affirming the judgment of dismissal should be affirmed.

KEATING, Judge (dissenting).

No one questions the proposition that the first duty of government is to assure its citizens the opportunity to live in personal security. And no one who reads the record of Linda's ordeal can reach a conclusion other than that the City of New York, acting through its agent, completely and negligently failed to fulfill this obligation to Linda.

Linda has turned to the courts of this State for redress, asking that the city be held liable in damages for its negligent failure to protect her from harm. . . . If a private detective acts carelessly, no one would deny that a jury could find such conduct unacceptable. Why then is the city not required to live up to at least the same minimal standards of professional competence which would be demanded of a private detective?

Linda's reasoning seems so eminently sensible that surely it must come as a shock to her and to every citizen to hear the city argue and to learn that this court decides that the city has no duty to provide police protection to any given individual. What makes the city's position particularly difficult to understand is that, in conformity to the dictates of the law, Linda did not carry any weapon for self-defense. Thus, by a rather bitter irony she was required to rely for protection on the City of New York which now denies all responsibility to her. . . .

The city invokes the specter of a "crushing burden" if we should depart from the existing rule and enunciate even the limited proposition that the State and its municipalities can be held liable for the negligent acts of their police employees in executing whatever police services they do in fact provide. The fear of financial disaster is a myth. . . . [I]n the past four or five years, New York City has been presented with an average of some 10,000 claims each year. The figure would sound ominous except for the fact the city has been paying out less than $8,000,000 on tort claims each year and this amount includes all those sidewalk defect and snow and ice cases about which the courts fret so often. . . . Certainly this is a slight burden in a budget of more than six billion dollars (less than two tenths of 1%) and of no importance as compared to the injustice of permitting unredressed wrongs to continue to go unrepaired. That Linda Riss should be asked to bear the loss, which should properly fall on the city if . . . her injuries resulted from the city's failure to provide sufficient police to protect Linda is contrary to the most elementary notions of justice. . . .

No one would claim that, under the facts here, the police were negligent when they did not give Linda protection after her first calls or visits to the police station in February of 1959. The preliminary investigation was sufficient. If Linda had been attacked at this point, clearly there would be no liability here. When, however, as time went on and it was established that Linda was a reputable person, that other verifiable attempts to injure her or intimidate her had taken place, that other witnesses were available to support her claim that her life was being threatened, something more was required—either by way of further investigation or protection—than the statement that was made by one detective to Linda that she would have to be hurt before the police could do anything for her. . . .

If the police force of the City of New York is so understaffed that it is unable to cope with the everyday problem posed by the relatively few cases where single, known individuals threaten the lives of other persons, then indeed we have reached the danger line and the lives of all of us are in peril. If the police department is in such a deplorable state that the city, because of insufficient manpower, is truly unable to protect persons in Linda Riss' position, then liability not only should, but must be imposed. It will act as an effective inducement for public officials to provide at least a minimally adequate number of police. . . .

[I]f we were to hold the city liable here for the negligence of the police, courts would no more be interfering with the operations of the police department than they "meddle" in the affairs of the highway department when they hold the municipality liable for personal injuries resulting from defective sidewalks, or a private employer for the negligence of his employees. In other words, all the courts do in these municipal negligence cases is require officials to weigh the consequences of their decisions. If Linda Riss' injury resulted from the failure of the city to pay sufficient salaries to attract qualified and sufficient personnel, the full cost of that choice should become acknowledged in the same way as it has in other areas of municipal tort liability. Perhaps officials will find it less costly to choose the alternative of paying damages than changing their existing practices. That may be well and good, but the price for the refusal to provide for an adequate police force should not be borne by Linda Riss and all the other innocent victims of such decisions. . . .

The methods of dealing with the problem of crime are left completely to the city's discretion. All that the courts can do is make sure that the costs of the city's and its employees' mistakes are placed where they properly belong. . . . The order of the Appellate Division should be reversed and a new trial granted.

ASSIGNMENT

13.6

a. Is it relevant that eight months after Burton Pugach was released from a fourteen-year prison term, he married Linda Riss? *Love Story: Part II,* N.Y. Times, Feb. 22, 1987, at 26.

b. Is the *Riss* case consistent with the *Soldano* case? Why or why not?

c. Smith is an informant who helps the police arrest a criminal. In a news interview, the police tell a reporter that Smith was helpful in making the arrest. Two weeks later, Smith tells the police that he needs special protection because his life has been threatened. He is denied this protection. When he is murdered, his estate sues the city for negligently failing to protect him. Does *Riss* apply?

PROTECTION FOR THE GOOD SAMARITAN

The Good Samaritan rules do not encourage people to come to the aid of their fellow citizens. "Try to do a good deed for someone and you end up being sued!" Some studies show that one in six potential volunteers refuses to become involved because of a fear of a lawsuit in the event that a mistake is made while trying to render aid. Even if the Good Samaritan wins the lawsuit, the embarrassment, time lost, and expense of defending oneself in court are enough to make many would-be rescuers conclude that the wiser course is to "mind my own business" rather than try to help a person in distress.

To combat this uncharitable inclination, a few states have passed laws *requiring* a citizen to become a Good Samaritan in emergency situations. Here is an example of this extreme approach:

Minnesota Statutes Annotated § 604A.01

Duty to assist. A person at the scene of an emergency who knows that another person is exposed to or has suffered grave physical harm shall, to the extent that the person can do so without danger or peril to self or others, give reasonable assistance to the exposed person. Reasonable assistance may include obtaining or attempting to obtain aid from law enforcement or medical personnel. A person who violates this subdivision is guilty of a petty misdemeanor.

Most states do not go this far. It is more common for a state to encourage rescue efforts by relieving Good Samaritans of civil liability for negligence in rendering emergency care or assistance. In such states, if a Good Samaritan makes a careless mistake, there is no negligence liability. In 1997, Congress passed the Volunteer Protection Act, which provides that "no volunteer of a nonprofit organization or governmental entity shall be liable for harm caused by an act or omission of the volunteer." There are exceptions, however, to this limitation of liability. For example, the volunteer *can* be liable for harm "caused by willful or criminal misconduct, gross negligence, reckless misconduct, or a conscious, flagrant indifference to the rights or safety of the individual harmed by the volunteer." (42 U.S.C. § 14503). This federal act applies to every state unless the state already provides protection for the volunteer or unless the state elects not to have the act apply. If a state "opts out" of the act and does not have its own program of protection, the old rules apply—a Good Samaritan can be sued for negligence in such states.

SUMMARY

Whenever one's conduct creates a foreseeable risk of injury or damage to someone else's person or property, a duty of reasonable care arises to take precautions to prevent that injury or damage. Under the Cardozo test, a duty is owed to a specific person who is foreseeably in the zone of danger. Under the Andrews test, a duty is owed to someone who suffers injury as a result of the defendant's unreasonable conduct toward anyone, even if the person injured was not in the zone of danger. Nonfeasance alone does not create a duty unless there is a special relationship between the parties. Among the special relationships are common carrier and passenger, innkeeper and guest, employer and employee, etc. If the defendant undertakes a task, he or she assumes a duty to perform it with reasonable care even though there was no initial duty to undertake it and even though the undertaking was gratuitous. If the defendant promises to undertake a task, he or she assumes a duty to perform it with reasonable care if the plaintiff relies on the promise, even though there was no initial duty to undertake it and even though the promise was gratuitous. Many states have laws that limit the liability of the Good Samaritan for simple negligence.

KEY TERMS

duty   214
general rule on duty   214
reasonable care   214
breach of duty   214
foreseeability   214
foreseeable plaintiff   215
unforeseeable plaintiff   215
Cardozo test   215

Andrews test   215
zone of danger   216
world at large   216
affirmative conduct   217
misfeasance   217
nonfeasance   217
malfeasance   217
special relationship   217

Good Samaritan   218
undertaking   222
gratuitous   222
consideration   222
promise   223
reliance   223

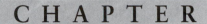

C H A P T E R

14

Negligence: Element II: Breach-of-duty (Unreasonableness)

CHAPTER OUTLINE

- Standard of Care: Reasonableness
- Breach-of-duty (Unreasonableness) Equation
- Objective or Subjective Standard?
- Res Ipsa Loquitur
- Custom and Usage
- Violation of a Statute
- Compliance with a Statute
- Gross Negligence (Unreasonableness) and Willful, Wanton, and Reckless Conduct
- Vicarious Liability

STANDARD OF CARE: REASONABLENESS

In Chapter 13, we studied the first element of negligence: duty. In the vast majority of cases, the duty is to use **reasonable care** to avoid injuring others, both bodily injury and property damage. Now we begin our examination of the second element of negligence: **breach of duty**. A breach of duty exists if the defendant engages in **unreasonable** conduct. When can we say that someone has acted unreasonably? One of the difficulties of tort law is to define what we mean by reasonableness as the **standard of care** by which to measure the breach of duty that leads to negligence liability. This difficulty will be our challenge in this chapter.

Totality of Circumstances

The beauty of reasonableness as a standard is that it is flexible enough to accommodate an infinite variety of situations. It is very versatile. On the other hand, the nightmare of reasonableness as a standard is that its determination requires a juggling act. All of the circumstances leading to the accident and injury must be assessed. At times, a slight change in any of the circumstances can produce a different result. Figure 14–1 identifies the **factors** that we must assess to determine whether someone acted reasonably. A factor is simply one of several circumstances or considerations that will be weighed in making a decision, no one of which is usually conclusive. (For more on factors, see Legal Analysis Guideline #12 in Chapter 2.) Note that the factors in Figure 14–1 cover a range of information such as data from the senses (e.g., what could be seen), identity and char-

FIGURE 14–1
Factors to be assessed in the determination of reasonableness.

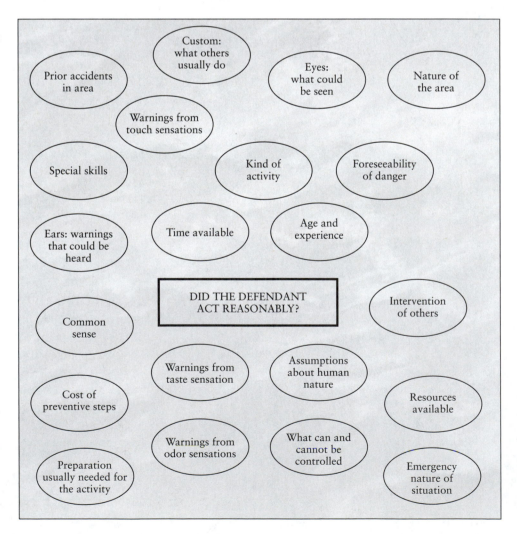

acteristics of the participants (e.g., their age and experience), earlier occurrences (e.g., prior accidents in the area), expectations (e.g., foreseeability of danger), and assessment of alternatives (e.g., cost of preventive steps). It is this mix of factors that will help us answer the question of whether the defendant was reasonable.

Comparative Standard

To establish a breach of duty by showing unreasonable conduct on the part of the defendant in a negligence case, five steps are necessary:

Step 1: State the injury the plaintiff claims to have suffered because of the defendant.

Step 2: Identify the specific acts or omissions of the defendant about which the plaintiff is complaining.

Step 3: Turn back the clock in your mind to the time just before the acts and omissions identified in step 2. Ask yourself what a reasonable person would have done under the same or similar circumstances *at that time*. (You answer this question by using your common sense of what a reasonable person would have done and, most important, by reading what court opinions have said a reasonable person would have done in such circumstances.)

Step 4: Compare the specific acts and omissions of the defendant identified in step 2 with what you said a reasonable person would have done in step 3.

Step 5: Reach your conclusion:

a. If the comparison in step 4 tells you that the defendant did exactly what a reasonable person would have done (or that there is a substantial similarity), then you can conclude that the defendant acted reasonably, and hence there was no breach of duty.

b. If the comparison in step 4 tells you that a reasonable person would have done the opposite of what the defendant did (or would have acted substantially differently from the defendant), then you can conclude that the defendant acted unreasonably, and hence there was a breach of duty.

In flowchart form, the comparative process is outlined in Figure 14–2.

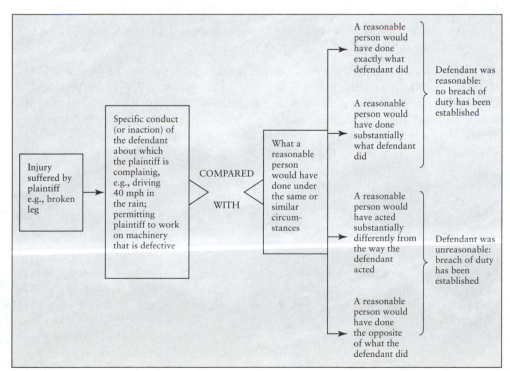

FIGURE 14–2
Reasonableness by comparison.

Examine the following excerpt from a memorandum of law that discusses the reasonableness of a truck driver who caused an accident on the road. Assume that one of the arguments against the truck driver was that he obviously acted unreasonably when he took his eyes off the road just before the accident. Here is the response of the truck driver. Excerpt B is a rewrite of Excerpt A.

Excerpt A:

The truck driver took his eyes off the road to look at his instrument panel and it was at this point that the truck collided with the other car. The driver did nothing unreasonable in taking his eyes off the road for a moment.

Excerpt B:

The truck driver took his eyes off the road to look at his instrument panel and it was at this point that the truck collided with the other car. It is not uncommon for truck drivers to take their eyes off the road. Reasonable drivers would not keep their eyes on the road at all times. For example, drivers glance at their gas gauge, their rear view mirror, etc. Trucks are designed with instrument panels that must be checked while the truck is moving. Drivers can't pull over every time they need to look away from the road. Hence, reasonable drivers must take their eyes off the road to look at their instrument panel, if only momentarily. It cannot be said, therefore, that the driver in this case was unreasonable simply because he took his eyes off the road momentarily.

Excerpt A does not demonstrate an understanding of the comparative nature of reasonableness. There is no comparison between what the truck driver did and what a reasonable truck driver would have done. All we have is a *conclusory* statement that he acted reasonably. The rewrite in Excerpt B, on the other hand, shows a very good grasp of the comparative nature of reasonableness. A major focus of the excerpt is on what a reasonable truck driver would have done under the same circumstances. This is compared to what the truck driver in this case actually did.

Reasonableness versus Perfection

What is a **reasonable person?** Unfortunately, it is easier to define what a reasonable person is *not* than to say definitively what one is. First, let us look at the traditional definition:

A reasonable person is an ordinary, prudent person who uses reasonable care to avoid injuring others.

This definition, although commonly used, is not very satisfactory. We are still left with the questions of what is "ordinary," what is "prudent," what is "reasonable care." We will focus on these questions in great detail later. For now, we need to confront the major myth that the reasonable person is a perfect person, or more narrowly, that a reasonable person does not injure other people. Figure 14–3 gives an overview of some of the basic differences among the perfect person, the reasonable person, and the unreasonable person.

BREACH-OF-DUTY (UNREASONABLENESS) EQUATION

To avoid injuring others, the reasonable person tries to avoid the dangers or risks of injury. How is this done? What mental process is used to decide what dangers to take precautions against? The reasonable person applies the **breach-of-duty equation** in Figure 14–4.

If the danger of a serious accident outweighs the burden or inconvenience of taking precautions to avoid the accident, the reasonable person would take those

Perfect Person	Reasonable Person	Unreasonable Person
1. Never causes an accident.	1. Does cause accidents, but they are never due to carelessness.	1. Causes accidents due to carelessness.
2. Never makes a mistake leading to an accident.	2. Does make mistakes leading to accidents, but the mistakes are never careless.	2. Makes careless mistakes leading to accidents.
3. Reacts perfectly in an emergency in order to prevent accidents.	3. Reacts as cautiously as possible in an emergency, but can still make a mistake in an emergency that causes an accident. These mistakes, however, are not careless.	3. Reacts carelessly in an emergency, causing accidents.
4. Has the right knowledge and experience needed to avoid accidents.	4a. Has the knowledge and experience common to everyone, and uses them to help avoid accidents. b. When more expert knowledge and experience are available, the reasonable person uses them to help avoid accidents. **Note:** even with the use of common or expert knowledge and experience, accidents can happen, but they are not due to carelessness.	4a. Does not have or fails to use the knowledge and experience common to everyone to help avoid accidents. b. When more expert knowledge and experience are available, the unreasonable person does not adequately use them to help prevent accidents.
5. Will undergo any inconvenience or burden to avoid an accident.	5. Will undergo only reasonable inconvenience or burden to avoid an accident.	5. Refuses to undergo even reasonable inconvenience or burden to avoid an accident.

FIGURE 14–3 Perfect/reasonable/unreasonable persons.

precautions. The failure of the defendant to do so would mean that the defendant was unreasonable and had committed a breach of duty in the law of negligence. If, on the other hand, the danger of a serious accident is so slight that the danger would not outweigh the relatively high burden or inconvenience of the precautions that would be needed to avoid the accident, then the reasonable person would *not* take these precautions. The failure of the defendant, therefore, to take these precautions would not amount to a breach of duty. The defendant is not deemed to be unreasonable even though the precautions would have prevented the accident the defendant caused.

To better understand the breach-of-duty equation, we need to explore the following topics:

- danger/caution hypothesis
- foreseeability
- burden or inconvenience
- importance or social utility

FIGURE 14–4
Breach-of-duty equation.

Foreseeability of the danger of an accident occurring		The burden or inconvenience on the defendant of taking precautions to avoid the accident
	balanced against	
Foreseeability of the kind of injury or damage that will result if an accident occurs		The importance or social utility of what the defendant was trying to do before the accident

Danger/Caution Hypothesis

A **hypothesis** is a theory or assumption. For every fact or group of facts, it is possible to state a hypothesis about the amount of danger that is present and the amount of caution that is needed to offset or eliminate the danger. The overriding principle is as follows: THE GREATER THE DANGER, THE GREATER THE CAUTION NEEDED. Here are some examples:

Facts: A sharp knife is on a table in a day care center.

Danger hypothesis: Knives are very attractive to children; knives are often easy for children to pick up; children do not appreciate the danger of knives; knives can seriously injure parts of the body with minimal force. Therefore, a sharp knife on a table in a day care center presents a VERY GREAT DANGER of SERIOUS injury to one of the children.

Caution: Given the high risk of potential danger, a GREAT DEAL of CAUTION is needed to avoid an injury from the knife. Precautions include removing the knife from the room or locking it away so that it is not reachable by any of the children.

Facts: A sharp knife is on a table in a factory.

Danger hypothesis: Factories are places for adults; adults know how to handle sharp knives, especially if the knife is used in a factory where the workers are skilled. Therefore, a sharp knife on a table in a factory poses ALMOST NO DANGER of injury to anyone.

Caution: Given the minimal and almost nonexistent danger posed by the knife, VERY LITTLE CAUTION is needed to avoid an injury from the knife.

ASSIGNMENT

14.1

Analyze the following fact situations. Assess the danger/caution hypothesis for each fact situation. Identify all possible dangers in each. How likely is each danger to lead to an injury? What kind of injury? In the light of your assessment of each danger, state how much caution is needed to avoid the injury. What precautions need to be taken? (See General Instructions for the Legal Analysis Assignment in Chapter 2.)

a. A sign on a busy three-lane street says, "USE TWO LANES GOING NORTH FROM 6 A.M. to 9:30 A.M. AND FROM 4:30 P.M. to 6:30 P.M. EXCEPT HOLIDAYS AND WEEKENDS. USE ONE LANE AT ALL OTHER TIMES."

b. Mary owns a motorcycle. Her friend, Leo, does not know how to drive it. Mary lets Leo drive the motorcycle while Mary is sitting right behind him, giving instructions as they drive in an empty lot.

c. The XYZ Chemical Company manufactures a new floor cleaner. On the label of the bottle containing the cleaner, there are very bright colors and a cartoon of a happy person cleaning the floor. The ingredients are listed on the label, plus a warning to keep the liquid away from eyes.

Of course, it can be argued that there is danger lurking in everything. It is possible to conceive of a set of acts in which any object (e.g., a tissue) could be used to injure someone in some way. This is not the kind of danger we are talking about in negligence law. It is not a breach of duty to fail to take precautions against every conceivable danger. Reasonableness does not require excessive caution.

How do we decide the amount of caution that *is* reasonable in a given set of circumstances? The answer depends on carefully weighing the elements of the breach-of-duty equation in Figure 14–4.

- **The FORESEEABILITY of an accident occurring.**
  The more foreseeable the accident is, the more caution a reasonable person would take to try to prevent the accident.
- **The FORESEEABILITY of the kind of injury or damage that would result from the accident if it occurs.**
  The more serious the kind of injury or damage that is foreseeable, the more caution a reasonable person would take to prevent the accident.
- **The BURDEN or INCONVENIENCE that would be involved in taking the precautions necessary to avoid the accident.**
  The greater the burden or inconvenience, the less likely a reasonable person would take the precautions to avoid the accident.
- **The IMPORTANCE or SOCIAL UTILITY of what the defendant was trying to do before the accident.**
  The more important or socially useful it is, the more likely a reasonable person would take risks in carrying it out.

Foreseeability

In Chapter 4 we took a detailed look at foreseeability and the methods by which it is determined. Review the foreseeability-determination formula in that chapter (see Figure 4–2). Our concern here is the foreseeability of the danger of an accident occurring (e.g., a customer slipping on a wet floor, a worker dropping a case of dynamite, an electric switch malfunctioning) and the danger of a particular kind of injury or damage occurring (e.g., death, crop destruction). As indicated in the formula in Figure 4–2, there are eight interrelated topics to be assessed:

- area analysis
- activity analysis
- people analysis
- preparation analysis
- assumptions about human nature
- historical data
- specific sensory data
- common sense

Assessing all of these topics will tell us what dangers a reasonable person would have foreseen. Once we know what a reasonable person would have foreseen, we know what the defendant *should* have foreseen.

Recall that we do not simply want to know *whether* the danger is foreseeable. The critical question is *how foreseeable* are the dangers. Review the foreseeability spectrum in Figure 4–1 in Chapter 4. Are we talking about a danger that is only a slight possibility? A slight probability? A highly unusual danger? A certainty?

Burden or Inconvenience

Next, we examine the *burden or inconvenience* that would have to be borne in order to avoid the danger. Our focus at this point is not *who* should bear the burden or inconvenience, but *what* precisely *is* this burden or inconvenience. Suppose that the danger under discussion is a customer falling on a wet floor in a supermarket on a rainy day, and that the kind of injury posed by this danger is a broken or bruised limb. After going through the foreseeability-determination formula, assume we conclude that both dangers are fairly probable. Now let us focus on the burden or inconvenience on the supermarket of eliminating the danger. Burdens or inconveniences fall into the interrelated categories of cost, time, and effectiveness:

- **Costs**
  How much money would have been needed to take the steps needed to prevent the accident from happening? The cost of a sign saying, "CAUTION, WET FLOOR"? The cost of an employee whose job on a rainy day is to mop the floor all day long? Every hour? The cost of a rug to absorb the water? The cost of closing the store on rainy days? Etc.
- **Time**
  How much time would have been lost in having the sign painted? How much time would have been lost in having an employee mop up all day? Every hour? Etc.
- **Effectiveness**
  By effectiveness, we do not mean the effectiveness of the precautions in preventing the accident. Rather, the question is what impact any of the precautions would have had on the overall effectiveness of what the defendant was doing. If the precautions had been taken, how would they have affected the defendant's operation or activity? Going through the modest trouble of making and using a "WET FLOOR" sign would certainly not alter the effectiveness of the supermarket's business very much. Closing every day that it rains, however, would substantially disrupt the effectiveness of the supermarket's business. Indeed, this burden might amount to having to go out of business.

Importance or Social Utility

Finally, we examine the *importance or social utility* of what the defendant was trying to do before the accident occurred. Was the defendant driving to work? Watching a football game? Playing a practical joke? Skydiving for fun? Trying to cure cancer? Saving a child from a fire? The more beneficial or socially useful the activity, the more likely it is that a reasonable person would take risks to accomplish the goals involved. This does not mean that a reasonable person would never take any risks of injury if engaged in a mundane or frivolous task. It simply means that reasonable persons would take fewer risks of injuring someone else (or themselves) while engaged in such tasks than they would in tasks that we would all agree are more important and socially beneficial.

The reasonable person, therefore, will juggle all four components of the equation in order to decide what risks should be taken and what precautions should be taken to avoid an accident. The foreseeability of an accident, the foreseeability of the kind of injury or damage, the burden or inconvenience of the precautions, and the importance or social utility of the defendant's conduct must all be properly assessed. *Defendants will be found to have breached their duty if these factors were not assessed in the same or in substantially the same manner as a reasonable person would have assessed them.* This weighing or balancing of risks and benefits through the breach-of-duty equation is known as a **risk-benefit analysis** (also called a cost-benefit analysis or a **risk-utility analysis**).

Cynics charge that some manufacturers go through a drastically different kind of risk-benefit analysis when they decide whether to add a safety feature to a product.

EXAMPLE: The XYZ Motor Company places the gas tank in the rear of its cars. Since rear-end collisions are common, this location of the tank increases the risk of fire explosion from such collisions when the tank is hit. A number of such explosions in fact occur, leading to judgments against XYZ. As the company prepares for next year's models, it must decide whether to keep the gas tank in the rear or to locate it in a place less likely to lead to such fire explosions. An XYZ engineer writes a memo that calculates how much future lawsuits might cost per vehicle if the tank is kept in the rear. To reach this figure, the cost of anticipated lawsuits is divided by the number of vehicles expected to be sold. This calculation leads to the conclusion that the litigation cost of keeping the tank in the rear would be only a few dollars per vehicle. Since this cost is less than what the company would have to spend to move the tank, the company decides to keep the tank in the rear for its new models.

Can you imagine how excited a personal-injury attorney would be to obtain a copy of such a memo? Ecstatic would be the more likely reaction. This is precisely what happened in 1999 when a California jury awarded $4.9 billion to six people who were severely burned when their General Motors car was rammed from behind by another vehicle. The verdict consisted of $107.6 million in compensatory damages and $4.8 billion in punitive damages. (The trial judge reduced the punitive damages to $1.09 billion, but allowed the compensatory award to stand. G.M. then announced that it would file an appeal.) The burns were caused by the explosion of the gas tank in the rear of the car in which the six plaintiffs were riding. Their attorney was able to introduce into evidence a "smoking-gun" memo written by Edward Ivey, a G.M. engineer. The memo estimated that the company would have to pay out $200,000 for each fatality caused by the placement of the gas tank. Based on the number of cars on the road, "Mr. Ivey came up with an estimate of the cost to G.M. of $2.40 per vehicle."[1] Other evidence showed that the cost of redesigning the car to prevent this kind of accident would have been $8.59 per vehicle. Although there was some controversy at the trial over what role the Ivey memo had in the design decisions of G.M., there was little doubt that the memo had a major impact on the decision of the jury. G.M. refused to spend $8.59 to prevent the kind of tragedy that occurred. The plaintiffs' attorney told the jury that under a risk-benefit analysis, G.M. felt it was cheaper to pay $2.40 to litigate and settle the cases arising from the anticipated fatalities.

This is *not* the kind of analysis a reasonable manufacturer would make in applying the breach-of-duty equation in Figure 14–4. As we will see in Chapter 19 on products liability, a company should not make safety decisions solely on the basis of the cost of litigation. The question should not be how much will a death or maiming cost the company through verdicts and settlements. In light of the value of the product, the question should be how likely (foreseeable) is severe injury and what burdens would have to be undertaken to add a safety feature that would prevent the injury. If the burdens are relatively low and the risk of severe injury is high, a reasonable manufacturer would add the safety feature. This is very different from concluding that it would be cheaper to pay injured plaintiffs than to fix the problem by redesigning the product.

OBJECTIVE OR SUBJECTIVE STANDARD?

It is important that you understand the distinction between a **subjective standard** and an **objective standard**. By "standard" we mean the method by which something is assessed or measured.

---

[1] Andrew Pollack, *Paper Trail Haunts G.M. After It Loses Injury Suit: An Old Memo Hinted at the Price of Safety*, N.Y. Times, July 12, 1999, at A12.

FIGURE 14–5
Objective and subjective standards.

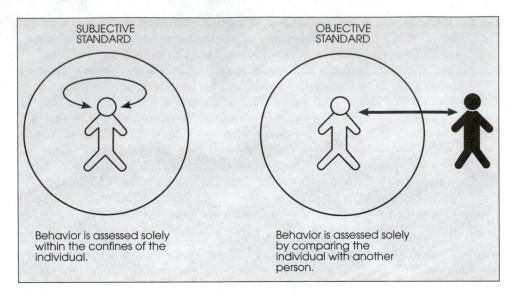

SUBJECTIVE STANDARD

OBJECTIVE STANDARD

Behavior is assessed solely within the confines of the individual.

Behavior is assessed solely by comparing the individual with another person.

A subjective standard is being used when something is measured solely by what one individual (e.g., the defendant) actually did, knew, believed, or understood. When Bob says, "that car is attractive," he is probably using a subjective standard: attractiveness *to Bob*. An objective standard is being used when something is defined or resolved solely by comparing one person to one or more other persons. When Bob says, "Jane is an excellent athlete," he is probably using an objective standard. Jane is excellent because she performs as well as or better than *other* athletes. The quality of her athletic skills is determined by comparing her to other athletes—an objective standard. See Figure 14–5.

We said earlier that reasonableness was a comparative standard: we compared what the defendant did to what a reasonable person would have done. This suggests that reasonableness is an objective standard. In the main, this is so. To at least some extent, however, reasonableness is also a subjective standard, as we shall see.

There is, of course, no actual human being who holds the title of "reasonable person." The concept of the reasonable person (sometimes called the "reasonable man") was invented in order to provide juries with guidance in trying to determine whether conduct that unintentionally caused injury was wrongful and hence negligent.[2] We now take a closer look at who this reasonable person is. We know that the reasonable person is not perfect. The reasonable person can and does cause accidents. Such accidents, however, are never due to carelessness or imprudent behavior. (See Figure 14–3.) What else do we know about this person? We examine first the physical characteristics and then the mental characteristics of the reasonable person.

Physical Characteristics

The reasonable person has the same physical strengths and weaknesses as the defendant. Hence, if a blind man causes an accident and is sued, the blind man's conduct will be measured against what a reasonable *blind* person would have done under the same or similar circumstances.

> **EXAMPLE:** Fred is blind. While walking down the corridor, he bumps into the plaintiff who falls and is injured. Fred was not using his cane at the time.

---

[2]If the defendant *intended* the contact or the injury that the plaintiff suffered, then we are not talking about negligence as the cause of action. The plaintiff may be able to use one of the intentional torts, e.g., battery. Intentional conduct may even lead to prosecution for a crime (e.g., criminal trespass, manslaughter).

Assume that if Fred did not have a sight handicap, the accident would not have happened. This does not necessarily mean that Fred was negligent. The question is not how a reasonable person with no physical disabilities would have acted. The question is how a reasonable person who is blind would have acted. Phrased another way, how would a reasonable person have acted under the circumstances when one of those circumstances is his or her blindness? It may be that Fred was not acting unreasonably in walking without a cane. Suppose, for example, that he was taking a short walk in an area he was very familiar with and that he had other means of sensing objects around him. A reasonable person who is blind, therefore, might not use a cane in such a case. Note that as to physical characteristics, the standard is both objective (the reasonable person) and subjective (a reasonable person with the same physical characteristics as the defendant).

Sometimes a physical handicap may require greater precautions than those expected of a person without such infirmities.

> **EXAMPLE:** Mary has two broken legs. Yet she continues to drive. While driving one day on the freeway, she causes an accident.

If Mary is sued for negligence, the question will not be whether she was driving as best she could. This would be a totally subjective standard. Rather, the issue will be what the reasonable person with two broken legs would have done. It may be that such a person would not have driven on the freeway or would drive only cars that are specially equipped for handicapped drivers. If Mary failed to use such precautions, she acted unreasonably.

Suppose, however, that the defendant had physical capacities *beyond* that of most people, e.g., superior vision, quicker reflexes. The test of reasonableness for this defendant is what a reasonable person *with these same physical strengths* would have done.

ASSIGNMENT
14.2

Fred is blind. While lighting a cigarette, he causes a fire because he did not know that he was in an area containing flammable materials. He could not see a sign that read, "Warning: Highly Flammable Vapors. No Smoking." Was Fred negligent? (See General Instructions for the Legal Analysis Assignment in Chapter 2.)

Mental Characteristics (When the Defendant Is an Adult)

Here we are talking about knowledge, intelligence, and overall mental ability that comes from experience and learning. In this regard, the reasonable person is neither exceptionally bright, nor of low intelligence. The reasonable person has the basic knowledge and intelligence needed in everyday life to handle the common occurrences of living. For example, a reasonable person would know that an exposed electrical wire can be very dangerous, but is not expected to know how to repair wire cables. A reasonable person would know that a child in a large body of water can drown, but is not expected to know how to perform complicated medical procedures on a drowning victim.

Suppose that the defendant has a mental illness or deficiency that prevents him or her from knowing that electricity is dangerous or that water can drown people. Is this defendant still held to the standard of the reasonable person who has no such illness or deficiency? Yes. Such defendants are therefore held to a standard that they cannot meet. The standard as to mental characteristics is very objective. For physical handicaps, discussed earlier, the test is what the reasonable person *with defendant's physical handicap* would have done. For mental disabilities in an adult, the test is what a reasonable person *without defendant's mental disabilities* would have done.

Suppose, however, that the defendant has mental strengths beyond that expected of everyone. For example, the defendant may be a doctor, an electrician, a police officer, etc. When this individual causes an injury, the standard of performance will be the reasonable person *with this special knowledge or skill.* Hence, the standard is subjective in the sense that we are talking about the special knowledge or skill *of the defendant,* but is objective in that we are comparing the defendant's conduct with that *of a reasonable person* with that knowledge or skill.

The special problems involving a doctor's skills (medical malpractice) and an attorney's skills (legal malpractice) will be discussed in Chapter 18.

Mental Characteristics (When the Defendant Is a Child)

An exception is made when the defendant is a child. When assessing breach of duty by a child, the standard is substantially subjective: What would a reasonable child of the age and intelligence of the defendant have done under the same or similar circumstances? Finally, however, there is an exception to this exception. When the child is engaging in an adult activity, such as driving a car, the child will be held to the standard of a reasonable *adult.*

RES IPSA LOQUITUR

Res ipsa loquitur (RIL) means "the event or thing speaks for itself." It is a doctrine used by a plaintiff having trouble proving the defendant's breach of duty—the defendant's unreasonableness. RIL is an evidentiary tool designed to give the plaintiff a break in certain kinds of situations.

> **EXAMPLE:** Plaintiff sues the owner of a building for negligence after being injured in an elevator that suddenly crashed to the basement from the second floor. The *only* evidence plaintiff is able to introduce is the fact of being in the elevator when it collapsed.

Without the aid of res ipsa, the plaintiff would lose because of the failure to establish the second element of negligence—breach of duty. Where is the specific evidence that the building owner was unreasonable in the maintenance of the elevator? There is none. All we know is that the accident happened. If res ipsa applies in such a case, the jury will be allowed to draw an inference of unreasonableness. In effect, res ipsa simply allows the plaintiff to get his or her case to the jury. It does not mean that the plaintiff has won the case.

What are the elements of a res ipsa case, in which the inference of unreasonableness can be drawn simply by reason of the fact that the accident happened? What does the plaintiff have to prove in order to get the case to the jury and require the latter to consider (but not necessarily accept) the inference of the defendant's unreasonableness? The three basic elements that must be established by the plaintiff are outlined in Figure 14–6.

More Likely Than Not Due to Someone's Unreasonableness

> **Example:** Tom is driving his car down the street. Suddenly, his front tire blows out. His car runs into plaintiff's car. Plaintiff sues Tom for negligence. The only evidence of unreasonableness introduced by the plaintiff is the fact of the tire blow out. Is this a res ipsa case?

No. The first element of a res ipsa case has not been satisfied. The most likely explanation of the tire blow out is *not* someone's unreasonableness. An equally likely explanation is that Tom unknowingly and quite innocently ran over a nail or other sharp object. To be sure, Tom's unreasonableness is a *possible* explanation. A mere possibility of unreasonableness, however, is not enough for the first element of a res ipsa case.

Traditional Statement of the Elements	Statement of the Elements as Applied
1. The event must be of a kind that ordinarily does not occur in the absence of someone's negligence.	1. It must be more likely than not that the accident was due to someone's unreasonableness.
2. The event must be caused by an agency or instrumentality within the exclusive control of the defendant.	2a. It must be more likely than not that the accident was due to the *defendant's* unreasonableness. b. The possibility, if any, that the unreasonableness of others caused the accident must be adequately eliminated.
3. The event must not have been due to any voluntary action or contribution on the part of the plaintiff.	3. Plaintiff must not be a responsible cause of the accident.

FIGURE 14–6 Elements of a res ipsa loquitur case.

Compare the tire blow out case with the elevator case mentioned earlier. Can it be said that it is more likely than not that the explanation for an elevator falling from the second floor is someone's unreasonableness? The answer in this case is yes. One might indeed go so far as to say that it is highly likely that someone was unreasonable. Here are some of the arguments that could be made in support of this conclusion:

- It is commonly known that elevators require frequent inspections.
- If the inspections are adequate, they should reveal defects.
- A falling elevator can cause severe damage to passengers.
- Given the severity of the potential damage, one would expect very careful maintenance by those in charge of the operation and safety of the elevator; when an elevator falls, the likelihood is that this kind of care was not given.
- Elevators have been in existence for a long time; they are not mysterious machines we know very little about; hence, we cannot say that the mishap was probably due to some unknown factor.
- There is safety equipment on an elevator system; if this equipment were being maintained properly (reasonably), it is unlikely that the collapse would occur.

The plaintiff does not have to prove that the *only* explanation for the accident was someone's unreasonableness. The plaintiff does not have to prove that no other cause is possible. The test for this first element is whether unreasonableness by someone is *more likely than not* the explanation. (See Figure 14–7.) Hence, a defendant does not defeat a res ipsa case simply by showing that it is *possible* that the accident was *not* due to unreasonableness.

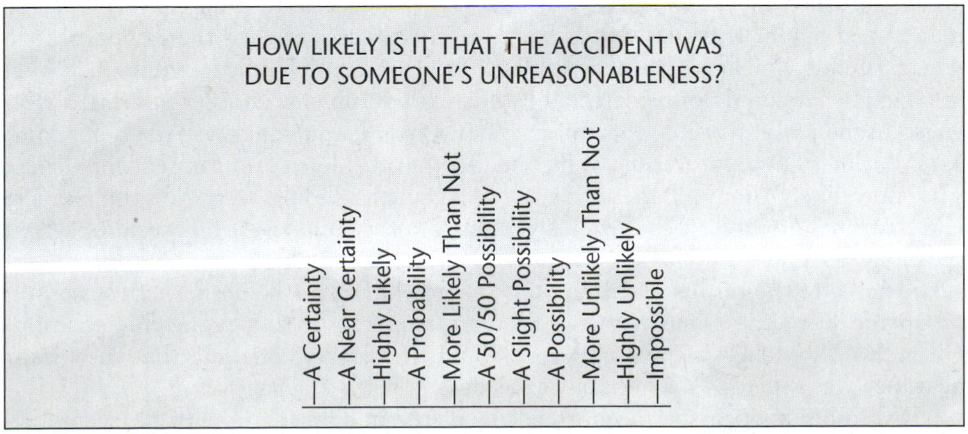

FIGURE 14–7 Spectrum of likelihood.

HOW LIKELY IS IT THAT THE ACCIDENT WAS
DUE TO SOMEONE'S UNREASONABLENESS?

A Certainty — A Near Certainty — Highly Likely — A Probability — More Likely Than Not — A 50/50 Possibility — A Slight Possibility — A Possibility — More Unlikely Than Not — Highly Unlikely — Impossible

ASSIGNMENT 14.3

Examine the following list of accidents. How likely is it that each accident was due to someone's unreasonableness? Where on the "spectrum of likelihood" does each accident fall? Give reasons for your answer. If more than one answer is possible, explain all the answers. In each case you can assume that the person injured is trying to get to the jury on a res ipsa theory. Assume that the only evidence available is the fact of the accident. (See the General Instructions for the Legal Analysis Assignment in Chapter 2.)

a. A passenger is injured when an airplane explodes on the runway before takeoff.
b. Electricity leaks from a wire and injures a child.
c. A small insect is found in a can of soup, injuring a consumer.
d. A large nail is found in a can of soup, injuring a consumer.
e. Two cars collide on the street, injuring a pedestrian.
f. A car collides into a parked car, damaging the latter.
g. A bottle of soda explodes, injuring a customer.
h. Cattle stray onto a road, damaging a parked car.

More Likely Than Not Due to Defendant's Unreasonableness

When the first element of res ipsa is established, we know that the accident was more likely than not due to *someone's* unreasonableness. In a lawsuit, of course, you do not sue a vague someone—you must sue the *defendant*. The second element of res ipsa requires the plaintiff to show that it is more likely than not that the accident was caused by the unreasonableness *of the defendant*. The "spectrum of likelihood" in Figure 14–7 for the first element applies here as well. If the unreasonableness of the defendant is a mere possibility, or if there is a 50/50 possibility that the accident was due to the unreasonableness of someone other than the defendant, then the second element of res ipsa has not been established.

> **EXAMPLE:** Mary is a passenger on XYZ Airlines, which manufactures and flies its own commercial planes. While Mary's plane is flying over the ocean, it disappears. Mary's estate sues XYZ for negligence and tries to get its case to the jury on a res ipsa theory. The only evidence of unreasonableness offered by the estate is the fact that the plane disappeared.

Can it be said that it is more likely than not that the defendant's (XYZ's) unreasonableness caused the disappearance of the plane, e.g., due to a defectively built or maintained plane? It is surely *possible* that other causes created the disappearance (e.g., a sudden violent storm that could not have been anticipated, a bomb concealed in luggage that could not be detected by current equipment, another passenger who went insane). It is possible that there was no unreasonableness by the defendant, XYZ Airlines. Yet, a jury could still conclude that the defendant's unreasonableness was more likely than not the cause of the accident leading to the disappearance. XYZ Airlines apparently had exclusive control of the plane—it built and operated the plane. Airplane travel is very common in our society. Crashes are thoroughly investigated and the results usually point to some defect in the design, construction, or operation of the plane—or at least one could reasonably argue this position. Given XYZ's exclusive control, a jury could, therefore, conclude that the disappearance was due to XYZ's unreasonableness in some respect.

Two other major issues need to be considered in connection with the second element of res ipsa: 1. What if the defendant was not in exclusive control of what caused the accident? 2. What if more than one person is sued and not all of them could have caused the accident?

1.   What if the defendant was not in exclusive control of what caused the acci-dent? In spite of the traditional way in which the second element of res ipsa is com-monly phrased (see first column of Figure 14–6), it is *not* always necessary for the defendant to be in exclusive control of what caused the accident. Exclusive control is simply *one* of the ways to prove that the unreasonableness causing the accident was that of the defendant. Assume that a soda bottle explodes in the plaintiff's hands. At the time of this accident, the bottle may no longer be in the exclusive control of the manufacturer. Yet, res ipsa loquitur is still possible in negligence suits of this kind.[3] It is true that before the bottle reached the consumer, it passed through several hands in addition to the manufacturer. A trucking company, for example, as well as one or more distributor/retailers may have made some contact with the bottle. It is admit-tedly difficult for the consumer to use res ipsa to show that it was the manufacturer's unreasonableness that was responsible for the explosion of the bottle. The law, how-ever, tends to be somewhat lenient on plaintiffs in such cases, knowing the tremen-dous problem of proof that they have. The second element of res ipsa can still apply if the plaintiff submits enough evidence to enable a jury to conclude that the explo-sion was *probably not* due to anyone else in the chain of distribution between the manufacturer and consumer. Examples of such evidence include:

- evidence of careful handling of the bottle once it left the manufacturer, or the absence of evidence of careless handling during this time
- no evidence the bottle was dropped once it left the manufacturer
- no evidence of cracks on the bottle
- no improper storage indicated

Such evidence, although fairly weak in itself, is usually sufficient to permit a jury to rationally eliminate other potential causes so as to conclude that it is more likely than not that the unreasonableness of the defendant (here, the manufacturer) caused the bottle to explode. If, of course, there is strong specific evidence to the contrary (e.g., evidence of vandalism or dropping since it left the hands of the manufacturer), the plaintiff will have great difficulty establishing the second element of res ipsa.

ROBERT FARRELL

---

[3]Additional theories of liability against the manufacturer include strict liability in tort and breach of warranty. See Chapter 19.

ASSIGNMENT **14.4**	In the following two cases, has the second element of res ipsa loquitur been established? (See General Instructions for the Legal Analysis Assignment in Chapter 2.) Be sure to include a discussion of possible explanations in each case. What further evidence would you try to obtain in both cases? (See General Instructions for the Investigation Strategy Assignment in Chapter 2.)

a. Richard is a customer in Karen's supermarket. He slips on a ripe, yellow banana peel and is injured.

b. Richard is a customer in Karen's supermarket. He slips on a black, moldy banana peel and is injured.

2. **What if more than one person is sued and not all of them could have caused the accident?** The classic res ipsa case involving multiple defendants is *Ybarra v. Spangard*,[4] in which a patient received an injury while unconscious. The patient sued all the doctors, nurses, and other hospital employees involved. Since the plaintiff was unconscious at the time of the injury, there was no way for the plaintiff to give direct testimony about which of the defendants was or was not responsible. No other evidence was available. Hence, according to our test on the second element of res ipsa, the plaintiff cannot show it is more likely than not that the unreasonableness of any of the individual defendants caused the injury. Remarkably, however, the court in *Ybarra* allowed the application of res ipsa loquitur against all of the defendants. This had the practical effect of forcing these defendants to decide among themselves who was responsible. Failing to do this, **joint and several liability** would result. This means each defendant is liable for all the damages suffered by the plaintiff, who can sue any or all of the defendants until 100 percent of the damages are recovered. (An individual defendant who is joint and severally liable cannot force the plaintiff to collect part of the damages from the other defendants.)

Not all states follow the *Ybarra* case. Many would deny the application of res ipsa in such cases because of the difficulty of establishing the second element of res ipsa. The unusual ruling in *Ybarra* may have been due to a special duty of care that medical personnel owe patients and to the fact that in *Ybarra* there was a pre-existing relationship among all the defendants.[5]

Plaintiff Is Not a Responsible Cause of the Accident

The final element of res ipsa the plaintiff must establish is that the plaintiff was not the responsible cause of the accident. In the vast majority of cases, this means little more than plaintiff's showing that there was no contributory negligence (or more accurately, showing that the plaintiff's own unreasonableness, if any, did not cause the accident). In the bottle explosion case, for example, the plaintiff must show that there is no evidence he or she mishandled or dropped the bottle while holding it.

ASSIGNMENT **14.5**	Select any of the eight fact situations (*a–h*) of Assignment 14.3. Draft a complaint covering the fact situation you select. (See General Instructions for the Complaint-Drafting Assignment in Chapter 2.)

---

[4]25 Cal. 2d 486, 154 P.2d 687 (1944).
[5]W. Page Keeton et al., *Prosser and Keeton on the Law of Torts* 252 (5th ed. 1984).

CASE

Ward v. Forrester Day Care, Inc.
547 So. 2d 410 (1989)
Supreme Court of Alabama

Background: *The parents of an 11-week-old child sued a day care center for negligently causing the child's broken arm. The trial court entered summary judgment for the center. The case is now on appeal before the Supreme Court of Alabama.*

Decision on Appeal: *Reversed and remanded. Res ipsa loquitur can apply.*

OPINION OF COURT

Justice MADDOX delivered the opinion of the court . . .

On April 29, 1987, Radney Garrett Ward, an 11-week-old baby boy, was left at Forrester day care center in Dothan, operated by the defendant. The parents of baby Garrett, Radney Ward, Sr., and Margaret Ward, did not see their child until approximately 5:30 or 6:00 that afternoon, when he was picked up by Radney Ward, Sr. When the child was lifted out of his chair that afternoon, he screamed "a very unusual scream," according to the plaintiffs, causing them to suspect that something was wrong with him. The Wards said they examined him to determine if something was wrong with him, but they could not discover what caused him to scream. The next day, the child was brought back to Forrester day care center and was left for the day. Mr. and Mrs. Ward said that when Garrett was taken home on the afternoon of April 30, they noticed swelling on his right wrist. The next morning, they took young Garrett to his pediatrician, Dr. Barron, who instructed them to take him to Dr. Owen, a local orthopedic surgeon, and have his arm X-rayed. Dr. Owen examined the child and discovered that his arm had been broken. The parents sued Forrester Day Care, Inc.

Mr. and Mrs. Ward both testified in depositions that their child was not injured while under their care and that the only other place he had been cared for was Forrester day care center. Employees of Forrester testified that the baby was not injured while at the Forrester day care center. The same employees also testified about the operations of the center, the tendencies of their evidence being to indicate that there was no negligence.

In contrast to the testimony of the Forrester employees, Mr. and Mrs. Ward both testified in their depositions that they had witnessed conditions at the center that they contend showed the Center was improperly operated. The Wards testified in their depositions concerning several conditions that they say were potentially dangerous and could have caused the injury to their child, or to any other child under the care of the Forrester day care center. However, there is no evidence that shows the exact cause of the child's broken arm.

The plaintiffs' position is that the defendant's employees have adopted a "conspiracy of silence" and that that conspiracy should not remove their legal remedy for the injury suffered by Garrett while at the day care center. The Wards ask us to apply the doctrine of *res ipsa loquitur*. . . .

Defendant argues that "[w]here the act or instrumentality causing the injury is unknown, there is no basis for the application of the doctrine of res ipsa loquitur," citing *McClinton v. McClinton*, 258 Ala. 542, 63 So. 2d 594 (1952), and *Viking Motor Lodge, Inc. v. American Tobacco Co.,* 286 Ala. 112, 237 So. 2d 632 (1970). Defendant correctly states the plaintiff's usual burden of proof, but a plaintiff is not required in every case to show a specific instrumentality that caused the injury. The drafters of comments (f) and (g) to the *Restatement (Second) of Torts* § 328D (1965) state that in making the negligence point to the defendant, this is usually done by showing that a specific instrumentality has caused the event, or that *"all reasonably probable causes were under the exclusive control of the defendant."* (Emphasis added.) The commentators note that "[i]t is not, however, necessary to the inference that the defendant have such exclusive control; and exclusive control is merely one way of proving his responsibility." *Restatement (Second) of Torts* § 328D.

In this case, the plaintiffs claim that the defendant was guilty of negligent supervision. As a general rule, a plaintiff who can prove his case by specific acts of negligence cannot avail himself of the doctrine of *res ipsa loquitur*. We do not believe that rule is applicable here.

In *Zimmer v. Celebrities, Inc.*, 44 Colo. App. 515, 519, 615 P.2d 76, 79-80 (1980), the Court addressed this question, as follows:

"Defendant also contends that res ipsa loquitur is inapplicable in this case because plaintiffs have argued and introduced some evidence that defendant was negligent in supervision of the nursery. Defendant reasons that negligent supervision would be a specific act of negligence and therefore res ipsa is not applicable. We do not agree. *Kitto v. Gilbert,* 39 Colo. App. 374, 570 P.2d 544 (1977), is dispositive of this issue. In that case we held that:

" 'Res ipsa loquitur is a rule which presumes evidence which applies when it is judicially determined that a particular unexplained occurrence creates a prima facie case of negligence without proof of specific misfeasance. . . . A corollary requirement is that no direct evidence exists establishing that a specific act of negligence was *the only likely cause* for the harm. . . . *The mere introduction of evidence as to how an accident could have occurred and its possible causes* does not necessarily preclude application of res ipsa loquitur so long as that evidence does not clearly resolve the issue of culpability.' "

39 Colo. App. at 379, 570 P.2d at 548 (emphasis added except the word 'possible'.)

"Even though evidence was offered concerning the probabilities of the injury being caused by a piece of equipment or by inadequate supervision on the premises, there was no direct evidence establishing a specific act of negligence which was the only likely cause of the injury, and the evidence presented did not resolve the issue of culpability."

44 Colo. App. at 519, 615 P.2d at 79-80.

We hold that the mere introduction of evidence as to how an accident could have occurred and its possible causes does not necessarily preclude the application of the doctrine of *res ipsa loquitur* so long as that evidence does not clearly resolve the issue of culpability.

Based on the foregoing, we hold that the trial court erred in entering summary judgment for the defendant. Reversed and remanded.

ASSIGNMENT 14.6

a. Who had exclusive control of the baby during the time of the injury? The Wards took the baby home and returned him to the center the next day after hearing the "very unusual scream" at the center. Was there exclusive control by the defendant? If not, how can the Wards use res ipsa loquitur?

b. The Smiths are about to go on a two-week vacation. They take their pet poodle to the Dog Vacation Home. When they return, the manager of the Home says that the dog unfortunately died and had to be cremated. The manager does not know why it died. The caretaker at the Dog Vacation Home came in one morning and found it dead in its cage. Does res ipsa loquitur apply?

CUSTOM AND USAGE

Often in a negligence case the plaintiff alleges that the defendant failed to take specific precautionary steps and that this failure led to the plaintiff's injury. For example:

- the failure to place a safety guard on a bicycle wheel
- the failure to build a fence alongside a railroad track
- the failure to place a rubber mat in front of a store
- the failure to have two-way radios in tugboats
- the failure to perform a medical test to detect a certain disease

A common response of the defendant in these cases is that no one else in the field takes these steps. The defendant is saying: "a reasonable person in my position would not have taken these steps; it is the custom in the field to act the way I acted." Hence, the question becomes: When is it reasonable to do what everyone else is doing or to fail to do something when everyone else fails to do it as well?

As indicated in Figure 14–1, what is reasonable depends on a wide variety of circumstances. One of these circumstances is what others are doing. It may be unreasonable, for example, to expect a defendant to take a very expensive precaution that no other person in the defendant's position has ever taken and that is designed to avoid the small risk of very minor injury. On the other hand, it may be that an entire industry or profession is being unreasonable in failing to take a certain precautionary step. They may be acting unreasonably in spite of the fact that everyone is acting in the same way. To let them off the hook would provide little incentive to raise their standards.

Recall the breach-of-duty equation: The foreseeability of injury must be balanced against the extent of the burden or inconvenience of taking precautions against the injury occurring. (See Figure 14–4.) The more foreseeable the danger of serious injury, the more reasonable it is for the defendant to bear the burden or inconvenience of trying to prevent the injury. This principle helps us assess the impact of **custom and usage.**

We need to ask *why* the business or profession acted or failed to act in a certain way. Suppose a company manufactures a product, but does not add a device that would protect the public against a particular kind of injury. Suppose further that this is the custom in the industry—no manufacturer adds the device. Why isn't the device added? Because the injury is very rare? If so, this is relevant to the foreseeability of danger in the breach-of-duty equation. Because of the cost of adding the device? Would the price to the consumer be so high that only the wealthy could afford the product with the device? Because of a loss of effectiveness? If the device were added, would the product be significantly less effective in its primary function? These questions are relevant to the burden/inconvenience component of the breach-of-duty equation.

In short, the most you can say is that custom and usage is *a* relevant factor in the law of negligence, but it almost never settles the question of what is reasonableness or unreasonableness.

VIOLATION OF A STATUTE

In a negligence case, the plaintiff will often include an allegation that the defendant violated a statute.

> **EXAMPLE:** Ron Davis carelessly drives his truck onto Ed Packard's land. Davis crashes into a lamppost. The impact causes a gasoline storage tank on the truck to flip over, spilling the contents on the ground. A spontaneous fire breaks out, causing extensive damage. Packard sues Davis for negligence. The complaint alleges that Davis was driving his truck carelessly (unreasonably) and that Davis violated a statute, § 200 of the state statutory code. This section prohibits the transportation of gasoline in the kind of storage container Davis was using.

What is the effect of the statute on the negligence claim? Does the violation of § 200 make it easier for Packard to establish breach of duty? How, if at all, is the violation relevant? We know that the standard of care in a negligence case is reasonableness as measured by the breach-of-duty equation of Figure 14–4. If the defendant violates a statute, does this violation, in effect, become the standard of care that determines the defendant's reasonableness? Can we conclude that the defendant was unreasonable *solely because* he or she violated the statute? Unfortunately, most statutes say nothing explicit about how a violation might be relevant to a negligence suit such as Packard's. The statute may impose a fine or other criminal penalties for a violation, but say nothing about whether the violation allows a victim to bring a tort action such as negligence. When the statute is silent on this point, we need a method of analyzing how a statutory violation might affect the standard of care in a negligence case.

In addition to statutes, there may also be an allegation that the defendant violated a local ordinance (e.g., a traffic ordinance) or an administrative regulation (e.g., an on-the-job safety regulation). Although the following discussion will focus on statutes, the same method of analysis can be used when the negligence case includes alleged violations of ordinances or administrative regulations.

There is an eight-part analysis you need to use to determine how to handle an alleged violation of a statute in a negligence case:

1. State what the defendant did or failed to do that the plaintiff claims was a breach of duty (unreasonableness).
2. State whether a statute might be involved. (The plaintiff's complaint may allege a violation of a statute. Your own legal research may uncover such statutes.)
3. If so, determine whether the statute was violated.
4. If so, determine whether the violation was excused.

5. If not, determine whether the violation of the statute caused the accident.
6. If so, determine whether the plaintiff was within the class of persons the statute was intended to protect.
7. If so, determine whether the statute was intended to avoid the kind of harm the plaintiff suffered.
8. If so, determine whether your state considers the violation to be negligence per se, a presumption of negligence, or simply some evidence of negligence.

In most states, when an unexcused violation of a statute causes harm to a person, the violation will constitute negligence per se (or unreasonableness per se) if the statute was intended to cover this class of victim and this kind of harm. Let us go through the steps to see how we reach this conclusion.

At the end of this section you will find a flowchart (Figure 14–8) on how these eight steps fit together.

It is important to keep in mind that a plaintiff's failure to establish the statute as the standard of care does *not* mean that the defendant wins the case. What the defendant did or failed to do may be found by a court to have been unreasonable *independent* of any statute. A given accident may involve hundreds or thousands of facts, only a small portion of which may be relevant to a particular statute. Suppose a statute requires farmers to place a fence around certain kinds of animals. No fence is erected and the plaintiff is injured by one of the farmer's animals. It may be that after we go through the eight-part analysis, we will come to the conclusion that a court would *not* adopt the statute as the standard of reasonable conduct. This would eliminate the statute from the case. It is *still* possible, however, that the court will find that the defendant acted unreasonably in failing to build the fence. If so, it will not be due to the violation of the statute; it will be due to the court's application of the breach-of-duty equation in which the absence of a fence is but one of the factors that enter into the balancing required by the equation (see Figure 14–4).

We now take a closer look at the steps used to analyze the impact of a statute in a negligence case. Assume that we have identified what the defendant allegedly did or failed to do (step 1) and have found a statute that might be applicable (step 2). The following discussion covers steps 3–8 of the eight-step process:

Was the Statute Violated?

> **EXAMPLE:** Tom is driving his motorcycle 30 mph downtown when he crashes into the car of the plaintiff, who sues Tom for negligence. There is a statute in the state (§ 100) that says, "No motor vehicle can travel more than 25 mph in a thickly settled district."

The first step of our analysis is to identify what the defendant did or failed to do that allegedly was unreasonable. (While driving 30 mph downtown, Tom hit the plaintiff's car.) The second step is to identify any statutes that might apply to the case. (Section 100 provides that "No motor vehicle can travel more than 25 mph in a thickly settled district.") Next we ask whether this statute was violated.

Recall our discussion of legal analysis in Chapter 2 on how to determine whether a statute or other rule has been violated. We break the rule into its elements, define the major terms in the elements in contention, connect the facts to the elements, etc. (See Legal Analysis Guidelines 2 to 14 in Chapter 2.) One of the elements of § 100 is "motor vehicle." Is a motorcycle a "motor vehicle" under the statute? It depends on how broadly or narrowly we can define "motor vehicle." Another element of § 100 is "thickly settled district." Tom was downtown at the time of the crash. The phrase "thickly settled district" needs to be defined in order to determine whether downtown is within such a district. These definition questions are answered by finding the **legislative intent** of § 100. What was the intent of the legislature when it enacted § 100? What was the purpose of this statute? Answering these questions through legal research (particularly by trying to find court opinions that have interpreted § 100 in the past) will help us find the definitions we need. Our conclusion might be that "motor vehicles" are those vehicles with four or more wheels and that "thickly settled district" refers to residential areas, not to downtown. If so, then Tom did not violate § 100.

This does not mean, however, that the plaintiff loses the case for failure to convince the court that the defendant violated a particular statute. Independent of the statute, the plaintiff may be able to show that the defendant was driving unreasonably, given the totality of the circumstances. In our motorcycle case, the plaintiff will argue that going 30 mph was unreasonable in light of all of the circumstances such as the road conditions, the level of traffic, the position of the plaintiff's car, etc. The statute—§ 100—may be out of the case, but the plaintiff may still be able to show that Tom was negligent.

Was the Violation Excused?

It is not enough to show that the defendant violated a statute. If the violation was excused, it cannot be used to show that the defendant was unreasonable.

> **EXAMPLE:** John causes an accident while driving at night. His car crashes into the plaintiff's car. John's front lights suddenly went out and he could not see the plaintiff's car in front of him. The plaintiff sues John for negligence.

Assume that there is a statute that requires headlights to be on at night. Clearly, John has violated this statute. But his violation was probably excused, particularly if he had no warning that the lights might be defective. This takes the violation out of the negligence case. When we ask whether the violation of a statute constitutes proof of the defendant's unreasonableness, we are referring to unexcused violations.

Did the Violation Cause the Accident?

There was a time when all American males of a certain age were required by statute to carry a draft card on their person. Suppose such a person injures someone in a car accident while he is not carrying his draft card. The defendant has clearly violated the draft card statute. But this is not relevant to the accident. Not having a draft card certainly did not cause the car accident.

Use the but-for test or the substantial-factor test to determine whether the violation of the statute caused the accident. (These tests are covered in Chapter 15.) If there had been no violation (i.e., "but for" the violation), would the accident still have occurred? If so, then the violation did not cause the accident. When more than one possible cause exists, the test is whether the violation was a substantial factor (along with other factors) in producing the accident. If not, then the violation did not cause the accident.

Licensing statutes often raise causation questions:

- You are in a traffic accident at a time when your driver's license has expired.
- You are a doctor whose license has been suspended and you are sued for a medical injury you caused while you were without a license.
- You are a contractor who fails to obtain the required permit to build a house; you are sued when the house collapses and injures someone.

In most license cases such as these, it cannot be said that the violation caused the harm. You may have had the same mishap if you had had the driver's license, doctor's license, or building permit. It is very weak to argue that because you did not have the license, you probably were incompetent in what you were doing. Competence is determined by a host of other factors, e.g., age, prior experience, training. It cannot be said that simply because you did not have a license, you acted unreasonably in doing what you did. Competent doctors, for example, do not automatically become incompetent the day after their medical licenses expire.

Assume that a statute requires handrails on the stairs of every restaurant facility. A customer at a restaurant slips and falls on the stairs where there are no handrails. There appears to be a clear violation of the statute. But did the violation *cause* the fall? The answer appears to be yes. Of course, we need to know more facts in order to determine whether the fall would have occurred even if there were handrails, or if their absence was a substantial factor in the fall. For example, how quickly did the accident happen? How wide were the steps, and where was the plaintiff at the time of the fall? If the plaintiff fell in the center of very wide steps, it may have been impossible to have reached handrails if they were available.

ASSIGNMENT

14.7

A statute requires department stores to report all accidents occurring on elevators to a city agency. Over the years, the XYZ department store has never reported accidents on some of its elevators. Recently, a customer was injured on one of the XYZ elevators. The customer sues the XYZ store for negligence. The customer bases the entire breach-of-duty claim on the violation of the statute. Discuss causation. (See General Instructions for the Legal Analysis Assignment in Chapter 2.)

Is Plaintiff Within the Class of Persons Protected by the Statute?

It is not enough that the plaintiff establishes a violation of a statute, which is the cause of the injury suffered by the plaintiff. More analysis of the statute is needed to determine whether the plaintiff is the kind of person the statute was designed to protect.

Suppose that you have a statute requiring factories to have certain safety devices on machines. A factory violates the statute by not installing these devices. One day a salesperson happens to be in the factory and is injured while walking past one of the machines. Assume that there is no difficulty establishing causation. The salesperson can prove that "but for" the failure to have the safety device, the accident would not have occurred. The question then becomes: Who was the statute designed to protect? Only factory employees? If so, the breach of statute cannot be the basis of the salesperson's claim that the factory was unreasonable (negligent). Was it designed to protect *anyone* who is in the factory on business? If so, the salesperson can use the statute.

ASSIGNMENT

14.8

A statute requires all vacant lots to be fenced at all times. Tom owns a vacant lot in the city, which has no fence. One day a stranger cuts through Tom's lot and injures himself by falling into a hole that is very difficult to see. The stranger sues Tom for negligence. What breach-of-duty argument will the stranger make based on the statute? What will Tom's response be? (See General Instructions for the Legal Analysis Assignment in Chapter 2.)

Was the Statute Intended to Avoid this Kind of Harm?

Closely related to the class-of-plaintiff problem just discussed is the question of whether the statute was meant to cover the kind of harm or injury the plaintiff suffered.

EXAMPLES:

- A statute requires all traffic to drive under 55 mph on the highways. Defendant crashes into plaintiff while defendant is driving 65 mph. *Is the purpose of statute* to:
  a. Save lives?
  b. Save gas?

- A statute requires employers to have sprinkler systems in good repair at all times. One day the sprinkler system at a plant malfunctions. It is activated even though no fire exists. The entire plant is flooded. An employee, who is laid off because of the flood, sues the employer for lost wages due to the breach of the statute. *Is the purpose of statute* to:
  a. Avoid personal injuries in case of fire?
  b. Avoid economic loss due to flooding?

- A statute requires that all commercial poison be stored in properly designated containers. A business fails to use the right containers. One day the box containing the poison explodes because it was stored too close to heat. The explosion would not have occurred if the correct containers had been used. A customer is injured by the explosion. *Is the purpose of statute* to:
  a. Prevent people (or animals) from being poisoned?
  b. Prevent explosions?

If the statute was not intended to cover the kind of harm that resulted, the plaintiff cannot use the breach of the statute as the basis of the breach-of-duty argument. As we said before, however, even if the statute was not intended to cover what happened, plaintiff should still try to establish unreasonableness as if the statute did not exist. In the poison example, even if the statute was not intended to cover explosions, a court could still find that the defendant was unreasonable in the method used to store the poison if, according to the breach-of-duty equation, the danger of explosion was highly foreseeable and the burden or inconvenience on the defendant of preventing this danger by proper storage was minimal.

Does the Violation of the Statute, in and of Itself, Constitute a Breach of Duty?

Finally, we come to the point of assessing the consequences of our analysis. Assume that you work for a law firm that represents the plaintiff in a negligence case. You have gone through all the hurdles and are able to show that:

- The defendant violated a statute.
- The violation was not excused.
- The violation caused the plaintiff's injury.
- The plaintiff is within the class of persons the statute was intended to protect.
- The injury suffered by the plaintiff was the kind of harm the statute was designed to include.

Does this mean that the plaintiff wins the case? Not quite. More analysis is needed. We need to determine whether the violation means that the defendant was unreasonable and, therefore, committed a breach of duty. Can we say that the defendant acted unreasonably *solely because* of the violation? In other words, if the plaintiff offers no evidence other than the violation, has the plaintiff established breach of duty? We need to do legal research to answer this question. There are different ways that states treat a violation of a statute in a negligence case. Here are the three options:

Negligence (Unreasonableness) Per Se The violation of the statute may be **negligence per se** (or unreasonableness per se). This means that the jury *must* find that the defendant acted unreasonably. The plaintiff does not have to introduce any evidence of unreasonableness other than the violation of the statute. The defendant will not be allowed to offer evidence that he or she acted reasonably in spite of the violation. (Negligence per se is also referred to as negligence *as a matter of law*.)

Presumption of Negligence (of Unreasonableness) The violation of the statute may amount to a **presumption** of negligence (of unreasonableness). This means that the jury must find that the defendant acted unreasonably *unless* the defendant offers convincing evidence that he or she acted reasonably in spite of the violation. (A presumption is an assumption of fact that can be drawn when another fact or set of facts is established. The presumption is *rebuttable* if a party is allowed to introduce evidence that the assumption is false.)

Evidence of Negligence (of Unreasonableness) The violation of the statute may simply amount to some evidence of negligence (of unreasonableness). The jury is free to reject this evidence if it does not find it convincing enough. The defendant can offer evidence that he or she acted reasonably in spite of the violation.

Most states choose the first option: a violation of a statute is negligence per se (unreasonableness per se). There are some states, however, that do not go this far. They will treat the violation as a presumption or simply as some evidence of negligence (of unreasonableness). Again, you need to do legal research to determine which option your state will use.

Figure 14–8 presents an overview of the eight-part analytical process we have been examining to determine whether a violation of a statute, in and of itself, constitutes a breach of duty.

CASE

Potts v. Fidelity Fruit & Produce Co., Inc.
165 Ga. App. 546, 301 S.E.2d 903 (1983)
Court of Appeals of Georgia

Background: *There are spiders on bananas of Fidelity Fruit & Produce Company in violation of the Georgia Food Act. An employee is bitten by one of the spiders while unloading them from a truck. He sues for negligence. The trial court enters a summary judgment in favor of the company. The employee, now the appellant, appeals to the Court of Appeals of Georgia.*

Decision on Appeal: *Judgment affirmed. Violation of the Georgia Food Act cannot be the basis of a negligence action by an employee.*

OPINION OF COURT

Judge BANKE delivered the opinion of the court. . . .

In determining whether the violation of a statute or ordinance is negligence *per se* as to a particular person, it is necessary to examine the purposes of the legislation and decide (1) whether the injured person falls within the class of persons it was intended to protect and

(2) whether the harm complained of was the harm it was intended to guard against. *Rhodes v. Baker,* 116 Ga. App. 157, 160, 156 S.E.2d 545 (1967); *Huckabee v. Grace,* 48 Ga. App. 621, 636, 173 S.E. 744 (1933). Having examined the provisions of the Georgia Food Act, we agree fully with the following analysis made by the trial court: "Clearly, the Act is a consumer protection act, designed not to render the workplace a safe environment, but to prevent the sale and distribution of adulterated or misbranded foods to consumers. While safety in the workplace, and compensation for injuries arising out of work activities, are indeed matters of contemporary concern, they are the subject of other legislative enactments on both the state and federal level." Because the appellant's alleged injuries did not arise incident to his consumption of the bananas, we hold that the trial court was correct in concluding that the Act affords him no basis for recovery.

Judgment affirmed.

FIGURE 14–8 How to determine whether the violation of a statute will become the standard of care in a negligence action.

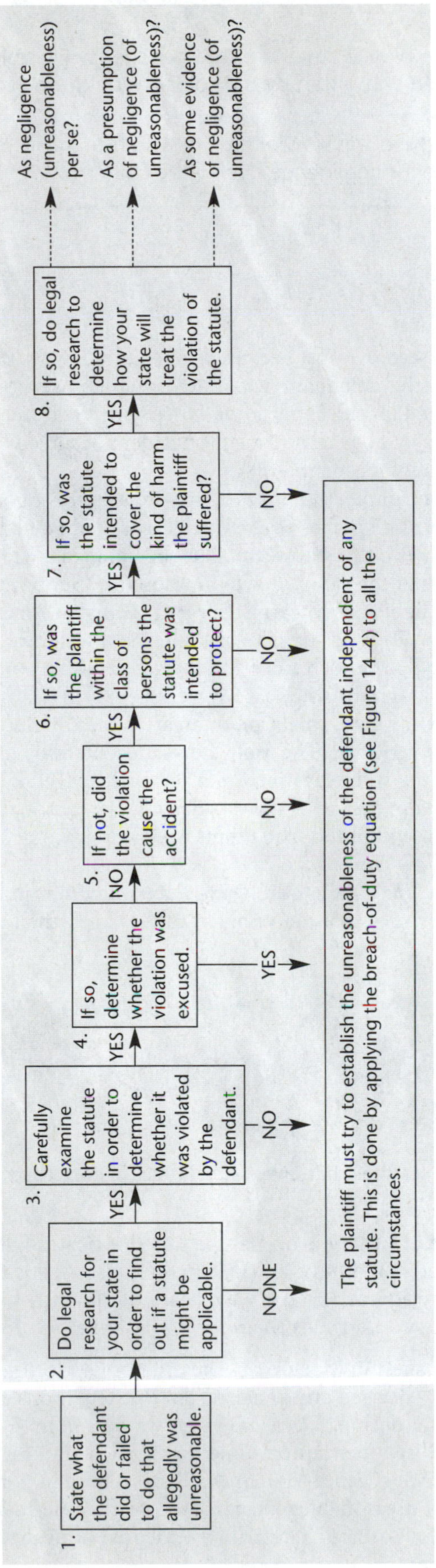

a. What if the employee ate one of the bananas while unloading them from the truck, and then was bitten by the spider. Would the *Potts* case reach the same result?

b. Assume that there was no violation of a statute in this case. Would the company be liable for negligence due to the spider bite?

COMPLIANCE WITH A STATUTE

Thus far we have seen that just because a defendant has *violated* a statute, it does not necessarily mean the defendant was unreasonable. We now look at the converse problem. If a defendant can show *compliance* with a statute, does it necessarily mean he or she acted reasonably at the time the accident occurred? *No,* but compliance can be strong evidence of reasonableness.

Suppose, for example, that a safety statute requires railroad companies to place flashing red lights at all points where tracks cross public highways. The fact that the railroad complies with this statute and has the lights in place does not guarantee that a court will find that the railroad acted reasonably. Suppose an accident occurs at a corner where the lights are working, but it is clear that much more is needed by the railroad to prevent injuries because of the large number of accidents in the past at this same intersection. In such a case, the statute amounts only to the *minimum* conduct expected of the railroad. Reasonableness may have called for additional precautions, e.g., a swing gate, an alarm, or an attendant on duty at the intersection during times of heavy traffic. The railroad is not off the hook simply by showing compliance with the statute. Similarly, a motorist traveling 30 mph who causes an accident cannot claim that he or she was driving at a reasonable speed simply because he or she was well within the speed limit of 45 mph. Compliance is evidence of reasonableness, but it is not conclusive.

To summarize, the statute merely sets the minimum standard of conduct, but reasonableness under the circumstances might call for more than what the statute requires.

GROSS NEGLIGENCE (UNREASONABLENESS) AND WILLFUL, WANTON, AND RECKLESS CONDUCT

Some states have statutes that cover special negligence cases, such as that of a *guest* injured in an automobile.

> **EXAMPLE:** Mary is on her way to the post office. Her neighbor asks Mary if he could have a ride, since he also needs to go to the post office. Mary agrees. On the way, Mary negligently hits a tree. The neighbor is injured and sues Mary for negligence.

The neighbor is a guest in Mary's car—he did not pay for the ride and there is no indication that Mary derived any benefit from the neighbor's presence in the car other than social companionship. There are **guest statutes** in many states that make it difficult for guests to sue their automobile hosts. Such statutes require guests to prove a greater degree of negligence (unreasonableness) than in non-guest/host suits. **Ordinary negligence** (unreasonableness) is not enough. The following are some of the terms used in guest statutes to describe the degree of negligence (unreasonableness) a guest must prove:

Gross Negligence (Gross Unreasonableness)

The failure to use even a small amount of care to avoid foreseeable harm.

Willful, Wanton, and Reckless Conduct

Having knowledge that harm will probably result from one's actions or inactions (harm is *very* foreseeable).

In our tree case involving Mary and the neighbor, if Mary simply failed to do what an ordinary, reasonable person would have done to avoid the tree, the neighbor would lose his negligence action in a state that imposes standards such as those just listed. To be grossly negligent or reckless, Mary would have had to be drunk at the time, or be traveling 60 mph in a 20 mph zone before hitting the tree.

As we shall see later, gross negligence (unreasonableness) or willful, wanton, and reckless conduct will often be the basis for awarding punitive damages in a negligence case.

ASSIGNMENT

14.10

Matthew is driving from one city to another in your state. The distance is 50 miles. His best friend, George, asks Matthew if he could drive him to a point midway between the two cities. Matthew is delighted to do him this favor, since he enjoys his company very much. When they reach the point where George is to get off, the latter gives Matthew $5 as a contribution toward the cost of gas. As George is getting out, Matthew sneezes and steps on the accelerator by mistake, injuring George. George sues Matthew for negligence. Discuss George's chances of winning this case. (See General Instructions for the Legal Analysis Assignment in Chapter 2.)

VICARIOUS LIABILITY

"Vicarious" means taking the place of another. Vicarious negligence, or more accurately, vicarious unreasonableness, means that one person will be found to be unreasonable solely because someone else is unreasonable. The unreasonableness of one person will be thrust upon or imputed to another person. Other terms used to mean the same thing include **vicarious liability** and **imputed negligence**. Again, since we are discussing only one element of negligence—breach of duty—it is more accurate to say: imputed unreasonableness. The unreasonableness of one person is charged or "credited" to another person, even though the latter did nothing wrong or unreasonable. The three types of vicarious unreasonableness we will consider are outlined in Figure 14–9. Vicarious liability is not automatic in the three situations of Figure 14–9. As we shall see, there are tests that must be applied before this liability can be imposed.

Two major points need to be kept in mind as we explore each of the three forms of vicarious unreasonableness. The first deals with who can be sued, and the second deals with the distinction between vicarious liability and independent liability:

Who Can Be Sued?

You will note in the three examples of Figure 14–9 that Sara, Joe, and Jessica were the defendants in the three negligence actions. What about the other three who, as the drivers, were more directly responsible for the accidents: Mary, Ed, and Bob? Can they also be sued for negligence? Yes. *Joint and several liability* exists. If a person is jointly and severally liable, he or she is individually responsible for 100 percent of the damages suffered by the plaintiff. The plaintiff can sue all of these persons

FIGURE 14–9 Vicarious unreasonableness.

VICARIOUS UNREASONABLENESS		
Employer/Employee (Master/Servant)	**Joint Enterprise**	**Family Purpose Doctrine**
Mary works for Sara as a truck driver. While making a delivery, Mary carelessly injures the plaintiff. The plaintiff sues <u>Sara</u> for negligence. Mary's unreasonableness will be imputed to Sara because of the *employer-employee relationship*.	Joe and Ed rent a car in order to buy some goods to be used in a business they are going to start together. They both contribute funds to rent the car. Ed is the driver. While driving, Ed carelessly hits the plaintiff. Joe is also riding in the car at the time. The plaintiff sues <u>Joe</u> for negligence. Ed's unreasonableness will be imputed to Joe because of the *joint enterprise*.	Jessica owns a car which she lets her son, Bob, drive. One day Bob is driving to the supermarket alone and carelessly hits the plaintiff. The plaintiff sues <u>Jessica</u> for negligence. Bob's unreasonableness will be imputed to Jessica because of the *family purpose doctrine*.

together or can sue any one or more of them until 100 percent of his or her damages are recovered. An individual defendant cannot force the plaintiff to collect part of the damages from other persons. (If a defendant is upset about paying all of the damages, he or she can seek **contribution** from the others in a separate action where the plaintiff is not a party.) Since all of the individuals in Figure 14–9 are jointly and severally liable, here are the actions that are possible:

Plaintiff v. Sara *or*	Plaintiff v. Joe *or*	Plaintiff v. Jessica *or*
Plaintiff v. Mary *or*	Plaintiff v. Ed *or*	Plaintiff v. Bob *or*
Plaintiff v. Sara and Mary	Plaintiff v. Joe and Ed	Plaintiff v. Jessica and Bob

Mary, Ed, and Bob are not off the hook simply because Sara, Joe, and Jessica are vicariously liable. Why then would the plaintiffs want to bring an action against Sara, Joe, and Jessica? The practical answer is the **deep pocket** reality: a plaintiff wants to go after the party with the deepest pocket, i.e., the one who probably has the financial resources from which a negligence judgment can be satisfied. If vicarious liability exists, the deep pocket strategy can be used. But again, this does not mean that the other parties cannot also be sued, or that both parties cannot be sued together.

Vicarious Liability and Independent Liability

In the three examples in Figure 14–9, there is no indication that the parties vicariously liable (Sara, Joe, and Jessica) did anything wrong, careless, or unreasonable themselves. They were not individually at fault. Suppose, however, that they were, as in the following scenarios.

Employer/Employee Case
- Sara knew that Mary was a poor driver, but let her drive anyway.
- Sara instructed Mary to make the delivery as fast as she could, even if it meant breaking the speed law.
- Sara never bothered to check to determine whether her drivers were properly trained.

Joint Enterprise Case
- Joe knew that Ed was a poor driver, but let him drive anyway.
- The accident happened because Joe carelessly distracted Ed.
- Joe knew that the car was defective; this defect contributed to the accident.

Family Purpose Doctrine Case
- Jessica knew that Bob was a poor driver, but let him drive anyway.
- Jessica instructed Bob to get to the supermarket and back as soon as possible, even if it meant breaking the speed law.
- Jessica knew that the car was defective; this defect contributed to the accident.

Now we have *individual* fault on the part of the parties who were not driving. Sara, Joe, and Jessica may be liable for their own negligence as well as vicariously liable.

In the discussion that follows, we will assume that the defendants are not independently liable because of any unreasonableness of their own. Our focus is on vicarious liability only. You should always keep in mind, however, the distinction between vicarious and **independent liability,** because in any given case a defendant may be legitimately faced with both theories of liability.

Employer/Employee Vicarious liability because of the **employer/employee relationship** (sometimes referred to as the **master/servant relationship**) is often given the Latin name, **respondeat superior,** meaning "look to the man higher up." The underlying principle has been phrased as follows: "He who does a thing through another does it himself."[6] The employer/employee relationship is one example of a broader category of relationships called **principal/agent.** Generally, an *agent* is someone who agrees to do something on behalf of another. A *principal* is the person on whose behalf the agent is acting and who has some authority or control over the agent while so acting.

Our study of the vicarious liability of an employer shall center on two questions: 1. When is an employee acting within the scope of employment so that the employer is vicariously liable? and 2. When is defendant vicariously liable for the negligence of his or her independent contractor?[7]

1. **When is an employee acting within the scope of employment?** The overriding principle is that the employer is vicariously liable for the torts of his or her employee if the latter was acting within the **scope of employment** at the time. A great deal of litigation has resulted from trying to define the phrase "scope of employment." (As we shall see in Chapter 28, the comparable phrase in the law of workers' compensation is, "arising out of and in the course of employment.")

There is no absolute definition of scope of employment. A working definition is as follows:

Scope of employment is that which is foreseeably done by the employee for the employer under the employer's specific or general control.

Scope of employment is not determined by what the employer has authorized the employee to do, although authorization is one factor a court will consider. Suppose that a boss tells her hardware clerk not to allow a customer to operate the automatic paint mixer. The employee violates this instruction, resulting in an injury to a customer. This violation does not mean respondeat superior will not apply. The boss will still be vicariously liable for the negligence of her employee if the latter was acting for the boss, under the latter's control, and if what the employee did should have been foreseeable to the boss because of prior conduct of the employee and the nature of the work.

---

[6]W. Page Keeton et al., *Prosser and Keeton on the Law of Torts* 499 (5th ed. 1984).

[7]The distinction between an employee and an independent contractor is also important for federal tax purposes. Social security and withholding taxes, for example, must be deducted from payments to employees, but not to independent contractors. The Internal Revenue Service has its own tests to determine when a worker is an employee. Employers can be fined for attempting to treat employees as independent contractors.

A major concern of the courts has been the so-called **frolic and detour** of an employee. There is no vicarious liability if the negligent act of the employee was committed while he or she was on a frolic and detour of his or her own.

> **EXAMPLE:** Bill is an employee of a delivery company. One morning while making a delivery for the company, he drives the company truck 25 miles out of the way to spend three hours with his girlfriend. While driving out of the girlfriend's drive in order to return to work, Bill rams the company truck into the plaintiff's fence.

It is highly unlikely that the plaintiff can win a negligence action against the employer; the accident was not within the scope of employment—the employee was on a frolic and detour of his own. The plaintiff will be limited to a suit against the employee (Bill). A major characteristic of a frolic and detour is that the employee is acting for his or her personal objectives rather than acting primarily for the employer's business.

There is a large gray area where courts have had difficulty determining what is within the scope of employment. A number of factors are considered in identifying this scope. The factors are outlined in the scope of employment checklist in Figure 14–10. No single factor is determinative; a court will weigh them all. Although our emphasis has been on negligence liability (vicarious unreasonableness), the factors in the checklist would also be used by a court to determine whether the employer would

FIGURE 14–10 Checklist of factors used to determine scope of employment.

A "yes" answer to any of the following interrelated questions would help support a conclusion that the employee did act within the scope of employment. A "no" answer helps support the conclusion that the act was outside this scope. A single yes or no answer is rarely conclusive. A court will weigh all of the factors before deciding what was within or outside of the scope of employment. The "conduct" referred to in the following eight categories of questions is what the employee did that accidently resulted in the plaintiff's injury, which is now the basis of the plaintiff's negligence suit against the employer.

1. Authorization
   Was the employee's conduct substantially within what the employer authorized the employee to do?
2. Purpose
   Was the employee acting to pursue the business interests of the employer? If the employee also had personal objectives in what was done, can it nevertheless be said that the employee was acting *primarily* to pursue the business interests of the employer?
3. Normalcy
   Was the employee's conduct common or usual in the job being performed?
4. Foreseeability
   Was the conduct of the employee foreseeable to the employer?
5. Time
   Was the employee's conduct undertaken substantially within the time of work for the employer?
6. Place
   Was the employee's conduct undertaken substantially within the place or locale authorized by the employer for such conduct?
7. Special Obligation
   Was the employer engaged in the kind of business on which the courts have historically placed a special obligation for the protection of its customers, e.g., common carriers, innkeepers?
8. Common Sense
   As a matter of common sense, can we say that the employee's conduct was within the scope of employment?

be liable for any intentional torts committed by the employee, such as battery, fraud, or false imprisonment.

Apply the scope of employment checklist of factors in Figure 14–10 to determine whether the employees in the following situations were acting within the scope of their employment at the time of the accident. Identify further fact investigation you may need. In each instance, the plaintiff is suing the employer on a respondeat superior theory. (See General Instructions for the Legal Analysis Assignment in Chapter 2.)

a. The ashes from the employee's cigarette fall onto the plaintiff's fur coat, causing substantial damage. The plaintiff sues for negligence.

b. While making a delivery in a company truck, the employee travels five miles out of the way to visit his ailing mother. He stays three hours. On his way back to the company plant to return the truck, he injures plaintiff in a traffic accident. The plaintiff sues for negligence.

c. The employee is a door-to-door salesperson. At one house, the employee gets into an argument with the plaintiff, who owns the house. The plaintiff calls the employee "stupid." The employee hits the plaintiff, who now sues for battery.

In Assignment 14.11, you examined three fact situations. Select any one of them. Draft a complaint for the fact situation you select. (See General Instructions for the Complaint-Drafting Assignment in Chapter 3.)

2. When is the defendant vicariously liable for the negligence of his or her independent contractor? Different rules apply when the defendant hires an **independent contractor.** The distinction between an employee and an independent contractor is not always easy to draw. Some of the significant points of difference include:

- The person doing the hiring has less control over the independent contractor than over the employee.
- The independent contractor has a great deal more discretion over the way the job is done than an employee.
- The employee is on the payroll of the employer, whereas the independent contractor is hired primarily to produce a certain product or result without being on the payroll.

For example, compare the following two ways in which a business hires an accountant:

- Gabe's Fine Furniture, Inc. pays an accountant an annual fee of $500 to prepare its federal and state tax returns. The accountant comes to Gabe's business about four times a year to collect data from the company's financial books. The data is used for the tax returns.
- Ace Trucking Co. pays an accountant $1,538.46 every two weeks ($40,000 a year) to keep its books, pay accounts receivable, prepare the payroll, prepare tax returns, and perform other accountancy tasks in the financial office of the company.

Gabe's accountant is an independent contractor, whereas Ace's accountant is an employee. The latter is on staff and is subject to as much supervision as the company's management decides to provide. Gabe's accountant, on the other hand, probably performs his or her task with relatively little supervision from anyone at the furniture company. Another example would be a company that pays an attorney a fee to bring a lawsuit or to handle some other specific legal problem. This attorney is an independent contractor. If, however, the company has attorneys on its permanent payroll staff, the attorney is an employee. (Employed attorneys are called *in-house attorneys,* whereas independent contractor attorneys are referred to as *outside counsel.*)

The general rule is that the person who hires independent contractors is *not* liable for their torts. (See Figure 14–11.) If you are injured by an independent contractor, your only recourse is to sue the independent contractor. Under this general rule, respondeat superior does not apply. There are, however, two major exceptions. Vicarious liability will continue to apply when someone is injured while the independent contractor is performing:

- a **non-delegable duty** (e.g., a city's duty to keep its streets in repair) or
- an **inherently dangerous** task (e.g., transporting dynamite).

(See other examples in Figure 14–11.) While performing work in either category, the independent contractor is treated as an employee for purposes of vicarious liability.

FIGURE 14–11 Liability for torts of independent contractors.

General Rule
A defendant is *not* vicariously liable for the torts of his or her independent contractor. If the independent contractor injures someone while working for the defendant, the victim is limited to suing the independent contractor.

Exceptions
There are two circumstances in which a defendant *will* be liable for the torts committed by his or her independent contractor:
1. the independent contractor is performing certain non-delegable duties of the defendant (e.g., a city's duty to keep its streets in repair, a landlord's duty to keep the leased premises safe for business visitors, a duty of a common carrier to transport passengers safely, and other special duties imposed by statute or regulation), or
2. the independent contractor is performing inherently dangerous work for the defendant (e.g., transporting dynamite, keeping vicious animals, conducting fireworks exhibitions).[8]

Recall the distinction made earlier between vicarious liability and independent liability. Assume that a defendant is careless in selecting an independent contractor such as by hiring someone who is obviously incompetent to perform a job that could injure someone. The defendant might be subject to independent liability for what is called **negligent hiring** to anyone injured by the independent contractor. The same is true if the person hired is an employee, although for employees the basis of the employer's liability would be both vicarious liability and independent liability.

ASSIGNMENT 14.13

a. A business hires a construction company to erect a commercial building. While one of the company's executives is driving back from the job site in her car, she carelessly hits Tom's car.
b. A month later, the company is transporting a gigantic derrick along a small county road on the back of a massive trailer. An accident occurs when the derrick falls off the trailer and damages Mary's barn.

---

[8]Some of these activities may also impose strict liability. See Chapter 11.

In each case, who can sue whom and on what theories? Be sure to discuss vicarious liability, if applicable. (See General Instructions for the Legal Analysis Assignment in Chapter 2). Prepare investigation strategies for each case. (See General Instructions for the Investigation Strategy Assignment in Chapter 3.)

Joint Enterprise   We come now to the second example of vicarious unreasonableness listed in Figure 14–9—the **joint enterprise**. For parties to be engaged in a joint enterprise, the following elements must be present:

1. an express or implied agreement to participate in the enterprise together
2. a common purpose (usually financial or business-related)
3. a mutual right to control the enterprise

In a few states, the agreement can be to go to a picnic or to the zoo. In most states, however, the common purpose must be financial or business-related.

The third element has caused the courts the most difficulty. How, for example, do you establish that two people riding in a car for a common business purpose have the same (mutual) right to control the direction and operation of the car?

Mutuality of the right of control is not established simply because both are riding together for a business purpose. There must be more concrete indications that the passenger has the same right to control the direction and operation of the car as the driver. Such indications would include: they rented the car with their joint funds; both own the car; they share expenses on the maintenance of the car; both have driven the car in the past; on this trip, they alternate the driving; the passenger is reading the road map and giving route instructions to the driver, etc. The court must be able to find that there was a clear understanding between the parties that both had an equal say in the operation of the car, even if only one party did all the driving at the time the car had the accident injuring the plaintiff. Taking all the factors into consideration, the question is whether it would have been odd, unusual, or presumptuous for the passenger to have exercised the same authority as the driver in the operation of the car. If so, there probably was no joint control.

Once a joint enterprise is established, vicarious liability comes into play. In automobile cases, the passenger is vicariously unreasonable if the driver's unreasonableness caused the accident. In a sense, the joint enterprise is treated as a partnership in which one partner becomes personally liable for the acts of all the other partners. Most joint enterprises, however, are usually more limited in their duration and less structured than the traditional partnership.

ASSIGNMENT

14.14

a. Husband and wife are in a car on their way to sign up for a motel training course in which couples are taught the motel business. The car is in both names. The wife is driving. An accident occurs. The third party sues the husband for negligence. How would you determine if there is a joint enterprise? Prepare an investigation strategy. (See General Instructions for the Investigation Strategy Assignment in Chapter 3.)

b. Dr. Jones and Dr. Smith practice medicine separately; they are not partners. During times of vacation, however, they cover for each other's patients. While Dr. Smith is on vacation, Dr. Jones sees one of Dr. Smith's patients. The patient suffers an injury because of negligent treatment by Dr. Jones. Assume that Dr. Jones, unlike Dr. Smith, has no liability insurance and almost no assets. Dr. Smith, therefore, is the "deep pocket." Vicarious liability? Can the patient sue Dr. Smith for the negligence of Dr. Jones? Assume that Dr. Smith had no reason to suspect that Dr. Jones would ever commit negligence. (See General Instructions for the Legal Analysis Assignment in Chapter 2.)

Once a joint enterprise is established, there can *also* be **imputed contributory negligence.** Compare the following two cases:

> **Case I (Imputed Negligence)** Dan and Paul are engaged in a joint enterprise. They are in a truck on a highway. Dan is driving and Paul is a passenger. Dan carelessly crashes into Mary's car. Mary sues Paul for negligence (Mary v. Paul). Because of the joint enterprise, the negligence (unreasonableness) of Dan is imposed upon (i.e., imputed to) Paul.
>
> **Case II (Imputed Contributory Negligence)** Same accident as in Case I except that this time Paul sues Mary for negligence (Paul v. Mary), claiming that her negligence caused the crash with Dan. Mary's defense is that Dan's negligence caused the accident and his contributory negligence should be imposed upon (i.e., imputed to) Paul because of the joint enterprise between them.

The same principle of imputed contributory negligence will apply in the employer-employee relationship discussed earlier. If the employer sues a third party for damages suffered by the employer arising out of an accident in which the employee was also negligent, the contributory negligence of the employee will be imputed to the employer in the employer's negligence action against the third party. For more on contributory negligence, see Chapter 17.

Family Purpose Doctrine   The final form of vicarious unreasonableness mentioned in Figure 14–9 is based on the **family purpose doctrine.** It makes a nondriver vicariously liable for an accident caused by a driver. Not all states have adopted the family purpose doctrine, and those that have, do not all agree on its elements. In general, the elements are as follows:

- Defendant must own the car, or have an ownership interest in it (e.g., co-owner), or control the use of the car.
- Defendant must make the car available for family use rather than for the defendant's business. (In some states, the defendant must make it available for general family use rather than just for a particular occasion.)
- The driver must be a member of the defendant's immediate household.
- The driver must be using the car for a family purpose at the time of the accident.
- The driver must have had the defendant's express or implied consent to be using the car at the time of the accident.

The defendant does not have to be the traditional head of the household and does not have to be in the car at the time of the accident. Again, individual states, by case law or by statute, may impose different elements to the doctrine or may reject it entirely.

ASSIGNMENT

14.15

Fred has just bought a used car, but it will not be ready for a week. During the week he is waiting, he rents a car. He pays a per-mile charge on the car. He tells his family that the car is to be used only to drive to work. One day while the car is at home and Fred is out of town, his child becomes sick. Fred's mother, who is staying with Fred until an opening comes up in a local nursing home, drives the child to the hospital. On the way, she has an accident, injuring the plaintiff, a pedestrian. The plaintiff sues Fred for negligence. Does the family purpose doctrine apply? (See General Instructions for the Legal Analysis Assignment in Chapter 2.)

Parent and Child   The traditional rule is that parents are not vicariously liable for the torts committed by their children. If a child commits negligence (or an intentional tort), the child is personally liable. The parent might be individually (not vicariously) liable for his or her own negligence in failing to use available opportunities to control a child with known **dangerous propensities** or for actually participating in the unreasonable conduct of the child. Similarly, there can be individual liability for **negligent entrustment** whenever a person carelessly allows someone such as a child to use a vehicle, tool, or any other object that poses an unreasonable risk of harm to others. This kind of liability is quite separate from the parent being vicariously liable simply because he or she is the parent of a child who commits a tort.

In some states, however, there are statutes that *do* impose vicarious liability on parents for the torts of their child, but only up to a limited dollar amount, e.g., $3,000. (See also Chapter 22 on torts against and within the family.)

SUMMARY

In most negligence cases, the standard of care is reasonableness, which is determined by assessing the totality of circumstances. The defendant has breached this standard if his or her acts and omissions are substantially different from those of a reasonable person under the same or similar circumstances. Reasonableness is determined by comparing what this person would have done to what the defendant did or failed to do. A reasonable person is someone who can make mistakes and cause injury, but never due to carelessness. If the danger of a foreseeably serious accident outweighed the burden or inconvenience of taking precautions to avoid the accident, the reasonable person would take those precautions. In assessing a burden or inconvenience, the court will consider cost, time, and effectiveness. The more important or socially useful the activity, the more likely it is that a reasonable person would take the risks involved in the activity.

Physically, a reasonable person has the same strengths and weaknesses as the defendant. Mentally, the reasonable person has the basic knowledge and intelligence needed in everyday life, even if the defendant does not. If the defendant has more than the minimum (e.g., has professional) knowledge and skills, then the reasonable person is deemed to have the same knowledge and skills. If the defendant is a child, the standard is a reasonable child of the age and intelligence of the defendant, unless the defendant was engaging in an adult activity, in which case the standard is the reasonable adult.

Res ipsa loquitur allows a jury to infer unreasonableness simply by reason of the fact that the accident happened, even if there is no direct or specific evidence of unreasonableness. It must be more likely than not that the accident was due to someone's unreasonableness—the defendant's—and the plaintiff must not be a responsible cause of the accident.

Custom and usage (what others in the business or industry are doing) is one of the factors a court will consider in assessing reasonableness. Following custom and usage does not necessarily make a defendant reasonable. Under the breach-of-duty equation, a defendant may be required to do more than what everyone else is doing.

If the defendant has violated a statute, the unexcused violation might be considered negligence per se, create a presumption of negligence, or simply be some evidence of negligence. We need to ask if the violation caused the accident, if the plaintiff is within the class of persons protected by the statute, and if the plaintiff has suffered the kind of harm the statute was intended to avoid. Conversely, the defendant's compliance with a statute does not automatically establish reasonableness. Compliance may merely constitute some evidence of reasonableness.

Reasonable care under the circumstances may call for more than the minimum requirements imposed by the statute.

Guest statutes often refuse to impose liability on hosts unless the latter have committed gross negligence or have been wilful, wanton, or reckless. Under the doctrine of respondeat superior, employers are vicariously liable for the negligence committed by their employees within the scope of employment. There is no vicarious liability for the negligence committed by independent contractors unless the latter are performing non-delegable duties or inherently dangerous work. Participants in a joint enterprise are vicariously liable for the negligence committed by each other in furtherance of the objective of the enterprise. Under the family purpose doctrine, the owner of a car who makes it available for family (nonbusiness) use will be vicariously liable for the negligence of a driver in the owner's immediate household who was using the car for a family purpose at the time of the accident with the express or implied consent of the owner. Unless modified by statute, parents are not vicariously liable for the torts of their children.

KEY TERMS

reasonable care   230
breach of duty   230
unreasonable   230
standard of care   230
factors   230
reasonable person   230
breach-of-duty equation   232
hypothesis   234
risk-benefit analysis   236
risk-utility analysis   236
subjective standard   237
objective standard   237
res ipsa loquitur   240
joint and several liability   244
custom and usage   246

legislative intent   248
negligence per se   251
presumption   252
guest statutes   254
ordinary negligence   254
gross negligence   255
wilful, wanton, and reckless conduct   255
vicarious liability   255
imputed negligence   255
contribution   256
deep pocket   256
independent liability   257
employer/employee relationship   257

master/servant relationship   257
respondeat superior   257
principal/agent   257
scope of employment   257
frolic and detour   258
independent contractor   259
non-delegable duty   260
inherently dangerous   260
negligent hiring   260
joint enterprise   261
imputed contributory negligence   262
family purpose doctrine   262
dangerous propensities   263
negligent entrustment   263

Negligence: Element III: Proximate Cause

CHAPTER OUTLINE

- Introduction
- Cause in Fact
- Cut-Off Test of Proximate Cause
- Overview of Steps Needed to Analyze Proximate Cause

INTRODUCTION

Proximate cause[1] involves two separate questions, only one of which deals with causation. The two questions are:

1. The causation question (*cause in fact*):
   Did the defendant cause the plaintiff's injury?
2. The policy question (a *cut-off test*):
   At what point will the law refuse to hold the defendant responsible for the injury or injuries that he or she has in fact caused?

In the vast majority of negligence cases, the policy question does not need to be considered. Defendant breaks plaintiff's leg in an automobile accident in which the defendant is driving at an excessive rate of speed. We do not need a cut-off test once we establish that the defendant in fact caused plaintiff's leg injury. There is no reason to refuse to hold the defendant responsible. The defendant is the proximate cause of the leg injury in this case. The two-fold questions of proximate cause become critical in two main situations:

- when the injury suffered by the plaintiff appears to be unusual or unexpected,
  or
- when other causes join the defendant in a chain-type sequence

Assume that Sam unreasonably drives his car down the street at an excessive rate of speed and hits the plaintiff, breaking the latter's leg. While the plaintiff is lying in the road, a second car runs over the plaintiff's arm, and disappears. When the ambulance finally arrives and takes the plaintiff to the hospital, a nurse carelessly treats the plaintiff, causing injury to the plaintiff's knee. Assume that *only* Sam is sued for negligence. The proximate cause issue is two-fold:

1. **Cause in Fact:**
   a. Did Sam cause the original leg injury by hitting the plaintiff?
   b. Did Sam cause the arm injury when the second car ran over the plaintiff's arm?
   c. Did Sam cause the knee injury that resulted from the nurse's carelessness?
2. **Policy (cut-off):**
   Should Sam be responsible for *all* the injury or injuries that he has in fact caused? Should Sam be liable for what the nurse did and for what the second car did, as well as for what he directly did himself when he hit the plaintiff? Did Sam proximately cause the arm and knee injuries as well as the original leg injury?

The tests of proximate cause, outlined in Figure 15–1, will answer all of these questions. We need to examine these tests as well as some important modifications or exceptions to them.

CAUSE IN FACT

The **but-for test** and the **substantial factor test** are alternative tests that courts often use to determine whether the defendant was the cause in fact of the plaintiff's injury. As we shall see, the substantial factor test is fully adequate and often easier for a plaintiff to establish. It is important, however, that you understand both tests.

The but-for test asks the following question: Would the plaintiff have been injured but for what the defendant did or failed to do? Under this test, if the plaintiff

---

[1]Sometimes referred to as **legal cause.**

FIGURE 15–1   The tests of
proximate cause.

> **1.** The Case-in-Fact Tests
>   **a.** But-for test[2] (used when there is only one alleged cause):
>   Is it more likely than not that but for the defendant's unreasonable acts or omissions, the injury would not have been suffered by the plaintiff?
>   **b.** Substantial factor test (used when there is more than one alleged cause): Is it more likely than not that the defendant's unreasonable acts or omissions had a significant role in producing the injury suffered by the plaintiff?
> **2.** The Cut-off Test:
>   Is the injury suffered by the plaintiff the *foreseeable consequence* of the *original risk* created by the defendant's unreasonable acts or omissions?

[2]Also referred to as the **sine qua non test.**

would have been injured regardless of what the defendant did or failed to do, the defendant did not cause the injury.

EXAMPLES:

- Dwayne is an ambulance driver. One day he gets a call from the plaintiff's home for an ambulance to take the plaintiff to the hospital. Dwayne takes the call at 9:00 A.M. Because of Dwayne's careless driving, he arrives at the plaintiff's home 45 minutes later than he would have arrived if he had not been careless. When he does arrive, the plaintiff is already dead. According to the coroner's report, the plaintiff died at 9:01 a.m. Dwayne was not the cause in fact of the death. Dwayne was careless and unreasonable in driving to the plaintiff, but the plaintiff would have died even if Dwayne had driven with great caution and skill. But for what Dwayne did or failed to do, the plaintiff would still have been dead when he arrived to take her to the hospital. Hence, there was not cause in fact.

- Mary is a doctor whose license to practice medicine has been suspended for a year because of the illegal prescription of drugs to several patients. In secret, however, Mary continues her practice. During this time, she performs a routine operation on George. George suffers serious complications following the operation and dies. His estate sues Mary for negligence. At the trial there is no evidence that Mary was careless or unreasonable in performing the operation. The estate introduces evidence that Mary performed the operation while her license was suspended. The lack of a license, however, was not the cause in fact of George's death. Even if Mary had had a license, the death would still have occurred. But for Mary's not having a license, it cannot be said that George would not have died. There was no evidence that Mary did not use adequate professional skill in performing the operation. It may be that a separate criminal proceeding can be brought against Mary for practicing without a license, but the estate loses its negligence action for failure to establish cause in fact.

- Sam carelessly drives his car into Fred's barn. But for the way Sam drove, the damage to the barn would not have occurred. Sam, therefore, is the cause in fact of the damage to Fred's property.

The but-for test is sufficient for most tort cases on the issue of causation. This includes negligence cases as well as those charging intentional torts or strict liability torts. There is, however, an alternative test: the defendant will be considered the cause in fact of the plaintiff's injury if the defendant was *a substantial factor* in producing the injury. Every time you establish cause in fact by the but-for test, you certainly have established that the defendant was a substantial factor. But the converse is not necessarily true:

> **EXAMPLE:** Helen and Jane carelessly shoot their hunting guns at the same time through some bushes, trying to hit an animal. Both bullets, however, hit plaintiff, who is killed instantly. Either bullet would have killed the plaintiff. Here, the but-for test leads to a bizarre result. Helen says, correctly, that but for her bullet, the plaintiff would have died anyway. Jane says, correctly, that but for her bullet, the plaintiff would have died anyway. Hence, both use the but-for test to show that she individually was not the cause in fact of the plaintiff's death.

The plaintiff's estate would not be able to win a negligence action against anyone if the but-for test were the only test to determine cause in fact in such a case. Hence the need for an alternative test. If either Helen or Jane was *a substantial factor* in producing the death, then either one is the cause in fact of the death. When two people fire a bullet at a person who is killed by the impacts, the law will say that they are both substantial factors in producing the death. In this case, therefore, the substantial factor test leads to the establishment of cause in fact, even though the but-for test would not do so.

It is usually easier for a plaintiff to establish cause in fact by the substantial factor test than by the but-for test, but in most cases, both tests will lead to the same result. In tort law, it is sufficient if the plaintiff proves cause in fact by the broader substantial factor test. *In analyzing any tort problem on the issue of cause in fact, you should apply both tests, but always keep in mind that the substantial factor test will be sufficient.* Plaintiffs will have a stronger case if they can show cause in fact by the but-for test. Hence, you should determine whether this can be done on the facts before you. If not, move on to the substantial factor test, particularly when more than one cause has contributed to the plaintiff's injury.

Note that the substantial factor test requires only that the defendant be *a* substantial factor. It is not necessary that the defendant be the *sole* or *only* cause of the plaintiff's injury in order to be the cause in fact of the injury. It is not even necessary to show that the defendant was the dominant factor in producing the injury. Being *a* substantial factor is enough.

ASSIGNMENT

15.1

Phrasing the causation means asking the question by using important facts along with the legal test for causation. For example, "But for the defendant's excessive speed on a slippery road at night, would the plaintiff's car have been struck by the defendant's car?" Re-read the fact situation at the beginning of this chapter about Sam and the plaintiff whose leg, arm, and knee were injured.

a. For each of these injuries, phrase the cause-in-fact question using the but-for test (one question per injury).

b. For each of these injuries, phrase the cause-in-fact question using the substantial factor test (one question per injury).

You do not have to answer the questions; simply phrase them

Evidence of Causation

What do we mean when we say that there is evidence of causation—whether we are using the but-for test or the substantial factor test? How does one establish a connection between cause and effect? For the vast majority of cases, our most sophisticated tool in assessing causation is common sense based upon everyday experience. Our common sense depends heavily on the factors of *time*, *space*, and *history*. These factors present us with some fundamental hypotheses about life and human nature.

Time: When did the injury occur? After the defendant's acts or omissions? The shorter the time between the plaintiff's injury and the acts or omissions of the defendant, the more convinced we are that those acts or omissions caused the injury. The more time that elapses between the defendant's acts or omissions and the injury of the plaintiff, the more skeptical we are that those acts or omissions caused the injury.

EXAMPLES:

- Tom becomes sick seconds after drinking a beer. Common sense tells us that drinking the beer may have caused the sickness since the two events (drinking and sickness) came so close together. We would be less inclined to reach this conclusion, however, if Tom's sickness occurred two weeks later.
- Mary and Claire belong to the same social club. Mary has a pet-walking business in which all of her clients are members of the club. (Every morning, an employee of Mary's business goes to the homes of clients to get their pets for walks.) Her business drops by 80 percent within one week after Claire tells many other club members that Mary is incompetent. Common sense tells us that Claire's derogatory statement may have caused some or all of Mary's decline in business, since the decline occurred so soon after Claire made the statement. We would be less inclined to reach this conclusion if the decline occurred a year later.

In the first example, notice that we did not say that the beer caused the sickness because the sickness occurred seconds after drinking it. Nor did we say that the beer could not have caused the sickness if it occurred two weeks later. Rarely can such definitive conclusions be made on the basis of time evidence alone. All we can say is that our common sense suggests these conclusions, although we are willing to look at any other evidence that may suggest different conclusions. In the second example, we did not say that the derogatory statement caused the decline in business because the decline occurred one week after the derogatory statement was made. Nor did we say that the statement could not have caused the decline if it occurred a year later. All we can say is that time evidence is one of the relevant pieces of information that we need to consider.

Space: Did the injury occur in the same area or vicinity where the defendant acted or failed to act? The closer we can pinpoint the defendant's acts or omissions to the area or vicinity of the plaintiff's injury, the more convinced we are that those acts or omissions caused the injury. The greater the distance between the area or vicinity of the injury and the area or vicinity of the defendant's acts or omissions, the more skeptical we are that those acts or omissions caused the injury.

EXAMPLES:

- One of Bob's jobs at a printing plant is to pour a certain ink, which has a heavy odor, into the presses. Bob develops a respiratory problem. He says that the problem is due to breathing the ink fumes. Common sense tells us that the ink fumes may have caused the respiratory problem since he worked so close to the ink. We would be less inclined to reach this conclusion, however, if Bob worked 500 yards away from the presses that use the ink.
- Lena is a department store clerk where she is in charge of one of the five cosmetics counters. Occasionally she works at the other four counters. The store suspects that she is stealing cosmetics (which would constitute the crime of larceny and the tort of conversion). All of the missing cosmetics were at Lena's main counter and at those counters where she occasionally has worked. Common sense tells us that Lena may have taken the cosmetics since she was physically present at those counters where the goods were missing. We would be less inclined to reach this conclusion, however, if Lena never worked at the counters that experienced the missing cosmetics.

These observations about time and space evidence are simply hypotheses or assumptions about life and human nature. They are nothing more than points of departure in our search for causation. We must never close our mind to evidence that may point to other conclusions. Some illnesses, for example, may not appear until months or years after an accident, yet we can still be convinced that one caused the other. So, too, we can be convinced that actions taken in New York can lead to damage or injury in California. There is nothing ironclad about the hypotheses. Just as we can be convinced that the defendant has caused an injury that is far removed in time and space from what the defendant did or failed to do, so too, cases may arise in which we can be convinced that the defendant did not cause an injury that occurred immediately after the defendant's acts or omissions. The facts of each individual case must be carefully scrutinized. The predisposition of our common sense, however, tells us to begin this scrutiny with the hypotheses on time and space.

Assume that for years a railroad has stationed a guard at a point where the track crosses a highway. One day, the railroad removes the guard. Two days later, a train crashes into a car at the intersection. Was the absence of the guard the cause in fact of the injury? Was the absence of the guard a substantial factor in producing the injury? Among the evidence to be introduced by the plaintiff's attorney are time and space evidence. The attorney will present evidence to show that the crash occurred soon after the guard was removed (time) and that the crash occurred at the very intersection where the guard was once stationed (space). Common sense tells us, according to this attorney, that the accident would not have happened if the guard had been there, or at the very least, that the absence of the guard was a substantial factor in producing the crash. Time-and-space evidence is critical on the issue of causation, but not necessarily determinative. Other evidence might show that the job function of the guard was not to try to prevent the kind of collision that occurred and that even if the guard had been present, the collision would have occurred anyway. Again, the time and space evidence is but a point of departure.

Another important source of causation evidence is *history*. Here again, a basic hypothesis is in play.

History: In the past, have the same or similar acts or omissions by the defendant or people like the defendant produced this kind of injury? The more often this kind of injury has resulted from such acts or omissions in the past, the more convinced we are that the acts or omissions of the defendant caused the injury. If this kind of injury has never or has rarely been produced by such acts or omissions, we are more skeptical that the defendant's acts or omissions caused the injury.

Of course, just because something has happened in the past does not necessarily mean that it happened in this particular case. The predisposition of our common sense, however, tells us that history does tend to repeat itself. Hence, our common sense leads us to inquire about the past. In the railroad crossing case, for example, the plaintiff's attorney may try to introduce evidence that collisions between trains and cars never occurred when the guard was on duty, as a way of proving that it is more likely than not that the absence of the guard caused the collision.

Hence, evidence of time, space, and history is critical in beginning to collect evidence of causation in fact. We are drawn to search out such evidence on the basis of some basic hypotheses about time, space, and history. Such evidence will not always be conclusive—either way—on the issue of causation in fact. All of the facts and circumstances of a given case must be examined. Start your examination, however, with the evidence of time, space, and history.

| ASSIGNMENT **15.2** | Re-read the fact situation at the beginning of this chapter about the plaintiff whose leg, arm, and knee were injured. Was Sam the cause in fact of each of these injuries? (Sam is the driver who initially hit the plaintiff while driving at an excessive rate of speed.) (See General Instructions for the Legal Analysis Assignment in Chapter 2.) |

FIGURE 15–2
To prove causation, attorneys often hire consultants to help explain why and how things went wrong. If they are engineers or scientists, they are sometimes called forensic engineers or scientists. Exponent, Inc. is a company consisting of these individuals. One of the cases for which they were hired involved the death of 113 people at the Hyatt Regency Hotel in Kansas City. An estimated 2,000 people had gathered in the lobby area to enjoy a tea dance. Suddenly, the two walkways that spanned the lobby collapsed. Forensic engineers from Exponent, Inc. sifted through the wreckage for four days. Speculation that the accident had been the result of "harmonic vibrations" caused by dancers on the walkway were disproved by mathematical models of walkways and by the sequence of events. Combined testing, materials, and stress analysis led the engineers to testify that the collapse had occurred when a bolt end on a rod that attached the walkways to the ceiling had pulled through a walkway beam.

Photo courtesy of Exponent, Inc.

Weight of the Evidence

Let us shift our focus for a moment away from the tests for causation in fact (but-for and substantial factor) to the **standard of proof** needed to establish causation in fact. (See Figure 15-2.) By standard of proof we mean how convincing the evidence of something must be before a fact finder can accept it as true. (The fact finder is the jury or, if there is no jury, the judge.) The amount and believability of evidence is referred to as the **weight of the evidence.** The standard of proof, therefore, can be phrased as the "weight" that evidence of something must have before a fact finder can accept it as true. Here our focus is on how convincing the plaintiff's evidence must be that the defendant was a cause in fact of the plaintiff's injury. There are several different "weights" that evidence can have. Evidence of something can be overwhelming, highly likely, more likely than not, fifty/fifty, possible, etc. In most tort cases, the minimum standard of proof that must be met is **preponderance of the evidence.** Under this standard, a party must prove that its version of a fact is more likely true than not. This preponderance-of-the-evidence standard ("more likely than not") is the minimum degree of believability (the minimum weight) that a plaintiff's evidence must have in order for a fact finder to be able to accept the plaintiff's version of who was the cause in fact of his or her injury. Using the two tests for cause in fact, the standard would be expressed as follows:

Plaintiff must produce evidence that is convincing enough for a fact finder to conclude it is *more likely than not* that the defendant was a substantial factor in producing the injury, *or*

Plaintiff must produce evidence that is convincing enough for a fact finder to conclude it is *more likely than not* that but for what the defendant did, the plaintiff's injury would not have occurred.

A mere *possibility* that the defendant was a substantial factor in producing the injury is not enough. (Or a mere possibility that but for what the defendant did, the plaintiff would not have been injured is not enough.) Anything is possible. A fifty/fifty possibility is also not enough. In mathematical terms, believability must be *at least* greater than 50 percent. This is what is meant by the more-likely-than-not standard. (See Figure 15–3.)

FIGURE 15–3 Weight of the evidence on cause in fact: Eight possibilities.

USING THE BUT-FOR TEST:	USING THE SUBSTANTIAL FACTOR TEST:	CONSEQUENCES
1. The evidence is overwhelming that but for what the defendant did, the plaintiff's injury would not have occurred.	1. The evidence is overwhelming that the defendant was a substantial factor in producing the injury.	*If the case falls into any one of these three categories (1–3) for the but-for test or the substantial factor test, the plaintiff has carried the burden of proving by a preponderance of the evidence that the defendant was the cause in fact of the plaintiff's injury.*
2. The evidence shows it is highly likely that but for what the defendant did, the plaintiff's injury would not have occurred.	2. The evidence shows it is highly likely that the defendant was a substantial factor in producing the injury.	
3. The evidence shows it is more likely than not that but for what the defendant did, the plaintiff's injury would not have occurred.	3. The evidence shows it is more likely than not that the defendant was a substantial factor in producing the injury.	
4. The evidence is overwhelming that but for what the defendant did, the plaintiff's injury would still have occurred.	4. The evidence is overwhelming that the defendant was not a substantial factor in producing the injury.	*If the case falls into any one of these five categories (4–8) for the but-for test or the substantial factor test, the plaintiff has failed to carry the burden of proving by a preponderance of the evidence that the defendant was the cause in fact of the plaintiff's injury. Causation, therefore, cannot be established.*
5. The evidence shows it is highly likely that but for what the defendant did, the plaintiff's injury would still have occurred.	5. The evidence shows it is highly likely that the defendant was not a substantial factor in producing the injury.	
6. The evidence shows it is more likely than not that but for what the defendant did, the plaintiff's injury would still have occurred.	6. The evidence shows it is more likely than not that the defendant was not a substantial factor in producing the injury.	
7. The evidence shows a fifty/fifty possibility that but for what the defendant did, the plaintiff's injury would not have occurred.	7. The evidence shows a fifty/fifty possibility that the defendant was a substantial factor in producing the injury.	
8. The evidence shows there is a possibility that but for what the defendant did, the plaintiff's injury would not have occurred.	8. The evidence shows there is a possibility that the defendant was a substantial factor in producing the injury.	

CASE

Parra v. Tarasco, Inc. d/b/a Jiminez Restaurant
230 Ill. App. 3d 819, 595 N.E.2d 1186 (1992)
Appellate Court of Illinois, First District

Background: *Ernest Parra died when he choked on a piece of food at Jiminez Restaurant. This suit alleges that the restaurant negligently failed to post instructions in the restaurant on how to aid a choking victim and negligently failed to summon emergency medical assistance. The Illinois Choke-Saving Methods Act requires every restaurant to "have posted in a conspicuous location that is visible to patrons and employees on the premises, but which location need not be in the actual dining areas, instructions concerning at least one method of first aid assistance to choking persons." Jiminez Restaurant failed to post these instructions. The trial court dismissed the complaint for failure to state a cause of action. The case is now on appeal before the Appellate Court of Illinois.*

Decision on Appeal: *Judgment affirmed. Plaintiff has not alleged causation.*

OPINION OF COURT

Justice GORDON delivered the opinion of the court . . .

[Plaintiff has] failed to adequately allege that failure to post the sign was the proximate cause of decedent's death. The violation of a statute or ordinance designed for the protection of human life or property can be *prima facie* evidence of negligence, but the injury must have a direct and proximate connection with the violation. Plaintiff must include sufficient factual allegations that such violation was the proximate cause of his injuries. It is not sufficient to merely plead conclusions. *Horcher v. Guerin*, 94 Ill. App. 2d 244, 248–50, 236 N.E.2d 576 (complaint merely alleges conclusion that violation of building code [requiring windows in operating condition] was proximate cause of injury from fire; however, nothing indicates causal connection between inoperative windows and actual injury of plaintiff).

In order to state a cause of action, plaintiff must allege the ultimate facts which give rise to the cause of action, and liberality of pleading will not relieve plaintiff of the requirement that the complaint contain sufficient, factual averments and set out every fact essential to be proved.

In determining whether proximate cause has been sufficiently set forth, it is important to "distinguish the causal connection between what the defendant did and the plaintiff's injury from the connection between the plaintiff's injury and the class of the injuries from which the statute was intended to afford protection [choking to death]." (N.J. Singer, 2B *Sutherland Statutory Construction,* sec. 55.05, at 287–88 (5th ed. 1992) (footnotes omitted).) While clearly decedent's choking to death is precisely the class of injury for which the statute intends to afford protection; however, the necessary causal connection here runs between what defendant allegedly did—failure to post the sign, and plaintiff's injury—choking to death on his food.

The complaint here merely alleges that defendant: "5a. failed to post in a conspicuous location that was visible to patrons and employees in the premises instructions concerning first aid assistance to choking persons in violation of Illinois Revised statute; b. failed to instruct their employees in first aid assistance to choking persons; c. failed to assist the plaintiff decedent who was choking after failing to post in a conspicuous place instructions concerning first aid assistance to choking persons. 6. That as a direct and proximate result of the aforesaid negligent acts or omissions of the defendants, the plaintiff decedent . . . suffered personal injuries and died on March 18, 1989."

This broad, conclusory language fails to provide the necessary factual allegations which would establish a causal relationship between not posting the sign and decedent's death. There is no allegation, for example, that anyone tried to perform the Heimlich Maneuver but performed it incorrectly because the sign was not posted, or failed to undertake such an attempt because of a failure to post the sign.

Plaintiff additionally alleges in the complaint that defendant "failed to promptly summon emergency medical personnel." . . . [But] there is no factual allegation in the complaint which even hints at a causal connection between decedent's death, and any action or inaction by defendant. In fact, there is no allegation that anyone in the restaurant had any knowledge that decedent was choking. There is no allegation that defendant's employees had discovered decedent choking and refused to call, or delayed calling, for medical assistance. There is no allegation that, but for the failure of defendant to summon an ambulance, decedent would have lived. Cf. *Acosta v. Fuentes,* 150 Misc. 2d 1013, 571 N.Y.S. 666, 669 (1991) (if the patron choking on his food was "already doomed to die" before the restaurant's employees called an ambulance and moved him outside, then no causal connection has been shown between defendants' action or inaction and decedent's death).

We conclude that the trial court properly found that plaintiff's allegations of negligence based on defendant's failure to post a sign, or failure to secure or render first aid, did not state a cause of action. . . .

ASSIGNMENT

15.3

a. Write a complaint for Parra that *adequately* alleges causation. Make up whatever facts you need to draft this complaint. Be sure that Justice Gordon would not have the same problems with your complaint that he had with the complaint actually used in the litigation, even if your state does not require the same kind of pleading specificity that Justice Gordon required. (See General Instructions for the Complaint-Drafting Assignment in Chapter 3.)

b. Assume that none of the employees in the Illinois restaurant spoke English, and that none of the customers in the restaurant at the time of the choking spoke English. Also assume that there are instructions clearly posted in the restaurant on what to do if someone chokes on food, but the instructions are in English. Would the result in the *Parra* case be the same? What would the complaint have to allege?

CUT-OFF TEST OF PROXIMATE CAUSE

As we said at the beginning of this chapter, there are two dimensions of proximate cause: a cause-in-fact question (using the but-for or substantial factor tests) and a policy question (using the cut-off test). See Figure 15–1. Once we have answered the first question by concluding that the defendant was the cause in fact of the plaintiff's injury, we then ask the policy question of whether there is a need for a cut-off of the defendant's liability. The policy question is whether the defendant should be able to avoid liability for what he or she has caused in fact. The cut-off test is whether the injury suffered by the plaintiff was the foreseeable consequence of the original risk created by the defendant's unreasonable acts or omissions. If the answer is no, liability is cut off; the defendant will *not* be liable for what he or she has caused in fact. If the answer is yes, liability is not cut off; the defendant is liable for what he or she has caused in fact.

Although the phrase "proximate cause" refers to both the cause-in-fact issue and the policy issue, you will often see the phrase used in reference to the policy issue only. In this usage, someone might ask whether the defendant was the cause in fact of the injury and whether the defendant was the proximate cause of that injury.

EXAMPLE: Cliff speeds through a red light in his truck. He hits a car proceeding on a green light in the intersection. The plaintiff in the car suffers a broken arm from the collision, and the car is demolished.

CAUSE IN FACT: "But for" the way Cliff drove, the plaintiff would not have suffered the broken arm nor the property damage to the car; Cliff was certainly a substantial factor in producing the personal and property damage. Cliff is the cause in fact of both.

PROXIMATE CAUSE: Cliff is also the proximate cause of the personal and property damage. The original risk created by speeding through a red light was the risk of hitting other cars and people. The plaintiff's broken arm and demolished car are foreseeable consequences of this original risk Cliff created. Hence, there is no need for a cut-off rule. Cliff is the proximate cause of what he caused in fact.

Let us look at another case:

EXAMPLE: Jim carelessly pushes Alice, who breaks a leg. Two weeks later, while walking on crutches, Alice falls and breaks her arm. Soon thereafter, she catches pneumonia because of her general rundown condition.

CAUSE IN FACT: "But for" Jim's push, Alice would not have suffered the leg injury, the arm injury, and the pneumonia. He is also a substantial factor in producing all three. He is the cause in fact of all three.

PROXIMATE CAUSE: When Jim pushed Alice, it was foreseeable that she could break a leg bone. This was within the original risk Jim created. It was also foreseeable that such an injury would require medical attention that would lead to the use of crutches. Everyone knows that walking on crutches is difficult. It is foreseeable that someone could fall on them and suffer further injury. Hence, the arm injury was also within the original risk created by Jim. Finally, it is foreseeable that an injured person would be in a rundown condition (initially created by the leg and arm injuries) and could contract an illness such as pneumonia. There is nothing unusual about this occurring. Jim, therefore, is the proximate cause of the leg injury, the arm injury, and the pneumonia. They are all foreseeable consequences of the original risk created by Jim's carelessness.

ASSIGNMENT

15.4

Peter is a passenger in a bus that is carelessly speeding. The bus crashes into another car. Peter is forced forward, injuring his arm. Moments after the crash, lightning strikes a tree, which falls on the part of the bus where Peter is sitting, injuring his leg. Is the bus company the proximate cause of the arm injury and the leg injury? (See General Instructions for the Legal Analysis Assignment in Chapter 2.)

The conclusion that defendants are liable for the injuries they proximately cause is subject to the requirement that the plaintiff must take reasonable steps to **mitigate the consequences** of those injuries. (This duty to mitigate damages is also referred to as the doctrine of **avoidable consequences,** which is discussed more fully in Chapter 16.) Plaintiff, for example, cannot refuse all medical attention and then hold the defendant responsible for the **aggravation** of the injury caused by the refusal to see a doctor.

There are two major exceptions to the general cut-off test of proximate cause. They pertain to the unforeseeability of the extent of the injuries and of the manner of their occurrence.

Exceptions to Test

"Eggshell Skull" Rule—Extent of Injury

If it is foreseeable that defendant's unreasonable acts or omissions will result in any *impact on plaintiff's body,* and this impact does occur, the defendant will be liable for the foreseeable *and the unforeseeable* personal injuries that follow. The cut-off test of proximate cause will not prevent liability for unforeseeable personal injuries that follow from any foreseeable impact on the plaintiff's body. Assume that the defendant is carelessly running down the corridor and bumps into the plaintiff as the latter is turning the corner. Plaintiff is one month pregnant at the time. The accidental bump causes a miscarriage. Or, assume the defendant is driving 15 mph in heavy traffic. For a second, the defendant carelessly takes his eyes off the road and runs into the rear of the plaintiff's car. Only a slight dent is put on the plaintiff's car. The plaintiff, however, dies because the collision activates a rare disease. In both of these examples, the plaintiff had an **eggshell skull,** meaning a very high vulnerability to injury to any part of the body. The extent of the injury was not foreseeable by the defendant. The extent of the injury was not within the risk originally created by the defendant. In both cases, it was foreseeable that the defendant would cause an impact on someone's body, but the injury itself that resulted was clearly not foreseeable. In such situations, however, the defendant "takes the plaintiff as he finds him." There is no cut-off of liability. Note again, however, that this exception to the cut-off test applies only when it is foreseeable that there will be at least some body impact on the plaintiff.

The eggshell-skull rule is not limited to impact caused by negligence or unreasonableness. If the defendant makes impact on the plaintiff's body through an intentional tort such as battery, the defendant will be liable for all resulting injuries, foreseeable or not.

Phrased another way, the eggshell-skull exception means that the defendant will be deemed to be the proximate cause of all foreseeable and unforeseeable personal injuries that result from any foreseeable impact due to unreasonable or intentional conduct by the defendant.

Often, the plaintiff with the eggshell skull has a pre-existing condition, disease, or injury that has been aggravated by the defendant. The latter, of course, will not be responsible for the original existence of the pre-existing condition, disease, or injury, but will be responsible for its *aggravation.*

Suppose that the plaintiff goes insane or commits suicide because of despair over the initial injuries caused by the defendant. Assume that there was a foreseeable impact on the plaintiff's person. Courts differ as to whether the defendant will be held responsible. Some courts would say that insanity or suicide is so extreme that the cut-off principle of proximate cause will prevent liability for such a drastic consequence. Other courts would consider the suicide to be a superseding cause (to be considered later in this chapter), which would cut off liability. Many courts, on the other hand, will carry the eggshell-skull rule to its logical extreme and hold that the defendant is the proximate cause of the insanity or the death by suicide as long as there was a foreseeable impact on the body that the defendant carelessly or intentionally created.

Unforeseeability of Manner of Injury

Frequently, the precise **manner** in which the damage or injury would occur is not foreseeable.

> **EXAMPLE:** Defendant is carelessly navigating a steamboat that rams into a bridge. The plaintiff was one of the workers repairing the bridge at the time. When the boat hit the bridge, the plaintiff fell onto a blowtorch he was using, resulting in blindness in both eyes.

In this case, it was foreseeable that some damage to the bridge and some kind of injury to someone on the bridge would occur from the careless navigation of a steamboat in the area of the bridge. Personal and property damage was foreseeable. But the *manner* in which the injury would result in this particular plaintiff—falling on the blowtorch—was not foreseeable to the defendant, who did not even know that the plaintiff was there working with a torch. Drowning or a severe concussion to anyone on the bridge may have been foreseeable to the defendant, but not the manner in which the injury in fact occurred in this case. The rule in such cases is as follows:

> The manner in which an injury occurs does not have to be foreseeable in order for the defendant to be the proximate cause of the injury, as long as the harm that resulted was within the risk originally created by the defendant's acts or omissions.

This then is the second major exception to the rule that you are not the proximate cause of an injury that is unforeseeable. You can be the proximate cause of a foreseeable injury that occurs in an unforeseeable manner.

The American Law Institute, in its *Restatement of Torts*, would agree that the particular manner of the occurrence of the harm need not be foreseeable in order for the defendant to be the proximate cause of the injury (or as the *Restatement* would phrase it, the "legal cause" of the injury). It is important to the *Restatement* (and to the courts that follow it) to assess whether the injury was a normal or ordinary consequence of the risk that the defendant created. Liability should be cut off, according to this view, only if we can say that the harm that resulted was in fact **highly extraordinary.**[3]

ASSIGNMENT	
15.5	Tom, an adult, gives a loaded gun to Bob, a young boy. Tom asks Bob to deliver the gun to Jack. Bob takes his friend Bill with him to make the delivery. Upon arrival, Bob accidentally drops the gun on Bill's toe. The toe breaks. When the gun falls, it discharges immediately, killing Jack. Bob suffers a nervous breakdown over the incident. Is Tom the proximate cause of Bill's broken toe? Of Jack's death? Of Bob's nervous breakdown? (See General Instructions for the Legal Analysis Assignment in Chapter 2. See also *Restatement (Second) of Torts* § 281, illustration 3 (1965).)

As we examine proximate cause, it is important that this element be kept in perspective with the other elements of negligence discussed thus far—duty (Chapter 13) and breach of duty (Chapter 14). A discussion of proximate cause assumes that the plaintiff has already been able to establish that a duty of reasonable care (the first element) exists between the plaintiff and defendant, and that the defendant has breached that duty (the second element) by unreasonable conduct. Note the role that foreseeability plays in each element:

Element I: Duty
Defendant owes plaintiff a duty of reasonable care if the defendant's act or omission has created a *foreseeable* risk of injury or damage to the plaintiff's person or property (the general rule; see Figure 13–1 in Chapter 13).

Element II: Breach of Duty
Defendant breaches a duty of reasonable care by failing to take precautions against injury to the plaintiff when the *foreseeability* of serious injury outweighs

---

[3]American Law Institute, *Restatement (Second) of Torts* § 435(2) (1965).

the burden or inconvenience of taking those precautions (see Figure 14–4 in Chapter 14).

Element III: Proximate Cause

Defendant is the proximate cause of every injury he or she in fact caused the plaintiff to suffer if those injuries were the *foreseeable* consequence of the original risk of injury created by the defendant's acts or omissions.

The foreseeability analysis that you must do to determine whether a duty exists (first element) is substantially the same foreseeability analysis that you must do to determine whether proximate cause exists (third element), or more accurately, whether the cut-off test of proximate cause will prevent the defendant from being liable for harm he or she has caused in fact. The very definition of the cut-off test requires you to refer back to the original risk created by the defendant. The relationship between the first element, duty, and the third element, proximate cause, is so close that you will sometimes see the proximate cause issue phrased in terms of duty: was the defendant under a duty to protect the plaintiff against the injury that resulted? Always keep in mind the two exceptions that operate to establish proximate cause for injuries that in extent or manner go beyond the original risk that was foreseeable. Aside from these two exceptions, you conduct the cut-off test of proximate cause by substantially repeating the same foreseeability analysis that you used to determine whether the first element of negligence (duty) applied.

Finally, we need to examine two special problem areas:

- the unforeseeable plaintiff
- intervening causes

Unforeseeable Plaintiff

We already looked at the problem of the **unforeseeable plaintiff** when we studied duty in Chapter 13. (See Figure 13–2.) What happens when injury to someone is foreseeable but not injury to the particular plaintiff who is injured? Is a duty (first element) owed to the unforeseeable plaintiff? As we saw in Figure 13–3, the Cardozo zone-of-danger test would say no, whereas the Andrews world-at-large test would say yes. If the Cardozo view is adopted in a state, the negligence case is over. The plaintiff loses for failure to establish one of the elements of negligence (duty). If the Andrews view is adopted in a state, the plaintiff will be successful in establishing the existence of a duty and must then move to the other elements of negligence, such as proximate cause. Because of the close relationship between duty and proximate cause, as we have seen, a plaintiff who successfully establishes duty is well on the way to establishing proximate cause as well. The cut-off principle of proximate cause will prevent liability only if the injury was beyond the scope of the foreseeable risk.

Intervening Causes

An **intervening cause** is a force that produces harm after the defendant's act or omission.

> **EXAMPLE:** Car #1 crashes into plaintiff's truck. While the plaintiff's truck is disabled in the middle of the road, car #2 crashes into the truck, but does not stop. Plaintiff sues car #1.

Car #2, the hit-and-run driver, is an intervening cause. The harm it caused occurred after the defendant's act or omission that led to the initial crash. Intervening causes operate subsequent to the involvement of the defendant. We need to examine the effect of an intervening cause on the defendant's liability. This is important because often the only party available to sue is the defendant; the person or entity that is the intervening cause may have disappeared, may have no assets (i.e., be **judgment proof**), or simply cannot be sued. The question, therefore, is whether the defendant is liable for the harm he or she originally caused *as well as* for the harm caused by what intervened. Phrased another way: is the defendant the proximate cause both of the harm he or she caused and of the harm produced by the intervening cause? First, we need to distinguish four different kinds of intervening causes:

- An **intervening force of nature** is a subsequent natural occurrence that is independent of human interference; it is an act of God. For example: The ABC Company carelessly builds a dam. Slight cracks become visible. A month after the dam is built, a severe tornado hits the area and the dam collapses. The tornado is an intervening force of nature.
- An **intervening innocent human force** is a subsequent occurrence caused by a human being who was not careless or wrongful. For example: Cynthia carelessly runs into the plaintiff crossing the street. While the plaintiff is on the ground, Tom's car hits the plaintiff. Tom was driving carefully when he hit the plaintiff. Tom is an intervening innocent human force.
- An **intervening negligent human force** is a subsequent occurrence negligently caused by a human being. For example: Alex carelessly runs into the plaintiff. Plaintiff is rushed to the hospital but is given negligent medical treatment by a nurse, causing further injury. The nurse is an intervening negligent human force.
- An **intervening intentional or criminal human force** is a subsequent occurrence caused intentionally or criminally by a human being. For example: George carelessly runs into the plaintiff. While at the hospital, the plaintiff sees his archenemy, who tries to poison him. The archenemy is an intervening intentional or criminal human force.

If any of these intervening forces can be classified as a **superseding cause,** the cutoff test of proximate cause will prevent the defendant from being responsible for the harm caused by the intervening force. If the intervening force is not a superseding cause, then the defendant will be found to be the proximate cause of the harm caused by the intervening force. Our question, therefore, becomes: when is an intervening force a superseding cause?

> An intervening force becomes a superseding cause when the harm caused by the intervening force is beyond the foreseeable risk originally created by the defendant's unreasonable acts or omissions, and/or when the harm caused by the intervening force is considered highly extraordinary.

Hence, foreseeability and the original risk created by the defendant again become critical factors. Alternatively, the "highly extraordinary" test of the *Restatement* that we saw earlier can be used as a guide.

Intervening intentional or criminal human forces are often considered superseding causes, because they are either outside the scope of the original risk or are highly extraordinary. Examine again the example just given involving the archenemy's attempt to poison the plaintiff in the hospital. George initially hit the plaintiff in an automobile collision and is the proximate cause of the plaintiff's injuries sustained in the collision, but he is not the proximate cause of the poisoning. The latter was highly extraordinary and far beyond the original risk that George created by his careless driving. The injuries are the natural and foreseeable consequence of bad driving. The intentional and criminal act of poisoning is not reasonably connected with George's bad driving.

Intervening intentional or criminal human forces are *not* always considered superseding causes. What the defendant does or fails to do may increase the risk of such an intervention, making the latter neither unforeseeable nor extraordinary. Suppose the defendant gives loaded guns to a group of juvenile delinquents, who intentionally shoot the plaintiff. Or suppose a motel fails to provide any security in a section of the motel where the burglary or robbery of patrons is highly likely, and such a burglary or robbery in fact occurs. In these cases, the intentional or criminal intervening force was part of the foreseeable risk created by the defendant's acts or omissions. Such intervening forces are not superseding; defendant is the proximate cause of the harm produced by them.

Intervening innocent or negligent human forces are treated the same way. If their intervention was part of the original risk, then they were foreseeable and do not become superseding causes. In those cases, for example, where the plaintiff is further injured in a hospital (whether innocently or negligently) after being brought there for treatment for the injury originally caused by the defendant, the hospital injuries are usually considered to be part of the original risk and not highly extraordinary. So, too, if the plaintiff receives a second injury by a third party (whether innocently or negligently) at the scene of the accident. In all these cases, the defendant has rendered the plaintiff highly vulnerable to further injury. It is not uncommon for individuals to receive injuries in hospitals or on the road after the first injury, although it may be highly unusual for such second injuries to be produced intentionally or criminally.

What about intervening forces of nature? Here it is important to ask whether the injury or damage is of the same kind as would have occurred if the intervening force of nature had not intervened at all. If the same kind of injury or damage results, the intervening force of nature is not a superseding cause. Suppose, for example, that the defendant carelessly leaves explosives in an area where people would be hurt by an explosion. Because of the manner of storage, assume that the explosives could detonate on their own. Hence, unreasonable storage creates a risk of serious personal and property damage to people in the area. One day, lightning strikes the explosives, leading to serious personal and property damage. The lightning may have been unforeseeable, but the damage or injury caused by the intervention of the lightning was the same kind of damage or injury that the defendant's method of storage risked. Defendant is the proximate cause of what the lightning produced. The resulting damage or injury is not highly extraordinary, even though it may have been unforeseeable that it would occur in this way.

A different result is reached in many, but not all, courts when the intervening force of nature causes a totally different kind of injury than that originally foreseeable by the defendant's act or omission. Suppose, for example, that a truck company carelessly delays the delivery of the plaintiff's food goods, and the goods are destroyed by a storm. The destruction was not within the original risk created by the defendant (spoilage due to the delay), and some courts would therefore say that the intervening force of nature was a superseding cause.

OVERVIEW OF STEPS NEEDED TO ANALYZE PROXIMATE CAUSE

- Cause in Fact
  Apply the two tests for cause in fact. First ask if the plaintiff's injury would have occurred but for the acts or omissions of the defendant. Then apply the substantial factor test, especially when more than one cause may have produced the plaintiff's injury. Was the defendant's act or omission *a* substantial factor in producing the plaintiff's injury? Plaintiff can establish cause in fact by *either* test.

- Burden of Proof
  Determine if there is enough evidence so that the fact finder (e.g., a jury) could at least say that it is more likely than not that the defendant's act or omission was a substantial factor in producing the plaintiff's injury. Or determine if there is enough evidence so that the fact finder could say it is more likely than not that but for the defendant's act or omission, the injury would not have occurred.

- Original Risk
  Turn the clock back to the time of the defendant's original act or omission. Identify the foreseeable risk as of that time. What kind of injury or damage was foreseeable or should have been foreseeable to the defendant?

- Eggshell Skull
  Determine whether the plaintiff has an "eggshell skull," or special vulnerability to injury. Was there a foreseeable impact on his or her body? If so, the resulting injuries are proximately caused by the defendant, even if the extent of the injuries was unforeseeable.
- Unforeseeable Manner
  Determine whether injury or damage was foreseeable because it was within the original risk created by the defendant and whether the only thing that was unforeseeable was the manner in which that injury or damage occurred. If so, the defendant is the proximate cause of the injury or damage, even though the manner of occurrence was unforeseeable.
- Intervening Human Force
  Determine whether any intervening human force was a causal factor in producing the injury or damage. If so, determine whether this human force was innocent, negligent, intentional, or criminal. Was the intervening human force within the scope of the original risk produced by the defendant? Was it foreseeable to the defendant? Did the human force proceed naturally out of what the defendant did or failed to do? Affirmative answers to these questions will make the defendant the proximate cause of what the intervening human force produced.
- Intervening Force of Nature
  Determine whether an intervening force of nature was a causal factor in producing the injury or damage. If so, ask whether the injury or damage that resulted was the same kind that would have occurred if the force of nature had not intervened. If so, the defendant is still the proximate cause of the injury or damage.
- Highly Extraordinary
  Can it be said that the injury or damage was highly extraordinary in view of what the defendant did or failed to do? If not, then the likelihood is that a court will find that the defendant was the proximate cause of the injury or damage.
- Causation v. Policy
  Make sure that your analysis has not confused the causation question with the policy question of proximate cause. The causation question involves a straightforward but-for or substantial factor assessment. The policy question involves the cut-off test that will prevent defendants from being responsible for injury or damage they have in fact caused. Do not worry about the policy question if cause in fact cannot be established.

ASSIGNMENT 15.6	Examine both issues of proximate cause (cause in fact and the cut-off principle) in the following situations:

- a. Tom carelessly drives his motorcycle into Dan's horse. The horse goes wild and jumps over a five-foot fence (which it has never done before) and runs into traffic. Henry tries to turn his car away from the horse and accidentally hits Pete, who is a pedestrian on the sidewalk at the time of the collision. Pete sues Tom for negligence.
- b. Same facts as in (a), except that Henry just misses Pete, rather than hitting him with his car. Pete and Henry begin an argument over Henry's driving. Henry hits Pete in the jaw. Pete sues Tom for negligence.
- c. Mary gives a loaded gun to a ten-year-old girl who is Mary's neighbor. The girl takes the gun home. The girl's father discovers the gun but fails to take it away from his daughter. The girl shoots Linda with the gun. Linda sues Mary for negligence.
- d. Harry carelessly hits Helen, a pedestrian, with his car in a busy intersection downtown. While Helen is lying on the ground, a person in another car accidentally hits Helen, causing further injuries. This other person is a hit-and-run driver who does not stop after hitting Helen. Helen sues Harry for negligence.

e. Pat carelessly leaves her keys in her car. A thief gets in the car and starts to speed away. Moments later, the thief hits Kevin with the car one block away from where Pat parked the car. Kevin sues Pat for negligence.

f. Same facts as in (e), except that the thief hits Kevin one month after he has stolen the car, in another section of the city.

(See General Instructions for the Legal Analysis Assignment in Chapter 2.)

CASE

Mussivand v. David
45 Ohio St. 3d 314, 544 N.E.2d 265 (1989)
Supreme Court of Ohio

Background: *George David has a venereal disease, but does not tell the woman he is having an affair with. She contracts the disease from him and then gives it to her husband, Tofigh Mussivand. The latter sues David for negligence in failing to tell his wife that he had the disease. This failure allegedly caused Mussivand to contract the disease. The trial court granted David's motion to dismiss. The case is now on appeal before the Supreme Court of Ohio.*

Decision on Appeal: *The case should not have been dismissed. A husband can bring an action against his wife's paramour (lover), alleging that the paramour was negligent in failing to notify the wife that the paramour was at risk of passing venereal disease to the wife, who in turn could (and did) pass it to the husband.*

OPINION OF COURT

Justice RESNICK delivered the opinion of the court. . . .

The complaint basically states that [Mussivand] contracted a venereal disease due to the acts of [David]. . . . A "venereal disease" is defined as "a contagious disease, most commonly acquired in sexual intercourse or other genital contact; the venereal diseases include syphilis, gonorrhea, chancroid, granuloma inguinale, lymphogranuloma venereum, genital herpesvirus infection, and balanitis gangraenosa." *Dorland's Illustrated Medical Dictionary* (26 Ed. 1985) 394. . . .

Recently several jurisdictions have allowed tort actions for negligent, fraudulent or intentional transmission of genital herpes where the person infected with genital herpes fails to disclose to his or her sexual partner that he or she is infected with such a disease. *Maharam v. Maharam* (1986), 123 A.D.2d 165, 510 N.Y.S.2d 104; *Long v. Adams* (1985), 175 Ga. App. 538, 333 S.E.2d 852. Thus, courts have placed upon persons who have a venereal disease such as genital herpes or gonorrhea the duty to protect others who might be in danger of being infected by such a disease. In other words, people with a venereal disease have a duty to use reasonable care to avoid infecting others with whom they engage in sexual conduct. . . .

David argues that possibly Mussivand's wife, not he, was the cause of Mussivand's injuries. "Whether an intervening act breaks the causal connection between negligence and injury, thus relieving one of liability for his negligence, depends upon whether that intervening cause was a conscious and responsible agency which could or should have eliminated the hazard, and whether the intervening cause was reasonably foreseeable by the one who is guilty of the negligence. . . ." *Cascone*

v. Herb Kay Co. (1983), 6 Ohio St. 3d 155, 451 N.E.2d 815.

In *Jeffers v. Olexo* (1989), 43 Ohio St. 3d 140, 144, 539 N.E.2d 614, 618, we equated foreseeability with proximate cause. This is misleading since they are not equatable. Rather, in order to establish proximate cause, foreseeability must be found. In determining whether an intervening cause "breaks the causal connection" between negligence and injury depends upon whether that intervening cause was reasonably foreseeable by one who was guilty of the negligence. If an injury is the natural and probable consequence of a negligent act and it is such as should have been foreseen in the light of all the attending circumstances, the injury is then the proximate result of the negligence. It is not necessary that the defendant should have anticipated the particular injury. It is sufficient that his act is likely to result in an injury to someone. Thus we do not equate foreseeability with proximate cause. Instead, if David knew his paramour was married, then it can be said that it was reasonably foreseeable that she would engage in sexual intercourse with her husband. In addition, if David did not inform her of the fact that he had a venereal disease, she could not be an intervening cause and, as such, David's liability to Mussivand would not be terminated. David's negligence would then be the proximate cause of Mussivand's injury.

We do not, however, mean to say that David, subsequent to his affair with Mussivand's wife, will be liable to any and all persons with whom she may have sexual contact. A spouse, however, is a foreseeable sexual partner. Furthermore, the liability of a person with a sexually transmissible disease to a third person, such as a spouse, would be extinguished as soon as the paramour spouse knew or should have known that he or she was exposed to or had contracted a venereal disease. She or he then would become a "conscious and responsible agency which could or should have eliminated the hazard." *Cascone,* supra. For example, if David told Mussivand's wife he had a venereal disease or if she noticed symptoms of the disease on herself, she then would have the duty to abstain from sexual relations or warn her sexual partner. Whether Mussivand's wife knew, or should have known, of her exposure to a venereal disease is a question of fact to be decided by the trier of fact. . . .

For the foregoing reasons we cannot say that Mussivand could not prove any set of facts entitling him to recover in negligence from David. Accordingly, the trial court erred in granting David's motion to dismiss. . . .

ASSIGNMENT

15.7

a. Why did the court say that Mrs. Mussivand may not have broken the chain of David's causation?

b. Suppose David does tell his paramour (Mrs. Mussivand) that he has VD. She tells him she doesn't care because this is the last time she will have sex with him before returning to her husband. She says, "I will never tell my husband about you or our affair." Mr. Mussivand contracts VD from her. Is David the proximate cause of Mr. Mussivand's VD?

c. Could Mr. Mussivand sue Mrs. Mussivand for negligence?

CASE

Gaines-Tabb v. ICI Explosives, USA, Inc.
160 F.3d 613 (1998)
United States Court of Appeals, Tenth Circuit

Background: *In 1995, a terrorist bomb killed 163 people when it exploded at the Alfred P. Murrah Federal Building in Oklahoma City. Timothy McVeigh and Terry Nichols were later convicted of murder for their role in the bombing. The material allegedly used to construct the bomb was ammonium nitrate (AN) that was manufactured by ICI Explosives and eventually sold as fertilizer by Mid-Kansas Co-op. It was purchased in Kansas from Mid-Kansas Co-op by either McVeigh or Nichols. This suit was brought on behalf of victims of the bombing. They sued ICI for negligence, among other theories. The trial court (district court) dismissed the negligence action. The case is now on appeal before the United States Court of Appeals for the Tenth Circuit.*

Decision on Appeal: *The judgment for ICI is affirmed. Proximate cause has not been established. The terrorist's act was a supervening cause that cut off the manufacturer's liability.*

OPINION OF COURT

Judge EBEL delivered the opinion of the court . . .:

Individuals injured by the April 19, 1995, bombing of the Alfred P. Murrah Federal Building ("Murrah Building") in Oklahoma City, Oklahoma, filed suit against the manufacturers of the ammonium nitrate allegedly used to create the bomb. . . . [The main cause of action asserted in the complaint was negligence.] The district court dismissed the complaint for failure to state a claim upon which relief may be granted, and the plaintiffs appealed. We affirm. Specifically, we hold that: plaintiffs cannot state a claim for negligence . . . because they cannot show, as a matter of law, that defendants' conduct was the proximate cause of their injuries. . . .

ICI manufactures ammonium nitrate ("AN"). Plaintiffs allege that AN can be either "explosive grade" or "fertilizer grade." According to plaintiffs, "explosive-grade" AN is of low density and high porosity so it will absorb sufficient amounts of fuel or diesel oil to allow detonation of the AN, while "fertilizer-grade" AN is of high density and low porosity and so is unable to absorb sufficient amounts of fuel or diesel oil to allow detonation.

Plaintiffs allege that ICI sold explosive-grade AN mislabeled as fertilizer-grade AN to Farmland Industries, who in turn sold it to Mid-Kansas Cooperative Association in McPherson, Kansas. Plaintiffs submit that a "Mike Havens" purchased a total of eighty 50-pound bags of the mislabeled AN from Mid-Kansas. According to plaintiffs, "Mike Havens" was an alias used either by Timothy McVeigh or Terry Nichols, the two men tried for the bombing. Plaintiffs further allege that the perpetrators of the Oklahoma City bombing used the 4000 pounds of explosive-grade AN purchased from Mid-Kansas, mixed with fuel oil or diesel oil, to demolish the Murrah Building. . . .

Plaintiffs allege that ICI was negligent in making explosive-grade AN available to the perpetrators of the Murrah Building bombing. Under Oklahoma law, the three essential elements of a claim of negligence are: "(1) a duty owed by the defendant to protect the plaintiff from injury, (2) a failure to properly perform that duty, and (3) the plaintiff's injury being proximately caused by the defendant's breach." *Lockhart v. Loosen,* 943 P.2d 1074, 1079 (Okla. 1997). . . .

"[W]hether the complained of negligence is the proximate cause of the plaintiff's injury is dependent upon the harm (for which compensation is being sought) being the result of both the natural and probable consequences of the primary negligence." *Lockhart,* 943 P.2d at 1079. . . . Under Oklahoma law, "the causal *nexus* between an act of negligence and the resulting injury will be deemed broken with the intervention of a new, independent and efficient cause which was neither anticipated nor reasonably foreseeable." *Minor v. Zidell Trust,* 618 P.2d 392, 394 (Okla. 1980). Such an intervening cause is known as a "supervening cause." Id. To be considered a supervening cause, an intervening cause must be: (1) independent of the original act; (2) adequate by itself to bring about the injury; and (3) not reasonably foreseeable. See id.; *Henry v. Merck and Co.,* 877 F.2d 1489, 1495 (10th Cir. 1989). "When the intervening act is intentionally tortious or criminal, it is more likely to be considered independent." Id.

"A third person's intentional tort is a supervening cause of the harm that results—even if the actor's negligent conduct created a situation that presented the opportunity for the tort to be committed—unless the actor realizes or should realize the likelihood that the third person might commit the tortious act." *Lockhart,* 943 P.2d at 1080. . . . If "the intervening act is a reasonably foreseeable consequence of the primary negligence, the original wrongdoer will not be relieved of liability." Id. at 1079. . . . "In determining questions relating to the foreseeability element of proximate cause, the courts have uniformly applied what might be termed a practical, common sense test, the test of common experience." *57A Am. Jur. 2d* Negligence § 489 (1989). Oklahoma has looked to the *Restatement (Second) of Torts* § 448 for assistance in determining whether the intentional actions of a third party constitute a supervening cause of harm. See *Lay v. Dworman,* 732 P.2d 455, 458–59 (Okla. 1986). Section 448 states:

> The act of a third person in committing an intentional tort or crime is a superseding cause of harm to another resulting therefrom, although the actor's negligent conduct created a situation which afforded an opportunity to the third person to commit such a tort or crime, unless the actor at the time of his negligent conduct realized or should have realized the likelihood that such a situation might be created, and that a third person might avail himself of the opportunity to commit such a tort or crime.

Comment b to § 448 provides further guidance in the case before us. It states:

> There are certain situations which are commonly recognized as affording temptations to which a recognizable percentage of humanity is likely to yield. So too, there are situations which create temptations to which no considerable percentage of ordinary mankind is likely to yield but which, if they are created at a place where persons of peculiarly vicious type are likely to be, should be recognized as likely to lead to the commission of fairly definite types of crime. If the situation which the actor should realize that his negligent conduct might create is of either of these two sorts, an intentionally criminal or tortious act of the third person is not a superseding cause which relieves the actor from liability.

Thus, under comment b, the criminal acts of a third party may be foreseeable if (1) the situation provides a temptation to which a "recognizable percentage" of persons would yield, or (2) the temptation is created at a place

where "persons of a peculiarly vicious type are likely to be." There is no indication that a peculiarly vicious type of person is likely to frequent the Mid-Kansas Co-op, so we shall turn our attention to the first alternative.

We have found no guidance as to the meaning of the term "recognizable percentage" as used in § 448, comment b. However, we believe that the term does not require a showing that the mainstream population or the majority would yield to a particular temptation; a lesser number will do. Equally, it does not include merely the law-abiding population. In contrast, we also believe that the term is not satisfied by pointing to the existence of a small fringe group or the occasional irrational individual, even though it is foreseeable generally that such groups and individuals will exist.

We note that plaintiffs can point to very few occasions of successful terrorist actions using ammonium nitrate, in fact only two instances in the last twenty-eight years—a 1970 bombing at the University of Wisconsin-Madison and the bombing of the Murrah Building.[1] Due to the apparent complexity of manufacturing an ammonium nitrate bomb, including the difficulty of acquiring the correct ingredients (many of which are not widely available), mixing them properly, and triggering the resulting bomb, only a small number of persons would be able to carry out a crime such as the bombing of the Murrah Building. We simply do not believe that this is a group which rises to the level of a "recognizable percentage" of the population. Cf. *Restatement (Second) of Torts* § 302B, comment d (1965) ("Even where there is a recognizable possibility of the intentional interference, the possibility may be so slight, or there may be so slight a risk of foreseeable harm to another as a result of the interference, that a reasonable man in the position of the actor would disregard it.").

As a result, we hold that as a matter of law it was not foreseeable to defendants that the AN that they distributed to the Mid-Kansas Co-op would be put to such a use as to blow up the Murrah Building. Because the conduct of the bomber or bombers was unforeseeable, independent of the acts of defendants, and adequate by itself to bring about plaintiffs' injuries, the criminal activities of the bomber or bombers acted as the supervening cause of plaintiffs' injuries. Because of the lack of proximate cause, plaintiffs have failed to state a claim for negligence.

We AFFIRM the dismissal of plaintiffs' complaint. . . .

---

[1] In the complaint, Plaintiffs allege in a general way the detonation of AN fertilizer bombs in "Europe and especially Northern Ireland" prior to 1970 and the unsuccessful attempt in the United States to use AN to bomb certain facilities in New York.

ASSIGNMENT 15.8

a. What negligent act was alleged against ICI?

b. Would the result in *Gaines-Tabb* have been different if McVeigh or Nichols told the clerk at the Mid-Kansas Co-op that the AN was going to be used to "make the government pay for its crimes"?

c. The *Mussivand* case held that proximate cause could be established. The *Gaines-Tabb* case held the opposite. Explain the difference. Are the two cases consistent?

SUMMARY

Proximate cause raises a causation issue (who caused what?) and a policy issue (is there a point at which the law should cut off liability for the harm we have caused?). There are two cause-in-fact tests. First, is it more likely than not that but for the defendant's unreasonable acts or omissions, the injury would not have been suffered by the plaintiff? (This test is used when there is only one alleged cause.) Second, is it more likely than not that the defendant's unreasonable acts or omissions were a substantial factor in producing the injury suffered by the plaintiff? (This test is used when there is more than one alleged cause.) The policy test used to determine whether to cut off liability is as follows: Was the injury suffered by the plaintiff the foreseeable consequence of the original risk created by the defendant's unreasonable acts or omissions?

In assessing cause in fact, our common sense relies on time (how soon after the defendant's act or omission did the injury occur?), space (how close was the defendant's act or omission to the area where the injury occurred?), and historical data (in the past, have acts or omissions similar to the defendant's led to this kind of injury?). The standard of proof used by the fact finder to decide the cause-in-fact issue is preponderance of the evidence.

If it is foreseeable that the defendant's unreasonable (or intentional) acts or omissions will result in any impact on the plaintiff's body, the plaintiff will be responsible for the foreseeable and the unforeseeable personal injuries that follow. The manner in which an injury occurs does not have to be foreseeable in order for the defendant to be the proximate cause of the injury as long as the harm that resulted was within the original risk created by the defendant's acts or omissions. Whether an intervening force is a superseding cause depends on whether the intervention was beyond the original risk or was highly extraordinary. Intervening intentional or criminal human forces are often considered superseding, unlike intervening innocent or negligent human forces. An intervening force of nature is not a superseding cause if it creates the same kind of injury or damage that the defendant's carelessness would have caused if nature had not intervened.

KEY TERMS

proximate cause 266
legal cause 266
cause in fact 266
but-for test 266
substantial factor test 266
sine qua non test 267
standard of proof 271
weight of the evidence 271
preponderance of the
  evidence 271

mitigate the consequences 275
avoidable consequences 275
aggravation 275
eggshell skull 275
manner 275
highly extraordinary 276
unforeseeable plaintiff 277
intervening cause 277
judgment proof 277

intervening force of nature 278
intervening innocent human
  force 278
intervening negligent human
  force 278
intervening intentional or
  criminal human force 278
superseding cause 278

Negligence: Element IV: Damages

CHAPTER OUTLINE

- Kinds of Damages
- Present Value
- Pain and Suffering
- Software
- Property Damage
- Doctrine of Avoidable Consequences
- Collateral Source Rule
- Joint Tortfeasors
- Release
- Contribution
- Indemnity

KINDS OF DAMAGES

The plaintiff in a negligence action must suffer actual harm or loss to person or property. It is not enough that the defendant has engaged in unreasonable or even reckless conduct. Without actual harm or loss, the negligence action fails. Although the focus of this chapter is on damages in a negligence action, most of the principles discussed here also apply to intentional and strict liability torts.

Damages are monetary payments awarded for a legally recognized wrong. (The word *damage* also refers to any harm or loss.) Damages are a *legal* remedy, unlike an injunction, for example, which is an *equitable* remedy.[1] There are three main categories of damages: compensatory, nominal, and punitive.

Compensatory Damages

Compensatory damages are monetary payments awarded to make the plaintiff whole, to compensate him or her for the actual loss suffered. An important purpose of tort law is to return the plaintiff to the position he or she was in before the loss. The payment of money, of course, cannot always accomplish this. The payment of compensatory damages is designed to come as close as possible to returning the plaintiff to the status quo before the accident.

Compensatory damages cover two kinds of losses: economic and non-economic. Economic losses are **out-of-pocket** items—those things the plaintiff has already had to pay for or will probably have to pay for in the future. Economic losses can be objectively verified by examining the dollar amounts you would have to pay to replace whatever was lost.

> **EXAMPLES:**
>
> - present and future medical expenses
> - burial costs
> - loss of the use of property
> - costs of repair
> - costs of obtaining substitute domestic services
> - present and future loss of earnings, loss of business or employment opportunities

Non-economic losses, on the other hand, are those losses for which no objective dollar amount can be identified. They are subjective to the plaintiff.

> **EXAMPLES:**
>
> - pain
> - mental anguish
> - inconvenience
> - loss of companionship
> - humiliation
> - injury to reputation

Collectively, these non-economic damages are sometimes referred to as **pain and suffering** damages.

Another important classification of compensatory damages is the distinction between general and special damages. **General damages** are those compensatory dam-

---

[1]Equity was once a court system that was separate from the common law court system. The equity courts administered equitable remedies that were based on a somewhat flexible sense of fairness as opposed to the more rigid legal remedies available in the common law courts. Today the two court systems have merged in most states so that equitable remedies and legal remedies are usually available in the same court.

ages that usually result from the kind of harm caused by the defendant's conduct. General damages naturally follow from the harm caused by such conduct. Pain and suffering, for example, naturally follow from a severe head injury. In most states, the complaint of the plaintiff does not have to allege general damages with specificity. The law will presume that general damages result from the wrong complained of. **Special damages,** on the other hand, are compensatory damages that are peculiar to the plaintiff. They would include medical expenses, loss of earnings, insanity, etc. The law does not presume that they exist. They must be specifically pleaded in the complaint. Special damages are also called **consequential damages.**

> **EXAMPLE:** Sam is seeing a psychiatrist to help him overcome the anxiety he feels over the negligent conduct of the defendant who almost killed Sam with scalding water in a freak accident. The cost of the psychiatrist is part of Sam's special damages. His pain and suffering due to the anxiety are part of his general damages.

Nominal Damages

Nominal damages are a small monetary payment (often $1) awarded when the defendant has committed a tort that has resulted in little or no harm so that no compensatory damages are due. Nominal damages are not awarded in negligence cases since one of the elements of negligence is actual damages. Nominal damages are awarded in intentional tort and strict liability tort cases when there has been a technical commission of the tort but no actual harm. Attorneys usually do not take cases that do not present the possibility of substantial damages since fees are often a percentage of the damages award. When nominal damages are likely, the plaintiff's incentive to bring the case is to vindicate a right, to make a public record of the defendant's misdeed, or to warn the defendant that future misconduct of the same kind will lead to further lawsuits. If the attorney is not taking such a case **pro bono** (for free), he or she is probably being paid an hourly or set fee rather than a percentage.

Punitive Damages

Punitive damages are noncompensatory damages that seek to punish the defendant and to deter similar conduct by others. Punitive damages are awarded when the defendant has acted maliciously, outrageously, recklessly, or in conscious disregard for the safety of others. Mere negligence or unreasonable conduct is not enough. Nor is intentional conduct enough unless the court can conclude that the defendant acted in a morally reprehensible way. Punitive damages are also called **exemplary damages.**

PRESENT VALUE

By the time a trial ends, the court will want to reach one number to cover all past *and future* damages in what is called a **lump sum judgment.** The alternative would be for the court to retain jurisdiction of the case to keep it open for the life of the plaintiff in order to take account of actual medical costs, loss of income, inflation, and other uncertainties of the economy. This would create chaos in the court system since no tort case would ever end. Hence, the court will want to have a lump sum judgment. Normally, this judgment is paid at one time, although some states allow the amount to be paid in periodic payments over a set time. This may be required in certain kinds of tort cases such as medical malpractice.

Parties have more flexibility when negotiating a settlement. A **structured settlement,** for example, would consist of periodic payments for a designated period of time such as the life of the victim. The periodic payments are often paid through an annuity that the defendant funds. The settlement might call for a reduced lump sum payment with the balance covered by future periodic payments through an annuity.

Whenever you are entitled to a payment now to cover something that will happen in the future, the payment must be reduced to **present value**. Suppose, for example, that on January 1, you win a bet that will entitle you to $1,000 by the end of the year, but you are to be paid on January 1. On January 1, you are *not* given $1,000. If you were given this amount on this date, you could immediately invest it so that you would end up with more than $1,000 at the end of the year. Assume that you could invest $1,000 at 6 percent. At this rate, you would have $1,060 at the end of the year (6 percent of $1,000 is $60). To give you $1,000 at the beginning of the year, therefore, would amount to a $60 overpayment or **windfall**, which is an extra amount to which you are not entitled under the original understanding of the parties.

To avoid this windfall, you are given the present value of $1,000 (also called its **present cash value**). Present value is the amount of money an individual would have to be given now to produce or generate, through prudent investment, a certain amount of money in a designated period of time. (An example of a prudent investment might be a risk-free certificate of deposit or U.S. treasury bill.) If you were given $943.39 at the beginning of the year and invested it at 6 percent, you would have $1,000 by the end of the year ($999.99). The present value of $1,000, therefore, is $943.39. This is the amount you would be given on January 1. The calculation is called *reducing $1,000 to present value*, or phrased another way, *discounting $1,000 to present value*. The amount given now depends on what rate of interest we assume would be earned. Our example used a 6 percent rate. If the rate were 8.5 percent, the present value of $1,000 would be $921.57. If you were given this amount and invested it at 8.5 percent, by the end of the year you would have $1,000 ($999.90). A computer can easily calculate present value once we know the period of time to cover and the rate of return to use. We also need to know whether to use simple interest—as in the preceding examples—or compound interest so that interest is earned on interest as the year unfolds. If compound interest is used, you earn more and therefore need less at the outset to reach a given outcome. The percentage by which you reduce the amount you want to reach is called the **discount rate**.

The same process applies in tort litigation in the award of future economic damages such as expected medical expenses and lost wages.

> **EXAMPLE:** Early in 2000, Ted negligently injures Mary. During 2000, Mary pays $15,000 in medical bills. For each year from 2001 to the end of 2004, she is expected to spend $12,500 a year in further medical expenses. Assume that the negligence trial against Ted takes place at the end of 2000, at which time her total past and future economic damages for medical expenses are $65,000.

2000:	$15,000	(past medical expenses)
2001–2004:	50,000	(future medical expenses; $12,500 × 4)
	$65,000	(calculated as of the end of 2000)

She has already incurred a $15,000 loss for 2000. There is no problem in giving her this amount. We do not need to reduce this amount to present value since it is not a future loss. But what about the $50,000 loss she is expected to incur in the future? If we give her $50,000 at the end of 2000, she could immediately invest this money and thereby have considerably more than $50,000 by the end of 2004.

To prevent this overcompensation or windfall, the future economic loss must be reduced to present value or present cash value. We discount the $50,000. What sum of money must be awarded today so that she will end up with $50,000 by the end of 2004? If we gave her $40,322.49 now and she invested it at 6 percent (simple interest), she would have $50,000 in four years ($49,999.88). In this example, therefore, the present value of $50,000 is $40,322.49, assuming a discount rate of 6 percent. The present value number would be lower if we used compound interest. Again, computer programs are available to make these calculations quickly. (For an example, see Figure 16–2 later in the chapter.)

Figure 16–1 contains an example of a jury instruction on damages. Notice that the trial judge tells the jury that it must use present value for all future economic losses. Anything lost up to the date of the trial, however, is not reduced to present value. Also note that the instructions do not tell the jury to reduce non-economic losses such as pain and suffering to present value.

FIGURE 16–1   Jury instructions on damages.

Adapted from David W. Robertson et al. *Torts* 349–350 (2d ed. 1998) and 2 *California Jury Instructions-Civil* §§ 14.00–14.13 (7th ed. 1986) (Book of Approved Jury Instructions (BAJI) of the Committee on Standard Jury Instructions, Civil, of the Superior Court of Los Angeles County, California); and Robert E. Keeton et al. *Tort and Accident Law* 449–450 (3d ed. 1998) and *Illinois Pattern Jury Instructions, Civil* §§ 30.01–30.07, 34.01, 34.02 (2d ed. 1971).

If you find that the plaintiff is entitled to a verdict against the defendant, you must then award the plaintiff damages in an amount that will provide reasonable and fair compensation for each of the following elements of loss proved by the evidence to have resulted from the negligence of the defendant:

(1) The reasonable value of medical, hospital, and nursing care, services, and supplies reasonably required and actually given in the treatment of the plaintiff to the present time, and the present cash value of the reasonable value of similar items reasonably certain to be required and given in the future.

(2) The reasonable value of working time lost to date. In determining this amount, you should consider evidence of plaintiff's earnings and earning capacity, how he or she ordinarily occupied him- or herself, and find what was reasonably certain to have been earned in the time lost if there had been no injury. One's ability to work may have a monetary value even though that person is not employed by another. In determining this amount, you should also consider evidence of the reasonable value of services performed by another in doing things for the plaintiff which, except for the injury, plaintiff would ordinarily have performed for him- or herself.

(3) The present cash value of earning capacity reasonably certain to be lost in the future as a result of the injury in question.

(4) In computing the damages arising from the future because of expenses and loss of earnings, you must not simply multiply the damages by the length of time you have found they will continue or by the number of years you have found that the plaintiff is likely to live. Instead, you must determine their present cash value. "Present cash value" means the sum of money needed now, which, when added to what that sum may reasonably be expected to earn in the future through prudent investment, will equal the amount of the expenses and earnings at the time in the future when the expenses must be paid and the earnings would have been received.

(5) Reasonable compensation for any pain, discomfort, fears, anxiety and other mental and emotional distress suffered by the plaintiff and of which the injury was a cause and for similar suffering reasonably certain to be experienced in the future from the same cause. No definite standard or method of calculation is prescribed by law by which to fix reasonable compensation for pain and suffering. Nor is the opinion of any witness required as to the amount of such reasonable compensation. Furthermore, the argument of counsel as to the amount of damages is not evidence of reasonable compensation. In making an award for pain and suffering, you shall exercise your authority with calm and reasonable judgment and the damages you fix shall be just and reasonable in the light of the evidence.

Let us look at lost future wages more closely through the case of *O'Shea v. Riverway Towing Co.* The case provides an excellent overview of other economic factors that go into a determination of damages in a personal injury case. As you will see in the case, the downward adjustment that results from the determination of present value is not the only adjustment made in an award of damages. Make careful note of all of the factors the court uses to reach the final award. In particular, note how the following factors affected the final award of damages for lost wages:

- federal taxes the plaintiff would have paid on the lost future wages
- projected annual wage increases the plaintiff would have received
- life expectancy of the plaintiff and the projected period during which the plaintiff would have continued to work
- discount rate
- inflation

CASE

O'Shea v. Riverway Towing Co.
677 F.2d 1194 (7th Cir. 1982)
United States Court of Appeals for the Seventh Circuit

Background: *Margaret O'Shea was a cook on a Mississippi towboat. After falling and breaking her leg getting off the boat, she sued her employer, Riverway, for negligently causing the fall. She won in the district court (the federal trial court), which awarded her over $86,033 in damages for lost future wages. The case is now on appeal before the United States Court of Appeals for the Seventh Circuit.*

Decision on Appeal: *The award of damages was proper.*

OPINION OF COURT

Judge POSNER delivered the opinion of the court. . . .

When the harbor boat reached shore it tied up to a seawall the top of which was several feet above the boat's deck. There was no ladder. The other passengers, who were seamen, clambered up the seawall without difficulty, but Mrs. O'Shea, a 57-year-old woman who weighs 200 pounds (she is five foot seven), balked. According to Mrs. O'Shea's testimony, which the district court believed, a deckhand instructed her to climb the stairs to a catwalk above the deck and disembark from there. But the catwalk was three feet above the top of the seawall, and again there was no ladder. The deckhand told her that she should jump and that the men who had already disembarked would help her land safely. She did as told, but fell in landing, carrying the assisting seamen down with her, and broke her leg. . . .

Mrs. O'Shea's job as a cook paid her $40 a day, and since the custom was to work 30 days consecutively and then have the next 30 days off, this comes to $7200 a year although, as we shall see, she never had earned that much in a single year. She testified that when the accident occurred she had been about to get another cook's job on a Mississippi towboat that would have paid her $60 a day ($10,800 a year). She also testified that she had been intending to work as a boat's cook until she was 70—longer if she was able. An economist who testified on Mrs. O'Shea's behalf used the foregoing testimony as the basis for estimating the wages that she lost because of the accident. He first subtracted federal income tax from yearly wage estimates based on alternative assumptions about her wage rate (that it would be either $40 or $60 a day); assumed that this wage would have grown by between six and eight percent a year; assumed that she would have worked either to age 65 or to age 70; and then discounted the resulting lost-wage estimates to present value, using a discount rate of 8.5 percent a year. These calculations, being based on alternative assumptions concerning starting wage rate, annual wage increases, and length of employment, yielded a range of values rather than a single value. The bottom of the range was $50,000. This is the present value, computed at an 8.5 percent discount rate, of Mrs. O'Shea's lost future wages on the assumption that her starting wage was $40 a day and that it would have grown

by six percent a year until she retired at the age of 65. The top of the range was $114,000, which is the present value (again discounted at 8.5 percent) of her lost future wages assuming she would have worked till she was 70 at a wage that would have started at $60 a day and increased by eight percent a year. The judge awarded a figure—$86,033—near the midpoint of this range. He did not explain in his written opinion how he had arrived at this figure, but in a preceding oral opinion he stated that he was "not certain that she would work until age 70 at this type of work," although "she certainly was entitled to" do so and "could have earned something"; and that he had not "felt bound by [the economist's] figure of eight percent increase in wages" and had "not found the wages based on necessarily a 60 dollar a day job." If this can be taken to mean that he thought Mrs. O'Shea would probably have worked till she was 70, starting at $40 a day but moving up from there at six rather than eight percent a year, the economist's estimate of the present value of her lost future wages would be $75,000.

There is no doubt that the accident disabled Mrs. O'Shea from working as a cook on a boat. The break in her leg was very serious: it reduced the stability of the leg and caused her to fall frequently. It is impossible to see how she could have continued working as a cook, a job performed mostly while standing up, and especially on a boat, with its unsteady motion. But Riverway argues that Mrs. O'Shea (who has not worked at all since the accident, which occurred two years before the trial) could have gotten some sort of job and that the wages in that job should be deducted from the admittedly higher wages that she could have earned as a cook on a boat.

The question is not whether Mrs. O'Shea is totally disabled in the sense, relevant to social security disability cases but not tort cases, that there is no job in the American economy for which she is medically fit. It is whether she can by reasonable diligence find gainful employment, given the physical condition in which the accident left her. Here is a middle-aged woman, very overweight, badly scarred on one arm and one leg, unsteady on her feet, in constant and serious pain from the accident, with no education beyond high school and no work skills other than cooking, a job that happens to require standing for long periods which she is incapable of doing. It seems unlikely that someone in this condition could find gainful work at the minimum wage. True, the probability is not zero; and a better procedure, therefore, might have been to subtract from Mrs. O'Shea's lost future wages as a boat's cook the wages in some other job, discounted (i.e., multiplied) by the probability—very low—that she would in fact be able to get another job. But the district judge cannot be criticized for having failed to use a procedure not suggested by either party. The question put to him was the dichotomous one, would she or would she not get another job if she made reasonable efforts to do so? This required him to decide whether there was a more than 50 percent probability that she would. We cannot say that the negative answer he gave to that question was clearly erroneous.

Riverway argues next that it was wrong for the judge to award damages on the basis of a wage not validated, as it were, by at least a year's employment at that wage. Mrs. O'Shea had never worked full time, had never in fact earned more than $3600 in a full year, and in the year preceding the accident had earned only $900. But previous wages do not put a cap on an award of lost future wages. If a man who had never worked in his life graduated from law school, began working at a law firm at an annual salary of $35,000, and was killed the second day on the job, his lack of a past wage history would be irrelevant to computing his lost future wages. The present case is similar if less dramatic. Mrs. O'Shea did not work at all until 1974, when her husband died. She then lived on her inheritance and worked at a variety of part-time jobs till January 1979, when she started working as a cook on the towboat. According to her testimony, which the trial judge believed, she was then working full time. It is immaterial that this was her first full-time job and that the accident occurred before she had held it for a full year. Her job history was typical of women who return to the labor force after their children are grown or, as in Mrs. O'Shea's case, after their husband dies, and these women are, like any tort victims, entitled to damages based on what they would have earned in the future rather than on what they may or may not have earned in the past.

If we are correct so far, Mrs. O'Shea was entitled to have her lost wages determined on the assumption that she would have earned at least $7200 in the first year after the accident and that the accident caused her to lose that entire amount by disabling her from any gainful employment. And since Riverway neither challenges the district judge's (apparent) finding that Mrs. O'Shea would have worked till she was 70 nor contends that the lost wages for each year until then should be discounted by the probability that she would in fact have been alive and working as a boat's cook throughout the damage period, we may also assume that her wages would have been at least $7200 a year for the 12 years between the date of the accident and her seventieth birthday. But Riverway does argue that we cannot assume she might have earned $10,800 a year rather than $7200, despite her testimony that at the time of the accident she was about to take another job as a boat's cook where she would have been paid at the rate of $60 rather than $40 a day. The point is not terribly important since the trial judge gave little weight to this testimony, but we shall discuss it briefly. Mrs. O'Shea was asked on direct examination what "pay you would have worked" for in the new job. Riverway's counsel objected on the ground of hearsay, the judge overruled his objection, and she answered $60 a day. The objection was not well taken. Riverway argues that only her prospective employer knew what her wage was, and hence when she said it was $60 she was testifying to what he had told her. But an employee's wage is as much in the personal knowledge of the employee as of the employer. If Mrs. O'Shea's prospective employer had testified that he would have paid her $60,

Riverway's counsel could have made the converse hearsay objection that the employer was really testifying to what Mrs. O'Shea had told him she was willing to work for. Riverway's counsel could on cross-examination have probed the basis for Mrs. O'Shea's belief that she was going to get $60 a day in a new job, but he did not do so and cannot complain now that the judge may have given her testimony some (though little) weight.

We come at last to the most important issue in the case, which is the proper treatment of inflation in calculating lost future wages. Mrs. O'Shea's economist based the six to eight percent range which he used to estimate future increases in the wages of a boat's cook on the general pattern of wage increases in service occupations over the past 25 years. During the second half of this period the rate of inflation has been substantial and has accounted for much of the increase in nominal wages in this period; and to use that increase to project future wage increases is therefore to assume that inflation will continue, and continue to push up wages. Riverway argues that it is improper as a matter of law to take inflation into account in projecting lost future wages. Yet Riverway itself wants to take inflation into account—one-sidedly, to reduce the amount of the damages computed. For Riverway does not object to the economist's choice of an 8.5 percent discount rate for reducing Mrs. O'Shea's lost future wages to present value, although the rate includes an allowance—a very large allowance—for inflation.

To explain, the object of discounting lost future wages to present value is to give the plaintiff an amount of money which, invested safely, will grow to a sum equal to those wages. So if we thought that but for the accident Mrs. O'Shea would have earned $7200 in 1990, and we were computing in 1980 (when this case was tried) her damages based on those lost earnings, we would need to determine the sum of money that, invested safely for a period of 10 years, would grow to $7200. Suppose that in 1980 the rate of interest on ultra-safe (i.e., federal government) bonds or notes maturing in 10 years was 12 percent. Then we would consult a table of present values to see what sum of money invested at 12 percent for 10 years would at the end of that time have grown to $7200. The answer is $2318. But a moment's reflection will show that to give Mrs. O'Shea $2318 to compensate her for lost wages in 1990 would grossly undercompensate her. People demand 12 percent to lend money risklessly for 10 years because they expect their principal to have much less purchasing power when they get it back at the end of the time. In other words, when long-term interest rates are high, they are high in order to compensate lenders for the fact that they will be repaid in cheaper dollars. In periods when no inflation is anticipated, the risk-free interest rate is between one and three percent. See references in *Doca v. Marina Mercante Nicaraguense, S.A.*, 634 F.2d 30, 39 n.2 (2d Cir. 1980). Additional percentage points above that level reflect inflation anticipated over the life of the loan. But if there is inflation it will affect wages as well as prices. Therefore to give Mrs. O'Shea $2318 today because that is the present value of $7200 10 years hence, computed at a discount rate—12 percent—that consists mainly of an allowance for anticipated inflation, is in fact to give her less than she would have been earning then if she was earning $7200 on the date of the accident, even if the only wage increases she would have received would have been those necessary to keep pace with inflation.

There are (at least) two ways to deal with inflation in computing the present value of lost future wages. One is to take it out of both the wages and the discount rate—to say to Mrs. O'Shea, "we are going to calculate your probable wage in 1990 on the assumption, unrealistic as it is, that there will be zero inflation between now and then; and, to be consistent, we are going to discount the amount thus calculated by the interest rate that would be charged under the same assumption of zero inflation." Thus, if we thought Mrs. O'Shea's real (i.e., inflation-free) wage rate would not rise in the future, we would fix her lost earnings in 1990 as $7200 and, to be consistent, we would discount that to present (1980) value using an estimate of the real interest rate. At two percent, this procedure would yield a present value of $5906. Of course, she would not invest this money at a mere two percent. She would invest it at the much higher prevailing interest rate. But that would not give her a windfall; it would just enable her to replace her lost 1990 earnings with an amount equal to what she would in fact have earned in that year if inflation continues, as most people expect it to do. (If people did not expect continued inflation, long-term interest rates would be much lower; those rates impound investors' inflationary expectations.)

An alternative approach, which yields the same result, is to use a (higher) discount rate based on the current risk-free 10-year interest rate, but apply that rate to an estimate of lost future wages that includes expected inflation. Contrary to Riverway's argument, this projection would not require gazing into a crystal ball. The expected rate of inflation can, as just suggested, be read off from the current long-term interest rate. If that rate is 12 percent, and if as suggested earlier the real or inflation-free interest rate is only one to three percent, this implies that the market is anticipating 9–11 percent inflation over the next 10 years, for a long-term interest rate is simply the sum of the real interest rate and the anticipated rate of inflation during the term.

Either approach to dealing with inflation is acceptable (they are, in fact, equivalent) and we by no means rule out others; but it is illogical and indefensible to build inflation into the discount rate yet ignore it in calculating the lost future wages that are to be discounted. That results in systematic undercompensation, just as building inflation into the estimate of future lost earnings and then discounting using the real rate of interest would systematically overcompensate. The former error is committed, we respectfully suggest, by those circuits, notably the Fifth, that refuse to allow inflation to be used in projecting lost future earnings but then use a discount rate that has built into it a large allowance for inflation. See, e.g., *Culver v. Slater Boat Co.,* 644 F.2d 460, 464 (5th Cir. 1981) (using a 9.125 percent discount rate). We align ourselves instead with those circuits (a majority, see *Doca v. Marina Mercante Nicaraguense, S.A.,* supra, 634 F.2d at 35-36), notably the Second, that require that inflation be treated consistently in choosing a discount rate and in estimating the future lost wages to be discounted to present value using that rate. . . .

Applying our analysis to the present case, we cannot pronounce the approach taken by the plaintiff's economist unreasonable. He chose a discount rate—8.5 percent—well above the real rate of interest, and therefore containing an allowance for inflation. Consistency required him to inflate Mrs. O'Shea's starting wage as a boat's cook in calculating her lost future wages, and he did so at a rate of six to eight percent a year. If this rate had been intended as a forecast of purely inflationary wage changes, his approach would be open to question, especially at the upper end of his range. For if the estimated rate of inflation were eight percent, the use of a discount rate of 8.5 percent would imply that the real rate of interest was only .5 percent, which is lower than most economists believe it to be for any substantial period of time. But wages do not rise just because of inflation. Mrs. O'Shea could expect her real wages as a boat's cook to rise as she became more experienced and as average real wage rates throughout the economy rose, as they usually do over a decade or more. It would not be outlandish to assume that even if there were no inflation, Mrs. O'Shea's wages would have risen by three percent a year. If we subtract that from the economist's six to eight percent range, the inflation allowance built into his estimated future wage increases is only three to five percent; and when we subtract these figures from 8.5 percent we see that his implicit estimate of the real rate of interest was very high (3.5–5.5 percent). This means he was conservative, because the higher the discount rate used the lower the damages calculated.

If conservative in one sense, the economist was most liberal in another. He made no allowance for the fact that Mrs. O'Shea, whose health history quite apart from the accident is not outstanding, might very well not have survived—let alone survived and been working as a boat's cook or in an equivalent job—until the age of 70. The damage award is a sum certain, but the lost future wages to which that award is equated by means of the discount rate are mere probabilities. If the probability of her being employed as a boat's cook full time in 1990 was only 75 percent, for example, then her estimated wages in that year should have been multiplied by .75 to determine the value of the expectation that she lost as a result of the accident; and so with each of the other future years. The economist did not do this, and by failing to do this he overstated the loss due to the accident.

But Riverway does not make an issue of this aspect of the economist's analysis. Nor of another: the economist selected the 8.5 percent figure for the discount rate because that was the current interest rate on Triple A 10-year state and municipal bonds, but it would not make sense in Mrs. O'Shea's federal income tax bracket to invest in tax-free bonds. If he wanted to use nominal rather than real interest rates and wage increases (as we said was proper), the economist should have used a higher discount rate and a higher expected rate of inflation. But as these adjustments would have been largely or entirely offsetting, the failure to make them was not a critical error.

Although we are not entirely satisfied with the economic analysis on which the judge, in the absence of any other evidence of the present value of Mrs. O'Shea's lost future wages, must have relied heavily, we recognize that the exactness which economic analysis rigorously pursued appears to offer is, at least in the litigation setting, somewhat delusive. Therefore, we will not reverse an award of damages for lost wages because of questionable assumptions unless it yields an unreasonable result—especially when, as in the present case, the defendant does not offer any economic evidence himself and does not object to the questionable steps in the plaintiff's economic analysis. We cannot say the result here was unreasonable. If the economist's method of estimating damages was too generous to Mrs. O'Shea in one important respect it was, as we have seen, niggardly in another. Another error against Mrs. O'Shea should be noted: the economist should not have deducted her entire income tax liability in estimating her future lost wages. While it is true that the damage award is not taxable, the interest she earns on it will be (a point the economist may have ignored because of his erroneous assumption that she would invest the award in tax-exempt bonds), so that his method involved an element of double taxation.

If we assume that Mrs. O'Shea could have expected a three percent annual increase in her real wages from a base of $7200, that the real risk-free rate of interest (and therefore the appropriate discount rate if we are considering only real wage increases) is two percent, and that she would have worked till she was 70, the present value of her lost future wages would be $91,310. This figure ignores the fact that she did not have a 100 percent probability of actually working till age 70 as a boat's cook, and fails to make the appropriate (though probably, in her bracket, very small) net income tax adjustment; but it also ignores the possibility, small but not totally negligible, that the proper base is really $10,800 rather than $7200.

So we cannot say that the figure arrived at by the judge, $86,033, was unreasonably high. But we are distressed that he made no attempt to explain how he had arrived at that figure, since it was not one contained in the economist's testimony though it must in some way have been derived from that testimony. Unlike many other damage items in a personal injury case, notably pain and suffering, the calculation of damages for lost earnings can and should be an analytical rather than an intuitive undertaking. Therefore, compliance with Rule 52(a) of the Federal Rules of Civil Procedure requires that in a bench trial the district judge set out the steps by which he arrived at his award for lost future earnings, in order to assist the appellate court in reviewing the award. The district judge failed to do that here. We do not consider this reversible error, because our own analysis convinces us that the award of damages for lost future wages was reasonable. But for the future we ask the district judges in this circuit to indicate the steps by which they arrive at damage awards for lost future earnings.

Judgment Affirmed.

ASSIGNMENT 16.1

a. What is meant by present value? What role does it play in an award of damages?

b. What tactical mistakes did the attorney representing the employer make in the trial of this case?

PAIN AND SUFFERING

Pain is often experienced when a tort is committed, at the time of medical treatment, and while recovering. During these periods, mental suffering or distress can also occur. For example:

- fright
- humiliation
- fear and anxiety
- loss of companionship
- unhappiness
- depression or other forms of mental illness

The amount recovered for pain and suffering will depend on the amount of time it was experienced and the intensity of the experience. Also considered are the age and condition of life of the plaintiff. It is, of course, very difficult to assign a dollar amount that will compensate the plaintiff for pain and suffering. The main guide available is the amount a reasonable person would estimate as fair. (See paragraph 5 in Figure 16–1.) A minority of states permit counsel to make a **per diem argument** to the jury whereby a certain amount is requested for every day the pain and suffering has been endured and is expected to continue. (The per diem argument is also called the **unit-of-time argument**.) Other states, however, do not allow such arguments on the ground that they are too arbitrary.

Damages for pain and suffering are controversial. The largest portion of an award of damages is usually the amount given for pain and suffering. Juries have been known to give amounts for pain and suffering that are fifty times the compensatory damages. It is sometimes said that pain and suffering "pays the attorney fees." Most attorneys in personal injury cases are paid a percentage of what the plaintiff receives. When the attorney walks away with a large fee, it is usually due to the pain and suffering portion of the final judgment or of the settlement if the case does not go to trial. Some states have passed reform proposals designed to set limits on damages for pain and suffering in certain categories of cases. For example, a state might pass a statute that limits (i.e., **caps**) damages for pain and suffering in medical malpractice cases at $250,000. As you might expect, trial attorneys are often vigorous opponents of such statutes.

Hedonic damages are compensatory damages that cover the victim's loss of pleasure or enjoyment for life's activities such as raising children, experiencing the morning sun, reading a good book, singing in a choir, and attending college. Some courts, however, say that an award of hedonic damages is improper because they are already provided for in the award of pain and suffering. If, however, the victim dies immediately, there may have been no pain and suffering. The concept of hedonic damages is relatively new; it is unclear how many states will allow juries to consider it.

| ASSIGNMENT 16.2 | Due to medical negligence during an operation, a patient becomes permanently comatose, although she did respond to certain stimuli such as light. What damages are possible? (See General Instructions for the Legal Analysis Assignment in Chapter 2.) |

Before a case goes to trial, a plaintiff will usually try to settle with the insurance company of the defendant, if any. How does a claims adjuster calculate damages? Although insurance companies do not all operate in the same way, there is a rough formula that many companies use as a starting point:

A claims adjuster begins with the medical expenses. Then the intangibles—pain and other non-economic losses—are multiplied by 1.5 to 2 times if the injuries are relatively minor, and up to 5 times if the injuries are particularly painful, serious, or long-lasting. Finally, lost income is added to that amount. Several factors raise the damages formula toward the 5-times end:

- more painful, serious, or long-lasting injuries
- more invasive or long-lasting injuries
- clearer medical evidence of extent of injuries
- more obvious evidence of the other person's fault[2]

The settlement precis and settlement brochure discussed in Chapter 29 are very important in the negotiation process. These documents, prepared by the plaintiff's attorney, can have a major impact on what an insurance company is willing to settle for.

SOFTWARE

Often a law office will use computer programs to help it calculate the damages that it will request. For example, Advocate Software, Inc. has software used in personal injury cases. It can be used to:

---

[2]Joseph Matthews, *Taking the Mystery Out of Personal Injury Claims*, Nolo News 9 (Fall 1994).

- convert future losses to present value
- calculate life expectancy
- calculate work life expectancy
- estimate average earnings for specific categories of work
- calculate household service values
- estimate fringe benefits a worker would have received
- prepare reports to be sent to insurers for settlement negotiations

See Figure 16–2, which provides damages projections for Robert Exemplar. When planning a case, the law office needs to calculate damages based on certain assumptions such as the discount rate and the rate of inflation. Software allows the office to change assumptions quickly and easily in order to assess alternatives.

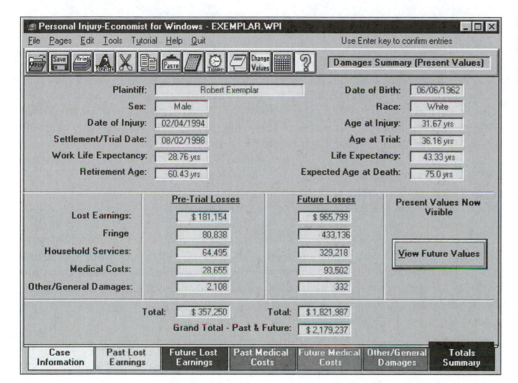

FIGURE 16–2
Software to help calculate damages.

Source: Advocate Software, Inc., Personal Injury-Economist.

PROPERTY DAMAGE

The defendant can inflict loss to property through the commission of a number of torts, such as negligence, trespass to chattels, and conversion. The measure of damages depends on the extent of the loss caused by the tort.

Property destroyed: The measure of damages is the fair market value of the property at the time of the destruction.

Property damaged but not destroyed: The measure of damages is the difference between the fair market value of the property before the damage was done and its fair market value after the damage was done.

Deprivation of the use of the property: The measure of damages is the fair market value of the use of the property during the time the plaintiff was wrongfully deprived of its use.

Fair market value is what the property could probably have been sold for in the ordinary course of a voluntary sale by a willing seller to a willing buyer.[3] The fair market value of the use of the property might be the cost that an unpressured lessee would have to pay to rent the property from a willing lessor.

There are times when the fair market value of property is not a proper measure of damages. For example, a family portrait may have no exchange value or a dog may be trained to answer only one master. In such cases, other measures of damage might be used, e.g., replacement value, original cost, value of the time spent producing it.[4]

In addition, the plaintiff can recover for any mental distress that accompanied the destruction, damage, or deprivation of the property.

DOCTRINE OF AVOIDABLE CONSEQUENCES

Once plaintiffs have been injured, they must take reasonable steps to **mitigate the consequences** of their original injury. A defendant will not be liable for any further injury that the plaintiff could have reasonably avoided. This doctrine of **avoidable consequences** is different from contributory negligence. The latter is unreasonable conduct by the plaintiff that bars all recovery. It occurs before or simultaneously with the wrong committed by the defendant. The doctrine of avoidable consequences refers to unreasonable conduct by the plaintiff *after* the defendant has wronged the plaintiff. All recovery is not barred. The amount of the recovery is reduced to cover those damages the plaintiff brought on him- or herself by failing to use reasonable care.

The most obvious example is the plaintiff who fails to obtain medical help after being injured by the defendant. The plaintiff has thereby aggravated his or her own injury. The defendant will be liable for the initial injury, but not for the **aggravation** of that injury if the failure to seek medical assistance was unreasonable under the circumstances (e.g., such assistance was available, the plaintiff knew about it, and it had a good chance of helping the plaintiff).

The same principles apply to property loss. Suppose that the defendant negligently sets fire to a small portion of the plaintiff's barn. The plaintiff cannot sit by and watch the entire farm burn up if some reasonable steps by the plaintiff could have mitigated the loss (e.g., throwing an available bucket of water on the fire or calling the fire department).

ASSIGNMENT

16.3

Mary negligently hits a pedestrian. The pedestrian is rushed to the hospital and told that a blood transfusion is necessary. The pedestrian refuses on religious grounds. The pedestrian dies. For what damages will Mary be responsible in the negligence action brought by the pedestrian's estate? (See General Instructions for the Legal Analysis Assignment in Chapter 2.)

---

[3]McCormick, *Handbook on the Law of Damages* 165 (1975).
[4]*Restatement (Second) of Torts* § 911, comment e (1979).

CASE

Keans v. Bottiarelli
35 Conn. App. 239, 645 A.2d 1029 (1994)
Appellate Court of Connecticut

Background: *In this action for dental malpractice, the plaintiff sued her oral surgeon for injuries resulting from a tooth extraction. The trial court found for the plaintiff, awarding her $20,000. Of this amount, $14,965.54 was for pain and suffering, and $5,034.46 was for the hospitalization the plaintiff needed because of the defendant's negligence. The trial court reduced the award by $5,034.46 after finding that the plaintiff was the cause of this hospitalization due to her failure to mitigate her damages. Both parties appealed the award of damages. The case is now before the Appellate Court of Connecticut.*

Decision on Appeal: *The judgment affirmed. There was a failure to mitigate. The award for pain and suffering was fair.*

OPINION OF COURT

Judge SCHALLER delivered the opinion of the court . . .:

The trial court could reasonably have found the following facts. On July 19, 1990, the plaintiff consulted the defendant, an oral surgeon, to have a tooth extracted. On the initial visit to the defendant, the plaintiff informed the defendant that she suffered from myelofibrosis, a rare blood disorder that inhibits production of red blood cells and platelets, thereby affecting the blood clotting ability of afflicted individuals. The plaintiff's condition requires her to receive frequent blood and platelet transfusions and to self-administer interferon injections. The plaintiff further informed the defendant that her platelet count was 39,000. The defendant performed the extraction without first consulting the plaintiff's hematologist, concluding that the plaintiff "looked good" and would not require a platelet transfusion. The plaintiff remained in the defendant's recovery room until the area around the extraction site stopped bleeding and was sent home with a prescription for penicillin and a pamphlet detailing postoperative instructions. After returning home, the extraction site began to bleed. The plaintiff's son called the defendant, who advised him that the plaintiff should bite down on a tea bag to release tannic acid to facilitate blood clotting. The plaintiff made no further effort to contact the defendant that day, despite worsening of her condition.

The next morning, the plaintiff contacted Richard Hellman, her hematologist, who admitted her to the hospital. The plaintiff, diagnosed with neutropenia, severe thrombocytopenia, severe anemia and myelofibrosis, was hospitalized for three days and was discharged on July 23, 1990, with no permanent injuries. . . .

The plaintiff's expert testified that the conduct of the defendant deviated from prudent and standard dental practice. He testified that because the plaintiff reported a low platelet count, the defendant should have consulted her hematologist prior to attempting the extraction. One of the defendant's experts reported that on the one occasion that he himself performed an extraction on a myelofibrotic patient he consulted with a hematologist. The trial court determined that the plaintiff's expert was more credible than that of the defendant, and that a causal connection existed between the deviation from prudent and standard dental practice and the plaintiff's initial injury. We conclude that the trial court's finding that the plaintiff had established the elements necessary to prove dental malpractice by the defendant was not clearly erroneous.

The trial court applied the doctrine of mitigation of damages and reduced the award by the amount of the plaintiff's hospitalization expense. Our Supreme Court has stated that "[w]e have long adhered to the rule that one who is injured by the negligence of another must use reasonable care to promote recovery and prevent any aggravation or increase of the injuries." (Internal quotation marks omitted.) *Preston v. Keith,* 217 Conn. 12, 15, 584 A.2d 439 (1991). "When there are facts in evidence that indicate that a plaintiff may have failed to promote his recovery and do what a reasonably prudent person would be expected to do under the same circumstances, the court, when requested to do so, is obliged to charge on the duty to mitigate damages." *Jancura v. Szwed,* 176 Conn. 285, 288, 407 A.2d 961 (1978). "[A]lthough the plaintiff need not specially plead [a duty to mitigate damages], the defendant 'must bring forward evidence that the plaintiff could reasonably have reduced his loss or avoided injurious consequences. . . .' " *Preston v. Keith,* supra, 217 Conn. at 22, 584 A.2d 439. To prevail, the wrongdoer " 'must show that the injured party failed to take reasonable action to lessen the damages; that the damages were in fact enhanced by such failure; and that the damages could have been avoided and can be measured with reasonable certainty.' " Id., quoting 2 M. Minzer, *Damages in Tort Actions* (1989) § 16.11, p. 16–18.

The trial court concluded that the three requirements to establish a failure to mitigate damages set forth in *Preston v. Keith,* supra, 217 Conn. at 22, 584 A.2d 439 were proven. The trial court found that the plaintiff's conduct exacerbated her initial injury. The trial court found that the plaintiff failed to take reasonable action to lessen the damages by neglecting to fill the prescription for penicillin and by not following the defendant's postoperative instructions. The trial court further found that this failure on the part of the plaintiff caused the need for her hospitalization. We conclude that the trial court's reduction of the damage award for this reason was not clearly erroneous. . . .

The defendant . . . contends that the plaintiff's damage award of $14,965.54 for her pain and suffering was excessive. At the outset, we note the "question of damages in personal injury cases . . . is always a difficult one." *Prosser v. Richman,* 133 Conn. 253, 256, 50 A.2d 85 (1946). The "amount of an award is a matter peculiarly within the province of the trier of facts." *Pisel v. Stamford Hospital,* 180 Conn. 314, 342, 430 A.2d 1 (1980); *Angelica v. Fernandes,* 174 Conn. 534, 535, 391 A.2d 167 (1978). Because we find that the amount of the damage award was properly within the bounds of fair and reasonable compensation and is far from "shock[ing to our] sense of justice"; *Herb v. Kerr,* 190 Conn. 136, 139, 459 A.2d 521 (1983); we find the lower court did not abuse its discretion in assessing the damages. . . .

The judgment is affirmed.

ASSIGNMENT

16.4

a. The dentist was negligent but the only damages he was held liable for were pain and suffering. Why?

b. In the next chapter, you will learn that, in some states, if the plaintiff was also negligent in contributing to his or her own injury, the plaintiff recovers nothing no matter how negligent the defendant was. If this rule applied in Connecticut where this case was decided, would the plaintiff have recovered anything?

COLLATERAL SOURCE RULE

When a person is injured or dies, he or she often receives funds or services from a variety of sources other than the defendant:

- the plaintiff's own medical or life insurance
- company insurance
- veteran's benefits
- Social Security
- wage continuation plans
- free medical care provided by a relative

These are all **collateral sources**—sources to which the defendant did not contribute. When the time comes to calculate the total amount in damages owed by the defendant to the plaintiff, should this amount be reduced by what the plaintiff has received through collateral sources? All states do not answer this question in the same way. Here are some of the approaches taken by different states:

- The damages are not reduced by collateral sources in any case even though the plaintiff, in effect, recovers twice for part or all of his or her injury. Furthermore, the defendant is not allowed to tell the jury about the collateral sources. The defendant is not given the benefit of the plaintiff's good luck or resourcefulness in obtaining benefits from collateral sources.
- The damages are not reduced by collateral sources in any case, but the defendant is allowed to tell the jury about the collateral sources in the hope that it might reduce the verdict because of them. (A reduction that is allowed but not required is called a **permissive offset**.)
- The damages are reduced by collateral sources, but only in certain kinds of cases such as medical malpractice. (A required reduction is called a **mandatory offset**.)
- The damages are reduced by collateral sources in all cases.
- The damages are reduced by some collateral sources. For example, the state may allow reduction of social security benefits, but not for life insurance proceeds or other death benefits.

JOINT TORTFEASORS

Joint tortfeasors fall into two categories:

- persons acting in concert to produce a wrong
- persons not acting in concert whose wrongs produce a single indivisible result[5]

---

[5]Some authorities feel that it is a mistake to include such persons in the category of joint tortfeasors. Joint tortfeasors, according to this view, should be limited to defendants who act in concert and should not extend to independent defendants who concurrently produce the wrong.

The significance of being a joint tortfeasor is that each joint tortfeasor is **jointly and severally liable** for the entire harm suffered by the plaintiff. This means that the plaintiff can sue any individual joint tortfeasor for the entire harm or can join them all to recover for the entire harm. It does not mean that the plaintiff receives a multiple recovery. The plaintiff can receive only one satisfaction. Yet the plaintiff chooses whether to go after all of them or one of them. If the plaintiff sues one, but is unable to collect the full judgment, the plaintiff can sue the remaining tortfeasors until the full amount of the damages is recovered. Suppose only one joint tortfeasor pays the entire judgment. Can this person then collect anything from the other joint tortfeasors as their "share"? We will consider this separate topic later when we discuss *contribution*. It is of no concern to the plaintiff that the joint tortfeasors did not pay the judgment equally. They are left to fight this out among themselves. The plaintiff's only interest is in recovering full damages.

Persons Acting in Concert

Persons who act in **concert** to produce the negligent or intentional wrong are joint tortfeasors, and hence are jointly and severally liable for the harm they caused while on their **joint venture.**

> **EXAMPLES:**
>
> - Mary and Jane buy a truck to make deliveries together. One day, they are late in making a delivery. Mary, the driver, starts speeding. Jane urges her to go even faster. The truck negligently hits the plaintiff. Both Mary and Jane are joint tortfeasors.
> - Al and Donald agree to steal the plaintiff's goods. Al takes the goods while Donald acts as lookout. Both are joint tortfeasors.

There must be an express agreement or a tacit understanding that each will participate in the activity that produces the wrong. No such agreement or understanding would exist, for example, with a hitchhiker in the truck of Mary and Jane at the time of the accident in the first case. The hitchhiker would not be a joint tortfeasor along with Mary and Jane. To be a joint tortfeasor, the person must cooperate in the wrong, encourage it, or otherwise be an active participant. Someone who approves or **ratifies** the wrong after it is done for his or her benefit can also be a joint tortfeasor.

Persons Not Acting in Concert

Assume that two individuals, acting independently of each other, cause an accident.

> **EXAMPLE:**   Two cars carelessly collide on the highway. They both run into and kill a pedestrian.

The two drivers acted concurrently, but they were not acting in concert. There was no joint venture between them since they were operating independently. Yet, each was a substantial factor in producing a harm (the death of the pedestrian) that is **indivisible.** A result that cannot be practically divided is considered indivisible. In our example, we cannot separate the harm by determining which driver caused which part of the death. When two persons cause an indivisible harm, they are jointly and severally liable for the harm even though they were not acting in concert. They are treated the same as if they acted in concert.

If the harm is divisible, there is no joint tortfeasorship and no joint and several liability. Suppose that two companies independently pollute a stream with different chemicals, which can be separately identified. In such a case, each company will be liable only for that portion of the damage it caused. Suppose, however, that it is difficult to apportion the damages, because the companies used the same chemicals or because the different chemicals cannot be separately identified. The plaintiff and the defendants are in difficult positions. The plaintiff must do more than show that "somebody caused me harm." How is the plaintiff to meet his or her burden of proving what the individual defendants caused? From the defendants' perspective, it is unfair to saddle any one of them with the harm caused by the other defendants. A few courts shift the burden to the defendants and require them to establish who caused what. Most courts do not go this far; yet, they will assist the plaintiff in such cases by accepting a rough approximation of the portion of the harm caused by each defendant.

ASSIGNMENT

16.5

Ten families live in an apartment complex. They are very unhappy with the maintenance service provided by the landlord. Nine of the families begin throwing their garbage in a pile in one of the alleys next to the main building. The garbage draws many rats, which infest the apartment of the tenth family. This family sues the other nine families for negligence when it is forced to move out because of the rats.

a. Are the nine families jointly and severally liable? (See General Instructions for the Legal Analysis Assignment in Chapter 2.)

b. Prepare an investigation strategy to help you determine whether the nine families are jointly and severally liable. (See General Instructions for the Investigation Strategy Assignment in Chapter 3.)

RELEASE

Satisfaction is the receipt of full payment or compensation by the plaintiff. If the satisfaction has been received from one joint tortfeasor, the others can no longer be sued by the plaintiff. A **release,** on the other hand, is the giving up of a claim. This may be done for "free" (**gratuitously**) or for money or something else of value (**consideration**).

> **EXAMPLE:** While Tim and Fred are fishing in a lake, they negligently destroy Diane's boat, which was moored at the dock. Because they were engaged in a joint enterprise, they are jointly and severally liable to her for the damage. Diane agrees, however, to give up (i.e., release) all her claims against Tim and Fred if they stop fishing in the lake where the accident occurred. They agree. If they abide by their agreement, Diane cannot later change her mind and sue them for the damage to her boat.

What happens if the plaintiff releases only one of the joint tortfeasors? Are the other joint tortfeasors likewise released? Yes. In most states, the release of one joint tortfeasor automatically releases the others. Statutes in some states change this result by providing that the release of one does not automatically discharge the others. The plaintiff under these statutes can still go after the other joint tortfeasors.

In states where the release of one discharges all the joint tortfeasors, there is a device designed to get around this result. The device works as follows: In the negotiation with one joint tortfeasor, the plaintiff does not provide a release. Rather, he or she makes a promise or **covenant not to sue** that joint tortfeasor. The covenant, unlike the release, does not act as a bar to go after the other joint tortfeasors.

CONTRIBUTION

Suppose that the plaintiff obtains satisfaction of the entire amount of damages from one of the joint tortfeasors. Can that tortfeasor now force the other joint tortfeasors to contribute their share of the amount paid? Can he or she obtain **contribution?**

(Contribution is the right of one tortfeasor who has paid a judgment to be proportionately reimbursed by other tortfeasors who have not paid their share of the damages caused by all the tortfeasors.) States answer this question differently:

- Some states deny contribution among joint tortfeasors.
- Some states allow contribution only among joint tortfeasors against whom the plaintiff has secured a judgment. Those not sued would not have to contribute.
- Some states allow contribution only among joint tortfeasors who were negligent. Intentional joint tortfeasors cannot obtain contribution.

When contribution is allowed, the allocation is usually pro rata, or proportionate to the number of joint tortfeasors: two would be responsible for 50 percent each, three for 33⅓ each, etc. A few states, however, make the allocation according to the relative fault of the joint tortfeasors. Again, contribution is not a concern of the plaintiff who has received satisfaction. Contribution is a battle among the tortfeasors.

INDEMNITY

Indemnity is a device whereby one party who has paid the plaintiff can force another party to reimburse him or her for the full amount paid. Unlike contribution, which usually calls for a proportionate sharing of the loss, indemnity shifts the entire loss from the defendant who has paid onto someone else. Indemnity can arise by contract, where one person agrees to indemnify the other for any loss that results if the latter is sued. Indemnity can also arise by operation of law independent of any agreement between the parties.

EXAMPLES:

- An employer, who is vicariously liable for the tort committed by his or her employee, can seek indemnity from the employee. (Vicarious liability exists when a person becomes responsible for the tort or other wrong committed by another.) Seeking indemnity, of course, would be impractical if the employee has **shallow pockets** (inadequate resources from which a judgment can be collected).
- The supermarket, which is strictly liable for a product it sold, can obtain indemnity from the negligent manufacturer who made the product.
- One who has been passively negligent may be able to obtain indemnity from the person who was actively negligent or who acted intentionally.

The person seeking indemnity is liable for the tort. This person, however, is allowed to make someone else reimburse him or her for the judgment he or she has paid when it appears equitable to do so. The relationship between the party who has paid and the party against whom indemnity is sought must be such that in fairness we can say that the latter should pay.

SUMMARY

Damages are monetary payments awarded for a legally recognized wrong. Compensatory damages are monetary payments awarded to make the plaintiff whole for the actual loss suffered. These damages cover two kinds of losses: economic (out-of-pocket) losses and non-economic for which no objective dollar amount can be identified, e.g., pain and suffering. General damages are those compensatory damages that generally result from the kind of harm caused by the defendant's conduct. Special damages are compensatory damages that are peculiar to the plaintiff. Nominal damages are a small monetary payment awarded when the defendant has committed a tort that has resulted in little or no harm so that no compensatory damages are due. Punitive damages are noncompensatory damages that seek to punish the defendant and to deter similar conduct by others.

Future economic losses such as lost wages and medical expenses must be reduced to present value, which is the amount of money an individual would have to be given now to produce or generate, through prudent investment, a certain amount of money in a designated period of time.

Damages for pain and suffering are sometimes capped in certain kinds of cases. Hedonic damages are compensatory damages that cover the victim's loss of pleasure or enjoyment in life. Insurance claims adjusters sometimes use a rough formula in calculating the damages they may be willing to settle for. Software programs exist to help a law office calculate the variables involved in damage assessment. The measure of damages to property is often the fair market value of the property before and after the wrong. Under the doctrine of avoidable consequences, a defendant will not be liable for the additional or aggravated damages that the victim's reasonable steps could have avoided. Under the collateral source rule, the amount in damages owed by the defendant is not reduced by the injury-related funds received by the plaintiff from sources independent of the trial.

Joint tortfeasors are jointly and severally liable for the harm they wrongfully cause. They may have acted in concert or independently to produce an indivisible result. If the plaintiff receives full payment (satisfaction) from one joint tortfeasor, the other joint tortfeasors cannot be sued by the plaintiff. The relinquishment (release) of a claim against one joint tortfeasor usually acts to discharge the others. States differ on whether and when joint tortfeasors can seek contribution and thereby allocate the damages among themselves. Indemnity is the device whereby one party who has paid the plaintiff can force another party to reimburse him or her for the full amount paid.

KEY TERMS

damages   286

compensatory damages   286

out-of-pocket   286

pain and suffering   286

general damages   286

special damages   287

consequential damages   287

nominal damages   287

pro bono   287

punitive damages   287

exemplary damages   287

lump sum judgment   287

structured settlement   287

present value   288

windfall   288

present cash value   288

discount rate   288

per diem argument   293

unit-of-time argument   293

caps   294

hedonic damages   294

fair market value   296

mitigate the consequences   296

avoidable consequences   296

aggravation   296

collateral sources   298

permissive offset   298

mandatory offset   298

joint tortfeasors   298

jointly and severally liable   299

concert   299

joint venture   299

ratifies   299

indivisible   299

satisfaction   300

release   300

gratuitously   300

consideration   300

covenant not to sue   300

contribution   300

indemnity   301

shallow pockets   301

C H A P T E R

17

Negligence: Defenses

CHAPTER OUTLINE

- Introduction
- Contributory Negligence
- Last Clear Chance
- Comparative Negligence
- Assumption of the Risk

INTRODUCTION

A **defense** is the response of a party to a claim of another party, setting forth the reason(s) the claim should be denied. In this chapter we consider the defenses of contributory negligence, last clear chance, assumption of risk, and the newest arrival, comparative negligence. Elsewhere in the book we examine other defenses to negligence such as the privileges and immunities covered in Chapter 27.

As we will see, the defenses of contributory negligence and assumption of risk are very harsh on the plaintiff. They nullify the effect of the defendant's negligence. To avoid the seeming unfairness of this result, doctrines such as last clear chance and, in particular, comparative negligence have been created. In many states, comparative negligence has merged into and led to the partial or total abolishment of contributory negligence and assumption of risk. We still need to cover contributory negligence and assumption of risk, however, since every state has not adopted comparative negligence, and even in states that have, contributory negligence and assumption of risk may still apply if the provisions of comparative negligence have not been met.

Here is an overview of comparative negligence and its impact on the other defenses:

Comparative negligence: The damages between the plaintiff and the defendant are allocated according to their relative fault. There is a formula that must be met before comparative negligence can apply. When the formula has been met, the damages are allocated.

Contributory negligence: *Before comparative negligence was adopted:* If the plaintiff's unreasonable conduct contributed to his or her own injury, the defendant paid no damages. Contributory negligence was a complete defense in spite of the defendant's negligence. *If comparative negligence applies:* Contributory negligence is not a complete bar to the plaintiff's recovery. The damages are allocated between the plaintiff and the defendant according to their relative fault.

Last clear chance: *Before comparative negligence was adopted:* The last-clear-chance doctrine offset the impact of contributory negligence. Contributory negligence was not a bar to the plaintiff's recovery if the defendant had the last clear chance to avoid the plaintiff's injury but failed to use this chance. *If comparative negligence applies:* There is no longer a need for the last-clear-chance doctrine since contributory negligence is no longer a complete bar to the plaintiff's recovery.

Assumption of the risk: *Before comparative negligence was adopted:* Assumption of risk was a complete defense. The plaintiff loses if he or she knowingly and voluntarily accepted the risk of being injured by the negligence of the defendant. This could occur in two ways: an express assumption of risk (the plaintiff knowingly and voluntarily accepts a risk by express agreement) and an implied assumption of risk (the plaintiff knowingly and voluntarily accepts a risk by reason of his or her knowledge and conduct). In either case, the defendant is not liable for the injury he or she negligently caused the plaintiff to suffer. *If comparative negligence applies:* The parties can still agree to an express assumption of risk. In a case of implied assumption of risk, the court will distinguish between primary assumption of risk and secondary assumption of risk. In primary assumption of risk, the plaintiff knowingly and voluntarily accepts a particular risk that the defendant did not have a duty to protect the plaintiff against. Hence the plaintiff recovers nothing. In secondary assumption of risk, the plaintiff knowingly and voluntarily accepts a particular risk that the defendant had a duty to protect the plaintiff against. The damages are allocated between the plaintiff and the defendant according to their relative fault.

We turn now to a closer examination of these principles.

CONTRIBUTORY NEGLIGENCE

Contributory negligence exists when the plaintiff's unreasonable conduct contributed to his or her own injury. Once established, the effect of this defense was drastic. It required the plaintiff to bear the full loss of his or her injury. The negligent defendant walked away without paying anything because the plaintiff was also negligent.

There were, however, limitations on the defense. The contributory negligence of the plaintiff prevented liability only when the defendant committed **ordinary negligence,** which is unreasonable conduct that is not reckless or gross. If the misdeed of the defendant went beyond ordinary negligence, the plaintiff's contributory negligence was not a defense. Conduct is **reckless** when a person acts with the knowledge that harm will probably result. **Gross negligence** is the failure to use even a small amount of care to avoid foreseeable harm. Contributory negligence was a defense to the defendant's ordinary negligence, but not to the defendant's recklessness or gross negligence. Also, contributory negligence was never a defense to any of the intentional torts the defendant might commit.

In most states, contributory negligence must be pleaded and proven by a preponderance of the evidence by the defendant. It is an affirmative defense. In a few states, however, the *plaintiff* had the burden of pleading and proving that the injury was not caused by his or her own negligence.

There are two major elements of contributory negligence:

- plaintiff's negligence (unreasonableness)
- cause in fact

Plaintiff's Negligence (Unreasonableness)

EXAMPLE: Ben is driving 40 mph in a 40 mph zone in rainy weather at night. Fred runs through a red light and hits Ben's car. Ben sues Fred for negligence. In Fred's answer, he raises the defense of contributory negligence.

In Chapter 14, we considered the standard that would apply to a defendant such as Fred who is sued for negligence: a defendant will be liable for acting unreasonably under the circumstances. This same test applies to determine whether a *plaintiff* has been contributorily negligent.

Plaintiffs must not take **unreasonable risks** of injuring themselves. There is a formula or equation that is used to determine whether someone has acted unreasonably. See Figure 17–1. This is the same equation used to determine whether the defendant was negligent or unreasonable. See Figure 14–4 in Chapter 14. The only difference between Figure 14–4 and Figure 17–1 is that in 17–1 our focus is on what a reasonable plaintiff would have done to prevent the injury to him- or herself, whereas in 14–4 the focus is on what a reasonable defendant would have done to prevent the injury to the plaintiff.

When you are charged with contributory negligence, the allegation is that you acted unreasonably for your own safety. To determine whether this was so, we apply the equation by asking a series of questions. How foreseeable was it to you that your conduct would contribute to an accident? How foreseeable should it have been to you? What kind of injury was foreseeable to you? What kind of injury should have been foreseeable to you? What were you trying to do before the accident? How important or socially beneficial was it? What kind of burden or inconvenience would you have had to endure in order to take added precautions to avoid injuring yourself? These are the questions that a reasonable person would ask.

If the danger of an accident causing serious injury to yourself outweighs whatever burden or inconvenience you would have had to go through to avoid this injury, then you were unreasonable and hence negligent in failing to take those preventive steps.

FIGURE 17-1 Breach-of-duty equation.

Foreseeability of the danger of an accident occurring		The burden or inconvenience on the plaintiff of taking precautions to avoid the accident
Foreseeability of the kind of injury or damage that will result if an accident occurs	balanced against	The importance or social utility of what the plaintiff was trying to do before the accident

The equation also considers the importance or social utility of what you were trying to do at the time. A reasonable person is more likely to take risks of injuring him- or herself when engaged in socially useful tasks than when engaged in minor or frivolous activities.

In the example involving Ben and Fred, was Ben contributorily negligent? He was driving 40 mph in a 40 mph zone in rainy weather at night. All of the circumstances of the accident would have to be considered in applying the equation. To determine the foreseeability of an accident, for example, we must know the condition of the road, the amount of traffic, visibility, etc. We have to *particularize* the event. (See Figure 3–5 in Chapter 3.) It may be that Ben's speed was not unreasonable under the circumstances. What was Ben trying to do at the time? Simply get home as fast as possible to watch a football game, or get to a hospital as soon as possible to take a passenger to the emergency room? The more important or socially useful the goal of Ben at the time, the more reasonable it would be for him to take risks of his own safety. What was the burden or inconvenience on Ben of driving slower and hence taking less risk of injuring himself? All he had to do was not press down so hard on the accelerator. A minimal burden. What was the inconvenience of doing this? Arriving a few seconds or minutes later? Whether this is much of an inconvenience may depend on where he was going and whether the extra time was needed for an important or socially useful purpose.

You will recall that special allowances are made for a defendant who has a physical defect or who is a child (see Chapter 14). The same allowances are made for a plaintiff who is alleged to be contributorily negligent. The test of reasonableness is what a reasonable person with the plaintiff's physical defects would have done under the circumstances, or what a reasonable person as young as the plaintiff would have done under the circumstances. Mental deficiencies of the party, however, are not taken into consideration. The standard of reasonableness is a mentally healthy person. Finally, if the plaintiff had any special knowledge or skills that would have helped to avoid the accident, the test of reasonableness is what a reasonable person with that knowledge or skill would have done under the circumstances.

In assessing the contributory negligence of a plaintiff, it is important to identify the particular risks that he or she undertook in order to determine whether these risks were in fact the risks that contributed to his or her injury. The general rule is that plaintiffs are contributorily negligent only if the risks they unreasonably created to their own safety are the *same* risks that eventually led to the injury.

> **EXAMPLE:** Tomas goes on Jim's land knowing that there are many dangerous animals on the land. While walking, Tomas falls into a concealed hole and breaks his leg. Tomas sues Jim for negligence. Jim raises the defense of contributory negligence.

Tomas was not contributorily negligent. Tomas may have created an unreasonable risk of injury to himself when he went on the land knowing dangerous animals were present, but this is not the particular risk that produced the broken leg—Tomas was not attacked by an animal. Nor is it significant that Tomas may have been a trespasser on Jim's land. Torts can be committed against trespassers (see Chapter 23).

Suppose that the plaintiff's negligence consists of a violation of a statute, ordinance, or regulation. A court will treat a violation by the plaintiff the same way that it will treat a violation by the defendant. The same analytical process is used whether we are assessing the negligence of the defendant (see Figure 14–8 in Chapter 14) or the contributory negligence of the plaintiff.

ASSIGNMENT
17.1

In the following situation, will the defendant be successful in raising the defense of contributory negligence? (See General Instructions for the Legal Analysis Assignment in Chapter 2.)

A trucking company uses a public alley to load and unload its trucks. The manager warns a pedestrian to keep out because of the danger. The pedestrian ignores the warning and walks through. Two of the trucks collide. The collision causes a tremor in the alley. The tremor causes a large shovel to fall off a truck and hit the pedestrian. This truck was parked and was not part of the collision. The pedestrian sues the trucking company for negligence. The company asserts contributory negligence.

Cause in Fact

Once it is determined that the plaintiff was negligent (unreasonable), the next question is whether the plaintiff was a **cause in fact** of his or her own injury, along with the defendant. The question is whether both the plaintiff and the defendant caused the plaintiff's injury. The substantial-factor test is used to answer this question. The plaintiff caused his or her own injury if he or she was a substantial factor in producing the injury. The same test is used to determine whether the defendant caused the injury (see Chapter 15).

If the plaintiff acted unreasonably regarding his or her own safety, and this unreasonableness was a substantial factor in producing that injury, contributory negligence is established. It does not matter that the plaintiff was only slightly unreasonable when compared to the unreasonableness of the defendant, unless, as indicated, the defendant's unreasonableness could be categorized as reckless or gross.

In Chapter 16, on damages, we considered the doctrine of **avoidable consequences.** Assume that the defendant is liable in a case where there is no contributory negligence. Once the accident occurs, the plaintiff must take reasonable steps to mitigate or avoid aggravated or increased damages (e.g., by seeking proper medical attention). If the plaintiff does not take these steps, the defendant will not be liable for the aggravated or increased damages that could have been avoided. This is more of a damages issue than a contributory negligence issue.

Finally, the adoption of comparative negligence completely alters the impact of the plaintiff's contributory negligence. Under comparative negligence, damages are allocated between the plaintiff and the defendant according to their relative fault. Contributory negligence is no longer a complete defense if the state's comparative negligence law—to be examined shortly—applies.

LAST CLEAR CHANCE

Last clear chance is a pro-plaintiff doctrine that counteracts the drastic consequences of contributory negligence. A plaintiff found to be contributorily negligent can still recover if he or she can show that the defendant had the last clear chance to avoid the injury and failed to do so. Unfortunately, the doctrine is surrounded by a good deal of confusion, so that it is sometimes unclear whether a court will apply it.

It is important to distinguish the different predicaments in which plaintiffs can find themselves:

Plaintiff in helpless peril: A plaintiff is in **helpless peril** when his contributory negligence has placed him in a predicament that he *cannot* get himself out of. Even if the plaintiff now used reasonable care, he could not get out of the danger (e.g., plaintiff's foot is carelessly caught in a machine or in a railroad track).

Plaintiff in inattentive peril: A plaintiff is in **inattentive peril** when her contributory negligence has placed her in a predicament that she *could* get herself out of by the use of reasonable care, but the plaintiff remains negligently unaware of her peril up to the time of the accident (e.g., in a noisy section of town, plaintiff carelessly fails to hear or see a bus coming right at her on the street).

Plaintiff in Helpless Peril

If the defendant discovered the plaintiff in helpless peril and had an opportunity to avoid the accident but did not take it, then the plaintiff's contributory negligence will not bar recovery. The reason is that the defendant had and failed to take the last clear chance to avoid the injury.

Suppose, however, that the defendant did *not* discover the helpless plaintiff. Theoretically, the defendant did not have the last clear chance to avoid the accident. How can the defendant avoid what he or she does not know? Many states say that it is impossible, and hence deny the plaintiff the use of the last-clear-chance doctrine. This results in the plaintiff's loss of the case because of contributory negligence. Other states, however, take a different position, but only if the defendant *could have discovered* the helpless peril if the defendant had used reasonable care in his or her observation of the situation. For example, as the defendant railroad engineer approached the scene of the accident, the engineer failed to see the helpless plaintiff because the engineer negligently failed to maintain proper attention to the track directly in front. A few states treat "should-have-discovered" in the same way as "did-discover" and permit the plaintiff to recover in spite of the latter's contributory negligence if the defendant would have had a reasonable opportunity to prevent the accident at the last moment. The defendant must have been negligent in failing to discover the plaintiff and must have had a reasonable opportunity to prevent the accident if the plaintiff had been discovered.

Plaintiff in Inattentive Peril

If the defendant discovered the plaintiff in inattentive peril and had a reasonable opportunity to avoid the accident but did not take it, then the plaintiff's contributory negligence will not bar his or her recovery. The reason is that the defendant had and failed to take the last clear chance to avoid the injury. In other words, discovery of plaintiff in inattentive peril is treated in the same way as discovery of the plaintiff in helpless peril. The defendant does not have to have definite knowledge that the plaintiff was unaware of his or her peril, but the situation must be such that the defendant did see the plaintiff and should have known that the plaintiff was unaware or inattentive.

The most troublesome case is when the defendant failed to discover the plaintiff in inattentive peril because of the defendant's negligence at the time of the accident. Very few courts would permit the plaintiff to recover here. The negligence of both plaintiff and defendant resulted in their being ignorant of each other. Neither had the last clear chance. In most courts, therefore, the plaintiff's contributory negligence would bar his or her recovery.

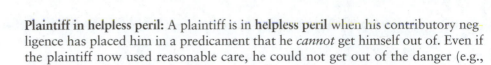

ASSIGNMENT

17.2

Peter is negligently driving his car, which collides with Bill's car at an intersection. Peter is not injured, but his car is thrown onto the other side of the road, upon which Dan's car is approaching from the opposite direction. Dan is driving carelessly. Dan sees Peter's car, but instead of stopping, unreasonably thinks he can cut around Peter's car. The space is too narrow and Dan collides with Peter's car, causing Peter to break his leg. Peter sues Dan for negligence. Dan raises the defense of contributory negligence.

a. Assess Dan's chances of succeeding with this defense. (See General Instructions for the Legal Analysis Assignment in Chapter 2.)

b. Prepare an investigation strategy. (See General Instructions for the Investigation Strategy Assignment in Chapter 3.)

A state that has adopted comparative negligence does not need the defense of last clear chance. When comparative negligence applies, contributory negligence is not a complete bar to recovery. Hence, there is no longer a need for a defense that offsets the all-or-nothing impact of contributory negligence.

COMPARATIVE NEGLIGENCE

Most states have adopted comparative negligence. The court first determines the total damages suffered by the plaintiff. Then it apportions these damages between the negligent plaintiff and the negligent defendant according to their relative fault. There are two main kinds of comparative negligence systems:

Pure Comparative Negligence

When the plaintiff sues the defendant for negligence and the defendant claims that the plaintiff's negligence contributed to the injury, a court will decide the percentage by which each side was negligent. Plaintiff's recovery is limited to that percentage of the award that was due to the defendant's negligence. If, for example, plaintiff suffered $100,000 in damages, and the court concludes that the defendant was 5 percent at fault and the plaintiff was 95 percent at fault in causing the injury, the plaintiff recovers $5,000 from the defendant—5 percent of $100,000. Plaintiff always recovers something if the injury was caused by the negligence of both parties, even if the plaintiff's fault was greater than the defendant's.

Restricted Comparative Negligence

Other states use different versions of comparative negligence that are not as comprehensive as the pure form. For example, some states will compare the negligence of the defendant and plaintiff in causing the plaintiff's injury and allow the plaintiff to recover only if the plaintiff's negligence was "slight" in comparison with the "gross" negligence of the defendant. Other states will compare the negligence of the defendant and that of the plaintiff in causing the plaintiff's injury and allow the plaintiff to recover only if the plaintiff's negligence is less than that of the defendant. In the latter states, if they are equally negligent, the plaintiff recovers nothing; if the plaintiff is 51 percent negligent and the defendant is 49 percent negligent, the plaintiff recovers nothing.

ASSUMPTION OF THE RISK

Assumption of the risk is the knowing and voluntary acceptance of the risk of being injured by someone's negligence. The plaintiff's conduct may amount to both contributory negligence and assumption of the risk. In a state that still has both defenses, the defendant can choose *either* to avoid liability. A basic difference between the two defenses, however, is that contributory negligence is determined by the **objective standard** of the reasonable person, whereas assumption of the risk is determined by a **subjective standard**—whether this particular plaintiff knowingly and voluntarily assumed the risk of the defendant's conduct.

Contributory negligence (objective test): The plaintiff *should have known* that he or she was creating an unreasonable risk of injuring him- or herself and *should have taken* greater precautions against this risk.

Assumption of the risk (subjective test): The plaintiff *actually knew* of the risk to his or her safety, but voluntarily chose to confront it.

There are two main elements of the defense of assumption of risk:

- Plaintiff understood the risks posed by the defendant's conduct to the plaintiff's safety.
- Plaintiff voluntarily chose to confront those risks.

Understanding the Risk

It is very easy to confuse assumption of the risk with contributory negligence. Suppose, for example, that Sam is injured in an electrical plant by coming into contact with large live wires that the plant negligently left on the floor. Sam never saw the wires in spite of their size. In Sam's negligence suit against the plant, can the plant use the assumption-of-the-risk defense? No. How could Sam have understood a risk in something that he did not see? If the plant says that Sam *should have seen* the wires because they were so large, the plant is confusing assumption of the risk with contributory negligence. If Sam did not see the wires but should have seen them if he had been acting reasonably as he walked, he was contributorily negligent, but it was impossible for him to have assumed the risk. Assumption of risk is subjective: the risk must be known and understood by a particular plaintiff before we can say that he or she assumed that risk. If all the defendant can say is that the plaintiff was stupid in failing to understand the risk, the defendant has conceded that assumption of the risk cannot apply.

To be sure, there will be some extreme cases in which no one will believe the plaintiff's claim that he or she did not understand the danger. A plaintiff, for example, who walks into a fire negligently set by the defendant would probably not be believed if the plaintiff says he or she did not know that the fire could cause serious injury.

ASSIGNMENT

17.3

Diane is a high school freshman. She has a part-time job at a convenience store in a run-down section of the city. There have been several robberies at the store, several of which Diane witnessed. The store manager carelessly fails to hire a guard or to install a security system. One day, a robber confronts Diane and demands all the cash in the register. Diane complies. She is traumatized by the incident and sues the store for negligently failing to have a guard or other security system. Can the store claim the defense of assumption of risk? (See General Instructions for the Legal Analysis Assignment in Chapter 2.)

Voluntarily Confronting the Risk

We need to examine two categories of assumption of risk:

- the plaintiff's **express assumption of risk** in which the plaintiff knowingly and voluntarily accepts a risk by express agreement; the express assumption must not violate public policy
- the plaintiff's **implied assumption of risk** in which the plaintiff knowingly and voluntarily accepts a risk by reason of his or her knowledge and conduct; the implied assumption must not violate public policy

Express Assumption People often enter into agreements limiting their liability to each other. For example, when someone stores a car or a coat in a warehouse or other business set up for this purpose, the parties may agree that the business will not be liable for certain kinds of damage to the car or coat. The owner of the car or coat in these situations is expressly assuming the risk of the damage.

But it must be clear that the parties agreed to such **limitation of liability.** The plaintiff must know about the limitation. A company may try to tell the customer that it will not be liable for negligence by putting a notice to this effect on a sign buried on a wall in the rear of a room, or in very small print on the back of a receipt check. Such communication will usually be insufficient. Customers do not agree to assume a risk of which they are unaware.

There are a number of situations in which the law will not permit or will restrict assumption-of-the-risk agreements even if the terms are made quite clear to both parties. This occurs mainly when there is a significantly unbalanced bargaining position between the parties. In such situations, the likelihood is that the weaker of the parties did not voluntarily agree to assume the risk. Considerable **coercion** or pressure took place. As a matter of **public policy,** the law will invalidate such "agreements."

> **EXAMPLES:**
>
> - An employer cannot ask an employee to assume all risks of injury on the job. The employer must provide a reasonably safe workplace.
> - Someone engaged in a public service (e.g., common carrier, innkeeper, public utility) cannot ask a customer to assume all risks of injury or damage while using the public service—but it can seek to limit its liability if the terms of the limitation are clearly communicated to the customer so that the latter knows what he or she is getting into.

Merchants often try to place a **release** clause in an agreement that they ask the consumer to sign. A release is the giving up or relinquishing of a claim. An agreement containing a release of liability for negligence or other wrongdoing is called an **exculpatory agreement.** Courts are often suspicious of such agreements, particularly when they are **adhesion contracts.** An adhesion contract is a standardized contract for goods or services offered on a take-it-or-leave-it basis without any realistic opportunity for bargaining between the buyer and seller.

All release clauses, however, are not necessarily invalid. A court will consider a number of factors to determine the validity of the release. The most important factors are illustrated in the case of *Wagenblast v. Odessa School District No. 105-157-166J.*

CASE

Wagenblast v. Odessa School District No. 105-157-166J
110 Wash.2d 845, 758 P.2d 968 (1988)
Supreme Court of Washington

Background: *Charles Wagenblast is a public school student. To participate in high school sports, all students and their parents must sign a standardized form releasing the school district from liability for negligence—an exculpatory agreement. They sued the school district in Superior Court, seeking an injunction to prevent the use of the release form as a condition of participating in school sports. The Superior Court granted the injunction. The case is now on appeal before the Supreme Court of Washington.*

Decision on Appeal: *The judgment is affirmed. The release violates public policy.*

OPINION OF COURT

Justice ANDERSEN delivered the opinion of the court . . . . :

Can school districts require public school students and their parents to sign written releases which release the districts from the consequences of all future school district negligence, before the students will be allowed to engage in certain recognized school related activities, here interscholastic athletics? We hold that the exculpatory releases from any future school district negligence are invalid because they violate public policy.

The courts have generally recognized that, subject to certain exceptions, parties may contract that one shall not be liable for his or her own negligence to another. As Prosser and Keeton explain: "It is quite possible for the parties expressly to agree in advance that the defendant is under no obligation of care for the benefit of the plaintiff, and shall not be liable for the consequences of conduct which would otherwise be negligent. There is in the ordinary case no public policy which prevents the parties from contracting as they see fit, as to whether the plaintiff will undertake the responsibility of looking out for himself." W. Keeton, D. Dobbs, R. Keeton & D. Owen, *Prosser and Keeton on Torts* § 68, at 482 (5th ed. 1984).

In accordance with the foregoing general rule, appellate decisions in this state have upheld exculpatory agreements where the subject was a toboggan slide, a scuba diving class, mountain climbing instruction, an automobile demolition derby, and ski jumping.

As Prosser and Keeton further observe, however, there are instances where public policy reasons for preserving an obligation of care owed by one person to another outweigh our traditional regard for the freedom to contract. Courts in this century are generally agreed on several such categories of cases. Courts, for example, are usually reluctant to allow those charged with a public duty, which includes the obligation to use reasonable care, to rid themselves of that obligation by contract. Thus, where the defendant is a common carrier, an innkeeper, a professional bailee, a public utility, or the like, an agreement discharging the defendant's performance will not ordinarily be given effect. Implicit in such decisions is the notion that the service performed is one of importance to the public, and that a certain standard of performance is therefore required.

Courts generally also hold that an employer cannot require an employee to sign a contract releasing the employer from liability for job-related injuries caused by the employer's negligence. Such decisions are grounded on the recognition that the disparity of bargaining power between employer and employee forces the employee to accept such agreements.

Consistent with these general views, this court has held that a bank which rents out safety deposit boxes cannot, by contract, exempt itself from liability for its own negligence, and that if the circumstances of a particular case suggest that a gas company has a duty to inspect the pipes and fittings belonging to the owner of the building, any contractual limitation on that duty would be against public policy.

This court has also gone beyond these usually accepted categories to hold future releases invalid in other circumstances as well. It has struck down a lease provision exculpating a public housing authority from liability for injuries caused by the authority's negligence and has also struck down a landlord's exculpatory clause relating to common areas in a multi-family dwelling complex.

In reaching these decisions, this court has focused at times on disparity of bargaining power, at times on the importance of the service provided, and at other times on other factors. In reviewing these decisions, it is apparent that the court has not always been particularly clear on what rationale it used to decide what type of release was and was not violative of "public policy". Undoubtedly, it has been much easier for courts to simply declare releases violative of public policy in a given situation than to state a principled basis for so holding.

Probably the best exposition of the test to be applied in determining whether exculpatory agreements violate public policy is that stated by the California Supreme Court. In writing for a unanimous court, the late Justice Tobriner outlined the factors in *Tunkl v. Regents of Univ. of Cal.,* 60 Cal. 2d 92,

383 P.2d 441, 32 Cal. Rptr. 33, 6 A.L.R.3d 693 (1963):

Thus the attempted but invalid exemption involves a transaction which exhibits some or all of the following characteristics. [1] It concerns a business of a type generally thought suitable for public regulation. [2] The party seeking exculpation is engaged in performing a service of great importance to the public, which is often a matter of practical necessity for some members of the public. [3] The party holds himself out as willing to perform this service for any member of the public who seeks it, or at least for any member coming within certain established standards. [4] As a result of the essential nature of the service, in the economic setting of the transaction, the party invoking exculpation possesses a decisive advantage of bargaining strength against any member of the public who seeks his services. [5] In exercising a superior bargaining power the party confronts the public with a standardized adhesion contract of exculpation, and makes no provision whereby a purchaser may pay additional reasonable fees and obtain protection against negligence. [6] Finally, as a result of the transaction, the person or property of the purchaser is placed under the control of the seller, subject to the risk of carelessness by the seller or his agents.

Tunkl, 60 Cal. 2d at 98-101.* We agree.

Obviously, the more of the foregoing six characteristics that appear in a given exculpatory agreement case, the more likely the agreement is to be declared invalid on public policy grounds. In the . . . [case] before us, *all* of the characteristics are present. . . .

1. The agreement concerns an endeavor of a type generally thought suitable for public regulation. Regulation of governmental entities usually means self-regulation. Thus, the Legislature has by statute granted to each school board the authority to control, supervise, and regulate the conduct of interscholastic athletics. In some situations, a school board is permitted, in turn, to delegate this authority to the Washington Interscholastic Activities Association (WIAA) or to another voluntary nonprofit entity. In the [case before us the school board looks] to the WIAA for regulation of interscholastic sports. The WIAA handbook contains an extensive constitution with rules for such athletic endeavors. These rules cover numerous topics, including student eligibility standards, athletic awards, insurance, coaches, officials, tournaments and state championships. Special regulations for each sport cover such topics as turnout schedules, regular season game or meet limitations, and various areas of regulation peculiar to the sport, including the rule book governing the sport. Clearly then, interscholastic sports in Washington are extensively regulated, and are a fit subject for such regulation.

2. The party seeking exculpation is engaged in performing a service of great importance to the public, which is often a matter of practical necessity for some members of the public. This court has held that public school students have no fundamental right to participate in interscholastic athletics. Nonetheless, the court also has observed that the justification

---

*Accord, *Jones v. Dressel,* 623 P.2d 370 (Colo. 1981). See generally 57 *American Jurisprudence 2d* Negligence § 28 (1971).

advanced for interscholastic athletics is their educational and cultural value. As the testimony of . . . School Superintendent Robert Nelson and others amply demonstrate, interscholastic athletics is part and parcel of the overall educational scheme in Washington. The total expenditure of time, effort and money on these endeavors makes this clear. The importance of these programs to the public is substantive; they represent a significant tie of the public at large to our system of public education. Nor can the importance of these programs to certain students be denied; as Superintendent Nelson agreed, some students undoubtedly remain in school and maintain their academic standing only because they can participate in these programs. Given this emphasis on sports by the public and the school system, it would be unrealistic to expect students to view athletics as an activity entirely separate and apart from the remainder of their schooling.**. . .

3. Such party holds itself out as willing to perform this service for any member of the public who seeks it, or at least for any member coming within certain established standards. Implicit in the nature of interscholastic sports is the notion that such programs are open to all students who meet certain skill and eligibility standards. . . .

4. Because of the essential nature of the service, in the economic setting of the transaction, the party invoking exculpation possesses a decisive advantage of bargaining strength against any member of the public who seeks the services. Not only have interscholastic sports become of considerable importance to students and the general public alike, but in most instances there exists no alternative program of organized competition. . . . While outside alternatives exist for some activities, they possess little of the inherent allure of interscholastic competition. Many students cannot afford private programs or the private schools where such releases might not be employed. In this regard, school districts have near-monopoly power. And, because such programs have become important to student participants, school districts possess a clear and disparate bargaining

_____

**This intimate relationship between interscholastic sports and other aspects of public education serves to distinguish this case from those involving private adult education for hazardous activities, e.g., skydiving and mountain climbing.

strength when they insist that students and their parents sign these releases.

5. In exercising a superior bargaining power, the party confronts the public with a standardized adhesion contract of exculpation, and makes no provision whereby a purchaser may pay additional reasonable fees and obtain protection against negligence. . . . Student athletes and their parents or guardians have no alternative but to sign the standard release forms provided to them or have the student barred from the program.

6. The person or property of members of the public seeking such services must be placed under the control of the furnisher of the services, subject to the risk of carelessness on the part of the furnisher, its employees or agents. A school district owes a duty to its students to employ ordinary care and to anticipate reasonably foreseeable dangers so as to take precautions for protecting the children in its custody from such dangers. This duty extends to students engaged in interscholastic sports. As a natural incident to the relationship of a student athlete and his or her coach, the student athlete is usually placed under the coach's considerable degree of control. The student is thus subject to the risk that the school district or its agent will breach this duty of care.

In sum, the attempted releases . . . before us exhibit all six of the characteristics denominated in *Tunkl v. Regents of Univ. of Cal.* Because of this, and for the aforesaid reasons, we hold that the releases. . .are invalid as against public policy. . . .

Another name for a release of the sort presented here is an express assumption of risk. If a plaintiff has released a defendant from liability for a future occurrence, the plaintiff may also be said to have assumed the risk of the occurrence. If the release is against public policy, however, it is also against public policy to say that the plaintiff has assumed that particular risk. This court has implicitly recognized that an express assumption of risk which relieves the defendant's duty to the plaintiff may violate public policy. Accordingly, to the extent that the release portions of these forms represent a consent to relieve the school districts of their duty of care, they are invalid whether they are termed releases or express assumptions of risk. . . .

The decision of the trial court in the Odessa School District case is affirmed. . . .

ASSIGNMENT 17.4

a. A fellow student asks you for a ride downtown. Is it legal for you to do this favor on the condition that he or she signs a release of liability for any injury that may result from the ride? Assume that the student has no other way to get downtown.

b. Can a public high school have a fencing class that is limited to students who, with their parents, sign a waiver of negligence liability? Why or why not? What about a furniture-making class that is similarly limited?

c. Tommy shows up for high school football. After about three weeks of practice, the coach tells Tommy that he is too thin to play football. If, however, he and his parents sign a waiver of negligence liability, he will be allowed to play. Is this waiver valid?

d. What remedy do the students have if the school district decides to cancel all school sports whether or not waivers are signed?

Implied Assumption The plaintiff can voluntarily assume the risk in ways other than by express agreement. An implied assumption of the risk arises because of the knowledge and conduct of the parties rather than because of an express agreement. If, for example, the plaintiff walks very close to the spot where fireworks are exploding and fully understands the dangers involved, the plaintiff has assumed the risk of injury due to the negligent setting off of the fireworks. This is an implied assumption of the risk. As with express assumption of the risk, however, there are some situations in which the law as a matter of public policy will not permit a plaintiff to impliedly assume the risk. Such a situation occurs, for example, when an employee works in an unsafe environment. The law may not permit express *or* implied assumption of the risk in such situations. With this qualification in mind, the rule on implied assumption of the risk, according to the *Restatement,* is as follows:

> A plaintiff who fully understands a risk of harm to himself or his things caused by the defendant's conduct or by the condition of the defendant's land, and who nevertheless voluntarily chooses to enter or remain, or to permit his things to enter or remain in the area of that risk, under circumstances that manifest his willingness to accept it, is not entitled to recover for harm within that risk.[1]

In effect, once you understand the risks and voluntarily proceed to confront them, you have decided to take your chances on injury or damage caused by the negligence of the defendant. Suppose that you buy a lawn mower, but before using it, you discover that it is defective. The blade has been negligently fastened to the body of the machine. You see the defect and understand the consequences of the blade's flying off while in use. If you decide to use it anyway, and are injured when the blade does come off, your negligence suit against the manufacturer will be defeated because of assumption of the risk. You have impliedly assumed the risk.

ASSIGNMENT

17.5

Examine the following situations to determine whether the plaintiff has voluntarily assumed the risk. (See General Instructions for the Legal Analysis Assignment in Chapter 2.)

a. Plaintiff runs out into the street in the path of cars that are exceeding the speed limit. One of the cars hits the plaintiff. Plaintiff sues the driver.

b. Plaintiff agrees to take a joy ride with the defendant, who will drive on the beach in very shallow water. Neither party knows that the brakes are defective. The brakes fail and the car goes out to deep water, almost drowning the plaintiff. Plaintiff sues the defendant.

There is a form of pressure that a defendant can place on the plaintiff that can negate what would otherwise be an assumption of the risk. The pressure comes in the form of negligently leaving the plaintiff no reasonable alternative in protecting the plaintiff's rights.

> **EXAMPLE:** Defendant negligently sets fire to the plaintiff's car. The plaintiff tries to put out the fire and is burned. Plaintiff sues defendant for damage to the car and for personal injuries due to the burn. As to the personal injuries, the defendant raises the defense of assumption of the risk.

If the plaintiff acted reasonably in trying to put out the fire, he or she has not assumed the risk of being burned *even though the plaintiff fully understood the risks of being burned.* The risks were not voluntarily assumed. Defendant's negligent conduct put the plaintiff in the predicament of either watching the fire destroy the car or trying to stop the fire. The essential question is whether the plaintiff was reasonable in the

---

[1]*Restatement (Second) of Torts* § 496C (1965).

course taken. This will depend on all the circumstances. How big was the fire at the time the plaintiff tried to put it out? How old was the car? What was its value? How close was a fire station, and how difficult or easy was it to contact the station? What was in the car? Nothing? Valuable papers? An infant? Would the plaintiff have been stranded in an inhospitable area if he or she were not able to use the car? Taking all of these factors into consideration, if the attempt to put out the fire was reasonable, there was no voluntary assumption of the risk. If, on the other hand, the attempt was foolhardy because of the extraordinary danger of being seriously burned to protect a car of relatively little value, a court will conclude that there was an assumption of the risk. The plaintiff's protection of his or her rights or property must not be out of all proportion to the danger that the plaintiff walks or leaps into.

ASSIGNMENT

17.6

In the following cases, determine whether the defendant can successfully raise the assumption-of-risk defense. (See General Instructions for the Legal Analysis Assignment in Chapter 2.)

a. Tony is building a new road in front of Alan's house. A ditch is dug in front of the house. Tony puts a thin piece of plywood across the ditch so that workers and Alan can cross over the ditch. A large "danger" sign is placed by Tony close to the plywood crossing. Alan sees the sign. While Alan is crossing over the plywood, it caves in, causing severe injuries. Alan sues Tony for negligence.

b. Bob's leg is injured in a hit-and-run accident. Along comes Tom in another car. Tom's car has defective brakes, and Bob knows this. Bob has no other way to get to a hospital for needed medical attention. Bob goes with Tom to the hospital. Along the way, the defective brakes cause another accident, in which Bob breaks his arm. Bob sues Tom for negligent injury to his arm.

We turn now to the effect of comparative negligence on assumption of risk.

First of all, express assumption of risk remains a defense, except in those cases where the court might rule that the agreement to limit liability is against public policy. All other assumption-of-risk cases fall into the category of implied assumption of risk. Does this category survive as a defense in states that have adopted comparative negligence? To answer this question, courts distinguish between two kinds of assumption of risk: primary and secondary.

Primary assumption of risk: The plaintiff knowingly and voluntarily accepts a particular risk that the defendant did not have a duty to protect the plaintiff against. The plaintiff recovers nothing in such cases.

> **EXAMPLE:** Paul buys an expensive season ticket to a professional basketball game. He sits in the front row, a few feet from the playing court. During play, a ball bounces off a player and hits Paul in the face, breaking his glasses. He sues the stadium for negligently failing to build a net in front of spectators to protect them from stray basketballs.

Paul loses. The stadium did not have a duty to protect spectators from being hit by a ricocheted basketball during an aggressive, but normally played, basketball game. The risk of serious injury from stray balls is relatively small. The burden on the stadium of preventing such accidents outweighs the risk of the injury. It would be impossible to keep the basketball in bounds at all times without fundamentally altering the competitive nature of the game. Stray balls are inevitable. Nets all around the court would impede vision. Spectators have the option of sitting further back from the playing court. In short, the stadium simply was not negligent. Another way of phrasing this conclusion is to say that a front-row spectator assumes the risk of being hit by stray basketballs during play even if the ball was carelessly thrown by a player before it ricocheted off the court. Yet, it would be more accurate to say that there was no negligence on the part of the defendant. Unfortunately, however, assumption-of-risk language is still used in these cases, but when the defendant had no duty to protect the plaintiff against a particular risk, many courts use the phrase *primary assumption of risk*.

If the state has comparative negligence, does the court compare the conduct of the parties and apportion liability? No. There is nothing to compare. The defendant simply was not negligent. Plaintiff recovers nothing in cases of primary assumption of risk because the defendant was not negligent—there is no reason to invoke the comparative fault principles of comparative negligence. This is so whether the plaintiff was reasonable or unreasonable in his or her own conduct.

Secondary assumption of risk: The plaintiff knowingly and voluntarily accepts a particular risk that the defendant had a duty to protect the plaintiff against.

> **EXAMPLE:** At a county fair, Mary agrees to ride in a horse-drawn carriage driven by a driver who is visibly drunk. Mary sees the driver's condition as he staggers onto the carriage, but decides to take the ride with him anyway. The driver carelessly drives too close to the edge of the road. The carriage tips over, injuring Mary.

This is a case of secondary assumption of risk. The driver had a duty to drive the carriage carefully and to protect passengers from injuries caused by unreasonable driving. Driving while intoxicated was certainly unreasonable. Mary, however, knew the driver was impaired and that this could affect the safety of the ride. She foolishly decided to ride with him. Arguably, she knowingly and voluntarily accepted the risk of injury from the ride. In cases of secondary assumption of risk, comparative negligence applies. Recovery is not barred because of assumption of risk. The court will compare the negligence of both parties and apportion the damages according to the comparative negligence rules in the state.

The case of *Knight v. Jewett* provides further clarification on the impact of comparative negligence on assumption of risk as well as on contributory negligence and last clear chance.

CASE

Knight v. Jewett
3 Cal. 4th 296, 834 P.2d 696, 11 Cal. Rptr. 2d 2 (1992)
Supreme Court of California

Background: *Kendra Knight had to have her finger amputated after Michael Jewett ran into her during a game of touch football. She sued him for negligence, assault, and battery. In the trial court, the defendant made a motion for summary judgment. It was sustained and the case was dismissed. The court ruled that plaintiff would not be able to win even if all the allegations made in the pleadings and during discovery were true. The Court of Appeal affirmed the dismissal. Knight has now appealed the dismissal to the California Supreme Court.*

Decision on Appeal: *The judgment is affirmed. Jewett did not owe a duty to Knight to protect her against the risk of injury she received.*

OPINION OF COURT

Justice GEORGE delivered the opinion of the court . . . :
On January 25, 1987, the day of the 1987 Super Bowl football game, plaintiff Kendra Knight and defendant Michael Jewett, together with a number of other social acquaintances, attended a Super Bowl party at the home of a

mutual friend. During half time of the Super Bowl, several guests decided to play an informal game of touch football on an adjoining dirt lot, using a "peewee" football. Each team had four or five players and included both women and men; plaintiff and defendant were on opposing teams. No rules were explicitly discussed before the game.

Five to ten minutes into the game, defendant ran into plaintiff during a play. According to plaintiff, at that point she told defendant "not to play so rough or I was going to have to stop playing." Her declaration stated that "[defendant] seemed to acknowledge my statement and left me with the impression that he would play less rough prospectively." In his deposition, defendant recalled that plaintiff had asked him to "be careful," but did not remember plaintiff saying that she would stop playing.

On the very next play, plaintiff sustained the injuries that gave rise to the present lawsuit. As defendant recalled the incident, his team was on defense on that play, and he jumped up in an attempt to intercept a pass. He touched the ball but did not catch it, and in coming down he collided with plaintiff, knocking her over. When he landed, he stepped backward onto plaintiff's right hand, injuring her hand and little finger.

Both plaintiff and Andrea Starr, another participant in the game who was on the same team as plaintiff, recalled the incident differently from defendant. According to their declarations, at the time plaintiff was injured, Starr already had caught the pass. Defendant was running toward Starr, when he ran into plaintiff from behind, knocked her down, and stepped on her hand. Starr also stated that, after knocking plaintiff down, defendant continued running until he tagged Starr, "which tag was hard enough to cause me to lose my balance, resulting in a twisting or spraining of my ankle."

The game ended with plaintiff's injury, and plaintiff sought treatment shortly thereafter. After three operations failed to restore the movement in her little finger or to relieve the ongoing pain of the injury, plaintiff's finger was amputated. Plaintiff then instituted the present proceeding, seeking damages from defendant on theories of negligence and assault and battery. . . .

[Defendant contended] he did not intend to step on plaintiff's hand or to injure her. Defendant also attached a copy of plaintiff's deposition in which plaintiff acknowledged that she frequently watched professional football on television and thus was generally familiar with the risks associated with the sport of football, and in which she conceded that she had no reason to believe defendant had any intention of stepping on her hand or injuring her. . . .

[P]laintiff maintained that . . . in view of the casual, social setting, the circumstance that women and men were joint participants in the game, and the rough dirt surface on which the game was played, she anticipated from the outset that it was the kind of "mock" football game in which there would be no forceful pushing or hard hitting or shoving. Plaintiff also asserted that the declarations and depositions of other players in the game, included in her opposition papers, demonstrated that the other participants, including defendant, shared her expectations and assumptions that the game was to be a "mellow" one and not a serious, competitive athletic event. Plaintiff claimed that there had been no injuries during touch football games in which she had participated on previous occasions, and that in view of the circumstances under which the game was played, "[t]he only type of injury which I reasonably anticipated would have been something in the nature of a bruise or bump.". . .

After considering the parties' submissions, the trial court granted defendant's motion for summary judgment. On appeal, the Court of Appeal . . . affirmed the judgment. . . .

As every leading tort treatise has explained, the assumption of risk doctrine long has caused confusion both in definition and application, because the phrase "assumption of risk" traditionally has been used in a number of very different factual settings involving analytically distinct legal concepts. (See, e.g., *Prosser & Keeton on Torts* (5th ed. 1984) pp. 480–481. . . .)

Prior to the adoption of comparative fault principles of liability, there often was no need to distinguish between the different categories of assumption of risk cases, because if a case fell into either category, the plaintiff's recovery was totally barred. With the adoption of comparative fault, however, it became essential to differentiate between the distinct categories of cases that traditionally had been lumped together

under the rubric of assumption of risk. This court's seminal comparative fault decision in *Li v. Yellow Cab Co.* (1975) 13 Cal. 3d 804, 119 Cal. Rptr. 858, 532 P.2d 1226, explicitly recognized the need for such differentiation, and attempted to explain which category of assumption of risk cases should be merged into the comparative fault system and which category should not. . . .

In *Li,* our court undertook a basic reexamination of the common law doctrine of contributory negligence. As *Li* noted, contributory negligence generally has been defined as "'conduct on the part of the plaintiff which falls below the standard to which he should conform for his own protection, and which is a legally contributing cause cooperating with the negligence of the defendant in bringing about the plaintiff's harm.'" (*Li,* supra, 13 Cal. 3d at p. 809, quoting *Restatement (Second) Torts,* § 463.) Prior to *Li,* the common law rule was that " '[e]xcept where the defendant has the last clear chance, the plaintiff's contributory negligence *bars recovery* against a defendant whose negligent conduct would otherwise make him liable to the plaintiff for the harm sustained by him.' " (*Li,* supra, at pp. 809–810, italics added, quoting *Restatement (Second) Torts,* § 467.). . .

[The *Li* court criticized the doctrine of contributory negligence because it fails to distribute responsibility in proportion to fault. The court concluded that contributory negligence] should be replaced in this state by a system under which liability for damage will be borne by those whose negligence caused it in direct proportion to their respective fault. . . .

After determining that the "all-or-nothing" contributory negligence doctrine should be replaced by a system of comparative negligence, the *Li* court went on to undertake a rather extensive discussion of the effect that the adoption of comparative negligence would have on a number of related tort doctrines, including the doctrines of last clear chance and assumption of risk.

Under the last clear chance doctrine, a defendant was rendered totally liable for an injury, even though the plaintiff's contributory negligence had played a role in the accident, when the defendant had the "last clear chance" to avoid the accident. With regard to that doctrine, the *Li* decision, observed: "Although several states which apply comparative negligence concepts retain the last clear chance doctrine, the better reasoned position seems to be that when true comparative negligence is adopted, the need for last clear chance as a palliative of the hardships of the 'all-or-nothing' rule disappears and its retention results only in a windfall to the plaintiff in direct contravention of the principle of liability in proportion to fault." (*Li* at p. 824) Accordingly, the court concluded that the doctrine should be "subsumed under the general process of assessing liability in proportion to fault." (Id. at p. 826.). . .

[As to assumption of risk, the *Li* court said that some categories of assumption of risk are really forms of contributory negligence. When this is so, the old all-or-nothing rule of contributory negligence does not apply. Comparative negligence principles take over. The conduct of the plaintiff is called secondary assumption of risk, which does not bar recovery. There are two kinds of assumption of risk: primary and secondary. In primary assumption of risk, the defendant was under no duty of care to protect the plaintiff from a particular risk. Primary assumption of risk, therefore, bars the plaintiff from any recovery for injuries resulting from that risk. In secondary assumption of risk, however, the defendant had a duty of care to protect the plaintiff from a particular risk, but the plaintiff knowingly and unreasonably encountered that risk. Secondary assumption of risk is merged into and becomes part of comparative negligence. The fault of the plaintiff and the defendant are compared for purposes of allocating responsibility. Hence, when the defense of assumption of risk is raised, we need to ask whether the defendant had a duty to protect the plaintiff from a particular risk. If not, recovery is barred because the case falls into the category of primary assumption of risk.]

As a general rule, persons have a duty to use due care to avoid injury to others, and may be held liable if their careless conduct injures another person. (See Civ. Code, § 1714.) Thus, for example, a property owner ordinarily is required to use due care to eliminate dangerous conditions on his or her property. (See, e.g., *Rowland v. Christian* (1968) 69 Cal. 2d 108, 70 Cal. Rptr. 97, 443 P.2d 561.) In the sports setting, however, conditions or conduct that otherwise might be viewed as dangerous often are an integral part of the sport itself. Thus, although moguls on a ski run pose a risk of harm to skiers that might not exist were these configurations removed, the challenge and risks posed by the moguls are part of the sport of skiing, and a ski resort has no duty to eliminate them. (See generally Annotation (1987) 55 *A.L.R.4th* 632.) In this respect, the nature of a sport is highly relevant in defining the duty of care owed by the particular defendant.

Although defendants generally have no legal duty to eliminate (or protect a plaintiff against) risks inherent in the sport itself, it is well established that defendants generally do have a duty to use due care not to increase the risks to a participant over and above those inherent in the sport. Thus, although a ski resort has no duty to remove moguls from a ski run, it clearly does have a duty to use due care to maintain its towropes in a safe, working condition so as not to expose skiers to an increased risk of harm. The cases establish that the latter type of risk, posed by a ski resort's negligence, clearly is not a risk (inherent in the sport) that is assumed by a participant. (See generally Annotation (1979) 95 *A.L.R.3d* 203.)

In some situations, however, the careless conduct of others is treated as an "inherent risk" of a sport, thus barring recovery by the plaintiff. For example, numerous cases recognize that in a game of baseball, a player generally cannot recover if he or she is hit and injured by a carelessly thrown ball (see, e.g., *Mann v. Nutrilite, Inc.* (1955) 136 Cal. App. 2d 729, 734-735, 289 P.2d 282), and that in a game of basketball, recovery is not permitted for an injury caused by a carelessly extended elbow (see, e.g., *Thomas v. Barlow* (1927) 5 N.J. Misc. 764, 138 A. 208). The divergent results of the foregoing cases lead naturally to the question how courts are to determine when careless conduct of another properly should be considered an "inherent risk" of the sport that (as a matter of law) is assumed by the injured participant. . . .

In the present case, defendant was a participant in the touch football game in which plaintiff was engaged at the time of her injury, and thus the question before us involves the circumstances under which a participant in such a sport may be held liable for an injury sustained by another participant.

The overwhelming majority of the cases, both within and outside California, that have addressed the issue of coparticipant liability in such a sport, have concluded that it is improper to hold a sports participant liable to a coparticipant for ordinary careless conduct committed during the sport—for example, for an injury resulting from a carelessly thrown ball or bat during a baseball game—and that liability properly may be imposed on a participant only when he or she intentionally injures another player or engages in reckless conduct that is totally outside the range of the ordinary activity involved in the sport. (See, e.g., *Gauvin v. Clark* (1989) 404 Mass. 450, 537 N.E.2d 94, 96-97 and cases cited.)

In reaching the conclusion that a coparticipant's duty of care should be limited in this fashion, the cases have explained that, in the heat of an active sporting event like baseball or football, a participant's normal energetic conduct often includes accidentally careless behavior. The courts have concluded that vigorous participation in such sporting events likely would be chilled if legal liability were to be imposed on a participant on the basis of his or her ordinary careless conduct. The cases have recognized that, in such a sport, even when a participant's conduct violates a rule of the game and may subject the violator to internal sanctions prescribed by the sport itself, imposition of *legal liability* for such conduct might well alter fundamentally the nature of the sport by deterring participants from vigorously engaging in activity that falls close to, but on the permissible side of, a prescribed rule.

A sampling of the cases that have dealt with the question of the potential tort liability of such sports participants is instructive. In *Tavernier v. Maes* (1966) 242 Cal. App. 2d 532, 51 Cal. Rptr. 575, for example, the Court of Appeal upheld a verdict denying recovery for an injury sustained by the plaintiff second baseman as an unintended consequence of the defendant baserunner's hard slide into second base during a family picnic softball game. Similarly, in *Gaspard v. Grain Dealers Mutual Insurance Company* (La. Ct. App. 1961) 131 So. 2d 831, the plaintiff baseball player was denied recovery when he was struck on the head by a bat which accidentally flew out of the hands of the defendant batter during a school game. (See also *Gauvin v. Clark* (1989) 404 Mass. 450, 537 N.E.2d 94, 96-97 [plaintiff hockey player injured when hit with hockey stick by opposing player; court held that defendant's liability should be determined by whether he acted "with reckless disregard of safety"]; *Marchetti v. Kalish* (1990) 53 Ohio St. 3d 95, 559 N.E.2d 699, 703 [child injured while playing "kick the can"; "we join the weight of authority . . . and require that before a party may proceed with a cause of action involving injury resulting from recreational or sports activity, reckless or intentional conduct must exist"]; *Kabella v. Bouschelle* (Ct. App. 1983) 100 N.M. 461, 465, 672 P.2d 290, 294 [plaintiff injured in informal tackle football game; court held that "a cause of action for personal injuries between participants incurred during athletic competition must be predicated upon recklessness or intentional conduct, 'not mere negligence' "]; *Ross v. Clouser* (Mo. 1982) 637 S.W.2d 11, 13-14 [plaintiff third baseman injured in collision with baserunner; court held that "a cause of action for personal injuries incurred during athletic competition must be predicated on recklessness, not mere negligence"]; *Moe v. Steenberg* (1966) 275 Minn. 448, 147 N.W.2d 587 [plaintiff ice skater denied recovery for injury incurred when another skater, who was skating backwards, accidentally tripped over her after she had fallen on the ice];. . .)

By contrast, in *Griggas v. Clauson* (1955) 6 Ill. App. 2d 412, 128 N.E.2d 363, the court upheld liability imposed on the defendant basketball player who, during a game, wantonly assaulted a player on the opposing team, apparently out of frustration with the progress of the game. And, in *Bourque v. Duplechin* (La. Ct. App. 1976) 331 So. 2d 40, the court affirmed a judgment imposing liability for an injury incurred during a baseball game when the defendant baserunner, in an ostensible attempt to break up a double play, ran into the plaintiff second baseman at full speed, without sliding, after the second baseman had thrown the ball to first base and was standing four to five feet away from second base toward the pitcher's mound; in upholding the judgment, the court stated that defendant "was under a duty to play softball in the ordinary fashion without unsportsmanlike conduct or wanton injury to his fellow players." (Id. at p. 42.) (See also *Averill v. Luttrell* (1957) 44 Tenn. App. 56, 311 S.W.2d 812 [defendant baseball catcher properly held liable when, deliberately and without warning, he hit a batter in the head with his fist]; *Hackbart v. Cincinnati Bengals, Inc.* (10th Cir. 1979) 601 F.2d 516 [trial court erred in absolving defendant football player of liability when, acting out of anger and frustration, he struck a blow with his forearm to the back of the head of an opposing player, who was kneeling on the ground watching the end of a pass interception play]; *Overall v. Kadella* (1984) 138 Mich. App. 351, 361 N.W.2d 352 [hockey player permitted to recover when defendant player intentionally punched him in the face at the conclusion of the game].)

In our view, the reasoning of the foregoing cases is sound. Accordingly, we conclude that a participant in an active sport breaches a legal duty of care to other participants—i.e., engages in conduct that properly may subject him or her to financial liability—only if the participant intentionally injures another player or engages in conduct

that is so reckless as to be totally outside the range of the ordinary activity involved in the sport.*

As applied to the present case, the foregoing legal principle clearly supports the trial court's entry of summary judgment in favor of defendant. The declarations filed in support of and in opposition to the summary judgment motion establish that defendant was, at most, careless or negligent in knocking over plaintiff, stepping on her hand, and injuring her finger. Although plaintiff maintains that defendant's rough play as described in her declaration and the declaration of Andrea Starr properly can be characterized as "reckless," the conduct alleged in those declarations is not even closely comparable to the kind of conduct—conduct so reckless as to be totally outside the range of the ordinary activity involved in the sport—that is a prerequisite to the imposition of legal liability upon a participant in such a sport.

Therefore, we conclude that defendant's conduct in the course of the touch football game did not breach any legal duty of care owed to plaintiff. Accordingly, this case falls within the primary assumption of risk doctrine, and thus the trial court properly granted summary judgment in favor of defendant. Because plaintiff's action is barred under the primary assumption of risk doctrine, comparative fault principles do not come into play.

The judgment of the Court of Appeal, upholding the summary judgment entered by the trial court, is affirmed.

---

*As suggested by the cases described in the text, the limited duty of care applicable to coparticipants has been applied in situations involving a wide variety of active sports, ranging from baseball to ice hockey and skating. Because the touch football game at issue in this case clearly falls within the rationale of this rule, we have no occasion to decide whether a comparable limited duty of care appropriately should be applied to other less active sports, such as archery or golf. We note that because of the special danger to others posed by the sport of hunting, past cases generally have found the ordinary duty of care to be applicable to hunting accidents. (See, e.g., *Summers v. Tice* (1948) 33 Cal. 2d 80, 83, 199 P.2d 1.)

ASSIGNMENT

17.7

a. What facts could Kendra have alleged about the touch football game that would have led the court to reach a different conclusion?

b. Ted and George are playing golf. Is Ted liable for negligence in any of the following situations:

   (i)   Ted is carelessly taking practice swings with his golf club while waiting to tee off. George says, "Watch out with that swing. You almost hit me." Laughing, Ted keeps swinging and accidently hits George in the head with the club.

   (ii) Ted and George have an argument over whether one of George's shots was over the foul line. In anger, Ted gets in the electric golf cart and drives away. Accidently, however, he drives the cart over George's foot.

   (iii) The golf course is next to a steep cliff. For fun, Ted and George decide to race the golf cart along the edge of the cliff. Ted is driving. The cart accidently goes over the cliff, injuring George.

c. The court also ruled that Jewett did not commit assault on Kendra. What facts could she have alleged to support her assault claim? (See Chapter 6 on assault.)

d. The court also ruled that Jewett did not commit battery on Kendra. What facts could she have alleged to support her battery claim? (See Chapter 5 on battery.)

SUMMARY

Under the defense of contributory negligence, the plaintiff's unreasonableness in taking risks for his or her own safety is a complete bar to recovery of damages if it was a substantial factor in causing the injury. If, however, the defendant was reckless or grossly negligent, the contributory negligence of the plaintiff did not bar recovery. Plaintiff's contributory negligence is determined by the same formula used to determine the defendant's negligence: the foreseeability of the accident and of the kind of injury or damage that could result is weighed against the importance or social utility of what plaintiff was doing at the time and the burden or inconvenience of taking precautions to avoid the accident. Under comparative negligence, damages are allocated according to the relative fault of the parties. Contributory negligence is no longer a complete defense.

Contributory negligence does not bar recovery of damages if the defendant had the last clear chance to avoid the injury but failed to take it. If the defendant discovers (or could discover) the plaintiff in helpless peril and fails to take reasonable steps to avoid the accident, the plaintiff's contributory negligence is not a bar. The same is true if the defendant discovers the plaintiff in inattentive peril. A state that has adopted comparative negligence does not need the defense of last clear chance. Since contributory negligence is no longer a complete bar, there is no longer a need for a defense that offsets the all-or-nothing impact of contributory negligence.

Comparative negligence apportions the damages between the plaintiff and the defendant based on the extent to which each acted unreasonably. In a state that has adopted pure comparative negligence, the plaintiff's recovery is limited to the percentage of the harm that was due to the defendant's negligence. In a state that has adopted restricted comparative negligence, there may be no recovery unless the plaintiff's negligence meets a designated standard, such as being "slight" as opposed to the "gross" negligence of the defendant.

The plaintiff recovers nothing if he or she knowingly and voluntarily accepted (i.e., assumed) the risk of being injured by the negligence of the defendant. There must be actual knowledge of the risk. Generally, parties are free to enter agreements that limit their liability with each other. In an express assumption of risk, the plaintiff knowingly and voluntarily accepts a risk by express agreement. In an implied assumption of risk, the plaintiff knowingly and voluntarily accepts a risk by reason of his or her knowledge and conduct. Both kinds of assumption must not violate public policy. Under comparative negligence the parties can still agree to an express assumption of risk. For implied assumption of risk, a further distinction is made. In primary assumption of risk, the plaintiff knowingly and voluntarily accepts a particular risk that the defendant did not have a duty to protect the plaintiff against. Plaintiff recovers nothing. In secondary assumption of risk, the plaintiff knowingly and voluntarily accepts a particular risk that the defendant had a duty to protect the plaintiff against. Damages are allocated between the plaintiff and the defendant according to their relative fault.

KEY TERMS

defense 304
comparative negligence 304
contributory negligence 304
last clear chance 304
assumption of the risk 304
ordinary negligence 305
reckless 305
gross negligence 305
unreasonable risks 305

cause in fact 307
avoidable consequences 307
helpless peril 308
inattentive peril 308
objective standard 309
subjective standard 309
express assumption of risk 310
implied assumption of risk 310
limitation of liability 311

coercion 311
public policy 311
release 311
exculpatory agreement 311
adhesion contracts 311
primary assumption of risk 315
secondary assumption of risk 316

18

Medical Malpractice and Legal Malpractice

CHAPTER OUTLINE

- Medical Malpractice
- Legal Malpractice

MEDICAL MALPRACTICE

Medical malpractice is often one of the major areas of a tort practice. It consists of professional misconduct or wrongdoing by medical practitioners such as doctors. A crusading personal injury attorney would say that there are many medical malpractice claims because there are many victims of medical incompetence. "Findings from several studies of large numbers of hospitalized patients indicate that each year a million or more people are injured and as many as 100,000 die as a result of errors in their care. This makes medical care one of the leading causes of death, accounting for more lost lives than automobile accidents, breast cancer or AIDS."[1] A cynic, on the other hand, would say the main reason medical malpractice is a large part of the practice of many attorneys is simply that doctors and hospitals are **deep pockets**—defendants who have resources (i.e., personal wealth and liability insurance) with which to pay a judgment.

According to a 1998 report of the Physician Insurers Association of America, just over 31 percent of all medical malpractice claims made between 1985 and 1998 resulted in a payout through settlement or litigation. (Almost a fourth of these payouts were OB-GYN claims.) When a payout did result, the average amount was $154,910. Payments of a million dollars or more rose from 8 percent of the claims in 1985 to 20 percent in 1997. The conditions leading to the largest number of medical malpractice claims are listed in Figure 18–1.[2]

Physician-Patient Relationship

A **physician-patient relationship** arises when a doctor undertakes to render medical services in response to an express or implied request for services by the patient or by the patient's guardian. The relationship does not come into existence simply because the doctor provides emergency medical care to an injured person. Yet, in providing such services, the doctor must use reasonable care.[3]

A doctor is not required to accept every patient. Once the physician-patient relationship exists, however, the doctor cannot withdraw at will. He or she must give reasonable notice of withdrawal so that the patient has an opportunity to find alternative treatment. On the other hand, the patient can end the relationship at any time by firing the doctor for any reason, but will remain responsible for the agreed-upon fee up to the time of termination.

Warranty

Normally a doctor does not warrant or promise a particular cure or other result. If such a **warranty** or promise is given, the patient has a breach-of-warranty or breach-of-contract action against the doctor if the result or cure is not produced. Although doctors are understandably reluctant to give express guarantees, they sometimes use language to their patients that a court will interpret as a guarantee. Suppose, for example, that a doctor makes the following statements to a patient about an operation:

---

[1]*Concerning Patient Safety and Medical Errors,* Statement of Harvard Professor Lucian Leape, M.D., before the Subcommittee on Labor, Health and Human Services, and Education, U.S. Senate, January 25, 2000 (http://www.apa.org/ppo/science/leape.html).
[2]Physician Insurers Association of America, *Risk Management Review of Malpractice* in *Special Section: Medical Malpractice Statistics,* 15 No. 11 Med. Malpractice L. & Strategy § 1 (Leader Publications, Sept. 1998) (WESTLAW cite in HTH-TP database: 15 No. 11 MED-MALLST S1). See also http://www.phyins.org.
[3]Office of the General Counsel, American Medical Association, *Medicolegal Forms with Legal Analysis* 1 (1973).

Condition Leading to Claim	Number of Claims	Average Payout
Brain-damaged infant	3,466	$477,968
Breast cancer	3,337	205,851
Pregnancy	2,417	127,959
Acute myocardial infarction	2,202	188,281
Displacement of intervertebral disc	2,087	185,484
Cancer of lung or bronchus	1,806	148,907
Fracture of femur	1,522	94,491
Appendicitis	1,519	89,885
Cataracts	1,459	108,267
Colorectal cancer	1,457	199,235
Back disorders	1,430	147,881
Abdominal/pelvic symptoms	1,355	130,871
Sterilization	1,341	53,634
Elective plastic surgery	1,216	59,629
Coronary atherosclerosis	1,199	161,352

FIGURE 18–1 Largest medical malpractice claims (1985–1998).

"The operation will take care of all your troubles."

"You'll be able to return to work in approximately three or four weeks at the most."

Such language could be interpreted as a promise to cure. If the patient is not cured, a breach-of-contract action may be successful against the doctor *even if the doctor was not negligent in performing the operation.*

A mere opinion by a doctor on the probable results of treatment is not a promise. It is sometimes very difficult, however, to distinguish between a prediction of probabilities and a promise.

Negligence

Doctors are not liable for every mistake they make that causes injury. There is no **strict liability,** or liability without fault, for the services of doctors, attorneys, or other professionals. Plaintiffs must show that their injury was wrongfully caused.

The main category of wrongful conduct in this area is **negligence,** which is harm caused by the failure to use reasonable care (see Chapters 12 and 14). Because doctors have specialized skill and knowledge, they are measured by what a reasonable doctor would have done with that specialized skill and knowledge. Simply stated, the standard is as follows:

A doctor must use the skill and learning commonly possessed by members of the profession in good standing.[4]

There is considerable controversy, however, as to whether this standard is to be gauged from a national or from a local perspective:

national standard: A doctor is required to have and use the equipment, knowledge, and experience that doctors have and use nationally.

local standard: A doctor is required to have and use the equipment, knowledge, and experience that doctors have and use locally or in localities similar to the community where the defendant-doctor practices.

In assessing reasonable care, one of the considerations of the court will be how other doctors commonly practice. What is the **custom** of sound medical practice

---

[4]W. Page Keeton et al., *Prosser and Keeton on the Law of Torts* 187 (5th ed. 1984).

for treating a particular ailment? To help a jury answer this question, expert witnesses are called, typically other doctors. If a state has adopted a national standard, an expert from anywhere in the country can testify. If, however, the state has adopted a local standard, a doctor from a big medical facility will not be allowed to give testimony on sound medical practice if the doctor being sued for malpractice is from a small rural town.

States that impose a local standard take the position that a doctor in a small community with limited resources should not be held to the standard of a doctor practicing in a large metropolitan area with access to state-of-the-art facilities and close to unlimited resources. Some doctors will understandably refuse to practice in rural areas of the country if they know that their mistakes will be judged by a standard they cannot meet because of the limited resources available to them.

There are strong arguments, however, in favor of a national standard, which a number of states impose. A national standard will tend to increase the quality of care a patient receives. Also a national standard is more likely to overcome a **conspiracy of silence,** which is the reluctance or refusal of one member of a group to testify against another member. In small communities where most doctors know each other and refer business to each other, an injured patient may find it difficult, if not impossible, to find a doctor willing to testify against another doctor. A national standard, on the other hand, would allow doctors from outside the community to testify. They arguably would be more willing to do so since they would not have the close personal and professional ties that doctors in the same small community have. Another argument in favor of a national standard is the fact that medical training for all doctors has become more standardized at a high level of skill. Furthermore, doctors everywhere are close to having equal access to the most current medical science through the Internet and other online resources.

Regardless of whether a state uses a local or a national standard, there still may be disagreement over the treatment that should be given in a given case. Schools of thought exist, as in any area. If there is more than one recognized method of diagnosis or treatment, and no one of them is used exclusively and uniformly by all practitioners in good standing, doctors, in the exercise of their best judgment, can select one of the approved methods. Negligence is not established simply because it turns out to be the wrong selection or because other doctors would have used other methods. Again, the test is reasonableness. If more than one approach is reasonable, doctors will not be liable if they make a mistake as long as diligence and good judgment were otherwise used in the method selected and applied.

Informed Consent

Doctors can commit a **battery** if they make physical contact with a part of the patient's body without consent or beyond the consent provided by the patient. Most cases, however, are decided under a negligence theory. The patient argues that there was no **informed consent** in that the doctor negligently failed to inform the patient of the risks involved in what was to be done. This failure allegedly prevented the patient from being able to make an intelligent decision on whether to seek the operation or treatment. The problem is serious. A recent study conducted by doctors reached the startling conclusion that only 1 of 10 patient decisions are based on informed consent. Patients were simply not told enough. In effect, something was missing from the doctor-patient discussions 90 percent of the time![5]

How much information on the benefits and risks of a proposed treatment must a doctor provide a patient? To tell the patient everything might take hours of explanation and reams of printed information. States differ on what a patient must be

---

[5]Clarence H. Braddock, et al., *Informed Decision Making in Outpatient Practice,* 282 Journal of the American Medical Association 2313 (December 22/29, 1999). *Study Shows Doctors are Lax in Giving Information to Patients,* N.Y. Times Nat'l Ed., Dec. 22, 1999, at A16.

told in order for his or her consent to be informed. Here are the two most commonly used tests:

reasonable patient standard: A doctor must disclose information on the risks and benefits of a proposed treatment that a reasonable patient with the plaintiff's condition would wish to know. In a state that adopts this standard, no expert witnesses would be needed on this issue since jurors are capable of concluding what a reasonable patient would want to know.

reasonable doctor standard: A doctor must follow the standards of the profession as to how much information on the risks and benefits of a proposed treatment would be disclosed to a patient in the plaintiff's condition. In a state that adopts this standard, expert witnesses would be needed to help the jury decide the standard practice of disclosure by doctors.

If a case is litigated, the two tests could lead to different results. It is possible for a reasonable doctor to withhold information that a reasonable patient would have wanted to know. When this occurs, the patient would lose in a state that has adopted the reasonable doctor standard.[6]

Consent forms are often used by doctors and hospitals as a way of providing information and avoiding liability. At times, however, these forms are inadequate. Suppose that a woman consents to a simple appendectomy. The surgeon, however, performs a total hysterectomy as a precautionary measure, because he feels that it would be a sound medical procedure even though no emergency existed. Before the operation, the woman signed the following statement:

"I hereby authorize the physician in charge to administer such treatment as found necessary to perform this operation which is advisable in the treatment of this patient."

A court would probably find this consent form to be invalid. It is very ambiguous. It does not designate the nature of the operation and therefore does not state what is being consented to. It is close to a blanket authorization to do whatever the doctor thinks is wise.

Suppose that the condition of the patient is such that it would be dangerous to inform him or her of all the details of a proposed treatment. Or suppose that the doctor discovers an unanticipated emergency after the patient is under anesthesia and an incision has been made. How is consent to be handled in these situations? A court will examine all of the circumstances in order to determine whether it was reasonable for the doctor not to obtain consent or even to ask for it. The factors to be considered include: the seriousness of the patient's condition, the patient's emotional stability, the availability of time, the extent of the emergency, the practice in the medical community in such cases. A court might conclude that it was reasonable for the doctor to proceed without consent.

Reform

In the 1980s, the country faced what was called a medical malpractice crisis; some feel that the crisis is still with us. One way to gauge whether this is so is to look at the cost of liability insurance that doctors and hospitals buy to protect themselves against medical malpractice suits. In 1960, doctors and hospitals paid under $100 million for liability insurance. In the late 1990s, they were paying nearly $10 billion annually, an increase of about 10,000 percent.[7] In some areas of the country, doctors have withdrawn from certain high-risk kinds of practice (e.g., delivering babies) because of the frequency of litigation and the high cost of malpractice insurance associated with those areas of practice.

---

[6]Kenneth S. Abraham, *The Forms and Functions of Tort Law* 77 (1997).
[7]Id. at 70.

Many blame the legal system for a large part of the skyrocketing cost of health care. Doctors, for example, allegedly order expensive tests solely to make them "look good" in court in the event of a later malpractice suit by a patient. This is known as the practice of **defensive medicine**—the ordering of precautionary tests and procedures intended primarily to shield doctors from possible lawsuits. Studies have shown that liability premiums and defensive medical measures are a significant part of the cost of every visit to a doctor or medical facility.[8]

Insurance companies are particularly angry about the system of compensating attorneys through the **percentage fee.** This kind of fee gives attorneys a percentage of any payout through settlement or litigation their clients obtain. The large amount of the percentage (e.g., 30–40 percent) arguably causes attorneys to be excessively aggressive in pursuing litigation for their clients. Attorneys, on the other hand, deny that there is a malpractice insurance crisis, arguing that if there is a problem, it is due primarily to greedy insurance companies and incompetent doctors and hospitals.

The turmoil has led to reform proposals in every state. There is a great diversity in the kinds of reforms that different states have enacted or considered. Here are some examples:

- Limiting damage awards (**damage caps**). The state would limit the amount of damages that can be awarded in a medical malpractice lawsuit. Typically, a state might limit the amount of a plaintiff's non-economic damages, such as pain and suffering, to between $250,000 and $500,000.
- Limiting attorney fees (**fee caps**). A state might limit the percentage of the recovery a plaintiff's attorney can receive as a fee.
- Allowing **collateral source** offsets. A collateral source is an amount of money an injured party receives independent of the tortfeasor (see Chapter 16). An example would be payments an injured plaintiff pedestrian receives from a medical insurance policy provided by an employer. Under the traditional rule, a tortfeasor cannot seek the reduction of damages by amounts received from collateral sources. Juries are not even allowed to be told that collateral sources exist. There are some states, however, that have changed this rule and now permit amounts received from some collateral sources to be deducted from (offset by) the total damages caused by the tortfeasor.
- Requiring cooling-off periods. To encourage negotiation and settlement between the parties, some states enforce a cooling-off period (e.g., ninety days) during which litigation cannot begin. A malpractice claimant must give the doctor or hospital a formal notice of intent to file a suit. During the cooling-off period, the **statute of limitations** does not run—it is **tolled**—so that the plaintiff is not placed at a disadvantage by waiting to file. The statute of limitations is a law that designates a time period within which a lawsuit must be commenced or it can never be brought.
- Requiring **alternative dispute resolution** (ADR). A state may require the parties to attempt to resolve their dispute by using alternative dispute resolution before being allowed to litigate in court. ADR can take a number of formats. The state might have a system of **screening panels** that try to weed out frivolous cases before they are brought to court for trial. A panel could consist of a group of neutral attorneys and physicians who examine the evidence, consult with medical experts, and decide whether the patient was a victim of negligence. The panel may encourage settlement or dismissal of the claim. More traditional forms of ADR are mediation and arbitration. In **mediation,** parties bring their dispute before a neutral third party—the mediator—who hears the arguments from both sides and encourages the parties to resolve the matter on their own. The mediator does not render a decision. In **arbitration,** on the other hand, the parties

---

[8]Physician Insurers Association of America, supra note 2.

bring their dispute before a neutral third party—the arbitrator—who hears the arguments from both sides and renders a decision. None of these ADR proceedings are binding. They are simply steps the parties are required to try before they are allowed to bring their medical malpractice case before a court.

- Providing more information about doctors. To keep track of (and to help weed out) incompetent or unprofessional doctors, particularly those who move from one state to another, a **National Practitioner Data Bank** was created to collect information about doctors who had been defendants in malpractice cases and who had paid claimants through settlement or litigation. A hospital is required to check the information in the Data Bank whenever a doctor seeks appointment or reappointment to its medical staff.

- Adopting the **English rule.** To discourage the filing of frivolous malpractice lawsuits, one state has adopted the English rule under which the party who loses the trial must pay both parties' attorney fees and other legal expenses. With some exceptions, most of our courts follow the American rule under which each side pays its own legal expenses.

- Imposing limited **no-fault systems** of medical malpractice. Under no-fault, a victim of medical incompetence (malpractice) receives compensation from insurance whether or not negligence or fault can be proven. In the few states that have experimented with no-fault, it is applied in only limited kinds of cases such as those involving brain-damaged newborns.

- Considering **enterprise liability.** One of the most radical proposals is called enterprise liability. It would allow injured patients to sue either the hospital where they were treated or the health plans to which doctors and other providers subscribe. Individual doctors would no longer be subject to malpractice lawsuits. One variation on this proposal would permit courts to hold health plans strictly liable for all medical injuries suffered by their beneficiaries, regardless of whether the injury was a result of negligent care. The more traditional enterprise liability proposal, however, would require a determination of negligence before a hospital's managed care organization would be held liable for a patient's injury. Enterprise liability has not been enacted to date.[9]

The turmoil—along with proposals for further change and reform—continues today.

CASE

Fein v. Permanente Medical Group
38 Cal. 3d 137, 211 Cal. Rptr. 368, 695 P.2d 665 (1985)
Supreme Court of California

Background: *A nurse practitioner and a doctor told the plaintiff that his chest pains were muscle spasms. Valium and other drugs were prescribed. In fact, the plaintiff was suffering a heart attack. In a medical malpractice action, he alleged negligence in the diagnosis. He was successful in the trial court. The case is now before the Supreme Court of California on appeal.*

Decision on Appeal: *Judgment affirmed.*

OPINION OF COURT
Justice KAUS delivered the opinion of the court . . .

On Saturday, February 21, 1976, plaintiff Lawrence Fein, a 34-year-old attorney employed by the Legislative Counsel Bureau of the California State Legislature in Sacramento, felt a brief pain in his chest as he was riding his bicycle to work. The pain lasted a minute or two. He noticed a similar brief pain the following day while he was jogging, and then, three days later, experienced another episode while walking after lunch. When the chest pain returned again while he was working at his office that evening, he became concerned for his health and, the following morning, called the office of his regular physician, Dr. Arlene Brandwein, who was employed by defendant Permanente Medical Group, an affiliate of the Kaiser Health Foundation (Kaiser).

[9]Risa B. Greene, *Federal Legislative Proposals for Medical Malpractice Reform: Treating the Symptoms or Effecting a Cure?* 4 Cornell Journal of Law and Public Policy 563 (Spring, 1995).

Dr. Brandwein had no open appointment available that day, and her receptionist advised plaintiff to call Kaiser's central appointment desk for a "short appointment." He did so and was given an appointment for 4 P.M. that afternoon, Thursday, February 26. Plaintiff testified that he did not feel that the problem was so severe as to require immediate treatment at Kaiser Hospital's emergency room, and that he worked until the time for his scheduled appointment.

When he appeared for his appointment, plaintiff was examined by a nurse practitioner, Cheryl Welch, who was working under the supervision of a physician-consultant, Dr. Wintrop Frantz; plaintiff was aware that Nurse Welch was a nurse practitioner and he did not ask to see a doctor. After examining plaintiff and taking a history, Nurse Welch left the room to consult with Dr. Frantz. When she returned, she advised plaintiff that she and Dr. Frantz believed his pain was due to muscle spasm and that the doctor had given him a prescription for Valium. Plaintiff went home, took the Valium, and went to sleep.

That night, about 1 A.M., plaintiff awoke with severe chest pains. His wife drove him to the Kaiser emergency room where he was examined by Dr. Lowell Redding about 1:30 A.M. Following an examination that the doctor felt showed no signs of a heart problem, Dr. Redding ordered a chest X-ray. On the basis of his examination and the X-ray results, Dr. Redding also concluded that plaintiff was experiencing muscle spasms and gave him an injection of Demerol and a prescription for a codeine medication.

Plaintiff went home but continued to experience intermittent chest pain. About noon that same day, the pain became more severe and constant and plaintiff returned to the Kaiser emergency room where he was seen by another physician, Dr. Donald Oliver. From his initial examination of plaintiff, Dr. Oliver also believed that plaintiff's problem was of muscular origin, but, after administering some pain medication, he directed that an electrocardiogram (EKG) be performed. The EKG showed that plaintiff was suffering from a heart attack (acute myocardial infarction). Plaintiff was then transferred to the cardiac care unit.

Following a period of hospitalization and medical treatment without surgery, plaintiff returned to his job on a part-time basis in October 1976, and resumed full-time work in September 1977. By the time of trial, he had been permitted to return to virtually all of his prior recreational activities—e.g., jogging, swimming, bicycling and skiing.

In February 1977, plaintiff filed the present action, alleging that his heart condition should have been diagnosed earlier and that treatment should have been given either to prevent the heart attack or, at least, to lessen its residual effects. The case went to judgment only against Permanente.

At trial, Dr. Harold Swan, the head of cardiology at the Cedars-Sinai Medical Center in Los Angeles, was the principal witness for plaintiff. Dr. Swan testified that an important signal that a heart attack may be imminent is chest pain which can radiate to other parts of the body. Such pain is not relieved by rest or pain medication. He stated that if the condition is properly diagnosed, a patient can be given Inderal to stabilize his condition, and that continued medication or surgery may relieve the condition.

Dr. Swan further testified that in his opinion any patient who appears with chest pains should be given an EKG to rule out the worst possibility, a heart problem. He stated that

the symptoms that plaintiff had described to Nurse Welch at the 4 P.M. examination on Thursday, February 26, should have indicated to her that an EKG was in order. He also stated that when plaintiff returned to Kaiser late that same night with his chest pain unrelieved by the medication he had been given, Dr. Redding should also have ordered an EKG. According to Dr. Swan, if an EKG had been ordered at those times it could have revealed plaintiff's imminent heart attack, and treatment could have been administered which might have prevented or minimized the attack.

Dr. Swan also testified to the damage caused by the attack. He stated that as a result of the attack a large portion of plaintiff's heart muscle had died, reducing plaintiff's future life expectancy by about one-half, to about 16 or 17 years. Although Dr. Swan acknowledged that some of plaintiff's other coronary arteries also suffer from disease, he felt that if plaintiff had been properly treated his future life expectancy would be decreased by only 10 to 15 percent, rather than half.

Nurse Welch and Dr. Redding testified on behalf of the defense, indicating that the symptoms that plaintiff had reported to them at the time of the examinations were not the same symptoms he had described at trial. Defendant also introduced a number of expert witnesses—not employed by Kaiser—who stated that on the basis of the symptoms reported and observed before the heart attack, the medical personnel could not reasonably have determined that a heart attack was imminent. Additional defense evidence indicated (1) that an EKG would not have shown that a heart attack was imminent, (2) that because of the severe disease in the coronary arteries which caused plaintiff's heart attack, the attack could not have been prevented even had it been known that it was about to occur, and finally (3) that, given the deterioration in plaintiff's other coronary arteries, the heart attack had not affected plaintiff's life expectancy to the degree suggested by Dr. Swan.

In the face of this sharply conflicting evidence, the jury found in favor of plaintiff on the issue of liability and, pursuant to the trial court's instructions, returned special verdicts itemizing various elements of damages. The jury awarded $24,733 for wages lost by plaintiff to the time of trial, $63,000 for future medical expenses, and $700,000 for wages lost in the future as a result of the reduction in plaintiff's life expectancy. Finally, the jury awarded $500,000 for "noneconomic damages," to compensate for pain, suffering, inconvenience, physical impairment and other intangible damages sustained by plaintiff from the time of the injury until his death. . . .

[One of the issues on appeal is whether the trial judge properly instructed the jury in the duty of care owed by a nurse practitioner. The judge] told the jury that "the standard of care required of a nurse practitioner is that of a physician and surgeon . . . when the nurse practitioner is examining a patient or making a diagnosis."*

---

*The relevant instruction read in full: "It is the duty of one who undertakes to perform the service of a trained or graduate nurse to have the knowledge and skill ordinarily possessed, and to exercise the care and skill ordinarily used in like cases, by trained and skilled members of the nursing profession practicing their profession in the same or similar locality and under similar circumstances. Failure to fulfill either of these duties is negligence. I instruct you that the standard of care required of a nurse practitioner is that of a physician and surgeon duly licensed to practice medicine in the state of California when the nurse practitioner is examining a patient or making a diagnosis." . . .

We agree with defendant that this instruction is inconsistent with recent legislation setting forth general guidelines for the services that may properly be performed by registered nurses in this state. Section 2725 of the Business and Professions Code . . . explicitly declares a legislative intent "to recognize the existence of overlapping functions between physicians and registered nurses and to permit additional sharing of functions within organized health care systems which provide for collaboration between physicians and registered nurses." Section 2725 also includes, among the functions that properly fall within "the practice of nursing" in California, the "[o]bservation of signs and symptoms of illness, reactions to treatment, general behavior, or general physical condition, and . . . determination of whether such signs, symptoms, reactions, behavior or general appearance exhibit abnormal characteristics. . . ." In light of these provisions, the "examination" or "diagnosis" of a patient cannot in all circumstances be said—as a matter of law—to be a function reserved to physicians, rather than registered nurses or nurse practitioners. Although plaintiff was certainly entitled to have the jury determine (1) whether defendant medical center was negligent in permitting a nurse practitioner to see a patient who exhibited the symptoms of which plaintiff complained and (2) whether Nurse Welch met the standard of care of a reasonably prudent nurse practitioner in conducting the examination and prescribing treatment in conjunction with her supervising physician, the court should not have told the jury that the nurse's conduct in this case must as a matter of law be measured by the standard of care of a physician or surgeon. (See *Fraijo v. Hartland Hospital* (1979) 99 Cal. App. 3d 331, 340–344, *White—New Approaches in Treating Nurses as Professionals* (1977) 30 Vand. Law Review 839, 871–879.)

But while the instruction was erroneous, it is not reasonably probable that the error affected the judgment in this case. As noted, several hours after Nurse Welch examined plaintiff and gave him the Valium that her supervising doctor had prescribed, plaintiff returned to the medical center with similar complaints and was examined by a physician, Dr. Redding. Although there was considerable expert testimony that the failure of the medication to provide relief and the continued chest pain rendered the diagnosis of muscle spasm more questionable, Dr. Redding—like Nurse Welch—failed to order an EKG. Given these facts, the jury could not reasonably have found Nurse Welch negligent under the physician standard of care without also finding Dr. Redding—who had more information and to whom the physician standard of care was properly applicable—similarly negligent. Defendant does not point to any evidence which suggests that the award in this case was affected by whether defendant's liability was grounded solely on the negligence of Dr. Redding, rather than on the negligence of both Dr. Redding and Nurse Welch, and, from our review of the record, we conclude that it is not reasonably probable that the instructional error affected the judgment. Accordingly, the erroneous instruction on the standard of care of a nurse practitioner does not warrant reversal. . . .

ASSIGNMENT

18.1

a. 1. What was the error committed by the trial judge on the standard of care of a nurse practitioner?

   2. Why was it an error?

   3. Why was this error harmless?

b. If an EKG had been administered the first time Lawrence Fein contacted the Permanente hospital system, could the hospital have been accused of practicing defensive medicine and thereby contributing to the cost of health care, now so high that millions of Americans are underinsured and uninsured?

c. Nurses have a relationship to doctors that is similar to the relationship of paralegals to attorneys. What implications does the *Fein* case have for paralegals?

Interrogatories

Once litigation has commenced, pretrial discovery is used by the parties to learn about each others' cases in order to prepare for trial (see Chapter 3). One of the major discovery devices is **written interrogatories,** which are a series of written questions sent by one party to another. The answers are given in writing under oath. See Figure 3–14 in Chapter 3.

Reading interrogatories is an excellent way to understand the kind of factual detail that parties seek in medical malpractice cases. Figure 18–2 contains a set of sample interrogatories that a hospital defendant might send to the plaintiff.[10]

---

[10]Uniform Medical Malpractice Interrogatories, 17B Arizona Revised Statutes.

FIGURE 18–2
Sample medical malpractice interrogatories sent by a defendant hospital to plaintiff(s).

These interrogatories should be answered to provide information regarding each person claiming damages in this action and also regarding the decedent if a wrongful death action.

I. GENERAL INFORMATION AND BACKGROUND

1. A. State your full name, address, and date of birth.
    B. State any and all other names which you have ever used or by which you have been known.
2. A. Which of the following is your present marital status: single, married, separated, widowed, or divorced.
    B. State the name and last known address of your spouse and every former spouse.
    C. State the date of each such marriage.
    D. As to previous marriages, please give the date, place, and manner of each termination.
    E. State the name, age, and address of each of your children.
3. Have you ever been a party to a civil lawsuit? _____ . If so, state:
    A. Were you plaintiff or defendant.
    B. What was the nature of the plaintiff's claim.
    C. When, where, and in what court was the action commenced.
    D. The names of all parties other than yourself.
4. Have you ever been convicted of a felony? _____ . If so, state:
    A. What was the original charge made against you.
    B. What was the charge of which you were convicted.
    C. Did you plead guilty to the charge, or were you convicted after trial.
    D. What was the name and address of the court where the proceedings took place.
    E. Date of conviction or date plea entered.

II. EDUCATION, EMPLOYMENT, ACTIVITIES, AND IMPAIRMENT

5. State the highest grade of formal schooling completed by you and any certificate or degrees received.
6. List each job or position of employment, including self-employment, held by you on the date of and since the incident in question, stating as to each:
    A. Name and address of employer.
    B. Date of commencement and date of termination.
    C. Nature of employment and duties performed.
    D. Name and address of immediate supervisor.
    E. Rate of pay or compensation received.
    F. The reason for termination.
7. List each job or position of employment, including self-employment, held by you for the five (5) years before the incident in question, stating as to each:
    A. Name and address of employer.
    B. Date of commencement and date of termination.
    C. Place of employment.
    D. Nature of employment and duties performed.
    E. Name and address of immediate supervisor.
    F. Rate of pay or compensation received.
    G. Reason for termination.
8. Do you claim to have lost any time from gainful employment as a result of the incident in question? _____ . If so, state:
    A. The specific condition which you claim caused the loss of time.
    B. The amount of time lost.
    C. The rate of pay or compensation regularly received from each such gainful employment.
    D. If you claim damage as a result of the time lost, the total amount and your method of computation.

FIGURE 18–2   Continued

E. Whether or not you have in your possession or control any records or other written memoranda which show or purport to show any or all of the amount of your income for the five (5) years preceding the incident complained of to the present time, including a brief description of each such record or memorandum and the person having possession or control of the same or any copy thereof.

9. Do you claim your earning capacity will be impaired as a result of the incident complained of? _____ . If so, state:

   A. The manner in which the condition will impair your ability to work.

   B. Name and address of each person who had advised you concerning the impairment.

10. Have you received any special education or training for any type of work? _____ . If so, state:

    A. The names and addresses of the training or education institutions attended and the dates of attendance.

    B. The names, addresses, and inclusive dates of employment by employers from whom you received on-the-job training.

11. Do you claim that as a result of the incident complained of you have lost any opportunities for advancement or promotion in your employment? _____ . If so, state:

    A. What opportunities would have been available had the incident complained of not occurred.

    B. When would each opportunity have been available.

    C. The amount of monetary damages you allege you have lost as a result of said lost opportunity.

III. INVESTIGATION

12. Have you or your attorney interviewed or spoken with any defendant, or its agents, servants, or employees, about the events in question? _____ . If so, state who was present, when and where such conversation took place and the substance of any such conversations including, but not limited to, any statement or admission made by a defendant.

13. Are you aware of the existence of any oral, written, or recorded statement or admission made or claimed to have been made, by any party or witness? _____ . If so, state:

    A. The name of each person making the statement or admission.

    B. The date of the statement or admission.

    C. The name, employer, occupation, and last known address of the person or persons taking or hearing the statement or admission.

    D. The name and last known address of the person now in possession of a written or recorded admission.

IV. INJURIES AND DAMAGES

14. Describe in detail all injuries, complaints, and symptoms, whether physical, mental, or emotional, each person claiming damages in this action has experienced since the alleged incident and which is claimed to have been caused, aggravated, or otherwise contributed to by the alleged incident.

15. Do you claim any of your injuries are permanent? _____ . If so, state:

    A. What, if any, pains do you contend such injuries will cause in the future.

    B. What do you contend will be the course of such pains.

    C. What, if any, disabilities do you contend such injuries will cause.

    D. What do you contend will be the course of such disabilities.

    E. The name, profession, and specialty, if any, of any medical practitioner who has provided you with any of the information given in answers (A) through (D).

V. PRIOR AND SUBSEQUENT INJURIES/TREATMENT

16. Have you been hospitalized since the occurrence? _____ . If so, state:

    A. The person [hospitalized].

FIGURE 18–2 Continued

B. The name and location of each hospital in which each was confined.

C. The dates of each hospitalization.

D. The conditions treated during each hospitalization.

E. The nature of the treatment rendered during each hospitalization.

17. Has any health care provider or any person claiming damages in this action criticized defendant's care or treatment given you? _____ . If so, for each criticism, state:

    A. A description of it.

    B. The name, address, and qualifications of the person who made the criticism.

    C. The date, time, and place it was made.

18. List each injury, symptom, or complaint for which damages are claimed in this action from which you suffered at any time before the incident complained of.

19. State:

    A. The name and address of each health care provider who examined or treated you for any physical or emotional condition during the past ten years.

    B. The conditions or complaints for which the examination or treatment was performed.

    C. The date of each examination or treatment performed.

    D. Whether or not the symptoms evidencing the conditions described in your answer to paragraph (B) of this interrogatory were completely relieved and, if so, the date of relief.

20. Since the incident complained of, have you suffered any injuries, accidental or otherwise? _____ . If so, state:

    A. The date and place.

    B. How the injury was sustained.

    C. A detailed description of each injury received.

    D. The name and address of each medical practitioner rendering treatment.

    E. If any permanent disability was suffered, its nature and extent.

    F. If you were compensated in any manner for any such injury, state the name and address of each person or organization against whom a claim was made or from whom payments were received.

21. Have you ever made any claim against anyone, group, organization, corporation, industrial commission, or any entity for any reason? _____ . If so, state:

    A. If the claim was filed as a lawsuit, what was the style of the case.

    B. If the claim was not filed in court, with whom was it filed.

    C. Has the claim been adjudicated or settled as yet.

    D. If the answer to (C) above is in the affirmative, how much money did you receive.

22. Please identify each health care provider who has records pertaining to plaintiff(s) for the period of seven years before the incident giving rise to plaintiff(s)' claims through the present.

    A. With respect to each provider identified above, state whether plaintiff(s) will obtain and produce the records. . . .

    B. With respect to any records plaintiff(s) will not obtain and produce. . ., state the specific reason or reasons for nonproduction.

VI. MATTERS CONCERNING THE CONDUCT OF DEFENDANT(S)

23. In your Complaint you have characterized certain acts or conduct on the part of the defendant(s) as below the standard of care. As to such acts and conduct, state:

    A. Each specific act or acts, failure or failures to act by the defendant(s) which fell below the standard of care.

    B. Specifically what conduct you claim would have complied with the standard of care.

FIGURE 18–2 Continued

   C. Each and every fact upon which you rely when you claim:
     1. That this defendant negligently performed its professional duties to you.
     2. That this defendant's negligent performance of its professional duties to you proximately caused your injury.

24. Do you allege that any agent, servant, or employee of this defendant violated or failed to follow any rule, regulation, policy, or procedure of the hospital or some other authority? _____ . If so, state:
   A. The identity of said rule, regulation, policy, or procedure.
   B. How and by whom you allege said rule, regulation, policy, or procedure was violated.
   C. How you allege said violation proximately caused injury to the plaintiff.

25. Do you contend that any agent, servant, or employee of this defendant neglected to inform, instruct, or warn you as to any matters relating to your condition, care, or treatment? _____ . If so, for each matter, state:
   A. A description of what agent, servant, or employee of this defendant neglected to inform, instruct, or warn you.
   B. Whether such failure or neglect contributed to any injury of which you complain, and if so, in what way and to what extent.

26. Do you know of any person who is skilled in any particular field or science whom you may call as a witness at trial of this action and who has expressed an opinion upon any issue of this action? _____ . If so, state:
   A. The name and address of each person.
   B. The field or science in which each such person is sufficiently skilled to enable him [or her] to express opinion evidence in this action.
   C. A complete list of all medical malpractice actions in which each person has rendered an opinion, whether by written report, deposition testimony, or trial testimony, including:
     1. The name of the case.
     2. The court in which filed.
     3. The docket number assigned.
     4. Whether each person rendered his [or her] opinion by written report, deposition testimony, trial testimony, or a combination thereof.
   D. Whether such person will base his [or her] opinion:
     1. In whole or in part upon facts acquired personally by him [or her] in the course of an investigation or examination of any of the issues of this case, or
     2. Solely upon information as to facts provided him [or her] by others.
   E. If your answer to Interrogatory No. 26(D) discloses that any such person has made a personal investigation or examination relating to any of the issues of this case, state the nature and dates of such investigation or examination.
   F. Each and every fact, and each and every document, item, photograph, or other tangible object supplied or made available to such person.
   G. The general subject upon which each person may express an opinion.
   H. The substance of the facts and opinions to which such person is expected to testify.
   I. Whether such persons have rendered written reports. If so, state:
     1. The dates of each report.
     2. The name and address of the custodian of such reports.

VII. DAMAGES

27. State each and every expense, debt, or obligation you have incurred, amount expended, and item of special damage you will claim at trial as a result of the injuries or conditions listed in your answer to these Interrogatories other than that itemized in your answer to the foregoing Interrogatories. This Interrogatory inquires as to, but is not limited to: medical expense, ambulance expense, transportation expense, physiotherapist expense, psychologist fees, psychiatric fees, laboratory charges, hospital costs, and x-ray costs.

FIGURE 18–2 Continued

VIII. WITNESSES AND EXHIBITS

28. With respect to every lay witness whom you intend to or may call to testify, please state:
    A. The name, address, occupation, and employer of each such person.
    B. What information or facts such person has provided or communicated to you.
    C. What knowledge or information do you believe the witness has with respect to the matters which are at issue in this lawsuit.
    D. The subject about which such witness will or may testify, i.e., liability, damages, injuries, etc.
    E. The substance of the testimony of each witness.
29. List the names, addresses, official titles, if any, and other identification of all witnesses not previously identified who, it is contemplated, will be called upon to testify in support of your claim in this action at trial indicating the nature and substance of the testimony which is expected will be given by each such witness, and stating the relationship, if any, to the plaintiff.
30. List specifically and in detail each and every exhibit you propose to utilize at trial in this matter. This interrogatory is directed both to exhibits you intend to use at trial and exhibits you may use.
31. At the time of trial, do you intend to use or refer to any medical textbook, periodical, or other medical publication during direct examination of your witnesses? _____ . If your answer is in the affirmative, provide the citation for any text or periodical you intend to use.

IX. COLLATERAL SOURCE

32. Have you received, are you now receiving, or are you entitled to receive, collateral source benefits?_____ If so, please state:
    A. The amount of each and every payment.
    B. Schedule or frequency of such payments/benefits.
    C. If the payments have stopped, the date and reason the payments stopped.
    D. If the payments are still being received, the length of time you expect to receive these payments.
    E. If the benefits are stopped at some future time, please state when and under what circumstances the payments will terminate.
    F. The amount of payments you expect to receive in the future.

X. MISCELLANEOUS

33. Has plaintiff entered into any agreement or agreements or covenants with any other person or entity in any way compromising, settling, or in any way limiting such person's or entity's liability or potential liability for any part of the claim arising out of the occurrence alleged in plaintiff's Complaint? _____ . If so, state:
    A. The name and address of each person or entity with whom such agreement or covenant was made.
    B. State the date of each such agreement or covenant.
    C. Are the agreements or covenants in writing? _____ . If so, state the name and address of the individual who has custody and control of a copy of each such agreement or covenant.
    D. What are the terms of each such agreement or covenant.
    E. What was the consideration paid for each such agreement or covenant.
34. Has plaintiff asserted any claim against any person or entity, not a named party to this lawsuit, for any part of the loss or damage arising out of the occurrence alleged in plaintiff's Complaint? _____ . If so, state:
    A. The name and last known address of each such person or entity.
    B. State briefly the basis upon which the claim was asserted.
35. Does any insurance company or any other person or organization have any interest in this action or any recovery herein by way of subrogation, assignment, trust receipt, or otherwise, or has any such claim been asserted? _____ . If so, state the name and address of each such company, other person, or organization and the nature and amount of any such claimed interest.

FIGURE 18–2   Concluded

36. Do you contend that any of this defendant's entries in the medical records are incorrect or inaccurate? _____ . If so, state:
    A. The precise entry (entries) that you think is incorrect or inaccurate.
    B. What you contend the correct or accurate entry (entries) should have been.
    C. The name, address, and employer of each and every person who has knowledge pertaining to (A) and (B).
    D. A description, including the author and title of each and every document that you claim supports your answers to (A) and (B).
    E. The name, address, and telephone number of each and every person you intend to call as a witness in support of your contention.

37. List the names, addresses, official titles, if any, and other identification of all persons, not previously identified, who:
    A. Were present at the events in question.
    B. Claim to have information concerning the events in question.
    C. Are reported to have information concerning the events in question.
    D. Have knowledge of any pre-existing medical problems or medical treatment received by plaintiff(s) prior to the events in question.
    E. Have knowledge of medical problems or medical treatment received by plaintiff(s) from the events in question up to the present time.
    F. Participated in any investigation concerning the incident in question or of any party or witness thereto.

    Please set forth the subject and substance of the information each such person claims to have.

LEGAL MALPRACTICE

Legal malpractice refers to professional misconduct or wrongdoing by attorneys, primarily negligence. As we have seen, negligence is the failure to use reasonable care (see Chapters 12 and 14). Because attorneys have specialized skill and knowledge, they are measured by what a reasonable attorney would have done with that skill and knowledge. Attorneys, like doctors, must use the skill and learning commonly possessed by members of the profession in good standing. Liability for negligence will not automatically result when an attorney makes a mistake or loses the case. Unless the attorney specifically guarantees a result, the standard of care will be reasonableness, not warranty. Expressed in greater detail, the standard is as follows:[11]

> Ordinarily when an attorney engages in the practice of the law and contracts to prosecute an action in behalf of his client, he impliedly represents that (1) he possesses the requisite degree of learning, skill, and ability necessary to the practice of his profession and which others similarly situated ordinarily possess; (2) he will exert his best judgment in the prosecution of the litigation entrusted to him; and (3) he will exercise reasonable and ordinary care and diligence in the use of his skill and in the application of his knowledge to his client's cause.

> An attorney who acts in good faith and in an honest belief that his advice and acts are well founded and in the best interest of his client is not answerable for a mere error of judgment or for a mistake in a point of law which has not been settled by the court of last resort in his State and on which reasonable doubt may be entertained by well-informed lawyers.

> Conversely, he is answerable in damages for any loss to his client which proximately results from a want of that degree of knowledge and skill ordinarily possessed by others of his profession similarly situated, or from the omission

---

[11]*Hodges v. Carter*, 239 N.C. 517, 519–20, 80 S.E.2d 144, 145–46 (1954).

FIGURE 18–3
Professional liability claims against law firms by error group.

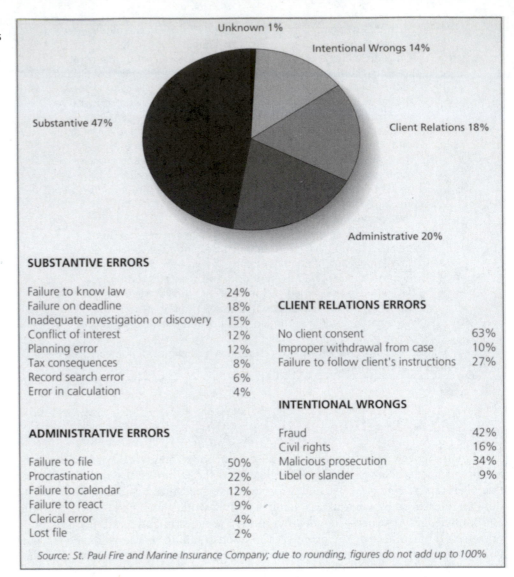

SUBSTANTIVE ERRORS

Failure to know law	24%
Failure on deadline	18%
Inadequate investigation or discovery	15%
Conflict of interest	12%
Planning error	12%
Tax consequences	8%
Record search error	6%
Error in calculation	4%

ADMINISTRATIVE ERRORS

Failure to file	50%
Procrastination	22%
Failure to calendar	12%
Failure to react	9%
Clerical error	4%
Lost file	2%

CLIENT RELATIONS ERRORS

No client consent	63%
Improper withdrawal from case	10%
Failure to follow client's instructions	27%

INTENTIONAL WRONGS

Fraud	42%
Civil rights	16%
Malicious prosecution	34%
Libel or slander	9%

Source: St. Paul Fire and Marine Insurance Company; due to rounding, figures do not add up to 100%

to use reasonable care and diligence, or from the failure to exercise in good faith his best judgment in attending to the litigation committed to his care.

If attorneys hold themselves out to the public as specialists in a particular area of the law (e.g., criminal law or patent law), the standard of competence is not the general practitioner handling such a case, but the specialist in good standing using the skill and knowledge normally possessed by such specialists. The *Restatement of Torts 2d* phrases the standard this way:[12]

> *Special representation.* An actor undertaking to render services may represent that he has superior skill or knowledge, beyond that common to his profession or trade. In that event he incurs an obligation to the person to whom he makes such a representation, to have, and to exercise, the skill and knowledge which he represents himself to have.

One way to gauge the kinds of malpractice with which attorneys have been charged is to examine the claims handled by insurance companies that sell liability insurance to attorneys. See Figure 18–3 for the breakdown in the categories of substantive errors, administrative errors, client relations errors, and intentional wrongs committed by attorneys.

---

[12]*Restatement (Second) of Torts* § 299A, comment d (1965).

Mistakes

A distinction should be made between:

- a reasonable mistake that could have been made by any attorney in good standing using the skill and knowledge normally possessed by attorneys, and
- an unreasonable mistake that would not have been made by an attorney in good standing using the skill and knowledge normally possessed by attorneys.

Only the latter kinds of mistakes will lead to liability for negligence. (See Figure 18–4.) The test is not whether the average attorney would have made the mistake. The focus is on the attorney in good standing using the knowledge and skill normally possessed by attorneys.[13]

It is important to keep in mind that the attorney is the agent of the client. While the attorney is representing the client (within the scope of the attorney's "employment"), the client is bound by what the attorney does. This includes both successes and mistakes. Hence, if the attorney makes a mistake and the client loses the case as a result, the recourse of the client is to sue the attorney and try to establish that an

FIGURE 18–4 Mistakes of attorneys.

Kind of Mistake	Examples	Negligence Consequences
1. Technical/mechanical mistake *not* involving the exercise of judgment.	• Attorney forgets to file an action and client is thereby barred by the statute of limitations. • Attorney forgets to appear in court and client thereby has a default judgment entered against him or her.	It is relatively easy for a client to win a negligence action against an attorney based on this kind of mistake. (See, however, the discussion on causation.)
2. Tactical mistake involving the exercise of judgment and discretion in a relatively uncomplicated area of the law.	• Attorney decides not to call a certain witness who would have been able to provide valuable testimony. • Attorney does not object to the introduction of certain evidence at trial from the other side and thereby waives the right to object on appeal.	It is difficult for a client to win a negligence action against an attorney based on this kind of mistake unless what the attorney did or failed to do was blatantly contrary to what would be considered good or competent practice. (See discussion on causation.)
3. Tactical mistake involving the exercise of judgment and discretion in a complicated area of the law.	• Attorney fails to challenge the constitutionality of a guest statute. • Attorney calls an expert witness on a design defect in a products liability case and the witness gives very damaging testimony to the attorney's own case.	It is almost impossible for a client to win a negligence action against an attorney based on this kind of mistake. This is so not only because of the complexity of the area of the law, but also because of the difficulty of proving causation, i.e., that the mistake caused the client any harm. (See discussion on causation.)

---

[13]*Restatement (Second) of Torts* § 229A, comment e (1965).

unreasonable mistake was made that would not have been made by an attorney in good standing using the skill and knowledge normally possessed by attorneys.[14]

There are three basic interrelated errors in the way an attorney practices law that often lead to successful negligence actions against the attorney. Errors in practicing law that can make an attorney vulnerable include:

- **Taking Too Many Cases**
  There are strong temptations to keep adding new cases to the attorney's caseload. Although one might admire "busy" attorneys, the danger exists that they have more than they can competently handle.
- **Failure to Do More Than Minimal Legal Research**
  Legal research can be difficult and time-consuming. It is much easier "to practice out of one's hip pocket." Courts, however, have warned attorneys that the failure to do needed legal research is a strong indication of incompetence.
- **Failure to Consult and/or Associate with More Experienced Attorneys**
  The tendency in legal practice is for an attorney to concentrate on certain kinds of cases—to specialize. Even many general practitioners will emphasize one or two categories of cases in their practice. What happens when the client with a new kind of case walks into the office? If the case is taken and the attorney does *not* have enough time to learn the theory and practicalities of a new area of the law, it is strong evidence of incompetence if the attorney fails to consult with attorneys who are experienced in that area of the law, and perhaps, with the client's consent, to work with such an attorney on the case.

Causation

To win a negligence case against an attorney, it is not enough to establish that the attorney made an unreasonable mistake; causation must also be proven. For certain kinds of attorney errors, a **trial within a trial** must occur.

> **EXAMPLE:**　George hires John Taylor, Esq. to represent him in a products liability case against XYZ Motor Company. The car George bought from XYZ exploded, causing $100,000 in injuries to George. John Taylor is so tied up with other cases that he neglects to file the action within the statute-of-limitations period. Hence, George can no longer sue XYZ Motor Company; the action is barred. George now sues John Taylor for negligence (malpractice) in letting the statute of limitations run. Assume that the error of John Taylor was quite unreasonable. What can George recover from John Taylor? $100,000? Is that what he lost? Did John Taylor *cause* $100,000 in damages? The answer is yes—but only if George can establish:
>
> 1. that he would have won his case against XYZ Motor Company, and,
> 2. that the recovery from XYZ would have been at least $100,000.
>
> In George's negligence suit against John Taylor, George must establish that he would have won the $100,000 suit against the XYZ Motor Company if the suit had not been barred by the statute of limitations. This, then, is the suit within the suit, or the trial within a trial.

The difficulty of establishing causation can be further complicated: Suppose XYZ Motor Company is bankrupt. Even if George could have won a $100,000 judgment against XYZ, he would have been able to collect nothing or very little. Hence, it can-

---

[14]Depending on the kind of mistake the attorney made, some courts might permit the client to "undo" the error by correcting it, e.g., permit a client to file a document even though the client's attorney had negligently allowed the deadline for its filing to pass. It is rare, however, that the courts will be this accommodating. A client will have to live with the mistakes of his or her attorney and seek relief solely by suing the attorney for negligence. See R. Mallen & V. Levit, *Legal Malpractice* 45ff (1977).

not be said that John Taylor's negligence in waiting too long to file the action caused George a $100,000 loss. In such circumstances, George would have to prove (in his action against John Taylor) that there would have been something to collect from XYZ Motor Company.

Indemnity

Indemnity is the right to have another person pay you the full amount you were forced to pay. In tort law, when one party is liable to a plaintiff solely because of what someone else has done (e.g., employer is liable because of what employee did), the party who is liable, and who pays as a result of the liability, can often receive indemnity from the person whose action produced the liability. Assume that an attorney is representing a *defendant* in a suit brought against the latter. Assume further that the defendant loses the suit and must pay the judgment solely because of the negligence of the attorney. In some states, the defendant can ask a court to force the attorney to *indemnify* him or her based upon the above definition of indemnity.[15]

ASSIGNMENT

18.2

Karen Smith, Esq. represents Jim Noonan in the preparation of a will. It was Jim's intent that his friend Ralph Skidmore receive a bequest of $10,000. Karen Smith drafts the will. After Jim dies, it is discovered that Karen Smith made a mistake in drafting the will that resulted in Ralph receiving nothing.

a. Make an argument that Karen Smith did not *cause a* $10,000 loss to Ralph. Assume that Jim died at the age of 35, one year after the will was drafted, and that his death was a surprise to everyone—including Jim.

b. Are there any other problems that might prevent Ralph from being able to bring a negligence action against Karen Smith?

(See General Instructions for the Legal Analysis Assignment in Chapter 2.)

CASE

Smith v. Lewis
13 Cal. 3d 349, 118 Cal. Rptr. 621, 530 P.2d 589 (1975)
Supreme Court of California

Background: *Rosemary Smith hired Jerome Lewis, Esq. to represent her in her divorce case. He advised her that her husband's state and federal retirement benefits were his separate property; they were not community property. Hence these benefits were not pleaded as items of community property, and therefore were not apportioned by the divorce court. After the divorce decree became final, Smith sued Lewis for legal malpractice in giving her negligent legal advice on the pensions. The trial court ruled for Smith (the plaintiff) against Lewis (the defendant). The case is now on appeal before the Supreme Court of California.*

Decision on Appeal: *Judgment affirmed. Lewis committed legal malpractice by failing to perform adequate research into the community property character of retirement benefits.*

OPINION OF COURT
Justice MOSK delivered the opinion of the court . . .

In determining whether defendant exhibited the requisite degree of competence in his handling of plaintiff's divorce action, the crucial inquiry is whether his advice was so legally deficient when it was given that he may be found to have failed to use "such skill, prudence, and diligence as lawyers of ordinary skill and capacity commonly possess and exercise in the performance of the tasks which they undertake." *Lucas v. Hamm* (1961) 364 P.2d 685, 689. We must, therefore examine the indicia of the law which were readily available to defendant at the time he performed the legal services in question.

The major authoritative reference works which attorneys routinely consult for a brief and reliable exposition of the law relevant to a specific problem uniformly indicated in

---

[15]R. Mallen & V. Levit, *Legal Malpractice* 124 (1977).

1967 that vested retirement benefits earned during marriage were generally subject to community [property] treatment. See, e.g., 38 *Cal. Jur. 2d*, Pensions, § 12, p. 325; 4 Witkin, *Summary of Cal. Law* (1960) pp. 2723–2724. . . .

Although it is true this court had not foreclosed all conflicts on some aspects of the issue at that time, the community character of retirement benefits had been reported in a number of appellate opinions often cited in the literature and readily accessible to defendant. *Benson v. City of Los Angeles* (1963) 384 P.2d 649; *French v. French* (1941) 112 P.2d 235. In *Benson,* decided four years before defendant was retained herein, we stated directly that "pension rights which are earned during the course of a marriage are the community property of the employee and his wife." 384 P.2d at p. 651. . . .

On the other hand, substantial uncertainty may have existed in 1967 with regard to the community character of [her husband's] *federal* pension. . . . [But] the fact that in 1967 a reasonable argument could have been offered to support the characterization of [her husband's] federal benefits as separate property does not indicate the trial court erred in submitting the issue of defendant's malpractice to the jury. The *state* benefits, the large majority of the payments at issue, were unquestionably community property according to all available authority and should have been claimed as such. As for the *federal* benefits, the record documents defendant's failure to conduct any reasonable research into their proper characterization under community property law. Instead, he dogmatically asserted his theory, which he was unable to support with authority, . . . that all noncontributory . . . retirement benefits, whether state or federal, were immune from community treatment upon divorce. The jury could well have found defendant's refusal to educate himself to the applicable principles of law constituted negligence which prevented him from exercising informed discretion with regard to his client's rights.

As the jury was correctly instructed, an attorney does not ordinarily guarantee the soundness of his opinions and, accordingly, is not liable for every mistake he may make in his practice. He is expected, however, to possess knowledge of those plain and elementary principles of law which are commonly known by well informed attorneys, and to discover those additional rules of law which, although not commonly known, may readily be found by standard research techniques. If the law on a particular subject is doubtful or debatable, an attorney will not be held responsible for failing to anticipate the manner in which the uncertainty will be resolved. But even with respect to an unsettled area of the law, we believe an attorney assumes an obligation to his client to undertake reasonable research in an effort to ascertain relevant legal principles and to make an informed decision as to a course of conduct based upon an intelligent assessment of the problem. In the instant case, ample evidence was introduced to support a jury finding that defendant failed to perform such adequate research into the question of the community character of retirement benefits and thus was unable to exercise the informed judgment to which his client was entitled.

We recognize, of course, that an attorney engaging in litigation may have occasion to choose among various alternative strategies available to his client, one of which may be to refrain from pressing a debatable point because potential benefit may not equal detriment in terms of expenditure of time and resources or because of calculated tactics to the advantage of his client. But, as the Ninth Circuit put it somewhat brutally in *Pineda v. Craven* (9th Cir. 1970) 424 F.2d 369, 372: "There is nothing strategic or tactical about ignorance. . . ." In the case before us it is difficult to conceive of tactical advantage which could have been served by neglecting to advance a claim so clearly in plaintiff's best interest, nor does defendant suggest any. The decision to forego litigation on the issue of plaintiff's community property right to a share of [her husband's] retirement benefits was apparently the product of a culpable misconception of the relevant principles of law, and the jury could have so found.

Furthermore, no lawyer would suggest the property characterization of [her husband's] retirement benefits to be so esoteric an issue that defendant could not reasonably have been expected to be aware of it or its probable resolution. *Lucas v. Hamm* (1961) 364 P.2d 685. In *Lucas* we held that the rule against perpetuities poses such complex and difficult problems for the draftsman that even careful and competent attorneys occasionally fall prey to its traps. The situation before us is not analogous. Certainly one of the central issues in any divorce proceeding is the extent and division of the community property. In this case the question reached monumental proportions, since [her husband's] retirement benefits constituted the only significant asset available to the community. In undertaking professional representation of plaintiff, defendant assumed the duty to familiarize himself with the law defining the character of retirement benefits; instead, he rendered erroneous advice contrary to the best interests of his client without the guidance through research of readily available authority. . . .

In any event, as indicated above, had defendant conducted minimal research into either hornbook or case law, he would have discovered with modest effort that [the husband's] state retirement benefits were likely to be treated as community property and that his federal benefits at least arguably belonged to the community as well. . . . Even as to doubtful matters, an attorney is expected to perform sufficient research to enable him to make an informed and intelligent judgment on behalf of his client. . . .

The judgment is affirmed.

a. Assume that Rosemary Smith's husband in *Smith v. Lewis* had a federal pension, but no state pension. Would the court still have found Lewis negligent?

b. To avoid a charge of negligence, is every attorney obligated to own a comprehensive law library?

Paralegals

Two questions should be kept in mind. First, when are paralegal employees *personally liable* for their torts? Second, when are employers *vicariously liable* for the torts of their paralegal employees? (As we saw in Chapter 14, **vicarious liability** simply means being liable because of what someone else has done or failed to do.) The short answer to the first question is: *always*. The short answer to the second question is: *when the wrongdoing by the paralegal was within the scope of employment*.

Several different kinds of wrongdoing are possible. The paralegal might commit:

- the tort of negligence
- an intentional tort, such as battery
- an act that is both a crime (such as embezzlement) *and* an intentional tort (such as conversion)

A client who is injured by any of these torts can sue the paralegal in the same manner that a patient in a hospital can sue a nurse. Paralegals are not relieved of liability simply because they work for, and function under the supervision of, an attorney. Every citizen is *personally* liable for the torts he or she commits. The same is true of the crimes they commit.

Next we turn to the employers of paralegals. Are they *also* liable for wrongdoing committed by their paralegals? Assume that the supervising attorneys did nothing wrong themselves. For example, the attorney did not commit the tort or crime as an active participant with the paralegal, or the attorney was not careless in selecting and training the paralegal. Our question is: Can an attorney be liable to a client solely because of the wrongdoing of a paralegal? As we noted, such *vicarious liability* exists when one person is liable solely because of what someone else has done or failed to do. The answer to our question is found in the doctrine of **respondeat superior,** which makes employers responsible for the torts of their employees or agents when the wrongdoing occurs within the **scope of employment.**[16]

Hence, if a paralegal commits a tort within the scope of employment, the client can sue the paralegal or the attorney, or both. This does not mean that the client recovers twice; there can be only one recovery. The client is simply given a choice in bringing the suit. In most cases, the primary target of the client will be the employer, who is the so-called deep pocket, the one who has resources from which a judgment can be satisfied.

Finally, we need to examine what is meant by "scope of employment." Not every wrongdoing of a paralegal is within the scope of employment simply because it is employment related. The test is as follows: Paralegals act within the scope of employment when they are furthering the business of their employer, which for our purposes is the practice of law. (See Figure 14–10 in Chapter 14 for more on scope of employment.) Slandering a client for failure to pay a law firm bill certainly

---

[16]We are talking here of vicarious *civil* liability, or more specifically, the tort liability of employers because of the torts committed by their employees. Employers are not subject to vicarious *criminal* liability. If a paralegal commits a crime on the job, only the paralegal goes to jail (unless the employer actually participated in the crime).

furthers the business of the law firm. But the opposite is probably true when a paralegal has an argument with a client over a football game and punches the client during their accidental evening meeting at a bar. In the latter example, the client could not sue the paralegal's employer for the intentional tort of battery under the doctrine of respondeat superior, because the battery was not committed while furthering the business of the employer. Only the paralegal would be liable for the tort under such circumstances.

When a paralegal commits negligence within the scope of employment, the attorney becomes as fully responsible for what the paralegal did as if the attorney had personally committed the negligence. The work product of the paralegal blends into the work product of the attorney. Clients hiring a law firm are led to believe that the services to be received would be of professional quality, regardless of what tasks might be delegated to employees within the firm. Hence, when a client is harmed by a negligent mistake committed by a paralegal and brings a negligence action against the attorney, negligence will be measured by what a reasonable attorney would have done, not by what a reasonable paralegal would have done.

ASSIGNMENT
18.4

Mary Smith is a paralegal at the XYZ law firm. One of her tasks is to file a document in court. She negligently fails to do so. As a result, the client loses the case through a default judgment entered against the client. What options are available to the client? (See General Instructions for the Legal Analysis Assignment in Chapter 2.)

There have not been many tort cases in which paralegals have been sued for wrongdoing in a law office. Yet as paralegals become more prominent in the practice of law, more are expected to be named as defendants. Michael Martz, General Counsel of the Mississippi Bar Association, makes the unsettling point that the prominence of paralegalism means there will be more suits against them. "As paralegals become more and more professional and proficient, they . . . will become better targets for disgruntled clients looking for someone to sue."[17] The most common kinds of cases involving paralegals have occurred when the paralegal was a notary and improperly notarized signatures under pressure from the supervising attorney.

SUMMARY

A physician-patient relationship arises when a doctor undertakes to render medical services in response to an express or implied request for services by the patient or by the patient's guardian. Doctors are not liable for breach of contract unless they guarantee a result. Nor is there strict liability. They are held to the standard of negligence: A doctor must use the skill and learning commonly possessed by members of the profession in good standing. States disagree on whether this standard of care is judged from a national or a local perspective. The failure of a doctor to provide informed consent on the treatment proposed may lead to a battery claim, although more often the claim is negligence. The amount of disclosure a doctor must provide is determined by a reasonable patient standard or by a reasonable doctor standard. Consent forms must not be so ambiguous as to amount to a blanket authorization of whatever the doctor thinks is wise to do.

---

[17]Michael Martz, *Ethics, Does a Paralegal Need Insurance?* The Assistant, p. 13 (Mississippi Ass'n of Legal Assistants, Fall 1993).

Critics say that medical malpractice law causes doctors to practice defensive medicine, increasing the cost and unavailability of coverage. Proposals for reform have included damage caps, fee caps (particularly on the contingent fee), collateral source offsets, cooling-off periods, alternative dispute resolution, a National Practitioner Data Bank, the English rule, limited no-fault systems, and enterprise liability.

Interrogatories are used as a pretrial discovery device for parties to learn about each others' cases and prepare for trial.

To determine an attorney's negligence liability, the standard of care is the skill and knowledge commonly possessed by attorneys in good standing. Every mistake made by an attorney will not necessarily lead to negligence liability. It must be an unreasonable mistake that actually causes the client a loss. If a paralegal commits a tort, such as negligence, he or she is personally liable to the defendant. Under the theory of respondeat superior, the supervising attorney is also liable for the wrong committed by the paralegal if it occurred within the scope of employment. When a client sues a law firm because of harm caused by paralegal negligence, the firm is held to the standard of what a reasonable attorney should have done, not what a reasonable paralegal should have done.

KEY TERMS

medical malpractice   322

deep pockets   322

physician-patient
    relationship   322

warranty   322

strict liability   323

negligence   323

national standard   323

local standard   323

custom   323

conspiracy of silence   324

battery   324

informed consent   324

reasonable patient standard   325

reasonable doctor standard   325

defensive medicine   326

percentage fee   326

damage caps   326

fee caps   326

collateral source   326

statute of limitations   326

tolled   326

alternative dispute
    resolution   326

screening panels   326

mediation   326

arbitration   326

National Practitioner
    Data Bank   327

English rule   327

no-fault systems   327

enterprise liability   327

written interrogatories   329

legal malpractice   335

trial within a trial   338

indemnity   339

vicarious liability   341

respondeat superior   341

scope of employment   341

CHAPTER

19

Products Liability

CHAPTER OUTLINE

- Products Liability in the Media
- Categories of Defects
- Negligence
- Misrepresentation
- Warranty and Strict Liability
- Express Warranty
- Sale versus Service
- Implied Warranties
- Strict Liability in Tort
- Reform
- Paralegal Roles

PRODUCTS LIABILITY IN THE MEDIA

Each year 29,000 deaths are associated with consumer products (not including automobiles and trucks). In addition, an estimated 33 million people are injured. The cost of injuries treated in hospital emergency rooms alone is about $10 billion a year. (See Figure 19–1.) Yet the law of **products liability** is often misunderstood, particularly by the public. In part this is due to the media's fascination with the apparently frivolous case. For example:

- A man convinces a court that he became impotent after being shocked by a Pepsi Cola vending machine.
- A jury awards $2.7 million (later reduced to $640,000) to a woman against McDonald's because its coffee was so hot that she burned herself when she spilled some of it on her lap.

Reading about such cases in the media had many shaking their heads in disbelief. Warning labels were also ripe for comment. A sign on a baby stroller read, "Remove Child Before Folding." A Batman toy set warned that "Cape Does Not Enable User to Fly." The president of a stepladder company recently told a press conference of a case in which a man placed his ladder on frozen horse manure so that he could do some shingle work on his barn. As the manure melted, the ladder slipped. He fell and was injured. He then sued the ladder manufacturer and was awarded $330,000 on the theory that the manufacturer failed to provide adequate warning of the viscosity of manure! What does the need for such a warning say about the mentality of the American consumer? One commentator wonders whether we will one day see ladder warnings like the following:

- Avoid contact with electrical current. Never attempt to plug in a ladder.
- This warning sticker gets slippery when wet. That's why we put it on the side. If you're standing on this sticker, you've got the ladder pointed the wrong way.
- Never drink and climb. Always have a designated climber on hand.[1]

What's going on? Is the field of products liability law coming apart in a sea of ridicule? Not quite, but attorneys and the legal system have been taking a pounding. Talk-show hosts, late-night comics, and cartoonists are ever-available to give us the details of the latest seemingly absurd products liability case. In this environment of attack, humor, and exaggeration, it would be an understatement to say that many are confused about the law of products liability. Our goal in the following two chapters is to place this area of the law in perspective. An understanding of the basics will help separate the reality from the ridicule.

---

[1]Andrew J. McClurg, *Rungful Suits*, 83 ABA Journal 98 (June, 1997).

FIGURE 19–1   Consumer products involved in injuries: Estimates of cases treated in hospital emergency rooms: 1996–1997.

Product Group	Total	Age Group			
		Under 5	5–24	25–64	65 and Over
1. Child Nursery Equipment and Supplies	86,428	72,479	6,530	6,734	685
2. Toys	137,151	64,944	50,680	19,684	1,843
3. Sports and Recreational Activities and Equipment	3,853,295	172,767	2,676,076	939,401	65,051
4. Home Communication, Entertainment, and Hobby Equipment	103,143	26,868	32,556	33,604	10,115
5. Personal Use Items	389,268	129,161	118,906	111,197	30,004
6. Packaging and Containers for Household Products	327,621	42,919	103,905	154,163	26,634
7. Yard and Garden Equipment	219,024	8,735	48,407	128,727	33,155
8. Home Workshop Apparatus, Tools, and Attachments	318,907	11,596	74,343	200,613	32,355
9. Home and Family Maintenance Products	115,734	27,988	30,137	49,564	8,045
10. General Household Appliances	134,137	28,213	28,041	60,092	17,791
11. Space Heating, Cooling, and Ventilating Appliances	125,531	33,495	34,207	46,907	10,922
12. Housewares	753,844	49,918	254,062	404,250	45,614
13. Home Furnishings and Fixtures	1,903,978	497,599	434,127	589,340	382,912
14. Home Structures and Construction Materials	3,083,776	438,569	912,245	1,130,726	600,236
15. Miscellaneous	201,104	44,974	86,081	53,117	16,932

Source: National Electronic Injury Surveillance System (NEISS) of the Consumer Product Safety Commission. Note: NEISS data indicate that a product was associated with an injury but not necessarily that the product caused the injury. ATVs (all terrain vehicles) are included in the data, but *not* most motor vehicles that are under the jurisdiction of the National Highway Transportation and Safety Administration.

CATEGORIES OF DEFECTS

The term *products liability* does not refer to a particular tort. Rather, it is a short-hand term that covers a variety of causes of action that can be raised when a **defective** product causes injury or other harm. The causes of action are:

- negligence
- misrepresentation
- breach of express warranty
- breach of implied warranty of merchantability
- breach of implied warranty of fitness for a particular purpose
- strict liability in tort

In this chapter we begin our study of these causes of action. In the next chapter, we continue the study with a focus on the problems that are peculiar to what is called *mass torts*.

The primary focus of a products liability case is on a product that is defective. Something is wrong with the product that makes it dangerous. As a result, someone is injured, property is damaged, or both. As we shall see, however, every product that causes injury or damage is not necessarily defective. A bottle of milk that falls and breaks a toe has caused an injury, but it is highly unlikely that the bottle fell because it was defective. The three broad categories of defectiveness are outlined in Figure 19–2.

Before we begin our study of negligence and the other causes of action based on these categories of defects, it is important to note that the status of the plaintiff or of

FIGURE 19–2 Categories of defects in products.

1. Manufacturing Defect

The product does not conform to its design. Something went wrong in the manufacturing process making the product dangerous. The defective product is different from the others. *Examples:* The screws on the wheels of the car were not tightened, a foreign substance was left in the soda bottle, a worker failed to follow instructions on the amount of a chemical to pour into the mold.

2. Design Defect

The product conforms to the design, but the design is defective. Something went wrong at the planning stage making the product dangerous. The defective product is exactly like all the others, but something is wrong with all of them because of the very design of the product. *Examples:* The kind of metal called for by the design is not strong enough to do the work of the product, a safety shield should have been built into the product, the driver's vision through the rear view mirror was blocked because of the amount and position of the paneling in the back of the car.

3. Warning Defect

There are no effective instructions or warnings to go with the product. This defect makes the product dangerous. The design of the product is otherwise reasonable and there are no manufacturing flaws in it, but the consumer should have been given more information about what the product can and cannot do. *Examples:* Consumers with a certain allergy should have been told not to use the drug, or should have been told to use it only under a doctor's supervision; consumers should have been told to keep the polish out of the reach of children.

the defendant can sometimes have a dramatic effect on the outcome of a case. The various combinations are presented in Figure 19–3. For some of the causes of action, as we will see, if the status of a party changes, the applicable law will change.

FIGURE 19–3 Status: Who is the plaintiff? Who is the defendant?

Status Possibilities of the Injured Plaintiff	Status Possibilities of the Defendant
• buyer of product • user of product • lessee (renter) of product • bailee of product • bystander	• manufacturer of entire product • manufacturer of a part of product • assembler of product • supplier/wholesaler of product • retail seller of product • lessor of product • bailor of product

NEGLIGENCE

If the plaintiff tries to assert a negligence cause of action, he or she must establish the elements that would apply to any negligence case:

1. duty
2. breach of duty
3. proximate cause
4. damages

The element of **duty** is rarely difficult to establish. According to the general rule on duty we examined in Figure 13–1 of Chapter 13, a defendant who brings a product on the market for sale has engaged in affirmative conduct, which gives rise to a duty to use reasonable care to prevent the product from causing injury. There was a time when this duty was owed only to plaintiffs who were buyers of the product. A buyer was said to be in **privity** of contract with the seller.

Privity simply means the relationship that exists between parties who have entered a contract with each other. The old rule was as follows: without privity there was no duty to use reasonable care.

> **EXAMPLE:**   Jones goes to Wal-Mart to buy a toaster manufactured by Sunbeam. While using the toaster one day, Jones is injured when it catches fire. Jones sues Sunbeam for negligence.

Under the old rule, the case would be dismissed. There was no contract and, therefore, no privity between Jones and Sunbeam. Jones was limited to a suit against Wal-Mart with whom he was in privity.

As we will see, the case of *MacPherson v. Buick Motor Co.* changed this privity rule. *MacPherson* is one of the most famous tort cases in American legal history. It was written by one of the giants in the field, New York State Court of Appeals Judge Benjamin Cardozo, later appointed to the United States Supreme Court. (Cardozo also wrote the majority opinion in the equally famous *Palsgraf* case we examined in Chapter 13.) The *MacPherson* case said that a duty of reasonable care is owed to all **foreseeable users** of the product (not just to those in privity) whenever it can be anticipated that harm will result if the product is defective. Noting the historical importance of this ruling, commentators have pointed out that *MacPherson* signaled the collapse of the "citadel of privity." In our example, Jones certainly was a foreseeable user of Sunbeam's toaster. A toaster, like almost any product, can cause serious harm if it is defectively made. Under the ruling in *MacPherson,* therefore, a duty of reasonable care would be owed by Sunbeam to Jones. As Judge Cardozo points out in *MacPherson,* this obligation is based on the law, not on whether a contract exists.

The model of the Buick purchased by Mr. MacPherson.

CASE

MacPherson v. Buick Motor Co.
217 N.Y. 382, 111 N.E. 1050 (1916)
Court of Appeals of New York

Background: *MacPherson was injured while driving his Buick because it had a defective wheel. He purchased the car from a retail dealer, not directly from the manufacturer, Buick Motor Company. Yet he sued Buick Motor Company for negligence. In the lower courts, Buick Motor Company argued that MacPherson could sue only the company with whom he was in privity—the retail dealer. Buick Motor Company also pointed out that it did not make the defective wheel itself; it purchased it from a wheel manufacturer and then assembled the wheel along with other component parts. The lower court (the Appellate Division) entered a judgment for MacPherson. The case is now on appeal before the Court of Appeals of New York.*

Decision on Appeal: *Judgment for MacPherson is affirmed. A consumer can sue a manufacturer for negligence even in the absence of privity.*

OPINION OF COURT

Judge CARDOZO delivered the opinion of the court.

The defendant is a manufacturer of automobiles. It sold an automobile to a retail dealer. The retail dealer resold to the plaintiff. While the plaintiff was in the car, it suddenly collapsed. He was thrown out and injured. One of the wheels was made of defective wood, and its spokes crumbled into fragments. The wheel was not made by the defendant; it was bought from another manufacturer. There is evidence, however, that its defects could have been discovered by reasonable inspection, and that inspection was omitted. There is no claim that the defendant knew of the defect and willfully concealed it. . . . The question to be determined is whether the defendant owed a duty of care and vigilance to any one but the immediate purchaser.

The foundations of this branch of the law, at least in this state, were laid in *Thomas v. Winchester* (6 N.Y. 397). A poison was falsely labeled. The sale was made to a druggist, who in turn sold to a customer. The customer recovered damages from the seller who affixed the label. "The defendant's negligence," it was said, "put human life in imminent danger." A poison falsely labeled is likely to injure any one who gets it. Because the danger is to be foreseen, there is a duty to avoid the injury. . . . *Thomas v. Winchester* became quickly a landmark of the law. . . . [Judge Cardozo then discusses prior court opinions in order to reject the position of Buick that *Thomas v. Winchester* applies only to inherently dangerous products like poison.]

We hold, then, that the principle of *Thomas v. Winchester* is not limited to poisons, explosives, and things of like nature, to things which in their normal operation are implements of destruction. If the nature of a thing is such that it is reasonably certain to place life and limb in peril when negligently made, it is then a thing of danger. Its nature gives warning of the consequences to be expected. If to the element of danger there is added knowledge that the thing will be used by persons other than the purchaser, and used without new tests then, irrespective of contract, the manufacturer of this thing of danger is under a duty to make it carefully. That is as far as we are required to go for the decision of this case.

There must be knowledge of a danger, not merely possible, but probable. . . . There must also be knowledge that in the usual course of events the danger will be shared by others than the buyer. . . . We are dealing now with the liability of the manufacturer of the finished product, who puts it on the market to be used without inspection by his customers. If he is negligent, where danger is to be foreseen, a liability will follow. . . . We have put aside the notion that the duty to safeguard life and limb, when the consequences of negligence may be foreseen, grows out of contract and nothing else. We have put the source of the obligation where it ought not be. We have put its source in the law. . . .

Beyond all question, the nature of an automobile gives warning of probable danger if its construction is defective. This automobile was designed to go fifty miles an hour. Unless its wheels were sound and strong, injury was almost certain. It was as much a thing of danger as a defective engine for a railroad. The defendant knew the danger. It knew also that the car would be used by persons other than the buyer. This was apparent from its size; there were seats for three persons. It was apparent also from the fact that the buyer was a dealer in cars, who bought to resell. The maker of this car supplied it for the use of purchasers from the dealer. . . . The dealer was indeed the one person of whom it might be said with some approach to certainly that by him the car would not be used. Yet the defendant would have us say that he was the one person whom it was under a legal duty to protect. The law does not lead us to so inconsequent a conclusion. . . .

We think the defendant was not absolved from a duty of inspection because it bought the wheels from a reputable manufacturer. It was not merely a dealer in automobiles. It was a manufacturer of automobiles. It was responsible for the finished product. It was not at liberty to put the finished product on the market without subjecting the component parts to ordinary and simple tests. . . . The obligation to inspect must vary with the nature of the thing to be inspected. The more probable the danger, the greater the need of caution. . . .

The judgment [for MacPherson] should be affirmed.

a. Four people or businesses are mentioned in this opinion: Buick Motor Company, the wheel manufacturer, the retail dealer, and Mr. MacPherson. From this list, identify who was in privity with whom.

b. How are the facts in *MacPherson v. Buick Motor Co.* similar to those in *Thomas v. Winchester?* How are they different? Were the differences strong enough to lead Judge Cardozo to conclude that the *Thomas* opinion should not apply?

c. Would Judge Cardozo have ruled the same way if the person injured in the car was a backseat passenger who was in privity with no one?

The second element of negligence in a products liability case is **breach of duty.** As we saw in Chapter 14, the duty is breached when the defendant engages in unreasonable conduct under the circumstances as measured by the breach-of-duty equation (see Figure 14–4 in Chapter 14.) The defendant is unreasonable when the foreseeability of serious injury outweighs the burden or inconvenience of trying to avoid the accident and the defendant fails to undergo that burden or inconvenience. Also, the more important or socially useful the defendant's objective or task, the more reasonable it is to take risks of injury. A wonder drug has considerable social importance. If, however, the drug has the potential of dangerous side effects, the defendant must act reasonably to test the drug and make it as safe as reasonably possible. Some risk may still exist—even if consumer warnings are also added. Given the social importance of the drug, however, the law is less inclined to call a manufacturer negligent (unreasonable) for taking such risks by putting the drug on the market.

The same analysis is used for a product such as a lawn mower. Is it foreseeable that rocks will be thrown from the blade onto a person? If so, reasonable steps, such as the addition of an extra safety guard, may be needed. Lawn mowers are arguably not as socially valuable as medicine, but they are not frivolous items, and it is important to have them on the market even though they pose some risk. In all these cases, we must ask how much of a burden or inconvenience it would be for the defendant to take steps to try to eliminate the danger. The greater the potential harm, the more burden or inconvenience the defendant should undergo. It may be unreasonable for a manufacturer to fail to take extra time to do more testing and perhaps to add a safety feature (even if this will increase the cost of the product) when the foreseeability of serious harm without this feature is very high. On the other hand, it might be unreasonable to go through considerable expense to avoid a small injury that has little chance of occurring.

It is important to remember that the defendant is not an insurer. Injury caused by a manufacturing defect, a design defect, or a warning defect will *not* impose negligence liability on the defendant if the latter has taken all reasonable precautions as to safety. Under the law of negligence, the defendant does not have an obligation to produce a safe product; the obligation is to provide a **reasonably safe** product. The defendant does not have an obligation to produce a product without defects; the obligation is to take reasonable steps to avoid defects.

Later in the chapter when we cover warranty and strict liability in tort, we will see that defendants are not always off the hook simply by showing that they acted reasonably. It is generally much easier to establish liability under these causes of action than under negligence.

We turn now to an examination of how the status of the defendant in a negligence action affects the determination of what is reasonable.

Manufacturer

A **manufacturer** is held to the standard of an expert in the product manufactured. It must use reasonable care to discover and correct manufacturing defects. This includes the requirement of inspection and testing. Reasonable care must be used in the training of employees and in the operation of machinery on the production line. If parts are used from other manufacturers, care must be used to be sure that the parts are safe. The packaging must also be reasonably safe with no misleading markings or advertising on it that could lead someone into a dangerous use. Defects that are discovered or that should have been discovered must be made known. A manufacturer cannot shift its inspection responsibility to someone else in the chain of distribution. For example, a manufacturer of a car is not relieved of its obligation to inspect simply because it knows that a dealer will later inspect the car before final sale.

Design defects pose more of a problem. There is no absolute answer to the question of when a design is unreasonable. What, for example, is a reasonable design of a teenager's bicycle? Each year these bicycles are involved in thousands of accidental injuries. How should the bicycles be designed to avoid this danger? Theoretically, they could be designed to be very heavy so that they would never go very fast or designed with a very low seat so that a fall would always be no more than a foot or so. It might even be possible to design them so that they can be operated only on softer surfaces such as grass. But what would such bicycles cost? Would these designs render the bicycle relatively useless for recreation or sports for the vast majority of teenagers? Would they stop buying them? A reasonable design does not require a manufacturer to do that which is ridiculous—even if it could be done. In short, the breach-of-duty equation (see Figure 14–4 in Chapter 14) must be applied to determine whether a product design is reasonable—particularly the part of the equation calling for an assessment of the burden or inconvenience on the defendant to take design precautions that would avoid or minimize injury.

ASSIGNMENT

19.2

Is a car manufacturer unreasonable (and therefore negligent) for making a car without side air bags as standard equipment for everyone in the front and rear seats? (See General Instructions for the Legal Analysis Assignment in Chapter 2.)

Warning defects also need to be considered. A manufacturer should provide reasonable instructions on the use of the product and reasonable warnings against dangers that may not be obvious. It must be emphasized, however, that a good warning is not a substitute for a reasonably safe product. Slapping a "danger" sign on an unreasonably dangerous product will not relieve the manufacturer from negligence liability. The product must be designed so that it is reasonably safe, even though it may still need a warning against dangers.

It is not always easy for a plaintiff to prove negligence, particularly in view of the difficulty of obtaining evidence about what occurred during the design and manufacturing process. (This difficulty is one of the reasons for the creation of the easier-to-establish warranty and strict liability causes of action we will consider shortly.) In negligence cases, as we saw in Chapter 14, the doctrine of **res ipsa loquitur** is sometimes available to a plaintiff as an aid in getting its negligence case to the jury. The elements of a res ipsa case (see Figure 14–6 in Chapter 14) require a showing that:

1. the accident is one that ordinarily does not occur in the absence of some-one's negligence (i.e., unreasonableness);
2. the accident was caused by an agency or instrumentality within the exclusive control of the defendant;
3. the accident was not due to any voluntary action or contribution of the plaintiff.

The doctrine helps the plaintiff in cases such as the following: a human toe is found in a soda bottle, an aspirin contains ten times the normal ingredients, a new car explodes while driving it off the dealer's lot. The special problems of applying the elements of res ipsa loquitur in a negligence case are discussed in Chapter 14.

Nonmanufacturer

A **merchant** who sells the product wholesale or retail directly to the consumer can also be liable for negligence when a defective product causes injury. The boundary line of liability is reasonableness. Again, the status of the defendant is relevant to our determination of what is reasonable. It may be unreasonable to ask a wholesaler or retailer to take certain safety precautions that would be quite reasonable for a manufacturer to take. A department store, for example, would not be under an obligation to safety-test every product it sells, whereas one would expect manufacturers to undertake safety tests for their products. The burden or inconvenience of this testing on a department store, a gas station, or a drugstore would be so great that it would probably mean going out of business.

Although reasonable merchants rarely need to test the products they sell, they do need to respond when injury becomes foreseeable. The following factors affect foreseeability:

Complaints   If merchants have received complaints of injury from customers, they are on notice that something should be done, e.g., remove the product from the shelf. A reasonable merchant would not take a business-as-usual attitude in the face of actual knowledge that the product is being attacked by prior customers, especially if they are claiming serious injury.

Reputation of the Manufacturer   A reasonable merchant who deals with a reputable manufacturer has less concern over the safety of the latter's product than when the manufacturer had had a history of problems or is relatively new on the market.

Packaging   A reasonable merchant is less likely to be concerned about packaged products than those that are sold without packaging. The package helps prevent damage. A merchant is not expected to open every package to make sure there are no dangers.

Custom in the Trade   Although what other merchants do is never conclusive on the issue of reasonableness (see Chapter 14), the **custom** in the trade is relevant to determining what is reasonable. Is it the practice of similar merchants, for example, to sell the product without any inspection or warning? If so, then this may help persuade a court that a particular merchant was not unreasonable when it did not inspect or warn.

Common Sense   A reasonable merchant uses common sense. Obvious defects in the product, for example, would call for caution, especially if it is clear that the danger would not be equally apparent to every consumer, e.g., a child. Merchants may not stick their heads in the sand and play dumb in the face of obvious danger.

ASSIGNMENT

19.3

a. Helen is the manager of the XYZ Supermarket. While talking to a neighbor one day, Helen is told that the neighbor began feeling dizzy after using a room deodorizer she bought from the XYZ Supermarket. Helen says, "You've got to be careful these days." Two weeks later, another customer dies while using the same product. Prepare an investigation strategy to help you determine if the XYZ Supermarket was negligent in selling the room deodorizer. (See General Instructions for the Investigation Strategy Assignment in Chapter 3.)

b. The ABC Company manufactures a chain saw. Assume that it is negligently designed because the blade comes off while the saw is in operation. Jones owns a hardware store that sells the saw. Many customers have complained to Jones about this defect in the saw. Jones, however, keeps selling the product, telling earlier customers to direct their complaints to ABC. A month later another customer buys the saw and is injured because of the defect. Can this customer successfully sue the ABC Company for negligence? (See General Instructions for the Legal Analysis Assignment in Chapter 2.)

Defenses

Contributory negligence of the plaintiff is a complete defense in states where the full force of this defense is still alive. If the state has adopted **comparative negligence** (see Chapter 17), the court will compare the fault of the plaintiff and defendant and apportion responsibility according to the applicable formula.

Plaintiffs must use reasonable care to protect themselves, particularly with respect to discovering reasonably detectable defects in the product. It is contributory negligence for a plaintiff to fail to discover a defect in a product if a reasonable person in the plaintiff's position would have discovered it. Assume, for example, that the plaintiff is injured by a lawn mower, which she kept using even though she heard loud, unusual noises from the motor. These noises would have alerted any reasonable user to the probability of serious malfunction. Consumers who have paid "good money" for a product tend to be reluctant to cease using it, even when danger signs exist. The consumer keeps using the product in the hope that the machine will correct itself. After the injury, the consumer says, "I didn't know it was dangerous." If a reasonable user would have discovered the danger, the plaintiff loses the case in a contributory-negligence state (or has his or her damages reduced in a comparative-negligence state) in spite of the fact that the product was negligently designed or manufactured. Of course, consumers are not expected to conduct elaborate tests on a product in order to discover defects. They are held only to what a reasonable user would have discovered and done. (It is important to note that this negligent failure on the part of the plaintiff to discover the danger will *not* be a defense when the plaintiff sues under a warranty or strict-liability-in-tort cause of action, as we shall see later.)

Suppose that the plaintiff *does* discover the defect in the product and fully appreciates the danger. Continuing to use the product under such circumstances is an **assumption of risk.** In most states, this is a defense to *any* cause of action in a products liability case. The plaintiff must have actual knowledge of the danger and voluntarily encounter it. There is a difference between suspecting that a problem might exist and knowing that it exists. The defense of assumption of risk requires the latter. As pointed out in Chapter 17, however, some states have abolished assumption of risk and rely on comparative negligence to allocate the damages between the plaintiff and defendant when the negligence of both has caused the plaintiff's injury.

MISREPRESENTATION

The tort of **misrepresentation** (also called deceit or fraud) is another cause of action that should be considered. Suppose a merchant knowingly makes a false statement of fact to a consumer about a product with the intent to deceive the consumer.

> **EXAMPLE:** Fred is a sales clerk in a department store where Mary is a prospective customer. She asks Fred if a particular mattress is flammable. Fred tells her it is not flammable. He knows this is not so, but feels that Mary would not make the purchase if she knew the truth. She buys the mattress. When she discovers the mattress is flammable, she sues the department store for misrepresentation.

If Mary is injured because of the false statement (e.g., being burned by the mattress), she can recover for her injury as well as for her loss in failing to get what she paid for. The critical element in the tort of misrepresentation is the intent to deceive—called **scienter.** This element exists when the defendant makes the statement knowing it is false, without a belief in its truth, or in reckless disregard of its truth or falsity, with the desire that the statement be believed and relied upon. This and other elements of misrepresentation will be examined in Chapter 26.

WARRANTY AND STRICT LIABILITY

A **warranty** action is a form of **strict liability,** meaning that a breach of the warranty will lead to liability whether the defendant acted intentionally, negligently, or innocently. The historical development of warranty shows that it has both contract and tort dimensions. The contract dimension is that the warranty grows out of a contract relationship. The major tort dimension is that there are consequences of violating or breaching the warranty that are imposed by law irrespective of what the parties to the contract agreed to do.

Three warranties need to be considered:

- express warranty
- implied warranty of merchantability
- implied warranty of fitness for a particular purpose

Since all three are strict liability causes of action, a plaintiff does not have to show that the defendant was negligent (or acted intentionally) in order to recover. Do not confuse the terms *strict liability* and *strict liability in tort.* "Strict liability" is a general term that means liability without fault—the imposition of liability without having to show negligence or intent. When we say that a cause of action imposes "strict liability," we are simply saying that there is no need to prove negligence or intent. The phrase "strict liability in tort," on the other hand, has a narrower meaning. It is an actual tort cause of action. Of course, the general meaning of liability without fault also applies to this tort. But since "strict liability in tort" is an actual cause of action, it has elements, as we shall see later in this chapter. Think of "strict liability" as a phrase applying to different causes of action, one of which being "strict liability in tort."

EXPRESS WARRANTY

The elements of an action for a breach of **express warranty** are as follows:

i.   a statement of fact that is false
ii. made with the intent or expectation that the statement will reach the plaintiff

   iii. reliance on the statement by the plaintiff

   iv. damage

   v. causation

Many states have passed § 2-313 of the **Uniform Commercial Code (UCC)**,[2] a statute on express warranties.[3]

False Statement of Fact

The first element of a breach-of-express-warranty cause of action is that there must be a statement of **fact** that is false. A fact is a concrete statement that can be objectively established as true (e.g., "it's raining today"). An **opinion,** on the other hand, is a communication containing a relatively vague or indefinite value judgment that is not objectively verifiable (e.g., "the weather is refreshing"). The statement must be reasonably understood to be a fact.

Seller's talk or **puffing** is an expected exaggeration of quality, and as such, does not communicate facts. For example:

"The car is a great buy."

"The tool is excellent."

"It is the best buy around."

It does state a fact, however, to say that the glass in the car is "shatter-proof," and the statement would be false if a rock broke the glass. Sometimes it is difficult to classify a statement as fact or as seller's talk. Suppose that a merchant says that a chain saw is "durable." Has a fact been stated? The answer depends on how a reasonable listener would interpret the statement. It would be unreasonable to interpret the statement to mean that it will last forever. Arguably, however, the statement communicates that the saw is safe for ordinary uses.

The creation of the express warranty does not require the use of the words "warranty" or "guarantee." Any words describing a product can be sufficient so long as the words communicate statements of fact. The warranty can also be created by showing the plaintiff a model or sample. The defendant is stating that the product conforms to the model or sample.

The plaintiff does not have to prove that the defendant knew that the statement was false; it simply must be false. (If the defendant knew it was false and had the intent to deceive, a tort suit for misrepresentation would also be available.) Nor does the plaintiff have to show that the defendant acted negligently or intentionally in communicating the false statement.

ASSIGNMENT 19.4	Which of the following statements, if any, communicate statements of fact? (See General Instructions for the Legal Analysis Assignment in Chapter 2.) a. "The ladder will last a lifetime." b. "The vaporizer is practically foolproof."

---

[2]The UCC is a set of statutes covering commercial transactions in areas where uniformity across state lines is desirable. (Section 2-313 is one of the statutes in the UCC.) The UCC was created by the National Conference of Commissioners on Uniform State Laws and the American Law Institute. The Conference then submitted it to each state's legislature, which was free to accept, modify, or reject its provisions. Although most legislatures adopted all of the UCC without significant modification, a researcher in any particular state must check the UCC in that state to determine its exact wording.

[3]See also § 402B of the *Restatement (Second) of Torts* on liability for misrepresentations of a material fact concerning the character or quality of a chattel that causes physical harm.

c. "These cigarettes are soothing."
d. "The detergent dissolves instantly."
e. "You can trust General Electric."
f. "If our tires save your life once, they are a bargain."

Intent or Expectation the Statement Will Reach the Plaintiff

The false statement of fact must be made to the plaintiff. If it is made to the public, the defendant must reasonably expect that the statement will reach someone like the plaintiff. Hence, statements made in general advertising would be covered. If the manufacturer makes statements in a manual that it distributes to retailers, the question will be whether the manufacturer could reasonably expect the retailer to tell consumers what is in the manual or to show the manual to them.

Reliance on Statement

Reliance means placing faith or confidence in someone or something. The statement of fact about the product must be **material** or important to the transaction. This is so when the plaintiff either buys the product or uses it because of what the defendant said about it. Of course, plaintiffs cannot rely on a statement unless they know about it. Hence, it must be shown that the plaintiff saw or heard the statement.

Damage and Causation

The reliance on the false statement of fact must cause the plaintiff's damage or injury. The plaintiff must show that "but for" the statement, the damage or injury would not have occurred, or that the statement was a substantial factor in producing the damage or injury.

SALE VERSUS SERVICE

The final three causes of action we will examine in this chapter are:

- breach of implied warranty of merchantability
- breach of implied warranty of fitness for a particular purpose
- strict liability in tort

A common component of all three is that they apply to **sales,** not to **services.** The distinction can be critical. If you are injured because of what the defendant *sold* you, the causes of action you can bring include negligence and the three strict-liability causes of action: breach of implied warranty of merchantability, breach of implied warranty of fitness for a particular purpose, and strict liability in tort. If, however, you are injured while the defendant is rendering a *service*, your cause of action is limited to negligence.[4] Phrased another way, if the defendant is engaged in a service, you must show that the defendant acted unreasonably; but if a sale is involved, you can use the strict-liability causes of actions without having to establish the defendant's unreasonableness, i.e., negligence. It is therefore to the plaintiff's advantage to be able to show that the defendant sold something.

---

[4]You can also sue for the tort of misrepresentation if you can establish intent (scienter). See Chapter 26. Of course, if the service provider has made express statements of fact about the service, a breach-of-express-warranty suit is a possibility as well. Express warranties can be made and breached in sales and in the rendering of services.

A sale is the passing of title to tangible goods or products from a seller to a buyer for a price.[5] Courts, however, do not always use this definition. For example, when you rent or lease property, title does not pass, but the courts treat such transactions as "sales" for purpose of using the strict-liability causes of action. Also, every sale does not qualify. The sale must be by a merchant—someone in the business of selling. Hence, the strict-liability causes of action would not apply to the sale of a car between neighbors who are not car merchants.

ASSIGNMENT 19.5	Is there a sale in the following situations? (See General Instructions for the Legal Analysis Assignment in Chapter 2.)

ASSIGNMENT 19.5

Is there a sale in the following situations? (See General Instructions for the Legal Analysis Assignment in Chapter 2.)

a. Fred is at a supermarket. He takes a bottle of catsup from the shelf, puts it in his cart, and heads for the checkout counter. While he is picking up the bottle from the cart to place it on the counter, it explodes, injuring Fred.

b. Mary is test driving a car that she is considering purchasing. She is alone in the car five blocks from the dealer. On her way back to the dealer, she decides against purchasing the car. Just as she drives in to the dealer's lot, the brakes malfunction, causing an accident, in which she is injured.

A service is an activity that is performed or a benefit that is provided as part of one's line of work, e.g., a doctor operating on a patient, an attorney conducting a trial, or a professor teaching a class. In general, if title does not pass, then what you have paid for is a service. The easiest services to recognize are the professional services of doctors, attorneys, and teachers. Such professionals are not strictly liable for the harm they cause. Suits against them must establish their negligence.[6]

A service does not become a sale simply because there is a sale dimension to what occurs. Suppose, for example, that a dentist uses a hypodermic needle in a patient's mouth. The needle is a product or "good" for which the patient is charged. Yet this does not change the character of the event from a service to a sale. There is no implied warranty that the needle is safe. There is no implied warranty that anything the dentist does is safe or effective. If the needle breaks in the patient's mouth, a suit against the dentist must show negligence.

What about a blood transfusion at a hospital? Assume that a hemophiliac contracts AIDS by receiving infected blood during a transfusion. Is the blood a "good" (a product) that has been purchased? Most courts say no. The blood transfusion is a service. (In some states this result is mandated by statute.) Negligence, therefore, must be shown, e.g., carelessness in the screening and testing procedures for those who donate blood.

Services are not limited to the professions. Hotels provide services, as do plumbers and carpenters. The gray area is again the situation where it appears that both a sale and a service exist. A beauty parlor, for example, provides a service. Yet, it uses and charges for products in rendering this service, e.g., a permanent-wave solution. Again, the general rule is that a service does not become a sale simply because a product is used or because there is a product component to what is predominantly

---

[5]Our focus here is on the sale of **personal property** rather than of **real property** or real estate. (Personal property, also called **chattels,** is movable property not attached to the land. Real property is land and anything permanently attached to the land.) There are some courts, however, that have allowed strict-liability causes of action in real estate transactions, particularly when the houses sold were mass-produced.

[6]Unless, of course, they have guaranteed their service (in which case they may be liable for a breach of express warranty) or lied about some critical aspect of their service (in which case they may be liable for the tort of misrepresentation). See also footnote 4.

a service. There are courts, however, that *are* willing to chip away at this rule when nonprofessional services are involved. In the beauty parlor case, for example, there is a well-known New Jersey opinion that held there was a sale of the permanent-wave solution by a beauty parlor. When the solution caused injury, strict liability was imposed without the need to prove negligence.[7] The same result would be reached if a plaintiff at a restaurant were injured by food or drink. They are sales.

Defendants understandably want to classify what they do as services in order to avoid any form of strict liability. If they are correct that they are engaged in a service, the plaintiff must prove that the injury was negligently produced.

ASSIGNMENT

19.6

Bob is an independent paralegal in your state. He is authorized to represent clients in cases before the Social Security Administration for which he can legally charge a fee. For $25 extra, he sells clients a packet of forms that they can use to fill out themselves. Mary is one of his clients. She pays him his fee plus $25 for the forms. When opening the packet of forms at home, she cuts herself on a small razor that Bob had carelessly left in the packet. Mary wants to sue Bob. Does she have to prove negligence? (See General Instructions for the Legal Analysis Assignment in Chapter 2.)

IMPLIED WARRANTIES

There are two implied warranties:

- implied warranty of merchantability
- implied warranty of fitness for a particular purpose

They are imposed by the law and not through agreement of the parties. You will find these warranties in state statutory codes. State legislatures created the warranties by modeling them on § 2-314 (merchantability) and § 2-315 (fitness) of the Uniform Commercial Code (UCC) (see footnote 2). Like the breach of an express warranty, the breach of these two implied warranties imposes strict liability, in that the plaintiff does not have to establish that the defendant intended to breach them nor that the defendant was negligent in breaching them.

Our discussion of the implied warranties will cover the following topics:

- elements of breach
- problems of privity
- defenses

Implied Warranty of Merchantability

The elements of a breach of an **implied warranty of merchantability** are:

i.   sale of goods
ii. by a merchant of goods of that kind
iii. the goods are not merchantable
iv. damage
v.   causation

---

[7]*Newmark v. Gimbel's Inc.* 102 N.J. Super. 279, 246 A.2d 11, *aff'd*, 54 N.J. 585, 258 A.2d 697 (1969).

Sale of Goods   Sales are covered, but not services. See the earlier discussion in this chapter on the problems of distinguishing a sale (which does carry an implied warranty of merchantability) and a service (which does not).

Merchant of Goods of that Kind   This warranty does not apply to the occasional seller of goods, such as a cab driver who sells a watch to a fellow cab driver or to a customer in the cab. The defendant must be a merchant in the business of selling goods of the kind in question. There is an implied warranty of merchantability in a car sold by a car dealer, but not in a rifle sold by the car dealer.

Goods Are Not Merchantable   Goods are **merchantable** when they are fit for the ordinary purposes for which the goods are used. (As we shall see in the next section, this is a broader test than that used for *strict liability in tort*, which requires that the product be unreasonably dangerous.) The following are examples of products that are not merchantable:

- vinegar bottles that contain particles of glass
- shoes with heels that break off with normal use soon after purchase
- aspirin that causes infertility

If, however, regular shoes fall apart when the plaintiff is mountain climbing, there is no implied warranty of merchantability, because the shoes were not being used for their ordinary purpose. If the plaintiff who bought the shoes can establish the elements of an implied warranty of fitness *for a particular purpose,* strict liability will be imposed on that theory. Otherwise, the defendant is not liable without a showing of negligence.

There is no requirement that plaintiffs prove they actually relied on the merchantability of the goods before purchase. This reliance is assumed. Suppose, however, that there are obvious defects in the product, which a reasonable inspection of the goods would reveal to the typical consumer. There is no implied warranty with respect to such defects so long as the consumer had full opportunity to inspect.

Damage and Causation   The damage or injury to the person or property of the plaintiff must be caused by the fact that the goods were not fit for their ordinary purpose. The traditional but-for or substantial factor test will be applied to establish causation.

ASSIGNMENT

19.7

There is a small fire in Mary's apartment. When she tries to smother it with a blanket, she is burned by the flames that come from the blanket, which caught fire the moment she placed it on the small fire. In a suit against the manufacturer of the blanket, can she claim breach of implied warranty of merchantability? (See General Instructions for the Legal Analysis Assignment in Chapter 2.)

Implied Warranty of Fitness for a Particular Purpose

Next we examine the **implied warranty of fitness for a particular purpose.** The elements of a breach of this warranty are:

   i. sale of goods
   ii. seller has reason to know the buyer's particular purpose in buying the goods
   iii. seller has reason to know that the buyer is relying on the seller's skill or judgment in buying the goods
   iv. the goods are not fit for the particular purpose
   v. damage
   vi. causation

Particular purposes must be distinguished from the ordinary purposes of a product. Ordinary purposes are the customary uses of the product. The following are examples of particular purposes:

- shoes to be used to climb mountains
- sunglasses to be used by a professional baseball player
- a dog chain to hold a 300-pound dog

The seller must know or have reason to know about the particular purpose, and know that the buyer is relying on the seller's skill and judgment. The buyer must in fact rely on this skill and judgment. A buyer who makes a careful inspection of the product may have difficulty proving reliance. A good deal will depend on the extent of the inspection and on the expertise of the buyer in the use of the product. If the buyer relies on his or her own skill and judgment rather than on that of the seller, the buyer cannot use this cause of action. Of course, if the product is also not fit for its *ordinary* purpose, the plaintiff can sue under the merchantability warranty. Otherwise, there is no recovery unless the plaintiff establishes negligence.

Privity

Earlier when we discussed negligence in a products liability case, we saw that all states now follow the ruling of *MacPherson v. Buick Motor Co.* that privity is not needed to bring a negligence action. Privity is the relationship that exists between parties who have entered a contract with each other.

> **EXAMPLE:**   Helen buys a General Electric blender from Macy's. One day in Helen's kitchen, the blender explodes, injuring Helen, her young daughter, and a visiting neighbor. When the accident occurred, they were all gathered around the blender ready to taste a new drink the blender was mixing.

Helen is in privity with Macy's, but not with General Electric. Her daughter and neighbor are in privity with no one. Yet, under the ruling in *MacPherson*, they can all sue General Electric for negligence. The absence of privity will not be a bar since they are all foreseeable users of the blender, which is dangerous if defectively made.

Suppose, however, that Helen, her daughter, and her neighbor want to sue General Electric for breach of any of the warranties. Will the lack of privity be a bar? States do not answer this question in the same way:

Who Can Sue for Breach of Warranty
- A few states cling to the old rule that there must be privity, which can exist only between an immediate buyer and the immediate seller.
- Some states permit the immediate buyer and members of the buyer's family or household to bring the warranty action.
- Some states permit the immediate buyer and any person who may reasonably be expected to be affected by the goods to bring the warranty action, e.g., a bystander who is hit by a car.

Who Can Be Sued for Breach of Warranty
- A few states cling to the old rule that there must be privity, which can exist only between an immediate buyer and the immediate seller.
- Some states permit designated nonprivity plaintiffs (see "Who Can Sue") to bring direct warranty actions against the manufacturer when the product is designed to come into contact with the body, e.g., food, home permanent solution.
- Some states permit designated nonprivity plaintiffs (see "Who Can Sue") to bring direct warranty actions against the manufacturer for any product.

Defenses to Warranty Actions

The following defenses will be briefly discussed:

- disclaimer
- notice
- contributory negligence
- assumption of the risk

Disclaimer of Warranty Under certain conditions, parties to a sales contract can agree that some or all warranties do not exist, i.e., the warranties are disclaimed. The **disclaimer** must be conspicuous and unambiguous so that it is clearly communicated to the buyer. A disclaimer buried in small print on the back of a standardized contract form will probably be held to be ineffective against the ordinary consumer. A court may rule that the disclaimer is invalid because it is **unconscionable.** Something is unconscionable when it is substantially unfair due to a highly unequal bargaining position of the parties. If the defendant is the seller or manufacturer of mass-produced goods, courts are likely to find that nonconspicuous disclaimers are unconscionable against the average consumer. Statutes may impose special requirements for disclaimers to be effective. For example, a disclaimer of the warranty of merchantability must mention the word "merchantability" in the language of the disclaimer. Finally, if a nonpurchaser is allowed to bring a warranty action (see the discussion on privity), disclaimers are generally ineffective against them.

Notice It is a defense to a warranty action that the injured plaintiff failed to give **notice** to the defendant of the breach of the warranty within a reasonable time after the breach was discovered or should have been discovered. Since many plaintiffs wait a good deal of time before taking action, they fall into the trap of this defense. Some courts, however, disregard the notice requirement when the breach of warranty causes personal injury or when the plaintiff is a nonpurchaser. Even if a court will not go this far, the tendency is to be lenient to plaintiffs in deciding whether they waited an unreasonable time to notify the defendant.

Contributory Negligence Generally, contributory negligence is not a defense to a breach-of-warranty action.

Assumption of Risk Assumption of the risk *is* a defense to a breach-of-warranty action. The defendant must show that the plaintiff had actual knowledge and an appreciation of the danger and yet still voluntarily proceeded to use the product.

CASE

Ressallat v. Burglar & Fire Alarms, Inc.
79 Ohio App. 3d 43, 606 N.E.2d 1001 (1992)
Court of Appeals of Ohio, Third District, Crawford County

Background: *Dr. Ressallat and his wife bought a home burglary alarm from BFA (Burglar & Fire Alarms, Inc.). The contract of sale disclaimed all implied warranties. After a burglary, the Ressallats sued BFA for breach of implied warranty of merchantability seeking recovery for loss of personal property resulting from the burglary. The position of BFA was that it had disclaimed all warranties in the contract of sale. The trial court agreed with BFA, ruling that the disclaimer was sufficiently conspicuous. The Ressallats (as appellants) appealed. The case is now on appeal before the Court of Appeals of Ohio.*

Decision on Appeal: *Judgment for BFA affirmed. Although the trial court erred in ruling that the disclaimer was conspicuous, the error was harmless because there was no breach of warranty that caused harm.*

OPINION OF COURT
Judge EVANS delivered the opinion of the court. . . .
[The] Ressallats ("appellants") entered into an agreement with BFA [Burglar & Fire Alarms, Inc.] for the purchase of a burglar alarm system for their home. The system was designed to alert the Ressallats, both via warning lights

and the sounding of a horn, when an unauthorized person had entered the house. The burglar alarm system was linked with the telephone system so that, simultaneous with the sounding of the alarm, a call was placed through the telephone lines to BFA's "central monitoring station." The Ressallats paid a monthly fee for these services.

On the advice of BFA's salesperson, the Ressallats arranged with the telephone company to have the phone cable, from the pole to the house, buried. However . . . the Ressallats began having problems with the telephone lines. Although General Telephone Company ("GTE") resolved the difficulties with the phone lines, the cable was not reburied. Instead, it was strung directly from the pole to the Ressallats' house, suspended just a few feet above the ground. Although Dr. Ressallat contacted GTE several times about reburying the phone cable, the company took no action until after the burglary.

[The] Ressallats' home was burglarized. The burglar apparently obtained unimpeded access to the house by cutting the exposed telephone wires so as to prevent transmission of the alarm. Inside the house, wires to the burglar alarm horn were severed at the electric service box. Jewelry and coins worth over $100,000 were stolen from the house. The Ressallats' insurance company, Physicians' Insurance Company of Ohio ("PICO"), reimbursed the Ressallats in the amount of $17,125.37, the maximum payable on their homeowners' policy. . . .

[In the Ressallats' suit against BFA for breach of warranty, the trial court ruled for BFA, concluding that all warranties had been validly disclaimed because they were conspicuous. On appeal the Ressallats argue that the disclaimer was "inconspicuous as a matter of law."]

Under R.C. [Ohio Revised Code] 1302.29, unless exclusions or disclaimers of warranty are part of the parties' "bargain in fact," a purchaser of goods in Ohio receives, in addition to any express warranty (which generally only provides for repair or replacement of defective goods), an implied warranty that the goods shall be merchantable and "fit" for their intended purpose. See R.C. 1302.27 and 1302.28. Although courts generally uphold disclaimers of implied warranties between parties who have equal bargaining power, they are reluctant to afford validity to such disclaimers when a purchaser is simply a consumer, rather than a commercial entity. As stated by the Supreme Court: ". . . [Disclaimers] of implied warranties. . . must be a part of the parties' bargain in fact. If it is contained in a printed clause which was not conspicuous or brought to the buyer's attention, the seller had no reasonable expectation that the buyer understood that his remedies were being restricted to repair and replacement." *Ins. Co. of N. Am. v. Automatic Sprinkler Corp.* (1981), 67 Ohio St. 2d 91, 96-97, 423 N.E.2d 151, 154-155.

Further, R.C. 1302.29(B) requires compliance with the following: ". . . to exclude or modify the implied warranty of merchantability or any part of it the language must mention merchantability and in case of a writing must be conspicuous, and to exclude or modify any implied warranty of fitness the exclusion must be by a writing and conspicuous. . . ."

The code itself defines "conspicuous," and provides that a determination of conspicuousness is a matter of law for the court to decide. R.C. 1301.01(J) provides:

". . . A term or clause is conspicuous when it is so written that a reasonable person against whom it is to operate ought to have noticed it. A printed heading in capitals (as: NONNEGOTIABLE BILL OF LADING) is conspicuous. Language in the body of a form is 'conspicuous' if it is in larger or other contrasting type or color . . . Whether a term is 'conspicuous' or not is for decision by the court."

The disclaimer of warranties at issue herein appears on the back page of the sales contract, which was signed on the front by both parties. The disclaimer is buried in the middle of a full page of small type, in a style identical to the rest of the text on the page. There are no outstanding headings alerting a purchaser to the disclaimer, and there is no mention of "merchantability" as required by R.C. 1302.29. Furthermore, Dr. Ressallat testified in his deposition that the disclaimer was not mentioned by the salesman at the time of the sale of the burglar alarm system, nor was it brought to his attention that anything was printed on the back page of the contract.

We believe the court erred in concluding that the disclaimer of warranties in these parties' contract was conspicuous. First, the disclaimer fails to mention "merchantability," a requirement of the code which must be fulfilled if a disclaimer of the implied warranty of merchantability is to be found valid. Additionally, we find that the trial court ignored the statutory language and applied an improper standard in determining that the disclaimer was conspicuous. In making that determination, the court stated: "These warranties and conditions are not hidden, but clearly spelled out in common understandable language which leaves no doubt as to what is and what is not covered, and when."

While we agree that the common, ordinary definition of "conspicuous" can be "not hidden," or "clearly spelled out," the code explicitly sets forth what the term means under the circumstances of this case. One's understanding of the terminology bears no relation to conspicuousness under the code. In the disclaimer at issue, there are no prominent headings, and there is no print of a different style or color that would draw one's attention. The disclaimer wording blends in with the surrounding "terms" and "conditions" and is in no way more noticeable. We find that the disclaimer in the contract is, as a matter of law, inconspicuous. . . .

However . . . we find that in this case the court's error was harmless, and not prejudicial to appellants. Absent evidence or testimony supporting the breach of warranty claims, the disclaimers are irrelevant, and thus provide no ground for reversal of the court's judgment. . . .

Dr. Ressallat himself testified that BFA had advised him at the time of the burglar alarm purchase to have the telephone lines buried for the sake of security. Further, after GTE had dug up the lines for repair purposes, it failed to rebury them despite several requests from appellants. Burial of the telephone cable was never a duty assumed by BFA. . . . Appellants present no evidence of failure or defect in the actual system or its components. There is simply no evidence that BFA breached any duty it could possibly have had to appellants. Appellants offer no facts evidencing how any warranty was breached, nor do the complaint, transcript, or affidavits indicate that any action of [BFA] was the proximate cause of the burglary. Furthermore, BFA's evidence that the alarm system was functioning properly immediately before and after the robbery was unrefuted.

Therefore . . . no reasonable person could find that BFA sold appellants a defective alarm system or failed in its duty to maintain and repair the system under the parties' contract, thereby becoming liable for appellants' loss of property. Indeed, sellers of goods are not required to be insurers of property, absent assumption of such a duty. . . . Having found no evidence as to BFA's . . . breach of warranties . . . we affirm the judgment of the trial court.

Judgment affirmed.

ASSIGNMENT

19.8

a. If the implied warranty on the burglar alarm was not validly disclaimed, why did the buyers of the alarm lose the case?

b. Would the result in this case have been different if the buyers had signed the contract of sale on the same page that contained the disclaimer of warranties?

c. Can the buyers sue GTE? If so, for what causes of action?

STRICT LIABILITY IN TORT

One of the most dramatic developments in the law of torts since the 1960s has been the creation of a new tort called **strict liability in tort.** As we will see, it provides considerable advantages to an injured consumer over the other products liability causes of action. We begin our study of this important tort by an overview that places it in context.

 Strict Liability in Tort Checklist:
Definitions, Relationships, Paralegal Roles, and Research References

Category
Strict liability in tort is a strict liability tort. There is no need to show intent or negligence. In many states, however, negligence concepts are relevant to design defects.

Interest Protected by This Tort
The right to be free from injuries due to products that are defective and unreasonably dangerous.

Elements of This Tort
    i. seller
    ii. a defective product that is unreasonably dangerous to person or property
    iii. user or consumer
    iv. physical harm (damages)
    v. causation

Definitions of Major Words/Phrases in These Elements
Seller: A person engaged in the business of selling products for use or consumption.
Defective product: At the time the product leaves the seller's hands, it has a manufacturing, design, or warning defect.
Unreasonably dangerous: The product is dangerous to an extent beyond that which would be contemplated by the ordinary consumer who purchases it, with the ordinary knowledge common to the community as to its characteristics. (Note: Some courts use other tests.)
User or consumer: Anyone who uses or consumes the product (some courts have extended the definition to cover bystanders).
Physical harm: Damage to person or property.

Strict Liability in Tort Checklist Continued

Causation: "But for" the defect, the physical harm would not have occurred, or the defect was a substantial factor in producing the physical harm.

Major Defenses and Counterargument Possibilities That Need to Be Explored

1. The defendant is not a seller.
2. The injury came from a service, not a product.
3. The product is not defective.
4. The product is not unreasonably dangerous.
5. The plaintiff is not a user or consumer.
6. There was no physical harm to person or property of the plaintiff.
7. The defendant did not cause the physical harm.
8. There was unforeseeable, extreme misuse of the product by the plaintiff.
9. The plaintiff assumed the risk of the danger in the product.
10. The plaintiff failed to take reasonable steps to mitigate the harm caused when the defendant committed strict liability in tort; therefore, damages should not cover the aggravation of the harm caused by the plaintiff (on the doctrine of avoidable consequences, see Chapter 16).

Damages

In most states, damages for strict liability in tort cover physical harm to persons or property, but not economic loss alone. Once physical harm to persons or property is established, compensatory damages can include medical bills, pain and suffering, etc. Punitive damages are also possible. (On the categories of damages, see Chapter 16.)

Relationship to Criminal Law

A state might impose criminal penalties on a company for selling designated products, e.g., drugs, explosives. The company would also be subject to civil liability—strict liability in tort—if the product is defective (unreasonably dangerous) and causes injury.

Relationship to Other Causes of Action

Breach of express warranty: Available if the product does not conform to a representation made by the seller of the product.
Breach of implied warranty of merchantability: Available if the product is not fit for its ordinary purpose.
Breach of implied warranty of fitness for a particular purpose: Available if the product is not suitable for a particular purpose when the buyer relied on the seller's skill or judgment on the product's suitability for that purpose.
Misrepresentation: Defendant must have knowingly made false statements of fact about the product that led to the injury and must have had the intent to deceive (scienter).
Negligence: Plaintiff must prove that the injury from the product was caused by the absence of reasonable care on the part of the seller.

Federal Law

a. Under the Federal Tort Claims Act, the United States Government will *not* be liable for a tort based on strict liability committed by one of its federal employees within the scope of employment. Sovereign immunity is not waived as to such torts. (See Figure 27–7 in Chapter 27.)
b. The United States Consumer Product Safety Commission (CPSC) has authority to protect the public against unreasonable risks of injury associated with designated consumer products. Penalties can be imposed for violation of CPSC mandates.
c. Other federal agencies also have jurisdiction over specific consumer products, e.g., the Food and Drug Administration, the National Highway Transportation and Safety Administration. Such agencies write administrative regulations that impose safety and other standards governing these products. These standards must be examined to assess their relevance to litigation on strict liability in tort.

Employer-Employee (Agency) Law

An employer who is a seller is strictly liable in tort for harm caused by a product sold by one of its employees within the scope of employment if the product is defective and unreasonably dangerous (respondeat superior). On the factors that determine the scope of employment, see Figure 14–10 in Chapter 14.

Strict Liability in Tort Checklist Continued

Paralegal Roles in Strict Liability in Tort Litigation
(See also Figures 3–1, 3–14, and 29–1 in Chapters 3 and 29.)

Fact finding (help the office collect facts relevant to prove the elements of strict liability in tort, the elements of available defenses, and extent of injuries or other damages):
- client interviewing
- field investigation
- online research (e.g., identity of board of directors of a manufacturer)

File management (help the office control the volume of paperwork in a strict liability in tort litigation):
- open client file
- enter case data in computer database
- maintain file documents

Litigation assistance (help the trial attorney prepare for a trial and appeal, if needed, of a strict liability in tort case):
- draft discovery requests
- draft answers to discovery requests
- draft pleadings
- digest and index discovery documents
- help prepare, order, and manage trial exhibits (visuals or demonstratives)
- prepare trial notebook
- draft notice of appeal
- order trial transcript
- cite check briefs
- perform legal research

Collection/enforcement (help the trial attorney for the judgment creditor to collect the damages award or to enforce other court orders at the conclusion of the strict liability in tort case):
- draft postjudgment discovery requests
- field investigation to monitor compliance with judgment
- online research (e.g., location of defendant's business assets)

Research References for Strict Liability in Tort

Digests
In the digests of West, look for case summaries of court opinions on this tort under key topics such as:

Products liability	Damages
Drugs and narcotics	Torts
Food	Negligence
Sales	Death

Corpus Juris Secundum
In this legal encyclopedia, look for discussions under topic headings such as:

Products liability	Damages
Drugs and narcotics	Torts
Food	Negligence
Sales	Death

American Jurisprudence 2d
In this legal encyclopedia, look for discussions under topic headings such as:

Products liability	Damages
Drugs, narcotics and poisons	Torts
Food	Negligence
Sales	Death

Strict Liability in Tort Checklist Continued

Legal Periodical Literature
There are two index systems to use to locate articles on this tort:

INDEX TO LEGAL PERIODICALS AND BOOKS (ILP)	CURRENT LAW INDEX (CLI)
See literature in *ILP* under subject headings such as:	See literature in *CLI* under subject headings such as:
Products Liability	Products Liability
Warranty	Insurance,
Strict Liability	Products Liability
Insurance,	Product Recall
Products Liability	Manufacturers
Product Recall	Torts
Manufacturers	Damages
Torts	Negligence
Damages	Warranty
Negligence	

Example of a legal periodical article you can locate on this tort by using *ILP* or *CLI:*

Strict Liability in Tort: Reliance on Circumstantial Evidence to Prove a Defect by Donald J. O'Meara, 27 Federation of Insurance Counsel Quarterly 129 (1977).

A.L.R., A.L.R.2d, A.L.R.3d, A.L.R.4th, A.L.R.5th, A.L.R. Fed.
Use the *ALR Index* to locate annotations on this tort. In this index, check subject headings such as:

Products liability	Negligence
Warranty	Torts
Warnings	Damages
Drugs and narcotics	Death
Absolute liability	Repairs and maintenance

Example of an annotation you can locate through this index on strict liability in tort:

Products Liability: Modern Cases Determining Whether Product is Defectively Designed by Kristine Cordier Karnezis, 96 A.L.R.3d 22.

Words and Phrases
In this multivolume legal dictionary, look up *strict liability, warranty, defect, dangerous,* and every other word or phrase connected with strict liability in tort discussed in this section of the chapter. The dictionary will give you definitions of these words or phrases from court opinions.

CALR: Computer-Assisted Legal Research

Example of a query you could ask on WESTLAW to try to find cases, statutes, or other legal materials on strict liability in tort: **"strict liability in tort"/p damages**

Example of a query you could ask on LEXIS to try to find cases, statutes, or other legal materials on strict liability in tort: **strict liability in tort/p damages**

Example of search terms you could use on an Internet legal search engine such as LawCrawler (http://lawcrawler.findlaw.com) to find cases, statutes, or other legal materials on this tort: **"strict liability in tort"**

Example of search terms you could use on an Internet general search engine such as Alta Vista (http://www.altavista.com) to find cases, statutes, or other legal materials on this tort: **"strict liability in tort"**

More Internet sites to check to find materials on strict liability in tort and other torts:
Jurist: (http://jurist.law.pitt.edu/sg_torts.htm)
LawGuru: (http://www.lawguru.com/search/lawsearch.html)
See also Tort Law Online at the end of Chapter 1.

In several significant ways, strict liability in tort is different from the products liability causes of action we have been considering thus far in this chapter: negligence, misrepresentation, implied warranty of merchantability, and implied warranty of fitness for a particular purpose. In an action for strict liability in tort:

- The plaintiff does not have to prove that the defendant was negligent (although negligence concepts may be relevant when the plaintiff alleges that the injury was caused by a design defect).
- The plaintiff does not have to prove that the defendant knew of the defect or intended to deceive the plaintiff.
- The plaintiff does not have to establish privity with the defendant.
- The defendant cannot disclaim the obligation of safety no matter how conspicuous the disclaimer.
- Before being able to sue, the plaintiff has no duty to notify the defendant of the injury caused by the product.

There are five elements to the strict liability in tort cause of action:

1. seller
2. a defective product that is unreasonably dangerous to person or property
3. user or consumer
4. physical harm (damages)
5. causation

These elements are based on the highly influential § 402A of the American Law Institute's *Restatement (Second) of Torts*. Most courts have adopted these five elements of § 402A. As we shall see, however, there are a number of courts that have modified some of the elements. Also, the American Law Institute has itself made significant changes in its more recent *Restatement (Third) of Torts,* particularly as to design defects. Yet, the principles that dominate this area of the law in most states continue to be those embodied in § 402A of *Restatement (Second) of Torts.*

Seller

The defendant must be a **seller.** Seller has a broad definition: any person engaged in the business of selling products for use or consumption. Not covered is the occasional seller of a product who is not engaged in selling as part of his or her business. If, for example, one student sells another student a defective car, there is no strict liability in tort, because the student is not in the business of selling products. If the student is liable at all, negligence will have to be shown. Isolated sales that are not part of the usual course of business of the seller are not covered.

The following would be sellers under the first element:

- manufacturer of entire product
- assembler
- wholesaler
- operator of a restaurant
- supplier of a part
- distributor
- retailer

Some states do not impose strict liability in tort on the manufacturer of a defective **component part** of a product. Its liability would have to be based on negligence. Other courts, however, treat the manufacturer of a component part like everyone else in the **chain of distribution** and impose strict liability in tort.

Assume that at a small neighborhood hardware store you buy a defective hammer that is manufactured by a company located a thousand miles away. Both the store (a retailer) and the manufacturer are subject to strict liability in tort. They are both in the chain of distribution to the plaintiff. The store manager cannot say, "I didn't make the hammer; go sue the manufacturer." The store is a seller engaged in the business of selling, and hence is subject to strict liability in tort. To recover, the plaintiff does not have to prove that the store manager was negligent.

Someone who *rents* products as a business is also considered a seller. A company that rents cars, planes, or other equipment, for example, can be strictly liable in tort. Section 402A does not cover sales of real property. As we saw with implied warranty of merchantability, however, some states are willing to extend strict liability to sellers of houses, particularly mass-produced structures. (See footnote 5.)

Strict liability in tort applies to the *sale of products,* not to *services.* See the earlier discussion of this distinction in this chapter, particularly with reference to the problem of transactions that have both sale and service components.

Defective Product That Is Unreasonably Dangerous

There are two requirements for this element under § 402A of *Restatement (Second) of Torts:* the product must be both defective *and* **unreasonably dangerous.** Earlier in Figure 19–2, we examined the three major categories of defects:

manufacturing defects: Something never intended went wrong when the product was being put together. The product does not conform to its design.

design defects: The product conforms to what the planners intended, but something is wrong with their design.

warning defects: The instructions or warnings for the product are either missing or are inadequate.

The plaintiff does not have to prove that the defendant was negligent in creating any of these defects. A defendant who has "sold" a defective product can be strictly liable in tort even if the defendant used all reasonable care. The problem, however, is that it is sometimes difficult to avoid discussing negligence concepts, particularly when the product is alleged to have design defects. Part of the confusion is the use of the phrase "unreasonably dangerous" in § 402A of *Restatement (Second) of Torts.* This phrase certainly suggests the reasonableness analysis that dominates any discussion of negligence. In theory, however, we need to separate negligence from strict liability in tort. They are different causes of action.

When is a product unreasonably dangerous? Section 402A uses the "ordinary consumer" test:

A product is unreasonably dangerous when it is dangerous to an extent beyond that which would be contemplated by the ordinary consumer who purchases it, with the ordinary knowledge common to the community as to its characteristics.

Note that the test is not whether the injured plaintiff thought the product was unreasonably dangerous. All injured plaintiffs undoubtedly would. The test is **objective:** what would an ordinary consumer think or expect?

In many cases there is little difficulty establishing unreasonable danger by using the test of the ordinary consumer. Such consumers, for example, would not expect a bottle of catsup to have arsenic in it and would expect a bus to be designed with handrails within easy reach during a sudden stop. They are also aware of the danger that is inherent in some products, e.g., knives, matches, bug sprays. If these products are not defectively made or designed, they are not unreasonably dangerous. Aware of the obvious danger, the ordinary consumer takes obvious precautions, e.g., lifts a knife by its handle rather than by its blade.

Other products, however, are not so easy to assess. Assume, for example, that the plaintiff eats a bowl of fish chowder at a New England restaurant and suffers severe injuries when a fish bone gets caught in the throat. Is the product unreasonably dangerous? Probably not. An ordinary consumer would expect to find some bones in this kind of soup. There is danger from bones in the soup, but not an unreasonable danger. Note that we do not ask whether the restaurant used reasonable care to re move bones from the fish chowder. The use of reasonable care is a negligence standard. The test here is the expectation of the ordinary consumer.

There are some courts that argue that a product is unreasonably dangerous if it contains a substance that is "foreign" to the product. Most courts, however, reject this view and say that even a substance that is "natural" to the product can be unreasonably dangerous.

A manufacturer or retailer is not required to sell a product that will never cause injury. Nor are they required to sell a product in the safest condition possible. A car built like a tank may be the safest vehicle on the road, but a car manufacturer is not strictly liable in tort for failing to build its cars to be as strong as tanks. Why? Because ordinary consumers do not expect cars to be built this way for their safety.

ASSIGNMENT **19.9**	Are the following products unreasonably dangerous? (See General Instructions for the Legal Analysis Assignment in Chapter 2.)

a. Linda goes into a bar and orders a martini. She breaks a tooth on an unpitted olive.

b. George chokes on a cherry pit in a pie he purchases from a school vending machine.

c. Sara chokes on a whole peanut found in "extra creamy" peanut butter she purchases at the supermarket.

d. Tom, age twelve, buys a bicycle from the Cycle and Sports Store. The bike does not have a headlight on it. While carefully driving the bike at night, Tom is hit by a car. Assume that the accident would not have occurred if the bike had a headlight on it.

Many products can become dangerous to a consumer who overuses or overconsumes them, but they are not necessarily unreasonably dangerous. Good, "wholesome" whiskey is not unreasonably dangerous because it can be deadly to alcoholics. Uncontaminated butter is not unreasonably dangerous because it can bring on heart attacks for people who need a low-cholesterol diet.

Nor is a product unreasonably dangerous because it fails to warn against every possible danger that could be caused by its use.

> The seller may reasonably assume that those with common allergies, as for example to eggs or strawberries, will be aware of them, and he is not required to warn against them. Where, however, the product contains an ingredient to which a substantial number of the population are allergic, and the ingredient is one whose danger is not generally known, or if known is one which the consumer would reasonably not expect to find in the product, the seller is required to give warning against it, if he has knowledge, or by the application of reasonable, developed human skills and foresight should have knowledge, of the presence of the ingredient and the danger. Likewise in the case of poisonous drugs, or those unduly dangerous for other reasons, warning as to use may be required. *Restatement (Second) of Torts* § 402A, comment j (1965).

Once a warning is clearly and conspicuously given, the seller can assume that it will be read and followed.

Unavoidably unsafe products are those that are incapable of being made safe due to the current state of technology and science. A certain drug, for example, may be extremely valuable, but have a high risk of dangerous side effects. If the drug is properly prepared and marketed, and an adequate warning is given of the risk, the drug is neither defective nor unreasonably dangerous. Properly prepared means that all feasible tests were conducted on the drug before it was placed on the market. Properly marketed might mean that it is sold only by prescription through a doctor.

Design defects pose the greatest headaches for the courts. The first problem is to make the distinction between the **intended use** and the **foreseeable use** of a product:

intended use: What the manufacturer wanted the product used for; the purpose for which the product was built and placed on the market.

foreseeable use: What the manufacturer anticipates or should be able to anticipate the product will be used for; a foreseeable use may not be the intended use.

A product must not be unreasonably dangerous both for its intended use *and* for its foreseeable use.

EXAMPLES:

- Chair
  Intended Use: To sit on
  Foreseeable Use: To stand on in order to store things in a closet
  Unforeseeable Use: To provide extra support for an elevated car while changing a tire
- Cleaning Fluid
  Intended Use: To clean floors
  Foreseeable Use: To be swallowed by children
  Unforeseeable Use: As a lighter fluid for a barbecue

If a plaintiff is injured when a chair on which he or she is standing collapses, the manufacturer cannot escape strict liability in tort by arguing that the plaintiff was not using the product for its intended purpose. It is foreseeable that at least a fair number of users will stand on chairs. Therefore, the product must not be unreasonably dangerous for this foreseeable purpose—the chair must be built strongly enough to accommodate this purpose, or adequate warnings against use for this purpose must be provided. An ordinary consumer would expect the product to be reasonably safe for all foreseeable purposes, including, of course, its intended purposes.

Nor will the defendant be able to raise the defense that the plaintiff misused the product. It is not a **misuse** of a product to use it for a purpose that the manufacturer should have anticipated. Or, viewed from another perspective, if it is a misuse, it is a foreseeable misuse that should have been guarded against in the design or through a warning. Similarly, it is foreseeable that small children will swallow cleaning liquid. Therefore, the manufacturer should provide safety precautions against such use, e.g., a warning on the bottle addressed to parents that the substance is toxic and should be kept out of the reach of children, or instructions on the bottle of what to do if someone swallows the contents.

Unforeseeable uses, however, are another matter. To make a manufacturer strictly liable in tort for injuries caused by products put to unforeseeable uses would be to make the manufacturer an insurer. Liability does not extend this far.

Of course, liability for unreasonably dangerous products put to foreseeable uses is not limited to the manufacturer that designed the defective product. The local department store is also strictly liable for such products. Anyone who is a "seller" in the chain of distribution has committed strict liability in tort.

ASSIGNMENT 19.10

For the following products, identify what you think are:
- the intended uses
- possible unintended uses that are foreseeable
- possible unintended uses that are unforeseeable
  a. a screwdriver
  b. shampoo for a dog
  c. a lawn mower
  d. bug spray

Assume that each time the product was used for one of the three categories of use, an injury occurred because the product was defective and dangerous for that use. (See General Instructions for the Legal Analysis Assignment in Chapter 2.)

ASSIGNMENT 19.11

The Smith family live in a hot neighborhood. To keep out insects, they have placed standard removable screens on the windows of their second floor apartment. One day their eleven-month-old, twenty-eight-pound child accidentally falls on the screen, pushing it out. The baby falls to the ground outside, sustaining severe injuries. The Smith's sue the screen manufacturer for strict liability in tort. What arguments will the Smiths make and what will be the response of the manufacturer? (See General Instructions for the Legal Analysis Assignment in Chapter 2.)

An important design defect issue concerns the **crashworthiness** of automobiles—the problem of the second injury or the second collision. An automobile accident often involves two events: the impact with the other car or object and the impact of the plaintiff *inside* the car with the steering wheel, window, dashboard, or car roof. The design of the car may have nothing to do with the initial accident, yet have a great deal to do with the extent of the injury suffered by the plaintiff. The question is: how crashworthy does the car have to be? Does the manufacturer have the responsibility of designing the car so that the plaintiff is not injured through internal impact with the car's steering wheel, dashboard, gas tank, or other component? It is highly foreseeable that a plaintiff will receive serious injury following an initial crash. This risk must be weighed against the cost of designing the car to minimize the risk. A court may conclude, for example, that a dashboard made out of a hard metal is unreasonably dangerous, or that the placement of the gas tank is unreasonably dangerous because alternative designs were feasible and would have lessened the danger of the second injury.

Many state and federal statutes and regulations exist on consumer products. Is a product that conforms to all of them automatically deemed to be reasonably safe even though it causes an injury? Yes, according to some courts, particularly if the statute explicitly exempts the defendant from liability when there is compliance. Many courts, however, say that a product that conforms to all of the statutes and regulations can still be unreasonably dangerous, because they may cover only what is minimally required for safety. Compliance is merely some evidence—or at most, raises a presumption—that the product is not defective or unreasonably dangerous.

Other Tests?

Thus far we have been focusing on the ordinary consumer test for unreasonable danger presented in § 402A of *Restatement (Second) of Torts*. Some states do not accept this test for determining all kinds of product defects. Everyone knows, for example, that products do not last forever. But how is an ordinary consumer supposed to identify the exact life of a particular product such as a tire, engine, or drug during which it should remain reasonably safe? Ordinary consumers (with the "ordinary knowledge common to the community") often do not know enough to be able to judge the amount of danger that should have been designed out of a particular product.

In part because of this difficulty, some states do not use the ordinary consumer test for all products, particularly when a design defect is alleged. Here is a sample of the language used in some states:

- The risks of the product's design outweigh its benefits.
- The risks of the product are so great that a reasonable seller, knowing the risks, would not place the product on the market.
- The product is defective and this defect caused injury in reasonably foreseeable use.

The focus of these tests is not the expectations of the ordinary consumer. Most of the tests require the kind of **risk-benefit analysis** that courts traditionally use when determining negligence:

The foreseeability of serious harm: The greater the foreseeability of serious harm, the more care, time, and expense are needed to design the product to avoid or minimize the harm.

The importance or social utility of the product: How valuable or significant is the product? The more importance or social utility it has, the more reasonable it is to take risks in putting the product on the market.

The burden or inconvenience on the manufacturer of redesigning the product to make it safer: What would have been the expense of adding an extra safety precaution? If it is slight, it probably should have been taken. If, however, the cost is so excessive as to make the product close to unmarketable, the precautions may not need to be taken. A warning might be sufficient. Note, however, that although warnings might be the cheapest and least burdensome precaution, they are not a substitute for reasonable design changes that would take the danger out of the product or significantly reduce it.

This kind of analysis is also referred to as **risk-utility analysis** or **risk-utility balancing.**

CASE

Riley v. Becton Dickinson Vascular Access, Inc.
913 F. Supp. 879 (1995)
United States District Court, Eastern District of Pennsylvania

Background: *Lynda Riley contracted Human Immuno Deficiency Virus (HIV) when she was stuck by a needle at the Community Hospital of Lancaster where she was a nurse. At the time of the accident, she was administering an intravenous (I.V.) conventional catheter. As she removed the needle from the catheter and was preparing to dispose of the needle, the patient's left arm moved. The nurse reacted to his movement by moving her hand, and the needle* *penetrated her left palm. She was using a conventional catheter, the Angiocath, manufactured by Becton Dickinson Vascular Access. She sued Becton for strict liability in tort, alleging that the catheter's design was defective, and that an alternative catheter, ProtectIV, would have prevented her accident. Becton made a motion for summary judgment, arguing that the court should rule without a trial that its product was not unreasonably dangerous. (This is a diversity of* *citizenship case brought in federal court because the parties are citizens of different states. The federal trial court in this diversity action applied the state tort law of Pennsylvania.)*

Decision of Court: *Judgment for Becton. Motion for summary judgment is granted. The conventional catheter, Angiocath, is not unreasonably dangerous.*

OPINION OF COURT

Judge Troutman delivered the opinion of the court. . . .

[W]hen presented with claims arising under § 402A of the *Restatement (Second) of Torts,* . . .Pennsylvania courts have adopted a risk/utility test which requires consideration of [seven] factors in aid of the determination whether a product is unreasonably dangerous, *Fitzpatrick v. Madonna,* 424 Pa. Super. 473, 623 A.2d 322, 324 (1993):

1. The usefulness and desirability of the product—its utility to the user and to the public as a whole. . . .

It is obvious that many medical procedures depend upon the use of sharp needles. . . . The evidence submitted by defendant demonstrates that the Angiocath is such a device and is particularly well suited for use in certain situations, such as emergencies, and with patients in whom accessing a vein is more difficult than usual, e.g., infants, small children and the elderly, since a different type of I.V. catheter is more difficult to use in those circumstances. The fact that an instrument such as the Angiocath is capable of causing injury to both the medical professional user and to the patient user does not in any way impair the usefulness of the product. Thus, we conclude that the product is both highly useful and that its availability is desirable to both the medical profession and to the public at large.

2. The safety aspects of a product—the likelihood that it will cause injury, and the probable seriousness of the injury. . . .

In analyzing this factor, we consider both the likelihood of injury from use of the product and the probable seriousness of the injury. . . . [A]lthough it is indisputable that all exposures to HIV which result in infection are terribly serious, and, because of the deadly consequences of infection, all needle stick exposures to HIV contaminated blood are serious, it does not follow that all needle stick incidents present a risk of serious injury. . . . [I]f we assume that there are 18.4 I.V. catheter needle sticks per 100,000 uses of such devices, assume an HIV contamination rate of 2%, and assume the highest likely infection rate, .47%, there could be 17 HIV infections per 1 billion I.V. catheters used . . . or between 8 and 9 infections per 500,000,000 uses of an I.V. catheter set. . . . From the available evidence and projections based thereon, the Court concludes that the risk of serious injury from use of an I.V. catheter such as the Angiocath is quite low.

3. The availability of a substitute product which would meet the same need and not be as unsafe. . . .

Plaintiff does not argue that there is an acceptable substitute for an I.V. catheter. Plaintiff points out, however, that there is an available substitute for a conventional I.V. catheter which leaves the introducing needle exposed after it is withdrawn from the flexible tube. The ProtectIV, an I.V. catheter manufactured by Critikon, a competitor of defendant, permits the needle to be retracted into a plastic

sheath as it is withdrawn from the tube attached to the patient's vein. . . .

A study of 1024 healthcare workers at nine hospitals in 6 states over a period of six months revealed that the incidence of needle sticks was lower with the ProtectIV, . . . Although a reduction in the total number of needle sticks would obviously lessen the likelihood of serious injury, the projected risks of HIV exposure and infection from any one such needle stick are identical to the risks associated with a needle stick from a conventional catheter, since the rate of HIV exposure and infection depend upon the patient population, not the type of I.V. catheter used. . . . [T]he projected risk of HIV infection from an I.V. catheter needle stick would be reduced from 3.5/500,000,000 uses with a conventional catheter to 2/1,000,000,000 uses or 1/500,000,000 uses with a protected catheter. Consequently, it appears that an already small risk might be somewhat reduced, but would not be eliminated, by use of a protected rather than a conventional I.V. catheter. . . .

[C]ontrary to plaintiff's argument that the ProtectIV provides "automatic" protection from an exposed needle, the record shows that the introducer needle is retracted into the protective sheath only if the person initiating the I.V. activates that mechanism by sliding the sheath front, over the needle, as the needle is withdrawn through the catheter. Failure to properly engage the mechanism by fully extending the sheath until it "clicks" allows the sharp tip of the needle to remain exposed, which can . . . result in a needle stick.*

Moreover, the available evidence also discloses that even if the incidence of needle sticks is ultimately somewhat reduced by using the ProtectIV, a healthcare worker's exposure to a patient's blood may not be significantly reduced since more blood escapes from the catheter as the needle is withdrawn than occurs with a conventional I.V. catheter. . . .

Other problems with the ProtectIV [include]. . . difficulty using the catheters on infants, small children, elderly patients and others with difficult veins. Many such problems would likely result in the need for additional I.V. initiations, thereby actually increasing the potential for a needle stick by increasing the number of times an I.V. introducer needle is used. . . .

We conclude, therefore, that although the small projected risk of a needle stick might be further reduced by substituting a protected I.V. catheter for a conventional device, assuming that the user is proficient with the new device, the danger of a needle stick cannot be eliminated. Moreover, a reduction in the incidence of needle

---

*As defendant points out, given the undisputed circumstances of plaintiff's accident and the operation of the ProtectIV, it is not at all certain that she could have avoided the needle stick if she had been using it, since she reacted to a patient's sudden movement by an apparently reflexive movement of her own. It is not possible, therefore, to infer that plaintiff would have been able to completely engage the protective mechanism of the ProtectIV before the incident occurred. Had the needle been suddenly withdrawn from the catheter in response to the patient's movement and the tip remained exposed, a needle stick could have occurred. . . . [by a failure] to fully engage the sheath of the ProtectIV. . . .

sticks is by no means assured, and, even if achieved, blood exposure may not be significantly reduced, if at all, due to a generally recognized "backflow" problem which occurs when the needle is withdrawn from the catheter and the I.V. connection is not completed quickly. We further conclude that other design features of the available substitute product render it less effective, in general, than the Angiocath for its intended purpose, since use of the protected catheter may not be appropriate in some situations due to difficulties that cannot be easily overcome, if at all, with certain patients.

Thus, although a substitute for a conventional I.V. catheter is available which may reduce the incidence of needle sticks, it is not entirely certain that such substitute is safer overall when other aspects of the alternative design are considered and it does not appear to be an alternative which can feasibly replace conventional I.V. catheters completely.

4. The manufacturer's ability to eliminate the unsafe character of the product without impairing its usefulness or making it too expensive to maintain its utility. . . .

[T]he cost of the protected catheter far exceeds that of the conventional device. At the time the Community Hospital of Lancaster first evaluated the ProtectIV in 1992, the cost was $1.40 per unit compared to $.78 for the Angiocath. Moreover, the unit cost of the catheters is not the only cost consideration. . . . [T]he evidence establishes the need for extensive training with the ProtectIV in order to gain the benefit of somewhat fewer needle sticks and to overcome the problems inherent in other aspects of the product to the greatest possible extent. The additional costs associated with training hundreds of hospital workers prior to introducing the protected device for general use, combined with the potential need for follow-up in-servicing . . . are also costs associated with use of the alternative product. . . .

[T]he unit cost of the ProtectIV . . . is very high in light of the small benefit likely to be derived from the possible reduction, but not elimination, of the risk of a needle stick. . . . Thus, we conclude that it is not possible to eliminate the unsafe feature of the Angiocath without impairing its utility since the costs of the only available alternative product are much higher; the risk associated with the allegedly unsafe design cannot be completely eliminated; and there are problems other than the risk of a needle stick associated with the use of the alternative design which require extensive training to diminish and which cannot be entirely eliminated.

5. The user's ability to avoid danger by the exercise of care in the use of the product.

Despite the suggestion by defendant that plaintiff might somehow have prevented her accident by more careful attention to proper procedures, we find nothing in the record which establishes that a lack of care on plaintiff's part contributed to her injury. Under the undisputed circumstances, it appears that anyone, using any type of sharp device, might have sustained a similar injury by reacting to a patient's unexpected movement.

Such conclusion with respect to the present accident, however, does not appear to the Court to be truly relevant to our inquiry into this aspect of the risk/utility

analysis. In making the required social policy determination, we are concerned with the ability of the users of conventional I.V. catheters, in general, to avoid the risks inherent in the product, not with the particular circumstances of plaintiff's accident. In that regard, it appears that although healthcare workers often fail to take the appropriate precautions, proper safety practices can, to some extent, enable healthcare workers to reduce the risk of needle sticks. . . . [J]ust as the design of the protected catheter cannot completely prevent needle sticks from the use of I.V. catheters, it is unlikely that even extreme caution and punctilious adherence to recommended procedures can enable a healthcare worker to completely avoid that danger. Nevertheless, it does appear that healthcare facilities and healthcare workers themselves have some ability to reduce the risk inherent in the use of any I.V. catheter by taking appropriate precautions.

6. The user's anticipated awareness of the dangers inherent in the product and their avoidability, because of general public knowledge of the obvious condition of the product, or of the existence of suitable warnings or instructions. . . .

[T]here is widespread knowledge of the potential danger of a needle stick accident among healthcare workers. Indeed, plaintiff does not contend that the danger inherent in an exposed needle is hidden, generally unknown to healthcare workers, or that she was personally unaware of such danger.

7. The feasibility, on the part of the manufacturer, of spreading the loss of setting the price of the product or carrying liability insurance. . . .

[A]lthough it is unquestionably true that a manufacturer is almost always able to spread the cost of an injured plaintiff's loss over all users of a product by raising the price thereof, the feasibility of doing so depends upon balancing the . . . factors in the risk/utility analysis. . . . [W]hen consideration of the preceding six factors leads to the conclusion that the utility of product in question outweighs its risks, such determination compels the further conclusion that shifting the cost of plaintiff's loss to the manufacturer of the product is not fair, and, therefore, not feasible. . . .

[C]ost-shifting to the supplier is not appropriate, and, therefore, not "feasible" in this case since we have concluded that the Angiocath is unquestionably a useful product in which a very small risk of injury is inherent in the alleged design defect, an exposed needle which has contacted a patient's blood. We have also concluded that an alternative design which can, but does not always, eliminate that feature of the product likewise reduces its utility because of much higher costs and because of problems associated with other aspects of the alternative design. Finally, we concluded that the danger of the alleged design defect is obvious, well-known to users thereof, and can be reduced with appropriate precautions. . . .

Moreover, we conclude that in this case, there would be no adverse effect to plaintiff or to the public in general as a result of not shifting the costs of plaintiff's injury to the manufacturer of the product, thereby allowing the costs to remain where they are currently allocated: on the plaintiff's employer via the Workmen's Compensation system. . . .

SUMMARY

Having examined each factor in the risk/utility analysis, . . . we conclude that the Angiocath, although dangerous because it is capable of causing serious injury, is not unreasonably dangerous. . . . [I]n most instances the danger inherent in a needle stick is not grave, since most needle sticks do not expose the injured party to a serious illness, and even when exposed to HIV, only a small percentage of injured parties become infected. Moreover, needle sticks from I.V. catheters, specifically, are relatively rare and the likelihood of a resulting serious injury, defined herein as exposure to HIV/HIV infection, is slight in comparison to the widespread use of the product.

Although a feasible design which appears to reduce the risk of a needle stick injury is available, the potential reduction of the risk of a needle stick comes at a greatly increased cost and it is by no means certain that such design is truly "safer" overall since the available product which incorporates the alternative design is not as well-suited as the Angiocath to the primary purpose of an I.V. catheter, quick and efficient piercing of the skin and subcutaneous tissue for access to a vein. . . .

Accordingly, defendant's motion for summary judgment will be granted and judgment will be entered in favor of the defendant.

ASSIGNMENT

19.12

a. Why did the court rule that the conventional catheter was not unreasonably dangerous?

b. What was the causation problem that the nurse had in this case?

c. What does cost shifting mean? If compensation for the nurse is limited to her workers' compensation benefits, who bears the cost? If she had won this case, who would have borne the cost?

d. Assume that another hospital, Midway Hospital, must decide whether to purchase the Angiocath catheter or the ProtectIV catheter. What legal advice should Midway be given in light of the *Riley* opinion?

Risk-utility analysis has recently been adopted by the American Law Institute, the creator of the *Restatements*. As indicated earlier, the American Law Institute has made a significant change in strict liability in tort. It no longer recommends that courts use the unreasonable danger and ordinary consumer test of § 402A of the *Restatement (Second) of Torts* as the exclusive test for design defects. The new *Restatement (Third) of Torts* (1997) on products liability now recommends a different test for design defects:

> The product is defective in design when the foreseeable risks of harm posed by the product could have been reduced or avoided by the adoption of a reasonable alternative design . . . and the omission of the alternative design renders the product not reasonably safe. § 2.

Hence, the new test on design defects is the availability of a **reasonable alternative design**. It replaces the "ordinary consumer" expectations test from § 402A of *Restatement (Second) of Torts*. Of course, the availability of an alternative design was also relevant under § 402A of *Restatement (Second) of Torts*. Yet, this availability was often judged from the perspective of the ordinary consumer's expectations.

Under the new test, how do you determine whether a reasonable alternative design was possible? By going through a risk-benefit analysis or risk-utility balancing. We just saw an example of how this is done in the *Riley* case on the competing catheter designs. The *Restatement's* new test does not mean that the expectations of the ordinary consumer are discarded. They are still considered. Under the new test, however, consumer expectations do not constitute an independent standard for judging the defectiveness of product designs.

This change has been controversial; it is unclear how many states will adopt the new test of *Restatement (Third) of Torts*. In a recent case, a court said that "the majority of jurisdictions *do not* impose upon plaintiffs an absolute requirement to prove a feasible alternative design."[8] Clearly, the law on this element of strict liability in tort is not settled. We can expect to see continued developments in the determination of what constitutes a product defect.

User or Consumer

The third element of a cause of action for strict liability in tort is that the plaintiff must be a user or consumer. The plaintiff does not have to be the purchaser of the product. A state that follows § 402A will require only that the plaintiff be a user or consumer.

> **EXAMPLE:**   Tom is driving a car that is unreasonably dangerous because of defective brakes. Jim is his passenger. There is an accident caused by the brakes. Tom and Jim are injured as well as Mary, who was a pedestrian crossing the street when the car hit her.

Tom is a user or consumer whether or not he is the purchaser of the car. So is Jim. Passengers certainly use cars. Mary, however, is not a user or consumer. She is a **bystander**. Under § 402A, Mary cannot sue the car manufacturer for strict liability in tort unless the state expands the tort to cover anyone who is foreseeably injured by the unreasonably dangerous product. There are a number of states that have done so. This would cover Mary. It is highly foreseeable that cars with defective brakes will go out of control and injure pedestrians or other bystanders.

ASSIGNMENT

19.13

In the fact situation just mentioned involving Tom, Mary, and the defective brakes, could Mary sue Tom for strict liability in tort? (See General Instructions for the Legal Analysis Assignment in Chapter 2.)

Physical Harm

The tort covers actual damage to property (e.g., demolished car) or to person (e.g., broken arm, death). If no such damage has occurred, and the plaintiff has suffered economic damage only, most courts do not allow recovery under strict liability in tort. If the plaintiff is the purchaser, he or she may be able to sue under some other cause of action. The plaintiff, for example, buys a boat that is defective and unreasonably dangerous because of the design of the motor. The boat cannot be used in the plaintiff's business. No one is injured and no damage occurs to the boat itself. Only an economic loss has been suffered. The plaintiff may be able to sue for breach of contract, for breach of warranty, or perhaps even for misrepresentation. Most courts, however, do not provide strict liability in tort as a remedy for purely economic loss.

Causation

The plaintiff must show that the product was defective at the time it left the hands of the defendant and that this defect caused the physical harm. Causation is established

---

[8]*Potter v. Chicago Pneumatic Tool Co.*, 694 A.2d 1319, 1331 (Conn. 1997)(emphasis in original).

by the but-for test (but for the defect, the harm would not have resulted), or the substantial factor test when more than one cause is involved (the defect was a substantial factor in producing the harm).

> The seller is not liable when he delivers the product in a safe condition, and subsequent mishandling or other causes make it harmful by the time it is consumed. . . . If the injury results from abnormal handling, as where a bottled beverage is knocked against a radiator to remove a cap, or from abnormal preparation for use, as where too much salt is added to food, or from abnormal consumption, as where a child eats too much candy and is made ill, the seller is not liable.[9]

Causation can sometimes be difficult to prove when the defendant is a remote manufacturer and the product has passed through many hands before it injured the plaintiff. A court will not allow causation to be established by mere speculation. This does not mean that the plaintiff must eliminate every possible cause other than the defendant. Where there is some evidence of other causes, however, the plaintiff must either negate them or show that the defendant was at least a substantial factor along with the other causes in producing the injury.

Causation by Market Share

In Chapter 14, we saw that the courts created the doctrine of res ipsa loquitur to help plaintiffs who would otherwise have great difficulty establishing the second element of negligence: breach of duty (unreasonableness). The doctrine allowed the jury to draw the inference of unreasonableness even though there was no direct or specific evidence of it.

We now look at a similar problem pertaining to the element of causation.

> **EXAMPLE:** During pregnancy a woman takes DES (diethylstilbestrol), a synthetic form of estrogen, designed to prevent miscarriage. She gives birth to a daughter. When the child grows up, she develops cervical cancer, which was caused by the DES taken by her mother. Which manufacturer of DES can the daughter sue? At least 200 manufacturers used an identical formula to produce DES. But the daughter cannot determine which manufacturer made the DES pills that her mother took. The pharmacist used by her mother is no longer in business, and no records are available.

The drug was obviously defective, and unreasonably so. A duty of reasonable care existed, the duty was breached, and an injury resulted. But *who caused the injury?* We know *what* caused the cancer, but we do not know *who* caused it. Under traditional rules, it is fundamental that the plaintiff establish which manufacturer made the defective pills taken by her mother. But she has no way of doing so on these facts.

In most states, she loses her case. A minority of states, however, are more sympathetic. In *Sindell v. Abbott Laboratories,*[10] for example, a California court held that if the plaintiff:

- established that DES caused the cancer, and
- sued a substantial share of the DES manufacturers who were selling in the market in which her mother purchased the drug,

---

[9]*Restatement (Second) of Torts* § 402A, comment g (1965).
[10]26 Cal. 3d 588, 607 P.2d 924, 163 Cal. Rptr. 132, 2 A.L.R.4th 1061 (1980).

then each defendant/manufacturer would be liable for the proportion of the plaintiff's damages represented by its share of that market unless it could prove that it could not have made the DES pill that caused plaintiff's injuries.[11] If a particular defendant/manufacturer could not prove this, then it would be liable for that part of the judgment that was proportional to its market share. This approach has been called **market share liability**.

Using this method of handling causation has been highly controversial. Some fear that it might open a floodgate of liability.

Although *Sindell* was dramatic in its approach, there are limitations to its use. The product made by the manufacturers must be identical, or nearly so. If the products are simply similar and are not made in the same dangerous way, this approach cannot be used. *Sindell* arguably would not apply, for example, if different manufacturers used different proportions of ingredients to make what would otherwise be considered the same product. Also, a large number of manufacturers must be sued so that it can be said that they constitute a significant or substantial share of the market. For a more extensive discussion of causation in mass tort cases, see Chapter 20.

Defenses to Strict Liability in Tort

Misuse   Every misuse of the product is not a defense. As indicated earlier, the simple fact that a consumer does not use a product for its intended purpose does not necessarily mean that it has been misused. A product must be reasonably safe for the foreseeable uses of the product. Furthermore, a manufacturer must plan for a certain amount of foreseeable misuse. Misuse is a defense when it is unforeseeable and when it is extreme. Such misuse occurs, for example, when the plaintiff knowingly violates the plain, unambiguous instructions on using the product or ignores the clear warnings provided.

Contributory Negligence   In most states, contributory negligence is *not* a defense when the plaintiff's conduct consists of failing to discover the danger. Assume the defendant rents a defective car to Bob Smith. On the dashboard, there is a red light signaling trouble to the driver. Smith does not see the light and keeps driving. An accident occurs because of the defect in the car that makes it unreasonably dangerous. It is no defense that Smith failed to discover the danger— even if a reasonable person would have discovered it by checking the dashboard and seeing the red light. Smith's own negligence in failing to discover the danger to himself is not a defense.

Contributory negligence is a defense only when it constitutes the extreme, unforeseeable misuse described above, or an assumption of the risk described below.

Comparative Negligence   There are some states that apply their comparative negligence rules to strict-liability-in-tort cases, even though there is no need for the plaintiff in such cases to establish the negligence of the defendant. The damages suffered by the plaintiffs are proportionately reduced by whatever percentage of the harm the plaintiffs caused themselves through carelessness.

Assumption of the Risk   If the plaintiff has actual knowledge of the danger and voluntarily proceeds to use the product in spite of the danger, there has been an assumption of the risk, which *is* a defense to strict liability in tort. The plaintiff must have actually discovered the danger. For a discussion of assumption of the risk, see Chapter 17.

---

[11]W. Page Keeton et al., *Prosser and Keeton on the Law of Torts* 271 (5th ed. 1984).

ASSIGNMENT 19.14

Tom buys a lawn mower from a department store. A string is tied around the top of the mower attached to a tag that says "WARNING: BEFORE USING, READ IN-STRUCTION BOOK CAREFULLY." Tom sees this sign but fails to read the instruction book. In the book, the consumer is told never to use the mower on a steep hill. Tom is injured while mowing on a steep hill in his yard. The mower tipped over and fell on him. Is the department store strictly liable in tort? (See General Instructions for the Legal Analysis Assignment in Chapter 2.)

REFORM

Federal involvement in this area of the law has been relatively minor, including the work of the Consumer Product Safety Commission, whose role has primarily been that of a monitor and information collector in spite of its authority to force companies to recall their products.

Most products liability law is created and applied at the state level, which is true for most of tort law. This, of course, means that each state is free to develop its own products liability law. Critics say that this system has produced chaos, and that we need a federal products liability law. Although Congress has considered a number of proposals to implement such a law, none has been enacted to date. Here are selected aspects of some of the proposed reforms:

- The creation of federal standards governing the litigation of disputes arising out of injuries caused by defective products. These standards would **preempt** (take the place of, be controlling over) state law.
- The creation of an expedited settlement system to be available at the outset of every case.
- The imposition of a cap on non-economic damages that can be awarded.
- The creation of standards for when punitive damages can be obtained from a defendant.
- A uniform statute of limitations for bringing a case.

PARALEGAL ROLES

The checklist that began our discussion of strict liability in tort contained a list of paralegal roles in litigation involving this tort. Paralegals often have a great deal of responsibility in products liability cases. "Every step of the way, from investigating the accident before suit is filed to assisting at trial, paralegals are essential in product liability litigation."[12] One of their important roles is to help prepare, order, and manage trial visuals or demonstratives that are designed to help juries understand the complexities of product defects. (See Figure 19–4 for examples of these trial visuals.) Paralegals also assist attorneys with pleadings such as complaints and answers. (See Figures 19–5 and 19–6 for a sample complaint and answer.) The assistance can include doing legal research in codes and legal treatises to find examples of complaints, answers, and other pleadings; summarizing or digesting the pleadings that are filed, helping to draft these pleadings, etc.

---

[12]Jan L'Hommedieu, *Products Liability: An Inhouse Perspective,* 23 National Paralegal Reporter 24, 25–6 (Winter 1998).

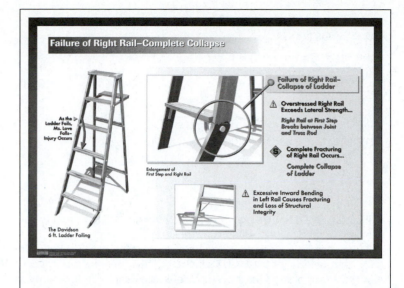

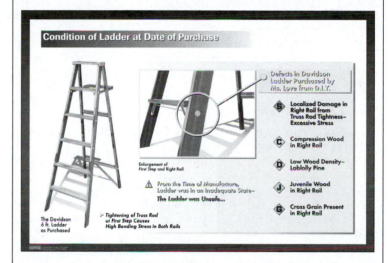

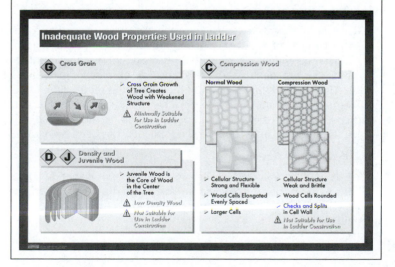

FIGURE 19–5 Sample products liability complaint.

Reprinted from *Trial of a Personal Injury Case—1984 Case Study,* copyright 1984 New York Bar Association.

SUPREME COURT OF THE STATE OF NEW YORK
COUNTY OF NASSAU

———————————————————————————X

STEVEN HURT   Index No.

                           Plaintiff,   VERIFIED
                                           COMPLAINT

                    v.

NICE CUT MOWER CORP., GETWELL
HOSPITAL, INC., AND SAMUEL BONZ, M.D.,

                            Defendants.

———————————————————————————X

    Plaintiff, STEVEN HURT, by his attorney, ADAM ABEL, as and for his complaint against the defendants, respectfully sets forth:

    1. That plaintiff was and is a resident of the State of New York, County of Nassau.

    2. That defendant NICE CUT MOWER CORP. (hereinafter "NICE CUT") was and is a New York corporation having a place of business in Suffolk County, New York.

    3. That defendant GETWELL HOSPITAL, INC. (hereinafter "HOSPITAL") was and is a New York proprietary hospital corporation having its principal place of business in Nassau County, New York.

    4. That defendant SAMUEL BONZ, M.D., (hereinafter "DOCTOR") was and is a physician duly licensed to practice medicine in the State of New York.

    5. That defendant DOCTOR was and is a resident of the State of New York, County of Suffolk.

First Cause of Action

    6. That defendant NICE CUT was and is engaged in the manufacture of lawn mowers and the sale of same to the public.

    7. That on or about May 1, 1991, plaintiff purchased a lawn mower from defendant NICE CUT at its retail store in Stony Brook, New York bearing Model No. A-1.

    8. That on June 13, 1992, while plaintiff was operating said mower in accordance with its instructions, plaintiff sustained personal injury.

    9. That defendant NICE CUT was negligent in the design, manufacture, and sale of said mower to the plaintiff.

    10. That the aforementioned occurrence was caused by the negligence, carelessness, and recklessness of the defendants.

    11. That by reason of the foregoing, plaintiff has been damaged.

Second Cause of Action

    12. Plaintiff repeats and realleges each and every allegation contained in paragraphs "6" through "8" of the complaint as if set forth more fully at length herein.

    13. That defendant NICE CUT expressly and impliedly warranted that said mower was fit for its intended use, was safe, and was of merchantable quality.

    14. That the plaintiff relied upon the warranties of defendant NICE CUT.

    15. That defendant NICE CUT breached its warranties in that said mower was unsafe and unsuitable for its intended purpose, and not of merchantable quality.

    16. That by reason of the foregoing, plaintiff has been damaged.

Third Cause of Action

    17. Plaintiff repeats and realleges each and every allegation contained in paragraphs "6" through "8" of the complaint as if set forth more fully at length herein.

    18. That said mower was manufactured and sold in a dangerous and defective condition.

FIGURE 19–5 Continued

19. That said mower was an inherently dangerous product.

20. That said defects resulted in injury to the plaintiff.

21. That by reason of the foregoing, defendant NICE CUT is strictly liable in tort to the plaintiff.

22. That by reason of the foregoing, plaintiff has been damaged.

23. That defendant NICE CUT knew or should have known that said mower was dangerous and that defendant NICE CUT engaged in conduct which amounted to a deliberate, reckless, and outrageous disregard and indifference to the lives and safety of the public.

24. That by reason of the foregoing, plaintiff is entitled to an award of punitive damages.

Fourth Cause of Action

25. Plaintiff repeats and realleges each and every allegation contained in paragraphs "6" through "8" of the complaint as if set forth more fully at length herein.

26. That on or about June 13, 1992, and after the plaintiff utilized his lawn mower, the plaintiff sought medical care and treatment at the emergency room of defendant HOSPITAL.

27. That on or about June 13, 1992, the plaintiff was admitted to defendant HOSPITAL and came under the care of defendant DOCTOR.

28. That defendant DOCTOR was an agent, servant, employee, or was otherwise an affiliate of defendant HOSPITAL.

29. That plaintiff remained under the care of defendant HOSPITAL and defendant DOCTOR until he was discharged on July 15, 1992.

30. That defendant HOSPITAL, defendant DOCTOR, and their agents, servants, and employees negligently, carelessly, and recklessly failed to diagnose, treat, and care for the plaintiff, failed to obtain the plaintiff's informed consent to treatment, and deviated from the reasonable and accepted standard of medical care and skill prevailing among other hospitals and physicians in the community.

31. That as a result of the negligence and medical malpractice of defendant HOSPITAL and defendant DOCTOR, the plaintiff was caused to sustain an injury.

32. That by reason of the foregoing, plaintiff has been damaged in a sum which exceeds the jurisdictional limit of all other courts which would otherwise have jurisdiction over this matter.

WHEREFORE, plaintiff demands judgment against the defendant as follows:

1. On the first Cause of Action, judgment against defendant NICE CUT for the sum of $2,000,000.

2. On the Second Cause of Action, judgment against defendant NICE CUT for the sum of $2,000,000.

3. On the Third Cause of Action, judgment against defendant NICE CUT for the sum of $2,000,000.

4. Judgment against defendant NICE CUT for the sum of $6,000,000 in punitive damages.

5. On the Fourth Cause of Action, judgment against defendant HOSPITAL and defendant DOCTOR for a sum in excess of the jurisdictional limit of all other courts which would otherwise have jurisdiction over this matter;

all together with the costs and disbursements of this action.

Dated: Mineola, New York
     August 21, 1994

Yours, etc.

ADAM ABEL, ESQ.
Attorney for Plaintiff
1 Retainer Plaza
Mineola, New York

FIGURE 19–6 Sample products liability answer.

Reprinted from *Trial of a Personal Injury Case—1984 Case Study,* copyright 1984 New York Bar Association.

SUPREME COURT OF THE STATE OF NEW YORK
COUNTY OF NASSAU

————————————————————————X

STEVEN HURT

Plaintiff,   VERIFIED ANSWER

v.

NICE CUT MOWER CORP., GETWELL
HOSPITAL, INC., AND SAMUEL BONZ, M.D.,

Defendants.

————————————————————————X

Defendant, NICE CUT MOWER CORP., by its attorneys, ROBERT BLACK, P.C., as and for its answer to the complaint of the plaintiff, respectfully sets forth:

1. Denies knowledge or information sufficient to form a belief as to the truth of the allegations contained in paragraphs "1", "3", "4", and "5" of the complaint.

Answer to the First Cause of Action

2. Denies the allegations contained in paragraphs "9", "10" and "11" of the complaint.

3. Denies knowledge or information sufficient to form a belief as to the truth of the allegations contained in paragraphs "7" and "8" of the complaint.

Answer to the Second Cause of Action

4. Repeats and reiterates the denials to each and every allegation contained in paragraph "12" of the complaint as if more fully set forth at length herein.

5. Denies the allegations contained in paragraphs "15" and "16" of the complaint.

6. Denies knowledge or information sufficient to form a belief as to the truth of the allegations contained in paragraphs "13" and "14" of the complaint.

Answer to the Third Cause of Action

7. Repeats and reiterates the denials to each and every allegation contained in paragraph "17" of the complaint as if more fully set forth at length herein.

8. Denies the allegations contained in paragraphs "18", "19", "20", "21", "22", "23" and "24" of the complaint.

Answer to the Fourth Cause of Action

9. Repeats and reiterates the denials to each and every allegation contained in paragraph "25" of the complaint as if more fully set forth at length herein.

10. Denies knowledge or information sufficient to form a belief as to the truth of the allegations contained in paragraphs "26", "27", "28", "29", "30", "31" and "32" of the complaint.

First Affirmative Defense

11. Upon information and belief, any damage or damages sustained by the plaintiff herein were not caused by the wrongdoing on the part of the answering defendant, his servants, agents or employees, but were caused solely by the wrongdoing of the plaintiff and that such conduct requires diminution of any award, verdict or judgment that plaintiff may recover against said answering defendant.

**Cross-Claim Against Co-Defendants
Getwell Hospital, Inc. and Samuel Bonz, M.D.**

12. That although NICE CUT MOWER CORP. has denied the allegations of plaintiff with respect to any wrongdoing on the part of said defendant, nevertheless, in the event that there is a verdict or judgment in favor of the plaintiff as against NICE CUT MOWER CORP., then, and in that event, said defendant demands judgment over and against co-defendants, GETWELL HOSPITAL, INC. and SAMUEL BONZ, M.D., by reason of their wrongful conduct being primary and/or active while any wrongdoing of NICE CUT MOWER CORP., if any, was secondary and/or passive and the indemnity is to be full and complete.

FIGURE 19–6   Continued

Second Cross Claim against Co-Defendants Getwell Hospital, Inc. and Samuel Bonz, M.D.

13. Although NICE CUT MOWER CORP. has denied allegations of plaintiff with respect to any alleged wrongdoing on the part of NICE CUT MOWER CORP., nevertheless, if it is found that NICE CUT MOWER CORP. is liable to the plaintiff-herein, all of which is denied, said defendant, on the basis of apportionment of responsibility for the alleged occurrence, is entitled to contribution from and judgment over and against co-defendants, GETWELL HOSPITAL, INC. and SAMUEL BONZ, M.D., for all or part of any verdict or judgment plaintiff may recover against NICE CUT MOWER CORP.

WHEREFORE, defendant, NICE CUT MOWER CORP., demands:

1. Judgment dismissing the complaint;

2. In the event that the complaint is not dismissed, then full indemnity with respect to the first cross-claim;

3. In the event that full indemnity is not granted, then contribution pursuant to the second cross-claim in accordance with degrees of wrongdoing; together with the costs and disbursements of this action.

Dated: Commack, New York
      September 5, 1994   Yours, etc.

                               ROBERT BLACK, P.C.
                               Attorneys for Defendant
                               NICE CUT MOWER CORP.
                               Defense Street
                               Commack, New York

SUMMARY

Products liability is not a cause of action. It is a general term that covers different causes of action based on products that cause harm. These causes of action are negligence, misrepresentation, breach of express warranty, breach of implied warranty of merchantability, breach of implied warranty of fitness for a particular purpose, and strict liability in tort. There are three categories of defects in products: manufacturing defects, design defects, and warning defects.

For purposes of a negligence suit, the defendant owes a duty of reasonable care to all foreseeable users of the product if it can be anticipated that substantial harm to person or property will result if the product is defective. Privity is not necessary. Breach of duty is established when the defendant fails to take reasonable steps to prevent injury caused by the product. Contributory negligence is a complete defense unless the state had adopted comparative negligence as the standard. Assumption of the risk is also a complete defense. Another traditional cause of action is misrepresentation, which can be used when the defendant makes a false statement about a product with the intent to mislead (scienter) that causes injury.

Breach of express warranty requires proof of a false statement of fact, the intent or expectation that the statement will reach the plaintiff, reliance on the statement by the plaintiff, and causation of damage or injury.

The following causes of action apply to sales rather than to services: breach of implied warranty of merchantability, breach of implied warranty of fitness for a particular purpose, and strict liability in tort. For a breach of implied warranty of merchantability, goods must be sold by a merchant of that kind. The goods are not merchantable and cause damage or injury. For a breach of implied warranty of fitness for a particular purpose, goods must be sold by a seller who has reason to know that the buyer has a particular purpose in buying the goods and is relying on the seller's skill or judgment. The goods cause damage or injury because they are not fit for that particular purpose.

To bring a warranty action, the general rule is that there must be privity, or a contractual relationship, between the defendant and the person injured. Some states have abolished the privity requirement in designated kinds of cases such as when the person injured is in the immediate family of the person who bought the product. Defenses to actions for breach of warranty include valid disclaimers, failure of the plaintiff to provide notice within a reasonable time after the breach was discovered or should have been discovered, and assumption of the risk. Contributory negligence is generally not a defense.

In an action for strict liability in tort, the defendant must be a seller, which includes most companies in the chain of distribution. Companies in the business of renting products are also included. The product must be defective and unreasonably dangerous for its intended use and its foreseeable use. States differ on the tests they use to determine when a defect is unreasonably dangerous. The, predominant test is the expectations of the ordinary consumer. Some states, however, use other tests, particularly for design defects. A recent proposal for such defects is the availability of a reasonable alternative design as determined by a risk-benefit analysis. The defect in the product must cause physical harm in the plaintiff, who is either a user or consumer of the product, or, in some states, anyone who is foreseeably injured, which could include a bystander. Misuse is a defense when it is unforeseeable and is extreme. Assumption of the risk is also a defense. Generally, contributory negligence is not. A state may compare the fault of the plaintiff and the defendant and apportion the damages according to its applicable formula.

KEY TERMS

products liability   346
defective   347
manufacturing defect   348
design defect   348
warning defect   348
duty   348
privity   348
foreseeable users   349
breach of duty   351
reasonably safe   351
manufacturer   352
res ipsa loquitur   352
merchant   353
custom   353
contributory negligence   354
comparative negligence   354
assumption of risk   354
misrepresentation   355
scienter   355
warranty   355

strict liability   355
express warranty   355
Uniform Commercial Code   356
fact   356
opinion   356
puffing   356
reliance   357
material   357
sales   357
services   357
personal property   358
real property   358
chattels   358
implied warranty of merchantability   359
merchantable   360
implied warranty of fitness for a particular purpose   360
disclaimer   362
unconscionable   362

notice   362
strict liability in tort   364
§ 402A   368
seller   368
component part   368
chain of distribution   368
unreasonably dangerous   369
objective   369
unavoidably unsafe products   370
intended use   371
foreseeable use   371
misuse   371
crashworthiness   372
risk-benefit analysis   373
risk-utility analysis   373
risk-utility balancing   373
reasonable alternative design   376
bystander   377
market share liability   379
preempt   380

CHAPTER

20

Mass Tort Litigation

CHAPTER OUTLINE

- Introduction
- Solicitation of Clients
- Class Actions
- Junk Science and Causation
- Asbestos
- Breast Implants
- Tobacco
- Paralegal Roles in Mass Tort Litigation

INTRODUCTION

We live in a society in which it is relatively easy to poison the environment, contaminate the food supply, and market products that endanger the life and limb of millions. In response, one of the most dramatic developments in tort law since the 1980s has been the increase in the litigation and settlement of **mass tort** cases. According to one commentator, "If litigation is war, mass torts are the legal system's version of a nuclear exchange: Thousands of complex claims. Huge potential damages. Massive discovery and expense."[1] These will be some of the major themes in this chapter.

There are four general categories of mass tort cases, although some overlap exists among the categories.[2] (See Figure 20–1.) As creative attorneys continue to find new ways to litigate these cases, we are likely to see additional categories emerge in the coming years.

FIGURE 20–1 Categories of mass tort litigation.

Kinds of Mass Tort Litigation	Examples
Mass accident: a large number of people are injured in a single catastrophic event	train wreck, plane crash, nightclub fire
Mass marketed product: a large number of people are injured by a widely marketed product	asbestos, contraceptives, breast implants, tobacco, lead paint, weight loss drug
Mass exposure: a large number of people are injured by exposure from the same toxic source	Agent Orange, nuclear plant leakage
Mass economic loss: a large number of people suffer monetary loss from misrepresentation or consumer fraud, usually not involving bodily injury	misleading car warranty; false representations made in a stock prospectus

A mass tort is tortious conduct involving the same event or product that has caused harm to many people. More precisely, it is a tort cause of action that is asserted by a large number of persons who have been harmed by the same or similar conduct or product of a relatively small number of defendants. In a mass tort case, an important concern of the legal system is to provide a remedy for those who have been harmed without destroying the industry that caused the harm. According to federal judge Jack B. Weinstein, the need is to find the best way to "protect and compensate people exposed to toxic substances and dangerous products—particularly those with latent, after-discovered dangers—at a reasonable cost, without unnecessarily destroying industries and unduly deterring development of new products."[3]

A mass tort is not a new cause of action. In the litigation of a mass tort case, plaintiffs typically assert traditional causes of action such as negligence, nuisance, misrepresentation, breach of warranty, and strict liability in tort. What is new is the scope of these cases. They often involve years of litigation, tens of thousands of plaintiffs, hundreds of millions of dollars, and extensive media publicity. Although there is no such thing as a typical mass tort case, several characteristics are common to many of them:[4]

---

[1]Michael Higgins, *Mass Tort Makeover?* 84 American Bar Association Journal 52 (November 1998).

[2]Anne E. Cohen, *Mass Tort Litigation After Amchem,* 57 ALI-ABA Course of Study Materials 269 (February 25, 1998).

[3]Jack B. Weinstein, *Notes for a Discussion of Mass Tort Cases and Class Actions,* 63 Brooklyn Law Review 581 (Summer 1997).

[4]American Law Institute, *Enterprise Responsibility for Personal Injury* 389 (Reporters' Study, 1991); Mark A. Peterson and Molly Selvin, *Resolution of Mass Torts* 31 (Rand, 1988).

- numerous victims who have filed or who might file damage claims against the same defendant(s);
- injuries that are widely dispersed over time, territory, and jurisdiction;
- large burdens on the court systems where cases are filed;
- inconsistent judgments from different courts involving the same or similar facts;
- legal issues (questions of law and fact) that are complex and expensive to litigate—frequently issues that are scientific and technological in nature;
- problems in establishing causation between the plaintiff's injury and the defendant's tortious conduct—especially in cases alleging toxic substance exposure where it may be difficult to identify the precise products to which there was exposure and where there is a long latency period between exposure to the toxic substance and the injury complained of;
- long delays in the resolution of claims; this may lead to conflict between claimants who need prompt compensation and claimants who are willing to hold out for the largest payout possible;
- huge litigation costs to plaintiffs and defendants; in some cases, attorneys fees, costs of expert witnesses, and other litigation expenses have exceeded the total compensation paid to victims;
- strong pressures on defendants to settle so that litigation costs do not consume all of their business energy and resources; some defendants may face so many claims that they agree to large settlements even though their liability may be doubtful; some file for bankruptcy;
- an inclination among multiple defendants to cooperate with each other even though they may not present a united defense; cooperation could include sharing experts and information;
- allegations of ethical impropriety by attorneys who solicit clients, send them to friendly doctors, and claim extraordinarily high legal fees.

Perhaps the most common characteristic of a mass tort case is its sheer size, as we will see when we examine paralegal roles in a toxic tort case at the end of the chapter. A mass tort case is called a "document case" because of the large volume of documents exchanged during discovery and trial. In a recent Minnesota tobacco case, for example, the attorney representing one of the cigarette companies (Lorillard) made the following comments in her closing arguments to the jury:

> Now as you know, this case has been what we refer to as a document case. You've seen many documents. You've heard some testimony on the documents. . . . There was testimony of some 30 million pages of documents being in a depository right here in the Twin Cities area. Lorillard has produced approximately 1.8 million pages of documents in this lawsuit. If you were to take those documents and stack them one on end—one on top of the other, they would be 666 feet high. That's the equivalent of a 66-story office building. That's how many documents Lorillard has produced in this lawsuit.[5]

This comment is not an exaggeration; the quantity of documents in a mass tort case is often staggering. (The Minnesota tobacco case was eventually settled; the state of Minnesota received $6.6 billion to cover the health costs it paid to treat sick smokers. We will examine the tobacco settlement later.)

Our primary focus in this chapter will be on personal injury from a mass marketed product, although many of the issues we will discuss apply to all of the categories listed in Figure 20-1. Hundreds of products have been the subject of mass tort litigation. The three we have selected for study (asbestos, breast implants, and tobacco) present vivid examples of a legal system striving to achieve justice while

---

[5] *State of Minnesota and Blue Cross And Blue Shield of Minnesota v. Philip Morris, Inc.,* Trial Transcript, Closing Statements, May 7, 1998, P.M. Session [1998 WL 242426].

seeming to be on the verge of collapse. Before beginning our examination of these three products, we need to cover some preliminary topics that apply throughout this area of the law. The topics are client solicitation, class actions, and junk science in the courtroom. At the end of the chapter, we will explore paralegal roles from the perspective of a paralegal project manager who helps the office oversee the large number of tasks that must be performed in a mass tort case.

ASSIGNMENT

20.1

a. What is a mass tort?

b. Is a mass tort a new tort? Explain.

c. What are some of the characteristics of mass tort cases?

SOLICITATION OF CLIENTS

Mass tort litigation can bring attorneys millions of dollars in fees. Understandably, therefore, competition for clients among personal injury attorneys can be fierce. One court recently painted the following unflattering picture of how some of these attorneys solicit clients:

> The familiar spectacle of lawyers and their agents preying on the victims of disaster has occasioned revulsion. . . . In the aftermath of the tragic release of poison gas at the Union Carbide plant in Bhopal, India, "American lawyers rushed to India in an attempt to retain clients and in their zeal brought shame and discredit to the American Bar." Eric S. Roth, *Confronting Solicitation of Mass Disaster Victims,* 2 Georgetown Journal of Legal Ethics 967, 972 (1989). The examples of abuse are chilling. Shortly after the crash of a Northwest airliner in Detroit on August 16, 1987, a man posing as a Catholic priest appeared on the scene to console the families of the victims. He "hugged crying mothers and talked with grieving fathers of God's rewards in the hereafter. He even sobbed along with dazed families. . . . Then he would pass out the business card of a Florida attorney . . . and repeatedly urge them to call the lawyer." Roth, supra, 2 Geo. J. Legal Ethics at 972. After the crash of Pan Am Flight 103 in Scotland, one victim's widow reported solicitation "by no less than 30 attorneys within 24 hours of the crash." Ibid. Other examples abound. "How much money would you like to get out of this case?" a letter asked the mother of a child who had recently suffered brain damage in an automobile accident. It was one of three letters she had received from attorneys within two weeks of her son's accident. In the same envelope was a police report with the lawyer's card stapled to it. In the view of an Oregon Bar Association commentator, "[s]uch a letter clearly offends common decency." Richard Sanders, *Lawyer Advertising and Solicitation: The Good, the Bad, the Unethical,* 50 Oregon State Bar Bulletin 5 (June 1990). An editorial cartoon in a Miami newspaper portrayed lawyers after the Delta 911 air crash disaster as " 'vultures, members of the law firm of Pickem, Pickem, Scavage & Bone . . . Don't Call Us—We'll Call You!' " Howard R. Messing, *The Latest Word on Solicitation,* Fla. Bar Journal, 17, May 1986 (quoting The Miami Herald, Aug. 16, 1985, at 20A). . . . A mother, faced with attorney solicitation shortly after her daughter's death in a car crash, reacted: "give me some time—I am still grieving." Allessandra Stanley, *Bronx Crash, Then Contest of Lawyers,* N.Y. Times, June 17, 1991, at B1.[6]

---

[6]*In the Matter of Magdy F. Anis,* 126 N.J. 448, 451, 599 A.2d 1265, 1266 (1992).

There are ethical rules governing the **solicitation** of prospective clients by attorneys and by those working for attorneys such as paralegals. The policy behind these rules is that prospective clients should not be placed under undue pressure at a time when they are vulnerable and unable to make clear decisions about whom to hire, if anyone.

The ethical rules make a distinction between **in-person solicitation** (i.e., on the phone or in a face-to-face contact such as at home or in the office) and solicitation through the mail:

a. Most in-person solicitation is unethical because of the pressure this places on prospective clients. The exception is if the attorney is not seeking fees or other financial gain from being hired or if the attorney already has a professional or family relationship with the prospective client.

b. Most solicitation by mail is ethical because the prospective client can easily treat the mail as junk mail and toss it in the trash without having to listen to an attorney's speech on why he or she should be hired.

Yet, even mail solicitation is subject to regulation. For example, a state might require that the phrase "Advertising Material" be printed prominently on the front of the envelope sent by the attorney seeking employment. In New Jersey and in many states that have adopted the *Model Rules of Professional Conduct* of the American Bar Association, Rule 7.3(b)(1) prohibits written communications through the mail if "the lawyer knows or reasonably should know that the physical, emotional or mental state of the person is such that the person could not exercise reasonable judgment in employing a lawyer."

This prohibition became an issue in an attorney solicitation letter sent to the parent of a child killed on Pan American Flight 103 over Lockerbie, Scotland. One of the victims was Alexander Lowenstein, a student at Syracuse University and resident of Morristown, New Jersey. His remains were identified on January 3, 1989. The following day, attorney Magdy F. Anis sent the following solicitation letter to Peter Lowenstein, Alexander's father:

Dear Mr. Lowenstein:

Initially, we would like to extend our deepest sympathy for the loss of your son, Mr. Alexander Lowenstein. We know that this must be a very traumatic experience for you, and we hope that you, along with your relatives and friends, can overcome this catastrophe which has not only affected your family but has disturbed the world.

As you may already realize, you have a legal cause of action against Pan American, among others, for wrongful death due to possible negligent security maintenance. If you intend to take any legal recourse, we urge you to consider to retain our firm to prosecute your case.

Both my partner and myself are experienced practitioners in the personal injury field, and feel that we can obtain a favorable outcome for you against the airline, among other possible defendants.

We would also like to inform you that if you do decide to retain our services, you will not be charged for any attorneys fees unless we collect a settlement or verdict award for you. Before retaining any other attorney, it would be worth your while to contact us, since we will substantially reduce the customary one-third fee that most other attorneys routinely charge.

Please call us to schedule an appointment at your earliest convenience. If you are unable to come to our office, please so advise us and we will have an attorney meet you at a location suitable to your needs.

Very truly yours,
(Mr.) Magdy F. Anis
MFA/seb
P.S. There is no consultation fee.

Outraged by the letter, the father immediately filed an ethics charge with the New Jersey Office of Attorney Ethics. The case was eventually resolved by the New Jersey Supreme Court, which ruled that Anis had crossed the ethical line in his mail solicitation. The attorney admitted that he did not know at the time that he mailed the letter whether Alexander's body had yet been identified. The court said, "We believe that an ordinarily prudent attorney would recognize that within the hours and days following a tragic disaster, families would be particularly weak and vulnerable." Any "reasonable lawyer" would conclude that an obsequious letter of solicitation delivered the day after a death notice would reach people when they 'could not exercise reasonable judgment in employing a lawyer' " under 7.3(b)(1). The court rejected the argument of Anis that his solicitation letter was protected by his commercial speech rights under the First Amendment of the United States Constitution. Reasonable restrictions on such rights, such as those found in ethical rule 7.3(b)(1), can be imposed on attorneys.

The New Jersey court acknowledged that its ruling cast doubt on when it is permissible to send solicitation letters to potential clients. "We realize" said the court "that there may be other cases in which it will be more difficult to draw the line of ethical propriety. Would a truthful solicitation letter sent fifteen or thirty days after a tragic loss reach people when they are no longer emotionally weak or vulnerable? We cannot say with certainty, since our assumptions in such cases are largely untested. It may be that there are degrees of loss or suffering. Common sense tells us that the mildly-injured survivors of an overturned-bus incident might be less vulnerable than were the Lockerbie families. Hence, we attempt no permanent bright-line rule in this opinion."[7]

Not all states follow New Jersey's reluctance to establish clear-cut (i.e., "bright-line") rules on the impropriety of solicitation. Some states, for example, prohibit attorneys from using direct mail to solicit potential personal injury or wrongful death clients within thirty days of the accident. And in 1996, Congress passed the Aviation Disaster Family Assistance Act, which provides that in the event of an air carrier accident, "no unsolicited communication concerning a potential action for personal injury or wrongful death may be made by an attorney or any potential party to the litigation to an individual injured in the accident, or to a relative of an individual involved in the accident, before the 30th day following the date of the accident." 49 U.S.C. § 1136(g)(2) (Supp. II 1996).

Nevertheless, the lure of mega-fees will continue to encourage some attorneys to take questionable risks in order to sign up tort victims, particularly those injured by mass torts. Paralegals need to be careful. There are unscrupulous attorneys, for example, who will hire paralegals of a certain race or ethnic background for the sole purpose of soliciting mass tort victims of the same race or background. This is no less illegal than the attorney who used the priest to hand out attorney business cards in the example quoted earlier.

ASSIGNMENT	
20.2	a. When is in-person solicitation ethical and unethical?
	b. When is mail solicitation ethical and unethical?

CLASS ACTIONS

In the vast majority of cases, a person injured by a mass tort can bring a solo or an individual lawsuit, by which we mean that the injured person is usually the only party bringing the litigation (sometimes with a relative or associate) against one or more defendants. This kind of litigation, however, can be expensive. Also, obtain-

---

[7]*In the Matter of Magdy F. Anis*, 126 N.J. at 460, 599 A.2d at 1271.

ing attorney representation can sometimes be a challenge. Most personal injury attorneys are paid a percentage of what the plaintiff receives through settlement or litigation. Unless the accident caused a death or a major disability, damages are likely to be modest. This will discourage many attorneys from taking the case, particularly if there are difficult causation issues or other problems of proof that must be litigated.

Once an attorney does become interested (often because of allegations of serious injuries), the traditional route is to launch an individual lawsuit. If there are several potential plaintiffs, they might all be joined in the lawsuit. Suppose, however, there are hundreds or thousands of injured persons due to a mass tort. Joining them all in one action may not be practical. "In the mass tort context . . . joinder is not feasible because it would create a 'zoo' of litigants in the courtroom, each seeking to pursue his cause of action."[8] An alternative is the **class action**, although as we will see, this kind of action has its own management problems.

A class action is a lawsuit in which one or more members of a class sue (or are sued) as representative parties on behalf of everyone in the class. All members of the class do not have to be joined individually in the lawsuit; they are not actually brought into court. The representative parties act on behalf of everyone. (Here the word *representative* does not refer to an attorney; it refers to named parties who act on behalf of the class. Of course, representative parties are almost always "represented" by attorneys who thereby become counsel for the class.) If the parties do not intend to litigate the claims made in the complaint because they have reached a settlement before trial, the action is called a **settlement class action.**

A class action can help prevent a court system from collapsing under the weight of individual lawsuits. Another benefit is that it can be attractive to injured persons who individually have not suffered greatly and hence might have difficulty attracting an attorney. As one court said:

> The policy at the very core of the class action mechanism is to overcome the problem that small recoveries do not provide the incentive for any individual to bring a solo action prosecuting his or her rights. A class action solves this problem by aggregating the relatively paltry potential recoveries into something worth someone's (usually an attorney's) labor.[9]

If all victims of a mass tort are part of the class action, the benefit to the defendants is achieving **global peace**—a final resolution of all claims. In many cases, this is achieved only partially since members of the class usually have the right to **opt out** of the class (called a "request for exclusion") by deciding that they would rather bring their own individual lawsuit than be a member of the class action. In some class actions, however, claimants are not allowed to opt out.[10]

Class actions in federal court are governed by Rule 23 of the Federal Rules of Civil Procedure (FRCP). State courts follow their own rules on class actions, although many states have patterned their state class action rules on Rule 23 of the FRCP. Yet, it is sometimes easier to bring a class action in a state court than in a federal court. (We will see an example of this later when we study tobacco litigation; a

---

[8]Kevin H. Hudson, *Catch-23(b)(1)(B): The Dilemma of Using the Mandatory Class Action to Resolve the Problem of the Mass Tort Case* 40 Emory Law Journal 665, 677 (1991).

[9]*Mace v. Van Ru Credit Corp.*, 109 F.3d 338, 344 (7th Cir. 1997).

[10]A class action in which a member of the class can opt out is a **permissive class action.** A class action in which a member of the class cannot opt out is a **mandatory class action.** The latter is often attempted if the defendant(s) have limited resources (constituting a so-called "limited fund") out of which to pay a judgment. Allowing individual lawsuits might quickly deplete the assets of the defendant(s), leaving little or nothing for others similarly injured. This is particularly true if the plaintiff in an individual lawsuit is allowed to collect punitive damages. For an example of a mandatory class action in a tobacco case, see Figure 20–4 later in the chapter.

federal court refused to allow a nationwide class of smokers while an Alabama state court approved one.)

The first step in bringing a class action in a federal court is to ask the court to **certify the class.** This petition for certification seeks the court's permission to allow a member of the class to be the representative party who will act on behalf of every other member of the class.

> **EXAMPLE:** Thousands of people develop skin diseases after washing their hair with a shampoo that contains the chemical ingredient, habberol. Bob Smith is one of them. He goes to federal court and files a class action on behalf of himself and every person who has been injured by the shampoo.

Before a court will certify a class such as this, a number of requirements must be met. Among the most important are four threshold requirements.

The first is called **numerosity.** This means that there must be so many potential claimants that it would be "impracticable" to join them all in one action as plaintiffs. In our shampoo case, there are thousands of people who claim to have been harmed by the shampoo. Bringing them all together in one courtroom would be a nightmare. Each would have his or her own attorney, each would require formal notice of every stage of the proceeding, etc. To say the least, litigating such a case would be extraordinarily cumbersome.

The second requirement is **commonality.** There must be common questions of law or fact among the members of the class. Suppose that one of the legal disputes in the shampoo case is whether the warning on the shampoo bottle violated regulations of the Food and Drug Administration. Since this question applies to every user of the shampoo, it is a question of law that is common to members of the class. Or suppose that the manufacturer of the shampoo says that its products do not contain the chemical ingredient, habberol. This would be a question of fact that is common among the class.

The third requirement is **typicality.** The claims or defenses of the proposed representative party must be typical of the claims or defenses of the members of the class. In our example, Bob Smith is the member of the class seeking certification of the class. It is important that his claims or defenses be typical of other members of the class. This is to ensure that he will not take advantage of his position to protect his own claims or defenses at the expense of those of the other members. This is less likely to occur if his claims and defenses are typical of those everyone has.

The fourth requirement is that the court must be convinced that the proposed representative party will provide **fair and adequate representation** of the entire class. The court must be satisfied that Bob Smith will fairly and adequately represent every member of the class, not just his own interest. Suppose that Smith needed money right away and was willing to settle for a lower amount now, whereas other members wanted a higher amount and were willing to wait longer to obtain it. This would be a conflict of interest between Smith and the other members. It could lead a court to refuse to certify the class.[11] For an overview of the four threshold requirements, see Figure 20–2.

A court must also be satisfied that adequate **notice** of the case will be given to every member of the class. In some mass tort cases, such as our shampoo case, there can be thousands of claimants. Many may be unaware of the proposed class action. Hence, extensive efforts must be made to notify everyone. Those who are known by name should be notified individually. A common method of reaching others is to place ads in general circulation newspapers that describe the action and provide an

---

[11]There are other requirements in addition to these four threshold requirements. For example, the court must find that separate actions might lead to incompatible standards of conduct for the defendant. The court may also have to conclude that a class action is superior to other available methods for a fair and efficient adjudication of the controversy.

1. numerosity	The class of potential claimants must be so *numerous* that joinder of all individual members in the same action as plaintiffs would be impracticable.
2. commonality	There must be questions of law or fact that are *common* to the members of the class.
3. typicality	The claims or defenses of the proposed representative party must be *typical* of the claims or defenses of the members of the class.
4. fairness and adequacy of representation	The proposed representative party must be able to *fairly* and *adequately* protect the interests of all members of the class.

FIGURE 20–2 Threshold requirements for a class action in federal court under FRCP 23.

800 number to obtain further information. (For an example, see Figure 20–4 later in the chapter.) A World Wide Web site might also be made available.

Future claimants pose particular notice problems, especially for people whose disease or other illness has a long latency period before symptoms appear. How are these people to be notified? Even if they hear about the class action, they may have no motivation to do anything since they are presently healthy. To protect them, courts have the power to appoint independent counsel who will look after their interests. A fund might be set aside to cover claims that will be filed in the future after the class action is over. If none of these measures are deemed adequate, the court may simply refuse to certify the class. Past, present, and future claimants, therefore, would have to bring their own individual lawsuits.

Meeting all the requirements of FRCP 23 is not easy, as we will see later when we examine the case of *Amchem Products, Inc. v. Windsor* in which the United States Supreme Court refused to certify a nationwide class action for asbestos claimants.

Some mass tort cases are so pervasive that they are filed in courts throughout the country. Lawsuits raising essentially the same issues could be filed in scores of different courts. Some might be individual lawsuits while others might be class actions. In our shampoo case, for example, a class action might be filed in a United States District Court in Texas on behalf of all users of the shampoo injured in Texas. Another class action might be filed in a United States District Court in New York on behalf of all users of the shampoo injured in New York. Other shampoo class actions might also be filed in other districts, in addition to individual lawsuits against the shampoo manufacturer. All of this litigation might lead to inconsistent judgments since it is unlikely that all of the cases will reach the same conclusion.

When similar cases have been filed in more than one federal district court, they can all be *temporarily* transferred to a single federal district for pretrial purposes such as completing discovery. There is a special federal body that has the power to order such a transfer. It is called the **Judicial Panel on Multidistrict Litigation** (J.P.M.L.). Once the pretrial matters are completed, the cases are transferred back to the districts where they were initially filed. This procedure saves resources, encourages settlement, and helps reduce inconsistent judgments once the cases are returned.

ASSIGNMENT

20.3

a. What is a class action?
b. Explain why a class action may not bring global peace.
c. Explain the threshold requirements for a class action in federal court under FRCP 23.
d. What is the function of the Judicial Panel on Multidistrict Litigation (J.P.M.L.)?

JUNK SCIENCE AND CAUSATION

For years, critics have accused clever trial attorneys of using dubious scientific evidence to persuade juries that the defendant's product caused a particular disease or other harm. The charge is that courts are allowing juries to consider **junk science**, which simply refers to unreliable and, therefore, potentially misleading scientific evidence. Many of the cases in court are extremely complex. Scores of experts and a maze of documents can sometimes overwhelm juries. Even judges can become confused. Jurors and judges are not trained in engineering or science, yet they often must sort through and interpret a mountain of technical evidence. In this environment, critics charge that junk science has dominated many cases.

> [E]xperts peddling junk science have [led to] billions of dollars in judgments, coerced settlements, and litigation costs on the basis of speculative, unscientific theories of liability.[12]

Suppose, for example, that a plaintiff's attorney calls an expert witness to the stand to give testimony on a university study showing that 80 percent of cancer patients in the study took a particular diet supplement. Arguably, this study is junk science when it is used to prove that the diet supplement caused the cancer. *Association is not causation.* If we notice that many overweight people drink ice tea, we cannot conclude that ice tea causes obesity. In a case we will read later in the chapter, the court complains that a plaintiff's argument "is a bit like saying that if a person has a scratchy throat, runny nose, and a nasty cough, that person has a cold; if, on the other-hand, that person has a scratchy throat, runny nose, nasty cough, and wears a watch, they have a watch-induced cold. Such reasoning is extremely suspect."

What guidelines have trial courts used in ruling on the admissibility of scientific evidence? For years, many federal courts followed the *Frye* **test** written by a lower federal court in the case of *Frye v. United States.* Under this test, expert opinion on a scientific principle or discovery is admissible only if it has "gained general acceptance" as being reliable in the relevant scientific community. In a famous quote, the *Frye* court said:

> Just when a scientific principle or discovery crosses the line between the experimental and demonstrable stages is difficult to define. Somewhere in this twilight zone the evidential force of the principle must be recognized, and while courts will go a long way in admitting expert testimony deduced from a well-recognized scientific principle or discovery, the thing from which the deduction is made must be sufficiently established to have gained general acceptance in the particular field in which it belongs.[13]

After the *Frye* decision was written, Congress passed the Federal Rules of Evidence (FRE). The FRE is broader and more liberal on admissibility than the *Frye* test. Under FRE 702, governing expert testimony:

> If scientific, technical, or other specialized knowledge will assist the trier of fact to understand the evidence or to determine a fact in issue, a witness qualified as an expert by knowledge, skill, experience, training, or education, may testify thereto in the form of an opinion or otherwise.

Under the *Frye* test, scientific evidence was admissible if it has "gained general acceptance." Under the FRE 702 test, such evidence is admissible if it "will assist the trier of fact." Many were concerned that the broader 702 test would do nothing to curb the use of junk science in the courtroom. In fact, it might make junk science

---

[12]Daniel J. Popeo, *Truth for Sale,* New York Times, September 21, 1998, at A23.
[13]*Frye v. United States,* 293 F. 1013, 1014 (D.C. Cir. 1923).

more prevalent since it would be relatively easy for a plaintiff's attorney to convince a trial court that a particular theory, study, or other item of evidence "will assist" the jury. The 702 test is so vague and broad that some feared it would lead to a free-for-all where absurd and irrational pseudoscientific assertions would continue to manipulate and confuse juries.

The time was ripe for the United States Supreme Court to clarify the scope of FRE 702. It did do in the case of *Daubert v. Merrell Dow Pharmaceuticals, Inc.*[14] In *Daubert,* the Court said that FRE 702 is not an open door. There are restrictions on the kind of scientific evidence that is admissible under FRE 702. Federal trial judges "must ensure that any and all scientific testimony or evidence admitted is not only relevant, but reliable." In applying Rule 702, the trial court has the responsibility of acting as a "gatekeeper." In this role, the court must carefully examine an expert's opinion before it allows a jury to hear it. It must assess whether the methodology, principles, and reasoning underlying the opinion:

- can be and have been empirically tested;
- have been subjected to peer review and publication;
- have a known or potential rate of error; and
- have gained general acceptance in the relevant scientific community.

Federal judges must exclude proposed scientific or other technical evidence under FRE 702 unless they are convinced that the evidence is reliable, speaks clearly and directly to an issue in dispute in the case, and will not mislead the jury. This interpretation of FRE 702 gives trial judges a very activist role in this aspect of a trial. Although the *Daubert* opinion is relatively recent, there is every reason to believe that it will cut down on the use of junk science, particularly in mass tort litigation brought in federal court.

ASSIGNMENT

20.4

a. What is junk science?
b. What is the *Frye* test and how does it compare with FRE 702?
c. What guidelines did *Daubert* impose on the kind of scientific evidence that is admissible in federal court?

ASBESTOS

Asbestos is a fibrous material known for its resistance to acid and fire. It was used in many products such as brake linings, water pipes, blankets, rope, wall insulation, caulking, and other building materials. The fibers in asbestos are invisible. They are easily dispersed into the air when products containing asbestos are installed or removed.

There is no safe level of exposure to asbestos. It can cause mesothelioma (an untreatable terminal cancer), asbestosis (a progressive untreatable disease of the lung), and pleural disease. There is some disagreement over whether it also causes gastrointestinal tract cancers. For most victims, there is a latency period between exposure and the manifestation of disease, although the length of this latency period can widely vary. Some will have a latency period as long as forty years. Since the 1940s, the number of people estimated to have been exposed to asbestos is between 11 and 30 million. Every year tens of thousands become ill or die from asbestos-related diseases. The number of people who will develop symptoms in the

---

[14]509 U.S. 579, 113 S. Ct. 2786, 125 L. Ed. 2d 469 (1993).

FIGURE 20–3   Asbestos cases in federal courts: 1993 to 1996.

TYPE OF CASE	CASES COMMENCED				CASES PENDING			
	1993	1994	1995	1996	1993	1994	1995	1996
Cases total[1]	**228,562**	**235,996**	**239,013**	**272,661**	**215,574**	**217,963**	**224,378**	**250,233**
Contract actions[1]	38,240	31,988	31,619	33,413	40,525	29,697	27,337	29,934
Recovery of overpayments[2]	7,255	2,591	2,099	3,583	5,995	1,227	1,041	2,379
Real property actions	8,436	7,468	7,282	6,276	7,743	5,855	5,073	4,554
Tort actions	40,939	48,067	44,511	67,029	45,148	47,186	52,334	69,309
Personal injury	37,409	44,734	41,102	63,222	41,324	43,638	48,789	65,527
Personal injury product liability[1]	16,545	23,977	17,631	38,170	15,208	20,694	24,166	37,261
Asbestos	4,900	7,111	6,821	6,760	7,154	3,704	3,524	4,503
Other personal injury	20,864	20,757	23,471	25,052	26,116	22,944	24,623	28,266
Personal property damage	3,530	3,333	3,409	3,807	3,824	3,548	3,545	3,782
Actions under statutes[1]	140,811	148,344	155,495	165,922	121,964	135,020	139,487	146,303
Civil rights[1]	26,483	31,521	35,566	40,476	26,477	33,271	37,512	42,961
Employment	12,221	15,256	18,225	22,150	12,530	17,359	20,375	24,428
Bankruptcy suits	6,192	5,675	5,138	4,737	4,203	4,705	4,541	4,087
Commerce (ICC rates, etc.)	1,475	1,228	613	1,622	1,238	693	446	795
Environmental matters	1,077	1,059	1,136	1,158	1,943	1,864	1,823	1,866
Prisoner petitions	52,454	56,283	62,597	69,352	39,512	45,417	47,382	51,428
Forfeiture and penalty	4,832	3,548	2,670	2,255	4,850	3,359	2,399	2,058
Labor laws	16,174	15,800	15,030	15,068	13,026	12,346	11,829	11,942
Protected property rights[3]	6,202	7,051	6,990	6,800	5,281	5,963	5,998	6,387
Securities commodities and exchanges	1,875	1,742	1,870	1,741	3,983	3,130	2,969	2,881
Social Security laws	11,602	11,142	10,168	8,517	8,304	12,302	11,310	9,226
Tax suits	2,267	2,275	2,144	2,078	2,255	1,884	1,692	1,669
Freedom of information	425	566	481	465	498	502	500	497

[1]Includes other types not shown separately.   [2]Includes enforcement of judgments in student loan cases, and overpayments of veterans benefits.   [3]Includes copyright, patent, and trademark rights.

Source: Administrative Office of the U.S. Courts, *Statistical Tables for the Federal Judiciary,* annual.

future is uncertain. Some predict the death toll will reach 500,000. Asbestos has been banned or declared hazardous by the Occupational Safety and Health Administration, the National Institute for Occupational Safety and Health, the Environmental Protection Agency, and the Surgeon General. Most manufacturers stopped making asbestos in the 1970s when the lawsuits began.

Thousands of asbestos personal injury claims have been filed in almost every court in the country. In a recent year, asbestos lawsuits consisted of more than 6 percent of all federal civil filings. (See Figure 20–3.) The United States Supreme Court has referred to all this litigation as an "elephantine mass of asbestos cases."

Litigation delays in asbestos cases have been double that of other civil cases. Transaction costs (e.g., attorney fees, witness fees, travel, court costs) consumed 61 cents of each asbestos-litigation dollar; plaintiffs have received only 39 cents from each litigation dollar.[15] One judge painted the following picture of the large number of asbestos cases that have been filed:

> Results of jury verdicts are capricious and uncertain. Sick people and people who die a terrible death from asbestos are being turned away from the courts, while people with minimal injuries who may never suffer severe asbestos disease are being awarded hundreds of thousands of dollars, and even in excess of a million dollars. The asbestos litigation often resembles the casinos . . . more than a court-room procedure.[16]

[15]Rand Corporation, *Annual Report,* April 1, 1990–March 31, 1991.
[16]Rand Corporation, *Asbestos in the Court* 42 (1985).

By 1991, the total cost to asbestos defendants was approximately $7 billion. Some estimate the final cost to go to $100 billion.

In 1982, the first major bankruptcy took place in a mass tort case when Johns-Manville Corporation, an asbestos manufacturer, filed for bankruptcy. Once bankruptcy had been filed, tort victims became creditors along with all the commercial creditors of the company. A bankruptcy trust was established to assume the liabilities of Johns-Manville. Within two years, however, the trust ran out of money. Over a dozen other asbestos companies have also sought bankruptcy protection "due to the deluge of asbestos-related personal injury litigation. These bankrupt companies collectively constitute well over 50 percent of the historical liability in asbestos personal injury cases."[17]

Many hoped that a proposed *nationwide* class action settlement would help end the chaos, at least in the federal courts. In 1997, however, the United States Supreme Court, in the case of *Amchem Products, Inc. v. Windsor,* refused to certify the proposed class.[18] This was a major event in mass tort cases. It was a signal that class actions were being overused in the federal courts.

The *Amchem* case began when eight federal judges who had handled asbestos cases asked the Judicial Panel on Multidistrict Litigation (J.P.M.L.) to transfer to one district all asbestos complaints then pending in federal courts. The Panel agreed and temporarily transferred all federal cases that had been filed (but were not yet in trial) to a single district, the United States District Court for the Eastern District of Pennsylvania.

Soon after the transfer, most of the parties reached a settlement that had an estimated value of over $1 billion. They asked the United States District Court for the Eastern District of Pennsylvania to certify the class solely for purposes of settlement. (As indicated earlier, this would be called a settlement class action.) The proposed class consisted of all persons who had been exposed—occupationally or through the occupational exposure of a spouse or household member—to asbestos attributable to one of the asbestos manufacturers in the case. Potentially hundreds of thousands, perhaps millions, of individuals would fit this description. The settlement agreement:

1. detailed an administrative mechanism and a schedule of payments to compensate class members who meet defined exposure and medical criteria;
2. described four categories of compensable cancers and nonmalignant conditions, and specified the range of damages to be paid qualifying claimants for each (mesothelioma claimants, for example, were scheduled to receive between $20,000 and $200,000);
3. did not adjust payments for inflation;
4. capped the number of claims payable annually for each disease;
5. denied compensation for family members who claim loss-of-consortium (see glossary and Chapter 22); and
6. proposed to settle claims not previously filed against the asbestos manufacturers in the case.

The District Court approved the settlement's plan for giving notice to the class and certified the proposed class for settlement only. Those who objected to the settlement and to the certification of the class appealed.

The United States Supreme Court in *Amchem* rejected the class certification. The Court held that the proposed class did not meet the standards of Rule 23 of the Federal Rules of Civil Procedure. (See Figure 20–2.)

The major objection was that the proposed class could not fairly protect the interests of those who had been exposed to asbestos but had not yet manifested injury

---

[17]Anne E. Cohen, *Mass Tort Litigation After Amchem* 57 ALI-ABA 269, 277–78 (1998).
[18]521 U.S. 591, 117 S. Ct. 2231, 138 L. Ed. 2d 689 (1997).

(called exposure-only members). Their interests clashed with those who had already manifested injury. The Supreme Court said that the requirements for Rule 23 cannot be met for a class so enormously diverse:

> Class members were exposed to different asbestos-containing products, for different amounts of time, in different ways, and over different periods. Some class members suffer no physical injury or have only asymptomatic pleural changes, while others suffer from lung cancer, disabling asbestosis, or from mesothelioma. . . . Each has a different history of cigarette smoking, a factor that complicates the causation inquiry. The plaintiffs [who have been exposed but who manifest no injuries] share little in common, either with each other or with the presently injured class members. It is unclear whether they will contract asbestos-related disease and, if so, what disease each will suffer. They will also incur different medical expenses because their monitoring and treatment will depend on singular circumstances and individual medical histories.[19]

The Court observed that no settlement class had ever been brought to its attention "as sprawling as this one."

Furthermore the named representative parties could not fairly and adequately protect the interests of the class. This requirement of Rule 23 serves to uncover conflicts of interest between named representative parties and the class they seek to represent. The Court felt that the conflict was blatant in this proposed class. The goal of the named parties is to obtain "generous immediate payments." On the other hand, the exposure-only members needed to ensure an ample, inflation-protected fund for the future.

Notice to the exposure-only members was also flawed. Many persons in the exposure-only category may not even know of their exposure, or realize the extent of the harm they may incur. Even if they fully appreciate the significance of class notice, those without current afflictions may not have the information or foresight needed to decide, intelligently, whether to stay in or opt out. Family members of asbestos-exposed individuals may themselves fall prey to disease or may ultimately have ripe claims for loss of consortium. Yet, large numbers of people in this category—future spouses and children of asbestos victims—could not be alerted to their class membership. And current spouses and children of the occupationally exposed may know nothing of that exposure.

Consequently, the proposed settlement class action was rejected by the Supreme Court. Many argued that Congress should pass legislation to set up an administrative claims procedure similar to the one established for black lung disease. Congress, however, has not seen fit to do so. The parties in the *Amchem* case, therefore, had to return to litigate their cases or to attempt far less ambitious settlement efforts.

The impact of *Amchem* is being felt far beyond asbestos cases since many mass tort plaintiffs seek class action certification under Rule 23 of the Federal Rules of Civil Procedure. Although it is still possible to have a class action certified under Rule 23, the general consensus is that certification will become much harder to obtain in the future, at least in the federal courts, particularly for the class that contains large and diverse potential members.

ASSIGNMENT

20.5

a. Describe the proposed class action settlement in *Amchem*.
b. Why did the Supreme Court refuse to certify the class?

---

[19]*Amchem,* 117 S. Ct. at 2250 (citing the lower court opinion in the case).

BREAST IMPLANTS

Between one and two million women have breast implants. Hundreds of thousands of these women believe the implants have caused connective-tissue diseases such as rheumatoid arthritis and other immune-system disorders. For example:

- In early 1975, after the birth of her son, Mildred Valentine consulted her doctor about having a "breast lift" or maximum mastopexy. The doctor explained that the procedure would involve hospitalization, general anesthesia, and two to three incisions in each breast. He also informed Mrs. Valentine of the alternative of the silicone breast implant, performed in the office with local anesthesia. She accepted this alternative and underwent the augmentation surgery with silicone breast implants manufactured by Heyer-Schulte Corporation. Shortly thereafter, she developed complications—capsular contracture in the left breast. Her doctor performed an open capsulotomy procedure, which entailed removing the implant, dividing the scar tissue, and inserting a new implant. Contracture, however, returned to the left side. Her doctor performed a closed capsulotomy, squeezing the breast to rupture the excess scar tissue. Four years later he again performed a closed capsulotomy, once on both sides, and a month later on one side. Mrs. Valentine was diagnosed with lupus around 1976. Lupus, or "systemic lupus erythematosus" is an autoimmune disease in which the body turns "against itself" by producing antinuclear antibodies. Characteristic manifestations of the disease include skin rashes, sensitivity to sun, hair loss, joint pain, stiffness, pleurisy, kidney involvement, nervous system involvement, lung involvement, and involvement of the gastrointestinal tract. In 1991, a pulmonary care specialist convinced her that due to the severity of her lung disease, the breast implants should be removed.

- In August 1985, as part of reconstructive surgery following a bilateral subcutaneous mastectomy, Charlotte Mahlum elected to receive silicone gel breast prostheses (breast implants). Dow Corning manufactured the two Silastic II breast implants that her surgeon implanted. The Silastic II implant is made up of several components. A clear outer shell of silicone rubber called an elastomer contains the silicone gel and is the protective barrier between the gel and the implant host. The silicone gel itself is comprised of 80 to 85 percent DC 360 silicone fluid. In 1990, her health began to deteriorate. In July 1993, one of the breast implants ruptured, requiring the surgical removal of both implants. The surgeon was unable to remove all of the silicone gel from her body, leaving approximately 10 percent of the silicone materials embedded in muscle, tissue, and blood vessels under her arms and ribs. Her health continued to deteriorate after the explantation surgery.

- In 1978, Nancy Jennings, age 51, received silicone gel breast implants following bilateral mastectomies. (The breast implants were manufactured by Heyer-Schulte, which obtained the silicone material from Dow Corning.) Subsequently, one implant partially deflated and was replaced in 1980. The other implant partially deflated after a mammogram was performed in 1992. In 1993, Jennings had surgery to remove the implants. She now alleges that as a direct result of silicone exposure from her silicone gel breast implants, she has suffered severe and permanent injuries including silicone invasion of her tissue and cells, migration of silicone particles through her body, local and systemic inflammatory reactions, impairment of the immune system, neurological disease, and damage to her inner ear and vestibular system. These injuries have caused her physical and mental pain and suffering associated with surgical removal of her silicone gel breast implants, itching breasts, aching joints and muscles, fatigue, dry eyes and mouth, skin changes, memory loss, sleep disturbance, hearing loss, dizziness and balance problems, numbness in the extremities, increased susceptibility to disease, and emotional distress including anxiety, nervousness, irritability, and fear of future injury and/or death.

- In 1974, Erin Page Tucker had silicone gel breast implants inserted. (The responsible manufacturer was Baxter Healthcare.) About two years later, she began to experience breast hardening from her implants. To relieve the hardening, her doctor performed a closed capsulotomy (squeezing the breast by hand to rupture the scar tissue). By 1986, breast hardening reoccurred. She also suffered from other health problems such as fatigue, pain and numbness (e.g., arm pain resulted in the inability to fully use her right arm), and cognitive dysfunction. In 1988, she was diagnosed with human adjuvant disease, an incurable autoimmune disorder. In October 1989, she had her silicone gel implants replaced with saline implants. The surgery revealed that one of her silicone gel implants had ruptured. In 1990, she joined a support group for women with breast implant problems. In group discussions she was told that the Food and Drug Administration (FDA) had never reviewed manufacturer safety data on breast implants and never approved breast implants for use in humans; that breast implant manufacturers did not perform any long-term safety tests on animals or humans; and that the manufacturers knew that silicone implants bled silicone oil into the body, and that silicone oil could stimulate the immune system. After learning of this misconduct, Erin Page Tucker believed that her breast implant manufacturer's wrongdoing was the cause of her autoimmune injuries.

In 1992, after several million-dollar verdicts were won by women, the FDA placed a moratorium on the sale of silicone breast implants for cosmetic or augmentation purposes because of doubts about their safety. This decision was given wide publicity. Soon manufacturers were facing thousands of products liability suits in state and federal courts throughout the country. In 1992, the federal Judicial Panel on Multidistrict Litigation (J.P.M.L.) ordered over 27,000 cases filed in federal courts to be transferred to a federal trial court (United States District Court) in Alabama where pretrial proceedings such as discovery would be coordinated. The largest manufacturer, Dow Corning, had over 30,000 claims filed against it. Dow and other manufacturers entered into extensive settlement negotiations. A proposed $4.2 billion class action settlement was abandoned because of the large number of women who sought payments under it; the amount available was simply not going to be enough. After the collapse of this settlement, the principal defendant, Dow Corning, filed for bankruptcy.

Throughout the controversy, many attorneys received considerable criticism. "Lawyers, who may take up to 40 percent of any compensation, have been advertising for clients with implants, encouraging them to believe they can get large sums of money. Some lawyers even recruit women with implants and send them to friendly physicians who will diagnose medical problems so they can participate in the lawsuits. The result has been one of the biggest legal messes in history."[20]

Perhaps the largest issue before the courts was causation. Substantial doubts were raised over whether implants caused the illnesses complained of. Thousands of women and their attorneys "have argued that exposure to silicone leaking from implants has caused serious disease like lupus. While there is little dispute that the implants can cause local inflammation and scar tissue buildup, implant manufacturers have rejected links between their products and more serious illnesses. A number of recent studies have supported that position."[21] One federal court appointed its own panel of scientific experts to study the data on causation. Their conclusions did *not* support the claim that the implants caused the illnesses. This did not stop the filing

---

[20]Joan Beck, *Hidden Agenda on Breast Implants,* San Diego Union-Tribune, March 2, 1996, at B6.
[21]Barry Meier, *Judges Set Up Panel for Lawsuits on Implants,* New York Times, April 4, 1996, at A12.

of new lawsuits. Even though manufacturers won many of these cases in court, the pressure to settle was enormous. It can cost a manufacturer up to $1 million in litigation costs alone to defend a single case that could drag on for years.

In 1995, implant makers Baxter International, Bristol-Myers Squibb, and 3M reached a settlement that resolved most of the claims against them.

In 1998, Dow Corning filed a bankruptcy reorganization plan proposing $3.1 billion to settle up to 170,000 claims from women over its silicone breast implants. The plan must be approved by claimants, creditors, and the bankruptcy court.[22] Under the plan, a woman has several options:

- She can accept a quick resolution by not filing a disease claim; she will receive up to $5,000 for implant removal surgery (explant surgery) and up to $20,000 for a ruptured implant.
- She can file a disease claim and, with medical documentation, receive between $10,000 and $250,000.
- She can opt out of the settlement and bring her own individual suit.

Hence, while settlement efforts continue, so does litigation, particularly over the causation issue. The following federal case of *In re Breast Implant Litigation* presents an excellent opportunity to study some of the basics of causation evidence in mass tort cases.

CASE

In re Breast Implant Litigation
11 F. Supp. 2d 1217 (1998)
United States District Court, Colorado

Background: *The plaintiffs claimed that their autoimmune diseases were caused by the silicone gel breast implants made by the defendants. During the trial, the plaintiffs asked the court to allow them to introduce testimony on causation. The defendants have made a motion to exclude this testimony.*

Decision of Court: *The motion to dismiss is granted. The proposed testimony on causation is not admissible under Federal Rules of Evidence 702.*

OPINION OF COURT

Judge SPARR delivered the opinion of the court . . .:

Plaintiffs assert tort claims for negligence and strict liability, as well as claims for breach of express and implied warranty. In Colorado, "[i]n order to prevail on a tort claim, a plaintiff must prove by a preponderance of the evidence [more likely than not] that a defendant committed an act which caused an injury to that plaintiff." *Renaud v. Martin Marietta Corp.*, 749 F. Supp. 1545, 1551 (D. Colo. 1990). Plaintiffs premise many of their alleged injuries on the existence of various kinds of "atypical connective tissue disease" ("ACTD"). This "disease" allegedly manifests itself through a "constellation" of symptoms and is allegedly caused by an autoimmune response to silicone from breast implants. . . .

The Federal Rules of Evidence govern the admission of expert scientific testimony in a federal trial. *Daubert v. Merrell*

Dow Pharmaceuticals, Inc., 509 U.S. 579 (1993). Federal Rules of Evidence 702, governing expert testimony, provides:

> If scientific, technical, or other specialized knowledge will assist the trier of fact to understand the evidence or to determine a fact in issue, a witness qualified as an expert by knowledge, skill, experience, training, or education, may testify thereto in the form of an opinion or otherwise.

Under the Rules, federal trial judges "must ensure that any and all scientific testimony or evidence admitted is not only relevant, but reliable." *Daubert*, 509 U.S. at 589. The Plaintiffs have the burden of proving that the testimony of their expert witnesses is admissible pursuant to Fed. R. Evid. 702 and the standards set forth in *Daubert* governing the admissibility of scientific evidence. In applying Rule 702, the trial court has the responsibility of acting as a gatekeeper. . . .

GENERAL AND SPECIFIC CAUSATION

Causation in toxic tort cases is discussed in terms of general and specific causation. See e.g., *Raynor v. Merrell Pharmaceuticals, Inc.*, 104 F.3d 1371, 1376 (D.C. Cir. 1997). General causation is whether a substance is capable of causing a particular injury or condition in the general population, while specific causation is whether a substance caused a particular individual's injury.

In order to establish their claims, Plaintiffs "must show both general and specific causation—that is, that breast

---

[22]For information about the settlement on the Internet, see <www.implantclaims.com> and <www.tortcomm.org>.

implants are capable of causing" the conditions complained of, and that "breast implants were the cause-in-fact" of the specific conditions. *Kelley v. American Heyer-Schulte Corp.,* 957 F. Supp. 873, 875 (W.D. Tex. 1997); . . . *Hall v. Baxter Healthcare Corp.,* 947 F. Supp. 1387, 1412–13 (D. Ore. 1996)(Courts "have recognized two levels of causation: general causation (i.e., can silicone gel cause disease in anyone?) and specific causation (i.e, did silicone gel breast implants cause disease in this plaintiff?)"); *Jones v. United States,* 933 F. Supp. 894, 900–01 (N.D. Cal. 1996) (plaintiff must show both "general causation," that defendant's conduct increased likelihood of injury, and "specific causation," that defendant's conduct was probable, not merely possible, cause of injury).

EPIDEMIOLOGY IS THE BEST EVIDENCE OF CAUSATION

The diseases and symptoms allegedly associated with breast implants occur in non-implanted women as well as implanted women. Many of the conditions that Plaintiffs attribute to breast implants appear in the general population. Without a controlled study, there is no way to determine if these symptoms are more common in women with silicone breast implants than women without implants. "The most important evidence relied upon by scientists to determine whether an agent (such as breast implants) cause disease is controlled epidemiologic studies. Epidemiology can be viewed as the study of the causes of diseases in humans." (Ory Affidavit, p. 7 to Defendants' Science Brief). Therefore, epidemiological studies are necessary to determine the cause and effect between breast implants and allegedly associated diseases. A valid epidemiologic study requires that study subjects, cases, and controls are chosen by an unbiased sampling method from a definable population. Epidemiology is the best evidence of causation in the mass torts context. Linda A. Bailey, et al., Reference Guide on Epidemiology, *Reference Manual on Scientific Evidence* at 126 (1994) ("In the absence of an understanding of the biological and pathological mechanisms by which disease develops, epidemiological evidence is the most valid type of scientific evidence of toxic causation"). . . .

MORE-PROBABLE-THAN-NOT BURDEN MEANS PLAINTIFFS MUST ESTABLISH A DOUBLING OF RISK

[I]f the available body of epidemiology demonstrates that breast implants do not double the risk of any known disease, then plaintiffs' causation evidence is inadmissible.

There exists in the context of breast implanted women a "background rate" of injury; that is, the injuries of which the breast implant plaintiffs complain are not unique, but occur frequently in women without breast implants. Because the injuries of which Plaintiffs complain occur commonly in women without breast implants, Plaintiffs must present expert testimony demonstrating that exposure to breast implants more than doubled the risk of their alleged injuries. *Hall v. Baxter Healthcare Corp.,* 947 F. Supp. 1387, 1403 (D. Ore. 1996). . . . If exposure to breast implants does not at least double the risk of injury, then more than half of the population suffering from the injuries allegedly caused by breast implants would be injured anyway (the background rate of injury), thereby disproving legal causation. . . .

The difference between groups is often expressed as the ratio between the incidence of the disease in the exposed group and the incidence in the unexposed group. Marcia Angell, M.D., *Science on Trial* (1996) at 164. The relative risk

simply indicates how high above the background level the risk is.

The threshold for concluding that an agent was more likely the cause of a disease than not is a relative risk greater than 2.0. . . . [A] relative risk of 1.0 means that the agent has no effect on the incidence of disease. When the relative risk reaches 2.0, the agent is responsible for an equal number of cases of disease as all other background causes. Thus, a relative risk of 2.0 implies a 50% likelihood that an exposed individual's disease was caused by the agent. *Hall,* 947 F. Supp. at 1403 (quoting *Reference Manual on Scientific Evidence* at 168).

For example, if the relative risk for a disease between women with breast implants and women without breast implants is 1.2, it means that for every 10 women without implants who develop the disease, 12 women with implants in an equal population would develop the disease. *Science on Trial* at 196.

It is important to realize that we do not know exactly what a relative risk of 1.2 means for each of those 12 women who develop connective tissue disease. It could mean that in 2 of them, the implants were the sole cause of their disease and in the other 10 they played no role. Or it could mean that implants played a major role in 3 or 4 women and a very small one in the others. Or it could mean that implants contributed a varying amount to the disease in all 12. . . . All we could say for sure with a relative risk of 1.2 is that on *average,* implants contributed about 17 percent (0.2/1.2) to the disease. For any one woman among the 12, then, we could not say that but for the implants, she would not have developed the disease. Further, we would have to say that some other factor or group of factors was the dominant cause. *Science on Trial* at 196–97 (emphasis in original).

THE EPIDEMIOLOGICAL EVIDENCE [IN THIS CASE] DEMONSTRATES THE ABSENCE OF A DOUBLING OF THE RISK

At least seventeen epidemiological studies of breast implants have been published in peer reviewed medical journals. (Ory Affidavit pp. 35, 36). Every controlled epidemiological study concludes that silicone breast implants do not double the risk of any known disease. None of these studies support a conclusion that breast implants cause rheumatic or connective tissue diseases, either classic or atypical, in breast implanted women. None of these studies reports a statistically significant elevation of risk of rheumatic or connective tissue disease, either classic or atypical, over 2.0. The reported results from every published controlled epidemiological study uniformly show the absence of a doubling of the risk of any known disease among breast implant recipients. . . . As a whole, these studies provide a solid body of epidemiologic evidence establishing that breast implants do not cause connective tissue disease, autoimmune disease or various symptoms. . . .

The largest study to date concluded that there is no doubling of the risk of connective tissue disease among women with breast implants. Hennekens, et al., "Self-Reported Breast Implants and Connective-Tissue Diseases in Female Health Professionals," 275 Journal of the American Medical Assoc. 616 (February 28, 1996) ("Hennekens Study"). The

Hennekens Study included almost 400,000 female health professionals who completed mailed questionnaires, including more than 10,000 who reported having breast implants and almost 12,000 who reported having connective-tissue diseases between 1962 and 1991. The relative risk for all connective-tissue diseases was estimated at 1.24 (95% confidence interval, 1.08 to 1.41). As the authors themselves noted, this study suffered from bias which probably explains the slight increased relative risk. . . .

To the extent that there are case or anecdotal reports noting various symptoms or signs in breast implanted women, without controls, these suggest only a potential, untested hypothesis that breast implants may be their cause. Such case reports are not reliable scientific evidence of causation, because they simply describe reported phenomena without comparison to the rate at which the phenomena occur in the general population or in a defined control group . . . [T]hey do not isolate and exclude potentially alternative causes . . . and do not investigate or explain the mechanism of causation. An untested hypothesis cannot be a scientifically reliable basis for an opinion on causation. . . .

The reports submitted by Plaintiffs' experts fail to present a single peer-reviewed, controlled epidemiologic study that support their causation theories. This is not to say that epidemiological studies are required in this type of tort action. Epidemiological studies are not the magical cure for legal disputes. In many instances, epidemiological data may be unavailable. A lack of epidemiology should not end the inquiry, but rather begin the inquiry into what other types of evidence a plaintiff can present to satisfy the burden of proof. There is a range of scientific methods for investigating questions of causation, for example, toxicology and animal studies, clinical research, and epidemiology, all of which have distinct advantages and disadvantages. The court's inquiry is whether reliable scientific evidence, based on sound methodology, has been presented. What is significant in this case is that the substantial body of epidemiological evidence demonstrates that silicone breast implants do not double the risk of any known disease.

DIFFERENTIAL DIAGNOSIS

Plaintiffs seek to introduce expert testimony from clinicians (i.e., treating physicians) who claim to be able to diagnose a patient with a disease caused by breast implants through the process of differential diagnosis. [A neurologist, for example, has provided a written opinion stating that he, as a treating physician of the Plaintiffs has used the medical procedure of differential diagnosis and has] determined to "a reasonable degree of medical certainty" that the illnesses and symptoms from which the Plaintiffs suffer are caused by the silicone from their silicone gel breast implants.

Such testimony is not scientifically reliable in the cases before the court because it confuses two distinct burdens. Plaintiffs must demonstrate two types of causation: general causation and specific causation. *Raynor,* 104 F.3d at 1376; *Hall,* 947 F. Supp. at 1412–1413. By using differential diagnosis, a clinician can identify possible diseases the patient may have and, through a process of elimination, rule out diseases until a disease or symptom is left as the diagnosis. Differential diagnosis is not a scientific method by which a physician can determine whether silicone

breast implants can cause disease in humans. As the court explained in *Hall,*

[d]ifferential diagnosis is a patient-specific process of elimination that medical practitioners use to identify the 'most likely' cause of a set of signs and symptoms from a list of possible causes. However, differential diagnosis does not by itself *prove* the cause, even for the particular patient. Nor can the technique speak to the issue of general causation. Indeed, differential diagnosis *assumes* that general causation has been proven for the list of possible causes it eliminates:

The process of differential diagnosis is undoubtedly important to the question of "specific causation." If other possible causes of an injury cannot be ruled out, or at least the probability of their contribution to causation minimized, then the "more likely than not" threshold for proving causation may not be met. But, it is also important to recognize that a fundamental assumption underlying this method is that the final, suspected "cause" remaining after this process of elimination must actually be capable of causing the injury. That is, the expert must "rule in" the suspected cause as well as "rule out" other possible causes. And, of course, expert opinion on this issue of "general causation" must be derived from a scientifically valid methodology.

947 F. Supp. at 1413 (emphasis in original) (quoting *Cavallo v. Star Enterprise,* 892 F. Supp. 756, 771 (E.D. Va. 1995)).

As a practical matter, the cause of many diseases remains unknown; therefore, a clinician who suspects that a substance causes a disease in some patients very well might conclude that the substance caused the disease in the plaintiff simply because the clinician has no other explanation. See Margaret A. Berger, "Evidentiary Framework," *Reference Manual on Scientific Evidence* at 81 (1994). The kind of causation testimony offered by Plaintiffs' experts was summarized and rejected by Judge Prado in *Kelley:*

[T]he witness admits that if the Plaintiff did not have breast implants but had the exact same symptoms and blood chemistry, then his diagnosis would have been non-implant-caused Sjogren's Syndrome. Essentially, this is a bit like saying that if a person has a scratchy throat, runny nose, and a nasty cough, that person has a cold; if, on the other-hand, that person has a scratchy throat, runny nose, nasty cough, and wears a watch, they have a watch-induced cold. Such reasoning is extremely suspect, which has prompted other courts to reject it as unscientific in the absence of convincing epidemiology evidence. 957 F. Supp. at 882 (citing *Brock v. Merrell Dow Pharmaceuticals, Inc.,* 874 F.2d 307, 310 n. 11 (5th Cir. 1989)).

The causation testimony offered by the Plaintiffs is precisely the kind of subjective testimony that is inadmissible pursuant to Rules 702 [of the Federal Rules of Evidence]. "Reasoning that a cause-and-effect relationship exists simply because a large number of individuals with a particular characteristic develop a particular disease is fallacious, because it totally fails to account for the fact that both characteristics and diseases are widely distributed among the general population." (Ory Affidavit p. 50). In short, "a single differential diagnosis is a scientifically invalid methodology" for the purpose of demonstrating general causation. *Hall,* 947 F. Supp. at 1414. Differential diagnosis may be utilized by a clinician to determine what recognized disease or symptom the patient has, but it is incapable of determining whether exposure to a substance caused disease in the legal sense.

TEMPORALITY

Plaintiffs' experts assert that causation may be inferred based upon the temporal sequence of implantation and the onset of illness. A temporal relationship by itself, provides no evidence of causation. Temporality at best addresses the issue of specific causation; therefore, evidence of temporality is inadmissible where no admissible evidence of general causation exists. . . . *Cavallo v. Star Enterprise,* 892 F. Supp. at 773 (a causation opinion based solely on a temporal relationship is not derived from the scientific method and is therefore insufficient to satisfy the requirements of Rule 702).

CONCLUSION

[The motion to exclude the testimony of the plaintiffs is granted].

ASSIGNMENT

20.6

a. What type of evidence of causation would this court find acceptable?
b. What is differential diagnosis and why does the court object to it?
c. What is wrong with case studies as evidence of causation?
d. What is temporality and why does the court object to it?

TOBACCO

"Vicious!" said the plaintiff's attorney when he saw a roadside billboard display in the city where he was suing a tobacco company. The display, paid for by tobacco companies, contained a photo of an obviously wealthy and obnoxious attorney sitting by a pool with his golf clubs and Mercedes in the background. The caption on the billboard read in large letters:

"1-800-I-Sue-4-You."

In response, anti-smoking ads were available in abundance in the same city. One TV ad showed a tobacco executive at a "Demon Award" ceremony. As he accepted the award, he said, "This is for all you smokers out there." Among the executive's admirers in the audience were murderers, drug dealers, Adolf Hitler, and Joseph Stalin.[23] Such ads and counter-ads are a not-very-subtle attempt to influence juries, judges, legislators, and the general public. The tobacco wars were being waged on all fronts.

For years, smokers lost their cases in court because they were portrayed as foolish people who wanted someone else to pay for their lack of self-control. They knew smoking was hazardous to their health; since 1966 every pack of cigarettes bluntly told them so. In legal terms, they assumed the risk of health problems by continuing to smoke. Juries consistently came to this conclusion, in part, because the general public had little sympathy for the smoker. A political cartoon by Signe Wilkinson in the Philadelphia Daily News shows a distraught but sincere woman on the witness stand telling the judge and jury, "The cigarette that I was forced to smoke dropped ashes on the silicone breasts I was forced to implant and they melted over the hamburger I hadn't cooked so that's why I deserve $325 million." So prevalent was this anti-consumer attitude that a number of states even passed statutes that banned most smoker lawsuits on the ground that the dangers of tobacco use were well known. Prior to the 1990s, tobacco companies (e.g., American Tobacco Company, Brown & Williamson, Liggett & Myers, Lorillard, Philip Morris, R.J. Reynolds, and United States Tobacco Company) were not concerned by individual lawsuits brought by

---

[23] *Blowing Smoke: Cigarette Maker Taunts Lawyers in Ad Campaign,* Wall Street Journal October 20, 1998, at B1.

smokers since few of them succeeded, the awards were small, and every victorious plaintiff was overturned on appeal.

Such legal victories by the tobacco industry were remarkable in the face of a drumbeat of news that over 400,000 people per year died in the United States from smoking-related diseases such as cancer, heart disease, and emphysema. The Secretary of the United States Department of Health and Human Services estimated that smoking-related health costs exceeded $45 billion a year, particularly through Medicare and Medicaid. If you include fire damage, absenteeism, and lost productivity, the total economic cost of tobacco use was said to exceed $145 billion a year. Nevertheless, the tobacco industry kept winning in the courtroom.

Since the mid-1990s, however, the tide has turned. For years, tobacco companies denied that their product was addictive, unhealthy, or targeted at young people. Internal documents, however, have dramatically shown otherwise. For example, extensive media attention has been given to reports that the tobacco industry considered teenagers to be "replacement smokers" for the hundreds of thousands of smokers dying each year from lung cancer and other smoking-related diseases. A 1975 memo (marked "secret") of R.J. Reynolds made the following stunning statement about children as young as fourteen:

> To ensure increased and long-term growth for CAMEL FILTER, the brand must increase its share penetration among the 14–24 age group which have a new set of more liberal values and which represent tomorrow's cigarette business.

A paralegal played a prominent role in this drama. Merrell Williams was a paralegal who once worked at Wyatt, Tarrant & Combs, the largest law firm in Kentucky. The firm represented Brown & Williamson (B&W), maker of Kool and Viceroy. While Merrell Williams worked at the firm, he secretly photocopied and distributed confidential internal memos, letters, and other documents between the law firm and its client. The documents demonstrated that the corporation knew about the danger of smoking, but tried to cover it up. The news media made extensive use of this material. Here is how a Los Angeles Times article described this development:

> Big tobacco is known as a formidable legal adversary, skilled and even ruthless in the courtroom. Yet the industry is being slowly undone by its former secrets. . . . Disclosure of documents [containing these secrets], many dating back 40 years, has done enormous damage, outraging citizens and forcing once-helpful politicians to climb on the anti-tobacco bandwagon. . . . The ground shifted in 1994, when an obscure paralegal, who had secretly stolen thousands of pages of documents from a [law firm representing] B&W, leaked the purloined papers to Congress and the media. The documents were an instant sensation. In one 1963 memo, for example, the [tobacco] company's former general counsel declared, "We are, then, in the business of selling nicotine, an addictive drug.". . . Now the blood was in the water, and so were the sharks. For 1994 also marked the formation of a powerful alliance of products liability lawyers and state attorneys general, who began filing immense new claims against the industry.[24]

Wyatt, Tarrant & Combs obtained an injunction against Merrell Williams to prevent him from continuing to reveal what he learned while he was a paralegal at the firm. The law firm says "Williams broke his employment contract which requires confidentiality, and stole photocopies of documents from the law office." An ex-smoker himself, Williams has undergone quadruple bypass surgery and has sued Brown & Williamson for his own health problems.[25]

---

[24]Myron Levin, *Years of Immunity and Arrogance Up in Smoke,* Los Angeles Times, May 10, 1998, at D1, D17.
[25]Mark Curriden, *DOJ (Department of Justice) Probes Law Firms: Paralegal Who Copied Documents Subpoenaed,* 80 American Bar Association Journal 14 (June 1994); *It Started with a Paralegal,* 13 Legal Assistant Today 18 (May/June 1996).

The onslaught of litigation against tobacco companies fell into several categories:

- states sued for the Medicaid costs they paid to treat smoking-related illnesses;
- private citizens who were smokers or ex-smokers brought class action suits in state and federal courts on behalf of large numbers of sick and deceased smokers;
- private citizens who were smokers or ex-smokers brought individual suits in state and federal courts for the illness or death brought on by smoking;
- private citizens who were not smokers or ex-smokers brought individual or class action suits in state and federal courts for the illness or death caused by second-hand smoking.

The largest number of these cases, many of which take years to litigate, were filed during the period when the media were revealing the contents of the internal tobacco documents.

Class actions in tobacco cases have not done well in federal courts, particularly since the United States Supreme Court decided not to approve the asbestos class in *Amchem Products, Inc. v. Windsor,* as we saw earlier. For example, a federal court refused to certify a nationwide class action on behalf of "all nicotine dependent persons in the United States." The class could have involved 50 million smokers. The court concluded that the criteria for a class action in federal court (see Figure 20–2) had not been met.

State courts, however, have not been as reluctant as federal courts to certify a nationwide class. In 1996, one of the smaller cigarette manufacturers, Liggett Group (maker of Chesterfield, L&M, and Eve), broke ranks and settled a class action that was filed in an Alabama state court on behalf of a nationwide class of smokers.[26] The Alabama court certified this action as a settlement class and preliminarily approved the proposed settlement. A nationwide campaign of notice then took place. See Figure 20–4 for the "official notice" of this settlement printed in newspapers across the country. Under the settlement, Liggett admitted that smoking causes various health problems and that nicotine is addictive. Liggett also agreed to pay 7.5 percent of its pre-tax income to a Settlement Fund for the next twenty-five years. To the dismay of the rest of the tobacco industry, Liggett also agreed to "cooperate fully" in "lawsuits against the other cigarette manufacturers." (See paragraph 2 in the Settlement Notice of Figure 20–4.)

In June of 1997, the front pages of every major newspaper in the country reported that cigarette makers and forty states had reached a settlement that would provide $368.5 billion over twenty-five years to cover Medicaid money that states have paid to treat sick smokers.[27] Although this settlement eventually collapsed, many were amazed at what the tobacco industry had agreed to do:

- give the United States Food and Drug Administration (FDA) expanded authority to regulate the level of nicotine in cigarettes;
- cease all outdoor tobacco advertising and eliminate cartoon characters and human figures, such as Joe Camel and the Marlboro Man, two tobacco icons, which the public health community had long assailed as advertising appealing to our nation's youth; and
- subject tobacco manufacturers to severe financial surcharges in the event underage tobacco use did not decline radically over the next decade.

This settlement required legislation by Congress since it involved major policy changes such as the scope of the FDA's regulatory power. Public health groups, however, attacked the deal as too weak since companies could simply pass on their added costs to smokers. The American Lung Association called it a "bailout for the industry." In the end, Congress failed to act, and the settlement fell apart.

Several states pursued their own actions against the tobacco industry to recover their Medicaid costs. Individually, the states of Mississippi, Florida, Texas, and Minnesota reached settlements. The total involved in these four states was over $40 billion.

(text continued on page 411)

---

[26]You can examine the court documents in this state case on the Internet at <www.liggett.net>.
[27]The details of the settlement were posted on the Internet at <http://stic.neu.edu/settlement/6-20-settle.htm> and also at <www.tobaccoresolution.com>.

FIGURE 20–4 Notice printed in newspapers of tobacco class action filed against Liggett Group in Alabama State Court on behalf of smokers nationwide.

IN THE CIRCUIT COURT OF MOBILE COUNTY, ALABAMA
OFFICIAL NOTICE

—ATTENTION—

ALL SMOKERS
and
ALL INDIVIDUALS OR ENTITIES WHICH MAY HAVE CLAIMS AGAINST CIGARETTE MANUFACTURERS

Your rights may be affected by a class action lawsuit pending in the Circuit Court of Mobile County, Alabama, **Fletcher, et al. v. Brooke Group, Ltd., Liggett Group Inc., and Liggett & Myers, Inc.,** Case No. 97-913. A settlement has been filed for this class action, and this settlement has been preliminarily approved by the Circuit Court.

If approved, the class action and settlement in **Fletcher** will resolve all smoking-related claims against Liggett Group, Inc. and its affiliates Brooke Group Ltd. and Liggett & Myers, Inc. (hereinafter referred to collectively as "Liggett"). Liggett is the manufacturer of Chesterfield, Eve, L & M, Lark, Pyramid, and various generic brands of cigarettes.

If you or some person or entity for whom you act as a legal representative is or was a smoker, has been exposed to cigarette smoke, or has incurred or claims to have incurred direct or indirect economic loss as a result of paying for the treatment of diseases, illnesses, or medical conditions allegedly caused by cigarettes, you may be covered by terms of the settlement as a member of the Settlement Class.

Among other things, the settlement provides for 1) compliance by Liggett with certain FDA regulations and other restrictions on Liggett's marketing and sale of cigarettes to minors and children; 2) a public statement by Liggett acknowledging that nicotine is addictive and that smoking causes various health problems; 3) placement of a prominent warning on each of Liggett's packages of cigarettes and in its advertising stating "Smoking is Addictive"; 4) cooperation with the Settlement Class and Settlement Class Counsel in pursuit of lawsuits against other cigarette manufacturers; and 5) monetary compensation—to the extent practicable given Liggett's troubled financial condition—to the Settlement Class for equitable distribution.

Liggett's assets are so limited in relation to the potential liability of Liggett for pending and potential smoking-related claims against it that even a relatively insignificant judgment could render Liggett insolvent, and members of the Settlement Class would be left unable to avail themselves of the valuable cooperation to be provided by Liggett under the settlement, and without any prospect of financial recovery from Liggett.

If the Settlement is approved and becomes effective, its main features will affect Settlement Class members as follows:

1. 7.5% of Liggett's annual pre-tax income, with a minimum yearly payment of $1 million, will be placed in a Settlement Fund for the next twenty-five (25) years. The allocation of the settlement fund to specific uses or among particular claimants has not been determined. Future allocation and distribution of the Settlement Fund will be administered by a Settlement Fund Board. The Settlement Fund Board shall be comprised of, among others, representatives of the public health community and by Settlement Class Counsel with the approval of the Court. The Settlement Fund Board shall be responsible for recommending and implementing guidelines and procedures for the administration of claims. The settlement agreement does not specify any particular allocation of settlement proceeds. Settlement Class members will be given notice and an opportunity to be heard and make suggestions regarding allocation before any final allocation or distribution decisions are made.

2. Liggett will cooperate fully with the Settlement Class and Settlement Class Counsel in their lawsuits against the other cigarette manufacturers. To that end, Liggett will make available to the Settlement Class and Settlement Class Counsel all relevant documents and information, including documents subject to

FIGURE 20–4 Continued

Liggett's own attorney-client privileges and work product protections and will assist those parties in obtaining prompt court adjudication of the joint defense privilege claims of the other cigarette manufacturers. Moreover, Liggett will offer their employees, and any and all other individuals over whom they have control, to provide witness interviews of such employees and to testify, in deposition and at trial.

3. Liggett will support and not challenge Food and Drug Administration regulations concerning the sale and distribution of nicotine-containing cigarettes and smokeless tobacco products to children and adolescents. Accordingly, Liggett has agreed to comply with many of these regulations and other advertising restrictions even before they apply to the tobacco industry generally.

4. All smoking-related claims against Liggett covered by the settlement will be cut off.

5. In the event that another tobacco company merges with or acquires Liggett or Brooke Group in the future, the merging tobacco company would participate in certain aspects of the Settlement Agreement.

On March 9, 1999, a hearing will be held in the Thirteenth Judicial Circuit Court, Courtroom 8600, Mobile Government Plaza, Mobile, Alabama and will continue, if necessary, at such times as the Court orders. The purpose of this hearing is to determine whether the settlement described herein is fair, reasonable, and adequate to members of the Settlement Class and should be approved. The Court will review all aspects of the settlement and the historical events leading up to the settlement. If the Court finds the terms proposed in the settlement to be fair, reasonable and adequate, the settlement may be approved. If the Court finds any of the provisions in the proposed settlement to be unfair, it may reject the settlement.

Although you may not exclude yourself from the class, you have a right at the hearing to comment on or object to the settlement, or to any of its terms. If you desire to object or to comment on the settlement prior to the hearing, you must

mail written objections or comments to Special Master John W. Sharbrough, Esq., 156 St. Anthony St., Mobile Alabama and place on your submission the case name and the number "***Fletcher, et al. v. Brooke Group, Ltd., et al.,*** Case No. 97-913," provided such written objections or comments are postmarked no later than March 1, 1999. If you desire to appear in person, or through counsel selected by you, at the March 9, 1999 hearing, you must mail a timely notice of intention to appear to Special Master Sharbrough on or before March 1, 1999. If you have no objections to this settlement and accept the terms of this settlement, you need not file anything with the Court. **YOU DO NEED TO MAKE ANY OBJECTIONS YOU MAY HAVE TO THE SETTLEMENT AT THIS TIME.**

You may also seek to intervene in this action as a party pursuant to either Rule 24(a) or Rule 24(b) of the Alabama Rules of Civil Procedure; however, there is no assurance that your application to intervene will be granted by the Court. A party who only objects to the settlement may not enjoy all the rights in the proceeding as a party who is permitted to intervene. For example, rights to engage in discovery may be greater for a party permitted to intervene, and there is precedent that a party who has not sought to intervene will not be permitted to appeal if dissatisfied with the outcome in the Circuit Court. If you have not intervened in this action or if you do not file a timely notice of objections or a timely intention to appear at the hearing, you will waive your right to object to the settlement.

If the Settlement Agreement is approved by the Court, and you or a person for whom you act as a legal representative fall within the definition of the Settlement Class, you will be bound by the Court's final orders and judgments. The Settlement Agreement is available for public inspection in the Court Clerk's office, 205 Government Street, Mobile, Alabama. Copies of the Settlement Agreement can be obtained from the Clerk's office by payment of the copying and mailing expense. The Settlement Agreement is also available on the World Wide Web of the Internet at www.liggett.net.

In the meantime, efforts to achieve a broader settlement continued. The break-through came in November of 1998 when the other forty-six states reached a settlement that called for the payment of $206 billion over 25 years for smoking-related health costs. Note that the claimants in these settlements were *not* smokers who arguably assumed the known risks of smoking. The claimants were the state governments who wanted to recoup the billions of dollars they spent for smoking-related diseases. The governments had not assumed any risks. States do not inhale!

The settlements did not increase the authority of the FDA to regulate nicotine in tobacco or other aspects of the manufacture and marketing of tobacco products. The courts have ruled that the FDA would have to obtain this authority through new legislation from Congress. Nor did the settlements put an end to individual lawsuits or class actions brought by smokers. They still had the right to prove their case in court. Individual smokers were not part of the settlements that the tobacco industry made with the fifty state governments.

In 1999, a San Francisco jury awarded a smoker $51.5 million from Philip Morris Company, fifty million of which was for punitive damages. The plaintiff was a 52-year-old woman who said she had inoperable lung cancer from 35 years of smoking. The size of the verdict frightened the tobacco companies. The punitive damages were more than three times the $15 million she asked for. She also was not expected to be a sympathetic plaintiff since she tried to stop smoking only once in 35 years. Yet, she walked away with a $51.5 million judgment. Although this amount was eventually cut in half on appeal, the size of the verdict has encouraged other individual smokers to bring their own cases. By the end of 1998, for example, Philip Morris said that it was defending over 500 smoking and health cases filed by individuals, an increase of just under 30 percent from the previous year. Class action filings had also jumped from 50 to 60 in the same period. This is the experience of only one manufacturer. In Florida, five of the largest tobacco manufacturers lost the first state class action case ever to be tried by a jury. It returned a staggering punitive damages award of $144 billion! Many feared that the judgments coming out of such suits may be so large that the tobacco companies will be forced into bankruptcy. And in 1999, the federal government sued the tobacco industry to recover the billions it spends treating smoking-related diseases of Medicare patients, military veterans, and federal employees. Clearly, the tobacco industry is not close to achieving global peace.

Manufacturers of other allegedly dangerous products have not been encouraged by what has happened to tobacco companies. Who is next? they wonder. Manufacturers and distributors of intoxicating liquor? Those who make and sell guns? Attempts to subject these other industries to mass tort litigation have not yet been successful, but the attempts are continuing. A few years ago, no one would have predicted that tobacco companies would be facing multibillion-dollar liability payments through settlements and judgments. There are a lot of mass tort attorneys in the United States looking around for other deep pockets.

PARALEGAL ROLES IN MASS TORT LITIGATION

Large mass tort cases present many opportunities for paralegal involvement, particularly in the area of document management. The following discussion of paralegal roles is by a paralegal with extensive experience in the field. Although it covers toxic torts, the task and organization principles apply to other kinds of mass tort cases as well.[28]

---

[28]Reprinted with permission from *Toxic Law Reporter,* vol. 4, no. 21, pp. 628–37, October 25, 1989 (as "The Administrative Legal Assistant: A Nuts and Bolts View of Complex Toxic Tort Litigation Management"). Copyright 1989 by the Bureau of National Affairs, Inc. (800-372-1033).

FIGURE 20–5 Paralegal as Project/Case Manager in Toxic Tort Litigation by Bert E. Gagnon Director of Paralegals and Litigation Support Services Thompson & Coburn.

Managing complex toxic tort litigation is one of the most difficult challenges for legal case assistant managers. Mountains of bewildering materials seemingly erupt in awesome magnitude during a marathon toxic tort case. The sheer volume of documents to sift and sort can appear insurmountable, so overwhelming that you want to run screaming into the morning sun. Do not take that step. A good legal assistant's expert organizational skills are often equal to the task at hand. With a sensible and cooperative paralegal team, a legal assistant can turn this nightmare into an efficient and effective gold mine of information easily accessible to the trial litigators.

There are many types of toxic exposure, ranging from a specific incident, such as a spill, to long-term exposure of a product, such as asbestos, which takes place over a period of many years. . . .

This author's experience in toxic tort litigation management has been for the defense in five multi-plaintiff cases involving a total of more than 300 plaintiffs, including *Kemner v. Monsanto,* the longest jury trial in the history of the United States (Ill CirCt, St. Clair Cnty, 2 TXLR 612, 1987). The systems outlined below are defense-oriented and were originally developed for a chemical spill case, but they can be applied to any type of toxic exposure litigation.

The following discussion is aimed at aiding you in mapping out the elements of your case and establishing reliable document control mechanisms for each of these elements. It assumes that your firm represents a defendant involved in a complex toxic tort litigation brought by multiple plaintiffs claiming personal injury and property damage. Your goal is a meticulous support system that will provide responsive informational backup to your trial counsel. The ideas outlined in this article are not rules carved in granite. They are merely suggestions. You should add your own creative powers to develop systems specifically tailored to the needs of your litigation.

An effective legal assistant case manager is aware that what he or she does is identified in the client's bills and is a direct reflection on his or her firm. All projects should be designed to bring your case closer to settlement or to trial; it goes without saying that none should be undertaken without the consent of your supervising attorney.

I. WHERE DO I BEGIN?

Where you come into the case will determine where you start. If you are afforded the luxury of being assigned to anticipated litigation immediately after an incident has happened, rather than the day before trial, you have the opportunity to lay solid groundwork on which to build the factual information of the case. Whether you are the legal assistant project manager or the newest legal assistant on the team, you are the keeper of the facts. Factual development is the key to what every litigation legal assistant does and is your team's primary responsibility.

You start at a disadvantage because the plaintiffs' legal assistants will have already begun factual development. They may have assisted in drafting the complaint. They will have collected the factual data necessary to determine the strength of the claim and to develop their case after the complaint was filed.

If your initial contact with the lawsuit is after it has commenced, read the complaint. Know who is suing who for what and gain an understanding of the legal causes of action as well as the factual background. As members of the defense team, this is where most of us will enter the litigation, shortly after receipt of the complaint.

Begin with the facts of the incident. Ask to be included in initial interviews with the client and keep communication with your attorneys and their secretaries open. If you cannot be at the initial interviews, then question the attorney who was and read the memos they prepare. Find out as much as you can about the exposure or accident and the nature of injuries as early as possible. What parties were involved in the incident? Who was in charge? Who organized the cleanup efforts? What is the nature of the toxic agent? Who are the witnesses to the incident? What local, state, or federal agencies are involved? Find out who has taken photographs of the incident and obtain copies.

This is a good time to start files on every individual and agency you identify and to note not only pertinent contact information, but, in general terms, the nature of their involvement in the incident. You can maintain an alphabetical listing of these individuals either on a computer or on separate index cards, noting name, address, phone number, and whether they are eye witnesses, defendants, plaintiffs, government officials, etc. . . .

It is also a sound idea to establish the same type of index for all other contacts you make regarding any and all aspects of the litigation. This could include plaintiffs' attorneys, secretaries and paralegals, government officials, librarians, photographers and graphic artists, police dispatchers and investigators, expert witnesses and their staff members, and many others. Keep their addresses and phone numbers and note who you speak with at each office or agency. The next time you call it will speed your process and assist you in getting results if you are known by the person you are calling.

Develop Checklists And Indices

Throughout the course of any complex toxic tort litigation you will continually be developing and updating various checklists and indices. Although it may seem time-consuming, these working tools are essential to the management of cases of this magnitude. . . .

Be creative in developing them and use them to monitor projects in progress or structure anticipated projects. Apply them to every project you institute that involves a review of more than a few items—such as witnesses, depositions, or medical records. Use them to coordinate project assignments and status. Use them when you are called upon to organize teams of attorneys. If your organizational skills are sharp (and you would not be doing this if they were not) you will frequently be called upon to work as the pivot point for teams of attorneys drafting outlines or motions, etc. Apply your checklists here, too. When preparing status reports for supervising attorneys or clients, you will know at a glance what has happened or needs to happen in each instance.

You should have indices for all aspects of the case. Develop them for expert witnesses, plaintiffs, factual witnesses, potential witnesses, witness statements, depositions, deposition exhibits, pleadings, production documents, trial transcripts, trial exhibits, scientific literature, medical literature, etc. Keep them close at hand because you will refer to them often.

At the front of every checklist or index identify all parties who have copies of that listing. When you update your listing, notify all identified parties of the update. It is much easier to update your checklists and indices as changes happen than to backtrack and try to develop them after the information is no longer fresh in your mind.

One practical checklist is a daily list of things to do. Keep one at hand at all times and note such things as changes or updates needing incorporation into your other lists, new projects, comments, memos to prepare or copies to obtain, or notes that need to be placed into your tickler system. As each of these duties is taken care of, cross it off the list or click it as "done" on your computer To-Do list. Seeing what you have accomplished at the end of the day will help you in completing your daily time sheet.

Tickler System

Each of us has our own method of noting upcoming events. It does not matter whether you use a calendar system in a computer or in your daily appointment book, a weekly flow chart, or a manual index card system. What matters is that you use a tickler system that prevents any important dates from "falling thru the cracks." When you file interrogatories or requests for production, note the date on which a response is due. If you make a call requesting copies, put a note in your system to follow up in two weeks to ensure that they were received. If a pleading or motion must be filed on a specific date, insert reminders a week to 10 days before and again on the day before as well as on the due date. Your tickler system will save you and your firm the embarrassment of missed deadlines. Be sure to check it every morning.

Coordination of Document Flow

Most attorneys and legal assistants involved in the case will generate or receive correspondence and memoranda as well as other miscellaneous materials and data relating to the issues and individuals involved. Different teams will be working with various witnesses or pleadings. Establish control mechanisms for document flow within your firm to guarantee that all information regarding this litigation is filtered through your team.

Your legal assistants and the attorneys' secretaries will usually be in position to direct documents to the proper files. Be sure all team members know who handles the pleadings, who files correspondence and memos, who codes or scans these documents into the

(Continued)

FIGURE 20–5 Continued

computer database for the case, who schedules depositions, who maintains the tickler system, who receives incoming records, etc. Make it your responsibility to orient any new team members to established procedures. Be sure to notify all team members whenever there is a change in these procedures. It is important to let the right hand know what the left hand is doing. You, as project manager, are in a pivotal position that obligates you to notify those persons involved in any changes in the team's established procedures.

II. Discovery

Typically, in a large case, there will be more than one set of interrogatories or requests for documents. Therefore, when filing interrogatories or production requests, be sure that the individuals drafting these documents number the sets within the title or first paragraph. A number in the title (e.g. Defendant's *First Set* of Interrogatories Directed to Plaintiffs, or Defendant's *Third* Request to Produce Directed to Plaintiffs) reduces confusion as to which interrogatories are being filed or for which request for production a response is being received. If opposing parties do not use numbered sets, simply add the appropriate number to the title described in your . . . index (e.g. Plaintiff's Request to Produce Directed to Defendant ABC Co. *Second*).

Production Requests

Plaintiffs' production requests can be extensive or even burdensome. Requests can be for documents, films, blueprints, photographs, drawings, video and audio recordings, etc. More than likely the plaintiffs will wish to review all data regarding such topics as knowledge of the incident, product testing, manufacture, toxicity, corporate reports or minutes relating to company positions on the incident, product design, and quality control. They may also request copies of all documents previously produced in other cases.

Your firm will notify the client of the types of documentation that need to be assembled for review and possible production. Coordination of this effort may be your responsibility. If your client is a large corporation and the production request is broad and not limited by the court, your client may be required to review hundreds or even thousands of paper and computer files to comply with the request. If you are fortunate, your client will arrive at your office with only a handful of files to be reviewed. Either way your team's task is the same.

Find out what kinds of documents are available regarding day-to-day business operations. Take extensive notes, recording names and respective job titles. Know if there are diaries, handwritten notes, email messages, calendars, or any special forms available, and find out how they are used. Identify any documents that may be considered confidential, privileged, or under protective order, and have stamps available for these documents. Segregate documents that are privileged or under protective order. Be sure you are not producing any documents whose production has been objected to. Determine which documents, if any, will need to be produced in camera and keep a separate index of them.

Discuss with your supervising attorney the time frame for production and the method to be used for production of documents. This could be either the order they are kept in during normal business, or by categories corresponding to the plaintiffs' production request. All documents produced should be numbered sequentially with an alpha-numerical stamp. Assign a letter and a seven-digit number for all production documents no matter who is the producing party. The letter designates the producing party. If plaintiffs or co-defendants do not wish to cooperate with your numbering system, renumber their production documents upon receipt.

Obtain signed and dated receipts from opposing counsel. This receipt should provide a brief description of the documents produced and indicate their number ranges. This can be beneficial in the future if opposing counsel claims never to have received a certain document. You will have a signed receipt indicating exactly when the document was produced to the opposition.

For documents produced or received, you will need to develop and maintain a master index of produced documents. If the documents received are not numbered, then establish and apply a numbering system to them. Record pertinent information such as the document's title and number range, requesting party, producing party, date produced, and the location of the document. This tool combined with clearly numbered production requests will alleviate later confusion as to when and where certain documents became available.

If at all possible, channel all production through one individual to assure consistency. If this is not possible, ensure that all persons handling production are fully knowledgeable as to established production procedures. Not knowing exactly what has and has not been produced can lead to severe problems. Proper handling of all aspects of production can help your client avoid possible sanctions.

Interrogatory Answers

When you receive the plaintiff's interrogatory responses, you are ready to begin building your plaintiff files. Your review of these answers will be your guide for obtaining a thorough history on each plaintiff in your case. Since you are dealing with multiple plaintiffs, it is helpful to set up a data summary for each one. The data summary should include the family history, educational history, prior residences, employment history, previous medical history, health care providers consulted, instances of exposure, problems attributed to exposure, and other relevant categories of information attainable from the interrogatory responses.

Record Discovery

Now it is time to start obtaining the plaintiffs' records, a process which can take days, weeks, or months, depending on the number of plaintiffs you are tracking and the number of places they have lived, worked, and obtained medical treatment. Medical records are the most obvious type of documents to obtain, but employment and military records are also important, as are school records if any of the plaintiffs are children (or adults claiming brain damage).

If most of your plaintiffs are from one area it may be beneficial to develop cross-indices by doctor, medical institution, school, and employer prior to sending out requests for records. This way when writing to one physician, you may request records for all of the plaintiffs who claim to have received treatment from that physician. The same goes for each of the other record sources.

Moreover, do not rely on the plaintiffs to tell you all the possible sources of records. We have found that often people overlook or forget where they have received medical attention. If your plaintiffs are from a small town with relatively few sources of medical treatment, it may be fruitful to canvas all doctors and health care facilities within the nearby geographical area to determine whether they have treated any of your plaintiffs. You may also canvas physicians near plaintiffs' previous residences. A surprising number of records can be obtained in this way.

Other informative sources are within the records already obtained. A cursory review of the records received from one doctor will often yield the names of other doctors who saw the patient previously, who have referred the patient or to whom the patient was referred. These sources should not be overlooked. The same principle, of course, applies to employment, school, and military records. They are a rich source of information for further record discovery and will often tell of other employers, schools, or record sources not identified by the plaintiffs in interrogatory responses. Limiting your discovery to only the sources identified by the plaintiffs is limiting the resources available to the defense of your client.

Establishing and maintaining an ongoing log for records requested is the surest way to know the current status of your record discovery procedures. A chart indicating a plaintiff's name, record sources, date records were requested, date received, summarized, and, if applicable, computerized, will provide an adequate control mechanism. Be sure to leave room for comments on record legibility or on specific problems encountered in gathering the records.

The type of file retrieval system you establish for discovered records does not matter as long as you are able to identify the plaintiff and the source of the record. We have found that a simple index and document numbering system works best. Each plaintiff is assigned a two- or three-digit code, and each record source is given a three-digit code. Then each document is given an eight- or nine-digit number based on the

(Continued)

FIGURE 20–5 Continued

plaintiff, record source, and page sequence. That way if a record is inadvertently removed from its file, it can easily be returned. For example, if plaintiff John Doe is plaintiff No. 5, Dr. Smith is record source No. 115, and there are 110 pages of records received from Dr. Smith on plaintiff John Doe, the last page of these records would be numbered 05-115-110. When future records are collected from Dr. Smith regarding plaintiff John Doe, they would start at page 111 (05-115-111).

Medical Summaries

Once obtained, an initial review and summarization of medical records is essential. . . . The medical summary should be updated as new records are received. It should also incorporate information obtained from plaintiff depositions and from expert medical examinations as these materials become available. It will prove to be an invaluable tool to your trial attorneys.

Appendix I is a suggested medical summary format. . . . The summarizers will need guidelines to help them identify contradictions in complaints and symptoms and allegations of ill health as well as a straightforward summary of the plaintiffs' medical, employment, and educational history. Be sure your summarizing team is using standardized medical and dental abbreviations.

APPENDIX I
Medical Summary

I. GENERAL INFORMATION AND PERSONAL DATA
(Name, address, age, employment, family history, etc.)
II. BRIEF SUMMARY OF PRE-EXPOSURE HISTORY
III. EXPOSURE
(from interrogatory answers, expert's reports and deposition testimony)
IV. PLAINTIFF'S COMPLAINTS AND EXPERT MEDICAL FINDINGS
   A. Plaintiff's Answers to Interrogatories
   B. Complaints and Symptoms Told to Expert Medical Witnesses
   C. Complaints and Symptoms From Plaintiff's Deposition
   D. Plaintiff's Expert's Positive Findings
V. DEFENDANT'S EXPERT'S MEDICAL FINDINGS
VI. MEDICAL RECORDS
   A. Doctor/Institution Index
   B. Detailed Chronological Summary of Doctor Visits and Hospitalizations
   C. Height, Weight, and Blood Pressure Charts
   D. Medications
VII. ADDITIONAL RECORDS
   A. School Records
      (including grades, attendance, teacher comments, athletic accomplishments, standardized test results)
   B. Employment Records
   C. Insurance or Military Records
VIII. LABORATORY CHARTS
   A. Blood Count/Blood Chemistry Charts
      (with applicable reference ranges)
   B. Urinalyses
   C. Electrodiagnostic: EKG, EMG, PNVC, EEG
   D. Audiometric
   E. Vision
   F. Other tests

As the paralegal case manager, it may be your job to recruit and interview the team of medical summarizers and monitor their progress. You or one of your team's legal assistants may work as a liaison between them and your staff of typists or word processors and the supervising attorneys. A simple chart indicating each plaintiff, assigned summarizer, and status of the summary will aid you in following the progress of this specialized team.

Plaintiff Depositions

Your trial counsel may decide to depose the plaintiffs prior to medical examinations by either plaintiff or defense experts. As case manager it will undoubtedly fall to you to schedule and prepare notices of depositions. If you are so authorized, try to develop a friendly working relationship with the opposing attorney or legal assistant who is coordinating deposition scheduling. This will make life easier for both of you.

If your lead counsel agrees, assign a member of your team to each plaintiff deposition scheduled and ensure that he or she will be available for organizing documents and other preparatory work with the attorney taking the deposition. The legal assistant can provide support at the deposition with document handling as well as taking detailed notes and keeping track of exhibits. The legal assistant can guarantee that copies of the deposition and all exhibits are obtained. He or she can also prepare the deposition summary and topical index. The work already invested in the deposition preparation and execution will have provided clear insight into what medical, physical, mental, and emotional problems the plaintiff has attributed to exposure and which conditions pre-existed exposure. The deposition information should be incorporated into the medical summaries.

The plaintiffs' depositions, together with the summaries of the depositions and the topical indices to the depositions, can then be added to the plaintiff files. It is important to make sure you develop a standard summary format for depositions (as well as trial testimony). When reviewing numerous deposition summaries, it increases the reviewer's speed and accuracy if all summaries are organized in the same manner. This of course applies to topical summaries as well.

Expert Medical Examinations

The plaintiffs will be examined by their team of medical experts, who will in turn issue their opinions as to the medical condition of each plaintiff. The experts' reports are, of course, discoverable and will need to be incorporated into the medical summaries previously discussed. They can be numbered and indexed into the plaintiff files in the same manner as other discovered documents. By comparing allegations of injury contained in these expert opinions with findings of the plaintiffs' treating physicians, the trial attorney will find invaluable defense ammunition. For example, an expert may attribute one condition to toxic exposure but a review of the plaintiff's records reveals that the condition pre-existed the exposure incident.

More than likely the defendant will also wish to have the plaintiffs undergo medical examinations by its own team of medical experts. As project manager you may play a more active role in these examinations by being charged with making all necessary scheduling arrangements for such examinations. Whether or not you schedule such events, it will be up to you to obtain the results and see that the defendant's medical expert reports are also numbered, incorporated into the medical summaries, and added to the plaintiff files.

Use Of Records

Obtaining, numbering, and summarizing the plaintiffs' medical, school, employment, and military records will not be your team's only contact with discovered records. You will come back to these records time and time again. . . .

You and your team will also be called upon to conduct numerous factual reviews of the plaintiffs' records. You might chart out statistics on property damage or loss of income. You might do comparative analysis of results of laboratory testing done by treating physicians, plaintiff experts, and defense experts. Whatever the various record reviews requested of you, it will be important for your team to have a thorough working knowledge of these records, how to read them, and what the myriad of tests stand for. Much of the factual development that you do here will ultimately be used at trial or in the preparation of trial exhibits. . . .

Other Discovery

Local, state, and federal government agencies are other sources of informative factual documents. The accident or exposure incident you are involved with will no doubt have been investigated or handled by various governmental agencies. You will need to locate each of the agencies involved and obtain copies of all related documentation

(Continued)

FIGURE 20–5 Continued

available. You may even have to file requests under the Freedom of Information Act, but it is essential to obtain everything possible. Documents from the Environmental Protection Agency, the Occupational Safety and Health Administration, state conservation organizations, local emergency teams, or the Centers for Disease Control can help to construct crucial chronologies of events as well as provide a record of government reactions and responses to the situation.

As with other production documents, number stamp any government agency documents received and add them to your master index of production.

Expert Depositions

Part of your team's trial preparation will be deposing the plaintiffs' expert medical witnesses to gain insight into their backgrounds, knowledge, and opinions. This will determine inconsistencies and help to develop trial strategies. Your team will function here in the same way they do for plaintiff depositions.

You will coordinate scheduling and noticing depositions, and your legal assistant team will compile and organize all relevant documentation needed for the deposition. They may be required to review available information regarding the deponent, and draft deposition outlines for the deposing attorneys. As with plaintiff depositions, it is helpful to have the same legal assistant that prepares for the deposition do the deposition summary and topical index.

The information gathered from medical experts relating to opinions on specific plaintiffs' conditions should be added into the medical summaries, and inconsistencies should be noted. Depositions and summaries should be added to the witness files, which will be discussed later. As with all other categories of this litigation, keep an index to depositions taken.

Non-Expert Depositions

In preparation for trial or settlement, your litigators may deem it necessary to take depositions or statements of many non-expert individuals. Eyewitness statements aid in the development of factual knowledge of the specific incident of exposure. Depositions of co-workers, health care providers, employers, and teachers provide keen insight to the moral character of the plaintiff and an excellent view of pre-existing complaints or problems versus post-exposure complaints or problems. Your team's function basically remains the same for these as for previously discussed depositions. However, legal assistants can be used effectively to take some witnesses' statements and thereby increase savings for the client. This, of course, is a choice to be made by your supervising attorneys. All statements and materials collected from record custodians will have to be numbered and produced as outlined above.

III. WITNESS FILES

By now you should be maintaining lists not only of plaintiffs and their treating physicians, schools, and employers, but also of plaintiff medical experts, plaintiff factual witnesses, defense medical experts, and other potential witnesses. These lists are the groundwork for and guide to your witness files.

Your witness files are the core of your litigation file support system. They are a compilation of the full cast of characters involved in the complex toxic tort litigation. Anything and everything you obtain on these individuals should be added to the indices and made a part of these core files.

Witness files are not limited strictly to those people expected to testify at trial. They should include all individuals who gave statements or depositions, who were involved in any way with the accident or exposure incident, who are identified anywhere throughout the production documents, who are potential witnesses, who are potential expert witnesses, who are knowledgable about some aspect of the product or incident, etc. Any individual or agency that you have information on should be included in the witness files.

The information gathered can include such things as curriculum vitae, depositions, deposition summaries, deposition exhibits, statements given, attorney's notes, relevant correspondence and memoranda, preparatory work product, related literature listings, examination outlines, relevant documents produced, chronological listings of events, proposed exhibits, testimony given in other cases, and more. Anything and everything that you gather relating to a potential witness should be kept here. . . .

IV. PRIOR TO TRIAL

Trial Notebooks

As the trial draws closer you will start to develop trial notebooks. . . . Whether or not your team is asked to draft them, the goal of each trial notebook at this point will be to develop the witness examination outline. Many sources of information available to legal assistants discuss methodology for establishing trial notebooks. The key is that they are organized in a consistent manner allowing the user immediate access to information contained. The materials you have gathered in the witness files will undoubtably go into these notebooks, but do not surrender your only copies. The notebooks will be used and marked on. Save your witness files and use only copies of necessary documents in the trial notebooks.

Review the draft examination outline and indicate, in the trial notebook, where each point counsel wishes to make is supported. Highlight relevant passages of deposition testimony or production documents that support these points. Be sure the trial notebooks include all production documents of which the witness has knowledge. Include depositions and previous trial testimony if applicable. If you have prepared any type of time lines that relate to this witness, include them as well. Be sure to discuss with the litigator what he or she will need in the trial notebook to prepare this witness for live testimony. If there are any working tools, charts, or reports needed to complete the trial notebook, develop them.

Witness Preparation Sessions

Preparatory sessions with expert witnesses on complex personal injury matters can be long and grueling. Medical experts, for example, will be required to review hundreds of treating physicians' medical records as well as their own and other expert reports regarding each plaintiff. They may need to develop a familiarity with the toxicological literature relating to their own area of medical expertise. Your team may be assigned to work with the litigator and witness in these prep sessions.

The legal assistant can function not only as a document handler during these sessions, but can take detailed notes of the expert's opinions and ensure that questions or problems that arise during preparation sessions are answered or dealt with before the next session. He or she can help to monitor which records, articles, charts, or documents are to be developed for trial exhibits and can continue to supplement the trial notebooks as needed. These notebooks, now armed with outlines and materials developed during the preparatory sessions, will provide everything necessary to examine the witness at trial.

Exhibit Preparation

During witness preparation sessions and throughout the pretrial period, certain records and documents will be designated as possible exhibits. Start an index of exhibits to be used during the trial testimony of each witness. These exhibits will not be limited to discovery and production documents. Your team may be called upon to design or draft various time lines, charts, graphs, or other compilations of data to be used as trial exhibits. Keep an index to all enlargements that are prepared. . . .

If your firm does not already have business relations with photographers, computer graphic companies, commercial printers, and reproduction services, it is time to establish them. Locate and interview vendors in your area who are cost-efficient and produce quality products. Find out what their turn-around times are for the kinds of exhibits you will be using. When you are in the trial situation and discover that you need a new exhibit in court within a few hours, you will not have time to find out who can provide that service. Do your footwork early and be prepared.

Establishing A Trial Office

Your trial may be in a distant city or even in another state. If your firm is not located within close proximity of the court conducting the trial, you may be required to open a trial office close to the trial site. In-depth discussion with both the client and your litigating attorneys will be necessary to determine how much of the litigating team needs to be at the trial office, what kind of support staff and equipment will be necessary, and what files and information will need to be duplicated for or relocated to the trial office.

(Continued)

FIGURE 20–5 Continued

If the support team is remaining at the home office with a small satellite team at the trial office, it may be necessary to establish two complete filing systems or a secure computer network on which files can be shared. Whatever scenario your firm plans, try to determine it early. See that a suitable space is located and supplied appropriately to accommodate your trial team's needs. If may be that as project manager you will move your entire team to the trial office. If, however, you remain at the home office, you will need to designate a legal assistant to manage the trial office. Establish a communication system between the trial office and the home office and funnel all information through your trial office legal assistant. He or she should be an individual with a full view of the issues and facts of the litigation and with a thorough working knowledge of all the systems established thus far. You will need to assure that this legal assistant has the authority to manage the trial office and has the complete support of the litigation team. As you go into trial, this individual's role becomes crucial.

Final Trial Preparation

In the last weeks prior to trial there are a great number of tasks to accomplish and loose ends to tie. Your checklists will help now more than ever as your team approaches the wire. It is especially important for you to maintain a clear-minded, calm, unflustered approach as you apply your skills to this final organizational pre-trial push. Check the status of all projects previously described and determine that they are ready for trial.

It may be your team's duty to maintain contact with and be responsible for witnesses. If necessary, arrange to serve subpoenaes to guarantee witnesses' appearance at trial. Set up necessary travel and hotel accommodations. Do everything possible to put your witnesses at ease.

Become familiar with the layout of the court and instruct witnesses as to the location of facilities. Know procedures for obtaining transcripts and copies of exhibits and pass this information to your trial team. Anticipate your litigator's needs.

Determine whether your trial attorneys prefer one specific legal assistant to provide support at trial or a team of legal assistants who rotate in and out of the position. Utilizing the same person in this role for the entire trial may maintain a small team image for the jury and provide a certain continuity. However, by rotating legal assistants, you can use the individual most familiar with the witness and proposed exhibits. Make sure that whoever functions as the legal assistant at trial develops a checklist of basic supplies (i.e. pens, pencils, legal pads, disks, change for copies, etc.) to take to trial.

Meet with your team and review the extra demands that will be placed on them during the course of the trial. This will include staggering hours to provide support prior to trial in the morning, during lunch hours, and after trial each evening. During the course of the trial, unexpected projects will be required in rapid turnaround time. Your team must be ready at all times to provide immediate response to the trial attorneys.

Establish a distribution list for both internal and out-of-firm recipients of exhibits, transcripts, and trial notes. Setting up a flow chart for their distributions prior to trial avoids confusion after it commences. Know who will obtain these materials and how they will be copied and disbursed.

You may also need to determine what kind of special requirements will be necessary for your computer equipment and exhibits at trial. If your attorneys are using unusually large or awkward exhibits, such as a scale model of the site, you may need to make prior arrangements with the court personnel to accommodate these exhibits.

In the last days prior to trial, it will be your team's obligation to search out whatever needs to be done to achieve trial readiness and do it. This is not the time to wait to be given assignments. If you or your team members see a problem area or have an idea for a needed project, take it to your supervising attorneys and present it assertively. Gain the authority and take the task to completion.

V. THE TRIAL

As project manager, it is your goal to maximize efficient litigation support and to minimize any obstacles to that goal. You must stay on top of every aspect of the trial and coordinate the smooth operation of all the components of your litigation team. The trial will challenge you and your team both at the courthouse and behind the scenes.

Be sure your legal assistant at the court knows what is expected of him or her. This person will be your pipeline of information. Establish a communication routine whereby you are available to talk with your trial legal assistant during court breaks to receive any comments or assignments from the in-trial team and relay it to the appropriate back-up team members.

Your trial legal assistant will be the team's source of daily information. He or she should take detailed notes of the proceedings, noting not only the witnesses' testimony, but other information such as starting and stopping times, reasons for late starts or early dismissals, objections by all parties, bench conferences, in-chambers proceedings, juror reactions, etc. He or she will also need to keep a roster not only of defense and plaintiff exhibits marked and admitted into evidence, but of previously marked exhibits that were used with each witness. These notes and indices are an essential source of information and should be distributed to appropriate parties on a daily basis. Use the rosters of exhibits to build a formal log showing the history and use of each exhibit.

Your trial legal assistant will also be responsible for obtaining copies of all exhibits on a daily basis, obtaining transcripts as soon as they are available, maintaining and handling documents for the trial litigators, managing trial notebooks and trial boxes, providing the necessary number of copies of all proposed exhibits needed for distribution to the jury and being available for any in-trial support needed by the trial litigators and witnesses.

Behind the scenes the entire litigation support team should be available to deal with projects on a crisis basis. There will be situations where your entire staff and every available attorney and legal assistant in your firm may be needed to help "put out fires." . . .

The demands of the trial team will be numerous in this type of litigation. Throughout the course of the trial new ideas will arise and new work product and further factual development will be the result. It is important to keep indices of all major projects, including reviews and searches that are conducted. When a new project is assigned, check to be sure that it is not something that was previously done. There will be ample "real work" during trial and you will have no need to waste your team's time and the client's resources recreating something that already exists.

You will need to have the trial transcripts summarized as fast as possible. For this purpose you can utilize either a core summarizing team or disburse the responsibility of transcript summarization throughout the entire support team. . . .

VI. CONCLUSION

We have taken a look at the inner workings of complex toxic tort litigation management. This discussion hopefully has inspired your own creative powers and induced ideas that you can apply to your own situation. Remember the main elements of this type of management are to define the nature of the materials you have to work with, develop standardized procedures for handling these materials, and educate all parties involved as to the established procedures.

Whether your title is administrative legal assistant or project manager or major case coordinator, it is essential to your success that you remember your own roots. You are still a legal assistant, and the skills you developed as a legal assistant should not be set aside. Do not ask any of your team members to perform a task that you would not do. The other legal assistants on your team today are the project managers of tomorrow. Try to maintain an even balance between being a task-oriented leader and a people-oriented leader. Your success as an administrator depends largely on the people on your litigation team. Without them you can do nothing. Shift their assignments and do not hesitate to delegate responsibilities. Mix the mundane or boring assignments with ones that really challenge their skills and help them to grow. Keep your team informed by scheduling periodic meetings to let them know what is happening with the litigation and what other team members are working on. Develop group leaders within the team and assign yourself to projects as a group member whenever time allows.

Above all, you are a proactive member of the litigation team, and it is your obligation to stay ahead of any crisis. Be accessible to both the lawyers and the legal assistants involved in your litigation. Remain open to suggestions and do not hesitate to use good ideas, whether or not they were yours. In accepting the position of administrator on a complex toxic tort litigation, you have accepted the responsibility for establishing clockwork organization and building a loyal and motivated support team. The challenge is big. The personal and professional satisfaction achieved by meeting that challenge is enormous. Good luck!

SUMMARY

There are four major categories of mass tort cases: mass accident, mass marketed product, mass exposure, and mass economic loss. A mass tort is a tort cause of action that is asserted by a large number of persons who have been harmed by the same or similar conduct or product of a relatively small number of defendants. In a mass tort case, the plaintiffs assert traditional causes of action such as negligence and strict liability in tort; mass tort is not a new tort cause of action.

Most in-person solicitation is unethical unless the attorney is not seeking fees or other financial gain or already has a professional or family relationship with the prospective client. Most solicitation by mail is ethical unless the lawyer knows or reasonably should know that the physical, emotional, or mental state of the person is such that the person could not exercise reasonable judgment in employing a lawyer.

A person injured by a mass tort may seek relief through an individual lawsuit. An alternative is a class action, in which one or more members of a class sue (or are sued) as representative parties on behalf of everyone in the class. If the parties do not intend to litigate because they have settled, the action is called a settlement class action. The first step is to ask the court to certify the class, which is the court's permission to allow a member of the class to be the representative party who will act on behalf of every other member of the class. In federal court, a class action must meet the threshold requirements of numerosity, commonality, typicality, and fairness/adequacy of representation. Notice to members of the class is important in order to give members the option to opt out if the class action is permissive. In federal court, the Judicial Panel on Multidistrict Litigation can transfer similar cases to one district for pretrial proceedings.

Junk science is unreliable and, therefore, potentially misleading scientific evidence. Under Federal Rule of Evidence 702, scientific evidence is admissible when offered by a qualified expert and "will assist the trier of fact." Federal trial judges must act as gatekeepers to ensure that only reliable, relevant, and nonmisleading scientific evidence is allowed before the jury.

Asbestos is a fibrous material used in products such as wall insulation and other building materials. Asbestos causes mesothelioma, asbestosis, etc. Millions of people have been exposed and hundreds of thousands of personal injury claims have been filed throughout the country. Over twelve asbestos manufacturers have filed for bankruptcy. An attempt at a nationwide class action settlement failed when the United States Supreme Court refused to certify the class. The proposed class did not meet the standards of Rule 23 of the Federal Rules of Civil Procedure. The members of the class were too diverse. In particular the class could not fairly protect the interests of those who have been exposed to asbestos but had not yet manifested injury. Their needs clashed with those who have already manifested injury. The named representative parties could not fairly and adequately protect the interests of the class. Also there were flaws in the plan to give notice to everyone in the class, particularly those who had not yet manifested injury.

Hundreds of thousands of women have sued breast implant manufacturers for diseases the implants have allegedly caused. So many claims were filed that manufacturers like Dow Corning sought bankruptcy protection. Causation was a big issue since many studies did not support the conclusion that the implants caused serious diseases. Yet, litigation costs pressured some manufacturers to settle.

For years, tobacco companies were very successful in court, particularly with the argument that smokers were assuming a known risk. The tide, however, has turned in large part because of leaked tobacco company documents that show that the companies knew about the danger of smoking and targeted young people. States sued for the Medicaid costs; private citizens brought class actions and individual lawsuits for the illnesses caused by direct and secondhand smoke. After

Liggett Group broke ranks and settled, forty-six states agreed to a $206 billion settlement. (Four other states reached individual settlements.) The settlements did not put an end to individual lawsuits or class actions brought by smokers. They still had the right to prove their case in court.

Paralegals play many roles in mass tort cases. They assist in drafting complaints, prepare extensive checklists and document indexes, maintain a tickler system, coordinate document flow and discovery, summarize medical records, keep witness files, develop trial notebooks, help prepare witnesses, coordinate trial exhibits, and respond to ongoing and emergency needs during the trial.

KEY TERMS

mass tort   388

solicitation   391

in-person solicitation   391

class action   393

settlement class action   393

global peace   393

opt out   393

permissive class action   393

mandatory class action   393

certify the class   394

numerosity   394

commonality   394

typicality   394

fair and adequate
        representation   394

notice   394

Judicial Panel on Multidistrict
        Litigation   395

junk science   396

Frye test   396

Daubert   397

Survival and Wrongful Death

CHAPTER OUTLINE

- Introduction
- Survival of Torts Unrelated to Death
- Wrongful Death
- Avoiding Double Recovery

INTRODUCTION

Distinguish between the following situations:

Case I.   Dan steals Paul's watch. Paul then sues Dan for the tort of conversion. Within two weeks of filing the suit, Paul dies in a car accident and Dan dies in an earthquake.

Case II. Barbara negligently drives her car into Sam's car. Sam dies from the injuries resulting from the crash.

In Case I, the plaintiff (Paul) died from a cause unrelated to Dan's tort of conversion; the tort did not cause Paul's death. The same is true of the defendant (Dan)—his death had nothing to do with the tort. Case II presents a very different situation. Barbara's negligence caused the death of Sam. It was a **wrongful death** because it was caused by a tort. (It, therefore, is also referred to as a **tortious** death.) We need to determine whether the tort action survives the death of either the victim or the **tortfeasor** in Cases I and II. (A tortfeasor is a wrongdoer who has committed a tort.) **Survival** is the continuation of a cause of action such as a tort after the death of either the victim or the alleged wrongdoer. As we will see, not all tort actions survive.

SURVIVAL OF TORTS UNRELATED TO DEATH

First, we examine the survival of a tort cause of action when a death has occurred that had nothing to do with the tort (Case I in the preceding example). The survival of the tort depends in part on the kind of injury or harm that the tort inflicts. Three main categories of torts exist: personal torts, personal property torts, and real property torts. **Personal torts** injure the person.

Tom invades Pete's privacy, defames Pete, or batters him. These are examples of torts against Pete's *person*.

Personal property torts damage movable property, which is any property not attached to the land.

Tom converts Pete's car or negligently damages Pete's livestock. These are examples of torts against Pete's *personal property*.

Real property torts damage land and anything attached to the land.

Tom trespasses on Pete's land or negligently damages Pete's house. These are examples of torts against Pete's *real property*.

In all of these examples, assume that Tom or Pete dies from a cause unrelated to the tort. What survives? Logically, you would think that the death of the victim or of the tortfeasor from an unrelated cause would not affect the litigation of the tort action. If the tortfeasor dies, the victim's **estate** should be able to bring the tort claim against the tortfeasor. (An estate consists of all the assets and debts left by a decedent. The estate can sue and be sued; it acts through a personal representative appointed by the decedent's will or by the court.) If, on the other hand, it is the tortfeasor who dies, the victim should be able to bring the tort action against the tortfeasor's estate. Logic, however, has not always ruled this area of the law.

Common Law and Statutory Law

First, we will examine survival of the three categories of torts (personal, personal property, and real property) at **common law.** (Common law is judge-made law in the absence of statutes or other higher law to the contrary.) Then, more important, we will examine what survives under statutory law that has changed the common law. Such statutes are often called *survival statutes*.

Personal Torts

Common law: At common law, torts against the person of the victim did not survive the death of either the victim or the tortfeasor. If the victim dies, the action could not be brought by the victim's estate. If the tortfeasor dies, the action could not be brought against the estate of the tortfeasor.

Statutory law: All states have passed survival statutes that have changed the common law, but not completely. In most states, the personal torts that are invasions of **tangible** interests survive, but the personal torts that are invasions of **intangible** interests do not. Something is tangible if we can make contact with it through our senses such as touch. For example, a human body is tangible. Since battery is a tort against the body, it is a tort that protects a tangible interest and, therefore, would survive. Something is intangible, however, if it cannot be perceived by the senses. For example, a person's reputation or privacy is intangible. Hence, personal torts that protect these interests such as defamation and invasion of privacy would not survive.

Personal Property Torts

Common law: At common law, torts against the personal property of the victim survived the death of the victim but did not survive the death of the tortfeasor.

Statutory law: Survival statutes have changed the common law. In all states, torts against personal property survive both the victim and the tortfeasor.

Real Property Torts

Common law: At common law, torts against the real property of the victim did not survive the death of the victim or the tortfeasor.

Statutory law: Survival statutes have changed the common law. In all states, torts against real property survive the death of either the victim or the tortfeasor.

Hence, if a tort action survives today, it is because the action is one of the few that survived at common law, or because a survival statute has established that it survives.

Characteristics of Actions That Survive

Let us focus on a tort action that survives the death of the victim, again keeping in mind that we are not yet talking about a death that is caused by the tort. Before the victim brings any action against the tortfeasor, the victim dies from a cause unrelated to the tort. The action is brought after this death. Note the following characteristics of this action:

- The action is brought by the estate of the victim through the personal representative of the estate.
- The action is not a new or independent action. It is the same action that the victim would have had if he or she had lived.
- The plaintiff in the action is not an heir or relative of the victim unless the heir or relative happens to be the personal representative of the victim's estate.
- Heirs or relatives do not directly receive any benefit from a damage award in the tort action that survives. If they benefit from the award, they do so through the estate as beneficiaries of a will or via **intestacy** (the distribution of a decedent's estate when no valid will exists).
- There is no recovery for the death of the victim, because we are examining a case in which the tort did not cause the death of the victim; the decedent was the victim of a tort that did not cause death.
- Any defenses the tortfeasor would have had against the victim, had the latter lived (e.g., contributory negligence, assumption of the risk, self-defense), are available to the tortfeasor in the action that survives.

WRONGFUL DEATH

Common Law

Now we move to the situation in Case II presented at the beginning of this chapter: what happens when the victim of a tort dies *because* of the tort? Here we are talking about a tortious or wrongful death. At common law, a tort action for this death could not be brought against the wrongdoer. If, however, the act that caused the death of the victim constituted a crime, the wrongdoer might be prosecuted in a criminal court, but no civil tort action could be brought. If the wrongdoer committed a non-deadly tort against the victim or a tort against the property of a victim who was still alive, there *could* be recovery against the wrongdoer, but not if the latter had killed the victim. It was cheaper, therefore, to kill the victim!

Needless to say, statutes were passed to change this absurdity. Every state now has a remedy for wrongful death. The remedy is not the same in each state. Although your primary concern will be the law of your state, you will need to be aware of the major remedies available in other states, because it is not uncommon for an office to work on a case involving the death of someone in another state.

Elsewhere in this book, we discuss the law of workers' compensation (Chapter 28). If an employee dies from an injury that arises out of and in the course of employment, compensation to heirs or relatives is received through the workers' compensation statute, whether or not the employer wrongfully caused the death. In most states, workers' compensation replaces any other civil remedy. Hence, the following discussion does not apply to death due to an employment accident or disease.

Recovery for Wrongful Death

States differ on how they allow recovery for wrongful death. Two common methods include:

- enlarging the survival statute to include death, and
- enacting a wrongful death statute (Lord Campbell's Act)

Enlarging the Survival Statute to Include Wrongful Death We saw earlier that survival statutes have been passed to permit most kinds of tort actions to survive the death of the victim of the tort. In some states, the death of the victim caused by the tort is handled as follows:

- The tort action of the victim survives his or her death and covers damages that accrued up to the moment of death.
- Damages resulting from the death can be recovered in the same survival action.

No new cause of action is created because of the death. The victim's cause of action is continued by the personal representative of his or her estate. In this action, any defense is available that could have been brought had the victim lived. The damages that are recoverable in this action usually include:

- pain and suffering of the victim from the time of the injury to the time of death
- medical, hospital, and funeral expenses
- lost net earnings and savings the victim would have accumulated if he or she had lived to his or her life expectancy

Enacting a Wrongful Death Statute (Lord Campbell's Act) Most states create a new cause of action for designated relatives of the deceased victim, e.g., spouse and children. A statute creating this wrongful death cause of action is usually modeled after **Lord Campbell's Act** in England and is sometimes referred to as a "pure" death action, as distinguished from the enlarged survival action, which continues the victim's claim. The new cause of action is brought by a representative for the benefit of the relatives or beneficiaries, or in some states, by the beneficiaries themselves. The damages that are recoverable in this action are usually limited to **pecuniary losses.** This covers the loss of the economic value of the support, services, and contributions that the beneficiaries would have received if the victim had lived to his or her life expectancy.

Damages are *not* recoverable in this action for:

- pain and suffering of the victim, medical bills, lost wages, or any other loss that the victim would have had against the tortfeasor (damages for such items are recoverable in a separate survival action, which is often brought along with the beneficiaries' action—see the following discussion on Avoiding Double Recovery)
- mental suffering and grief experienced by the survivor-beneficiaries because of the death of the victim, and loss of consortium rights (see Chapter 22), particularly the right to the companionship and society of the deceased (some states, however, have changed this rule and allow recovery for such **nonpecuniary losses**)

Under most wrongful death statutes, the defendant can raise any defense he or she would have had against the victim if death had not occurred. For example, the defendant may assert that the death was not wrongful. The defendant may have caused the death—but not tortiously. There must be an underlying intentional, negligence, or strict-liability tort before the beneficiaries can recover anything in the wrongful death action. Also, defenses of contributory negligence, assumption of the risk, or any of the privileges will usually defeat the wrongful death action. In most states, the statute of limitations runs from the time of death and not from the date of the injury.

AVOIDING DOUBLE RECOVERY

Some states have both a survival statute (covering the victim's pain and suffering, loss of earnings, medical expenses up to death, etc.) *and* a wrongful death statute (covering the beneficiaries' pecuniary loss of the support, services, and contributions that the victim would have provided them if he or she had not died). The survival action and the wrongful death action can usually be brought concurrently. When both actions are possible, there is a fear of double recovery, especially with respect to the lost earnings of the victim. The following describes the basic conflict and how it may be handled:

An injured person's own cause of action in tort, which at common law would have ended abruptly at death, is now preserved and vested in his personal representative by means of a survival statute, one of which obtains in every jurisdiction. The existence of such a measure side by side with a wrongful death provision has proved to be a source of concern arising from fear that a duplication of damages could result. Indeed such a fear is not without foundation: Whenever an injured victim while still alive can demonstrate that the impairment of his bodily condition is sufficiently serious to shorten his life expectancy he will become entitled to damages sufficient to replace the lost earnings that otherwise would have been in prospect for him. It is not to be expected that this right would be expunged in the event that death does indeed foreshorten his life before the award has been made. In theory, this element of loss should persist and remain available to his personal representative under a survival statute. If, however, to this survived claim for lost future earnings there were superadded a separate award for his dependents' loss of support under a [wrongful] death statute, the prospect of a duplication of damages would face the defendant. This dilemma has been dealt with in a bewildering variety of ways. In a few states a binding election must be made between a survival claim and an action for wrongful death (e.g., Ky. and Wyo.). Occasionally the survival suit is arbitrarily restricted to those claims of the deceased that were unrelated to his death (e.g., W.Va.). In other states the lawmakers have deliberately omitted a separate death statute, and lost future earnings in full are provided under the survival measure (e.g., Conn.). There are numerous other varieties in approach. The one that is most satisfactory and which has been most widely adopted is that of affording recognition of both the survival claim and the wrongful death claims but with damages for loss of earnings under the survival suit limited exclusively to those earnings that were lost between the time of accident and the moment of death. All pecuniary loss accruing thereafter must be recovered solely under the [wrongful] death statute. It is noteworthy, however, that funeral expenses, which do not accrue, of course, during the lifetime of the deceased, are frequently made recoverable by express provision in the survival statute.[1]

ASSIGNMENT

21.1

Bill negligently kills George in an automobile accident. A wrongful death action is brought in your state. Draft a complaint for this action. Select any plaintiff or plaintiffs who would be able to sue in your state. (See General Instructions for the Complaint-Drafting Assignment in Chapter 3.)

CASE

Cassano v. Durham
180 N.J. Super. 620, 436 A.2d 118 (1981)
Superior Court of New Jersey, Law Division, Passaic County

Background: *The plaintiff had a "live-in" relationship with decedent; they never married. He died intestate—without leaving a valid will. Following his death, she claimed benefits as the equivalent of a "surviving spouse" under the New Jersey intestacy statute and Wrongful Death Act. In the trial court, a motion for summary judgment has been made that would strike plaintiff's claim.*

Decision of Court: *The motion is granted. Only spouses can claim benefits under the Wrongful Death Act.*

OPINION OF COURT

Judge SCHWARTZ delivered the opinion of the court . . .

In this case the [plaintiff] had lived with decedent for seven years and they intended to get married. The court is asked to permit her to recover for her pecuniary loss as if she qualified as a "surviving spouse" under N.J.S.A. 3A:2A-34 of the intestacy statute. . . .

The "palimony" cases* which have been decided in various states . . . have not been of aid to the court because they were not determined on the basis of the status of the live-in partner but on entirely contractual grounds.

In *Wood v. State Farm Mutual Automobile Ins. Co.,* 178 N.J. Super. 607, 429 A.2d 1082 (App. Div. 1981) the court held that an economically independent companion who lived in the same home as the insured for three and one-half years before he suffered a vehicular accident and who married her almost two years later, had not been a member of her "family" residing in her household and therefore was not entitled to coverage under the personal injury protection provision of the insurance policy.

But even when a claimant relies upon the companion for support, the issue of dependency is irrelevant since the right of the spouse to partake of the benefits of the Wrongful Death Act is not conditioned on dependency. In this respect, it differs from the Worker's Compensation Act in which our Supreme Court in *Parkinson v. J. & S. Tool Co.,* 64 N.J. 159, 313 A.2d 609 (1974) recognized as a proper peti-

---

*Palimony is a nonlegal term for payments made by one nonmarried party to another after they cease living together, usually because they had an express or implied contract to do so while they were living together or cohabiting.

---

[1]W. Malone, *Injuries to Family, Social and Trade Relations* 44–45 (1979).

tioner a live-in partner who had previously been married to and divorced from the decedent and who became entitled to the benefits of that statute having proved dependency upon the decedent who suffered death during and arising out of employment.

In *Bulloch v. United States,* 487 F. Supp. 1078 (1980) the U.S. District Court recognized the right of recovery for loss of consortium as residing in one who had intended to resume cohabitation with the injured party after having been previously married to and divorced from the injured party. The court reasoned that the intended cohabitant suffered as much as a consequence of the injuries suffered by her mate as a spouse did.

The court concluded that since the right of consortium is judge-made law, the court could readily expand it. The law of intestacy, however, is statutorily created and not subject to judicial amendment. . . .

Is it arbitrary to provide a remedy for a surviving spouse and to deny a like remedy for a live-in companion who may equally suffer as the result of the tort? There is no constitutional impediment to the legislative determination to designate one, who has entered into the bonds of matrimony with decedent, as a beneficiary under the Wrongful Death Act among those who will inherit under the intestacy statute. That is solely a legislative function and the court cannot enlarge the reach of the statute.

Changed attitudes toward marriage are temporal, reflecting the temper of the times as they may still relate to the permissiveness of the 1960s and the early '70s. But the reaction to freedom of thought as it extends to consensual sexual conduct outside of the family tradition has not found ready acceptance by the Legislature in areas where the stability and responsibility of family life may be affected.

It was in 1939 that the Legislature determined (now N.J.S.A. 37:1–10) that no marriage subsequently contracted shall be valid unless the contracting parties obtained a marriage license and the marriage was legally solemnized. This was an expression of public policy which precluded common law marital relationships acquired through cohabitation and matrimonial repute, and the statute has not been amended. . . .

The family has been the genesis of our society since the birth of civilization, and the laws of inheritance were intended to buttress the stability and continuance of the family unit. The preservation of familial law is so essential that where questions of inheritance, property, legitimacy of offspring and the like are involved, an adherence to conventional doctrine is demanded.

Since the live-in plaintiff cannot be classified as a "surviving spouse" under the legislative designation in the intestacy laws, and the Wrongful Death Act was intended to apply for the exclusive benefit of persons eligible to inherit under the succession provisions of the statute, the motion for summary judgment striking the claim of plaintiff shall be granted.

ASSIGNMENT

21.2

a. Would this case be decided in the same way if the decedent died the moment before he was scheduled to say "I do" to the plaintiff at the altar?
b. Is this opinion consistent with *Bulloch v. United States* discussed in the opinion?
c. Is it consistent with *Parkinson v. J. & S. Tool Co.* discussed in the opinion?
d. Why did the court say that it could change the law of consortium (see Chapter 22) but not the law of intestacy?

SUMMARY

An action for a personal tort that does not cause death, such as defamation, does not survive the death of either the tortfeasor or the victim when the tort protects an intangible interest such as reputation or privacy. A personal tort that does not cause death, such as battery, and that protects tangible interests, does survive the death of either the tortfeasor or the victim. A personal property tort or a real property tort that does not cause death also survives the death of either. The tort action that survives is the same action that the victim would have brought if he or she had lived.

When the tort causes the death of the victim, a state might enlarge its survival statute to allow the personal representative of the deceased's estate to recover damages for wrongful death in the survival action. On the other hand, the state might create a separate cause of action for wrongful death for designated relatives of the deceased. Special provisions are often necessary to avoid double recovery for lost earnings (in the survival action) and loss of support (in the wrongful death action).

KEY TERMS

wrongful death   426

tortious   426

tortfeasor   426

survival   426

personal torts   426

personal property torts   426

real property torts   426

estate   426

common law   426

tangible   427

intangible   427

intestacy   427

Lord Campbell's Act   428

pecuniary losses   429

nonpecuniary losses   429

palimony   430

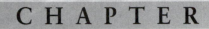

Torts Against and Within the Family

CHAPTER OUTLINE

- Torts Derived from Other Torts
- Torts Not Derived from Other Torts
- Prenatal Injuries
- Wrongful Life, Birth, Pregnancy
- Wrongful Adoption
- Intrafamily Tort Immunity

TORTS DERIVED FROM OTHER TORTS

Loss of Consortium

Consortium is the companionship, love, affection, sexual relationship, and services (e.g., cooking, making repairs around the house) that one spouse provides another. There can be a recovery for a tortious injury to consortium. At one time, only the husband could recover for **loss of consortium.** In every state, this view has been changed by statute or has been ruled unconstitutional as a denial of the equal protection of the law. Either spouse can now recover for loss of consortium.

> **EXAMPLE:**
>
> - Rich and Ann are married.
> - Paul, a stranger, injures Ann by negligently hitting her with his car.
> - Ann sues Paul for negligence. She receives damages to cover her medical bills, lost wages, and pain and suffering.
> - Rich then brings a *separate* suit against Paul for loss of his wife's consortium. He receives damages to compensate him for whatever loss or impairment he can prove to the companionship he had with Ann before the accident—to the love, affection, sexual intercourse, and services that she gave him as his wife before the accident.

In Rich's action against Paul, Rich cannot recover for injuries sustained by Ann. Ann must recover for such injuries in her own action against Paul. Paul's liability to Rich is limited to the specific injuries sustained by Rich—the loss or impairment of his wife's consortium. If Ann loses her suit against Paul, e.g., because she was contributorily negligent, Rich will not be able to bring his consortium suit. To recover for loss of consortium, there must be an underlying successfully litigated tort.

Most states deny recovery for loss of consortium to individuals who are not married.

> **EXAMPLES:**
>
> - Jim and Rachel are engaged to be married. The defendant negligently incapacitates Rachel the day before the wedding. Rachel sues the defendant to recover for her injuries.
> - Mary and John have lived together for forty years. They have never married and do not live in a state that recognizes common law marriage. The defendant negligently incapacitates John, who sues the defendant to recover for his injuries.
> - George and Bob are homosexuals who have lived together as a couple for ten years. The defendant negligently incapacitates Bob, who sues the defendant to recover for his injuries.

Clearly, Jim, Mary, and George have experienced a loss of consortium. They arguably have suffered in the same manner as Rich, whose wife, Ann, was negligently hit by Paul. The difference, however, is that Jim, Mary, and George (unlike Rich) were not married at the time their consortium was damaged. Most states deny an unmarried person the right to sue for loss of consortium. This may seem unfair, particularly to a couple who is hours away from being married. The law, however, must draw a line somewhere. A court would have a difficult time distinguishing between Jim and Rachel (a day away from their wedding) and an engaged couple whose wedding is one or two years away. What about someone six months or six weeks away? The practical problem of drawing the line plus the bias of the law in favor of marriage has led courts to limit the action for loss of consortium to married individuals.

The word *consortium* sometimes also refers to the normal companionship and affection that exists between a parent and a child. The right of a child to the companionship and affection of a parent is referred to as **parental consortium.** The right of a parent to the companionship and affection of a child is referred to as **filial consortium.**

EXAMPLES:

- Bill is the father of Sam.
- The defendant negligently incapacitates Bill, who sues the defendant to recover for Bill's injuries.
- The defendant negligently incapacitates Sam, who sues the defendant to recover for Sam's injuries.

In the first case, Sam has also suffered a loss—a loss of parental consortium. Yet, most states do *not* allow suits for damage to this kind of consortium. Suppose, however, that the parent (Bill) dies from the defendant's negligence. There are some states whose wrongful death statute gives children the right to damages for the loss of companionship and affection they had with their parent (in addition to the financial losses caused by the death). But most states would *not* allow a suit for loss of parental consortium when the injured parent is still alive. (On wrongful death, see Chapter 21.)

In the second case, Bill has also suffered a loss—a loss of filial consortium. As we will see in a moment, parents can sue someone who interferes with their right to receive the services of their children such as doing household chores. States differ, however, on the parent's right to recover for interference with the companionship and affection the parent has with a child—filial consortium. Many states deny such recovery. There are, however, a fair number of states that take a different position and allow recovery for interference with filial consortium.

Loss of Services

A parent has the right to the services of his or her **unemancipated** child. This would include tasks such as cutting the grass and running errands for the household. (Unemancipated means legally dependent on one's parent or legal guardian. A child is **emancipated** if he or she becomes legally independent such as by marrying.)

EXAMPLE: Mary is the twelve-year-old child of Victor and Helen. The defendant negligently injures Mary in a car accident. In a negligence action against the defendant, Mary can recover damages for her injuries.

Victor and Helen can also recover damages from the defendant for causing a **loss of services** by Mary to them. As a twelve-year-old who is dependent on her parents, Mary is unemancipated. She probably helps around the house. The parents can recover for any interference with these services that are wrongfully caused.

> *more successful to recover loss of services rather than filial consortium*

TORTS NOT DERIVED FROM OTHER TORTS

Other tort actions that can be brought by one family member because of what the defendant did with or to another family member include the following:

- **alienation of affections**
- **criminal conversation**
- **enticement of spouse**
- **abduction or enticement of a child**
- **seduction**

To establish one of these causes of action, there is no need to prove an underlying tort; they are torts in their own right. A number of states, however, have passed statutes (sometimes called **heart-balm statutes**) that have abolished some or all of these tort actions.

Alienation of Affections

Elements

    i. The defendant intended to diminish the marital relationship (love, companionship, and comfort) between the plaintiff and the latter's spouse.

    ii. Affirmative conduct by the defendant.

    iii. Affections between the plaintiff and spouse were in fact alienated.

    iv. The defendant caused the alienation (but for the defendant, the alienation would not have occurred, or the defendant was a substantial factor in producing the alienation).

Criminal Conversation

Element

The defendant had sexual relations with the plaintiff's spouse (adultery).

Enticement of Spouse

Elements

    i. The defendant intended to diminish the marital relationship between the plaintiff and the latter's spouse.

    ii. Affirmative conduct by the defendant either:

        a. to entice or encourage the spouse to leave the plaintiff's home, or

        b. to harbor the spouse and encourage the latter to stay away from the plaintiff's home.

    iii. The plaintiff's spouse left home.

    iv. The defendant caused the plaintiff to leave home or to stay away (but for what defendant did, the plaintiff would not have left home or stayed away; or, the defendant was a substantial factor in the spouse's leaving or staying away).

Abduction or Enticement of a Child

Elements

    i. The defendant intended to interfere with the parent's custody of the child.

    ii. Affirmative conduct by the defendant:

        a. to abduct or force the child from the parent's custody,

        b. to entice or encourage the child to leave the parent, or

        c. to harbor the child and encourage the latter to stay away from the parent's custody.

    iii. The child left the custody of the parent.

    iv. The defendant caused the child to leave or to stay away (but for what the defendant did, the child would not have left or stayed away; or, the defendant was a substantial factor in the child's leaving or staying away).

ASSIGNMENT

22.1

Olivia is the mother of Irene, who is married to George. Olivia begged Irene not to marry George—to no avail. After the marriage and the birth of a son, Olivia warns Irene that George has a violent disposition. Irene and George separate. Irene takes their son to live with Olivia. Has Olivia committed any torts? (See General Instructions for the Legal Analysis Assignment in Chapter 2.)

Seduction

Element

The defendant had sex with the plaintiff's minor daughter by force or with the consent of the daughter.

CASE

Franklin v. Hill
264 Ga. 302, 444 S.E.2d 778 (1994)
Supreme Court of Georgia

Background: *Nancy Franklin sued her daughter's high school teacher, Andrew Hill, when he seduced her daughter. His defense was that the tort of seduction is unconstitutional because it applied to men only. The trial court agreed and dismissed the case. The mother appealed to the Supreme Court of Georgia.*

Decision on Appeal: *The tort is unconstitutional. Judgment of dismissal is affirmed.*

OPINION OF COURT

Justice FLETCHER delivered the opinion of the court:

This case involves the constitutionality of the state statute that gives parents a cause of action for the seduction of their unmarried daughter. We hold that OCGA [the Official Code of Georgia] § 51-1-16 is a gender-based classification that violates the equal protection clause of the Georgia Constitution because only men may be civilly liable for seduction under the statute.

Nancy Franklin sued her daughter's former high school teacher, Andrew Hill, seeking damages for Hill's alleged seduction of the daughter under OCGA § 51-1-16.[1] . . . Hill moved for summary judgment, challenging the constitutionality of the statute on equal protection grounds. The trial court declared the statute violated the equal protection clauses of the United States and Georgia constitutions and granted summary judgment. We affirm.

The protection of the equal protection clause in the State Constitution is similar to the protection provided in the Federal Constitution.[2] To withstand constitutional challenge, a gender-based classification " 'must serve important governmental objectives and must be substantially related to achievement of those objectives.' " *Lamar v. State,* 243 Ga. 401, 254 S.E.2d 353 (1979) (quoting *Orr v. Orr,* 440 U.S. 268, 99 S. Ct. 1102, 59 L. Ed. 2d 306 (1979)). Applying this standard, this court has held unconstitutional several state laws that created a gender classification in violation of the federal equal protection clause. We have relied on the state's equal protection guarantee to invalidate a state statute that treated children differently based on the sex of their deceased parents. See *Tolbert v. Murrell,* 253 Ga. 566, 571, 322 S.E.2d 487 (1984) (finding wrongful death act violated equal protection by denying to children of deceased fathers rights granted to children of deceased mothers).

Hill argues that the seduction statute establishes a gender classification in three ways. First, only unmarried daughters, not sons, are protected from seduction; second, mothers are permitted to bring a seduction action only if the father is unable or unwilling to sue; and third, only men are liable for seduction. Because Hill limits his challenge to the third classification where his rights as a male are implicated, we do not address the constitutionality of the first two classifications. . . .

Seduction is defined as the "[a]ct of man enticing woman to have unlawful intercourse with him by means of persuasion, solicitation, promises, bribes, or other means without employment of force." *Black's Law Dictionary* p. 1218 (5th ed. 1979). This court has defined "seduction" as a term substantially similar to "debauchery." *Mosley v. Lynn,* 172 Ga. 193, 201, 157 S.E. 450 (1930). " 'Seduction, as a civil injury, may generally be defined as the act of a man in inducing a virtuous woman to commit unlawful sexual intercourse with him.' " Id. at 201, 203, 157 S.E. 450 (quoting *Dwire v. Stearns,* 44 N.D. 199, 172 N.W. 69). Therefore, by definition the statute makes a gender classification in that only men may be liable for the seduction of unwed daughters. . . .

A gender-based classification violates equal protection only if it fails to serve important government interests that are substantially related to those interests. The mother argues that the seduction statute advances the important state interests of "protect[ing] females from the emotional and physical consequences of non-marital sexual intercourse," including unwanted pregnancies and the physical and emotional scars of seduction.

Although preventing unwanted pregnancies, particularly of minors, is a legitimate government interest, the seduction statute is not substantially related to that goal. First, the statute has no age limitation, such as restricting the claim to parents of minor children. Second, the statute does not give the cause of action to the girl or woman who has the unwanted pregnancy and endured the "scars," but instead gives the right only to the parent. Third, the statute does not restrict the claim to parents whose daughters become pregnant, but extends the claim to seduction "whether followed by pregnancy or not.". . . [T]he statute is aimed at compensating a father or mother for personal injuries suffered by the daughter's seduction.[3]

Rather than seeking to prevent the pregnancy of unwed daughters, the statute was passed to hold men civilly liable for corrupting the morals and compromising the chastity of unmarried women. Passed in 1863 at a time when women and children were the legal property of their husbands or fathers, the statute vindicates the outraged feelings of the father whose daughter's virtue has been

---

[1]The challenged statute provides: The seduction of a daughter, unmarried and living with her parent, whether followed by pregnancy or not, shall give a right of action to the father or to the mother if the father is dead, or absent permanently, or refuses to bring an action. No loss of services need be alleged or proved. . . . OCGA § 51-1-16.

[2]The equal protection clause in the Georgia Constitution provides: "Protection to person and property is the paramount duty of government and shall be impartial and complete. No person shall be denied the equal protection of the laws." Ga. Const. Art. I, Sec. I, Para. II (1983).

---

[3][As to the argument that the statute is] . . . related to the deterrence of unwanted pregnancies,. . . [note that] it does not cover the seduction of married women or any woman living in a household away from her parents, but does include single, divorced, and widowed women who are past child-bearing age.

ruined. See *Mosley,* 172 Ga. at 199, 157 S.E. 450. As Justice Lumpkin explained:

> Never, so help me God, while I have the honor to occupy a seat upon this bench, will I consent to control the Jury, in the amount of compensation which they may see fit to render a father for the dishonor and disgrace thus cast upon his family; for this atrocious invasion of his household peace. There is nothing like it, since the entrance of Sin and Death into this lower world.

Kendrick v. McCrary, 11 Ga. 603, 606 (1852) (quoted with approval in *Mosley,* 172 Ga. at 200, 157 S.E. 450). Based on the language, history, and judicial interpretation of the seduction statute, we conclude it does not bear a substantial relationship to any important government objective.

We hold that the statute, which by definition applies only to men, violates the equal protection of laws and must be struck down as unconstitutional. . . .

Judgment affirmed.

ASSIGNMENT 22.2

a. Rewrite the Georgia statute (§ 51-1-16 found in footnote 1 of the case) so that it will not be subject to any constitutional objection mentioned by the court.

b. Are there any other tort actions against the coach that should be considered?

PRENATAL INJURIES

It is possible to commit a tort against an unborn child.

> **EXAMPLE:** Mary is pregnant. While on the freeway one day, Tom negligently drives his car into Mary's car. The impact causes a head injury to the unborn child Mary is carrying.

Mary, of course, can sue for her own injuries and for damage to her car caused by the defendant's negligence. Also, if the child is later born alive, an action can be brought on its behalf to cover the head injury. Suppose, however, the prenatal injury results in the death of the child. In such cases, many states will allow a wrongful death action to be brought (see Chapter 21), but only if the child was **viable** at the time of death. (*Viable* means able to live indefinitely outside the womb by natural or artificial support systems.)

WRONGFUL LIFE, BIRTH, PREGNANCY

Doctors and pharmaceutical companies have been sued for negligence that results in the birth of an unwanted child. When the child is born deformed or otherwise impaired, two categories of suits have been attempted:

Wrongful life: An action by or on behalf an unwanted child who is impaired; the child seeks its own damages in this action.

Wrongful birth: An action by the parents of an unwanted child who is impaired; the parents seek their own damages in this action.

Suppose, for example, a woman contracts German measles early in her pregnancy. Her doctor negligently advises her that the disease will not affect the health of the child. In fact, the child is born with severe defects caused by the disease. If the woman had known the risks, she would have had an abortion.

In such cases, a small number of states allow suits for wrongful life to cover the child's damages. The vast majority of states, however, do not. Courts are very reluctant to recognize a right not to be born. Several reasons account for this result. One is the enormous difficulty of calculating damages. According to the New Jersey court in a case we will examine in a moment, it is literally impossible to measure the difference in value between life in an impaired condition and the "utter void of nonexistence." Some courts also feel that allowing the suit might encourage unwanted children to sue for being born to a poverty-stricken family or to parents with criminal records. Finally, anti-abortion activists have argued that no one should be allowed to sue for missing the opportunity to have been aborted.

Wrongful birth cases, on the other hand, have been more successful. Here the parents sue for their own damages to cover their emotional distress, the cost of prenatal care and delivery, and other expenses attributed to the child's impaired condition.

Finally, we examine negligence that leads to the birth of an unwanted *healthy* child:

Wrongful pregnancy: An action by the parents of an unwanted child who is healthy; the parents seek their own damages in this action.

Cases of wrongful pregnancy (also called wrongful conception) are allowed in most states. The most common example is a suit against a doctor for negligently performing a vasectomy or against a pharmaceutical company for producing defective birth control pills. Damages are limited to the expenses of prenatal care and delivery; they rarely extend to the costs of raising a healthy child. Furthermore, the unwanted healthy child is usually not allowed to bring the same kind of action in his or her own right.

CASE

Berman v. Allen
80 N.J. 421, 404 A.2d 8 (1979)
Supreme Court of New Jersey

Background: *Sharon Berman was born with Down's Syndrome, a genetic defect commonly referred to as mongolism. The mother would have had an abortion if she had known this before birth. Doctors Allen and Attardi, specialists in gynecology and obstetrics, failed to tell her about the availability of amniocentesis as a technique to discover the presence of Down's Syndrome. In this medical malpractice action, the parents sue for wrongful life on behalf of Sharon and for wrongful birth on their own behalf. The trial court granted the doctors a summary judgment because the plaintiffs failed to state a cause of action. The case is now on appeal before the Supreme Court of New Jersey.*

Decision on Appeal: *The child cannot sue for wrongful life, but the parents can sue for wrongful birth.*

OPINION OF COURT

Justice PASHMAN delivered the opinion of the court . . .

Plaintiffs allege that defendants deviated from accepted medical standards by failing to inform Mrs. Berman during her pregnancy of the existence of a procedure known as amniocentesis. This procedure involves the insertion of a long needle into a mother's uterus and the removal therefrom of a sample of amniotic fluid containing living fetal cells. Through "karyotype analysis" a procedure in which the number and structure of the cells' chromosomes are examined, the sex of the fetus as well as the presence of gross chromosomal defects can be detected. Prenatal diagnosis of genetic abnormalities is potentially available for approximately 60 to 90 metabolic defects, including Tay-

Sachs Disease and Down's Syndrome. Recent studies indicate that amniocentesis is highly accurate in predicting the presence of chromosomal defects, and that the risk of even minor damage to mother or fetus deriving from the procedure is less than one percent.

Due to Mrs. Berman's age at the time of her conception [38], plaintiffs contend that the risk that her child, if born, would be afflicted with Down's Syndrome was sufficiently great that sound medical practice at the time of pregnancy required defendants to inform her both of this risk and the availability of amniocentesis as a method of determining whether in her particular case that risk would come to fruition. Had defendants so informed Mrs. Berman, the complaint continues, she would have submitted to the amniocentesis procedure, discovered that the child, if born, would suffer from Down's Syndrome, and had the fetus aborted.

As a result of defendants' alleged negligence, the infant Sharon, through her Guardian *ad litem,* seeks compensation for the physical and emotional pain and suffering which she will endure throughout life because of her mongoloid condition. Mr. and Mrs. Berman, the child's parents, request damages in their own right both for the emotional anguish which they have experienced and will continue to experience on account of Sharon's birth defect, and the medical and other costs which they will incur in order to properly raise, educate and supervise the child. . . .

The claim for damages asserted on behalf of the infant Sharon has aptly been labeled a cause of action grounded upon "wrongful life." Sharon does not contend that absent defendants' negligence she would have come into the world in a normal and healthy state. There is no suggestion in either the pleadings below or the medical literature which we have scrutinized that any therapy could have been prescribed which would have decreased the risk that, upon birth, Sharon would suffer from Down's Syndrome. Rather, the gist of the infant's complaint is that had defendants informed her mother of the availability of amniocentesis, Sharon would never have come into existence.

As such, this case presents issues different from those involved in malpractice actions where a plaintiff asserts that a defendant's deviation from sound medical practices *increased* the probability that an infant would be born with defects. Nor are we here confronted with a situation in which an individual's negligence while a child was in gestation caused what otherwise would have been a normal and healthy child to come into the world in an impaired condition. Here, defendants' alleged negligence neither caused the mongoloid condition nor increased the risk that such a condition would occur. . . . In essence, Sharon claims that her very life is "wrongful. . . ."

The primary purpose of tort law is that of compensating plaintiffs for the injuries they have suffered wrongfully at the hands of others. As such, damages are ordinarily computed by "comparing the condition plaintiff would have been in, had the defendants not been negligent, with plaintiff's impaired condition as a result of the negligence." *Gleitman v. Cosgrove,* 49 N.J. 22, 28, 227 A.2d 689, 692. In the case of a claim predicated upon wrongful life, such a computation would require the trier of fact to measure the difference in value between life in an impaired condition and the "utter void of nonexistence." *Gleitman,* supra. Such an endeavor, however, is literally impossible. As Chief Justice Weintraub noted, man, "who knows nothing of death or nothingness," simply cannot affix a price tag to non-life. *Gleitman* at 63.

Nevertheless, although relevant to our determination, we would be extremely reluctant today to deny the validity of Sharon's complaint solely because damages are difficult to ascertain. The courts of this and other jurisdictions have long held that where a wrong itself is of such a nature as to preclude the computation of damages with precise exactitude, it would be a "perversion of fundamental principles of justice to deny all relief to the injured [party], and thereby relieve the wrongdoer from making any amend for his acts." *Story Parchment Co. v. Paterson Parchment Paper Co.,* 282 U.S. 555, 563 (1931). To be sure, damages may not be determined by mere speculation or guess and, as defendants emphasize, placing a value upon non-life is not simply difficult—it is humanly impossible. Nonetheless, were the measure of damages our sole concern, it is possible that some judicial remedy could be fashioned which would redress plaintiff, if only in part, for injuries suffered.

Difficulty in the *measure* of damages is not, however, our sole or even primary concern. Although we conclude, as did the . . . majority [in *Gleitman v. Cosgrove*] that Sharon has failed to state an actionable claim for relief, we base our result upon a different premise [:] that Sharon has not suffered any damage cognizable at law by being brought into existence.

One of the most deeply held beliefs of our society is that life whether experienced with or without a major physical handicap is more precious than non-life. See *In re Quinlin,* 70

N.J. 10, 19 & n. 1, 355 A.2d 647 (1976). Concrete manifestations of this belief are not difficult to discover. The documents which set forth the principles upon which our society is founded are replete with references to the sanctity of life. The federal constitution characterizes life as one of three fundamental rights of which no man can be deprived without due process of law. U.S. Const., Amends. V and XIV. Our own state constitution proclaims that the "enjoying and defending (of) life" is a natural right. N.J. Const. (1947), Art. I, § 1. The Declaration of Independence states that the primacy of man's "unalienable" right to life is a "self-evident truth." Nowhere in these documents is there to be found an indication that the lives of persons suffering from physical handicaps are to be less cherished than those of non-handicapped human beings.

State legislatures and thus the people as a whole have universally reserved the most severe criminal penalties for individuals who have unjustifiably deprived others of life. Indeed, so valued is this commodity that even one who has committed first degree murder cannot be sentenced to death unless he is accorded special procedural protections in addition to those given all criminal defendants. Moreover, it appears that execution is constitutionally impermissible unless the crime which a defendant has perpetrated was one which involved the taking of another's life. Again, these procedural protections and penalties do not vary according to the presence or absence of physical deformities in the victim or defendant. It is life itself that is jealously safeguarded, not life in a perfect state.

Finally, we would be remiss if we did not take judicial notice of the high esteem which our society accords to those involved in the medical profession. The reason for this is clear. Physicians are the preservers of life.

No man is perfect. Each of us suffers from some ailments or defects, whether major or minor, which make impossible participation in all the activities the world has to offer. But our lives are not thereby rendered less precious than those of others whose defects are less pervasive or less severe.

We recognize that as a mongoloid child, Sharon's abilities will be more circumscribed than those of normal, healthy children and that she, unlike them, will experience a great deal of physical and emotional pain and anguish. We sympathize with her plight. We cannot, however, say that she would have been better off had she never been brought into the world. Notwithstanding her affliction with Down's Syndrome, Sharon, by virtue of her birth, will be able to love and be loved and to experience happiness and pleasure[,] emotions which are truly the essence of life and which are far more valuable than the suffering she may endure. To rule otherwise would require us to disavow the basic assumption upon which our society is based. This we cannot do.

Accordingly, we hold that Sharon has failed to state a valid cause of action founded upon "wrongful life."

The validity of the parents' claim for relief calls into play considerations different from those involved in the infant's complaint. As in the case of the infant, Mr. and Mrs. Berman do not assert that defendants increased the risk that Sharon, if born, would be afflicted with Down's Syndrome. Rather, at bottom, they allege that they were tortiously injured because Mrs. Berman was deprived of the option of making a meaningful decision as to whether to abort the fetus, a decision which, at least during the first trimester of pregnancy, is not subject to state interference. See *Roe v. Wade*, 410 U.S. 113, 93 S. Ct. 705, 35 L. Ed. 2d 147 (1973). They thus claim that Sharon's "birth" as opposed to her "life" was wrongful.

Two items of damage are requested in order to redress this allegedly tortious injury: (1) the medical and other costs that will be incurred in order to properly raise, supervise and educate the child; and (2) compensation for the emotional anguish that has been and will continue to be experienced on account of Sharon's condition.

The . . . majority [in *Gleitman v. Cosgrove*] refused to recognize as valid a cause of action grounded upon wrongful birth. Two reasons underlay its determination. The first related to measure of damages should such a claim be allowed. In its view,

In order to determine [the parents'] compensatory damages a court would have to evaluate the denial to them of the intangible, unmeasurable, and complex human benefits of motherhood and fatherhood and weigh these against the alleged emotional and money injuries. Such a proposed weighing is . . . impossible to perform. . . . [*Gleitman*, 49 N.J. at 29, 227 A.2d at 693]

Second, even though the Court's opinion was premised upon the assumption that Mrs. Gleitman could have legally secured an abortion, the majority concluded that "substantial [public] policy reasons" precluded the judicial allowance of tort damages "for the denial of the opportunity to take an embryonic life." 49 N.J. at 30, 227 A.2d at 693.

In light of changes in the law which have occurred in the 12 years since *Gleitman* was decided, the second ground relied upon by the *Gleitman* majority can no longer stand in the way of judicial recognition of a cause of action founded upon wrongful birth. The Supreme Court's ruling in *Roe v. Wade* clearly establishes that a woman possesses a constitutional right to decide whether her fetus should be aborted, at least during the first trimester of pregnancy. Public policy now supports, rather than militates against, the proposition that she not be impermissibly denied a meaningful opportunity to make that decision.

As in all other cases of tortious injury, a physician whose negligence has deprived a mother of this opportunity should be required to make amends for the damage which he has proximately caused. Any other ruling would in effect immunize from liability those in the medical field providing inadequate guidance to persons who would choose to exercise their constitutional right to abort fetuses which, if born, would suffer from genetic defects. Accordingly, we hold that

a cause of action founded upon wrongful birth is a legally cognizable claim.

Troublesome, however, is the measure of damages. As noted earlier, the first item sought to be recompensed is the medical and other expenses that will be incurred in order to properly raise, educate and supervise the child. Although these costs were "caused" by defendants' negligence in the sense that but for the failure to inform, the child would not have come into existence, we conclude that this item of damage should not be recoverable. In essence, Mr. and Mrs. Berman desire to retain all the benefits inhering in the birth of the child, i.e., the love and joy they will experience as parents while saddling defendants with the enormous expenses attendant upon her rearing. Under the facts and circumstances here alleged, we find that such an award would be wholly disproportionate to the culpability involved, and that allowance of such a recovery would both constitute a windfall to the parents and place too unreasonable a financial burden upon physicians.

The parents' claim for emotional damages stands upon a different footing. In failing to inform Mrs. Berman of the availability of amniocentesis, defendants directly deprived her and, derivatively, her husband of the option to accept or reject a parental relationship with the child and thus caused them to experience mental and emotional anguish upon their realization that they had given birth to a child afflicted with Down's Syndrome. We feel that the monetary equivalent of this distress is an appropriate measure of the harm suffered by the parents deriving from Mrs. Berman's loss of her right to abort the fetus. . . .

[W]e do not feel that placing a monetary value upon the emotional suffering that Mr. and Mrs. Berman have and will continue to experience is an impossible task for the trier of fact. . . . [C]ourts have come to recognize that mental and emotional distress is just as "real" as physical pain, and that its valuation is no more difficult. Consequently, damages for such distress have been ruled allowable in an increasing number of contexts. Moreover . . . to deny Mr. and Mrs. Berman redress for their injuries merely because damages cannot be measured with precise exactitude would constitute a perversion of fundamental principles of justice.

Consequently, we hold that Mr. and Mrs. Berman have stated actionable claims for relief. Should their allegations be proven at trial, they are entitled to be recompensed for the mental and emotional anguish they have suffered and will continue to suffer on account of Sharon's condition. Accordingly, the judgment of the trial court is affirmed in part and reversed in part, and this case remanded for a plenary trial.

ASSIGNMENT 22.3

a. Did the two doctors owe a duty of care to Sharon Berman? Why or why not?

b. Assume that the doctors owed Sharon a duty and that it was breached by a failure to render competent medical advice and services in connection with the pregnancy. What harm did the doctors cause? They clearly did not cause the Down's Syndrome. What was Sharon's loss?

WRONGFUL ADOPTION

Suppose that an adoption agency misrepresents the physical or mental health of a child or misrepresents the medical history of the child's birth family.

> **EXAMPLE:** Alice and Stan Patterson want to adopt a child. They go to the Riverside Adoption Agency (RAA), which introduces them to Irene, an infant available for adoption. The Pattersons adopt Irene. Before the adoption, RAA told the Pattersons that Irene did not have any genetic disorders. This turned out to be false. Also, RAA knew that Irene had been sexually abused, but they did not inform the Pattersons of this. After Irene has been living with the Pattersons for a while, they discover that she has severe medical and psychological problems.

Can the Pattersons sue RAA for damages covering the increased cost of child rearing? The period for challenging the adoption itself may have passed. Furthermore, the adoptive parents may have bonded with the child and do not want to "send" the child back even if it were possible to annul or abrogate the adoption. In such cases, some states have allowed the adoptive parents to sue, particularly when they made clear to the agency that they did not want to adopt a problem child. Their argument is that they would not have adopted the child if they had been presented with all the facts. They cannot expect a guarantee that the child will be perfect. But they are entitled to available information that might indicate a significant likelihood of future medical or psychological problems. The failure to provide such information may constitute the tort of **wrongful adoption.** In an action for this tort, the adoptive parents seek damages from the adoption agency for wrongfully stating or failing to disclose available facts on the health or other condition of the child (the adoptee) that would have been relevant to their decision of whether to adopt.

INTRAFAMILY TORT IMMUNITY

Finally, we consider **intrafamily torts,** which are torts committed by one family member against another. Historically, an intrafamily **immunity** existed for most of these torts. (An immunity is a defense that prevents someone from being sued for what would otherwise be wrongful conduct.) Courts have always been reluctant to permit tort actions among any combination of wife, husband, and unemancipated child. (If a state refuses to allow one spouse to sue another for a specific category of tort, the immunity is referred to as **interspousal immunity.**) This reluctance to allow family members to sue each other is based on the theory that family harmony will be threatened if members know they can sue each other in tort. If the family carries liability insurance, there is also a fear that family members will fraudulently try to collect under the policy by fabricating tort actions against each other. A more technical and brutal reason was given at common law for why husbands and wives could not sue each other—the husband and wife were considered to be one person, and that one person was the husband! Hence, to allow a suit between spouses would theoretically amount to one person suing himself. With the passage of the Married Women's Property Acts and the enforcement of the laws against sex discrimination, a wife now retains her separate identity so that she can sue and be sued like anyone else.

Reform in the law, however, has not meant that **intrafamily tort immunity** no longer exists. A distinction must be made between a suit against the person (such as battery) and a suit against property (such as conversion). For torts against property, most states allow suits between spouses and between parent and child. Many states, however, retain the immunity in some form when the suit involves a tort against the person. The state of the law is outlined in Figure 22–1.

FIGURE 22–1
Intrafamily torts.

Spouse against Spouse

1. In most states, spouses can sue each other for intentional or negligent injury to their property, e.g., negligence, trespass, conversion.
2. In some states, spouses cannot sue each other for intentional or negligent injury to their person—a personal tort action, e.g., negligence, assault, battery.
3. Some states will permit personal tort actions if the man and woman are divorced or if the tort is covered by liability insurance.
4. Some states will permit intentional tort actions against the person to be brought by spouses against each other, but continue to forbid negligence actions for injury to the person.

Child against Parent(s)

1. In all states, a child can sue the parent for intentional or negligent injury caused by the parent to the child's property, e.g., negligence, trespass, conversion.
2. In many states, a child cannot sue a parent for intentional or negligent injury caused by the parent to the child's person, e.g., negligence, assault, battery, particularly in cases where the parent was disciplining the child. Parents have a privilege to discipline their children.
3. If the child is emancipated (e.g., married, member of the armed forces, self-supporting), the child in all states can sue the parent for intentional or negligent injury caused by the parent to the child's person, e.g., negligence, assault, battery.
4. Some states will permit any child (emancipated or not) to sue the parent for intentional torts causing injury to the person, but continue to forbid actions for negligence causing injury to the person.
5. A few states allow the child to sue the parent for all intentional torts causing injury to the person, except where a tort arises out of the parent's exercise of discipline over the child.

Other Related Persons

Brothers and sisters, aunts and uncles, grandparents and grandchildren, and other relatives can sue each other in tort. The restrictions imposed on spouse suits and child suits do not apply to tort actions involving other relatives.

ASSIGNMENT

22.4

Dave knows that he has contagious genital herpes, but does not tell Alice, who contracts the disease from Dave. Can Alice sue Dave for battery? For intentional infliction of emotional distress? For deceit or fraud? Does it make any difference whether the disease was communicated before or after Dave and Alice were married? Does it make any difference that they are now divorced? (See General Instructions for the Legal Analysis Assignment in Chapter 2.)

SUMMARY

Loss of consortium is an independent action brought by a person whose spouse has been tortiously injured. The action covers the loss of love, affection, sexual relationship, and services that one spouse normally provides another. When a parent is injured, most states do not recognize an action for loss of parental consortium in which a child sues for the tortious interference with the normal companionship and affection children have with their parents. When a child is injured, states differ on whether parents can sue for tortious interference with filial consortium, the normal companionship and affection parents have with their children. An action for loss of services can be brought by a parent against a defendant who has tortiously injured a child to the extent that the child cannot render services that rightfully are due the parent.

Other torts against the family include alienation of affections (the defendant causes the deprivation of love, companionship, and comfort between the plaintiff and the plaintiff's spouse); criminal conversation (the defendant has sex with the plaintiff's spouse); enticement of spouse (the defendant causes the plaintiff's spouse to leave home or to stay away); abduction or enticement of a child (the defendant causes the plaintiff's child to leave home or to stay away); and seduction (the defendant has sex with the plaintiff's minor daughter, with or without the latter's consent). Many states have abolished these torts.

Unborn children can sue for prenatal injuries. If the child dies from the injuries, many states allow a wrongful death action if the child was viable at the time of death. Courts are reluctant to allow an unwanted impaired child to bring an action for wrongful life for his or her own damages in being negligently born. Wrongful birth actions in which parents seek damages for the negligent birth of an unwanted impaired child are usually permitted, as are wrongful pregnancy actions, in which parents seek damages for the negligent birth of an unwanted healthy child. The failure of an adoption agency to give prospective adoptive parents available information about the health or other condition of the prospective adoptee may constitute the tort of wrongful adoption.

Intrafamily torts that damage property are often treated differently from torts that injure the person. Generally, spouses can sue each other for negligent or intentional damage to property. The same is true for such damage caused by the parent to a child's property. There is no immunity for property torts. For torts against the person, in some states, one spouse cannot sue another, and an unemancipated child cannot sue a parent; immunity does apply to torts against the person in such states. There are some exceptions. For example, many states grant this immunity only for negligent injury to the person; thus, any family member can sue another for intentional injury to the person in such states. Other family members such as siblings and other relatives do not have intrafamily tort immunity.

KEY TERMS

consortium   434

loss of consortium   434

parental consortium   435

filial consortium   435

unemancipated   435

emancipated   435

loss of services   435

heart-balm statutes   435

alienation of affections   436

criminal conversation   436

enticement of spouse   436

abduction or enticement of a
    child   436

seduction   436

viable   438

wrongful life   438

wrongful birth   438

wrongful pregnancy   439

wrongful adoption   442

intrafamily torts   442

immunity   442

interspousal immunity   442

intrafamily tort immunity   442

Torts Connected with Land

CHAPTER OUTLINE

- Introduction
- Trespass to Land
- Nuisance
- Traditional Negligence Liability

INTRODUCTION

An **interest** is a right, claim, or legal share of or in something. There are a variety of interests you can have in land based on your relationship to the land. You can be:

- an owner who is occupying the land
- a nonoccupying owner who is the landlord (i.e., lessor) of a tenant (i.e., lessee) who is occupying the land
- a nonoccupying owner of vacant land
- a tenant (lessee) of the land
- a subtenant (sublessee) who is renting the land from the tenant
- a trespasser who now claims to own the land as an adverse possessor

This chapter is primarily about the torts that can be committed by and against individuals with these relationships to—these interests in—land. The topics we will consider are:

- trespass to land
- nuisance due to trespass, negligence, or strict liability
- negligence

In Chapter 11, we examined a separate tort called strict liability of abnormally dangerous conditions or activities, which is often committed by occupiers of land.

We begin with an overview of **trespass to land.**

TRESPASS TO LAND

 Trespass to Land Checklist

Definitions, Relationships, Paralegal Roles, and Research References

Category
Trespass to land is an intentional tort.

Interest Protected by This Tort
The interest in the exclusive possession of land in its present physical condition.

Elements of This Tort
- i. An act
- ii. Intrusion on land
- iii. In possession of another
- iv. Intent to intrude
- v. Causation of the intrusion

Definitions of Major Words/Phrases in These Elements
Act: A voluntary movement of the body that leads to the intrusion.
Intrusion: a. Physically going on the land,
 b. Remaining on the land,
 c. Going to a prohibited portion of the land, or
 d. Failing to remove goods from the land.
Possession: a. Actual occupancy with intent to have exclusive control over the land, or
 b. The right to immediate occupancy when no one else is actually occupying it with intent to control it.
Intent to Intrude: The desire to intrude on the land or the knowledge with substantial certainty that an intrusion will result from what you do or fail to do.
Causation: But for what the defendant did, the intrusion would not have occurred, or the defendant was a substantial factor in producing the intrusion.

Trespass to Land Checklist Continued

Major Defenses and Counterargument Possibilities That Need to Be Explored

1. The defendant did not voluntarily go on the land, remain on the land, go to a prohibited portion of the land, or fail to remove goods from the land.
2. The plaintiff did not have possession of the land.
3. The plaintiff had no reasonably beneficial use of the land that the defendant entered (e.g., the air space over the land).
4. There was no intent to intrude: the defendant did not desire to intrude or know with substantial certainty that an intrusion would result from what the defendant did.
5. The defendant did not cause the intrusion (but for what the defendant did or failed to do, the intrusion would have occurred anyway; the defendant was not a substantial factor in bringing about the intrusion).
6. The plaintiff consented to the defendant's intrusion (on the defense of consent, see Chapter 27).
7. The intrusion occurred while the defendant was defending property (on necessity and other self-help privileges, see Chapter 27).
8. The intrusion occurred while the defendant was abating a nuisance (see discussion of this self-help privilege later in this chapter).
9. The plaintiff's suit against the government for trespass committed by a government employee may be barred by sovereign immunity (on sovereign immunity, see Chapter 27).
10. The plaintiff's suit against the government employee for trespass may be barred by public official immunity (on official immunity, see Chapter 27).
11. The plaintiff's suit against the charitable organization for trespass committed by someone working for the organization may be barred by charitable immunity (on charitable immunity, see Chapter 27).

Damages

If actual harm or damage was done to the land, the plaintiff can recover compensatory damages, e.g., cost or repair. If no harm or damage was done (a technical violation only), nominal damages can be recovered. If the defendant acted out of hatred and malice, punitive damages are possible. (On the categories of damages, see Chapter 16.)

Relationship to Criminal Law

It may be a crime in certain states to enter designated land, e.g., government property.

Relationship to Other Torts

Negligence: If the defendant does not intentionally enter the plaintiff's land, the defendant may have entered negligently, e.g., due to an unreasonable mistake. The tort of negligence is committed if actual damage results from the negligent entry.

Nuisance: The defendant may commit a private or public nuisance while entering the plaintiff's land.

Strict Liability for Abnormally Dangerous Activities: The defendant may enter the land while engaged in abnormally dangerous activities, which could be the basis of strict liability.

Federal Law

a. Under the Federal Tort Claims Act, the United States Government *will* be liable for trespass to land committed by one of its federal employees within the scope of employment (respondeat superior). (See Figure 27–7 in Chapter 27.)
b. There may be liability under the Civil Rights Act if the trespass to land was committed while the defendant was depriving the plaintiff of federal rights under color of law. (See Figure 27–9 in Chapter 27.)

Employer-Employee (Agency) Law

An employee who commits a trespass to land is personally liable for this tort. His or her employer will *also* be liable for trespass to land if the conduct of the employee was within the scope of employment (respondeat superior). The employee must be furthering a business objective of the employer at the time. Intentional torts such as trespass to land, however, are often outside the scope of employment. If so, only the employee is liable for the trespass to land. (On the factors that determine the scope of employment, see Figure 14–10 in Chapter 14.)

Trespass to Land Checklist Continued

Paralegal Roles in Trespass to Land Litigation
(See also Figures 3–1, 3–14, and 29–1 in Chapters 3 and 29.)

Fact finding (help the office collect facts relevant to prove the elements of trespass to land, the elements of available defenses, and extent of injuries or other damages):
- client interviewing
- field investigation
- online research (e.g., identity of owners of land)

File management (help the office control the volume of paperwork in a trespass to land litigation):
- open client file
- enter case data in computer database
- maintain file documents

Litigation assistance (help the trial attorney prepare for a trespass trial and appeal, if needed):
- draft discovery requests
- draft answers to discovery requests
- draft pleadings
- digest and index discovery documents
- help prepare, order, and manage trial exhibits (visuals or demonstratives)
- prepare trial notebook
- draft notice of appeal
- order trial transcript
- cite check briefs
- perform legal research

Collection/enforcement (help the trial attorney for judgment creditor to collect the damages award or to enforce other court orders at the conclusion of the trespass case):
- draft postjudgment discovery requests
- field investigation to monitor compliance with judgment
- online research (e.g., location of defendant's business assets)

Research References for Trespass to Land

Digests
In the digests of West, look for case summaries on trespass to land under key topics such as:

Trespass	Torts
Forcible Entry and Detainer	Damages
Ejectment	Adverse Possession
Landlord and Tenant	Animals

Corpus Juris Secundum
In this legal encyclopedia, see the discussions under topic headings such as:

Trespass	Landlord and Tenant
Forcible Entry and Detainer	Torts
Ejectment	Damages
	Adverse Possession

American Jurisprudence 2d
In this legal encyclopedia, see the discussions under topic headings such as:

Trespass	Ejectment
Property	Landlord and Tenant
Damages	Torts
Forcible Entry and Detainer	Adverse Possession
	Animals

Legal Periodical Literature
There are two index systems to use to locate legal periodical literature on trespass to land:

Trespass to Land Checklist Continued

INDEX TO LEGAL PERIODICALS AND BOOKS (ILP)	*CURRENT LAW INDEX (CLI)*
See literature in *ILP* under subject headings such as:	See literature in *CLI* under subject headings such as:
Trespass	Trespass
Forcible Entry and Detainer	Torts
Real Property	Riparian Rights
Air Law	Real Property
Torts	Damages
Damages	
Adjoining Landowners	

Example of a legal periodical article you will find using *ILP* or *CLI*:

Invasion of Radioactive Particulates as a Common Law Trespass 3 Urban Law Review 206 (1980).

A.L.R., A.L.R.2d, A.L.R.3d, A.L.R.4th, A.L.R.5th, A.L.R. Fed.
Use the *Index to Annotations* to locate annotations on trespass to land. In this index, check subject headings such as:

Trespass	Adverse possession
Forcible Entry and Detainer	Torts
Real property	Damages
	Air Space

Example of an annotation on trespass to land you can locate through this index:

Liability for Personal Injury or Death Caused by Trespassing or Intruding Livestock by James L. Rigelhaupt, 49 A.L.R.4th 710 (1987).

Words and Phrases
In this multivolume legal dictionary, look up *trespass to land, intrusion, land, real property, ejectment, detainer,* and every other word or phrase connected with trespass to land discussed in this section of the chapter. The dictionary will give you definitions of these words or phrases from court opinions.

CALR: Computer-Assisted Legal Research
Example of a query you could ask on WESTLAW or on LEXIS to try to find cases, statutes, or other legal materials on trespass to land: **trespass /s damages**

Example of search terms you could use on an Internet legal search engine such as LawCrawler (http://lawcrawler.findlaw.com) to find cases, statutes, or other legal materials on trespass to land: **"trespass to land"**

Example of search terms you could use on an Internet general search engine such as Alta Vista (http://www.altavista.com) to find cases, statutes, or other legal materials on trespass to land: **"trespass to land"**

More Internet sites to check for materials on trespass to land and other torts:
Jurist: (http://jurist.law.pitt.edu/sg_torts.htm)
LawGuru: (http://www.lawguru.com/search/lawsearch.html)
See also Tort Law Online at the end of Chapter 1.

Plaintiffs in a Trespass Action

You do not have to own land to bring a suit against someone who is trespassing on the land. Plaintiffs in trespass cases can include tenants and anyone else who has a present or future right to possess the land (referred to as someone with a **possessory interest**). A major reason to bring a trespass action is to prevent someone from taking it away by **adverse possession.** This is a method of acquiring title to land without buying it or receiving it as a gift through a will or other traditional means. The law allows a trespasser to obtain title to land by occupying it in a hostile and visible manner for a designated number of continuous years. This method of acquiring title is designed to prevent speculators from buying land and leaving it vacant for long periods of time until its price increases. If these speculators want to avoid losing their land, they must bring trespass actions against anyone claiming it by adverse possession.

The elements of trespass to land are act, intrusion on land, in possession of another, intent to intrude, and causation of the intrusion. See the definition of these elements in the checklist at the beginning of this chapter. (See also the example of how to apply these elements in Figure 2–2 of Chapter 2 on connecting facts to elements.) Before leaving the relatively uncomplicated tort of trespass to land, we need to explore briefly the nature of the required intent, the definition of land, and the issue of damages in a trespass case.

Intent

The intent required for this tort is the intent to enter upon the particular piece of land in question. The defendant does not have to show that the plaintiff intended to violate defendant's rights. Hence, it is no defense for the plaintiff to be able to show that he or she was reasonable in thinking there was a right to enter. For example, the defendant has committed trespass to land even though the defendant reasonably, but mistakenly, believed that he or she owned the land. "The defendant is liable for an intentional entry although he acted in good faith, under the mistaken belief, however reasonable, that he was committing no wrong."[1]

Although this element is called the "intent to intrude," intrude or intrusion simply means physically going on the land, remaining on the land, going to a prohibited portion of the land, or failing to remove goods from the land.

Land

Land does not consist solely of ground. It also includes that portion of the air space above the ground over which the plaintiff can claim a **reasonable beneficial use.** If a defendant throws a brick over the plaintiff's land, a trespass has occurred even if the brick never touches the plaintiff's home or ground. Assume that it finally lands beyond the plaintiff's property line. The plaintiff has the use of the air space immediately above the ground. Hence, there has been a trespass to land. The case is different, however, for the space one mile above the ground that is used by airplanes. The latter do not commit trespass.

Damages

Actual destruction or harm to the land does not have to be shown. The actual entry is damage enough. If nothing more has occurred, the plaintiff can at least recover **nominal damages** and prevent someone else from obtaining title by adverse possession.

ASSIGNMENT **23.1**	Has a trespass to land been committed in the following cases? (See General Instructions for the Legal Analysis Assignment in Chapter 2.) a. Jim sells automobiles on the Internet. He obtains Dan's e-mail address and sends Dan a message announcing an automobile sale. Dan sends an e-mail back telling Jim not to send him any unsolicited messages (spam). Jim responds by sending Dan another automobile sale message. b. Same facts as in (a) except that the spam contains an ad for a pornographic site on the Internet and a new ad is sent every day.

---

[1] W. Page Keeton et al., *Prosser and Keeton on the Law of Torts* 74 (5th ed. 1984).

NUISANCE

The first obstacle in understanding this topic is to realize that the word **nuisance** has been very loosely used throughout the law. There is *no* separate tort of nuisance, although the language of many opinions would appear to indicate otherwise. Nuisance is a word that describes two different kinds of harm that are produced by some other tortious or wrongful conduct. The two kinds of harm are **private** and **public nuisance**:

Private nuisance: An unreasonable interference with the use and enjoyment of private land.

Public nuisance: An unreasonable interference with a right common to the general public.

There are a variety of ways that these interferences can be brought about:

- The interferences may be due to negligence.
- The interferences may be due to abnormally dangerous conditions or activities that impose strict liability.
- The interferences may be intentional.
- The interferences may be due to a violation of a statute.

Although nuisance is often thought to apply to land, only private nuisance is primarily concerned with land. In the main, public nuisance is a separate category of injury that often has nothing to do with land. As we shall see, however, there are some public nuisances that can also constitute private nuisances.

Private Nuisance

A private nuisance is different from a trespass to land in that the latter protects one's interest in the exclusive possession of land, whereas the former protects one's right to the reasonable use and enjoyment of land. Of course, the same conduct of the defendant may constitute a private nuisance and a trespass to land, e.g., building a fence on the plaintiff's land. In such cases, the plaintiff can sue either for trespass to land or for a private nuisance.

We approach the subject of private nuisance through five basic questions:

1. What is the nature of a private nuisance? What type of harm does it cover?
2. How is it created?
3. Who can sue?
4. What remedies are available?
5. What defenses are available?

See Figure 23–1 for an overview of the law governing these questions.

1. What Is the Nature of a Private Nuisance and What Type of Harm Does It Cover?   There are a number of forms that the interference can take:

- loud noises
- vibrations from blasting
- odors or gases
- pollution of air, land, or water
- flooding
- damage to crops or to structures on the land
- keeping a house of prostitution next door
- bringing insects into the area
- constant knocking on the door, constant telephone calls

Any of these examples can interfere with the use and enjoyment of one's land. It is not necessary that the physical condition of the land be altered or damaged, although

FIGURE 23–1
Private nuisance: An overview.

1. What type of harm does private nuisance cover?	**1.** Unreasonable interference with the use and enjoyment of private land.
2. What are the ways in which a private nuisance can be created?	**2.** a. Negligently causing the unreasonable interference with the use and enjoyment of land. b. Intentionally causing the unreasonable interference with the use and enjoyment of land. c. Strict liability in maintaining an abnormally dangerous condition or activity, which causes an unreasonable interference with the use and enjoyment of land.
3. Who can sue for the private nuisance?	**3.** Anyone who has a right to the use and enjoyment of the land, e.g., owner, tenant.
4. What remedies can be obtained when a private nuisance has been committed?	**4.** a. Damages (money). b. Injunction—if the reasonable interference is threatened or is continuous. c. The plaintiff may be able to exercise the privilege to abate the nuisance (self-help).
5. What defenses are available?	**5.** a. Contributory negligence. This may be a defense if the defendant negligently created the unreasonable interference with the use and enjoyment of the land. Contributory negligence is not a defense if the defendant recklessly or intentionally created this interference. b. Assumption of the risk. This is a defense no matter how the defendant produced the unreasonable interference. c. Failure to mitigate damages. A plaintiff must mitigate damages no matter how the defendant produced the unreasonable interference. d. Official authorization. The government authorized or required the defendant's activity that caused the interference.

this will certainly qualify. Interference with use and enjoyment of land also occurs when the plaintiff's **peace of mind** is disturbed while on the land because of what the defendant has done or failed to do.

Of course, every interference with the use and enjoyment of land is not a private nuisance. It is not a private nuisance for one's relative to move into the state, no matter how upsetting this might be! The interference must be **unreasonable.** The determination of when this is so has caused the greatest difficulty in this area of the law. The difficulty arises from the fact that *both* plaintiff and defendant are claiming the reasonable use and enjoyment of their own land. A delicate balancing process must be used to determine unreasonableness. There are a number of factors that a court will consider.

Factors to Consider When Determining Unreasonableness

- the gravity and character of the harm
- the social value of the use that the plaintiff is making of the land
- the character of the locality
- the extent of the burden on the plaintiff of avoiding or minimizing the interference
- the motive of the defendant

- the social value of the defendant's conduct that led to the interference
- the extent of the burden on the defendant of avoiding or minimizing the interference

The gravity and character of the harm   The interference must be substantial. There is a certain level of annoyance that we are all required to endure in society. A restaurant next door that occasionally makes noises or a neighbor whose garden sprinkler occasionally throws drops of water on someone else's land does not constitute substantial interference with the use and enjoyment of land.

It is important to know the extent of the harm in order to assess its gravity. Has there been serious physical damage done to the land? Even if the physical condition of the land has not been altered, is the plaintiff experiencing significant mental discomfort as a result of what the defendant has done? Can such discomfort be passed off as the whining of a grouchy neighbor, or would most people agree that plaintiff's adverse reaction is understandable? The duration of the harm is also important to measure. Is the interference momentary or is it continuous?

The spectrum of the gravity and character of harm can be viewed in Figure 23–2. Of course, something less than total interruption can qualify as a private nuisance. How much less? This question can never be answered in isolation. All of the other factors, to be discussed, would also have to be examined.

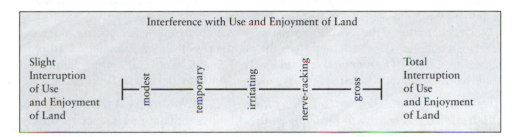

FIGURE 23–2
Spectrum of interference.

When the physical condition of the land has been damaged, a court will usually have little trouble measuring the gravity of the interference. When, however, the interference involves personal discomfort or annoyance alone, the difficulties of assessment are sometimes acute. A rough objective standard is used in such cases. The test is: How would a normal person in that locality view the interference? Would a person who is not unduly sensitive be substantially annoyed or disturbed? Suppose that a halfway house is opened next door to the plaintiff. The halfway house will provide rehabilitation services for men just released from prison as a transition to parole. The plaintiff fears that his children may be molested and that property values in the area will go down as a result of the halfway house. Has there been a substantial interference with the use and enjoyment of the plaintiff's land? This question is answered by determining how a normal person, who is not hypersensitive, would react to the halfway house. If the fears of the plaintiff are based on sheer speculation on what *might* happen, then a normal person would not consider the interference to be a serious one. If, however, the fears are based on substantive data, e.g., the fact that the men in the house will receive very little supervision from trained staff, or the fact that many of the ex-inmates have a history of child molestation, or the fact that property assessments have actually gone down due to the halfway house, then a normal person might agree that the interference is a substantial one.

The social value of the use that the plaintiff is making of the land   For what purpose is the plaintiff using his or her land? How valuable is that use to society? What is the **social value** of the use? (Social value means quality as measured by the general public good.) The following uses have considerable social value: use as a residence, use for business purposes, and use for recreational purposes. This is not to say that vacant or unoccupied land has no social value. In balancing all of the factors, however, a court is less likely to conclude that an interference with such land is unreasonable than an interference with land actively used for residential, commercial, or recreational purposes.

The character of the locality This factor is one of the most important in determining the reasonableness or unreasonableness of the interference. How suitable is the use the plaintiff is making of his or her land to the environment? Zoning ordinances are one measure of suitability. Even if no such ordinances exist, however, a court will still ask whether an area is used primarily or exclusively for residences, for heavy industry, for small businesses, for agriculture, etc. Having made this determination, a court will then use the following rough equation:

> If the plaintiff's use of his or her land is suitable to the locality, a court will be more likely to conclude that an interference with this use by the defendant is unreasonable than if the use is not suitable or compatible.

If, for example, the plaintiff is using land as a home in an area that is predominantly residential, a court will be more inclined to find that noise, odor, or other pollution from a nearby business is unreasonable than if the area is predominantly commercial. Of course, the equation becomes more difficult to apply when an area consists of a significant mixture of residential, commercial, and recreational structures, such as in many of our cities where use patterns change over the years. When there is such a mixture, it simply means that a plaintiff cannot be as sensitive to interferences as a plaintiff living in a purer or more homogeneous area.

The character of the locality can also be looked at from the perspective of the defendant's conduct. How compatible is the conduct with the predominant nature of the environment? The more incompatible it is, the more likely that a court would find that the interference with the plaintiff's use and enjoyment of land is unreasonable.

The extent of the burden on the plaintiff of avoiding or minimizing the interference A court will probably be unwilling to find an interference by the defendant to be unreasonable if the burden on the plaintiff of avoiding or minimizing the interference is modest. The plaintiff, in effect, has an obligation to avoid the consequences of the defendant's tort when it is practical to do so. Suppose, for example, that all the plaintiff had to do to prevent occasional factory odors from coming into the house was to close some of the windows a few times during the week. The minor nature of this burden would weigh against calling the interference unreasonable. On the other hand, if the only way for the plaintiff to minimize or avoid the interference were to rebuild the house or business or to move away, then the substantial nature of the burden might help to tip the scale toward concluding that the interference is unreasonable.

The motive of the defendant Why has the defendant interfered with the use and enjoyment of the plaintiff's land? If it can be shown that the defendant acted out of spite to harm the plaintiff, then it is highly likely that a court will conclude that any significant interference is unreasonable. On the other hand, if the interference is simply the product of the defendant's pursuit of his or her own self-interest, unreasonableness may be more difficult to establish.

The social value of the defendant's conduct that led to the interference Just as we needed to ask about the social value of the plaintiff's use of his or her land, so too we must ask about the social utility of the defendant's conduct that produced the interference. Conduct can have social utility even if the defendant is acting for his or her own private interests, e.g., using his or her backyard for a barbecue or running a machine in a farm or other business. The question is rarely: does the defendant's conduct have social value or utility? Rather, the question is: *how much* social value or utility does it have? How much is the general public good advanced by the conduct? Operating a hospital or school has high social value. Operating a farm or living in a home also has social value. The court must assess where on the scale the activity falls. The greater the social value, the less likely that a court will conclude that the conduct or condition causing the interference is unreasonable. This does not mean, however, that a cancer-curing hospital cannot commit a private nuisance. Again, all of the factors must be considered. The ultimate test is whether the social value or utility of the defendant's conduct outweighs the hardship of the interference the plaintiff is suffering.

The extent of the burden on the defendant of avoiding or minimizing the interference   What would the defendant have to do to stop or minimize the interference? Install an inexpensive shield? Close down? Radically change the nature of the business? The more minimal the burden, the more likely the court will find the continued interference to be unreasonable. This does not mean, however, that the defendant is home free simply by showing that the burden of avoiding or minimizing the interference would be great. The extent of the burden is but one factor that must be weighed.

ASSIGNMENT

23.2

Examine the following situations. What questions would you want answered in order to determine whether there has been an unreasonable interference with the use and enjoyment of land for purposes of establishing a private nuisance? (See General Instructions for the Investigation Strategy Assignment in Chapter 3.)

a. The plaintiff lives next door to a small nursing home. The home has a large air conditioner motor in the backyard. The plaintiff is very upset about the noise given off by this motor.

b. The defendant is an excellent mechanic. She works on cars as a hobby after her regular job hours. She frequently works on her car and the cars of her friends until late at night. The plaintiff, a neighbor, is bothered by the bright lights the defendant uses while working on the cars and by the constant coming and going of her friends who visit to talk about cars.

c. The local church runs a bingo game every Thursday night. This is extremely upsetting to the plaintiff, who lives next door to the church.

d. A factory employing five hundred people has a chimney that sends black smoke into the air. Particles in the smoke sometimes fall on the plaintiff's house. The plaintiff is worried that the particles will damage her property.

e. Tom lives two floors above Mary's apartment in a four-story apartment building. Mary is a cigarette smoker and her boyfriend smokes a cigar. Whenever either of them smokes, the secondhand smoke travels up through the walls into Tom's apartment. It also goes into several of Tom's windows when they are open.

---

2. What Are the Ways in Which a Private Nuisance Can Be Committed?

First, the unreasonable interference can be created negligently. Here, there is no intent to interfere. The defendant creates an unreasonable risk of interfering. Suppose, for example, the defendants dump what they think is harmless waste into a stream that flows through the plaintiff's land before going out to sea. In fact, the waste is not harmless. As a result, the plaintiff's land becomes totally useless. If the defendants had taken reasonable precautions, they would have discovered the harmful nature of the waste. The defendants have negligently created an unreasonable interference with the plaintiff's use and enjoyment of land.

Second, the unreasonable interference can be created intentionally. Intent here means that the defendant knows the interference will occur or has knowledge with substantial certainty that the interference will result from what the defendant does or fails to do. If the defendant, for example, knows that foul pollutants are coming from its factory to the plaintiff's land, the defendant, in the eyes of the law, has intended this interference.

Finally, the unreasonable interference can be created through conduct that would impose strict liability—an abnormally dangerous condition or activity, such as blasting.

3. Who Can Sue for a Private Nuisance?

Since private nuisance protects the use and enjoyment of private land, anyone who has rights to the use and enjoyment of the land can sue for a private nuisance. This includes individuals in possession of the land who are claiming an interest in the land as well as their families. Landlords who do not live on or use the land themselves can bring the suit when the damages caused by the defendant are permanent.

4. What Remedies Can Be Obtained When a Private Nuisance Has Been Committed?

Damages can be awarded for the harm caused by the private nuisance. The measure of damages is usually the difference between the value of the land before the harm and its value after the harm. Some courts will permit a plaintiff to choose as the measure of damages the **cost of restoration.** Additional compensatory damages include the loss in the rental value of the land, the loss of the plaintiff's own personal use of the land, and an amount to compensate the plaintiff for any discomfort or annoyance that has been experienced.

There are times when an award of damages is not adequate, particularly when the interference is threatened or is continuous. The issue will be whether the plaintiff can obtain an **injunction** against the defendants to prevent or stop the interference. (An award of damages is a legal remedy; an injunction is an equitable remedy. A court will not consider equitable remedies unless it determines that there are no adequate legal remedies, referred to as "no adequate remedy at law.") Most courts are reluctant to grant the equitable relief of an injunction because of its drastic nature. The court must first be satisfied that an award of damages will not be adequate to remedy the problem. If the interference is threatened, the court will want to be convinced that there is a high likelihood that the interference will in fact occur. The effect of an injunction could be to close down a defendant's business. This may lead to the loss of many jobs. Hence, before a court will grant an injunction, it will weigh (a) the economic hardship that will be suffered by the defendant due to an injunction, and (b) the nature of the interference the plaintiff is suffering. The court will also consider the hardship that the entire community might suffer if the injunction is granted. In short, the court will go through a similar kind of analysis on the injunction issue that it went through to determine whether the interference was unreasonable. A court may decide that the interference is unreasonable, but that injunctive relief against it is unwarranted because it is too drastic. If so, the court will permit the defendant to proceed, but require damages to be paid to the plaintiff. This is an unsatisfactory result, because the practical effect of refusing to grant the injunction is a kind of court "permission" to continue with an unreasonable interference with the plaintiff's land.

Another remedy that might be available is **self-help** in which the victim of a tort takes corrective steps on his or her own without resort to the courts. This would include the common law privilege to **abate the nuisance.** This is the privilege to take reasonable steps to correct a nuisance that is interfering with the use and enjoyment of your land.

> **EXAMPLE:** Tom and Mary live next to each other. When Tom returns late one evening from a two-month business trip, he is surprised to find Mary's car parked in his driveway, preventing him from getting into his garage. Tom goes over to Mary's house to complain, but no one is home. He then gets in Mary's car, releases the emergency brake, and rolls it into the street curb away from the front of his driveway entrance.

Tom has properly exercised his privilege to abate a nuisance. Aggrieved parties, such as Tom, must act within a reasonable amount of time after they discover interference with the use and enjoyment of their land. If practical, they must give notice to the wrongdoers to determine whether they will remove the interference on their own. Only reasonable force can be used to abate the nuisance. One cannot blow up a polluting factory in order to stop the flow of offending smoke.

5. What Defenses Are Available to a Defendant?

Contributory negligence   The **contributory negligence** of the plaintiff in helping to cause his or her own injury or interference is a defense if the defendant produced the private nuisance negligently. It normally would not be a defense, however, if the defendant acted recklessly or intentionally in causing the nuisance. If the state has adopted **comparative negligence,** the damages would be apportioned according to the extent of the defendant's negligence and the plaintiff's negligence as determined by the comparative negligence formula followed in the state. (On comparative negligence, see Chapter 17.)

Assumption of the risk   **Assumption of the risk** is a defense if the plaintiff voluntarily accepted a risk from the nuisance that he or she fully understands. It is not often that a defendant can establish that the plaintiff assumed the risk of a private nuisance. The defense is more frequently raised in cases of a public nuisance, to be discussed shortly.

Suppose that the plaintiff has "moved to the nuisance," e.g., the plaintiff moves to an industrial town knowing that a lot of noise and pollution exists in that town. Hasn't the plaintiff assumed the risk of the private nuisance? No. A plaintiff is not barred from complaining about a nuisance simply because the nuisance was there before the plaintiff arrived. To say that someone has "moved to the nuisance" may beg the question of whether there is in fact a private nuisance. All of the factors discussed previously must be analyzed to determine whether there is an unreasonable interference, e.g., the suitability of the activity to the locale.

An interference may be unreasonable in an exclusively residential area, but quite reasonable in an industrial area. On the separate question of whether a court will grant an injunction against what it has found to be a nuisance, the fact that the plaintiff has "come to the nuisance" will be a factor to be weighed *against* the granting of the injunction. This is different, however, from the problem of whether a private nuisance in fact exists.

Mitigation of damages   If the plaintiff knows that the defendant's private nuisance has resulted in the poisoning of the plaintiff's drinking water, the plaintiff cannot proceed to drink the water anyway or continue to let his or her animals drink it. The defendant will be responsible for the poisoning of the water, but not for the consequences of the poisoning that the plaintiff could have eliminated. The plaintiff has failed to **mitigate the consequences** or to mitigate the damages. The rule of **avoidable consequences** requires the plaintiff to take reasonable steps to avoid the damages or other harmful consequences of the defendant's tort.

Official authorization   Special statutes, ordinances, or regulations may exist that either authorize or require the defendant to engage in the activity that is later being challenged as a nuisance. For example, zoning ordinances authorize certain kinds of activities and structures, and statutes may exist requiring public utilities to transport dangerous substances. Such official sanction, however, is never an authorization to carry on the activity carelessly or negligently. Damages and injunctive relief will be granted only to the extent that harm is caused or threatened by carrying on the activity in an unreasonable manner. The entire operation will rarely be enjoined, because that would have the effect of rescinding the official authorization.

Even if the defendant is not conducting the activity unreasonably, a plaintiff may have an argument that the official sanction of the activity has, in effect, resulted in a **taking of property** for which the government is responsible and therefore liable for just compensation.

Public Nuisance

We examine public nuisance by the same five basic questions we used to discuss a private nuisance:

1. What is the nature of a public nuisance? What type of harm does it cover?
2. How is it created?
3. Who can sue?
4. What remedies are available?
5. What defenses are available?

For some of the questions, the answers are very similar to those given for private nuisance. The answers to the first and third questions, however, are substantially different.

1. What Is the Nature of a Public Nuisance and What Type of Harm Does It Cover?

A public nuisance often has nothing to do with the use and enjoyment of land. It is an unreasonable interference with a right that is common to the public.

EXAMPLES:

- keeping diseased animals that will be sold for food
- operating a house of prostitution
- operating an illegal gambling parlor
- obstructing a public highway
- polluting a public river
- wiretapping conversations in a judge's chambers or in a jury room
- maintaining unsafe apartment buildings used by many people
- using public profanity

Very often, the conduct of the defendant constitutes a crime.

To be a public nuisance, there must be some public right involved. Every member of the public does not have to be actually affected by it. If only a small number of people are affected, however, there is usually no public nuisance. To obstruct a public highway, e.g., by leaving a truck on it or by causing boulders to be placed on it, is a public nuisance, because there is a public right to use the highway, and this right is taken away from everyone who tries to use it.

The interference with the public right must be unreasonable. If the defendant has violated a specific statute, ordinance, or regulation, there is usually little difficulty establishing unreasonableness. Otherwise, many of the same factors described earlier to determine the reasonableness of an alleged private nuisance must also be used to determine the reasonableness of an alleged public nuisance, e.g., the gravity of the interference and the burden of removal or mitigation.

ASSIGNMENT
23.3

Three gun manufacturers make 95 percent of the guns used in the commission of a crime in a large city. They spend a great deal of money advertising the guns in this city even though they know about the high crime rate with guns in the city. They also know that many individuals there buy hundreds of guns at one time even though these individuals are not connected to gun stores. The police believe that they sell the guns to minors, ex-felons, and others who cannot obtain a gun permit. Have the manufacturers committed a public nuisance? (See General Instructions for the Legal Analysis Assignment in Chapter 2.)

2. What Are the Ways in Which a Public Nuisance Can Be Created?

Negligence: The defendant can negligently create the public nuisance, e.g., carelessly allowing logs to fall off a truck, which obstruct a public highway.

Intent: Here the defendant knows that the interference with a public right will occur or is substantially certain that it will occur based on what the defendant does or fails to do, e.g., the defendant knows that the pollutants being poured into a lake will make the lake unusable by the public for fishing.

Abnormally dangerous condition or activity: The defendant, for example, conducts blasting in an area, which causes substantial damage to all surrounding buildings through vibrations.

Violation of a statute, ordinance, or regulation: The defendant, for example, opens a house of prostitution.

3. Who Can Sue for the Public Nuisance?

Because public rights are involved, a public official can always either bring a civil action or a criminal prosecution against the defendant.

When can a *private* citizen bring a suit for a public nuisance? A private person can sue only when he or she suffered in a way that is different from every other member of the public affected by the public nuisance. The plaintiff must have suffered special or particular damage. The harm must be different in kind. If the plaintiff has "only" suffered more of the same harm everyone else has suffered (a difference in degree only), very few courts will allow the plaintiff to bring an independent action for the public nuisance. If the defendant obstructs a public highway resulting in the need for a substantial detour, the citizens who must suffer this inconvenience have *not* suffered an inconvenience that is different in kind from everyone else. Hence, a private suit cannot be brought. All that a citizen can do is ask the public authorities to take the defendant to court. Suppose, however, that one citizen crashes into the obstruction. This individual has suffered personal or property damage that is different in kind from having to make a detour. Such an individual, therefore, *can* bring a private action for the public nuisance. Also, if the plaintiff can show special financial damage that other members of the public do not suffer, the plaintiff will often be able to bring the public nuisance action.

Some public nuisances are also private nuisances when the conduct of the defendant interferes with a public right *and* interferes with the use and enjoyment of a particular plaintiff's land. For example, the defendant builds a dam that prevents the public from using the water that would otherwise flow into a lake used for recreational purposes, and the dam also floods the plaintiff's land; or the defendant opens a gambling hall next door to the plaintiff, whose peace of mind is substantially disrupted as a result.

The violation of some environmental statutes may constitute a public nuisance. It is important to check whether such statutes allow a private citizen to sue whoever caused the violation. If so, the private citizen has **standing,** which is the right to bring an action because of the sufficiency of one's personal interest in the outcome of proposed litigation or because of a special statute that gives this right. The private citizen may be able to act on behalf of a class or group of similarly situated citizens. (On class actions, see Chapter 20.)

4. What Remedies Can Be Obtained When a Public Nuisance Has Been Committed?

When a public official brings the public nuisance action, the remedies often include a fine or imprisonment. The government may also be able to collect damages for harm that may have been done to public property.

As with a private nuisance, it is sometimes difficult to obtain an injunction against a public nuisance, particularly when a crime has been committed or is threatened. There is an elaborate trial procedure governing crimes that a court cannot bypass through an injunction against a public nuisance allegedly involving criminal behavior. Where this problem does not exist, a court will go through a balancing analysis similar to the one it uses to decide whether to issue an injunction against a private nuisance.

Self-help is also a possible remedy—the privilege to abate a nuisance. Only reasonable force can be used, and the steps taken by the plaintiff to stop the nuisance must occur very soon after the nuisance is discovered and after notice is given to the defendant, unless such notice is impractical under the circumstances.

Statutes in some states allow officials to remove vehicles and other objects that constitute a public nuisance. In Michigan, for example, a man's car was forfeited as a public nuisance after he engaged in sexual activity in the car with a prostitute. The man's wife, who was a co-owner of the car, argued unsuccessfully that her half ownership in the car should not have been forfeited since she never knew her wayward husband used the car for this purpose.[2]

5. What Defenses Are Available to a Defendant in a Public Nuisance Case?

The four main categories of defenses discussed under private nuisance apply equally to public nuisances:

- contributory negligence (or comparative negligence)

- assumption of the risk

- mitigation of damages

- official authorization

CASE

Armory Park Neighborhood Assn v. Episcopal Community Services
148 Ariz. 1, 712 P.2d 914 (1985)
Supreme Court of Arizona

Background: *St. Martin's Center is run by Episcopal Community Services (ECS). The Center operates a free food distribution program for indigent persons in Tucson. The Armory Park Neighborhood Association sought an injunction against this program as a public nuisance. Although the program did not violate any zoning or health codes, the trial court granted a preliminary injunction against the Center on the ground that its activities constituted a public and a private nuisance. The case is now on appeal before the Supreme Court of Arizona.*

Decision on Appeal: *The injunction against the Center's free meal program is appropriate.*

OPINION OF COURT

Justice FELDMAN delivered the opinion of the court . . .

Before the Center opened, the area had been primarily residential with a few small businesses. When the Center began operating in December 1982, many transients crossed the area daily on their way to and from the Center. Although the Center was only open from 5:00 to 6:00 P.M., patrons lined up well before this hour and often lingered in the neighborhood long after finishing their meal. The Center rented an adjacent fenced lot for a waiting area and organized neighborhood cleaning projects, but the trial judge apparently felt these efforts were inadequate to control the activity stemming from the Center. Transients frequently trespassed onto residents' yards, sometimes urinating, defecating, drinking and littering on the residents' property. A few broke into storage areas and unoccupied homes, and some asked residents for handouts. The number of arrests in the area increased dramatically. Many residents were frightened or annoyed by the transients and altered their lifestyles to avoid them. . . .

We have previously distinguished public and private nuisances. In *City of Phoenix v. Johnson,* 51 Ariz. 115, 75 P.2d 30 (1938), we noted that a nuisance is public when it affects rights of "citizens as a part of the public, while a private nuisance is one which affects a single individual or a definite number of persons on the enjoyment of some private right which is not common to the public." Id. at 123, 75 P.2d 34. A public nuisance must also affect a considerable number of people. . . .

---

[2]*Michigan ex rel. Wayne County Prosecutor v. Bennis,* 447 Mich. 719, 527 N.W.2d 483 (1994); *Bennis v. Michigan,* 516 U.S. 442, 116 S. Ct. 994, 134 L. Ed. 2d 68 (1996).

Defendant claims that its business should not be held responsible for acts committed by its patrons off the premises of the Center. It argues that since it has no control over the patrons when they are not on the Center's premises, it cannot be enjoined because of their acts. We do not believe this position is supported either by precedent or theory.

In *Shamhart v. Morrison Cafeteria Co.,* 159 Fla. 629, 32 So. 2d 727 (1947), the defendant operated a well frequented cafeteria. Each day customers waiting to enter the business would line up on the sidewalk, blocking the entrances to the neighboring establishments. The dissenting justices argued that the defendant had not actually caused the lines to form and that the duty to prevent the harm to the plaintiffs should be left to the police through regulation of the public streets. The majority of the court rejected this argument, and remanded the case for a determination of the damages. See, also, *Reid v. Brodsky,* 397 Pa. 463, 156 A.2d 334 (1959) (operation of a bar enjoined because its patrons were often noisy and intoxicated; they frequently used the neighboring properties for toilet purposes and sexual misconduct); *Barrett v. Lopez,* 57 N.M. 697, 262 P.2d 981, 983 (1953) (operation of a dance hall enjoined, the court finding that "mere possibility of relief from another source [e.g., the police] does not relieve the courts of their responsibilities"); *Wade v. Fuller,* 12 Utah 2d 299, 365 P.2d 802 (1961) (operation of drive-in cafe enjoined where patrons created disturbances to nearby residents); *McQuade v. Tucson Tiller Apartments,* 25 Ariz. App. 312, 543 P.2d 150 (1975) (music concerts at mall designed to attract customers enjoined because of increased crowds and noise in residential area). . . .

Since the rules of a civilized society require us to tolerate our neighbors, the law requires our neighbors to keep their activities within the limits of what is tolerable by a reasonable person. However, what is reasonably tolerable must be tolerated; not all interferences with public rights are public nuisances. As Dean Prosser explains, "[t]he law does not concern itself with trifles, or seek to remedy all of the petty annoyances and disturbances of everyday life in a civilized community even from conduct committed with knowledge that annoyance and inconvenience will result." Prosser, W. and W. P. Keeton, *Handbook on the Law of Torts,* § 88, at 626 (5th ed. 1984). Thus, to constitute a nuisance, the complained-of interference must be substantial, intentional and unreasonable under the circumstances. *Restatement (Second) of Torts,* § 826 comment c and § 821F. Our courts have generally used a balancing test in deciding the reasonableness of an interference. The trial court should look at the utility and reasonableness of the conduct and balance these factors against the extent of harm inflicted and the nature of the affected neighborhood. We noted in the early case of *MacDonald v. Perry:*

> What might amount to a serious nuisance in one locality by reason of the density of the population, or character of the neighborhood affected, may in another place and under different surroundings be deemed proper and unobjectionable. What amount of annoyance or inconvenience caused by others in the lawful use of their property will constitute a nuisance

depends upon varying circumstances and cannot be precisely defined.

32 Ariz. 39, 50, 255 P. 494 (1927).

The trial judge did not ignore the balancing test and was well aware of the social utility of defendant's operation. His words are illuminating:

> It is distressing . . . [that this activity] should be restrained. Providing for the poor and the homeless is certainly a worthwhile, praisworthy [sic] activity. It is particularly distressing to this Court because it [defendant] has no control over those who are attracted to the kitchen while they are either coming or leaving the premises. However, the right to the comfortable enjoyment of one's property is something that another's activities should not affect, the harm being suffered by the Armory Park Neighborhood and the residents therein is irreparable and substantial, for which they have no adequate legal remedy. . . .

We believe that a determination made by weighing and balancing conflicting interests or principles is truly one which lies within the discretion of the trial judge. We defer to that discretion here. The evidence of the multiple trespasses upon and defacement of the residents' property supports the trial court's conclusion that the interference caused by defendant's operation was unreasonable despite its charitable cause.

The common law has long recognized that the usefulness of a particular activity may outweigh the inconveniences, discomforts and changes it causes some persons to suffer. We, too, acknowledge the social value of the Center. Its charitable purpose, that of feeding the hungry, is entitled to greater deference than pursuits of lesser intrinsic value. It appears from the record that ECS purposes in operating the Center were entirely admirable. However, even admirable ventures may cause unreasonable interferences. See e.g., *Assembly of God Church of Tahoka v. Bradley,* 196 S.W.2d 696 (Tex. Civ. App. 1946). We do not believe that the law allows the costs of a charitable enterprise to be visited in their entirety upon the residents of a single neighborhood. The problems of dealing with the unemployed, the homeless and the mentally ill are also matters of community or governmental responsibility.

ECS argues that its compliance with City of Tucson zoning regulations is a conclusive determination of reasonableness. We agree that compliance with zoning provisions has some bearing in nuisance cases. . . . We decline, however, to find that ECS' compliance with the applicable zoning provisions precludes a court from enjoining its activities. The equitable power of the judiciary exists independent of statute. Although zoning and criminal provisions are binding with respect to the type of activity, they do not limit the power of a court acting in equity to enjoin an unreasonable, albeit permitted, activity as a public nuisance. . . .

The trial court's order granting the preliminary injunction is affirmed. By affirming the trial court's preliminary orders, we do not require that he close the Center permanently. It is of course, within the equitable discretion of the trial court to fashion a less severe remedy, if possible. . . .

a. Suppose that a church operated the same kind of free meal program in New York City. Would the result be the same?

b. What is the logical consequence of this opinion? That programs such as those operated by St. Martin's Center will always be kept in the inner city and never be allowed in the suburbs?

TRADITIONAL NEGLIGENCE LIABILITY

In this section, we consider negligence liability to persons who are injured on someone's premises or in the immediate environment. In Chapters 13 through 16, we studied the elements of negligence:

- duty
- breach of duty
- proximate cause
- damages

The major headache in the area of **premises liability** is the first element: duty. In Chapter 13 the general rule on duty is stated as follows:

> Whenever one's conduct creates a foreseeable risk of injury or damage to someone else's person or property, a duty of reasonable care arises to take precautions to prevent that injury or damage.

When discussing the negligence liability of occupiers of land, this general rule on duty is unfortunately riddled with exceptions depending on the status of the plaintiff:

- adult trespasser
- child trespasser
- licensee
- invitee

and the status of the defendant:

- owner-seller
- owner-buyer
- tenant

Every time the status of the plaintiff or defendant changes, we must ask whether the court will apply a different standard of duty (other than the general duty of reasonable care) for purposes of negligence liability.

A few courts have recently discarded all these special rules and exceptions, and have declared that the duty is reasonable care for all categories of plaintiffs and defendants. The status of the plaintiff or defendant is simply one of the factors to be taken into consideration in deciding whether there has been a breach of this duty. The status of the plaintiff as trespasser, licensee, or invitee, for example, would be relevant solely in determining the extent to which their presence on the land was foreseeable to the defendant. A separate duty would not exist for each category of plaintiff under this minority view. Because most courts, however, do not take this position, we must examine each status separately.

Throughout the discussion, we will be asking whether a duty of **reasonable care** is owed by the defendant, and if not, what *lesser standard of care* is owed. In some situations, it may be that *no duty* of care is owed, so that the defendant will not be liable for the injury suffered by the plaintiff.

The following themes will guide our discussion:

1. the duty of occupiers of land to persons outside the land
2. the duty of occupiers of land to trespassers, licensees, and invitees on the land
3. the special problems of the seller and buyer of land (vendor and vendee)
4. the special problems of the landlord and tenant (lessor and lessee)

By **occupier** we mean anyone in possession of the land claiming a right to possession, e.g., an owner personally using the premises, a tenant, or an adverse possessor.

1. Persons Outside the Land

A person traveling in front of the defendant's land or living close by can be injured in a number of ways. The injury can come from a natural condition on the defendant's land (e.g., a tree limb falls on the plaintiff who is walking on a sidewalk), or from a non-natural condition on the defendant's land (e.g., a building collapses on a car parked on a street in front of the defendant's land), or from some business or personal activity taking place on the defendant's land (e.g., a bucket falls from a plank used by painters, and the bucket hits a pedestrian). See Figure 23–3 for the defendant's duty with respect to each category.

The Condition or Activity	The Duty Owed
1. *Natural conditions on the defendant's land* (e.g., natural lakes, trees, rocks)	1. Generally, the defendant owes *no* duty of care to prevent injury to persons outside the land who might be injured by natural conditions on the defendant's land. If, however, the defendant owns *trees* in an *urban* area, he or she does owe a *duty of reasonable care* to inspect the trees and make sure that they are safe to persons outside the land. In most states, there is *no* duty owed if the trees are in a *rural* area.
2. *Non-natural or artificial conditions on the defendant's land* (e.g., fence, swimming pool, building)	2. The defendant owes a *duty of reasonable care* to prevent injury to persons outside the land who might be injured by non-natural or artificial conditions on the defendant's land.
3. *Business or personal activity taking place on the defendant's land* (e.g., steam blasting the wall of a building)	3. The defendant owes a *duty of reasonable care* to prevent injury to persons outside the land who might be injured by business or personal activities being conducted by the defendant on the land.

FIGURE 23–3
Standard of care owed by occupiers of land to persons outside the land.

The rules in Figure 23–3 apply if the injury results from anything that the defendant's employees do or fail to do within the scope of their employment. Suppose, however, the defendant hires an **independent contractor** over whom the defendant usually has little control concerning the manner in which the work is done. If injury occurs to plaintiffs not on the land due to the activity of independent contractors on the land, the independent contractor and not the defendant will be liable for the negligence. An exception exists when the defendant hires the independent contractor to do inherently dangerous work. The defendant will be liable for injuries resulting from such activities. When, however, the injury results from the manner or method of work of the independent contractor not involved in inherently dangerous work, the defendant-occupier of the land is not liable.

FIGURE 23–4
Trespasser, licensee, and invitee.

Trespasser: A person who enters the land without the consent of the occupier and without any privilege to do so.

Licensee: A person who enters the land for his or her own purposes, but with the express or implied consent of the occupier. A licensee does not enter to pursue a purpose of the occupier.

Invitee: A person who enters the land upon the express or implied invitation of the occupier in order to use the land for the purposes for which it is held open to the public or to pursue the business of the occupier.

2. Trespassers, Licensees, and Invitees

Everyone who comes on the land will fall into one of the three categories of trespasser, licensee, or invitee. (See the definitions in Figure 23–4.) The highest standard of care is owed the invitee, who must be accorded full reasonable-care treatment by the land occupier. Although the trespasser is given the lowest standard of care of the three, there are important exceptions that have the effect of elevating the amount of care owed the trespasser.

Trespassers

Trespassers have neither consent nor privilege to be on the land or on designated portions of the land. The privileges would include necessity, recapture of chattels (for a discussion of these self-help privileges, see Chapter 27), and abatement of a nuisance.

The general rule is that the occupier owes *no duty of care* to a trespasser unless the trespasser falls into one of the following categories:

- discovered trespasser anywhere on the land
- foreseeable constant trespassers on limited areas of the land
- child trespasser anywhere on the land

Discovered trespasser anywhere on the land   An occupier cannot commit any *intentional* harm on a known trespasser unless the occupier has a privilege (e.g., self-defense, defense of others) to use such force. A spring gun, for example, cannot be used to catch an unsuspecting trespasser. (See *Katko v. Briney* in Chapter 27 on the use of such guns.) What about *negligence* liability? A known trespasser is owed a duty of reasonable care by the occupier. If, for example, a railroad engineer sees a trespasser ahead, reasonable care must be used to avoid hitting the trespasser. Actual knowledge of the trespasser is not necessary as long as the occupier has enough information to lead a reasonable person to know that a trespasser is present.

Reasonable care does not mean that the occupier must make the land safe for the trespasser. It simply means that once discovered, the occupier must use reasonable care to avoid injuring the trespasser. Ordinary care under the circumstances will be sufficient. A warning, for example, may be required to alert the trespasser to dangerous activities or conditions on the land, which the trespasser might not be expected to notice. No such warning would be needed, however, for natural conditions on the land such as a lake or clearly visible ice.

A few courts take a more simplistic view and argue that the only duty of the occupier to the known trespasser is to avoid injuring the trespasser by willful or wanton conduct.

Foreseeable constant trespassers on limited portions of the land   The occupier has a duty of reasonable care to discover and provide protection for trespassers who frequently enter limited areas of the land. For example, a railroad may know (or should know) that large numbers of people regularly walk across the track at a designated spot. The area must be limited and the trespassing in that area must be constant. As with the known trespasser, the occupier does not have a duty to inspect his or her land in order to make it injury-proof. The duty is to use reasonable care under the circumstances, which may include a warning, fencing, extra lighting—but only on the limited area where constant trespassers are foreseeable. The more dangerous the condition or activity in that area, the greater the precaution the occupier must take to prevent the injury. No such precautions are usually needed for natural conditions on the limited area of the land that the trespassers can be expected to protect themselves against. If the trespasser is injured in spite of the reasonable steps taken by the occupier, the latter will not be liable for negligence.

Child trespassers anywhere on the land   Children are given special protection in the law of premises liability. A **child** is usually defined as someone who is too young to appreciate the dangers that could be involved in a given situation. There is no age limit that sets the boundary line for the level of immaturity that is required, but in the vast majority of cases that have provided this special protection, the plaintiff has been under fifteen.

The special protection is embodied in the **attractive nuisance doctrine,** which says a duty of reasonable care is owed to prevent injury:

1. to a trespassing child unable to appreciate the danger
2. from an artificial condition or activity on land
3. to which the child can be expected to be drawn or attracted

The word "nuisance" is used in its generic sense of something that is mischievous; it has no reference to the rules on private and public nuisance discussed earlier.

A more modern statement of the "attractive nuisance" rule or doctrine has been provided by the *Restatement of Torts*[3], which provides that an occupier of land is liable for physical harm caused by artificial conditions on the land if:

1. the artificial condition is on a place on the land that the occupier knows or has reason to know that children will trespass upon, and
2. the occupier knows or has reason to know that the artificial condition will involve an unreasonable risk of serious injury to the trespassing children, and
3. the trespassing children are too young to discover the artificial condition or to appreciate the danger within it, and
4. the utility to the occupier of maintaining the condition and the burden or inconvenience of eliminating the danger are slight when compared to the risk to the trespassing children, and
5. the occupier fails to take those reasonable steps that would protect the child.

This list is a specific application of the traditional breach-of-duty equation we examined in Chapter 14, which balances the factors that help the court determine what is and is not unreasonable conduct. (See Figure 14–4 in Chapter 14 and Figure 23–5 here.)

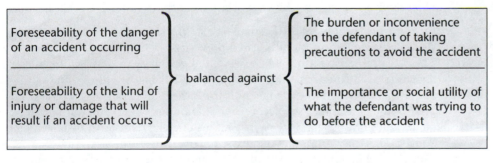

FIGURE 23–5
Breach-of-duty equation.

The foreseeability of serious injury to the child is measured or weighed against what the defendant was trying to accomplish by the artificial condition, and the burden or inconvenience on the defendant to protect the child against this condition.

[3]*Restatement (Second) of Torts* § 339 (1965).

Artificial conditions include tracks, vehicles, rope, fences, barns, and factories. Under the *Restatement*'s formula, the attractiveness of the condition is important mainly on the issue of the foreseeability of the child's presence.

The duty of reasonable care is usually not applied when the child is injured by natural conditions on the land (e.g., lakes, rivers, and natural rock formations) unless the defendant has significantly altered these conditions through strip-mining or other processes.

ASSIGNMENT

23.5

What questions would you investigate to decide whether the defendant in the following cases owed and breached a duty of reasonable care to the plaintiff? (See General Instructions for the Investigation Strategy Assignment in Chapter 3.)

a. A ten-year-old boy is trespassing on the defendant's land. He leans against a fence on the land and badly injures his back against a protruding nail.

b. A nine-year-old girl is trespassing on the defendant's land. She watches workers climb a pole on the land. After the workers leave, the girl puts on a pair of spiked or cleated shoes that she owns and tries to climb the pole. She falls and severely injures herself.

Licensees

Licensees are on the land with the express or implied permission of the occupier. The licensees, however, are present for their own purposes.

> **EXAMPLES:**
>
> - someone taking a shortcut through the land
> - someone soliciting money for charity
> - a trespasser who has been allowed to remain, e.g., a loiterer
> - a person who comes to borrow a tool
> - a social guest, even if invited

The last example has caused some difficulty. Because **social guests** are invited, one would normally tend to classify them as invitees. Only a few courts, however, take this position. In most states, a social guest is a mere licensee, no matter how much urging the occupier may have used to get the guest to come and even though the guest may perform some incidental chores or tasks for the occupier while there. A **business guest,** however, who comes for the purpose of doing business with the occupier, *is* an invitee.

What standard of care is owed by the occupier to the licensee?

1. First, the occupier owes the licensee at least the same duty of care that he or she owes the trespasser, as discussed previously.
2. The occupier must warn the licensee of dangerous natural *or* artificial conditions (a) if the owner knows about these conditions or has reason to know about them—actual knowledge, and (b) if they are **latent** so that the occupier should expect that the licensee would not discover them. (Note: the occupier does not have a duty to inspect his or her premises to discover such danger. This duty to inspect *will* exist for the protection of an invitee.)
3. Third, if the condition is extremely dangerous, the occupier's duty may be to take active, reasonable precautions to protect the licensee rather than to simply warn him or her of the condition.
4. Fourth, for any activities being conducted on the land, the occupier owes the licensee a duty of reasonable care to avoid injuring the licensee, which may call for a warning or for more active safety precautions.

Suppose that there is a fence on the land in a state of disrepair. The occupier does not know or have reason to know about this artificial condition but should know about it if he or she were acting reasonably. The licensee is injured when the fence falls on him or her. On these facts, the occupier would not be liable to the licensee for negligence. The occupier has no duty to inspect for dangerous *conditions.* If the occupier has actual knowledge of the dangerous condition (artificial or natural), then he or she must either warn the licensee of it or make it safe, depending on the nature of the danger. *Activities,* such as operating machinery on the land, however, call for reasonable care.

If the occupier knows that third persons are on the land who are likely to injure the licensee, the occupier has a duty to at least warn the licensee of the presence of such third persons, e.g., known criminals or individuals who have told the occupier that they want to harm the licensee.

An analogous situation involves automobiles. If the social guest is a licensee in an automobile, the same rules apply: the driver has a duty to use reasonable care in driving the car (an activity), but has no duty to inspect the car to make sure that it is safe. When the driver knows of defective conditions in the car, he or she must warn the guest of them. As indicated in Chapter 14, however, there are automobile guest statutes in some states that change this common law, often making the driver liable only for wanton or reckless conduct in driving the car. A **passenger**, however, is often treated differently than a mere social guest. In many states, a duty of reasonable care is owed passengers. To be a passenger, the plaintiff's presence must confer some benefit on the driver other than the benefit of his or her company or the mere sharing of expenses, although the latter can be a factor to show that the plaintiff is a passenger if other benefit to the driver is also shown. If the plaintiff is paying for the ride, or if the driver is trying to solicit business from the plaintiff, the latter is a passenger to whom a duty of reasonable care is owed.

ASSIGNMENT

23.6

A door-to-door salesperson slips and falls on a child's skate upon approaching the front door of a residence. What standard of care would the occupier owe this person? (See General Instructions for the Legal Analysis Assignment in Chapter 2.)

Invitees

The highest degree of care by the occupier of land is owed an invitee. An invitee is someone present on the land with the express or implied invitation of the occupier to use the land for a purpose for which it is open to the public or to use the land to pursue the business of the occupier.

EXAMPLES:

- a customer in a department store
- someone browsing in a department store, even if nothing is purchased
- a user of a laundromat to wash clothes (a person who is present in the laundromat to wait for a bus or to get out of the rain, however, is probably a licensee only)
- someone attending a free public lecture on religion
- a user of a library (a person who is there to meet a friend, however, is probably only a licensee)
- a patron at a restaurant, theater, amusement park, or similar establishment
- someone who goes to a garage to find out if it sells a certain part for a car

There must be an element of invitation that is much stronger than mere permission or consent that the person be on the land. The invitation is an implied or direct statement of a desire by the occupier that the person be present. A greater standard of care is owed to an invitee than to a trespasser or a licensee because the invitation justifies the invitee's belief that the premises are safe.

Public employees injured on the premises often pose a problem. They include police officers, fire fighters, sanitation workers, postal workers, and meter readers. What is their status? If they are not present in their official capacity within working hours, their status is determined like that of any other citizen. Indeed, they could have the status of trespasser. When present in an *official* role, are they invitees or licensees?

In most states, police officers and fire fighters are licensees only, to whom a duty of reasonable care is owed for activities conducted on the premises, but no duty concerning dangerous conditions unknown to the occupier. The theory behind this position is that these public employees are likely to go to parts of the premises that the occupier has no reason to expect, especially in emergency situations. As to such areas, the occupier has made no implied or direct representation that they are safe. Other public official entrants, however, are given the status of invitees on the somewhat strained theory they are present for a business purpose of the occupier.

A few states disregard this distinction and classify all public entrants as invitees.

ASSIGNMENT

23.7

Are the following individuals invitees, licensees, or trespassers? (See General Instructions for the Legal Analysis Assignment in Chapter 2.)

a. Tom enters a restaurant solely to use its bathroom. He slips on the bathroom floor.

b. Mary wants to visit a friend who is staying at a hotel. She goes to the room of the friend. While there, she is assaulted by another guest.

c. Fred goes to a railroad station to meet a passenger. While there, he falls over a hose on the ramp.

d. Linda goes to a soccer game to pass out religious literature. She falls down a flight of steps.

e. Jim is in a restaurant eating. He notices that there are cries of distress coming from the kitchen. He passes through the kitchen door on which a sign is posted reading, "Authorized Personnel Only." He discovers that nothing is wrong, but slips on the kitchen floor.

What is the duty of care owed by an occupier to an invitee?

1. First, the occupier owes the invitee at least the same standard of care owed the trespasser, as discussed previously.
2. Second, the occupier owes the invitee at least the same standard of care owed the licensee, as discussed previously.
3. Third, the occupier owes the invitee a duty of reasonable care to inspect *and discover* dangerous artificial conditions on the land, dangerous natural conditions on the land, and dangerous activities on the land.
4. Fourth, depending on the extent of the danger in the condition or activity, the occupier must either warn the invitee or make the condition or activity safe.

Again, no more than reasonable care is required to discover the danger and protect the invitee from it. The occupier is not the insurer of the invitee.

CASE

Donnell v. California Western School of Law
200 Cal. App. 3d 715, 246 Cal. Rptr. 199 (1988)
California Court of Appeal, Fourth District, Division 1

Background: *William Donnell is a law student at California Western School of Law in San Diego. While going home from school late one night, he was attacked at night on a dark city-owned sidewalk adjoining the school. He sued the law school for negligence. The trial court denied the claim. Donnell has now appealed to the Court of Appeals.*

Decision on Appeal: *The judgment is affirmed. The law school did not have a duty to place lights or monitors on the exterior of its building.*

OPINION OF COURT

Justice KREMER delivered the opinion of the court . . .:

Donnell's complaint alleged: Cal Western runs a law school at 350 Cedar Street in a San Diego building it owns, possesses and controls. Cal Western provides no parking for its students at or near its law school. On January 30, 1984, Cal Western's library and school grounds were open for student use until midnight. About 10 P.M., Cal Western law student William Donnell left Cal Western's building after studying in its library and headed toward his parked car. While walking along the west side of Cal Western's building, William was attacked, stabbed and injured by an unknown assailant. William called for help, but no security personnel came to his assistance. Cal Western's building had no exterior lights on its west side. No security guards patrolled the building's west side.

Donnell further alleged: Defendants knew criminal activity had occurred in the immediate area but negligently failed to provide adequate lighting and security around the law school building. Students, including William, going to and from the law school were forced to traverse the dangerous area because Cal Western did not provide parking for its students. Despite knowing about prior criminal activity perpetrated on persons and property around its law school premises, defendants did not warn William of the dangerous conditions, provide adequate security forces or otherwise safeguard law school students from criminal acts. . . .

We decline . . . to impose on Cal Western a duty to insure its adult students' safety once they have left Cal Western's premises. Mature students are generally considered business invitees. . . . [N]othing in the record suggests Cal Western voluntarily assumed a duty to protect its students from criminal acts outside its premises.

A right to protection from the dangerous conduct of another may arise from the special relationship between a landholder and its invitees. (*Peterson v. San Francisco Community College Dist.,* (1984) 36 Cal. 3d 799, 806, 685 P.2d 1193.) Thus, the issue here is the extent of Cal Western's premises liability to its invitee William.

"A defendant cannot be held liable for the defective or dangerous condition of property which it [does] not own, possess, or control. Where the absence of ownership, possession, or control has been unequivocally established,

summary judgment is proper." (*Isaacs v. Huntington Memorial Hospital* (1985) 38 Cal. 3d 112, 134, 695 P.2d 653.)

Donnell contends Cal Western had a duty to take reasonable steps to protect its invitees from foreseeable criminal assaults on sidewalks giving immediate access to its building. Donnell seeks to hold Cal Western liable for a dangerous condition of a City-owned sidewalk adjoining Cal Western's property, asserting Cal Western had the power to "control" the sidewalk by placing lights on its own building to shine on the sidewalk. Donnell also asserts Cal Western should perhaps have mounted exterior monitors on its building walls to permit its students to view the dangerous area before traversing it. However, Donnell attempts to expand the principle of "control" of property to include situations where an adjoining landowner merely has the ability to influence or affect such property. Donnell in effect attempts to hold Cal Western responsible for the dangerous condition of "something with which [its] only connection is the fact of [its] ownership or use of the abutting land." (*Kopfinger v. Grand Central Pub. Market* (1964) 60 Cal. 2d 852, 858, 389 P.2d 529.) The law of premises liability does not extend so far as to hold Cal Western liable merely because its property exists next to adjoining dangerous property and it took no action to influence or affect the condition of such adjoining property.

In *Kopfinger,* as a result of the defendant merchant's business operation, meat fell to the sidewalk in the course of defendant's activities rendering the walkway dangerous to pedestrians. . . . [T]he court held the defendant could be held liable because its business activities *affirmatively* created a dangerous physical condition on the adjacent public sidewalk which was not timely remedied by the defendant. The court specifically distinguished the "numerous cases to the effect that in the absence of statute there is no common-law duty on the occupant of land abutting a sidewalk to repair or maintain the sidewalk." (Id. at p. 858.) Unlike the plaintiff in *Kopfinger,* Donnell has presented no evidence Cal Western's business activities affirmatively created a dangerous physical condition on the City-owned sidewalk. . . .

[Nor has he offered evidence that] Cal Western had any right to control the City-owned sidewalk where Donnell was assertedly injured. At most Cal Western merely had the ability to influence or affect the condition of the City's property. Further, Donnell presented no evidence Cal Western assumed any responsibility for or exercised control over the means of lighting the City-owned sidewalk where Donnell was injured. Indeed, Donnell asserts Cal Western should be liable precisely because it did not assume responsibility over the City-owned sidewalk.

Donnell's heavy reliance on *Schwartz v. Helms Bakery Limited* (1967) 67 Cal. 2d 232, 235, 430 P.2d 68, is misplaced. In *Schwartz* the court . . . [held] that by undertaking to direct a child to an assigned rendezvous with a dough-nut truck the defendants assumed a duty to exercise due care for the child's safety. In discussing earlier cases involving premises liability, the court stated: "The physical area encompassed by the term 'the premises' does not, however, coincide with the area to which the invitor possesses a title or a lease." (Id. at p. 239.) However, this language in *Schwartz* did not expand the law of premises liability beyond those premises owned, possessed or controlled by the defendant. . . . The court in *Schwartz* stated the "premises" may be greater than the invitor's property: "The premises may include such means of ingress and egress as a customer may reasonably be expected to use. The crucial element is *control*." (Id. at p. 239, italics added.). . . "An invitor bears a duty to warn an invitee of a dangerous condition existing on a public street or sidewalk adjoining his business which, because of the invitor's special benefit, convenience, or use of the public way, creates a danger." (Id. pp. 239–240.)

The court in *Schwartz* also emphasized it was applying established premises liability law to the unique facts before it involving the mobile doughnut truck:

> "It may be argued that defendants, as business invitors, cannot incur a duty to protect invitees from injury on a public street. We have pointed out, however, that the jury could have found that the dangerous circumstances which caused the injury were *created* by defendants. Moreover, . . . the concept of 'business premises' may no longer be mechanically defined by the geographical area in which the invitor holds a property interest. An invitor may be liable for an injury, whether it occurs on his property or on a common passageway or on an adjacent sidewalk or street being used for his special benefit, if, and only if, the injury is caused by a dangerous condition, or unreasonable risk of harm, within the invitor's *control*. [Citation.] Defendants' business consisted of selling bakery goods from a truck. In coming to the truck for the convenience of defendants, patrons used the public streets and sidewalks as means of access for the special benefit of defendants' business. Defendants may therefore be held liable for an injury occurring to their customer in the immediate vicinity of the truck if the circumstances causing the injury are within the range of defendants' *reasonable supervision and control*. Obviously, defendants are not insurers for all accidents occurring in areas through which their truck passes. They may not be held liable, for example, for a fall caused by an unobserved defect in a sidewalk next to which their truck stops. They may be responsible, however, for harm occurring in the immediate vicinity of the truck, wherever it may be stopped at a given time, if the harm is of the kind that defendants could have prevented by exercising reasonable care for the safety of their customers." (*Schwartz*, supra, 67 Cal. 2d at p. 243, fn. 10, italics added.)

Donnell also relies on *O'Hara v. Western Seven Trees Corp.* (1977) 75 Cal. App. 3d 798, 142 Cal. Rptr. 487. However, [this case does] not help Donnell. *O'Hara* involved a landlord-tenant relationship not involved here. Alleging she was raped in her apartment, plaintiff tenant sued her landlord for not providing adequate security and not warning her of the danger of rape. The court held the plaintiff had stated a cause of action. The court noted "the landlord-tenant relationship, at least in the urban, residential context, has given rise to liability under circumstances where landlords have failed to take reasonable steps to protect tenants from criminal activity. . . . It has been held that since *only the landlord is in the position to secure common areas,* he has a duty to protect against types of crimes of which he has notice and which are likely to recur if the common areas are not secure." (Id. at pp. 802–803, italics added.) Cal Western's position was unlike the landlord's in *O'Hara*. Here the City could remedy any dangerous condition of its sidewalk.

Donnell's asserted premises liability case against Cal Western fails under the analysis of *Steinmetz v. Stockton City Chamber of Commerce* (1985) 169 Cal. App. 3d 1142, 214 Cal. Rptr. 405. In a case involving "a landowner's liability for a criminal assault by a third person upon an invitee which occurs off the landowner's premises," the court in *Steinmetz* affirmed summary judgment favoring defendant tenant. (Id. at p. 1144.) The court found "the record establishes without question the decedent was murdered off the premises leased by [defendant tenant] on property not within the possession or control of [defendant tenant], but rather on the premises of another tenant in the industrial park. . . . Plaintiffs have not cited nor are we aware of any case where a *landowner* was held responsible for injuries to an invitee from criminal activity occurring off the landowner's premises." (Id. at p. 1146, italics in original.) Discussing *Schwartz v. Helms Bakery Limited,* supra, 67 Cal. 2d 232, the court stated *Schwartz's* "elastic concept of business premises is uniquely appropriate to the vendor whose commercial activities are conducted from a mobile vehicle at shifting locations on the public streets. However, we know of no decision which has applied this standard to one whose business is conducted on private property in a fixed location. Indeed, it is difficult to perceive how such a rule could be fashioned." (*Steinmetz*, supra, at p. 1146.). . .

[P]remises liability is based on ownership, possession or control. The mere possibility of influencing or affecting the condition of property owned or possessed by others does not constitute "control" of such property. . . .

The judgment is affirmed.

a. Assume that Cal Western holds a forum at the law school on prison re-form. The speakers include ex-felons discussing their experiences. Would the *Donnell* case have reached the same result if a law student was as-saulted by one of the ex-felons (i) in a restroom at the law school during the forum, or (ii) on a City-owned sidewalk adjacent to the law school af-ter the forum?

b. Assume that two days after the attack on William Donnell, another student is assaulted on the adjacent sidewalk by an unknown stranger. Would the *Donnell* case reach the same result when the student attacked sues the law school?

c. Assume that two days after the attack on William Donnell, another student is assaulted on the adjacent sidewalk by a fellow law student. Would the *Donnell* case reach the same result when this student sues the law school?

d. In the *Armory Park* case we read earlier in the chapter, the landowner (Epis-copal Community Services) said that it should not be held responsible for the criminal acts committed by its patrons off the premises of the food dis-tribution center. The landowner lost this argument. Is *Armory Park* consis-tent with the *Donnell* case, which held that the landowner (Cal Western) was not responsible for the criminal act that was committed off the school premises?

3. The Special Problems of the Seller and Buyer of Land (Vendor and Vendee)

When land is sold, the general rule is that the seller (**vendor**) has no further tort lia-bility for injuries that occur on the land, either to the buyer (**vendee**) or to a third per-son. The buyer, under the theory of **caveat emptor** (buyer beware), takes the land as he or she finds it. The buyer is expected to make an inspection of the premises before purchasing. The seller will not be liable if the buyer is injured by a condition on the land, even if the condition was present when the land was sold. Third parties injured by such conditions must look to the new owner for liability.

A number of exceptions exist to this rule. If there is a hidden or latent condi-tion on the land that is dangerous and if the seller knows about the condition (or has reason to know about it), the seller has a duty either to warn the buyer of the condition or to repair it before turning the land over to the buyer. Examples of la-tent conditions include deep holes in the yard covered by thin plywood, and ceilings infested with termites not visible on the surface. A seller does not have a duty to in-spect the premises to discover defects that are latent. There is a duty to warn or re-pair only when the seller knows about such defects or has reason to believe they ex-ist. If this duty is breached, injuries sustained by the buyer can lead to negligence liability against the seller. The buyer may also be able to assert the tort of fraud or misrepresentation.

Another exception concerns conditions on the land that are dangerous to per-sons *outside the land* at the time of the sale. These conditions sometimes amount to a public or private nuisance, although the seller's liability for injury caused to a plain-tiff outside the land is not dependent on the existence of a nuisance. The seller's lia-bility exists only for a reasonable time to enable the buyer to discover such condi-tions and therefore assume responsibility for them.

4. The Special Problems of the Landlord and Tenant (Lessor and Lessee)

Normally, a landlord (**lessor**) is not entitled to possession of the land, but has a **reversionary interest** in the land, which comes into effect after the tenancy is over. (A reversionary interest is a right to the future enjoyment of land that is presently occupied by another). The general rule is that the tenant (**lessee**) assumes all liability for injuries caused by conditions or activities on the land. There are a number of exceptions to this general rule.

Statutes may exist in a state requiring the landlord to maintain the premises, particularly apartment houses, in a safe condition. The violation of such statutes may impose negligence (and in severe cases, criminal) liability on the landlord.

The landlord will be liable to the tenant and to third parties for injuries caused by latent dangerous conditions on the land at the time of the lease which the landlord has actual knowledge of or has reason to believe exist. In most states, the landlord has no duty to inspect and discover such conditions, but must know of them or have reason to believe that they are present. The conditions must be latent or concealed—not obvious to the tenant.

Often the landlord does not lease the entire building or land to the tenant(s). The landlord may retain control over certain **common areas,** such as hallways, stairways, elevators, boiler rooms. The landlord has a duty of reasonable care to inspect these common areas and make sure that they are safe for those who are entitled to use them, e.g., the tenants and people using the land as invitees.

Another exception occurs when the landlord leases the premises for a purpose that involves the admission of the public, e.g., theater, pier, hotel, and department store. In such cases, the landlord has a duty to inspect the premises and to repair any dangerous conditions that exist at the time of the lease, *before* the tenant takes over. Reasonable care must be used to make sure that the land is not turned over in a dangerous condition. If a member of the public is injured by such a condition that was unreasonably not discovered and repaired by the landlord before the tenant took over, the landlord will be liable, even if the lease agreement provides that the tenant shall assume all responsibility for repairs. The landlord cannot shift the responsibility to the tenant in this way. The duty is nondelegable.

Suppose that the dangerous condition arises *after* the land is leased. The general rule is that injured third parties must look to the tenant for liability rather than to the landlord. If, however, the landlord is obligated to make repairs by the terms of the lease, failure to do so will lead to negligence liability in most states. In such cases, the tenant can argue that the tenant did not make the repairs because of reasonable reliance on the landlord's contract obligation to do so. There are some states, however, that do not impose tort liability on the landlord for a failure to make agreed-upon repairs. In such states, only the tenant is liable in tort to injured third parties. The tenant's recourse in such states is a breach-of-contract action against the landlord. If the landlord does undertake the repairs but performs them negligently, the landlord will be liable in tort.

SUMMARY

Trespass to land is an intentional intrusion on land in possession of another. The intent to enter does not require proof of an intent to enter wrongfully. Land includes the ground and the air space above the ground over which the plaintiff has reasonable beneficial use. Actual harm to the land does not have to be shown.

A private nuisance is an unreasonable interference with the reasonable use and enjoyment of private land. This occurs when one's peace of mind is disturbed while on the land. In determining whether the interference is unreasonable, the court will consider a number of factors: the gravity and character of the harm, the social value of the use the plaintiff is making of the land, the character of the locality, the extent of the burden on the plaintiff of avoiding or minimizing the interference, the motive of the defendant, the social value of the defendant's conduct, and the extent of the burden on the defendant of avoiding or minimizing the interference. A private nuisance can be created negligently, intentionally, or through an abnormally dangerous condition or activity. Any person who has the right to the use and enjoyment of the land can bring the action. The remedies might include money (damages,) injunction, and self-help via the privilege to abate the nuisance. Depending on how the nuisance was created, the defenses include contributory negligence (or comparative negligence), assumption of the risk, the failure to mitigate damages, and official authorization.

A public nuisance is an unreasonable interference with a right common to the general public. It can be created negligently; intentionally; through an abnormally dangerous condition or activity; or by violating a statute, ordinance, or regulation. A public official can sue the wrongdoer. A private citizen can also sue if he or she has suffered in a way that is different in kind from every other member of the public affected by the public nuisance. The remedies are similar to those for a private nuisance, and the government may also be able to impose a fine or imprisonment. The defenses to a public nuisance are similar to those available in private nuisance cases.

Traditional negligence liability may depend on the status of the parties. To persons outside the land, occupiers owe a duty of reasonable care as to non-natural or artificial conditions on the land and as to business or personal activity taking place on the land. No duty of care is owed to trespassers unless they are discovered on the land, are constant trespassers on limited areas of the land, or are trespassing children (under the attractive nuisance doctrine). Licensees must be warned of dangerous natural or artificial conditions on the land if the occupier knows or has reason to know about the conditions and if they are latent so that the licensee is not expected to discover them. More than a warning is needed if the condition is extremely dangerous. Licensees must be accorded reasonable care as to activities on the land. For invitees, the occupier must take reasonable steps to inspect and discover dangerous artificial or natural conditions and dangerous activities on the land. The occupier must then use reasonable care to protect the invitee from such conditions and activities. The seller of land can be liable for known latent defects that injure the buyer or a third person on the land. A landlord can be liable to tenants and others injured by latent dangerous conditions on the land that the landlord knows about or should know about. The landlord must use reasonable care to make common areas safe.

KEY TERMS

interest 446	nominal damages 450	unreasonable 452
trespass to land 446	nuisance 451	social value 453
possessory interest 449	private nuisance 451	damages 456
adverse possession 449	public nuisance 451	cost of restoration 456
reasonable beneficial use 450	peace of mind 452	injunction 456

self-help 456

abate the nuisance 456

contributory negligence 457

comparative negligence 457

assumption of the risk 457

mitigate the consequences 457

avoidable consequences 457

taking of property 457

standing 459

premises liability 462

reasonable care 462

occupier 463

independent contractor 463

trespasser 464

licensee 464

invitee 464

child 465

attractive nuisance doctrine 465

social guests 466

business guest 466

latent 466

passenger 466

vendor 471

vendee 471

caveat emptor 471

lessor 472

reversionary interest 472

lessee 472

common areas 472

C H A P T E R

24

Defamation

CHAPTER OUTLINE

- Introduction
- Defamatory Statement
- Extrinsic Facts
- Falsity of the Statement
- Of and Concerning the Plaintiff
- Publication
- Republication
- Cyberspace Defamation
- Damages
- Privilege
- SLAPP Suits
- "Veggie Libel"

INTRODUCTION

In Shakespeare's *Othello*, Iago says to Othello:

> Good name in man and woman, dear my lord,
> Is the immediate jewel of their souls.
> Who steals my purse steals trash;
> 'Tis something, nothing;
> 'Twas mine, 'tis his, and has been slave to thousands;
> But he that filches from me my good name
> Robs me of that which not enriches him,
> And makes me poor indeed. Act III, scene 3.

Iago, however, is not without a remedy. He can bring a suit for **defamation,** which covers injuries to a person's good name and reputation. There are two defamation torts: libel and slander. **Libel** consists of defamation that is written (e.g., in a book) or embodied in a physical form (e.g., a photograph, a film, an effigy). **Slander** consists of defamation that is spoken (e.g., a conversation) or gestured as a substitute for speech (e.g., a nod of the head, a wave of the hand). Defamation on a television program would be considered libel since it has relative permanence in the physical form of film or video.[1] The elements of libel and slander are the same with the major exception of the element of damages.

For a sample defamation complaint alleging both libel and slander, see Figure 3–12 in Chapter 3.

The United States Supreme Court significantly changed the common law of defamation when the alleged defamer is a newspaper, a television program, or other member of the media. To preserve the freedom-of-the-press protection under the First Amendment of the *United States Constitution*, the Court made it considerably harder to win a defamation suit against the media than against any other category of defendant. Some believe that the Court will eventually impose the same or similar rules in all defamation suits. To date, however, the Court has not constitutionalized all of defamation law. Hence, we need to examine both the common law of defamation (covering primarily non-media defendants) and the constitutional law of defamation (covering primarily media defendants). Constitutional law will be covered throughout the chapter, but primarily when we study the falsity of a defamatory statement. This is where the most significant changes have been made.

 Defamation Checklist

Definitions, Relationships, Paralegal Roles, and Research References

Category
At common law, defamation was a strict-liability tort except for the element of publication. For media defendants, this has been changed by constitutional law. For such defendants, defamation is now a tort that requires a showing of fault.

Interest Protected
The right to one's good name and reputation.

Elements
Defamation consists of two torts: libel and slander. The elements of these torts are the same. When we study the first and fourth elements, however, we will find that there can be important differences depending on the identity of the parties and the kind of defamation alleged.

---

[1] At one time, defamation on radio or television was referred to as **defamacast.**

Defamation Checklist Continued

   i. A defamatory statement by the defendant
   ii. Of and concerning the plaintiff
  iii. Publication
  iv. Damages
   v. Causation

Definitions of Major Words/Phrases in These Elements

Defamatory Statement: A statement of fact that would tend to harm the reputation of the plaintiff in the eyes of at least a substantial and respectable minority of people by lowering the plaintiff in the estimation of those people or by deterring them from associating with the plaintiff.

Of and Concerning the Plaintiff: A statement reasonably understood to refer to the plaintiff.

Publication: A communication of the statement to someone other than the plaintiff.

Damages (in non-media cases): Slander:
   a. Special damages are not required if the slander is *slander per se.*
   b. Special damages must be proven if the slander is *slander per quod.*
     Libel:
   a. In some states, libel never requires special damages.
   b. In other states, only libel on its face does not require special damages. In such states, libel per quod requires special damages.

Causation: But for the defendant's statement, the plaintiff would not have suffered harm to reputation; or, the defendant's statement was a substantial factor in bringing about the harm to the plaintiff's reputation.

Major Defenses and Counterargument Possibilities That Need to Be Explored

(Constitutional law has changed a good deal of the common law of defamation as it applies to the media. In the following list, if the item has been applied only to media defendants, it will so indicate.)

1. The statement did not tend to harm the reputation of the plaintiff in the eyes of at least a respectable and substantial minority of the community.

2. Only the plaintiff thought that the statement harmed his or her reputation, or that it had a tendency to do so.

3. The defendant's statement cannot reasonably be understood in a defamatory sense.

4. The defendant's statement was not in fact understood in a defamatory sense.

5. The defendant merely stated an opinion, which did not expressly or impliedly communicate any statements of fact.

6. The defendant's statement could not reasonably be understood to refer to the plaintiff.

7. The group the defendant defamed was too large for the plaintiff (who was part of the group) to be able to reasonably say that the statement was of and concerning the plaintiff.

8. The defendant neither intended to refer to the plaintiff nor was negligent in referring to the plaintiff (for media defendants only).

9. The defendant's statement was not communicated to someone other than the plaintiff.

10. The defendant neither intended to communicate the statement to someone other than the plaintiff nor was negligent in this regard.

11. The defendant's oral defamatory statement is not slander per se and the plaintiff has failed to prove special damages.

12. The defendant's statement is libel per quod and the plaintiff has failed to prove special damages.

13. The harm suffered by the plaintiff was not caused by the defendant's defamatory statement.

14. The defendant's defamatory statement was true.

15. The defamatory statement pertained to a matter of public concern about a public official or a public figure and the plaintiff has not shown actual malice by clear and convincing evidence (for media defendants only).

Defamation Checklist Continued

16. The defamatory statement pertained to a matter of private concern about a public official or a public figure and the plaintiff has not shown the defendant's fault as to truth or falsity by clear and convincing evidence (for media defendants only).

17. The defamatory statement pertained to a matter of public or private concern about a private person and the plaintiff has not shown the defendant's fault as to truth or falsity by clear and convincing evidence (for media defendants only).

18. The defendant had an absolute privilege to utter the defamatory statement.

19. The defendant had a qualified or conditional privilege to utter the defamatory statement and the privilege was not lost by abusing it.

20. The defendant consented to the publication of the defamatory statement (on the defense of consent, see Chapter 27).

21. The plaintiff's defamation suit is a "slapp" suit that should be dismissed.

22. The plaintiff's suit against the government for defamation committed by a government employee may be barred by sovereign immunity (on sovereign immunity, see Chapter 27).

23. The plaintiff's suit against the government employee for defamation may be barred by public official immunity (on official immunity, see Chapter 27).

24. The plaintiff's suit against the charitable organization for a defamation committed by someone working for the organization may be barred by charitable immunity (on charitable immunity, see Chapter 27).

25. The plaintiff's suit against a family member for defamation may be barred by intrafamily immunity (on intrafamily immunity, see Chapter 22).

26. The plaintiff failed to take reasonable steps to mitigate the harm caused when the defendant committed defamation; therefore, damages should not cover the aggravation of the harm caused by the plaintiff (on the doctrine of avoidable consequences, see Chapter 16).

Damages
At common law, defamation plaintiffs can receive presumed damages; special damages do not have to be proven. (Special damages are actual monetary or pecuniary losses.) In many states, special damages must be proven if the defamation is slander per quod. In some states, libel never requires special damages. In others, this is so only for libel on its face. For media defendants, in almost all cases there can be no presumed damages.

Relationship to Criminal Law
Certain forms of defamation are crimes in some states if the defamatory statement is intentionally published. Truth is usually not a defense to the crime of criminal defamation.

Relationship to Other Torts
Abuse of Process: While abusing legal process, the defendant may also defame the plaintiff.
Alienation of Affections: While alienating the affections of a spouse, the defendant may also defame the plaintiff.
Assault: While assaulting the plaintiff, the defendant may also defame the plaintiff.
Battery: While battering the plaintiff, the defendant may also defame the plaintiff.
Disparagement: Defamation protects the personal reputation of the plaintiff. Disparagement is an attack against the goods or property of the plaintiff beyond ordinary commercial competition. While committing disparagement, the defendant may also defame the plaintiff if the attack against the plaintiff's goods or property is also an express or implied personal attack on the reputation of the plaintiff.
False Imprisonment: While falsely imprisoning the plaintiff, the defendant may also defame the plaintiff.
Intentional Infliction of Emotional Distress: The defendant's defamatory statement may not be actionable because it is true or because it is not communicated to a third person. Yet, the statement might be so outrageous as to constitute the tort of intentional infliction of emotional distress.
Invasion of Privacy: The facts that give rise to false light invasion of privacy often also give rise to an action for defamation.

Defamation Checklist Continued

Malicious Prosecution: While committing malicious prosecution, the defendant may also defame the plaintiff.

Federal Law

a. Under the Federal Tort Claims Act, the United States Government will *not* be liable for libel or slander committed by one of its federal employees within the scope of employment (respondeat superior). (See Figure 27–7 in Chapter 27.)

b. There may be liability under the Civil Rights Act if the libel or slander was committed while the defendant was depriving the plaintiff of federal rights under color of law. (See Figure 27–9 in Chapter 27.)

Employer-Employee (Agency) Law

An employee who commits libel or slander is personally liable for this tort. His or her employer will *also* be liable for libel or slander if the conduct of the employee was within the scope of employment (respondeat superior). The employee must be furthering a business objective of the employer while defaming the plaintiff. (On the factors that determine scope of employment, see Figure 14–10 in Chapter 14.)

Paralegal Roles in Defamation Litigation

(See also Figures 3–1, 3–14, and 29–1 in Chapters 3 and 29.)

Fact finding (help the office collect facts relevant to prove the elements of libel or slander, the elements of available defenses, and extent of injuries or other damages):
- client interviewing
- field investigation
- online research (e.g., locating news stories about the defendant)

File management (help the office control the volume of paperwork in a libel or slander litigation):
- open client file
- enter case data in computer database
- maintain file documents

Litigation assistance (help the trial attorney prepare for a libel or slander trial and appeal, if needed):
- draft discovery requests
- draft answers to discovery requests
- draft pleadings
- digest and index discovery documents
- help prepare, order, and manage trial exhibits (visuals or demonstratives)
- prepare trial notebook
- draft notice of appeal
- order trial transcript
- cite check briefs
- perform legal research

Collection/enforcement (help the trial attorney for the judgment creditor to collect the damages award or to enforce other court orders at the conclusion of the libel or slander case):
- draft postjudgment discovery requests
- field investigation to monitor compliance with judgment
- online research (e.g., location of defendant's business assets)

Research References for Defamation

Digests

In the digests of West, look for case summaries on defamation under key topics such as:

Libel and Slander	Damages
Constitutional Law (90)	Torts

Corpus Juris Secundum

In this legal encyclopedia, see the discussions under topic headings such as:

Libel and Slander	Damages
Constitutional Law (585)	Torts

Defamation Checklist Continued

American Jurisprudence 2d
In this legal encyclopedia, see the discussions under topic headings such as:

Libel and Slander	Constitutional Law
Damages	Torts

Legal Periodical Literature
There are two index systems to use to try to locate articles on defamation:

Index to Legal Periodicals and Books (ILP)	**Current Law Index (CLI)**
See literature in *ILP* under subject headings such as:	See literature in *CLI* under subject headings such as:
Libel and Slander	Libel and Slander
Constitutional Law	Liberty of the Press
Freedom of the Press	Constitutional Law
Liability without Fault	Strict Liability
Radio and Television	Torts
Torts	Damages
Damages	

Examples of legal periodical articles on defamation you will find by using *ILP* or *CLI*:

Pornography as Defamation and Discrimination by Catherine MacKinnon, 71 Boston University Law Review 793 (1991)

Old Doctrines on a New Frontier: Defamation and Jurisdiction in Cyberspace by R. Timothy Muth, Wisconsin Lawyer 10 (Sept. 1995) [also available on WESTLAW at 68-SEP WILAW 10]

A.L.R., A.L.R.2d, A.L.R.3d, A.L.R.4th, A.L.R.5th, A.L.R. Fed.
Use the *ALR Index* to find annotations on defamation. In this index, check subject headings such as:

Libel and Slander	Radio and Television
Freedom of Speech and Press	Damages
	Torts
Privileges and Immunities	New York Times Rule
Newspapers	

Example of an annotation on defamation you will find by using this index:

Who Is "Public Figure" for Purposes of Defamation Action by Tracy A. Bateman, 19 A.L.R.5th 1 (1995).

Words and Phrases
In this multivolume legal dictionary, look up *slander per se, libel per quod, defamatory statement, publication, special damages,* and every other word or phrase connected with defamation discussed in this chapter. The dictionary will give you definitions of these words or phrases from court opinions.

CALR: Computer-Assisted Legal Research
Example of a query you could ask on WESTLAW to try to find cases, statutes, or other legal materials on defamation: **"defamatory statement" /p slander**

Example of a query you could ask on LEXIS to try to find cases, statutes, or other legal materials on defamation: **defamatory statement /p slander**

Example of search terms you could use on an Internet legal search engine such as LawCrawler (http://lawcrawler.findlaw.edu) to find cases, statutes, or other legal materials on defamation: **defamation AND tort**

Example of search terms you could use on an Internet general search engine such as Alta Vista (http://www.altavista.com) to find cases, statutes, or other legal materials on defamation: **+defamation tort**

Defamation Checklist Continued

More Internet sites to check for materials on defamation and other torts:
Jurist: (http://jurist.law.pitt.edu/sg_torts.htm)
LawGuru: (http://www.lawguru.com/search/lawsearch.html)
See also Torts Law Online at the end of Chapter 1.

DEFAMATORY STATEMENT

Introduction

A **defamatory statement** is a statement of fact that would tend to harm the reputation of the plaintiff in the eyes of at least a substantial and respectable minority of
people by lowering the plaintiff in the estimation of those people or by deterring them
from associating with the plaintiff. More specifically, it is a statement of fact that
tends to disgrace a person by holding him or her up to hatred or ridicule, or by causing others to avoid him or her. The people who express this hatred or ridicule must
not be extreme or antisocial in their reaction. For example, although it is possible to
find people who hate members of a particular race, it is not defamatory for someone
to say that you like or support the rights of members of that race, even if a large number of bigots hold you in contempt for this position.

Facts and Opinions

Defamatory opinions are rarely actionable. An **opinion** is defined as a relatively
vague or indefinite value judgment that is not objectively verifiable. ("The speaker
was boring.") Opinions are often the basis of endless debate. A **fact,** on the other
hand, is a concrete statement that can be objectively established as true or false.
("The speaker lied about his credentials.") There is a difference between saying,
"Helen's behavior is disgraceful" and saying, "Helen stole $100." Only the latter
is a statement of fact. In general, you cannot sue someone for expressing a defamatory opinion unless the opinion implies the existence of undisclosed defamatory
facts as the basis for the opinion. The statement, "The food at the City Deli is un-
eatable" is an opinion, but it is arguably based on the unstated defamatory fact that
the speaker has eaten spoiled food at this restaurant. According to the United States
Supreme Court:

> [E]xpressions of "opinion" may often imply an assertion of objective fact. If a
> speaker says, "In my opinion John Jones is a liar," he implies a knowledge of
> facts which lead to the conclusion that Jones told an untruth. Even if the speaker
> states the facts upon which he bases his opinion, if those facts are either incor-
> rect or incomplete, or if his assessment of them is erroneous, the statement may
> still imply a false assertion of fact. Simply couching such statements in terms of
> opinion does not dispel these implications. . . .[2]

The statement, "In my opinion John Jones is a liar," communicates a fact because
you can objectively verify whether someone has told the truth. On the other hand,
the following statement does not communicate undisclosed facts: "In my opinion
Mayor Jones shows his abysmal ignorance by accepting the teachings of Marx and
Lenin." It would be impossible to prove that someone is ignorant because of a belief
in a particular political or social philosophy.

There is no doubt that opinions can be derogatory and harmful. Yet, it is very
difficult to win suits that grow out of defamatory opinions. There are two main reasons for this. First, everyone has a privilege to express opinions on matters of public

---

[2]*Milkovich v. Lorain Journal Co.,* 497 U.S. 1, 19, 110 S. Ct. 2695, 2706, 111 L. Ed. 2d 1 (1990).

interest, even if the opinions are defamatory. ("The contest is rigged.") This privilege is known as **fair comment.** It prevents liability for defamation so long as the comment, no matter how unreasonable, was the actual opinion of the critic and was not made solely for the purpose of causing harm to the person about whom the comment was made. Second, when the media is the defendant, the First Amendment of the *United States Constitution* gives wide latitude in the expression of ideas and opinions. In a famous line in *Gertz v. Welch,* the United States Supreme Court said,

> Under the First Amendment, there is no such thing as a false idea. However pernicious an opinion may seem, we depend for its correction not on the conscience of judges and juries but on the competition of other ideas.[3]

This does not mean that the media has a constitutional right to express any opinion. As we have seen, opinions based on undisclosed defamatory facts can lead to liability for defamation. Yet, winning a defamation suit based on such an opinion is extremely difficult for reasons we will examine shortly.

ASSIGNMENT 24.1

Are any of the following statements defamatory? Assume that each of the statements is made in front of third persons. (See General Instructions for the Legal Analysis Assignment in Chapter 2.)

a. Vince calls Nick a "closet Republican." Nick is a registered Democrat.
b. Tom calls Juanita a "Socialist."
c. Ed calls Bill a "tree-hugger."
d. Rich is a member of a union who returns to work during a strike. Hank, another union member, calls Rich a traitor.
e. Mary is the ex-wife of John, now married to Linda. Mary says she had a dream last night and knows it is going to come true. In the dream, Linda wanted to "murder me."
f. Don Adams is the sports announcer for the city's major league baseball team. Sam says, "Adams is the only sportscaster in town who is enrolled in a course for remedial speaking."

CASE

Van Duyn v. Smith
173 Ill. App. 3d 523, 527 N.E.2d 1005 (1988)
Appellate Court of Illinois, Third District

Background: *Margaret Van Duyn directs an abortion clinic. Smith is a pro-life activist who distributed a "Wanted" poster and a "Face The American Holocaust" poster to Van Duyn's friends, neighbors and acquaintances living in the three block area surrounding Van Duyn's residence. She sued Smith for defamation and other causes of action. Her complaint was dismissed by the trial court for failure to state a cause of action. The case is now before the Third District Appellate Court of Illinois.*

Decision on Appeal: *Defamation was not committed because there was no statement of fact; the posters contained opinions.*

OPINION OF COURT
Justice SCOTT delivered the opinion of the court . . .
Plaintiff claims that the "Wanted" poster . . . resembling those used by the Federal bureau of Investigation and seen on bulletin boards in public places, states: that plaintiff is a wanted person "for prenatal killing in violation of the Hip-

---

[3]418 U.S. 323, 339, 94 S. Ct. 2997, 3007, 41 L. Ed. 2d 789, 805 (1974).

pocratic oath and Geneva Code"; that plaintiff uses the alias "Margaret the Malignant"; that plaintiff has participated in killing for profit and has presided over more than 50,000 killings; and the plaintiff's modus operandi is a small round tube attached to a powerful suction machine that tears the developing child limb from limb. The poster further contains a statement at the bottom which indicates in part, that "(n)othing in this poster should be considered unethical. Once abortion was a crime but it is not now considered a crime."

The "Face The American Holocaust" poster . . . contains pictures of fetuses between 22 and 29 weeks gestational age that have been aborted. Under each picture the "cause of death" of the fetus is listed; referring to the method used to perform the abortion. Among the techniques listed are dismemberment, salt poisoning, and massive hemorrhaging. The poster also contains four paragraphs of information regarding the discovery of some 17,000 fetuses stored in a 3 1/2 ton container in California, the number of abortions performed per day in "America's abortion mills", and how "America's Holocaust is the responsibility of us all." The poster additionally gives the name and address of Pro-Life Action League and lists the defendant's name and telephone number for those who choose to call locally. . . . [Plaintiff alleges] that as a result of defendant's actions, her good name, character and reputation were impaired and brought into disrepute before her friends and acquaintances. . . .

Generally, defamation, which consists of the identically treated branches of libel and slander, is the publication of anything injurious to the good name or reputation of another, or which tends to bring him into disrepute. Illinois courts have held that a statement is defamatory if it impeaches a person's integrity, virtue, human decency, respect for others, or reputation and thereby lowers that person in the estimation of the community or deters third parties from dealing with that person. Each defamation case must be decided on its own facts. . . .

Plaintiff maintains that the "Wanted" poster, when read alone, or in conjunction with the "Face the American Holocaust" poster, contains false statements of fact that are libelous. . . . In particular, plaintiff argues that defendant's use of the word "killing" would cause the average reader to believe that plaintiff has committed a criminal offense. . . . .

We acknowledge, however, that the Supreme Court has recognized a constitutional privilege for expressions of opinion. (*Gertz v. Welch*, 418 U.S. 323.) Whether a statement is one of opinion or fact is a matter of law. Moreover, the alleged defamatory language must be considered in context to determine whether or not it is an expression of opinion. . . .

In *Ollman v. Evans*, the court drew upon theories used in prior cases to devise the totality of the circumstances analysis for determining whether a publication is a statement of fact or an expression of opinion. The four part analysis is explained as follows: "First, we will analyze the common usage or meaning of the specific language of the challenged statement itself. Our analysis of the specific language under scrutiny will be aimed at determining whether the statement has a precise core of meaning for which a consensus of understanding exists or, conversely, whether the statement is indefinite and ambiguous. Readers are, in our judgment, considerably less likely to infer facts from an indefinite or

ambiguous statement than one with a commonly understood meaning. Second, we will consider the statement's verifiability—is the statement capable of being objectively characterized as true or false? Insofar as a statement lacks a plausible method of verification, a reasonable reader will not believe that the statement has specific factual content. And, in the setting of litigation, the trier of fact obliged in a defamation action to assess the truth of an unverifiable statement will have considerable difficulty returning a verdict based upon anything but speculation. Third, moving from the challenged language itself, we will consider the full context of the statement—the entire article or column, for example—inasmuch as other, unchallenged language surrounding the allegedly defamatory statement will influence the average reader's readiness to infer that a particular statement has factual content. Finally, we will consider the broader context or setting in which the statement appears. Different types of writing have . . . widely varying social conventions which signal to the reader the likelihood of a statement's being either fact or opinion. . . ." *Ollman v. Evans*, 750 F.2d 970, 979 (D.C. Cir. 1984).

We believe defendant's statement that plaintiff is involved in "killing" can be commonly understood as meaning that plaintiff has terminated a life of something or someone that was previously living. In itself the accusation that plaintiff is involved with "killing the unwanted and unprotected" is a potentially damaging fact. Our difficulty, however, is that the type of killing being referred to in this instance is not, in our opinion, objectively capable of being proven or disproven. This is especially true when the allegedly defamatory statements are read in the context in which the statements occur. It becomes apparent when looking at the "Wanted" poster in its entirety that defendant's use of the word "killing" is his description of what takes place during an abortion procedure. We are not prepared to find that the word "killing" in this context is verifiable and, thus, a defamatory statement of fact. Additionally, when the statements are considered within the social context, it becomes quite clear that defendant's use of the word "killing" merely describes his opinion of the results of an abortion procedure. Since the Supreme Court decision of *Roe v. Wade* (1973), 410 U.S. 113, wherein a woman's right to have an abortion was determined to be constitutionally protected, one of the primary issues has been, and still is, whether or not there is an actual killing of a human life as the result of an abortion. Pro-life activists certainly maintain that abortion is a killing, however, pro-choice activists believe the contrary, especially before the fetus has reached viability. Regardless of which position may ultimately be considered correct, at the present we find that the average reasonable reader of the "Wanted" poster would not believe as an actual fact that plaintiff has been involved in killing, as that word is commonly understood by our society. In fact, we believe that the average reader would quickly realize that the central theme of the "Wanted" poster is that abortion is a killing, to which plaintiff plays a part, and should be a crime in the opinion of those siding with the pro-life movement.

Although we consider the "Wanted" poster repulsive, explicit, unnecessary and in bad taste, we adhere to the belief that "(u)nder the First Amendment there is no such thing as a false idea. However pernicious an opinion may seem, we depend for its correction not on the conscience of judges and juries but on the competition of other ideas." (*Gertz v. Welch,* 418 U.S. at 339-40.) As elaboration, we cite *Sloan v. Hatton,* wherein the court stated: "Free speech is not restricted to compliments. Were this not so there could be no verbal give and take, no meaningful exchange of ideas, and we would be forced to confine ourselves to platitudes and compliments. But members of a free society must be able to express candid opinions and make personal judgments. And those opinions and judgments may be harsh or critical—even abusive—yet still not subject the speaker or writer to civil liability." (*Sloan v. Hatton* (1978), 383 N.E.2d 259, 260.)

We consider the above rationale applicable to all the other allegedly defamatory statements with the exception of the allegedly false statement that plaintiff performs abortions on 29 week gestationally old fetuses. This alleged statement requires reading the two posters in conjunction. In this regard we perceive plaintiff's reasoning to be that the two posters were distributed at the same time, therefore, the average reader would look at the pictures of apparently aborted fetuses on the "Face the American Holocaust" poster and infer that plaintiff was involved with abortions involving fetuses as old as 29 weeks gestationally. Without more information, we note that an abortion at 29 weeks may be a crime. (Ill. Rev. Stat. 1987, ch. 38, ¶ 81–21 et seq. . . .) [Yet defendant did not state] that plaintiff performs abortions on 29 week gestationally old fetuses. . . . First, there is absolutely no cross-referencing between the two posters which would lead the average reader to infer that the two posters should be read and considered together. Second, the "Face the American Holocaust" poster tells the story of how 17,000 fetuses were found in a 3 1/2 ton container in Los Angeles, California. Nowhere does it state that plaintiff was responsible for any of the fetuses found in the container. . . .

The average reasonable reader would realize that the "Wanted" poster is referring to the practice of abortion and that the basis for defendant's opinion that plaintiff is "killing for profit the unwanted and unprotected" is that plaintiff is somehow involved in the abortion process. Moreover, the average reader of the "Wanted" poster would recognize that it is merely another restatement of the pro-life movement's opinion regarding abortion; an opinion that has been publicized since at least the *Roe v. Wade* decision in 1973. The "Wanted" poster does not imply that plaintiff has been involved in any "killing for profit" outside of her involvement with abortions. The "Face the American Holocaust" poster simply does not refer to plaintiff and cannot be read in conjunction with the "Wanted" poster for reasons previously stated. Accordingly, we affirm the trial court's dismissal. . . .

ASSIGNMENT

24.2

Has defamation been committed in the following circumstances?

a. Sam is the mayor. Because he refuses to say in advance that he will never raise taxes, Alice calls him a "coward and a fraud." "It's highway robbery what you're doing," she says to him in a corridor in front of many people.

b. George Harrison is a doctor who performs abortions. Ed carries a poster in front of Harrison's office that reads, "Dr. Harrison is a murderer who pressures young women to kill their babies."

EXTRINSIC FACTS

Some statements are not defamatory on their face because you cannot understand the defamatory meaning simply by examining the words or images used. For example, to say that "Mary gave birth to a child today" is not defamatory **on its face** because you need to know the **extrinsic fact** that Mary has been married only a month. When extrinsic facts are needed, they are alleged in the part of the complaint called the **inducement.** The explanation of the defamatory meaning of words alleged by inducement is called the **innuendo.**

FALSITY OF THE STATEMENT

At common law, the plaintiff did not have to prove the statement was false. It was assumed to be false. Truth was an **affirmative defense,** which meant that the defendant had to allege and prove it. (An affirmative defense to a claim or charge is a response that is based on new factual allegations by the defendant not contained in the complaint of the plaintiff.) Also, there was no need at common law to show **fault** in the defendant. The mere fact that the statement was defamatory was enough to establish liability. A plaintiff did not have to show that the defendant knew the statement was false, or was reckless or negligent as to the truth or falsity of the statement.

The United States Supreme Court, however, has dramatically changed the common law when the defendant is part of the media. When the media publishes a defamatory statement, the common law on falsity does *not* apply. The statement is not assumed to be false; the defendant does not have the burden of proving that the statement is true as an affirmative defense. The plaintiff has the burden of proving the falsity of the statement and must do so by showing fault. There are three possible standards of fault: the media knew the statement was false, was reckless as to its truth or falsity, or was negligent as to its truth or falsity. There can be no strict liability against the media in defamation cases.

> **EXAMPLE:**   A local newspaper publishes a story that Jim Franklin recently sold a stolen Picasso painting. Unfortunately, this statement turns out to be false. Examine the following four possibilities.
>
> A. The editor knew that the painting was not stolen.
> B. The editor did not know the story was false. An anonymous source told the editor that the painting was stolen. This is the basis of the story. The editor was told that three other sources would cast serious doubt on whether the painting was stolen. The editor, however, decides not to check these sources or any other evidence.
> C. The editor did not know the story was false. An anonymous source told the editor that the painting was stolen. This is the basis of the story. The editor does no more checking to find out if there are any other sources that will confirm or deny the claim that the painting was stolen.
> D. The editor did not know the story was false. An anonymous source told the editor that the painting was stolen. Three other sources, however, cast serious doubt on whether the painting was stolen. The editor carefully checks all of these sources as well as others.

In Case A, the editor knew the story was false. In Case B, the editor printed the story in reckless disregard for the truth or falsity of the story. Not checking three known sources seems to be extraordinarily poor judgment. Recklessness means an egregious or blatant disregard of what should appear to be an obvious step to take to determine the accuracy of a story. To rely on one anonymous source and to disregard known contrary sources is reckless. In Case C, the editor is negligent. There was no checking to determine if there were other sources. Negligence means sloppiness or carelessness in disregarding reasonable steps to determine the accuracy of a story. In Case D, the editor was innocently wrong. There was no fault involved. All sources were carefully checked.

We said that a plaintiff suing a media defendant for a defamatory statement must prove fault. We now address the question of which standard of fault must be established. This depends on the answer to two questions:

- What is the status of the plaintiff?
- Is the defamatory statement about a matter of public concern or about a private matter?

Status.   There are three categories of plaintiffs in media cases: public officials, public figures, and private persons. A **public official** is a government employee who has significant authority, e.g., mayor, police officer. A **public figure** is a nongovernment employee who has assumed special prominence in the affairs of society. There are two categories of public figures. An all-purpose public figure is a person of general power, influence, or notoriety (e.g., a prominent actor). A limited-purpose public figure is a person who has voluntarily become involved in a controversy of interest to the general public (e.g., a death-penalty activist). A **private person** is everyone else. Private persons are those who are neither public officials nor public figures. An example might be your retired Uncle Ed or the local supermarket clerk.

Public concern/private matter. Defamatory statements about a plaintiff fall into two main categories: those that involve public issues or matters of public concern and those that involve private matters.

> **EXAMPLES:**
>
> - The Detroit Daily News prints a story that says Sam Smith tried to pour poison into the drinking reservoir of the city.
> - A TV show called *Revelations* says that Sam Smith once took a male impotency pill.

Assume that both statements are false and defamatory. For the moment, we will not concern ourselves with whether Smith is a public official, public figure, or private person. Let us simply classify the category of defamatory statement in each example. The statement about the poison clearly involves a matter of public concern. The public has an interest in the safety of its drinking water. The statement about impotency medication, however, appears to be little more than barnyard gossip. The kind of medication someone may have taken for a sexual problem is a private matter, not a public one.

Once we identify the category of the plaintiff and the category of the defamatory statement about the plaintiff, we now turn to the law that applies to the media defendant. There are three main kinds of cases:

1. *The plaintiff is a public official or a public figure who is suing the media for a defamatory statement about the plaintiff that pertains to a matter of public concern.* The plaintiff must prove by clear and convincing evidence that:

- the media knew the statement was false *or*
- the media was reckless in determining the truth or falsity of the statement

Either standard of fault is sufficient. Knowledge of falsity or recklessness is referred to as **actual malice** or **constitutional malice.**[4] Negligence is not enough. There is no liability if the media negligently publishes a defamatory falsehood of this kind about a public official or public figure. Nor is there any liability if it was innocently published.

2. *The plaintiff is a public official or a public figure who is suing the media for a defamatory statement about the plaintiff that pertains to a private matter.* The plaintiff must prove by clear and convincing evidence that:

- the media knew the statement was false *or*
- the media was reckless in determining the truth or falsity of the statement *or*
- the media was negligent in determining the truth or falsity of the statement

A state is free to select one of these three standards. Fault must be established. There is no liability if the media innocently publishes a defamatory falsehood of this kind about a public official or public figure.

3. *The plaintiff is a private person who is suing the media for a defamatory statement about the plaintiff that pertains to a public or a private matter.* The plaintiff must prove by clear and convincing evidence that:

---

[4]It is also called **New York Times malice** because the standard was first announced in the case of *New York Times v. Sullivan,* 376 U.S. 254, 84 S. Ct. 710, 11 L. Ed. 2d 686 (1964).

- the media knew the statement was false *or*
- the media was reckless in determining the truth or falsity of the statement, *or*
- the media was negligent in determining the truth or falsity of the statement

The state is free to select one of these three standards. Fault must be established. There is no liability if the media innocently publishes a defamatory falsehood about a private person. Most states have chosen the negligence standard, making it somewhat easier for private persons in these states to win defamation cases than public officials or public figures alleging defamation on matters of public concern.

Suppose that the defendant in a defamation case is not part of the media, e.g., your neighbor calls you a thief, a bank teller accuses you of forging a check. The common law of defamation applies. The defamatory statement is assumed to be false and there is no need for the plaintiff to prove that the defendant knew the statement was false, or was reckless as to its truth or falsity, or was negligent as to its truth or falsity.

As indicated earlier, however, some believe that the United States Supreme Court will eventually change defamation law for non-media defendants in the same way it has revolutionized the law governing media defendants. The law of defamation is still evolving. Our society places a high value on robust debate in the free exchange of ideas. Making defamation suits harder to win arguably supports this value. Yet, there is still a need for individuals to be able to protect their name and reputation. As the Court tries to balance these interests, it is unclear whether the trend toward narrowing the torts of libel and slander will continue.

ASSIGNMENT 24.3

Explain why the following statement is true: The media has a constitutional right to negligently publish defamatory statements about public officials or public figures on matters of public concern.

ASSIGNMENT 24.4

In the following cases, what is the standard of fault that the plaintiff must prove in order to win the defamation case against the defendant? (See General Instructions for the Legal Analysis Assignment in Chapter 2.)

a. A national television news report says that the president of the United States is a "philanderer."

b. Dr. Adams is a twenty-five-year-old biologist who teaches at the local community college. He applies for and is given a $1,500 government grant to study whether fleas can understand Italian. A columnist in a local newspaper awards him the "Golden Fleece Award of the Month" for the absurd use of public funds.

ASSIGNMENT 24.5

The front page of a newspaper contains a story that the mayor illegally grants city contracts to his "cronies and friends." The mayor sues for defamation. You are a paralegal who works for the law firm that represents the mayor. What facts would you try to investigate in order to determine whether the newspaper published the story with constitutional malice? (See General Instructions for the Investigation Strategy Assignment in Chapter 3.)

OF AND CONCERNING THE PLAINTIFF

The defamatory statement must be **of and concerning the plaintiff**. This requires proof by the plaintiff that a recipient of the statement reasonably understood that it referred to the plaintiff. Occasionally, extrinsic facts are needed to make this determination. Suppose the defendant says that "the head guard at Fulton Prison has stolen state funds." On the face of this statement, we cannot identify who was defamed. We need to know who was the head guard at the time the statement was made. The plaintiff can introduce the extrinsic fact that he or she was the head guard at the time, and that, therefore, the statement was reasonably understood to refer to the plaintiff. The part of the complaint in which the plaintiff alleges that the defamatory statement was of and concerning the plaintiff is called the **colloquium**.

Suppose that the defendant defames a group, e.g., "all Italians are thieves" or "Boston doctors are quacks." The groups defamed here are too large; no individual Italian or Boston doctor can say that the statement can be reasonably understood to refer to him or her as an individual. The larger the group, the less reasonable such an understanding would be.

ASSIGNMENT	
24.6	Can defamation actions be brought because of the following statements? If so, by whom? (See General Instructions for the Legal Analysis Assignment in Chapter 2.) a. "The jury that acquitted John Gotti was bribed." b. "Cab drivers always cheat." c. "The Titon University football players take steroids." d. "The money was stolen by Tom or Fred."

PUBLICATION

There must be a **publication** of the defamatory statement by the defendant. Publication means that the statement is communicated to someone other than the plaintiff. Publication has always been a fault element. The defendant must intentionally or negligently allow someone else to read or hear the statement.

> **EXAMPLE:** Ted telephones Paulette in order to accuse her of being a thief.

There is no publication if Paulette is the only person who heard the statement.

> **EXAMPLES:** Ted telephones Paulette in order to accuse her of being a thief. He knows that she has her speakerphone on.
>
> Ted sends Paulette a postcard in which he accuses her of being a thief.

In both of these cases, Paulette can try to prove that Ted knew or should have known that someone other than Paulette would hear or see the statement, e.g., evidence that Ted knew that Paulette had roommates who would probably listen to all phone messages, or that others picked up her mail for her and could easily read a postcard. If such evidence does not exist, the publication of the defamatory statement was unintentional or innocent and therefore not actionable.

> **EXAMPLE:** Alice sends Dan a letter in which she says he is a child molester. On the cover of the envelope, Alice prints the words, "PERSONAL AND CONFIDENTIAL." Unknown to Alice, however, Dan has asked his mother to open and sort all his mail. Or, Dan's neighbor steals the letter and reads it.

In both instances, Alice was not at fault in communicating the statement to a third person. She did not intend someone else to read it and there is no indication that she was careless or negligent in allowing this to occur. She sealed the letter in an envelope, using language alerting everyone that the letter was for Dan's eyes only. Hence, the element of publication has not been established.

ASSIGNMENT
24.7

Nina writes a note on a piece of paper in which she says that George's divinity degree is a fake. She intends to hand the note to George in person. She places the note in her purse and boards a bus. Carelessly, however, she leaves her purse on the bus. A bus driver finds the purse and reads everything in it, including the note to George. Has Nina published the note? (See General Instructions for the Legal Analysis Assignment in Chapter 2.)

REPUBLICATION

Someone who repeats another's defamatory statement has *republished* it and can sometimes be subject to the same tort liability as the person who originated the statement.

> **EXAMPLE:** Ted works for the Ajax Company in the town of Salem. At a staff meeting, he hears Thomas Sanford, another employee, say that "Senator Bill Crowley is a crook." The next morning, Ted says to a friend, "Thomas Sanford said that Senator Bill Crowley is a crook."

If Sanford made this statement, he published a defamatory statement at the meeting. But Ted *also* published (or republished) the defamatory statement the next morning when he repeated the statement to a friend. Ted's **republication** is treated as a publication. Crowley can sue Sanford and Ted for defamation.

The media can also be a republisher.

> **EXAMPLE:** The Salem News prints a news article on a staff meeting held at the Ajax Company in Salem. The article reports that Thomas Sanford told the assembled employees that "Senator Bill Crowley is a crook."

The newspaper has republished the defamatory statement. Winning a defamation case against the media, however, can be difficult. As we have seen, a public figure like Senator Crowley must establish that a defamatory falsehood on a matter of public concern was published with actual malice. Also, many states give the media a **fair report privilege**. This privilege allows the media to publish fair and accurate stories on government reports and proceedings, even if the stories contain defamatory statements made in the government reports or proceedings. This privilege would not apply to the Salem News case in our example since the news story was not about a government report or proceeding. Yet, Senator Crowley would still have a difficult time suing Salem News because he would have to prove actual malice.

Other individuals and businesses are also engaged in republication. Examples include bookstores, news carriers, libraries, message deliverers, and printers. Are they liable for the defamatory statements contained in the products that they deliver or transmit? Since it would be too burdensome for them to check the content of everything they distribute, they are *not* liable for defamation unless they have reason to know that the book, article, message, or other communication contains defamatory material. The same is true of telephone and telegraph companies.

CYBERSPACE DEFAMATION

The coming of the Internet has raised the issue of defamation in cyberspace through the Internet. **Cyberspace** "refers to the interaction of people and businesses over computer networks, electronic bulletin boards, and commercial online services. The largest and most visible manifestation of cyberspace is the Internet."[5] Over 100 million regular users of the Internet exist. One of the main Internet service providers is America Online (AOL), which allows its subscribers to send and receive information through AOL's computer network. This is done in a variety of ways, including:

- electronic mail or e-mail, which consists of private electronic communications addressed to specific recipients
- message boards, which are topical forums where subscribers post messages that may be read by all other subscribers
- chat rooms, which are forums in which two or more subscribers may conduct real-time, computer-to-computer conversations, with the statements of each speaker briefly appearing on the computer screens of other participating subscribers[6]

The quantity of material exchanged through these methods is staggering. AOL alone processes over 30 million e-mail messages a day and oversees over 19,000 chat rooms.

What happens when one subscriber defames another through one of these vehicles?

> **EXAMPLE:** Mary and George are AOL subscribers. On a message board, Mary sends a message to George that says, "Jim Thompson beats his wife." Thousands of other subscribers read this.

Mary has published a defamatory statement to George. Clearly, Thompson can sue her for defamation. What about AOL? Hasn't it *also* published the defamatory statement?

Congress has definitively answered *no* to this question. In 1996, it passed a law that prohibited tort actions that seek to treat an entity such as AOL as the "publisher or speaker" of messages transmitted over its service by third parties:

> "No provider . . . of an interactive computer service shall be treated as the publisher or speaker of any information provided by another information content provider. . . . No cause of action may be brought and no liability may be imposed under any State or local law that is inconsistent with this section." 47 U.S.C. § 230(c)(1) & (d)(3).

In our example, AOL is a "provider" of an "interactive computer service." Mary is an "information content provider"; she provided the "information" that "Thompson beats his wife." Under the protection granted by Congress, the victim of defamation delivered in this manner cannot sue the interactive computer service. The victim must go after the originator of the defamatory speech. Online providers such as AOL will not be treated as newspapers, magazines, and television and radio stations that have more control over the content of their products. In effect, Congress granted tort **immunity** to Internet intermediaries that are providers of interactive computer services. This was done to encourage further robust development of the Internet:

> The purpose of this statutory immunity is not difficult to discern. Congress recognized the threat that tort-based lawsuits pose to freedom of speech in the new and burgeoning Internet medium. The imposition of tort liability on service providers for the communications of others represented, for Congress, simply another form of intrusive government regulation of speech. [The immunity] was

---

[5]R. Timothy Muth, *Old Doctrines on a New Frontier: Defamation and Jurisdiction in Cyberspace*, Wisconsin Lawyer 10, 11 (Sept. 1995).
[6]*Doe v. America Online, Inc.*, 25 Media L. Rep. 2112, 1997 WL 374223 (Fla. Cir. Ct. 1997).

enacted, in part, to maintain the robust nature of Internet communication and, accordingly, to keep government interference in the medium to a minimum.[7]

The immunity is also a recognition of the near impossibility of requiring providers of online services to edit the vast quantity of information passed between the millions of connected computers all over the world.

DAMAGES

At common law, once the plaintiff proved that the defendant published a defamatory statement, the jury was allowed to presume that the plaintiff suffered humiliation or harm to reputation. There was no need for the plaintiff to offer specific evidence of these consequences. Such damages were called **presumed damages.** If, in addition, the plaintiff suffered actual dollar losses such as medical expenses or lost income, they could be recovered as **special damages.** These are actual economic or pecuniary losses. Today, there can be no presumed damages against media defendants charged with making defamatory statements on matters of public concern *unless* the plaintiff can prove actual malice—the defendant knew the statement was false or was reckless as to its truth or falsity.[8]

The following discussion of damages in libel and slander is limited to suits against non-media defendants.

Libel

In most categories of libel, presumed damages can be awarded and there is no need to prove that special damages were suffered. In some states, however, if the plaintiff is alleging **libel per quod,** special damages must be shown. Libel per quod is a written statement that requires the reader to know extrinsic facts (see earlier section on extrinsic facts) to understand its defamatory meaning. Special damages in libel cases are not required in any state if the statement is defamatory on its face.

Slander

Slander per se does not require proof of special damages, but slander per quod does.

Slander per se is an oral statement that is defamatory in one of the following four ways:

- It accuses the plaintiff of a crime (e.g., "Ed stole a car").
- It accuses the plaintiff of having a loathsome communicable disease (e.g., "Ed has venereal disease").
- It accuses the plaintiff of sexual misconduct (e.g., "Ed is an adulterer").
- It adversely affects the plaintiff's trade, profession, or office (e.g., "Ed forged his license to sell liquor").

Most states have all of these categories, although some states have made modifications. (The *Becker* case printed below, for example, refers to a different third category for Illinois.) A slanderous statement that does *not* fall into one of these four categories (e.g., "Ed is illegitimate") is called **slander per quod.** In a few states, this phrase has the additional meaning of an oral statement that requires extrinsic facts to understand its defamatory meaning.

The *Becker* case raises the question of whether an attorney committed slander per se against three independent paralegals that the attorney hired for work on specific

---

[7]*Zeran v. America Online, Inc.,* 129 F.3d 327, 330 (4th Cir. 1997).

[8]A private person, however, can obtain presumed damages if the defamatory statement did not involve an issue of public concern. *Dun & Bradstreet,* 472 U.S. 749, 105 S. Ct. 2939, 86 L. Ed. 2d 593 (1985).

FIGURE 24–1 From left to right: Steven Becker, Thomas Becker, and Jeffrey Becker. Independent paralegals in Illinois who sued an attorney for slander per se in the case of *Becker v. Zellner.*

cases. The paralegals are the Becker brothers of Monroe, Illinois—Steven, Thomas, and Jeffrey Becker. They were not salaried employees of the attorney; they were independent paralegals, sometimes called freelance paralegals. Such individuals often work for more than one attorney on a short-term basis. Their work for Kathleen Zellner, Esq. in the Chicago area did not go well, as you will see in the case of *Becker v. Zellner.*

CASE

Jeffrey Becker, Steven Becker, and Thomas Becker
v.
Kathleen Zellner and Associates
292 Ill. App. 3d 116, 684 N.E.2d 1378
Appellate Court of Illinois, Second District (1997)

Background: *Jeffrey, Steven, and Thomas Becker (the plaintiffs) are independent paralegals in Illinois. Among the attorneys for whom they worked were Kathleen Zellner and Associates (the defendants). The Beckers brought a defamation complaint against the defendants for saying:*

- *the plaintiffs submitted "a $45,000 bill for five pages of worthless memorandum,"*
- *a client should not contact the plaintiffs,*
- *the plaintiffs were "devious" in how they conducted their independent paralegal business, and would "try to get into the back door" when charging for their paralegal services.*

The trial court dismissed the complaint. The case is now on appeal before the Appellate Court of Illinois, Second District where the paralegal brothers are representing themselves (pro se).

Decision on Appeal: *The judgment dismissing the complaint is reversed. The attorney's statements about the paralegals were defamatory per se and the case should proceed to trial.*

OPINION OF COURT

Justice BOWMAN delivered the opinion of the court. . . .:
On May 6, 1996, plaintiffs filed a . . . complaint against defendants in which they alleged that, as paralegals, they assisted defendants in their representation of Frank Lyons dur-

ing the fall of 1994. On May 9, 1995, Sharon Wendt, a friend of Lyons, called defendants in order to obtain plaintiffs' telephone number for Lyons. Lyons apparently wanted plaintiffs to work with his new attorney. In the presence of an associate of her firm, defendant Zellner accepted Wendt's call and placed it on a speakerphone. Zellner then allegedly told Wendt (1) that during plaintiffs' employment with her, they had submitted "a $45,000 bill for five pages of worthless memorandum"; (2) that Lyons should not contact plaintiffs; and (3) that plaintiffs were "devious" and that they would try to "get into the back door" when charging Lyons for their services. Plaintiffs' complaint further alleged that later on May 9, 1995, Lyons "left a message on their answering machine stating that he wanted to know whether Plaintiffs were going to stick him with a $45,000.00 bill." Lyons did not hire plaintiffs to assist him in the preparation of his case, and their "business relationship and reputation" with Lyons were "never the same" after Zellner's telephone conversation with Wendt. . . . [The] defendants filed a motion to dismiss . . . [the paralegals' defamation complaint, which] the trial court granted. . . .

Defendants' motion to dismiss . . . sought the dismissal of plaintiffs' complaint for "failure to make a claim for which relief may be granted." Accordingly, the question on review is "whether sufficient facts are contained in the pleadings which, if established, could entitle [plaintiffs] to relief." *Illinois Graphics v. Nickum,* 159 Ill. 2d 469, 488, 639

N.E.2d 1282 (1994). A cause of action should be dismissed when it is apparent that no set of facts can be proved that would entitle the nonmovant to relief.

In . . . their complaint, plaintiffs alleged that Zellner had committed slander *per se* during her conversation with Wendt. Specifically, plaintiffs pointed to Zellner's alleged statements that they had submitted "a $45,000 bill for five pages of worthless memorandum," that Lyons should not contact them, and that they were "devious" and "would try to get into the back door." According to plaintiffs, these alleged statements constituted slander *per se* because they pertained to plaintiffs' "profession and employment." The trial court found the statements "susceptible of an innocent construction as a matter of law" and dismissed the *per se* [cause of action].

The four categories of statements which are considered actionable *per se* [in Illinois] include: "(1) [W]ords that impute the commission of a criminal offense; (2) words that impute infection with a loathsome communicable disease; (3) words that impute an inability to perform or want of integrity in the discharge of duties of office or employment; or (4) words that prejudice a party, or impute lack of ability, in his or her trade, profession or business." *Bryson v. News America Publications, Inc.,* 174 Ill. 2d 77, 88, 672 N.E.2d 1207 (1996).

Even if words fall into a *per se* category, the claim will not be actionable if the words are capable of an innocent construction. *Bryson,* 174 Ill. 2d at 90. Under the innocent construction rule, courts consider the statement "in context, giving the words, and their implications, their natural and obvious meaning." *Bryson,* 174 Ill. 2d at 90. Importantly, only a *reasonable* innocent construction will negate the *per se* effect of an allegedly defamatory statement. Courts decide, as a matter of law, whether an allegedly defamatory statement is reasonably capable of being innocently construed.

Plaintiffs argue that Zellner's alleged statements fall into the fourth *per se* category, as words that impute their lack of abilities as paralegals. We agree. In context, Zellner's allegedly defamatory statements were obviously intended to describe and denigrate plaintiffs' abilities as paralegals. She allegedly called plaintiffs' work product "worthless," labeled them as "devious," and, in an apparent attempt to further impugn their character, told Wendt that they would try to "get into the back door" during their billing process. The natural and obvious meaning of these words prejudices plaintiffs and imputes a lack of ability in their profession as paralegals.

Despite counsel's . . . creative attempt at oral argument to the contrary, the natural and obvious meanings of "worthless" and "devious" are negative. Webster's Dictionary defines "devious" as "hard to pin down or bring to agreement" and lists as synonyms "shifty, tricky, unscrupulous, [and] unfair." *Webster's Third New International Dictionary* 619 (1986). Moreover, Webster's defines "worthless" as "lacking value or material worth" and lists "useless" as a synonym. *Webster's Third New International Dictionary* 2637 (1986). Counsel's alternative definitions of these words at oral argument were accurate, but the mere existence of other dictionary definitions does not automatically indicate an innocent construction. Rather, under the innocent construction rule, we are neither required to "strain to find an unnatural but possibly innocent meaning for words where the defamatory meaning is far more reasonable," nor are we required to "espouse a naïveté unwarranted under the circumstances." *Bryson,* 174 Ill. 2d at 94. Thus, we reject defendants' contention that Zellner's alleged statements can be innocently construed. . . .

For the foregoing reasons, the judgment [dismissing the slander *per se* complaint] is . . . reversed . . . and the cause is remanded for proceedings consistent with this opinion.

ASSIGNMENT

24.8

a. The attorney tried to argue that the words "worthless" and "devious" are not necessarily negative. What meanings do you think the attorney tried to offer?

b. Chris Eagan is a paralegal who works for David Vinson, Esq. Both live in the same neighborhood. One day, Vinson tells a neighbor that Chris "is barely making it" at the office. Is this slander per se under the *Becker* case?

c. Same facts as (c), only this time Vinson makes this comment to his law partner.

PRIVILEGE

There are a number of situations in which a defendant has, in effect, a **privilege** to defame. A privilege is the right to act contrary to another individual's right without being subject to tort or other liability. The existence of a privilege is a defense to the tort action. Two kinds of privileges exist: absolute and qualified.

Absolute Privilege

An **absolute privilege** is a privilege that cannot be lost because of the bad motives of the party asserting the privilege. The holder of such a privilege is not subject to defamation liability even though he or she knows the statement is false and has personal ill will toward or intends to harm the subject of the defamation. In short, the privilege is absolute.

> **EXAMPLE:** Judge Smith says to attorney Jones during a trial, "your incompetence knows no equal among the practicing bar in the state."

Judge Smith has an absolute privilege to utter this defamatory statement even if the judge knows it is false and utters it solely out of hatred of Jones.

There are several categories of individuals who can assert this absolute privilege:

1. Judges, attorneys, parties, witnesses, and jurors while performing their functions during judicial proceedings.
2. Members of Congress, the state legislature, and city councils or other local legislative bodies while the members are performing their functions during legislative proceedings. Witnesses testifying before these bodies also have an absolute privilege to defame.
3. High executive or administrative officers of the government while performing their official duties.

Qualified Privilege

A **qualified privilege** (also called a *conditional privilege*) is a privilege that can be lost if it is not exercised in a reasonable manner for a proper purpose.[9] Some states are more specific on how this privilege can be lost in defamation cases. For example, some states say it is lost if the defamer did not believe the statement was true or did not have reasonable grounds to believe the statement was true. Other states say that the privilege is lost only if the defamer was reckless in determining its truth or falsity.

Who can assert qualified privileges? As we saw earlier, everyone has a right to make a *fair comment* on a matter of public interest. This is a qualified privilege that can be lost if it is abused. We also saw that many states have a *fair report* privilege that allows the media to publish stories on government reports and proceedings, even if the stories contain defamatory statements made in the government reports or proceedings. This privilege can be lost if the media's story is not fair and accurate.

The most common qualified privilege is the privilege to protect your own legitimate interests.

> **EXAMPLE:** Tony calls Diane a "liar" after Diane says Tony stole her money.

Tony has defamed Diane. If she sues him for defamation, his defense is the qualified privilege of protecting his interest in his own integrity. The privilege would be lost, however, if Tony goes beyond the scope of protecting his interest such as by calling Diane a prostitute or by responding solely out of revenge to hurt Diane.

Under limited circumstances, a person also has a qualified privilege to defame in order to protect *others*. The defamer must be under a legal or moral obligation to protect the other and must act reasonably in believing the protection is necessary.

> **EXAMPLE:** Lena tells her daughter that it would be disastrous for her to marry "a bum and a gigolo like Paul."

Finally, people who share a *common interest* have a qualified privilege to communicate about matters that will protect or advance that interest.

> **EXAMPLE:** One employee of a company says to another, "don't buy anything from the Eagle Supplier Corp. since all of its goods are stolen."

---

[9]W. Page Keeton et al., *Prosser and Keeton on the Law of Torts* 832 (5th ed. 1984).

In the following cases, what defenses, if any, can the defendant raise in the defamation action? (See General Instructions for the Legal Analysis Assignment in Chapter 2.)

a. Alex calls ABC Insurance Company and says that Jackson, his neighbor, has filed fraudulent automobile-accident claims against the company. The neighbor sues Alex for defamation.

b. Same facts as in (a). ABC Insurance Company tells a different insurance company that Jackson has been charged with filing fraudulent claims. Jackson sues ABC Insurance Company for defamation.

SLAPP SUITS

It is relatively easy to sue someone. All you need is an allegation and court filing fees. Many defendants, however, are quite upset when they find out they are being sued, particularly after a process server formally hands them the official documents that signal the beginning of litigation. In this environment of tension, some individuals use defamation suits to intimidate those who have complained about something.

> **EXAMPLE:**   Mary Adams tries to organize fellow trailer-home owners against the fees imposed by the park where the trailers are located. She writes a newsletter in which she says that the park owner, Ron Ullson, should be reported to the government for imposing "greedy" fees. Ullson then sues Adams for defamation.

Arguably, the defamation suit is meritless and Ron Ullson is simply trying to use the suit to intimidate Mary Adams—to scare her off. Even if he loses the defamation suit, he may cause her so much agony that she will drop her efforts to organize the trailer-home owners. Emotional and financial costs of defending the defamation action can be overwhelming.

If this is Ullson's motive, his suit is known as an intimidation suit. It is also called a **SLAPP suit,** which stands for "strategic lawsuit against public participation." They are meritless suits brought primarily for the purpose of chilling the defendant's exercise of the right to free speech and to petition the government for a redress of grievances. The cause of action in these suits is usually defamation, but other causes of action are also common such as the tort of interference with economic advantage, which we will consider in Chapter 26.

What can a defendant do in such cases, particularly the defendant who does not have the economic resources of the party who "slapped" the defendant with the intimidation suit? As we discussed in Chapter 8, the defendant can sue the plaintiff for the tort of malicious prosecution, but this can be a cumbersome and expensive remedy.[10] A more direct method of relief is to use the anti-SLAPP statute that about eight states have passed to help curb the use of intimidation suits to muzzle citizens. In California, for example, victims of SLAPP suits can assert a special motion to strike the defamation or other suit. The motion will be granted unless there is a probability that the plaintiff will prevail on the claim. This can end a meritless suit well before the full ordeal of a trial is played out. Furthermore, the defendant may be able to recover his or her attorney fees and costs in defending the SLAPP suit.

---

[10]A party can also file an ethics charge against the attorney who helped the plaintiff bring the SLAPP suit. It is unethical for an attorney to assert a frivolous claim for a client. The ethics charge, however, is resolved later; it does not stop the SLAPP suit.

"VEGGIE LIBEL"

Occasionally, people will make unflattering comments about certain consumer products, e.g., "there are dangerous pesticides in Idaho potatoes." Can you defame a potato? Several states have enacted statutes that allow suits for maligning or disparaging certain products. The media has labeled such suits "veggie libel cases." We will consider them later in Chapter 26.

SUMMARY

There are two defamation torts: libel (written or embodied in a physical form) and slander (spoken or gestured). A statement of fact is defamatory if it would tend to harm the reputation of the plaintiff in the eyes of at least a substantial and respectable minority of people by lowering the plaintiff in the estimation of those people or by deterring them to associate with the plaintiff. In general, defamatory opinions are not actionable unless they imply the existence of defamatory facts, i.e., facts that can be objectively established as true or false. The privilege of fair comment and the media's First Amendment rights make defamation suits based on derogatory opinions difficult to win.

When extrinsic facts had to be alleged for the explanation of the defamatory statement (the innuendo), the facts were pleaded in the inducement. At common law, the falsity of the statement was assumed; truth was an affirmative defense. Constitutional law has changed this for media defendants. Fault must be proven. If the defamatory statement pertained to a matter of public concern about a public official or a public figure, the plaintiff must show by clear and convincing evidence that the defendant knew the statement was false or was reckless as to its truth or falsity (actual malice). If the defamatory statement pertained to a matter of private concern about a public official or a public figure, the plaintiff must show by clear and convincing evidence that the defendant knew the statement was false or was reckless or negligent as to its truth or falsity. If the defamatory statement pertained to a matter of public or private concern about a private person, the plaintiff must show by clear and convincing evidence that the defendant knew the statement was false or was reckless or negligent as to its truth or falsity.

The defamatory statement must be of and concerning the plaintiff. Extrinsic facts may need to be pleaded in the colloquium of the complaint to establish that the defamatory statement was of and concerning the plaintiff. Publication of the statement occurs when it is intentionally or negligently communicated to someone other than the plaintiff. The repetition or republication of a defamatory statement by someone else is treated as a publication of the statement. The media, however, has the protection of the new constitutional law of defamation and, in some states, a fair report privilege. Entities that merely deliver or transmit the defamatory statement such as bookstores and telephone companies, however, are not liable for defamation unless they have reason to know that they are transmitting defamatory material. Providers of interactive computer services on the Internet have an immunity from tort liability based on defamatory statements made by others on the online service of the providers.

In non-media cases, most libel on its face does not require special damages. Libel per quod does in some states, slander per se does not, and slander per quod does.

Judges, attorneys, parties, witnesses, and jurors have an absolute privilege to make defamatory statements while performing their duties in judicial proceedings. The same is true of legislators, legislative witnesses, and high executive officers. An absolute privilege cannot be lost by bad motives. Under certain circumstances, defendants have a qualified privilege to defame in order to protect their own legitimate interests, the interests of others, or common interests. Everyone has the qualified privilege of fair comment on a matter of public interest or concern, and in some states, the media has the qualified fair report privilege. A qualified privilege can be lost if it is not exercised in a reasonable manner for a proper purpose.

Plaintiffs sometimes "slapp" defendants with meritless defamation suits solely to intimidate them. Several states give SLAPP victims the right to assert special motions designed to end such suits quickly.

KEY TERMS

defamation   476
libel   476
slander   476
defamacast   476
defamatory statement   481
opinion   481
fact   481
fair comment   482
on its face   484
extrinsic fact   484
inducement   484
innuendo   484
affirmative defense   484

fault   485
public official   485
public figure   485
private person   486
actual malice   486
constitutional malice   486
New York Times malice   486
of and concerning the
    plaintiff   488
colloquium   488
publication   488
republication   489
fair report privilege   489

cyberspace   490
immunity   490
presumed damages   491
special damages   491
libel per quod   491
slander per se   491
slander per quod   491
privilege   493
absolute privilege   493
qualified privilege   494
SLAPP suit   495

CHAPTER

25

Invasion of Privacy

CHAPTER OUTLINE

- Four Torts
- Intrusion
- Appropriation
- Public Disclosure of Private Fact
- False Light
- Media Defendants

FOUR TORTS

Invasion of privacy consists of four torts: intrusion, appropriation, public disclosure of private fact, and false light. Each has its own elements. In general, the torts are designed to protect an individual's interest in being left alone that is violated because of an unreasonable form of attention or publicity.

 Invasion-of-Privacy Checklist

Definitions, Relationships, Paralegal Roles, and Research References

Interests Protected by These Torts

Intrusion: The right to be free from unreasonable intrusions into a person's private affairs or concerns. This tort is also called *intrusion on seclusion.*

Appropriation: The right to prevent the unauthorized use of a person's name, likeness, or personality for someone else's benefit.

Public Disclosure of Private Facts: The right to be free from unreasonable disclosures of private facts about a person's life that are not matters of legitimate public concern.

False Light: The right to be free from false statements that unreasonably place a person in a false light in the public eye.

Elements of These Torts

1. Intrusion:
    i. an act of intrusion into someone's private affairs or concerns
    ii. highly offensive to a reasonable person
2. Appropriation:
    i. the use of the plaintiff's name, likeness, or personality
    ii. for the benefit of the defendant
3. Public disclosure of private fact:
    i. publicity
    ii. concerning the private life of the plaintiff
    iii. highly offensive to a reasonable person
4. False light:
    i. publicity
    ii. placing the plaintiff in a false light
    iii. highly offensive to a reasonable person

Definitions of Major Words/Phrases in These Elements

Intrusion: Prying, peering, or probing.

Private: Pertaining to facts about an individual's personal life that have no reasonable or logical connection to what the person does in public and that the person does not consent to reveal.

Reasonable Person: An ordinary person who is not unduly sensitive.

Benefit: Deriving some advantage.

Publicity: Communication to the public at large or to a large group of people.

Major Defense and Counterargument Possibilities That Need to Be Explored

1. There was no prying, peering, or probing (for Intrusion).
2. What the defendant did related to the public activities of the defendant (for Intrusion, Public Disclosure of Private Fact, and False Light).
3. The defendant did not use plaintiff's name, likeness, or personality (for Appropriation).
4. The defendant did not derive benefit from the use of the plaintiff's name, likeness, or personality—or derived only incidental benefit from such use (for Appropriation).
5. The statement about the plaintiff was not communicated to the public at large nor to a large group of people (for Public Disclosure of Private Fact and False Light).
6. No inaccurate impression or statement was made about the plaintiff (for False Light).
7. The plaintiff consented to what the defendant did (for all four torts)(on the defense of consent, see Chapter 27).
8. The defendant's conduct occurred while the defendant was arresting the plaintiff, protecting the defendant's own property, or giving testimony in a public proceeding

Invasion-of-Privacy Checklist Continued

(for Intrusion, Public Disclosure of Private Fact, and False Light)(on the privilege of arrest, see Chapter 7; on defense of property and other self-help privileges, see Chapter 27).

9. The plaintiff's suit against the government employee for invasion of privacy may be barred by public official immunity (for all four torts)(on official immunity, see Chapter 27).
10. The plaintiff's suit against the charitable organization for invasion of privacy committed by someone working for the organization may be barred by charitable immunity (for all four torts)(on charitable immunity, see Chapter 27).
11. The plaintiff's suit against a family member for invasion of privacy may be barred by intrafamily immunity (for all four torts)(on intrafamily immunity, see Chapter 27).
12. The plaintiff failed to take reasonable steps to mitigate the harm caused by the defendant's invasion of privacy; therefore, damages should not cover the aggravation of the harm caused by the plaintiff (for all four torts) (on the doctrine of avoidable consequences, see Chapter 16).

Damages

The plaintiff can recover compensatory damages for humiliation or embarrassment caused by the defendant. If the plaintiff suffered mental or physical illness due to the tort committed by the defendant, recovery can also include damages for the illness. If the defendant's conduct constituted more than one of the four torts, there can be only one recovery. If the defendant acted with a malicious motive to harm or injure the plaintiff, punitive damages are possible. (On the categories of damages, see Chapter 16.)

Relationship to Criminal Law

If the defendant committed Intrusion by wiretapping or other electronic devices, the conduct may also violate the criminal law.

Relationship to Other Torts

Defamation: Libel or slander may be committed along with False Light if the statement is also derogatory (harms the plaintiff's reputation).

Intentional Infliction of Emotional Distress: This tort is committed along with any of the four invasion-of-privacy torts if the defendant committed an outrageous act with the intent to cause severe emotional distress.

Malicious Prosecution: One example of Intrusion is to pry into the plaintiff's private affairs through procedural devices such as subpoenas. In such cases, malicious prosecution may also be committed.

Misrepresentation: Misrepresentation may be committed along with False Light when the following elements can be established: a false statement of fact, intent to deceive, intent that the plaintiff rely on the statement, justifiable reliance, and actual damages.

Prima Facie Torts: If the plaintiff cannot establish the elements of any of the four invasion-of-privacy torts, the plaintiff should check prima facie tort in those states that recognize it.

Federal Law

a. Under the Federal Tort Claims Act, the United States Government can be liable for invasion of privacy committed by one of its federal employees within the scope of employment (respondeat superior) (see Figure 27–7 in Chapter 27).
b. There may be liability under the Civil Rights Act if the invasion of privacy was committed while the defendant was depriving the plaintiff of federal rights under color of law (see Figure 27–9 in Chapter 27).

Employer-Employee (Agency) Law

An employee who commits an invasion of privacy is personally liable for this tort. His or her employer will *also* be liable for invasion of privacy if the conduct of the employee was within the scope of employment (respondeat superior). The employee must be furthering a business objective of the employer at the time. (On the factors that determine scope of employment, see Figure 14–10 in Chapter 14.)

Paralegal Roles in Invasion-of-Privacy Litigation

(See also Figures 3–1, 3–14, and 29–1 in Chapters 3 and 29.)

Invasion-of-Privacy Checklist Continued

Fact finding (help the office collect facts relevant to prove the elements of the four invasion-of-privacy torts, the elements of available defenses, and extent of injuries or other damages):
- client interviewing
- field investigation
- online research (e.g., obtaining public records)

File management (help the office control the volume of paperwork in an invasion-of-privacy litigation):
- open client file
- enter case data in computer database
- maintain file documents

Litigation assistance (help the trial attorney prepare for an invasion-of-privacy trial and appeal, if needed):
- draft discovery requests
- draft answers to discovery requests
- draft pleadings
- digest and index discovery documents
- prepare trial notebook
- draft notice of appeal
- order trial transcript
- cite check briefs
- perform legal research

Collection/enforcement (help the trial attorney for the judgment creditor to collect the damages award or to enforce an injunction or other court order at the conclusion of the invasion-of-privacy case):
- draft postjudgment discovery requests
- field investigation to monitor compliance with judgment
- online research (e.g., location of defendant's business assets)

Research References for Invasion-of-Privacy Torts

Digests
In the digests of West, look for case summaries on these torts under key topics such as:

Torts	Constitutional Law (274)
Damages	

Corpus Juris Secundum
In this legal encyclopedia, see the discussions under topic headings such as:

Constitutional Law (582)	Torts
Right of Privacy	Damages

American Jurisprudence 2d
In this legal encyclopedia, see the discussions under topic headings such as:

Privacy	Damages
Constitutional Law (503)	Fright, Shock, and
Torts	Mental Disturbance

Legal Periodical Literature
There are two index systems to use to locate articles and other legal periodical literature on these torts:

INDEX TO LEGAL PERIODICALS (ILP)	CURRENT LAW INDEX (CLI)
See literature in *ILP* under subject headings such as:	See literature in *CLI* under subject headings such as:
Right of Privacy	Privacy, Right of Liberty of the Press
Eavesdropping	Torts
Torts	Damages
Freedom of the Press	
Damages	

Invasion-of-Privacy Checklist Continued

Example of a legal periodical article you can find by using *ILP* or *CLI*:

Invasion of Privacy: New Guidelines for the Public Disclosure Tort by Greg Trout, 6 Capitol University Law Review 95 (1976).

A.L.R., A.L.R.2d, A.L.R.3d, A.L.R.4th, A.L.R.5th, A.L.R. Fed.

Use the *ALR Index* to locate annotations on these torts. In this index, check subject headings such as:

Privacy	Newspapers
Harassment	Torts
Eavesdropping	Damages

Example of an annotation you can locate through this index on these torts:

Publication of Address as well as Name of Person as Invasion of Privacy by Phillip E. Hassman, 84 A.L.R.3d 1159 (1978).

Words and Phrases

In this multivolume legal dictionary, look up *invasion of privacy, intrusion, appropriation, false light,* and every other word or phrase connected with the four invasion-of-privacy torts discussed in this chapter. The dictionary will give you definitions of these words or phrases from court opinions.

CALR: Computer-Assisted Legal Research

Example of a query you could ask on WESTLAW to try to find cases, statutes, or other legal materials on these four torts: **"invasion of privacy"/p damages**

Example of a query you could ask on LEXIS to try to find cases, statutes, or other legal materials on these four torts: **invasion of privacy/p damages**

Example of search terms you could use on an Internet legal search engine such as LawCrawler (http://lawcrawler.findlaw.com) to find cases, statutes, or other legal materials on these four torts: **"invasion of privacy" AND tort**

Example of search terms you could use on an Internet general search engine such as Alta Vista (http://www.altavista.com) to find cases, statutes, or other legal materials on these four torts: **+invasion of privacy" +tort**

More Internet sites to check for materials on invasion of privacy and other torts:
Jurist: (http://jurist.law.pitt.edu/sg_torts.htm)
LawGuru: (http://www.lawguru.com/search/lawsearch.html)
See also Tort Law Online at the end of Chapter 1.

INTRUSION

The elements of the tort of **intrusion** (also called *intrusion on seclusion*) are:

1. an act of intrusion into someone's private affairs or concerns
2. highly offensive to a reasonable person

Intrusion consists of prying, peering, or probing of some kind, e.g., wiretapping, opening mail, filing subpoenas that require disclosure of records, making persistent phone calls. Such methods of intrusion must be directed at something that is considered one's **private affairs.** It is usually not an intrusion to follow the plaintiff in a department store or to photograph him or her in a park. In these settings, the plaintiff is engaging in public activity. There are a number of factors a court will consider in determining whether something is private, none of which is usually conclusive alone. These factors are outlined in Figure 25–1.

Not every intrusion into private matters is tortious. The intrusion must be highly offensive to a **reasonable person.** The test is objective—what the reasonable person considers **highly offensive.** The plaintiff may be greatly offended by a call from a bill collector at the plaintiff's workplace. But a reasonable person would probably not be highly offended by such a call. The case may be different, however, if calls are made every fifteen minutes starting at midnight while the plaintiff is trying to sleep at home.

FIGURE 25–1
Factors a court will consider when deciding whether plaintiff was engaged in a private activity.

A. "Yes" answers to the following questions will help persuade a court that the activity was *not* private:

- Was the plaintiff in a public place at the time?
- Was the activity of the plaintiff observable by normal methods of observation?
- Was the activity of the plaintiff already a matter of public record before the defendant became involved?
- Was the plaintiff drawing attention to him- or herself?

B. "Yes" answers to the following questions will help persuade a court that the activity *was* private:

- Was the plaintiff caught off guard through no fault of his or her own?
- Did the defendant take advantage of a vulnerable position that the plaintiff was in?
- Was the activity of the plaintiff something that society would consider none of anyone else's business?

ASSIGNMENT

25.1

Has the tort of intrusion been committed in any of the following situations? (See General Instructions for the Legal Analysis Assignment in Chapter 2.)

a. Tim photographs Karla at an amusement park in the fun house at the moment an air vent on the floor blows up her dress.

b. At a bus terminal, a wall television camera is clearly visible in the men's room.

c. General Motors hires a prostitute to solicit Ralph Nader to engage in sexual activities. Ralph refuses.

CASE

Hamberger v. Eastman
106 N.H. 107, 206 A.2d 239, 11 A.L.R.3d 1288 (1964)
Supreme Court of New Hampshire

Background: *The Hambergers are husband and wife. They are weekly tenants of Eastman. When they discovered that he had installed a concealed listening and recording device in their bedroom, they sued him for invasion of privacy. The defendant moved to dismiss on the ground that the plaintiffs had not stated a cause of action. The trial court transferred the case to the Supreme Court without making a ruling, probably because the privacy cause of action had not yet been recognized in the state. The case is now before the Supreme Court of New Hampshire.*

Decision on Appeal: *Motion to dismiss should be denied. The plaintiffs have stated an invasion of privacy cause of action for intrusion. The case is sent back (remanded) to the trial court for the trial.*

OPINION OF COURT

Justice Kenison delivered the opinion of the court:

The question presented is whether the right of privacy is recognized in this state. There is no controlling statute and no previous decision in this jurisdiction which decides the question. . . . In capsule summary the invasion of the right of privacy developed as an independent and distinct tort from the classic and famous article by Warren and Bran-

deis, *The Right to Privacy,* 4 Harvard Law Review 193 (1890). . . . It is not one tort, but a complex of four. The law of privacy comprises four distinct kinds of invasion of four different interests of the plaintiff which are tied together by the common name, but otherwise have almost nothing in common except that each presents an interference with the right of the plaintiff "to be let alone." Prosser, *Torts,* § 112, p. 832 (3d ed. 1964).

The four kinds of invasion comprising the law of privacy include: (1) intrusion upon the plaintiff's physical and mental solitude or seclusion; (2) public disclosure of private facts; (3) publicity which places the plaintiff in a false light in the public eye; (4) appropriation, for the defendant's benefit or advantage, of the plaintiff's name or likeness. In the present case, we are concerned only with the tort of intrusion upon the plaintiffs' solitude or seclusion. . . .

The tort of intrusion upon the plaintiff's solitude or seclusion is not limited to a physical invasion of his home or his room or his quarters. As Prosser points out, the principle has been carried beyond such physical intrusion "and extended to eavesdropping upon private conversations by means of wire tapping and microphones." Prosser, supra, p. 833. . . . The right of privacy has been upheld in situations where microphones have been planted to overhear private conversations. *Roach v. Harper,* 143 W. Va. 869, 105 S.E.2d 564.

We have not searched for cases where the bedroom of husband and wife has been "bugged" but it should not be necessary—by way of understatement—to observe that this is the type of intrusion that would be offensive to any person of ordinary sensibilities. What married "people do in the privacy of their bedroom is their own business so long as they are not hurting anyone else." Ernst and Loth, *For Better or Worse,* 79 (1952). The *Restatement, Torts* § 867 provides that "a person who unreasonably and seriously interferes with another's interest in not having his affairs known to others . . . is liable to the other." As is pointed out in comment d "liability exists only if the defendant's conduct was such that he should have realized that it would be offensive to persons of ordinary sensibilities. It is only where the intrusion has gone beyond the limits of decency that liability accrues. These limits are exceeded where intimate details of the life of one who has never manifested a desire to have publicity are exposed to the public. . .".

The defendant contends that the right of privacy should not be recognized on the facts of the present case as they appear in the pleadings because there are no allegations that anyone listened or overheard any sounds or voices originating from the plaintiffs' bedroom. The tort of intrusion on the plaintiffs' solitude or seclusion does not require publicity and communication to third persons although

this would affect the amount of damages, as Prosser makes clear. Prosser, supra, 843. The defendant also contends that the right of privacy is not violated unless something has been published, written or printed and that oral publicity is not sufficient. Recent cases make it clear that this is not a requirement. *Carr v. Watkins,* 227 Md. 578, 177 A.2d 841.

If the peeping Tom, the big ear and the electronic eavesdropper (whether ingenious or ingenuous) have a place in the hierarchy of social values, it ought not to be at the expense of a married couple minding their own business in the seclusion of their bedroom who have never asked for or by their conduct deserved a potential projection of their private conversations and actions to their landlord or to others. Whether actual or potential such "publicity with respect to private matters of purely personal concern is an injury to personality. It impairs the mental peace and comfort of the individual and may produce suffering more acute than that produced by a mere bodily injury." III Pound, *Jurisprudence* 58 (1959). The use of parabolic microphones and sonic wave devices designed to pick up conversations in a room without entering it and at a considerable distance away makes the problem far from fanciful. . . . [T]he invasion of the plaintiffs' solitude or seclusion, as alleged in the pleadings, was a violation of their right of privacy and constituted a tort for which the plaintiffs may recover damages to the extent that they can prove them. . . .

The motion to dismiss should be denied. Remanded.

ASSIGNMENT

25.2

a. Would the *Hamberger* court have reached a different result if the landlord installed the listening devices because of his suspicion that the married couple was planning to set fire to his building?

b. How would the *Hamberger* court have decided the bus terminal case in Assignment 25.1(b)?

CASE

Smyth v. The Pillsbury Co.
914 F. Supp. 97 (1996)
United States District Court, Eastern District, Pennsylvania

Background: *Michael Smyth was an at-will employee of The Pillsbury Company. (At-will employees can be terminated at any time for any reason that does not violate public policy.) Smyth was fired after sending an e-mail that contained threats to "kill the backstabbing bastards" and that referred to a planned holiday party as the "Jim Jones Koolaid affair." (Jim Jones was a cult leader who persuaded hundreds of his followers to commit mass suicide by drinking poison-laced Koolaid.) Smyth sued the company in District Court for wrongful termination. He argued that the reading of his e-mail messages constituted the tort of intrusion and that a firing that resulted from this invasion of privacy was*

wrongful. At the trial, the defendant moved to dismiss on the ground that the plaintiff has failed to state a claim on which relief can granted. In effect, the company denied that there was an invasion of privacy. The portions of the opinion excerpted below pertain to this tort claim.

Decision of Court: *The District Court granted the motion to dismiss. The firing for transmitting inappropriate and unprofessional comments over Pillsbury's e-mail system was not wrongful since there was no invasion of privacy.*

OPINION OF COURT
Judge WEINER delivered the opinion of the court. . . .

[P]laintiff, an at-will employee, claims he was wrongfully discharged from his position as a regional operations manager by the defendant [Pillsbury]. Defendant maintained an electronic mail communication system ("e-mail") in order to promote internal corporate communications between its employees. Defendant repeatedly assured its employees, including plaintiff, that all e-mail communications would remain confidential and privileged. Defendant further assured its employees, including plaintiff, that e-mail communications could not be intercepted and used by defendant against its employees as grounds for termination or reprimand.

In October 1994, plaintiff received certain e-mail communications from his supervisor over defendant's e-mail system on his computer at home. In reliance on defendant's assurances regarding defendant's e-mail system, plaintiff responded and exchanged e-mails with his supervisor. At some later date, contrary to the assurances of confidentiality made by defendant, defendant, acting through its agents, servants and employees, intercepted plaintiff's private e-mail messages made in October 1994. On January 17, 1995, defendant notified plaintiff that it was terminating his employment effective February 1, 1995, for transmitting what it deemed to be inappropriate and unprofessional comments over defendant's e-mail system in October, 1994. . . . [The e-mails concerned sales management and contained threats to "kill the backstabbing bastards" and referred to the planned holiday party as the "Jim Jones Koolaid affair."]

Plaintiff claims that his termination was [improper because it was based on an invasion of privacy.]. . . [O]ne of the torts which Pennsylvania recognizes as encompassing an action for invasion of privacy is the tort of "intrusion upon seclusion.". . . [T]he *Restatement (Second) of Torts* defines the tort as follows: One who intentionally intrudes, physically or otherwise, upon the solitude or seclusion of another or his private affairs or concerns, is subject to liability to the other for invasion of his privacy, if the intrusion would be highly offensive to a reasonable person. *Restatement (Second) of Torts* 652B. Liability only attaches when the [intrusion is substantial]. . . .

Applying the *Restatement* definition of the tort of intrusion upon seclusion to the facts, . . . we find that plaintiff has failed to state a claim upon which relief can be granted. In the first instance, . . . we do not find a reasonable expectation of privacy in e-mail communications voluntarily made by an employee to his supervisor over the company e-mail system notwithstanding any assurances that such communications would not be intercepted by management. Once plaintiff communicated the alleged unprofessional comments to a second person (his supervisor) over an e-mail system which was apparently utilized by the entire company, any reasonable expectation of privacy was lost. Significantly, the defendant did not require plaintiff, . . . to disclose any personal information about himself. Rather, plaintiff voluntarily communicated the alleged unprofessional comments over the company e-mail system. We find no privacy interests in such communications.

In the second instance, even if we found that an employee had a reasonable expectation of privacy in the contents of his e-mail communications over the company e-mail system, we do not find that a reasonable person would consider the defendant's interception of these communications to be a substantial and highly offensive invasion of his privacy. Again, we note that by intercepting such communications, the company is not, . . ., requiring the employee to disclose any personal information about himself or invading the employee's person or personal effects. Moreover, the company's interest in preventing inappropriate and unprofessional comments or even illegal activity over its e-mail system outweighs any privacy interest the employee may have in those comments.

In sum, we find that the defendant's actions did not tortiously invade the plaintiff's privacy. . . . As a result, the motion to dismiss is granted.

ASSIGNMENT **25.3**	a. What legitimate business reasons might exist that could make it reasonable for a company to monitor and read all e-mail correspondence on its system? b. Is the court's conclusion in the *Hamberger* case consistent with the conclusion reached in the *Smyth* case? c. Suppose that in the *Smyth* case the director of the personnel department at Pillsbury sends all employees the following e-mail message: "As you know the Red Cross will be here next week to collect blood. We want 100% participation." Michael Smyth sends an e-mail back that says he cannot contribute blood because of a rare disease he has. The director sends a copy of this response to Smyth's supervisor and to a co-worker, neither of whom knew about this health problem. Would the *Smyth* court say it was an invasion of privacy for the personnel director to have allowed these individuals to read the e-mail?

Several states have passed statutes that are designed to curb some of the most blatant kinds of intrusion, particularly by *paparazzi,* photographers who stalk celebrities for photographs. For example, the Hollywood community cheered the enactment of the following California law in 1998 that they argued was long overdue:

California Civil Code § 1708.8 (1998)

(a) A person is liable for physical invasion of privacy when the defendant knowingly enters onto the land of another without permission or otherwise committed a trespass, in order to physically invade the privacy of the plaintiff with the intent to capture any type of visual image, sound recording, or other physical impression of the plaintiff engaging in a personal or familial activity and the physical invasion occurs in a manner that is offensive to a reasonable person.

(b) A person is liable for constructive invasion of privacy when the defendant attempts to capture, in a manner that is offensive to a reasonable person, any type of visual image, sound recording, or other physical impression of the plaintiff engaging in a personal or familial activity under circumstances in which the plaintiff had a reasonable expectation of privacy, through the use of a visual or auditory enhancing device, regardless of whether there is a physical trespass, if this image, sound recording, or other physical impression could not have been achieved without a trespass unless the visual or auditory enhancing device was used.

(c) A person who commits physical invasion of privacy or constructive invasion of privacy, or both, is liable for up to three times the amount of any general and special damages that are proximately caused by the violation of this section. This person may also be liable for punitive damages. . . . If the plaintiff proves that the invasion of privacy was committed for a commercial purpose, the defendant shall also be subject to disgorgement to the plaintiff of any proceeds or other consideration obtained as a result of the violation of this section. . . .

(i) It is not a defense to a violation of this section that no image, recording, or physical impression was captured or sold. . . .

(k) For the purposes of this section, "personal and familial activity" includes, but is not limited to, intimate details of the plaintiff's personal life, interactions with the plaintiff's family or significant others, or other aspects of plaintiff's private affairs or concerns. . . .

APPROPRIATION

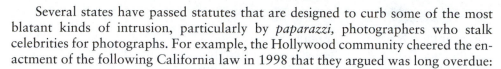

The elements of the tort of **appropriation** are:

1. the use of the plaintiff's name, likeness, or personality
2. for the benefit of the defendant

The first element is present if the plaintiff is specifically identifiable through the use of his or her name, likeness, or personality. To make a statue or mannequin of the plaintiff is not sufficient unless the plaintiff is clearly recognizable.

The defendant must derive benefit from the use. In some states, the benefit must be commercial or pecuniary, e.g., impersonating the plaintiff to obtain credit, or using the plaintiff's name or picture in a business ad to give the appearance of an endorsement. But in most states the benefit does not have to be financial. The second element would be met, for example, if the defendant pretended to be a famous photographer as part of his effort to seduce women.

ASSIGNMENT

25.4

The plaintiff is a "human cannonball" who shoots himself out of a cannon at county fairs. Do either of the following situations constitute appropriation? (See General Instructions for the Legal Analysis Assignment in Chapter 2.)

a. The defendant tapes a video of the stunt and shows it at home to friends and relatives.

b. The defendant is a television station. One of its employees videotapes the stunt and shows it both on the evening news and on its "Incredible People" variety show. (See the last section of this chapter on Media Defendants.)

PUBLIC DISCLOSURE OF PRIVATE FACT

The elements of the tort of **public disclosure of private fact** are:

1. publicity
2. concerning the private life of the plaintiff
3. highly offensive to a reasonable person

For purposes of this tort, "publicity" has a different meaning from "publication" in the law of defamation. **Publication** is the communication of the defamatory statement to at least one person other than the plaintiff. **Publicity,** however, means communication to the public at large. More than a few people must hear or read the statement.

Review the factors mentioned in the section on intrusion that are used to determine whether something is private (see Figure 25–1). Most of these factors are also relevant to determine whether there has been a public disclosure of a private fact.

There is no disclosure of a private fact when publicity is given to something that is already a matter of public record (e.g., a document filed in court, the names of contributors to a political candidate). Some subject matter, however, is clearly private, either by law or by custom. Data provided on income tax returns and census forms, for example, are protected from disclosure by law. Also legally protected are confidential communications between attorney and client, doctor and patient, and minister and penitent. One's sexual inclinations are also private, because in our society such matters are considered no one's business. Of course, if a plaintiff flaunts such information, he or she may be considered to have consented to the disclosure.

If there has been a disclosure of a private fact, it is no defense that the fact is true. Falsity is not one of the elements of this tort.

It is not enough that the plaintiff considers the publicity discomforting or embarrassing. It must be highly offensive to a reasonable person. A reasonable person, for example, would not be highly offended by a story about an individual's having his deceased dog cremated, but would probably be offended by a story about the individual's three unsuccessful operations to cure his impotency. Here are some other disclosures that might be highly offensive to a reasonable person:

- a sign placed in the defendant's window that the plaintiff does not pay his or her debts
- an interoffice memo sent to thirty employees that a fellow employee is a homosexual
- a video shown in a tavern of a woman nursing her baby on her backyard porch

For a sample complaint alleging public disclosure of private fact, see Figure 3–13 in Chapter 3.

Tom is an ex-convict who served time for murder twenty-five years ago. He is now a reformed citizen living an outstanding life in a new community. Bill finds out about Tom's past and lets everyone know at a town meeting. Does Tom have a cause of action against Bill? (See General Instructions for the Legal Analysis Assignment in Chapter 2.)

FALSE LIGHT

The elements of the tort of **false light** are:

1. publicity
2. placing the plaintiff in a false light
3. highly offensive to a reasonable person

The first element of false light is publicity. It has the same meaning as publicity in the tort of public disclosure of private fact: communication to the public at large—not just to a few people.

False light is similar to defamation in that the statement about the plaintiff must be false. Unlike defamation, however, false light can be established without the statement harming the plaintiff's reputation, although most usually do. When is a person placed in a false light? Broadly speaking, whenever an impression or conclusion is given about a person that is not accurate.

EXAMPLES:

- falsely stating in a report that a doctor has given AIDS to one of his patients during an operation
- falsely claiming that the plaintiff has written a pornographic novel
- signing the name of a pro-choice plaintiff on a pro-life petition without permission.

These cases of false light would be considered highly offensive by a reasonable person. Not all false light, however, falls into this category. Misspelling the plaintiff's name on a notice places him or her in a false light, but this would hardly be deemed highly offensive, even if the plaintiff was very embarrassed by the incident. A reasonable person would not take such offense.

a. At a banquet honoring the retirement of Linda, her boss rises to make a speech. The boss gives some details of Linda's life, including the fact that she was married on June 26, 1968 and gave birth to her first child on July 1, 1968. In fact, the child was born on June 30, 1969. Linda sues her boss for false light. What result? (See General Instructions for the Legal Analysis Assignment in Chapter 2.)

b. George Jones is a practicing attorney. He decides to hire two attorneys as associates (not partners). The name of the firm is "Jones & Associates." Jones decides to take out a Yellow Pages listing under this name. When the Yellow Pages come out, his firm is listed as "Jones & Ass." Have any torts been committed? (See General Instructions for the Legal Analysis Assignment in Chapter 2.)

MEDIA DEFENDANTS

Special protections exist for the press, television, radio, or other members of the media who are defendants in invasion-of-privacy tort suits. The media has a constitutional right under the First Amendment to publicize **newsworthy** people and events. This covers a broad range of matters of **legitimate public interest**. Media defendants are often charged with false light invasion of privacy, particularly by a **public official** or a **public figure**. (A public figure is someone who has assumed special prominence in the affairs of society because of power, influence, or voluntary involvement in a controversy of interest to the general public.) In such a case, there must be proof that the media defendant either knew that the publication placed the plaintiff in a false light or acted in reckless disregard of whether it did so. (This is known as **constitutional malice** or **actual malice**.) These rules also apply to defamation cases against the media. See Chapter 24 where the rules are more fully discussed.

CASE

Peoples Bank and Trust Co. of Mountain Home, Conservator of the Estate of Nellie Mitchell, an Aged Person

v.

Globe International Publishing, Inc. doing business as "Sun"

978 F.2d 1065 (1992)

United States Court of Appeals for the Eighth Circuit

Background: *The* Sun, *a supermarket tabloid owned by Globe International, published photographs of Nellie Mitchell to illustrate a story about a 101-year-old pregnant woman. Mitchell sued for false light invasion of privacy and won a jury verdict in federal district court. Globe now appeals to the United States Court of Appeals for the Eighth Circuit.*

Decision on Appeal: *Globe committed false light invasion of privacy. A judgment against Globe does not violate the First Amendment.*

OPINION OF COURT

Judge HEANEY delivered the opinion of the court . . .

Plaintiff Mitchell is a ninety-seven-year-old woman from the city of Mountain Home, in Baxter County, Arkansas. After having operated a newsstand and delivered newspapers in Mountain Home for almost fifty years, Mitchell has become a well-recognized figure in her community and something of a local legend. She was recognized for her long service in 1980 when major newspapers ran human interest stories about her and she appeared for interviews on television talk shows.

Defendant Globe publishes several supermarket tabloids, including the *National Examiner* and the *Sun*. Globe published a fairly accurate account of Mitchell in the November 25, 1980, issue of the *National Examiner*. A photograph of Mitchell, purchased from the Baxter County News, accompanied that story.

The same photograph appeared again on the cover page of the October 2, 1990, edition of the *Sun* with the headline "Pregnancy forces granny to quit work at age 101." Customers at supermarket checkout lines in Baxter County who scanned the cover page of the *Sun* saw only that Nellie Mitchell was featured next to a headline about a "granny" forced to quit work because of pregnancy. Purchasers of the tabloid who turned to the story on page eleven also would have seen a second photograph of Mitchell next to a fictitious story about a woman named "Audrey Wiles," living in Australia, who quit her paper route at the age of 101 because an extramarital affair with a millionaire client on her route had left her pregnant.

Word spread quickly in Mountain Home that Nellie Mitchell, "the paper lady," was featured in the offending edition of the *Sun*. This edition of the *Sun* was a "sell-out" in the northern region of Arkansas where Mitchell lives. . . .

The district court gave the following instruction regarding "false light" invasion of privacy:

> to prevail on this claim, the plaintiff has the burden of proving by clear and convincing evidence the following: one, that the false light in which she was placed by the publicity would be highly offensive to a reasonable person; and two, that the defendant acted with actual malice in publishing the statements at issue in this case. Actual malice means that Globe International intended, or recklessly failed to anticipate, that readers would construe the publicized matter as conveying actual facts or events concerning Mrs. Mitchell. A finding of actual malice requires a showing of more than mere negligence.

Globe does not dispute that the published story was false; indeed, its principal defense is that the story was "pure fiction." Nor does Globe dispute that the story would be highly offensive to a reasonable person, or that it was in fact highly offensive to Mitchell. The central issue on appeal is the existence of actual malice: whether Globe intended, or recklessly failed to anticipate, that readers would construe the story as conveying actual facts or events concerning Mitchell. Globe contends that, as a matter of law, no reader reasonably could construe the story as conveying actual facts about Mitchell, and that no evidence supports a finding that Globe intended that result.

Globe . . . asserts it is biologically impossible for a woman of either 101 or 95 years of age to become pregnant, and therefore, as a matter of law, no reasonable reader could have believed the story represented true facts about Mitchell. . . .

Every other aspect of the charged story, however—such as the implication of sexual impropriety and that Mitchell was quitting her life-long profession—is subject to reasonable belief. Even the report of the pregnancy—a physical condition, not an opinion, metaphor, fantasy, or surrealism—could be proved either true or false. In the context of this case, therefore, we cannot say as a matter of law that readers could not reasonably have believed that the charged story portrayed actual facts or events concerning Mitchell. . . .

The circumstances of the instant case suggest the story in the *Sun* may well be believed by readers as conveying actual facts about Mitchell despite the apparent absurdity of a pregnant centenarian. Indeed, there is more than sufficient evidence to conclude that Globe intends its readers to believe the *Sun* generally. Although there is less evidence to conclude that Globe intended its readers to believe facts specifically about Mitchell, we conclude there is sufficient evidence to find that it recklessly failed to anticipate that result. . . .

The format and style of the *Sun* suggest it is a factual newspaper. Globe advertises the *Sun* as publishing "the weird, the strange, and the outlandish *news* from around the globe," and nowhere in the publication does it suggest its stories are false or exaggerated. The *Sun* also mingles factual, fictional, and hybrid stories without overtly identifying one from the other. At trial, even its own writers could not tell which stories were true and which were completely fabricated.

In the October 2, 1990, issue submitted as evidence, the *Sun* consistently alerted its readers to advertisements with small-print caveats above the text of those advertisements. The *Sun* even published a disclaimer above certain personal advertisements warning its readers that those notices had not been investigated—implying that other advertisements and the news stories *had* been investigated. These disclaimers and caveats on advertisements, and the absence of any warning or explanation on the admittedly fictional "news" stories, bolster our conclusion that Globe intends for its 366,000 readers to believe the *Sun* prints factual material. It is the kind of *calculated* falsehood against which the First Amendment can tolerate sanctions without significant impairment of its function. See *Time, Inc. v. Hill,* 385 U.S. 374 (1967).

Globe was on notice that the photographs of Mitchell it published in its October 2, 1990, issue of the *Sun* were purchased from Baxter County, Arkansas—an area where Globe circulated the *Sun.* Counsel at oral argument conceded that the photographs were identified on the back as having been purchased from the Baxter County Bulletin. The editor who chose the photograph testified that he knew the individual pictured in the photograph was a real person, but that he assumed she was dead. This was the same editor who, ten years before, had worked for the Examiner when it published the essentially truthful story about Mitchell.

Although Globe's failure to investigate and confirm its assumption of Mitchell's death will not alone support a finding of actual malice, the purposeful avoidance of the truth is in a different category. Globe contends it made a simple mistake, and that it was not on notice that Mitchell was alive. The jury, however, had sufficient evidence to determine that Globe purposefully avoided the truth about Mitchell.

[Judgment affirmed. The case is remanded, however, to reconsider the issue of damages.]

ASSIGNMENT

25.7

a. Was Nellie Mitchell a public figure? If so, would it be relevant to her invasion-of-privacy claim?

b. Was the case correctly decided? Some may think that tabloids deserve to be sued, but is it accurate to say that readers could interpret the photos and story as conveying actual facts or events concerning Mrs. Mitchell?

c. What other torts do you think Globe may have committed?

SUMMARY

There are four invasion-of-privacy torts that protect an individual's interest in being left alone: intrusion, appropriation, public disclosure of private fact, and false light.

Intrusion is prying, peering, or probing into the plaintiff's private affairs or concerns when it is considered highly offensive to a reasonable person. Appropriation is the use of the plaintiff's name, likeness, or personality for the benefit of the defendant. In most states, this benefit does not have to be pecuniary. Public disclosure of private fact is a communication of a statement to the public at large (publicity) concerning the private life of the plaintiff when such publicity is considered highly offensive to a reasonable person. False light is publicity that inaccurately portrays the plaintiff when such publicity is considered highly offensive to a reasonable person.

Media defendants in an action for appropriation or for public disclosure of private fact often have the defense that the information was a matter of legitimate public interest, which the media has a constitutional right to make public. In an action for false light against a media defendant, the plaintiff who is a public official or a public figure must prove that the defendant knew the statement placed the plaintiff in a false light or acted in reckless disregard of whether it did so.

KEY TERMS

intrusion   503

private affairs   503

reasonable person   503

highly offensive   503

appropriation   507

public disclosure of private
     fact   508

publication   508

publicity   508

false light   509

newsworthy   510

legitimate public interest   510

public official   510

public figure   510

constitutional malice   510

actual malice   510

Misrepresentation, Tortious Interference, and Other Torts

CHAPTER OUTLINE

- Misrepresentation
- Interference with Contract Relations
- Interference with Prospective Advantage
- Tortious Interference with Employment (Wrongful Discharge)
- Disparagement
- Injurious Falsehood
- Prima Facie Tort
- Bad Faith Liability
- Dram Shop Liability

MISREPRESENTATION

The tort of **misrepresentation** (sometimes called **deceit** or **fraud**) primarily covers **pecuniary loss** caused by false statements. A pecuniary loss is a loss of money.

> **EXAMPLE:** When George sells Brenda a used computer for $500, he tells her that it has a modem. He knows that this is not true.

George lied about the features of the computer. Contrary to his statement, it does not have a modem. He probably has committed the tort of misrepresentation, although we must examine all of the elements of this tort to be sure. Brenda has suffered a pecuniary loss. She received a computer that is worth less than the one George described.

There has been no property damage or bodily injury as a result of what George did. If such damage or injury does result from a false statement (e.g., Sam becomes ill after drinking what Mary told him was a healthy fruit drink when she knew there was poison in it), many courts will allow recovery for the property damage or bodily injury in the misrepresentation suit. It would be more common, however, for this kind of recovery to be sought under other torts such as battery, conversion, or negligence.

 Misrepresentation Checklist

Definitions, Relationships, Paralegal Roles, and Research References

Category
Misrepresentation is an intentional tort. (In many states, however, negligence is also a basis for liability—negligent misrepresentation.)

Interest Protected by This Tort
The right to be free from pecuniary loss resulting from false statements.

Elements of This Tort
  i. Statement of fact
  ii. Statement is false
  iii. Scienter (intent to mislead)
  iv. Justifiable reliance
  v. Actual damages

Definitions of Major Words/Phrases in These Elements
Fact: An express or implied communication containing concrete information that can be objectively established as true or false. (An opinion is an express or implied communication containing a relatively vague or indefinite value judgment that rarely, if ever, is objectively verifiable.)
Intent to Mislead (Scienter): Making a statement knowing it is false, or without a belief in its truth, or in reckless disregard of its truth or falsity—with the desire that the statement be believed and relied upon.
Justifiable Reliance: Being reasonable in taking action (or in refraining from taking action) because of something such as what someone has said or done.

Major Defense and Counterargument Possibilities That Need to Be Explored
  1. The defendant made no statement of past or present fact.
  2. The defendant concealed no past or present fact.
  3. The defendant had no duty to disclose the fact; there was no fiduciary or other relationship of trust and confidence between the parties.
  4. The statement was not false, incomplete, ambiguous, or misleading.
  5. The defendant did not have a state of mind that differed from what he or she expressed.
  6. The defendant did not know or believe the statement was false or inaccurate.
  7. The defendant did not act in reckless disregard of the truth or falsity of his or her statement.

Misrepresentation Checklist Continued

8. The defendant did not intend the plaintiff to rely on the defendant's statement, and had no reason to expect that the plaintiff would rely on it.
9. The plaintiff did not in fact rely on the defendant's statement.
10. The defendant's statement was not a substantial factor in the plaintiff's action or inaction.
11. The plaintiff's reliance was not justifiable.
12. The defendant did not take advantage of idiosyncrasies of the plaintiff.
13. A cursory investigation by the plaintiff would have revealed the truth or falsity of the defendant's statement.
14. The plaintiff suffered no actual damages.
15. The plaintiff's suit against the government for misrepresentation committed by a government employee may be barred by sovereign immunity (on sovereign immunity, see Chapter 27).
16. The plaintiff's suit against the government employee for misrepresentation may be barred by public official immunity (on official immunity, see Chapter 27).
17. The plaintiff's suit against the charitable organization for misrepresentation committed by someone working for the organization may be barred by charitable immunity (on charitable immunity, see Chapter 27).
18. The plaintiff failed to take reasonable steps to mitigate the harm caused when the defendant committed misrepresentation; therefore, damages should not cover the aggravation of the harm caused by the plaintiff (on the doctrine of avoidable consequences, see Chapter 16).

Damages

Actual damages must be proved. Some courts use the out-of-pocket measure of damages, whereas other courts allow a benefit-of-the-bargain measure of damages. Traditionally, misrepresentation covered only pecuniary or economic damages. Many courts now also allow recovery for injury to person or property caused by the false statement. Punitive damages are also possible. (On the categories of damages, see Chapter 16.)

Relationship to Criminal Law

In all states, embezzlement is a crime. In many states there is a crime called false pretenses. False statements of fact are often made by the defendant in the commission of both crimes.

Other Torts and Related Actions

Battery: One way to commit battery is to induce the plaintiff to give consent to a touching by falsely stating facts (e.g., defendant falsely claims to be a doctor and examines the plaintiff).

Breach of Express Warranty: Under the Uniform Commercial Code (UCC), a cause of action for breach of an express warranty is possible if the defendant makes a false statement of fact with the intent that the plaintiff rely on the statement, which in fact occurs, to the detriment of the plaintiff.

Conversion: One way to commit this tort is to take possession of the plaintiff's property by falsely stating the authority to do so.

Defamation: Defendant can defame the character of the plaintiff by making false statements about the plaintiff.

False Imprisonment: One way to commit this tort is to confine the plaintiff by falsely stating the authority to do so.

Intentional Infliction of Emotional Distress: One way to commit this tort is to tell a particularly vicious lie to an unsuspecting plaintiff.

Negligence: The tort of negligence can be committed when the defendant causes injury to plaintiff's person or property by carelessly stating facts (e.g., carelessly telling the plaintiff that the milk is safe to drink when in fact it is not).

Trespass to Land: One way to commit this tort is to get someone to go onto the plaintiff's land by making false statements about who owns the land.

Federal Law

a. Under the Federal Tort Claims Act, the United States Government will *not* be liable for misrepresentation committed by one of its federal employees within the scope of employment. (See Figure 27–7 in Chapter 27.)

Misrepresentation Checklist Continued

b. There may be liability under the Civil Rights Act if the misrepresentation was committed while the defendant was depriving the plaintiff of federal rights under color of law. (See Figure 27–9 in Chapter 27.)

Employer-Employee (Agency) Law

An employee who commits a misrepresentation is personally liable for this tort. His or her employer will *also* be liable for misrepresentation if the conduct of the employee was within the scope of employment (respondeat superior). The employee must be furthering a business objective of the employer at the time. Many times, intentional torts such as misrepresentation, however, are outside the scope of employment. If so, only the employee is liable for the misrepresentation. (On the factors that determine scope of employment, see Figure 14–10 in Chapter 14.)

Paralegal Roles in Misrepresentation Litigation

(See also Figures 3–1, 3–14, and 29–1 in Chapters 3 and 29.)

Fact finding (help the office collect facts relevant to prove the elements of misrepresentation, the elements of available defenses, and the extent of injuries or other damages):
- client interviewing
- field investigation
- online research (e.g., identification of financial data relevant to the defendant's alleged misrepresentation)

File management (help the office control the volume of paperwork in a litigation of a misrepresentation case):
- open client file
- enter case data in computer database
- maintain file documents

Litigation assistance (help the trial attorney prepare for a trial and appeal, if needed, of a misrepresentation case):
- draft discovery requests
- draft answers to discovery requests
- draft pleadings
- digest and index discovery documents
- help prepare, order, and manage trial exhibits (visuals or demonstratives)
- prepare trial notebook
- draft notice of appeal
- order trial transcript
- cite check briefs
- perform legal research

Collection/enforcement (help the trial attorney for the judgment creditor to collect the damages award or to enforce other court orders at the conclusion of the misrepresentation case):
- draft postjudgment discovery requests
- field investigation to monitor compliance with judgment
- online research (e.g., location of defendant's business assets)

Research References for Misrepresentation

Digests
In the digests of West, look for case summaries on this tort under the following key topics:

Fraud	Torts
Vendor and Purchaser	Damages
Negligence	

Corpus Juris Secundum
In this legal encyclopedia, see the discussion under topic headings such as:

Fraud	Torts
Vendor and Purchaser	Damages
Negligence	

Misrepresentation Checklist Continued

American Jurisprudence 2d
In this legal encyclopedia, see the discussion under topic headings such as:

Fraud and Deceit	Sales
Fraudulent Conveyances	Damages
Vendor and Purchaser	Torts
Negligence	

Legal Periodical Literature
There are two index systems to use to locate legal periodical articles on this tort:

INDEX TO LEGAL PERIODICALS AND BOOKS (ILP)	CURRENT LAW INDEX (CLI)
See Literature in *ILP* under subject headings such as:	See literature in *CLI* under subject headings such as:
Fraud	Fraud
Damages	Fraudulent
Fraudulent	Conveyance
Conveyance	Debtor and Creditor
Negligence	Negligence
Torts	Torts
Debtor and Creditor	Damages

Example of a legal periodical article you can find by using *ILP* or *CLI*:

Misrepresentation of Sterility or of Use of Birth Control by J. Mann, 26 Journal of Family Law 623 (1987–88).

A.L.R., A.L.R.2d, A.L.R.3d, A.L.R.4th, A.L.R.5th, A.L.R. Fed.
Use the *ALR Index* to locate annotations on this tort. In this index, check subject headings such as:

Fraud and Deceit	Negligence
Fraudulent Conveyance	Torts
Vendor and Purchaser	Damages
Debtors and Creditors	

Example of an annotation you can find through this index:

Consumer Class Action Based on Fraud or Misrepresentations by Mary J. Cavins, 53 A.L.R.3d 534.

Words and Phrases
In this multivolume legal dictionary, look up *misrepresentation, deceit, fraud, scienter, fact, opinion, justifiable reliance,* and every other word or phrase connected with misrepresentation discussed in this chapter. The dictionary will give you definitions of these words or phrases from court opinions.

CALR: Computer-Assisted Legal Research
Example of a query you could ask on WESTLAW or on LEXIS to try to find cases, statutes, or other legal materials on misrepresentation: **misrepresentation /p damages**

Example of search terms you could use on an Internet legal search engine such as LawCrawler (http://lawcrawler.findlaw.com) to find cases, statutes, or other legal materials on misrepresentation: **misrepresentation AND tort**

Example of search terms you could use on an Internet general search engine such as Alta Vista (http://www.altavista.com) to find cases, statutes, or other legal materials on misrepresentation: **+misrepresentation +tort**

More Internet sites to check for materials on misrepresentation and other torts:
Jurist: (http://jurist.law.pitt.edu/sg_torts.htm)
LawGuru: (http://www.lawguru.com/search/lawsearch.html)
See also Tort Law Online at the end of Chapter 1.

Statement of Fact That Is False

The first element of misrepresentation is that the defendant has made a statement of **fact.** The second element is that the fact is false. (Sometimes the first element is expressed as a statement of material fact. In this chapter, however, we will cover materiality under a different element of the tort—the element of justifiable reliance.) A fact is an express or implied communication containing concrete information that can be objectively established as true or false. When I tell you that a particular pen has red ink in it, I have communicated a fact. There is an objective way to find out if my statement is true: we simply write with the pen to check the color of its ink. An **opinion,** on the other hand, is an express or implied communication containing a relatively vague or indefinite value judgment that is not objectively verifiable. When I tell you that a particular product is "wonderful," I have communicated an opinion. Whether something is "wonderful" could be the subject of endless debate. There is no way to prove—objectively—that the statement is true or false.

Controversy often arises in sales transactions where **puffing** is common. Puffing is an expected exaggeration of quality. An example would be a seller telling a buyer that the XYZ brand of shampoo is "fabulous." Such comments are mere puffing, not statements of fact. Furthermore, there cannot be justifiable reliance (an element we will consider later) on puffing.

Some opinions contain implied statements of fact.

> **EXAMPLE:** Vince is trying to sell Linda an automobile. He tells her that the car is in "excellent condition." Once Linda buys the car, she discovers that it has no engine.

Vince's comment about the car is an opinion, but it implied the fact that the car had at least the basic equipment in it—such as an engine!

If you state an opinion that you do not believe, you have lied about your state of mind. When you communicate your state of mind, you are communicating a fact. While an opinion itself is not a fact, a communication about your state of mind is a fact.

> **EXAMPLE:** A stock broker says, "I believe this stock is a dream come true." The broker, however, knows that the stock is worthless and highly unlikely to appreciate in value or to earn income.

The statement that the stock is a "dream come true" is an opinion. It is a vague value judgment that cannot be objectively proven or disproved. But whether the broker believes the statement at the time he or she made it is a fact that can be proven or disproved. He either thinks highly of the stock or he doesn't. A false representation of a state of mind is a false representation of a fact.

Words are not always necessary to communicate a fact. Someone who turns back the odometer without saying a word, for example, is making a factual statement about the number of miles a vehicle has traveled to date. Occasionally, the active concealment of a fact can lead to liability for misrepresentation. For example, the defendant paints over cracks in an engine in order to conceal its defects from a potential buyer.

Silence can also communicate facts, e.g., not telling someone that a house has termites could constitute a communication that the house is termite-free. Communicating facts through silence, however, is not sufficient to impose liability for misrepresentation unless there is an obligation to disclose the facts. Two strangers usually do not have this obligation to each other. Suppose, however, that two people have a **fiduciary relationship,** sometimes called a **confidential relationship.** A fiduciary relationship exists when one of the parties owes the other loyalty, candor, and fair treatment. Examples would be business partners, doctor and patient, bank and depositor, and husband and wife. When this relationship exists, silence can be the basis for the tort of misrepresentation when the fact should have been communicated because of the fiduciary relationship.

CASE

Dushkin and Others v. Desai
18 F. Supp. 2d 117 (1998)
United States District Court, D. Massachusetts

Background: *This is a misrepresentation action brought against a yoga guru, Amrit Desai, by some of his former followers. The complaint in the United States District Court in Massachusetts alleges that Desai "misrepresented his celibacy, honesty, and status as an authentic guru." Desai has made a motion to dismiss on the grounds that he made no statements of fact to the plaintiffs. To rule on this motion, the court must assume that the allegations in the complaint are true and decide whether the allegations contain facts that constitute a cause of action—here, the tort of misrepresentation.*

Decision of Court: *Motion to dismiss is denied. Desai did make statements of fact. The complaint alleges sufficient facts that, if proved, entitle the plaintiffs to succeed in their misrepresentation action.*

OPINION OF COURT

Judge PONSOR delivered the opinion of the court . . . :

Fourteen former "disciples" of self-proclaimed yoga guru Amrit Desai have brought this suit against their former leader for losses suffered when Desai was (according to their allegations) revealed to be a charlatan. Plaintiffs resided and labored for many years at the Kripalu Ashram, a yoga retreat center in Lenox, Massachusetts, where Desai, plaintiffs' revered spiritual leader, presented himself as a "true and authentic guru." [The quotes are from the complaint of the plaintiffs.] Plaintiffs devoted themselves to emulating Desai, who promoted a celibate and ascetic lifestyle to which he himself outwardly proclaimed to adhere. . . .

After coming to the United States in the 1960s to study at the Philadelphia College of Art, defendant Amrit Desai formed the Kripalu Yoga Ashram, a small intentional living community, sometime in 1974. Desai appointed himself as the Kripalu Ashram's "guru," or spiritual leader. The ashram included approximately twenty resident members and operated a small public center for the purpose of teaching yoga. In the late 1970s, Desai's ashram became a Pennsylvania nonprofit charitable corporation called the Kripalu Yoga Fellowship ("KYF").

In 1983, KYF moved to a 350-acre site in Lenox, Massachusetts. KYF began to operate a large-scale retreat center for holistic health and education at the Lenox site, which contained several large facilities that housed up to 500 people. Over 15,000 paying guests per year visited KYF "to relax, take yoga classes, meditate, have massages, and otherwise take a break from the routine of their daily lives." Approximately 250 resident members of the ashram (including the plaintiffs) operated the facility, working for room and board and a small monthly stipend in exchange for the opportunity to live at the Kripalu Ashram as Desai's "disciples."

Plaintiffs allege that the resident members, paying guests, and KYF donors were attracted to the facility precisely because of Desai's presence. Desai's picture hung throughout the facilities, his videos ran continuously in the public areas, and his books, tapes, and other items were offered for sale by KYF. Publicly, Desai claimed to be an authentic guru—a "teacher and object of veneration" who attains his status in part through several forms of abstinence, including refraining from sexual activity and material pursuits. Desai outwardly professed to live the proper life of an authentic guru, which he identified as demanding "honesty, selfless devotion to the well-being of his followers," and "absolute personal trust" between guru and followers, in addition to celibacy and commitment to a non-material, physically and financially simple lifestyle. As resident guru at KYF, he conducted a combination of life counseling, spiritual leadership, and health and educational services.

Plaintiffs characterize Desai as cultivating in his followers an intense emotional dependence. The plaintiffs, as "disciples," were told to identify themselves and their well-being with Desai's personality and integrity, and to regard Desai as the most important person in their lives. Desai deemed himself the plaintiffs' "personal life counselor," and frequently offered guidance with respect to the most intimate aspects of the plaintiffs' personal lives. Plaintiffs state that over many years, each of them developed a "close and deeply personal relationship" with Desai.

Plaintiffs claim that during their years at the ashram they strove to emulate Desai's professed lifestyle, in that they endeavored to be celibate or chaste, honest, selfless, and devoted to the well-being of others, within the framework of a simple, non-material way of life. In addition, on numerous occasions, Desai allegedly urged the plaintiffs to donate literally all of their possessions to KYF. One plaintiff claims to have donated more than $30,000, and another more than $100,000 in earnings to KYF upon Desai's instruction.

Behind his carefully cultivated image, plaintiffs charge, Desai was in fact a fraud. Plaintiffs' complaint alleges that, from the 1970s until 1994, KYF entered into a series of lucrative contractual relationships with Desai, the purpose of which was "to induce Desai to remain physically present at KYF, teaching yoga courses, meeting with guests and visitors, serving as advisor, mentor and exemplar to the residents," and performing the role of guru at KYF. In exchange, Desai, as an independent contractor, received an annual fee, free housing, free transportation (both domestic and international), a percentage of the proceeds from literature, video, and audiotape sales, and free sponsorship of Desai's seminars throughout the world, all revenue from which he retained. Plaintiffs aver that Desai secretly received payments and benefits from KYF totaling many hundreds of thousands of dollars.

Moreover, between 1974 and 1994, Desai engaged in a series of secret sexual relationships with several female "disciples" in the KYF community (none of whom is a party to this litigation). Plaintiffs assert that these relationships, like his material self-enrichment, were deliberately concealed by

Desai in order to preserve his reputation as a true and authentic guru. In 1985, a woman apparently revealed to KYF officers and directors that Desai had had abusive sexual relations with her. Desai accused the woman of deceit and mental illness, and "prevailed on KYF and its residents and members, including each of the plaintiffs, to ostracize, expel, or otherwise usher her out of the KYF community." In 1994, another woman brought similar accusations against Desai, at which time he publicly admitted to some past sexual activities. In an audiotaped statement, Desai apologized for his behavior and acknowledged that it had caused his disciples much emotional pain and suffering. KYF ended its contractual relationship with Desai, who moved to Florida. The Kripalu Ashram still operates in Lenox, Massachusetts, but without any connection to Desai.

[The complaint of the plaintiffs asserts fraud and misrepresentation in that] Desai knowingly misrepresented his celibacy, honesty, and status as an authentic guru, and that plaintiffs reasonably relied on these misrepresentations to their detriment. In essence, plaintiffs contend that they were induced by defendant's misrepresentations to devote years of their lives—and in some cases, large sums in personal savings—to Desai and the overall interests of KYF. . . .

Defendant argues that his alleged misrepresentations did not concern matters of fact—that they were merely promissory in nature, or simple expressions of opinion—and therefore could not form the basis of an action for fraud. If the allegations of the complaint are accepted, as they must be at this stage of the litigation, this contention is manifestly untrue. Desai's representations regarding his manner of living—especially his celibacy and lack of interest in material things—concerned verifiable facts regarding his life habits. Furthermore, his representations regarding these habits and attitudes were . . . the kinds of representations to which potential disciples such as the plaintiffs would attach importance in distinguishing a "true and authentic guru" from an ordinary layperson, or even an ordinary teacher of yoga. . . . [T]he complaint . . . depicts that Desai and KYF depended on the virtually free labor provided by the plaintiffs and other resident members of the Kripalu Ashram in order to keep the center operating for outside paying visitors. The court may readily infer that it was in Desai's interest to perpetuate his image as an authentic guru in order to retain the plaintiffs' devotion and free labor, continue to attract a steady stream of outside customers, and thereby maintain the benefits that flowed to him from his status.

In short, plaintiffs have offered sufficient allegations from which the court reasonably may infer that Desai made false representations with respect to his status . . . and that plaintiffs in fact relied on defendant's representations, as evidenced by their significant donations of time, labor, and money to the facility. . . .

For the foregoing reasons, defendant's motion [to dismiss the misrepresentation claim is] DENIED. . . .

ASSIGNMENT 26.1

a. Is it relevant that none of the women with whom Desai was sexually intimate are plaintiffs in this case?
b. Make specific arguments that communications about a person's manner of living, celibacy, honesty, selflessness, devotion to the well-being of others, and lack of interest in material things:
   (i) are matters of opinion,
   (ii) are not matters of opinion.

Scienter

Scienter is the intent to mislead. This means that the defendant knows the statement is false, or does not believe in its truth, or acts in **reckless disregard** for its truth or falsity. Scienter also includes an intent that the audience of the statement believe it and act in reliance on its truth. The audience consists of those individuals the defendant intends to reach with the statement. Some states go further and extend liability to those individuals the defendant has reason to expect will learn about and act on the statement, even though the defendant never actually intended to reach them.

Negligent Misrepresentation

Suppose the defendant's misrepresentation does not encompass scienter because there was no knowledge of the statement's falsity, no lack of belief in its truth, or no reckless disregard for truth or falsity. The defendant may simply have been careless in making the false statement, such as by not taking reasonable steps to check the accuracy of the statement before making it. If this leads to physical harm (e.g., plaintiff is injured because the car brakes failed after defendant carelessly told the plaintiff that the brakes were safe), a traditional negligence suit can be brought. If, however, only pecuniary harm results (e.g., the plaintiff loses $10,000 because of a careless statement by the defendant on the value of a painting), many states will allow the plaintiff to sue for **negligent misrepresentation** as long as he or she was one of the individuals the defendant intended to reach by the careless statement. In many states, individuals within a relatively small group can also sue if the defendant knows that at least someone in a group will learn about the statement and rely on it, even if the defendant does not know which specific individual will do so.

Justifiable Reliance

To recover, the plaintiff must rely on the statement of the defendant, and it must be a **justifiable reliance.** If the plaintiff is foolish in believing and acting on the defendant's statement, recovery for misrepresentation may be denied unless the defendant knew about and took advantage of the plaintiff's intellectual vulnerabilities. The fact on which the plaintiff relies must be **material,** meaning that it was important to the transaction. In selling the plaintiff a car, for example, it is not material that the defendant falsely tells the plaintiff that the defendant likes bananas, if all the statements about the car itself are accurate. If, however, the defendant knows that the plaintiff attaches significance to a peculiar fact and intentionally misleads him or her as to that fact, recovery may be allowed.

ASSIGNMENT

26.2

Diane has just been hired as a telemarketer for a museum. She calls Harry, a stranger, to solicit a contribution. She tells Harry that the museum has important works of art in it and therefore deserves the support of the community. In fact, none of the works of art is valued over $500. During the conversation, Diane learns that Harry is a Catholic. She tells Harry that she too is a Catholic. In fact, she has always been a practicing Lutheran. She is married to a Catholic and attends Catholic church services once or twice a year. Harry tells his wife about the museum. His wife decides to donate $10,000. When she finds out that the museum has a very weak collection and that Diane is not a Catholic, she sues Diane for misrepresentation. What result? (See General Instructions for the Legal Analysis Assignment in Chapter 2.)

CASE

Vokes v. Arthur Murray, Inc.
212 So. 2d 906 (1968)
District Court of Appeal of Florida, Second District

Background: *After spending over $31,000 for 2,302 hours of dancing lessons, Audry Vokes sued the dancing school for misrepresentation. The trial dismissed the complaint for failure to state a cause of action. The case is now before the Florida District Court of Appeal.*

Decision on Appeal: *The dismissal is reversed. Audry Vokes has alleged enough to state a cause of action.*

OPINION OF COURT

Judge PIERCE delivered the opinion of the court . . .

Defendant Arthur Murray, Inc., a corporation, authorizes the operation throughout the nation of dancing schools under the name of "Arthur Murray School of Dancing" through local franchised operators, one of whom was defendant J. P. Davenport whose dancing establishment was in Clearwater.

Plaintiff Mrs. Audry E. Vokes, a widow of 51 years and without family, had a yen to be "an accomplished dancer" with the hopes of finding "new interest in life". So, on February 10, 1961, a dubious fate, with the assist of a motivated acquaintance, procured her to attend a "dance party" at Davenport's "School of Dancing" where she whiled away the pleasant hours, sometimes in a private room, absorbing his accomplished sales technique, during which her grace and poise were elaborated upon and her rosy future as "an excellent dancer" was painted for her in vivid and glowing colors. As an incident to this interlude, he sold her eight 1/2-hour dance lessons to be utilized within one calendar month therefrom, for the sum of $14.50 cash in hand paid, obviously a baited "comeon".

Thus she embarked upon an almost endless pursuit of the terpsichorean art during which, over a period of less than sixteen months, she was sold fourteen "dance courses" totalling in the aggregate 2302 hours of dancing lessons for a total cash outlay of $31,090.45, all at Davenport's dance emporium. All of these fourteen courses were evidenced by execution of a written "Enrollment Agreement—Arthur Murray's School of Dancing" with the addendum in heavy black print, "No one will be informed that you are taking dancing lessons. Your relations with us are held in strict confidence", setting forth the number of "dancing lessons" and the "lessons in rhythm sessions" currently sold to her from time to time, and always of course accompanied by payment of cash of the realm.

These dance lesson contracts and the monetary consideration therefor of over $31,000 were procured from her by means and methods of Davenport and his associates which went beyond the unsavory, yet legally permissible, perimeter of "sales puffing" and intruded well into the forbidden area of undue influence, the suggestion of falsehood, the suppression of truth, and the free exercise of rational judgment, if what plaintiff alleged in her complaint was true. From the time of her first contact with the dancing school in February, 1961, she was influenced unwittingly by a constant and continuous barrage of flattery, false praise, excessive compliments, and panegyric encomiums, to such extent that it would be not only inequitable, but unconscionable, for a Court exercising inherent chancery power to allow such contracts to stand.

She was incessantly subjected to overreaching blandishment and cajolery. She was assured she had "grace and poise"; that she was "rapidly improving and developing in her dancing skill"; that the additional lessons would "make her a beautiful dancer, capable of dancing with the most accomplished dancers"; that she was "rapidly progressing in the development of her dancing skill and gracefulness", etc., etc. She was given "dance aptitude tests" for the ostensible purpose of "determining" the number of remaining hours [of] instructions needed by her from time to time.

At one point she was sold 545 additional hours of dancing lessons to be entitled to award of the "Bronze Medal" signifying that she had reached "the Bronze Standard", a supposed designation of dance achievement by students of Arthur Murray, Inc. Later she was sold an additional 926 hours in order to gain the "Silver Medal", indicating she had reached "the Silver Standard", at a cost of $12,501.35. At one point, while she still had to her credit about 900 unused hours of instructions, she was induced to purchase an additional 24 hours of lessons to participate in a trip to Miami at her own expense, where she would be "given the opportunity to dance with members of the Miami Studio". She was induced at another point to purchase an additional 123 hours of lessons in order to be not only eligible for the Miami trip but also to become "a life member of the Arthur Murray Studio", carrying with it certain dubious emoluments, at a further cost of $1,752.30. At another point, while she still had over 1,000 unused hours of instruction she was induced to buy 151 additional hours at a cost of $2,049.00 to be eligible for a "Student Trip to Trinidad", at her own expense as she later learned. Also, when she still had 1100 unused hours to her credit, she was prevailed upon to purchase an additional 347 hours at

a cost of $4,235.74, to qualify her to receive a "Gold Medal" for achievement, indicating she had advanced to "the Gold Standard". On another occasion, while she still had over 1200 unused hours, she was induced to buy an additional 175 hours of instruction at a cost of $2,472.75 to be eligible "to take a trip to Mexico". Finally, sandwiched in between other lesser sales promotions, she was influenced to buy an additional 481 hours of instruction at a cost of $6,523.81 in order to "be classified as a Gold Bar member, the ultimate achievement of the dancing studio".

All the foregoing sales promotions, illustrative of the entire fourteen separate contracts, were procured by defendant Davenport and Arthur Murray, Inc., by false representations to her that she was improving in her dancing ability, that she had excellent potential, that they were developing her into a beautiful dancer, whereas in truth and in fact she did not develop in her dancing ability, she had no "dance aptitude", and in fact had difficulty in "hearing that musical beat". The complaint alleged that such representations to her "were in fact false and known by the defendant to be false and contrary to the plaintiff's true ability, the truth of plaintiff's ability being fully known to the defendants, but withheld from the plaintiff for the sole and specific intent to deceive and defraud the plaintiff and to induce her in the purchasing of additional hours of dance lessons". It was averred that the lessons were sold to her "in total disregard to the true physical, rhythm, and mental ability of the plaintiff". In other words, while she first exulted that she was entering the "spring of her life", she finally was awakened to the fact there was "spring" neither in her life nor in her feet.

The complaint prayed that the Court decree the dance contracts to be null and void and to be cancelled, that an accounting be had, and judgment entered against, the defendants "for that portion of the $31,090.45 not charged against specific hours of instruction given to the plaintiff". The Court held the complaint not to state a cause of action and dismissed it with prejudice. We disagree and reverse.

The material allegations of the complaint must, of course, be accepted as true for the purpose of testing its legal sufficiency. Defendants contend that contracts can only be rescinded for fraud or misrepresentation when the alleged misrepresentation is as to a material fact, rather than an opinion, prediction or expectation, and that the statements and representations set forth at length in the complaint were in the category of "trade puffing", within its legal orbit.

It is true that "generally a misrepresentation, to be actionable, must be one of fact rather than of opinion". *Tonkovich v. South Florida Citrus Industries, Inc.,* Fla. App. 1966, 185 So. 2d 710. But this rule has significant qualifications, applicable here. It does not apply where there is a fiduciary relationship between the parties, or where there has been some artifice or trick employed by the representor, or where the parties do not in general deal at "arm's length" as we understand the phrase, or where the representee does not have equal opportunity to become apprised of the truth or falsity of the fact represented. As stated by Judge Allen of this Court in *Ramel v. Chasebrook Construction Company,* Fla. App.1961, 135 So. 2d 876: "A statement of a party having . . . superior knowledge may be regarded as a statement of fact although it would be considered as opinion if the parties were dealing on equal terms."

It could be reasonably supposed here that defendants had "superior knowledge" as to whether plaintiff had "dance potential" and as to whether she was noticeably improving in the art of terpsichore. And it would be a reasonable inference from the undenied averments of the complaint that the flowery eulogiums heaped upon her by defendants as a prelude to her contracting for 1944 additional hours of instruction in order to attain the rank of the Bronze Standard, thence to the bracket of the Silver Standard, thence to the class of the Gold Bar Standard, and finally to the crowning plateau of a Life Member of the Studio, proceeded as much or more from the urge to "ring the cash register" as from any honest or realistic appraisal of her dancing prowess or a factual representation of her progress.

Even in contractual situations where a party to a transaction owes no duty to disclose facts within his knowledge or to answer inquiries respecting such facts, the law is if he undertakes to do so he must disclose the *whole truth*. From the face of the complaint, it should have been reasonably

apparent to defendants that her vast outlay of cash for the many hundreds of additional hours of instruction was not justified by her slow and awkward progress, which she would have been made well aware of it they had spoken the "whole truth".

In *Hirschman v. Hodges, etc.,* 1910, 59 Fla. 517, 51 So. 550, it was said that—"what is plainly injurious to good faith ought to be considered as a fraud sufficient to impeach a contract", and that an improvident agreement may be avoided—"because of surprise, or mistake, *want of freedom, undue influence, the suggestion of falsehood, or the suppression of truth*". (Emphasis supplied.)

We repeat that where parties are dealing on a contractual basis at arm's length with no inequities or inherently unfair practices employed, the Courts will in general "leave the parties where they find themselves". But in the case sub judice, from the allegations of the unanswered complaint, we cannot say that enough of the accompanying ingredients, as mentioned in the foregoing authorities, were not present which otherwise would have barred the equitable arm of the Court to her. In our view from the showing made in her complaint, plaintiff is entitled to her day in Court.

It accordingly follows that the order dismissing plaintiff's . . . complaint . . . is reversed.

ASSIGNMENT
26.3

a. If you owned a small struggling business, how would you feel about *Vokes v. Arthur Murray, Inc.?* Consumers love it. What do you think the business community feels about this opinion?

b. What could the defendants have done to avoid losing their dance sales agreements because of misrepresentation? Should they have told Audry Vokes that she has two left feet? (Wouldn't she then be able to sue for slander?) Should they have refused to take her money for more lessons? (Wouldn't she then charge them with some form of discrimination or violation of her consumer right to spend her money as she pleased?) Assume that she is determined to become a good dancer no matter how much it costs. Where is she supposed to turn? Is it true that Arthur Murray, Inc. can continue to take her money forever as long as it explicitly insults her by telling her that she is wasting her time and money?

c. Ted Smith has a problem losing weight. He attends the Avis Weight Reduction Center. The literature of the Center says, "We guarantee nothing, but eventually, we will help you lose it all." The Center costs $1,000 a week. Ted has been attending every week for the past six years. Center personnel work regularly with Ted. They encourage him to keep a good attitude and never give up. Is the Center liable under the reasoning of *Vokes v. Arthur Murray, Inc.?*

INTERFERENCE WITH CONTRACT RELATIONS

Suppose that Fred has a contract to build a bridge for Sam. If Fred fails to build the bridge, Sam can sue Fred in a contract action—for breach of contract. Now suppose that a third party, Dan, persuades Fred not to build Sam's bridge so that Fred can build one for Dan. At this point two legal actions are possible:

- a *contract* action (Sam v. Fred) for breaching the contract to build a bridge for Sam
- a *tort* action (Sam v. Dan) for inducing a breach of the contract Sam had with Fred

The tort is called **interference with contract relations.** Its elements are as follows:

i. an existing contract
ii. interference with the contract by defendant
iii. intent
iv. damages
v. causation

Existing Contract

There must be a contract with which the defendant interferes. The enforcement of the contract must not violate public policy. A contract to marry, for example, cannot be the subject of a breach of contract action. It is against **public policy** to enforce such contracts by requiring someone to go through with a marriage he or she no longer wants. Therefore, it would not be a tort to induce someone to breach a contract to marry. So too, it is not a tort to induce the breach of an illegal gambling contract or a prostitution contract.

Suppose that the contract is **voidable,** i.e., unenforceable at the option of one of the parties. A voidable contract remains in effect if the option to terminate is not exercised. A contract might be voidable because it is not in writing or because one of the parties is a minor. Is it a tort to interfere with such a contract? Yes, as long as the contract is in existence and is not contrary to public policy as just discussed. The contract does not have to be enforceable to be the foundation of this tort. There is always the possibility that the party to the contract will *not* exercise his or her option to get out of it; hence, it is a wrong (a tort) for a third party (the defendant) to induce its breach.

Many contracts, particularly employment contracts, are **terminable at will,** meaning that either party can get out at any time for any reason. Some courts conclude that it is not a tort to induce the termination of a contract at will since the parties to the contract are always free to terminate it without committing a breach of contract to each other. Most courts, however, disagree. It is a tort in most states to interfere with a contract at will. The injured party to the contract had a valuable expectation that the other party would not terminate—until the defendant came along. It is a tort to upset the contract relationship that existed.

Interference

The interference with the contract can take a number of forms:

- inducing one party to the contract to breach it
- making it impossible for one party to perform the contract
- making it substantially more difficult for one party to perform the contract

Intent

The plaintiff must show that the defendant intended to interfere with the contract relation by inducing the breach, or by rendering performance impossible or more burdensome. The defendant must desire this interference or know with substantial certainty that the interference will result from what the defendant does or fails to do. Negligence is not enough. Suppose that the XYZ Company has a contract to supply lake water to a city, and the defendant (a third party) negligently pollutes this water before delivery. The defendant has surely interfered with XYZ's contract with the city, but no intentional tort has been committed by the defendant because there was no intent to interfere with the contract. The XYZ Company or the city may be able to sue the defendant for negligence in polluting the water, but there can be no suit for interference with contract. The defendant must know about the contract and intend to interfere with it.

Damages

The damages for this tort cover the loss of the contract or the diminished value of its performance. Most courts require a showing of actual damages, even though they may be nominal. In addition, damages for mental suffering are usually allowed, and if malice is shown, punitive damages can be awarded. As indicated in the bridge example at the beginning of this section involving Fred, Sam, and Dan, the plaintiff may have a breach of contract action against the other party to the contract *and* a tort action against the third party for inducing the breach or for diminishing the value of performance. To avoid double recovery, however, the amount recovered in the tort action is reduced by whatever the plaintiff recovers in the contract action. When the defendant has threatened an interference with the contract, or when the interference is continuing, many courts will grant an **injunction** against the defendant because of the inadequacy of damages as a remedy.

Causation

The plaintiff must show that either:

- but for the action or inaction of the defendant, the plaintiff would not have suffered the damages that are provable, or

- the defendant was a substantial factor in producing these damages

Privilege to Interfere

One of the major defenses to this tort is the privilege to interfere in order to protect one's own interest. Assume, for example, that Len has a contract to furnish goods to Ted. Len will obtain these goods from Mary with whom Len has a separate contract. If Mary feels that Len is violating his contract with her, she can take steps to protect her own interest. This might include stopping delivery of the goods to Len. This, of course, would have the effect of interfering with Ted's contract with Len. Mary has not committed a tort, however, as long as she is acting reasonably to protect her own interest.

There may also be a privilege to interfere in order to protect the interest of someone else if there is a legal or moral duty to protect this other person (e.g., a doctor caring for a patient, an attorney advising a client). The interference could take the form of a recommendation that the person remove him- or herself from certain contract obligations that are reasonably thought to be detrimental to the welfare of that person. For example, the doctor might tell the patient that continuing to work at a particular plant could lead to a further deterioration of the patient's health.

This privilege is lost if the interference was **malicious.** In this context, malice means not acting reasonably—acting for a purpose other than to protect a legitimate interest, e.g., interfering with someone's contract in order to seek revenge.

ASSIGNMENT

26.4

Helen works for Linda. One day, Helen borrows $500 from Linda to repair a fence at Helen's home. Linda has difficulty collecting this money from Helen. Linda tells her father, Ed, about the loan. He advises Linda to fire Helen if she does not repay the loan. Linda tells Helen that she will lose her job if she does not repay the loan within a week. Helen is fired when she does not make the payment within the time designated. Does Helen have a cause of action against Ed? (See General Instructions for the Legal Analysis Assignment in Chapter 2.)

CASE

Texaco, Inc. v. Pennzoil Co.
729 S.W.2d 768 (1987)
Court of Appeals of Texas, Houston (1st District)

Background: *This case involves a multibillion dollar verdict for committing the tort of interference with contract relations. In 1984 Getty Oil was for sale. It agreed "in principle" to be purchased by Pennzoil in a leveraged buyout for $110 per share (plus a $5 "stub," payable later). Although there was no formal contract between Getty and Pennzoil, both issued a "news release" that announced an "agreement in principle" based on a Memorandum of Agreement. The day after this announcement, Texaco offered to buy Getty for $125 per share. Getty withdrew from its relationship with Pennzoil and agreed to merge with Texaco. Pennzoil then sued Texaco for the tort of interfering with its contract with Getty. A Houston jury found that: (1) at the end of a board meeting on January 3, 1984, the Getty entities intended to bind themselves to an agreement providing for the purchase of Getty Oil stock by Pennzoil; (2) Texaco knowingly interfered with the agreement between Pennzoil and the Getty entities; (3) as a result of Texaco's interference, Pennzoil suffered damages of $7.53 billion; (4) Texaco's actions were intentional, willful, and in wanton disregard of Pennzoil's rights; and, (5) Pennzoil was entitled to punitive damages of $3 billion. The case is now on appeal before the Court of Appeals of Texas.*

Decision on Appeal: *The Court of Appeals affirmed the trial court and held that Texaco did commit the tort. Following this opinion, the parties negotiated to try to settle the case. After further court proceedings (including a Chapter 11 bankruptcy by Texaco) Pennzoil and Texaco agreed to a settlement of $3 billion dollars to be paid by Texaco.*

OPINION OF COURT

Justice WARREN delivered the opinion of the court. . . .

Texaco argues first that there was no evidence [Getty intended to bind itself] to an agreement with Pennzoil. . . . Second, Texaco asserts that the evidence is legally and factually insufficient to support the . . . [finding that] it had actual knowledge of a legally enforceable contract, or that Texaco actively induced a breach of the alleged contract. . . . Pennzoil contends that the evidence showed that the parties intended to be bound to the terms in the Memorandum of Agreement plus price terms of $110 plus a $5 stub, even though the parties may have contemplated a later, more formal document to memorialize the agreement already reached. . . .

[If] parties do not intend to be bound to an agreement until it is reduced to writing and signed by both parties, then there is no contract until that event occurs. If there is no understanding that a signed writing is necessary before the parties will be bound, and the parties have agreed upon all substantial terms, then an informal agreement can be binding, even though the parties contemplate evidencing their agreement in a formal document later. . . .

Texaco states that the use of the term "agreement in principle" in the press release was a conscious and deliberate choice of words to convey that there was not yet any binding agreement. . . . There was sufficient evidence at trial on the common business usage of the expression "agreement in principle" and on its meaning in this case for the jury reasonably to decide that its use in the press release did not necessarily establish that the parties did not intend to be bound before signing a formal document. . . . There was sufficient evidence for the jury to conclude that the parties had reached agreement on all essential terms of the transaction with only the mechanics and details left to be supplied by the parties' attorneys. Although there may have been many specific items relating to the transaction agreement draft that had yet to be put in final form, there is sufficient evidence to support a conclusion by the jury that the parties did not consider any of Texaco's asserted "open items" significant obstacles precluding an intent to be bound. . . .

Texaco asserts that Pennzoil failed to prove that Texaco had actual knowledge that a contract existed. [There must be] knowledge by a defendant of the existence of contractual rights as an element of the tort of inducing a breach of that contract. However, the defendant need not have full knowledge of all the detailed terms of the contract. . . . Since there was no direct evidence of Texaco's knowledge of a contract in this case, the question is whether there was legally and factually sufficient circumstantial evidence from which the trier of fact reasonably could have inferred knowledge. . . .

Pennzoil responds that there was legally and factually sufficient evidence to support the jury's finding of knowledge, because the jury could reasonably infer that Texaco knew about the Pennzoil deal from the evidence of (1) how Texaco carefully mapped its strategy to defeat Pennzoil's deal by acting to "stop the train" or "stop the signing"; (2) the notice of a contract given by a January 5 Wall Street Journal article reporting on the Pennzoil agreement—an article that Texaco denied anyone at Texaco had seen; [and] (3) the knowledge of an agreement that would arise from comparing the Memorandum of Agreement with the Getty press release. . . . Pennzoil contends that these circumstances indicated Texaco's knowledge of Pennzoil's deal too strongly to be overcome by Texaco's "self-serving verbal protestations at trial" that Texaco was told and believed that there was no agreement. . . . We find that an inference could arise that Texaco had some knowledge of Pennzoil's agreement with the Getty entities, given the evidence of Texaco's detailed studies of the Pennzoil plan, its knowledge that some members of the Getty board were not happy with Pennzoil's price, and its subsequent formulation of strategy to "stop the [Pennzoil] train". . . .

The second major issue Texaco raises . . . is that the evidence was legally and factually insufficient to show that Texaco actively induced breach of the alleged Pennzoil/Getty contract. A necessary element of the plaintiff's cause of action is a showing that the defendant took an active part in persuading a party to a contract to breach it. Merely entering into a contract with a party with the knowledge of that party's contractual obligations to someone else is not the same as inducing a breach. It is necessary that there be some act of interference or of persuading a party to breach, for example by offering better terms or other incentives, for tort liability to arise. . . .

The evidence . . . on Texaco's calculated formulation and implementation of its ideal strategy to acquire Getty is . . . inconsistent with its contention that it was merely the passive target of Getty's aggressive solicitation campaign and did nothing more than to accept terms that Getty Oil . . . proposed. The evidence showed that Texaco knew it had to act quickly, and that it had "24 hours" to "stop the train." . . .

[The judgment of the trial court is affirmed.]

ASSIGNMENT 26.5

You and Bob are applying for the job of president of a major corporation. The contract will be for three years. Both of you are equally qualified. After the chairman of the board of the corporation meets with Bob, the chairman tells the press that the board is very impressed with Bob and that "no one should be surprised if the formality of an announcement is made soon that Bob will be joining us very soon." This announcement troubles you. You immediately call the chairman and tell him that Bob is not serious about joining the corporation. "He is really using an offer by you as leverage to negotiate better employment terms with a rival company where he really wants to work." The chairman investigates and finds out that in fact Bob is actively pursuing a position at the rival company. The corporation decides to give you the job. Have you committed the tort of interference with contract relations? Does the *Texaco* case apply?

INTERFERENCE WITH PROSPECTIVE ADVANTAGE

Next, we consider the tort called **interference with prospective advantage,** which has the following elements:

   i. reasonable expectation of an economic advantage
  ii. interference with this expectation
 iii. intent
 iv. damages
  v. causation

In this tort, there is no existing contract with which the defendant has interfered. All that is needed is a reasonable expectation of some economic advantage. The defendant usually has committed other torts that have led to this interference, e.g., misrepresentation, defamation, assault, and battery.

In the business world, most of the cases that have arisen under the tort of interference with prospective advantage have involved what is loosely called **unfair competition.**

EXAMPLES:

- The plaintiff is trying to lure ducks at a public pond, which he or she will then kill and try to sell. The defendant intentionally fires a gun into the air in order to scare the ducks out of the plaintiff's range. The defendant is a competitor of the plaintiff in the sale of ducks.
- The defendant threatens a third party not to go to work for the plaintiff (no employment contract yet exists). The goal of the defendant is to get the third party to go to work for the defendant.
- The defendant pours some foul-smelling chemicals on his or her own property, which is next door to the plaintiff's, in order to scare the latter's potential customers away. The defendant wants the plaintiff to leave the area so that the defendant can rent the premises now occupied by the plaintiff.

The defendant has a privilege to protect his or her own business interests by engaging in fair competitive practices. Deceptive advertising and monopolistic steps, of course, constitute unfair (and illegal) competition. When these devices are not used, the defendant is free to use tactics such as high pressure advertising, price cutting, and rebates in order to lure prospective customers away from other merchants.

Courts are often reluctant to allow the tort of interference with prospective advantage when business or commercial interests are not involved, e.g., a defendant pressures a person to remove the plaintiff as the beneficiary of a will. There are a few courts, however, that will allow recovery in such situations, when there is a reasonable degree of certainty that the plaintiff would have received the expected benefit if there had been no interference by the defendant. In most cases of interference with prospective advantage, causation is a problem. It can be very difficult to prove that the benefit would have been obtained but for what the defendant did, or that the defendant was a substantial factor in the loss of the benefit. This is because the plaintiff had no contract right to the benefit at the time of the interference. Yet, if causation can be shown with reasonable certainty, recovery is allowed.

TORTIOUS INTERFERENCE WITH EMPLOYMENT (WRONGFUL DISCHARGE)

Most people are employed "at will," which, as indicated earlier, simply means that either the employee or the employer can terminate the relationship at any time and for any reason. There is no obligation to explain why or to state a cause. If, on the other hand, an express contract of employment exists for a designated period of time (e.g., a one-year union contract), the termination of the relationship within this period must comply with the terms of the contract. This usually means that terminations are allowed only for **cause;** employees with contract protection cannot be fired at will. In this context, cause means a justifiable reason such as incompetence.

The traditional rule on **employment at will** has been undergoing some modification. There are now some circumstances in which the law *will* protect the employee at will. Suppose, for example, that the employer fires the employee because the latter reported fire hazards in the employer's building to the city, or because the employee filed a workers' compensation claim. This **retaliatory discharge** violates public policy, because it obviously discourages employees from engaging in important activity such as fire prevention and in exercising rights such as those provided by the workers' compensation system.

What is the remedy for such retaliation? It is difficult to categorize the remedy within the traditional causes of action. A breach of contract action is somewhat strained, because there is no express contract that was violated. Some courts say that in the employment relationship there is an implied condition that forbids the employer from terminating the relationship for a reason that violates public policy. Most courts take a different approach by concluding that a tort has been committed—the **tortious interference with employment** (also called **wrongful discharge**). This tort differs from the tort of interference with contract relations (discussed earlier), in which a *third party* has wrongfully caused the interference.

For a case that unsuccessfully alleged wrongful discharge based on information revealed through an invasion of privacy, see *Smyth v. The Pillsbury Co.* in Chapter 25.

DISPARAGEMENT

The tort of **disparagement** covers attacks made against the business or property of the plaintiff. The elements of this tort are as follows:

   i. false statement of fact
   ii. disparaging the plaintiff's business or property
   iii. publication
   iv. intent
   v. special damages
   vi. causation

The attack might cast doubt on the plaintiff's title to property (called **slander of title**) or attribute a quality to goods that make them undesirable for sale or other commercial use (called **trade libel**). The effect of the disparaging statement is to cause others not to deal with the plaintiff or to cause some other similar disadvantage.

> **EXAMPLES:**
>
> - Sam falsely states that he holds a mortgage on the plaintiff's farm, which the latter has on the market for sale.
> - Tom falsely says that he owns the land that Jim is trying to sell.
> - Sarah falsely states that the tires being sold by XYZ as radials are not radials.

Some statements constitute the tort of disparagement and the tort of defamation. Disparagement discredits the quality of or title to *goods or property.* Defamation consists of a derogatory statement about the *person* of the plaintiff (see Chapter 24). Compare the following statements:

"Prostitutes regularly use the XYZ Hotel for their clients."
"Fred, the manager of the XYZ Hotel, takes a cut of the fee charged by prostitutes in exchange for the use of the hotel for their clients."

The first statement disparages the hotel—the business. The second statement disparages the hotel *and* personally defames the manager.

The plaintiff must plead and prove **special damages,** which are specific economic or pecuniary losses. It is usually not enough for the plaintiff to prove that there was a general loss of business following the disparaging statements of the defendant. The plaintiff must show specifically identified contracts or customers that were lost. Or, the plaintiff must show he or she had to sell goods at a lower price to specific customers as a result of the disparagement.

Defendants have a privilege to protect their own interest. For example, a defendant can state that he or she owns property the plaintiff is trying to sell. This disparages the property of the plaintiff, but it is privileged as long as the defendant is acting in the honest belief that he or she is protecting his or her own interest. Malice, however, defeats the privilege.

There is also a general privilege to compete in the business world by exaggerating the qualities of your own products compared to the products of others. There is a privilege, for example, to say that "no car is more economical" than the car being offered for sale. As indicated earlier, such statements are viewed either as nonfactual statements (hence not qualifying as the first element of disparagement) or as **fair competition.**

Special Statutes: "Veggie Libel"

Some statements about consumer products can have a major impact on their sale. Suppose, for example, that a guest, a reporter, or a host on a national talk show or newsmagazine says, "The pesticides used on all broccoli cause cancer in children." This could devastate the broccoli market.

Several states have passed special statutes that give producers of perishable food products a cause of action when they lose business because of false statements that disparage the safety of their products. The media has called such actions "**veggie libel.**"

> **EXAMPLES:**
>
> - Ranchers sued television talk-show host, Oprah Winfrey, and a guest who said American beef was largely infected with bovine spongiform encephalopathy, or "mad cow disease." (WINFREY: "You said this disease could make AIDS look like the common cold?" GUEST: "Absolutely." WINFREY: "Now doesn't that concern you-all a little bit right here, hearing that? It has just stopped me cold from eating another burger. I'm stopped.")
> - Washington State apple growers sued the CBS television show *60 Minutes* for alleging in a segment called, "*A* Is for Apple" that Alar, a chemical growth regulator, dramatically increased cancer risks.
> - Emu ranchers sued Honda Motor Company for a Honda advertisement that said the emu was the "pork of the future."

Almost all cases of this kind are lost by the plaintiffs who bring them. It is often very difficult to prove that the statements are false. This is particularly true in those states where the plaintiff must prove that the defendant knew the statement was false. Also some courts are not receptive to an allegation of group disparagement that is not directed at a particular grower or food producer. Furthermore, there is reason to believe that the United States Supreme Court will eventually impose severe constitutional limitations on disparagement suits of this kind against the media as it has in the area of defamation. The inclination of the Court is to interpret the First Amendment as encouraging robust speech. "Veggie libel" laws arguably do the opposite.

ASSIGNMENT

26.6

Did President George Bush commit a tort when he told the media, "I hate broccoli and we don't serve it here at the White House"? (See General Instructions for the Legal Analysis Assignment in Chapter 2.)

INJURIOUS FALSEHOOD

The phrase **injurious falsehood** is sometimes used interchangeably with the word "disparagement," but injurious falsehood is a broader concept. Disparagement is an example of an injurious falsehood. An injurious falsehood can consist of a statement of fact that injures someone economically in a way other than disparaging goods or a business.

> **EXAMPLES:**
>
> - a false statement to the immigration officials that results in the deportation of the plaintiff
> - a false statement by an employer of the income paid to an employee, resulting in tax evasion charges against the employee

The same elements for disparagement are required for injurious falsehood, except for the second element: disparaging the plaintiff's business or property. Instead of showing that the statement disparages the business or products of the plaintiff, the broader tort of injurious falsehood requires only that the statement be harmful to the interests of the plaintiff. The other elements are the same: false statement of fact, publication, intent, special damages, and causation.

ASSIGNMENT

26.7

Tom dies intestate, i.e., without a valid will. There are only two survivors: Mary, a daughter, and George, a nephew. Under the intestate law of the state, all property goes to legitimate children. If no legitimate children survive, the property goes to other relatives. George claims that Mary is illegitimate. Mary hires an attorney who helps establish that she is legitimate. What tort or torts, if any, has George committed? (See General Instructions for the Legal Analysis Assignment in Chapter 2.)

PRIMA FACIE TORT

Negligence is a catchall tort that encompasses a very wide variety of wrongful conduct that is considered unreasonable. There is no comparable catchall tort for conduct that is intentional. We cannot say that all intentional conduct causing harm is tortious. If the defendant's actions or inactions do not fall within the elements of negligence, the plaintiff must look to the approximately thirty other torts, e.g., battery, deceit, malicious prosecution, and others listed in Figure 1–3 of Chapter 1. If these torts do not fit, then the plaintiff must suffer the loss, unless, of course, workers' compensation and no-fault insurance (see Appendix G) provide some form of relief.

Some consider it unfortunate that the law does not provide a clear tort remedy for a defendant's intentional conduct that harms someone even though the facts do not fit within the traditional torts. In a sense, the torts of injurious falsehood and interference with prospective advantage try to fill some of the holes left by the traditional torts. Yet, as we have seen, even these torts have limitations on what intentional conduct they will or will not cover.

In a few states (including New York), small efforts toward the creation of a generic intentional tort have been made in the form of the **prima facie tort.** Although this tort is not limited to the business world, most of the cases applying it have involved commercial matters. The elements of the prima facie tort are:

   i. infliction of harm
  ii. intent to do harm (malice)
 iii. special damages
 iv. causation

It is sometimes said that the tort does not exist unless the defendant acted "maliciously and without justification." It is not always clear whether malice means a desire to harm someone or simply an intentional act or omission.

In theory, the prima facie tort is available when the facts of the case do not fit the pigeonholes of any of the traditional torts. It does not follow, however, that the prima facie tort will apply every time the other torts do not. The requirement of special damages, for example, tends to limit the applicability of the prima facie tort, due to the difficulty of proving specific economic or pecuniary loss (i.e., special damages).

The vast majority of states do *not* recognize the prima facie tort. Too many problems exist in defining it and in defining the defenses to it. Rather than create a new tort, most states would prefer to try to stretch the boundaries of the existing torts so that plaintiffs will not be without a remedy when defendants have intentionally caused injury.

BAD FAITH LIABILITY

A relatively recent basis of liability against insurance companies is called **bad faith liability**. It consists of an unreasonable denial or delay in paying an insurance claim within policy limits.

> **EXAMPLE:** Jackson has a $100,000 liability policy with an insurance company. He has an accident and is sued for $250,000 by Pamela. The latter offers to settle for $80,000. Jackson's attorney notifies the insurance company of the offer, but the company takes an unreasonable amount of time to respond. Pamela proceeds with litigation and obtains a $200,000 judgment against Jackson. The insurance company pays $100,000 of this judgment, the maximum under the policy.

Jackson can now sue the company for the tort of bad faith in handling the insurance claim. His argument is that the company's unreasonable delay in processing his claim led to a judgment far in excess of policy limits. For a discussion of bad faith liability in an automobile case, see Appendix I within the settlement brochure presented in full in Chapter 29 (page 599).

DRAM SHOP LIABILITY

A number of states have what is called a Civil Liability Act or Dram Shop Act that imposes liability on those who give liquor to someone who is visibly intoxicated when the intoxication causes an injury to a third person. The basis of **dram shop liability** can differ from state to state. Negligence may have to be shown: the person giving the liquor created an unreasonable risk that the person receiving the liquor might injure others. Some states impose strict liability, especially if the person receiving the liquor is a minor. In such states there is no need for the injured third party to show that the person giving the liquor was negligent.

Many states impose dram shop liability only when the liquor is *sold* and only when the buyer is already visibly intoxicated. In a few states, however, liability is not dependent on a sale. A social host can also be held to dram shop liability when a *gift* of intoxicating liquor causes an injury.

> **EXAMPLE:** Bob holds a high school graduation party in his home for his daughter and her friends. He serves liquor at the party. One of the guests is Kelly, who is intoxicated. While driving home from the party, Kelly hits a pedestrian. Kelly became intoxicated at the party and the intoxication was a substantial factor in causing the pedestrian's injury. The latter can now seek dram shop liability against Bob.

ASSIGNMENT

26.8

The XYZ Supermarket has a liquor section. Davidson, an adult, buys a six-pack of beer at XYZ. At the time of the purchase, his speech was slightly slurred from drinking earlier in the day. He goes to his car in the parking lot of XYZ and drinks all the beer he just bought. Would dram shop liability apply in the following cases? (See General Instructions for the Legal Analysis Assignment in Chapter 2.)

a. After Davidson drives out of the XYZ Supermarket parking lot, he goes to a nearby parking lot. He has a fist fight with another driver in an argument over a parking space. Davidson knocks the other driver unconscious. This driver now wants to sue the XYZ Supermarket for selling Davidson the beer.

b. After Davidson drives out of the XYZ Supermarket parking lot, he hits a tree and is killed. His family now wants to sue the XYZ Supermarket for selling Davidson the beer.

SUMMARY

Misrepresentation covers pecuniary loss caused by false statements of fact, by the active concealment of a fact, by the nondisclosure of a fact that someone had a duty to disclose, and by the statement of opinion containing false implied facts. There must be scienter, the intent to mislead, which is established by showing that the defendant made a statement knowing it is false, without a belief in its truth, or in reckless disregard of its truth or falsity, with the desire that the statement be believed and relied upon. An action for negligent misrepresentation can be brought in many states for the careless communication of a false statement of fact brought by someone whom the statement was intended to reach. There must be justifiable reliance, which means that the plaintiff was reasonable in taking action because of the plaintiff's statement. The exception is when the defendant knows the plaintiff is particularly vulnerable to whatever the defendant says.

It is a tort to interfere with contract relations by intentionally inducing another to breach a contract or to make it impossible or more difficult to perform. There must be an existing contract with which the defendant intends to interfere. The plaintiff's damages include compensation to cover the loss of the contract or the diminished value of its performance. One of the defenses to this tort is the privilege to protect one's own interest or the interest of another. If the plaintiff does not have a contract, but the defendant interferes with the plaintiff's reasonable expectation of an economic advantage, the defendant may have committed the tort of interference with prospective advantage. Most cases raising this tort in the business world involve unfair competition. Some states will allow an employee at will to sue an employer for tortious interference with an employment relationship through a retaliatory discharge. When the employment is at will, this tort is an exception to the traditional rule that at-will employees can be fired at any time for any reason.

To commit the tort of disparagement, the defendant must publish a false statement of fact that casts doubt on the plaintiff's title to property (slander of title) or attributes a quality to the plaintiff's goods that makes them undesirable for commercial use (trade libel). A defendant has the privilege to protect his or her own interest and to engage in fair competition in the business world. Some states have passed "veggie libel" statutes that give producers of perishable food products a cause of action when they lose business because of false statements that disparage the safety of their products. These cases are difficult to prove and are subject to constitutional challenge.

In a few states, if the defendant causes special damages by intentionally inflicting harm, the plaintiff may be able to bring an action for prima facie tort when the conduct does not fit within any of the traditional torts.

Insurance companies that unreasonably delay acting on insurance claims within policy limits may be subject to bad faith liability when the litigated claim results in a judgment against the plaintiff that is over the limits of the policy. Businesses that sell liquor to intoxicated persons who then injure others can be subject to dram shop liability. Some states also impose this liability on hosts who serve liquor to intoxicated guests at social gatherings.

KEY TERMS

misrepresentation 514

deceit 514

fraud 514

pecuniary loss 514

fact 518

opinion 518

puffing 518

fiduciary relationship 518

confidential relationship 518

scienter 520

reckless disregard 520

negligent misrepresentation 521

justifiable reliance 521

material 521

interference with contract
relations 524

public policy 524

voidable 524

terminable at will 524

injunction 525

malicious 525

interference with prospective
advantage 527

unfair competition 527

cause 528

employment at will 528

retaliatory discharge 528

tortious interference with
employment 528

wrongful discharge 528

disparagement 529

slander of title 529

trade libel 529

special damages 529

fair competition 529

veggie libel 530

injurious falsehood 530

prima facie tort 531

bad faith liability 532

dram shop liability 532

CHAPTER

27

Additional Tort Defenses

CHAPTER OUTLINE

- Introduction
- Consent in Tort Law
- Self-Help Privileges
- Sovereign Immunity
- Official Immunity: The Personal Liability of Government Employees
- Charitable Immunity
- Intrafamily Tort Immunity

INTRODUCTION

A **defense** is the response of a party to a claim of another party, setting forth the reason(s) the claim should not be granted. Sometimes the defense is a simple denial ("I didn't do it"). More often the response is more specific (e.g., "the law allowed me to do what I did because. . . ."). Throughout this text, we have studied defenses to specific torts, e.g., Chapter 17 (defenses to negligence) and Chapter 24 (defenses to defamation). In this chapter, almost all the defenses we will study apply to more than one tort.

Many defenses are privileges or immunities. A **privilege** is a justification for what would otherwise be wrongful or tortious conduct. A privilege is the right of an individual to act contrary to the right of another individual without being subject to tort or other liability. Self-defense is an example. Using physical force against another usually constitutes a battery. If, however, you used this force to protect yourself against attack, you may have a defense when you are sued for battery—the privilege of self-defense. Technically, a tort cannot exist if the defendant had a privilege to do what the plaintiff is now complaining about. An **immunity,** on the other hand, is a special protection given to someone who *has* committed a tort. Sovereign immunity is an example. Suppose, for example, that a government employee defames you. The defense of sovereign immunity may prevent you from suing the government for this tort, and the defense of official immunity may prevent you from suing the employee for this tort. The practical effect of privileges and immunities is the same: they both are defenses that prevent liability for damage or injury. Because of this similarity of effect, you will sometimes see the words "privilege" and "immunity" used interchangeably.

Privileges that are defenses to tort actions are different from evidentiary privileges that operate to prevent a jury from considering otherwise admissible evidence. Examples of evidentiary privileges are attorney-client privilege, doctor-patient privilege, and privilege against self-incrimination. In this chapter, we are concerned with the privileges that prevent tort liability.

CONSENT IN TORT LAW

A central principle of the law is **volenti non fit injuria:** no wrong is done to one who consents. If the plaintiff consented to the defendant's conduct, the defendant should not be liable for the resulting harm. When the defendant is charged with negligence or strict liability in tort, the consent defense is the closely related concept of assumption of risk, which we examined in Chapters 17 and 19. Here, our focus is consent as a defense to intentional torts such as assault, battery, and trespass.

The basic elements of **consent** are presented in Figure 27–1.

Capacity to Consent

The person giving consent must have the capacity to consent. A young girl, for example, may agree to sexual intercourse with an older male, but the latter can still be guilty of statutory rape. If the girl later sues the male for battery in a civil case, the male cannot raise the defense of consent, just as he could not raise it in the criminal case. The young girl does not have the capacity to consent if she is below the age designated by law. So too, there are statutes intended to protect children from working in dangerous conditions. If a child is injured in working conditions that violate the statute, the employer will not be able to say that the child consented to work there and took the risk of being injured—even if the child understood those risks and willingly proceeded. The statutes will probably be interpreted as taking away the child's capacity to consent.

FIGURE 27–1
Elements of consent.

> **1.** Plaintiff (P) must have the capacity to consent to the conduct of Defendant (D).
> **2.** There is an express or implied manifestation from P of a willingness to let the conduct of D occur.
> **3.** P's willingness is voluntary.
> **4.** D reasonably believes that P is willing to let D's conduct occur.
> **5.** P has knowledge of the nature and consequences of D's conduct.
> **6.** D's conduct is substantially the same as the conduct P agreed to.

A person can also lack the capacity to consent by being too young or ill to understand the conduct involved. Unless an authorized parent or guardian gives consent for this person, the consent is invalid.

Suppose that the conduct to which consent is given is criminal conduct. Paul and Dan agree to a duel or boxing match that is illegal. Both are prosecuted under criminal law. Paul then sues Dan for damages in a civil battery case. Dan's defense is that Paul consented to being hit. Courts differ on how they handle this problem. Some hold that the consent will be a good defense, barring the civil action. Other courts, however, do not recognize the consent as valid on the theory that no one has the power or capacity to consent to a crime. Since the consent is invalid, the civil battery action can be brought. As a consequence, a plaintiff can receive damages growing out of a criminal act in which the plaintiff willingly participated. Of course, if both Paul and Dan were injured in their illegal fight with each other, each of them could sue the other for civil battery in a state where the consent will not be recognized.

ASSIGNMENT

27.1

Henry and Fred are having an argument. Henry is about to hit Fred with a baseball bat. In response, Fred punches Henry with his fist and breaks Henry's jaw. While Henry is unconscious on the ground, Fred stabs him in the leg. Henry later sues Fred for injury to his leg in a civil battery case. Fred raises the defense of consent. What result and why? (See General Instructions for the Legal Analysis Assignment in Chapter 2.)

Manifestation of Willingness

A person can demonstrate or manifest willingness in a variety of ways. There can be an express manifestation such as telling someone he or she can enter the land or use a car. Written or verbal manifestation is not always needed. The wave of a hand can indicate consent to come on one's land. Consent by silence is also common if the person would normally be expected to speak if he or she objected to conduct about to occur. If a trespasser enters your yard and you fail to object or fail to take steps to remove the individual, your silence or nonaction is strong evidence that you do not object. This is an **implied consent.** If you voluntarily agree to play football, you are implying consent to the kind of rugged contact that is usually associated with this sport. If you walk downtown into a crowded store, you are implying consent to the kind of everyday contact that is normal in crowds.

ASSIGNMENT

27.2

At a college dance, Jessica asks Dan, a stranger, to dance. After the dance, Jessica kisses Dan on the cheek and walks away. Dan sues Jessica for battery. Does she have a defense? (See General Instructions for the Legal Analysis Assignment in Chapter 3.)

Voluntariness

If the plaintiff has been coerced into agreeing to the defendant's conduct, the consent is invalid. **Coercion** is the use of such strength or pressure to secure compliance that the compliance is not the product of a free will. Coercion renders consent involuntary, invalidating the defense. Suppose that a foreign passenger about to enter port does not want to be vaccinated, but nevertheless rolls up her sleeve to the doctor injecting the needle. Her conduct led the doctor to believe that she consented. She may have been under pressure to be vaccinated in order to avoid the hassle of being detained at port, yet the consent was still the product of a free will. The consent was voluntary.

Extreme or drastic pressure, however, can be enough to invalidate consent, e.g., a threat of force against the plaintiff or a member of the plaintiff's family, or a threat against the valuable property of the plaintiff. The plaintiff's agreement as a result of such pressure would probably not be voluntary.

ASSIGNMENT
27.3

Tom calls Linda on the phone and tells her that he has her very valuable painting, which he will destroy if she does not come to his apartment and engage in sexual intercourse. Linda is frantic about the painting. She goes to his apartment and has sex with him. He then gives her the painting. Later, she brings a civil battery action against him. Does he have a defense? Would it make any difference if his threat was to harm Linda's neighbor? (See General Instructions for the Legal Analysis Assignment in Chapter 2.)

Reasonable Belief

The defendant must be reasonable in believing that the plaintiff has consented to the conduct in question. Problems often arise when the defendant claims to have relied on the plaintiff's implied consent. Suppose that the defendant has always played practical jokes on the plaintiff, to the latter's great amusement, e.g., squirting the plaintiff with a water pistol or pretending to steal the plaintiff's hat. It would be reasonable for the defendant to believe that the plaintiff would continue to agree to such jokes as long as they were of the same kind as practiced in the past. If the plaintiff has decided that enough is enough and does not want to be subjected to such jokes anymore, he or she must communicate this to the defendant. Otherwise, the defendant is justified in believing that plaintiff continues to consent. The test of consent is not what the plaintiff subjectively thinks, but what someone reasonably interprets the plaintiff to be communicating based upon the latter's words, actions, silence, and any relevant cultural customs in the area on how people normally interpret each other's behavior.

ASSIGNMENT
27.4

Mary is riding in her car when she spots Alex injured on the side of the road. Mary pulls over to try to help. She sees that his arm is broken and puts it in a sling. Later, Alex sues Mary for battery. Does she have a defense? Does it make any difference that Mary is a doctor? Why or why not? (See General Instructions for the Legal Analysis Assignment in Chapter 2.)

Knowledge

The plaintiff must know what conduct is being consented to and its probable consequences in order for the consent to be an effective bar to a later tort action against the defendant. If a doctor obtains the consent of a patient to undergo an operation, but fails to tell the patient of the very serious probable side effects of the operation, the patient has not consented to the operation. The defendant has not provided the patient with the basic knowledge to enable the patient to give an **informed consent.** As we saw in Chapter 18, if an emergency exists, the doctor can proceed with treatment to save the patient's life or to avoid serious further injuries if it is not possible or practical to obtain the patient's consent and the doctor does not have an express prior direction to the contrary from the patient.

Consent obtained by trickery or misrepresentation is not effective. The classic case is the plaintiff who buys candy that turns out to be poisoned. The implied representation of the seller is that the candy is wholesome. The plaintiff consented to eat candy, not poison. So too if the defendant entices the plaintiff to play a game of ice hockey in order to get the plaintiff into a position where the defendant can intentionally cut the plaintiff with skates, the defendant cannot later claim that the plaintiff consented to such contact. The plaintiff's consent was obtained by misrepresentation.

When the plaintiff has made a mistake about what he or she is consenting to, it is important to know whether the defendant caused the plaintiff's mistake and whether the defendant knew about it. If the mistake was not caused by and was not known to the defendant, the consent is still valid as long as the defendant was reasonable in believing that the plaintiff consented. If, for example, the plaintiff agrees to let the defendant ride a truck over one parcel of land, but makes a mistake and lets the defendant ride over a different parcel of land, the consent is valid and defeats a trespass action as long as the defendant neither knew about nor procured the error that the plaintiff made. The consent is invalid if the defendant either knew about or caused the plaintiff to make the mistake, as through misrepresentation.

Substantially the Same Conduct

If the defendant's conduct deviates in a minor way from the conduct the plaintiff consented to, the consent is still effective. The deviation must be substantial for the consent to be invalid. If, for example, the plaintiff agrees to let the defendant throw a bucket of water on him or her, the consent is still effective if the same approximate amount of water is poured on the plaintiff by using a garden hose. The defendant's conduct is substantially different, however, if the bucket of water contains rocks, unknown to the plaintiff.

Sexual fidelity can sometimes raise consent issues.

> **EXAMPLE:** In the case of *Neal v. Neal,* Thomas and Mary Neal are married. They engage in sexual relations during a time that Thomas is having an affair. When Mary finds out about the affair, she brings a battery action against Thomas for those times they had sexual relations while the affair was going on. Tom's defense is that Mary consented to these relations.

If Mary had known of Thomas's sexual involvement with another woman, she says she would not have consented to continue having sex with him since sexual relations under those circumstances "would have been offensive to her." Therefore, she contends that his failure to disclose the fact of the affair rendered her consent ineffective and subjects him to liability for battery. In *Neal v. Neal,* the trial court ruled in favor of Thomas on the ground that Mary's consent was valid since sexual relations with her husband "was not actually offensive at the time it occurred." The appellate court reversed because the ruling of the trial court

> ignores the possibility that Mary Neal may have engaged in a sexual act based upon a substantial mistake concerning the nature of the contact or the harm to be expected from it, and that she did not become aware of the offensiveness until well after the act had occurred. . . . To accept that the consent, or lack thereof, must be measured by only those facts which are known to the parties at the time of the alleged battery would effectively destroy any exception for consent induced by fraud or deceit. Obviously if the fraud or deceit were known at the time of the occurrence, the 'consented to' act would never occur. *Neal v. Neal,* 125 Idaho 617, 622, 873 P.2d 871, 876 (1994).

ASSIGNMENT

27.5

In the case of Thomas and Mary Neal, assume that several weeks after Mary found out about Thomas's affair, she resumed sexual relations with her husband. Later, however, she still sues him for battery to cover the time they had sexual relations when she was unaware of the affair. Does Thomas now have a better argument that her consent was valid during this time? (See General Instructions for the Legal Analysis Assignment in Chapter 2.)

The defendant must substantially comply with any restrictions or conditions imposed on the consent by the plaintiff that are communicated to the defendant. If, for example, the plaintiff tells the defendant that he or she can cut one truckload of timber from the plaintiff's land on January 3 or 4, the defendant will be liable for trespass to land if he or she cuts three truckloads on those dates, or if any timber is cut on January 10.

ASSIGNMENT

27.6

Ted and Maureen agree to have sexual intercourse. Maureen gets venereal disease from Ted and sues him for battery. How, if at all, would the following factors affect Ted's defense of consent? (See General Instructions for the Legal Analysis Assignment in Chapter 2.)

a. Ted was a prostitute and Maureen knew it.

b. Ted led Maureen to believe that he was a virgin.

c. Ted and Maureen confided to each other that both had had many lovers before.

d. Ted lied to Maureen about wanting to marry her.

e. Maureen lied to Ted about wanting to marry him.

f. This was the first time Ted and Maureen met.

g. Ted and Maureen are married to each other.

CASE

Peterson v. Sorlien
299 N.W.2d 123 (1980)
Supreme Court of Minnesota

Background: *Susan Jungclaus Peterson joined a religion called The Way Ministry. Her father, Norman Jungclaus, enlisted the support of Susan's former minister, Paul Sorlien, and of deprogrammers to try to separate her from what the father believed was a cult. Later Susan sued for false imprisonment. The lower courts dismissed the suit. The case is now on appeal in the Supreme Court of Minnesota.*

Decision on Appeal: *Judgment affirmed. There was no false imprisonment.*

OPINION OF COURT

Chief Justice SHERAN delivered the opinion of the court. . . .

This action by plaintiff Susan Jungclaus Peterson for false imprisonment . . . arises from an effort by her parents . . . to prompt her disaffiliation from an organization known as The Way Ministry. . . . [T]his case marks the emergence of a new cultural phenomenon: youth-oriented religious or pseudo-religious groups which utilize the techniques of what has been termed "coercive persuasion" or "mind control" to cultivate an uncritical and devoted following. Commentators have used the term "coercive persuasion," originally coined to identify the experience of American prisoners of war during the Korean conflict to describe the cult-induction process. The word "cult" is not used pejoratively but in its dictionary sense to describe an unorthodox system of belief characterized by "[g]reat or excessive devotion or dedication to some person, idea, or thing." Webster's *New International Dictionary of the English Language Unabridged* 552 (1976). Coercive persuasion is fostered through the creation of a controlled environment that heightens the susceptibility of a subject to suggestion and manipulation through sensory deprivation, physiological depletion, cognitive dissonance, peer pressure, and a clear assertion of authority and dominion. The aftermath of indoctrination is a severe impairment of autonomy and the ability to think independently, which induces a subject's unyielding compliance and the rupture of past connections, affiliations and associations. See generally Delgado, *Religious Totalism: Gentle and Ungentle Persuasion under the First Amendment,* 51 Southern California Law Review 1 (1977). One psychologist characterized the process of cult indoctrination as "psychological kidnapping." Id. at 23.

At the time of the events in question, Susan Jungclaus Peterson was 21 years old. For most of her life, she lived with her family on a farm near Bird Island, Minnesota. In 1973, she graduated with honors from high school, ranking second in her class. She matriculated that fall at Moorhead State College. A dean's list student during her first year, her academic performance declined and her interests narrowed after she joined the local chapter of a group organized internationally and identified locally as The Way of Minnesota, Inc.

The operation of The Way is predicated on the fund-raising activities of its members. The Way's fund-raising strategy centers upon the sale of pre-recorded learning programs. Members are instructed to elicit the interest of a group of ten or twelve people and then play for them, at a charge of $85 per participant, a taped introductory course produced by The Way International. Advanced tape courses are then offered to the participants at additional cost, and training sessions are conducted to more fully acquaint recruits with the orientation of the group and the obligations of membership. Recruits must contribute a minimum of 10 percent of their earnings to the organization; to meet the tithe, student members are expected to obtain part-time employment. Members are also required to purchase books and other materials published by the ministry, and are encouraged to make larger financial contributions and to engage in more sustained efforts at solicitation.

By the end of her freshman year, Susan was devoting many hours to The Way, listening to instructional tapes, soliciting new members and assisting in training sessions. As her sophomore year began, Susan committed herself significantly, selling the car her father had given her and working part-time as a waitress to finance her contributions to The Way. Susan spent the following summer in South Dakota, living in conditions described as appalling and overcrowded, while recruiting, raising money and conducting training sessions for The Way.

As her junior year in college drew to a close, the Jungclauses grew increasingly alarmed by the personality changes they witnessed in their daughter; overly tired, unusually pale, distraught, and irritable, she exhibited an increasing alienation from family, diminished interest in education and decline in academic performance. The Jungclauses, versed in the literature of youth cults and based on conversations with former members of The Way, concluded that through a calculated process of manipulation and exploitation Susan had been reduced to a condition of psychological bondage.

On May 24, 1976, defendant Norman Jungclaus, father of plaintiff, arrived at Moorhead to pick up Susan following the end of the third college quarter. Instead of returning to their family home, defendant drove with Susan to Minneapolis to the home of Veronica Morgel. Entering the home of Mrs. Morgel, Susan was greeted by Kathy Mills and several young people who wished to discuss Susan's involvement in the ministry. Each of those present had been in some way touched by the cult phenomenon. Kathy Mills, the leader of the group, had treated a number of former cult members, including Veronica Morgel's son. It was Kathy Mills, a self-styled professional deprogrammer, to whom the Jungclauses turned, and intermittently for the next sixteen days, it was in the home of Veronica Morgel that Susan stayed.

The avowed purpose of deprogramming is to break the hold of the cult over the individual through reason and confrontation. Initially, Susan was unwilling to discuss her involvement; she lay curled in a fetal position, in the downstairs bedroom where she first stayed, plugging her ears and crying while her father pleaded with her to listen to what was being said. This behavior persisted for two days during which she intermittently engaged in conversation, at one point screaming hysterically and flailing at her father. But by Wednesday Susan's demeanor had changed completely; she was friendly and vivacious and that night slept in an upstairs bedroom. Susan spent all day Thursday reading and conversing with her father and on Saturday night went roller-skating. On Sunday she played softball at a nearby park, afterwards enjoying a picnic lunch. The next week Susan spent in Columbus, Ohio, flying there with a former cult member who had shared with her the experiences of the previous week. While in Columbus, she spoke every day by telephone to her fiance who, playing tapes and songs from the ministry's headquarters in Minneapolis, begged that she return to the fold. Susan expressed the desire to extricate her fiance from the dominion of the cult.

Susan returned to Minneapolis on June 9. Unable to arrange a controlled meeting so that Susan could see her fiance outside the presence of other members of the ministry, her parents asked that she sign an agreement releasing them from liability for their past weeks' actions. Refusing to do so, Susan stepped outside the Morgel residence with the puppy she had purchased in Ohio, motioned to a passing police car and shortly thereafter was reunited with her fiance in the Minneapolis headquarters of The Way. Following her return to the ministry, she was directed to counsel and initiated the present action.

Plaintiff [alleges] that defendants unlawfully interfered with her personal liberty by words or acts which induced a reasonable apprehension that force would be used against her if she did not otherwise comply. The jury, instructed that an informed and reasoned consent is a defense to an allegation of false imprisonment and that a nonconsensual detention could be deemed consensual if one's behavior so indicated, exonerated defendants with respect to the false imprisonment claim.

The period in question began on Monday, May 24, 1976, and ceased on Wednesday, June 9, 1976, a period of 16 days. The record clearly demonstrates that Susan willingly remained in the company of defendants for at least 13 of those days. During that time she took many excursions into the public sphere, playing softball and picnicking in a city park, roller-skating at a public rink, flying aboard public aircraft and shopping and swimming while relaxing in Ohio. Had Susan desired, manifold opportunities existed for her to alert the authorities of her allegedly unlawful detention; in Minneapolis, two police officers observed at close range the softball game in which she engaged; en route to Ohio, she passed through the security areas of the Twin Cities and Columbus airports in the presence of security guards and uniformed police; in Columbus she transacted business at a bank, went for walks in solitude and was interviewed by an F.B.I. agent who sought assurances of her safety. At no time during the 13-day period did she complain of her treatment or suggest that defendants were holding her against her will. If one is aware of a reasonable means of escape that does not present a danger of bodily or material harm, a restriction is not total and complete and does not constitute unlawful imprisonment. Damages may not be assessed for any period

of detention to which one freely consents.

In his summation to the jury, the trial judge instructed that to deem consent a defense to the charge of false imprisonment for the entire period or for any part therein, a preponderance of the evidence must demonstrate that such plaintiff voluntarily consented. The central issue for the jury, then, was whether Susan voluntarily participated in the activities of the first three days. The jury concluded that her behavior constituted a waiver.

We believe the determination to have been consistent with the evidence. See *Faniel v. Chesapeake & Potomac Telephone Co.*, 404 A.2d 147 (D.C. 1979); *Schneckloth v. Bustamonte*, 412 U.S. 218, 93 S. Ct 2041, 36 L. Ed. 2d 854 (1973); F. Harper & F. James, *The Law of Torts* § 3.10, at 235 (1956). Were the relationship other than that of parent and child, the consent would have less significance.

To determine whether the findings of the jury can be supported upon review, the behavior Susan manifested during the initial three days at issue must be considered in light of her actions in the remainder of the period. Because, it is argued, the cult conditioning process induces dramatic and non-consensual change giving rise to a new temporary identity on the part of the individuals whose consent is under examination, Susan's volitional capacity prior to treatment may well have been impaired. Following her readjustment, the evidence suggests that Susan was a different person, "like her old self." As such, the question of Susan's consent becomes a function of time. We therefore deem Susan's subsequent affirmation of defendants' actions dispositive.

In *Weiss v. Patrick*, 453 F. Supp. 717 (D. R.I.), aff'd, 588 F.2d 818 (1st Cir. 1978), the federal district court in Rhode Island confronted a situation similar to that which faces us. Plaintiff, a devotee of the Unification Church, brought an action for false imprisonment against individuals hired by her parents to prompt her disassociation from the church. Because plaintiff's mother was dying of cancer, the church authorities permitted her to join her family for the Thanksgiving holiday. Met at the airport by her mother, she testified that she was restrained against her will in the home of one of the defendants and subjected to vituperative attacks against the church until she seized an opportunity to flee. Despite the evidently traumatic experience sustained by plaintiff, the district court found that she failed to demonstrate a meaningful deprivation of personal liberty, reasoning that "any limitation upon personal mobility was not her primary concern." Id. at 722. In so reasoning, the court underscored a parental right to advocate freely a point of view to one's child, "be she minor or adult." To assure freedom, the court observed, "the right of every person 'to be left alone' must be placed in the scales with the right of others to communicate." Id. (quoting *Rowan v. United States Post Office Department*, 397 U.S. 728, 736, 90 S. Ct. 1484, 1490, 25 L. Ed. 2d 736 (1970)).

In light of our examination of the record and rules of construction providing that upon review the evidence must be viewed in a manner most favorable to the prevailing party, we find that a reasonable basis existed for the verdict exonerating defendants of the charge of false imprisonment. Although carried out under colorably religious auspices, the method of cult indoctrination, viewed in a light most favorable to the prevailing party, is predicated on a strategy of coercive persuasion that undermines the capacity for informed consent. While we acknowledge that other social institutions may utilize a degree of coercion in promoting their objectives, none do so to the same extent or intend the same consequences. Society, therefore, has a compelling interest favoring intervention. The facts in this case support the conclusion that plaintiff only regained her volitional capacity to consent after engaging in the first three days of the deprogramming process. As such, we hold that when parents, or their agents, acting under the conviction that the judgmental capacity of their adult child is impaired, seek to extricate that child from what they reasonably believe to be a religious or pseudo-religious cult, and the child at some juncture assents to the actions in question, limitations upon the child's mobility do not constitute meaningful deprivations of personal liberty sufficient to support a judgment for false imprisonment. But owing to the threat that deprogramming poses to public order, we do not endorse self-help as a preferred alternative. In fashioning a remedy, the First Amendment requires resort to the least restrictive alternative so as to not impinge upon religious belief. *Cantwell v. Connecticut,* 310 U.S. 296, 60 S. Ct. 900, 84 L. Ed. 2d 1213 (1940). . . .*

Affirmed.

Justice WAHL (dissenting in part).

I must respectfully dissent. In every generation, parents have viewed their children's religious and political beliefs with alarm and dismay if those beliefs were different from their own. Under the First Amendment, however, adults in our society enjoy freedoms of association and belief. In my view, it is unwise to tamper with those freedoms and with longstanding principles of tort law out of sympathy for parents seeking to help their "misguided" offspring, however well-intentioned and loving their acts may be. . . .

Any imprisonment "which is not legally justifiable" is false imprisonment, *Kleidon v. Glascock,* 215 Minn. 417, 10

N.W.2d 394 (1943); therefore, the fact that the tortfeasor acted in good faith is no defense to a charge of false imprisonment. . . .

The majority opinion finds, in plaintiff's behavior during the remainder of the 16-day period of "deprogramming," a reasonable basis for acquitting [her father] of the false imprisonment charge for the initial three days, during which time he admittedly held plaintiff against her will. Under this theory, plaintiff's "acquiescence" in the later stages of deprogramming operates as consent which "relates back" to the events of the earlier three days, and constitutes a "waiver" of her claim for those days. . . . Certainly, parents who disapprove of or disagree with the religious beliefs of their adult offspring are free to exercise their own First Amendment rights in an attempt, by speech and persuasion without physical restraints, to change their adult children's minds. But parents who engage in tortious conduct in their "deprogramming" attempts do so at the risk that the deprogramming will be unsuccessful and the adult children will pursue tort remedies against their parents. To allow parents' "conviction that the judgmental capacity of their [adult] child is impaired [by her religious indoctrination]" to excuse their tortious conduct sets a dangerous precedent.

Here, the evidence clearly supported a verdict against Norman Jungclaus on the false imprisonment claim. . . .

_____

*While we decline at this time to suggest a particular alternative, we observe that some courts have permitted the creation of temporary guardianships to allow the removal of cult members to therapeutic settings. If the individuals desire, at the end of the conservatorship they may return to the cult. Actions have also been initiated against cult leaders on the basis of criminal liability. See generally Delgado, supra, at 73–97.

ASSIGNMENT

27.7

a. Explain why the court said Susan consented to the confinement during the first three days. Or is the court saying that she did not have the capacity to consent during these three days? Or is the court saying that there really was no confinement during these three days?

b. Susan's parents asked her to sign an agreement releasing them from liability for their past weeks' actions. Suppose she had signed. Would the agreement have had legal effect?

c. Can you falsely imprison someone who is mentally retarded?

d. Does this opinion set good social policy? Why or why not?

SELF-HELP PRIVILEGES

When serious conflict arises, our society encourages people to use the legal system—the courts—to resolve the conflict. In effect, we say, "don't take the law into your own hands; tell it to a judge!" There are situations, however, where it simply is not practical to ask the courts to intervene. A person may need to act immediately to protect an interest or a right. Such immediate, protective action is called **self-help.** Self-help is justified when there is a privilege to act without first obtaining the permission or involvement of the legal system.

We shall consider nine self-help privileges:

1. self-defense
2. defense of others
3. necessity
4. abating a nuisance
5. defense of property
6. recapture of chattels
7. retaking possession of land forcibly
8. discipline
9. arrest

The question often arises whether a defendant loses the protection of a privilege because the defendant has made a *mistake*. As we shall see, some reasonable mistakes do not destroy the privilege, whereas other mistakes—even if reasonably made—do destroy it.

Self-Defense

The privilege of **self-defense** is the use of reasonable force to prevent an immediate harmful or offensive contact against you by someone who is making an apparent threat of this contact. In short, it is the right to protect yourself from immediate physical harm. The threat must be immediate (today, you cannot hit someone who has threatened to hurt you tomorrow) and the force used to prevent the threat must be reasonable (you cannot shoot someone who has threatened to blow smoke in your face).

What happens if you make a mistake in trying to protect yourself?

> **EXAMPLE:** Nathan sees Diana running toward him with a raised baseball bat. Thinking that she is going to hit him, Nathan throws a brick at Diana, breaking her leg. In fact, unknown to Nathan, Diana was simply expressing jubilation after just coming from a baseball game that her team won.

Nathan acted in self-defense, but he made a mistake. There was no actual threat to him from Diana. In most states, the defense is not lost if this mistake was reasonable as to the amount of force needed for self-protection or, indeed, as to whether any protection was needed. Figure 27–2 presents an overview of the elements of the privilege of self-defense, examples of the kinds of torts to which this privilege can be used as a defense, examples of paralegal interviewing and investigation tasks to uncover facts that are relevant to proving that the privilege applies (including the reasonableness of mistakes), and a list of facts that could make it impossible to use the privilege.

ASSIGNMENT 27.8	In the following situations, assess whether the defendant can successfully raise the privilege of self-defense. (See General Instructions for the Legal Analysis Assignment in Chapter 2.)

a. Richard raises his cane over his head and shouts at Gary, saying, "If my daughter wasn't here with me, I'd smash you in the head." Gary is afraid. He grabs Richard's cane and knocks him down. Richard then sues Gary for battery.

b. Jane asks Clayton to leave Jane's store because she does not like the color of Clayton's clothes. Clayton refuses to leave. Jane comes at Clayton with a broom. Jane is over twenty-five feet away and is on crutches. As Jane approaches, Clayton shoots her. Jane sues Clayton for battery.

c. Lou is in Robin's home. Lou starts yelling obscenities at Robin in front of Robin's family. Lou spits in Robin's face and throws Robin's coat out the window. Just as Lou is about to spit in Robin's face again, Robin stabs Lou. Lou sues Robin for battery.

FIGURE 27–2   An overview of the privilege of self-defense.

Elements of the Privilege of Self-Defense	The Torts Involved (Examples)	Paralegal Tasks: What to Find Out Through Interviewing and Investigation	Facts That Destroy the Privilege
a. Reasonable belief by D that P will immediately inflict harmful or offensive contact on D. **b.** Reasonable force used by D to prevent P from carrying out the apparent threat of an immediate harmful or offensive contact on D. (See the notes on mistakes, deadly force, and attacks in a residence.)	• *Battery* P is about to hit D. To prevent this, D knocks P down. P sues D for battery. D can raise the defense of self-defense. • *Assault* P is about to hit D. To prevent this, D threatens to hit P. P sues D for assault. D can raise the defense of self-defense. • *False Imprisonment* P is about to hit D. To prevent this, D locks P in a room. P sues D for false imprisonment. D can raise the defense of self-defense.	• Has P threatened D in the past? • Has P hit D in the past? • Does P have a reputation for aggressiveness? • What age and strength differences appear to exist between P and D? • How close was P to D at the time of the threat? • What did P threaten D with? • Did the threat occur in D's residence? • Did P say anything to indicate how serious the threat was? • How much time did D have before P would carry out P's threat? • Was P's threat to inflict future or present harm on D? • Did D know or believe that P was only bluffing? • Did D have time to warn P that D would inflict force on P? • In the past, has D ever consented to the kind of contact that P threatened?	• D's response to the threat of P was disproportionate to the danger posed by P. (D cannot kill P to prevent a shove by P when the shove does not threaten D's life or limb with serious bodily harm.) • P's threat was to inflict future harm on D. • P was merely insulting D and not threatening D with bodily harm or offensive contact. • D was acting solely to protect D's honor and not to prevent a harmful or offensive contact by P. • D was acting out of revenge and not to prevent immediate harm to D. • D was not threatened at D's residence and could have retreated without responding with deadly force or force calculated to impose serious bodily harm on P. • D knew or believed that P was only bluffing.

Notes:

• If D makes a mistake on whether P is about to inflict an immediate harmful or offensive contact on D, or if D makes a mistake on the amount of force needed to prevent the immediate threat, the privilege of *self-defense* is still valid if the mistake was reasonable under the circumstances.

• Reasonable force can include deadly force or force calculated to cause serious bodily harm *only if* D reasonably believes D is threatened with death or serious bodily harm from P.

• If D is in his or her residence, D does not have to retreat before inflicting deadly force or force calculated to cause serious bodily harm if such force is otherwise reasonable.

• States differ on whether such retreat is needed if D is *not* in his or her residence.

Defense of Others

We are also allowed to defend others. The privilege of the **defense of others** is the use of reasonable force to prevent an immediate harmful or offensive contact against a third person by someone who is making an apparent threat of this contact. This privilege is similar to self-defense in that the threat must be immediate and the use of force must be proportionate to the threat. A major distinction between the two privileges concerns the effect of a mistake. As we just saw, the privilege of self-defense is not lost if you make a reasonable mistake in what you thought was needed to protect yourself. Suppose, however, you make a mistake when trying to protect a third person.

> **EXAMPLE:** Dan sees that Paul is about to knock Bill down. To prevent this, Dan runs over and pushes Paul away. Paul sues Dan for battery. Dan raises the defense of the defense of others—Dan was trying to prevent Paul from harming Bill. Unknown to Dan, however, Bill had just pulled a knife on Paul. Paul was acting in self-defense when he was about to knock Bill down. Hence, Paul had a privilege to harm Bill.

In this case, the third person—Bill—was the aggressor against Paul. Dan didn't know this. He made a mistake. Does this mistake mean that Dan loses the defense of defense of others? Yes, in most states. Even a reasonable mistake will not save Dan. When you intervene to protect a third person, you take the risk that this third person has no right to be protected. In a minority of states, however, a reasonable mistake *will* preserve the defense. In our example, if Dan was reasonable in thinking that Bill needed protection, Dan can use the defense of defense of others to defeat Paul's battery action against him. But this is so only in a minority of states.

Figure 27–3 presents an overview of the elements of this privilege, examples of the kinds of torts to which this privilege can be used as a defense, examples of paralegal interviewing and investigation tasks to uncover facts that are relevant to proving that the privilege applies, and a list of facts that could make it impossible to use the privilege.

Necessity

Necessity is the privilege to make a reasonable use of the property of others to prevent immediate harm or damage to persons or property. The property can be **chattels** (personal property) or land.

> **EXAMPLES:** Without permission, you use a stranger's car to drive a member of your family to the emergency room of a hospital.
>
> Without permission, you burn the crops of a neighbor in order to stop the spread of a fire that is headed toward the town on the other side of the neighbor's field containing the crops.

When you use someone's property in this way, do you have to compensate them for any damage that you do? The answer depends on the kind of necessity that existed. You must provide compensation if a **private necessity** existed. This is the privilege to make a reasonable use of someone's property to prevent immediate private harm or damage. The use of the car in the first example demonstrates a private necessity. You were trying to protect a member of your family. A **public necessity,** on the other hand, is the privilege to make a reasonable use of someone's property to prevent immediate public harm or damage. This was the case in the second example. There was a danger of the town going up in flames—clearly a public danger. There is no requirement to provide compensation to someone whose property is used to prevent public harm or danger. In many states, however, special statutes exist that provide compensation in these cases, particularly when the damage is done by public employees such as the police or fire department.

Figure 27–4 presents an overview of the elements of the privilege of necessity, examples of the kinds of torts to which the privilege can be used as a defense, examples of paralegal interviewing and investigation tasks to uncover facts that are relevant to proving that the privilege applies, and a list of facts that could make it impossible to use the privilege.

FIGURE 27–3   An overview of the privilege of defense of others.

Elements of the Privilege of Defense of Others	The Torts Involved (Examples)	Paralegal Tasks: What to Find Out Through Interviewing and Investigation	Facts That Destroy the Privilege
a. Belief by D that P will immediately inflict harmful or offensive contact on a third person. **b.** Reasonable force used by D with the intent to prevent P from carrying out the apparent threat of an immediate harmful or offensive contact on the third person. **c.** P did not have a privilege to threaten the third person. (See the notes on the minority rule on the third element, the use of deadly force, and the identity of the third person.)	• *Battery* P is about to hit a third person. D sees this and hits P to prevent P's attack on the third person. P sues D for battery. D can raise the defense of the defense of others. • *Assault* P is about to hit a third person. D sees this and threatens to hit P if P does not stop. P sues D for assault. D can raise the defense of defense of others. • *False Imprisonment* P is about to hit a third person. D sees this and locks P in a "bear hug" until the third person can escape. P sues D for false imprisonment (and for battery). D can raise the defense of the defense of others.	• Has P threatened the third person in the past? • Has P hit the third person in the past? • Does P have a reputation for aggressiveness? • What age and strength differences appear to exist between P and the third person? Between P and D? • How close was P to the third person at the time of P's threat? • What gestures or words were used by P to the third person that D could observe or hear? • How much time appeared to exist before P would carry out P's threat against the third person? • Was P's threat against the third person immediate or for the future? • Did P appear to be bluffing? • Did D have time to warn P that D would use force against P if the latter did not stop trying to harm the third person? • Did the third person appear to be consenting to contact from P, e.g., in a football game?	• D's response was disproportionate to the harm P was threatening the third person with. • P's threat was to impose future harm on the third person. • P was merely insulting the third person and not threatening the latter with immediate harm. • D knew P was bluffing. • D was acting out of revenge and not to prevent immediate harm to the third person. • In most states, D loses the privilege if D made a mistake and the third person turns out to have been the aggressor against P. This is so even if the mistake was reasonable. In a minority of states, however, the privilege is *not* lost if D's mistake was reasonable.

Notes:

• A minority of states do not include the third element listed in the first column (c) as long as D was reasonable in what turns out to be a mistake as to the third party's right to be protected.

• As to the amount of force that is reasonable, D stands in the shoes of the third person. D can use the amount of force that the third person could have reasonably used to protect him- or herself. This could include deadly force *only if* the third person was in danger of death or serious bodily harm from P.

• The third person does not have to be a member of D's family. In most states, the third person whom D tried to protect can be a stranger.

ASSIGNMENT 27.9

Tom has a contagious disease. He has no money to buy medicine and no hospitals are in the area. Tom breaks into a doctor's office at night and steals what he thinks is medicine that will help. In fact, he takes the wrong medicine. The doctor sues Tom for conversion. Does Tom have a defense? If Tom has a defense, does he still have to pay the doctor for losses sustained due to the break-in? (See General Instructions for the Legal Analysis Assignment in Chapter 2.)

FIGURE 27–4 An overview of the privilege of necessity.

Elements of the Privilege of Necessity	The Torts Involved (Examples)	Paralegal Tasks: What to Find Out Through Interviewing and Investigation	Facts That Destroy the Privilege
a. Reasonable belief by D that persons or property will be immediately harmed or damaged. **b.** Reasonable use by D of P's chattels (personal property) or land to prevent the immediate harm or damage.	• *Conversion* D destroys P's liquor to prevent it from getting into the hands of an invading army. P sues D for conversion. D can raise the defense of public necessity and avoid paying P for the loss D caused. • *Conversion* D is injured in a car accident and uses P's scarf as a tourniquet. The scarf is ruined. P sues D for conversion. D can raise the defense of private necessity, but must compensate P for any damage done to P's scarf. • *Trespass to Land* D runs onto P's land to escape a bear. P sues D for trespass to land. D can raise the defense of private necessity but must compensate P for any damage D does to P's land, e.g., to a fence.	• What alternatives, if any, were available to D and how realistic were they? • How much time did D have to act? • How much damage did D do? • What were the indications that the public was in danger (for public necessity)? • Did D seek advice on what to do—if any time was available?	• D's belief in the existence of the danger was unreasonable. • D's use of P's chattels or land was disproportionate to the danger. (For example, D cannot blow up P's house to prevent the spread of a fire when the fire is minor and water is easily available to put it out.)

Abating a Nuisance

There are times when a defendant has a privilege to enter someone's land in order to **abate a nuisance.** This is the privilege to take reasonable steps to correct a nuisance that is interfering with the use and enjoyment of your land. The privilege is a defense to the tort of trespass to land. For a discussion of this privilege, see page 456.

Defense of Property

The privilege of the **defense of property** is the right to use reasonable force to prevent an immediate interference with your property or to end an interference that has begun. The property can be land or chattels (personal property). You cannot use deadly force, however, to protect your property. This kind of force was one of the main issues in the *Katko* case we will examine shortly.

There are two major kinds of mistakes possible in trying to use this privilege:

- mistake on the amount of force needed to protect your possession, and
- mistake on whether you had the right to possess the property you protected.

A reasonable mistake on the amount of force needed will not defeat the privilege. Any mistake, however, on your right to possession *will* defeat the privilege, regardless of how reasonable your mistake might have been.

> **EXAMPLE:** Dan buys a painting from Kevin, a reputable art dealer, not knowing that Kevin stole the painting from Peter. When Peter sees the painting on Dan's wall, Peter starts to take the painting off the wall. To prevent this, Dan pushes Peter away. Peter sues Dan for battery.

FIGURE 27–5 Overview of the privilege of defense of property.

Elements of the Privilege of Defense of Property	The Torts Involved (Examples)	Paralegal Tasks: What to Find Out Through Interviewing and Investigation	Facts That Destroy the Privilege
a. D has possession of land or chattels (personal property). b. D's right to possession is superior to P's claim of possession, if any. c. D has a reasonable belief that immediate force is needed to prevent P's present threat to or continued interference with D's possession. d. D requests that P cease the threatened or continued interference with D's possession, unless the request would be unsafe or impractical for D. e. D uses reasonable force against P to prevent the threatened or continued interference by P of D's possession.	• *Battery* P enters D's land and refuses to leave when D asks him to do so. D takes P by the collar and pushes him out. P sues D for battery. D can raise the defense of defense of property. • *Assault* P reaches for D's purse on the table. D raises her fist at P and shouts at him to keep away from her purse. P sues D for assault. D can raise the defense of defense of property.	• Did D have possession of the land or chattel? • What indications were there that P was going to interfere immediately or was going to continue the interference? • What did P say or do? • What alternatives to force, if any, were available to D? • What age and strength differences existed between P and D? • What harm was P subjected to by D's use of force to prevent P's threatened or continued interference? • Did D ask P to stop the interference? Would such a request have been realistic? • Did P's interference with D's land or chattel in any way threaten D's personal safety or that of others?	• P had a privilege to be on the land or to possess the chattel. • P's right to possession was superior to D's. • P's threat to interfere was in the future—it was not an immediate threat. • D's use of force was disproportionate to the threat posed by P to D's possession. • D was motivated solely by hatred and revenge. D was not trying to prevent interference by P. • D knew that P was bluffing when P threatened interference. • D did not ask P to cease the threatened or actual interference by P. The request would have been reasonable or practical. • D used deadly force or force calculated to cause serious bodily harm even though neither D nor anyone else was threatened with death or serious bodily harm by P.

Notes:

• In most states, D cannot use deadly force or force calculated to cause serious bodily harm (e.g., shoot P), even if D adequately warns P that such force will be used. D has a privilege to use great force *only if* P's interference with property also threatens life or limb of others.

• D is still protected by the privilege if D makes a reasonable mistake on the amount of force needed, but not if D makes even a reasonable mistake on D's right to possession of the land or the chattel, unless P caused D to make the mistake.

• In this privilege, we are not talking about D's privilege to *recapture* possession from P. Recapture will be considered later in Figure 27–6.

In the battery action, Dan cannot use the defense of defense of property. He made a reasonable mistake in believing that he had a right to possess the painting since he bought it from a reputable dealer without knowing the dealer was a thief. Mistakes on the right to possession, however, destroy the privilege to defend property—even reasonable mistakes. The only exception would be if the person with the superior right to possession caused the other person to make the mistake.

Figure 27–5 presents an overview of the elements of this privilege, examples of the kinds of torts to which this privilege can be used as a defense, examples of paralegal interviewing and investigation tasks to uncover facts that are relevant to proving that the privilege applies, and a list of facts that could make it impossible to use the privilege.

CASE

Katko v. Briney
183 N.W.2d 657 (1971)
Supreme Court of Iowa

Background: *The Brineys own an unoccupied farm house that had been broken into several times. Boarding up the windows and posting no-trespassing signs did not deter the break-ins. On June 11, 1967 Mr. Briney set "a shotgun trap" in the north bedroom. He secured the gun to an iron bed with the barrel pointed at the bedroom door. It was rigged with wire from the doorknob to the gun's trigger so it would fire when the door was opened. He first pointed the gun so an intruder would be hit in the stomach. At Mrs. Briney's suggestion, however, it was lowered to hit the legs. He admitted he did so "because I was mad and tired of being tormented" but "he did not intend to injure anyone." Tin was nailed over the bedroom window. The spring gun could not be seen from the outside and no warning of its presence was posted. When Katko and a companion tried to break in, Katko was seriously injured when he triggered the gun. Much of his leg, including part of the tibia, was blown away. In a criminal proceeding, Katko pled guilty to larceny, was fined $50, and was paroled during good behavior from a sixty-day jail sentence. He then brought a civil suit against the Brineys for damages. At the trial, the jury returned a verdict for Katko for $20,000 actual and $10,000 punitive damages. The case is now on appeal before the Supreme Court of Iowa.*

Decision on Appeal: *Judgment affirmed. Deadly force cannot be used to protect uninhabited property.*

OPINION OF COURT

Chief Justice MOORE delivered the opinion of the court.

The primary issue presented here is whether an owner may protect personal property in an unoccupied boarded-up farm house against trespassers and thieves by a spring gun capable of inflicting death or serious injury. We are not here concerned with a man's right to protect his home and members of his family. Defendants' home was several miles from the scene of the incident. . . .

In the statement of issues the trial court stated plaintiff and his companion committed a felony when they broke and entered defendants' house. In instruction 2 the court referred to the early case history of the use of spring guns and stated under the law their use was prohibited except to prevent the commission of felonies of violence and where human life is in danger. The instruction included a statement [that] breaking and entering is not a felony of violence.

Instruction 5 stated: "You are hereby instructed that one may use reasonable force in the protection of his property, but such right is subject to the qualification that one may not use such means of force as will take human life or inflict great bodily injury. Such is the rule even though the injured party is a trespasser and is in violation of the law himself."

Instruction 6 stated: "An owner of premises is prohibited from willfully or intentionally injuring a trespasser by means of force that either takes life or inflicts great bodily injury; and therefore a person owning a premise is prohibited from setting out 'spring guns' and like dangerous devices which will likely take life or inflict great bodily injury, for the purpose of harming trespassers. The fact that the trespasser may be acting in violation of the law does not change the rule. The only time when such conduct of setting a 'spring gun' or a like dangerous device is justified would be when the trespasser was committing a felony of violence or a felony punishable by death, or where the trespasser was endangering human life by his act." . . .

The overwhelming weight of authority, both textbook and case law, supports the trial court's statement of the applicable principles of law.

Prosser on Torts, Third Edition, pages 116–118, states: "the law has always placed a higher value upon human safety than upon mere rights in property. [It] is the accepted rule that there is no privilege to use any force calculated to cause death or serious bodily injury to repel the threat to land or chattels, unless there is also such a threat to the defendant's personal safety as to justify a self-defense. . . . [S]pring guns and other mankilling devices are not justifiable against a mere trespasser, or even a petty thief. They are privileged only against those upon whom the landowner, if he were present in person would be free to inflict injury of the same kind." . . .

Affirmed.

ASSIGNMENT

27.10

a. Do you agree with the result in this case? Why or why not?

b. Would the case have been decided differently if the Brineys had posted a large sign on the farm property saying, "WARNING: Property Protected by Spring Guns"?

c. Smith owns a liquor store that has been burglarized often. He buys a pit bull dog to stay in the store after he closes. A midnight burglar is mauled by the dog. Does *Katko* apply?

Mr. and Mrs. Briney in front of the vacant farmhouse they tried to protect with a spring gun, leading to the famous case of *Katko v. Briney*.

In the following situations, examine what defenses, if any, can be raised in the suits brought. (See General Instructions for the Legal Analysis Assignment in Chapter 2.)

a. George is invited to Henry's house for dinner. They have an argument and Henry asks George to leave. George refuses. Henry pushes George through a glass window. George sues Henry for battery.

b. Tom is terrified by dogs. Leo's little dog starts barking at Tom in the street. Tom picks up a stick and is about to hit the dog. Leo sees this and clubs Tom with a baseball bat. Tom sues Leo for battery.

c. Helen is in her boat when a storm suddenly begins. Helen takes the boat to Kevin's private dock in order to prevent the destruction of her boat. When Kevin sees Helen's boat at his dock, he tells her to leave immediately or he will punch her in the nose. Helen leaves even though the storm is still raging. Helen sues Kevin for assault.

Recapture of Chattels

The defense-of-property privilege is used when you have possession of property with which someone is interfering. Suppose, however, you no longer have possession. Someone has wrongfully dispossessed you of a chattel and you want to recapture it. The privilege you need to try to use in this situation is called **recapture of chattels**. It is the right to use reasonable force to obtain the return of personal property (chattels) shortly after someone obtains them wrongfully. Before force is used, a request for the return of the chattel must be made unless such a request would be impractical or unsafe. Like the defense of property, you cannot use deadly force to recapture the chattels. Also, the privilege of recapture does not apply unless the chattel was taken from you wrongfully.

> **EXAMPLE:** David lets his friend, Paul, use David's bike for a brief ride in the playground. When Paul is on the bike for a few moments, he decides not to return it and tells David this. David immediately pushes Paul off the bike and retrieves it. Paul sues David for battery.

Paul wins. David cannot use the defense of recapture of chattels because Paul initially obtained possession of the bike rightfully—David agreed to let him use it. The privilege does not apply unless it is being used to obtain it back from someone who obtained it wrongfully. Paul rightfully obtained possession, but he has wrongfully kept it. To get the bike back in such a case, David must resort to the courts. The case would be different if Paul took the bike without permission. Then David would have the privilege to recapture.

You must be sure that you have the right to possess the chattel you want to recapture. If you make a mistake—even a reasonable one—the privilege is destroyed and you can be liable for any torts resulting from your use of force. To demonstrate this, let us change the facts of our bike example:

> **EXAMPLE:** David sees Paul, a total stranger, take a bike out of the playground. David immediately pushes Paul off the bike and retrieves it. In fact, Paul was riding his own bike, which looked exactly the same as David's bike. Paul sues David for battery.

Paul wins. David made a mistake about his right to possess the bike. Even though the mistake may have been reasonable since the bikes looked alike, the mistake is fatal. If you use force to recapture a chattel, you must have the right to possess that chattel. The only exception would be if the person with the superior right to possession caused the other person to make the mistake.

Figure 27–6 presents an overview of the elements of this privilege, examples of the kinds of torts to which this privilege can be used as a defense, examples of paralegal interviewing and investigation tasks to uncover facts that are relevant to proving that the privilege applies, and a list of facts that could make it impossible to use the privilege.

ASSIGNMENT **27.12**

In the following situations, determine whether the defendant can claim the defense of recapture of chattels. (See General Instructions for the Legal Analysis Assignments in Chapter 2.)

a. Tom is playing football. He asks Fred to hold his watch. While Tom is on the field, Fred suddenly must leave. Fred asks Joe to hold the watch for Tom. Fred does not know that Joe is Tom's archenemy. When Tom finds out that Joe has the watch, he asks for it back. Joe refuses. Tom hits Joe over the head with a football helmet and takes the watch back. Joe sues Tom for battery.

b. Sam steals John's ring and sells it for $1 in a dark alley to Fred, who knows neither John nor Sam. Two weeks after John finds out that Fred has the ring, John breaks into Fred's house and takes the ring from Fred's jewelry box. Fred sues John for trespass to land.

Retaking Possession of Land Forcibly

Only under limited circumstances is a defendant entitled to retake possession of *land* from a plaintiff with the use of force, e.g., the plaintiff him- or herself has directly and wrongfully dispossessed the defendant. State statutes exist in most states governing the repossession of land through the use of court proceedings, particularly when a landlord is trying to remove (evict) a tenant.

Discipline

Parents have the privilege of disciplining their children. This can include physically hitting and confining the children, as long as such force is reasonable. (Teachers and others who stand in the place of parents—*in loco parentis*—also have this privilege unless it has been restricted by special statute.) Suits within the family are discussed elsewhere. See Figure 22–1 in Chapter 22.

Arrest

When a public officer or a private citizen tries to arrest someone, the latter might respond with a suit for battery, assault, or false imprisonment. The privilege of **arrest** can be raised as a defense to such suits. The elements of this privilege and its special circumstances are considered in Chapter 7 on false imprisonment and false arrest.

FIGURE 27–6   Overview of the privilege of recapture of chattels (personal property).

Elements of the Privilege of Recapture of Chattels	The Torts Involved (Examples)	Paralegal Tasks: What to Find Out Through Interviewing and Investigation	Facts That Destroy the Privilege
a. P acquired possession of the chattel wrongfully, e.g., by fraud or force. **b.** D has the right to immediate possession. **c.** D requests that P return the chattel. This request is made before D uses force to recapture it unless the request would be unrealistic or unsafe for D. **d.** D's use of force to recapture the chattel occurs promptly after P took possession of the chattel (sometimes referred to as **fresh pursuit**), or promptly after D discovered that P took possession. **e.** D uses reasonable force (not force calculated to cause death or serious bodily injury) with the intent to recapture the chattel from P.	• *Battery* P has just stolen D's television, and refuses to return it. D pushes P aside in order to take the television back. P sues D for battery. D can raise the defense of recapture of chattels. • *Assault* Same facts as above, except that instead of pushing P, D raises his fist and threatens to hit P if P does not return the television. P sues D for assault. D can raise the defense of recapture of chattels. • *Trespass to Land* Same facts as above on the television. P has the television in his garage. When D finds out, D immediately goes into the garage to recapture the television. P sues D for trespass to land. D can raise the defense of recapture of chattels.	• How did P get possession of the chattel? • Did P claim P had a right to possession? If so, on what basis? • What is D's basis for the claim that D had a right to possess the chattel? • Did either P or D claim that they owned the chattel, that they had properly rented it, or that they were properly holding it for someone else? • Did P originally get possession with the consent of D? • Did D request P to return the chattel? Was such a request realistic and safe? • When did D discover that P had possession, and how long after discovery did D try to recapture it? • Could D have discovered that P had possession sooner? Why or why not? • Could D have acted sooner to recapture the chattel? Why or why not? • How much force was necessary to take the chattel back from P? Could less force have been used? Why or why not? • What did P and D say to each other just prior to D's use of force?	• P did not have actual possession nor did P control possession. • P in fact got possession rightfully (even though P's *continued* possession may now be wrongful, in which case D does not have the privilege of recapture—D must use the courts to get the chattel back). • D has no right to possession. • D failed to request a return when such a request was practical and safe. • D took too long to discover that P had possession. • D took too long to recapture after D knew or should have known that P had possession. • D used a disproportionate amount of force to recapture the chattel. • D was acting solely from the motive of hatred and revenge and did not limit the force to what was necessary to recapture the chattel.

Notes:

• D's mistake about P's right to possession destroys the privilege even if the mistake was reasonable (unless P caused D to make the mistake).

• The **shopkeeper privilege** allows a merchant to detain a person for a reasonably short time for the purpose of investigating whether there has been a theft. The merchant must reasonably believe the person detained is a thief. (See Chapter 7 on false imprisonment.)

• For each example in the second column, D must establish compliance with the five elements of the privilege listed in the first column, e.g., the demand for a return is made when realistic and safe.

The arrest of an individual can also raise issues of defamation, invasion of privacy, malicious prosecution, and abuse of process. Finally, the arrested person might claim a violation of his or her civil rights.

SOVEREIGN IMMUNITY

When is a government liable for the torts committed on its behalf? The old answer was: never. The King cannot be sued because the King can do no wrong. This was the essence of the doctrine of **sovereign immunity**. Over the years, however, the government (i.e., the sovereign) has agreed to be sued for torts in limited situations. In this section, we will discuss the boundaries of what is now a limited sovereign immunity. Government, of course, acts only through its agents or employees. Hence, when the government is liable, it will be on a theory of **respondeat superior**: let the master answer for the acts of its servant. The servant is the government employee. We also need to explore when this employee is *personally* liable for the torts he or she commits while carrying out governmental functions. In summary, the issues are:

1. When has the *federal* government agreed to be liable for the torts of its employees?
2. When has the *state* government agreed to be liable for the torts of its employees?
3. When have *local* governments agreed (on their own or on order from the state government) to be liable for the torts of their employees?
4. When is a federal, state, or local government employee independently and personally liable for the torts he or she commits on the job? As we will see later, when government employees are not personally liable for such torts, it is because they enjoy what is called **official immunity**, which is separate from sovereign immunity.

If you are the victim of a tort committed by a government employee (e.g., slander, conversion), you will have no one to sue if both sovereign immunity and official immunity apply.

Before we examine these immunities, two closely related issues need to be mentioned. First, legislatures sometimes pass special legislation that allows a private individual to sue the government when the individual's suit would otherwise be barred by sovereign immunity. This waiver from immunity is more narrow than the general waiver for designated classes of torts or other claims that are our concern here. Second, if the government forces you to give up your land for a public purpose (e.g., to build a road through it), you must receive **just compensation**. This is because the constitution forbids government **taking of property** from a private individual without just compensation. To the extent that the government is forced by the constitution to provide compensation for a "taking," the government is waiving its sovereign immunity.

Federal Government

The basic law containing the federal government's consent to be sued is the **Federal Tort Claims Act** (FTCA).[1] By no means does the FTCA abolish sovereign immunity for the federal government. The general rule established by the FTCA is as follows: The United States (this phrase refers to the federal government) will be liable for its torts in the same manner as a private individual would be liable according to the local law in the place where the tort occurs, *unless* the United States is specifically exempted for that tort in the FTCA.

Assume that a federal employee in Delaware commits a tort such as negligence against you. According to the general rule, if the negligence law of the state of Delaware would make a private person liable for negligence for doing what the fed-

---

[1]28 U.S.C. §§ 2671-80 (1994).

eral employee did, then the federal government will be liable for the tort—unless there is a specific exemption for that tort in the FTCA. Hence, we need to know what the FTCA specifically excludes and covers. Figure 27–7 tells us.

FIGURE 27–7 Federal Tort Claims Act.

Exclusions

(Claims for which the United States will *not* be liable; sovereign immunity is *not* waived)

I. Explicitly Excluded Torts

Claims arising out of
1. assault
2. battery
3. false imprisonment
4. false arrest
5. malicious prosecution
6. abuse of process
7. libel
8. slander
9. misrepresentation
10. deceit
11. interference with contract rights

A limited exception to this list of exclusions is created for investigative or law enforcement officers. The United States government *will* be liable when such officers commit the torts of assault, battery, false imprisonment, false arrest, abuse of process, or malicious prosecution.

II. Discretion

Claims arising out of the non-negligent or negligent exercise of discretion by an employee at the *planning* level, involving policy decisions and judgment on whether to perform a government task. Also excluded are claims arising out of acts performed with due care in the execution of a statute or regulation, even if invalid.

III. Strict Liability

Claims based on liability without fault, such as acts or omissions involving ultrahazardous activities. To make the federal government liable for such activities, fault (i.e., negligence or intent) must be shown.

IV. Other Exclusions

1. Claims arising out of the following activities: war, mail delivery, admiralty, customs, tax collection. (Government liability for some of these activities may be covered under *other* waiver-of-immunity statutes.)
2. Claims by members of the armed forces in the course of their duties.

Coverage

(Claims for which the United States *will* be liable; sovereign immunity *is* waived)

I. Covered Torts

1. Trespass to land, trespass to chattels, conversion, invasion of privacy, or other tort, as long as the claim does not also arise out of one of the eleven excluded torts or involve any of the other exclusions mentioned in the "Exclusions" column.
2. Assault, battery, false imprisonment, false arrest, abuse of process, or malicious prosecution committed by investigative or law enforcement officers.

II. Ministerial/Operational Level

Claims (usually negligence) arising out of acts or omissions of an employee at the *ministerial* level, where no discretion is involved, or at the *operational* level, where the discretion involved, if any, relates only to the carrying out of the planning decisions.

There is an important distinction under the FTCA between torts committed at the *planning* level and those committed at the *operational* level. Sovereign immunity is not waived for torts at the planning level; it is waived for torts at the operational (or ministerial) level. Planning involves policy decisions and judgment (for which considerable discretion is used) on whether to perform a government task. (An example of a planning task would be the decision of the government to raise taxes.) Something is operational if it involves the carrying out of a plan for which very little discretion is needed. (An example of an operational task would be making a delivery in a government truck.) Even less discretion is involved in *ministerial* tasks. (An example would be sending out a standard government form in response to a citizen phone request.)

The federal government may try to avoid liability by claiming that a tort committed by one of its employees involved planning discretion. Suppose that the United States Coast Guard negligently maintains a lighthouse, causing a private ship to crash into rocks. Do we have planning or operational negligence? Surely the initial decision to install the lighthouse involves a great deal of planning discretion, for which the government will not be liable, even if the Coast Guard was negligent in that planning. But the maintenance of the lighthouse itself is an operational function. To be sure, discretion is needed in running the lighthouse, but this discretion is at the operational level. Negligence at this level *will* impose liability under the Act. The same would be true of negligent operation of government motor vehicles.

Before a citizen tries to bring a claim under the Federal Tort Claims Act, the administrative agency involved must be given the chance to settle the case on its own within certain dollar limits. If the citizen is still dissatisfied, he or she can sue under the Act in a federal court. (See a sample complaint in Figure 27–8.)

Federal employees themselves are generally excluded as claimants under the Federal Tort Claims Act. Injuries that they receive on the job are covered by other statutory schemes, such as the Federal Employees' Compensation Act.

State Government

The state government consists of the governor's office, state agencies such as the state police, state hospitals, and state commissions and boards. To what extent has a state government waived its own sovereign immunity so that citizens can sue the state for the torts of state employees? States differ in their answers to this question. Some states have come close to abolishing sovereign immunity. Other states have schemes modeled in whole or in part on the Federal Tort Claims Act. Finally, other states have retained most of the traditional immunity.

Special protection is always given to agencies and offices when they are carrying out policy deliberations involving considerable judgment and discretion. It is sometimes said that it is not a tort for a government to govern! Rarely, for example, will any government waive immunity for tortious injury caused a citizen by a judge, legislator, or high administrative officer. Negligence by a lower-level employee in the judicial, legislative, or executive branches, however, may constitute an act or omission for which the state will waive immunity, e.g., a court clerk negligently loses a pleading that was properly filed. Acts that do not involve much discretion and that do not involve the formulation of policy will often subject the state to tort liability because the state has waived immunity for such acts.

Keep in mind that we are not talking about individual or personal liability of the government employee at this point. Personal liability will be discussed later. Our focus is on the government's liability via respondeat superior for the torts its employees commit within the scope of their employment.

Local Government

Local government units have a variety of names: cities, municipalities, municipal corporations, counties, towns, villages, etc. Also part of local government are the schools, transportation agencies, hospitals, recreational agencies, and some utilities. Whether any of these local units of government can be sued in tort is again a problem of sovereign immunity. A number of possibilities exist:

FIGURE 27–8   Sample Federal Tort Claims Act complaint.

**IN THE UNITED STATES DISTRICT COURT FOR THE
WESTERN DISTRICT OF _____**

_____ , Plaintiff

v.

[U.S.], Defendant

Complaint[2]

Plaintiff for his claim for relief states:

1. The action arises under the Federal Tort Claims Act, 60 Stat. 842, 843, 28 U.S.C.A. § 1346(b) and § 2671 et. seq.

2. Plaintiff resides in the City of _____ , _____ County, State of _____ , the same being within the Western District of _____ .

3. On July 1, 1967, in a public highway called _____ Street in _____ , _____ , _____ , an employee of defendant, negligently drove a motor vehicle against plaintiff who was then crossing said highway.

4. At the above time and place the said _____ was acting within the scope of his employment as an employee of the United States _____ Department, one of the departments of defendant, in that he was operating a truck owned by that Department.

5. On November 4, 1967, plaintiff presented to the Secretary of the Department in _____ a claim for his personal injuries on Standard Form 95 in the amount of ten thousand dollars.

6. On February 7, 1968, such claim was finally denied by the _____ Department of the United States.

7. As a result of said accident plaintiff was thrown down and had his leg broken and was otherwise injured, was prevented from transacting his business, suffered great pain of body and mind, and incurred expenses for medical attention and hospitalization in the sum of six thousand dollars.

Wherefore plaintiff demands judgment against defendant in the sum of sixteen thousand dollars and costs.

_____ ,
Attorney for Plaintiff,
_____ Building,
_____ , _____ ,

[2]*West's Federal Practice Manual, § 2031 (1970).*

- Sovereign immunity has been completely or almost completely waived.
- The sovereign immunity of the units of local government is the same as that enjoyed by the state government.
- The sovereign immunity of the units of local government is different from that of the state government.
- Different units of local government have different sovereign immunity rules.

In short, extensive legal research must be done every time you sue a unit of local government. You must determine its category or status. What is it called? Who created it? Why was it created? What are its powers? Is it really part of the state government? Is it separate from the state government? Is it a hybrid combination of both state and local government? Many cities and counties receive substantial state aid. Does such aid entitle them to the same sovereign immunity protection as the state? You may find that for some purposes, the unit of government is considered part of the state, whereas for other purposes it is considered entirely separate and local. Over the years, a great deal of litigation has dealt with the problem of determining the nature of the unit of government in order to decide what sovereign immunity principles apply.

Units of local government perform many different kinds of functions. These functions are often grouped into two classifications: **governmental** and **proprietary.** The sovereign immunity rules may differ depending on what category of function the employee was carrying out when the tort was committed. The general rule is that sovereign immunity is *not* waived when the tort grows out of a *governmental* function, whereas it *is* waived when it grows out of a *proprietary* function. (An important exception is when the city, county, town, or other unit has created a public or a private nuisance. Even if this nuisance grows out of a governmental function, sovereign immunity will usually not prevent the suit.) Of course, there is always the possibility that a government will waive its sovereign immunity for torts arising out of both governmental and proprietary functions. The waiver, however, is usually limited to proprietary functions.

Unfortunately, there are few clear rules on the distinction between a governmental and a proprietary function.

Governmental Functions A governmental function is one that can be performed adequately only by the government. The operation of local courts and local legislatures (e.g., a city council) is considered governmental. The same is true of the chief administrative offices of the local government (e.g., office of the mayor, office of the county commissioner) where basic policy is made. Police and fire departments, jails, schools, and sanitation also fall into the category of governmental functions where sovereign immunity will prevent suits for the torts that grow out of these functions.[3]

Proprietary Functions These are functions that generally cannot be performed adequately *only* by the government. Examples include government-run airports, docks, garages, and utilities such as water and gas. For some of these functions, the local government often collects special fees or revenue. The test for a proprietary function, however, is not whether a "profit" is made. This is simply one factor that tends to indicate a proprietary function. Some functions are very difficult to classify, such as the operation of a city hospital. You will find courts going both ways for these and similar functions.

There are courts that do not rely totally on the distinction between governmental and proprietary functions to decide whether sovereign immunity prevents the suit against the local government. Some courts make the same distinction we saw earlier under the Federal Tort Claims Act between a claim arising out of planning decisions made by the government (for which sovereign immunity will not be waived), and claims arising out of the implementation of the planning decisions at the operational or ministerial level (for which sovereign immunity will be waived). For example, a city may be immune from liability for damages resulting from its negligent decision on where to construct sewers, but would be liable for damages resulting from the negligent construction or repair of a particular sewer.

Finally, some governments have purchased liability insurance and have waived sovereign immunity, but only to the extent of this coverage.

ASSIGNMENT 27.13

Select any three agencies: one that is part of the federal government, one that is part of your state government, and one that is part of your local government. For each agency, assume that one of its employees has committed a tort against you. For example, while in a government car, the employee negligently hit your car. Contact each agency. Ask that you be sent any forms that must be used to file a claim against the agency. Attach the forms to three reports in which you explain the process of bringing such a tort claim as described in what is sent to you.

---

[3]W. Page Keeton et al., *Prosser and Keeton on the Law of Torts* 1053 (5th ed. 1984). See also *Restatement (Second) of Torts* § 895C (1965).

OFFICIAL IMMUNITY: THE PERSONAL LIABILITY OF GOVERNMENT EMPLOYEES

What about a suit against the *individual* government employee as opposed to one against the sovereign, or the government itself? If the employee is sued *personally,* any judgment is paid out of the employee's own pocket. Although there are circumstances in which **personal liability** is imposed on government employees, it should be pointed out that the law is reluctant to impose such liability. Public employees must be "free to exercise their duties unembarrassed by the fear of damage suits in respect of acts done in the course of those duties—suits which would consume time and energies which would otherwise be devoted to governmental service and the threat of which might appreciably inhibit the fearless, vigorous, and effective administration of policies of government."[4] On the other hand, critics argue that public employees should not be treated differently from employees in the private sector. When an employee of a business commits a tort, the employer is **vicariously liable** if the tort was committed within the scope of employment, but the employee may also be *personally liable*. The critics say that the same rule should apply to government employees. For the most part, however, it does not.

When government employees are *not* liable, it is because of *official immunity.* This is a defense under which government employees are not personally liable for torts they commit within the scope of their employment. Three questions need to be asked in this area of the law. First, was a tort committed? It may be that the government employee had a privilege to act so that there was no tort. For example, a police officer has the privilege to arrest someone. (See Figure 7–1 in Chapter 7.) The privilege prevents liability for torts such as battery and false imprisonment. If, however, a tort was committed, the second question is whether it was committed within the scope of employment. (See Figure 14–10 in Chapter 14 on the factors that determine scope of employment.) Judges may have official immunity for defamation they commit from the bench against attorneys or defendants, but not for defamation they commit against their neighbor in an argument over a football game. The latter is clearly outside the judge's scope of employment. A government employee is as liable for torts outside the scope of employment as any citizen would be. If a tort was committed by the government employee and if it was within the scope of employment, we then ask a third question: is the official immune from personal liability under the doctrine of official immunity?

A citizen who has been the victim of a government tort may face one of several scenarios in looking for a defendant to sue:

- Sovereign immunity may prevent a suit against the government, and official immunity may prevent a suit against the employee; the citizen is without remedy.
- Sovereign immunity may have been waived so that the government can be sued, but official immunity may prevent a suit against the employee; the citizen can sue only the government.
- Sovereign immunity may have been waived so that the government can be sued, and official immunity may not apply so that the employee can also be sued; the citizen can sue either or both.

If the citizen can sue both the government and the employee, and successfully does so, the citizen does not receive double damages for the same injury. There is one recovery only. The plaintiff can usually collect from either defendant until there has been a satisfaction of the judgment.

Official immunity must be examined under two main categories: the employee's personal liability for a traditional common law tort (e.g., negligence, battery,

---

[4]*Barr v. Matteo,* 360 U.S. 564, 571, 79 S. Ct. 1335, 3 L. Ed. 2d 1434 (1959).

defamation), and the employee's personal liability for a civil rights violation. First, let us examine civil rights violations.

Section 1983 of the **Civil Rights Act** of 1871 provides as follows:

"Every person who, under color of any statute, ordinance, regulation, custom, or usage, of any State . . . subjects . . . any citizen . . . to the deprivation of any rights, privileges, or immunities secured by the Constitution and laws, shall be liable to the party injured in an action at law,. . ." 42 U.S.C. § 1983.

Under this statute, a person who acts or pretends to act as a state official in a governmental capacity is said to be acting under **color of law,** or, to be specific, under color of *state* law. If that person deprives someone of a federal civil right, a special cause of action arises.

> **EXAMPLE:** Fred Jamison is a state police officer. He sees Loretta Walker driving down the street. Jamison decides to give Walker a speeding ticket solely because she is Black. Jamison knows that she was not speeding at the time.

Such racial discrimination is forbidden by the Equal Protection Clause of the United States Constitution. Since Jamison was charging Walker with violating the speeding law (a state law), the police officer was acting under color of law when he deprived Walker of the constitutional right not to be subjected to racial discrimination. Walker can sue Jamison under § 1983 of the Civil Rights Act. A civil rights suit seeking damages under this Act is called a **1983 action,** which asserts a federal cause of action called a **1983 tort.** The phrase **constitutional tort** refers to a special cause of action that arises when someone is deprived of federal civil rights.

Liability for a traditional common law tort such as battery is separate from liability for a constitutional tort. It is possible for a government employee to commit a constitutional tort that is not, in addition, a common law tort. An example is the Jamison/Walker case just discussed. There is no indication that the police officer committed a common law tort when he wrote the ticket, but he did commit a constitutional tort for which he might be liable in a 1983 action. Sometimes, however, the wrong committed by the employee is both a common law tort and a constitutional tort as in the following examples:

- A police officer punches a citizen (battery) to prevent him or her from voting.
- A government tax auditor destroys the flag of a citizen (conversion) in order to stop him or her from participating in a lawful demonstration.

A plaintiff can assert the common law tort and the constitutional tort in the same lawsuit. A major benefit of winning a constitutional tort is that attorney fees can be awarded, whereas for common law torts, the parties pay their own attorneys.

When will a government employee be personally liable for common law torts and for civil rights violations (constitutional torts)? As Figure 27–9 demonstrates, the answer often depends on whether the employee has an **absolute official immunity,** a **qualified official immunity,** or no immunity at all. An immunity is qualified if it can be lost because of malice; it is absolute if malice will not defeat it. Whether the government employee can claim the protection of one of these immunities depends in large measure on the nature of his or her job. The more ministerial or operational the job, the less protection the employee is given. Of course, it is difficult to think of any job that does not involve at least some measure of discretion. The difference between a job that is primarily judgmental and discretionary, on the one hand, and a job that is primarily ministerial or operational, on the other, is often a matter of degree. Some jobs clearly involve a great deal of discretion, e.g., a high administrative officer, judge, or legislator. Jobs such as repairing roads, driving trucks, and collecting taxes also pose little difficulty; they are clearly ministerial jobs. The gray area between these two extremes has produced a good deal of litigation.

Congress and the state legislatures are always free to pass special legislation that changes the basic rules outlined in Figure 27–9, on the official's immunity for com-

FIGURE 27–9   Official immunity of government employees for common law torts and for violations of the Civil Rights Act.

The Government Employees	Official Immunity for Common Law Torts	How the Official Immunity for Common Law Torts Can Be Lost	Official Immunity for Violations of the Civil Rights Act (Constitutional Torts)
Judges and legislators	Absolute official immunity for torts committed in the course of their employment even if they acted maliciously.	a. They did not commit the tort while performing their judicial or legislative role. b. They acted totally outside their authority or jurisdiction. **Note:** The immunity is not lost if they acted merely in excess of their authority.	Absolute official immunity for violations of the Act committed under color of law even if they acted maliciously. (The immunity is lost, however, for the same two reasons listed in the third column: *a* and *b*.)
High administrative officials	Same as for judges and legislators.	Same as for judges and legislators. In some states, however, they have a qualified immunity that is defeated by malice.	Qualified official immunity, which is lost if a reasonable official would have believed that the conduct violated a "clearly established" constitutional or statutory right.
Lower administrative officials who exercise considerable discretion in their job	Qualified official immunity for torts committed in the course of their employment.	a. They did not commit the tort in the course of their employment. b. They acted totally outside their authority. c. They acted maliciously or not in good faith.	Qualified official immunity. Same as for high administrative officials.
Lower administrative officials who function at the ministerial level with little or no discretion	No immunity in many states. They are personally liable for their torts, whether or not they acted in good faith or without malice. Statutes may have been passed, however, that provide absolute or qualified immunity for such employees.		Qualified official immunity. Same as for high administrative officials.

Note: As indicated earlier, the words "immunity" and "privilege" are sometimes used interchangeably in this area of the law. Absolute immunity, for example, is often referred to as absolute privilege, and qualified immunity as qualified privilege. In this chapter, we use the word "immunity" as a doctrine that prevents liability for a tort that was committed, and the word "privilege" as a doctrine that prevents the defendant's conduct from being a tort. The practical effect of either word, however, is the same with respect to the ultimate question of whether the government official will be personally liable.

mon law torts. For example, a statute might be passed to extend the qualified immunity to employees who act at the ministerial or operational level. The Federal Employees Liability Reform and Tort Compensation Act of 1988 is an important federal statute that grants extensive official immunity to federal employees who commit common law torts within the scope of employment.

In Figure 27–9, note that when high administrative officials are charged with a violation of the Civil Rights Act (see the fourth column), they have a qualified immunity that is lost if a reasonable official would have believed that his or her conduct violated a "clearly established" constitutional or statutory right. In the case of *Conn and Najera v. Gabbert* on the practice of law, we will examine an allegation by an attorney that such a right was violated.

CASE

Conn and Najera v. Gabbert
119 S. Ct. 1292, 143 L. Ed. 2d 399 (1999)
United States Supreme Court

Background: *Paul Gabbert was an attorney for Traci Baker, a witness appearing before the grand jury in a nationally-publicized state criminal trial involving two brothers accused of murdering their wealthy parents in Beverly Hills. While Baker was being questioned, the prosecutors searched Gabbert for evidence Baker may have given him earlier. Gabbert then brought a § 1983 action against the prosecutors for damages, claiming that their search interfered with his "clearly established" constitutional right to practice law. The Fourteenth Amendment says that no state shall "deprive any person of life, liberty, or property without due process of law." Part of the "liberty" protected by this clause is the right to practice one's employment. If the state unreasonably interferes with this liberty right, the victim can sue for damages under § 1983. Government officials such as prosecutors have a qualified immunity against such suits as long as they have not violated a "clearly established" right. Gabbert argued that his right to practice law without unreasonable interference was "clearly established" at the time the prosecutors violated it. The trial court (a Federal District Court) disagreed and dismissed the § 1983 action. Gabbert appealed to the Court of Appeals. During oral argument at the Court of Appeals, one of the judges expressed shock at what had occurred: "If you described what happened in this case to a stranger and didn't [say] what country it had happened in, America is not the first place that would come to mind." The Court of Appeals reversed the District Court and held that the prosecutors had violated Gabbert's right to practice law, thus reinstating his § 1983 action. The prosecutors then petitioned to the United States Supreme Court to reverse the Court of Appeals. They are the petitioners; Gabbert, the respondent, is responding to their petition.*

Decision on Appeal: *Judgment reversed. Gabbert's Fourteenth Amendment right to practice his calling was not violated by the search ordered by the prosecutors. His client had no right to have him present during the grand jury proceeding. An attorney has a Fourteenth Amendment right to practice his profession, but this right can be restricted by reasonable government regulation. Since Gabbert was subjected to no more than reasonable regulation when he was forced to submit to a search warrant, his right to practice law was not violated. This defeats the basis of the § 1983 action. There is no need, therefore, to decide whether the prosecutors lost their qualified immunity by violating a "clearly established" right.*

OPINION OF COURT

Chief Justice REHNQUIST delivered the opinion of the court . . .:

This case arises out of the high-profile California trials of the "Menendez Brothers," Lyle and Erik Menendez, for the murder of their parents. Petitioners David Conn and Carol Najera are Los Angeles County Deputy District Attorneys, and respondent Paul Gabbert is a criminal defense attorney. In early 1994, after the first Menendez trial ended in a hung jury, the Los Angeles County District Attorney's Office assigned Conn and Najera to prosecute the case on retrial. Conn and Najera learned that Lyle Menendez had written a letter to Traci Baker, his former girlfriend, in which he may have instructed her to testify falsely at trial. Gabbert represented Baker, who had testified as a defense witness in the first trial. Conn obtained and served Baker with a subpoena directing her to testify before the Los Angeles County grand jury and also directing her to produce at that time any correspondence that she had received from Lyle Menendez. After Gabbert unsuccessfully sought to quash the portion of the subpoena directing Baker to produce the Menendez correspondence, Conn and Najera obtained a warrant to search Baker's apartment for any such correspondence. When police tried to execute the warrant, Baker told the police that she had given all her letters from Menendez to Gabbert.

Three days later, on March 21, 1994, Baker appeared as directed before the grand jury, accompanied by Gabbert. Believing that Gabbert might have the letter on his person, Conn directed a police detective to secure a warrant to search Gabbert. . . . California law provides that a warrant to search an attorney must be executed by a court-appointed special master. When the Special Master arrived, Gabbert requested that the search take place in a private room. He did not request that his client's grand jury testimony be postponed. The Special Master searched Gabbert in the private room, and Gabbert produced two pages of a three-page letter from Lyle Menendez to Baker.

At approximately the same time that the search of Gabbert was taking place, Najera called Baker before the grand jury and began to question her. After being sworn, Najera asked Baker whether she was acquainted with Lyle Menendez. Baker replied that she had been unable to speak with her attorney because he was "still with the special master." A short recess was taken during which time Baker was unable to speak with Gabbert. He was aware that Baker sought to speak with him, but apparently stated that the prosecutors would simply have to delay the questioning until they finished searching him. Baker returned to the grand jury room and declined to answer the question "upon the advice of my counsel" on the basis of her Fifth Amendment privilege against self-incrimination.

Najera asked a follow-up question, and Baker again asked for a short recess to confer with Gabbert. Baker was again unable to locate Gabbert, and she again returned to the grand jury room and asserted her Fifth Amendment privilege. At this point, the grand jury recessed.

Believing that the actions of the prosecutors were illegal, Gabbert brought suit against them and other officials in Federal District Court under 42 U.S.C. § 1983. Relevant to this appeal by Conn and Najera, he contended that his Fourteenth Amendment right to practice his profession without unreasonable government interference was violated when the prosecutors executed a search warrant at the same time his client was testifying before the grand jury. [The District Court ruled for the prosecutors on the basis that their actions were protected by qualified immunity.]

The Court of Appeals reversed in part, holding that Conn and Najera were not entitled to qualified immunity on Gabbert's Fourteenth Amendment claim. 131 F.3d 793 (C.A.9 1997). Relying on *Board of Regents of State Colleges v. Roth*, 408 U.S. 564 (1972), and earlier cases of this Court recognizing a right to choose one's vocation, the Court of Appeals concluded that Gabbert had a right to practice his profession without undue and unreasonable government interference. The Court of Appeals also held that . . . the right allegedly violated in this case was clearly established, and as a result, Conn and Najera were not entitled to qualified immunity: "The plain and intended result [of the prosecutors' actions] was to prevent Gabbert from consulting with Baker during her grand jury appearance. These actions were not objectively reasonable, and thus the prosecutors are not protected by qualified immunity from answering Gabbert's Fourteenth Amendment claim." Id., at 802–803. We granted certiorari and now reverse.

Section 1983 provides a federal cause of action against any person who, acting under color of state law, deprives another of his federal rights. 42 U.S.C. § 1983. In order to prevail in a § 1983 action for civil damages from a government official performing discretionary functions, the defense of qualified immunity that our cases have recognized requires that the official be shown to have violated "clearly established statutory or constitutional rights of which a reasonable person would have known." *Harlow v. Fitzgerald*, 457 U.S. 800 (1982). Thus a court must first determine whether the plaintiff has alleged the deprivation of an actual constitutional right at all, and if so, proceed to determine whether that right was clearly established at the time of the alleged violation. See *Siegert v. Gilley*, 500 U.S. 226, 232–233 (1991).

We find no support in our cases for the conclusion of the Court of Appeals that Gabbert had a Fourteenth Amendment right which was violated in this case. The Court of Appeals relied primarily on *Board of Regents v. Roth*. In *Roth*, this Court repeated the pronouncement in *Meyer v. Nebraska*, 262 U.S. 390, 399 (1923) that the liberty guaranteed by the Fourteenth Amendment " 'denotes not merely freedom from bodily restraint but also the right of the individual to contract, to engage in any of the common occupations of life, to acquire useful knowl-

edge, to marry, establish a home and bring up children, to worship God according to the dictates of his own conscience, and generally to enjoy those privileges long recognized . . . as essential to the orderly pursuit of happiness by free men.' " *Roth*, supra, at 572 (quoting *Meyer*, supra, at 399). But neither *Roth* nor *Meyer* even came close to identifying the asserted "right" violated by the prosecutors in this case. *Meyer* held that [a state could not pass a law] that prohibited teaching in any language other than English. And *Roth* . . . held that an at-will college professor had no "property" interest in his job within the meaning of the Fourteenth Amendment so as to require the university to hold a hearing before terminating him. . . . Neither case supports the conclusion that the actions of the prosecutors in this case deprived Gabbert of a liberty interest in practicing law.

Similarly, none of the other cases relied upon by the Court of Appeals or suggested by Gabbert provide any more than scant metaphysical support for the idea that the use of a search warrant by government actors violates an attorney's right to practice his profession. In a line of earlier cases, this Court has indicated that the liberty component of the Fourteenth Amendment's Due Process Clause includes some generalized due process right to choose one's field of private employment, but a right which is nevertheless subject to reasonable government regulation. See, e.g., *Dent v. West Virginia*, 129 U.S. 114 (1889) (upholding a requirement of licensing before a person can practice medicine); *Truax v. Raich*, 239 U.S. 33 (1915) (invalidating on equal protection grounds a state law requiring companies to employ 80% United States citizens). These cases all deal with a complete prohibition of the right to engage in a calling, and not the sort of brief interruption which occurred here.

Gabbert also relies on *Schware v. Board of Bar Examiners of N.M.*, 353 U.S. 232, 238–239, 77 S. Ct. 752, 1 L. Ed. 2d 796 (1957), for the proposition that a State cannot exclude a person from the practice of law for reasons that contravene the Due Process Clause. *Schware* held that former membership in the Communist Party and an arrest record relating to union activities could not be the basis for completely excluding a person from the practice of law. Like *Dent*, supra, and *Truax*, supra, it does not deal with a brief interruption as a result of legal process. No case of this Court has held that such an intrusion can rise to the level of a violation of the Fourteenth Amendment's liberty right to choose and follow one's calling. That right is simply not infringed by the inevitable interruptions of our daily routine as a result of legal process which all of us may experience from time to time. . . .

We hold that the Fourteenth Amendment right to practice one's calling is not violated by the execution of a search warrant, whether calculated to annoy or even to prevent consultation with a grand jury witness. In so holding, [there is no need to address] the question of whether such a right was "clearly established" as of a given day. The judgment of the Court of Appeals holding to the contrary is therefore reversed.

It is so ordered.

a. Why didn't the Court have to decide whether the prosecutors had lost their qualified immunity?

b. Would the Court have reached a different result and ruled in favor of Gabbert if the state had revoked his license to practice law because he had the letter?

CHARITABLE IMMUNITY

There was a time when a charitable, educational, religious, or other benevolent organization enjoyed an immunity for the torts it committed in the course of its work. The law was reluctant to allow the resources of such organizations to be depleted in a suit brought against the organization because of a tort committed by one of its employees or volunteers. **Charitable immunity,** however, was never complete. An organization, for example, was liable for its negligence in selecting personnel and in raising money. Most states, however, have abolished the immunity altogether, and other states have severely restricted its applicability.

INTRAFAMILY TORT IMMUNITY

Suppose that one family member wrongfully injures another. Can they sue each other in tort? If they are not allowed to do so, it is because of the **intrafamily tort immunity.** This topic is covered in Figure 22–1 at the end of Chapter 22 on Torts Against and Within the Family.

SUMMARY

A defense is the response of a party to a claim of another party, setting forth the reason(s) the claim should not be granted. The defense of immunity is that there should be no liability for the tort that was committed. The defense of privilege is that there should be no liability since there was no tort committed.

Consent is a defense to most torts. The plaintiff must have the capacity to consent and must voluntarily manifest the consent. The test is the reasonableness of the defendant's belief that the plaintiff consented, not the plaintiff's subjective state of mind. For the consent to be valid, the plaintiff must know the nature and consequences of what the defendant wants to do; gaining consent by misrepresentation renders the consent invalid.

There are several self-help privileges. The defendant can use reasonable force to protect him- or herself in the reasonable belief that the plaintiff will immediately inflict harmful or offensive contact on the defendant (self-defense). The defendant can use reasonable force to prevent the plaintiff from immediately inflicting on a third person harmful or offensive contact which the plaintiff does not have the privilege to inflict (defense of others). If the defendant reasonably believes that persons or property will be immediately injured or damaged, he or she can make reasonable use of the plaintiff's chattels or land to prevent it (necessity). If the defendant possesses land or chattels and this right of possession is superior to the plaintiff's claim of possession, the defendant can use reasonable force to prevent the plaintiff's immediately threatened or continued interference with the defendant's possession (defense of property). If the plaintiff wrongfully acquires possession of a chattel and the defendant has the immediate right to possession, the defendant can use reasonable force to recapture it promptly after the plaintiff takes possession or promptly after discovering that the plaintiff has taken possession. There must be a request that it be returned before force is used, unless this would be unrealistic or unsafe (recapture of chattels).

Under the Federal Tort Claims Act, the federal government has waived sovereign immunity for designated torts. Examples include negligence at the ministerial or operational level, trespass to land or invasion of privacy committed by any federal employee, and battery or false arrest committed by a federal law enforcement officer.

State governments differ on the extent to which sovereign immunity is waived. The state often retains its immunity to cover the conduct of its judges, legislators, and high administrative officers. The less discretion and policy involvement a state employee has, the more likely the state will waive its sovereign immunity for harm caused by that employee. Local governments often waive their sovereign immunity for the proprietary functions they perform, but not for their governmental functions.

Government employees with official immunity cannot be personally liable for the common law or constitutional torts they commit within the scope of their employment. (A constitutional tort is a special cause of action, such as a 1983 action, that arises when someone is deprived of federal civil rights.) Generally, judges, legislators, and high administrative officers have an absolute official immunity; lower officials who exercise considerable discretion in their jobs have a qualified official immunity; lower officials who exercise little or no discretion in their jobs have no official immunity unless changed by statute.

Most states have eliminated the charitable immunity that once relieved charities and similar organizations of liability for their torts.

KEY TERMS

defense 536	public necessity 546	governmental 557
privilege 536	abate a nuisance 548	proprietary 557
immunity 536	defense of property 548	personal liability 559
volenti non fit injuria 536	recapture of chattels 551	vicariously liable 559
consent 536	*in loco parentis* 552	Civil Rights Act 560
implied consent 537	arrest 552	color of law 560
coercion 538	fresh pursuit 553	1983 action 560
informed consent 539	shopkeeper privilege 553	1983 tort 560
self-help 543	sovereign immunity 554	constitutional tort 560
self-defense 544	respondeat superior 554	absolute official immunity 560
defense of others 545	official immunity 554	qualified official immunity 560
necessity 546	just compensation 554	charitable immunity 564
chattels 546	taking of property 554	intrafamily tort immunity 564
private necessity 546	Federal Tort Claims Act 554	

CHAPTER

28

Workers' Compensation

CHAPTER OUTLINE

- Introduction
- On-the-Job Injuries at Common Law
- Workers' Compensation Statutes
- Injuries and Diseases Covered
- Filing a Claim
- Benefits Available
- Tort Claims Against Third Parties
- Reform

INTRODUCTION

The estimated cost of on-the-job injuries and illnesses is between $70 billion and $170 billion a year. According to the United States Bureau of Labor Statistics, in 1997:

- 6.1 million injuries and illnesses were reported in private industry workplaces.
- This consisted of 7.1 cases per 100 full-time workers.
- Over 93 percent of the reported cases resulted in lost work time, medical treatment, loss of consciousness, or transfer to another job.[1]

Under the common law, the major remedy of the worker was to sue the employer for negligence. This was not a satisfactory option. Not only was negligence difficult to prove, but also, as we will see, the employer could use some powerful defenses that effectively defeated the vast majority of such negligence suits. After 1910, however, a strict liability system was created under which the cost of worker injuries was spread over an entire industry or enterprise regardless of who was negligent or at fault. This no-fault system of enterprise responsibility was called **workers' compensation**.[2] Before examining its scope, we need to take a closer look at the common law fault system that workers' compensation was designed to replace for most workers.

ON-THE-JOB INJURIES AT COMMON LAW

When an employee was injured on the job, his or her traditional remedy was a negligence suit, brought on the theory that the employer unreasonably failed to provide a safe work environment. This was, of course, a common law tort remedy (on negligence, see Chapters 12 to 17). For years, there was widespread criticism of this remedy, primarily because it was difficult for an employee to win a negligence case.

The difficulty was due to the employer's ability to establish one or more of the following three defenses:

---

[1]*Workplace in Brief,* San Francisco Chronicle, December 18, 1998, at B3; *Report: Job-Related Injury, Illness Costly,* San Diego Union-Tribune, July 28, 1997, at A6.
[2]For legal materials on workers' compensation on the Internet, see http://www.law.cornell.edu/topics/workers_compensation.html. See also Tort Law Online at the end of Chapter 1.

Contributory negligence: The employee acted unreasonably, which contributed to his or her own injury, along with the negligence of the employer. The contributory negligence of the employee prevented recovery against the employer (unless the latter's negligence was willful or wanton, or unless the employer failed to take the last clear chance (see Chapter 17) to avoid the injury).

Assumption of the risk: The employee knew about the hazards of the job and voluntarily took the job or voluntarily remained on the job, even though the employee understood the dangers involved. Assumption of the risk defeated the employee's recovery for the employer's negligence.

Fellow-employee rule: The employer was not liable for the injuries received by an employee if the injury was caused by the negligence of a fellow employee. An exception existed when the fellow employee was a **vice principal,** i.e., an employee with supervisory authority over other employees or an employee of any rank who has been given some responsibility for the safety of the work environment; the employer *will* be liable if the employee is injured because of the negligence of a fellow employee who is a vice principal.

WORKERS' COMPENSATION STATUTES

Throughout the country, workers' compensation statutes have been passed by the legislatures as an alternative to the common law negligence system. Under these statutes, an employee will receive compensation for an industrial accident without having to prove that the employer was negligent. Hence, the liability of the employer under such a statute is a form of **strict liability.** This means there is no need to prove that the employer caused the injury negligently. It is a **no-fault system.** The defenses of contributory negligence, assumption of the risk, and the fellow-servant rule are abolished. See Figure 28–1 for an overview of the advantages and disadvantages of workers' compensation.

Not all employers and employees are covered under workers' compensation. When employees are not covered, they are left with a traditional negligence action in which they must face the "unholy trinity" of defenses: contributory negligence,[3] assumption of risk, and the fellow-servant rule.

The primary way in which the workers' compensation system is financed is through insurance. An employer must either purchase insurance or prove that it is financially able to cover any risks on its own. The latter is called **self-insurance.** When insurance is purchased, it comes either from a state-operated insurance fund or from a private insurer or carrier.

Every state has an agency or commission that administers the workers' compensation law for employees in the private sector. It may be an independent entity or be part of the state's department of labor. Government employees have a separate workers' compensation system to cover their employment. Workers' compensation for nonmilitary employees of the federal government, for example, is administered by the Office of Workers' Compensation Programs within the United States Department of Labor.[4] In this chapter, our focus is workers' compensation for employees in the private sector.

The statutory code of your state will list the categories of employers and employees covered by workers' compensation in the private sector. It is important to note the definitions of employer, employee, employment, and any other word that will tell you who is and who is not covered. Some codes may say that everyone is covered except those specifically excluded, such as domestic workers, farm workers, casual workers, independent contractors, or people who work for employers with fewer than a certain number of employees.

---

[3]Or comparative negligence if the state has abolished contributory negligence. See Chapter 17.
[4]See Federal Employees' Compensation Act, 5 U.S.C. §§ 8101 et seq.

FIGURE 28–1 Benefits/disadvantages of workers' compensation (WC).

ADVANTAGES

To Employee

- In a WC case, there is no need to prove the employer was negligent.
- Contributory negligence, assumption of risk, and fellow-servant rule cannot defeat a WC case—they are not defenses in a WC case.
- The WC administrative procedure is quicker and less costly than a suit for negligence in court.
- Recovery of benefits in a WC case is usually quicker than filing an action for negligence in court.

To Employer

- Limited liability: the cash benefits awarded an employee under WC are limited to set amounts specified by statute, whereas a negligence judgment in court against the employer could be much higher.
- The WC administrative procedure is quicker and less costly than a negligence suit in court.

DISADVANTAGES

To Employee

- Recovery of cash benefits in a WC case is usually smaller than damages awarded in a successful negligence case in court.

To Employer

- Critics charge that the WC system is riddled with fraud. The temptation to fabricate a WC claim is large. Consequently, WC insurance premiums paid by employers are very high.

ASSIGNMENT

28.1

What is the name, address, phone number, e-mail address, and World Wide Web address of the central office of the agency in your state that administers the workers' compensation law for employees in the private sector? You can obtain this information in a number of ways: Check with the personnel department of any large employer in the private sector in your state, ask any union officer in your state, call information for your state government, contact the office of a politician, ask any library if it has an organizational chart or a list of state agencies (e.g., *The National Directory of State Agencies*). Write or call this agency to request a brochure describing benefits and other information about the system. Also request the application forms used by the agency.

INJURIES AND DISEASES COVERED

Not every on-the-job misfortune is covered under workers' compensation. A few states, for example, do not cover certain diseases that occur as a result of long-term exposure to conditions or hazards at a job. In most states, however, diseases as well as accidents are covered.

The basic requirement is that the employee's injury must **arise out of** and occur **in the course of** employment. "Arising out of" refers to the causal connection between the injury and the employment; "in the course of" refers to the time, place, and circumstances of the injury in connection with the employment. We will explore both issues through the following themes:

In the Course of Employment
1. while clearly at work
2. while going to or coming from work
3. during trips
4. during horseplay and misconduct
5. while engaged in personal comfort

Arising Out of Employment
1. causal connection tests
2. acts of nature
3. street risks
4. assault and battery
5. personal risks

In the Course of Employment

1. While Clearly at Work The vast majority of injuries pose little or no difficulty, e.g., a hand is injured while operating a printing press, or death results from an explosion while the worker is in a mine. Liability under the workers' compensation statute is clear for most cases of this kind.

2. While Going to and Coming from Work A **going-and-coming rule** exists in most states: workers' compensation is denied if the employee is injured "off the premises" while going to or coming back from work or while going to or coming back from lunch. The company parking lot is usually considered part of the employer's premises, so that there *is* coverage if the employee is injured while on the lot. A number of exceptions have been created to the going-and-coming rule. For example, if the route to work exposes the worker to special dangers or risks (e.g., passing through a "rough" neighborhood to get to the plant), the injury will be considered within the "course of employment" even though it technically occurred beyond the premises owned or leased by the employer. Such risks are said to be **incident to the job.** The court will conclude that there is a close association between the access route and the premises of the employer.[5] Some courts also make an exception if the injury occurs when the employee is on a public sidewalk or street that is close to the premises of the employer.

3. During Trips Of course, any trip made by the employee that is part of a job responsibility is within the course of employment, and an injury that occurs on such a trip will be covered by workers' compensation, e.g., injury while making a sales trip or a delivery. Even if the employee is going to or from work, the trip will be considered part of the employment if the trip is a special assignment from or service to the employer, e.g., an employee is injured when asked to return to the shop after work hours to check on an alarm or to let someone in. It is not always necessary to show that the employee is paid extra compensation for such a trip, but when such compensation is paid, the argument is strengthened that the trip is within the course of employment.

Suppose, however, that the trip serves a *personal* purpose of the employee as well as a business purpose of the employer. This is a **mixed-purpose trip,** also called a **dual-purpose trip.**

> **EXAMPLE:** Helen is asked to deliver a package to a certain city. She rents a car for the purpose at company expense. She takes along two of her friends so that the three of them can attend a party after Helen makes the delivery. While on her way to the city, Helen is injured in a traffic accident.

Helen had a business purpose for the trip (make the delivery) and a personal purpose (go to a party with her friends). The criteria a court will use to determine whether the trip is business (and hence covered by workers' compensation) or personal (and not covered) are as follows:

- The trip is considered a business trip if it would have been made even if the personal objective did not exist.
- The trip is considered a personal trip if it would have been made even if the business objective did not exist.

---

[5] Arthur Larson, *Workmen's Compensation Law* § 15.13, p. 4–22 (1978).

Therefore, the characterization of the trip depends on what would have happened if one of the purposes failed or did not materialize. The business nature of the trip is established once it can be said that the trip must be made at some time by someone, whether or not the person making the trip will also attend to some personal matters.

Suppose that an employee is on a purely business trip. While on the trip, however, the employee decides to take a detour for personal reasons, e.g., to visit a relative or to inquire into another job. The general rule is that the employee is not covered by workers' compensation if injured while on a personal detour. Once the personal detour has been completed and the employee is once more attending to the business purpose of the trip, coverage under the compensation statute resumes.

4. During Horseplay and Misconduct   It is not uncommon for workers on the job to be playful with each other or to engage in horseplay. What happens if an employee is injured during such horseplay? If the employee is the innocent victim of the horseplay, he or she will be covered by workers' compensation, e.g., the employee is hit on the head by a hard aluminum-foil ball that other employees were using to "play catch," in which the injured employee was not participating.

Suppose, however, that one of the employees participating in or instigating the horseplay is injured. Such injuries are often not covered by workers' compensation unless it can be shown that the horseplay was a very minor departure from normal work responsibilities, or that the horseplay had been occurring over a long period of time and had, in effect, become customary.

The employee's injury may be caused by his or her own misconduct on the job. Recall what was said earlier about the defense of contributory negligence: the employee's own negligence is not a defense to recovery under workers' compensation. Some workers' compensation statutes, however, provide that if the employee is injured while engaged in **willful** misconduct, such as the willful failure to use a safety device, workers' compensation benefits *will* be denied or reduced.

It is important to distinguish between the following:

- what the employee has been asked to do—the **objective** of the job, and
- the **method** that the employee uses to carry out the objective

The general rule is that employee misconduct related to the objective of a job leads to no coverage under workers' compensation, but misconduct related to method is still covered.

Objective: A bus ticket clerk violates specific instructions never to drive a bus, and is injured. The injury is not covered under workers' compensation.

Method: A bus driver is injured because of careless operation of the bus. The injury is covered by workers' compensation.

Other examples of injuries that grow out of the method of doing the job and hence are covered under workers' compensation include reaching into a machine before stopping it, climbing over a fence rather than walking around it, repairing a machine while it is still operating, and using a machine with its safety guard removed.[6] Even if these methods of doing the job were specifically prohibited by the employer, workers' compensation will still be allowed unless the statute has an exception for certain willful violations, as already mentioned.

5. While Engaged in Personal Comfort   Simply because an employee is injured while taking care of a personal need on the job does not mean that coverage is denied under workers' compensation. Here is how one court described this aspect of the law:

For the purposes of the [workers'] compensation act the concept of course of employment is more comprehensive than the assigned work at the lathe. It includes an employee's ministrations to his own human needs: he must eat; concessions to his

---

[6]Arthur Larson, *Workmen's Compensation Law* § 31.22, p. 6–20 (1978).

own human frailties: he must rest, must now and then have a break, and he sometimes, even on the job, plays practical jokes on his fellows. Course of employment is not scope of employment. The former, as the cases so clearly reveal, is a way of life in a working environment. If the injury results from the work itself, or from the stresses, the tensions, the associations of the working environments, human as well as material, it is compensable [under workers' compensation]. Why? because those are the ingredients of the product itself. It carries to the market with it, on its price tag stained and scarred, its human as well as its material costs.[7]

When an injury occurs while a worker is taking a lunch break, going to the restroom, or stepping out for a moment of fresh air, workers' compensation usually applies. Factors that will be considered in reaching this result include whether the accident occurred on the premises and within an authorized area for the activity, whether it occurred within working hours, whether the hazard that led to the accident is considered normal for that work environment, and whether the employer prohibited the activity that led to the accident. (On factor analysis, see Legal Analysis Guideline #12 in Chapter 2.)

Suppose that the employee is injured while engaged in a sports contest at a picnic or other social event involving coworkers. Workers' compensation is applicable if the activity is sponsored by the employer or if the workers are otherwise encouraged to participate by the employer. The more benefit the employer is likely to derive from the activity, the more inclined an agency or a court will be to conclude that the activity was within the course of employment and hence covered by workers' compensation.

ASSIGNMENT

28.2

Examine the following situations to determine whether the injury was within the "course of employment." (See General Instructions for the Legal Analysis Assignment in Chapter 2.)

a. An employee is killed while crossing a public street immediately in front of her office. She is on her way home when hit by the car of another employee on the way to work.

b. The street in front of the company building is over 50 feet wide and is heavily traveled. An employee, walking to a restaurant during a lunch break, is hit by a car on this street. Another route to the restaurant is available through the rear of the company building. If the employee had used this other route, the trip would have taken an extra twelve minutes.

c. An employee is injured in a public parking lot 800 feet from his place of work. The company parking lot has spaces for only 200 of its 500 employees. The public parking lot is the closest alternative parking lot available.

d. During the work day, the employee is given an old company radio and allowed to take it home on company time. While putting the radio in her car in the company parking lot, she drops the radio and injures her foot.

e. An employee is a company salesperson who travels extensively throughout the city. At 6:00 P.M., the employee makes the last call and is on the way home. The employee is killed in an automobile collision one mile from home.

f. A teacher attends an evening PTA meeting and is on the way home. The teacher stops for a few minutes at a tavern and has half a glass of beer. After leaving the tavern, the teacher is injured in an automobile collision one mile from home.

g. An employee is a lawyer who works for a title insurance company. She usually takes a bus to work. On Tuesday, her employer asks her to come to work

---

[7]*Crilly v. Ballou*, 353 Mich. 303, 326, 91 N.W.2d 493, 505 (1958). See also Malone, Plant, & Little, *Workers' Compensation and Employment Rights* 126 (2d. ed. 1980).

as soon as possible. The lawyer takes her car and has a collision on the way to work.

h. A real estate appraiser leaves home to inspect property listed by his employer. On the way, he stops at a jewelry store to buy a present for his wife. He slips in the store and injures his back.

i. An employee is a salesperson. While on a sales trip, she stops at a store to buy some groceries for that evening. The stop takes her ten miles out of the way. While in the store buying her groceries, she meets a prospective customer. After a brief discussion about a possible sale, she injures herself in a fall just outside the store.

j. An employee injures his back while putting out a cigarette in the lunchroom during his lunch break. The employee was leaning down to extinguish the cigarette in a bucket that had sand in it.

k. An employee has a heart attack while dancing at a Christmas party in the company hall.

l. An employee is injured while playing handball in the rear of the plant during a break. Employees have been playing handball there for months in spite of a company sign forbidding play in that area.

m. The elevator door in a company building is broken. All employees are forbidden to use it until it is repaired. Two employees use this elevator and are both injured during a friendly wrestling match while the elevator is in motion.

CASE

Colvin v. Industrial Indemnity
83 Or. App. 73, 730 P.2d 585
Court of Appeals of Oregon (1986)

Background: *Leslie Colvin was a paralegal at a fifty-attorney law firm. While on a law firm picnic, she suffered low back and neck injuries after a fall. No one saw the incident, but she told Ms. Kreft, the firm's senior paralegal, about her injury shortly after it happened. She also told Mr. Lilly, an associate attorney of the firm for whom she frequently worked. Although claimant missed two days of work following the fall, she did not file a workers' compensation claim because she thought the pain would go away. Two years after the party, however, she filed for workers' compensation because of recurring symptoms during this period. The Workers' Compensation Board denied her claim because she failed to inform her employer about the injury and to file her claim in a timely manner. It also ruled that the injury was not work-related. She appealed to the Court of Appeals, which affirmed the Board's decision. She further appealed to the Supreme Court of Oregon, which reversed and sent the case back (remanded it) to the Court of Appeals. The case is now before the Court of Appeals of Oregon for the second time.*

Decision on Appeal: *Reversed and remanded. The paralegal did give timely notice of her claim to the employer and the injury was in the course of employment.*

OPINION OF COURT

Judge WARDEN delivered the opinion of the court . . . :

We first address the issue of whether the persons claimant told of her injury had supervisory authority over her. [Under the workers' compensation statute in Oregon, a claim is barred if the claimant fails to give a formal notice of injury to the employer unless someone with supervisory authority over the claimant already "had knowledge of the injury." Oregon Revised Statutes 656.265(4)(a).] Claimant was a paralegal in a large law firm. Her injury occurred at a firm picnic. She told Kreft, the firm's senior paralegal, about her injury shortly after it occurred. The next week she mentioned to Lilly, an associate attorney of the firm, that she had fallen and injured her back at the picnic. After reviewing the record, we find that both Kreft and Lilly had supervisory authority over claimant. Both testified that the firm's organization was loosely structured at the time of claimant's injury. Kreft's uncontroverted testimony was that she was the senior paralegal, that she had interviewed claimant before the firm had hired her and that she always represented the paralegals when speaking with the firm's partners concerning issues such as salaries and the need for more secretaries. Lilly . . . said that he worked at least weekly, and often daily, with claimant on cases assigned to him. Both Kreft and Lilly therefore exercised a degree of supervisory authority over claimant. Claimant's failure to give [formal notice of the injury] does not bar her claim, because her employer had knowledge of the injury.

Employer's knowledge, however, is not determinative, by itself, of the issue of compensability. To be compensable, the injury must be one "arising out of and in the course of employment." Oregon Revised Statutes (ORS) 656.005(8)(a). Some discussion of the facts is required for an analysis of whether the picnic at which the injury occurred was sufficiently work-related to make the injury compensable. The facts are undisputed. The picnic was an annual affair, sponsored and paid for entirely by the firm. The organizing committee planned it on company time. It started at noon on a regular workday and lasted until late in the evening. Only the firm's legal and paralegal staff and their spouses were allowed to participate. No clients were present. The paralegals perceived the picnic as one of their job benefits. Attendance was not compulsory, but people were encouraged to attend. If those eligible to attend did not, they were expected to be at work that afternoon. Business was discussed only on an informal and casual basis. Some humorous or "fun" awards were made by the firm to those who participated in athletic events in the afternoon. Claimant was injured at the picnic between 6:30 and 7:00 P.M.

We address the issue of whether "the relationship between the injury and the employment [is] sufficient that the injury should be compensable." *Rogers v. SAIF,* 289 Or. 633, 642, 616 P.2d 485 (1980). [We accept the tests proposed by the commentator, Larson]:

> "Recreational or social activities are within the course of employment when
> "(1) They occur on the premises during a lunch or recreation period as a regular incident of the employment; or
> "(2) The employer, by expressly or impliedly requiring participation, or by making the activity part of the services of an employee, brings the activity within the orbit of the employment; or
> "(3) The employer derives substantial direct benefit from the activity beyond the intangible value of improvement in employee health and morale that is common to all kinds of recreation and social life." 1A. Larson, *Workmen's Compensation Law,* 5-52, § 22.00 (1985).

The three tests are stated in the disjunctive. If claimant's attendance at the picnic satisfies any one of them, it would be within the course of her employment. She concedes that Larson's first test is not met, because the picnic occurred off the firm's premises.

The second test involves the extent to which an employer requires participation or makes the activity part of the services of an employee. We find Larson's analysis helpful: "When the degree of employer involvement descends from compulsion to mere sponsorship or encouragement, the questions become closer, and it becomes necessary to consult a series of tests bearing on work-connection. The most prolific illustrations of this problem are company picnics and office parties. Among the questions to be asked are: Did the employer in fact sponsor the event? To what extent was attendance really voluntary? Was there some degree of encouragement to attend in such factors as taking a record of attendance, paying for the time spent, requiring the employee to work if he did not attend, or maintaining a known custom of attending? Did the employer finance the occasion to a substantial extent? Did the employees regard it as an employment benefit to which they were entitled as a right? Did the employer benefit from the event, not merely in a vague way through better morale and good will, but through such tangible advantages as having an opportunity to make speeches and awards?" 1A. Larson, supra, 5-110, § 22.23 (1985).

The law firm sponsored the picnic and allowed it to be organized on company time. Although attendance was voluntary, the firm did provide encouragement to attend by requiring staff members to work if they did not attend and by paying those who did attend. The firm financed the picnic in its entirety, including box lunches, barbecue dinners and cocktails. The paralegal staff regarded the picnic as one of their employment benefits. Although the firm presumably derived intangible benefits from the picnic through better morale among its employees, we cannot say that it received any more tangible benefits. [We note that under Larson's third test, the picnic does not fall within the course of employment, because the firm gained no benefit from the picnic other than boosting employee morale.] Nevertheless, consideration of all of the factors that Larson lists leads us to conclude that the picnic was an "activity within the orbit of employment."

Employer's insurer argues that, because the injury occurred between 6:30 and 7:00 P.M. and because the normal workday at the firm ended at 5:00 P.M., the injury occurred after any work-connection had terminated. We reject that argument. We hold that claimant's injury arose out of and was within her course of employment. . . . Reversed and remanded to the Workers' Compensation Board with instructions to accept the claim and for determination of compensation.

ASSIGNMENT

28.3

a. How, if at all, do you think the following facts would have affected the outcome of the *Colvin* case?

  i. The picnic where the claimant fell was held at the home of the senior partner at the firm.

  ii. The picnic where the claimant fell was held at the home of the paralegal claimant.

b. Assume that the only person the claimant told about the fall was a fellow paralegal, Ed Davis, who had just applied for the job of senior paralegal. He was told a week before the picnic that he would get the promotion effective the day after the picnic. Would this change the result in *Colvin*?

c. Assume that the claimant fell at a Tuesday afternoon meeting of the local paralegal association. The dues for membership are paid by the employer. Would this change the result in *Colvin*?

Arising Out of Employment

1. Causal Connection Tests   "Arising out of employment" refers to the workers' compensation requirement that the injury must be caused by the employment. Various tests have been used by the courts to determine whether the requisite causal connection exists between the conditions under which the employee works and the injury sustained.[8]

> **Peculiar-risk test:** The source of the harm is peculiar to the employment. The danger must be incidental to the character of the business and dependent on the existence of an employer-employee relationship. The risk must not be one that the employee shares with every citizen, e.g., injury due to cold weather. The risk must differ in quality.
>
> **Increased-risk test:** The risk of injury to the employee is quantitatively greater than the risk of injury to nonemployees. The employment must increase the risk of an injury, even if others are also exposed to the risk of the injury.
>
> **Positional-risk test:** The injury of the employee would not have occurred but for the fact that the job placed the employee in a position where the employee could be injured.
>
> **Proximate-cause test:** The injury is foreseeable, and no intervening factor breaks the chain of causation between the conditions of employment and the injury.
>
> **Actual-risk test:** The injury is a risk of this particular employment. Whether or not the employment increases the risk, there is causation if the injury comes from a risk that is actually present in this employment.

Most states use the increased-risk test to determine whether the injury arises out of the employment. You must be aware of the other tests, however, because they are used by some states as sole tests, and they are sometimes used along with the increased-risk test.

2. Acts of Nature   There is usually no problem showing that an injury arose out of (was caused by) the employment when it was due to an **act of God** such as a storm or freezing weather that occurred during work. The increased-risk test is most often applied to reach this result. An injury received by an employee by lightning, for example, arises out of the employment if the job places the employee on an elevation, near metal, or in any place where there is an increased risk of this injury's occurring.

Suppose, however, that the act of nature delivers the same harm to everyone, e.g., a tornado levels an entire town. In such a case, it cannot be said that the employee was subjected to any increased risk by being on the job as opposed to being at home. Workers' compensation will be denied, because the injury did not arise out of the employment. Many courts make an exception to this rule if there is contact with the premises: if the act of God produces a force that makes actual contact with the employment premises, e.g., the hurricane blows down a company pole that hits the employee.

Exposure to the elements may bring on diseases such as Rocky Mountain spotted fever, which many people in an area may contract. If the employment increases the employee's chances of getting the disease, causation is established.

3. Street Risks   Traveling salespersons and employees making deliveries or soliciting sales are sometimes injured by falls or traffic accidents. Even though everyone is exposed to the risk of such injuries, most states will say that if the job increases the risk of their occurring, compensation will be allowed. Other courts will go even further and say that workers' compensation will be awarded simply by the plaintiff's showing that the job requires that public streets be used.

4. Assault and Battery   What happens if the employee is injured because of an assault or a battery? If the employee is the aggressor and the quarrel is personal,

---

[8]Arthur Larson, *Workmen's Compensation Law* § 6, p. 3–1 (1978).

having nothing to do with the job, the injury does not arise out of the employment and workers' compensation is denied. It does not take much, however, for the assault or battery to be connected with the employment. The following are examples of injuries due to assault or battery that are sufficiently connected with the employment so that it can be said that the injury arises out of the employment:

- A police officer is hit by someone under arrest.
- A cashier is killed in a robbery attempt.
- A lawyer is raped in an office located in a dangerous area.
- A supervisor is struck by a subordinate being disciplined.
- A worker is struck by a coworker in an argument over who is supposed to perform a certain task.
- A union member and a nonunion member have a fight over whether the latter should join the union.

Fights on the job pose some difficulty. It is not always easy to determine whether a fight is due solely to personal animosity or vengeance (not compensable under workers' compensation) or whether the fight has its origin in the employment, so that it can be said that the employment is a contributing factor to the fight (compensable under workers' compensation). In most states, the fact that the injured employee is the aggressor in the fight does not mean that compensation will be denied to him or her, as long as the employment itself contributed to the fight.

5. Personal Risks   Some employees are more susceptible to injury or disease than others, e.g., someone with a heart condition or epilepsy. An on-the-job injury or disease suffered by such an employee will be said to arise out of the employment only if it can be shown that the employment increased the risk of the injury or disease occurring, or if the employment **aggravated** the extent of the harm resulting from the injury or disease. Workers' compensation, of course, cannot be awarded for any **pre-existing injuries or diseases** that the employee brings to the job, because the job did not cause them. Such injuries or diseases are personal to the employee, unrelated to the occupation. Workers' compensation will be granted, however, when the job contributes to the risk or aggravates the resulting injury or disease. For example, if an employee falls on a machine after blacking out due to a pre-existing condition, the dangerous consequences of a blackout have been increased by the employer because the employee was stationed next to such a machine. Since the employer increased the risk of serious injury, workers' compensation will be awarded. Most courts, however, would reach a different result if the injury resulted from a fall onto the floor (without hitting any objects) while the employee was standing on a level surface. The injury following the blackout was not increased by the employment; it is the same injury that would have occurred if the employee had blacked out at home.

An employer cannot insist that all employees be fully healthy or normal at the time of employment. The employer takes employees as he or she finds them. If the employment produces stress, exertion, or strain that activates or aggravates a pre-existing condition, the resulting injury or disease is said to arise out of the employment. Workers' compensation will be awarded.

ASSIGNMENT

28.4

Examine the following situations to determine whether the injury "arises out of the employment." (See General Instructions for the Legal Analysis Assignment in Chapter 2.)

a. A caddie is struck by lightning while under a tree on a golf course during a sudden storm.

b. While digging a ditch, an employee is stung by a wasp, resulting in a severe fever.

c. A professor contracts infectious hepatitis due to exposure to an infected student.

    d. An employee is killed in an airplane explosion on the way to a business meeting. The plane exploded because of a bomb planted by another passenger.

    e. An employee had an ulcer before taking her job. She becomes worried about being laid off. The employee is hospitalized for further treatment on the ulcer during a period of depression about the possible loss of the job.

    f. An employee is a door-to-door salesperson. While at a home trying to make a sale, he asks the prospective customer if she would go out with him to a dance that evening. She breaks his arm.

    g. Two employees have an intense argument on the job over which employee is entitled to go to lunch first. Thirty minutes after the argument, one of the employees walks up behind the other and hits him over the head.

    h. An employee has a weak leg due to an injury sustained before she began her present employment. As part of her job, she is required to use a ladder to store supplies on shelves. While on the second rung of the ladder, she falls due to the weak condition of her bad leg.

CASE

Seitz v. L&R Industries, Inc.
437 A.2d 1345 (1981)
Supreme Court of Rhode Island

Background: *Beulah Seitz (referred to in the opinion as "the employee") sought worker's compensation for mental distress allegedly caused by her job. Under § 28-33-1 of the Rhode Island statutory code, benefits can be awarded if there has been a "personal injury arising out of and in the course of employment." The Rhode Island Worker's Compensation Commission awarded her compensation. The case is now before the Supreme Court of Rhode Island on appeal.*

Decision on Appeal: *Her mental injury was the result of the ordinary stresses of her job, not a physical or unexpected emotional trauma. Worker's compensation, therefore, is denied.*

OPINION OF COURT

Justice WEISBERGER delivered the opinion of the court. . . .

The employee had worked as secretary to the vice president and general manager of the Worcester Pressed Aluminum Corporation (Worcester) for approximately six years. The place of employment during this period was Worcester, Massachusetts. In 1975 portions of the Worcester enterprise were placed on the market for sale. One of the divisions known as Palco Products Division was sold to L&R Industries, Inc. (employer). At some time during the month of September 1975, the employer ordered the Palco operations to be moved from Worcester, Massachusetts, to Smithfield, Rhode Island. This change necessitated physical movement of office equipment, furniture, inventory, records, invoices, and machinery. The moving operation began on a Friday afternoon and was completed in a thirty-six-hour period. The employee and a former vice president of Palco Products Division, one Francis Maguire, were active in supervising and implementing the moving activities.

When Palco Products, under the new ownership, began operation on the following Monday, conditions in the new location were confusing and abnormal to a marked degree. Records were unavailable, the telephone service was inadequate, the previous tenants had not vacated the premises, and personnel were untrained. The employee sought to perform duties as office manager and secretary to Mr. Maguire but was also required to do janitorial and cleaning work and to protect office equipment from potential damage due to a leaking roof. She encountered difficulties in interpersonal relations with other employees in the new location. Her authority as office manager was not recognized, and office protocol was not satisfactory to her. She attempted to arrange a meeting with Mr. Maguire and other key personnel in order to work out these difficulties and to improve the organization of the employer's business at the new location. The meeting was scheduled for October 3, 1975, but because of the intervention of another employee, the meeting did not take place. As a result, the employee became so upset that she terminated her employment on the afternoon of October 3, 1975, and has not returned to work since that time.

Dr. Elliot R. Reiner, a psychiatrist who practices in the city of Worcester, had earlier begun treatment of the employee on June 10, 1967, for a condition he described as a depressive neurosis. After three office visits, the employee was discharged. The employee next visited the doctor on October 9, 1975, and described the emotional disruption she had experienced in association with occupational problems and conflicts during the period she had worked with the employer in Smithfield. The doctor diagnosed the employee's condition as an "obsessive compulsive personality disorder." The doctor stated, and the [workers' compensation] commission found, that the employee's rigid personality characteristic had been of long standing but had been aggravated by her employment from September 15, 1975 to October 3, 1975. The doctor testified that the employee had sustained an emotional trauma but had not experienced any physical trauma as the result of her employment.

The commission found that this aggravation qualified within the terms of G.L. 1956 (1979 Reenactment) § 28-33-1 as a "personal injury arising out of and in the course of [her] employment." Although the commission determined the aggravation to be entirely psychic, it found as a matter of fact and held as a matter of law that the conditions under which the employee had been required to work resulted in a malfunction of the body which gave rise to an incapacity to perform her customary work. Therefore, the appellate commission, with one dissenting member, sustained the decree of the trial commissioner and ordered that compensation for total disability be paid to the employee. We reverse.

Professor Larson in this treatise . . . has set forth an analysis of three broad types of psychic injury. 1B Larson, *The Law of Workmen's Compensation* §§ 42.21-.23 (1980). The first type is a physical injury caused by mental stimulus. An analysis of case law on this subject leads Professor Larson to conclude that the "decisions uniformly find compensability." . . . The second broad type of psychic injury is that caused by physical trauma. The courts, including this court, have almost universally awarded compensation for this type of physically produced psychic injury upon an appropriate showing of causal connection. *Greenville Finishing Co. v. Pezza,* 81 R.I. 20, 98 A.2d 825 (1953) (neurosis produced by traumatic loss of eye). . . .

The third type of psychiatric injury mentioned by Professor Larson is a mental injury produced by mental stimulus in which there are neither physical causes nor physical results. Professor Larson finds "a distinct majority position supporting compensability in these cases" but concedes that "[t]he contra view, denying compensation in the 'mental-mental' category continues, however, to command a substantial following." 1B Larson, *The Law of Workmen's Compensation* §§ 42.23 at 7-628 (1980). In this field, of course, it is difficult to compare holdings in various jurisdictions because of the variation among the statutory provisions. Some statutes require accidental injuries. Other statutes, such as that of Rhode Island, require "personal injury" without the necessity of an accident. . . .

The Supreme Court of Wisconsin has succinctly encapsulated the distinction in *School District No. 1 v. Department of Industry, Labor & Human Relations,* 62 Wis. 2d 370, 215 N.W.2d 373 (1974), in which it stated: "Thus it is the opinion of this court that mental injury nontraumatically caused must have resulted from a situation of greater dimensions than the day-to-day emotional strain and tension which all employees must experience. Only if the 'fortuitous event unexpected and unforeseen' can be said to be so out of the ordinary from the countless emotional strains and differences that employees encounter daily without serious mental injury will liability . . . be found." Id. at 377-78, 215 N.W.2d at 377.

In *School District No. 1 v. Department of Industry, Labor & Human Relations,* compensation was denied to a school guidance teacher who suffered psychic injury in the form of an acute anxiety reaction upon seeing a recommendation from a group of students that she be dismissed from her position as a member of the guidance counseling staff of the school. . . .

The courts are reluctant to deny compensation for genuine disability arising out of psychic injury. However, since screening of such claims is a difficult process, the courts recognize the burden that may be placed upon commerce and industry by allowing compensation for neurotic reaction to the ordinary everyday stresses that are found in most areas of employment. Indeed, it is a rare situation in which some adverse interpersonal relations among employees are not encountered from time to time. Employers and managers must admonish their subordinates and correct perceived shortcomings. The stress of competitive enterprise is ever present and attendant upon all types of commercial and industrial activity.

Great care must be taken in order to avoid the creation of voluntary "retirement" programs that may be seized upon by an employee at an early age if he or she is willing or, indeed, even eager to give up active employment and assert a neurotic inability to continue.

It is all very well to say that the adversary system will expose the difference between the genuine neurotic and the malingerer. We have great fears that neither the science of psychiatry nor the adversary judicial process is equal to this task on the type of claim here presented. An examination of the evidence in the instant case discloses that the employee's psychiatrist largely accepted her statement that she was unable to return to work. The patient, who had exhibited neurotic tendencies, arising out of family relationships as early as 1967, apparently suffered an aggravation during her sixteen-day period of employment with the employer. An analysis of the testimony in the case would clearly indicate that this stressful period contained conditions that, though scarcely tranquil did not exceed the intensity of stimuli encountered by thousands of other employees and management personnel every day. If psychic injury is to be compensable, a more dramatically stressful stimulus must be established. . . .

[The decision of the Worker's Compensation Commission is reversed.]

KELLEHER, Justice, with whom BEVILACQUA, Chief Justice, joins, dissenting. . . .

An overriding objective of worker's compensation legislation is to impose upon the employer the burden of caring for the casualties occurring in its employment by preventing an employee who has suffered a job-related loss of earning capacity from becoming a public charge. . . . An employer takes its workers as it finds them, and when the employee aggravates an existing condition and the result is an incapacity for work, the employee is entitled to compensation for such incapacity. Here, the commission, in awarding Beulah compensation, believed her psychiatrist when he testified that the office chaos that ensued following her employer's weekend move from Massachusetts to Rhode Island aggravated a preexisting psychiatric condition. Credibility and fact-finding are part of the commission's job. However, this award goes for naught because of the . . . imposition by my brother of a standard calling for a "more dramatically stressful stimulus." With all due deference to my learned associate, this standard represents judicial legislation. . . .

ASSIGNMENT

28.5

Can workers' compensation be granted in the following situations?

a. Smith and Jones are working on a scaffold when one end gives way. Jones falls to his death as Smith watches. Smith had the sensation that he might fall himself, but he didn't. After this experience, Smith is unable to continue in this employment as a structural steelworker. He blanks out and freezes, experiencing complete paralysis when attempting work in a high place.

b. Edward works as an assistant manager at a food processing plant. The last year has been very stressful. For three months he was temporarily laid off because of a small fire that seriously damaged the plant's electrical system. He was accused of stealing and of sexually harassing another worker. (After an investigation, the owners of the plant concluded that he was innocent of both charges.) Due to declining profits, the plant seriously considered filing for bankruptcy. All of these events led to Edward's having a mental breakdown requiring hospitalization.

FILING A CLAIM

States differ on the steps involved in making a workers' compensation claim. (See Figure 28–2 for an example.) The basic procedure is often as follows:

1. The worker reports the injury or disease to the supervisor and/or to the insurance carrier.
2. The worker receives medical attention.
3. The doctor, worker, and employer fill out forms provided by the workers' compensation agency and/or insurance carrier.
4. The worker receives disability benefits after a waiting period following the injury, e.g., seven days.

Each state has a statute of limitations within which the worker must make a claim, e.g., two years from the date of the injury or accident.

Most claims for workers' compensation are uncontested. No questions of liability for compensation arise. The employer or insurance carrier and the employee sign an agreement on the benefits to be received consistent with any state laws on the extent of such benefits. The state workers' compensation agency will usually approve such agreements as a matter of course. Some states do not use this agreement system. In such states, the employer or insurance carrier simply begins to make direct payments to the employee or to the dependents of the employee.

If there is a dispute, it will be resolved by the agency responsible for the workers' compensation program, often a board or commission. The procedure is frequently as follows:

- A hearing is held before a hearing officer, arbitrator, or referee of the agency. The proceeding is usually informal, unlike a court trial. Paralegals are often allowed to represent claimants at these hearings.
- A decision is made by the hearing officer, arbitrator, or referee. A party disagreeing with the decision can appeal it to the agency's commission or board.
- The commission or board makes the final decision of the agency. This decision can then be appealed to a court.

FIGURE 28–2 Filing a claim.

WORKERS'
COMPENSATION NOTICE
And instructions to
Employers & Employees

All employees of this establishment, entitled to benefits under the provisions of the Arkansas Workers' Compensation Law, are hereby notified that their Employer has secured the payment of such compensation as may at any time be due a disabled employee or his dependents.

IN CASE OF JOB-RELATED INJURIES OR OCCUPATIONAL DISEASES
The Employer Shall:

1. Provide all necessary medical, surgical and hospital treatment, as required by the Law, following the disability and for such additional time as ordered by the Commission.

2. Keep a record of all injuries received by his employees, and make a prompt report thereof in writing to the Arkansas Workers' Compensation Commission on blanks procured for this purpose.

3. Determine the average weekly wage of the employee and provide compensation in accordance with the provisions of the Act. The first installment of compensation becomes due on the 15th day after the employer has notice of the injury or death, except in those cases where liability has been denied by the employer. Additional compensation shall be paid every two weeks, except where the Commission directs that installment payments be made at other periods.

The Employee Should:

1. Immediately give or cause to be given to the employer notice in writing of disability or upon the first distinct manifestation of an occupational disease and request medical services. Failure to give notice within sixty (60) days after an accident or injury or ninety (90) days after the first distinct manifestation of an occupational disease, or to accept the medical services provided, may deprive the employee of the right to compensation.

2. Give promptly to the employer and to the Workers' Compensation Commission, on forms approved by the latter, notice of any claim for compensation for the period of disability. In case of fatal injuries, notice must be given by one or more dependents of the deceased or by a person in their behalf. (Act, Sec. 17.)

ARKANSAS WORKERS' COMPENSATION COMMISSION
Justice Building
State Capitol Grounds
Little Rock, Ark. 72201

All employers, who come within the operation of the Arkansas Workers' Compensation Law, and have complied with its provisions, MUST POST THIS NOTICE IN A CONSPICUOUS PLACE in or about his place or places of business, in addition to the prescribed notice as required by the Commission for insured employers.

ALLYN C. TATUM, Chairman
JOHN E. COWNE, JR., Commissioner
JIMMIE D. CLARK, Commissioner
OGDEN BERRY, Executive Director

INSURED EMPLOYERS make all reports to the insurance carrier in all cases where the employee loses time or is sent to the doctor. The insurance carrier then makes the necessary reports to the Commission. SELF-INSURED employers, State agencies, counties and cities under the State Plan, and public schools shall report directly to the Workers' Compensation Commission.

REVISED 6-1-76

FIGURE 28–3
Example of a schedule of
weeks of benefits.

Injury	Weeks of Compensation Benefits
Loss of thumb	60
Loss of first finger	35
Loss of second finger	30
Loss of third finger	25
Loss of fourth finger	20
Loss of hand	190
Loss of arm	250
Loss of great toe	40
Loss of any other toe	15
Loss of foot	150
Loss of leg	220
Loss of eye	140
Loss of hearing in one ear	50
Loss of hearing in both ears	175
Permanent disfigurement, face or head	150

Note: The schedule of weeks is based on a 100 percent loss of the body member indicated. If the disability rating is less than 100 percent, the percentage rated should be multiplied by the number of weeks shown. For example, a 20 percent loss of function of a thumb would be computed as 20 percent of sixty weeks, or twelve weeks of compensation benefits.

BENEFITS AVAILABLE

Most statutes are very specific on the number of weeks of disability benefits that are available to an employee who establishes a workers' compensation claim. For an example, see Figure 28–3.

The weekly disability benefit is usually based on a percentage of the employee's weekly pay over a designated period of time. The percentage is often 66⅔ percent. This benefit is in addition to the cost of medical services. Different benefit periods, percentages, and amounts are provided depending on which of the following the employee has suffered:

- permanent total disability
- temporary total disability
- permanent partial disability
- temporary partial disability
- disfigurement
- death

TORT CLAIMS AGAINST THIRD PARTIES

As we have seen, a covered injured worker cannot sue his or her employer for negligence when the benefits of workers' compensation are available. Tort litigation between employer and employee is barred in such cases. This does not mean, however, that all tort cases are eliminated. It still may be possible to bring a tort action against a third party involved in the worker's injury. For example:

- A worker is injured on defective machinery. Although a suit against the employer is not possible, a products liability suit (see Chapter 19) against the machinery's manufacturer is possible.

- An injured worker files a workers' compensation claim. The workers' compensation insurance carrier fails to process the worker's claim in a reasonable and timely manner. A bad faith action (see Chapter 26) against the carrier is possible.

Attorney fees in workers' compensation are often not large enough to entice attorneys to take workers' compensation cases. Yet, an attorney may become very interested in handling a workers' compensation case if the attorney sees the possibility of suing a deep pocket third party in a related tort case that is not barred by the workers' compensation statute.

REFORM

Every state has expressed concern about the high cost of workers' compensation insurance. There are companies that leave a state that has a reputation for excessive costs. Employers may feel that a particular state is too generous in the amount of workers' compensation benefits available and too lax in preventing fraud in the filing of workers' compensation claims. Some states have responded by enacting a variety of reforms[9] such as:

- no longer awarding benefits for mental or psychological disorders unless they are the result of an injury
- eliminating cost-of-living adjustments
- denying benefits to a worker who cannot identify the day and time of injury
- establishing a special fund to pay for teams that go after fraudulently filed applications

Although many of these reforms are the result of deep frustration, no one is thinking about eliminating workers' compensation. A return to the tort system as the sole vehicle to obtain compensation for injured workers is out of the question.

SUMMARY

Traditional negligence actions brought by employees injured on the job were often won by employers who used the defenses of contributory negligence, assumption of the risk, or the fellow-employee rule. An alternative remedy is workers' compensation, which is a form of strict liability, because recovery is not dependent on establishing the negligence of the employer. To be covered, the injury or disease must arise out of and occur in the course of employment.

Generally, injuries off the premises while going to or coming back from work or lunch are not within the course of employment and hence are not covered. Injuries that occur while on a mixed-purpose trip are covered if the trip is primarily business, because the trip would have been made even if the employee did not also have a personal purpose in making the trip. But an injury that occurs during a personal detour while on a business trip is not covered.

An employee who is the innocent victim of horseplay is covered, but not the employee who participated in or instigated the horseplay, unless the horseplay was a very minor departure from normal work responsibility or had become customary. The employee's own misconduct is usually not a bar to recovery unless it amounted to a willful failure to use a safety device. An injury that results from misconduct in the method of doing a job is covered, whereas one that results from

---

[9]Michael Quint, *Crackdown on Job-Injury Costs*, N.Y. Times, March 16, 1995, at C1.

misconduct in what the employee has been asked to do, or the objective of the job, is not. Whether there is coverage for an injury that occurs while an employee is engaged in personal comfort on the job, e.g., during a break, depends on factors such as whether the injury occurred on the premises, within an authorized area for the activity, and within working hours.

Courts use different tests to determine whether the injury arose out of, and hence was caused by, the employment. The most common is the increased-risk test, whereby the risk of injury to the employee is quantitatively greater than the risk of that injury to nonemployees. An injury that results from an act of nature is covered if the job increased the risk of that injury occurring. The same is true of injuries incurred from street risks. An employee who is injured from an assault and battery or a fight is covered if the event was connected with the employment. Workers' compensation does not cover pre-existing injury or disease, but does cover their aggravation due to the job.

Claims are made to the employer, to the insurance carrier, or both. If the claim is disputed, the workers' compensation agency will attempt to resolve it. If this is unsuccessful, the claim can be appealed in court.

When workers' compensation applies, tort actions between employer and employee are barred. There may, however, be tort actions that can still be brought against third parties such as a products liability suit against the manufacturer of a machine that caused the worker's on-the-job injury. Most of the efforts to reform workers' compensation have centered on reducing the number of fraudulent claims filed by workers.

KEY TERMS

workers' compensation   568
contributory negligence   569
assumption of the risk   569
fellow-employee rule   569
vice principal   569
strict liability   569
no-fault system   569
self-insurance   569
arise out of   570

in the course of   570
going-and-coming rule   571
incident to the job   571
mixed-purpose trip   571
dual-purpose trip   571
willful   571
objective   572
method   572
peculiar-risk test   576

increased-risk test   576
positional-risk test   576
proximate-cause test   576
actual-risk test   576
act of God   576
aggravated   577
pre-existing injuries or
    diseases   577

C H A P T E R

29

Settlement

CHAPTER OUTLINE

- Introduction
- Paralegal Roles During Settlement
- Settlement Precis
- Settlement Brochure

INTRODUCTION

The vast majority of legal disputes are settled in one form or another without the need for a complete trial. In fact, the moment a case is initiated, the opposing attorneys are usually thinking about the possibilities of **settlement**. There are substantial incentives for the parties to settle, such as the enormity of the cost of a trial and of the amount of time needed to complete the litigation through the appeal process.

This chapter presents two documents used by attorneys to encourage settlement—the settlement precis[1] and the settlement brochure. They are documents presented by one attorney to the other side and to the insurance company in an effort to settle the case. A **settlement precis** is a relatively brief document used by a party to advocate a settlement. It states an amount the party is willing to settle the case for. To support this request, the precis summarizes facts, theories of recovery, medical expenses, lost wages or profits, and other components of damages. If the document is more elaborate, it is often called a **settlement brochure.**

PARALEGAL ROLES DURING SETTLEMENT

There are a number of important roles that a paralegal can play to assist the attorney during settlement efforts. For an overview, see Figure 29–1.

SETTLEMENT PRECIS

Lawyers are constantly reminded that theirs is "a profession, not a business." Unfortunately, this plea for competence and high ethical standards has been interpreted by some to mean that lawyers should give no thought to the economic realities of their profession. Obviously, a case with a potential settlement value of less than ten thousand dollars cannot be handled in the same fashion as one with a settlement value of ten or twenty times that much. The client is concerned with the net amount of the settlement. A lawyer who diverts a substantial percentage of that settlement for photographs, plats, etc., when the potential of the case does not deserve it, is guilty of dissipating his or her time and the money of his or her client. Neither client nor lawyer can afford to swat flies with sledgehammers.

But the smaller case has the same need of effective presentation as the larger one. Some format should be adopted that will have the advantages of a persuasive disclosure without the expense of time and money in its preparation.

The use of a *settlement precis* seeks to meet that need. Its primary purpose is to present the claim in as persuasive a fashion as possible. It is divided into six main sections:

- identity of the plaintiff
- facts of the case
- theories of liability
- medical
- expenses
- analysis of evaluation

The preparation of such a precis has two secondary advantages: it will discipline lawyers to analyze their liability, marshall their evidence, and appraise the case; and it will provide a dress rehearsal for trial in the event that efforts at settlement are fruitless.

---

[1]The discussion and illustration of a settlement precis is taken in large part from J. Jeans, *Trial Advocacy* 549–53 (2d ed. 1993).

- Make sure you have the name, address, phone number, fax number, and e-mail address of the insurance adjuster assigned to your case.
- Make sure the insurance adjuster has the name, address, social security number, and phone number of the client.
- Maintain the office tickler system containing reminder calendar dates such as the date the statute of limitations is scheduled to run, deposition appointments, and important medical appointments of the client.
- Obtain waiver of confidentiality letters or forms from client that will authorize you to obtain medical files and other personal records of the client.
- Continue collecting medical records from client's past medical history and for the current case.
- Collect records relevant to the client's loss of income, e.g., current wage stubs, salary and fringe benefits history, past tax returns.
- Arrange for witness statements to be taken.
- Arrange for photographs to be taken of client's injury, accident scene, and property damage.
- Every few weeks send a brief letter to the insurance adjuster explaining the status of the case, particularly the client's medical condition and care received. (Attach copies of bills.)
- Contact the client regularly to ensure that he or she is following the prescribed medical treatment.
- Authenticate all medical records and bills.
- Research jury verdict awards to assess settlement range for this kind of case. (Check the Internet as well as commercial databases of organizations such as the American Trial Lawyers Association available on WESTLAW and LEXIS.)
- Help prepare or design life activity charts that provide a graphic presentation of the kinds of activities the client enjoyed before the injury as opposed to now.
- Help draft the demand package through the settlement precis or settlement brochure.
- Draft the cover letter for the settlement precis or settlement brochure.
- Contact insurance adjuster to confirm his or her receipt of documents sent such as medical reports, settlement precis, or settlement brochure.
- Contact the insurance adjuster to request a status report on the insurer's response to the settlement demand.

FIGURE 29–1 Paralegal roles during settlement.[2]

Settlement Precis—Illustration

Identity of the Plaintiff

Social History   Sharon Williams was born July 10, 1985, the fourth of four children born to John and Virginia Williams. The family lives at 2305 Grand Vista, Columbus, Missouri. Mr. Williams is employed as a machinist at Eagle Air Craft Co., a position he has held for six years.

Sharon is a student in the second grade of Middleton Grade School. She is a member of Girl Scout Troop 378 and is a member of the YMCA girl's swimming team.

Medical History   Sharon had a normal prenatal history and a normal birth. She has been attended by Dr. Grant Fry, a pediatrician, from birth. She has suffered from the childhood diseases of chicken pox and measles. She has never suffered any disability to her lower limbs and has never sustained any injuries to her legs, back, or spine. Dr. Fry's medical report is attached.

---

[2]Adapted from Melynda Hill-Teter, *Building the Perfect PI Settlement Demand Package*, 15 Legal Assistant Today 70 (July/August 1998) and Lori R. Hoesing, *The Settlement Brochure*, 10 In Brief 5 (Nebraska Association of Legal Assistants, May, 1990).

Facts of the Case On April 5, 1992, Sharon was en route from her home to school. The attached police report confirms that the day was clear and warm and the streets were dry. Sharon was by herself and crossing Grand Avenue at its intersection with Washington Street moving westwardly from the southeast to the southwest corner approximately six feet south of the south curb line and within the designated crosswalk. Grand Avenue is forty feet wide with two lanes of traffic moving in each direction. It is straight and level and surfaced with asphalt. There were no cars parked within sixty feet of the intersection. A sign located one hundred feet south of the intersection on Grand has a legend "Caution Children." A police report confirming the description of the scene of the accident is attached.

Sharon was struck by the north bound automobile of defendant at a point five feet from the center line. The attached photographs show the following:

Photo 1: skid marks ten feet long, blood on street.

Photo 2: damage to left headlight.

Sharon states that when she left the southeast corner of the intersection the light was in her favor. She never looked at the light again. She walked at a normal pace until she was hit. She was looking forward and never saw or heard the defendant's automobile. The accident occurred at 8:35 A.M. The school is two blocks away and convenes at 8:45 A.M.

A statement taken from the defendant, a copy of which is attached, acknowledges that he didn't see the plaintiff until she was fifteen feet from him and that his automobile came to a stop twenty feet after impact.

Theories of Recovery The plaintiff has three theories of recovery:

1. that defendant violated a red light
2. that defendant failed to keep a lookout
3. that defendant failed to exercise the highest degree of care to bring his automobile to a stop or slacken after plaintiff came into a position of immediate danger

The proof of the first theory is supported by plaintiff's testimony that when she left the curb the light was green for westbound traffic. By reason of the plaintiff's age, the court might decide not to permit her to testify. In that event, the defendant's failure to keep a lookout could be submitted as an alternate theory of recovery. Defendant has acknowledged that he didn't see plaintiff until he was fifteen feet away from her and she was already in his path. This would place Sharon at least twelve feet from the curb. The court will judicially notice that the pace of walk is approximately two or three miles an hour or 2.9 to 4.4 feet per second. *Wofford v. St. Louis Public Service Co., Mo.,* 252 S.W.2d 529. Sharon was in the street and visible to defendant for almost three seconds before the accident. At defendant's acknowledged speed of twenty-five miles per hour, he was traveling at approximately thirty-six feet per second or was approximately one hundred feet away when he should have seen Sharon. He was further alerted by the warning sign as he approached the intersection.

By reason of her age, it is questionable whether Sharon would be held responsible for her own actions. *Mallot v. Harvey,* 199 Mo. App. 615, 204 S.W. 940; *Quirk v. Metropolitan St. Ry. Co.,* 200 Mo. App. 585, 210 S.W. 103.

In the event Sharon could be held accountable for not maintaining a proper lookout, a third theory of recovery is available: defendant's failure to stop or slacken after plaintiff came into a position of immediate danger. By defendant's admission, he came to a stop twenty feet after the impact and he did not attempt evasive action until he was fifteen feet from Sharon; therefore, his overall stopping distance was thirty-five feet. A jury could find that by reason of Sharon's obliviousness that she was in immediate danger as she approached the path of the vehicle and when defendant's automobile was more than the thirty-five feet that was available to bring his vehicle to a stop.

The skid marks indicate that no slackening took place until the defendant's vehicle was within ten feet of the impact. The damage to the automobile indicates it was the left front headlight which struck Sharon. Sharon was within two feet of safety beyond the path of the car when she was struck. Moving at 4.4 feet per second, in one-half second she would have escaped injury. From this the jury could assume that a failure to slacken at an earlier time was the proximate cause of the injury.

Medical The police report states that Sharon was "bleeding about the face and mouth" complaining of "pain in the right hip." She was taken by police cruiser to Welfare Hospital where it was discovered that she had suffered the loss of a front upper left tooth which was permanent, a laceration of the lip necessitating six stitches, and a bruise of the right hip. Portions of the hospital record are attached. She was examined by her pediatrician, Dr. Fry, who referred her to Dr. William Jones, a dentist, for examination. He confirms the loss of the permanent tooth and outlines the dental prostheses which will be needed throughout her growth stage and into adulthood. His report is attached. The stitches were removed after six days by Dr. Fry, leaving a hairline scar one-fourth inch long near the upper lip.

Expenses

Emergency room Welfare Hospital	$1,250
Dr. Grant Fry	$750
Dr. William Jones	$550
Anticipated treatment	$4,000

Analysis of Evaluation

The loss of the tooth is permanent and will necessitate special prophylactic care to maintain the prosthetic devices which must be employed. The scar above the lip is discernible and will be permanent.

It is anticipated that a jury verdict could fall within the $25,000 to $28,000 range. If the case could be settled without further legal procedure, I would recommend a settlement of $17,500.

SETTLEMENT BROCHURE

Larger cases often require more than a settlement precis. If the case is of sufficient potential to warrant the necessary time and expense, a settlement brochure should be utilized in pretrial settlement negotiations. It will attempt to serve the same functions as outlined for the settlement precis, but on a larger scale.

A settlement brochure presents the plaintiff's case in a relatively extensive documentary form consisting of statements, reports, and exhibits. Generally, there is little oratorical flourish or emotional argument. The claims agent or representative of the insurance company receives the information "in cold blood" and can appraise the case rationally.

A well-ordered, carefully planned settlement brochure carries with it an aura of importance. The bulk alone suggests value. Plaintiff files might not be sold by the pound, but there seems to be some correlation between the bigness of the file and the bigness of the case. The preparation of a brochure demonstrates that the plaintiff has sufficient confidence in the magnitude of the case to warrant a detailed presentation. It immediately creates an impression of importance.

Settlement Brochure—
Illustration

DEMAND FOR SETTLEMENT

TO: ALL-RISK INSURANCE COMPANY

IN THE MATTER OF THE CLAIM OF

SARAH ANDERSON

CLAIMANT AND POTENTIAL PLAINTIFF

VERSUS

DONALD M. SWANSON

AND

JACK G. SWANSON D/B/A
SWANSON LOGGING

PRESENTED BY:
REX PALMER
ATTORNEYS, INC., P.C.
126 E. BROADWAY
MISSOULA, MT 59802
(406) 738-4514
ATTORNEY FOR CLAIMANT

TABLE OF CONTENTS

Disclaimer 2
Summary 2
Statement of Facts 3
— Family Background 3
— Prior Medical History 3
— The Collision 4
— The Injuries 6
— Medical Expenses 6
Evaluation of the Case 6
— Legal issues 6
— Damages 7
Conclusion 9
Appendix I: Good Faith and Fair Claims Practices
   in Montana 10
Appendix II: Diagnostic Pain Clinic Reports 12
Appendix III: Witnesses and Testimony 29
Exhibit A: Sid Silker, M.D., letter of Sept. 23,
   1986 34
Exhibit B: Keith Makie, Ph.D.
   Pain Clinic Director, letter of January 21, 1987 35
Exhibit C: Photographs Relevant to the Accident 36
— Photographs 1–9
Exhibit D: Accident Report, Montana Highway
   Patrol 40
Exhibit E: Oil Paintings by Sarah Anderson 41
Exhibit F: Newspaper Clipping Showing
   Sarah Anderson Painting Miniature
   Figures on Fingernails 41

DISCLAIMER

The matters set forth herein are stated solely for purposes of expediting possible settlement at this stage of this claim, and as such, are not to be used or referred to in any way should these matters proceed to trial, except as set forth in the paragraph immediately below. All photographs, attachments, and other exhibits set forth herein shall remain the property of Claimant and Claimant's attorney, the originals of which are to be returned promptly upon oral or written request. All figures utilized herein are subject to change without notice, as discovery and investigation are continuing, medical attention continues to be required, and all figures will accordingly require supplementation and updating at or prior to trial, and are not to be construed as final figures should these matters proceed to trial.

Potential plaintiff, Sarah Anderson, and her legal counsel, reserve the right to present a copy of this Settlement Brochure as evidence in a secondary action directly against All-Risk Insurance Company to recover compensatory and punitive damages if the Claimant and her legal counsel, in their sole discretion, deem that All-Risk has violated the provisions of the Montana Fair Claims Practices Act, Sec. 33-18-201(6), MCA (Montana Code Annotated), or the Montana common law obligation of good faith and fair dealing in insurance claims settlement practices. A review of applicable statutory and case law on settlement practices is set forth in Appendix I to this brochure.

SUMMARY

This is a personal injury claim resulting from an automobile collision in Yellowstone County, Montana. On August 20, 1985, Sarah Anderson was making a left turn off a secondary highway into her driveway. Donald Swanson, who was delivering a check for his father's logging company, Swanson Logging, tried to pass Sarah Anderson's vehicle in a no-passing zone as she was completing her turn. Swanson's pickup hit

Anderson's Datsun station wagon in the left rear corner, knocking it sideways and off the roadway into a power pole. In the wreck, Sarah Anderson was injured. For the direct medical costs resulting from these injuries, for the pain and suffering, for her continued impairment and future losses, she demands compensation in the amount of One Hundred Eighty-five Thousand and no/100 Dollars ($185,000.00).

Liability, jointly and severally, of the prospective defendants is clearly demonstrated by the facts set forth in this brochure. All-Risk, the insurer for the potential defendants, is therefore under a legal obligation to effectuate a settlement at or near the figure set forth above, or the policy limits of their insurance policies, whichever is less, within a reasonable period of time.

If All-Risk disagrees with the evaluation of this claim as set forth herein, it should respond within a reasonable period of time by providing Sarah Anderson's counsel with a written statement of its analysis and evaluation of this claim, together with its payment of the sum supported by its own evaluation.

For the purposes of this brochure, we consider thirty (30) days a reasonable period of time. This period will end on the 20th day of April, 1987. Thereafter, no further settlement negotiations will be initiated by Claimant, and Claimant will initiate legal action against the insurance carrier and its insured under the provisions of Montana statutory and case law, in an action for compensatory, general, and punitive damages in courts of appropriate jurisdiction.

STATEMENT OF FACTS

Family Background

Sarah Anderson was born March 10, 1941. At the time of this collision, Sarah was 44 years old. She resides with her husband, Ross and her family approximately one mile east of Laurel, Montana, on Devlin Road. Sarah and Ross have two (2) daughters, namely: Marsha, age 17, who still resides in the family home, and Teresa, age 20, who is currently residing in the family home but has lived outside the home on occasion. Sarah has two (2) other children from a prior marriage which ended in divorce: Jerry Landquer, who has been on his own for the past ten (10) years, and Roxanne Aist, who is married and resides in Red Lodge, Montana. Sarah has a close relationship with Roxanne and generally sees her once each week. Sarah also enjoys her relationship with her grandchild, Roxanne's daughter.

Prior Medical History

Sarah has had a complex medical history including surgeries on her pituitary gland, bladder, and colon. As well, she has had bilateral carpel tunnel repairs and a complete hysterectomy. In spite of this checkered medical history, she has always been able to return to her normal activities without restriction after a reasonable healing period.

The Collision

On August 20, 1985, Sarah Anderson drove her house guests, Lisa Weston and Lisa's children, Samuel and Laura, to visit a friend. After this visit, Sarah and her guests drove to the grocery store. After purchasing groceries, Sarah and her guests returned to the car and drove away from Laurel east on Devlin Road toward home, which is a little over one mile from Superior. (See Appendix III, Witnesses and Testimony.)

Devlin Road is a paved two-lane secondary highway. Sarah's home is immediately north of Devlin Road so that she must cross over the center line to turn into her driveway whenever she is returning home from town. When traveling east from town, Devlin Road dips down to cross a bridge, then immediately develops an uphill grade throughout the approach to Sarah Anderson's driveway and beyond. These physical characteristics of the road make passing very unsafe. The Highway Department has marked the entire area with solid double yellow lines, indicating that this is a no-passing zone.

On the day of this collision, it was daylight, approximately 5:00 P.M. Though the sky was somewhat overcast with patchy clouds, the road was dry. (See Highway Patrol's Accident Report in Exhibit D.)

At the time of the collision, Sarah was driving a 1975 Datsun 710 station wagon. She had driven this vehicle for some time and was completely familiar with its operation.

She is a cautious driver, and as a matter of practice she turns on her left turn indicator several hundred feet before turning into her driveway from Devlin Road. She is so regular in this practice that, a few days before this collision, Laura Weston asked Sarah why she began signaling her turn so early, referring to the fact that Sarah turns on her blinker before crossing the bridge.

On the day of this collision, Sarah followed her normal routine and triggered her left-turn indicator before crossing the bridge and before beginning the uphill grade to her driveway. Sarah slowed from approximately 45 m.p.h. at the bridge to approximately 3–4 m.p.h. at the immediate approach to her driveway. Immediately before initiating her turn, she checked her rear-view mirrors for approaching vehicles and saw none. (See Appendix III Witnesses and Testimony.)

After she had completely crossed the center line with the front tires of her compact vehicle completely off the paved roadway, Donald Swanson smashed into the left rear corner of Sarah's car with the left front corner of his 1980 four-wheel-drive Chevrolet pickup. (See photos 1–5 in Exhibit C.)

Donald Swanson was traveling at an excessive rate of speed (passing speed) with his vehicle traveling east in the passing lane when he collided with Sarah Anderson's vehicle. At the time of the collision, he was on an errand, delivering a check for his father Jack G. Swanson, d/b/a Swanson Logging.

If Donald Swanson had remained in his own lane of traffic, there would have been no collision even at his excessive rate of speed.

Donald Swanson left skid marks of over 60 feet prior to the point of impact. After impact, his vehicle continued to skid, leaving skid marks with a total length of approximately 119 feet. The impact of the collision threw Sarah Anderson's vehicle into a violent spin, off the roadway, and into a telephone pole approximately 65 feet from the point of impact. The force of the impact and the sudden stop against the telephone pole was so great that it broke the front passenger's seat belt and threw Lisa Weston completely out of the vehicle. Fortunately for Sarah Anderson, her seat belt did not break. Nevertheless, she was seriously injured when the car smashed into the telephone pole at precisely the point where her shoulder and left side were inside the car.

The Anderson vehicle was a total loss. (See photos 1–4 in Exhibit C.)

The Injuries

The hospital records and medical reports now in your possession, as well as the medical reports that have been furnished to you herewith, are self-explanatory as to the injuries received. Basically, Sarah sustained musculo-skeletal strain and chronic myofascitis of the left shoulder and neck region. As well, her dentures were broken, and she suffered an injury to her left side temporomandibular joint. The above were apparently the direct result of the rear-end collision and her subsequent left side contact with the telephone pole. She also required the surgical repair of a rectocele. Sarah had suffered a previous rectocele which had required surgical repair, and this recurrence was apparently due to the pressure exerted on her abdomen by her seat belt.

Immediately following the accident, Sarah was admitted to Billings Community Hospital on August 20, 1985, and was discharged five (5) days later on August 25, 1985. She was subsequently admitted to Deaconess Hospital on October 2, 1985 for repair of her rectocele. She was discharged five (5) days later on October 7, 1985. Over the eighteen (18) months since the accident, she has undergone an extensive regimen of physical therapy in an attempt to control her pain and return to her normal activities. Her primary treating physician, Sid Silker, M.D., was not satisfied with Sarah's progress and referred her to the Pain Center at Billings Community Rehabilitation Center for evaluation. (See Dr. Silker's Sept. 23, 1986 letter, Exhibit A.)

Sarah appeared for evaluation at the Billings Community Hospital Diagnostic Pain Clinic on December 9, 1986. She was evaluated by a team of six (6) professionals: Physiatric evaluation by Sandy T. Bickett, M.D.; Psychological evaluation by Keith

Makie, Ph.D.; Neurologic evaluation by Edward B. Runk, M.D.; Orthopedic evaluation by W. J. McConnell, M.D.; Physical Therapy evaluation by Todd Rockler, R.P.T.; and Social Service Intake Interview by Rick Wysil, B.S.W. The results of this diagnostic evaluation are attached hereto in full as Appendix II. In addition to the diagnostic team's results, the Pain Clinic Director, Keith Makie, Ph.D., provided a letter dated January 21, 1987, summarizing the process and costs of the Pain Clinic program. (See attached letter, Exhibit B.)

The Pain Clinic team unanimously recommends that Sarah seek out a highly structured, interdisciplinary, chronic pain treatment program such as that offered by the Billings Community Hospital Pain Clinic.

Prior to the accident, Sarah and her family routinely engaged in such activities as camping, gold mining, digging crystals, hiking, and searching for arrowheads. Through all these activities, whether summer or winter, Sarah would bring her easel and create portrait paintings. (See photos of her paintings in Exhibit E.) She particularly excelled in painting miniatures. Until the accident, Sarah usually entered the Yellowstone County Art Fair. One year she even painted small figures on people's fingernails at the art and craft show in Laurel. (See Exhibit F.) Often she sold and bartered her art work.

The pain, stiffness, and muscle spasms resulting from Sarah's injuries preclude her participation in the family's outdoor activities described above. The injuries also interfere with her indoor activities.

Now, Sarah is almost entirely unable to engage in her art work. The muscle spasms and stiffness in her shoulder and neck interfere with the delicate work generally required in her paintings. Aside from these physical restrictions, her ongoing pain substantially precludes the intricate detail and concentration required by her art work. As well, these restrictions and pain make it impossible to enjoy her art work even when she is physically able to do it.

Before the accident, Sarah was constantly sewing. She sewed for her family as well as for others. Sarah not only enjoyed sewing as an activity, her sewing saved her family clothing expense and provided her income from the sale of some of her work. This in turn gave her satisfaction and fulfillment from contributing to her family's welfare. Now, Sarah cannot even bend over the sewing machine and concentrate on her sewing work in any meaningful fashion.

The same is true of her cake decorating activities. Before the accident, she was able to engage in such activities to augment her family's income and to fulfill her creative desires. Now, her pain and physical limitations simply preclude any substantial participation in such activities.

Sarah has calculated that her income from cake decorating, paintings, jewelry, and sewing of shirts and coats for sale and barter has grown from between $700–$800 in 1982 to approximately $2,000 in 1985. From this we have calculated that her injuries have diminished her income by approximately $2,000 to date. These losses will continue into the future unless the Pain Clinic program is as successful as expected by Dr. Makie.

To date, Sarah has been primarily a housewife. Through her services she has nurtured and cared for her children and husband. Now that her children have reached adulthood, she could easily begin to pursue her sewing, cake decorating, and art as full-time occupations, or even work outside the home if she chose. But this is not possible because of the pain and restrictions she suffers from the accident.

Sarah's current diagnosis remains: musculo-skeletal strain and chronic myofascitis of the left shoulder and neck region, and chronic pain syndrome. We understand that the proposed treatment at the Pain Clinic will not relieve her of ongoing pain. The muscle problem and pain are probably a fact of life for her. However, with the treatment recommended by the pain evaluation team, the pain should no longer dominate her life. She should be able to substantially return to her previous active lifestyle by learning to manage her pain.

The next Pain Clinic starts April 27, 1987. As is evident from Dr. Keith Makie's January 21st letter, it is urgent that she receive the funds to participate in this or a similar program.

All indications are that Sarah's pain and physical limitations are a direct result of the accident, which either caused the particular condition or significantly aggravated a pre-existing condition such as with the aggravation of her prior depression and the recurrence of her rectocele.

Medical Expenses (through 1987)

As a result of the injuries sustained by Sarah Anderson, the following medical expenses were incurred:

Billings Community Hospital	$ 1,786.75
Yellowstone Co. Hospital	1,921.14
Laurel Vol. Fire Dept.	177.30
Jason Pharmacy	135.95
Doug Bard (dentures 1 TMJ)	850.00
Billings Radiology	125.70
Matterson Surgical Supply	40.00
Dr. B. J. Halst (glasses)	288.00
John Raysmer (dentist)	35.00
R. K. Hersh, M.D., P.C. (Radiologist)	16.00
Billings Medical Clinic	273.00
Deaconess Hosp. (Rectocele)	1,841.75
Family Practice Clinic	906.90
Vern Chase, M.D., (Anesthesiologist)	330.00
Neurological Associates	180.00
Medical reports	45.00
Billings Clinic Pharmacy	163.60
Edward B. Runk, M.D.	148.00**
Community Hosp., Diag. Pain Clinic	845.00**
Yellowstone Co. Hospital	253.50**
Yellowstone Co. Hospital	122.50**
Yellowstone Co. Hospital	45.00**
Billings Medical Clinic	20.00**
TOTAL:	$10,550.09

The sums indicated "**" have not yet been paid. In addition, as stated in Dr. Makie's letter of January 21st (see Exhibit B), Sarah is in urgent need of enrollment in the Pain Clinic program at a cost of between $25,000.00–$27,000.00 for a seven (7) week treatment program.

EVALUATION OF THE CASE

Legal Issues

From our investigation and our understanding of the facts, we feel that we will obtain a directed verdict in this case in favor of the Plaintiff, leaving only the issue of damages for the jury. We base this upon our research and briefing of the law.

Under Sec. 61-8-326 MCA (Montana Code Annotated), your insured should not have been driving on the left side of the roadway within the no-passing zone as indicated by the double yellow striping on the pavement. Furthermore, your insured was very familiar with this particular area; he knew that it was a low-visibility area with a no-passing zone throughout, and that several homes adjoined the roadway, requiring residents to enter and leave the highway to reach their homes. In this instance, the Andersons' driveway was clearly marked by their mailbox, which would call for additional caution on the part of a would-be passing vehicle. (See photos 6–9 in Exhibit C.)

It has been held repeatedly that the primary duty of avoiding a collision rests upon the following driver (*Custer Broadcasting Corp. v. Brewer,* 163 Mont. 519, 518 P.2d 257 (1974)). In a case directly on point with the present claim, a jury entered a verdict for the defendant where the defendant rear-ended the plaintiff while the plaintiff was turning into his driveway. *Garza v. Peppard,* 51 St. Rptr. 1922 (Mont.). In *Garza,* as with this claim, both vehicles were proceeding in the same direction, and both vehicles had passed over the double yellow lines on the pavement. The District Court entered judgment for the plaintiff notwithstanding the verdict. On appeal the Supreme Court affirmed the District Court and found that the defendant, who had been driving the following vehicle, was guilty of negligence as a matter of law for failing to keep a proper lookout. The Court stated:

Under Montana law, a motorist has a duty to look not only straight ahead but laterally ahead as well and to see that which is in plain sight. Furthermore, a motorist is presumed to see that which he could see by looking, and he will not be permitted to escape the penalty of his negligence by saying that he did not see that which is in plain view. *Nissen v. Johnson,* 135 Mont. 329, 333, 339 P.2d 651, 653 (1959); *Sorrells v. Ryan,* 129 Mont. 29, 289 P.2d 1028 (1955); *Koppang v. Sevier,* 106 Mont. 79, 75 P.2d 790 (1938).

Clearly, a person is negligent in either not looking or looking but not seeing if he claims not to have seen an object which is so clearly visible that all reasonable minds would agree the person must see the object if he were to look with reasonable diligence. *Payne v. Sorenson,* 183 Mont. 323, 326-327, 599 P.2d 362, 364 (1979).

Having these cases and other cases in mind, we strongly feel that this is a case in which the only issue will be the amount of damages to be awarded the plaintiff.

Damages

As to the question of damages, we have taken into consideration the initial hospitalization as well as the subsequent hospitalization for surgical repair of the rectocele, the extreme pain at the outset and during the initial recovery period, the continuing pain in therapy as well as the permanent pain, which Sarah hopes to manage with the assistance of the Pain Clinic program. We have also considered Sarah's lost income and changed course of life.

Sarah still receives treatment in connection with this injury, and even if the Pain Clinic program is successful in managing the pain, it is expected that she will continue to require intermittent physical therapy indefinitely. She will continue to suffer the effects of this injury, and we have considered her life expectancy, which at the present age of 46 is 34.5 years.

We have considered the substantial medical testimony indicating the relationship between Sarah's injuries and the automobile accident. We have considered the magnitude of medical expenses already incurred and those immediately required. We have adjusted our calculations downward to recognize the preexisting nature of her rectocele problem and intermittent depression.

We feel that in our evaluation of this matter, a probable jury verdict in this case would be the sum of Two Hundred Thousand Dollars ($200,000.00). This figure includes the following:

Pain and suffering: PAST:

10 days or 240 hours for the 2
hospital stays of 5 days each:

Physical Pain at $25.00/hour (muscular and
skeletal strain and sprain, tempormandibular joint
injury, headaches, surgical rectocele repair): $ 6,000.00

7

Mental anguish at $25.00/hour (restricted to hospital and trauma of surgery):	$ 6,000.00
Lost pleasure at $5.00/hour (inability to perform any activities):	$ 3,000.00
Remaining 18 months since the accident, approx. 12,960 hours:	
Physical pain at $2.00/hour (therapy, rehabilitation, pain related to muscle and skeletal strain and sprain, TMJ and surgery, etc.):	$25,920.00
Mental anguish at $3.00/hour (depression from pain and inability to pursue normal activities, 16 waking hours/day = 8,640 hours):	$17,280.00
Lost pleasure at $2.00/hour (limitations 8 hours/day = 4,320 hours, on sports, physical activities with friends, and self-fulfillment in pursuing established course of life, etc.):	$ 8,640.00
TOTAL PAST PAIN AND SUFFERING:	$66,840.00

Pain and suffering: FUTURE:

Sarah Anderson is 46 years old and has a life expectancy of 34.5 years pursuant to the life expectancy tables prepared by the U.S. Department of Health & Human Services. 34.5 years is 12,592 days or 302,220 hours:

Physical pain at $.10/hour (muscular and skeletal strain and sprain, myofascitis syndrome and chronic pain syndrome, future arthritis, etc.):	$30,222.00
Mental anguish at $.10/hour (includes concerns for diminished active physical relationship with immediate family and grandchildren, etc., for 16 waking hours/day = 199,465 hours):	$19,946.00
Lost pleasure at $.10/hour (this recognizes partial limitations in active sports and intricate detail work, and the need to be careful due to the injury, for 16 waking hours each day):	$19,946.00
TOTAL FUTURE PAIN AND SUFFERING:	$70,114.00

MEDICAL SPECIALS:

Past:	$10,550.00
Future—Pain Clinic:	$27,000.00
—Occasional physical therapy etc., @ $500.00/year:	$17,250.00
TOTAL MEDICAL SPECIALS:	$54,800.00

INCOME AND PRODUCTIVITY LOSSES:

Past—outside earnings and barter:	$ 2,000.00
—household activities:	6,000.00
TOTAL INCOME AND PRODUCTIVITY LOSSES:	$ 8,000.00

The calculations of pain, suffering, medical expenses, income, and productivity losses anticipate successful pain management by the Pain Clinic program as is expected by Dr. Makie in his January 21, 1987 letter.

8

Conclusion

As we have stated, our investigation discloses that the liability of your insured is certain in our opinion, and the injuries and actual damages sustained by our client are in excess of the amount of One Hundred Eighty-five Thousand Dollars ($185,000.00) for which we now offer to settle. In the event that you do not notify us to the contrary, we will proceed on the assumption that the offer of settlement made in this case is within the coverage of your insurance contract with your insured.

This offer and material is submitted in good faith and we expect you to carefully examine the material contained and honestly evaluate the same, responding to it in the same good faith with which it is submitted to you. Thank you for your cooperation.

Sincerely yours,

Rex Palmer

Rex Palmer
ATTORNEYS, INC., P.C.

Encs.

APPENDIX I: GOOD FAITH AND FAIR CLAIMS PRACTICES IN MONTANA

Public policy in the State of Montana encourages timely settlement of insurance claims without litigation. Montana statutory and case law history support this conclusion. Sec. 33-18-201(6), MCA, states:

> Unfair claims settlement practices prohibited. No person may, with such frequency as to indicate a general business practice, do any of the following: . . . (6) neglect to attempt in good faith to effectuate prompt, fair, and equitable settlements of claims in which liability has become reasonably clear. . . .

The above statute creates a duty that runs from the insurer to the insured as well as to third party claimants. The duty includes an obligation to negotiate in good faith and promptly settle claims when liability has become "reasonably clear." An action based upon a breach of this obligation by the insurer may be prosecuted by a third-party claimant after an action against the insured to determine liability.

The case generally cited for the above proposition is *Klaudt v. Flink,* 658 P.2d 1065 (Mont. 1983). Justice Daley for the majority wrote:

> We therefore hold that Sec. 33-18-201(6), MCA, does create an obligation running from the insurer to the claimant. When such an obligation is breached, the claimant has a basis for a civil action.
>
> The obligation to negotiate in good faith and to promptly settle claims does not mean that liability has been determined. Sec. 33-18-201(6) states that the insurer's obligation arises when liability has become "reasonably clear". . . . 658 P.2d 1065, 1067.

The *Klaudt* result was to be expected. In Montana, the State District Courts and Supreme Court have accepted the principle of third-party liability and the duty to deal in good faith in *Fowler v. State Farm Mutual Automobile Ins. Co.,* 153 Mont. 74, 454 P.2d 76 (1969), and *Thompson v. State Farm Mutual Automobile Ins. Co.,* 161 Mont. 207, 505 P.2d 423 (1973). *Klaudt* was immediately followed by *St. Paul Fire & Marine Ins. Co. v. Kumiskey,* 665 P.2d 223 (Mont. 1983); *Reno v. Erickstein,* 679 P.2d 1204 (Mont. 1984); and *Gibson v. Western Fire Ins. Co.,* 682 P.2d 725 (Mont. 1984).

In this rapidly expanding area of tort law, the relatively old federal case of *Jensen v. O'Daniel,* 210 F. Supp. 317 (D. Mont. 1962), hereinafter *Jensen,* establishes six (6) "elements of bad faith." In that case by an insured against his carrier, the carrier refused a pretrial settlement offer below policy limits.

The six (6) elements examined in *Jensen* and cited with approval by the court in *Gibson v. Western Fire Insurance Co., supra,* are as follows:

1. the likelihood of a verdict in excess of policy limits
2. whether a defendant's verdict is doubtful
3. the company's trial counsel's own recommendations
4. whether insured has been informed of all settlement offers
5. whether there has been a demand for settlement within policy limits, and
6. whether any offer of contribution has been made by the insured.

The *Gibson* court easily discarded the *Jensen* factors that were inapplicable, and relied upon as many of them as are clearly applicable.

> As the court said in *Jensen,* no one factor is decisive, and all of the circumstances must be considered as to whether the insurance company acted in good faith . . . [T]he failure of *Western* through its agents to follow established standards of investigation, evaluation, negotiation, and communication with its insured are the deciding factors upon which we base this conclusion . . . (682 P.2d 725, 737).
>
> Among the "standards of evaluation" mentioned in the *Gibson* decision is the fact that the insured's attorney evaluated the claim as being reasonably worth the amount demanded by the claimant in the insured's malpractice case.

10

The second issue is raised by the statute, namely, the requirement that bad faith be shown to be "general business practice" of that particular company.

[I]t is possible that multiple violations occurring in the same claim could be sufficient to show a frequent business practice, as would violations by the same company in different cases. (*Klaudt v. Flink,* 658 P.2d 1065, 1068).

The court concedes that its ruling in *Klaudt* could be viewed by many as "harsh," but offers the following rationale:

[T]he legislature has reacted to what it perceives to be an important problem. Insurance companies have, and are able to exert, leverage against individual claimants because of the disparity in resource base. Justice delayed is often justice denied. Public policy calls for a meaningful solution. The legislature has spoken and we, by this decision, breathe life into the legislative product. (*Ibid.*)

11

Billings Community Hospital Rehabilitation Center

Gregory M. Wies, EXECUTIVE DIRECTOR

January 9, 1987

Sid R. Silker, M.D.
Post Office Box 1045
Laurel, Montana 59248

Dear Dr. Silker:

Sarah Anderson was evaluated at Billings Community Rehabilitation Center's Outpatient Diagnostic Pain Clinic on December 9, 1986, by the following clinic team members: Keith Makie, Ph.D., Psychologist; Sandy Bickett, M.D., Physiatrist; Todd Rockler, R.P.T., Physical Therapist; Rick Wysil, B.S.W., Social Worker; and the following consultants: Edward B. Runk, M.D., Neurologist, and W. J. McConnell, M.D., Orthopedist.

Enclosed for your review are their reports, together with the Summary and Recommendations. If you wish to follow through with the recommendations, please contact the Pain Program Secretary at 248-2400 extension 3634 or by letter.

Thank you for referring your patient to the Billings Community Rehabilitation Center's Outpatient Diagnostic Pain Clinic.

Sincerely,

Keith Makie

Keith Makie, Ph.D.
Pain Program Director

KCM:pdr
enclosures
xc: Rex Palmer, Attorney

REPORTS

Billings Community Rehabilitation Center
OUTPATIENT DIAGNOSTIC PAIN CLINIC

December 9, 1986

SUMMARY AND RECOMMENDATIONS	Keith Makie, Ph.D.
	Albert Fremont, M.D.
PHYSIATRIC EVALUATION	Sandy Bickett, M.D.
PSYCHOLOGICAL EVALUATION	Keith Makie, Ph.D.
NEUROLOGIC EVALUATION	Edward Runk, M.D.
ORTHOPEDIC EVALUATION	W. J. McConnell, M.D.
PHYSICAL THERAPY EVALUATION	Todd Rockler, R.P.T.
SOCIAL SERVICE INTAKE INTERVIEW	Rick Wysil, B.S.W.

**SUMMARY AND RECOMMENDATIONS
(DIAGNOSTIC PAIN CLINIC)**

Billings Community Rehabilitation Center

PATIENT: Sarah Anderson
MEDICAL RECORD NUMBER: 0113075
DATE OF EVALUATION: 12-9-86
PROGRAM: Diagnostic Pain Clinic

On December 9, 1986 Sarah Anderson and her husband, Ross, participated in a comprehensive pain evaluation. Sarah was seen by an orthopedic surgeon, a psychiatrist, a psychologist, a physical therapist, and a neurologist; Ross was seen by a social worker. The reports from these various people are included; this will serve as a summary of their findings and the recommendations of the Diagnostic Pain Clinic Team.

It was the consensus of the individuals who examined Sarah from a physical standpoint that she was suffering from a rather long-standing problem with chronic shoulder, neck, and headache pain. Those who examined her agreed that the pain was of a musculo-skeletal chronic myofascitis origin and there was a consensus that Sarah was in the midst of what they would term chronic pain syndrome. Upon examination there was evidence of rather marked limitation and range of motion in her neck due to pain. There was a good deal of evidence of muscle tightness and some tenderness. There was no evidence of radiculopathy or other neurologic involvement upon examination and in general those who examined her from a physical standpoint saw her problem as mainly musculoskeletal with resultant problems in muscle tightness, deconditioning, and general inactivity. There were comments upon the large number of treatments that had been tried with Sarah to no avail and suggestions that an interdisciplinary, highly structured, intensive treatment program would be necessary to turn around the problem.

The Psychological Evaluation indicates that Sarah is a woman who, at the present time, is in a great deal of obvious psychological distress. She reports being extremely agitated and nervous. She clearly states that the stresses in her life that are enumerable at this time tend to directly contribute to her pain. She has many, many family and relationship problems with her husband, from her standpoint. She gave the impression during the psychological evaluation of being distressed to the point of

13

being desperate and not being in control of her life and this very high level of general psychological distress was definitely reflected on the MMPI. She appeared to be very motivated to do something about her problem because, as she said in the evaluation, she was coming to the "end of her rope," and very much wanted something to change.

In the social worker's interview with Ross, there was a marked discrepancy between Ross's report of the problem situation with Sarah's chronic pain and Sarah's own report. Ross appeared to be a rather poor historian and to be relatively uninvolved in Sarah's chronic pain problem. He continued to have past expectations of her even though she reports to be in great pain and is unable to do many things physically. The social worker commented that their relationship is quite traditional with Ross's expectations being that Sarah carry her load as a traditional wife. The social worker noted that Ross was quite ambivalent about supporting an intensive treatment program that could remove her from home, even if Sarah decided that was the best thing for her. The social worker questioned Ross's involvement and motivation to work with Sarah on solving this problem.

It was the overwhelming consensus of the Diagnostic Pain Clinic Team that Sarah seek out an inpatient, interdisciplinary, behaviorally oriented, chronic-pain treatment program. The team felt it was imperative that such a program be implemented very soon. They were concerned not only with Sarah's obvious decline physically and lack of ability to engage in most activities in her daily life, but also about the extreme degree of psychological distress reflected in the evaluation. The Team agreed that unless such an interdisciplinary, highly structured pain treatment program were implemented, Sarah's situation would continue to deteriorate to the point where she became more and more distressed psychologically and already serious family concerns would become even more serious. The Team felt that given Sarah's level of motivation to do something about her problem, she would be a good candidate for chronic pain treatment.

Keith Makie

Keith Makie, Ph.D.
Pain Program Director

Albert Fremont

Albert Fremont, M.D.
Medical Director
Community Rehabilitation Center

KCM/brm
dic 1/8/87
tran 1/8/87

PHYSIATRIC EVALUATION
(SANDY BICKETT, M.D.)

Billings Community Hospital

DIAGNOSTIC PAIN CLINIC

NAME: Sarah Anderson
MEDICAL RECORD NUMBER: 0113075
EVALUATION: Physiatrist Evaluation
EVALUATOR: Sandy Bickett, M.D.
DATE OF EVALUATION: December 9, 1986

Sarah is a 45-year-old woman who was involved in a motor vehicle accident in August of 1985. She reports that at that time she was pulling into her driveway when a four-wheel-drive pickup truck was passing in a no-passing zone and struck the rear of her car going approximately 80 to 90 miles an hour. The impact was sufficient to break the seat belt that the passenger was wearing and the passenger was thrown from the car. Sarah stayed in the car; she did have her seat belt on. The car was spun around and wrapped around the telephone pole on the driver's side and Sarah was wedged in the car and found herself wrapped around the telephone pole as well. She reports that she lost consciousness briefly and when she came to, the daughter of the woman who had been thrown from the car was calling out for her mother. Sarah reports being able to get out of the car though she felt like she was in slow motion and walked over to her friend who was injured and there passed out. They were taken initially to the Emergency Room in Laurel and from there to the Emergency Room in Billings. She remembers having no feeling in her left leg or foot at the time of the accident and for the rest of that night. She was initially seen by Dr. Coots who evaluated her and managed her during that stay, which he reports as a few days. She reports that from the moment she began to be fully conscious she had numbness in her left leg, but an aching feeling as well; she had an aching, burning pain in her left arm and shoulder and neck. She reports having been bruised over that entire shoulder and upper-arm region. She was sent home from the hospital and the pain was still there. She reports that the pain has continued to be present continuously ever since. It may wax and wane in intensity, but is always present in her shoulder and neck. Her leg and low back pain has subsided and only recurs once in a while. She notices pain in her lower back and leg when she has to do any bending or stooping. She attempted to pick some strawberries this summer and had the recurrence of her back and leg pain. She was unable to have a garden as she usually does.

When Sarah describes her shoulder and neck pain, which is her chief complaint, she reports that the pain is always present. It has a nagging, burning quality as well as a deep itching. It is not an itch which can be scratched on the surface, but is an itch or a tingle deep within. When she moves or stretches, she has a pulling, burning pain throughout that area that is being stretched. She has currently been instructed in some exercises for stretching her neck and shoulder and when she does those it brings on the pulling, burning pain, which does not subside during that hour. She also reports having headaches since the time of the accident, at least one a day. She reports she cannot remember a day since the accident when she did not have a headache. There are days when it is worse than others and some days where she is unable to function because of the headache and neck pain, but in general, the intensity waxes and wanes.

Sarah reports that things that increase the intensity of her pain include activity and stress. Activities that she describes that are particularly painful or pain-producing include doing paperwork, when she leans forward and concentrates. Vacuuming is particularly painful. She reports having been an avid seamstress prior to her accident and would finish two or three garments per day. Now, if she sews a half a garment she will hurt for the entire week. She does not do heavy housekeeping including mopping or vacuuming, but does do dishes, cooking, baking, and washing. Her husband is self-employed, so she does some of his bookwork on a daily basis. Sarah reports having tried multiple medications at the recommendation of her physicians and this includes Valium, which she reports "put her in outer space," but helped the pain. She discontinued that because although it reduced the pain she was unable to function. Xanax she will take on occasion when the pain is particularly severe and she is unable to relax and go to sleep at night. The Xanax causes her bad dreams and so she takes it only rarely, but will take it when the pain is severe. She reports having tried Naprosyn, which was not helpful, and is now taking Clinoril, which she finds somewhat better than Tylenol. In addition to the medications which she has tried, she has also tried physical therapy. The ultrasound helped and made her feel better and lasted approximately one-half an hour. She has tried hot baths and hot showers and finds that if she can lie down in the tub and relax and get the water as hot as possible, this will help for a short period of time. She had a Cortisone injection into

15

her left shoulder by Dr. Todd on two occasions, both of which helped; however, she is fearful of having too much Cortisone and Dr. Todd warned against having too many injections. She was seen by Dr. Dowell, who placed her on exercises for stretching, which she is supposed to do on an hourly basis. However, the exercise consistently makes her worse and so she is reluctant to do it hourly and does it somewhat less than that.

Sarah Anderson reports that her sleeping has been poor since the time of the accident. She reports she cannot remember sleeping through a whole night and is up three or four times a night because of the pain waking her, and she cannot get back to sleep. At these times, she will get up, read a little or walk around, or have a glass of warm milk in an attempt to go back to bed and go to sleep. She is finding that she will fall asleep during the day if she is sitting, because of her fitful night sleep. She reports occasionally staying in bed the whole day and sleeping essentially all day. This has only begun to occur in the last two months and she feels that this is an indication of her becoming worn out by the pain. She reports a bad appetite, comments that this seems unreasonable given her overweight condition, but reports not really having a good appetite or enjoying food, but that she considers herself a nervous eater and that when she is in pain, in order to make herself feel better she begins to eat and eat and not even taste what she is eating. She reports that after the injury, her weight got down to 155 pounds for a period of time; however, her usual weight is between 172 and 184 and has remained there for the last several years, and she is in that range at the present time. Sarah also reports that her social life and recreational life have taken a real reduction since her accident. She went to a Bible study both Tuesday and Wednesday nights and to church on Sunday regularly before her accident and now occasionally gets to Sunday services, which is a dramatic reduction for her. She used to visit people regularly; however, now she reports being anxious and hating to be around people. She finds they make her nervous and she thinks she rattles on. She also does not like to talk about her pain and yet people will comment on how bad she looks and this makes her feel worse. She also reports that she dislikes being around people because she has lost touch with the activities that she used to do and to do with them, and feels like she has nothing to talk about anymore. Prior to her accident, she liked to do a variety of activities, including camping, some gold mining, searching for arrowheads, hiking. She reports that she usually does a lot of activities with her family in the summer. However, last summer after the accident, she was left at home alone frequently while they went off to do their usual activities. She has done oil painting in the past, doing both miniatures and canvas. Since the time of the accident, she is unable to do miniatures because she cannot lean forward and concentrate or do the fine work. She has been unable to do her canvas oil painting because of the pain and the nervousness. Sewing was one of Sarah Anderson's other areas of release and enjoyment, as well as substantially contributing to the family's well-being. She finds she cannot do that anymore. She not only made her own clothing and that of her children, she also made jeans for her husband and did the winter coats for her adult daughters, as well as undergarments. The cost of doing it herself was so much less than the cost of purchasing that she and her family are experiencing a substantial burden by her inability to continue to do this activity and she is feeling a particular loss because this was an area of outlet for her.

Physical examination reveals a very short, stout woman in no apparent distress.

HEENT: The pupils are equal and react to light and accommodate. Extraocular muscles are intact. Sensation over the face is intact as are facial movements.
BACK: Back was examined and though there is no back deformity, the left shoulder is carried approximately an inch lower than the right without causing a spinal curve. Hips and pelvis are equal and level. Palpation of the back, neck, and shoulders reveals multiple areas of tautness of muscle and trigger point tenderness as demonstrated on the attached diagram.
NECK: Neck range of motion is limited in flexion to chin one inch from the chest. Extension is essentially normal. Rotation is approximately 60 degrees in both directions.

16

UPPER EXTREMITIES: Upper extremity strength is Grade V minus on the right and IV on the left including grip. These are all reduced because of the pain that they reportedly produce in the left shoulder. Range of motion of the left upper extremity is also limited by pain produced in the left shoulder area and limited to 120 degrees of flexion, 100 degrees of abduction, external rotation lacks 45 degrees.

NEUROLOGIC: Deep tendon reflexes and coordination are intact in both upper and lower extremities as is sensation to pin prick and light touch.

IMPRESSION:

1. Musculo-skeletal strain and chronic myofascitis of the left shoulder and neck region.
2. Chronic pain syndrome.

RECOMMENDATIONS: Sarah Anderson has had good episodic physical therapy, which produced short-term relief. All of the previous persons who have examined her have recommended physical therapy and stretch which have produced some positive results, but have not fully resolved this problem. For this reason, it is recommended that she become involved in an inpatient program that combines treatment for her myofascitis, tenseness, tightness as well as her chronic pain syndrome in order to achieve maximal results.

Sandy Bickett

Sandy Bickett, M.D.

STB: ajf

PSYCHOLOGICAL EVALUATION
(KEITH MAKIE, PH.D.)

Billings Community Rehabilitation Center

Psychological Evaluation

PATIENT: Sarah Anderson
DATE OF EVALUATION: 12/9/86
EVALUATION PROCEDURES: Review of records and questionnaires, interview, Minnesota Multiphasic Personality Inventory (MMPI)
STATUS: outpatient
AGE: 45
PROGRAM: Diagnostic Pain Clinic
EVALUATOR: Keith Makie, Ph.D.

Background Information

Sarah is a 45-year-old married woman who lives with her husband and family in Laurel, Montana. She was referred for this Psychological Evaluation, which is part of a larger interdisciplinary pain evaluation because of her long-standing debilitating problem with chronic shoulder, neck, and headache pain. It was obvious from the onset of the interview part of this evaluation that Sarah was extremely agitated and distressed. She came into the interview reporting that she was very nervous, that her pain is getting worse, that she had numerous family and personal problems, and was even having a hard time concentrating on the evaluation. She talked at a rapid rate, much of her thinking was confused, her speech was forced at times, she became quite emotional in several parts of the interview and in general presents herself as someone who is operating under a great deal of pressure and that pressure was steadily mounting to the point where she was feeling out of control.

17

She presented a history of her injury which happened in August of 1985 as a result of a motor vehicle accident. She indicated that since that time she has had rather excruciating and constant pain in her shoulder and neck and has had headaches. She says that this pain increases with any kind of activity, but definitely increases when she has problems with anxieties and worries at home. She said that nothing really helps the pain, other than taking medication and getting rest and quiet, which she never gets in her rather crisis-filled, tumultuous life. At the present time she takes Xanax, Tylenol Extra-Strength, and Clinoril. She says that these medications tend to help her somewhat, although the pain is usually there. She says that the pain does disturb her sleep but is not sure whether the disturbance is due to the pain, per se, or the many other worries and rapid thoughts she has going through her mind most of the time.

I did not have to ask her how the chronic pain had affected her life because she quickly launched into a long description of how out of control she feels and how awful her life has become since the accident. She indicated that before the accident she still had a number of concerns and problems, but was able to "roll with the punches" and handle the situations as they arose. She said that since the accident, her physical limitations, and the constant pain, she is just unable to handle the pressures in her life and finds herself wishing things like going to sleep and never waking up and then her family just all going away, which are very disturbing to her. She describes herself as a very responsible, caring, caretaking kind of person who watches out for the needs of everybody else before she takes care of her own needs. She again said that it was fine for her to operate that way before the chronic pain situation, but now she is finding she is "at her wit's end," she is losing control of her emotions, she feels that her life is a mass of confusion and she doesn't know which way to turn. All of this was presented in a rather distressed, agitated manner with Sarah shifting around in her chair, talking rapidly, and in general appearing as if she was having a difficult time. At several points during the interview she commented on the fact that she didn't know why she was telling me all these details because usually she presents a rather calm, stoic front when underneath she is seething with distress and agitation.

One of the things that came out clearly in the interview is that Sarah is a woman who takes responsibility for almost everybody she comes in contact with. She described her relationship with her husband as extremely problematic. She said that she does the work around the house, even though she has days where she cannot get out of bed; her husband still pretty much demands that she keep up the pace. She says at times she feels like a slave in her own home, and then again feels very badly for even having those unacceptable thoughts. She says there has been some recent trouble in her home because of a 21-year-old who has been living with them because he has nowhere else to go; this individual has gotten in trouble with the law and caused a great deal of stress and conflict in her life. She described her home as a motel for anybody who wants to stay there.

She doesn't feel like she has control over who impinges on her life. She said that she constantly works hard and doesn't seem to get anywhere and is feeling quite desperate. In general, it appeared that she was unable to draw any limits on what people in her life could expect from her and she did not know how she was going to get out of a situation that she definitely saw herself as getting into because of her wanting to help other people and meet their needs. There was a definite tone in the whole interview of her being trapped in a situation that she does not know how to get out of.

We talked about alternative treatments to chronic pain, including structured chronic pain treatment. She said she had heard about such a program and thought that would be exactly what she needed. She thought she needed to be removed from the very stressful environment she now lives in. She thought her family needed to learn more about her pain and the effects of stress on her pain and she seemed very interested in anything that could relieve what she describes as a desperate, intolerable situation.

18

TEST RESULTS: The Welsh Code for Sarah's MMPI is as follows: 83**1*76"429'0/5# F'K/L:

The first thing about this Welsh Code is the significantly elevated 'F' Scale, suggesting that Sarah is in a good deal of general psychological distress, which she is openly admitting. There are a number of extremely elevated clinical scales, suggesting a number of themes for this profile. The two high points suggest an individual who appears to be in a great deal of psychological turmoil. These individuals report feeling anxious, tense, nervous, fearful, and worried. They tend to be very dependent in interpersonal relationships and seek attention and affection; they tend to be depressed with feelings of hopelessness. They tend to present a large number of physical complaints of a vague nature. There tends to be a disturbance in their thinking and they often report memory lapses, poor concentration, and intrusive thoughts. A second theme is that of someone who is overly involved in her physical complaints and bodily functions; these complaints tend to increase in times of stress. There is also a suggestion of an individual who tends to convert psychological problems into physical symptoms. Other suggestions from the profile are someone who is quite distrustful and suspicious of the motives of others. There is a suggestion from this profile of an individual who is quite dependent in interpersonal relationships and tends to defer in decision-making matters, especially to males. This MMPI Profile fits in very well with my interview observations of Sarah, that of an extremely distressed, obviously upset, rather desperate woman who sees herself as trapped in a situation that she cannot solve with her own resources.

SUMMARY AND RECOMMENDATIONS: This evaluation indicates that Sarah has a rather long-standing, complicated, chronic pain problem that is made even more complicated by an obviously stressful family and social situation. She comes across as quite desperate, confused, and psychologically distressed. This distress definitely worsens her chronic pain, which then, in a circular fashion, increases her distress. My main recommendation at this point is that she seek out an inpatient, interdisciplinary, behaviorally oriented, chronic pain treatment program. Only in such a program could the multiplicity of factors contributing to her chronic pain problem be reasonably addressed. I would think without such an intervention she will continue to deteriorate and eventually the family situation will most likely collapse.

Keith Makie

Keith Makie, Ph.D.
Licensed psychologist

KCM/brm
dic 12/12/86
tran 12/16/86

**NEUROLOGIC EVALUATION
(EDWARD RUNK, M.D.)**

*Billings Community
Rehabilitation Center*

HX: This 45 YOWF is referred via the Pain Clinic for evaluation. Apparently she was injured in a MVA in 8/85. She was a driver wearing a belt, but apparently it was not tight. She was struck from behind by another vehicle that caused her vehicle to go into a spin and strike a tree. Apparently the tree was struck on the driver's door. The patient feels that her head struck a telephone pole through the open window and her shoulder was pinched between the seat and the door. The patient thinks she may have been unconscious for one minute, and was subsequently hospitalized for four days.

19

She had a CAT scan that was reportedly negative. The patient had residual neck, shoulder, and trapezius pain on the left, with continued symptoms until this time. This consists of a burning in the left arm, with some numbness in the hand. This is called a constant nagging pain. This is worse with bending, vacuuming, and other activity and better with rest. Heat seems to help, such as in the bath.

The patient has had an ultrasound, heat, massage, etc. via PT, without any continued benefit. Shoulder injection seems to help temporarily. Various checks in the past have shown spasm but no clear neurologic changes. The patient had nightmares on Xanax and amitriptyline. Imipramine apparently helped some, but it was DC'd for reasons that are unclear to the patient. Of the anti-inflammatories, she has had the best response on Clinoril but currently is only taking it intermittently, about three times per week. The patient is not currently in PT, and has never had a TENS unit.

PMH: The patient has had a transphenoidal hypophysectomy for a micropituitary tumor. She has had a prior hysterectomy, bil. carpal tunnel repairs, Marshall-Marketti procedure, and T and A. She has been treated in the past for depression. Current meds include the Clinoril, HCTZ, Premarin, K+, and occasional Xanax or Tylenol. The patient has no allergies. The patient had a grade eight education, but later received a GED. She is right-handed.

PH: Neg.

SH: The patient did sewing and painting for work in the past, is having difficulty pursuing these at the current time due to her problems. The patient's husband is out of work and currently is trying to get SSI for secondary to low-back pain and reported emotional problems. The patient denies use of tobacco and drinks alcohol rarely.

EXAM: Weight is 183 pounds. Height is 4'11". BP is 120-78. General: pleasant, obese 45 YOWF who appears quite comfortable at rest. Head: normocephalic, atraumatic without bruits. ENT: unremarkable. Neck: reasonably supple with full active ROM. Carotids 2+ without bruits. Lhermitte's sign was negative. Chest: clear. Cor: S1, S2 without murmur. Abdomen: soft. The patient had bil. CTS scars. The patient was very tight and tender throughout the left trapezius area.

Mental Status: The patient was alert and oriented ×3. She knew the recent presidents, was minimally right-left confused, but had normal praxis and naming skills. She read a grade 6 passage well with good recall. Serial 3's were well done. The patient remembered two of three objects after five minutes and confabulated on the third. With a hint she came up with it. The patient's speech was normal. The patient had a lot of nervous laughter. Cranial nerves: 1. intact. 2. fields and OKN's were normal. Fundi: benign. PERRL. The patient had full EOM's but seemed to have a minimal right exotropia at rest. Remaining cranial nerves are unremarkable. On motor exam, the patient has pain around the left shoulder girdle, leading to difficulty testing the biceps, deltoids. There was no winging of the scapula or other clear weakness. Sensation was intact to fine touch, sharp/dull, vibration, position, and graphesthesia testing throughout. A Romberg test was neg.

On coordination testing, the patient performed finger to nose, heel to shin, and rapid alternating movement tests well. Gait including toe and tandem was normal. Reflexes were 2–3+ and symmetrical with down going toes.

A: 45 YOWF seems to have a myofascial pain syndrome. I see no evidence of specific radiculopathy or other neurologic involvement at this time. The patient might respond to another round of PT, especially including such modalities as a TENS Unit. She might benefit additionally from imipramine as it has been used in the past. More frequent use of Clinoril might be of value as well. I will discuss the situation further with other members of the Pain Clinic team.

Edward Runk

Edward Runk, MD/jh
trans: 12/12/86

ORTHOPEDIC EVALUATION
(W. J. McCONNELL, M.D.)

Billings Community Rehabilitation Center

OUTPATIENT DIAGNOSTIC PAIN CLINIC
NAME: Sarah Anderson
MEDICAL RECORD NUMBER: 0113075
AGE: 45
PROGRAM: Outpatient Diagnostic Pain Clinic
EVALUATION: Orthopedic Evaluation
EVALUATOR: W. J. McConnell, M.D., Orthopedic Surgeon
EVALUATION: December 9, 1986

Sarah Anderson, a 45-year-old, Caucasian female, was evaluated on December 9, 1986 for purpose of the Pain Clinic Evaluation Unit.

She reported that on August 20, 1985, she was the driver of a Datsun pickup which was rear-ended by a 4 × 4 Chevy while she was turning into her driveway near Laurel, Montana. She reported injuring her left shoulder, neck and head as well as her left leg. According to her, she went to the Laurel Hospital where Dr. Gosten saw her and then was transferred to Billings Community Hospital. She further reported that Dr. Coots saw her upon her entrance to the Community X-Ray Department. She further stated that since that time she has been bothered by a lot of headaches, left neck, and shoulder pain extending down into the posterior aspect of the left arm to above the elbow; also to the front of her chest, indicating the anterior pectoral region.

In addition to being seen by Dr. Coots, she has also had neurosurgical consultation by Dr. Dowell, orthopedic consultation by Dr. Todd, and has also been seen by Dr. Sid Silker of Laurel. Dr. Silker is her doctor of record, according to her.

Past medical history is quite complex surgically as she reported that she has had a brain tumor removed by Dr. Grost in Seattle. She has had bilateral carpal tunnel three to four years ago, a number of D & C's, followed by a complete hysterectomy.

PRESENT CONDITION: According to her, she continues having frequent headaches, which she localizes by placing the palm of her hand to the occipital region, which she indicated progressed upwards and forwards, indicating the parietal-temporal regions, continuing into the frontal area. She characterized the pain as dull, deep, aching pain that she can partially alleviate when severe, by taking Xanax or Tylenol. She also reported other medical intake, including blood pressure medications and Premarin.

In regards to her headaches she denied any oral or auditory auras and denied any memory loss, type of seizures, dizziness, or syncope. She also indicated that the left shoulder bothered her and here, again, placing the palm of her hand onto the trapezii areas, extending up into the cervical region to the occiput on the left. She also reported that this pain extended into the posterior arm area, by her description and stopping at a level just above the elbow. She further related that the pain also extended forward, indicating the pectoralis area on the left. She also indicated that her upper back, and here indicated the infrascapular region, mainly on the left paraspinal musculature, bothers her at times when she is tense or with extended arm use.

She also indicated to this evaluator that actually her back is doing pretty well now and that she is not having any particular leg problem currently, at the time she was being seen here.

According to her, her last medical attention was provided by Dr. Silker who saw her approximately one month to her being seen here. Examination revealed a rather short, moderately obese female of stated age who did not appear in acute or chronic distress. She appeared awake, alert, and oriented and proved to be a good historian.

21

She was noted to move about without a visible gait disturbance and offered no complaints during the interview, with her sitting on the examining table throughout.

She was able to stand in the mode of attention upon request and the spine appeared to be in good alignment when viewed posteriorly and laterally. The scapular angles were noted to be level and scapular motion was full in all planes, as was range of motion of the upper extremities and the cervical spine. She produced forward flexion to approximately 60°, extension to 15°, right and left lateral flexion and rotation to 25° each. Motor power of the upper extremities, including grip, was considered to be within normal limits throughout. Digit dexterity was opinioned to be intact. There was no atrophy, in opinion noted, with special reference to the hand intrinsics.

She was able to stand and walk on toes and heels and tandem walk without apparent difficulty or complaint. Sitting straight-leg raise was negative, bilaterally, to beyond 90°. Passive ankle dorsiflexion was performed readily. Motor power of the lower extremities was considered to be within normal limits throughout, with special reference to the great toe extensors and feet evertors.

Deep tendon reflexes of the upper and lower extremities were considered to be bilaterally equal and active and produced without clonus. There were no sensory changes elicited to pin involving the upper extremities, with special reference to the left upper extremity.

It should be noted that while passive range of motion of the left shoulder was able to be performed fully, she was unable, according to her, to lift her arm in lateral elevation to above 90° and was able to forward elevate to approximately 120° with complaints of pain and pulling. At this point in time, palpation of this shoulder was accomplished and she indicated that the greatest amount of tenderness lay in the specific region of the bicipital groove on this side.

The question of left bicipital tendonitis is unanswered at this point and it may prove beneficial to form appropriate injection(s). Other than this suggestion, no other opinions to any further treatment, medically or surgically are able to be projected by this evaluator.

Following further X-ray reviews and file review, will discuss at the appropriate scheduled conference.

W. J. McConnell

W. J. McConnell, M.D.
Orthopedic Surgeon

WJM/brm
dic 12/16/86
tran 12/22/86

PHYSICAL THERAPY EVALUATION
(TODD ROCKLER, R.P.T.)

Billings Community Rehabilitation Center

PHYSICAL THERAPY EVALUATION
NAME: Sarah Anderson
MEDICAL RECORD NUMBER: 113075
AGE: 45
DIAGNOSIS: Chronic left arm and cervical pain.
PHYSICIAN ORDERS: Evaluation
PHYSICIAN: Dr. Sandy Bickett

FREQUENCY/DURATION: one time only
DATE OF EVAL: 12/9/86
STATUS: Outpatient Diagnostic Pain Clinic

HISTORY: This is a 45-year-old woman who was involved in a motor vehicle accident in August of 1985 in which she was hit from behind and spun around and struck a telephone pole. The patient stated she had immediate onset of shoulder and neck pain, and left upper extremity pain. She describes this pain as a nagging, dull, constant pain. She is worse with forward bending and doing desk work, lifting over 5 pounds. Patient said she is better with heat and ultrasound temporarily side bending to the right. She stated her upper extremity pain comes and goes, and that she has a problem sleeping and is up walking around, three to four times a night. She has been treated with stretching exercises, hot packs, ultrasound, and massage. Isometric exercises made her worse. She has been treated by an osteopath who gave her acupressure which temporarily helped relieve her pain. She has had two cortisone shots in the cervical area which she stated helped her pain for approximately one month. She currently has hypertension and is on medication for this. She feels that her pain is staying about the same over the last several months.

SUBJECTIVE: Patient's chief complaint is of dull, nagging, constant pain in her cervical area and left shoulder with intermittent radiations down her left upper extremity.

OBJECTIVE: Evaluation of patient showed her to have good posture with a slightly forward head. Range of motion of her cervical spine was approximately 75% in backward bending, approximately 90% in forward bending, within normal limits in left rotation and left side bending, approximately 75% of right rotation and right side bending. Palpation of patient's upper cervical and thoracic area showed her to be sore over her left sterno-clavicular joint and over the left clavicle, the subacrominal triangle, the sterno-cleidomastoids, and the scalenes on the left were all tender to palpation. The facet joints, bilaterally were tender to palpation and patient had a difficult time swallowing. Passive mobility of her cervical spine was difficult due to muscle guarding, but did show some significant tightness in the muscles on the left cervical and thoracic area. Temporomandibular test showed patient to have a late opening click on the left with a late closing click. She also had a late opening click on the right with an early closing click on the right. The patient has dentures and has had dentures since she was fifteen years old. Soft tissue testing showed her to be extremely tight on the left upper thoracic area and cervical area. Upper extremity range of motion was decreased on the left, both actively and passively, and internal and external rotation and abduction. Her strength was decreased to good-minus and sensation seemed to be increased on the left. Evaluation of her cervical spine was difficult due to her obesity.

PROBLEMS: Soft tissue tightness on the left in her upper thoracic and cervical area. Decreased strength. Decreased range of motion and increased sensation in the left upper extremity. Possible TMJ problems and slightly poor posture with a forward head.

GOALS: Not applicable.

TREATMENT RECOMMENDATIONS: Patient would probably do well with an intensive physical therapy program for stretching, strengthening, and mobilization of her left upper extremity. It is recommended that patient would do well with inpatient, behavioral modification pain program with extensive physical therapy.

Todd Rockler

Todd Rockler, RPT
12/10/86

TR/brm
dic 12/10/86
tran 12/12/86

23

Billings Community
Rehabilitation Center

OUTPATIENT DIAGNOSTIC PAIN CLINIC EVALUATION

NAME: Sarah Anderson

MEDICAL RECORD NUMBER:
   113075

PROGRAM: Chronic Pain Program
   DATE OF INTAKE: 12/9/86

EVALUATION: Social Services

EVALUATOR: Rick Wysil, BSW

SIGNIFICANT OTHER: Ross Anderson,
   husband

DESCRIPTIVE STATEMENT: The following information was obtained from a personal interview with Sarah's husband, Ross Anderson. He was a poor historian; he had particular trouble providing details or estimation of dates. Ross shared he is hard of hearing. He also stated he is "absent-minded" and if he is required to "think fast" he gets confused. Sarah Anderson, a 45-year-old married female, was injured in a two-vehicle accident during the summer of 1985. According to Ross, the other driver was at fault. Ross stated that Sarah was hospitalized for a number of days following this accident. He said she suffered injury to her left shoulder, neck, and upper back. As a result of the accident, Ross said she has had numerous surgeries and suffers from headaches.

Ross said Sarah has had a complicated medical history for the past twenty years, which has included surgeries on her bladder, intestines, and pituitary gland (he said she has had many other surgeries, but he couldn't remember them all).

FAMILY COMPOSITION AND SUPPORT NETWORK: Sarah and her 49-year-old husband, Ross, have been married between 20 and 25 years; this is the second marriage for both people. Ross indicated their attraction for each other was the cause of dissolvement of both their first marriages. He indicated this was a traumatic period for all parties involved; in fact, Sarah's husband somehow convinced her to go to Warm Springs State Mental Hospital for a month or so. Sarah has two adult children from her first union: Jerry Landquer, and Roxanne Aist, who is married and resides in Red Lodge (Ross adopted her). Ross and Sarah see Roxanne at least once a week. Roxanne has one daughter. Ross stated Sarah is very close to her daughter and grandchild and enjoys spending time with them. Sarah's son by her first marriage, Jerry Landquer, is in the Service and has been out of the family home for the past ten years. Ross had two children from his first marriage: his son died in an accident shortly after the divorce; his daughter Jolene, lives in Florida. He has little contact with his daughter. Ross and Sarah have two daughters, Theresa, age 20 who occasionally still resides in the family home and Marsha, age 17 who is still in the family home. Ross reports Sarah has close relationships with both daughters. He added they are having typical trouble with Marsha that one would expect from a teenager; he indicated he and Sarah both believe in physical punishment when they cannot manage Marsha in any other manner. Ross described Sarah as a good mother and stated she has very close family ties.

Ross stated his relationship with Sarah has had the "usual ups-and-downs," but "nothing terrible." He added they have always been able to overcome their problems. As far as communication between the two, Ross admitted Sarah probably feels he does not talk to her enough. He shared he tends not to discuss his feelings, but instead tends to keep things to himself. Ross said he and Sarah believe in traditional male/female values in their marriage, i.e., her place is in the home caring for the children and he is responsible for providing for their financial security. Ross added, "I'm in charge, I don't believe in a woman leading a family."

Sarah's father is deceased, her mother, Lisa Scoon, lives in Laurel. Ross stated Sarah sees her mother weekly, but does not believe they are terribly close; he stated Sarah's relationship with her mother has improved over the years. Ross said he believes Sarah's childhood was difficult. He said because her parents were divorced, the children (he did not know how many siblings she has) were "shoved around in the family." He believes Sarah's mother was physically and mentally abusive to her. He stated Sarah came from an extremely poor family. Sarah was born and raised in Wyoming. Ross said Sarah married at age 15 or 16; he suspects she married at such a young age as a means of getting out of her family situation.

Ross's father is deceased, his mother, Donna Anderson, resides in Laurel except during the summer when she lives with her daughter in Oregon. Ross believes his mother provides Sarah with much emotional support, but does not interfere.

Sarah apparently receives good emotional support from her sister, Lena Morgal, who lives in Laurel. Ross stated that she sees her at least weekly and they talk on the phone frequently.

According to Ross, Sarah has many friends, but none of them are particularly close. He has noticed her friends seem to come over less often; Sarah also does less with friends because of her pain.

Ross stated he has no one that he confides in; probably for emotional support he depends on Sarah.

CURRENT LIVING ARRANGEMENTS: Sarah and her family reside approximately one mile east of Laurel, Montana, on Devlin Road. They have lived in this home for the past ten years. Ross stated it is a two-bedroom, single-story home with a basement. They use the basement for storage, particularly of their canned goods; Sarah is able to go up and down the basement stairs without problems. They are buying their home.

Prior to her injury, Sarah was responsible for all homemaking tasks, including housework, laundry, meal preparation, and grocery shopping. Ross stated, as far as her homemaking duties, he always felt she enjoyed this work but now she asks the girls to share more in the chores. Ross stated the children do assist with cooking, dishes, and are responsible for their own rooms. He has noticed they are doing more of the home chores than they did before Sarah's accident. Ross stated, "I have never done housework, and never changed a baby's diapers."

Ross stated Sarah typically gets up around 7 A.M., at which time she may cook breakfast for Marsha (Teresa often does her own). After Marsha goes to school, Sarah may go back to bed. She then gets up around 8:30 and prepares Ross's breakfast. After that she does housework and may work on sewing projects for the children. Ross has noticed her housework is not at the level it used to be and he added, "she is not the greatest housekeeper." At noon Sarah prepares lunch for Ross. After lunch he is uncertain what she does with her time; he suspects she may lie down if the pain is severe. The evening meal is prepared by either Sarah or one of the daughters. Sarah tends to spend her evening time reading, watching television, or working on a craft project. She usually retires by 10:30 P.M.

Ross has noticed since her accident Sarah is less "energetic." He explained she still does the day-to-day tasks, but not all the extras she used to do. He has noticed she has given more responsibility to their daughters. When the daughters prepare a meal she usually sits in the kitchen with them and provides instructions.

EFFECT OF CHRONIC PAIN: Ross said Sarah's pain is constant; however, he has noticed the degree does vary. He is uncertain what makes her pain worse, but has noticed that when she uses her left arm during housework, her pain seems to increase. Ross believes Sarah's pain has progressively worsened. Ross said it is hard to know what her pain level is because she is not a complainer. He stated, "she doesn't tell me that much, and I haven't tried to find out." He believes Sarah continues to do her homemaking tasks even when she is in a lot of pain. He stated that Sarah has "an iron constitution." He added, "I don't try to keep her from doing her tasks, because I think she needs to as things would fall apart if she didn't." Ross stated her pain is primarily in her shoulders and neck area and that she is also bothered with extreme headaches.

25

He was uncertain how often she gets the headaches, but they are frequent. Unless Sarah has had an extremely bad day as far as her pain goes, she does not talk about it. Ross believes she has a very high pain tolerance.

Ross stated he can tell when Sarah's pain is worse because she becomes short-tempered with him and the girls, she grimaces, or she may hold the back of her neck or put her hand on her forehead.

Ross believes Sarah attempts to manage her pain by lying down with a pillow under her neck and a cold washcloth on her forehead, and with the use of medication. Ross was uncertain what type of medication Sarah is on, but he believes it is a muscle relaxant. He stated she is not taking any pain medication, as she does not wish to be "zonked out."

Ross stated there is little he does to assist Sarah when she is in pain. He said he seldom waits on her. Occasionally he will ask if there is something she needs. However, for the most part, he will ask the children to assist her. Ross shared it is emotionally difficult for him to provide the comfort she may wish.

Sarah is suffering from sleep disturbance due to her chronic pain. Ross said she changes position often during the night and she is up and down frequently. When she is up she may sit and have a cup of tea. Ross said she has been bothered with sleep disturbance for many years, but since the accident it has gotten worse. She is unable to sleep on her left side, due to the shoulder pain.

Ross was uncertain if Sarah's injury has affected her appetite. He stated he does not know what she weighs, but she may be losing some weight. He stated she has always had a weight problem and diets frequently. He believes she is 4'11" tall.

Ross believes the only way Sarah's chronic pain has changed her relationship with their daughters is that she is shorter-tempered with them. He stated the girls often complain to him about this, but he reminds them of what Sarah is going through. He said when Sarah is particularly upset with Marsha, she may slap her or hit her with a belt. Ross stated Sarah does not overuse physical punishment, nor does he believe this has increased since her injury. He stated when Sarah physically punishes Marsha, he believes Marsha "has it coming." He stated, "I sit in the background to see if it is justified." Ross believes Sarah has difficulty with Marsha because Marsha is "headstrong and talks back."

Ross believes he is able to understand Sarah's chronic pain because of the pain he has suffered in his back since he injured it skiing when he was in his twenties. Apparently because of his back injury, Ross has been self-employed for the past ten years so he is able to work at his own pace and for the number of hours he feels physically capable. Ross said when his back pain becomes severe he may be down for two or three days; however, this does not happen very often. He stated, "I have learned to live with it and know when to take it easy." He added he is uncertain whether Sarah has learned her physical limitations. Ross also senses because of his back pain he, too, is shorter-tempered. He stated, "If people leave me alone I get over it fast." When he is upset he tends to yell, swear, and throw objects. He stated he does not physically abuse Sarah when he is upset. He explained they used to fight a lot and in the early days occasionally hit each other; he added that this was many years ago.

When this worker asked Ross what he would do if their situation does not change, he indicated he can continue to cope and he does not plan to leave Sarah. He added he tends to look at the situation a day at a time, and does not plan ahead.

COMMUNITY AGENCIES AND TRANSPORTATION: Ross stated their family is receiving assistance through County Social Services and Human Resources.

Sarah is capable of driving; however, she often has one of the daughters run errands for her. Ross has noticed she does not want to go out of the house as much as she used to; he stated he is unsure why.

INCOME, FINANCIAL RESOURCES, AND MEDICAL COVERAGE:
- Ross stated his income varies from month to month, but probably averages around $500 a month.

- The family receives $100+ a month in food stamps.
- They are receiving energy assistance for their utility costs through Human Resources.
- Sarah's medical costs that relate to the accident are covered by the other driver's insurance, All-Risk.
- Ross thinks Sarah is considering applying for Social Security.
- Ross said their finances are extremely tight, and it is a stress area for the couple—he said that it tends to create friction between them.
- Sarah manages the family's finances; however, Ross oversees their money and makes the decisions as to how it will be spent.

EDUCATION AND MILITARY SERVICE:
- Sarah did not complete high school; Ross believes she was an average student; she quit school to get married.
- Sarah has her GED.
- Ross completed the ninth grade.
- Ross served in the Air Force for three years and received an Honorable Discharge.
- Sarah has no military experience.

EMPLOYMENT:
- Sarah has primarily been a homemaker throughout their marriage. Ross stated she has on several occasions worked as a waitress. This lasted for a short period of time as he was opposed to her working outside the home. Ross believes Sarah enjoyed working as a waitress, but stated, "a woman's place is in the home raising children."
- Ross has been self-employed as a "handyman" for the past ten years. He works four to five hours a day doing such things as plumbing, carpentry, welding, and furniture construction.
- Until ten years ago he worked as a welder. He held this position until he could no longer tolerate the pain. Prior to working as a welder he worked in the sawmills.

LEISURE ACTIVITIES AND ORGANIZATIONS: Sarah enjoys the following:
- cards (Pinochle)
- board games with the children
- sewing
- reading (romance novels)
- television
- knitting and crocheting
- listening to music (classical and country-western)
- working crossword puzzles

Prior to her injury she also enjoyed spending her time camping, going on short car trips, rock hunting, painting (oil and acrylics), and making jewelry. Ross has attempted to encourage her to do her art work, but stated, "mentally she can't get into it." Ross shared they do little as a couple. He said he tends to watch television a lot.

Sarah is a member of the Jehovah's Witnesses; she attends meetings at least once a week. Prior to her accident she attended Jehovah's Witnesses meetings five times a week.

PATIENT AND FAMILY COPING HISTORY: Ross described Sarah in the following terms:
- friendly and easy to get along with
- even-tempered
- optimistic
- poorly organized in housework and generally; this has been a friction area for the couple
- has always "bounded back" from surgeries; seems to endure "a lot"
- a humanitarian
  Ross has noticed the following changes in Sarah since her accident:
- mentally seems less able to tolerate the pain; Ross believes it may be too much after all of the medical problems she has had to deal with
- cries much more easily

27

- more irritable
- moody
- seems withdrawn

Ross believes Sarah copes with her situation through the support she receives from her family and her strong religious faith. Ross indicated he has always relied strongly on Sarah's optimistic attitude to help him get through difficult times. Ross shared he often feels anxious due to the amount of stress in his life caused by his inability to work, their limited financial resources and during peak work times, the number of jobs he has to do. Ross stated he had a mild heart attack some time after Sarah's accident; he believes it was brought on by stress.

HISTORY OF DRUG AND ALCOHOL USE: Ross stated Sarah does not have a problem with drugs or alcohol. He said at times he has been concerned that she may "get hooked on prescription drugs." However, he does not believe this has, as yet, been a problem. Ross shared that in the past he has been a heavy drinker; he believes in the past year or so he has decreased his amount of consumption. He stated, he at times uses alcohol to relax. When he drinks it is beer or whiskey.

Sarah drinks approximately three to four cups of coffee a day, and also often drinks black tea; she is not a smoker.

Ross indicated both his father and Sarah's mother were problem drinkers.

ASSESSMENT OF CURRENT SOCIAL SITUATION AND PROBLEMS:
From this report, Ross adamantly believes in traditional male and female roles within the marriage. He very clearly views himself as the head of the family and the individual who makes the major decisions. According to Ross it is out of the question that Sarah will work outside of the home because he does not approve of it. Apparently when Sarah has worked in the past she has acquiesced to his wishes for her to quit. Ross believes they have a strong relationship, although the communication is limited. He indicated there are some problems regarding their 17-year-old daughter; however, he minimized these problems by indicating they are typical teenage concerns. Ross and Sarah both subscribe to physical punishment when they feel their youngest daughter is out of line. This family does appear to be experiencing financial stress. Nonetheless, Ross does not consider it appropriate for Sarah to work to help ease the financial burden.

Sarah has apparently dealt with many medical problems over the last twenty years. Ross described her as highly resilient through all of her medical concerns. However, at this point he does not feel she is dealing with her injuries from the accident with the same mental strength and attitude she has demonstrated in the past. Ross is concerned she may "give up." Ross has noticed the following changes in Sarah since her accident: increased irritability, moodiness, more withdrawn behavior, and a change in her mental attitude (less optimistic). These changes, particularly the mental attitude, are probably very frightening to Ross as he indicated he has always depended on her to help him manage his own stress. By Ross's admission, his use of alcohol in the past has been heavy; it's possible he may revert back to that if he feels overwhelmed with the situation.

GOALS OF CLIENT AND FAMILY: Ross stated his primary goal for Sarah is for her to be more comfortable and for her to again pursue past projects such as her painting. Ross strongly indicated he does not plan for her to go to work (even though she has indicated a desire to). As far as her working goes, he said, "I just wouldn't let her; what I say is what happens."

Ross said they hope to receive a settlement from the other driver's insurance company.

SOCIAL SERVICE PLAN: This worker provided Ross with information on a residential chronic pain program. Ross was particularly troubled by the thought of Sarah being out of their home for six to seven weeks. He said it would be extremely hard on both of them. He was unwilling to commit himself to supporting such a program, even if Sarah would choose to participate. Unless Sarah is highly motivated to work in such a program (if one is deemed appropriate) and is able to solicit Ross's support, I suspect her chances of succeeding are slim. If Ross's perception is accurate of his being the final decision-maker, his support is crucial. If Ross's concern about Sarah's mental attitude and thus her inability to provide him with the kind of support he found uplifting is strong enough, this may be an issue that would push him to seek change. In general, I believe Ross would find the separation and the program highly threatening.

If Sarah takes part in the pain program, weekly sessions with Ross and occasional sessions with their daughters would be necessary to:

1. assist them to understand Sarah's chronic pain and behavior
2. assist them to understand their roles in Sarah's chronic pain
3. help them to understand the program's goals and expectations
4. help promote generalization of progress Sarah would make in a pain program to their home environment

Rick Wysil

Rick Wysil, BSW
Medical Social Services
12/18/86

RW/brm
dic 12/18/86
tran 12/29/86

APPENDIX III: WITNESSES AND TESTIMONY

Transcript of Telephone Interview Between All-Risk Insurance Agent and Sarah Anderson

This is Tim Taner recording a telephone interview with Sarah Anderson who is speaking from her attorney's office in Missoula, Montana. The date of this conversation is September 4, 1985. The time is 9:50 A.M. and we're going to be talking about an accident that Mrs. Anderson was involved in on or about August 20, 1985.

Q. Mrs. Anderson, would you give me your full name and spell your last name?
A. Sarah Anderson. A-n-d-e-r-s-o-n

Q. And Mrs. Anderson, you're aware that I'm recording this conversation?
A. Yes.

Q. It's being done with your consent?
A. Yes.

Q. Your age?
A. 44.

Q. You're married. Your husband's first name?
A. Ross.

Q. And what is your home address and phone number?
A. It's Box 336, Laurel, Montana, 59044. And my phone number's 248-6733.

Q. Are you employed other than as a housewife?
A. No.

Q. And were you operator of a car involved in this accident?
A. Yes, I was.

Q. What kind of a car is it and who is the owner of it?
A. It's a 1975 Datsun 710 station wagon, and my husband and I own it.

Q. What was the purpose of your trip that day? Where had you been? Where were you going?
A. Okay, we were, we went to a friend's house. Then we went to the store to get groceries and came home. And we were on the way home when this happened.

Q. What was the date and time of this accident as near as you can recollect?
A. It was on a Tuesday, August 20th.

Q. This year?
A. 1985.

Q. And the time?
A. About 5:00.

Q. And where did this accident occur?
A. Just right near my driveway on Devlin Road as we were, as I was almost turned in to go into the drive.

Q. All right. Where is this accident location relative to Laurel, Montana?
A. It's a mile-and-three-tenths from the Town Pump station.

Q. It's not in the city limits then?
A. No.

Q. It's in the county?
A. Um huh.

Q. And the county is?
A. Yellowstone.

Q. Devlin Road at this point, what direction does it run?
A. East and west.

Q. Is this a two-lane, two-way road or is it wider than that?
A. It's a two-lane road.

Q. Paved?
A. Yes.

Q. Were there any traffic controls in the immediate vicinity that regulated the flow of traffic, like stop signs?
A. There was no stop signs. There was a double yellow line.

Q. The double yellow line which indicated no passing?
A. Right.

Q. Is there a speed limit in the area?
A. Yes, it's 50.

Q. At the time this accident occurred, what other traffic was in the vicinity?
A. Coming to the town of Laurel, there was none. But going out, there was myself and there was a semi behind us, way behind us. And that's all I could see.

Q. All right. The terrain where this happened, is it level or is there a hill crest or curve involved?
A. Well there's a hill crest, but it's, uh, oh, how many—about 2200 feet to the crest of the hill. Oh it's more than that, but you can see. You can see the crest of the hill from my drive real easy.

Q. The road isn't level then. Are you going uphill or downhill?
A. It's going uphill as you turn into my drive.

Q. All right.
A. Just starting to go uphill.

Q. Would you classify this as a business, residential, or rural area?
A. A rural area.

Q. Were there any obstructions to your view either in your vehicle or outside it which would cause you or the other driver to fail to see each other?
A. No. My mirror was, I even looked in my rear-view mirror, and there was a truck coming just over the crest of the hill, but it was a semi.

Q. This was an oncoming vehicle or one that . . .
A. It was an oncoming one behind me. And my side mirror, there was nothing coming from it when I turned either.

30

Q. I see. This was a vehicle behind you, not coming at you?
A. Right.

Q. All right.
A. And it's not the vehicle that hit us.

Q. Yes. We've established that you were the driver of the car you were in. Would you indicate your passengers and their position in the vehicle?
A. Okay. Mrs. Weston was in the front seat with a seat belt on. And I had my seat belt on. And her son, Samuel, was behind her and her daughter, Laura, was behind me.

Q. So you had a total of three people besides yourself?
A. Right.

Q. Who was the operator of the other vehicle involved in this accident?
A. Donald Swanson.

Q. Was he alone in his vehicle?
A. Yes.

Q. And what kind of a vehicle was he operating?
A. It was a pickup truck, and I have no idea what kind. It's a four-wheel-drive, but what the make was I don't know.

Q. What was the weather like that day?
A. Clear.

Q. Pavement's dry?
A. Um huh.

Q. And at that time of day, it's still daylight?
A. Oh yeah.

Q. What was your direction of travel and speed?
A. Okay, I was going east. At the time of the accident, I wasn't going, oh maybe, three or four miles an hour because I had to turn in.

Q. Okay. You were making a turn, what direction?
A. To the left.

Q. Were you signaling for that turn?
A. Yes, I was.

Q. For what interval of time did you give your signal?
A. It started at the, the other side of the bridge, and, how far was the bridge from there?. . .

Q. That would be adequate for me. The other side of the bridge?
A. Um huh.

Q. All right. That's as you approach the bridge and before you crossed it you started . . .
A. I started signaling.

Q. And what was your speed at the time you started signaling and then again as you were in your turn?
A. Well, I started, well I started slowing it down right at the bridge to about, oh 45 maybe. And then I slowed continually down till I came to where we turn in. And then I looked and nobody's coming up. And then as I turned in I don't think I was going more than two or three miles an hour.

Q. Did you at any time reduce your speed suddenly?
A. No. It was just all gradual.

Q. When were you first aware of the Swanson's vehicle?
A. I never was.

Q. You didn't see it before the impact?
A. No, I didn't. And I had looked behind me and I looked in my rear-view mirror, too, and I didn't see him at all. I, in the side mirror I looked.

31

Q. How far into your turn or, well, you indicated that your intention was to turn. Had you started that turn?

A. Yes, I'd started the turn and I was almost down into my driveway. I was across the double yellow line.

Q. All right, so your car would be, would you say entirely in the left-hand lane or westbound lane when it was hit?

A. Well, I think part of my wheels were on my own driveway.

Q. So you had completed more than half of your turn?

A. Oh yeah.

Q. When were you first aware, you said you weren't aware of the other vehicle. Were you aware of it at impact?

A. Well, yes (inaudible).

Q. You didn't lose consciousness?

A. I did. I heard a crash and glass breaking. And um, I saw my friend going past me through my window. And then I must have hit the telephone pole because I blacked out completely.

Q. The Swanson vehicle as far as you're able to deduce at this time was traveling what direction?

A. East towards Billings.

Q. Overtaking you then, apparently?

A. Um huh.

Q. To your knowledge, was it apparent that Swanson had done anything to try and avoid this impact?

A. Well, no. As a matter of fact, I felt that he was going so fast, he'd have to have been going so fast that there's no way he could have avoided it except staying in his own lane. Staying in the right lane instead of turning into my passing lane.

Q. On what basis do you come to the conclusion that he was traveling too fast or that he was traveling fast?

A. Because I hadn't seen him as I turned. And he'd have to have been coming at a tremendous amount of speed in order for him to get up on us so close and so fast.

Q. Was there anything going on inside of the car that might have been a momentary distraction to you?

A. No, cause I don't play the radio or the, I don't even have a tape deck in the car, so I don't play that when I'm driving cause I don't like. . .

Q. Any conversation going on at the time?

A. No, nothing heavy. Just, in fact I can't even remember anything with it going on as far as conversations go that would even begin to cause a distraction.

Q. What was the point of impact on your car?

A. Okay. It was on the driver's side in the rear.

Q. Did you observe the other vehicle, the Swanson pickup, after the accident?

A. Yes, I've been down to see it.

Q. Where was the impact on it?

A. Okay, the right front fender on his.

Q. Following . . .

A. (Is that right?)

Q. Following this impact, where did your vehicle end up?

A. Well, just a minute. It's the left front fender.

Q. On the Swanson truck?

A. Yes.

Q. All right.

A. And where did my vehicle end up?

Q. Um huh.

A. Against the telephone pole.

Q. It actually came in contact with the pole?
A. Yes, and it dented the car. And the pole pushed it in quite a bit.

Q. Are you completely off the road?
A. Yes.

Q. And headed what direction?
A. Okay, headed north, nope, just a minute. I think south.

Q. All right, if you're not sure.
A. Okay.

Q. Yet, this would be on the right or left side of the road?
A. On the left side.

Q. Are you beyond your driveway?
A. Yes, well, a few feet off of the driveway if that. Yeah, a few feet off the driveway.

Q. Where was the Swanson pickup when it came to rest?
A. I have no idea because I didn't see it.

Q. Did you have any conversation with Mr. Swanson after the accident?
A. I didn't, no.

Q. To your knowledge, was it, had Mr. Swanson had anything intoxicating to drink?
A. No.

Q. Had you or your passengers?
A. No.

Q. Do you know of any witnesses to this accident other than the people involved?
A. My daughter seen a car get hit, but it was down in our yard. And she, she just knew there was an accident because our yard sits down a ways from where the highway was.

Q. You mentioned a semi.
A. Um huh.

Q. Is there, has that party been identified?
A. I don't think so. It was chip truck from, uh, . . .

Q. I see. Would it have been in a position to have seen the accident?
A. I think so, yes.

Q. Mrs. Anderson, I still have a few questions. I'm coming to the end of this side of the tape. I'll have to stop the recorder and turn over to the other side. Before I do, you are aware that I've recorded the entire conversation thus far? And it's been done with your consent?
A. Yes.

Mr. Taner: If you will hold, I'll change over the tape.

(End Tape, Side 1)

This is Tim Taner recording an in-person interview with Sarah Anderson on September 4, 1985. It concerns her accident on August 20, '85.

Q. All right, Mrs. Anderson, you're still with me?
A. Yes.

Q. And you're aware I'm once again recording?
A. Right.

Q. Was either car driveable following this accident?
A. I don't know if his was, but I know mine is completely totaled out.

Q. All right. Were, what injuries were sustained in your car to you and your passengers? Now that, anything that you're actually aware of by personal knowledge. Doesn't have to be anything too great.
A. Okay, I had a concussion, um, all my left side is bruised internally, all the soft tissue is bruised, um, my shoulder and my neck. Okay, and then I'm going to go in today and I think there's been damage to my bladder and to my colon. And then, um, Mrs. Weston, she had three broken ribs. Her leg was broke in two places. She has a

broken clavical, a concussion, and problems with her neck, too, I think. I'm not, I'm not sure. Then to Laura Weston, she had a whiplash and Samuel did also. And Laura had bruises, a concussion too.

Q. Following the accident, where did you receive your first medical attention?
A. At Yellowstone County Hospital.

Q. Your doctor there?
A. Dr. Gosten.

Q. And how did you get to the hospital?
A. Ambulance.

Q. You had subsequent medical attention, you personally. Where did you receive that?
A. They put an I.V. in me in the emergency room and got Mrs. Weston ready, and they took some X-rays of me there. And then they took us both into Billings.

Q. Did the, the police were at the scene?
A. I think they were, yes.

Q. You don't recall them specifically?
A. Yeah, I do. I recall Alice, um, Pracel there.

Q. The vehicles to your knowledge had not been moved by the time the police arrived?
A. Oh no, nothing had been.

Q. What relation is Mrs. Weston to you?
A. She's just a good friend.

Q. I see. Does she live in this area?
A. No, she lives in Spokane, Washington.

Q. She had come to visit you?
A. Right.

Q. A social-type visit?
A. Yes. She just came for a vacation.

Q. Had your passengers registered any kind of complaint about your driving prior to this accident?
A. No.

Q. Mrs. Anderson, I think that completes my interview, but is there anything further you would comment on? Something we haven't discussed to this point?
A. No, there isn't.

Q. You are aware that I've recorded this entire conversation using one side of a tape and part of another?
A. Yes, I have.

Q. It was done with your full knowledge and consent?
A. Right.

Q. Everything you've told me in the course of this interview is true?
A. Yes.

Q. Then that completes the recording and I'll turn off the machine.

EXHIBIT A: SID SILKER, M.D., LETTER OF SEPTEMBER 23, 1986

September 23, 1986

Attorneys, Inc. P.C.
126 E Broadway, Suite 25
P.O. Box 7742
Missoula, MT 59807

RE: Sarah Anderson

To Whom It May Concern:

I have referred Sarah Anderson to the Pain Center at Billings Community Rehabilitation Center for evaluation of her shoulder pain and neck pain. This pain she initially began experiencing as the result of a rear end automobile collision in the summer of 1985.

Despite multiple modalities of treatment locally, we have not succeeded in reducing her pain to an acceptable degree, either for her or for us. It is my belief that the pain that she is currently experiencing is the result of the motor vehicle accident that occurred last year.

If you have any other questions please feel free to contact me.

Sincerely,

Sid Silker

Sid Silker, M.D.
P.O. Box 1045
Laurel, MT 59248

SRS/bd
C: File

EXHIBIT B: KEITH MAKIE, PH.D. PAIN CLINIC DIRECTOR, LETTER OF JANUARY 21, 1987

January 21, 1987

Mr. Rex Palmer
Attorneys, Inc.
126 East Broadway
Missoula, Montana
59802

RE: Sarah Anderson

Dear Mr. Palmer:

The purpose of this letter is to answer your questions about the program we have recommended for your client, Sarah Anderson and the cost of that program. Sarah, as you know, was evaluated in our Diagnostic Pain Clinic on 12/9/86; it was the unanimous recommendation of the Evaluation Team that she seek out a highly structured, interdisciplinary, chronic pain treatment program. The evaluation suggested that not only does Sarah have an extremely complicated physical pain problem, but this physical pain problem is exacerbated by a great deal of general emotional distress and enumerable family problems.

Your specific question about our program was what exactly would we be recommending for Sarah and what would the cost be, and what outcomes might be expected. Our program is truly interdisciplinary and residential. We have the best of both worlds in that we have a highly trained interdisciplinary team affiliated with Billings Community Rehabilitation Center to do the treatment while we have the people stay in a home-like residential facility with twenty-four hour nursing care. Our program is aimed specifically at increasing activity level, returning people to as much of their function, prior to the injury, as possible, given the physical effects of the injury. Our goal is to get people active, to strengthen, stretch their muscles, to get them back into activities of daily living, and to eventually, in most cases, return them to work. Our program is seven weeks in length, involves a large vocational component, and addresses not only physical factors, but also psychological and family factors. The cost of the program at the present time is between $25,000 and $27,000 for the seven-week program. By the end of the program the Evaluation Team felt that Sarah would very likely be able to return to her former, fairly active lifestyle, and even work outside the home, if she chose to. The Evaluation Team predicted that by the end of the program the chronic pain and its attendant problems would cease to dominate Sarah's life. Much of the psychological upheaval we found in the evaluation would be reduced and we would also be able to improve her family situation. There was no doubt in the minds of the Evaluation Team that Sarah would not only find some relief from her seemingly unrelenting pain, but she would also be able to resume the activities of her life very close to what they had been before the accident.

The Evaluation Team was also unanimous in their prediction that unless Sarah took advantage of such an interdisciplinary, highly structured, intensive pain treatment program, she would continue to deteriorate. The Team felt this deterioration not only would manifest itself in decreased activity level, increased deconditioning, lack of mobility, but also that the great deal of psychological distress she reports at the present time, would worsen; her family situation would worsen to the point where the prediction was that the family would break down.

I hope this general description provides you with the information you need. If you need any more specific information I would be more than happy to provide it to you. You can either write to me or call me at 248-2400, extension 3634.

Sincerely,

Keith C. Makie

Keith C. Makie, Ph.D.
Pain Clinic Director
KCM/brm

EXHIBIT C: PHOTOGRAPHS RELEVANT TO THE ACCIDENT

Photo 1: Sarah Anderson's Vehicle

Photos 2–5: Sarah Anderson's Vehicle; Donald Swanson's Vehicle

Photo 2

Photo 3

Photo 4

Photo 5

Photos 6–9: Devlin Road

Photo 6

Photo 7

Photo 8

Photo 9

EXHIBIT D: ACCIDENT REPORT, MONTANA HIGHWAY PATROL

Exhibit D: Accident Report, of Montana Highway Patrol

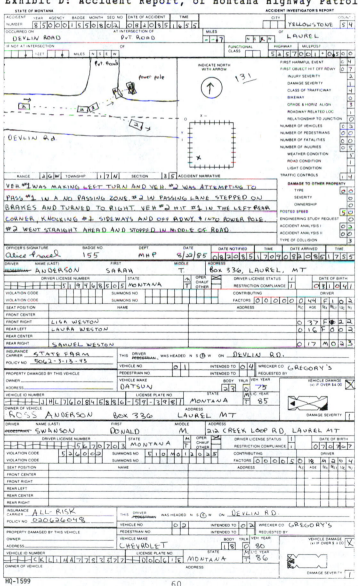

EXHIBIT E: OIL PAINTINGS BY SARAH ANDERSON

Four (4) Original Oil Paintings by Sarah Anderson

EXHIBIT F: NEWSPAPER CLIPPING SHOWING SARAH ANDERSON PAINTING MINIATURE FIGURES ON FINGERNAILS

PAGE TWELVE-THURSDAY, NOVEMBER 10, 1983

Jacki Sander took home a miniature souvenir from the Art and Craft show over the weekend. Sarah Anderson paints a very small figure on her finger nail. A continuous slide show, toys, stained glass work and other beautiful examples of county crafts were on display.

41

SUMMARY

A settlement is a resolution of a legal dispute without the need for a complete trial. To achieve this goal, a party may use a settlement precis. This is an advocacy document that tries to persuade the opponent (or the insurance company of the opponent) to settle the case in a certain way—or more accurately, for a certain amount. The precis presents the facts of the case, the theories of liability, the nature of past and anticipated expenses, and other matters that pertain to damages. If the case is more complex or elaborate, the advocacy document is often called a settlement brochure.

KEY TERMS

settlement 586

settlement precis 586

settlement brochure 586

A

Basic Medical Anatomy

Association of Trial Lawyers of America, *Anatomy of a Personal Injury Lawsuit*. Reprinted with the permission of the Association of Trial Lawyers of America and West Group. For additional information, please contact a West Group Customer Services representative at 1-800-328-4880. Material also adapted from Bureau of Medicine and Surgery, *Handbook of the Hospital Corps* (1959). Illustrations adapted from Richard Sloane, *The Sloan-Dorland Annotated Medical-Legal Dictionary* (1987). Reprinted with permission of West Group and W. B. Saunders.

TERMINOLOGY

Medical terms are derived mainly from Greek and Latin. In learning a relatively small number of roots, suffixes, and prefixes, you can acquire a basic understanding of medical terms. For example, the root for nerve is "neur" and the suffix, "itis," means inflammation. Thus, the term "neuritis" means inflammation of nerves.

A facet of the medical language which must be mastered at the outset is the terminology related to the positions, directions, and movements of the body. The following describe positions:

1. Anterior, posterior; front, back.
2. Ventral, dorsal; front, back.
3. Lateral, medial; away from the midline, toward the midline.
4. Proximal, distal; toward the source, away from the source.
5. Cranial, caudal; toward the head, toward the tail.
6. Superior, inferior; above, below.

The following describe movements of various portions of the body.

1. Abduction, adduction; away from the center of the body, toward the center of the body.
2. Flexion, extension; bending of a joint, straightening of a joint.
3. Supination, pronation; turning upward, turning downward.
4. Eversion, inversion; turning outward, turning inward.

"Anatomical planes" identify "views" of the body. The more common anatomical planes include:

1. Frontal: A section to the side of the body, passing at right angles to the median plane. This divides the body into anterior and posterior portions.
2. Median or midline: An imaginary plane which passes from the front to the back through the center of the body, dividing the body into right and left equal portions.
3. Sagittal: A section parallel to the long axis of the body or parallel to the median plane, dividing the body into right and left unequal parts.
4. Transverse: A horizontal plane, passing at right angles to both the frontal and median planes, dividing the body into cranial and caudal parts.

Some anatomical postures to which doctors have frequent reference are as follows:

1. Erect: the body is in a standing position.
2. Supine: the body is lying flat on the back.
3. Prone: the body is lying face and trunk down.
4. Laterally recumbent: the body is lying horizontally, either on the right or left side.

BASIC UNITS OF THE BODY

The human body is made up of four basic units: cells, tissues, organs, and systems. Cells are the building blocks of the body; they are the ultimate unit of the body, and are not of immediate importance. Tissues are masses of cells which are similar in structure and function. The primary tissues are:

1. Epithelial: These cover internal and external surfaces of the body.
2. Connective: These hold organs in place and bind all parts of the body together.
3. Muscular: These largely carry out activities of motion.

4. Nervous: These are the most highly specialized in the body; they convey impulses from and to the central nervous system.

Organs are combinations of groups of different tissues, e.g., the liver, the heart, lungs, pancreas, etc. Organs do not function independently, for they operate within the framework of systems. Systems are groupings of organs which perform specific functions. The body may be divided into ten basic systems:

1. Skeletal;
2. Muscular;
3. Nervous;
4. Cardiovascular;
5. Lymphatic;
6. Gastrointestinal;
7. Genitourinary;
8. Respiratory;
9. Endocrine; and
10. Integumentary.

The greater part of those injuries the lawyer and paralegal will deal with have their primary effect upon one, or all, of the first four systems.

SKELETAL SYSTEM

A. General Considerations:

The skeletal system is the jointed framework of the body which makes movement possible. This system is made up of some 200 bones and connective fibers. The purpose of the skeletal system is to give support and shape to the body, and provide attachment points for bones, muscles, and ligaments.

B. Anatomical Classification of Skeletal System:

1. The axial skeleton is comprised of those bones lying near the midline of the body, such as the skull and spinal column.
2. The appendicular skeleton is comprised of those bones which support the limbs.

C. Major Bones:

Lawyers and paralegals should learn the following portions of the skeletal systems:
1. The skull:
   a. Frontal;
   b. Temporal;
   c. Parietal;
   d. Occipital;
   e. Maxilla; and
   f. Mandible.
2. Vertebral column and associated structures:
   The importance of understanding the basic anatomy of the vertebral column and its associated structures cannot be over-emphasized. There are three major areas of the vertebral column: The cervical area, the thoracic or dorsal area, and the lumbar area. The bony structures which make up the vertebral column are known as vertebrae.
   The cervical area contains seven vertebrae. The first of these is termed the "atlas." This structure supports the skull. The second cervical vertebra is

called the "axis." This provides a point of rotation of the skull on the neck. The thoracic or dorsal area of the vertebral column is made up of twelve vertebrae. The lumbar area has five vertebrae. It is the lumbar area which is responsible for carrying most of the weight of the trunk. Immediately below the lumbar area is the sacrum. This structure consists of five fused vertebrae. Immediately below the sacrum is the coccyx, or "tail bone."

Between each pair of vertebrae there is an intervertebral disc. The outer portion of the disc, or the annulus fibrosus, is made up of cartilaginous substance. Within the annulus fibrosus is a jelly-like substance known as the nucleus pulposus. Intervertebral discs serve a highly important, cushioning function.

3. Upper trunk:
The ribs are made up of twelve pairs of flat curved bones which are attached posteriorly to the thoracic portion of the vertebral column. Anteriorly the first seven pairs are attached to the sternum, the broad flat bone located in the midline of the chest (the "breast bone"). The eighth, ninth, and tenth ribs are joined to the cartilage of the seventh rib. The eleventh and twelfth are unattached anteriorly and are the so called "floating ribs." Basically, the ribs, plus the sternum, comprise the thoracic cage. This bony structure protects the vital organs of the chest and makes possible the movement which permits expansion and contraction in breathing.

4. Upper extremities:
   a. Clavicle, the collar bone;
   b. Scapula, the shoulder blade;
   c. Humerus, the upper arm bone;
   d. Ulna and Radius, bones of the lower arm;
   e. Carpals, eight wrist bones;
   f. Metacarpals, bones of the palm and posterior hand; and
   g. Phalanges, finger bones.

5. Lower extremities:
   a. Pelvis: The pelvis may be divided into three principal parts: The ilium, the ischium, and the pubis. These three bones join to form the pelvic girdle.
   b. Acetabulum: This is not actually bone, but a large cup-shaped socket in the lateral aspect of the hip, into which the head of the femur fits.
   c. Greater and Lesser Trochanters: These are bony prominences located on the lateral and medial sides of the femur. These prominences are for the purpose of attachment of muscles.
   d. Femur: This is the longest bone in the body; it is the bone of the upper leg.
   e. Patella: This is the kneecap.
   f. Tibia and Fibula: These are the bones of the lower leg. The tibia is the larger, and is located medially.
   g. The Lateral Malleolus is the lower end of the fibula; the Medial Malleolus is the lower end of the tibia.
   h. Tarsals: These are the seven bones of the ankle.
   i. Metatarsals: These are the five bones in the sole and instep of the foot.
   j. Phalanges: These are the bones of the toes.

D. Joints:

A joint may be defined as a structure which holds bones together, permitting certain movements while prohibiting others. There are three types of joints:

1. Fibrous: united by Fibrous tissues; there are two types:
   a. Sutures: connected by several fibrous layers;
   b. Syndesmoses: a fibrous joint in which the intervening connective tissue is much more than in a suture;

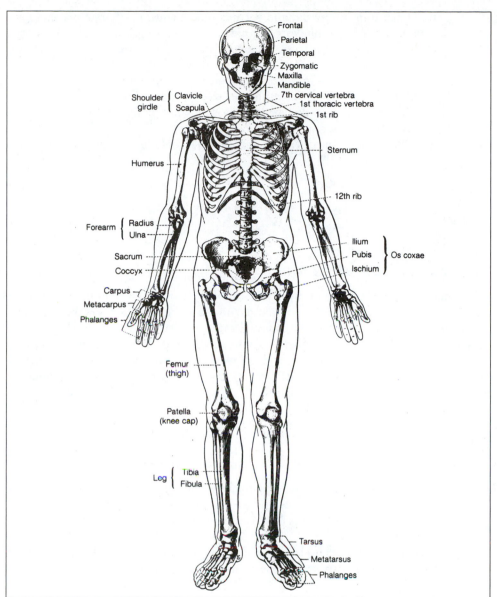

FIGURE A–1
The human skeleton.

2. Cartilaginous: united by fibrocartilage;
3. Synovial: often termed diathrodial joints; these possess a fluid filled space and are specialized to permit more or less free movements. The articular surfaces are covered with cartilage and the bones are united by the joint capsule and ligaments.

In classifying the joints with respect to movement, there are also three major classifications:

1. Synarthroses: These are immovable;
2. Amphiarthroses: These have limited movement; and
3. Diarthroses:
   a. Plane Joint (articular surfaces are slightly curved, and permit gliding or slipping in any direction).

b. Hinge Joint (uni-axial and permits movement in only one place: an example is an interphalangeal joint).
c. Condylar Joint (articular area consists of two district articular surfaces: knee joint is an example).
d. Ball and Socket Joint (shoulder joint is an example).
e. Ellipsoidal Joint (articulating surfaces are much longer in one direction than in another; radiocarpal joint is an example).
f. Pivot Joint (uni-axial; axis is vertical).
g. Saddle Joint (biaxial joint carpometacarpal joint of the thumb is an example).

MUSCULAR SYSTEM

A. General Considerations:

All human activity is carried on by operation of the muscles. The human body contains five hundred muscles which are large enough to be seen by the naked eye, and thousands more which are capable of visualization only through a microscope. Muscles constitute about one-half of the weight of the body; the form of the body is largely due to the muscle covering of the skeletal framework. Muscles are made up of tissues composed of long slender cells. In considering the muscular system, one should also consider tendons. There are strong bands which attach muscles to bones or to other structures.

B. Movement of Muscles:

Basically, muscles fall into the following categories with respect to movement:

1. Prime movers: These muscles actively produce movement.
2. Antagonists: These muscles operate in opposition to prime movers.
3. Fixation muscles: These muscles steady a part while others execute movement.
4. Synergists: These muscles control movement of a proximal joint so that a prime mover may obtain movement of a distal joint.

C. Primary Muscles:

1. The neck:
   a. Sternocleidomastoid: This muscle is frequently involved in cervical sprains.
   b. Paravertebral: These muscles run the length of the spine.
2. The Upper Trunk:
   a. Trapezius: The triangular-shaped muscle located in the back of the neck and the upper trunk.
   b. Pectoralis Major and Minor: These muscles are located on the chest.
   c. Latissimus: This is the broadest muscle on the back.
   d. Deltoid: This is a muscle capping the shoulder.
   e. Triceps: This is a muscle located on the posterior aspect of the upper arm.
   f. Biceps: This is a muscle located on the anterior aspect of the upper arm.
3. Thoracic Wall and Abdomen:
   a. Intercostals;
   b. Subcostals;
   c. Sternocostals;

FIGURE A–2
Muscles of trunk, anterior view.

Sternohyoid
Hyoid bone
Sternocleidomastoid
Omohyoid
Trapezius
Clavicle
Biceps:
Short head
Long head
Deltoid
Sternum
Head of humerus
Pectoralis major
Pectoralis minor
2
3
4
Coraco-brachialis
5
6
Pectoralis major (cut insertion)
Biceps
7
Latissimus dorsi
Rectus
8
Latissimus dorsi
9
Serratus anterior
10
Serratus anterior
Linea alba
Transversus
Umbilicus
External oblique
Internal oblique
Linea arcuata
Inguinal ligament
Gluteus medius
Superficial inguinal ring
Deep inguinal ring
Femoral ring
Spermatic cord
Femoral vein
Tensor fasciae latae
Great saphenous vein
Sartorius

   d. External and Internal Obliques;
   e. Rectus Abdominus; and
   f. Transversus Abdominus.
4. Hip and Thigh:
   a. Gluteus Minimus, Medius and Maximus;
   b. Pectineus;
   c. Adductur, Longus, Brevis and Magnus;
   d. Quadriceps Femoris;
   e. Sartorius;
   f. "Ham Strings":
      (1) Semimembranosus,
      (2) Semitendinosus,
      (3) Biceps Femoris; and
5. Lower Leg and Foot:
   a. Tibialis Anterior and Posterior;
   b. Peroneus Longus and Brevis;
   c. Soleus;
   d. Gastrocnemius.

FIGURE A–3
Muscles of trunk, posterior view.

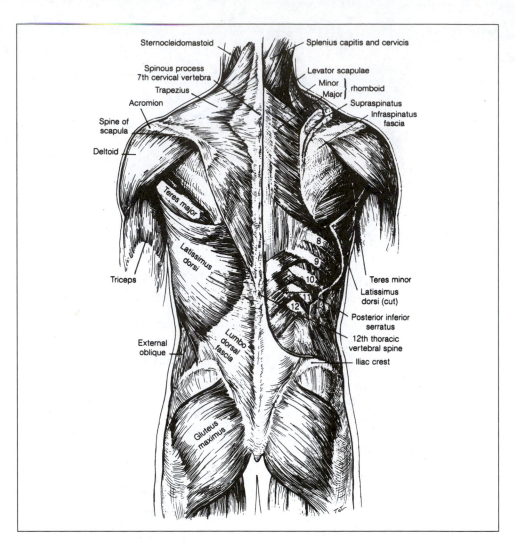

NERVOUS SYSTEM

The human body has a "central authority" which issues orders to the rest of the body. The function of the nervous system, then, is to coordinate all of the activities of the body. The basic functional units of the nervous system are known as neurons. These are specifically designed to carry impulses or messages rapidly over relatively long distances. There are basically two types of neurons: sensory neurons, which conduct impulses from sense organs to the spinal cord and brain; and motor neurons, which conduct impulses from the brain and spinal cord to the muscles and glands.

The nervous system may be divided into three main parts: the central nervous system, the peripheral nervous system, and the autonomic nervous system.

A. Central Nervous System:

There is no more important part of the body than the central nervous system. When one sustains serious trauma to this system, damage will be gross. The basic components of the central nervous system are the brain and spinal cord. Three membranes, known as the meninges, ensheath the central nervous system. The meninges serve supportive and protective roles. The meninges, from the outer- to the innermost, are designated as the dura, the arachnoid, and the pia.

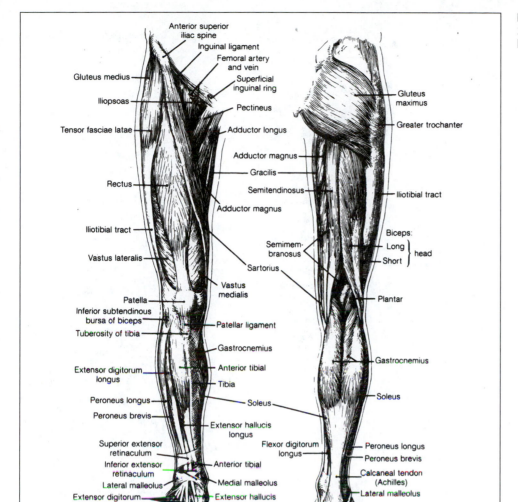

ANTERIOR   POSTERIOR

1. The Brain: The brain comprises 98% of the central nervous system, and lies
   within the bony protection of the skull. One may designate the following
   major divisions of the brain:
   a. Medulla Oblongata: A truncated cone of nervous tissue continuous
      above with the pons and below with the spinal cord. It lies anterior to
      the cerebellum. The medulla contains highly specialized nerve centers
      regulating heart action, breathing, circulation, and control of body
      temperature. It is in this area that many of the nerves cross over to the
      other side of the body. Thus, the right side of the brain controls the
      left side of the body, while the left side of the brain controls the right
      side.
   b. Pons (meaning bridge): This connects the medulla and the midbrain.
   c. Midbrain: This is the upper part of the brain stem, located just above
      the pons.
   d. Cerebellum: This is the second largest portion of the brain; it is located
      in the posterior aspect of the skull. The chief function of the cerebellum
      is to bring balance, harmony, and coordination to motions of the body
      initiated by the cerebrum. The cerebellum integrates and correlates
      nerve impulses.

FIGURE A–5
Superficial muscles of right upper extremity.

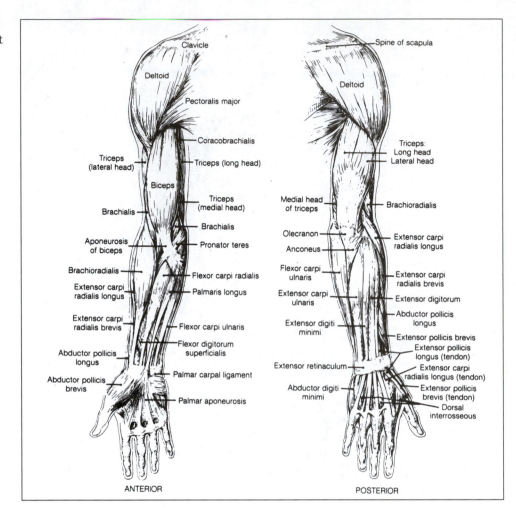

e. Diencephalon: This is the portion of the brain lying between the midbrain and cerebrum. It contains the following:
   (1) Thalamus: The integrating center of the brain, where tactile, olfactory, painful, and gustatory impulses are correlated with motor reactions.
   (2) Epithalamus.
   (3) Subthalamus: This regulates the muscles of emotional expression.
   (4) Hypothalamus: This controls emotions that affect the heartbeat and blood pressure, as well as body temperature, carbohydrate metabolism, food metabolism, appetite, and sexual reflexes.
f. Cerebrum: This occupies most of the cranial cavity; it may be divided into cerebral hemispheres, and each hemisphere is, in turn, divided into four lobes:
   (1) Occipital: This is visual in function.
   (2) Frontal: This is the center of voluntary movement and is also the seat of intellect and memory.
   (3) Temporal: This is auditory in function.
   (4) Parietal: This is sensory and motor in function.
2. The Cerebral Spinal Fluid: a clear transparent fluid found in the spinal canal. When a history of central nervous system pathology is suspected, physicians will draw out, or "tap," some of the fluid for the purpose of analysis. This fluid surrounds the brain and spinal cord, and is in large measure protective in function.
3. The Spinal Cord: One may compare the spinal cord to a highly complex telephone cable. It is enclosed in the vertebral column and has the three membranous coverings: the dura, the pia, and the arachnoid. Cerebral spinal fluid also surrounds the spinal cord.

One may demonstrate an "ascending tract" (responsible for conducting impulses to the brain), and a "descending tract" (responsible for conducting impulses from the brain). It is through the spinal cord that the brain maintains its intimate functional relationship with the organs of the body. Thirty-one pairs of spinal nerves which protrude from the lateral aspects of the cord, through the vertebral foramina, and into the peripheral areas of the body, constitute the specific means of accomplishing this highly complex system of intra-communication. Spinal nerves are attached to the spinal cord by anterior and posterior roots. The nerves, after leaving the cord, are named after their corresponding vertebrae. Thus, the first eight spinal nerves are known as cervical; the next twelve, dorsal; the next five, lumbar; the next five, sacral; and the last pair, coccygeal.

Actual trauma to the cord itself may produce serious injury. If there is any severing of the cord, the body will function normally above the level of the injury, while the portion below the injury will be paralyzed.

B. Peripheral Nervous System:

The peripheral nervous system is made up of nerves outside of the brain and spinal column. The thirty-one pairs of spinal nerves and twelve pairs of cranial nerves which branch out into the body for the purpose of sending and receiving messages to and from the brain are known as the peripheral nerves.

There are twelve pairs of cranial nerves which arise on each side of the brain. They are as follows:

1. First cranial nerve: This is olfactory in function; i.e., it is the nerve for the sense of smell.
2. Second cranial nerve: This is the optic nerve.
3. Third cranial nerve: This is oculomotor in function.
4. Fourth cranial nerve (also called the trochlear nerve): This serves the eye muscles.
5. Fifth cranial nerve: This is the largest of the cranial nerves. It serves both a sensory and a motor function. It has three portions:
    a. Ophalmic, serving the forehead;
    b. Maxillary, serving the upper cheek; and
    c. Mandibular, innervating the jaw and lower face.
6. Sixth cranial nerve (also called the abducens): This is visual in function and serves a purely motor function.
7. Seventh cranial nerve: This is both sensory and motor in function, and controls the muscles of the face, ears, and scalp.
8. Eighth cranial nerve: This is primarily acoustic or auditory. This is the sensory nerve of hearing and equilibrium.
9. Ninth cranial nerve: Known as glossopharyngeal nerve: it serves both a motor and sensory function, carrying messages from the pharynx and back part of the tongue to the brain.
10. Tenth cranial nerve: This is the vagus nerve, serving both a motor and sensory function to the thorax and abdomen.
11. Eleventh cranial nerve: It is a motor nerve which supplies the muscles of the neck and shoulders.
12. Twelfth cranial nerve: This is the hypoglossal nerve. It is a motor nerve controlling the muscles of the tongue.

C. Autonomic Nervous System:

The autonomic nervous system functions automatically; it activates involuntary, smooth, and cardiac muscles, as well as glands. It serves the vital systems which function automatically, i.e., the digestive, circulatory, respiratory, urinary, and endocrine systems.

The autonomic nervous system is broken down into two major divisions: sympathetic nervous system and parasympathetic nervous system. These two systems work in opposition and maintain balanced activity in the body mechanisms. For example, the sympathetic system will dilate the pupils, while the parasympathic system contracts them.

The trunk of the sympathetic system lies in close proximity to the vertebral bodies and is composed of a series of ganglia on either side of the spinal column. The ganglia extend from the base of the skull to the coccyx.

The ganglia of the parasympathetic system are located in the mid-portion of the brain, and the sacral region of the spinal cord.

CARDIOVASCULAR SYSTEM

There are five principal components of the cardiovascular system: heart, arteries, veins, capillaries, and blood.

A. Blood:

Blood is a tissue fluid pumped by the heart, which courses through miles of arteries, veins, and capillaries. The function of blood is to carry oxygen, food, and water to all of the cells of the body, and to return carbon dioxide to the lungs for disposal.

B. The Heart:

The heart is a hollow, muscular pump. It is located in the front of the chest, slightly to the left, between the lungs. A large portion of the heart is located directly behind the sternum. The heart is enclosed in a membranous sac called the pericardium.

The heart is divided longitudinally into left and right chambers by the septum passing through the apex at the base of the heart. Each side of the heart is subdivided into chambers; an atrium above, and a ventricle below.

C. Arteries:

Blood is carried from the heart to all of the structures of the body by arteries; these are elastic tubes. The arteries branch and rebranch as they course through the body becoming smaller and smaller, until they finally are called arterioles. The arterioles feed blood directly into the capillaries. As the blood circulates through the capillary net, it gives off oxygen and picks up waste products.

The aorta is the largest artery in the body. It arises directly from the left ventricle of the heart, arches upward, and passes down along the spinal column through the diaphragm. All along its route, the aorta branches off into other arteries which supply blood to the head, neck, arms, chest, abdomen, and then it divides into arteries supplying the legs. Some of the larger arteries include the following:

1. Innominate artery;
2. Right subclavian, which supplies the right arm;
3. Right carotid, which supplies the right side of the head;
4. Internal carotid, which supplies the brain and eyes;
5. External carotid, which supplies the muscles and skin of the face;
6. Left carotid, which supplies the left side of the head;
7. Left subclavian, which supplies the left arm;
8. Axillary, which is an artery supplying the arm;
9. Brachial, which supplies the upper arm;
10. Radial and Ulnar, which supply the lower arm;
11. Coronary, which supplies the heart;
12. Pulmonary, which takes blood to be oxygenated;
13. Gastric, which supplies the stomach;
14. Splenic, which supplies the spleen;

15. Hepatic, which supplies the liver;
16. Superior mesenteric, which supplies the small intestine and proximal colon;
17. Inferior mesenteric, which supplies the lower half of the colon and rectum;
18. Renal, which supplies the kidneys;
19. Abdominal aorta, which divides into the right and left common iliacs which supply blood to the lower extremities;
20. Femoral, which supplies the thigh;
21. Popliteal, which is located just behind of, and supplies, the knee;
22. Anterior and posterior tibial, which supplies the area of the tibia;
23. Peroneal, which supplies blood to the lower leg; and
24. Dorsalis pedis, which supplies blood to the foot.

D. Veins:

The veins carry blood back to the heart. They are hollow tubes, like arteries, though their walls are much thinner and less muscular. The small veins are known as venules; these venules collect blood from the capillary nets, join larger veins, and finally return to the heart. There are two major systems of veins:

1. Pulmonary System:
   This is comprised of four veins which carry blood from the lungs to the left atrium of the heart. These veins are the only ones in the entire body which carry freshly oxygenated blood. The systemic venous system carries deoxygenated blood to the right atrium of the heart. The blood then flows into the right ventricle from which it is pumped into the lungs. The pulmonary veins then carry the blood to the left atrium. From the left atrium, the blood flows to the left ventricle, from whence it is pumped into the aorta for distribution throughout the body.
2. Systemic Venous System:
   This system returns blood to the right atrium from the entire body.

LYMPHATIC SYSTEM

The lymphatic system is closely associated and confluent with the vascular system. Lymph is an almost colorless fluid which is rich in white blood cells. It is circulated throughout the body by the lymph vessels, which are located in every part of the body except the brain, spinal cord, eyeball, internal ear, nails, and hair.

The lymph vessels and lymph glands form a vast network throughout the body; they collect the lymph and carry it toward the heart, eventually opening into the thoracic duct and right lymphatic duct, which in turn empty into the left internal jugular and right subclavian veins. Lymph vessels, like blood vessels, carry nourishment to the organs of the body and in turn collect waste products from them.

The lymph glands serve a filtering function; that is, they remove bacteria from the lymph stream. Lymph glands are also important in the production of white blood cells (lymphocytes). The lymphatic system is highly important in defense against infection. The lymphoid organs include the spleen, tonsils, and thymus, and lymph nodes (glands).

RESPIRATORY SYSTEM

Respiration refers to the interchange of oxygen and carbon dioxide between humans and their external world.

The principal structures of the respiratory system are:

A. Nose:

This serves both respiratory and sensory functions.

FIGURE A–6
Principal arteries of the
body and pulmonary veins.

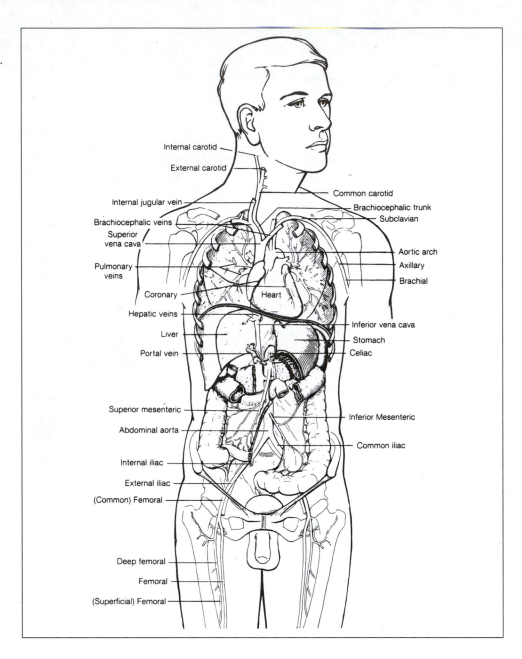

B. Pharynx:

This serves as an airway between the nasal chambers, the mouth, and larynx. It aids in both respiration and digestion.

C. Larynx:

This is the "voice box." It is located just below the pharynx, and serves as a passageway for air, aids in swallowing, and serves in the phonation or vocalization function.

D. Trachea:

This is the "windpipe." It is a tube, approximately four inches long, formed of cartilaginous rings.

FIGURE A–7
Principal veins of the body.

Internal jugular

External jugular

Subclavian

Brachiocephalic

Superior
vena cava

Aortic arch

Pulmonary
arteries

Axillary

Great cardiac

Left gastroepiploic

Liver

Stomach

Right gastroepiploic

Portal

Left gastric

Pancreaticoduodenal

Splenic

Renal

Superior mesenteric

Inferior mesenteric

Right colic

Left colic

Ileocolic

Inferior vena cava

Abdominal aorta

Sigmoid

Appendicular

Superor rectal

External iliac

Deep femoral

Great saphenous

(Superficial) Femoral

E. Bronchi:

These are the branches of the trachea which carry air into the lungs. As the bronchi further branch within the lungs, they are known as bronchioles.

F. Lungs:

The lungs are two large, closed membranous sacs located on either side of the chest; they are enclosed in a sac called the pleura.

G. Mediastinum:

This separates the chest into two cavities. It is, actually, a space between the two plural cavities.

H. Diaphragm:

This is a thin, muscular tendinous partition separating the thoracic cavity from the abdominal cavity; it is the chief muscle of respiration.

GASTROINTESTINAL SYSTEM

The gastrointestinal or digestive system includes the alimentary canal and its accessory organs. It extends from the mouth to the anus. The two major functions of the system are the digestion of food and the elimination of waste.

The principal components of the gastrointestinal system are as follows:

A. Mouth.

B. Pharynx:

This is an oval, fibromuscular sac about five inches long. It serves a dual function as a passageway for food and an air passageway.

C. Esophagus:

This is a narrow muscular tube about ten inches long. It connects the pharynx with the stomach.

D. Stomach:

This is the widest part of the alimentary canal. It digests masticated food to a fluid consistency and passes it along to the duodenum. There are millions of gastric glands in the stomach and these secrete juices which aid in the chemical breakdown of food.

E. Small Intestine:

This is a coiled twenty-foot tube which occupies the center and lower parts of the abdominal cavity. The greater part of digestion is completed in the small intestine, with three major divisions:

1. Duodenum: This is the widest, shortest, and most fixed part. Three accessory organs bear consideration at this point.
   a. Pancreas: This is a gland extending across the posterior aspect of the abdomen. It empties an alkaline digestive juice into the duodenum.
   b. Liver: This is the largest gland in the body. It lies in the upper abdomen, under the diaphragm and above the duodenum. It secretes bile into the duodenum.
   c. Gallbladder: This is a sac adhering to the lower aspect of the liver in a hollow space. The main function of the gallbladder is storage and concentration of bile.
2. Jejunum: The first part of the small intestine.
3. Ileum: This is the longest part of the small intestine. Most of the absorption of food takes place in the ileum.

F. Large Intestine:

This organ is about five feet long. The large intestine receives the products of digestion from the small intestine. The major divisions of the large intestine include the following:

1. Cecum: This is a blind sac located on the lower right side of the abdomen.
2. Vermiform Appendix: This is a narrow projection attached to the cecum.
3. Ascending Colon: This long tubular structure is fixed in the right flank.
4. Transverse Colon: This structure runs across the upper portion of the abdominal cavity.

5. Descending Colon: This structure runs down the left flank of the brim of the true pelvis.
6. Sigmoid Colon: The sigmoid colon communicates with the rectum.
7. Rectum: This communicates with the anus.
8. Anus.

GENITOURINARY SYSTEM

The genitourinary system is comprised of two major parts: urinary organs and reproductive organs.

A. Urinary Organs:

The urinary organs are common to both male and female, and are essentially similar in both. The major components of the urinary system are as follows:

1. Kidneys: These are bean-shaped organs situated in the posterior part of the abdomen on either side of the vertebral column.
2. Ureters: These are tubes about fifteen to eighteen inches long, extending from the kidneys down the back of the abdominal cavity and emptying into the urinary bladder.
3. Urinary Bladder: This is a musculo-membranous sac lying in the pelvis. It serves as a reservoir for urine.
4. Urethra: This structure serves a different function in the male and female:
   a. In the male, this is a membranous tube running from the urinary bladder to the penis and ending in a foramina. The urethra conveys both urine and the produce of the male reproductive organs.
   b. The female urethra opens near the front of a slit in the middle of the vulva. The function of the urethra in the female is solely for voiding.

B. Reproductive Systems:

1. The Male Reproductive System:
   The essential organs of the male reproductive system are as follows:
   a. Testes: These are two organs suspended in a sack of skin (the scrotum). The epithelial cells of the testes produce sperm.
   b. Epididymis: This is a cord-like, elongated structure located outside of, but hugging the posterior portion of the testis. Its function is to store sperm.
   c. Vas Deferens: This tiny tube extends from the epididymis up through the inguinal canal toward the bladder. Its function is to carry sperm to the ejaculatory duct.
   d. Spermatic Cord: Two spermatic cords comprise the vas deferens, arteries, veins, lymphatic ducts, and nerves. The ejaculatory duct is formed by union of the ductus deferens and the duct of the seminal vesicle.
   e. Ejaculatory Duct: This is a short, narrow tube, less than an inch long, which is formed just above the prostate by the union of seminal vesicles and the vas deferens.
   f. Prostate Gland: This gland secretes a thin alkaline substance which precedes the sperm and secretion of the vesicles during sexual intercourse.
   g. Cowper's Gland: These two structures are yellowish, rounded, lobulated, pea-size bodies on each side of the membranous urethra opening into the urethra.
   h. Urethra: This is a canal about eight inches long which extends from the urinary bladder to the external foramina of the penis.
   i. Penis: This is made up of three masses of tissue.

FIGURE A–8
Thoracic and abdominal
viscera.

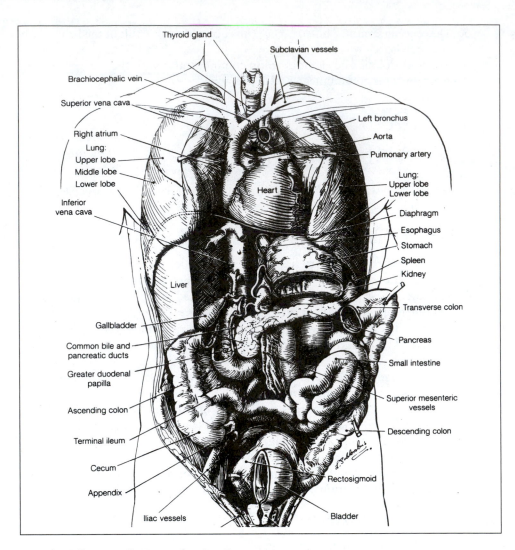

2. The Female Reproductive System:
   The essential organs of the female reproductive system include:
   a. Ovaries: These almond-shaped organs are approximately an inch and one-half in length, and an inch thick. They lie on each side of the pelvis and are responsible for the production of the germ cells.
   b. Uterus (womb): This is a thick-walled, hollow, pear-shaped organ about three inches long and three inches wide at the upper, widest portion. It lies between the bladder and the rectum. It tapers to a lower part called the cervix and projects into the anterior wall of the vagina.
   c. Fallopian Tubes: These are two musculo-membranous tubes about four inches long. They transmit the egg to the uterus where it meets the sperm.
   d. Vagina: This is a fibromuscular tube which extends from the cervix or neck of the uterus to the external genitalia part of the vagina.
   e. External Genitalia or Vulva.

ENDOCRINE SYSTEM

The complex activities of the body are carried on by the operation of the central nervous system and the endocrine system. The central nervous system is keyed to act instantaneously through the operation of the nerve impulses. The action of endocrine glands is more subtle, however; they slowly discharge secretions into blood and control the activities of the body more by "inference." The endocrine system is comprised of ductless glands of internal secretion; these glands secrete hormones.

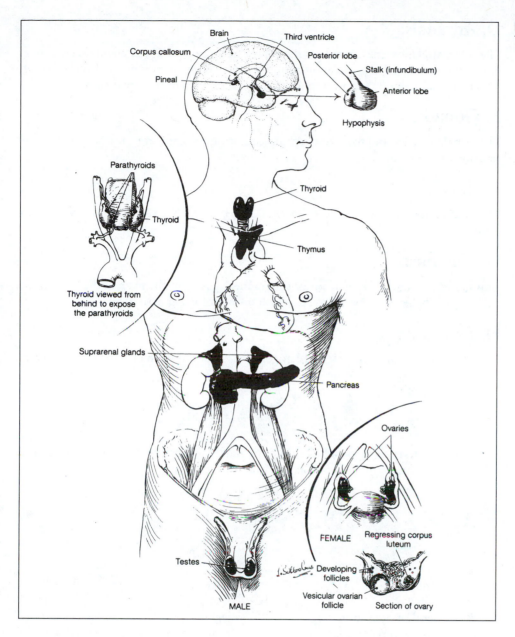

The principal endocrine glands include:

A. Thyroid:

The thyroid is composed of two pear-shaped lobes separated by a strip of tissue; it is located immediately in front of the trachea. The main function of the thyroid gland is in the secretion of the Thyroid Hormone. The thyroid functions within the framework of growth and metabolism.

B. Parathyroids:

These are four glands, two on each side, lying posterior to the thyroid gland and usually found embedded in the thyroid. The parathyroid's function is to secrete hormones which regulate the calcium and phosphorus content of blood and bone.

C. Pituitary:

The pituitary gland exercises control over all of the other glands. It is attached to the base of the brain and is divided into an anterior and posterior lobe.

D. Adrenals:

The adrenal glands are located on the top of each kidney. These glands secrete hormones which are active in metabolism and sex development; adrenalin also is secreted. This is one of the body's most important hormones, since it is a great stimulant.

E. Gonads:

The female ovaries and male testes produce hormones important for function of the reproductive system.

F. Pineal:

This gland is located near the base of the brain: its exact functions are not understood.

G. Thymus:

This gland is situated in the front of the trachea, partly in the neck and partly in the thorax. It is believed to be associated with immunological activities.

H. Pancreas:

Specialized cells, called the Islets of Langerhans, secrete insulin into the blood stream.

INTEGUMENTARY SYSTEM

The Integumentary System includes the skin, hair, nails, mammary glands, sweat and sebaceous glands. Its main function is protective.

MEDICAL SYMBOLS

Symbol	Meaning	Symbol	Meaning
@	at	℞	prescription
Ⓛ	left	2x	twice
Ⓜ	murmur	x2	twice
Ⓡ	right	lx	once
x	end of operation	°	degree
ø	assisted respiration	′	foot; minute
⊗	controlled respiration	″	inch; second
♂	male	/	per; ratio
♀	female	bn:	ratio
p̄	after	+	positive
ā	before	−	negative
c̄	with	∝	is proportional to
s̄	without	=	equals
x̄	except	≠	does not equal
?	question of	>	greater than
~	approximate	<	less than
±	not definite	μ	micron; micro
↓	decreased, down	Ø	none
↑	increased, elevated	&	and
→	causes	⊥	direct arterial diastolic blood pressure
∨	systolic blood pressure	∴	therefore
∧	distolic blood pressure	#	guage; number; pounds

B

Survey of Negligence Law in the United States

State	Code Section	Uniform Act	Comparative Negligence	Contributory Negligence—Limit to Plaintiff's Recovery	Judicial Imposition of Comparative Negligence	Contribution Among Tortfeasors
ALABAMA	None	No		Plaintiff's negligence is a bar to recovery. Contributory negligence is an affirmative defense. ARCP, Rule 86(c) *Jackson v. Waller*, 410 So. 2d 98 (1982)	No.	No. *Gobble v. Bradford*, 147 So. 619 (1933); Con instrument with joint payees or indorsers, see §7-3-116
ALASKA	23.25.000 (Employer's liability for negligence)	No	Yes, §09.17.060 Contributory fault diminishes proportionately the award based on claimant's fault, but does not bar recovery ("Pure" comparative negligence)	See Comparative Negligence	*Kaatz v. Alaska*, 540 P.2d 1037 (1975); "Pure" form adopted and codified herein	§09.17.080(d)
ARIZONA	12-2505	Yes; § 12-2501, et seq.	"Pure" comparative negligence			§12-2501, *et seq.*
ARKANSAS	16-64-122	Yes; 16-61-201 to 212	Yes	If Plaintiff's fault is of less degree than defendant's, he may recover amount diminished in proportion to degree of his own fault (§16-64-122); if plaintiff's fault is equal to or greater than defendant, he may not recover at all		Yes; §§16-61-201 to 212
CALIFORNIA	None	No	"Pure" form adopted by *Li v. Yellow Cab Co.*, 532 P.2d 1226 (1975).		*Li v. Yellow Cab Co.*, 532 P.2d 1226 (1975)	No.
COLORADO	13-21-111	Yes. §§13-50.5-101 to 13.50.5-106	Plaintiff's negligence not as great as that of defendant	If plaintiff's percentage of negligence is as great as defendant's, no recovery		Yes; §§13-50.5-101 to 13.50.5-106
CONNECTICUT	52-572h		Plaintiff's negligence not greater than combined negligence of defendants	If plaintiff's negligence is greater than defendant's		Yes; §52-572(e); also §52-572(h). Must be brought within one year
DELAWARE	Tit. 10 §8132	Yes; Tit. 10 §§6301 to 6308	Plaintiff's negligence not greater than the combined negligence of defendants; Tit. 10 §8132	If plaintiff's negligence is greater than defendant's		Yes; Tit. 10 §§6301 to 6308

State						
DISTRICT OF COLUMBIA	None	No		Plaintiff's negligence is a bar to recovery except the liability of common carriers for injuries to employees, when plaintiff's negligence is slight and employer's is gross. See §44-402		No
FLORIDA	768.81, et seq.	Yes; §768.31	Any contributory fault chargeable to claimant diminishes proportionately the amount awarded as economic or uneconomic damages; §768.81	Percentage of own fault	Hoffman v. Jones, 280 So. 2d 431 (1973)	Yes; §768.31
GEORGIA	51-11-7	No	Yes; plaintiff's negligence not greater than aggregate negligence of defendants; §663-31. Union Camp Corp. v. Helmy 258 Ga. 263, 367 SE.2d 796 (1988)	If plaintiff by ordinary care could have avoided defendant's negligence, he is barred		Yes; §51-12-32
HAWAII	663-31	663-11 to 663-17	Plaintiff's negligence not greater than aggregate negligence of defendants; §663-31	If plaintiff's negligence is as great as defendant's		§§663-11 to 663-17
IDAHO	6-801	No	Plaintiff's negligence not as great as defendant's	If plaintiff's negligence is greater than defendant's		Yes; §6-803.
ILLINOIS	735 ILCS 5/2-1116	No	If plaintiff is more than 50% negligent, he is barred from recovery (735 ILCS 5/2-1116; passed 1986 in response to the "insurance crisis")	Over 50% negligence attributed to plaintiff; under 50% damages diminished in proportion to plaintiff's percentage of fault		Yes; 740 ILCS 100/0.01, et seq.
INDIANA	34-4-33-3, 4	No	Plaintiff's fault not greater than defendants' aggregate fault	Plaintiff's fault greater than defendant's		No; §34-4-33-7, but section does not affect indemnity rights
IOWA	668.3; 668.5	No	Barred if claimant's fault is greater than combined fault of defendant (§668.3, enacted 1984)	If claimant's fault is greater than aggregate of defendant's	Goetzman v. Wichern, 327 N.W. 2d 742 (1982)	Yes; §668.5
KANSAS	60-258a	No	Plaintiff's negligence less than causal negligence of defendants	Plaintiff's negligence greater than defendant's		No

(Continued)

State	Code Section	Uniform Act	Comparative Negligence	Contributory Negligence—Limit to Plaintiff's Recovery	Judicial Imposition of Comparative Negligence	Contribution Among Tortfeasors
KENTUCKY	None	No	No; Failure to put child in safety restraint is statutorily not contributory negligence. (§189.125).	Plaintiff's negligence is a bar to recovery. Contributory negligence will not bar employee's recovery when railroad violated any safety statute (§277.320)		Yes; §412.030
LOUISIANA	La-Civ. Code Art 2323	No	"Pure" comparative negligence (La. Civ. Code Art. 2323)			No
MAINE	Tit. 14 §156	Plaintiff's negligence less than defendant's (Tit. 14 §156)	If plaintiff's negligence is equal to or greater than defendant's, then no recovery			No
MARYLAND	None	Uniform Contribution Among Tortfeasors Act Md. Ann. Code Art. 50 §16-24 (1957)	Not using seatbelt is not contributory negligence (Transp. §§22-412.3 & 4)	Plaintiff's negligence is a bar to recovery		Yes; Md. Ann. Code Art. 50 §16-24
MASSACHUSETTS	Ch. 231 §85	Ch. 231B §§1-4	Plaintiff's negligence not greater than defendant's (Ch. 231 §85)	Plaintiff's negligence greater than defendant's		Ch. 231B §§1-4
MICHIGAN	None		"Pure" comparative negligence	Percentage of his own negligence	Placek v. City of Sterling Heights, 275 N.W.2d 511 (1979)	Yes; MCL 600.2925c
MINNESOTA	604.01, et seq.		Plaintiff's fault not greater than defendant's, but damages are diminished in proportion to fault	Plaintiff's fault greater than defendant's		No
MISSISSIPPI	11-7-15	No	"Pure" comparative negligence	Plaintiff's percentage of negligence		No
MISSOURI	None				Gustafson v. Benda, 661 S.W. 2d 11 (1983)	Yes; §537.060
MONTANA	27-1-702	No	Plaintiff's negligence not greater than combined negligence of defendants (§27-1-702)	Plaintiff's negligence greater than defendant's		Yes; §27-1-703

State	Comparative Negligence Statute	Contribution Statute	Comparative Negligence Rule	Contribution Among Joint Tortfeasors?
NEBRASKA	25-21, 185.07 to 185.12		Plaintiff's award diminishes proportionally with negligence, but negligence equal to or greater than defendant's is a total bar.	No
NEVADA	41.141	17.225 to 17.305	Plaintiff's negligence not greater than defendant's	Yes; §§17.225 to 17.305
NEW HAMPSHIRE	507:7d	No	Plaintiff's negligence not greater than causal negligence of defendant	Yes; §507.7f
NEW JERSEY	2A:15-5.1, et seq.		Plaintiff's negligence not greater than defendant's (§2A: 15-5.1)	Yes; 2A:15-5.3 & 2A:53A-2
NEW MEXICO	None	41-3-1 to 41-3-8	"Pure" comparative negligence — Scott v. Rizzo, 634 P.2d 1234 (1981)	Yes; §§41-3-1 to 41-3-8
NEW YORK	N.Y. Civ. Prac. L. & R. §§1411, et seq.	N.Y. Civ. Prac. L. & R. §§1411, et seq.	"Pure" comparative negligence	Yes; N.Y. Civ. Prac. L. & R. §§1401 et seq.
NORTH CAROLINA	None	§1B-1 to 1B-6	Plaintiff's negligence bar to recovery; Defendant has burden of proving plaintiff was comparatively negligent (§1-139)	Yes; G.S. §§1B-1 to 1B-6
NORTH DAKOTA	None	32-38-01 to 04	Plaintiff's negligence as great as defendant's	Yes; §§32-38-01 to 04
OHIO	2315.19	2307.31, 2307.33	Plaintiff's negligence greater than defendant's; Plaintiff's negligence no greater than combined negligence of defendants; award diminished proportionately with fault (§2315.19)	Yes; §§2307.31, 33
OKLAHOMA	Tit. 23 §13-14	Tit. 12 §832	Plaintiff's negligence greater than defendant's; Plaintiff's negligence is not of greater degree than defendant's	Yes; Tit. 12 §832
OREGON	18.470	No	Plaintiff's negligence greater than defendant's; Plaintiff's negligence not greater than combined fault of defendants	Yes; §18.440
PENNSYLVANIA	Tit. 42 §7102	Tit. 42 §§8321-8327	Plaintiff's negligence cannot be greater than defendant's; Plaintiff's negligence not greater than causal negligence of defendants (§7102)	Yes; Tit. 42 §§8321-8327
RHODE ISLAND	9-20-4	§§10-6-1 to 11	"Pure" comparative negligence; Only percentage of negligence attributable to plaintiff; award diminished proportionately (9-20-4)	Yes; §§10-6-1 to 11

(Continued)

State	Code Section	Uniform Act	Comparative Negligence	Contributory Negligence—Limit to Plaintiff's Recovery	Judicial Imposition of Comparative Negligence	Contribution Among Tortfeasors
SOUTH CAROLINA	None	§§15-38-10 to 70	Does not exist in South Carolina except by statute for railroad employer's liability	Plaintiff's negligence bar to recovery		Yes; §§15-38-10 to 70
SOUTH DAKOTA	20-9-2	15-8-11, et seq.	Plaintiff's negligence slight in comparison to defendant's; he may then recover in proportion to comparative fault (§20-9-2)	Plaintiff's negligence is found to be more than slight in comparison to defendant's negligence		Yes; SDCL §§15-8-11 to 22
TENNESSEE	None	29-11-101	No; Last Clear Chance Doctrine (See Street v. Calvert, 541 S.W. 2d 576 (1976))	Plaintiff's negligence is a bar to recovery (See Street v. Calvert, 541 S.W. 2d 576 (1976) for discussion of "remote" contributory negligence.)		Yes; TCA §§29-11-101 to 106
TEXAS	Civ. Prac. & Rem. §33.001	No	Plaintiff's negligence not greater than defendant's; award diminished in proportion to negligence (Civ. Prac. & Rem. §33.001)			Yes; Civ. Prac. & Rem. §33.012
UTAH	78-27-37, et seq.	No	Plaintiff's negligence not as great as defendant's (§78-27-38)			No; but §78-27-40 will not affect any right to comparative negligence arising from statute, contract, or agreement

State					
VERMONT	Tit. 12 §1036		Plaintiff's negligence not greater than causal total negligence of defendants.		No
VIRGINIA	8.01-58 (Contributory negligence is no bar to recovery in certain employee-railroad disputes.)	No	In an action against a common carrier, comparative negligence will not bar recovery and if carrier violated a safety code, the injured party won't be found comparatively negligent (8.01-58)	Plaintiff's negligence bar to recovery	8.01-34; Contributory negligence may be applied when the wrong results from negligence and involves no moral turpitude
WASHINGTON	4.22.005 to 925	Yes; 4.22.005 to 925	"Pure" comparative negligence (§4.22.005); Amount of reward reduced proportionately with fault		Yes; §4.22.040
WEST VIRGINIA	None	No	Plaintiff's negligence does not exceed or equal defendant's	Bradley v. Appalachian Power Co., 256 S.E.2d 879 (1979), at 885.	Yes; §55-7-13
WISCONSIN	895.045	No	Plaintiff's negligence not greater than defendant's (§895.045)		Yes; common law right based on equitable principles (State Farm Mutual Auto Ins. v. Continental Cas. Co., 59 N.W. 2d 425)
WYOMING	1-1-109	No	Plaintiff's negligence must not be over 50% of the total fault (§1-1-109)	Over 50% fault ascribed to plaintiff	No

(Concluded)

Automobile Accident and Investigation Checklist

Thomas W. Elliott and Agnes M. Elliott, *Tort Resume for Use in Prosecution and Defense of All Damage Claims.*

Parties—General Information
( ) Plaintiff _____ Age _____ Sex _____ Phone _____
( ) Address _____ City _____ County _____ State _____ Z.Code _____
( ) Bus. Address _____ City _____ County _____ State _____ Phone _____
( ) Ins. Carrier _____ Address _____ Phone _____
      Amount of Insurance: Liability _____ Property Damage _____
      Medical _____ Collision _____ Uninsured Motorist _____
      Any Coverage Deductible? Which? _____

      _____

( ) Defendant 1. _____ Age _____ Sex _____ Phone _____
( ) Address _____ City _____ County _____ State _____ Z.Code _____
( ) Bus. Address _____ City _____ County _____ State _____ Phone _____
( ) Ins. Carrier _____ Address _____ Phone _____
      Amount of Insurance: Liability _____ Property Damage _____
      Medical _____ Collision _____ Uninsured Motorist _____
      Any Coverage Deductible? Which? _____

      _____

( ) Co-Defendants 2. _____ Age _____ Sex _____ Phone _____
                      3. _____   _____   _____   _____
( ) Address 2. _____ City _____ County _____ State _____ Z.Code _____
              3. _____   _____   _____   _____   _____
( ) Bus. Address 2. _____ City _____ County _____ State _____ Phone ___
                    3. _____   _____   _____   _____   ___
( ) Ins. Carrier 2. _____ Address _____ Phone _____
                  3. _____   _____   _____
      Amount of Insurance:
      Liability 2. _____ Property Damage _____ Medical _____ Collision _____
                3. _____   _____   _____   _____
      Uninsured Motorist 2. _____ Any Coverage Deductible? Which?
                          3. _____
      2. _____
      3. _____

Facts of Accident
( ) Date of Accident _____ Time _____ Material Facts _____
      _____
      _____
      _____

( ) Statements Made Immediately Prior to, During, or After the Incident _____
      _____

( ) Type of Case (Check Applicable Subject Matter)
      ( ) Animals ( ) Assault & Battery ( ) Drainage & Pollution
      ( ) Employer, Employee and Independent Contractor ( ) False
      Imprisonment ( ) Fraud and Deceit ( ) Invitees and Licensees
      ( ) Malicious Arrest or Prosecution ( ) Malpractice ( ) Municipal
      ( ) Products Liability ( ) Real Estate ( ) Slander or Libel
      ( ) Transportation—Airplane, Automobile, or Train ( ) Trespass
      ( ) Wrongful Death ( ) Workers' Compensation ( ) Other _____

( ) Attach Diagram of Accident Scene if Physical Facts are Important
      _____

      _____
( ) Indicate and Note on Diagram:
      ( )   Width of Streets or Roads Measured _____

(   )   Number of Lanes _____ Any Peculiar Curves or Hills _____
(   )   Yellow Lines _____ Stop Signs or Traffic Devices _____
(   )   Skid Marks _____ Position of Vehicles after Accident _____
(   )   Type of Road Surface. Asphalt or Concrete _____
(   )   Dry or Wet _____ Weather—Fog, Rain, Drizzle, Sleet, or Snow
_____
_____

(   )   Visibility—Good or Bad _____ Day, Night, Dusk, or Dawn _____
_____

(   )   Clear or Cloudy _____ Other _____
(   )   Were Pictures Taken of Accident Scene? _____
(   )   When? _____ By Whom? _____
(   )   Address _____ Phone _____
(   )   If Not, Take Pictures of Accident Scene Immediately
(   )   Place Pictures Obtained or Taken in Evidence File
(   )   Miscellaneous Comments _____
_____

(   )   Automobile Information
    (   )   Plaintiff Vehicle
        (   ) Year _____ Make _____ Model _____ Color _____
        (   ) Cylinders _____ Horsepower _____ Weight _____
               Manuf. I.D. _____
        (   ) Tag No. _____ Power or Regular Steering _____
               Brakes _____
        (   ) Defects of Vehicles—Brakes _____ Lights _____
               Motor _____ Steering _____ Tires _____
               Other _____
               Comments as to Condition _____
        (   ) Seat Belts in Use at Time? _____
               Air Bags Available and Functioning? _____
        (   ) Location of Vehicle—Garage _____
               Address _____ Phone _____
               Were Pictures Taken of Automobile? _____
               When? _____ By Whom? _____
               Address _____ Phone _____
        (   ) If Not, Take Pictures at Garage and Place in Evidence File
               Taken By _____ When _____ Address _____
        (   ) Note Alleged Speed Prior to Collision _____

        (   ) Indicate Impact Points on Vehicle Diagram and Note Interior
               Damage

Right Side
Length ____ ft.   Front
Width ____ ft.   Rear   Left Side

        (   ) Owner of Plaintiff Vehicle _____ Age _____ Sex _____
        (   ) Address _____ City _____ State _____ Phone _____
        (   ) Business Address _____ City _____
               State _____ Phone _____
        (   ) Ins. Carrier _____ Address _____
               Phone _____
               Amount of Insurance: Liability _____
               Property Damage _____
               Medical _____ Collision _____
               Uninsured Motorist _____ Any Coverage

Deductible? Which? _____
_____

( ) Driver Plaintiff Vehicle _____
( ) Relationship to Owner _____
Driving with Permission? _____
( ) Destination and Purpose _____
( ) Impediments of Driver—Intoxication _____
Glasses _____
( ) Hearing _____ Other Physical Defects _____
( ) **Passengers   Seat Location in Vehicle**
_____
_____
_____

( ) Defendant Vehicle
( ) Year _____ Make _____ Model _____ Color _____
( ) Cylinders _____ Horsepower _____ Weight _____
Manuf. I.D. _____
( ) Tag No. _____ Power or Regular Steering _____
Brakes _____
( ) Defects of Vehicle—Brakes _____ Lights _____
Motor _____ Steering _____ Tires _____
Other _____
Comments as to Condition _____
( ) Seat Belts in Use at Time?_____
Air Bags Available and Functioning?_____
( ) Location of Vehicle—Garage _____
Address _____ Phone _____
( ) Were Pictures Taken of Automobile? _____
When? _____ By Whom? _____
Address _____ Phone _____
( ) If Not, Take Pictures at Garage and Place in Evidence File
Taken By _____ When? _____
( ) Note Alleged Speed Prior to Collision _____
( ) Indicate Impact Points on Vehicle Diagrams & Note Interior
Damage

Right Side
Length ____ ft.   Front
Width ____ ft.   Rear   Left Side

( ) Owner of Defendant Vehicle _____ Age _____ Sex _____
( ) Address _____ City _____ State _____ Phone _____
( ) Business Address _____ City _____ State _____
Phone _____
( ) Ins. Carrier _____ Address _____ Phone _____
Amount of Insurance: Liability ___ Property Damage _____
Medical _____ Collision _____ Uninsured Motorist _____
Any Coverage Deductible? Which? _____
_____
( ) Driver Defendant Vehicle _____
( ) Relationship to Owner _____
( ) Driving with Permission? _____
( ) Destination and Purpose _____
( ) Impediments of Driver—Intoxication _____ Glasses _____
Hearing _____ Other Physical Defects _____

Passengers   Seat Location in Vehicle

_____

_____

_____

(   ) Traffic Violations by Plaintiff and Defendant

Charges Against   Court   Hearing Date   Result

_____

_____

(   ) Get Copy of Traffic Court Testimony if Recorded and Place
        in Evidence File

(   ) Witnesses to Accident, Including Parties

Witnesses   Address   County   State   Age   Phone

_____

_____

_____

_____

_____

(   ) Statements Taken from Witnesses, Including Parties

Name   Who Took   When?   Do We Have a Copy?
        Statement?

_____

_____

_____

_____

_____

_____

_____

(   ) Place All Statements in Evidence File

(   ) Impeachment of Parties and Witnesses (Note Unfavorable Military Record)

Name   Crime Conviction   Date   Good or Bad Character

_____

_____

_____

_____

(   ) Parties' Prior Accidents

Plaintiff _____

_____

Defendant _____

_____

Medical

(   ) Plaintiff—Summary of Injuries (Indicate Degree of Disability) (Restriction of
Activities in Work, Sports, Etc.) _____

_____

_____

_____

_____

_____

_____

_____

_____

_____

_____

_____

_____

_____

_____

_____

_____

_____

_____

_____

_____

_____

_____

_____

( ) Note Injuries on Diagram

( ) Indicate Plaintiff's
Area of Pain

( ) Symptoms
   ( ) Headaches
   ( ) Dizziness
   ( ) Nausea
   ( ) Nervousness
   ( ) Insomnia
   ( ) Appetite

( ) Head
   ( ) Brain
   ( ) Forehead
   ( ) Ears
   ( ) Eyes
   ( ) Nose
   ( ) Mouth
   ( ) Teeth

( ) Neck
   ( ) Muscles
   ( ) Spine
   ( ) Throat

( ) Chest
   ( ) Heart
   ( ) Lungs
   ( ) Ribs

( ) Abdomen

( ) Internal Injuries

( ) _____

_____

( ) Arms (Right or Left)
   ( ) Upper
   ( ) Forearms
   ( ) Elbows
   ( ) Wrists
   ( ) Hands
   ( ) Fingers

( ) Trunk
   ( ) Shoulders
   ( ) Spine
   ( ) Thoracic
   ( ) Scapula
   ( ) Lumbar
   ( ) Sacrum
   ( ) Coccyx
   ( ) Pelvis
   ( ) Hips

( ) Legs (Right or Left)
   ( ) Thighs
   ( ) Upper
   ( ) Lower
   ( ) Knees
   ( ) Ankles
   ( ) Feet
   ( ) Toes

(   ) Indicate Radiations of Pain.

(   ) Indicate Cuts, Bruises, Burns, Bumps, Sutures, Fractures, Missing Teeth, Swelling, Contusions, Points of Bleeding, Unconsciousness, etc.

(   ) Same Information for Defendant's Injuries (if any)

(   ) Ambulance, Hospital and Doctor Service, Findings, and Treatment

    (   ) Ambulance Service—By Whom? _____ Other _____

    Any First Aid Administered? If So, What? _____

    Note Time Ambulance Arrived at Accident Scene _____

    (   ) **Hospitals   Address   Phone   Period of Treatment   Surgery**

    1. _____

    Treatment _____

    _____ X-Rays Taken? When? _____

    2. _____

    Treatment _____

    _____ X-Rays Taken? When? _____

    3. _____

    Treatment _____

    _____ X-Rays Taken? When? _____

    (   ) **Doctors   Address   Phone   Period of Treatment   Surgery**

    1. _____

    Diagnosis, Treatment, and Prognosis _____

    _____ X-Rays Taken? When? _____

    2. _____

    Diagnosis, Treatment, and Prognosis _____

    _____ X-Rays Taken? When? _____

    3. _____

    Diagnosis, Treatment, and Prognosis _____

    _____ X-Rays Taken? When? _____

    4. _____

    Diagnosis, Treatment, and Prognosis _____

    _____ X-Rays Taken? When? _____

(   ) Summary Comments as to Percent of Disability and Patient Prognosis

_____

_____

_____

Prior Medical Treatment—Plaintiff and Defendant

(   ) Plaintiff—Prior Medical Treatment

Doctors and Hospitals   Address   Phone   Period of Treatment

1. _____

2. _____

3. _____

Treatment _____

_____

    (   ) Note Relationship of Prior to Present Injuries _____

    _____

    (   ) Prior Claims of any Nature? When? Where? _____

    _____

(   ) Defendant—Prior Medical Treatment

Doctors and Hospitals   Address   Phone   Period of Treatment

1. _____

2. _____

3. _____

Treatment _____

_____

    (   ) Note Relationship of Prior to Present Injuries _____

    _____

    _____

(   ) Prior Claims of any Nature? When? Where? _____
_____
_____

(   ) Summary Degree of Prior Disability
(   ) Plaintiff _____
(   ) Defendant _____

Damages—Plaintiff
(   ) Plaintiff Employment Subsequent and Prior to Accident

Subsequent to	**Dates**	**Position**	**Annual Earnings**	**Per Diem**

Prior to (Last 2 Yrs.)	**Dates**	**Position**	**Annual Earnings**	**Per Diem**

(   ) Education and Job Training—(   ) Elementary (   ) High School
(   ) College (   ) Graduate (   ) Other _____

(   ) Family

Spouse and Children	**Relationship**	**Age**

(   ) Computation of General Damages—Note Age of Injured Party _____
(   ) Pain and Suffering (Past, Present, and Future) Estimate
        of Party—
        Value Assessed Per Day $ _____ × _____ Days
        $ _____ × Life Expectancy _____ $ _____
(   ) Diminution Capacity to Labor as Element of Pain and Suffering
        (Past, Present, and Future) Estimate of Party—
        Value Assessed Per Day $ _____ × _____
(   ) Days $ _____ × Life Expectancy _____ $ _____
        Loss of Consortium—Estimate of Party—
        Value Assessed Per Day $ _____ × _____
        Days $ _____ × Life Expectancy _____ $ _____

(   ) Computation of Special Damages (Date Accident _____)
(   ) Loss of Earnings
        (   ) Past and Present to Date of Trial—(Days
               in Hospital _____)
        (   ) Past and Present Continued—(At Home
               _____ Returned To Work—
               Date _____)
               Total Days _____ × Per Diem
               Wages
               $ _____ $ _____
        (   ) Annual Average Earnings $ _____
               (Capacity Reduced _____ % Disability
               $ _____) × _____(Use Annuity
               table _____% Column to Reduce to
               Present Cash Value) or × _____ Life
               Expectancy (For Gross when Reduction
               not Required)
                                                            $ _____
        (   ) Hospitals, Nurses, Doctors, Drugs (Supports and
               Braces), and Ambulance Expenses

Hospitals	**Period**	**Amount**
		$ _____

_____
_____
_____

| Nurses | Period | $ _____ | Amount | $ _____ |
| | | $ _____ | | |

| Doctors | Period | $ _____ | Amount | $ _____ |
| | | $ _____ | | |

_____
_____
_____
_____
_____

| Pharmacy | Period | $ _____ | Amount | $ _____ |
| | | $ _____ | | |

| Ambulance | Period | $ _____ | Amount | $ _____ |
| | | $ _____ | | |

(   ) Funeral Expenses—Mortician's
Name and Address _____
_____ $ _____

(   ) Property Damage
    (   ) Automobile—Fair
        Market Value before
        Accident $ _____
        Less Fair Market
        Value after Accident $ _____
        Diminution in Value $ _____ $ _____
    (   ) Reasonable Hire _____
        Days × Rental Value $ _____ $ _____
    (   ) Real Estate—
        Fair Market Value
        before Accident $ _____
        Less Fair Market Value
        after Accident $ _____
        Diminution in Value $ _____ $ _____
    (   ) Damages to Building—
        Reasonable Repair
        Repairs by _____
        Address _____
        Estimate $ _____
        Repairs Completed $ _____ $ _____

(   ) Punitive Damages
(   ) Attorney Fees
(   ) Court Costs _____
_____ $ _____

(   ) Other Miscellaneous Damages
_____
_____ $ _____

(   ) Total Damages Sued For $ _____
_____

Summary Reminder

(   ) Client
    (   ) Obtain a Fee Contract (Retainer) from Client
    (   ) Obtain Signed Medical Authorizations from Client

( ) Obtain Financial Statements to Support Special Damages
( ) Obtain Income Tax Returns for Last Two Years
( ) Remind Client to Notify Own Insurance Carrier and File Accident Reports Required by Law
( ) Investigation
   ( ) Obtain Medical Information from Doctors, Hospitals, and Other Sources ·
   ( ) Take Statements from All Witnesses
   ( ) Obtain or Take Pictures and Place Newspaper Clippings in Evidence File of:
      ( ) Accident Scene
      ( ) Vehicles
      ( ) Visible Injuries To Client
      ( ) Other _____
   ( ) Obtain Appraisals of Property, Warranty Deeds, Plats, and Surveys
   ( ) Obtain Engineer's Drawing of Accident Scene
   ( ) Obtain Copy of Accident Reports and Testimony of Traffic Hearing
   ( ) Obtain Copy of Death Certificate Where Applicable
   ( ) Notice Preparatory to Filing Suit
      ( ) Write Letter of Notice to Opposite Party or Party's Insurance Carrier if Known
   ( ) Office Information
      ( ) File Handled This Office _____
      ( ) Associate Attorney _____
          Address _____ Phone _____
      ( ) Referral by _____
          Address _____ Phone _____
   ( ) Obtain Letter in File as to Fee Arrangement in Associate and Referral Matters

D

Sample Accident Report Filed with Police Department

SAN DIEGO POLICE DEPARTMENT TRAFFIC COLLISION REPORT

Page _____ of _____

PRIMARY CAUSE	NO. INJURED	H & R FELONY ☐	CITY			BEAT	COLLISION NUMBER
SECTION _____	NO. KILLED	H & R MISD. ☐	COUNTY SAN DIEGO	NCIC # 3711	OFFICER I.D. #		

LOCATION

COLLISION OCCURRED ON		MO.	DAY	YR.	TIME	DAY OF WEEK S M T W T F S	EMERGENCY VEH. ☐
		INJURY, FATAL OR TOW AWAY ☐ YES ☐ NO				STATE HIGHWAY RELATED ☐ YES ☐ NO	

☐ AT INTERSECTION WITH
☐ OR: _____ FEET/MILES _____ OF _____

			NO. VEH'S. INVL'D.	PHOTOGRAPHS ☐ YES ☐ NO

CLASS OF COLLISION

☐ 1. Fatal
☐ 2. Injury
☐ 3. Prop. Damage Only

☐ 1. At Intersection
☐ 2. Not at Intersection
☐ 3. On Public Property
☐ 4. On Private Property

ON STREET
OFF STREET

INVESTIGATED
☐ AT SCENE
☐ NOT AT SCENE

FOR OFFICE USE

IMD. FORM SENT ☐

	FOR OFFICE USE					TOTAL
HR	GAR	SAC	TRAN			
SAF	SSP	PRO	COR			
		INS				

PARTY 1

DRIVER ☐
PEDES-TRIAN ☐
PARKED VEH. ☐
BICY-CLIST ☐
OTHER ☐

DRIVER'S LICENSE NUMBER	STATE	CLASS	SAFETY EQUIP.	VEH. YR.	MAKE/MODEL/COLOR	LICENSE NUMBER	STATE

NAME (FIRST, MIDDLE, LAST)

OWNER'S NAME/ADDRESS ☐ SAME AS DRIVER

STREET ADDRESS

DIR. OF TRAVEL | ON STREET OR HIGHWAY | SPEED | SPEED LIMIT

CITY/STATE/ZIP

SEX	HAIR	EYES	HEIGHT	WEIGHT	BIRTHDATE MO. DAY YR.	RACE

V-1

DESCRIBE VEHICLE DAMAGE
☐ UNKN. ☐ NONE ☐ MINOR
☐ MOD. ☐ MAJOR ☐ TOTAL

DISPOSITION OF VEHICLE ON ORDERS OF: ☐ OFFICER ☐ DRIVER ☐ OTHER

HOME PHONE ( ) BUSINESS PHONE ( )

VIOLATION CHARGED
1. _____ 2. _____
3. _____ Form _____

INSURANCE CARRIER | POLICY NUMBER

PARTY 2

DRIVER ☐
PEDES-TRIAN ☐
PARKED VEH. ☐
BICY-CLIST ☐
OTHER ☐

DRIVER'S LICENSE NUMBER	STATE	CLASS	SAFETY EQUIP.	VEH. YR.	MAKE/MODEL/COLOR	LICENSE NUMBER	STATE

NAME (FIRST, MIDDLE, LAST)

OWNER'S NAME/ADDRESS ☐ SAME AS DRIVER

STREET ADDRESS

DIR. OF TRAVEL | ON STREET OR HIGHWAY | SPEED | SPEED LIMIT

CITY/STATE/ZIP

SEX	HAIR	EYES	HEIGHT	WEIGHT	BIRTHDATE MO. DAY YR.	RACE

V-2

DESCRIBE VEHICLE DAMAGE
☐ UNKN. ☐ NONE ☐ MINOR
☐ MOD. ☐ MAJOR ☐ TOTAL

DISPOSITION OF VEHICLE ON ORDERS OF: ☐ OFFICER ☐ DRIVER ☐ OTHER

HOME PHONE ( ) BUSINESS PHONE ( )

VIOLATION CHARGED
1. _____ 2. _____
3. _____ Form _____

INSURANCE CARRIER | POLICY NUMBER

SKETCH

◯ INDICATE NORTH

INITIAL CONTACT POINT _____

INVESTIGATION NARRATIVE/ADDITIONAL WITNESSES

COLLISION NUMBER:

PD-154 (Rev. 1-88)

*EXPLAIN IN NARRATIVE

Page _____ of _____

DESCRIPTION OF DAMAGE	ADDRESS OF DAMAGED PROPERTY

OWNER'S NAME	ADDRESS	PHONE	NOTIFIED ☐ YES ☐ NO

INJURED / WITNESS

EXTENT OF INJURY — **INJURED WAS** (CHECK ONE)

WITNESS ONLY	AGE	RACE	FATAL INJURY	SEVERE WOUND DISTORTED MEMBER	OTHER VISIBLE INJURIES	COMPLAINT OF PAIN	DRIVER	PASS.	PED.	BI-CYCLIST	OTHER	IN VEHICLE NUMBER
☐			☐ DESCRIBE INJURY:	☐	☐	☐	☐	☐	☐	☐	☐	

NAME		HAIR	EYES	HEIGHT	WEIGHT	MO.	BIRTH DATE DAY	YEAR	YES	BELT	HELMET
ADDRESS	HOME PHONE	WORK PHONE	TAKEN TO (INJURED ONLY) BY	SAFETY DEVICE IN USE* NO ☐ ☐ CHILD RESTRAINT							

☐ DESCRIBE INJURY:	☐	☐	☐	☐	☐	☐	☐	☐

NAME		HAIR	EYES	HEIGHT	WEIGHT	MO.	BIRTH DATE DAY	YEAR	YES	BELT	HELMET
ADDRESS	HOME PHONE	WORK PHONE	TAKEN TO (INJURED ONLY) BY	SAFETY DEVICE IN USE* NO ☐ ☐ CHILD RESTRAINT							

☐ DESCRIBE INJURY:	☐	☐	☐	☐	☐	☐	☐	☐

NAME		HAIR	EYES	HEIGHT	WEIGHT	MO.	BIRTH DATE DAY	YEAR	YES	BELT	HELMET
ADDRESS	HOME PHONE	WORK PHONE	TAKEN TO (INJURED ONLY) BY	SAFETY DEVICE IN USE* NO ☐ ☐ CHILD RESTRAINT							

☐ DESCRIBE INJURY:	☐	☐	☐	☐	☐	☐	☐	☐

NAME		HAIR	EYES	HEIGHT	WEIGHT	MO.	BIRTH DATE DAY	YEAR	YES	BELT	HELMET
ADDRESS	HOME PHONE	WORK PHONE	TAKEN TO (INJURED ONLY) BY	SAFETY DEVICE IN USE* NO ☐ ☐ CHILD RESTRAINT							

SSP:

SCHOOL NAME: _____ GRADE: _____

PRIMARY CAUSE

	1	2
1. SPEED		
2. VIOLATED PED. RT. OF WAY		
3. VIOLATED RT. OF WAY AUTO		
4. PED. IN VIOLATION		
5. FOLLOWING CLOSE		
6. WRONG SIDE OF RD.		
7. IMPROPER PASSING		
8. IMPROPER TURN		
9. DISREGARDED STOP		
10. DISREGARDED TRAF. SIGNAL		
11. IMPROPER SIGNAL		
12. IMPROPER START		
13. NO LIGHTS		
14. OTHER*_____		

VEHICLE DEFECTS

1.	
2.	

OTHER ASSOCIATED FACTORS

VC SECTION
1. VIOLATION _____

VC SECTION
2. VIOLATION _____

VISION OBSCUREMENTS
3. _____

4. INATTENTION

5. STOP AND GO TRAFFIC

6. NON-CONTACT VEHICLE

7. PREVIOUS COLLISION

8. AVOIDING OBJECT

9. OTHER

10. NONE APPARENT

TYPE

	1	2

COLLISION OF MOTOR VEH. WITH

	1	2
1. RAN OFF ROAD		
2. OVERTURNED IN ROAD		
3. PED.		
4. MOTOR VEH. IN TRAFFIC		
5. PARKED MOTOR VEH.		
6. TRAIN		
7. BICYCLIST		
8. ANIMAL		
9. FIXED OBJECT		
10. OTHER*_____		
11. OTHER NON-COLLISION		

VEHICLE ACTION

1. GOING STRAIGHT AHEAD
2. CHANGING LANES
3. MAKING RIGHT TURN
4. MAKING LEFT TURN
5. MAKING U TURN
6. SLOWING OR STOPPING
7. STARTING IN TRAFFIC
8. STARTING FROM PARKED POSITION
9. STOPPED IN TRAFFIC
10. PARKED
11. BACKING
12. DRIVERLESS MOVING VEH.

CONSTRUCTION ZONE

1. BARRICADES PRESENT
2. ROAD CONSTR.
3. OTHER CONSTR.

TRAFFIC CONTROL

1. TRAFFIC SIGNAL FUNC.
2. TRAF. SIG. NOT FUNC.
3. STOP SIGN
4. WARNING ON YIELD
5. FLASHING SIGNAL
6. RR SIGNAL
7. OFFICER OR WATCHMAN
8. NO CONTROL PRESENT
9. OTHER*_____

WEATHER

1. CLEAR	
2. RAIN	
3. FOG OR MIST	
4. OTHER*_____	

ROAD CONDITION

1. DRY
2. WET
3. SLIPPERY
4. OTHER*_____

LIGHT CONDITION

1. DAYLIGHT
2. DAWN, DUSK
3. DARKNESS

SOBRIETY – DRUG

	1	2
1. HAD NOT BEEN DRINKING		
1. HBD – UNDER INFLUENCE		
2. HBD – NOT UNDER INFLU.		
3. HBD – IMPAIRMENT UNK.		
1. UNDER DRUG INFLUENCE		
2. SOBRIETY NOT KNOWN		

TEST ADM.

	1	2
1. BLOOD/URINE		
2. BREATH		
3. COORDINATION		

PHYSICAL DEFECT

	1	2
1. DEF. EYES/HEARING		
2. PHYSICAL HANDICAP		
3. ILL		
4. SLEEPY/FATIGUED		
5. OTHER *_____		
6. APPARENTLY NORMAL		

PED'S CONDITION

	1	2
1. HAD NOT BEEN DRINKING		
2. HAD BEEN DRINKING		
3. UNDER DRUG INFLU.		
1. PHYSICAL HANDICAP _____		
2. APPARENTLY NORMAL		
3. NOT KNOWN		
4. OTHER *_____		

PED'S ACTION

1. WALKING
2. RUNNING
3. STANDING
4. SITTING OR LAYING
5. WALKING BICYCLE
6. ON TRICYCLE
7. ON SKATEBOARD
8. OTHER*_____

DRIVER'S VISION OF PEDESTRIAN LIMITED BY:

1. STANDING TRAFFIC
2. PARKED CAR OR TRUCK
3. BUS AT BUS STOP
4. NO STREET LIGHTS
5. HEADLIGHT GLARE
6. SUN GLARE
7. OTHER*

PED ATTEMPTED EVASIVE ACTION
YES ☐ NO ☐ UNK ☐

DRIVER ATTEMPTED EVASIVE ACTION
YES ☐ NO ☐ UNK ☐

PED CROSSING IN

1. LEGAL UNMARKED CROSSWALK
2. MARKED CROSSWALK
3. MARKED SCHOOL CROSSWALK
4. NOT IN CROSSWALK
5. OTHER* _____

WHERE WAS PED STRUCK?

1. IN ROADWAY AT INTERSECTION
2. IN ROADWAY NOT AT INTERSECTION
3. IN ALLEY
4. ON SIDEWALK
5. ON SHOULDER
6. OTHER* _____

WHAT WAS PED DOING?

1. CROSSING WITH SIGNAL
2. CROSSING AGAINST SIGNAL
3. CROSSING UNSIGNALIZED INTERSECTION
4. CROSSING INT. DIAGONALLY
5. WALKING ALONG ROAD:
   A. FACING TRAFFIC
   B. NOT FACING TRAFFIC
6. GETTING ON/OFF VEHICLE
7. PUSHING OR WORKING ON VEHICLE
8. OTHER WORKING IN ROAD
9. GOING TO OR FROM BUS
10. GOING TO OR FROM ICE CREAM VENDOR
11. PLAYING IN STREET
12. PLAYING NEXT TO STREET
13. ACCIDENTLY ENTERED STREET
14. ENTERING BEHIND PARKED VEHICLE
15. OTHER* _____

REPORTING OFFICER	I.D. NUMBER	DIVISION	DATE – TIME	APPROVED

Resources: State Agencies Relevant to a Torts Practice

Abbreviations:

www: World Wide Web site of the state (most states have links to state laws and administrative agencies)

ac: accident records (where to obtain records covering accidents on the road)

oc: occupational safety (state agency that enforces safety in the workplace)

wc: Workers' Compensation agency

Alabama

www.state.al.us

ac:	334-242-4241	(Department of Public Safety)
oc:	334-269-4914	(Department of Labor)
wc:	334-242-8980	(Workers' Compensation Division)

Alaska

www.state.ak.us

ac:	907-463-5860	(Department of Public Safety)
oc:	907-269-4914	(Division of Labor Standards and Safety)
wc:	907-465-2790	

Arizona

www.state.az.us

ac:	602-223-2236	(Department of Public Safety)
oc:	602-542-4411	(Industrial Commission)
wc:	602-631-2050	(State Compensation Fund)

Arkansas

www.state.ar.us

ac:	501-221-8236	(State Police, Accidents Records Section)
oc:	501-682-4500	(Department of Labor)
wc:	501-682-3930	(Workers' Compensation Commission)

California

www.state.ca.us

oc:	415-972-8500	(Division of Occupational Safety and Health)
wc:	415-703-4600	(Division of Workers' Compensation)

Colorado

www.state.co.us

ac:	303-205-5613	(Department of Motor Vehicles)
oc:	303-866-3848	(Risk Management Division)
wc:	303-620-4700	(Department of Labor and Employment)

Connecticut

www.state.ct.us

ac:	860-685-8250	(Department of Public Safety)
oc:	860-566-4550	(Occupational Safety and Health)
wc:	860-493-1500	(Workers' Compensation Commission)

Delaware

www.state.de.us

ac:	302-739-5931	(State Police Traffic Section)
oc:	302-761-8176	(Division of Industrial Affairs)
wc:	302-761-8200	(Industrial Accident Board)

District of Columbia

www.state.dc.us

ac:	202-727-5986	(Insurance Operations Branch, Accident Report Section)
oc:	202-576-6339	(Occupational Safety and Health Office)
wc:	202-576-6265	(Office of Workers' Compensation)

Florida

www.state.fl.us

ac:	904-488-5017	(Crash Records)
oc:	850-488-1188	(Labor and Employment Security)
wc:	850-488-2514	(Division of Workers' Compensation)

Georgia

www.state.ga.us

ac:	404-624-7660	(Accident Reporting Section)
oc:	404-656-2966	(Safety Engineering)
wc:	404-656-2034	(State Board of Workers' Compensation)

Hawaii

www.state.hi.us

oc:	808-586-9116	(Occupational Safety and Health Division)
wc:	808-586-9151	(Disability Compensation Division)

Idaho

www.state.id.us

ac:	208-334-8100	(Transportation Department, Accident Records)
wc:	208-334-6000	(State Industrial Commission)

Illinois

www.state.il.us

ac:	217-782-6992	(Vehicle Record Inquiry)
oc:	217-782-9386	(Department of Labor)
wc:	312-814-6556	(State Industrial Commission)

Indiana

www.state.in.us

ac:	317-232-8286	(Vehicle Crash Records)
oc:	317-232-2378	(Department of Labor)
wc:	317-232-3808	(Workers' Compensation Board)

Iowa

www.state.ia.us

ac:	515-237-3070	(Department of Transportation, Office of Driver Services)
oc:	515-281-3606	(Occupational Safety and Health)
wc:	515-281-5934	(Industrial Services Division)

Kansas

www.state.ks.us

ac:	913-296-3671	(Driver Control Bureau)
wc:	785-296-3441	(Division of Workers' Compensation)

Kentucky

www.state.ky.us

ac:	502-227-8734	(Department of State Police, Records Section)
oc:	502-564-3070	(Labor Cabinet)
wc:	502-564-5550	(Workers' Compensation Board)

Louisiana

www.state.la.us

ac:	504-925-6156	(State Police, Accident Records)
oc:	504-342-7556	(Department of Labor, Safety and Health)
wc:	504-342-7561	(Office of Workers' Compensation)

Maine

www.state.me.us

ac:	207-624-8944	(State Police, Traffic Section)
oc:	207-624-6400	(Bureau of Labor Standards)
wc:	207-287-3751	(Workers' Compensation Board)

Maryland

www.state.md.us

ac:	410-298-3390	(State Police, Central Records Division)
oc:	410-767-2196	(Occupational Safety and Health)
wc:	410-767-0829	(Workers' Compensation Commission)

Massachusetts

www.state.ma.us

ac:	617-351-9434	(Registry of Motor Vehicles)
oc:	617-727-3452	(Division of Occupational Safety)
wc:	617-727-6477	(Industrial Accident Board)

Michigan

www.state.mi.us

ac:	517-322-5509	(Department of State Police, Record Look-Up Unit)
oc:	517-322-1814	(Bureau of Safety and Regulation)
wc:	517-373-3480	(Bureau of Workers' Compensation)

Minnesota

www.state.mn.us

ac: 612-296-2060   (Driver and Vehicle Services, Accident Records)

oc: 612-296-2116   (Occupational Safety and Health Division, OSHA Management Team)

wc: 612-296-7958   (Workers' Compensation Division)

Mississippi

www.state.ms.us

ac: 601-987-1260   (Safety Responsibility, Accident Records)

oc: 601-987-3981   (Center for Safety and Health)

wc: 601-987-4200   (Workers' Compensation Commission)

Missouri

www.state.mo.us

ac: 573-526-6113   (Highway Patrol, Traffic Division)

oc: 573-751-3403   (Division of Labor Standards)

wc: 573-751-4231   (Division of Workers' Compensation)

Montana

www.state.mt.us

ac: 406-444-3278   (Highway Patrol, Accident Records)

oc: 406-444-1605   (Safety Bureau)

wc: 406-444-6501   (State Compensation Insurance Fund)

Nebraska

www.state.ne.us

ac: 402-479-4645   (Department of Roads, Accident Records Bureau)

oc: 402-471-4712   (Labor and Safety Standards Division)

wc: 402-471-3923   (Workers' Compensation Court)

Nevada

www.state.nv.us

ac: 702-687-5300   (Department of Motor Vehicles)

oc: 702-687-3032   (Occupational Safety and Health)

wc: 702-886-1000   (State Industrial Insurance System)

New Hampshire

www.state.nh.us

ac: 603-271-2128   (Department of Safety, Accident Reproduction Section)

oc: 603-271-3176   (Department of Labor)

wc: 603-271-3176   (Workers' Compensation Division)

New Jersey

www.state.nj.us

ac: 609-882-2000   (State Police, Records)

oc: 609-777-0249   (Labor Standards and Safety Enforcement)

wc: 609-292-2414   (Division of Workers' Compensation)

New Mexico

www.state.nm.us

ac:	505-827-9300	(Department of Public Safety)
oc:	505-827-4230	(Occupational Safety and Health Bureau)
wc:	505-841-6000	(Workers' Compensation Administration)

New York

www.state.ny.us

ac:	518-474-0710	(Department of Motor Vehicles, Accident Report Section)
oc:	518-457-2741	(Department of Labor)
wc:	518-474-6670	(Workers' Compensation Board)

North Carolina

www.state.nc.us

ac:	919-733-7250	(Department of Motor Vehicles, Collision Reports Section)
oc:	919-733-7166	(Department of Labor)
wc:	919-733-4820	(Industrial Commissioner)

North Dakota

www.state.nd.us

ac:	701-328-2553	(Driver License and Traffic Safety Division, Accident Report Section)
oc:	701-328-3886	(Loss Prevention)
wc:	701-328-3820	(Workers' Compensation Bureau)

Ohio

www.state.oh.us

ac:	614-752-1575	(Department of Public Safety, Traffic Crash Records)
oc:	614-644-2246	(Occupational Safety and Health)
wc:	614-728-8428	(Workers' Compensation Bureau)

Oklahoma

www.state.ok.us

ac:	405-425-2192	(Department of Public Safety, Accident Reports)
oc:	405-521-2413	(Safety Standards Division)
wc:	405-557-7600	(Workers' Compensation Committee)

Oregon

www.state.or.us

ac:	503-945-5098	(Motor Vehicle Division, Accident Reports and Information)
oc:	503-378-3272	(Occupational Safety and Health Administration)
wc:	503-945-7500	(Workers' Compensation Division)

Pennsylvania

www.state.pa.us

ac:	717-783-5516	(Police Headquarters, Accident Records Unit)
oc:	717-787-3323	(Occupational and Industrial Safety)
wc:	717-783-5421	(Bureau of Workers' Compensation)

Rhode Island
www.state.ri.us

ac:	401-444-1143	(State Police, Accident Record Division)
oc:	401-457-1800	(Occupational Safety and Health)
wc:	401-277-3097	(Workers' Compensation Commission)

South Carolina
www.state.sc.us

ac:	803-251-2969	(Accident Reports)
oc:	803-734-9644	(Occupational Safety and Health)
wc:	803-737-5744	(Workers' Compensation Commission)

South Dakota
www.state.sd.us

ac:	605-773-3868	(Department of Transportation, Accident Records)
oc:	605-772-3681	(Department of Labor)
wc:	605-773-3681	(Division of Labor and Management)

Tennessee
www.state.tn.us

ac:	615-741-3954	(Financial Responsibility Section, Accident Reports/Records Unit)
oc:	615-741-2793	(Compliance Division)
wc:	615-532-1468	(Workers' Compensation)

Texas
www.state.tx.us

ac:	512-424-2600	(Department of Public Safety, Accident Reports)
oc:	512-458-7375	(Department of Health)
wc:	512-448-7962	(Workers' Compensation Commission)

Utah
www.state.ut.us

ac:	801-965-4428	(Driver's License Division, Accident Reports Section)
oc:	801-530-6898	(Occupational Safety and Health Division)
wc:	801-530-6880	(Labor Commission)

Vermont
www.state.vt.us

ac:	802-828-2050	(Department of Motor Vehicles, Accident Report Section)
oc:	802-828-2765	(Division of Occupational Safety and Health Administration)
wc:	802-828-2288	(Department of Labor and Industry)

Virginia
www.state.va.us

ac:	804-367-0538	(Department of Motor Vehicles, Customer Record Requests)
oc:	804-786-2377	(Department of Labor and Industry)
wc:	804-367-8657	(Workers' Compensation Commission)

Washington

www.state.wa.us

ac:	360-902-3900	(Department of Licensing, Accident Reports)
oc:	360-902-5495	(Department of Labor and Industries)
wc:	360-902-5800	(Workers' Compensation Division)

West Virginia

www.state.wv.us

ac:	304-746-2128	(Department of Public Safety, Traffic Records Section)
oc:	304-558-7890	(Bureau of Employment Programs)
wc:	304-558-2630	(Workers' Compensation Division)

Wisconsin

www.state.wi.us

ac:	608-266-8753	(Department of Motor Vehicles, Traffic Accident Section)
oc:	608-266-3151	(Division of Safety and Buildings)
wc:	608-266-1340	(Workers' Compensation Division)

Wyoming

www.state.wy.us

ac:	307-777-4450	(Department of Transportation, Accident Records Section)
oc:	307-777-7700	(Occupational Safety and Health Administration)
wc:	307-777-6750	(Workers' Compensation Division)

F

Verdicts and Settlements

Legal newspapers often print information on recent litigation. Here are some tort cases from the "Verdicts & Settlements" feature of the *Los Angeles Daily Journal* and the *San Francisco Daily Journal*.[1] One of the interesting aspects of these summaries is the relationship between the settlement discussions and the final outcome of the case, either a verdict or a negotiated settlement. Parties are always concerned with questions such as: Should I settle? If so, how much should I demand or accept? Should I refuse to settle in order to try to do better in a trial verdict? With the benefit of hindsight, the following summaries allow you to determine how well the parties gambled on the answers to such questions.

PERSONAL INJURY

Auto v. Auto
Rear-End Collision

CASE/NUMBER: Carlos Bustamante v. Oz's Apparel, et al. / BC167799.

INJURIES: The plaintiff claimed soft tissue neck and back injury, bulging L5-S1 disc, Grade III tear left knee interior medical meniscus. The plaintiff claimed the meniscus would require arthroscopic surgery.

FACTS: On April 9, 1996, plaintiff Carlos Bustamante, a 43-year-old dress pattern cutter, alleged he was stopped at a red light at the intersection of San Pedro Street and Washington Boulevard behind a 1996 Nissan Sentra. He claimed defendant, Ernesto Zuniga driving a 1994 Ford GMC truck owned by his employer, defendant Oz's Apparel, ran into the plaintiff's Dodge Ram van pushing him into the Nissan. The plaintiff brought this action against the defendants based on a negligence theory of recovery.

CONTENTIONS: The plaintiff contended that he was rear-ended and pushed into the vehicle in front of him by the defendant's vehicle, which resulted in his knee striking the dashboard and his driver's seat breaking and throwing him to the floor.

The defendants contended that plaintiff ran into the Nissan first; that the collision from the rear was of insufficient force to have caused the $8,000 in property damage previously paid; and the force of the impact could not have pushed plaintiff forward into the Nissan. The defendants further contended that the force was insufficient to cause the ruptured disc and the alleged torn meniscus; there was no torn meniscus, and the disc was a consequence of aging and degeneration.

SETTLEMENT DISCUSSIONS: Plaintiff made a settlement demand for $80,000. The defendants made an offer of compromise for $15,001.

OUTCOME: Verdict of $25,000 for plaintiff.

SPECIALS IN EVIDENCE: MEDS, $25,000; Future MEDS, $12,000; LOE (loss of earnings), $3,500; Future LOE, $500.

JURY TRIAL: Length, seven days; Poll, 11-1 (liability); 9-3 (damages); Deliberation, four hours.

OTHER INFORMATION: The verdict was reached approximately one year after the case was filed.

PERSONAL INJURY

Medical Malpractice
Lack of Informed Consent

CASE/NUMBER: My Thi Pham; Toai Tan Huynh v. Habib Girgis, M.D. / BC113362.

INJURIES: The plaintiff claimed the removal of her uterus resulted in sterility.

FACTS: On Oct. 2, 1993, plaintiff My Thi Pham, a 28-year-old woman, went into labor under the care of defendant Dr. Habib Girgis. Postpartum, the plaintiff began bleeding heavily. The defendant ultimately performed a hysterectomy to stop the bleeding. The plaintiffs brought this action against the defendant based on negligence.

CONTENTIONS: The plaintiff contended the defendant negligently cut her cervix; and failed to repair or reoperate sooner, necessitating a hysterectomy.

The defendant contended the plaintiff's cervix was not cut; she had uterine atony; and other measures short of hysterectomy were attempted without success. The defendant also contended a hysterectomy was necessary to save the plaintiff's life.

SETTLEMENT DISCUSSIONS: The plaintiff made a settlement demand for $150,000. The defendant made an offer of $15,000.

OUTCOME: Verdict for defendant.

JURY TRIAL: Length, six days; Poll, 10-2; Deliberation, four hours.

PERSONAL INJURY

Medical Malpractice
Negligent Surgery

CASE/NUMBER: Case I.D. Confidential.

INJURIES: The plaintiff claimed she was forced to undergo a second operation to remove the surgical clip and repair any damage to the common bile duct. The plaintiff had a T-tube placed during the performance of that second operation. The T-tube remained in place for a period of several months until plaintiff's biliary tree had healed accordingly. As a result of being forced to undergo a second surgical procedure which could not be accomplished via a laparoscope, claimant now has an unsightly surgical scar of approximately seven or eight inches in length.

FACTS: The plaintiff underwent a laparoscopic cholecystectomy (removal of the gallbladder) which was performed by the defendant surgeon. Approximately one week post-operatively, the plaintiff began to experience itching and jaundice and was reevaluated by a gastroenterologist. An endoscopic retrograde cholangiopancreatography (ERCP) was performed which revealed a complete obstruction of the common bile duct secondary to a surgical clip. Immediately thereafter, the plaintiff was hospitalized and an exploratory laparotomy was performed to remove the clip and insert a T-tube for drainage of bile from the biliary tree. A T-tube is a catheter which extends from the patient's biliary tract outside of their body and which collects bile on a continuous basis until removed. The plaintiff brought this action against the defendant based on a negligence theory of recovery.

CONTENTIONS: The plaintiff contended that the defendant was negligent with respect to his respective care and treatment of her. The plaintiff also contended that it was negligent of the defendant to injure her common bile duct during the performance of the laparoscopic cholecystectomy by placement of a surgical clip across the common bile duct.

The defendant surgeon contended that, at all times, he acted within the applicable standard of care with respect to his care and treatment of the plaintiff.

SETTLEMENT DISCUSSIONS: The plaintiff made a settlement demand for $125,000. The defendant made an offer of $75,000.

OUTCOME: Case settled for $75,000.

OTHER INFORMATION: The settlement was reached approximately two years after the case was filed. The case was settled before designation of expert witnesses.

PERSONAL INJURY

Product Liability
Manufacturing Defect

CASE/NUMBER: Jim Hildebrandt v. Marker USA / 743684.

INJURIES: The plaintiff suffered injury to his right brachial plexus, requiring surgery, and to his right hand, requiring surgery. He underwent physical therapy, pain centers, psychiatric treatment, and he alleged loss of motor function in his right major arm, continued pain, possible reflex sympathetic dystrophy and psychiatric depression. He also claimed an inability to work. Plaintiff worked in real estate leasing and electric motor research and development.

FACTS: Plaintiff Jim Hildebrandt, a 40-year-old expert skier, purchased new Marker MISC bindings for his skies from a private party, took them to Newport Ski Company to be mounted, signed a release of liability form and went skiing on March 19, 1994 at Mammoth Mountain. As he skied over a mogul, he alleged that he stepped out of his left binding, lost his balance and fell putting his right hand in front of him to catch his fall. This caused injury to his right hand and his right brachial plexus. The plaintiff brought this product liability action against the binding manufacturer, alleging defective design, manufacture and warnings. The ski shop, an independent contractor and Marker authorized dealer, was named as a defendant but later prevailed on a motion for summary judgment.

CONTENTIONS: The plaintiff contended the instruction manual and certification program given to shop personnel regarding mounting procedures was defective; there was a manufacturing and design defect in the binding; and there was manufacturing defect in the defendant's ski-boot-binding system which was a separate and distinct product.

The defendant contended there was no defect in the instructions, and that the manual and certification program clearly advised as to proper mounting procedure; that shop personnel specifically testified they knew the proper procedure; that any mistake in the mounting was that of the shop; however, there still was no causation as the binding would still function properly as to release and retention; there was no defect in the binding or the system; and any mistake by the shop in mounting affected performance only and not release and retention.

SETTLEMENT DISCUSSIONS: Plaintiff says he offered to settle for $250,000. Defendant says plaintiff asked for $1 million. The defendant made no offer.

OUTCOME: Verdict for defendant.

JURY TRIAL: Length, 11 days; Poll, 12-0; Deliberation, one hour.

OTHER INFORMATION: The verdict was reached approximately three years after the case was filed.

ATTORNEYS

Legal Malpractice
Failure to File

CASE/NUMBER: Case I.D. Confidential.

DAMAGES: The plaintiff claimed $40,000 in lost earnings, per year, plus emotional distress and punitive damages.

FACTS: The plaintiff plead guilty to felony charges, and he asked his attorney to file a motion so that the judge who had sentenced him to home confinement would allow him to travel outside his restricted area for job related training. The attorney did not do this, and the plaintiff was fired. The plaintiff brought this action against the defendant based on a negligence theory of recovery.

CONTENTIONS: The plaintiff contended that he was fired because the motion was not filed and he was unable to mitigate his damages due to his status as a convicted felon.

The defendant contended that the plaintiff was planning to quit his job anyway and was able to mitigate damages through self-employment. The defendant also contended that the plaintiff had agreed with his attorney not to file the motion.

SETTLEMENT DISCUSSIONS: The plaintiff made a settlement demand for $85,000. The defendant made offers of $20,000, $35,000 and $37,000.

OUTCOME: Case settled for $40,000.

OTHER INFORMATION: The settlement was reached approximately two years and three months after the case was filed.

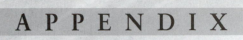

APPENDIX

G

Automobile Insurance

INTRODUCTION

Liability insurance protects others who are injured by your vehicle.[1] Every state requires motorists to demonstrate "financial responsibility" by carrying a minimum level of liability insurance or proving an ability to pay a tort judgment at this level without insurance. For example, the minimum level might be $25,000/$50,000/$10,000. (This means that for a single bodily injury in one accident, the coverage is $25,000; for multiple bodily injuries in one accident, the coverage is $50,000; and for property damage in one accident, the coverage is $10,000.) Motorists must apply for liability insurance on their own. The cost depends on factors such as the applicant's driving record, where the applicant lives, the sex and age of the applicant, and anticipated use of the vehicle. If no company agrees on its own to sell liability insurance to a particular motorist in the voluntary market (e.g., because of the applicant's bad driving record), he or she becomes an *assigned risk* in the involuntary market. Insurance companies are required to write liability insurance for assigned risks (at higher rates) in proportion to the amount of business they do in the state.

Under our tort system, an injured party sues a defendant in court in order to prove that the defendant was at fault in causing the accident. Most liability insurance, on the other hand, is based on a *no-fault* system. Under no-fault, each person's own insurance company pays for covered injury or damage up to policy limits, regardless of who was at fault in causing the accident.[2]

Liability insurance has not replaced the tort system. No state has a no-fault scheme that eliminates the option of bringing a tort suit in court for all automobile injury cases. Some states have what is called *add-on no-fault*. Here, liability insurance is simply added onto, but does not replace, the tort system. The injured party can recover under his or her liability insurance policy and can bring a tort suit in court against the person who caused the accident. If, however, the plaintiff wins anything in court, his or her insurance company is reimbursed for whatever benefits it paid the plaintiff. Other states have a *modified no-fault*. There are several versions of modified no-fault among the states. In general, the right of a victim to collect certain kinds of tort damages in court depends on whether a threshold has been met. There are two kinds of thresholds: a *dollar threshold* covering medical costs and a *verbal threshold* covering the kind of injury involved such as death, serious disfigurement, or dismemberment. Meeting a threshold means that the medical expenses of the victim exceed a designated amount (in a dollar threshold state) or that the victim's injury was of a designated severity (in a verbal threshold state). If the threshold has been met, the injured party can sue the other party in court for a tort. If, however, the threshold has not been met, the courts cannot be used; the parties are limited to the insurance coverage.

STATE NO-FAULT MOTOR VEHICLE INSURANCE LAWS[3]

---

[1]*Collision insurance* covers damage to your vehicle from a collision with an object. *Comprehensive insurance* covers a variety of other risks to your vehicle such as theft, vandalism, and fire. *Medical-payments insurance* covers medical costs for each person injured in your vehicle. *Uninsured/underinsured motorist insurance* protects you and the occupants of your car for bodily injury and property damage caused by someone who is uninsured or underinsured. These forms of insurances (unlike liability insurance) can be subject to deductibles.

[2]Liability insurance is *third-party insurance* in the sense that the insurance company pays a third party—someone other than the insured—who has been wrongfully injured by the insured. Fire insurance and collision insurance are examples of *first-party insurance* because the insurance company pays the insured for a covered loss; third parties are not directly involved.

[3]Copyright 1998 The Council of State Governments. Reprinted with permission from *The Book of States*. Source: State Farm Insurance Companies, *No Fault Press Reference Manual*.

State or other jurisdiction	Purchase of first-party benefits	Minimum tort liability threshold (a)	Maximum first-party (no-fault) benefits			
			Medical	Income loss	Replacement services	Survivors/funeral benefits
Arkansas	O (optional)	None	$5,000 if incurred within 2 yrs. of accident.	70% of lost income up to $140/wk. beginning 8 days after accident, for up to 52 wks.	Up to $70/wk. beginning 8 days after accident, for up to 52 wks.	$5,000 (if death occurs within one yr. of accident).
Colorado	M (mandatory)	$2,500 (b)	$50,000 (additional $50,000 for rehabilitation expenses incurred within 10 yrs. of accident).	100% of first $125/wk., 70% of next $125/wk., 60% of remainder up to $400/wk., for up to 52 wks.	Up to $25/day for up to 52 wks.	$1,000
Delaware	M	None, but amt. of no-fault benefits received cannot be used as evidence in suits for general damage.	$15,000 per person, $30,000 per accident overall max. on first-party benefits — Limited only by total benefits limit, but must be incurred within 2 yrs. of accident.	Limited only by total benefits limit, but must be incurred within 2 yrs. of accident.	Limited only by total benefits limit, but must be incurred within 2 yrs. of accident.	Funeral benefit: $3,000 (must be incurred within 2 yrs. of accident).
Florida	M	No dollar threshold. (c)	80% of all costs.	$10,000 overall max. on first-party benefits — 60% of lost income.	Limited only by total benefits limit.	Funeral benefit: $5,000
Hawaii (d)	M	Amount set annually by state insurance commissioner. (b)	Limited only by total benefits limit.	$20,000 overall max. on first-party benefits — Up to $1,200/mo.	Up to $800/mo.	Funeral benefit: $1,500
Kansas	M	$2,000 (b)	$4,500 (additional $4,500 for rehabilitation).	Up to $900/mo. for one yr. (if benefits not subject to taxes, max. 85% of lost income).	$25/day for 365 days.	Up to $900/mo. for lost income and replacement services for up to one yr., less disability payments received before death. Funeral benefit: $2,000.
Kentucky	(e)	$1,000 (b)	Limited by total benefits limit.	$10,000 overall max. on first-party benefits — Up to $200/wk. (If not subject to taxes, benefits can be reduced max. 15%).	Up to $200/wk.	Up to $200/wk. each for survivors' economic loss and survivors' replacement services loss. Funeral benefit: $1,000.
Maryland	M	None	Limited only by total benefits limit.	$2,500 overall max. on first-party benefits — for expenses incurred within 3 yrs. of accident — Limited only by total benefits limit.	Limited only by total benefits limit.	Funeral benefit: limited only by total benefits limit.
Massachusetts	M	$2,000 (b)	Limited only by total benefits limit, if incurred within 2 yrs.	$8,000 overall max. on first-party benefits — Up to 75% of lost income.	Up to 75% of actual loss.	Funeral benefit: limited only by total benefits limit.

(Continued)

State or other jurisdiction	Purchase of first-party benefits	Minimum tort liability threshold (a)	Maximum first-party (no-fault) benefits			
			Medical	Income loss	Replacement services	Survivors/funeral benefits
Michigan (d,f)	M	No dollar threshold. (c)	No dollar limits.	Up to $1,475/mo. up to 3 yrs.	$20/day for up to 3 yrs.	Up to $1,475/30-day period for lost income for up to 3 yrs. and $20/day for replacement services. Funeral benefits: not less than $1,750 nor more than $5,000.
Minnesota	M	$4,000 (b)	$20,000	85% of lost income up to $250/wk.	$20,000 max. for first-party benefits other than medical $200/wk., beginning 8 days after accident.	Up to $200/wk. ea. for survivors' economic loss and survivors' replacement service loss. Funeral benefit: $2,000.
New Jersey	M	(g)	Max. $250,000. Subject to $250 deductible and 20% co-payment between $250 and $5,000.	Up to $100/wk. for one yr.	Up to $12/day for a max. of $4,380/person.	Max. amount of benefits victim would have received. Funeral benefit: $1,000.
New York	M	No dollar threshold. (c)	Limited only by total benefits limit.	$50,000 overall max. on first-party benefits — 80% of lost income up to $2,000/mo. for up to 3 yrs.	$25/day for up to one yr.	$2,000 in addition to other benefits.
North Dakota	M	$2,500 (b)	Limited only by total benefits limit.	$30,000 overall max. on first-party benefits — 85% of lost income up to $150/wk.	Up to $15/day.	Up to $150/wk. for survivors' income loss and $15/day for survivors' replacement services. Funeral benefit: $3,500.
Oregon	M	None	$10,000	If victim is disabled at least 14 days, 70% of lost income up to $1,250/mo. for up to one year.	If victim is disabled at least 14 days up to $30/day for up to one yr. $15/day for child care, up to $450.	Funeral benefit: $2,500.
Pennsylvania	M	(h)	$5,000	(i)	(i)	(i)
South Dakota	O	None	$2,000 if incurred within 2 yrs. of accident.	$60/wk. for up to 52 wks. for disability extending beyond 14 days of date of accident.	None	$10,000 if death occurs within 90 days of accident.
Texas	O	None	$2,500 overall max. on first-party benefits — Limited only by total benefits limit if incurred within 3 yrs. of accident.	Limited only by total benefits limit if incurred within 3 yrs. of accident.	Limited only by total benefits limit if incurred within 3 yrs. of accident. Payable only to non-wage earners.	Limited only by total benefits limit if incurred within 3 yrs. of accident.

State or other jurisdiction	Purchase of first-party benefits	Minimum tort liability threshold (a)	Maximum first-party (no-fault) benefits			
			Medical	Income loss	Replacement services	Survivors/funeral benefits
Utah	M	$3,000 (b)	$3,000	85% of lost income up to $250/wk. for up to 52 wks., subject to 3-day waiting period which does not apply if disability lasts longer than 2 wks.	$20/day for up to 365 days subject to 3-day waiting period which does not apply if disability lasts longer than 2 wks.	$3,000 survivors benefit. Funeral benefit: $1,500.
Virginia	O	None	$2,000 if incurred within one yr. of accident.	Up to $100/wk. for max. 52 wks.	None	Funeral benefit: included in medical benefit.
Washington	O	None	Up to $35,000.	Up to $35,000.	Up to $5,000.	Funeral benefit: $2,000.
Dist. of Columbia	O	(j)	$50,000 or $100,000 (medical and rehabilitation).	$12,000 or $24,000.	Max. of $24,000.	Funeral benefit: $4,000.

Key:
O—Optional
M—Mandatory

(a) Refers to minimum amount of medical expenses necessary before victim can sue for general damages ("pain and suffering"). Lawsuits allowed in all states for injuries resulting in death and permanent disability. Some states allow lawsuits for one or more of the following: serious and permanent disfigurement; certain temporary disabilities, loss of body member, loss of certain bodily functions, certain fractures, or economic losses (other than medical) which exceed state limits.

(b) Victim cannot recover unless economic loss exceeds amount or injury results in condition(s) cited in legislation (e.g., permanent disfigurement, disability, dismemberment, fractures, etc.).

(c) Victim cannot recover unless injury results in condition(s) cited in legislation (e.g., permanent disfigurement, disability, dismemberment, fractures, etc.).

(d) Pending legislation.

(e) Accident victim is not bound by tort restriction if (1) he has rejected the tort limitation in writing or (2) he is injured by a driver who has rejected the tort limitation in writing. Rejection bars recovery of first-party benefits.

(f) Liability for property damage for all states with no-fault insurance under the state tort system. Michigan has no tort liability for vehicle damage, except in cases where damage does not exceed $400.

(g) Motorist chooses one of two optional limitations.

(h) Motorist chooses between full-tort option, with no limit on general damages, and a limited-tort option.

(i) Optional coverages are available to $177,500 maximum, including income loss benefits, accidental death benefits, and funeral benefits, in addition to medical benefits. An extraordinary medical benefits coverage to maximum $1.1 million is available.

(j) If person chooses "personal injury protection" option, victims who are covered by no-fault benefits have up to 60 days after accident to decide whether to receive no-fault benefits. Victims who choose to get no-fault benefits cannot recover damages unless injury resulted in substantial permanent scarring or disfigurement; substantial and medically demonstrable permanent impairment which has significantly affected the victim's ability to perform professional activities or usual and customary daily activities; a medically demonstrable impairment that prevents victim from performing substantially all of his usual customary daily activities for more than 180 continuous days; or medical and rehabilitation expenses or work loss exceeding the amount of no-fault benefits available.

H

Legal Nurse

Recently, many attorneys have begun hiring nurses to provide full- or part-time assistance in personal injury litigation. They are called *legal nurses* or *legal nurse consultants*. Although most traditional litigation paralegals do not have formal medical training, many of them perform duties that are similar to those of legal nurses. The American Association of Legal Nurse Consultants is anxious to point out, however, that there are differences between paralegals and legal nurses.[1]

---

[1]Reprinted with permission of the American Association of Legal Nurse Consultants: (AALNC), 4700 W. Lake Avenue, Glenview, IL 60025-1485. Copyright 1999.

AALNC Position Statement on the Role of the Legal Nurse Consultant as Distinct from the Role of the Paralegal and Legal Assistant

The American Association of Legal Nurse Consultants (AALNC) has defined legal nurse consulting as a specialty practice of the nursing profession. AALNC does not recognize legal nurse consultants (LNCs) as a special category of paralegals.

Attorneys and others in the legal arena consult with psychologists and engineers, for example, because of their expertise in their respective professions; similarly, they consult with LNCs because of their expertise in nursing and health care. Many LNCs have bachelor's and advanced degrees in nursing and other health-related fields. Some LNCs practice as independent consultants; others are employed by law firms, insurance companies, and other institutions in a wide variety of roles.

While many legal nurse consultants have acquired knowledge of the legal system through such experience as consulting with attorneys and attending seminars, legal education is not prerequisite to the practice of legal nurse consulting. (In contrast, legal education is frequently a requirement for paralegals.) Professional nursing education and healthcare experience make LNCs unique and valuable partners in legal processes.

The *Code of Ethics and Conduct*,[1] *AALNC Scope of Practice for the Legal Nurse Consultant*,[2] and *Standards of Legal Nurse Consulting Practice and Professional Performance*[3] describe the specialty of legal nurse consulting. The primary role of the legal nurse consultant is to evaluate, analyze, and render informed opinions on the delivery of health care and the resulting outcomes. The following list of activities helps to distinguish the practice of legal nurse consulting;

- facilitating communications and thus strategizing with the legal professional for successful resolutions between parties involved in healthcare-related litigation or other medical-legal or healthcare-legal matters
- educating attorneys or others involved in the legal process regarding the healthcare facts and issues of a case or a claim
- researching and integrating healthcare and nursing literature, guidelines, standards, and regulations as related to the healthcare facts and issues of a case or claim
- reviewing, summarizing, and analyzing medical records and other pertinent healthcare and legal documents and comparing them with and correlating them to the allegations
- assessing issues of damages and causation relative to liability with the legal process
- identifying, locating, evaluating, and conferring with expert witnesses
- interviewing witnesses and parties pertinent to the healthcare issues in collaboration with legal professionals
- drafting legal documents in medically related cases under the supervision of an attorney

- developing collaborative case strategies with those practicing within the legal system
- providing support during discovery, depositions, trial, and other legal proceedings
- testifying at depositions, hearings, arbitrations, or trials as expert healthcare witnesses
- supporting the process of adjudication of legal claims
- contacting and conferring with vendors to develop demonstrative evidence or to collect costs of healthcare services, supplies, or equipment
- supervising and educating other nurses in the practice of legal nurse consulting

Confusion about roles arises because in some settings, LNCs do some of the same work that legal assistants and paralegals do, particularly in small law offices where they are the only staff available to assist the attorneys.

Legal education programs offered for nurses by legal assistant or paralegal education programs also cause confusion about roles. To the extent that legal education is provided to nurses by legal assistant or paralegal education programs, it should be considered separate from the education of paralegals and legal assistants because of the differences in their practice in the legal arena.

In March 1998, the Standing Committee on Legal Assistants of the American Bar Association (ABA) decided that " . . . legal nurses and legal nurse consultants fall squarely within the ABA definition of 'paralegal/legal assistant' . . ."[4]. In contrast, AALNC recognizes a clear distinction between the roles of the legal nurse consultant and the paralegal . . . . AALNC does not support required ABA approval of legal nurse consulting education programs.

AALNC has defined legal nurse consulting as a specialty practice of nursing. AALNC's position, therefore, is that legal nurse consulting education should be developed and presented as specialty nursing curricula by nurse educators in partnership with legal educators.

References

[1] American Association of Legal Nurse Consultants. (1992). *Code of ethics and conduct of the American Association of Legal Nurse Consultants.* Glenview, IL: Author.
[2] American Association of Legal Nurse Consultants. (1995). *AALNC scope of practice for the legal nurse consultant.* Glenview, IL: Author.
[3] American Association of Legal Nurse Consultants. (1995). *Standards of legal nurse consulting practice and professional performance.* Glenview, IL: Author.
[4] American Bar Association Standing Committee on Legal Assistants. (Winter 1999). *More on legal nurse programs SCOLA update.* Chicago: Author.

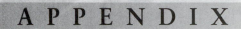

Disabling Injuries and Death: Some Statistics

All unintentional injuries, 1997				
Class	1997 Deaths	Change from 1996	Deaths per 100,000 Persons	Disabling Injuries[a]
All Classes[b]	**93,800**	**(c)**	**35.0**	**19,300,000**
Motor-Vehicle	43,200	(c)	16.1	2,300,000
Public nonwork	*40,900*			*2,200,000*
Work	*2,100*			*100,000*
Home	*200*			*(d)*
Work	5,100	+2%	1.9	3,800,000
Nonmotor-vehicle	*3,000*			*3,700,000*
Motor-vehicle	*2,100*			*100,000*
Home	28,400	+3%	10.6	6,800,000
Nonmotor-vehicle	*28,200*			*6,800,000*
Motor-vehicle	*200*			*(d)*
Public	19,400	−4%	7.2	6,500,000

Source: National Safety Council, Accident Facts™, *1998 Edition. The estimates (rounded) are based on data from the National Center for Health Statistics, Bureau of Labor Statistics, state departments of health, state traffic authorities, and state industrial commissions. The National Safety Council adopted the Bureau of Labor Statistics' Census of Fatal Occupational Injuries count for work-related unintentional injuries retroactive to 1992 data. See the Glossary for definitions and the Technical Appendix for revised estimating procedures.*

[a]*Disabling beyond the day of injury. Injuries are not reported on a national basis, so the totals shown are approximations based on ratios of disabling injuries to deaths developed each year by the National Safety Council. The totals are the best estimates for the current year. They should not, however, be compared with totals shown in previous editions of* Accident Facts™, *to indicate year-to-year changes or trends. See the Glossary for definitions and the Technical Appendix for estimating procedures.*

[b]*Deaths and injuries above for the four separate classes add to more than the All Classes figures due to rounding and because some deaths and injuries are included in more than one class. For example, 2,100 work deaths involved motor vehicles in transport and are in both the Work and Motor-vehicle totals, and 200 motor-vehicle deaths occurred on home premises and are in both Home and Motor-vehicle. The total of such duplication amounted to about 2,300 deaths and 100,000 injuries in 1997.*

[c]*Less than 0.5%.*

[d]*Less than 10,000.*

Deaths and Death Rates From Accidents, by Type: 1980 to 1995

Type of Accident	Deaths (number)					Rate per 100,000 Population				
	1980	1990	1993	1994	1995	1980	1990	1993	1994	1995
Total	**105,718**	**91,983**	**90,523**	**(NA)**	**(NA)**	**46.7**	**37.0**	**35.1**	**(NA)**	**(NA)**
Motor vehicle accidents	53,172	46,814	41,893	42,524	43,363	23.5	18.8	16.3	16.3	16.5
Traffic	51,930	45,827	40,899	41,507	42,331	22.9	18.4	15.9	15.9	16.1
Nontraffic	1,242	987	994	1,017	1,032	0.5	0.4	0.4	0.4	0.4
Water-transport accidents	1,429	923	763	723	762	0.6	0.4	0.3	0.3	0.3
Air and space transport accidents	1,494	941	859	1,075	851	0.7	0.4	0.3	0.4	0.3
Railway accidents	632	663	670	635	569	0.3	0.3	0.3	0.2	0.2
Accidental falls	13,294	12,313	13,141	13,450	13,986	5.9	5.0	5.1	5.2	5.3
Accidental drowning	6,043	3,979	3,807	3,404	3,790	2.7	1.6	1.5	1.3	1.4
Accidents caused by—										
Fire and flames	5,822	4,175	3,900	3,986	3,761	2.6	1.7	1.5	1.5	1.4
Firearms, unspecified and other	1,667	1,175	1,261	1,123	992	0.7	0.5	0.5	0.4	0.4
Handguns	288	241	260	233	233	0.1	0.1	0.1	0.1	0.1
Electric current	1,095	670	548	561	559	0.5	0.3	0.2	0.2	0.2
Accidental poisoning by—										
Drugs and medicines	2,492	4,506	7,382	7,828	8,000	1.1	1.8	2.9	3.0	3.0
Other solid and liquid substances	597	549	495	481	461	0.3	0.2	0.2	0.2	0.2
Gases and vapors	1,242	748	660	685	611	0.5	0.3	0.3	0.3	0.2
Complications due to medical procedures	2,282	2,669	2,724	2,616	2,712	1.0	1.1	1.1	1.0	1.0
Inhalation and ingestion of objects	3,249	3,303	3,160	3,065	3,185	1.4	1.3	1.2	1.2	1.2

NA Not available.
Source: U.S. National Center for Health Statistics, *Vital Statistics of the United States*, annual; and unpublished data.

Death Rates, by Leading Cause—States: 1995

[**Deaths per 100,000 resident population enumerated as of April 1.** By place of residence. Excludes nonresidents of the United States. Causes of death classified according to ninth revisions of International Classification of Diseases]

State	Total	Heart disease	Cancer	Cerebro-vascular diseases[1]	Accidents and adverse effects	Motor vehicle accidents	Chronic obstructive pulmonary diseases[1]	Diabetes mellitus	HIV[2]	Suicide	Homicide
U.S.	**880.0**	**280.7**	**204.9**	**60.1**	**35.5**	**16.5**	**39.2**	**22.6**	**(NA)**	**11.9**	**8.7**
AL	996.1	314.2	221.4	65.2	52.5	26.8	39.5	27.3	9.2	13.2	12.5
AK	423.0	90.6	95.1	24.0	56.2	16.1	17.7	9.3	5.0	17.1	8.9
AZ	837.9	242.6	190.1	51.8	47.0	23.5	48.3	19.5	11.5	19.1	12.7
AR	1,075.1	339.8	244.7	91.5	48.8	26.3	45.0	22.4	6.8	14.5	11.6
CA	709.8	216.3	162.8	51.4	29.3	14.1	34.2	16.2	20.4	11.7	11.6
CO	667.6	172.1	145.9	42.7	39.8	18.6	42.3	14.3	10.9	17.5	5.7
CT	899.5	298.9	215.6	57.2	32.9	10.7	35.5	18.1	18.4	9.9	—
DE	875.9	276.1	227.3	47.8	37.1	17.6	36.0	26.9	22.7	11.2	5.9
DC	1,244.2	302.4	267.2	66.8	34.8	12.3	24.2	39.5	117.8	7.0	56.8
FL	1,081.3	351.6	263.5	69.9	38.1	19.8	52.9	26.0	30.8	15.3	8.8
GA	810.8	242.4	177.3	56.2	41.1	21.4	34.2	16.7	22.0	11.5	10.3
HI	643.1	196.0	156.4	51.5	27.6	12.0	20.4	14.2	10.4	12.0	4.9
ID	732.1	212.3	172.4	54.8	45.2	22.7	38.2	17.7	3.7	16.0	4.0
IL	916.9	304.4	212.2	63.3	33.9	14.7	38.0	22.5	12.1	9.5	11.0
IN	918.2	294.3	216.3	68.9	38.0	17.1	41.3	24.8	6.7	12.0	7.8
IA	986.0	332.0	219.1	77.5	41.1	19.2	48.3	22.4	—	11.8	—
KS	933.0	297.7	205.9	70.6	38.7	17.6	44.9	22.5	5.6	11.3	6.3
KY	963.7	315.8	229.2	63.9	44.2	22.0	48.1	25.1	5.6	12.4	6.5
LA	914.4	279.4	214.3	58.6	42.4	21.0	32.7	34.4	16.8	12.5	17.6
ME	946.8	293.9	242.9	59.9	32.1	14.7	54.3	25.4	6.1	13.0	—
MD	829.8	236.4	201.9	52.5	27.6	13.5	31.6	27.0	25.6	10.1	12.7
MA	913.4	275.8	231.9	57.0	20.1	8.0	38.8	21.8	15.5	8.1	3.7
MI	876.1	294.8	203.5	61.4	33.2	17.0	37.5	23.4	8.4	10.3	9.9
MN	813.7	225.2	188.6	67.8	36.1	14.4	36.3	18.7	5.6	11.3	—
MS	1,002.0	356.0	213.1	69.3	59.6	33.5	37.9	18.1	9.5	11.8	15.9

MO	1,021.9	345.3	230.7	72.9	43.5	20.6	46.1	23.4	8.8	13.5	8.9
MT	876.6	230.3	203.4	68.3	43.7	22.4	55.2	24.1	—	23.1	5.4
NE	932.6	312.0	206.2	71.2	35.2	15.5	44.6	17.5	—	11.4	—
NV	818.6	246.9	194.5	46.4	36.0	19.9	52.0	15.4	13.2	25.8	11.2
NH	803.6	256.9	205.2	55.2	25.0	11.8	41.5	22.6	4.1	11.9	—
NJ	932.5	303.3	231.9	53.4	29.1	10.6	34.5	30.1	30.7	7.3	5.4
NM	744.3	196.1	159.5	42.7	54.6	26.7	41.5	26.1	9.1	17.6	10.1
NY	928.4	350.2	213.3	44.8	27.5	9.9	33.8	19.4	44.1	7.6	8.7
NC	902.2	269.5	206.8	72.3	41.0	20.7	39.7	24.3	14.1	12.6	9.6
ND	931.6	304.3	214.4	77.3	32.7	13.1	37.9	24.3	—	14.7	—
OH	950.1	317.4	226.1	60.0	29.1	12.4	44.2	30.0	7.9	9.7	—
OK	1,002.3	340.4	217.9	72.5	44.9	22.1	48.1	19.5	7.1	15.3	13.5
OR	898.4	240.1	214.7	77.7	43.5	18.9	45.4	21.7	9.2	15.8	4.7
PA	1,059.2	359.7	250.7	68.6	35.3	13.1	43.9	28.2	11.5	12.1	6.5
RI	975.7	334.1	250.4	64.8	21.9	8.1	42.0	24.7	10.0	9.0	—
SC	912.7	277.6	201.9	75.2	44.5	23.1	38.4	27.4	15.2	11.9	8.9
SD	948.5	312.3	214.5	73.2	44.4	22.1	44.4	23.0	—	11.8	—
TN	976.1	308.2	220.9	79.8	47.3	24.5	41.9	23.4	9.7	13.0	11.1
TX	736.1	222.9	168.9	52.3	34.3	17.8	33.3	24.4	14.8	11.9	9.6
UT	560.6	148.1	108.6	39.9	32.4	17.2	24.1	21.3	4.8	14.8	3.9
VT	846.7	278.2	198.9	57.1	32.8	16.1	41.2	24.5	4.6	13.0	—
VA	799.9	240.2	190.4	57.5	33.4	13.9	34.1	17.6	12.6	12.5	7.8
WA	751.0	208.6	183.0	60.7	34.9	13.7	39.7	19.4	10.9	14.4	5.5
WV	1,107.0	378.9	259.4	67.9	40.4	21.2	60.0	32.8	—	15.1	5.5
WI	880.1	281.4	206.3	69.8	35.6	15.1	36.7	21.6	—	12.1	4.7
WY	774.7	203.3	186.6	55.8	50.0	27.1	55.4	22.1	—	17.1	—

— Represents or rounds to zero. NA Not available.   [1]Includes allied conditions.   [2]Human immunodeficiency virus.

Source: U.S. National Center for Health Statistics, *Monthly Vital Statistics Report*; and unpublished data.

J

"Do you *seldomly* swear . . ?"

When it comes to examining witnesses, some attorneys are brilliant.[1] The lawyer who asked if the witness had the same nose he broke as a child was not. Recently, journalists from the *Baltimore Sun, Tampa Tribune, Fresno Bee, Dayton Daily News,* and *Salt Lake Tribune* hauled out their favorite examples of courtroom gaffes (the reporters swear they're true) and offered them to readers. A study of these bloopers reveals that most fall into one of five categories.

GOOD QUESTION

"Now doctor, isn't it true that when a person dies in his sleep he doesn't know about it until the next morning?"

_____

"The youngest son, the 20-year-old, how old is he?"

_____

"Were you alone or by yourself?"

_____

"Was it you or your younger brother who was killed in the war?"

_____

"Were you present when your picture was taken?"

_____

"Did he kill you?"

_____

"How far apart were the vehicles at the time of collision?"

_____

"You were there until the time you left, is that true?"

_____

"How many times have you committed suicide?"

ROCKET SCIENCE

Q: So the date of conception (of the baby) was August 8?
A: Yes.
Q: And what were you doing at that time?

_____

Q: She had three children, right?
A: Yes.
Q: How many were boys?
A: None.
Q: Were there any girls?

_____

_____

[1] William T.G. Litant, "And, were you present when your picture was taken?" Lawyers Journal, © Massachusetts Bar Association, May 1996.

Q: You say the stairs went down to the basement?
A: Yes.
Q: And these stairs, did they go up also?

Q: Mr. Slatery, you went on a rather elaborate honeymoon, didn't you?
A: I went to Europe, sir.
Q: And you took your new wife?

Q: How was your first marriage terminated?
A: By death.
Q.   And by whose death was it terminated?

Q: Can you describe the individual?
A: He was about medium height and had a beard.
Q: Was this a male or a female?

MAKES SENSE

Q: Is your appearance here this morning pursuant to a deposition notice which I sent to your attorney?
A: No, this is how I dress when I go to work.

Q: Doctor, how many autopsies have you performed on dead people?
A: All of my autopsies are performed on dead people.

Q: All of your responses must be oral, okay? What school did you go to?
A: Oral.

Q: You were shot in the fracas?
A: No, I was shot midway between the fracas and the navel.

Q: Are you qualified to give a urine sample?
A: I have been since early childhood.

JUST PLAIN HONEST

Q: Are you sexually active?
A: No, I just lie there.

Q: Did you ever stay all night with this man in New York?
A: I refuse to answer the question.
Q: Did you ever stay all night with this man in Chicago?
A: I refuse to answer the question.
Q: Did you ever stay all night with this man in Miami?
A: No.

FINALLY

Q: Okay, we've talked at length about how the accident happened, what people said as to how the accident happened, is there anything we haven't covered that you can think of, anything in your mind that you're thinking about how the accident happened that I haven't asked you and you're thinking "he hasn't asked me that" and "I'm not going to tell him because he hasn't asked me," is there anything?

A: Have you lost your mind?

When these quotes appeared on the Internet and were passed around by e-mail, someone offered the following variation on the autopsy exchange between an attorney and a witness:

Q. Doctor, is it possible that the patient was alive when you began the autopsy?

A. No.

Q. How can you be sure?

A. Because his brain was sitting on my desk in a jar.

Q. But could the patient have still been alive nevertheless?

A. It is possible that he could have been alive and practicing law somewhere.

A

abate a nuisance. To use the privilege of taking reasonable steps to correct a nuisance that is interfering with the use and enjoyment of your land.

abduction or enticement of a child. A tort involving serious interference with a parent's custody over his or her child.

abnormally dangerous conditions or activities. Unusual or non-natural conditions or activities that create a substantial likelihood of causing great harm that cannot be eliminated by the use of reasonable care.

absolute liability. *See* strict liability.

absolute official immunity. A defense to tort liability available to high government officials; the immunity cannot be lost even if the official acts with malice.

absolute privilege. *See* privilege.

abuse of process. The proper initiation of legal proceedings for an improper purpose.

act. A voluntary movement of the body.

actionable. Furnishing a legal basis for a cause of action.

act of God. A natural occurrence that is independent of human interference; a force of nature.

actual malice. *See* constitutional malice.

actual-risk test. The injury is a risk of this particular employment (a causal connection test for workers' compensation).

ad damnum clause. The clause stating the amount of damages claimed in a complaint.

additur. The power of a trial court to increase the amount of a jury's award of damages. The defendant is told that a new trial will be ordered if the defendant does not agree to the increase.

adequate remedy at law. Money damages will be sufficient to make the plaintiff whole. There is no need for an equitable remedy such as an injunction.

adhesion contract. A standardized contract for goods or services offered on a take-it-or-leave-it basis without any realistic opportunity for bargaining.

Note: See also William Statsky, *Legal Thesaurus/Dictionary* (West 1985); "Glossary of Insurance Terms," *No Fault Press Release Manual* (State Farm Insurance Companies, 1977–   ).

adjudication. The process by which a court or administrative agency resolves a legal dispute through litigation.

administrative code. A collection of administrative regulations organized by subject matter. Also called code of regulations.

administrative decision. An administrative agency's resolution of a controversy involving the application of the administrative regulations, statutes, or executive orders that govern the agency.

administrative regulation. A law of an administrative agency designed to explain or carry out the statutes and executive orders that govern the agency.

admissible. Allowed by a trial judge to be considered by a jury.

administrative agency. A governmental body whose primary function is to carry out or administer the statutes passed by the legislature and enacted into law.

ADR. *See* alternative dispute resolution.

adverse possession. A method of acquiring title to land without buying it or receiving it as a gift through a will or other traditional means: a trespasser obtains title to the land by occupying it in a hostile and visible manner for a designated number of continuous years.

adverse possessor. Someone who obtained title to land by adverse possession.

affirmative conduct. Activity, action, or conduct; the opposite of inaction or nonfeasance.

affirmative defense. A plaintiff's response to a claim of the defendant, setting forth new factual allegations by the defendant that were not contained in the complaint of the plaintiff.

agency hearing. A proceeding, similar to a trial, in which the hearing examiner of an administrative agency listens to evidence and legal arguments before deciding the case. *See also* administrative agency.

agent. Someone who agrees to do something on behalf of another.

aggravated. Made worse.

aggravation. An increase in the severity of the original injury, usually because of a failure to take reasonable steps to prevent the increase.

alienation of affections. The tort of causing a person to become alienated from his or her spouse.

alternative dispute resolution (ADR). A formal method of resolving a legal dispute without litigation in administrative agencies or courts.

American rule. Each party pays its own attorney fees and other legal expenses. There are exceptions to this such as when a judge has special statutory authority to award attorney fees to the winning party. *See also* English rule.

Andrews test. A duty is owed to anyone in the world at large if the plaintiff was injured as a result of unreasonable conduct toward anyone, whether or not the plaintiff who sues was in the zone of danger (from the *Palsgraff* case).

annotated statutes. A collection of statutes organized by subject matter, along with notes and commentary. Annotate means to provide notes and commentary.

annotation. The notes and commentary on issues in selected opinions. The annotations and opinions are published in *A.L.R., A.L.R.2d, A.L.R.3d, A.L.R.4th, A.L.R.5th,* and *A.L.R. Fed.*

answer. A pleading containing the defendant's response to the plaintiff's complaint.

apparent present ability. Appearing reasonably able to do something now or very shortly.

appellant. The party bringing an appeal.

appellate brief. A document submitted to an appellate court containing arguments on whether a lower court made errors of law.

appellate court. A court of appeals; any court that hears appeals from decisions of lower tribunals such as trial courts.

appellee. The party against whom an appeal is brought. Also called the respondent.

application. An explanation of the extent to which a rule governs (applies to) the facts. Connecting facts to the elements of a rule in order to determine whether the rule applies to the facts.

apprehension. An understanding, awareness, anticipation, belief, or knowledge of something.

appropriation. The unauthorized use of a person's name, likeness, or personality for the benefit of someone other than that person.

arbitration. A method of alternative dispute resolution in which the parties submit their dispute to a neutral third person who renders a decision that resolves the dispute. *See also* alternative dispute resolution.

arise out of. A causal connection between an injury or disease and the employment. *See also* workers' compensation.

arrest. Take another into custody or bring before the proper authorities.

assault. An act that intentionally causes an apprehension of a harmful or offensive contact.

assignment. The transfer of rights.

assumption of risk. The knowing and voluntary acceptance of the risk of being injured by someone's negligence. There are different categories of assumption of risk: *express assumption of risk:* the plaintiff knowingly and voluntarily accepts a risk by express agreement; *implied assumption of risk:* the plaintiff knowingly and voluntarily accepts a risk by reason of his or her knowledge and conduct; *primary assumption of risk:* the plaintiff knowingly and voluntarily ac-

cepts a particular risk that the defendant did not have a duty to protect the plaintiff against; and *secondary assumption of risk:* the plaintiff knowingly and voluntarily accepts a particular risk that the defendant had a duty to protect the plaintiff against.

at common law. (1) The case law and statutory law that existed during the Colonial period of American history. (2) The common law that existed before changed by statute. *See also* common law.

attachment. The taking of control or seizure of the property or assets of someone. The court may order it through a writ of attachment.

attestation clause. A statement that a person personally observed a witness sign something.

attorney work-product rule. Opposing parties are not allowed access to ideas, memos, etc. prepared in anticipation of litigation by attorneys and their assistants.

attractive nuisance doctrine. A duty of reasonable care is owed to a trespassing child unable to appreciate the danger from an artificial condition or activity on land to which the child can be expected to be drawn or attracted.

at will employment. *See* employment at will.

authority. Any written material a court could rely on to reach its decision. *Primary* authority is any law and *secondary* authority is any nonlaw that a court could rely on to reach its decision. *See also* legal authority.

avoidable consequences. Harm or injury that could have been avoided by taking reasonable steps. *See also* aggravation.

B

bad faith. (1) The opposite of good faith and fair dealing. (2) The absence of a reasonable basis for denying or delaying the payment of an insurance policy claim. A frivolous or unfounded refusal to pay the proceeds of a policy.

bad faith liability. Wrongfully acting on an insurance claim. *See also* bad faith.

bailee. *See* bailment.

bailment. The delivery of personal property to someone under an express or implied agreement to accept and later redeliver the property. The *bailor* delivers the property; the *bailee* receives it.

bailor. *See* bailment.

battery. A harmful or offensive contact with a person resulting from the defendant's intent to cause this contact or to cause an imminent apprehension of this contact.

benefit of the bargain. A measure of damages that gives the plaintiff the benefit of what he or she was promised.

bias. A leaning in favor of or against someone; a prejudgment; a lack of open-mindedness.

bill. A proposed statute.

boilerplate. Standard language commonly used in a particular kind of document such as a pleading.

bona fide purchaser. One who purchases property for value without notice of defects in the title of the seller.

breach of duty. Unreasonable conduct endangering someone to whom you owe a duty of care. The *breach-of-duty equation* is as follows: the foreseeability of an accident causing injury outweighed the burden or inconvenience on the defendant to take precautions against the injury, and the defendant failed to take those precautions.

breach of the peace. An offense committed by violence or by acts likely to cause immediate disturbance of the public order.

breach of warranty. *See* the entries under *warranty.*

brief. A summary of a court opinion. *See also* appellate brief.

burden of proof. The standard that tells the trier of fact how believable a party's evidence must be on a fact in order to accept that fact as true.

business guest. Someone who has been expressly or impliedly invited to be present, primarily for a business purpose.

but-for test. One of the tests to determine causation: Without (i.e., "but for") the act or omissions, the event in question would not have occurred. Also referred to as the *sine qua non test.*

bystander. One who stands near; one present but not taking part; one injured by a product but who was not a seller, buyer, user, or consumer of the product.

C

CALR. computer-assisted legal research.

camera. *See* in camera.

caps. Limitations; ceilings. *See also* damage caps; fee caps.

caption. The heading of a pleading or other document that identifies what it is, to whom it is submitted, who wrote it, etc.

Cardozo test. A duty is owed a specific person who is in the zone of danger as determined by the test of foreseeability (from the *Palsgraff* case).

case. (1) A court opinion. *See also* opinion. (2) A client matter.

causation. Bringing something about. *See also* causation in fact; but-for test; proximate cause; substantial factor test.

causation in fact. "But for" the act or omission, the event in question would not have occurred. The act or omission was a substantial factor in bringing about the event in question.

cause. (1) Justifiable reason. (2) Bring something about; causation.

cause in fact. *See* causation in fact.

cause of action. A legally acceptable reason for bringing a suit. When you *state a cause of action,* you list the facts that give you a right to judicial relief against the wrongdoer. When you *state a tort cause of action,* you list the facts that give you a right to judicial relief against the tortfeasor.

caveat emptor. Buyer beware. Protect yourself. If you make a mistake, the courts will not be sympathetic.

certify the class. The court's permission to allow a member of a class to represent every other member of the class in a class action.

certiorari. "To be more fully informed." When an appellate court has discretion on whether to hear an appeal, its decision to hear an appeal is announced by granting certiorari, or more accurately, by granting a writ of certiorari.

chain of distribution. All persons or businesses who had a role in making or selling a product that reached the person injured by that product.

charge. The judge's instructions to the jury on how to reach a verdict.

charitable immunity. A tort victim's loss of the right to bring a tort suit against the charitable organization that committed the tort.

charter. The fundamental law of a municipality or other local unit of government authorizing it to perform designated governmental functions.

chattel. Personal property; property other than land or things attached to land.

child. (1) Someone too young to appreciate the dangers that could be involved in a given situation. (2) Someone below a designated age.

civil arrest. Arrest for the purpose of treatment or protection, not because of the alleged commission of a crime.

civil law. (1) The law that governs rights and duties between private persons or between private persons and the government concerning matters other than the commission of a crime. (2) The law that applies in many Western European countries other than England.

Civil Rights Act. A federal statute that gives a citizen a right to sue a government employee who deprives the citizen of a federal right under color of state law.

class action. A lawsuit in which one or more members of a class sue (or are sued) as representative parties on behalf of everyone in the class, all of whom do not have to be joined in the lawsuit. If a prospective class member can decide not to join the class (i.e., can opt out), it is a *permissive class action;* if he or she cannot opt out, it is a *mandatory class action.*

closing argument. The final presentation to the jury (or to the judge if there is no jury) in which an attorney states what he or she believes the evidence has demonstrated.

Code Napoléon. The law that is the basis of civil law systems such as that of France.

code of regulations. The text containing administrative regulations.

coercion. The use of strength or pressure to secure compliance. If strong enough, the coercion can invalidate certain acts.

cognizable. Capable of being examined or tried by a court; being within the jurisdiction of the court.

cohabitant. One person who lives together with another as husband or wife without being married.

collateral source. Financial help to the victim of a tort that comes from a source that is independent of the trial of the tortfeasor. Examples include a health insurance policy of the victim and an employer who continues to pay the victim's salary. The collateral source rule is that the amount of the damages caused by the tortfeasor is not reduced by any injury-related funds received by the plaintiff from collateral sources.

colloquium. The part of the complaint in which the plaintiff alleges that the defamatory statement was of and concerning the plaintiff.

color of law. Acting or pretending to act in an official, governmental capacity.

commercial speech. Communications made in the pursuit of business, e.g., product advertising.

commonality. There must be questions of law or fact that are common to members of the class.

common area. An area controlled by the landlord that is used by more than one tenant.

common law. Judge-made law created to cover a dispute before the court that is not governed by statute or other controlling law. *See also* at common law.

comparative negligence. In a negligence action against the defendant, if the injury was caused in part by the plaintiff's own negligence, the damages will be reduced in proportion to the plaintiff's negligence.

compensatory damages. Money compensation designed to make plaintiffs whole, to compensate them for actual loss or injury. They are designed to restore an injured party to his or her position prior to the injury or wrong.

competent. Able to understand the obligation to tell the truth, has a basic ability to communicate, and has knowledge of the topic of the proposed testimony.

complaint. A pretrial document filed in court by the plaintiff that tries to state a claim or cause of action against the defendant. (Also called the *petition*.) It is one of the pleadings in the case.

complete. Total; confinement is complete if the victim knows of no safe or inoffensive means of escape from the boundaries set by the defendant.

component part. A part of a consumer product that is often manufactured by a company other than the assembler of the final product.

concert. An activity undertaken by mutual agreement.

conditional privilege. *See* privilege.

conditional threat. A threat to do something in the future if a specified event occurs.

confidential relationship. *See* fiduciary relationship.

confinement. The restraint of the plaintiff's physical movement.

consent. Express or implied agreement that something should happen or not happen.

consequential damages. See special damages.

consideration. Something of value that is exchanged between parties, e.g., an exchange of money for accounting services; an exchange of promises to do something or to refrain from doing something.

consortium. Love, affection, sexual relationship, and services that one spouse provides another.

conspiracy of silence. The reluctance or refusal of one member of a group to testify against another member.

constitution. The fundamental law that creates the branches of government and identifies basic rights and obligations.

constitutional malice. Knowledge that a defamatory statement is false, or recklessness as to its truth or falsity. Also called *actual malice*.

constitutional tort. A special cause of action that arises when someone is deprived of federal civil rights. Also called a § 1983 tort.

contention interrogatories. *See* interrogatories.

contingent fee. A plaintiff's attorney fee that is dependent on the outcome of the case.

contract at will. *See* terminable at will.

contribution. The right of one tortfeasor who has paid a judgment to be proportionately reimbursed by other tortfeasors who have not paid their share of the damages caused by all the tortfeasors.

contributory negligence. The failure of the plaintiff to take reasonable precautions for his or her safety, helping to cause his or her own injury.

conversion. An intentional interference with personal property that is serious enough to force the wrongdoer to pay its full value.

cost of restoration. The amount of money damages that will restore property to its condition before the defendant's tort.

covenant not to sue. An agreement not to sue one of the joint tortfeasors, provided in lieu of a release.

crashworthiness. The design of the interior of a motor vehicle so that it can avoid or minimize injury after the vehicle has been hit from outside.

counterclaim. A statement (often found in an answer) containing the defendant's claim or cause of action against the plaintiff.

course of. *See* in the course of.

court rules. *See* rules of court.

credibility. Believability; the extent to which something can be believed.

criminal conversation. The tort that occurs when the defendant has sexual relations with the plaintiff's spouse.

criminal law. The law that governs crimes alleged by the government.

cross-claim. A pleading containing the defendant's claim against a co-defendant.

cross-examination. Questioning the witness called by the other side after direct examination.

cut-off test. A policy test to determine whether a person should be liable for what he or she has caused in fact. *See also* proximate cause.

culpability. Fault, blameworthiness, wrongfulness.

custom. What is commonly done. Also called *custom and usage*.

custom and usage. *See* custom.

cyberspace. The Internet and World Wide Web.

D

damage caps. Limitations on the amount of damages that can be awarded in tort cases.

damages. (1) Monetary payments awarded for a legally recognized wrong. (2) Actual harm or loss. *See also* compensatory damages, general damages, hedonic damages, nominal damages, punitive damages, and special damages.

dangerous propensities. A tendency to cause damage or harm because of prior acts or omissions causing damage or harm.

Daubert. The United States Supreme Court opinion of *Daubert v. Merrell Dow Pharmaceuticals, Inc.* that defined the gatekeeper role of federal trial judges on the admissibility of scientific evidence under Federal Rules Evidence 702 (designed to limit admissibility of junk science).

deceit. *See* misrepresentation.

deep pocket. An individual who has resources with which to pay a judgment. *See also* shallow pockets.

defamacast. Defamation communicated on the radio or TV.

defamation. The publication of a written defamatory statement (libel) or an oral defamatory statement (slander) of and concerning the plaintiff that causes damages. *See also* defamatory statement, disparagement.

defamatory statement. A statement of fact that would tend to harm the reputation of the plaintiff in the eyes of at least a substantial and respectable minority of people by lowering the plaintiff in the estimation of those people or by deterring them from associating with the plaintiff.

default judgment. A judgment granted against a party who fails to appear, file an answer, or otherwise defend the action before the deadline.

defective. Lacking in some essential; not meeting standards.

defense. The response of a party to a claim of another party, setting forth the reason(s) the claim should be denied.

defense of others. The use of reasonable force to prevent an immediate harmful or offensive contact against a third person by someone who is making an apparent threat of this contact.

defense of property. The right to use reasonable force to prevent an immediate interference or to end an interference with the possession of your personal property or land.

defensive medicine. Ordering precautionary tests and procedures intended primarily to shield doctors (or others in the medical field) from possible lawsuits.

demurrer. A party's statement to a court that even if all the facts alleged by the other side can be proven at trial, those facts do not constitute the necessary elements of a claim or cause of action.

deponent. The person who is questioned in a deposition; the person deposed.

deposition. A method of discovery in which parties and their prospective witnesses are questioned before trial. Depositions are oral (when the attorneys are present asking the questions) or written (when the questions are submitted in writing and read by a reporter or stenographer). *See also* discovery.

derivative action. A plaintiff's action against a defendant to recover for a loss that is dependent on an underlying tort committed by that defendant against another plaintiff.

derogation of common law, statutes in. Statutes that change the common law.

design defect. The product is dangerous because of the way in which it was conceived and planned.

differential diagnosis. A method by which a clinician can identify possible diseases the patient may have and, through a process of elimination, rule out diseases until a disease or symptom is left as the diagnosis.

digest. (1) (n.) A set of volumes of small-paragraph summaries of court opinions. (2) (v.) To summarize a document according to a given organizational principle.

directed verdict. An order by the trial court that the jury return a verdict for the party making the motion for the directed verdict.

direct examination. The first questioning of a witness you have called.

disclaimer. Words or conduct that negate or limit a warranty. Repudiation of a claim.

discoverable. Obtainable through deposition, request for production, or other method of discovery.

discovery. Methods by which one party obtains information from the other party before trial. *See also* deposition; interrogatories.

disparagement. The intentional discrediting of a plaintiff's business (sometimes called *trade libel*) or title to property (sometimes called *slander of title*).

dispossession. Taking physical control of a chattel without the consent of the person who has possession but without exercising dominion over the chattel.

domestic animal. An animal that has been domesticated or habituated to live among humans.

dram shop liability. Civil liability imposed on the seller of intoxicating liquor to a buyer who then injures a third person. Sometimes applied also to a social host who gives intoxicating liquor.

dual-purpose trip. *See* mixed-purpose trip.

duress. Coercion; acting under the pressure of an unlawful act or threat.

duty. An obligation to conform to a standard of conduct prescribed by law. In most negligence cases, duty is the obligation to use reasonable care to avoid risks of injuring the person or property of others.

E

economic loss. An objectively verifiable monetary loss such as medical expense, burial expense, loss of earnings, and cost of repair. *See also* non-economic loss.

eggshell skull. An unusually high vulnerability to injury.

element. A portion of a rule that is one of the preconditions of the applicability of the entire rule. A cause of action is also a rule. Hence, a cause of action has elements. *See also* factor.

emancipated. Married or otherwise living independently from a parent or former legal guardian.

emotional distress. Mental anguish such as fright, worry, and humiliation.

employer/employee relationship. Employment. A work relationship between a person who hires someone and controls the goals and manner of his or her work. The person hiring is the employer; the person hired is the employee. A master/servant relationship.

employment. A work relationship in which the person hiring (the employer) controls the goals and manner of work of the person hired (the employee). *See also* scope of employment.

employment at will. An employment relationship that either the employee or the employer can terminate at any time for any reason without liability. An exception is that an employer cannot fire an employee at will for a reason that violates public policy such as a retaliatory discharge.

English rule. The party who loses the trial must pay the other side's attorney fees and other legal expenses. *See also* American rule.

enterprise liability. A system of spreading the costs of injuries over an entire industry or enterprise.

enticement of child. A tort involving serious interference with a parent's custody over his or her child.

enticement of spouse. A tort in which the defendant encourages the plaintiff's spouse to leave or to stay away from the plaintiff.

entrustment. The transfer of possession to someone's care. *See also* negligent entrustment.

epidemiology. The study of the causes of diseases in humans.

equitable remedy. A form of relief or remedy granted by a court of equity. An example is an injunction.

equity. (1) The system of justice administered in courts of equity. (2) Fairness.

estate. All the assets and debts left by a decedent.

evidence. Anything offered to help establish or disprove a fact. (An argument or reasoning, however, is not evidence.)

exculpation. Exoneration; release from liability.

exculpatory agreement. An agreement releasing a person from liability for wrongdoing.

execution. The process of carrying something out. In a writ of execution, the sheriff takes possession of the judgment debtor's assets, sells them, deducts the costs of execution, pays the judgment creditor, and gives anything left over back to the judgment debtor.

executive order. A law issued by the chief executive (e.g., president, governor, mayor) pursuant to specific statutory authority or to the executive's inherent authority (e.g., to direct the operation of governmental agencies).

exemplary damages. *See* punitive damages.

exempt. Not reachable to satisfy a debt or other obligation.

exhaustion of administrative remedies. Using all available methods of resolving a dispute within an administrative agency before asking a court to take action.

exhibit. An item of physical or tangible evidence offered to the court for inspection.

express assumption of risk. *See* assumption of risk.

express warranty. *See* warranty, breach of express.

extreme or outrageous conduct. Atrocious, totally intolerable, shocking behavior.

extrinsic fact. A fact not evident on the face of a statement that is needed to establish the defamatory meaning of the statement.

F

FACE. Free Access to Clinic Entrances Act. A federal statute that provides a remedy for victims of assault or other attack while trying to obtain reproductive health services.

fact. A concrete statement that can be objectively established as true or false. An express or implied communication containing concrete information that can be objectively shown to be true or false.

factor. One of the circumstances or considerations that will be weighed in making a decision, no one of which is usually conclusive. One of the considerations a court will examine to help it make a decision on whether a rule applies. Unlike elements, factors are not preconditions to the applicability of a rule.

fact particularization. A technique designed to help you list numerous factual questions in order to obtain a specific and comprehensive picture of all available facts that are relevant to a legal matter.

fact pleading. A statement of every ultimate (i.e., essential) fact in the complaint.

factual issue. A question of fact; a question of what happened. *See also* legal issue.

fair and adequate representation. In a class action in federal court, the representative of the class must be able to provide fair and adequate representation of the class.

fair comment. An observation or opinion on a matter of public interest. Fair comment is a qualified privilege to a defamation action.

fair competition. Honest, nonfraudulent rivalry in trade and commerce.

fair market value. What something would probably sell for in the ordinary course of a voluntary sale by a willing seller and a willing buyer.

fair on its face. No obvious or blatant flaws or irregularities.

fair report privilege. A newspaper or other media entity is not liable for defamation when it publishes fair and accurate stories on government reports and proceedings even if the stories contain defamatory statements made in the government reports or proceedings.

false arrest. An arrest for which the person taking someone into custody has no privilege.

false imprisonment. An intentional confinement within fixed boundaries set by the defendant.

false light. An inaccurate impression made by publicity about a person. It is highly offensive to a reasonable person.

family purpose doctrine. The owner of a car or person controlling the use of a car is liable for the negligence committed by a family member using the car for a family purpose.

fault. Wrongfulness, blameworthiness.

Federal Tort Claims Act. The federal statute that specifies the torts for which the federal government waives sovereign immunity.

fee caps. Limitations on the fees that attorneys can be paid in designated categories of cases.

fellow-employee rule. An employer is not liable for injuries caused by the negligence of one employee against another employee (unless the negligent employee was a vice principal).

felony. A crime that is punishable by incarceration for a term exceeding a year.

fiduciary relationship. The relationship that exists when one party (called the fiduciary) owes another loyalty, candor, and fair treatment. Also called a *confidential relationship*.

filial consortium. The right of a parent to the normal companionship and affection of a child.

financial responsibility law. Law requiring an operator or owner of a motor vehicle to give evidence of financial ability to meet claims for damages when he or she is involved in an accident.

first-party coverage. An insurance coverage under which policyholders collect compensation for their losses from their own insurer rather than from the insurer of the person who caused the accident.

fitness for a particular purpose. *See* warranty of fitness for a particular purpose.

foreseeable. Having the quality of being seen or known beforehand.

foreseeable use. *See* use.

foreseeable users. Those persons who a manufacturer or retailer can reasonably anticipate will use the product.

foreseeable plaintiff. Someone who the defendant can anticipate will be within the zone of danger.

fraud. *See* misrepresentation.

Freedom of Information Act. The statute that gives citizens access to specified categories of government information.

fresh pursuit. Going after someone or something promptly, without undue delay.

frolic and detour. Acts of an employee performed for the employee's personal objectives rather than primarily for the employer's business.

***Frye* test.** Expert opinion on a scientific principle or discovery is admissible if it has "gained general acceptance" as reliable in the relevant scientific community. Based on the holding of *Frye v. United States*.

G

garnishment. Reaching the assets of a debtor in the possession of a third party in order to satisfy a debt.

general damages. Compensatory damages that usually result from the kind of harm caused by the conduct of the defendant. Damages that usually and naturally flow from this wrong, e.g., pain and suffering. The law implies or presumes that such damages result from the wrong complained of. General damages differ from special damages, which are awarded for actual economic loss, such as medical costs and loss of income.

general rule on duty. Whenever your conduct creates a foreseeable risk of injury or damage to someone else's person or property, you owe a duty to take reasonable precautions to prevent that injury or damage.

global peace. A final resolution of all claims that binds all parties, usually through a class action.

going-and-coming rule. Workers' compensation is denied if the employee is injured "off the premises" while going to or coming back from work or lunch.

Good Samaritan. A person who comes to the aid of another without a legal obligation to do so.

governmental function. A function that can be performed adequately *only* by the government. Unlike a proprietary function.

gratuitous. Not involving payment or consideration; free.

gross negligence. The failure to use even a small amount of care to avoid foreseeable harm.

guest. Someone invited or allowed to be present for a non-business reason.

H

harmful. Involving physical or actual damage, impairment, pain, or illness in the body.

harmless. Not affecting substantial rights.

hearing. A proceeding in court or in an administrative agency. *See also* agency hearing.

hearing memorandum. *See* memorandum of law.

heart-balm statute. A statute that has abolished actions for breach of promise to marry, alienation of affections, criminal conversation, enticement, and seduction of a person under the age of consent.

hedonic damages. Damages that cover the victim's loss of pleasure or enjoyment.

helpless peril. A predicament created by the plaintiff's contributory negligence that he or she cannot get him- or herself out of.

highly offensive. Extremely distasteful or unpleasant to a reasonable person.

highly extraordinary. Unusually rare.

hiring. *See* negligent hiring.

hypothesis. An assumption that is subject to be verified or proven.

hypothetical. (1) (n.) A set of facts that are assumed to exist for the purposes of discussion. (The teacher asked the students to analyze the hypothetical she gave them.) (2) (adj.) Assumed or based on conjecture. (The lawyer asked the witness a hypothetical question.)

I

imminent. Immediate in the sense of no significant or undue delay.

immunity. A defense that renders otherwise tortious conduct nontortious. The right to be free from civil or criminal prosecution.

impeach. Discredit or attack.

implied assumption of risk. *See* assumption of risk.

implied warranty. *See* entries under *Warranty*.

imputed. Attributed to or imposed on someone or something.

imputed contributory negligence. The contributory negligence of a person involved in an accident is attributed to and imposed on the plaintiff.

imputed negligence. Negligence liability attributed or imposed solely because of the wrongdoing of others.

inattentive peril. A predicament created by the plaintiff's contributory negligence that he or she could get him- or herself out of by the use of reasonable care but the plaintiff is negligently unaware of this peril.

in camera. In chambers; in private.

incident to the job. Sufficiently connected to employment.

increased-risk test. The risk of injury to the employee is quantitatively greater than the risk of injury to nonemployees (a causal connection test for workers' compensation).

indemnity. The right to have another person pay you the full amount you were forced to pay. In the law of insurance, indemnity is the transfer of loss from an insured to an insurer to the extent of the agreed-upon insurance proceeds to cover the loss.

independent contractor. Someone who is hired or retained to produce a certain product or result. This person has considerable discretion in the methods used to achieve that product or result. The person is not an employee.

independent liability. Personal liability based on what an individual did or failed to do him- or herself. The opposite of vicarious liability.

indivisible. Not separable into parts; pertaining to that which cannot be divided.

inducement. The part of the complaint alleging extrinsic facts in a defamation action.

informed consent. Sufficient information provided so that the person can weigh the benefits and liabilities of taking certain action.

inherently dangerous. Being susceptible to harm or injury in the nature of the product, service, or activity itself.

initiate. To instigate, urge on, or incite.

injunction. A court order requiring a person to do or to refrain from doing a particular thing.

injurious falsehood. The publication of a false statement that causes special damages.

injury. *See* physical injury.

in loco parentis. "In the place of the parent"; assuming some or all the duties of a parent.

innocently. Done without negligence, intent, recklessness, malice, or other wrongful state of mind.

innuendo. The explanation of the defamatory meaning of words alleged by inducement in the complaint.

in-person solicitation. Seeking employment on the phone or in a face-to-face setting such as at home or in the office.

instigation. Insisting, directing, or encouraging.

instructions to jury. The explanation given by the judge to the jury on how it is to apply the law to the facts to reach a verdict.

insurance. A contract (called an insurance policy) under which a company agrees to compensate a person (up to a specific amount) for a loss caused by designated perils. *See also* liability insurance.

insured. The person designated as being protected against specified loss under an insurance policy.

intangible. *See* tangible.

intended use. *See* use.

intent. The desire to bring about the consequences of an act (or omission), or the substantially certain knowledge that the consequences will follow from the act (or omission).

intentional infliction of emotional distress. Intentionally causing severe emotional distress by an act of extreme or outrageous conduct. This tort is also called the tort of *outrage*.

intentionally. Knowingly; done with desire or substantially certain knowledge. *See also* intent.

intentional tort. A tort in which a person either desired to bring about the result or knew with substantial certainty that the result would follow from what the person did or failed to do.

interest. (1) A right, claim, or legal share of or in something. (2) The object of any human desire.

interference with contract relations. The tort of inducing a breach of contract.

interference with prospective advantage. The tort of interfering with a reasonable expectation of an economic advantage.

intermeddling. Making physical contact with a chattel.

Internet. A self-governing network of networks to which millions of computer users all over the world have access.

interoffice memorandum of law. *See* memorandum of law.

interrogatories. A pretrial discovery device consisting of written questions sent by one party to another to assist the sender of the questions in preparing for trial.

interspousal immunity. Spouses cannot sue each other for designated categories of torts.

intervening cause. A force that produces harm after the defendant's act or omission. An *intervening force of nature* is a subsequent natural occurrence that is independent of human interference; it is an act of God. An *intervening innocent human force* is a subsequent occurrence caused by a human being who was not careless or wrongful. An *intervening intentional or criminal force* is a subsequent occurrence caused intentionally or criminally by a human being. An *intervening negligent human force* is a subsequent occurrence negligently caused by a human being.

intervening force of nature. *See* intervening cause.

intervening innocent human force. *See* intervening cause.

intervening intentional or criminal human force. *See* intervening cause.

intervening negligent human force. *See* intervening cause.

interviewing. *See* legal interviewing.

intestacy. Dying without leaving a valid will.

in the course of. Occurring while at work or in the service of the employer; pertaining to the time, place, and circumstances of the injury or disease in connection with the employment. *See also* workers' compensation.

intra-agency hearing. A review within the agency of an earlier decision to determine if that decision was correct. *See also* agency hearing.

intrafamily tort. A tort committed by one family member against another.

intrafamily tort immunity. Family members cannot sue each other for designated categories of torts.

intrusion. (a) An unreasonable encroachment into an individual's private affairs or concerns. One of the invasion of privacy torts. Also called *intrusion on seclusion*. (b) Physically going on land, remaining on the land, going to a prohibited portion of the land, or failing to remove goods from the land. One of the elements of trespass to land.

invasion of privacy. *See* appropriation, false light, intrusion, and public disclosure of private fact.

investigation. *See* legal investigation.

invitee. One who enters the land upon the express or implied invitation of the occupier of the land, in order to use the land for the purposes for which it is held open to the public or to pursue the business of the occupier.

IRAC. A structure for legal analysis. An acronym that stands for the components of legal analysis. Issue (I), rule (R), application of the rule to the facts (A), and conclusion (C).

issue. *See* factual issue; legal issue.

J

joint and several liability. Each wrongdoer (defendant) is liable for all the damages suffered by the plaintiff, who can sue any or all of the defendants until 100 percent of his or her damages are recovered.

joint enterprise. An express or implied agreement to participate in a common enterprise (usually of a financial or business nature) in which the participants have a mutual right of control. A joint venture.

joint tortfeasors. Persons who together produce a tortious wrong.

joint venture. A mutually undertaken activity in which each person participates. *See* joint enterprise.

judgment. The final conclusion of a court resolving a legal dispute.

judgment creditor. The person to whom a money judgment is owed.

judgment debtor. The person who owes a money judgment to another.

judgment proof. Having few or no assets from which a money judgment can be satisfied.

Judicial Panel on Multidistrict Litigation (J.P.M.L.). A special federal judicial body with the power to order that similar cases filed in different districts be transferred to a single district for pretrial proceedings.

junk science. Unreliable and, therefore, potentially misleading scientific evidence. *See also Daubert*.

jurisdiction. The power of a court. Its *personal* jurisdiction is its power to order a particular defendant to do or to refrain from doing something. Its *subject matter* jurisdiction is its power to hear certain kinds of cases.

just compensation. The fair payment for property "taken" by the government for a public purpose.

justifiable reliance. Being reasonable in taking action (or in refraining from taking action) because of what someone has said or done.

K

knowledge with substantial certainty. A high degree of knowledge; having no more than very minimal doubt about a result that will flow from what you do or fail to do.

L

last clear chance. The opportunity to avoid the accident at the last moment in spite of the contributory negligence of the plaintiff.

latent. Not readily visible; hidden.

law journals. *See* law reviews.

law reviews. Legal periodicals published by law schools. Also called law journals.

legal analysis. The application of one or more rules to the facts presented by a client in order to answer a legal question that will help (1) avoid a legal dispute from arising, (2) resolve a legal dispute that has arisen, or (3) prevent a legal dispute from becoming worse. Also called *legal reasoning*.

legal authority. (1) The power of the government; the right to do something. (2) Any law (primary authority) or nonlaw (secondary authority) on which a tribunal can rely to help it resolve a legal dispute before it.

legal cause. *See* proximate cause.

legal encyclopedia. A multivolume set of books that alphabetically summarizes almost every legal topic.

legal interviewing. The process of gathering facts from a client (or from a prospective client if the office has not yet decided to take the case) in order to solve or avoid a legal problem.

legal investigation. The process of gathering additional facts and verifying presently known facts in order to solve or avoid a legal problem.

legal issue. A question of whether one or more rules apply to the facts. Also called *question of law*. *See also* factual issue.

legal malpractice. Professional misconduct or wrongdoing by attorneys. *See also* malpractice.

legal memorandum. *See* memorandum of law.

legal periodical. An ongoing publication (often published four or six times a year) containing articles, case notes or studies, and other information on legal topics.

legal reasoning. *See* legal analysis.

legal remedy. A method of enforcing a legal right or redressing the violation of a legal right. *See also* adequate remedy at law; remedy.

legal treatise. A book written by a private individual (or by a public official writing as a private citizen) that provides an overview, summary, or commentary on a legal topic.

legislative intent. The purpose of the legislature in enacting a particular statute.

legislative history. All the events that occur in the legislature before a bill is enacted into law as a statute.

legitimate public interest. Newsworthy; information the general public would like to have.

lessee. Person renting property from another.

lessor. Person renting property to another.

liability. The imposition of legal responsibility for something.

liability insurance. Insurance in which the insurer agrees to pay, on behalf of an insured, damages the latter is obligated to pay to a third party because of his or her legal liability to the third person for committing a tort or other wrong. *See also* insurance.

liability without fault. *See* strict liability.

liable. Legally responsible; under an obligation to pay for a wrong committed.

libel. Defamation that is written or embodied in a physical form. *See also* defamation.

libel per quod. A written statement that requires extrinsic facts to understand its defamatory meaning.

libel per se. A written defamatory statement that is actionable without proof that the plaintiff suffered special damages.

licensee. One who enters the land for his or her own purposes, but with the express or implied consent of the occupier.

limitation of liability. A modification of responsibility that would otherwise apply to harm that is caused.

listserv. A program that manages computer mailing lists automatically. This includes receiving and distributing messages from and to members of the list.

local standard. (1) A doctor is required to have and use the equipment, knowledge, and experience that doctors have and use locally or in localities similar to the community where the defendant-doctor practices. (2) Evaluation based on what is acceptable locally rather than nationally.

Lord Campbell's Act. A statute that allowed a separate cause of action for a tort that caused the death of the victim.

loss of consortium. See consortium; derivative action.

loss of services. An action by a parent for interference with an unemancipated child's ability to perform household chores and other tasks for the parent. *See also* derivative action.

lump sum judgment. One payment at the end of the trial to cover all past and future damages.

M

made whole. Restored to the condition before the wrong was committed against the victim insofar as this is possible.

malfeasance. Wrongful or illegal actions by a public official.

malice. (1) Ill will, hatred, or a desire to harm. (2) Recklessness. (3) Knowledge of consequences. (4) Improper motive.

malicious. Acting with malice. *See also* malice.

malicious prosecution. The initiation or procurement of legal proceedings without probable cause and with an improper motive. The proceedings terminate in favor of the accused.

malpractice. Professional misconduct or wrongdoing consisting of ethical violations, criminal conduct, negligence, battery, or other tort. *See also* legal malpractice, medical malpractice.

mandatory authority. Whatever a court must rely on in reaching its decision.

mandatory class action. *See* class action.

mandatory offset. A required reduction of damages by a designated amount. A *permissive offset* is a reduction of damages that is allowed but not required.

manner. A method or way of performing a task.

manufacturer. A business that makes a product.

manufacturing defect. The product is dangerous because of the way in which it was assembled; the product does not conform to its design.

market share. The proportion of the market attributable to the sales of a particular company.

market share liability. Legal responsibility according to the proportion of the market attributable to the sales of a particular company.

mass tort. A tort cause of action asserted by a large number of persons who have been harmed by the same or similar conduct or product of a relatively small number of defendants.

master/servant relationship. A work association in which one person (the master or principal) hires another (the servant or agent) to perform work, the master controls the goals and manner of the servant's work. An employer/employee relationship.

material. Important to a transaction or event.

med-arb. A method of alternative dispute resolution in which the parties first try mediation, and if it does not work, they try arbitration. *See also* alternative dispute resolution; arbitration; mediation.

mediation. A method of alternative dispute resolution in which the parties submit their dispute to a neutral third person who helps the parties reach their own decision to resolve the dispute. *See also* alternative dispute resolution.

medical malpractice. Professional misconduct or wrongdoing by doctors. *See also* malpractice.

memo. Shorthand for memorandum.

memorandum of law. A written explanation of how the law might apply to a set of facts. Also called a *legal memorandum.* (The shorthand word is *memo.*) If the audience of the memo is someone in the office such as a supervisor, the memo is called an *interoffice memorandum of law.* If the audience of the memo is someone outside the office, it might be called a *hearing memorandum* (submitted to an administrative law judge in an administrative agency), a *points and authorities* *memorandum* (submitted to a trial judge or hearing officer), or a *trial memorandum* (submitted to a trial judge).

merchant. Someone in the business of selling.

merchantable. Fit for the ordinary purposes for which the goods are used. *See also* warranty of merchantability.

merits. *See* on the merits.

method. The means used to accomplish something; the manner of performing a task.

misdemeanor. A crime that is punishable by incarceration for a term of a year or less.

misfeasance. Improper or unreasonable action.

misrepresentation. A false statement of fact made with the intent to mislead and to have the plaintiff rely on the statement. The plaintiff suffers actual damage due to justifiable reliance on the statement. Also called deceit and fraud.

mistake. An error; an unintentional act or omission.

misuse. The improper use of a product. Misuse is not a defense if the product was being used for its intended or foreseeable use.

mitigate the consequences. Take steps to lessen the damages or other impact of an injury.

mixed-purpose trip. A trip taken by an employee that has both a business and a personal purpose. Also called a *dual-purpose trip*.

movant. The party making a motion to the court.

motion. A formal request to a court.

motion for directed verdict. *See* directed verdict.

motion for judgment notwithstanding the verdict. *See* NOV.

motion for summary judgment. *See* summary judgment.

motion to dismiss. A request that the case be dismissed prior to the completion of the trial because the party initiating the suit has engaged in misconduct or cannot win even if it proves the facts alleged.

motive. The emotion, feeling, or need that induces a particular action or inaction.

N

National Practitioner Data Bank. A collection of information about doctors who have been defendants in malpractice cases and have paid claimants through settlement or litigation.

national standard. (1) A doctor is required to have and use the equipment, knowledge, and experience that doctors have and use nationally. (2) Evaluation based on what is acceptable nationally rather than locally.

necessity. The privilege to make a reasonable use of someone's property to prevent immediate threat of harm or damage to persons or property. If the threat is to private interests, the privileged use is a *private necessity*. If the threat is to the public, the privileged use is a *public necessity*.

negligence. Harm caused by the failure to use reasonable care. *Ordinary negligence* consists of unreasonable conduct that is not egregious or reckless. *Wilful, wanton, or*

reckless negligence consists of unreasonable conduct that creates a very great risk that harm will result; acting with the knowledge that the harm will probably result. *See also* gross negligence.

negligent entrustment. Carelessly allowing someone to use a vehicle, tool, or other object that poses an unreasonable risk of harm to others.

negligent hiring. Carelessly (rather than intentionally) hiring an incompetent person who poses an unreasonable risk of harm to others.

negligent infliction of emotional distress (NIED). Carelessly causing someone to suffer emotional distress.

negligently. Taking unreasonable risks. *See also* negligence.

negligent misrepresentation. An action for the careless communication of a false statement of fact brought by someone to whom the statement was intended to reach.

negligent per se. Negligent as a matter of law. There is no need to present evidence that the acts and omissions were unreasonable.

neighborhood justice center (NJC). A government or private center where community disputes can be resolved by mediation or other method of alternative dispute resolution.

newsworthy. Pertaining to information the general public would like to have; pertaining to matters of legitimate public interest.

NIED. *See* negligent infliction of emotional distress.

1983 action. A suit based on § 1983 of the Civil Rights Act of 1871 against a government employee who deprives someone of federal rights under color of state law. The deprivation is called a 1983 tort.

1983 tort. *See* 1983 action.

no-fault insurance. A motor vehicle insurance plan in which each person's own insurance company pays for injury or damage up to a certain limit, regardless of whether its insured was at fault.

no-fault system. A method of providing compensation for damage or injury that is not based on which side carelessly or wrongfully caused the damage or injury. Compensation is based on proving causation and the loss being within prescribed limits.

nolle prosequi. A statement by the district attorney that he or she is unwilling to prosecute an individual for the commission of a crime.

nominal damages. A small monetary payment (often $1) awarded when the defendant has committed a tort that has resulted in little or no harm so that no compensatory damages are due.

nondelegable duty. A task considered so important or critical that you are liable for injury or damage caused by performing the task even if you hire an independent contractor to perform it.

non-economic loss. A non-monetary harm such as emotional pain, suffering, inconvenience, mental anguish, loss of enjoyment of life, loss of companionship, damage to reputation, and humiliation. A nonpecuniary loss.

nonfeasance. The failure to act; an omission.

nonpecuniary losses. Mental suffering and grief. *See also* non-economic loss.

nonsuit. The termination or dismissal of a court action, usually not on the merits.

notice. (1) Formal notification sent or otherwise communicated. (2) Information or knowledge obtained by observation.

notice of appeal. A formal statement by a party to an appellate court that he or she is appealing a judgment.

notice pleading. A short and plain statement of a claim showing that the pleader is entitled to relief. Pleading that gives adequate notice of the nature of the claim.

NOV. Judgment notwithstanding the verdict. A judgment ordered by the court that is contrary to the verdict reached by the jury.

nuisance. A *private nuisance* is a substantial interference with the reasonable use and enjoyment of private land. A *public nuisance* is an unreasonable interference with a right common to the general public.

numerosity. The class must be so large that joinder of all members is impractical.

O

objective. Goal or purpose. *See also* objective standard.

objective standard. Measuring something by comparing it to something else. Assessing the behavior of a person by comparing what he or she did with what another person or persons would have done. In negligence, comparing what the defendant did or failed to do with what a reasonable person would have done under the same or similar circumstances. A *subjective standard* measures something solely by what one individual (e.g., the defendant) actually did, knew, believed, or understood.

occupier. Anyone in possession of land claiming a right to possession.

of and concerning the plaintiff. One of the elements of defamation that requires the defamatory communication to be reasonably understood by the recipient to refer to the plaintiff.

offensive. Offending the personal dignity of an ordinary person who is not unduly sensitive.

official immunity. Government employees are not personally liable for torts or other wrongdoing they commit within the scope of their employment.

offset. (1) A deduction. (2) A contrary claim.

on its face. Without reference to extrinsic facts. *See also* extrinsic fact.

online. Being connected to a host computer or information service—usually through telephone lines.

on the merits. Based on a substantive decision of who is in the right as opposed to being based on a preliminary, technical, or procedural matter.

opening statement. The statement by an attorney to the jury (or to the judge if there is no jury) at the beginning of a trial of the evidence the party expects to present during the trial and what that evidence will demonstrate.

opinion. (1) An express or implied communication containing a relatively vague or indefinite value judgment that is not objectively verifiable. (2) A court's written explanation of its decision. Also called a *case*.

opt out. To bring an individual lawsuit rather than become a member of a class action. *See also* class action.

oral deposition. *See* deposition.

ordinance. A law passed by the local legislative branch of government (e.g., city council, county commission) that declares, commands, or prohibits something. (Same as a statute, but at the local level.)

ordinary negligence. *See* negligence.

out-of-pocket. Pertaining to amounts actually paid or to be paid to cover losses.

out-of-pocket rule. A measure of damages that gives the plaintiff the difference between the value of what he or she parted with and the value of what was received.

outrage, tort of. *See* intentional infliction of emotional distress.

outrageous and extreme conduct. Atrocious, totally intolerable, shocking behavior.

P

pain and suffering. Emotional distress; disagreeable mental or emotional experience. Part of general damages.

palimony. A nonlegal term for payments to be made by one nonmarried party to another after they cease living together, usually because the payments were based on an express or implied contract they made while they were living together or cohabiting.

parasitic. Attached to something else, e.g., another tort.

parasitic damages. Damages for mental anguish (pain and suffering) that attach to a physical injury.

parental consortium. The right of a child to the normal companionship and affection of a parent.

passenger. Someone riding in a car who confers a benefit on the driver, other than the benefit of social company.

peace officer. A person appointed by the government to keep the peace.

peace of mind. The lack of anguish due to serious interference.

pecuniary loss. A money loss. Examples include cost of repair and the amount needed to replace the loss of support and services that would have been received.

peculiar-risk test. The source of the harm is peculiar to the employment (a causal connection test for workers' compensation).

percentage fee. Payment in the form of a percentage of the amount involved in the award, settlement, or transaction.

per diem argument. A certain amount is requested as damages for every day that pain and suffering has been endured and is expected to continue. Also called the *unit-of-time argument*.

permissive class action. *See* class action.

permissive offset. *See* mandatory offset.

person. (1) A human being or a business. (2) For purposes of battery, one's body, something attached to the body, or something so closely associated with the body as to be identified with it.

personal jurisdiction. *See* jurisdiction.

personal liability. Damages paid by the wrongdoer out of his or her own pocket.

personal property. *See* property.

personal property tort. *See* tort.

personal tort. *See* tort.

persuasive authority. Whatever a court relies on in reaching its decision that it is not required to rely on.

petition. *See* complaint.

physical impact. Actual contact.

physical injury. A wound, cut, or other detrimental change to the body. *See also* emotional distress.

physical or mental examination. A medical examination of a party ordered as part of discovery.

physician-patient relationship. The relationship that arises when a doctor undertakes to render medical services in response to an express or implied request for services by the patient or by the patient's guardian.

PI. Personal injury.

pleading. A pretrial paper or document filed in court stating the position of one of the parties on the cause(s) of action or on the defense(s).

plenary trial. A complete trial.

points and authorities memorandum. *See* memorandum of law.

polling. Asking each juror if he or she agrees with the verdict read.

positional-risk test. The injury of the employee would not have occurred but for the fact that the job placed the employee in a position where the employee could be injured (a causal connection test for workers' compensation).

possessory interest. Anyone who has a present or future right to possess land.

posttrial discovery. Formal methods of obtaining information from a judgment debtor relevant to enforcing the judgment.

prayer for relief. A statement in a complaint asking for a specific amount of damages or other form of relief.

preempt. Be controlling over.

pre-existing injuries or diseases. The injuries or diseases that existed prior to the time in question, e.g., prior to the employment of someone claiming workers' compensation benefits.

premises liability. The liability of landowners and others with possessory interests in land for injuries suffered in connection with the land.

preponderance of the evidence. The standard of proof according to which a party must prove that its version of a fact is more likely true than not.

present cash value. *See* present value.

present value. The amount of money an individual would have to be given now in order to produce or generate, through prudent investment, a certain amount of money within a designated period of time. Also called present cash value.

presumed damages. Damages that a jury is allowed to assume were suffered by the plaintiff, who does not have to introduce specific evidence that these damages were in fact suffered.

presumption. An assumption of fact that can be drawn when another fact (or set of facts) is established. The presumption is *rebuttable* if a party is allowed to introduce evidence that the assumption is false.

prima facie case. Enough factual allegations by a party to cover every element of a cause of action.

prima facie tort. Intentionally inflicting harm that causes special damages.

primary assumption of risk. *See* assumption of risk.

primary authority. Any law that a court could rely on to reach a decision. *See also* authority.

primary insurance. Insurance that pays compensation for a loss ahead of any other insurance coverage the policyholder may have.

principal/agent. The principal is the person on whose behalf an agent is acting; the principal has authority or control over the agent while the agent is acting for the principal.

private affairs. Information that is not of legitimate public concern. Non-newsworthy facts.

private citizen. Someone who is not employed by, an agent of, or acting for the government.

private necessity. *See* necessity.

private person. Someone who is not a public official or a public figure.

private nuisance. *See* nuisance.

privilege. (1) The right of an individual to act contrary to the right of another individual without being subject to tort or other liability. A defense to a tort. An *absolute privilege* is a privilege that cannot be lost because of the bad motives of the party asserting the privilege. A *qualified privilege* (also called a *conditional privilege*) is a privilege that can be lost if it is improperly asserted. (2) The right to exclude otherwise admissible evidence.

privileged competition. Business competition that uses no unfair or illegal methods.

privilege to recapture. The right to use reasonable force to obtain the return of personal property (chattels) shortly after someone obtained them wrongfully.

privity. The relationship that exists between two parties who directly enter a contract with each other.

probable cause. (a) A suspicion based upon the appearance of circumstances that are strong enough to allow a reasonable person to believe that a criminal charge against a person is true. (b) Reasonable cause to believe that good grounds exist to initiate a civil proceeding.

probative. Tending to prove or disprove a fact.

pro bono. Free.

production of documents and things, entry on land for inspection and other purposes. A pretrial discovery device designed to provide a party with information on physical items relevant to the litigation.

products liability. A general term that covers different causes of action based on products that cause harm: negligence, breach of express warranty, misrepresentation, breach of implied warranty of fitness for a particular purpose, breach of implied warranty of merchantability, and strict liability in tort.

promise. A declaration asserting that something will or will not be done.

property. *Real property* is land and anything attached to the land. *Personal property* is every other kind of property. *See also* tangible.

proprietary. Concerning a function that cannot be performed adequately *only* by the government—unlike a governmental function.

prosecution. (1) Bringing any court action, civil or criminal. (2) Bringing a criminal action. (3) The government attorney bringing a criminal action.

proximate cause. The defendant is the cause in fact of the plaintiff's injury, the injury was the foreseeable consequence of the original risk, and there is no policy reason why the defendant should not be liable for what he or she caused in fact. Proximate cause is also referred to as the *legal cause*.

proximate-cause test. The injury is foreseeable and no intervening factor breaks the chain of causation between the conditions of employment and the injury (a causal connection test for workers' compensation).

publication. Communication of a statement to someone other than the plaintiff.

public disclosure of private fact. Unreasonable disclosure of private facts about an individual's life that are not matters of legitimate public concern.

public figure. A non-government employee who has assumed special prominence in the affairs of society. A public figure for all purposes is a person of general power, influence, or notoriety. A public figure for a limited purpose is a person who has voluntarily become involved in a controversy of interest to the general public.

public necessity. *See* necessity.

public official. A government employee who has significant authority.

public policy. The principle inherent in the customs, morals, and notions of justice in a state. Principles that are naturally right and just.

public nuisance. *See* nuisance.

publicity. Communication to the public at large, to more than a few people.

puffing. An expected exaggeration of quality.

punitive damages. Non-compensatory damages designed to punish the defendant and deter similar conduct by others. Also called *exemplary damages*.

Q

qualified official immunity. A government employee will not be personally liable for his or her torts or other wrongdoing committed within the scope of employment so long as he or she does not act with malice. Also called conditional official immunity.

qualified privilege. *See* privilege.

quash. To terminate or make void; to suppress.

question of fact. *See* factual issue.

question of law. *See* legal issue.

R

real property. *See* property.

real property tort. *See* tort.

reasonable. Pertaining to what a reasonable person would or would not do. *See also* reasonable person. Pertaining to someone who is not unduly sensitive.

reasonable alternative design. An available design that a manufacturer could have reasonably used that would have been less dangerous than the design that caused the injury.

reasonable beneficial use. Space above and below the surface of land to which reasonable use can be made.

reasonable care. Conduct that a reasonable person would follow to avoid injury or harm to others.

reasonable doctor standard. A doctor must follow the standards of the profession as to how much information about the risks and benefits of a proposed treatment would be disclosed to a patient with the plaintiff's condition.

reasonable patient standard. A doctor must disclose information about the risks and benefits of a proposed treatment that a reasonable patient with the plaintiff's condition would wish to know.

reasonable person. An ordinary, prudent person who uses reasonable care to avoid injuring others. An ordinary person who is not unduly sensitive.

reasonably safe. As free from danger as is reasonably possible.

rebuttal. A response to an argument or position of another.

recapture. To obtain the return of possession. *See also* privilege to recapture.

recapture of chattels. *See* privilege to recapture.

reckless. Creating a very great risk that something will happen. Acting with the knowledge that harm will probably result. Totally outside the range of the ordinary activity.

reckless disregard. Consciously ignoring something such as whether a fact is true or false.

recklessly. Acting in conscious disregard of something.

recklessness. A very high degree of carelessness.

re-direct examination. Questioning your own witness after cross-examination by the other side of that witness.

release. The giving up or relinquishing of a claim.

reliance. (1) Placing faith or confidence in someone or something. (2) Forming a belief, taking action, or refraining from action in part due to confidence in someone or something. *See also* justifiable reliance.

remedy. (1) A means by which the enforcement of a right is sought or the violation of a right is compensated for or otherwise redressed. (2) Relief; a solution.

remedy at law. A remedy available in a court of law (e.g., damages) as opposed to one available in a court of equity (e.g., injunction).

remittitur. The power of a trial court to decrease the amount of a jury's award of damages. The plaintiff is told that a new trial will be ordered if the plaintiff does not agree to the decrease.

rent-a-judge. A method of alternative dispute resolution in which the parties hire a retired judge to arbitrate their dispute.

reply. A pleading containing the plaintiff's response to the affirmative allegations in the defendant's answer to the plaintiff's complaint.

reply brief. An appellate brief filed in response to the brief of the opposing side.

reporter. A volume containing the full text of court opinions.

republication. Repetition of a defamatory statement originally made by someone else. *See also* publication.

request for admissions. A request by one party of another that the latter admit or deny certain facts; the facts admitted do not then have to be established at trial.

respondeat superior. "Let the master answer." Rule by which an employer is liable for the torts of the employee committed within the scope of employment.

respondent. The party against whom an appeal is brought. Also called the *appellee*.

retainer. An agreement to hire someone.

retaliatory discharge. Dismissing someone from a job for a reason that violates public policy, e.g., for reporting a fire hazard at work.

reversionary interest. The right to the future enjoyment of land that is presently occupied by another.

risk-benefit analysis. Do the risks outweigh the benefits? The determination of whether the foreseeability of serious harm outweighs the burden or inconvenience of avoiding that harm in light of the value or social utility of the product. Also called *risk-utility analysis*.

risk-utility analysis. *See* risk-benefit analysis.

rule. A law or other governing principle.

rules of court. The procedural laws that govern the mechanics of litigation (practice and procedure) before a particular court. Also called *court rules*.

Rylands v. Fletcher. The case holding that if the defendant knows he or she is engaging in a non-natural or abnormal use of land that creates an increased danger to persons or property, the defendant will be strictly liable for harm caused by this use.

S

sale. The passing of title to property from a seller to a buyer for a price.

satisfaction. Full payment or compensation.

scienter. The intent to mislead. Making a statement while knowing it is false, or without a belief in its truth, or in reckless disregard of its truth or falsity—with the desire that the statement be believed and relied upon.

scope of employment. That which is foreseeably done by an employee for the employer under the employer's specific or general control.

screening panel. A group of individuals who will examine a case before it can be litigated in court. The panel can often make recommendations and encourage the parties to settle.

secondary assumption of risk. *See* assumption of risk.

secondary authority. *See* authority.

second chair. The law office employee who is allowed to sit at counsel's table during the trial to provide assistance to the lead attorney.

§ 402A. The main section on strict liability in tort from *Restatement (Second) of Torts*.

seduction. The tort of engaging in sexual relations with the plaintiff's daughter.

self-defense. The use of reasonable force to prevent an immediate harmful or offensive contact against you by someone who is making an apparent threat of this contact.

self-help. Preventive or corrective steps taken by the victim of a tort or other wrong on his or her own without resort to the courts.

self-insurance. The ability to pay workers' compensation benefits out of one's own funds rather than through an insurance policy.

seller. (1) Anyone in the business of selling. *See also* merchant. (2) A person who sells something. *See also* sale.

servant. *See* master/servant relationship.

service of process. A formal notification to a defendant that a suit has been instituted against him or her and that he or she must respond to it.

services. (1) Activities performed or benefits provided as part of one's line of work. (2) Household chores and other tasks an unemancipated child owes his or her parent. *See also* loss of services.

settlement. A resolution of the dispute, making the trial unnecessary.

settlement brochure. A written presentation by a party to an insurance company on the merits of a cause of action in an effort to encourage settlement. The presentation is called a *settlement precis* if the case is relatively uncomplicated.

settlement class action. A class action that the parties do not intend to litigate because they have reached a settlement on the claims made in the complaint.

settlement precis. *See* settlement brochure.

shadow trial. A mock trial designed to give the participants practice and feedback.

shallow pockets. Individuals without resources from which a judgment can be collected. *See also* deep pockets.

shopkeeper's privilege. The right of a merchant to detain someone temporarily for the sole purpose of investigating whether the person has committed any theft against the merchant.

sic [sic]. The error was in the quoted text.

sine qua non test. *See* but-for test.

slander. Defamation that is spoken or gestured. *See also* defamation.

slander of title. *See* disparagement.

slander per quod. (1) An oral defamatory statement that does not fit into one of the four categories that constitute slander per se. (2) An oral defamatory statement that requires extrinsic facts to understand its defamatory meaning.

SLAPP suit. Strategic Lawsuit Against Public Participation. A meritless suit brought primarily for the purpose of chilling the defendant's exercise of the right to free speech and to petition the government for a redress of grievances.

social guest. Someone who has express or implied permission to be present, primarily for a nonbusiness purpose.

social value. Quality as measured by the general public good.

solicitation. Actively seeking something such as to be hired. *See also* in-person solicitation.

sovereign immunity. The government cannot be sued without its permission.

special damages. Actual economic or pecuniary losses, such as medical expenses and lost wages. Also called *consequential damages.*

special relationship. A relationship that the law considers sufficiently important to impose a duty of reasonable care even in the absence of affirmative conduct.

spectrum of foreseeability. The extent to which something can be anticipated.

speech. *See* commercial speech.

standing. The right to bring a court action because of the sufficiency of one's personal interest in the outcome of the proposed court action or because of a special statute that gives this right.

standard of care. The degree of care that the law requires in a particular case. In most cases, the standard is what a reasonably prudent person would exercise under the same or similar circumstances. *See also* local standard, national standard.

standard of proof. The degree to which evidence of something must be convincing before a fact finder can accept it as true.

state a cause of action. *See* cause of action.

state a tort cause of action. *See* cause of action.

statement of fact. *See* fact.

statute. A law passed by the legislature declaring, commanding, or prohibiting something.

statute of limitations. A law that designates a time period within which a lawsuit must be commenced or it can never be brought.

statutory code. A collection of state or federal statutes organized by subject matter. *See* statute.

statutory law. Law created by the legislature. *See* statute.

stay. To stop or halt; a stoppage or suspension.

stay execution. To stop the process of enforcing the judgment.

strict liability. Liability or responsibility for harm whether or not the person causing the harm displayed any fault or moral impropriety. Also called *absolute liability* and *liability without fault.*

strict liability for abnormally dangerous conditions or activities. Liability for harm caused by abnormally dangerous conditions or activities whether the person causing the harm acted intentionally, negligently, or innocently.

strict liability in tort. Physical harm caused by a defective product that is unreasonably dangerous.

structured settlement. An agreement in which the defendant pays for damages he or she caused by making periodic payments for a designated period of time such as during the life of the victim. The payments are often funded through an annuity.

subjective standard. *See* objective standard.

subject matter jurisdiction. The power or authority of a court to resolve a particular kind of legal dispute. *See also* jurisdiction.

sub judice. Before the court; under judicial consideration.

subpoena. A command to appear at a certain time and place to give testimony.

subpoena duces tecum. A command that specific documents or other items be produced.

subrogation. The process by which one insurance company seeks reimbursement from another company or person for a claim it has already paid.

subscription. (a) The act of writing one's name. (b) The signature of the attorney who prepared the complaint.

substantial factor. A significant role.

substantial factor test. A person has caused something if his or her act or omission had a significant role in bringing it about.

substantially certain knowledge. *See* knowledge with substantial certainty.

summary judgment. A decision based on the pleadings, facts revealed through discovery, and other facts placed in the record, without going through a trial, because there is no genuine dispute on any material facts.

summary jury trial. A method of alternative dispute resolution in which the parties present their evidence to an advisory jury, which renders a non-binding verdict.

summons. A court notice requiring the defendant to appear and answer the complaint.

superseding cause. An intervening cause that is beyond the foreseeable risk originally created by the defendant's unreasonable acts or omissions. An intervening cause that creates a highly extraordinary harm.

survival. The continuation of a cause of action such as a tort after the death of either the victim or the alleged wrongdoer.

T

taking of property. The forced acquisition of private property by the government for a public purpose for which the government must pay just compensation.

tangible. Pertaining to that with which we can make contact with our senses such as touch. Having a physical form that can be seen or touched. Intangible refers to what cannot be perceived by the senses; property without physical form. Rights are intangible.

terminable at will. Something (e.g., a contract) that can be ended at any time for any reason without liability.

term of art. A word or phrase that has a special or technical meaning.

testate. Die leaving a valid will.

third-party complaint. A pleading that is a complaint filed by the defendant against a third party (who is not now in the suit) alleging that the third party may be liable for all or part of the damages the plaintiff may win from the defendant.

tickler. A system of reminders of important dates.

tolled. Suspended or stopped temporarily.

tort. A civil wrong (other than a breach of contract) that causes injury or other damage for which our legal system deems it just to provide a remedy such as compensation. A *personal tort* injures the person. A *personal property tort* damages movable property not attached to the land. A *real property tort* damages land and anything attached to the land.

tortfeasor. A person who has committed a tort.

tortious. Involving the commission of a tort.

tortious interference with employment. A wrongful discharge. Terminating employment for a reason that violates public policy.

toxic tort. Personal injury or property damage wrongfully caused by chronic or repeated exposure to toxic substances such as chemicals, biological agents, or radiation.

trade libel. *See* disparagement.

transcribe. To provide a word-for-word account or recording of what was said.

transferred intent. The defendant's intent to commit a tortious act against one person is transferred to the person who was in fact the object of this intent. Also, if the defendant intends to commit one tort but in fact commits another, the law may transfer the intent to cover the tort that was committed.

treatise. *See* legal treatise.

trespasser. One who enters land without the consent of the occupier and without any privilege to do so.

trespass to chattels. An intentional interference with personal property resulting in dispossession or intermeddling.

trespass to land. An intentional intrusion on land in possession of another.

trial memorandum. *See* memorandum of law.

trial notebook. A collection of documents, arguments, and strategies that an attorney plans to use during the trial.

trial within a trial. To win a legal malpractice case against an attorney, the plaintiff must establish that he or she would have won the case that the attorney lost if the attorney had not acted negligently.

typicality. The claims or defenses of the representative parties must be typical of the claims or defenses of the members of the class.

U

ultimate facts. Facts that are essential to the establishment of an element of a cause of action.

unavoidably unsafe product. A product that cannot be made safe by using current technology and science.

unconscionable. Substantially unfair because of highly unequal bargaining positions of the parties.

undertaking. Doing something; a task.

unemancipated. Still under the control of a parent.

unfair competition. Dishonest or fraudulent rivalry in trade and commerce.

unforeseeable plaintiff. A plaintiff who was not in the zone of danger. A plaintiff whose presence could not have been reasonably anticipated.

Uniform Commercial Code. The statute that governs commercial transactions in most states.

unit-of-time argument. *See* per diem argument.

unreasonable. *See* unreasonableness.

unreasonable conduct. *See* unreasonableness.

unreasonableness. The failure to act as a reasonable person would have acted under the same or similar circumstances. A breach of the duty of care.

unreasonable risks. Those risks that a reasonable person would not undertake because of the danger of harm.

unreasonably dangerous. Containing a risk of injury that a reasonable person would take reasonable precautions against.

upon information and belief. To the best of my knowledge; with a good faith recollection or understanding.

use. The *intended* use of a product is what the manufacturer wanted the product used for; its *foreseeable* use is what the manufacturer anticipates or should anticipate the product will be used for.

United States. Any entity of the federal government.

V

veggie libel. A cause of action created by statute that allows producers of perishable food products to sue when they lose business because of false statements that disparage the safety of their products.

vendee. Buyer.

vendor. Seller.

venue. The place of a trial.

verdict. The decision of a jury.

verification. An affidavit signed by a party stating that he or she has read the complaint or other pleading and that it is accurate to the best of his or her knowledge, information, and belief.

viable. Capable of surviving indefinitely outside the womb of the mother by natural or artificial support systems.

vicariously liable. Being responsible for a tort solely because of what someone else has done.

vice principal. An employee with supervisory authority over other employees.

voidable. Terminable and unenforceable at the option of someone.

voir dire. A preliminary examination to assess someone's qualifications to be a juror or witness. ("To speak the truth.")

volenti non fit injuria. "No wrong is done to one who consents."

W

waiver. The loss of a right or privilege because of an explicit rejection of it or because of a failure to claim it at the appropriate time.

wanton. Extreme recklessness.

warning defect. The product is dangerous because its instructions or warnings are ineffective.

warrant. A written order issued by an authorized government body directing the arrest of a person.

warranty. A guarantee; a commitment imposed by contract or by law that a product or service will meet a specified standard.

warranty, breach of express. Damage caused by a false statement of fact relied on by the plaintiff and made with the intention or expectation that the statement will reach the plaintiff.

warranty of fitness for a particular purpose, breach of implied. Damage caused by a sale of goods by a seller who had reason to know the buyer was relying on the expertise of the seller in selecting the goods for a particular purpose. The goods were not fit for that purpose.

warranty of merchantability, breach of implied. Damage caused by a sale of goods by a merchant of goods of that kind. The goods were not fit for the ordinary purposes for which they are used.

weight of the evidence. The amount and believability of the evidence.

whole. *See* made whole.

wild animal. An animal in the state of nature.

willful. (1) Knowing. (2) Acting with the knowledge that the harm will probably result. (3) Malicious.

willful, wanton, and reckless conduct. Actions or omissions of a person who knowingly creates a great risk of harm, or consciously ignores obvious risks of harm, or who is being malicious.

windfall. An extra amount to which you are not entitled under the original understanding of the parties.

witness statement. Information provided by a person who knows something relevant to the litigation.

workers' compensation. A no-fault system of covering the cost of medical care and weekly income payments of an insured employee if he or she is injured or killed on the job, regardless of blame for the accident.

work-product rule. *See* attorney work-product rule.

world at large. The Andrews test of duty. *See* Andrews test.

World Wide Web. A tool that allows you to navigate locations on the Internet that are often linked by hypertext.

writ of certiorari. *See* certiorari.

written deposition. *See* deposition.

written interrogatories. *See* interrogatories; discovery.

wrongful adoption. Wrongfully stating or failing to disclose to prospective adoptive parents any available facts on the health or other condition of a child that would be relevant to their decision to adopt the child.

wrongful birth. An action by parents of an unwanted deformed or impaired child for their own damages in the birth of the child.

wrongful civil proceedings. The initiation or procurement of civil legal proceedings without a reasonable belief that good grounds exist for the proceedings, which ultimately terminate in favor of the person against whom they were brought.

wrongful death. A death caused by a tort. *See also* Lord Campbell's Act.

wrongful discharge. Terminating employment for a reason that violates public policy. Tortious interference with employment.

wrongful life. An action by or on behalf of an unwanted deformed or impaired child for its own damages in being born.

wrongful pregnancy. An action by parents of a healthy child they did not want. Also called *wrongful conception.*

Z

zone of danger. The area within which it is foreseeable that someone may be injured.

1983 Action, 560
1983 Tort, 560
A.L.R., A.L.R.2D, A.L.R.3D, A.L.R.4th, A.L.R.5th,
    A.L.R. Fed, 20, 109, 123, 135, 151, 164, 183,
    198, 211, 367, 449, 480, 503, 517
Abate a Nuisance, 548, 705
Abate the Nuisance, 456
Abduction, 634
    of a child, 436
Abnormally Dangerous Condition or Activity, 199–200
Absolute Liability, 9, 192
Absolute Liability for Abnormally Dangerous Conditions
    or Activities, 195–204
Absolute Official Immunity, 560
Absolute Privilege to Defame, 493–494
Abuse of Process, 148, 149, 156–157, 162, 478
Accident Internet Sites, 21–22
Accident Records by State, 676–682
Accident Reporting Section, 677
Accident Reports, 681
Act, 41
    of assault, 123
    of battery, 110
Act of God, 201, 278, 576
Acting in Concert, 299
    not, 299–300
Activity Analysis of Foreseeability, 100
Acts of Nature, 576
Actual Malice, 171–172, 486, 510
Actual-risk Test, 576
Ad Damnum Clause, 66
Add-on No-fault, 688
Adduction, 634
Adhesion Contracts, 311
Administrative Code, 15
Administrative Regulations, 15
ADR (Alternative Dispute Resolution), 52–53
Adrenals, 652
Adultery, 436
Adverse Possession, 449
Advocacy, Legal Analysis and, 28
Advocacy Principles, Arguments on Foreseeability, 98–99
Affirmative Conduct, 217
Affirmative Defense, 484
Aggravated Assault, 107
Aggravated Injury or Disease, 577

Aggravation, 275
Aggravation of Injury, 296
Alienation of Affections, 436, 478
All-purpose Public Figure, 485–486
Allen v. Walker, 126
Alternative Dispute Resolution (ADR), 52–53, 326
Amchem Products, Inc. v. Windsor, 395, 399, 408
American Association of Legal Nurse Consultants, 693,
    694
American Digest System, 39, 151
American Jurisprudence 2d, 16, 17, 39, 109, 122, 135,
    151, 163, 182, 198, 210, 366, 448, 480, 502,
    517
American Law Reports, 20
Analysis, 44
Andrews Test, 215, 217, 277
Andrews v. Piedmont Air Lines, 142
Animals, Strict Liability for, 192–195
Annotations, 20
Answer, 63
Anterior, 634
Anti-SLAPP Statute, 495
Apparent Present Ability, 124
Appeal, 90–91
Application, 31–46
Apprehension in Assault, 120, 123–124
Appropriation, 507–508
Arbitration, 53
Arbitration in Medical Malpractice, 326–327
Area Analysis of Foreseeability, 100
Arising out of Employment, 570, 576
*Armory Park Neighborhood Assn v. Episcopal
    Community Services,* 460–461
Arrest, 144, 552, 553
Arteries, 644–645, 646
Asbestos, 397–400
Assault, 106, 107, 120, 133, 162, 478
    checklist for, 120–123
    civil rights and, 126–127
Assault and Battery, 10, 106, 107
    of employee, 576–577
Assault with Intent to Kill, 107
Assigned Risk, 688
Assumption of Risk, 354, 362
Assumption of the Risk, 202, 304, 309, 379, 569
    in private nuisance, 457

Assumptions about Human Nature in Analysis of
    Foreseeability, 101
Attestation Clause, 62
Attorney's Mistakes, 337–338
Attractive Nuisance Doctrine, 465
Automobile Accident and Investigation Checklist,
    662–670
Automobile Insurance, 688–691
Autonomic Nervous system, 643–644
Aviation Disaster Family Assistance Act, 392
Avoidable Consequences, 275, 296, 307
Avoidable Consequences in Private Nuisance, 457

Background facts, 54
Bad Faith Liability, 532
Battery, 8, 10, 106, 121, 125, 133, 149, 162, 342, 478,
    515
    by doctors, 324
    checklist for, 106–109
Behavior Modification Purpose, 3
Believability, spectrum of, 58
Benefits Available from Workers' Compensation, 582
Berman v. Allen, 439–441
Blood, 644
Body of Complaint, 64
Bona Fide Purchaser, 187
Bones in Skeletal System, 635–636
Breach of Contract, 322–323, 377
Breach of Duty, 214, 230, 251
    and negligence, 206
    of reasonable care, 276–277
Breach-of-Duty Equation, 232–237, 306, 351, 465
Breach of Express Warranty, 365, 515
    cause of action, 356
Breach of Implied Warranty, 357
    of fitness for particular purpose, 357, 365
    of merchantability, 365
Breach of the Peace, 145
Breach-of-Warranty, 322, 377
    who can be sued for, 361
    who can sue for, 361
Breast Implants, 401–406
Bronchi, 647
Brzoska v. Olson, 114–116
Burden of Proof, 57, 279
Burden on Defendant of Avoiding Interference by
    Private Nuisance, 455
Burden on Plaintiff of Avoiding Interference by Private
    Nuisance, 454
Burden or Inconvenience of Precautions, 235–236
Burden or Inconvenience on Manufacturer of
    Redesigning, 373
Bureau of Employment Programs, 682
Bureau of Labor Standards, 678
Bureau of Safety and Regulation, 678
Bureau of Workers' Compensation, 678, 680
Business Guest, 466
But for, 201

But-for-Test, 10, 249, 266–267, 268, 378
Buyer of Land, 471
Bystander, 377

CALR. *See* Computer-assisted Legal Research
Caption of Complaint, 64
Cardiovascular System, 644–645
Cardozo Test, 215, 217, 277
Case Law, 12
Case Valuation in Discovery, 73–74
Cassano v. Durham, 430–431
Categories of Defects, 347–348
Caudal, 634
Causal Connection Tests for Workers' Compensation,
    576
Causation, 201, 357, 360, 377–378
    and breast implants, 402
    by market share, 378
    evidence of, 268–270
    in false imprisonment, 140
    in intentional infliction of emotional distress, 167
    in interference with contract relations, 525
    in legal malpractice, 338–339
    introduction to, 10
    junk science and, 396
    of the intrusion, 42
Causation Question, 266
Causation v. Policy in Proximate Cause, 280
Cause in Fact, 10, 201, 266–273, 279, 307
Cause of Action, 4, 52
Caution Hypothesis, 234
Caveat Emptor, 471
Center for Safety and Health, 679
Central Nervous System, 640–643
Chain of Distribution, 368
Character of Land Locality, 454
Charitable Immunity, 564
Chattel, 180, 358, 546
    recapture of, 551–552, 553
Checklist for Automobile Accident and Investigation,
    662–670
Child, 465
Child Trespassers, 465–466
Citadel of Privity, 349
Civil Arrest, 144, 145
Civil Battery, 106, 107
Civil Disputes, 3
Civil Law, 3
Civil Liability Act, 532
Civil Procedure Law, 11
Civil Rights Act, 126, 560, 561
Claim, Filing for Workers' Compensation,
    580–581
Class Actions, 392–395
Class-of-Plaintiff Protected, 250–251
Clinton, Bill, 167
Code of Justinian, 12
Code of Napoléon, 12

Code of Regulations, 15
Coercion, 538
Collateral Source Offsets, 326
Collateral Sources, 298
Collectibility, 52
Colloquium, 488
Color of Law, 560
Color of State Law, 560
Colvin v. Industrial Indemnity, 574–575
Common Areas, 472
Common Interest, 494
Common Law, 12, 14, 137, 426, 427, 428
Common Law Fault System, 568
Common Law Tort, 560
Common Sense, 56
   and product liability, 353
   in analysis of foreseeability, 101
Commonality, 394
Comparative Negligence, 304, 309, 316, 354, 379
   in private nuisance, 457
Comparative Standard, 231–232
Compensatory Damages, 286–287
Complaint, 63
Complaint-Drafting Assignment in Personal Injury
      Litigation, general instructions for, 69
   sample, 70–71, 72
Complaints and Product Liability, 353
Complete Confinement, 132
Compliance Division, 681
Compliance with a Statute, 254
Component Part, Defective, 368
Comprehensiveness in Fact Gathering, 56
Computer-assisted Legal Research (CALR), 39, 109, 122,
      135, 152, 163, 183, 198, 211, 367, 449, 480,
      503, 517
Concert, Acting in, 299
   not, 299–300
Conclusion of Legal Analysis, 46–48
Conclusory Legal Analysis, 45–46
Conditional Privilege to Defame, 494
Confidential Relationship, 518
Confine in False Imprisonment, 132
Confinement, 136–138
   by asserted legal authority, 137
   by physical barrier, 136
   by physical force, 136
   by present threat of physical force, 136–137
   by refusal to release, 137
Conn and Najera v. Gabbert, 561, 562–563
Connective, 634
Consciousness
   in battery, 110
   of confinement, 141
Consent, 117, 536, 537
   capacity to, 536
   in tort law, 536
Consent forms, 325
Consequential Damages, 287

Consideration, 223
   release for, 300
Consortium, 434
Conspiracy of Silence, 324
Constitutional Law, 11
Constitutional Malice, 486, 510
Constitutional Tort, 560
Consumer, 377
Consumer Product Safety Commission, 380
Contingent Fee, 52
Contract Action, 524
Contract Law, 10
Contribution, 256, 299, 300–301
Contributory Negligence, 201, 304, 305–307, 354, 379,
      569
   objective test, 310
   subjective test, 310
Contributory Negligence in Private Nuisance, 457
Conversion, 162, 180–189, 515
   checklist for, 180–183
Cooling-off Periods in Medical Malpractice, 326
Corpus Juris Secundum, 16, 17, 39, 109, 122, 135, 151,
      163, 182, 198, 210, 366, 448, 479, 502, 516
Cost-benefit Analysis, 236
Cost of Restoration, 456
Counteranalysis, 45
Counterclaim, 63
Courtroom Gaffes, 702–703
Covenant Not to Sue, 300
Cranial, 634
Crash Records, 677
Credibility of Facts, 57
Crime, 3
Criminal Arrest, 144
Criminal Battery, 107
Criminal Conversation, 436
Criminal Disputes, 3
Criminal Law, 3, 10–11
Cross-claim, 63
Current Law Index, 19, 109, 122, 135, 151, 163, 183,
      198, 210–211, 367, 449, 480, 502, 517
Custom and Usage, 246–247
Custom in the Trade and Product Liability, 353
Cut-off Test, 266
   of proximate cause, 273–279
Cyberspace Defamation, 490–491

Damage, 357, 360
Damage Caps, 326
Damages, 3, 52
   for assault, 121
   for battery, 107
   for defamation, 478, 491–492
   for false imprisonment, 133
   for intentional infliction of emotional distress, 161
   for interference with contract relations, 525
   for invasion of privacy, 501
   for misrepresentation, 515

for negligence, 208
for private nuisance, 456–457
for strict liability for abnormally dangerous conditions
or activities, 196
for strict liability in tort, 365
for trespass to land, 447, 450
in conversion and trespass to chattels, 181, 183
jury instructions on, 289
kinds of, 286–287
software to calculate, 294–295
Danger Hypothesis, 234
Dangerous Propensities, 263
Daubert v. Merrell Dow Pharmaceuticals, Inc., 397
Death Rates
by leading cause, 698–699
from accidents, 697
Deaths from Accidents, 697
Deceit, 355, 514
Deep Pockets, 52, 106, 256, 322, 341
Defamacast, 476
Defamation, 149, 162, 476–496, 501, 515
checklist for, 476–481
in cyberspace, 490–491
in false arrest, 133
Defamatory Statement, 481
of and concerning the plaintiff, 488
Default Judgment, 66
Defective Product, Unreasonably Dangerous, 369–371
Defects, Categories of, 347–348
Defendant, Motive in Private Nuisance, 454
Defense, 304, 536
Defense of Others, 545, 547
Defense of Property, 548–549
Defenses in Strict Liability, 201–202
Defenses to and Product Liability, 354
Defenses to Strict Liability in Tort, 379
Defenses to Warranty Actions, 362
Defensive Medicine, 326
Definitions, Techniques of Locating, 38–39
Demonstrative Analysis, 46
Demurrer, 63
Department of Health, 681
Department of Labor, 676, 677, 679, 680, 681
Department of Labor, Safety and Health, 678
Department of Labor and Employment, 676
Department of Labor and Industry, 681, 682
Department of Labor and Management, 681
Department of Licensing, Accident Reports, 682
Department of Motor Vehicles, 679
Department of Motor Vehicles, Accident Report Section,
681
Department of Motor Vehicles, Collision Reports Section,
680
Department of Motor Vehicles, Customer Record
Requests, 681
Department of Motor Vehicles, Traffic Accident Section,
682
Department of Public Safety, 676, 680, 682
Department of Public Safety, Accident Reports, 680, 681

Department of Public Safety, Traffic Crash Records, 680
Department of Public Safety, Traffic Records Section, 681
Department of Roads, Accident Records Bureau, 679
Department of Safety, Accident Reproduction Section,
679
Department of State Police, Record Look-Up Unit, 678
Department of State Police, Records Section, 678
Department of Transportation, Accident Records, 681,
682
Department of Transportation, Office of Driver Services,
678
Deprivation of Use of Property, 295
Derogation of the Common Law, 13
DES (diethylstilbestrol), 378
Design Defects, 369
and Product Liability, 352
Designation of Pleading, 64
Deterrence, 3
Diaphragm, 647
Digests, 108, 122, 135, 151, 163, 182, 198, 210, 366,
448, 479, 516
Directed Question, 31
Disability Compensation Division, 677
Discipline, 552
Disclaimer of Warranty, 362
Discounting to Present Value, 288
Discovered Trespasser, 464
Discovery, 73–88
Discredit a Witness, 73
Diseases Covered under Workers' Compensation,
570–580
Disparagement, 149, 478, 529–530
Dispossession, 184
Distal, 634
Division of Industrial Affairs, 677
Division of Labor Standards and Safety, 676
Division of Occupational Safety, 678
Division of Occupational Safety and Health, 676
Division of Occupational Safety and Health
Administration, 681
Division of Safety and Buildings, 682
Division of Workers' Compensation, 676, 677, 678, 679
Doctrine of Avoidable Consequences, 296
Document Case, 389
Dollar Threshold, 688
Domestic Animals, Strict Liability for, 193
Donnell v. California Western School of Law, 469–470
Dorsal, 634
Double Recovery, Avoiding, 429–430
Dram Shop Liability, 532
Driver and Vehicle Services, Accident Records, 679
Driver Control Bureau, 678
Driver License and Traffic Safety Division, Accident
Report Section, 680
Driver's License Division, Accident Reports Section,
681
Dual-purpose Trip, 571
Duress, 136
Dushkin and Others v. Desal, 519–520

Duty, 214–228
    in negligence, 348
    in premises liability, 462
Duty of Care Owed by Occupier, 468
Duty of Reasonable Care, 276

Economic Losses, 286
Eggshell Skull Rule, 275, 280
Elements of a Rule, 4, 33–35
    analysis, 33–35
    connecting facts with, 39–43
    definitions of, 4, 36–39
Emancipated, Child, 435
Emotional Distress, 160
Employer-Employee (Agency) Law, 108, 121, 134, 150,
      162, 181–182, 197, 209, 365–366, 447, 479,
      501, 516
Employer/Employee Relationship, 257
Employment at Will, 528
Endocrine System, 650–652
Enforcement of Judgment, 91, 93
English Rule in Medical Malpractice, 327
Enterprise Liability in Medical Malpractice, 327
Enticement of a Child, 436
Enticement of Spouse, 436
Entry on Land for Inspection for Discovery, 73
Environmental Law, 11
Environmental Protection Agency, 398
Epithelial, 634
Equal Protection Clause, 560
Equitable Remedy, 286
Erect, 634
Esophagus, 648
Estate Law, 11
Estate of Victim, 426
Eversion, 634
Evidence Law, 55
Evidence of Causation, 268–270
Evidence of Negligence, 252
Evidence of Unreasonableness, 252
Evidentiary Privileges, 536
Exceptions to Proximate Cause Test, 276–277
Exculpatory Agreement, 311
Exemplary Damages, 287
Existing Contract, 524
Expectation Statement Will Reach Plaintiff, 357
Express Assumption of Risk, 310–311
Express Warranty, 355–356
Extension, 634
Extreme or Outrageous Conduct, 164–165
Extrinsic Facts, 484

FACE. *See* Free Access to Clinic Entrances Act
Fact, 518
    as defamatory statement, 481
    false statement of, 518
    statement of, 356
Fact Finding, Legal Analysis and, 28
Fact Gathering, 53–56

Fact Particularization, 58–61
Fact Pleading, 64
Fact Versions, 57
Factor, 44
Factor Analysis, 44
Factors in Reasonableness, 230
Factual Research Internet Sites, 22–23
Fair and Adequate Representation, 394
Fair Comment, 482, 494
Fair Competition, 529
Fair Market Value, 296
Fair on Its Face Warrant, 143
Fair Report Privilege, 489, 494
False Arrest, 143–145
False Imprisonment, 107, 121, 125, 132, 150, 162, 478,
      515
    checklist for, 132–136
False Light, 162, 509
False Statement of Fact, 356
Family Law, 11
Family Purpose Doctrine, 262
Fault, 206
    in Defamation, 485, 486
Federal Employees Liability Reform and Tort
      Compensation Act of 1988, 561
Federal Government, 554–556
Federal Rules of Civil Procedure (FRCP), 74
Federal Rules of Evidence (FRE), 396
Federal Tort Claims Act (FTCA), 554–556, 557, 558
Fee Caps, 326
Fein v. Permanente Medical Group, 327–329
Fellow-employee Rule, 569
Fellow-servant Rule, 569
Felony, 144
Fiduciary Relationship, 518
Filial Consortium, 435
Financial Responsibility, 688
Financial Responsibility Section, Accident
      Reports/Records Unit, 681
First Chair, 90
Flexion, 634
Foreseeability, 96, 214, 276–277
    of danger, 235
    of serious harm, 373
    steps to determine, 103
Foreseeability Determination Formula, 99–102, 236
Foreseeability Spectrum, 96–97
Foreseeable, 98–99
Foreseeable Consequences, 277
Foreseeable Constant Trespassers, 464–465
Foreseeable Plaintiff, 215–217
Foreseeable Risk, 276
Foreseeable Use of Product, 371
Foreseeable Users of Product, 349
Foster v. Preston Mill, 201, 202–203
Franklin v. Hill, 437–438
Fraud, 355, 514
FRE 702 test, 396
Free Access to Clinic Entrances Act (FACE), 126–127

Fresh Pursuit, 145
Frolic and Detour Negligence, 258
Frontal, 634
Frye test, 396
Frye v. United States, 396

Gaines-Tab V. ICI Explosives, USA, Inc., 282–283
Garratt v. Dailey, 111
Gastrointestinal System, 648–649, 650
General Damages, 286–287
General Legal Internet Sites, 23–24
General Phrasing of Foreseeability Question, 98, 100, 102
General Rule on Duty, 214
Genitourinary System, 649–650
Gertz v. Welch, 482
Global Peace in Class Action, 393
Going-and-Coming Rule, 571
Gonads, 652
Good Samaritan, 218
    protection for, 227
Goods Not Merchantable, Implied Warranty in, 360
Governmental Functions, 557–558
Gratuitous, 223
Gratuitous Release, 300
Gratuitous Undertaking, 223–224
Gravity of Harm, 453
Gross Negligence, 254–255, 305
Gross Unreasonableness, 255
Guest Statutes, 254

Hamberger v. Eastman, 504–505
Handwritten Witness Statement, 62
Harm in False Imprisonment, 141
Harmful, 120, 124
Harmful Contact and Battery, 113
Hearing Memorandum, 29
Heart, 644
Heart-balm Statutes, 435
Hedonic Damages, 294
Helpless Peril, 308
Highly Extraordinary Harm, 276, 280
Highly Offensive to Reasonable Person, 503
Highway Patrol, Accident Records, 679
Historical Data in Analysis of Foreseeability, 101
History in Causation, 270
Horseplay, Injuries during, 572
Hypothesis, 234
Hypothetical, 31

Imminent, 120
Imminent Harmful Contact, 124
Immunity, 536
Immunity, Intrafamily, 442
Immunity to Internet, 490
Impeach a Witness, 73
Implied Assumption of Risk, 310, 314–316
Implied Consent, 537
Implied Warranties, 359

of fitness for particular purpose, 360–361
of merchantability, 359–360
Importance or Social Utility, 236–237
of product, 373
Imputed Contributory Negligence, 262
Imputed Negligence, 255–263
Imputed Unreasonableness, 255–263
In-house Attorneys, 260
In Loco Parentis, 552
In-person Solicitation, 391
In Possession of Another, 41
In re Breast Implant Litigation, 402–406
In the Course of Employment, 570, 571–573
Inattentive Peril, 308
Incident-to-the-Job Risks, 571
Increased-risk Test, 576
Indemnity, 301, 339
Independent Contractor, 463
    negligence, 259–260
Independent Liability, 256–263
Index to Legal Periodicals and Books, 19, 109, 122, 135, 151, 163, 183, 198, 210–211, 367, 449, 480, 502, 517
Inducement, 484
Industrial Accident Board, 677, 678
Industrial Commission, 676
Industrial Commissioner, 680
Industrial Services Division, 678
Informal Investigative Techniques, 91
Information Gathering in Discovery, 73
Informed Consent, 324–325, 539
Inherently Dangerous Task, 260
Initiate, 152
Injunction, 456, 525
Injuries Covered under Workers' Compensation, 570–580
Injuries Internet Sites, 21–22
Injurious Falsehood, 530–531
Innuendo, 484
Instigation, 140–141
Insurance and Negligence, 206–207
Insurance Law, 11, 206
Insurance Operations Branch, Accident Report Section, 677
Intangible Interests, 427
Integumentary system, 652
Intended Use of Product, 371
Intent, 9, 97, 357, 524–525
    in intentional infliction of emotional distress, 165–166
    of assault, 120
    of battery, 106
Intent in False Imprisonment, 140
Intent of Battery, 110–111
Intent to Intrude, 41, 450
Intentional Infliction of Emotional Distress, 121, 133, 150, 160–167, 478, 501, 515
    checklist for, 160–164
Intentional Torts, 4, 8–9, 106
Interest, 446

Interference, 184, 524
  with contract relations, 523–527
  with prospective advantage, 527–528
Intermeddling, 184
Internet, 20
Internet Sites, 21
Interoffice Memorandum of Law, 29
  See also Legal Memorandum
Interrogatories, 329–335
Interspousal Immunity, 442
Intervening Cause, 201, 277–279
Intervening Force of Nature, 278, 279, 280
Intervening Innocent Human Force, 278, 279, 280
Intervening Intentional or Criminal Human Force, 278, 280
Intervening Negligent Human Force, 278, 279, 280
Interviewing, 32–33, 44
Intestacy, 427
Intimidation Suit, 495
Intrafamily Tort Immunity, 442–443, 564
Intrusion, 162, 503–507
  on land, 41
  on seclusion, 503
Invasion of Privacy, 162, 478, 500–511
  checklist for, 500–503
Inversion, 634
Investigation, 32–33, 44
Investigation Strategy Assignment, General Instructions for, 60–61
Invitees, 464, 467–468
IRAC, 28–29
Issue, Rule, Application, and Conclusion (IRAC), 28–29

Jeffrey Becker, Steven Becker, and Thomas Becker v. Kathleen Zellner and Associates, 492–493
Johns-Manville Corporation, 399
Joint and Several Liability, 244, 255
Joint Enterprise, 261–262
Joint Tortfeasors, 298–300
Jointly and Severally Liable Tortfeasor, 299
Joints in Skeletal System, 636–638
Jones, Paula Corbin, 167
Jones v. Clinton, 160, 168–170
Judgment, 3
Judgment Proof, 277
Judicial Panel on Multidistrict Litigation (J.P.M.L.), 395, 399, 402
Junk Science, 396
Jurisdiction, 3
Jury Instructions on Damages, 289
Jury Trial, 88
Just Compensation, 554
Justice, 4
Justifiable Reliance, 518, 521

Katko v. Briney, 548, 550
Keans v. Bottiarelli, 297
Knight v. Jewett, 316–319
Knowledge of Condition or Activity, 201

Knowledge with Substantial Certainty, 97, 111

Labor and Employment Security, 677
Labor and Safety Standards Division, 679
Labor Cabinet, 678
Labor Commission, 681
Labor Standards and Safety Enforcement, 679
Land, 450
  persons outside the, 463
  retaking possession forcibly, 552
Landlord, 472
Large Intestine, 648–649
Larynx, 646
Last Clear Chance, 304, 307–308
Latent Conditions, 466
Later Physical Harm or Injury, 173
Lateral, 634
Laterally Recumbent, 634
Law Journals, 19
Law Reviews, 19
Laying Foundation for Summary Judgment in Discovery, 74
Legal Analysis, 28, 32–33, 44
  conclusion of, 46–48
  length of, 45–46
Legal Analysis Assignment, General Instructions for, 47–48
Legal Analysis Guidelines, 28, 29, 30, 32, 34, 35, 36, 37, 38, 40, 42, 44, 45, 46, 47
Legal Encyclopedia, 16
Legal Interviewing, 44, 55
Legal Investigation, 44, 55
Legal Issue, 29–30
Legal Malpractice, 335–342
Legal Memorandum, 29, 43, 44
Legal Nurse, 693
  role of, 694
Legal Periodical Literature, 19, 109, 122, 135, 151, 163, 182–183, 198, 210, 367, 448–449, 480, 502, 517
Legal Reasoning, 28
Legal Remedy, 286
Legal Research, 32, 44
Legal Treatise, 18
Legitimate Public Interest, 510
Lessee, 472
Lessor, 472
LEXIS-NEXIS, 20
Liability, 51–52
Liability Insurance, 688
Liability without Fault, 9, 192
  medical, 323
Liable, 9, 28, 52
Libel, 476, 491
Libel Per Quod, 491
Licensees, 464, 466
Limitation of Liability, 311
Limited-purpose Public Figure, 486
Listservs, 25

Local Government, 556–558
Local Government Law, 11
Local Standard of Medical Care, 323
Lord Campbell's Act, 428–429
Loss of Consortium, 434
Loss of Services, 435
Loss Prevention, 680
Lucero v. Trosch, 127
Lump Sum Judgment, 287
Lungs, 647
Lymphatic System, 645

Made Whole, 4
Malice, 152–153
Malicious Civil Prosecution, 148
Malicious Interference, 525
Malicious Prosecution, 134, 148–154, 162, 479, 501
    checklist for, 148–152
    initiation of criminal proceedings for, 152
Mandatory Authority, 16
Mandatory Offset, 298
Manifestation of Willingness, 537
Manufacturer, 352
Manufacturing Defects, 369
Market Share Liability, 379
Married Women's Property Acts, 442
Mass Tort Cases, 388
    characteristics of, 388–389
Master/Servant Relationship, 257
Material Fact, 521
Material Statement, 357
McPherson v. Buick Motor Co., 349, 350, 361
Med-Arb, 53
Media, Products Liability in, 346
Media Defamation Cases, 485
Media Defendants
    in intentional infliction of emotional distress, 171–172
    in invasion-of-privacy torts, 510
Medial, 634
Median, 634
Mediastinum, 647
Mediation, 53
    in medical malpractice, 326
Medical Internet Sites, 24–25
Medical Malpractice, 322–335
Medical Malpractice Liability Insurance, 325–327
Medical Malpractice Reform, 325–327
Medical Symbols, 652
Medical Terminology, 634
Memo, 29
    See also Legal Memorandum
Memorandum of Law, 29
    See also Legal Memorandum
Mental Characteristics of Reasonable (Adult) Person, 239–240
Mental Characteristics of Reasonable (Child) Person, 240
Mental Examination for Discovery, 73
Merchant, 353

Merchant of Goods of that Kind, Implied Warranty in, 360
Merchantable Goods, 360
Method of Doing Job, 572
Midline, 634
Ministerial Tasks, 556
Misconduct, Injuries during, 572
Misdemeanor, 144
Misfeasance, 217, 218, 219
Misrepresentation, 181, 355, 365, 377, 501, 514–523
    checklist for, 514–517
Mistake Defense, 186–187
Mistakes by Attorneys, 337–338
Misuse, 379
Misuse of Product, 371
Mitigate Consequences, 275, 296
    in private nuisance, 457
Mitigation of Damages in Private Nuisance, 457
Mixed-purpose Trip, 571
Mock Trial, 90
Model Rules of Professional Conduct, 391
Modified No-fault, 688
Moore v. The Regents of the University of California, 187–188
More Likely Than Not Due to Unreasonableness
    defendant's, 242–244
    someone's, 240–242
Motion for Summary Judgment, 74
Motive of Battery, 113
Motor Vehicle Division, Accident Reports and Information, 680
Mouth, 648
Muscles, Primary, 638–639
Muscular, 634
Muscular System, 638–640
Mussivand v. David, 281

Nardi v. Gonzalez, 193–195
Narrowing Focus of Trial in Discovery, 74
National Institute for Occupational Safety and Health, 398
National Practitioner Data Bank, 327
National Standard of Medical Care, 323
Neal v. Neal, 540
Necessity, 546–548
Negligence, 9, 108, 111, 121, 134, 162, 181, 197, 206–212, 342, 365, 447, 515
    and breach of duty, 206
    and insurance, 206–207
    as a matter of law, 252
    checklist for, 207–211
    definition of, 207
    in false imprisonment, 140
    in product liability, 348–354
    medical, 323–324
Negligence Complaint, Structure of, 65
Negligence Law in U.S., Survey of, 654–659
Negligence Liability, 201
    traditional, 462–472

Negligence Per Se, 251–252
Negligent Entrustment, 263
Negligent Hiring, 260
Negligent Infliction of Emotional Distress (NIED), 172–174
Negligent Misrepresentation, 520–521
Neighborhood Justice Center (NJC), 53
Nervous System, 640–644
New York Times Malice, 486
Newsworthy People and Events, 510
NJC (Neighborhood Justice Center), 53
No Duty of Care, 464
No-fault Liability Insurance, 688
No-fault Motor Vehicle Insurance Laws by State, 688–691
No-fault System, 569
No-fault Systems of Medical Malpractice, 327
Nolle Prosequi, 153
Nominal Damages, 52, 287, 450
Non-delegable Duty, 260
Non-economic Losses, 286
Nonfeasance, 217–220
Nonjury Trial, 88
Nonmanufacturer and Product Liability, 353
Nonpecuniary Losses, 429
Nose, 645–646
Notes to Decisions, 38
Notice, 394
    to defendant, 362
Notice Pleading, 64, 66
Nuisance, 197, 447, 450–461
Numerosity, 394

Objective of a Job, 572
Objective Standard, 97, 237–240, 309
    for battery, 113
    test, 310
Occupational and Industrial Safety, 680
Occupational Safety and Health, 676, 678, 679, 680, 681
Occupational Safety and Health Administration, 398, 680, 682
Occupational Safety and Health Bureau, 680, 681
Occupational Safety and Health Division, 677, 679
Occupational Safety by State, 676–682
Occupier, 463
Of and Concerning the Plaintiff, 488
Offensive, 120, 124
Offensive Contact and Battery, 113
Offensive Harmful Contact, 124
Office of Workers' Compensation, 677, 678
Office of Workers' Compensation Programs, 569
Official Immunity, 554, 559–561
On Its Face, 484
Online, Tort Law, 20–21
On-the-Job Injuries at Common Law, 568–569
Open-ended Question, 31
Operational Level Torts, 555–556
Opinion, 356, 518

defamatory, 481–482
Opinions, 12
Opt Out of Class Action, 393
Oral Deposition for Discovery, 73
Ordinary Negligence, 254, 305
Ordinary Unreasonableness, 254
Original Risk in Proximate Cause, 279
O'Shea v. Riverway Towing Co., 289, 290–293
Out-of-Pocket Items, 286
Outrage, tort of, 160
Outrageous Conduct, 164–165
Outside Counsel, 260

Packaging and Product Liability, 353
Pain and Suffering, 160, 172
Pain-and-Suffering Damages, 286, 293–294
Palimony, 430
Palsgraff v. Long Island R.R., 215, 217, 349
Pancreas, 652
Paparazzi, 132, 507
Paralegal Investigation Tasks in Privilege to Arrest, 145
Paralegal Roles
    as project/case manager in toxic tort litigation, 412
    during settlement, 586, 587
    in assault litigation, 122
    in battery litigation, 108
    in defamation, 479
    in false imprisonment litigation, 134
    in intentional infliction of emotional distress, 162–163
    in invasion-of-privacy litigation, 301–302
    in malicious prosecution litigation, 150
    in mass tort litigation, 411–421
    in misrepresentation, 516
    in negligence, 209–210
    in strict liability for abnormally dangerous conditions or activities, 197
    in strict liability in tort, 366, 380–381
    in trespass to land litigation, 448
Paralegals, 341–342
    in ADR, 53
Parathyroid, 651
Parent and Child Liability, 263
Parental Consortium, 435
Parra v. Tarasco, Inc. d/b/a Jiminez Restaurant, 272–273
Particular Phrasing of Foreseeability Question, 98, 100, 102
Particularizing an event, 306
Passenger, 467
Peace, 3
Peace of Mind, 452
Peace Officer, 144
Peace Officer's Privilege to Arrest, 145
Peculiar-risk Test, 576
Pecuniary Losses, 429
People Analysis of Foreseeability, 101
Per Diem Argument, 293
Percentage Fee for Attorneys, 326
Perfect Person, 232, 233
Peripheral Nervous System, 643

Permissive Offset, 298
Person, 110
Personal Injury (PI) Attorney, 52
Personal Liability of Government Employees, 559–561
Personal Liability of Paralegals, 341
Personal Property, 358
Personal Property Torts, 426, 427
Personal Risks to Employee, 577
Personal Torts, 426, 427
Personally Liable Employee, 559
Persuasive Authority, 16
Peterson v. Sorlien, 541–543
Petition, 63
Pharynx, 646, 648
Physical Characteristics of Reasonable Person, 238–239
Physical Examination for Discovery, 73
Physical Harm, 377
Physical Harm or Injury, 173
Physical Impact, 173
Physical Injury In Intentional Infliction Of Emotional Distress, 161
Physician Insurers Association of America, 322
Physician-Patient Relationship, 322
PI (Personal Injury) Attorney, 52
Pineal, 652
Pituitary, 651
Plaintiff in Helpless Peril, 308
Plaintiff in Inattentive Peril, 308
Plaintiff not Responsible for Accident in Res Ipsa, 244
Plaintiffs in Trespass Action, 449–450
Plaintiff's Negligence, 305–307
Planning Level Torts, 555–556
Pleadings, 63
Points and Authorities Memorandum, 29
Police Headquarters, Accident Records Unit, 680
Policy Question, 266
Positional-risk Test, 576
Possessory Interest, 449
Posterior, 634
Posttrial Deposition, 91
Potts v. Fidelity Fruit & Produce Co., Inc., 252
Prayer for Relief, 66
Prediction, Legal Analysis and, 28
Pre-existing Injuries or Diseases, 577
Preliminary Assessment, 31–32
Premises Liability, 462
Prenatal Injuries, 438
Preparation Analysis of Foreseeability, 101
Preponderance of the Evidence, 57, 271
Present Cash Value, 288
Present Value, 287–289
Preserving Evidence in Discovery, 74
Presumed Damages for Defamation, 491
Presumption of Negligence, 252
Presumption of Unreasonableness, 252
Pretrial Discovery Devices with Paralegal Roles, 75–78
Prima Facie Case, 55
Prima Facie Tort, 501, 531
Primary Assumption of Risk, 315–316

Primary Authority, 12, 28, 30
    categories of, 13
Principal/Agent Relationship, 257
Private Affairs, 503
Private Citizen's Privilege to Arrest, 145
Private Matter Defamation, 486
Private Necessity, 546
Private Nuisance, 451–457
    defenses to defendant in, 457
    harm in, 451
    nature of, 451
    remedies for, 456
    ways of committing, 455–456
    who can sue for, 456
Private Person, 486
Private Wrong, 3
Privilege, 536
Privilege to Arrest
    peace officer's, 143
    peace officer's and private citizen's compared, 144–145
    private citizen's, 145
    without warrant, 144–145
Privilege to Defame, 493–494
Privilege to Interfere, 525
Privilege to Recapture, 136
Privity, 361–362
Privity of Contract, 348–349
Pro Bono, 287
Probable Cause, 152, 153
Product Liability
    reform in, 380
Production of Documents and Things for Discovery, 73
Production of Documents by Debtor, 91, 93
Products Liability, 346–386
    categories of defects, 347–348
    in the media, 346
Professionalism in Fact Gathering, 59
Promise, 223
Pronation, 634
Prone, 634
Property Damage, 295–296
Property Damaged, 295
Property Damaged but not Destroyed, 295
Proprietary Functions of Local Government, 557–558
Prosser and Keeton on the Law of Torts, 18
Proximal, 634
Proximate Cause, 201, 266–284
    steps to analyze, 279–280
Proximate-cause Test, 576
Public Concern Defamation, 486
Public Disclosure of Private Fact, 508
Public Employees as Invitees or Licensees, 468
Public Figure, 485, 510
Public Necessity, 546
Public Nuisance, 451, 458–460
    defenses for defendant in case of, 460
    harm in, 458
    nature of, 458

remedies for, 459–460
ways of creating, 459
who can sue for, 459
Public Official, 485, 510
Public Policy, 311, 524
Public Wrong, 3
Publication, 508
of defamatory statement, 488–489
Publicity, 508
Puffing, 356, 508
Punitive Damages, 287
Pure Comparative Negligence, 309

Qualified Official Immunity, 560
Qualified Privilege to Defame, 494
Question of Law, 29–30
Questionnaire Witness Statement, 62

Racial Discrimination, 560
Raine and Highfield v. Drasin and Fadel, 155–156
Real Property, 358
Real Property Law, 11
Real Property Torts, 426, 427
Reasonable, 124
Reasonable Alternative Design, 376
Reasonable Belief, 538
Reasonable Beneficial Use, 450
Reasonable Care, 214, 219, 230
Reasonable Doctor Standard in Informed Consent, 325
Reasonable Patient Standard in Informed Consent, 325
Reasonable Person, 97–98, 232, 233, 238, 503
Reasonableness by Comparison, 231–232
Recapture of Chattels, 551–552, 553
Reckless Conduct, 305
Reckless Disregard, 520
Recklessness, 165
Recorded Witness Statement, 62
Reducing to Present Value, 288
Reform in Product Liability Law, 380
Reform of Workers' Compensation, 583
Registry of Motor Vehicles, 678
Release, 300
Release Clause, 311
Reliance, 223
Reliance on Statement, 357
Remedy, 3
Rent-a-Judge, 53
Reply, 63
Reporters, 12
Representative Parties, 393
Reproductive Systems, 649–650
Republication of Defamatory Statement, 489
Reputation of Manufacturer and Product Liability, 353
Request for Admission for Discovery, 73
Request for Exclusion, 393
Res Ipsa Loquitur (RIL), 200, 240–246, 352–353
Research, 44
Research References
for assault, 122–123

for battery, 108–109
for false imprisonment, 135–136, 198
for invasion-of-privacy torts, 502
for misrepresentation, 516–517
for trespass to land, 448–449
Respiratory System, 645–647
Respondeat Superior, 108, 121, 134, 150, 162, 182, 197, 209, 257, 260, 341, 366, 447, 479, 501, 516, 554
Ressallat v. Burglar & Fire Alarms, Inc., 362–364
Restatement of Torts, 18–19, 200, 220, 276, 314, 336, 368, 369, 373, 376, 465
Restoration, 4
Restricted Comparative Negligence, 309
Retaliatory Discharge, 528
Reversionary Interest in Land, 472
Riley v. Becton Dickinson Vascular Access, Inc., 373–376
Risk Management Division, 676
Risk-benefit Analysis, 236, 373, 376
Risk-utility Analysis, 236, 376
Riss v. City of New York, 224–226
Routh Wrecker Service, Inc. v. Washington, 157–158
Rule, 28, 30
breaking down into elements, 33–35
Russell-Vaughn Ford, Inc. v. E. W. Rouse, 185–186
Rylands v. Fletcher, 199

Safety Bureau, 679
Safety Engineering, 677
Safety Responsibility, Accident Records, 679
Sagittal, 634
Sale of Goods, Implied Warranty in, 360
Sale Versus Service in Product Liability, 357–359, 369
Sales, 357, 369
Sample Accident Report Filed with Police Department, 672–673
Sample Interrogatories, 79–87
Satisfaction, 300
Scienter, 355, 520
Scope of Employment, 559
Scope of Employment and Negligence, 257
checklist for, 258
Scope of Employment and Paralegals, 341
Screening Panels in Medical Malpractice, 326
Second Chair, 90
Secondary Assumption of Risk, 316–317
Secondary Authority, 16
Seduction, 436
Seitz v. L&R Industries, Inc., 578–580
Self-defense, 536, 544, 545
Self-help, 456
Self-help Privileges, 543–554
Self-insurance, 569
Seller in Strict Liability in Tort, 368–369
Seller of Land, 471
Services, 357, 358
Settlement, 586
Settlement Brochure, 586, 589
illustration, 590–630

Settlement Class Action, 393

Settlement of Legal Dispute, 586–630
    paralegal roles during, 586

Settlement Precis, 586–589
    illustration, 587–589

Settlements, Examples of, 684–686

Severe Emotional Distress, 166

Shadow Trial, 90

Shallow Pockets, 52, 106, 301

Shephard's Citations, 38

Shephardize, 38

Shopkeeper's Privilege, 137, 553

Sindell v. Abbott Laboratories, 378, 379

Skeletal System, 635–638

Slander, 342, 476, 491–492

Slander of Title, 529

Slander Per Quod, 491

Slander Per Se, 491

SLAPP Suits, 495

Small Intestine, 648

Smith v. Lewis, 339–340

Smyth v. The Pillsbury Co., 505–506, 528

Social Guests, 466

Social Utility, 236–237

Social Value of Defendant's Conduct, 454–455

Social Value of Land Use, 453–454

Software To Calculate Damages, 294–295

Soldano v. O'Daniels, 220–222

Solicitation of Clients, 390–392

Sovereign Immunity, 554–558, 559

Space in Causation, 269–270

Special Damages, 287, 529

Special Damages for Defamation, 491

Special Relationships, 217–220

Special Representation, 336

Specific Sensory Data in Analysis of Foreseeability, 101

Specificity In Fact Gathering, 56

Standard Forms, 66

Standard of Care, 14–15, 463
    reasonableness, 230–232

Standard of Competence in Legal Malpractice, 336

Standard of Proof, 271

Standing, 459

State a Tort Cause of Action, 4

State Agencies Relevant to Torts Practice, 676–682

State Board of Workers' Compensation, 677

State Compensation Fund, 676

State Compensation Insurance Fund, 679

State Government Law, 11

State Government Liability, 556

State Industrial Commission, 677

State Industrial Insurance System, 679

State Police, Accident Record Division, 681

State Police, Accidents Records, 678

State Police, Accidents Records Section, 676

State Police, Central Records Division, 678

State Police, Records, 679

State Police Traffic Section, 677, 678

Statement of Jurisdiction of Complaint, 64

Status of Plaintiff in Defamation Case, 485

Statute, Violation of
    eight-step analysis of, 247–252, 253

Statute of Limitations in Medical Malpractice, 326

Statutes, 13–15

Statutory Codes, 15

Statutory Law, 427

Stomach, 648

Strategic Lawsuit Against Public Participation (SLAPP), 495

Strategy Formulation in Discovery, 73

Street Risks, 576

Strict Liability, 9, 192, 201, 355
    medical, 323
    of employer, 569

Strict Liability for Abnormally Dangerous Activities, 447

Strict Liability for Abnormally Dangerous Conditions or Activities, 195–204
    checklist for, 195–199

Strict Liability in Tort, 192, 355, 357, 360, 364–380
    checklist for, 364–367
    checklist for cause of action, 368
    defenses to, 379

Structured Settlement, 287–288

Subject Matter Jurisdiction, 64

Subjective Standard, 97, 237–240, 309
    test, 310

Subscription, 66

Substantial Certainty of Harm, 9

Substantial Factor, 201

Substantial Factor Test, 10, 249, 266, 267–268

Substantially Same Conduct, 539–540

Summary Judgment, Motion for, 74

Summary Jury Trial, 53

Superseding Cause, 278

Supination, 634

Supine, 634

Surgeon General, 398

Survival, 426
    of torts unrelated to death, 426–427

Survival Statute, Enlarging to Include Wrongful Death, 428

Survival Statutes, 427, 429

Taking of Property, 554
    in private nuisance, 457

Tangible Interests, 427

Tarasoff v. Regents of University of California, 220

Tenant, 472

Terminable at Will, 524

Terms of Art, 38

Texaco, Inc. v. Pennzoil Co., 526–527

The Limited Stores, Inc. v. Wilson-Robinson, 138–139

Thing v. La Chusa, 160, 175–176

Third Chair, 90

Third-party Complaint, 63

Threshold Requirements for Class Action, 394, 395

Thymus, 652

Thyroid, 651
Time in Causation, 268–269
Tobacco Companies, Suits Against, 406–411
Tolled Statute of Limitations, 326
Tort, 3
    and related causes of action, 5–8
    categories of, 4–9
Tort Action, 524
Tort Actions That Survive, Characteristics of, 427
Tort Cause of Action, 4
Tort Claims Against Third Parties in Workers'
        Compensation, 582–583
Tort Complaints, 63–66
Tort Internet Sites, 21–22
Tort Law, 3, 55
    consent in, 536
    impeachment of president and, 167
    purposes of, 3–4
    sources of, 12–25
Tort Law Online, 20–21
Tort Litigation, Overview with Paralegal Roles,
        50–51
Tort Litigation Planning Internet Sites, 23
Tortfeasor, 4, 426
Tortious Death, 426
Tortious Injury to Consortium, 434
Tortious Interference with Employment, 528
Torts Derived from Other Torts, 434–435
Torts Not Derived from Other Torts, 435–438
Totality of Circumstances, 230
Toxic Tort Litigation, Paralegal as Project/Case Manager
        in, 412–421
Trachea, 646
Trade Libel, 529
Traditional Negligence, 172–173
Traditional Negligence Liability, 462–472
Transferred Intent In Intentional Infliction Of Emotional
        Distress, 166
Transferred Intent of Assault, 125
Transferred Intent of Battery, 112–113
Transferred Intent of False Imprisonment, 140
Transportation Department, Accident Records, 677
Transverse, 634
Trespass to Chattels, 125, 180–189
    checklist for, 180–183
Trespass to Land, 125, 162, 197, 446–450, 515
    checklist for, 446–449
Trespasser
    child, 465–466
    discovered, 464
    foreseeable constant, 464–465
Trespassers, 464–466
Trial, 88–90
    role of paralegals at, 88–89
Trial Demonstratives, 380
Trial Memorandum, 29
Trial Visuals, 380
Trial within a Trial, 338
Typicality, 394

Unavoidably Unsafe Products, 370–371
Unconscionable Disclaimer, 362
Undertaking, 223
Unemancipated Child, 435
Unfair Competition, 527
Unforeseeability of Manner of Injury, 275–276, 280
Unforeseeable, 98–99
Unforeseeable Plaintiff, 215–217, 277
Unholy Trinity of Defenses, 569
Uniform Commercial Code (UCC), 356, 359
Unintended Plaintiff, 125
Unintended Tort, 125
Unintentional Injuries, 2, 696
United States Department of Labor, 569
Unit-of-Time Argument, 293
Unjustified Civil Proceedings, 154
Unreasonable Conduct, 230
Unreasonable Interference, 452
    factors in, 452–453
Unreasonable Person, 232, 233
Unreasonable Risk of Harm, 9
Unreasonable Risks, 305
Unreasonableness, 206, 305–307
Unreasonableness Equation, 232–237
Unreasonableness Per Se, 251–252
Unreasonably Dangerous Product, 369–371
Urinary Organs, 649
User, 377

Van Duyn v. Smith, 482–484
Veggie Libel Cases, 496, 529–530
Vehicle Crash Records, 677
Vehicle Record Inquiry, 677
Veins, 645, 646
Vendee, 471
Vendor, 471
Ventral, 634
Venue, 64
Verbal Threshold, 688
Verdicts, Examples of, 684–686
Verification, 66
Viable, 438
Vicarious Liability, 255–263
Vicarious Liability of Paralegals, 341
Vicarious Unreasonableness, 255–263
Vicariously Liable Employer, 559
Vice Principal, 569
Violation of Statute, 247–252
Voidable Contract, 524
Vokes v. Arthur Murray, Inc., 521–523
Volenti Non Fit Injuria, 536
Voluntariness, 538
Volunteer Protection Act, 227

Wagenblast v. Odessa School District No. 105-157-166J,
        311–313
Ward v. Forrester Day Care, Inc. 245–246
Warning Defects, 352, 369
Warrant, 144

Warranty, 322
Warranty Action, 355
  defenses to, 362
Weight of the Evidence, 270–271
WESTLAW, 20, 39
Wild Animals, Strict Liability for, 193
Willful, Wanton, and Reckless Conduct, 254–255
Willful Misconduct, 572
Williams, Merrell, 407
Windfall, 288
With Malice, 152–153
Without Probable Cause, 152
Witness Statement, 62–63
Witnessing Injury, 173–174
Workers' Compensation, 568–583, 681
Workers' Compensation Administration, 680
Workers' Compensation Agency by State, 676–682
Workers' Compensation Board, 677, 678
Workers' Compensation Bureau, 680
Workers' Compensation Commission, 676, 678, 679, 681
Workers' Compensation Committee, 680
Workers' Compensation Court, 679
Workers' Compensation Division, 676, 679, 680, 682

Workers' Compensation Statutes, 569–570
  benefits from, 582
  filing a claim for, 580–581
World Wide Web, 20
World-at-Large Test, 215, 217, 277
Written Deposition for Discovery, 73
Written Interrogatories, 93, 329–335
Written Interrogatories for Discovery, 73
Wrongful Adoption, 442
Wrongful Birth, 438
Wrongful Civil Proceedings, 148, 150, 154
Wrongful Criminal Proceedings, 148
Wrongful Death, 108, 121, 162, 197, 426, 428–429
  enacting statute, 428–429
  enlarging survival statute to include, 428
  recovery for, 428
Wrongful Discharge, 528
Wrongful Life, 438
Wrongful Pregnancy, 439

Ybarra v. Spangard, 244

Zone of Danger, 173
Zone-of-Danger Test, 215, 217, 277

ALSO BY WILLIAM P. STATSKY

Essentials of Torts, 2d ed., due out fall of 2000

Legal Research and Writing: Some Starting Points, 5th ed., 1999

Essentials of Paralegalism, 3rd ed., 1997

Family Law: The Essentials, 1997

Introduction to Paralegalism: Problems, Perspectives and Skills, 5th ed., 1997

Family Law, 4th ed., 1996

Case Analysis and Fundamentals of Legal Writing, 4th ed., 1995

Legal Desk Reference, 1991 (with B. Hussey, M. Diamond & R. Nakamura)

Paralegal Employment: Facts and Strategies for the 1990s, 2d ed., 1993

Paralegal Ethics and Regulations, 2d ed., 1993

Legal Thesaurus/Dictionary: A Resource for the Writer and Computer Researcher, 1985

Legislative Analysis and Drafting, 2d ed., 1984